COLLINS
FRENCH SCHOOL DICTIONARY
AND
GRAMMAR

FRENCH ▸ ENGLISH ENGLISH ▸ FRENCH

HarperCollins*Publishers*

First published in this edition 1994

© HarperCollins Publishers 1994

Latest reprint 1998

ISBN 0 00 766016 2

Pierre-Henri Cousin
Lorna Sinclair Knight Lesley Robertson

contributors
Claude Nimmo Philippe Patry
Hélène Lewis   Elizabeth Campbell
Renée Birks   Jean-François Allain
Christine Penman Sabine Citron

editorial staff
Catherine Love Angela Campbell
Stephen Clarke Joyce Littlejohn Megan Thomson
Linda Chestnutt

editorial management
Vivian Marr

*A catalogue record for this book is
available from the British Library*

*Dictionary text typeset by Morton Word Processing Ltd, Scarborough
Grammar text typeset by Tradespools Ltd, Frome, Somerset*

Printed and bound in Germany by Elsnerdruck, Berlin

Introduction

We are delighted you have decided to buy the **Collins French School Dictionary and Grammar**. This book is designed to give you, in one handy volume, comprehensive and authoritative answers to all your vocabulary and grammar queries.

In the Dictionary section you will find:

- in-depth vocabulary coverage which will more than meet your examination needs
- clear signposting of meanings and subject areas to guide you to the most appropriate translation
- modern, idiomatic phrases showing words in their context
- the most common words in each language are highlighted and treated in depth

The Grammar section contains further essential information on:

- all the basic rules and structures of French
- French verbs
- avoiding pitfalls in translation

We hope you will enjoy using this book and that it will be an invaluable reference tool for all your French language studies.

Contents

Using the Dictionary	iv-v
Abbreviations	vi-vii
Phonetics	viii-ix
FRENCH-ENGLISH	1-218
ENGLISH-FRENCH	219-436
Using the Grammar	3
Contents	4
Grammar	6-255

Using the Dictionary

The various typefaces, type sizes, symbols, abbreviations and brackets used throughout this dictionary all convey useful information. Take time to establish what they indicate and this will help you get the most out of your dictionary.

Finding the word you want

The information above the line at the top of each page helps you to locate, quickly and easily, the entry you want to consult. At the outside margin, the first and last entries on that page are shown, separated by an arrow. Information about which side of the dictionary you are using is shown at the inside margin.

Headwords

The words you look up in a dictionary are called headwords and are printed in **bold** type. The phonetic spelling is given in square brackets immediately after the headword. An explanation of these symbols is given on pages viii-ix. Information about the usage or form of certain headwords is given in brackets after the phonetic spelling. This usually appears in abbreviated form and in italics eg (*fam*), (*comm*). Explanations of these are given on pages vi-vii.

Where appropriate, words related to headwords are grouped in the same entry in a slightly smaller type than the headword.

> **passion** [...] *nf* passion; **passionant, e** *adj* fascinating;...

> **explosion** [...] *n* explosion *f*; **explosive** [...] *adj* explosif (ive)...

Common expressions in which the headword appears are shown in a smaller bold type.

> **autre** [...] *adj* **1** (*différent*) other, different; **je préférerais un ~ verre** I'd prefer another *ou* a different glass

Translations

Headword translations are given in ordinary type and, where more than one meaning or usage exists, these are separated by a semicolon. You will often find bracketed words in italics appearing before the translations. These are called "indicators" and they offer suggested contexts in which the headword might appear or provide synonyms for the headword to guide you to the most appropriate translation.

> **opposer** [...] vt (*personnes, armées, équipes*) to oppose, (*couleurs, termes, tons*) to contrast; .
>
> **relation** [...] n (*person*) parent (e); (*link*) rapport m, lien m;
>
> **superposer** [...] vi (*faire chevaucher*) to superimpose;
>
> **retire** [...] vi (*give up work*) prendre sa retraite; ...

Key words

Special status is given to certain French and English words which are considered "key" words in each language. These words occur very frequently in French or English, or have several types of usage (eg **vouloir, plus; get, that**). A combination of lozenges and numbers helps you to distinguish different parts of speech and meanings

Grammatical information

Parts of speech are given in abbreviated form in italics after the phonetic spellings of headwords (eg *vt, adv, conj*) A lozenge indicates a change in part of speech and different meanings are split into separate categories and numbered accordingly Genders of French nouns are indicated as follows *nm* for a masculine and *nf* for a feminine noun Feminine and irregular plural forms of nouns and adjectives, along with any change in pronunciation, are also shown

> **directeur, trice** [ ] *nm/f*
> (*d'entreprise*) director,
>
> **cheval, aux** [ ] *nm* horse,

Note on trademarks

Words which we have reason to believe constitute trademarks have been designated as such However, neither the presence nor the absence of such designation should be regarded as affecting the legal status of any trademark

v

Abbreviations

adjectif, locution adjective	**adj**	adjective, adjectival phrase
abréviation	**ab(b)r**	abbreviation
adverbe, locution adverbiale	**adv**	adverb, adverbial phrase
administration	**ADMIN**	administration
agriculture	**AGR**	agriculture
anatomie	**ANAT**	anatomy
architecture	**ARCHIT**	architecture
article défini	**art déf**	definite article
article indéfini	**art indéf**	indefinite article
l'automobile	**AUT(O)**	the motor car and motoring
auxiliaire	**aux**	auxiliary
aviation, voyages aériens	**AVIAT**	flying, air travel
biologie	**BIO(L)**	biology
botanique	**BOT**	botany
anglais de Grande-Bretagne	**Brit**	British English
commerce, finance, banque	**COMM**	commerce, finance, banking
comparatif	**compar**	comparative
informatique	**COMPUT**	computing
chimie	**CHEM**	chemistry
conjonction	**conj**	conjunction
construction	**CONSTR**	building
nom utilisé comme adjectif, ne peut s'employer ni comme attribut, ni après le nom qualifié	**cpd**	compound element: noun used as an adjective and which cannot follow the noun it qualifies
cuisine, art culinaire	**CULIN**	cookery
article défini	**def art**	definite article
diminutif	**dimin**	diminutive
économie	**ECON**	economics
électricité, électronique	**ELEC**	electricity, electronics
exclamation, interjection	**excl**	exclamation, interjection
féminin	**f**	feminine
langue familière (! emploi vulgaire)	**fam(!)**	colloquial usage (! particularly offensive)
emploi figuré	**fig**	figurative use
(verbe anglais) dont la particule est inséparable du verbe	**fus**	(phrasal verb) where the particle cannot be separated from main verb
dans la plupart des sens; généralement	**gén, gen**	in most or all senses; generally
géographie, géologie	**GEO**	geography, geology
géométrie	**GEOM**	geometry
impersonnel	**impers**	impersonal
article indéfini	**indef art**	indefinite article
langue familière (! emploi vulgaire)	**inf(!)**	colloquial usage (! particularly offensive)
infinitif	**infin**	infinitive
informatique	**INFORM**	computing
invariable	**inv**	invariable

irrégulier	*irreg*	irregular
domaine juridique	*JUR*	law
grammaire, linguistique	*LING*	grammar, linguistics
masculin	*m*	masculine
mathématiques, algèbre	*MATH*	mathematics, calculus
médecine	*MÉD, MED*	medical term, medicine
masculin ou féminin, suivant le sexe	*m/f*	either masculine or feminine depending on sex
domaine militaire, armée	*MIL*	military matters
musique	*MUS*	music
nom	*n*	noun
navigation, nautisme	*NAVIG, NAUT*	sailing, navigation
adjectif ou nom numérique	*num*	numeral adjective or noun
	o.s.	oneself
péjoratif	*péj, pej*	derogatory, pejorative
photographie	*PHOT(O)*	photography
physiologie	*PHYSIOL*	physiology
pluriel	*pl*	plural
politique	*POL*	politics
participe passé	*pp*	past participle
préposition	*prép, prep*	preposition
pronom	*pron*	pronoun
psychologie, psychiatrie	*PSYCH*	psychology, psychiatry
temps du passé	*pt*	past tense
quelque chose	*qch*	
quelqu'un	*qn*	
religions, domaine ecclésiastique	*REL*	religions, church service
	sb	somebody
enseignement, système scolaire et universitaire	*SCOL*	schooling, schools and universities
singulier	*sg*	singular
	sth	something
subjonctif	*sub*	subjunctive
sujet (grammatical)	*su(b)j*	(grammatical) subject
superlatif	*superl*	superlative
techniques, technologie	*TECH*	technical term, technology
télécommunications	*TEL*	telecommunications
télévision	*TV*	television
typographie	*TYP(O)*	typography, printing
anglais des USA	*US*	American English
verbe	*vb*	verb
verbe ou groupe verbal à fonction intransitive	*vi*	verb or phrasal verb used intransitively
verbe ou groupe verbal à fonction transitive	*vt*	verb or phrasal verb used transitively
zoologie	*ZOOL*	zoology
marque déposée	®	registered trademark
indique une équivalence culturelle	~	introduces a cultural equivalent

Phonetic Transcription

Consonnes / Consonants

poupée	p	puppy
bombe	b	baby
tente thermal	t	tent
dinde	d	daddy
coq qui képi	k	cork kiss chord
gag bague	g	gag guess
sale ce nation	s	so rice kiss
zéro rose	z	cousin buzz
tache chat	ʃ	sheep sugar
gilet juge	ʒ	pleasure beige
	tʃ	church
	dʒ	judge general
fer phare	f	farm raffle
valve	v	very rev
	θ	thin maths
	ð	that other
lent salle	l	little ball
rare rentrer	ʀ	
	r	rat rare
maman femme	m	mummy comb
non nonne	n	no ran
agneau vigne	ɲ	
	ŋ	singing bank
hop!	h	hat reheat
yeux paille pied	j	yet
nouer oui	w	wall bewail
huile lui	ɥ	
	x	loch

Divers / Miscellaneous

pour l'anglais: précède la syllabe accentuée	'	in French wordlist and transcription: no liaison
pour l'anglais: le r final se prononce en liaison devant une voyelle	*	

Phonetic Transcription

Voyelles		*Vowels*

NB. The pairing of some vowel sounds only indicates approximate equivalence.

*ic*i *v*ie lyre	i iː	heel bead
	ɪ	hit pity
jou*e*r *été*	e	set tent
l*ai*t jou*et* m*e*rci	ɛ	
pl*a*t *a*mour	a æ	bat apple
b*a*s p*â*te	ɑ ɑː	after car calm
	ʌ	fun cousin
l*e* pr*e*mier	ə	over above
b*eu*rre p*eu*r	œ	
p*eu* d*eu*x	ø ɜː	urn fern work
*o*r h*o*mme	ɒ	wash pot
m*o*t *eau* g*au*che	o ɔː	born cork
gen*ou* r*ou*e	u ʊ	full soot
	uː	boon lewd
r*ue* *u*rne	y	

Diphtongues		*Diphthongs*
	ɪə	beer tier
	ɛə	tear fair there
	eɪ	date plaice day
	aɪ	life buy cry
	aʊ	owl foul now
	əʊ	low no
	ɔɪ	boil boy oily
	ʊə	poor tour

Nasales		*Nasal Vowels*
mat*in* pl*ein*	ɛ̃	
br*un*	œ̃	
s*ang* *an* d*ans*	ɑ̃	
n*on* p*on*t	ɔ̃	
	ix	

—— *Dictionary* ——

FRANÇAIS - ANGLAIS
FRENCH - ENGLISH

A a

A *abr* = **autoroute**

a *vb voir* **avoir**

┌─────────────── *MOT CLÉ*

à [a] (*à* + *le* = **au**, *à* + *les* = **aux**) *prép* **1** (*endroit, situation*) at, in; **être ~ Paris/au Portugal** to be in Paris/Portugal; **être ~ la maison/~ l'école** to be at home/at school; **~ la campagne** in the country; **c'est ~ 10 km/~ 20 minutes (d'ici)** it's 10 km/20 minutes away

2 (*direction*) to; **aller ~ Paris/au Portugal** to go to Paris/Portugal; **aller ~ la maison/~ l'école** to go home/to school; **~ la campagne** to the country

3 (*temps*): **~ 3 heures/minuit** at 3 o'clock/midnight; **au printemps/mois de juin** in the spring/the month of June

4 (*attribution, appartenance*) to; **le livre est ~ Paul/~ lui/~ nous** this book is Paul's/his/ours; **donner qch ~ qn** to give sth to sb

5 (*moyen*) with; **se chauffer au gaz** to have gas heating; **~ bicyclette** on *ou* by bicycle; **~ la main/machine** by hand/machine

6 (*provenance*) from; **boire ~ la bouteille** to drink from the bottle

7 (*caractérisation, manière*): **l'homme aux yeux bleus** the man with the blue eyes; **~ la russe** the Russian way

8 (*but, destination*): **tasse ~ café** coffee cup; **maison ~ vendre** house for sale

9 (*rapport, évaluation, distribution*): **100 km/unités ~ l'heure** 100 km/units per *ou* an hour; **payé ~ l'heure** paid by the hour; **cinq ~ six** five to six

└───────────────

abaisser [abese] *vt* to lower, bring down; (*manette*) to pull down; (*fig*) to debase; to humiliate; **s'~** *vi* to go down; (*fig*) to demean o.s.

abandon [abɑ̃dɔ̃] *nm* abandoning; giving up; withdrawal; **être à l'~** to be in a state of neglect

abandonner [abɑ̃dɔne] *vt* (*personne*) to abandon; (*projet, activité*) to abandon, give up; (*SPORT*) to retire *ou* withdraw from; (*céder*) to surrender; **s'~** *vi* to let o.s. go; **s'~ à** (*paresse, plaisirs*) to give o.s. up to

abasourdir [abazuʀdiʀ] *vt* to stun, stagger

abat-jour [abaʒuʀ] *nm inv* lampshade

abats [aba] *nmpl* (*de bœuf, porc*) offal *sg*; (*de volaille*) giblets

abattement [abatmɑ̃] *nm* (*déduction*) reduction; **~ fiscal** ≈ tax allowance

abattoir [abatwaʀ] *nm* slaughterhouse

abattre [abatʀ(ə)] *vt* (*arbre*) to cut down, fell; (*mur, maison*) to pull down; (*avion, personne*) to shoot down; (*animal*) to shoot, kill; (*fig*) to wear out, tire out; to demoralize; **s'~** *vi* to crash down; **s'~ sur** to beat down on; to rain down on

abbaye [abei] *nf* abbey

abbé [abe] *nm* priest; (*d'une abbaye*) abbot

abcès [apsɛ] *nm* abscess

abdiquer [abdike] *vi* to abdicate ♦ *vt* to renounce, give up

abeille [abɛj] *nf* bee

aberrant, e [abɛʀɑ̃, -ɑ̃t] *adj* absurd

abêtir [abetiʀ] *vt* to make morons of (*ou* a moron of)

abîme [abim] *nm* abyss, gulf

abîmer [abime] *vt* to spoil, damage; **s'~** *vi* to get spoilt *ou* damaged

ablation [ablɑsjɔ̃] *nf* removal

abois [abwa] *nmpl*: **aux ~** at bay

abolir [abɔliʀ] *vt* to abolish

abondance [abɔ̃dɑ̃s] *nf* abundance; (*richesse*) affluence

abondant, e [abɔ̃dɑ̃, -ɑ̃t] *adj* plentiful, abundant, copious

abonder [abɔ̃de] *vi* to abound, be plentiful; **~ dans le sens de qn** to concur with sb

abonné, e [abɔne] *nm/f* subscriber; season ticket holder

abonnement [abɔnmɑ̃] *nm* subscription; *(transports, concerts)* season ticket

abonner [abɔne] *vt*: **s'~ à** to subscribe to, take out a subscription to

abord [abɔR] *nm*: **être d'un ~ facile** to be approachable; **~s** *nmpl (environs)* surroundings; **au premier ~** at first sight, initially; **d'~** first

abordable [abɔRdabl(ə)] *adj* approachable; reasonably priced

aborder [abɔRde] *vi* to land ♦ *vt (sujet, difficulté)* to tackle; *(personne)* to approach; *(rivage etc)* to reach; *(NAVIG: attaquer)* to board

aboutir [abutiR] *vi (négociations etc)* to succeed; **~ à/dans/sur** to end up at/in/on

aboyer [abwaje] *vi* to bark

abrégé [abReʒe] *nm* summary

abréger [abReʒe] *vt* to shorten

abreuver [abRœve] *vt (fig)*: **~ qn de** to shower *ou* swamp sb with; **s'~** *vi* to drink; **abreuvoir** *nm* watering place

abréviation [abRevjasjɔ̃] *nf* abbreviation

abri [abRi] *nm* shelter; **à l'~** under cover; **à l'~ de** sheltered from; *(fig)* safe from

abricot [abRiko] *nm* apricot

abriter [abRite] *vt* to shelter; *(loger)* to accommodate; **s'~** *vt* to shelter, take cover

abroger [abRɔʒe] *vt* to repeal

abrupt, e [abRypt] *adj* sheer, steep; *(ton)* abrupt

abrutir [abRytiR] *vt* to daze; to exhaust; to stupefy

absence [apsɑ̃s] *nf* absence; *(MÉD)* blackout; mental blank

absent, e [apsɑ̃, -ɑ̃t] *adj* absent; *(distrait: air)* vacant, faraway ♦ *nm/f* absentee; **s'~er** *vi* to take time off work; *(sortir)* to leave, go out

absolu, e [apsɔly] *adj* absolute; *(caractère)* rigid, uncompromising; **absolument** *adv* absolutely

absorber [apsɔRbe] *vt* to absorb; *(gén MÉD: manger, boire)* to take

absoudre [apsudR(ə)] *vt* to absolve

abstenir [apstəniR] : **s'~** *vi (POL)* to abstain; **s'~ de qch/de faire** to refrain from sth/from doing

abstraction [apstRaksjɔ̃] *nf* abstraction; **faire ~ de** to set *ou* leave aside

abstrait, e [apstRɛ, -ɛt] *adj* abstract

absurde [apsyRd(ə)] *adj* absurd

abus [aby] *nm* abuse; **~ de confiance** breach of trust

abuser [abyze] *vi* to go too far, overstep the mark ♦ *vt* to deceive, mislead; **s'~** *vi* to be mistaken; **~ de** to misuse; *(violer, duper)* to take advantage of; **abusif, ive** *adj* exorbitant; excessive; improper

acabit [akabi] *nm*: **de cet ~** of that type

académie [akademi] *nf* academy; *(ART: nu)* nude; *(SCOL: circonscription)* ≈ regional education authority

acajou [akaʒu] *nm* mahogany

acariâtre [akaRjɑtR(ə)] *adj* cantankerous

accablant, e [akablɑ̃, -ɑ̃t] *adj (témoignage, preuve)* overwhelming

accablement [akabləmɑ̃] *nm* despondency

accabler [akable] *vt* to overwhelm, overcome; *(suj: témoignage)* to condemn, damn; **~ qn d'injures** to heap *ou* shower abuse on sb

accalmie [akalmi] *nf* lull

accaparer [akapaRe] *vt* to monopolize; *(suj: travail etc)* to take up (all) the time *ou* attention of

accéder [aksede]: **~ à** *vt (lieu)* to reach; *(fig)* to accede to, attain; *(accorder: requête)* to grant, accede to

accélérateur [akseleRatœR] *nm* accelerator

accélération [akseleRasjɔ̃] *nf* acceleration

accélérer [akseleRe] *vt* to speed up ♦ *vi* to accelerate

accent [aksɑ̃] *nm* accent; *(inflexions expressives)* tone (of voice); *(PHONÉTIQUE, fig)* stress; **mettre l'~ sur** *(fig)* to stress; **~ aigu/grave** acute/grave accent

accentuer [aksɑ̃tɥe] *vt (LING)* to accent; *(fig)* to accentuate, emphasize; **s'~** *vi* to become more marked *ou* pronounced

acceptation [akseptasjɔ̃] *nf* acceptance

accepter [aksɛpte] *vt* to accept; *(tolérer)*: **~ que qn fasse** to agree to sb doing; **~ de faire** to agree to do

accès [aksɛ] *nm (à un lieu)* access; *(MÉD)* attack; fit, bout; outbreak ♦ *nmpl (routes etc)* means of access, approaches; **d'~ facile** easily accessible; **~ de colère** fit of anger

accessible [aksesibl(ə)] *adj* accessible; *(livre, sujet)*: **~ à qn** within the reach of sb; *(sensible)*: **~ à** open to

accessoire [akseswaR] *adj* secondary; incidental ♦ *nm* accessory; *(THÉÂTRE)* prop

accident [aksidɑ̃] *nm* accident; **par ~** by chance; **~ de la route** road accident; **~ du travail** industrial injury *ou* accident; **~é, e** *adj* damaged; injured; *(relief, terrain)* uneven; hilly

acclamer [aklame] *vt* to cheer, acclaim

accolade [akɔlad] *nf (amicale)* embrace; *(signe)* brace

accommodant, e [akɔmɔdɑ̃, -ɑ̃t] *adj* accommodating; easy-going

accommoder [akɔmɔde] *vt (CULIN)* to prepare; *(points de vue)* to reconcile; **s'~ de** *vt* to put up with; to make do with

accompagnateur, trice [akɔ̃paɲatœR, -tRis] *nm/f (MUS)* accompanist; *(de voyage: guide)* guide; *(: d'enfants)* accompanying adult; *(de voyage organisé)* courier

accompagner [akɔ̃paɲe] *vt* to accompany,

be *ou* go *ou* come with; (*MUS*) to accompany

accompli, e [akɔpli] *adj* accomplished

accomplir [akɔpliʀ] *vt* (*tâche, projet*) to carry out; (*souhait*) to fulfil; **s'~** *vi* to be fulfilled

accord [akɔʀ] *nm* agreement; (*entre des styles, tons etc*) harmony; (*MUS*) chord; **d'~!** OK!; **se mettre d'~** to come to an agreement; **être d'~** to agree

accordéon [akɔʀdeɔ̃] *nm* (*MUS*) accordion

accorder [akɔʀde] *vt* (*faveur, délai*) to grant; (*harmoniser*) to match; (*MUS*) to tune; **s'~** *vi* to get on together; to agree

accoster [akɔste] *vt* (*NAVIG*) to draw alongside ♦ *vi* to berth

accotement [akɔtmɑ̃] *nm* verge (*BRIT*), shoulder

accouchement [akuʃmɑ̃] *nm* delivery, (child)birth; labour

accoucher [akuʃe] *vi* to give birth, have a baby; (*être en travail*) to be in labour ♦ *vt* to deliver; ~ **d'un garçon** to give birth to a boy

accouder [akude]: **s'~** *vi* to rest one's elbows on/against; **accoudoir** *nm* armrest

accoupler [akuple] *vt* to couple; (*pour la reproduction*) to mate; **s'~** *vt* to mate

accourir [akuʀiʀ] *vi* to rush *ou* run up

accoutrement [akutʀəmɑ̃] (*péj*) *nm* (*tenue*) outfit

accoutumance [akutymɑ̃s] *nf* (*gén*) adaptation; (*MÉD*) addiction

accoutumé, e [akutyme] *adj* (*habituel*) customary, usual

accoutumer [akutyme] *vt*: **s'~ à** to get accustomed *ou* used to

accréditer [akʀedite] *vt* (*nouvelle*) to substantiate

accroc [akʀo] *nm* (*déchirure*) tear; (*fig*) hitch, snag

accrochage [akʀɔʃaʒ] *nm* (*AUTO*) collision

accrocher [akʀɔʃe] *vt* (*suspendre*): ~ **qch à** to hang sth (up) on; (*attacher: remorque*): ~ **qch à** to hitch sth (up) to; (*heurter*) to catch; to catch on; to hit; (*déchirer*): ~ **qch (à)** to catch sth (on); (*MIL*) to engage; (*fig*) to catch, attract; **s'~** (*se disputer*) to have a clash *ou* brush; **s'~ à** (*rester pris à*) to catch on; (*agripper, fig*) to hang on *ou* cling to

accroître [akʀwatʀ(ə)] *vt* to increase; **s'~** *vi* to increase

accroupir [akʀupiʀ]: **s'~** *vi* to squat, crouch (down)

accru, e [akʀy] *pp de* **accroître**

accueil [akœj] *nm* welcome; **comité d'~** reception committee

accueillir [akœjiʀ] *vt* to welcome; (*loger*) to accommodate

acculer [akyle] *vt*: ~ **qn à** *ou* **contre** to drive sb back against

accumuler [akymyle] *vt* to accumulate, amass; **s'~** *vi* to accumulate; to pile up

accusation [akyzɑsjɔ̃] *nf* (*gén*) accusation; (*JUR*) charge; (*partie*): **l'~** the prosecution; **mettre en ~** to indict

accusé, e [akyze] *nm/f* accused; defendant; ~ **de réception** acknowledgement of receipt

accuser [akyze] *vt* to accuse; (*fig*) to emphasize, bring out; to show; ~ **qn de** to accuse sb of; (*JUR*) to charge sb with; ~ **qch de** (*rendre responsable*) to blame sth for; ~ **réception de** to acknowledge receipt of

acerbe [asɛʀb(ə)] *adj* caustic, acid

acéré, e [aseʀe] *adj* sharp

achalandé, e [aʃalɑ̃de] *adj*: **bien ~** well-stocked; well-patronized

acharné, e [aʃaʀne] *adj* (*lutte, adversaire*) fierce, bitter; (*travail*) relentless, unremitting

acharner [aʃaʀne]: **s'~** *vi* to go at fiercely; **s'~ contre** to set *ou* s. against; to dog; **s'~ à faire** to try doggedly to do; to persist in doing

achat [aʃa] *nm* buying *no pl*; purchase; **faire des ~s** to do some shopping

acheminer [aʃmine] *vt* (*courrier*) to forward, dispatch; (*troupes*) to convey, transport; (*train*) to route; **s'~ vers** to head for

acheter [aʃte] *vt* to buy, purchase; (*soudoyer*) to buy; ~ **qch à** (*marchand*) to buy *ou* purchase sth from; (*ami etc: offrir*) to buy sth for; **acheteur, euse** *nm/f* buyer; shopper; (*COMM*) buyer

achever [aʃve] *vt* to complete, finish; (*blessé*) to finish off; **s'~** *vi* to end

acide [asid] *adj* sour, sharp; (*CHIMIE*) acid(ic) ♦ *nm* acid

acier [asje] *nm* steel; **aciérie** *nf* steelworks *sg*

acné [akne] *nf* acne

acolyte [akɔlit] (*péj*) *nm* associate

acompte [akɔ̃t] *nm* deposit; (*versement régulier*) instalment; (*sur somme due*) payment on account

à-côté [akote] *nm* side-issue; (*argent*) extra

à-coup [aku] *nm* (*du moteur*) (hic)cough; (*fig*) jolt; **par ~s** by fits and starts

acoustique [akustik] *nf* (*d'une salle*) acoustics *pl*

acquéreur [akeʀœʀ] *nm* buyer, purchaser

acquérir [akeʀiʀ] *vt* to acquire

acquis, e [aki, -iz] *pp de* **acquérir** ♦ *nm* (accumulated) experience; **être ~ à** (*plan, idée*) to fully agree with; **son aide nous est ~e** we can count on her help

acquit [aki] *vb voir* **acquérir** ♦ *nm* (*quittance*) receipt; **par ~ de conscience** to set one's mind at rest

acquitter [akite] *vt* (*JUR*) to acquit; (*facture*) to pay, settle; **s'~ de** *vt* to discharge, fulfil

âcre [ɑkʀ(ə)] adj acrid, pungent

acrobate [akʀɔbat] nm/f acrobat

acte [akt(ə)] nm act, action; (THÉÂTRE) act; **~s** nmpl (compte-rendu) proceedings; **prendre ~ de** to note, take note of; **faire ~ de candidature** to apply; **faire ~ de présence** to put in an appearance; **~ de naissance** birth certificate

acteur [aktœʀ] nm actor

actif, ive [aktif, -iv] adj active ♦ nm (COMM) assets pl; (fig): **avoir à son ~** to have to one's credit; **population active** working population

action [aksjɔ̃] nf (gén) action; (COMM) share; **une bonne ~** a good deed; **~naire** nm/f shareholder; **~ner** vt to work; to activate; to operate

activer [aktive] vt to speed up; **s'~** vi to bustle about; to hurry up

activité [aktivite] nf activity

actrice [aktʀis] nf actress

actualiser [aktɥalize] vt to actualize; to bring up to date

actualité [aktɥalite] nf (d'un problème) topicality; (événements): **l'~** current events; **les ~s** nfpl (CINÉMA, TV) the news

actuel, le [aktɥɛl] adj (présent) present; (d'actualité) topical; **actuellement** adv at present; at the present time

acuité [akɥite] nf acuteness

adaptateur [adaptatœʀ] nm (ÉLEC) adapter

adapter [adapte] vt to adapt; **s'~** (à) (suj: personne) to adapt (to); **~ qch à** (approprier) to adapt sth to (fit); **~ qch sur/dans/à** (fixer) to fit sth on/into/to

additif [aditif] nm additive

addition [adisjɔ̃] nf addition; (au café) bill; **~ner** [adisjɔne] vt to add (up)

adepte [adɛpt(ə)] nm/f follower

adéquat, e [adekwa, -at] adj appropriate, suitable

adhérent, e [adeʀɑ̃, -ɑ̃t] nm/f (de club) member

adhérer [adeʀe] **~ à** vi (coller) to adhere ou stick to; (se rallier à) to join; to support; **adhésif, ive** adj adhesive, sticky ♦ nm adhesive; **adhésion** nf joining; membership; support

adieu, x [adjø] excl goodbye ♦ nm farewell; **dire ~ à qn** to say goodbye ou farewell to sb

adjectif [adʒɛktif] nm adjective

adjoindre [adʒwɛ̃dʀ(ə)] vt: **~ qch à** to attach sth to; to add sth to; **s'~** vt (collaborateur etc) to take on, appoint; **adjoint, e** nm/f assistant; **adjoint au maire** deputy mayor; **directeur adjoint** assistant manager

adjudant [adʒydɑ̃] nm (MIL) warrant officer

adjudication [adʒydikasjɔ̃] nf sale by auction; (pour travaux) invitation to tender (BRIT) ou bid (US)

adjuger [adʒyʒe] vt (prix, récompense) to award; (lors d'une vente) to auction (off); **s'~** vt to take for o.s.

adjurer [adʒyʀe] vt: **~ qn de faire** to implore ou beg sb to do

admettre [admɛtʀ(ə)] vt (laisser entrer) to admit; (candidat: SCOL) to pass; (tolérer) to allow, accept; (reconnaître) to admit, acknowledge

administrateur, trice [administʀatœʀ, -tʀis] nm/f (COMM) director; (ADMIN) administrator; **~ judiciaire** receiver

administration [administʀasjɔ̃] nf administration; **l'A~** ≈ the Civil Service

administrer [administʀe] vt (firme) to manage, run; (biens, remède, sacrement etc) to administer

admirable [admiʀabl(ə)] adj admirable, wonderful

admirateur, trice [admiʀatœʀ, -tʀis] nm/f admirer

admiration [admiʀasjɔ̃] nf admiration

admirer [admiʀe] vt to admire

admis, e pp de **admettre**

admissible [admisibl(ə)] adj (candidat) eligible; (comportement) admissible, acceptable

admission [admisjɔ̃] nf admission; acknowledgement; **demande d'~** application for membership

adolescence [adɔlesɑ̃s] nf adolescence

adolescent, e [adɔlesɑ̃, -ɑ̃t] nm/f adolescent, teenager

adonner [adɔne]: **s'~ à** vt (sport) to devote o.s. to; (boisson) to give o.s. over to

adopter [adɔpte] vt to adopt; (projet de loi etc) to pass; **adoptif, ive** adj (parents) adoptive; (fils, patrie) adopted

adorer [adɔʀe] vt to adore; (REL) to worship

adosser [adose] vt: **~ qch à ou contre** to stand sth against; **s'~ à ou contre** to lean with one's back against

adoucir [adusiʀ] vt (goût, température) to make milder; (avec du sucre) to sweeten; (peau, voix) to soften; (caractère) to mellow

adresse [adʀɛs] nf (voir adroit) skill, dexterity; (domicile) address; **à l'~ de** (pour) for the benefit of

adresser [adʀese] vt (lettre: expédier) to send; (: écrire l'adresse sur) to address; (injure, compliments) to address; **s'~ à** (parler à) to speak to, address; (s'informer auprès de) to go and see; (: bureau) to enquire at; (suj: livre, conseil) to be aimed at; **~ la parole à** to speak to, address

adroit, e [adʀwa, -wat] adj skilful, skilled

adulte [adylt(ə)] nm/f adult, grown-up ♦ adj (chien, arbre) fully-grown, mature; (attitude) adult, grown-up

adultère [adyltɛʀ] nm (acte) adultery

advenir [advəniʀ] vi to happen

adverbe [advɛʀb(ə)] nm adverb

adversaire [advɛʀsɛʀ] *nm/f* (*SPORT*, *gén*) opponent, adversary; (*MIL*) adversary, enemy

adverse [advɛʀs(ə)] *adj* opposing

aération [aeʀɑsjɔ̃] *nf* airing; ventilation

aérer [aeʀe] *vt* to air; (*fig*) to lighten

aérien, ne [aeʀjɛ̃, -jɛn] *adj* (*AVIAT*) air *cpd*, aerial; (*câble*, *métro*) overhead; (*fig*) light

aéro... [aeʀɔ] *préfixe*: ~**bic** *nm* aerobics *sg*; ~**gare** *nf* airport (buildings); (*en ville*) air terminal; ~**glisseur** *nm* hovercraft; ~**naval, e** *adj* air and sea *cpd*; ~**phagie** [aeʀɔfaʒi] *nf* (*MÉD*) wind, aerophagia (*TECH*); ~**port** *nm* airport; ~**porté, e** *adj* airborne, airlifted; ~**sol** *nm* aerosol

affable [afabl(ə)] *adj* affable

affaiblir [afebliʀ] *vt* to weaken; **s'~** *vi* to weaken

affaire [afɛʀ] *nf* (*problème*, *question*) matter; (*criminelle*, *judiciaire*) case; (*scandaleuse etc*) affair; (*entreprise*) business; (*marché*, *transaction*) deal; business *no pl*; (*occasion intéressante*) bargain; ~**s** *nfpl* (*intérêts publics et privés*) affairs; (*activité commerciale*) business *sg*; (*effets personnels*) things, belongings; **ce sont mes ~s** (*cela me concerne*) that's my business; **ceci fera l'~** this will do (nicely); **avoir ~ à** to be faced with; to be dealing with; **les A~s étrangères** Foreign Affairs; **affairer: s'affairer** *vi* to busy o.s., bustle about

affaisser [afese]: **s'~** *vi* (*terrain*, *immeuble*) to subside, sink; (*personne*) to collapse

affaler [afale]: **s'~** *vi*: **s'~ dans/sur** to collapse *ou* slump into/onto

affamé, e [afame] *adj* starving

affecter [afɛkte] *vt* to affect; (*telle ou telle forme etc*) to take on; ~ **qch à** to allocate *ou* allot sth to; ~ **qn à** to appoint sb to; (*diplomate*) to post sb to

affectif, ive [afɛktif, -iv] *adj* emotional

affection [afɛksjɔ̃] *nf* affection; (*mal*) ailment; ~**ner** *vt* to be fond of

affectueux, euse [afɛktɥø, -øz] *adj* affectionate

afférent, e [afeʀɑ̃, -ɑ̃t] *adj*: ~ **à** pertaining *ou* relating to

affermir [afɛʀmiʀ] *vt* to consolidate, strengthen

affichage [afiʃaʒ] *nm* billposting; (*électronique*) display

affiche [afiʃ] *nf* poster; (*officielle*) notice; (*THÉÂTRE*) bill; **tenir l'~** to run

afficher [afiʃe] *vt* (*affiche*) to put up; (*réunion*) to put up a notice about; (*électroniquement*) to display; (*fig*) to exhibit, display

affilée [afile]: **d'~** *adv* at a stretch

affiler [afile] *vt* to sharpen

affilier [afilje]: **s'~ à** *vt* (*club*, *société*) to join

affiner [afine] *vt* to refine

affirmatif, ive [afiʀmatif, -iv] *adj* affirmative

affirmation [afiʀmɑsjɔ̃] *nf* assertion

affirmer [afiʀme] *vt* (*prétendre*) to maintain, assert; (*autorité etc*) to assert

affligé, e [afliʒe] *adj* distressed, grieved; ~ **de** (*maladie*, *tare*) afflicted with

affliger [afliʒe] *vt* (*peiner*) to distress, grieve

affluence [aflyɑ̃s] *nf* crowds *pl*; **heures d'~** rush hours; **jours d'~** busiest days

affluent [aflyɑ̃] *nm* tributary

affluer [aflye] *vi* (*secours*, *biens*) to flood in, pour in; (*sang*) to rush, flow

affolement [afɔlmɑ̃] *nm* panic

affoler [afɔle] *vt* to throw into a panic; **s'~** *vi* to panic

affranchir [afʀɑ̃ʃiʀ] *vt* to put a stamp *ou* stamps on; (*à la machine*) to frank (*BRIT*), meter (*US*); (*fig*) to free, liberate; **affranchissement** *nm* postage

affréter [afʀete] *vt* to charter

affreux, euse [afʀø, -øz] *adj* dreadful, awful

affront [afʀɔ̃] *nm* affront

affrontement [afʀɔ̃tmɑ̃] *nm* clash, confrontation

affronter [afʀɔ̃te] *vt* to confront, face

affubler [afyble] (*péj*) *vt*: ~ **qn de** to rig *ou* deck sb out in; (*surnom*) to attach to sb

affût [afy] *nm*: **à l'~ (de)** (*gibier*) lying in wait (for); (*fig*) on the look-out (for)

affûter [afyte] *vt* to sharpen, grind

afin [afɛ̃]: ~ **que** *conj* so that, in order that; ~ **de faire** in order to do, so as to do

africain, e [afʀikɛ̃, -ɛn] *adj*, *nm/f* African

Afrique [afʀik] *nf*: **l'~** Africa; **l'~ du Sud** South Africa

agacer [agase] *vt* to pester, tease; (*involontairement*) to irritate

âge [ɑʒ] *nm* age; **quel ~ as-tu?** how old are you?; **prendre de l'~** to be getting on (in years); **l'~ ingrat** the awkward age; **l'~ mûr** maturity; **âgé, e** *adj* old, elderly; **âgé de 10 ans** 10 years old

agence [aʒɑ̃s] *nf* agency, office; (*succursale*) branch; ~ **de voyages** travel agency; ~ **immobilière** estate (*BRIT*) *ou* real estate (*US*) agent's (office); ~ **matrimoniale** marriage bureau

agencer [aʒɑ̃se] *vt* to put together; to arrange, lay out

agenda [aʒɛ̃da] *nm* diary

agenouiller [aʒnuje]: **s'~** *vi* to kneel (down)

agent [aʒɑ̃] *nm* (*aussi*: ~ **de police**) policeman; (*ADMIN*) official, officer; (*fig*: *élément*, *facteur*) agent; ~ **d'assurances** insurance broker; ~ **de change** stockbroker

agglomération [aglɔmeʀɑsjɔ̃] *nf* town; built-up area; **l'~ parisienne** the urban area of Paris

aggloméré [aglɔmeʀe] *nm* (*bois*) chipboard; (*pierre*) conglomerate

agglomérer [aglɔmeʀe] vt to pile up; (TECH: bois, pierre) to compress

aggraver [agʀave] vt to worsen, aggravate; (JUR: peine) to increase; **s'~** vi to worsen

agile [aʒil] adj agile, nimble

agir [aʒiʀ] vi to act; **il s'agit de** it's a matter ou question of; it is about; (il importe que): **il s'agit de faire** we (ou you etc) must do

agitation [aʒitɑsjɔ̃] nf (hustle and) bustle; agitation, excitement; (politique) unrest, agitation

agité, e [aʒite] adj fidgety, restless; agitated, perturbed; (mer) rough

agiter [aʒite] vt (bouteille, chiffon) to shake; (bras, mains) to wave; (préoccuper, exciter) to perturb

agneau, x [aɲo] nm lamb

agonie [agɔni] nf mortal agony, death pangs pl; (fig) death throes pl

agrafe [agʀaf] nf (de vêtement) hook, fastener; (de bureau) staple; **agrafer** vt to fasten, to staple; **agrafeuse** nf stapler

agraire [agʀɛʀ] adj land cpd

agrandir [agʀɑ̃diʀ] vt to enlarge; (magasin, domaine) to extend, enlarge; **s'~** vi to be extended; to be enlarged; **agrandissement** nm (PHOTO) enlargement

agréable [agʀeabl(ə)] adj pleasant, nice

agréé, e [agʀee] adj: **concessionnaire ~** registered dealer

agréer [agʀee] vt (requête) to accept; **~ à** to please, suit; **veuillez ~ ...** (formule épistolaire) yours faithfully

agrégation [agʀegɑsjɔ̃] nf highest teaching diploma in France; **agrégé, e** nm/f holder of the agrégation

agrément [agʀemɑ̃] nm (accord) consent, approval; (attraits) charm, attractiveness; (plaisir) pleasure

agrémenter [agʀemɑ̃te] vt to embellish, adorn

agresser [agʀese] vt to attack

agresseur [agʀesœʀ] nm aggressor, attacker; (POL, MIL) aggressor

agressif, ive [agʀesif, -iv] adj aggressive

agricole [agʀikɔl] adj agricultural

agriculteur [agʀikyltœʀ] nm farmer

agriculture [agʀikyltyʀ] nf agriculture; farming

agripper [agʀipe] vt to grab, clutch; (pour arracher) to snatch, grab; **s'~ à** to cling (on) to, clutch, grip

agrumes [agʀym] nmpl citrus fruit(s)

aguerrir [ageʀiʀ] vt to harden

aguets [agɛ] nmpl: **être aux ~** to be on the look out

aguicher [agiʃe] vt to entice

ahuri, e [ayʀi] adj (stupéfait) flabbergasted; (idiot) dim-witted

ai vb voir **avoir**

aide [ɛd] nm/f assistant; carer ♦ nf assistance, help; (secours financier) aid; **à l'~ de** (avec) with the help ou aid of; **appeler (qn) à l'~** to call for help (from sb); **~ judiciaire** nf legal aid; **~ sociale** nf (assistance) state aid; **~-mémoire** nm inv memoranda pages pl; (key facts) handbook; **~-soignant, e** nm/f auxiliary nurse

aider [ede] vt to help; **s'~ de** (se servir de) to use, make use of; **~ à qch** (faciliter) to help (towards) sth

aie etc vb voir **avoir**

aïe [aj] excl ouch

aïeul, e [ajœl] nm/f grandparent, grandfather(mother); forebear

aïeux [ajø] nmpl grandparents; forebears, forefathers

aigle [ɛgl(ə)] nm eagle

aigre [ɛgʀ(ə)] adj sour, sharp; (fig) sharp, cutting; **aigreur** nf sourness; sharpness; **aigreurs d'estomac** heartburn sg; **aigrir** vt (personne) to embitter; (caractère) to sour

aigu, ë [egy] adj (objet, arête, douleur, intelligence) sharp; (son, voix) high-pitched, shrill; (note) high (-pitched)

aiguille [eguij] nf needle; (de montre) hand; **~ à tricoter** knitting needle

aiguiller [eguije] vt (orienter) to direct

aiguilleur du ciel [eguijœʀ] nm air-traffic controller

aiguillon [eguijɔ̃] nm (d'abeille) sting; **~ner** vt to spur ou goad on

aiguiser [egize] vt to sharpen; (fig) to stimulate; to excite

ail [aj] nm garlic

aile [ɛl] nf wing; **aileron** nm (de requin) fin; **ailier** nm winger

aille etc vb voir **aller**

ailleurs [ajœʀ] adv elsewhere, somewhere else; **partout/nulle part ~** everywhere/nowhere else; **d'~** (du reste) moreover, besides; **par ~** (d'autre part) moreover, furthermore

aimable [ɛmabl(ə)] adj kind, nice

aimant [ɛmɑ̃] nm magnet

aimer [eme] vt to love; (d'amitié, affection, par goût) to like; (souhait): **j'~ais ...** I would like ...; **bien ~ qn/qch** to like sb/sth; **j'aime mieux** ou **autant vous dire que** I may as well tell you that; **j'~ais autant y aller maintenant** I'd rather go now; **j'~ais mieux faire** I'd much rather do

aine [ɛn] nf groin

aîné, e [ene] adj elder, older; (le plus âgé) eldest, oldest ♦ nm/f oldest child ou one, oldest boy ou son/girl ou daughter; **aînesse** nf: **droit d'aînesse** birthright

ainsi [ɛ̃si] adv (de cette façon) like this, in this way, thus; (ce faisant) thus ♦ conj thus, so; **~ que** (comme) (just) as; (et aussi) as well as; **pour ~ dire** so to speak; **et ~ de suite** and so on

air [ɛʀ] nm air; (mélodie) tune; (expression) look, air; **prendre l'~** to get some (fresh) air; (*avion*) to take off; **avoir l'~** (*sembler*) to look, appear; **avoir l'~ de** to look like; **avoir l'~ de faire** to look as though one is doing, appear to be doing

aire [ɛʀ] *nf* (*zone, fig, MATH*) area

aisance [ɛzɑ̃s] *nf* ease; (*richesse*) affluence

aise [ɛz] *nf* comfort ♦ *adj*: **être bien ~ que** to be delighted that; **être à l'~** *ou* **à son ~** to be comfortable; (*pas embarrassé*) to be at ease; (*financièrement*) to be comfortably off; **se mettre à l'~** to make o.s. comfortable; **être mal à l'~** *ou* **à son ~** to be uncomfortable; to be ill at ease; **en faire à son ~** to do as one likes; **aisé, e** *adj* easy; (*assez riche*) well-to-do, well-off

aisselle [ɛsɛl] *nf* armpit

ait *vb voir* **avoir**

ajonc [aʒɔ̃] *nm* gorse *no pl*

ajourner [aʒuʀne] *vt* (*réunion*) to adjourn; (*décision*) to defer, postpone

ajouter [aʒute] *vt* to add; **~ foi à** to lend *ou* give credence to

ajusté, e [aʒyste] *adj*: **bien ~** (*robe etc*) close-fitting

ajuster [aʒyste] *vt* (*régler*) to adjust; (*vêtement*) to alter; (*coup de fusil*) to aim; (*cible*) to aim at; (*TECH, gén: adapter*): **~ qch à** to fit sth to

alarme [alaʀm(ə)] *nf* alarm; **donner l'~** to give *ou* raise the alarm; **alarmer** *vt* to alarm; **s'~r** *vi* to become alarmed

album [albɔm] *nm* album

albumine [albymin] *nf* albumin; **avoir** *ou* **faire de l'~** to suffer from albuminuria

alcool [alkɔl] *nm* ~ alcohol; **un ~** a spirit, a brandy; **~ à brûler** methylated spirits (*BRIT*), wood alcohol (*US*); **~ à 90°** surgical spirit; **~ique** *adj, nm/f* alcoholic; **~isé, e** *adj* alcoholic; **~isme** *nm* alcoholism

alco(o)test (®) [alkɔtɛst] *nm* Breathalyser (®); (*test*) breath-test

aléas [alea] *nmpl* hazards; **aléatoire** *adj* uncertain; (*INFORM*) random

alentour [alɑ̃tuʀ] *adv* around (about); **~s** *nmpl* (*environs*) surroundings; **aux ~s de** in the vicinity *ou* neighbourhood of, around about; (*temps*) around about

alerte [alɛʀt(ə)] *adj* agile, nimble; brisk, lively ♦ *nf* alert; warning; **alerter** *vt* to alert

algèbre [alʒɛbʀ(ə)] *nf* algebra

Alger [alʒe] *n* Algiers

Algérie [alʒeʀi] *nf*: **l'~** Algeria; **algérien, ne** *adj, nm/f* Algerian

algue [alg(ə)] *nf* (*gén*) seaweed *no pl*; (*BOT*) alga

alibi [alibi] *nm* alibi

aliéné, e [aljene] *nm/f* insane person, lunatic (*péj*)

aligner [aline] *vt* to align, line up; (*idées, chiffres*) to string together; (*adapter*): **~ qch sur** to bring sth into alignment with; **s'~** (*soldats etc*) to line up; **s'~ sur** (*POL*) to

align o.s. on

aliment [alimɑ̃] *nm* food

alimentation [alimɑ̃tasjɔ̃] *nf* feeding; supplying; (*commerce*) food trade; (*produits*) groceries *pl*; (*régime*) diet; (*INFORM*) feed

alimenter [alimɑ̃te] *vt* to feed; (*TECH*): **~ (en)** to supply (with); to feed (with); (*fig*) to sustain, keep going

alinéa [alinea] *nm* paragraph

aliter [alite]: **s'~** *vi* to take to one's bed

allaiter [alɛte] *vt* to (breast-)feed, nurse; (*suj: animal*) to suckle

allant [alɑ̃] *nm* drive, go

allécher [aleʃe] *vt*: **~ qn** to make sb's mouth water; to tempt *ou* entice sb

allée [ale] *nf* (*de jardin*) path; (*en ville*) avenue, drive; **~s et venues** comings and goings

alléger [aleʒe] *vt* (*voiture*) to make lighter; (*chargement*) to lighten; (*souffrance*) to alleviate, soothe

allègre [alɛgʀ(ə)] *adj* lively, cheerful

alléguer [alege] *vt* to put forward (as proof *ou* an excuse)

Allemagne [aləmaɲ] *nf*: **l'~** Germany; **allemand, e** *adj, nm/f* German ♦ *nm* (*LING*) German

aller [ale] *nm* (*trajet*) outward journey; (*billet: aussi: ~ simple*) single (*BRIT*) *ou* oneway (*US*) ticket ♦ *vi* (*gén*) to go; **~ à** (*convenir*) to suit; (*suj: forme, pointure etc*) to fit; **~ avec** (*couleurs, style etc*) to go (well) with; **je vais y ~/me fâcher** I'm going to go/to get angry; **~ voir** to go and see, go to see; **allez!** come on!; **allons!** come now!; **comment allez-vous?** how are you?; **comment ça va?** how are you?; (*affaires etc*) how are things?; **il va bien/mal** he's well/not well, he's fine/ill; **ça va bien/mal** (*affaires etc*) it's going well/not going well; **~ mieux** to be better; **cela va sans dire** that goes without saying; **il y va de leur vie** their lives are at stake; **s'en ~** (*partir*) to be off, go, leave; (*disparaître*) to go away; **~ (et) retour** return journey (*BRIT*), round trip; (*billet*) return (ticket) (*BRIT*), round trip ticket (*US*)

allergique [alɛʀʒik] *adj*: **~ à** allergic to

alliage [aljaʒ] *nm* alloy

alliance [aljɑ̃s] *nf* (*MIL, POL*) alliance; (*mariage*) marriage; (*bague*) wedding ring

allier [alje] *vt* (*métaux*) to alloy; (*POL, gén*) to ally; (*fig*) to combine; **s'~** to become allies; to combine

allô [alo] *excl* hullo, hallo

allocation [alɔkasjɔ̃] *nf* allowance; **~ (de) chômage** unemployment benefit; **~ (de) logement** rent allowance; **~s familiales** ≈ child benefit

allocution [alɔkysjɔ̃] *nf* short speech

allonger [alɔ̃ʒe] *vt* to lengthen, make longer; (*étendre: bras, jambe*) to stretch (out);

s'~ *vi* to get longer; (*se coucher*) to lie down, stretch out; **~ le pas** to hasten one's step(s)

allouer [alwe] *vt* to allocate, allot

allumage [alymaʒ] *nm* (*AUTO*) ignition

allume-cigare [alymsigaʀ] *nm inv* cigar lighter

allumer [alyme] *vt* (*lampe, phare, radio*) to put *ou* switch on; (*pièce*) to put *ou* switch the light(s) on in; (*feu*) to light; **s'~** *vi* (*lumière, lampe*) to come *ou* go on

allumette [alymet] *nf* match

allure [alyʀ] *nf* (*vitesse*) speed, pace; (*démarche*) walk; (*maintien*) bearing; (*aspect, air*) look; **avoir de l'~** to have style; **à toute ~** at top speed

allusion [alyzjɔ̃] *nf* allusion; (*sous-entendu*) hint; **faire ~ à** to allude *ou* refer to; to hint at

aloi [alwa] *nm*: **de bon ~** of genuine worth *ou* quality

―――――――――― *MOT CLÉ* ――――――――――

alors [alɔʀ] *adv* **1** (*à ce moment-là*) then, at that time; **il habitait ~ à Paris** he lived in Paris at that time

2 (*par conséquent*) then; **tu as fini? ~ je m'en vais** have you finished? I'm going then; **et ~?** so what?

~ que *conj* **1** (*au moment où*) when, as; **il est arrivé alors que je partais** he arrived as I was leaving

2 (*pendant que*) while, when; **~ qu'il était à Paris, il a visité ...** while *ou* when he was in Paris, he visited ...

3 (*tandis que*) whereas, while; **~ que son frère travaillait dur, lui se reposait** while his brother was working hard, HE would rest

―――――――――――――――――――――――――――

alouette [alwɛt] *nf* (sky)lark

alourdir [aluʀdiʀ] *vt* to weigh down, make heavy

alpage [alpaʒ] *nm* pasture

Alpes [alp(ə)] *nfpl*: **les ~** the Alps

alphabet [alfabe] *nm* alphabet; (*livre*) ABC (book); **alphabétiser** *vt* to teach to read and write; to eliminate illiteracy in

alpinisme [alpinism(ə)] *nm* mountaineering, climbing; **alpiniste** *nm/f* mountaineer, climber

Alsace [alzas] *nf* Alsace; **alsacien, ne** *adj, nm/f* Alsatian

altercation [alteʀkɑsjɑ̃] *nf* altercation

altérer [alteʀe] *vt* to falsify; to distort; to debase; to impair

alternateur [alteʀnatœʀ] *nm* alternator

alternatif, ive [alteʀnatif, -iv] *adj* alternating; **alternative** *nf* (*choix*) alternative; **alternativement** *adv* alternately

Altesse [altɛs] *nf* Highness

altitude [altityd] *nf* altitude, height

alto [alto] *nm* (*instrument*) viola

altruisme [altʀɥism(ə)] *nm* altruism

aluminium [alyminjɔm] *nm* aluminium (*BRIT*), aluminum (*US*)

amabilité [amabilite] *nf* kindness, amiability

amadouer [amadwe] *vt* to coax, cajole; to mollify, soothe

amaigrir [amegʀiʀ] *vt* to make thin(ner)

amalgame [amalgam] *nm* (*alliage pour les dents*) amalgam

amande [amɑ̃d] *nf* (*de l'amandier*) almond; (*de noyau de fruit*) kernel; **amandier** *nm* almond (tree)

amant [amɑ̃] *nm* lover

amarrer [amaʀe] *vt* (*NAVIG*) to moor; (*gén*) to make fast

amas [amɑ] *nm* heap, pile

amasser [amɑse] *vt* to amass

amateur [amatœʀ] *nm* amateur; **en ~** (*péj*) amateurishly; **~ de musique/sport** *etc* music/sport *etc* lover

amazone [amazon] *nf*: **en ~** sidesaddle

ambages [ɑ̃baʒ]: **sans ~** *adv* plainly

ambassade [ɑ̃basad] *nf* embassy; (*mission*): **en ~** on a mission; **ambassadeur, drice** *nm/f* ambassador(dress)

ambiance [ɑ̃bjɑ̃s] *nf* atmosphere

ambiant, e [ɑ̃bjɑ̃, -ɑ̃t] *adj* (*air, milieu*) surrounding; (*température*) ambient

ambigu, ë [ɑ̃bigy] *adj* ambiguous

ambitieux, euse [ɑ̃bisjø, -øz] *adj* ambitious

ambition [ɑ̃bisjɔ̃] *nf* ambition

ambulance [ɑ̃bylɑ̃s] *nf* ambulance; **ambulancier, ière** *nm/f* ambulance man(woman) (*BRIT*), paramedic (*US*)

ambulant, e [ɑ̃bylɑ̃, -ɑ̃t] *adj* travelling, itinerant

âme [ɑm] *nf* soul

améliorer [ameljɔʀe] *vt* to improve; **s'~** *vi* to improve, get better

aménagements [amenaʒmɑ̃] *nmpl* developments; **~ fiscaux** tax adjustments

aménager [amenaʒe] *vt* (*agencer, transformer*) to fit out; to lay out; (: *quartier, territoire*) to develop; (*installer*) to fix up, put in; **ferme aménagée** converted farmhouse

amende [amɑ̃d] *nf* fine; **mettre à l'~** to penalize; **faire ~ honorable** to make amends

amender [amɑ̃de] *vt* (*loi*) to amend; **s'~** *vi* to mend one's ways

amener [amne] *vt* to bring; (*causer*) to bring about; (*baisser: drapeau, voiles*) to strike; **s'~** *vi* to show up (*fam*), turn up

amenuiser [amənɥize]: **s'~** *vi* to grow slimmer, lessen; to dwindle

amer, amère [amɛʀ] *adj* bitter

américain, e [ameʀikɛ̃, -ɛn] *adj, nm/f* American

Amérique [ameʀik] *nf* America; **l'~**

centrale/latine Central/Latin America; l'~ **du Nord/du Sud** North/South America

amerrir [amerir] *vi* to land (on the sea)

amertume [amertym] *nf* bitterness

ameublement [amœbləmã] *nm* furnishing; *(meubles)* furniture

ameuter [amøte] *vt (badauds)* to draw a crowd of; *(peuple)* to rouse

ami, e [ami] *nm/f* friend; *(amant/maîtresse)* boyfriend/girlfriend ♦ *adj:* **pays/groupe** ~ friendly country/group; **être** ~ **de l'ordre** to be a lover of order; **un** ~ **des arts** a patron of the arts

amiable [amjabl(ə)]: **à l'**~ *adv (JUR)* out of court; *(gén)* amicably

amiante [amjãt] *nm* asbestos

amical, e, aux [amikal, -o] *adj* friendly; **amicale** *nf (club)* association; **amicalement** *adv* in a friendly way; *(formule épistolaire)* regards

amidon [amidɔ̃] *nm* starch

amincir [amɛ̃sir] *vt (objet)* to thin (down); **s'**~ *vi* to get thinner *ou* slimmer; ~ **qn** to make sb thinner *ou* slimmer

amincissant, e *adj:* **régime** ~ (slimming) diet; **crème** ~**e** slenderizing cream

amiral, aux [amiral, -o] *nm* admiral

amitié [amitje] *nf* friendship; **prendre en** ~ to befriend; **faire** *ou* **présenter ses** ~**s à qn** to send sb one's best wishes

ammoniac [amɔnjak] *nm:* **(gaz)** ~ ammonia

ammoniaque [amɔnjak] *nf* ammonia (water)

amoindrir [amwɛ̃drir] *vt* to reduce

amollir [amɔlir] *vt* to soften

amonceler [amɔ̃sle] *vt* to pile *ou* heap up; **s'**~ *vi* to pile *ou* heap up; *(fig)* to accumulate

amont [amɔ̃]: **en** ~ *adv* upstream; *(sur une pente)* uphill

amorce [amɔrs(ə)] *nf (sur un hameçon)* bait; *(explosif)* cap; primer; priming; *(fig: début)* beginning(s), start

amorphe [amɔrf(ə)] *adj* passive, lifeless

amortir [amɔrtir] *vt (atténuer: choc)* to absorb, cushion; *(bruit, douleur)* to deaden; *(COMM: dette)* to pay off; *(: mise de fonds, matériel)* to write off; ~ **un abonnement** to make a season ticket pay (for itself); **amortisseur** *nm* shock absorber

amour [amur] *nm* love; *(liaison)* love affair, love; **faire l'**~ to make love; **amouracher: s'amouracher de** *(péj) vt* to become infatuated with; **amoureux, euse** *adj (regard, tempérament)* amorous; *(vie, problèmes)* love *cpd; (personne):* **amoureux (de qn)** in love (with sb) ♦ *nmpl* courting couple(s); **amour-propre** *nm* self-esteem, pride

amovible [amɔvibl(ə)] *adj* removable, detachable

ampère [ɑ̃pɛr] *nm* amp(ere)

amphithéâtre [ɑ̃fiteatr(ə)] *nm* amphitheatre; *(d'université)* lecture hall *ou* theatre

ample [ɑ̃pl(ə)] *adj (vêtement)* roomy, ample; *(gestes, mouvement)* broad; *(ressources)* ample; **ampleur** *nf (importance)* scale, size; extent

amplificateur [ɑ̃plifikatœr] *nm* amplifier

amplifier [ɑ̃plifje] *vt (son, oscillation)* to amplify; *(fig)* to expand, increase

ampoule [ɑ̃pul] *nf (électrique)* bulb; *(de médicament)* phial; *(aux mains, pieds)* blister

ampoulé, e [ɑ̃pule] *(péj) adj* pompous, bombastic

amputer [ɑ̃pyte] *vt (MÉD)* to amputate; *(fig)* to cut *ou* reduce drastically

amusant, e [amyzɑ̃, -ɑ̃t] *adj (divertissant, spirituel)* entertaining, amusing; *(comique)* funny, amusing

amuse-gueule [amyzgœl] *nm inv* appetizer, snack

amusement [amyzmɑ̃] *nm* amusement; *(jeu etc)* pastime, diversion

amuser [amyze] *vt (divertir)* to entertain, amuse; *(égayer, faire rire)* to amuse; *(détourner l'attention de)* to distract; **s'**~ *vi (jouer)* to amuse o.s., play; *(se divertir)* to enjoy o.s., have fun; *(fig)* to mess around

amygdale [amidal] *nf* tonsil

an [ɑ̃] *nm* year; **le jour de l'**~, **le premier de l'**~, **le nouvel** ~ New Year's Day

analogique [analɔʒik] *adj* analogical; *(INFORM, montre)* analog

analogue [analɔg] *adj:* ~ **(à)** analogous (to), similar (to)

analphabète [analfabet] *nm/f* illiterate

analyse [analiz] *nf* analysis; *(MÉD)* test; **analyser** *vt* to analyse; to test

ananas [anana] *nm* pineapple

anarchie [anarʃi] *nf* anarchy

anathème [anatem] *nm:* **jeter l'**~ **sur** to curse

anatomie [anatɔmi] *nf* anatomy

ancêtre [ɑ̃sɛtr(ə)] *nm/f* ancestor

anchois [ɑ̃ʃwa] *nm* anchovy

ancien, ne [ɑ̃sjɛ̃, -jen] *adj* old; *(de jadis, de l'antiquité)* ancient; *(précédent, ex-)* former, old ♦ *nm/f (dans une tribu)* elder; **anciennement** *adv* formerly; **ancienneté** *nf* oldness; antiquity; *(ADMIN: length of) service; seniority

ancre [ɑ̃kr(ə)] *nf* anchor; **jeter/lever l'**~ to cast/weigh anchor; **à l'**~ at anchor; **ancrer** [ɑ̃kre] *vt (CONSTR: câble etc)* to anchor; *(fig)* to fix firmly; **s'**~**r** *vi (NAVIG)* to (cast) anchor

Andorre [ɑ̃dɔr] *nf* Andorra

andouille [ɑ̃duj] *nf (CULIN)* sausage made of chitterlings; *(fam)* clot, nit

âne [ɑn] *nm* donkey, ass; *(péj)* dunce

anéantir [aneɑ̃tir] *vt* to annihilate, wipe

out; (*fig*) to obliterate, destroy; to overwhelm
anémie [anemi] *nf* anaemia; **anémique** *adj*
anaemic
ânerie [ɑnʀi] *nf* stupidity; stupid *ou* idiotic
comment *etc*
anesthésie [anɛstezi] *nf* anaesthesia; **faire
une ~ locale/générale à qn** to give sb a
local/general anaesthetic
ange [ɑ̃ʒ] *nm* angel; **être aux ~s** to be
over the moon
angélus [ɑ̃ʒelys] *nm* angelus; evening bells
pl
angine [ɑ̃ʒin] *nf* throat infection; **~ de poitrine** angina
anglais, e [ɑ̃glɛ, -ɛz] *adj* English ♦ *nm/f*:
A~, e Englishman(woman) ♦ *nm* (*LING*)
English; **les A~** the English; **filer à l'~e** to
take French leave
angle [ɑ̃gl] *nm* angle; (*coin*) corner; **~
droit** right angle
Angleterre [ɑ̃glətɛʀ] *nf*: **l'~** England
anglo... [ɑ̃glo] *préfixe* Anglo-, anglo (-);
~phone *adj* English-speaking
angoissé, e [ɑ̃gwase] *adj* (*personne*) full of
anxieties *ou* hang-ups (*inf*)
angoisser [ɑ̃gwase] *vt* to harrow, cause anguish to ♦ *vi* to worry, fret
anguille [ɑ̃gij] *nf* eel
anicroche [anikʀɔʃ] *nf* hitch, snag
animal, e, aux [animal, -o] *adj, nm* animal
animateur, trice [animatœʀ, -tʀis] *nm/f*
(*de télévision*) host; (*de groupe*) leader, organizer
animation [animɔsjɔ̃] *nf* (*voir animé*) busy-
ness; liveliness; (*CINÉMA: technique*) animation
animé, e [anime] *adj* (*lieu*) busy, lively;
(*conversation, réunion*) lively, animated; (*opposé à in~*) animate
animer [anime] *vt* (*ville, soirée*) to liven up;
(*mettre en mouvement*) to drive
anis [ani] *nm* (*CULIN*) aniseed; (*BOT*) anise
ankyloser [ɑ̃kiloze]: **s'~** *vi* to get stiff
anneau, x [ano] *nm* (*de rideau, bague*)
ring; (*de chaîne*) link
année [ane] *nf* year
annexe [anɛks(ə)] *adj* (*problème*) related;
(*document*) appended; (*salle*) adjoining ♦ *nf*
(*bâtiment*) annex(e); (*de document, ouvrage*)
annex, appendix; (*jointe à une lettre*) enclosure
anniversaire [anivɛʀsɛʀ] *nm* birthday;
(*d'un événement, bâtiment*) anniversary
annonce [anɔ̃s] *nf* announcement; (*signe,
indice*) sign; (*aussi: ~ publicitaire*) advertisement; **les petites ~s** the classified adverti-
sements, the small ads
annoncer [anɔ̃se] *vt* to announce; (*être le
signe de*) to herald; **s'~ bien/difficile** to
look promising/difficult; **annonceur, euse**
nm/f (*TV, RADIO*: *speaker*) announcer;

(*publicitaire*) advertiser
annuaire [anɥɛʀ] *nm* yearbook, annual; **~
téléphonique** (telephone) directory, phone
book
annuel, le [anɥɛl] *adj* annual, yearly
annuité [anɥite] *nf* annual instalment
annuler [anyle] *vt* (*rendez-vous, voyage*) to
cancel, call off; (*mariage*) to annul; (*jugement*) to quash (*BRIT*), repeal (*US*); (*résultats*) to declare void; (*MATH, PHYSIQUE*) to
cancel out
anodin, e [anɔdɛ̃, -in] *adj* harmless; insignificant, trivial
anonyme [anɔnim] *adj* anonymous; (*fig*)
impersonal
ANPE *sigle f* (= *Agence nationale pour
l'emploi*) national employment agency
anse [ɑ̃s] *nf* (*de panier, tasse*) handle; (*GÉO*)
cove
antan [ɑ̃tɑ̃]: **d'~** *adj* of long ago
antarctique [ɑ̃taʀktik] *adj* Antarctic ♦ *nm*:
l'A~ the Antarctic
antécédents [ɑ̃tesedɑ̃] *nmpl* (*MÉD etc*) past
history *sg*
antenne [ɑ̃tɛn] *nf* (*de radio*) aerial;
(*d'insecte*) antenna, feeler; (*poste avancé*)
outpost; (*petite succursale*) sub-branch; **passer à l'~** to go on the air; **prendre l'~** to
tune in; **2 heures d'~** 2 hours' broadcasting time
antérieur, e [ɑ̃teʀjœʀ] *adj* (*d'avant*) previous, earlier; (*de devant*) front
anti... [ɑ̃ti] *préfixe* anti...; **~alcoolique** *adj*
anti-alcohol; **~atomique** *adj*: **abri ~ato-
mique** fallout shelter; **~biotique** *nm* anti-
biotic; **~brouillard** *adj*: **phare ~brouillard**
fog lamp (*BRIT*) *ou* light (*US*)
anticipation [ɑ̃tisipasjɔ̃] *nf*: **livre/film d'~**
science fiction book/film
anticipé, e [ɑ̃tisipe] *adj*: **avec mes remerciements ~s** thanking you in advance *ou*
anticipation
anticiper [ɑ̃tisipe] *vt* (*événement, coup*) to
anticipate, foresee
anti: ~conceptionnel, le *adj* contraceptive; **~corps** *nm* antibody; **~dote** *nm*
antidote
antigel [ɑ̃tiʒɛl] *nm* antifreeze
antihistaminique [ɑ̃tiistaminik] *nm* antihistamine
Antilles [ɑ̃tij] *nfpl*: **les ~** the West Indies
antilope [ɑ̃tilɔp] *nf* antelope
anti: ~mite(s) *adj, nm*: (*produit*) **~mite(s)**
mothproofer; moth repellent; **~parasite**
adj (*RADIO, TV*): **dispositif ~parasite** sup-
pressor; **~pathique** *adj* unpleasant, disagreeable; **~pelliculaire** *adj* anti-dandruff
antipodes [ɑ̃tipɔd] *nmpl* (*GÉO*): **les ~** the
antipodes; (*fig*): **être aux ~ de** to be the
opposite extreme of
antiquaire [ɑ̃tikɛʀ] *nm/f* antique dealer
antique [ɑ̃tik] *adj* antique; (*très vieux*) an-

cient, antiquated

antiquité [ãtikite] *nf (objet)* antique; **l'A~** Antiquity; **magasin d'~s** antique shop

anti: **~rabique** *adj* rabies *cpd*; **~rouille** *adj inv* anti-rust *cpd*; **traitement** **~rouille** rustproofing; **~sémite** *adj* anti-Semitic; **~septique** *adj, nm* antiseptic; **~vol** *adj, nm*: **(dispositif)** **~vol** anti-theft device

antre [ãtʀ(ə)] *nm* den, lair

anxieux, euse [ãksjø, -øz] *adj* anxious, worried

AOC *sigle f (= appellation d'origine contrôlée)* label guaranteeing the quality of wine

août [u] *nm* August

apaiser [apeze] *vt (colère, douleur)* to soothe; *(faim)* to appease; *(personne)* to calm (down), pacify; **s'~** *vi (tempête, bruit)* to die down, subside

apanage [apanaʒ] *nm*: **être l'~ de** to be the privilege *ou* prerogative of

aparté [aparte] *nm (THÉÂTRE)* aside; *(entretien)* private conversation

apathique [apatik] *adj* apathetic

apatride [apatʀid] *nm/f* stateless person

apercevoir [apɛʀsəvwaʀ] *vt* to see; **s'~ de** *vt* to notice; **s'~ que** to notice that

aperçu [apɛʀsy] *nm (vue d'ensemble)* general survey; *(intuition)* insight

apéritif [apeʀitif] *nm (boisson)* aperitif; *(réunion)* drinks *pl*

à-peu-près [apøpʀɛ] *(péj) nm inv* vague approximation

apeuré, e [apœʀe] *adj* frightened, scared

aphone [afɔn] *adj* voiceless

aphte [aft(ə)] *nm* mouth ulcer

apiculture [apikyltyʀ] *nf* beekeeping, apiculture

apitoyer [apitwaje] *vt* to move to pity; **s'~ (sur)** to feel pity (for)

aplanir [aplaniʀ] *vt* to level; *(fig)* to smooth away, iron out

aplatir [aplatiʀ] *vt* to flatten; **s'~** *vi* to become flatter; to be flattened; *(fig)* to lie flat on the ground

aplomb [aplɔ̃] *nm (équilibre)* balance, equilibrium; *(fig)* self-assurance; nerve; **d'~** steady; *(CONSTR)* plumb

apogée [apɔʒe] *nm (fig)* peak, apogee

apologie [apɔlɔʒi] *nf* vindication, praise

apostrophe [apɔstʀɔf] *nf (signe)* apostrophe

apostropher [apɔstʀɔfe] *vt (interpeller)* to shout at, address sharply

apothéose [apɔteoz] *nf* pinnacle (of achievement); *(MUS)* grand finale

apôtre [apotʀ(ə)] *nm* apostle

apparaître [apaʀɛtʀ(ə)] *vi* to appear

apparat [apaʀa] *nm*: **tenue/dîner d'~** ceremonial dress/dinner

appareil [apaʀɛj] *nm (outil, machine)* piece of apparatus, device; appliance; *(politique, syndical)* machinery; *(avion)* (aero)plane,

aircraft *inv*; *(téléphonique)* phone; *(dentier)* brace *(BRIT)*, braces *(US)*; **"qui est à l'~?"** "who's speaking?"; **dans le plus simple ~** in one's birthday suit; **~ler** [apaʀeje] *vi (NAVIG)* to cast off, get under way ♦ *vt (assortir)* to match up; **~(-photo)** [apaʀej(fɔtɔ)] *nm* camera

apparemment [apaʀamã] *adv* apparently

apparence [apaʀãs] *nf* appearance

apparent, e [apaʀã, -ãt] *adj* visible; obvious; *(superficiel)* apparent

apparenté, e [apaʀãte] *adj*: **~ à** related to; *(fig)* similar to

apparition [apaʀisjɔ̃] *nf* appearance; *(surnaturelle)* apparition

appartement [apaʀtəmã] *nm* flat *(BRIT)*, apartment *(US)*

appartenir [apaʀtəniʀ]: **~ à** *vt* to belong to; **il lui appartient de** it is up to him to, it is his duty to

apparu, e *pp de* **apparaître**

appât [apɑ] *nm (PÊCHE)* bait; *(fig)* lure, bait

appauvrir [apovʀiʀ] *vt* to impoverish

appel [apɛl] *nm* call; *(nominal)* roll call; *(: SCOL)* register; *(MIL: recrutement)* call-up; **faire ~ à** *(invoquer)* to appeal to; *(avoir recours à)* to call on; *(nécessiter)* to call for, require; **faire ~** *(JUR)* to appeal; **faire l'~** to call the roll; to call the register; **sans ~** *(fig)* final, irrevocable; **~ d'offres** *(COMM)* invitation to tender; **faire un ~ de phares** to flash one's headlights; **~ (téléphonique)** (tele)phone call

appelé [aple] *nm (MIL)* conscript

appeler [aple] *vt* to call; *(faire venir: médecin etc)* to call, send for; *(fig: nécessiter)* to call for, demand; **s'~:** **elle s'appelle Gabrielle** her name is Gabrielle, she's called Gabrielle; **comment ça s'appelle?** what is it called?; **être appelé à** *(fig)* to be destined to; **~ qn à comparaître** *(JUR)* to summon sb to appear; **en ~ à** to appeal to

appendice [apɛ̃dis] *nm* appendix; **appendicite** *nf* appendicitis

appentis [apɑ̃ti] *nm* lean-to

appesantir [apzãtiʀ]: **s'~** *vi* to grow heavier; **s'~ sur** *(fig)* to dwell on

appétissant, e [apetisã, -ãt] *adj* appetizing, mouth-watering

appétit [apeti] *nm* appetite; **bon ~!** enjoy your meal!

applaudir [aplodiʀ] *vt* to applaud ♦ *vi* to applaud, clap; **applaudissements** *nmpl* applause *sg*, clapping *sg*

application [aplikasjɔ̃] *nf* application

applique [aplik] *nf* wall lamp

appliquer [aplike] *vt* to apply; *(loi)* to enforce; **s'~** *vi (élève etc)* to apply o.s.

appoint [apwɛ̃] *nm (extra)* contribution *ou* help; **avoir/faire l'~** *(en payant)* to have/ give the right change *ou* money; **chauffage d'~** extra heating

appointements [apwɛtmɑ̃] *nmpl* salary *sg*
appointement [apɔtmɑ̃] *nm* landing stage, wharf
apport [apɔʀ] *nm* supply; contribution
apporter [apɔʀte] *vt* to bring
apposer [apoze] *vt* to append; to affix
appréciable [apʀesjabl(ə)] *adj* appreciable
apprécier [apʀesje] *vt* to appreciate; (*évaluer*) to estimate, assess
appréhender [apʀeɑ̃de] *vt* (*craindre*) to dread; (*arrêter*) to apprehend
apprendre [apʀɑ̃dʀ(ə)] *vt* to learn; (*événement, résultats*) to learn of, hear of; ~ **qch à qn** (*informer*) to tell sb (of) sth; (*enseigner*) to teach sb sth; ~ **à faire qch** to learn to do sth; ~ **à qn à faire qch** to teach sb to do sth; **apprenti, e** *nm/f* apprentice; (*fig*) novice, beginner; **apprentissage** *nm* learning; (*COMM, SCOL: période*) apprenticeship
apprêté, e [apʀete] *adj* (*fig*) affected
apprêter [apʀete] *vt* to dress, finish
appris, e *pp de* **apprendre**
apprivoiser [apʀivwaze] *vt* to tame
approbation [apʀɔbasjɔ̃] *nf* approval
approche [apʀɔʃ] *nf* approaching, approach
approcher [apʀɔʃe] *vi* to approach, come near ♦ vi to approach; (*rapprocher*): ~ **qch (de qch)** to bring *ou* put sth near (to sth); **s'~ de** to approach, go *ou* come near to; ~ **de** to draw near to; (*quantité, moment*) to approach
approfondir [apʀɔfɔ̃diʀ] *vt* to deepen; (*question*) to go further into
approprié, e [apʀɔpʀije] *adj*: ~ **(à)** appropriate (to), suited to
approprier [apʀɔpʀije]: **s'~** *vt* to appropriate, take over
approuver [apʀuve] *vt* to agree with; (*autoriser: loi, projet*) to approve, pass; (*trouver louable*) to approve of
approvisionner [apʀɔvizjɔne] *vt* to supply; (*compte bancaire*) to pay funds into; **s'~ en** to stock up with
approximatif, ive [apʀɔksimatif, -iv] *adj* approximate, rough; vague
appui [apɥi] *nm* support; **prendre ~ sur** to lean on; to rest on; **l'~ de la fenêtre** the windowsill, the window ledge; **appui(e)-tête** *nm inv* headrest
appuyer [apɥije] *vt* (*poser*): ~ **qch sur/contre** to lean *ou* rest sth on/against; (*soutenir: personne, demande*) to support, back (up) ♦ vi: ~ **sur** (*bouton, frein*) to press, push; (*mot, détail*) to stress, emphasize; (*suj: chose: peser sur*) to rest (heavily) on, press against; **s'~ sur** to lean on; to rely on; ~ **à droite** to bear (to the) right
âpre [ɑpʀ(ə)] *adj* acrid, pungent; (*fig*) harsh; bitter; ~ **au gain** grasping
après [apʀɛ] *prép* after ♦ *adv* afterwards; **2**

heures ~ 2 hours later; ~ **qu'il est parti** after he left; ~ **avoir fait** after having done; **d'~** (*selon*) according to; ~ **coup** after the event, afterwards; ~ **tout** (*au fond*) after all; **et** (*puis*) ~? so what?; **après-demain** *adv* the day after tomorrow; **après-guerre** *nm* post-war years *pl*; **après-midi** *nm ou nf* (*inv*) afternoon
à-propos [apʀopo] *nm* (*d'une remarque*) aptness; **faire preuve d'~** to show presence of mind
apte [apt(ə)] *adj* capable; (*MIL*) fit
aquarelle [akwaʀɛl] *nf* (*tableau*) watercolour; (*genre*) watercolours *pl*
aquarium [akwaʀjɔm] *nm* aquarium
arabe [aʀab] *adj* Arabic; (*désert, cheval*) Arabian; (*nation, peuple*) Arab ♦ *nm/f*: **A~** Arab ♦ *nm* (*LING*) Arabic
Arabie [aʀabi] *nf*: **l'~ (Saoudite)** Saudi Arabia
arachide [aʀaʃid] *nf* (*plante*) groundnut (plant); (*graine*) peanut, groundnut
araignée [aʀeɲe] *nf* spider
arbitraire [aʀbitʀɛʀ] *adj* arbitrary
arbitre [aʀbitʀ(ə)] *nm* (*SPORT*) referee; (: *TENNIS, CRICKET*) umpire; (*fig*) arbiter, judge; (*JUR*) arbitrator; **arbitrer** *vt* to referee; to umpire; to arbitrate
arborer [aʀbɔʀe] *vt* to bear, display
arbre [aʀbʀ(ə)] *nm* tree; (*TECH*) shaft; ~ **de transmission** (*AUTO*) driveshaft; ~ **généalogique** family tree
arbuste [aʀbyst(ə)] *nm* small shrub
arc [aʀk] *nm* (*arme*) bow; (*GÉOM*) arc; (*ARCHIT*) arch; **en ~ de cercle** semi-circular
arcade [aʀkad] *nf* arch(way); ~**s** *nfpl* (*série*) arcade *sg*, arches
arcanes [aʀkan] *nmpl* mysteries
arc-boutant [aʀkbutɑ̃] *nm* flying buttress
arceau, x [aʀso] *nm* (*métallique etc*) hoop
arc-en-ciel [aʀkɑ̃sjɛl] *nm* rainbow
arche [aʀʃ(ə)] *nf* arch; ~ **de Noé** Noah's Ark
archéologie [aʀkeɔlɔʒi] *nf* archeology; **archéologue** *nm/f* arch(a)eologist
archet [aʀʃɛ] *nm* bow
archevêque [aʀʃəvɛk] *nm* archbishop
archipel [aʀʃipɛl] *nm* archipelago
architecte [aʀʃitɛkt(ə)] *nm* architect
architecture [aʀʃitɛktyʀ] *nf* architecture
archive [aʀʃiv] *nf* file; ~**s** *nfpl* (*collection*) archives
arctique [aʀktik] *adj* Arctic ♦ *nm*: **l'A~** the Arctic
ardemment [aʀdamɑ̃] *adv* ardently, fervently
ardent, e [aʀdɑ̃, -ɑ̃t] *adj* (*soleil*) blazing; (*fièvre*) raging; (*amour*) ardent, passionate; (*prière*) fervent
ardoise [aʀdwaz] *nf* slate
ardt *abr* = **arrondissement**
ardu, e [aʀdy] *adj* (*travail*) arduous; (*pro-*

blème) difficult; (*pente*) steep

arène [aʀɛn] *nf* arena; ~**s** *nfpl* (*amphithéâtre*) bull-ring *sg*

arête [aʀɛt] *nf* (*de poisson*) bone; (*d'une montagne*) ridge; (*GÉOM etc*) edge

argent [aʀʒɑ̃] *nm* (*métal*) silver; (*monnaie*) money; ~ **de poche** pocket money; ~ **liquide** ready money, (ready) cash; **argenterie** *nf* silverware; silver plate

argentin, e [aʀʒɑ̃tɛ̃, -in] *adj* (*son*) silvery; (*d'Argentine*) Argentinian, Argentine

Argentine [aʀʒɑ̃tin] *nf*: **l'~** Argentina, the Argentine

argile [aʀʒil] *nf* clay

argot [aʀgo] *nm* slang; **argotique** *adj* slang *cpd*; slangy

arguer [aʀgɥe]: ~ **de** *vt* to put forward as a pretext *ou* reason

argument [aʀgymɑ̃] *nm* argument

argumentaire [aʀgymɑ̃tɛʀ] *nm* sales leaflet

argumenter [aʀgymɑ̃te] *vi* to argue

argus [aʀgys] *nm* guide to second-hand car *etc* prices

aristocratique [aʀistɔkʀatik] *adj* aristocratic

arithmétique [aʀitmetik] *adj* arithmetic(al) ♦ *nf* arithmetic

armateur [aʀmatœʀ] *nm* shipowner

armature [aʀmatyʀ] *nf* framework; (*de tente etc*) frame

arme [aʀm(ə)] *nf* weapon; (*section de l'armée*) arm; ~**s** *nfpl* (*armement*) weapons, arms; (*blason*) (coat of) arms; ~ **à feu** firearm

armée [aʀme] *nf* army; ~ **de l'air** Air Force; ~ **de terre** Army

armement [aʀməmɑ̃] *nm* (*matériel*) arms *pl*, weapons *pl*; (: *d'un pays*) arms *pl*, armament

armer [aʀme] *vt* to arm; (*arme à feu*) to cock; (*appareil-photo*) to wind on; ~ **qch de** to fit sth with; to reinforce sth with

armistice [aʀmistis] *nm* armistice; **l'A~** ≈ Remembrance (*BRIT*) *ou* Veterans (*US*) Day

armoire [aʀmwaʀ] *nf* (tall) cupboard; (*penderie*) wardrobe (*BRIT*), closet (*US*)

armoiries [aʀmwaʀi] *nfpl* coat of arms

armure [aʀmyʀ] *nf* armour *no pl*, suit of armour; **armurier** [aʀmyʀje] *nm* gunsmith; armourer

arnaquer [aʀnake] *vt* to swindle

aromates [aʀɔmat] *nmpl* seasoning *sg*, herbs (and spices)

aromatisé, e [aʀɔmatize] *adj* flavoured

arôme [aʀom] *nm* aroma; fragrance

arpenter [aʀpɑ̃te] *vt* (*salle, couloir*) to pace up and down

arpenteur [aʀpɑ̃tœʀ] *nm* surveyor

arqué, e [aʀke] *adj* bandy; arched

arrache-pied [aʀaʃpje]: **d'~** *adv* relentlessly

arracher [aʀaʃe] *vt* to pull out; (*page etc*)

to tear off, tear out; (*légumes, herbe*) to pull up; (*bras etc*) to tear off; **s'~** *vt* (*article recherché*) to fight over; ~ **qch à qn** to snatch sth from sb; (*fig*) to wring sth out of sb

arraisonner [aʀɛzɔne] *vt* (*bateau*) to board and search

arrangeant, e [aʀɑ̃ʒɑ̃, -ɑ̃t] *adj* accommodating, obliging

arrangement [aʀɑ̃zmɑ̃] *nm* agreement, arrangement

arranger [aʀɑ̃ʒe] *vt* (*gén*) to arrange; (*réparer*) to fix, put right; (*régler*) to settle, sort out; (*convenir à*) to suit, be convenient for; **s'~** *vi* (*se mettre d'accord*) to come to an agreement; **je vais m'~** I'll manage; **ça va s'~** it'll sort itself out

arrestation [aʀɛstɑsjɔ̃] *nf* arrest

arrêt [aʀɛ] *nm* stopping; (*de bus etc*) stop; (*JUR*) judgment, decision; **rester ou tomber en ~ devant** to stop short in front of; **sans ~** non-stop; continually; ~ **de mort** capital sentence; ~ **de travail** stoppage (of work)

arrêté [aʀete] *nm* order, decree

arrêter [aʀete] *vt* to stop; (*chauffage etc*) to turn off, switch off; (*fixer: date etc*) to appoint, decide on; (*criminel, suspect*) to arrest; **s'~** *vi* to stop; ~ **de faire** to stop doing

arrhes [aʀ] *nfpl* deposit *sg*

arrière [aʀjɛʀ] *nm* back; (*SPORT*) fullback ♦ *adj inv*: **siège/roue** ~ back *ou* rear seat/wheel; **à l'~** behind, at the back; **en ~** behind; (*regarder*) back, behind; (*tomber, aller*) backwards; **~-goût** *nm* aftertaste; **~-grand-mère** *nf* great-grandmother; **~-grand-père** *nm* great-grandfather; **~-pays** *nm inv* hinterland; **~-pensée** *nf* ulterior motive; mental reservation; **~-plan** *nm* background; **~-saison** *nf* late autumn; **~-train** *nm* hindquarters *pl*

arrimer [aʀime] *vt* to stow; to secure

arrivage [aʀivaʒ] *nm* arrival

arrivée [aʀive] *nf* arrival; (*ligne d'~*) finish; ~ **d'air** air inlet

arriver [aʀive] *vi* to arrive; (*survenir*) to happen, occur; **il arrive à Paris à 8h** he gets to *ou* arrives in Paris at 8; ~ **à** (*atteindre*) to reach; ~ **à faire qch** to succeed in doing sth; **il arrive que** it happens that; **il lui arrive de faire** he sometimes does; **arriviste** *nm/f* go-getter

arrogant, e [aʀɔgɑ̃, -ɑ̃t] *adj* arrogant

arroger [aʀɔʒe]: **s'~** *vt* to assume (without right)

arrondir [aʀɔ̃diʀ] *vt* (*forme, objet*) to round; (*somme*) to round off; **s'~** *vi* to become round(ed)

arrondissement [aʀɔ̃dismɑ̃] *nm* (*ADMIN*) ≈ district

arroser [aʀoze] *vt* to water; (*victoire*) to celebrate (over a drink); (*CULIN*) to baste; **ar-rosoir** *nm* watering can

arsenal, aux [arsənal, -o] *nm* (*NAVIG*) naval dockyard; (*MIL*) arsenal; (*fig*) gear, paraphernalia

art [ar] *nm* art; **~s ménagers** home economics *sg*

artère [arter] *nf* (*ANAT*) artery; (*rue*) main road

arthrite [artrit] *nf* arthritis

artichaut [artiʃo] *nm* artichoke

article [artikl(ə)] *nm* article; (*COMM*) item, article; **à l'~ de la mort** at the point of death; **~ de fond** (*PRESSE*) feature article

articulation [artikylɑsjɔ̃] *nf* articulation; (*ANAT*) joint

articuler [artikyle] *vt* to articulate

artifice [artifis] *nm* device, trick

artificiel, le [artifisjɛl] *adj* artificial

artificieux, euse [artifisjø, -øz] *adj* guileful, deceitful

artisan [artizɑ̃] *nm* artisan, (self-employed) craftsman; **artisanal, e, aux** *adj* of *ou* made by craftsmen; (*péj*) cottage industry *cpd*, unsophisticated; **artisanat** *nm* arts and crafts *pl*

artiste [artist(ə)] *nm/f* artist; (*de variétés*) entertainer; performer; **artistique** *adj* artistic

as¹ [a] *vb voir* **avoir**

as² [as] *nm* ace

ascendance [asɑ̃dɑ̃s] *nf* (*origine*) ancestry

ascendant, e [asɑ̃dɑ̃, -ɑ̃t] *adj* upward ♦ *nm* influence

ascenseur [asɑ̃sœr] *nm* lift (*BRIT*), elevator (*US*)

ascension [asɑ̃sjɔ̃] *nf* ascent; climb; **l'A~** (*REL*) the Ascension

aseptiser [asɛptize] *vt* to sterilize; to disinfect

asiatique [azjatik] *adj, nm/f* Asiatic, Asian **Asie** [azi] *nf*: **l'~** Asia

asile [azil] *nm* (*refuge*) refuge, sanctuary; (*POL*): **droit d'~** (political) asylum; (*pour malades etc*) home

aspect [aspɛ] *nm* appearance, look; (*fig*) aspect, side; **à l'~ de** at the sight of

asperge [aspɛrʒ(ə)] *nf* asparagus *no pl*

asperger [aspɛrʒe] *vt* to spray, sprinkle

aspérité [aspɛrite] *nf* excrescence, protruding bit (of rock *etc*)

asphalte [asfalt(ə)] *nm* asphalt

asphyxier [asfiksje] *vt* to suffocate, asphyxiate; (*fig*) to stifle

aspirateur [aspiratœr] *nm* vacuum cleaner

aspirer [aspire] *vt* (*air*) to inhale; (*liquide*) to suck (up); (*suj: appareil*) to suck up; **~ à** to aspire to

aspirine [aspirin] *nf* aspirin

assagir [asaʒir] *vt* to quieten down; **s'~** *vi* to quieten down, sober down

assaillir [asajir] *vt* to assail, attack

assainir [asenir] *vt* to clean up; to purify

assaisonner [asɛzɔne] *vt* to season

assassin [asasɛ̃] *nm* murderer; assassin; **~er** [asasine] *vt* to murder; (*esp POL*) to assassinate

assaut [aso] *nm* assault, attack; **prendre d'~** to storm, assault; **donner l'~** to attack; **faire ~ de** (*rivaliser*) to vie with each other in

assécher [aseʃe] *vt* to drain

assemblée [asɑ̃ble] *nf* (*réunion*) meeting; (*public, assistance*) gathering; assembled people; (*POL*) assembly

assembler [asɑ̃ble] *vt* (*joindre, monter*) to assemble, put together; (*amasser*) to gather (together), collect (together); **s'~** *vi* to gather

assener [asene] *vt*: **~ un coup à qn** to deal sb a blow

asséner [asene] *vt* = **assener**

assentiment [asɑ̃timɑ̃] *nm* assent, consent; approval

asseoir [aswar] *vt* (*malade, bébé*) to sit up; to sit down; (*autorité, réputation*) to establish; **s'~** *vi* to sit (o.s.) down

assermenté, e [asɛrmɑ̃te] *adj* sworn, on oath

asservir [asɛrvir] *vt* to subjugate, enslave

assez [ase] *adv* (*suffisamment*) enough, sufficiently; (*passablement*) rather, quite, fairly; **~ de pain/livres** enough *ou* sufficient bread/books; **vous en avez ~?** have you got enough?

assidu, e [asidy] *adj* assiduous, painstaking; regular; **assiduités** *nfpl* assiduous attentions

assied *etc vb voir* **asseoir**

assiéger [asjeʒe] *vt* to besiege

assiérai *etc vb voir* **asseoir**

assiette [asjɛt] *nf* plate; (*contenu*) plate(ful); **~ à dessert** dessert plate; **~ anglaise** assorted cold meats; **~ creuse** (soup) dish, soup plate; **~ de l'impôt** basis of (tax) assessment; **~ plate** (dinner) plate

assigner [asiɲe] *vt*: **~ qch à** (*poste, part, travail*) to assign sth to; (*limites*) to set sth to; (*cause, effet*) to ascribe sth to; **~ qn à** to assign sb to

assimiler [asimile] *vt* to assimilate, absorb; (*comparer*): **~ qch/qn à** to liken *ou* compare sth/sb to; **s'~** *vi* (*s'intégrer*) to be assimilated *ou* absorbed

assis, e [asi, -iz] *pp de* **asseoir** ♦ *adj* sitting (down), seated; **assise** *nf* (*fig*) basis, foundation; **~es** *nfpl* (*JUR*) assizes; (*congrès*) (annual) conference

assistance [asistɑ̃s] *nf* (*public*) audience; (*aide*) assistance

assistant, e [asistɑ̃, -ɑ̃t] *nm/f* assistant; (*d'université*) probationary lecturer; **~e sociale** social worker

assisté, e [asiste] *adj* (*AUTO*) power assisted

assister [asiste] *vt* to assist; ~ **à** (*scène, événement*) to witness; (*conférence, séminaire*) to attend, be at; (*spectacle, match*) to be at, see

association [asɔsjasjɔ̃] *nf* association

associé, e [asɔsje] *nm/f* associate; partner

associer [asɔsje] *vt* to associate; **s'~** *vi* to join together ♦ *vt* (*collaborateur*) to take on (as a partner); **s'~ à qn pour faire** to join (forces) with sb to do; **s'~ à** to be combined with; (*opinions, joie de qn*) to share in; ~ **qn à** (*profits*) to give sb a share of; (*affaire*) to make sb a partner in; (*joie, triomphe*) to include sb in; ~ **qch à** (*joindre, allier*) to combine sth with

assoiffé, e [aswafe] *adj* thirsty

assombrir [asɔ̃bʀiʀ] *vt* to darken; (*fig*) to fill with gloom

assommer [asɔme] *vt* to batter to death; (*étourdir, abrutir*) to knock out; to stun

Assomption [asɔ̃psjɔ̃] *nf*: **l'~** the Assumption

assorti, e [asɔʀti] *adj* matched, matching; (*varié*) assorted; ~ **à** matching

assortiment [asɔʀtimɑ̃] *nm* assortment, selection

assortir [asɔʀtiʀ] *vt* to match; **s'~ de** to be accompanied by; ~ **qch à** to match sth with; ~ **qch de** to accompany sth with

assoupi, e [asupi] *adj* dozing, sleeping; (*fig*) (be)numbed; dulled; stilled

assouplir [asupliʀ] *vt* to make supple; (*fig*) to relax

assourdir [asuʀdiʀ] *vt* (*bruit*) to deaden, muffle; (*suj: bruit*) to deafen

assouvir [asuviʀ] *vt* to satisfy, appease

assujettir [asyʒetiʀ] *vt* to subject

assumer [asyme] *vt* (*fonction, emploi*) to assume, take on

assurance [asyʀɑ̃s] *nf* (*certitude*) assurance; (*confiance en soi*) (self-) confidence; (*contrat*) insurance (policy); (*secteur commercial*) insurance; (*maladie*) health insurance; ~ **tous risques** (*AUTO*) comprehensive insurance; ~**s sociales** ≈ National Insurance (*BRIT*), ≈ Social Security (*US*); ~ **vie** *nf* life assurance *ou* insurance

assuré, e [asyʀe] *adj* (*certain*): ~ **de** confident of ♦ *nm/f* insured (person); **assurément** *adv* assuredly, most certainly

assurer [asyʀe] *vt* to insure; (*stabiliser*) to steady; to stabilize; (*victoire etc*) to ensure; (*frontières, pouvoir*) to make secure; (*service, garde*) to provide; to operate; **s'~** (*contre*) (*COMM*) to insure o.s. (against); **s'~ de/que** (*vérifier*) to make sure of/that; **s'~ (de)** (*aide de qn*) to secure; ~ **qch à qn** (*garantir*) to secure sth for sb; (*certifier*) to assure sb of sth; ~ **à qn que** to assure sb that; ~ **qn de** to assure sb of

asthme [asm(ə)] *nm* asthma

asticot [astiko] *nm* maggot

astiquer [astike] *vt* to polish, shine

astre [astʀ(ə)] *nm* star

astreignant, e [astʀɛɲɑ̃, -ɑ̃t] *adj* demanding

astreindre [astʀɛ̃dʀ(ə)] *vt*: ~ **qn à qch** to force sth upon sb; ~ **qn à faire** to compel *ou* force sb to do

astrologie [astʀɔlɔʒi] *nf* astrology

astronaute [astʀɔnot] *nm/f* astronaut

astronomie [astʀɔnɔmi] *nf* astronomy

astuce [astys] *nf* shrewdness, astuteness; (*truc*) trick, clever way; (*plaisanterie*) wisecrack; **astucieux, euse** *adj* clever

atelier [atəlje] *nm* workshop; (*de peintre*) studio

athée [ate] *adj* atheistic ♦ *nm/f* atheist

Athènes [atɛn] *n* Athens

athlète [atlɛt] *nm/f* (*SPORT*) athlete; **athlétisme** *nm* athletics *sg*

atlantique [atlɑ̃tik] *adj* Atlantic ♦ *nm*: **l'(océan) A~** the Atlantic (Ocean)

atlas [atlas] *nm* atlas

atmosphère [atmɔsfɛʀ] *nf* atmosphere

atome [atom] *nm* atom; **atomique** *adj* atomic, nuclear; (*nombre, masse*) atomic

atomiseur [atɔmizœʀ] *nm* atomizer

atone [atɔn] *adj* lifeless

atours [atuʀ] *nmpl* attire *sg*, finery *sg*

atout [atu] *nm* trump; (*fig*) asset; trump card

âtre [ɑtʀ(ə)] *nm* hearth

atroce [atʀɔs] *adj* atrocious

attabler [atable] : **s'~** *vi* to sit down at (the) table

attachant, e [ataʃɑ̃, -ɑ̃t] *adj* engaging, lovable, likeable

attache [ataʃ] *nf* clip, fastener; (*fig*) tie

attacher [ataʃe] *vt* to tie up; (*étiquette*) to attach, tie on; (*souliers*) to do up ♦ *vi* (*poêle, riz*) to stick; **s'~ à** (*par affection*) to become attached to; **s'~ à faire** to endeavour to do; ~ **qch à** to tie *ou* attach sth to

attaque [atak] *nf* attack; (*cérébrale*) stroke; (*d'épilepsie*) fit

attaquer [atake] *vt* to attack; (*en justice*) to bring an action against, sue; (*travail*) to tackle, set about ♦ *vi* to attack

attardé, e [ataʀde] *adj* (*passants*) late; (*enfant*) backward; (*conceptions*) old-fashioned

attarder [ataʀde] : **s'~** *vi* to linger; to stay on

atteindre [atɛ̃dʀ(ə)] *vt* to reach; (*blesser*) to hit; (*émouvoir*) to affect

atteint, e [atɛ̃, -ɛ̃t] *adj* (*MÉD*): **être ~ de** to be suffering from; **atteinte** *nf* attack; **hors d'atteinte** out of reach; **porter atteinte à** to strike a blow at; to undermine

atteler [atle] *vt* (*cheval, bœufs*) to hitch up; (*wagons*) to couple; **s'~ à** (*travail*) to buckle down to

attelle [atɛl] *nf* splint

attenant, e [atnã, -ãt] *adj*: ~ **(à)** adjoining

attendant [atãdã] *adv*: **en** ~ meanwhile, in the meantime

attendre [atãdʀ] *vt* (*gén*) to wait for; (*être destiné ou réservé à*) to await, be in store for ♦ *vi* to wait; **s'~ à (ce que)** to expect (that); ~ **un enfant** to be expecting a baby; ~ **de faire/d'être** to wait until one does/is; ~ **que** to wait until; ~ **qch de** to expect sth of; **en attendant** meanwhile, in the meantime; be that as it may

attendrir [atãdʀiʀ] *vt* to move (to pity); (*viande*) to tenderize

attendu, e [atãdy] *adj* (*visiteur*) expected; ~ **que** considering that, since

attentat [atãta] *nm* assassination attempt; ~ **à la bombe** bomb attack; ~ **à la pudeur** indecent exposure *no pl*; indecent assault *no pl*

attente [atãt] *nf* wait; (*espérance*) expectation

attenter [atãte] *vt*: ~ **à** (*liberté*) to violate; ~ **à la vie de qn** to make an attempt on sb's life

attentif, ive [atãtif, -iv] *adj* (*auditeur*) attentive; (*travail*) scrupulous; careful; ~ **à** mindful of; careful to

attention [atãsjõ] *nf* attention; (*prévenance*) attention, thoughtfulness *no pl*; **à l'~ de** for the attention of; **faire** ~ **(à)** to be careful (of); **faire** ~ **(à ce) que** to be *ou* make sure that; ~**!** careful!, watch out!; **attentionné, e** *adj* thoughtful, considerate

atténuer [atenɥe] *vt* to alleviate, ease; to lessen

atterrer [ateʀe] *vt* to dismay, appal

atterrir [ateʀiʀ] *vi* to land; **atterrissage** *nm* landing

attestation [atɛstasjõ] *nf* certificate

attester [atɛste] *vt* to testify to

attirail [atiʀaj] *nm* gear; (*péj*) paraphernalia

attirant, e [atiʀã, -ãt] *adj* attractive, appealing

attirer [atiʀe] *vt* to attract; (*appâter*) to lure, entice; ~ **qn dans un coin/vers soi** to draw sb into a corner/towards one; ~ **l'attention de qn (sur)** to attract sb's attention (to); to draw sb's attention (to); **s'~ des ennuis** to bring trouble upon o.s., get into trouble

attiser [atize] *vt* (*feu*) to poke (up)

attitré, e [atitʀe] *adj* qualified; accredited; appointed

attitude [atityd] *nf* attitude; (*position du corps*) bearing

attouchements [atuʃmã] *nmpl* touching *sg*; (*sexuels*) fondling *sg*

attraction [atʀaksjõ] *nf* (*gén*) attraction; (*de cabaret, cirque*) number

attrait [atʀɛ] *nm* appeal, attraction; lure

attrape-nigaud [atʀapnigo] *nm* con

attraper [atʀape] *vt* (*gén*) to catch; (*habi-*

tude, amende) to get, pick up; (*fam: duper*) to con

attrayant, e [atʀɛjã, -ãt] *adj* attractive

attribuer [atʀibɥe] *vt* (*prix*) to award; (*rôle, tâche*) to allocate, assign; (*imputer*): ~ **qch à** to attribute sth to; **s'~** *vt* (*s'approprier*) to claim for o.s.

attribut [atʀiby] *nm* attribute; (*LING*) complement

attrister [atʀiste] *vt* to sadden

attroupement [atʀupmã] *nm* crowd, mob

attrouper [atʀupe]: **s'~** *vi* to gather

au [o] *prép* +*dét* = **à** +**le**

aubade [obad] *nf* dawn serenade

aubaine [obɛn] *nf* godsend; (*financière*) windfall

aube [ob] *nf* dawn, daybreak; **à l'~** at dawn *ou* daybreak

aubépine [obepin] *nf* hawthorn

auberge [obɛʀʒ(ə)] *nf* inn; ~ **de jeunesse** youth hostel

aubergine [obɛʀʒin] *nf* aubergine

aubergiste [obɛʀʒist(ə)] *nm/f* inn-keeper, hotel-keeper

aucun, e [okœ̃, -yn] *dét* no, *tournure négative* +any; (*positif*) any ♦ *pron* none, *tournure négative* +any; any(one); **sans** ~ **doute** without any doubt; **plus qu'~ autre** more than any other; ~ **des deux** neither of the two; ~ **d'entre eux** none of them; **d'~s** (*certains*) some; **aucunement** *adv* in no way, not in the least

audace [odas] *nf* daring, boldness; (*péj*) audacity; **audacieux, euse** *adj* daring, bold

au-delà [odla] *adv* beyond ♦ *nm*: **l'~** the hereafter; ~ **de** beyond

au-dessous [odsu] *adv* underneath; below; ~ **de** under(neath), below; (*limite, somme etc*) below, under; (*dignité, condition*) below

au-dessus [odsy] *adv* above; ~ **de** above

au-devant [odvã]: ~ **de** *prép*: **aller** ~ **de** (*personne, danger*) to go (out) and meet; (*souhaits de qn*) to anticipate

audience [odjãs] *nf* audience; (*JUR*: *séance*) hearing

audio-visuel, le [odjovizɥɛl] *adj* audio-visual

auditeur, trice [oditœʀ, -tʀis] *nm/f* listener

audition [odisjõ] *nf* (*ouïe, écoute*) hearing; (*JUR*: *de témoins*) examination; (*MUS, THÉÂTRE*: *épreuve*) audition

auditoire [oditwaʀ] *nm* audience

auge [oʒ] *nf* trough

augmentation [ɔgmãtasjõ] *nf*: ~ **(de salaire)** rise (in salary) (*BRIT*), (pay) raise (*US*)

augmenter [ɔgmãte] *vt* (*gén*) to increase; (*salaire, prix*) to increase, raise, put up; (*employé*) to increase the salary of ♦ *vi* to increase

augure [ɔgyʀ] *nm* soothsayer, oracle; **de bon/mauvais** ~ of good/ill omen; ~**r** [ɔgyʀe] *vt*: ~**r bien de** to augur well for

aujourd'hui [oʒuʀdɥi] *adv* today

aumône [omon] *nf inv* alms *sg*; **faire l'~ (à qn)** to give alms (to sb)

aumônier [omonje] *nm* chaplain

auparavant [oparavɑ̃] *adv* before(hand)

auprès [opʀɛ]: ~ **de** *prép* next to, close to; *(recourir, s'adresser)* to; *(en comparaison de)* compared with

auquel [okɛl] *prép +pron* = **à +lequel**

aurai *etc vb voir* **avoir**

auréole [oʀeɔl] *nf* halo; *(tache)* ring

auriculaire [oʀikylɛʀ] *nm* little finger

aurons *etc vb voir* **avoir**

aurore [oʀoʀ] *nf* dawn, daybreak

ausculter [oskylte] *vt* to sound

aussi [osi] *adv (également)* also, too; *(de comparaison)* as ♦ *conj* therefore, consequently; ~ **fort que** as strong as; **moi** ~ me too; ~ **bien que** *(de même que)* as well as

aussitôt [osito] *adv* straight away, immediately; ~ **que** as soon as

austère [ostɛʀ] *adj* austere; stern

austral, e [ostʀal] *adj* southern

Australie [ostʀali] *nf*: **l'~** Australia; **australien, ne** *adj, nm/f* Australian

autant [otɑ̃] *adv* so much; *(comparatif)*: ~ **(que)** as much (as); *(nombre)* as many (as); ~ **(de)** so much *(ou* many); as much *(ou* many); ~ **partir we** *(ou* you *etc)* may as well leave; ~ **dire que** ... one might as well say that ...; **pour** ~ for all that; **pour** ~ **que** assuming, as long as; **d'~ plus/mieux (que)** all the more/the better (since)

autel [otɛl] *nm* altar

auteur [otœʀ] *nm* author

authentique [otɑ̃tik] *adj* authentic, genuine

auto [oto] *nf* car

auto: ~**biographie** *nf* autobiography; ~**bus** *nm* bus; ~**car** *nm* coach

autochtone [otoktɔn] *nm/f* native

auto: ~**collant, e** *adj* self-adhesive; *(enveloppe)* self-seal ♦ *nm* sticker; ~**couchettes** *adj*: **train** ~**couchettes** car sleeper train; ~**cuiseur** *nm* pressure cooker; ~**défense** *nf* self-defence; **groupe d'~défense** vigilante committee; ~**didacte** *adj nm/f* self-taught person; ~**école** *nf* driving school; ~**gestion** *nf* self-management; ~**graphe** *nm* autograph

automate [otomat] *nm (machine)* (automatic) machine

automatique [otomatik] *adj* automatic ♦ *nm*: **l'~** direct dialling; **automatiser** *vt* to automate

automne [otɔn] *nm* autumn *(BRIT)*, fall *(US)*

automobile [otomobil] *adj* motor *cpd* ♦ *nf* (motor) car; **l'~** motoring; the car industry; **automobiliste** *nm/f* motorist

autonome [otonɔm] *adj* autonomous; **autonomie** *nf* autonomy; *(POL)* self-

government, autonomy

autopsie [otopsi] *nf* post-mortem (examination), autopsy

autoradio [otoʀadjo] *nm* car radio

autorisation [otoʀizasjɔ̃] *nf* permission, authorization; *(papiers)* permit

autorisé, e [otoʀize] *adj (opinion, sources)* authoritative

autoriser [otoʀize] *vt* to give permission for, authorize; *(fig)* to allow (of), sanction

autoritaire [otoʀitɛʀ] *adj* authoritarian

autorité [otoʀite] *nf* authority; **faire** ~ to be authoritative

autoroute [otoʀut] *nf* motorway *(BRIT)*, highway *(US)*

auto-stop [otostɔp] *nm*: **faire de l'~** to hitch-hike; **auto-stoppeur, euse** *nm/f* hitch-hiker

autour [otuʀ] *adv* around; ~ **de** around; **tout** ~ all around

— **MOT CLÉ**

autre [otʀ(ə)] *adj* **1** *(différent)* other, different; **je préférerais un** ~ **verre** I'd prefer another *ou* a different glass

2 *(supplémentaire)* other; **je voudrais un** ~ **verre d'eau** I'd like another glass of water

3: ~ **chose** something else; ~ **part** somewhere else; **d'**~ **part** on the other hand

♦ *pron*: **un** ~ another (one); **nous/vous** ~**s** us/you; **d'**~**s** others; **l'**~ the other (one); **les** ~**s** the others; *(autrui)* others; **l'un et l'**~ both of them; **se détester l'un l'**~/**les uns les** ~**s** to hate each other *ou* one another; **d'une semaine à l'**~ from one week to the next; *(incessamment)* any week now; **entre** ~**s** among other things

autrefois [otʀəfwa] *adv* in the past

autrement [otʀəmɑ̃] *adv* differently; in another way; *(sinon)* otherwise; ~ **dit** in other words

Autriche [otʀiʃ] *nf*: **l'~** Austria; **autrichien, ne** *adj, nm/f* Austrian

autruche [otʀyʃ] *nf* ostrich

autrui [otʀɥi] *pron* others

auvent [ovɑ̃] *nm* canopy

aux [o] *prép +dét* = **à +les**

auxiliaire [oksiljɛʀ] *adj, nm/f* auxiliary

auxquelles [okɛl] *prép +pron* = **à +lesquelles**

auxquels [okɛl] *prép +pron* = **à +lesquels**

avachi, e [avaʃi] *adj* limp, flabby

aval [aval] *nm (accord)* endorsement, backing; *(GÉO)*: **en** ~ downstream, downriver; *(sur une pente)* downhill

avalanche [avalɑ̃ʃ] *nf* avalanche

avaler [avale] *vt* to swallow

avance [avɑ̃s] *nf (de troupes etc)* advance; progress; *(d'argent)* advance; *(opposé à retard)* lead; being ahead of schedule; ~**s** *nfpl (ouvertures)* overtures; *(amoureuses)* advances; **(être) en ~** (to be) early; (*sur un programme*) (to be) ahead of schedule; **à l'~, d'~** in advance

avancé, e [avɑ̃se] *adj* advanced; well on, well under way

avancement [avɑ̃smɑ̃] *nm* (*professionnel*) promotion

avancer [avɑ̃se] *vi* to move forward, advance; (*projet, travail*) to make progress; (*être en saillie*) to overhang; to jut out; (*montre, réveil*) to be fast; to gain ♦ *vt* to move forward, advance; (*argent*) to advance; (*montre, pendule*) to put forward; **s'~** *vi* to move forward, advance; (*fig*) to commit o.s.; to overhang; to jut out

avant [avɑ̃] *prép* before ♦ *adv*: **trop/plus ~** too far/further forward ♦ *adj inv*: **siège/roue ~** front seat/wheel ♦ *nm* (*d'un véhicule, bâtiment*) front; (*SPORT: joueur*) forward; **~ qu'il parte/de faire** before he leaves/doing; **~ tout** (*surtout*) above all; **à l'~** (*dans un véhicule*) in (the) front; **en ~** forward(s); **en ~ de** in front of

avantage [avɑ̃taʒ] *nm* advantage; **~s sociaux** fringe benefits; **avantager** *vt* (*favoriser*) to favour; (*embellir*) to flatter; **avantageux, euse** *adj* attractive; attractively priced

avant-: **~-bras** *nm inv* forearm; **~coureur** *adj inv*: **signe ~coureur** advance indication *ou* sign; **~-dernier, ière** *adj, nm/f* next to last, last but one; **~-goût** *nm* foretaste; **~-hier** *adv* the day before yesterday; **~-première** *nf* (*de film*) preview; **~-projet** *nm* (preliminary) draft; **~-propos** *nm* foreword; **~-veille** *nf*; **l'~** two days before

avare [avaʀ] *adj* miserly, avaricious ♦ *nm/f* miser; **~ de** (*compliments etc*) sparing of

avarié, e [avaʀje] *adj* rotting

avaries [avaʀi] *nfpl* (*NAVIG*) damage *sg*

avec [avɛk] *prép* with; (*à l'égard de*) to(wards), with

avenant, e [avnɑ̃, -ɑ̃t] *adj* pleasant; **à l'~** in keeping

avènement [avɛnmɑ̃] *nm* (*d'un roi*) accession, succession; (*d'un changement*) advent, coming

avenir [avniʀ] *nm* future; **à l'~** in future; **politicien d'~** politician with prospects *ou* a future

Avent [avɑ̃] *nm*: **l'~** Advent

aventure [avɑ̃tyʀ] *nf* adventure; (*amoureuse*) affair; **aventurer**: **s'aventurer** to venture; **aventureux, euse** *adj* adventurous, venturesome; (*projet*) risky, chancy

avenue [avny] *nf* avenue

avérer [avere]: **s'~** *vb +attrib* to prove (to be)

averse [avɛʀs(ə)] *nf* shower

averti, e [avɛʀti] *adj* (well-)informed

avertir [avɛʀtiʀ] *vt*: **~ qn (de qch/que)** to warn sb (of sth/that); (*renseigner*) to inform sb (of sth/that); **avertissement** *nm* warning; **avertisseur** *nm* horn, siren

aveu, x [avø] *nm* confession

aveugle [avœgl(ə)] *adj* blind; **aveuglément** *adv* blindly; **~r** *vt* to blind

aviateur, trice [avjatœʀ, -tʀis] *nm/f* aviator, pilot

aviation [avjasjɔ̃] *nf* aviation; (*sport*) flying; (*MIL*) air force

avide [avid] *adj* eager; (*péj*) greedy, grasping

avilir [aviliʀ] *vt* to debase

avion [avjɔ̃] *nm* (aero)plane (*BRIT*), (air)plane (*US*); **aller (quelque part) en ~** to go (somewhere) by plane, fly (somewhere); **par ~** by airmail; **à réaction** jet (plane)

aviron [aviʀɔ̃] *nm* oar; (*sport*): **l'~** rowing

avis [avi] *nm* opinion; (*notification*) notice; **changer d'~** to change one's mind; **jusqu'à nouvel ~** until further notice

avisé, e [avize] *adj* sensible, wise

aviser [avize] *vt* (*voir*) to notice, catch sight of; (*informer*): **~ qn de/que** to advise *ou* inform sb of/that ♦ *vi* to think about things, assess the situation; **s'~ de qch/que** to become suddenly aware of sth/that; **s'~ de faire** to take it into one's head to do

avocat, e [avɔka, -at] *nm/f* (*JUR*) barrister (*BRIT*), lawyer ♦ *nm* (*CULIN*) avocado (pear); **~ général** assistant public prosecutor

avoine [avwan] *nf* oats *pl*

─────────── MOT CLÉ

avoir [avwaʀ] *nm* assets *pl*, resources *pl*; (*COMM*) credit

♦ *vt* **1** (*posséder*) to have; **elle a 2 enfants/une belle maison** she has (got) 2 children/a lovely house; **il a les yeux bleus** he has (got) blue eyes

2 (*âge, dimensions*) to be; **il a 3 ans** he is 3 (years old); **le mur a 3 mètres de haut** the wall is 3 metres high; *voir aussi* **faim; peur** *etc*

3 (*fam: duper*) to do, have; **on vous a eu!** you've been done *ou* had!

4: en ~ contre qn to have a grudge against sb; **en ~ assez** to be fed up; **j'en ai pour une demi-heure** it'll take me half an hour

♦ *vb aux* **1** to have; **~ mangé/dormi** to have eaten/slept

2 (*avoir +à +infinitif*): **~ à faire qch** to have to do sth; **vous n'avez qu'à lui demander** you only have to ask him

♦ *vb impers* **1**: **il y a** (+ *singulier*) there is; (+ *pluriel*) there are; **qu'y-a-t-il?, qu'est-ce qu'il y a?** what's the matter?, what is it?; **il doit y avoir une explication** there must be an explanation; **il n'y a qu'à ...** we (*ou* you *etc*) will just have to ...

2 (*temporel*): **il y a 10 ans** 10 years ago; **il**

y a 10 ans/longtemps que je le sais I've known it for 10 years/a long time; **il y a 10 ans qu'il est arrivé** it's 10 years since he arrived

avoisiner [avwazine] *vt* to be near *ou* close to; *(fig)* to border *ou* verge on

avortement [avɔRtəmɑ̃] *nm* abortion

avorter [avɔRte] *vi (MÉD)* to have an abortion; *(fig)* to fail

avoué, e [avwe] *adj* avowed ♦ *nm (JUR)* ≈ solicitor

avouer [avwe] *vt (crime, défaut)* to confess (to); ~ **avoir fait/que** to admit *ou* confess to having done/that

avril [avRil] *nm* April

axe [aks(ə)] *nm* axis; *(de roue etc)* axle; *(fig)* main line; ~ **routier** main road, trunk road; **axer** *vt*: axer qch sur to centre sth on

ayons *etc vb voir* **avoir**

azote [azɔt] *nm* nitrogen

B b

babines [babin] *nfpl* chops

babiole [babjɔl] *nf (bibelot)* trinket; *(vétille)* trifle

bâbord [babɔR] *nm*: **à** *ou* **par** ~ to port, on the port side

baby-foot [babifut] *nm* table football

bac [bak] *abr m* = **baccalauréat**; ♦ *nm (bateau)* ferry; *(récipient)* tub; tray; tank

baccalauréat [bakalɔRea] *nm* high school diploma

bachelier, ière [baʃəlje, -jɛR] *nm/f holder of the baccalauréat*

bachoter [baʃɔte] *(fam) vi* to cram (for an exam)

bâcler [bakle] *vt* to botch (up)

badaud, e [bado, -od] *nm/f* idle onlooker, stroller

badigeonner [badiʒɔne] *vt* to distemper; to colourwash; *(barbouiller)* to daub

badin, e [badɛ̃, -in] *adj* playful

badiner [badine] *vi*: ~ **avec qch** to treat sth lightly

baffe [baf] *(fam) nf* slap, clout

bafouer [bafwe] *vt* to deride, ridicule

bafouiller [bafuje] *vi, vt* to stammer

bagage [bagaʒ] *nm*: ~**s** luggage *sg*; ~**s à main** hand-luggage

bagarre [bagaR] *nf* fight, brawl; **bagarrer:**

se bagarrer *vi* to have a fight *ou* scuffle, fight

bagatelle [bagatɛl] *nf* trifle

bagne [baɲ] *nm* penal colony

bagnole [baɲɔl] *(fam) nf* car

bagout [bagu] *nm*: **avoir du** ~ to have the gift of the gab

bague [bag] *nf* ring; ~ **de fiançailles** engagement ring; ~ **de serrage** clip

baguette [bagɛt] *nf* stick; *(cuisine chinoise)* chopstick; *(de chef d'orchestre)* baton; *(pain)* stick of (French) bread; ~ **magique** magic wand

baie [bɛ] *nf (GÉO)* bay; *(fruit)* berry; ~ **(vitrée)** picture window

baignade [bɛɲad] *nf* bathing

baigner [beɲe] *vt (bébé)* to bath; **se** ~ *vi* to have a swim, go swimming *ou* bathing; **baignoire** *nf* bath(tub)

bail [baj] *(pl* **baux)** *nm* lease

bâiller [baje] *vi* to yawn; *(être ouvert)* to gape

bâillon [bajɔ̃] *nm* gag; **bâillonner** *vt* to gag

bain [bɛ̃] *nm* bath; **prendre un** ~ to have a bath; **se mettre dans le** ~ *(fig)* to get into it *ou* things; ~ **de foule** walkabout; ~ **de soleil: prendre un** ~ **de soleil** to sunbathe; ~**s de mer** sea bathing *sg*; **bain-marie** *nm*: **faire chauffer au bain-marie** *(boîte etc)* to immerse in boiling water

baiser [beze] *nm* kiss ♦ *vt (main, front)* to kiss; *(fam!)* to screw *(!)*

baisse [bɛs] *nf* fall, drop; "~ **sur la viande**" "meat prices down"

baisser [bese] *vt* to lower; *(radio, chauffage)* to turn down; *(AUTO: phares)* to dip *(BRIT)*, lower *(US)* ♦ *vi* to fall, drop, go down; **se** ~ *vi* to bend down

bal [bal] *nm* dance; *(grande soirée)* ball; ~ **costumé** fancy-dress ball

balader [balade] *vt (traîner)* to trail round; **se** ~ *vi* to go for a walk *ou* stroll; to go for a drive

baladeur [baladœR] *nm* personal stereo, Walkman (®)

balafre [balafR(ə)] *nf* gash, slash; *(cicatrice)* scar

balai [balɛ] *nm* broom, brush; **balai-brosse** *nm* (long-handled) scrubbing brush

balance [balɑ̃s] *nf* scales *pl*; *(de précision)* balance; *(signe)*: **la B~** Libra

balancer [balɑ̃se] *vt* to swing; *(lancer)* to fling, chuck; *(renvoyer, jeter)* to chuck out ♦ *vi* to swing; **se** ~ *vi* to swing; to rock; to sway; **se** ~ **de** *(fam)* not to care about; **balancier** *nm (de pendule)* pendulum; *(perche)* (balancing) pole; **balançoire** *nf* swing; *(sur pivot)* seesaw

balayer [baleje] *vt (feuilles etc)* to sweep up, brush up; *(pièce)* to sweep; *(chasser)* to sweep away; to sweep aside; *(suj: radar)* to scan; **balayeur, euse** *nm/f* roadsweeper;

balayeuse nf (machine) roadsweeper

balbutier [balbysje] vi, vt to stammer

balcon [balkɔ̃] nm balcony; (THÉÂTRE) dress circle

baleine [balɛn] nf whale; (de parapluie, corset) rib; **baleinière** nf whaleboat

balise [baliz] nf (NAVIG) beacon; (marker) buoy; (AVIAT) runway light, beacon; (AUTO, SKI) sign, marker; **baliser** vt to mark out (with lights etc)

balivernes [balivɛrn(ə)] nfpl nonsense sg

ballant, e [balɑ̃, -ɑ̃t] adj dangling

balle [bal] nf (de fusil) bullet; (de sport) ball; (paquet) bale; (fam: franc) franc; ~ **perdue** stray bullet

ballerine [balrin] nf ballet dancer

ballet [balɛ] nm ballet

ballon [balɔ̃] nm (de sport) ball; (jouet, AVIAT) balloon; (de vin) glass; ~ **de football** football

ballot [balo] nm bundle; (péj) nitwit

ballottage [balɔtaʒ] nm (POL) second ballot

ballotter [balɔte] vi to roll around; to toss ♦ vt to shake about; to toss

balnéaire [balneɛr] adj seaside cpd

balourd, e [balur, -urd(ə)] adj clumsy ♦ nm/f clodhopper

balustrade [balystrad] nf railings pl, handrail

bambin [bɑ̃bɛ̃] nm little child

ban [bɑ̃] nm cheer; ~**s** nmpl (de mariage) banns; **mettre au** ~ **de** to outlaw from

banal, e [banal] adj banal, commonplace; (péj) trite

banane [banan] nf banana

banc [bɑ̃] nm seat, bench; (de poissons) shoal; ~ **d'essai** (fig) testing ground; ~ **de sable** sandbank

bancaire [bɑ̃kɛr] adj banking, bank cpd

bancal, e [bɑ̃kal] adj wobbly; bow-legged

bandage [bɑ̃daʒ] nm bandage

bande [bɑ̃d] nf (de tissu etc) strip; (MÉD) bandage; (motif) stripe; (magnétique etc) tape; (groupe) band; (: péj) bunch; **par la** ~ in a roundabout way; **faire** ~ **à part** to keep to o.s.; ~ **dessinée** comic strip; ~ **sonore** sound track

bandeau, x [bɑ̃do] nm headband; (sur les yeux) blindfold; (MÉD) head bandage

bander [bɑ̃de] vt (blessure) to bandage; (muscle) to tense; ~ **les yeux à qn** to blindfold sb

banderole [bɑ̃drɔl] nf banner, streamer

bandit [bɑ̃di] nm bandit; **banditisme** nm violent crime, armed robberies pl

bandoulière [bɑ̃duljɛr] nf: **en** ~ (slung ou worn) across the shoulder

banlieue [bɑ̃ljø] nf suburbs pl; **lignes/quartiers de** ~ suburban lines/areas; **trains de** ~ commuter trains

bannière [banjɛr] nf banner

bannir [banir] vt to banish

banque [bɑ̃k] nf bank; (activités) banking; ~ **d'affaires** merchant bank; ~**route** [bɑ̃krut] nf bankruptcy

banquet [bɑ̃kɛ] nm dinner; (d'apparat) banquet

banquette [bɑ̃kɛt] nf seat

banquier [bɑ̃kje] nm banker

banquise [bɑ̃kiz] nf ice field

baptême [batɛm] nm christening; baptism; ~ **de l'air** first flight

baquet [bakɛ] nm tub, bucket

bar [bar] nm bar

baraque [barak] nf shed; (fam) house; ~ **foraine** fairground stand

baraqué, e [barake] adj well-built, hefty

baraquements [barakmɑ̃] nmpl (pour réfugiés, ouvriers) huts

baratin [baratɛ̃] (fam) nm smooth talk, patter; **baratiner** vt to chat up

barbare [barbar] adj barbaric

barbe [barb(ə)] nf beard; **quelle** ~! (fam) what a drag ou bore!; **à la** ~ **de qn** under sb's nose; ~ **à papa** candy-floss (BRIT), cotton candy (US)

barbelé [barbəle] nm barbed wire no pl

barboter [barbɔte] vi to paddle, dabble; **barboteuse** [barbɔtøz] nf rompers pl

barbouiller [barbuje] vt to daub; **avoir l'estomac barbouillé** to feel queasy

barbu, e [barby] adj bearded

barda [barda] (fam) nm kit, gear

barder [barde] (fam) vi: **ça va** ~ sparks will fly, things are going to get hot

barème [barɛm] nm scale; table

baril [baril] nm barrel; keg

bariolé, e [barjɔle] adj gaudily-coloured

baromètre [barɔmɛtr(ə)] nm barometer

baron [barɔ̃] nm baron; **baronne** nf baroness

baroque [barɔk] adj (ART) baroque; (fig) weird

barque [bark(ə)] nf small boat

barquette [barkɛt] nf (pour repas) tray; (pour fruits) punnet

barrage [baraʒ] nm dam; (sur route) roadblock, barricade

barre [bar] nf bar; (NAVIG) helm; (écrite) line, stroke

barreau, x [baro] nm bar; (JUR): **le** ~ the Bar

barrer [bare] vt (route etc) to block; (mot) to cross out; (chèque) to cross (BRIT); (NAVIG) to steer; **se** ~ vi (fam) to clear off

barrette [barɛt] nf (pour cheveux) (hair) slide (BRIT) ou clip (US)

barricader [barikade] vt to barricade

barrière [barjɛr] nf fence; (obstacle) barrier; (porte) gate

barrique [barik] nf barrel, cask

bas, basse [bɑ, bɑs] adj low ♦ nm bottom, lower part; (vêtement) stocking ♦ adv low;

(parler) softly; **au ~ mot** at the lowest estimate; **en ~** down below; at (ou to) the bottom; (dans une maison) downstairs; **en ~ de** at the bottom of; **mettre ~ to** give birth; **à ~ ...!** down with ...!; **~ morceaux** nmpl (viande) cheap cuts

basané, e [bazane] adj tanned, bronzed

bas-côté [bakote] nm (de route) verge (BRIT), shoulder (US)

bascule [baskyl] nf: (jeu de) **~ seesaw**; (balance à) **~ scales** pl; **fauteuil à ~ rocking chair**

basculer [baskyle] vi to fall over, topple (over); (benne) to tip up ♦ vt to topple over; to tip out, tip up

base [bɑz] nf base; (POL) rank and file; (fondement, principe) basis; **de ~** basic; **à ~ de café** etc coffee etc -based; **~ de données** database; **baser** vt to base; **se ~r sur** vt (preuves) to base one's argument on

bas-fond [bafɔ̃] nm (NAVIG) shallow; **~s** nmpl (fig) dregs

basilic [bazilik] nm (CULIN) basil

basket [basket] nm trainer (BRIT), sneaker (US); (aussi: **~-ball**) basketball

basque [bask(ə)] adj, nm/f Basque

basse [bɑs] adj voir **bas** ♦ nf (MUS) bass; **~-cour** nf farmyard

bassin [basɛ̃] nm (cuvette) bowl; (pièce d'eau) pond, pool; (de fontaine, GÉO) basin; (ANAT) pelvis; (portuaire) dock

bassine [basin] nf (ustensile) basin; (contenu) bowl(ful)

basson [basɔ̃] nm bassoon

bas-ventre [bavɑ̃tʀ(ə)] nm (lower part of the) stomach

bat vb voir **battre**

bât [bɑ] nm packsaddle

bataille [bataj] nf battle; fight

bâtard, e [bɑtaʀ, -aʀd(ə)] nm/f illegitimate child, bastard (pej)

bateau, x [bato] nm boat, ship; **bateau-mouche** nm passenger pleasure boat (on the Seine)

batelier, ière [batəlje, -jeʀ] nm/f (de bac) ferryman(woman)

bâti, e [bɑti] adj: **bien ~** well-built

batifoler [batifɔle] vi to frolic about

bâtiment [bɑtimɑ̃] nm building; (NAVIG) ship, vessel; (industrie) building trade

bâtir [bɑtiʀ] vt to build

bâtisse [bɑtis] nf building

bâton [bɑtɔ̃] nm stick; **à ~s rompus** informally

bats vb voir **battre**

battage [bataʒ] nm (publicité) (hard) plugging

battant [batɑ̃] nm (de cloche) clapper; (de volets) shutter, flap; (de porte) side; (fig: personne) fighter; **porte à double ~** double door

battement [batmɑ̃] nm (de cœur) beat; (intervalle) interval (between classes, trains); **10 minutes de ~** 10 minutes to spare; **~ de paupières** blinking no pl (of eyelids)

batterie [batʀi] nf (MIL, ÉLEC) battery; (MUS) drums pl, drum kit; **~ de cuisine** pots and pans pl; kitchen utensils pl

batteur [batœʀ] nm (MUS) drummer; (appareil) whisk

battre [batʀ(ə)] vt to beat; (suj: pluie, vagues) to beat ou lash against; (blé) to thresh; (passer au peigne fin) to scour ♦ vi (cœur) to beat; (volets etc) to bang, rattle; **se ~** vi to fight; **~ la mesure** to beat time; **~ en brèche** to demolish; **son plein** to be at its height, be going full swing; **~ des mains** to clap one's hands

battue [baty] nf (chasse) beat; (policière etc) search, hunt

baume [bom] nm balm

baux [bo] nmpl de **bail**

bavard, e [bavaʀ, -aʀd(ə)] adj (very) talkative; gossipy; **bavarder** vi to chatter; (indiscrètement) to gossip; to blab

bave [bav] nf dribble; (de chien etc) slobber; (d'escargot) slime; **~r** vi to dribble; to slobber; **en ~r** (fam) to have a hard time (of it); **~tte** nf bib; **baveux, euse** adj (omelette) runny

bavure [bavyʀ] nf smudge; (fig) hitch; blunder

bayer [baje] vi: **~ aux corneilles** to stand gaping

bazar [bazaʀ] nm general store; (fam) jumble; **~der** (fam) vt to chuck out

B.C.B.G. sigle adj (= bon chic bon genre) preppy, smart and trendy

B.C.G. sigle m (= bacille Calmette-Guérin) BCG

bd. abr = **boulevard**

B.D. sigle f = **bande dessinée**

béant, e [beɑ̃, -ɑ̃t] adj gaping

béat, e [bea, -at] adj showing open-eyed wonder; blissful; **béatitude** nf bliss

beau(bel), belle [bo, bɛl] (mpl **~x**) adj beautiful, lovely; (homme) handsome ♦ adv: **il fait ~** the weather's fine; **un ~ jour** one (fine) day; **de plus belle** more than ever, even more; **on a ~ essayer** however hard we try; **bel et bien** well and truly; **faire le ~** (chien) to sit up and beg

────────── **MOT CLÉ** ──────────

beaucoup [boku] adv 1 a lot; **il boit ~** he drinks a lot; **il ne boit pas ~** he doesn't drink much ou a lot

2 (suivi de plus, trop etc) much, a lot, far; **il est ~ plus grand** he is much ou a lot ou far taller

3: **~ de** (nombre) many, a lot of; (quantité) a lot of; **~ d'étudiants/de touristes** a lot of ou many students/tourists; **~ de courage** a lot of courage; **il n'a pas ~ d'argent**

he hasn't got much *ou* at lot of money
4: de ~ by far

beau: **~-fils** *nm* son-in-law; *(remariage)*
stepson; **~-frère** *nm* brother-in-law; **~-
père** *nm* father-in-law; *(remariage)* step-
father
beauté [bote] *nf* beauty; **de toute ~** beautiful; **en ~** brilliantly
beaux-arts [bozar] *nmpl* fine arts
beaux-parents [boparɑ̃] *nmpl* wife's (*ou*
husband's) family, in-laws
bébé [bebe] *nm* baby
bec [bɛk] *nm* beak, bill; *(de récipient)* spout;
lip; *(fam)* mouth; **~ de gaz** (street) gas-
lamp; **~ verseur** pouring lip
bécane [bekan] *(fam) nf* bike
bec-de-lièvre [bɛkdəljɛvr(ə)] *nm* harelip
bêche [bɛʃ] *nf* spade; **bêcher** *vt* to dig
bécoter: **se ~** *vi* to smooch
becqueter [bɛkte] *(fam) vt* to eat
bedaine [bədɛn] *nf* paunch
bedonnant, e [bədɔnɑ̃, -ɑ̃t] *adj* potbellied
bée [be] *adj:* **bouche ~** gaping
beffroi [befʀwa] *nm* belfry
bégayer [begeje] *vt, vi* to stammer
bègue [bɛg] *nm/f:* **être ~** to have a stammer
béguin [begɛ̃] *nm:* **avoir le ~ de** *ou* **pour**
to have a crush on
beige [bɛʒ] *adj* beige
beignet [bɛɲɛ] *nm* fritter
bel [bɛl] *adj voir* **beau**
bêler [bele] *vi* to bleat
belette [bəlɛt] *nf* weasel
belge [bɛlʒ(ə)] *adj, nm/f* Belgian
Belgique [bɛlʒik] *nf:* **la ~** Belgium
bélier [belje] *nm* ram; *(signe):* **le B~** Aries
belle [bɛl] *adj voir* **beau** ♦ *nf (SPORT)* de-
cider; **~-fille** *nf* daughter-in-law; *(remariage)* stepdaughter; **~-mère** *nf* mother-in-
law; stepmother; **~-sœur** *nf* sister-in-law
belliqueux, euse [belikø, -øz] *adj* aggressive, warlike
belvédère [bɛlvedɛʀ] *nm* panoramic viewpoint *(or small building there)*
bémol [bemɔl] *nm (MUS)* flat
bénédiction [benediksjɔ̃] *nf* blessing
bénéfice [benefis] *nm (COMM)* profit;
(avantage) benefit; **bénéficier de** *vt* to enjoy; to benefit by *ou* from; to get, be given;
bénéfique *adj* beneficial
benêt [bənɛ] *nm* simpleton
bénévole [benevɔl] *adj* voluntary, unpaid
bénin, igne [benɛ̃, -iɲ] *adj* minor, mild;
(tumeur) benign
bénir [beniʀ] *vt* to bless; **bénit, e** *adj* con-
secrated; **eau bénite** holy water
benjamin [bɛ̃ʒamɛ̃, -in] *nm/f* youngest
child
benne [bɛn] *nf* skip; *(de téléphérique)*
(cable) car; **~ basculante** tipper *(BRIT)*,

dump truck *(US)*
B.E.P.C. *sigle m* = **brevet d'études du premier cycle**
béquille [bekij] *nf* crutch; *(de bicyclette)*
stand
berceau, x [bɛʀso] *nm* cradle, crib
bercer [bɛʀse] *vt* to rock, cradle; *(suj: musique etc)* to lull; **~ qn de** *(promesses etc)* to
delude sb with; **berceuse** *nf* lullaby
béret (basque) [beʀɛ(bask(ə))] *nm* beret
berge [bɛʀʒ(ə)] *nf* bank
berger, ère [bɛʀʒe, -ɛʀ] *nm/f* shep-
herd(ess)
berlingot [bɛʀlɛ̃go] *nm (emballage)* carton
(pyramid shaped)
berlue [bɛʀly] *nf:* **j'ai la ~** I must be seeing
things
berner [bɛʀne] *vt* to fool
besogne [bəzɔɲ] *nf* work *no pl*, job
besoin [bəzwɛ̃] *nm* need; *(pauvreté):* **le ~**
need, want; **faire ses ~s** to relieve o.s.;
avoir ~ de qch/faire qch to need sth/to
do sth; **au ~** if need be
bestiaux [bɛstjo] *nmpl* cattle
bestiole [bɛstjɔl] *nf* (tiny) creature
bétail [betaj] *nm* livestock, cattle *pl*
bête [bɛt] *nf* animal; *(bestiole)* insect, creature ♦ *adj* stupid, silly; **il cherche la petite
~** he's being pernickety *ou* overfussy; **~
noire** pet hate
bêtise [betiz] *nf* stupidity; stupid thing (to
say *ou* do)
béton [betɔ̃] *nm* concrete; **(en) ~** *(alibi, argument)* cast iron; **~ armé** reinforced concrete; **bétonnière** *nf* cement mixer
betterave [bɛtʀav] *nf* beetroot *(BRIT)*, beet
(US); **~ sucrière** sugar beet
beugler [bøgle] *vi* to low; *(radio etc)* to
blare ♦ *vt (chanson)* to bawl out
Beur [bœʀ] *nm/f person of North African origin living in France*
beurre [bœʀ] *nm* butter; **beurrer** *vt* to butter; **beurrier** *nm* butter dish
beuverie [bœvʀi] *nf* drinking session
bévue [bevy] *nf* blunder
Beyrouth [beʀut] *n* Beirut
bi... [bi] *préfixe* bi..., two-
biais [bjɛ] *nm (moyen)* device, expedient;
(aspect) angle; **en ~, de ~** *(obliquement)* at
an angle; *(fig)* indirectly; **biaiser** *vi (fig)* to
sidestep the issue
bibelot [biblo] *nm* trinket, curio
biberon [bibʀɔ̃] *nm* (feeding) bottle; **nourrir
au ~** to bottle-feed
bible [bibl(ə)] *nf* bible
biblio... *préfixe:* **~bus** *nm* mobile library
van; **~phile** *nm/f* booklover; **~thécaire**
nm/f librarian; **~thèque** *nf* library; *(meuble)* bookcase
bicarbonate [bikaʀbɔnat] *nm:* **~ (de soude)** bicarbonate of soda
biceps [bisɛps] *nm* biceps

biche [biʃ] *nf* doe
bichonner [biʃɔne] *vt* to groom
bicolore [bikɔlɔʀ] *adj* two-coloured
bicoque [bikɔk] (*péj*) *nf* shack
bicyclette [bisiklɛt] *nf* bicycle
bide [bid] *nm* (*fam: ventre*) belly; (*THÉÂTRE*) flop
bidet [bidɛ] *nm* bidet
bidon [bidɔ̃] *nm* can ♦ *adj inv* (*fam*) phoney
bidonville [bidɔ̃vil] *nm* shanty town
bidule [bidyl] (*fam*) *nm* thingumajig
bielle [bjɛl] *nf* connecting rod

MOT CLÉ
---

bien [bjɛ̃] *nm* **1** (*avantage, profit*): **faire du ~ à qn** to do sb good; **dire du ~ de** to speak well of; **c'est pour son ~** it's for his own good
2 (*possession, patrimoine*) possession, property; **son ~ le plus précieux** his most treasured possession; **avoir du ~** to have property; **~s (de consommation etc)** (consumer *etc*) goods
3 (*moral*): **le ~** good; **distinguer le ~ du mal** to tell good from evil
♦ *adv* **1** (*de façon satisfaisante*) well; **elle travaille/mange ~** she works/eats well; **croyant ~ faire, je/il ...** thinking I/he was doing the right thing, I/he ...; **c'est ~ fait!** it serves him (*ou* her *etc*) right!
2 (*valeur intensive*) quite; **~ jeune** quite young; **~ assez** quite enough; **~ mieux** (very) much better; **j'espère ~ y aller** I do hope to go; **je veux ~ le faire** (*concession*) I'm quite willing to do it; **il faut ~ le faire** it has to be done
3: **~ du temps/des gens** quite a time/a number of people
♦ *adj inv* **1** (*en bonne forme, à l'aise*): **je me sens ~** I feel fine; **je ne me sens pas ~** I don't feel well; **on est ~ dans ce fauteuil** this chair is very comfortable
2 (*joli, beau*) good-looking; **tu es ~ dans cette robe** you look good in that dress
3 (*satisfaisant*) good; **elle est ~, cette maison/secrétaire** it's a good house/she's a good secretary
4 (*moralement*) right; (: *personne*) good, nice; (*respectable*) respectable; **ce n'est pas ~ de ...** it's not right to ...; **elle est ~, cette femme** she's a nice woman, she's a good sort; **des gens ~s** respectable people
5 (*en bons termes*): **être ~ avec qn** to be on good terms with sb
♦ *préfixe*: **~-aimé** *adj, nm/f* beloved; **~-être** *nm* well-being; **~faisance** *nf* charity; **~faisant, e** *adj* (*chose*) beneficial; **~fait** *nm* act of generosity, benefaction; (*de la science etc*) benefit; **~faiteur, trice** *nm/f* benefactor/benefactress; **~-fondé** *nm* soundness; **~-fonds** *nm* property; **~heureux, euse** *adj* happy; (*REL*) blessed, blest;

~ que *conj* (al)though; **~ sûr** *adv* certainly

bienséant, e [bjɛ̃seɑ̃, -ɑ̃t] *adj* seemly
bientôt [bjɛ̃to] *adv* soon; **à ~** see you soon
bienveillant, e [bjɛ̃vejɑ̃, -ɑ̃t] *adj* kindly
bienvenu, e [bjɛ̃vny] *adj* welcome; **bienvenue** *nf*: **souhaiter la ~e à** to welcome; **~e à** welcome to
bière [bjɛʀ] *nf* (*boisson*) beer; (*cercueil*) bier; **~ (à la) pression** draught beer; **~ blonde** lager; **~ brune** brown ale
biffer [bife] *vt* to cross out
bifteck [biftɛk] *nm* steak
bifurquer [bifyʀke] *vi* (*route*) to fork; (*véhicule*) to turn off
bigarré, e [bigaʀe] *adj* multicoloured; (*disparate*) motley
bigorneau, x [bigɔʀno] *nm* winkle
bigot, e [bigo, -ɔt] (*péj*) *adj* bigoted
bigoudi [bigudi] *nm* curler
bijou, x [biʒu] *nm* jewel; **bijouterie** *nf* jeweller's (shop); jewellery; **bijoutier, ière** *nm/f* jeweller
bilan [bilɑ̃] *nm* (*COMM*) balance sheet(s); end of year statement; (*fig*) (net) outcome; (: *de victimes*) toll; **faire le ~ de** to assess; to review; **déposer son ~** to file a bankruptcy statement
bile [bil] *nf* bile; **se faire de la ~** (*fam*) to worry o.s. sick
bilieux, euse [biljø, -jøz] *adj* bilious; (*fig: colérique*) testy
bilingue [bilɛ̃g] *adj* bilingual
billard [bijaʀ] *nm* billiards *sg*; billiard table; **c'est du ~** (*fam*) it's a cinch
bille [bij] *nf* (*gén*) ball; (*du jeu de billes*) marble; (*de bois*) log
billet [bijɛ] *nm* (*aussi*: **~ de banque**) (bank)note; (*de cinéma, de bus etc*) ticket; (*courte lettre*) note; **~ circulaire** round-trip ticket
billetterie [bijɛtʀi] *nf* ticket office; (*distributeur*) ticket machine; (*BANQUE*) cash dispenser
billion [biljɔ̃] *nm* billion (*BRIT*), trillion (*US*)
billot [bijo] *nm* block
bimensuel, le [bimɑ̃sɥɛl] *adj* bimonthly
binette [binɛt] *nf* hoe
binocle [binɔkl(ə)] *nm* pince-nez
bio... *préfixe* bio...; **~graphie** *nf* biography; **~logie** *nf* biology; **~logique** *adj* biological
Birmanie [biʀmani] *nf* Burma
bis¹, e [bi, biz] *adj* (*couleur*) greyish brown
bis² [bis] *adv*: **12 bis** 12a *ou* A ♦ *excl, nm* encore
bisannuel, le [bizanɥɛl] *adj* biennial
biscornu, e [biskɔʀny] *adj* twisted
biscotte [biskɔt] *nf* (*breakfast*) rusk
biscuit [biskɥi] *nm* biscuit; sponge cake
bise [biz] *nf* (*baiser*) kiss; (*vent*) North wind
bissextile [bisɛkstil] *adj*: **année ~** leap year

bistouri [bistuʀi] *nm* lancet
bistro(t) [bistʀo] *nm* bistro, café
bitume [bitym] *nm* asphalt
bizarre [bizaʀ] *adj* strange, odd
blafard, e [blafaʀ, -aʀd(ə)] *adj* wan
blague [blag] *nf* (*propos*) joke; (*farce*) trick; **sans ~!** no kidding!; **~ à tabac** tobacco pouch
blaguer [blage] *vi* to joke ♦ *vt* to tease
blaireau, x [blɛʀo] *nm* (*ZOOL*) badger; (*brosse*) shaving brush
blairer [blere] (*fam*) *vt*: **je ne peux pas le ~** I can't bear *ou* stand him
blâme [blɑm] *nm* blame; (*sanction*) reprimand
blâmer [blɑme] *vt* to blame
blanc, blanche [blɑ̃, blɑ̃ʃ] *adj* white; (*non imprimé*) blank; (*innocent*) pure ♦ *nm/f* white, white man(woman) ♦ *nm* (*couleur*) white; (*espace non écrit*) blank; (*aussi: ~ d'œuf*) (egg-)white; (: **~ de poulet**) breast, white meat; (: **vin ~**) white wine; **~ cassé** off-white; **chèque en ~** blank cheque; **à ~** (*chauffer*) white-hot; (*tirer, charger*) with blanks; **~-bec** *nm* greenhorn; **blanche** *nf* (*MUS*) minim (*BRIT*), half-note (*US*); **blancheur** *nf* whiteness
blanchir [blɑ̃ʃiʀ] *vt* (*gén*) to whiten; (*linge*) to launder; (*CULIN*) to blanch; (*fig: disculper*) to clear ♦ *vi* to grow white; (*cheveux*) to go white
blanchisserie *nf* laundry
blason [blazɔ̃] *nm* coat of arms
blazer [blazɛʀ] *nm* blazer
blé [ble] *nm* wheat; **~ noir** (*nm*) buckwheat
bled [blɛd] (*péj*) *nm* hole
blême [blɛm] *adj* pale
blessé, e [blese] *adj* injured ♦ *nm/f* injured person; casualty
blesser [blese] *vt* to injure; (*délibérément: MIL etc*) to wound; (*suj: souliers etc, offenser*) to hurt; **se ~** to injure o.s.; **se ~ au pied** *etc* to injure one's foot *etc*
blessure [blesyʀ] *nf* injury; wound
bleu, e [blø] *adj* blue; (*bifteck*) very rare ♦ *nm* (*couleur*) blue; (*novice*) greenhorn; (*contusion*) bruise; (*vêtement: aussi: ~s*) overalls *pl*; **~ marine** navy blue
bleuet [bløɛ] *nm* cornflower
bleuté, e [bløte] *adj* blue-shaded
blinder [blɛ̃de] *vt* to armour; (*fig*) to harden
bloc [blɔk] *nm* (*de pierre etc*) block; (*de papier à lettres*) pad; (*ensemble*) group, block; **serré à ~** tightened right down; **en ~** as a whole; wholesale; **~ opératoire** operating *ou* theatre block; **~ sanitaire** toilet block; **~age** [blɔkaʒ] *nm* blocking; jamming; freezing; (*PSYCH*) hang-up
bloc-notes [blɔknɔt] *nm* note pad
blocus [blɔkys] *nm* blockade
blond, e [blɔ̃, -ɔ̃d] *adj* fair; blond; (*sable, blés*) golden; **~ cendré** ash blond
bloquer [blɔke] *vt* (*passage*) to block; (*pièce mobile*) to jam; (*crédits, compte*) to freeze
blottir [blɔtiʀ]: **se ~** *vi* to huddle up
blouse [bluz] *nf* overall
blouson [bluzɔ̃] *nm* blouson jacket; **~ noir** (*fig*) ≈ rocker
bluff [blœf] *nm* bluff
bluffer [blœfe] *vi* to bluff
bobard [bɔbaʀ] (*fam*) *nm* tall story
bobine [bɔbin] *nf* reel; (*ÉLEC*) coil
bocal, aux [bɔkal, -o] *nm* jar
bock [bɔk] *nm* glass of beer
bœuf [bœf, *pl* bø] *nm* ox, steer; (*CULIN*) beef
bof! [bɔf] (*fam*) *excl* don't care!; (*pas terrible*) nothing special
bohème [bɔɛm] *adj* happy-go-lucky, unconventional; **bohémien, ne** [bɔemjɛ̃, -jɛn] *nm/f* gipsy
boire [bwaʀ] *vt* to drink; (*s'imprégner de*) to soak up; **~ un coup** to have a drink
bois [bwa] *nm* wood; **de ~, en ~** wooden
boisé, e [bwaze] *adj* woody, wooded
boisson [bwasɔ̃] *nf* drink; **pris de ~** drunk, intoxicated
boîte [bwat] *nf* box; (*entreprise*) place, firm; **aliments en ~** canned *ou* tinned (*BRIT*) foods; **~ à gants** glove compartment; **~ aux lettres** letter box; **~ d'allumettes** box of matches; (*vide*) matchbox; **~ (de conserve)** can *ou* tin (*BRIT*) (of food); **~ de nuit** night club; **~ de vitesses** gear box; **~ postale** PO Box
boiter [bwate] *vi* to limp; (*fig*) to wobble; to be shaky
boîtier [bwatje] *nm* case
boive *etc vb voir* **boire**
bol [bɔl] *nm* bowl; **un ~ d'air** a breath of fresh air; **j'en ai ras le ~** (*fam*) I'm fed up with this
bolide [bɔlid] *nm* racing car; **comme un ~** at top speed, like a rocket
bombance [bɔ̃bɑ̃s] *nf*: **faire ~** to have a feast, revel
bombarder [bɔ̃baʀde] *vt* to bomb; **~ qn de** (*cailloux, lettres*) to bombard sb with; **bombardier** *nm* bomber
bombe [bɔ̃b] *nf* bomb; (*atomiseur*) (aerosol) spray
bomber [bɔ̃be] *vi* to bulge; to camber ♦ *vt*: **~ le torse** to swell out one's chest

---

— MOT CLÉ

bon, bonne [bɔ̃, bɔn] *adj* **1** (*agréable, satisfaisant*) good; **un ~ repas/restaurant** a good meal/restaurant; **être ~ en maths** to be good at maths
2 (*charitable*): **être ~ (envers)** to be good (to)
3 (*correct*) right; **le ~ numéro/moment** the

right number/moment
4 (souhaits): ~ **anniversaire** happy birthday; ~ **voyage** have a good trip; **bonne chance** good luck; **bonne année** happy New Year; **bonne nuit** good night
5 (approprié): ~ **à/pour** fit to/for
6: ~ **enfant** adj inv accommodating, easygoing; **bonne femme** (péj) woman; **de bonne heure** early; ~ **marché** adj inv cheap ♦ adv cheap; ~ **mot** witticism; ~ **sens** common sense; ~ **d'essence** jovial chap; **bonnes œuvres** charitable works, charities ♦ nm **1** (billet) voucher; (aussi: ~ **cadeau**) gift voucher; ~ **d'essence** petrol coupon; ~ **du Trésor** Treasury bond
2: **avoir du** ~ to have its good points; **pour de** ~ for good
♦ adv: **il fait** ~ it's ou the weather is fine; **sentir** ~ to smell good; **tenir** ~ to stand firm
♦ excl good!; **ah** ~? really?; voir aussi **bonne**

---

bonbon [bɔ̃bɔ̃] nm (boiled) sweet
bonbonne [bɔ̃bɔn] nf demijohn
bond [bɔ̃] nm leap; **faire un** ~ to leap in the air
bonde [bɔ̃d] nf bunghole
bondé, e [bɔ̃de] adj packed (full)
bondir [bɔ̃diʀ] vi to leap
bonheur [bɔnœʀ] nm happiness; **porter** ~ (à qn) to bring (sb) luck; **au petit** ~ haphazardly; **par** ~ fortunately
bonhomie [bɔnɔmi] nf goodnaturedness
bonhomme [bɔnɔm] (pl **bonshommes**) nm fellow; ~ **de neige** snowman
bonification [bɔnifikasjɔ̃] nf bonus
bonifier [bɔnifje] vt to improve
boniment [bɔnimɑ̃] nm patter no pl
bonjour [bɔ̃ʒuʀ] excl, nm hello; good morning (ou afternoon)
bonne [bɔn] adj voir **bon** ♦ nf (domestique) maid; ~ **à tout faire** general help; ~ **d'enfant** nanny; ~**ment** adv: **tout** ~**ment** quite simply
bonnet [bɔnɛ] nm bonnet, hat; (de soutiengorge) cup; ~ **d'âne** dunce's cap; ~ **de bain** bathing cap
bonneterie [bɔnɛtʀi] nf hosiery
bonshommes [bɔ̃zɔm] nmpl de **bonhomme**
bonsoir [bɔ̃swaʀ] excl good evening
bonté [bɔ̃te] nf kindness no pl
bonus [bɔnys] nm no-claims bonus
bord [bɔʀ] nm (de table, verre, falaise) edge; (de rivière, lac) bank; (de route) side; (monter) à ~ (to go) on board; **jeter par-dessus** ~ to throw overboard; **le commandant de** ~/**les hommes du** ~ the ship's master/crew; **au** ~ **de la mer** at the seaside; **être au** ~ **des larmes** to be on the verge of tears
bordeaux [bɔʀdo] nm Bordeaux (wine) ♦

adj inv maroon
bordel [bɔʀdɛl] nm brothel; (fam!) bloody mess (!)
border [bɔʀde] vt (être le long de) to border; to line; (garnir): ~ **qch de** to line sth with; to trim sth with; (qn dans son lit) to tuck up
bordereau, x [bɔʀdəʀo] nm slip; statement
bordure [bɔʀdyʀ] nf border; **en** ~ **de** on the edge of
borgne [bɔʀɲ(ə)] adj one-eyed
borne [bɔʀn(ə)] nf boundary stone; (aussi: ~ **kilométrique**) kilometre-marker, ≈ milestone; ~**s** nfpl (fig) limits; **dépasser les** ~**s** to go too far
borné, e [bɔʀne] adj narrow; narrow-minded
borner [bɔʀne] vt to limit; to confine; **se** ~ **à faire** to content o.s. with doing; to limit o.s. to doing
Bosnie-Herzégovine [bɔzni-ɛʀtzegɔvin] nf Bosnia (and) Herzegovina
bosquet [bɔskɛ] nm grove
bosse [bɔs] nf (de terrain etc) bump; (enflure) lump; (du bossu, du chameau) hump; **avoir la** ~ **des maths** etc to have a gift for maths etc; **il a roulé sa** ~ he's been around
bosser [bɔse] (fam) vi to work; to slave (away)
bossu, e [bɔsy] nm/f hunchback
bot [bo] adj m: **pied** ~ club foot
botanique [bɔtanik] nf botany ♦ adj botanic(al)
botte [bɔt] nf (soulier) (high) boot; (gerbe): ~ **de paille** bundle of straw; ~ **de radis** bunch of radishes; ~**s de caoutchouc** wellington boots; ~**r** [bɔte] vt to put boots on; to kick; (fam): **ça me botte** I fancy that
bottin [bɔtɛ̃] nm directory
bottine [bɔtin] nf ankle boot
bouc [buk] nm goat; (barbe) goatee; ~ **émissaire** scapegoat
boucan [bukɑ̃] nm din, racket
bouche [buʃ] nf mouth; **le** ~ **à** ~ the kiss of life; ~ **d'égout** manhole; ~ **d'incendie** fire hydrant; ~ **de métro** métro entrance
bouché, e [buʃe] adj (temps, ciel) overcast; (péj: personne) thick
bouchée [buʃe] nf mouthful; ~**s à la reine** chicken vol-au-vents
boucher, ère [buʃe, -ɛʀ] nm/f butcher ♦ vt (pour colmater) to stop up; to fill up; (obstruer) to block (up); **se** ~ vi (tuyau etc) to block up, get blocked up; **se** ~ **le nez** to hold one's nose; ~**rie** [buʃʀi] nf butcher's (shop); (fig) slaughter
bouche-trou [buʃtʀu] nm (fig) stop-gap
bouchon [buʃɔ̃] nm stopper; (en liège) cork; (fig: embouteillage) holdup; (PÊCHE) float; ~ **doseur** measuring cap
boucle [bukl(ə)] nf (forme, figure) loop;

(*objet*) buckle; ~ **(de cheveux)** curl; ~ **d'oreilles** earring

bouclé, e [bukle] *adj* curly

boucler [bukle] *vt* (*fermer: ceinture etc*) to fasten; (: *magasin*) to shut; (*terminer*) to finish off; (: *budget*) to balance; (*enfermer*) to shut away; (: *quartier*) to seal off ♦ *vi* to curl

bouclier [buklije] *nm* shield

bouddhiste [budist(ə)] *nm/f* Buddhist

bouder [bude] *vi* to sulk ♦ *vt* to turn one's nose up at; to refuse to have anything to do with

boudin [budɛ̃] *nm* (*CULIN*) black pudding

boue [bu] *nf* mud

bouée [bwe] *nf* buoy; ~ **(de sauvetage)** lifebuoy

boueux, euse [bwø, -øz] *adj* muddy ♦ *nm* refuse collector

bouffe [buf] (*fam*) *nf* grub (*fam*), food

bouffée [bufe] *nf* puff; ~ **de fièvre/de honte** flush of fever/shame

bouffer [bufe] (*fam*) *vi* to eat

bouffi, e [bufi] *adj* swollen

bouge [buʒ] *nm* (low) dive; hovel

bougeoir [buʒwar] *nm* candlestick

bougeotte [buʒɔt] *nf*: **avoir la** ~ to have the fidgets

bouger [buʒe] *vi* to move; (*dent etc*) to be loose; (*changer*) to alter; (*agir*) to stir ♦ *vt* to move

bougie [buʒi] *nf* candle; (*AUTO*) spark(ing) plug

bougon, ne [bugɑ̃, -ɔn] *adj* grumpy

bougonner [bugɔne] *vi, vt* to grumble

bouillabaisse [bujabɛs] *nf* type of fish soup

bouillant, e [bujɑ̃, -ɑ̃t] *adj* (*qui bout*) boiling; (*très chaud*) boiling (hot)

bouillie [buji] *nf* gruel; (*de bébé*) cereal; **en ~** (*fig*) crushed

bouillir [bujir] *vi, vt* to boil

bouilloire [bujwar] *nf* kettle

bouillon [bujɔ̃] *nm* (*CULIN*) stock *no pl*; ~**ner** [bujɔne] *vi* to bubble; (*fig*) to bubble up; to foam

bouillotte [bujɔt] *nf* hot-water bottle

boulanger, ère [bulɑ̃ʒe, -ɛr] *nm/f* baker

boulangerie [bulɑ̃ʒri] *nf* bakery

boule [bul] *nf* (*gén*) ball; (*pour jouer*) bowl; (*de machine à écrire*) golf-ball; **se mettre en ~** (*fig: fam*) to fly off the handle, to blow one's top; ~ **de neige** snowball

bouleau, x [bulo] *nm* (silver) birch

boulet [bulɛ] *nm* (*aussi*: ~ **de canon**) cannonball

boulette [bulɛt] *nf* ball

boulevard [bulvar] *nm* boulevard

bouleversement [bulvɛrsəmɑ̃] *nm* upheaval

bouleverser [bulvɛrse] *vt* (*émouvoir*) to overwhelm; (*causer du chagrin*) to distress; (*pays, vie*) to disrupt; (*papiers, objets*) to turn upside down

boulier [bulje] *nm* abacus

boulon [bulɔ̃] *nm* bolt

boulot, te [bulo, -ɔt] *adj* plump, tubby ♦ *nm* (*fam: travail*) work

boum [bum] *nm* bang ♦ *nf* (*fam*) party

bouquet [bukɛ] *nm* (*de fleurs*) bunch (of flowers), bouquet; (*de persil etc*) bunch; (*parfum*) bouquet

bouquin [bukɛ̃] (*fam*) *nm* book; **bouquiner** (*fam*) *vi* to read; to browse around (in a bookshop); **bouquiniste** *nm/f* bookseller

bourbeux, euse [burbø, -øz] *adj* muddy

bourbier [burbje] *nm* (quag)mire

bourde [burd(ə)] *nf* (*erreur*) howler; (*gaffe*) blunder

bourdon [burdɔ̃] *nm* bumblebee

bourdonner [burdɔne] *vi* to buzz

bourg [bur] *nm* small market town

bourgeois, e [burʒwa, -waz] *adj* (*péj*) ≈ (upper) middle class; bourgeois; ~**ie** [burʒwazi] *nf* ≈ upper middle classes *pl*; bourgeoisie

bourgeon [burʒɔ̃] *nm* bud

Bourgogne [burgɔɲ] *nf*: **la** ~ Burgundy ♦ *nm*: **b**~ burgundy (wine)

bourguignon, ne [burgiɲɔ̃, -ɔn] *adj* of ou from Burgundy, Burgundian

bourlinguer [burlɛ̃ge] *vi* to knock about a lot, get around a lot

bourrade [burad] *nf* shove, thump

bourrage [buraʒ] *nm*: ~ **de crâne** brainwashing; (*SCOL*) cramming

bourrasque [burask(ə)] *nf* squall

bourratif, ive [buratif] (*fam*) *adj* filling, stodgy (*pej*)

bourré, e [bure] *adj* (*rempli*): ~ **de** crammed full of; (*fam: ivre*) plastered, tanked up (*BRIT*)

bourreau, x [buro] *nm* executioner; (*fig*) torturer; ~ **de travail** workaholic

bourrelet [burlɛ] *nm* draught excluder; (*de peau*) fold ou roll (of flesh)

bourrer [bure] *vt* (*pipe*) to fill; (*poêle*) to pack; (*valise*) to cram (full)

bourrique [burik] *nf* (*âne*) ass

bourru, e [bury] *adj* surly, gruff

bourse [burs(ə)] *nf* (*subvention*) grant; (*porte-monnaie*) purse; **la B**~ the Stock Exchange

boursoufler [bursufle] *vt* to puff up, bloat

bous *vb voir* **bouillir**

bousculade [buskylad] *nf* rush; crush; **bousculer** [buskyle] *vt* to knock over; to knock into; (*fig*) to push, rush

bouse [buz] *nf* dung *no pl*

boussole [busɔl] *nf* compass

bout [bu] *vb voir* **bouillir** ♦ *nm* bit; (*d'un bâton etc*) tip; (*d'une ficelle, table, rue, période*) end; **au** ~ **de** at the end of, after; **pousser qn à** ~ to push sb to the limit; **venir à** ~ **de** to manage to finish; **à** ~ **por-**

tant at point-blank range; ~ **filtre** filter tip
boutade [butad] *nf* quip, sally
boute-en-train [butɑ̃trɛ̃] *nm inv* (*fig*) live wire
bouteille [butɛj] *nf* bottle; (*de gaz butane*) cylinder
boutique [butik] *nf* shop
bouton [butɔ̃] *nm* button; (*BOT*) bud; (*sur la peau*) spot; (*de porte*) knob; ~ **de manchette** cuff-link; ~ **d'or** buttercup; **boutonner** *vt* to button up; **boutonnière** *nf* buttonhole; **bouton-pression** *nm* press stud
bouture [butyʀ] *nf* cutting
bovins [bɔvɛ̃] *nmpl* cattle *pl*
bowling [bɔliŋ] *nm* (tenpin) bowling; (*salle*) bowling alley
box [bɔks] *nm* lock-up (garage); (*d'écurie*) loose-box
boxe [bɔks(ə)] *nf* boxing
boyau, x [bwajo] *nm* (*galerie*) passage(way); (narrow) gallery; ~**x** *nmpl* (*viscères*) entrails, guts
B.P. *abr* = **boîte postale**
bracelet [braslɛ] *nm* bracelet; **bracelet-montre** *nm* wristwatch
braconnier [brakɔnje] *nm* poacher
brader [brade] *vt* to sell off; ~**ie** [bradʀi] *nf* cut-price shop *ou* stall
braguette [bragɛt] *nf* fly *ou* flies *pl* (*BRIT*), zipper (*US*)
brailler [braje] *vi* to bawl, yell
braire [brɛʀ] *vi* to bray
braise [brɛz] *nf* embers *pl*
brancard [brɑ̃kaʀ] *nm* (*civière*) stretcher; **brancardier** *nm* stretcher-bearer
branchages [brɑ̃ʃaʒ] *nmpl* boughs
branche [brɑ̃ʃ] *nf* branch
branché, e [brɑ̃ʃe] (*fam*) *adj* trendy
brancher [brɑ̃ʃe] *vt* to connect (up); (*en mettant la prise*) to plug in
branle [brɑ̃l] *nm*: **donner le** ~ **à, mettre en** ~ to set in motion
branle-bas [brɑ̃lba] *nm inv* commotion
braquer [brake] *vi* (*AUTO*) to turn (the wheel) ♦ *vt* (*revolver etc*): ~ **qch sur** to aim sth at, point sth at; (*mettre en colère*): ~ **qn** to put sb's back up
bras [bra] *nm* arm ♦ *nmpl* (*fig: travailleurs*) labour *sg*, hands; **à** ~ **raccourcis** with fists flying; ~ **droit** (*fig*) right hand man
brasier [brazje] *nm* blaze, inferno
bras-le-corps [bralkɔʀ] : **à** ~ *adv* (a)round the waist
brassard [brasaʀ] *nm* armband
brasse [bras] *nf* (*nage*) breast-stroke; ~ **papillon** butterfly
brassée [brase] *nf* armful
brasser [brase] *vt* to mix; ~ **l'argent/les affaires** to handle a lot of money/business
brasserie [brasʀi] *nf* (*restaurant*) café-restaurant; (*usine*) brewery

brave [brav] *adj* (*courageux*) brave; (*bon, gentil*) good, kind
braver [brave] *vt* to defy
bravo [bravo] *excl* bravo ♦ *nm* cheer
bravoure [bravuʀ] *nf* bravery
break [brɛk] *nm* (*AUTO*) estate car
brebis [brəbi] *nf* ewe; ~ **galeuse** black sheep
brèche [brɛʃ] *nf* breach, gap; **être sur la** ~ (*fig*) to be on the go
bredouille [brəduj] *adj* empty-handed
bredouiller [brəduje] *vi, vt* to mumble, stammer
bref, brève [brɛf, brɛv] *adj* short, brief ♦ *adv* in short; **d'un ton** ~ sharply, curtly; **en** ~ in short, in brief
Brésil [brezil] *nm* Brazil
Bretagne [brətaɲ] *nf* Brittany
bretelle [brətɛl] *nf* (*de fusil etc*) sling; (*de vêtement*) strap; (*d'autoroute*) slip road (*BRIT*), entrance/exit ramp (*US*); ~**s** *nfpl* (*pour pantalon*) braces (*BRIT*), suspenders (*US*)
breton, ne [brətɔ̃, -ɔn] *adj, nm/f* Breton
breuvage [brœvaʒ] *nm* beverage, drink
brève [brɛv] *adj voir* **bref**
brevet [brəvɛ] *nm* diploma, certificate; ~ **d'études du premier cycle** school certificate (*taken at age 16*); ~ (**d'invention**) patent; **breveté, e** *adj* patented; (*diplômé*) qualified
bribes [brib] *nfpl* bits, scraps; snatches; **par** ~ piecemeal
bricolage [brikɔlaʒ] *nm*: **le** ~ do-it-yourself
bricole [brikɔl] *nf* trifle; small job
bricoler [brikɔle] *vi* to do DIY jobs; to potter about ♦ *vt* to fix up; to tinker with; **bricoleur, euse** *nm/f* handyman(woman), DIY enthusiast
bride [brid] *nf* bridle; (*d'un bonnet*) string, tie; **à** ~ **abattue** flat out, hell for leather; **laisser la** ~ **sur le cou à** to give free rein to
bridé, e [bride] *adj*: **yeux** ~**s** slit eyes
bridge [bridʒ(ə)] *nm* bridge
brièvement [brijɛvmɑ̃] *adv* briefly
brigade [brigad] *nf* (*POLICE*) squad; (*MIL*) brigade; (*gén*) team
brigadier [brigadje] *nm* sergeant
brigandage [brigɑ̃daʒ] *nm* robbery
briguer [brige] *vt* to aspire to
brillamment [brijamɑ̃] *adv* brilliantly
brillant, e [brijɑ̃, -ɑ̃t] *adj* brilliant; bright; (*luisant*) shiny, shining ♦ *nm* (*diamant*) brilliant
briller [brije] *vi* to shine
brimer [brime] *vt* to harass; to bully
brin [brɛ̃] *nm* (*de laine, ficelle etc*) strand; (*fig*): **un** ~ **de** a bit of; ~ **d'herbe** blade of grass; ~ **de muguet** sprig of lily of the valley
brindille [brɛ̃dij] *nf* twig

brio [bʀijo] *nm*: **avec ~** with panache
brioche [bʀijɔʃ] *nf* brioche (bun); (*fam*: *ventre*) paunch
brique [bʀik] *nf* brick ♦ *adj inv* brick red
briquer [bʀike] *vt* to polish up
briquet [bʀike] *nm* (cigarette) lighter
brise [bʀiz] *nf* breeze
briser [bʀize] *vt* to break; **se ~** *vi* to break
britannique [bʀitanik] *adj* British ♦ *nm/f*: **B~** British person, Briton; **les B~s** the British
brocante [bʀɔkɑ̃t] *nf* junk, second-hand goods *pl*
brocanteur, euse [bʀɔkɑ̃tœʀ, -øz] *nm/f* junkshop owner; junk dealer
broche [bʀɔʃ] *nf* brooch; (*CULIN*) spit; (*MÉD*) pin; **à la ~** spit-roasted
broché, e [bʀɔʃe] *adj* (*livre*) paper-backed
brochet [bʀɔʃɛ] *nm* pike *inv*
brochette [bʀɔʃɛt] *nf* skewer
brochure [bʀɔʃyʀ] *nf* pamphlet, brochure, booklet
broder [bʀɔde] *vt* to embroider ♦ *vi* to embroider the facts; **broderie** *nf* embroidery
broncher [bʀɔ̃ʃe] *vi*: **sans ~** without flinching; without turning a hair
bronches [bʀɔ̃ʃ] *nfpl* bronchial tubes; **bronchite** *nf* bronchitis
bronze [bʀɔ̃z] *nm* bronze
bronzer [bʀɔ̃ze] *vt* to tan ♦ *vi* to get a tan; **se ~** to sunbathe
brosse [bʀɔs] *nf* brush; **coiffé en ~** with a crewcut; **~ à cheveux** hairbrush; **~ à dents** toothbrush; **~ à habits** clothesbrush; **brosser** *vt* (*nettoyer*) to brush; (*fig*: *tableau etc*) to paint; to draw; **se brosser les dents** to brush one's teeth
brouette [bʀuɛt] *nf* wheelbarrow
brouhaha [bʀuaa] *nm* hubbub
brouillard [bʀujaʀ] *nm* fog
brouille [bʀuj] *nf* quarrel
brouiller [bʀuje] *vt* to mix up; to confuse; (*rendre trouble*) to cloud; (*désunir*: *amis*) to set at odds; **se ~** *vi* (*vue*) to cloud over; (*détails*) to become confused; (*gens*) to fall out
brouillon, ne [bʀujɔ̃, -ɔn] *adj* disorganised; unmethodical ♦ *nm* draft
broussailles [bʀusaj] *nfpl* undergrowth *sg*; **broussailleux, euse** *adj* bushy
brousse [bʀus] *nf*: **la ~** the bush
brouter [bʀute] *vi* to graze
broutille [bʀutij] *nf* trifle
broyer [bʀwaje] *vt* to crush; **~ du noir** to be down in the dumps
bru [bʀy] *nf* daughter-in-law
brugnon [bʀyɲɔ̃] *nm* (*BOT*) nectarine
bruiner [bʀɥine] *vb impers*: **il bruine** it's drizzling, there's a drizzle
bruire [bʀɥiʀ] *vi* to murmur; to rustle
bruit [bʀɥi] *nm*: **un ~** a noise, a sound; (*fig*: *rumeur*) a rumour; **le ~** noise; **sans ~**

without a sound, noiselessly; **~ de fond** background noise
bruitage [bʀɥitaʒ] *nm* sound effects *pl*
brûlant, e [bʀylɑ̃, -ɑ̃t] *adj* burning; (*liquide*) boiling (hot); (*regard*) fiery
brûlé, e [bʀyle] *adj* (*fig*: *démasqué*) blown ♦ *nm*: **odeur de ~** smell of burning
brûle-pourpoint [bʀylpuʀpwɛ̃] : **à ~** *adv* point-blank
brûler [bʀyle] *vt* to burn; (*suj*: *eau bouillante*) to scald; (*consommer*: *électricité, essence*) to use; (*feu rouge, signal*) to go through ♦ *vi* to burn; (*jeu*) to be warm; **se ~** to burn o.s.; to scald o.s.; **se ~ la cervelle** to blow one's brains out
brûlure [bʀylyʀ] *nf* (*lésion*) burn; (*sensation*) burning (sensation); **~s d'estomac** heartburn *sg*
brume [bʀym] *nf* mist
brun, e [bʀœ̃, -yn] *adj* brown; (*cheveux, personne*) dark; **brunir** *vi* to get a tan
brusque [bʀysk(ə)] *adj* abrupt; **brusquer** *vt* to rush
brut, e [bʀyt] *adj* raw, crude, rough; (*COMM*) gross; (*données*) raw; (*pétrole*) **~** crude (oil)
brutal, e, aux [bʀytal, -o] *adj* brutal; **brutaliser** *vt* to handle roughly, manhandle
Bruxelles [bʀysɛl] *n* Brussels
bruyamment [bʀɥijamɑ̃] *adv* noisily
bruyant, e [bʀɥijɑ̃, -ɑ̃t] *adj* noisy
bruyère [bʀɥjɛʀ] *nf* heather
bu, e *pp de* **boire**
buccal, e, aux [bykal, -o] *adj*: **par voie ~e** orally
bûche [byʃ] *nf* log; **prendre une ~** (*fig*) to come a cropper; **~ de Noël** Yule log; **~r** [byʃe] *nm* pyre; bonfire ♦ *vi* (*fam*) to swot (*BRIT*), slave (away) ♦ *vt* to swot up (*BRIT*), slave away at; **~ron** [byʃʀɔ̃] *nm* woodcutter
budget [bydʒɛ] *nm* budget
buée [bɥe] *nf* (*sur une vitre*) mist; (*de l'haleine*) steam
buffet [byfɛ] *nm* (*meuble*) sideboard; (*de réception*) buffet; **~ (de gare)** (station) buffet, snack bar
buffle [byfl(ə)] *nm* buffalo
buis [bɥi] *nm* box tree; (*bois*) box(wood)
buisson [bɥisɔ̃] *nm* bush
buissonnière [bɥisɔnjɛʀ] *adj*: **faire l'école ~** to skip school
bulbe [bylb(ə)] *nm* (*BOT, ANAT*) bulb; (*coupole*) onion-shaped dome
Bulgarie [bylgaʀi] *nf* Bulgaria
bulle [byl] *nf* bubble
bulletin [byltɛ̃] *nm* (*communiqué, journal*) bulletin; (*papier*) form; (*SCOL*) report; **~ d'informations** news bulletin; **~ de salaire** pay-slip; **~ (de vote)** ballot paper; **~ météorologique** weather report
bureau, x [byʀo] *nm* (*meuble*) desk; (*pièce*,

service) office; ~ **de change** (foreign) exchange office *ou* bureau; ~ **de location** box office; ~ **de poste** post office; ~ **de tabac** tobacconist's (shop); ~ **de vote** polling station; **bureaucratie** *nf* bureaucracy

bureautique [byʀɔtik] *nf* office automation

burin [byʀɛ̃] *nm* cold chisel; (*ART*) burin

burlesque [byʀlɛsk(ə)] *adj* ridiculous; (*LITTÉRATURE*) burlesque

bus¹ [by] *vb voir* **boire**; **bus²** [bys] *nm* bus

busqué, e [byske] *adj* (*nez*) hook(ed)

buste [byst(ə)] *nm* (*ANAT*) chest; bust

but [by] *vb voir* **boire** ♦ *nm* (*cible*) target; (*fig*) goal; aim; (*FOOTBALL etc*) goal; **de ~ en blanc** point-blank; **avoir pour ~ de faire** to aim to do; **dans le ~ de** with the intention of

butane [bytan] *nm* butane; Calor gas (®)

buté, e [byte] *adj* stubborn, obstinate

buter [byte] *vi*: ~ **contre/sur** to bump into; to stumble against ♦ *vt* to antagonize; **se** ~ *vi* to get obstinate; to dig in one's heels

butin [bytɛ̃] *nm* booty, spoils *pl*; (*d'un vol*) loot

butte [byt] *nf* mound, hillock; **être en ~ à** to be exposed to

buvais *etc vb voir* **boire**

buvard [byvaʀ] *nm* blotter

buvette [byvɛt] *nf* bar

buveur, euse [byvœʀ, -øz] *nm/f* drinker

C c

c' [s] *dét voir* **ce**

CA *sigle m* = **chiffre d'affaires**

ça [sa] *pron* (*pour désigner*) this; (: *plus loin*) that; (*comme sujet indéfini*) it; ~ **va?** how are you?; how are things?; (*d'accord?*) OK?, all right?; ~ **alors!** well really!; ~ **fait 10 ans (que)** it's 10 years (since); **c'est** ~ that's right

çà [sa] *adv*: ~ **et là** here and there

cabane [kaban] *nf* hut, cabin

cabaret [kabaʀɛ] *nm* night club

cabas [kaba] *nm* shopping bag

cabillaud [kabijo] *nm* cod *inv*

cabine [kabin] *nf* (*de bateau*) cabin; (*de plage*) (beach) hut; (*de piscine etc*) cubicle; (*de camion, train*) cab; (*d'avion*) cockpit; ~ **d'essayage** fitting room; ~ **spatiale** space capsule; ~ **(téléphonique)** call *ou* (tele)phone box

cabinet [kabinɛ] *nm* (*petite pièce*) closet;

(*de médecin*) surgery (*BRIT*), office (*US*); (*de notaire etc*) practice; (: *clientèle*) practice; (*POL*) Cabinet; ~**s** *nmpl* (*w.-c.*) toilet *sg*; ~ **d'affaires** business consultants' (bureau), business partnership; ~ **de toilette** toilet; ~ **de travail** study

câble [kɑbl(ə)] *nm* cable

cabrer [kabʀe]: **se** ~ *vi* (*cheval*) to rear up; (*avion*) to nose up; (*fig*) to revolt, rebel

cabriole [kabʀijɔl] *nf* caper; somersault

cacahuète [kakayɛt] *nf* peanut

cacao [kakao] *nm* cocoa (powder); (*boisson*) cocoa

cache [kaʃ] *nm* mask, card (for masking) ♦ *nf* hiding place

cache-cache [kaʃkaʃ] *nm*: **jouer à** ~ to play hide-and-seek

cachemire [kaʃmiʀ] *nm* cashmere

cache-nez [kaʃne] *nm inv* scarf, muffler

cacher [kaʃe] *vt* to hide, conceal; **se** ~ *vi* to hide; to be hidden *ou* concealed; ~ **qch à qn** to hide *ou* conceal sth from sb; **il ne s'en cache pas** he makes no secret of it

cachet [kaʃɛ] *nm* (*comprimé*) tablet; (*sceau: du roi*) seal; (: *de la poste*) postmark; (*rétribution*) fee; (*fig*) style, character; **cacheter** *vt* to seal

cachette [kaʃɛt] *nf* hiding place; **en** ~ on the sly, secretly

cachot [kaʃo] *nm* dungeon

cachotterie [kaʃɔtʀi] *nf*: **faire des** ~**s** to be secretive

cactus [kaktys] *nm* cactus

cadavre [kadɑvʀ(ə)] *nm* corpse, (dead) body

caddie [kadi] *nm* (supermarket) trolley

caddy *nm* = **caddie**

cadeau, x [kado] *nm* present, gift; **faire un** ~ **à qn** to give sb a present *ou* gift; **faire** ~ **de qch à qn** to make a present of sth to sb, give sb sth as a present

cadenas [kadna] *nm* padlock

cadence [kadɑ̃s] *nf* (*MUS*) cadence; (: *tempo*) rhythm; (*de travail etc*) rate; **en** ~ rhythmically; in time

cadet, te [kadɛ, -ɛt] *adj* younger; (*le plus jeune*) youngest ♦ *nm/f* youngest child *ou* one, youngest boy *ou* son/girl *ou* daughter

cadran [kadʀɑ̃] *nm* dial; ~ **solaire** sundial

cadre [kadʀ(ə)] *nm* frame; (*environnement*) surroundings *pl*; (*limites*) scope ♦ *nm/f* (*ADMIN*) managerial employee, executive; **dans le** ~ **de** (*fig*) within the framework *ou* context of; **rayer qn des** ~**s** to dismiss sb

cadrer [kadʀe] *vi*: ~ **avec** to tally *ou* correspond with ♦ *vt* to centre

caduc, uque [kadyk] *adj* obsolete; (*BOT*) deciduous

cafard [kafaʀ] *nm* cockroach; **avoir le** ~ to be down in the dumps

café [kafe] *nm* coffee; (*bistro*) café ♦ *adj inv* coffee(-coloured); ~ **au lait** white coffee; ~

noir black coffee; **~ tabac** *tobacconist's or newsagent's serving coffee and spirits;* **cafetière** *nf* (*pot*) coffee-pot

cafouillage [kafujaʒ] *nm* shambles *sg*

cage [kaʒ] *nf* cage; **~ (des buts)** goal; **~ d'escalier** (stair)well; **~ thoracique** rib cage

cageot [kaʒo] *nm* crate

cagibi [kaʒibi] *nm* shed

cagneux, euse [kaɲø, -øz] *adj* knock-kneed

cagnotte [kaɲɔt] *nf* kitty

cagoule [kagul] *nf* cowl; hood; (*SKI etc*) cagoule

cahier [kaje] *nm* notebook; **~ de brouillons** roughbook, jotter; **~ d'exercices** exercise book

cahot [kao] *nm* jolt, bump

caïd [kaid] *nm* big chief, boss

caille [kɑj] *nf* quail

cailler [kɑje] *vi* (*lait*) to curdle; (*sang*) to clot

caillot [kɑjo] *nm* (blood) clot

caillou, x [kaju] *nm* (little) stone; **caillouteux, euse** *adj* stony; pebbly

Caire [kɛʀ] *nm*: **le ~** Cairo

caisse [kɛs] *nf* box; (*où l'on met la recette*) cashbox; till; (*où l'on paye*) cash desk (*BRIT*), check-out; (*de banque*) cashier's desk; (*TECH*) case, casing; **~ d'épargne** savings bank; **~ de retraite** pension fund; **~ enregistreuse** cash register; **caissier, ière** *nm/f* cashier

cajoler [kaʒɔle] *vt* to wheedle, coax; to surround with love

cake [kɛk] *nm* fruit cake

calandre [kalɑ̃dʀ(ə)] *nf* radiator grill

calanque [kalɑ̃k] *nf* rocky inlet

calcaire [kalkɛʀ] *nm* limestone ♦ *adj* (*eau*) hard; (*GÉO*) limestone *cpd*

calciné, e [kalsine] *adj* burnt to ashes

calcul [kalkyl] *nm* calculation; **le ~** (*SCOL*) arithmetic; **~ (biliaire)** (gall)stone; **~ (rénal)** (kidney) stone; **calculateur** *nm* calculator; **calculatrice** *nf* calculator

calculer [kalkyle] *vt* to calculate, work out; (*combiner*) to calculate

calculette [kalkylɛt] *nf* pocket calculator

cale [kal] *nf* (*de bateau*) hold; (*en bois*) wedge; **~ sèche** dry dock

calé, e [kale] (*fam*) *adj* clever, bright

caleçon [kalsɔ̃] *nm* pair of underpants, trunks *pl*

calembour [kalɑ̃buʀ] *nm* pun

calendes [kalɑ̃d] *nfpl*: **renvoyer aux ~ grecques** to postpone indefinitely

calendrier [kalɑ̃dʀije] *nm* calendar; (*fig*) timetable

calepin [kalpɛ̃] *nm* notebook

caler [kale] *vt* to wedge; **~ (son moteur/véhicule)** to stall (one's engine/vehicle)

calfeutrer [kalføtʀe] *vt* to (make) draught-

proof; **se ~** *vi* to make o.s. snug and comfortable

calibre [kalibʀ(ə)] *nm* (*d'un fruit*) grade; (*d'une arme*) bore, calibre; (*fig*) calibre

califourchon [kalifuʀʃɔ̃]: **à ~** *adv* astride

câlin, e [kɑlɛ̃, -in] *adj* cuddly, cuddlesome; tender

câliner [kɑline] *vt* to fondle, cuddle

calmant [kalmɑ̃] *nm* tranquillizer, sedative; (*pour la douleur*) painkiller

calme [kalm(ə)] *adj* calm, quiet ♦ *nm* calm(ness), quietness

calmer [kalme] *vt* to calm (down); (*douleur, inquiétude*) to ease, soothe; **se ~** *vi* to calm down

calomnie [kalɔmni] *nf* slander; (*écrite*) libel; **calomnier** *vt* to slander; to libel

calorie [kalɔʀi] *nf* calorie

calorifuge [kalɔʀifyʒ] *adj* (heat-) insulating, heat-retaining

calotte [kalɔt] *nf* (*coiffure*) skullcap; (*gifle*) slap; **calotte glaciaire** *nf* (*GÉO*) icecap

calquer [kalke] *vt* to trace; (*fig*) to copy exactly

calvaire [kalvɛʀ] *nm* (*croix*) wayside cross, calvary; (*souffrances*) suffering

calvitie [kalvisi] *nf* baldness

camarade [kamaʀad] *nm/f* friend, pal; (*POL*) comrade; **camaraderie** *nf* friendship

cambouis [kɑ̃bwi] *nm* dirty oil *ou* grease

cambrer [kɑ̃bʀe] *vt* to arch

cambriolage [kɑ̃bʀijɔlaʒ] *nm* burglary; **cambrioler** [kɑ̃bʀijɔle] *vt* to burgle (*BRIT*), burglarize (*US*); **cambrioleur, euse** *nm/f* burglar

came [kam] *nf*: **arbre à ~s** camshaft

camelote [kamlɔt] *nf* rubbish, trash, junk

caméra [kameʀa] *nf* (*CINÉMA, TV*) camera; (*d'amateur*) cine-camera

caméscope *nm* camcorder

camion [kamjɔ̃] *nm* lorry (*BRIT*), truck; (*plus petit, fermé*) van; **~ de dépannage** breakdown (*BRIT*) *ou* tow (*US*) truck; **camion-citerne** *nm* tanker; **camionnette** *nf* (small) van; **camionneur** *nm* (*entrepreneur*) haulage contractor (*BRIT*), trucker (*US*); (*chauffeur*) lorry (*BRIT*) *ou* truck driver; van driver

camisole [kamizɔl] *nf*: **~ (de force)** straitjacket

camomille [kamɔmij] *nf* camomile; (*boisson*) camomile tea

camoufler [kamufle] *vt* to camouflage; (*fig*) to conceal, cover up

camp [kɑ̃] *nm* camp; (*fig*) side

campagnard, e [kɑ̃paɲaʀ, -aʀd(ə)] *adj* country *cpd*

campagne [kɑ̃paɲ] *nf* country, countryside; (*MIL, POL, COMM*) campaign; **à la ~** in the country

camper [kɑ̃pe] *vi* to camp ♦ *vt* to sketch; **se ~ devant** to plant o.s. in front of; **cam-**

peur, euse nm/f camper

camphre [kɑ̃fʀ(ə)] nm camphor

camping [kɑ̃piŋ] nm camping; **(terrain de)** ~ campsite, camping site; **faire du** ~ to go camping

Canada [kanada] nm: **le** ~ Canada; **canadien, ne** adj, nm/f Canadian; **canadienne** nf (veste) fur-lined jacket

canaille [kanɑj] (péj) nf scoundrel

canal, aux [kanal, -o] nm canal; (naturel) channel; **canalisation** [kanalizɑsjɔ̃] nf (tuyau) pipe; **canaliser** [kanalize] vt to canalize; (fig) to channel

canapé [kanape] nm settee, sofa

canard [kanaʀ] nm duck

canari [kanaʀi] nm canary

cancans [kɑ̃kɑ̃] nmpl (malicious) gossip sg

cancer [kɑ̃sɛʀ] nm cancer; (signe): **le C~** Cancer; ~ **de la peau** skin cancer

cancre [kɑ̃kʀ(ə)] nm dunce

candeur [kɑ̃dœʀ] nf ingenuousness, guilelessness

candidat, e [kɑ̃dida, -at] nm/f candidate; (à un poste) applicant, candidate; **candidature** nf candidature; application; **poser sa candidature** to submit an application, apply

candide [kɑ̃did] adj ingenuous, guileless

cane [kan] nf (female) duck

caneton [kantɔ̃] nm duckling

canette [kanɛt] nf (de bière) (flip-top) bottle

canevas [kanva] nm (COUTURE) canvas

caniche [kaniʃ] nm poodle

canicule [kanikyl] nf scorching heat

canif [kanif] nm penknife, pocket knife

canine [kanin] nf canine (tooth)

caniveau, x [kanivo] nm gutter

canne [kan] nf (walking) stick; ~ **à pêche** fishing rod; ~ **à sucre** sugar cane

cannelle [kanɛl] nf cinnamon

canoë [kanɔe] nm canoe; (sport) canoeing

canon [kanɔ̃] nm (arme) gun; (HISTOIRE) cannon; (d'une arme: tube) barrel; (fig) model; (MUS) canon; ~ **rayé** rifled barrel

canot [kano] nm ding(h)y; ~ **de sauvetage** lifeboat; ~ **pneumatique** inflatable ding(h)y; ~**age** nm rowing; ~**ier** [kanɔtje] nm boater

cantatrice [kɑ̃tatʀis] nf (opera) singer

cantine [kɑ̃tin] nf canteen

cantique [kɑ̃tik] nm hymn

canton [kɑ̃tɔ̃] nm district consisting of several communes; (en Suisse) canton

cantonade [kɑ̃tɔnad] : **à la** ~ adv to everyone in general; from the rooftops

cantonner [kɑ̃tɔne] vt (MIL) to quarter, station; **se** ~ **dans** to confine o.s. to

cantonnier [kɑ̃tɔnje] nm roadmender

canular [kanylaʀ] nm hoax

caoutchouc [kautʃu] nm rubber; ~ **mousse** foam rubber

cap [kap] nm (GÉO) cape; headland; (fig) hurdle; watershed; (NAVIG): **changer de** ~ to change course; **mettre le** ~ **sur** to head ou steer for

C.A.P. sigle m (= Certificat d'aptitude professionnelle) vocational training certificate taken at secondary school

capable [kapabl(ə)] adj able, capable; ~ **de qch/faire** capable of sth/doing

capacité [kapasite] nf (compétence) ability; (JUR, contenance) capacity; ~ **(en droit)** basic legal qualification

cape [kap] nf cape, cloak; **rire sous** ~ to laugh up one's sleeve

C.A.P.E.S. [kapɛs] sigle m (= Certificat d'aptitude pédagogique à l'enseignement secondaire) teaching diploma

capillaire [kapilɛʀ] adj (soins, lotion) hair cpd; (vaisseau etc) capillary

capitaine [kapitɛn] nm captain

capital, e, aux [kapital, -o] adj major; of paramount importance; fundamental ♦ nm capital; (fig) stock; asset; voir aussi **capitaux**; ~ **(social)** authorized capital; ~**e** nf (ville) capital; (lettre) capital (letter); ~**iser** vt to amass, build up; ~**isme** nm capitalism; ~**iste** adj, nm/f capitalist; **capitaux** [kapito] nmpl (fonds) capital sg

capitonné, e [kapitɔne] adj padded

caporal, aux [kapɔʀal, -o] nm lance corporal

capot [kapo] nm (AUTO) bonnet (BRIT), hood (US)

capote [kapɔt] nf (de voiture) hood (BRIT), top (US); (fam) condom

capoter [kapɔte] vi to overturn

câpre [kɑpʀ(ə)] nf caper

caprice [kapʀis] nm whim, caprice; passing fancy; **capricieux, euse** adj capricious; whimsical; temperamental

Capricorne [kapʀikɔʀn] nm: **le** ~ Capricorn

capsule [kapsyl] nf (de bouteille) cap; (BOT etc, spatiale) capsule

capter [kapte] vt (ondes radio) to pick up; (eau) to harness; (fig) to win, capture

captivant, e [kaptivɑ̃, ɑ̃t] adj captivating; fascinating

captivité [kaptivite] nf captivity

capturer [kaptyʀe] vt to capture

capuche [kapyʃ] nf hood

capuchon [kapyʃɔ̃] nm hood; (de stylo) cap, top

caquet [kakɛ] nm: **rabattre le** ~ **à qn** to bring sb down a peg or two

caqueter [kakte] vi to cackle

car [kaʀ] nm coach ♦ conj because, for

carabine [kaʀabin] nf carbine, rifle

caractère [kaʀaktɛʀ] nm (gén) character; **avoir bon/mauvais** ~ to be good-/ill-natured; **en** ~**s gras** in bold type; **en petits** ~**s** in small print; ~**s d'imprimerie**

(block) capitals; **caractériel, le** *adj* (of) character ♦ *nm/f* emotionally disturbed child

caractérisé, e [kaʁakteʁize] *adj*: **c'est une grippe ~e** it is a clear (-cut) case of flu

caractéristique [kaʁakteʁistik] *adj, nf* characteristic

carafe [kaʁaf] *nf* decanter; carafe

caraïbe [kaʁaib] *adj* Caribbean ♦ *n*: **les C~s** the Caribbean (Islands); **la mer des C~s** the Caribbean Sea

carambolage [kaʁãbɔlaʒ] *nm* multiple crash, pileup

caramel [kaʁamɛl] *nm* (*bonbon*) caramel, toffee; (*substance*) caramel

carapace [kaʁapas] *nf* shell

caravane [kaʁavan] *nf* caravan; **caravaning** *nm* caravanning; (*emplacement*) caravan site

carbone [kaʁbɔn] *nm* carbon; (*feuille*) carbon, sheet of carbon paper; (*double*) carbon (copy); **carbonique** [kaʁbɔnik] *adj*: **neige carbonique** dry ice; **carbonisé, e** [kaʁbɔnize] *adj* charred

carburant [kaʁbyʁɑ̃] *nm* (motor) fuel

carburateur [kaʁbyʁatœʁ] *nm* carburettor

carcan [kaʁkɑ̃] *nm* (*fig*) yoke, shackles *pl*

carcasse [kaʁkas] *nf* carcass; (*de véhicule etc*) shell

cardiaque [kaʁdjak] *adj* cardiac, heart *cpd* ♦ *nm/f* heart patient

cardigan [kaʁdigɑ̃] *nm* cardigan

cardiologue [kaʁdjɔlɔg] *nm/f* cardiologist, heart specialist

carême [kaʁɛm] *nm*: **le C~** Lent

carence [kaʁɑ̃s] *nf* incompetence, inadequacy; (*manque*) deficiency

caresse [kaʁɛs] *nf* caress

caresser [kaʁese] *vt* to caress, fondle; (*fig: projet*) to toy with

cargaison [kaʁgɛzɔ̃] *nf* cargo, freight

cargo [kaʁgo] *nm* cargo boat, freighter

carie [kaʁi] *nf*: **la ~ (dentaire)** tooth decay; **une ~** a bad tooth

carillon [kaʁijɔ̃] *nm* (*d'église*) bells *pl*; (*de pendule*) chimes *pl*; (*de porte*) door chime *ou* bell

carlingue [kaʁlɛ̃g] *nf* cabin

carnassier, ière [kaʁnasje, -jɛʁ] *adj* carnivorous

carnaval [kaʁnaval] *nm* carnival

carnet [kaʁnɛ] *nm* (*calepin*) notebook; (*de tickets, timbres etc*) book; (*d'école*) school report; (*journal intime*) diary; **~ de chèques** cheque book

carotte [kaʁɔt] *nf* carrot

carpette [kaʁpɛt] *nf* rug

carré, e [kaʁe] *adj* square; (*fig: franc*) straightforward ♦ *nm* (*de terrain, jardin*) patch, plot; (*MATH*) square; **mètre/ kilomètre ~** square metre/kilometre

carreau, x [kaʁo] *nm* (*en faïence etc*)

(floor) tile; (*wall*) tile; (*de fenêtre*) (window) pane; (*motif*) check, square; (*CARTES: couleur*) diamonds *pl*; (: *carte*) diamond; **tissu à ~x** checked fabric

carrefour [kaʁfuʁ] *nm* crossroads *sg*

carrelage [kaʁlaʒ] *nm* tiling; (tiled) floor

carrelet [kaʁlɛ] *nm* (*poisson*) plaice

carrément [kaʁemɑ̃] *adv* straight out, bluntly; completely, altogether

carrière [kaʁjɛʁ] *nf* (*de roches*) quarry; (*métier*) career; **militaire de ~** professional soldier

carriole [kaʁjɔl] (*péj*) *nf* old cart

carrossable [kaʁɔsabl(ə)] *adj* suitable for (motor) vehicles

carrosse [kaʁɔs] *nm* (horse-drawn) coach

carrosserie [kaʁɔsʁi] *nf* body, coachwork *no pl*; (*activité, commerce*) coachbuilding

carrure [kaʁyʁ] *nf* build; (*fig*) stature, calibre

cartable [kaʁtabl(ə)] *nm* (*d'écolier*) satchel, (school)bag

carte [kaʁt(ə)] *nf* (*de géographie*) map; (*marine, du ciel*) chart; (*de fichier, d'abonnement etc, à jouer*) card; (*au restaurant*) menu; (*aussi*: **~ postale**) (post)card; (: **~ de visite**) (visiting) card; **à la ~** (*au restaurant*) à la carte; **~ bancaire** cash card; **~ de crédit** credit card; **~ d'identité** identity card; **~ de séjour** residence permit; **~ grise** (*AUTO*) ≈ (car) registration book, logbook; **~ routière** road map; **~ téléphonique** phonecard

carter [kaʁtɛʁ] *nm* sump

carton [kaʁtɔ̃] *nm* (*matériau*) cardboard; (*boîte*) (cardboard) box; (*d'invitation*) invitation card; **faire un ~** (*au tir*) to have a go at the rifle range; to score a hit; (**à dessin**) portfolio; **cartonné, e** *adj* (*livre*) hardback, cased; **carton-pâte** *nm* pasteboard

cartouche [kaʁtuʃ] *nf* cartridge; (*de cigarettes*) carton

cas [kɑ] *nm* case; **faire peu de ~/grand ~ de** to attach little/great importance to; **en aucun ~** on no account; **au ~ où** in case; **en ~ de** in case of, in the event of; **en ~ de besoin** if need be; **en tout ~** in any case, at any rate; **~ de conscience** matter of conscience

casanier, ière [kazanje, -jɛʁ] *adj* stay-at-home

cascade [kaskad] *nf* waterfall, cascade; (*fig*) stream, torrent

cascadeur, euse [kaskadœʁ, -øz] *nm/f* stuntman(girl)

case [kɑz] *nf* (*hutte*) hut; (*compartiment*) compartment; (*pour le courrier*) pigeonhole; (*sur un formulaire, de mots croisés etc*) box

caser [kɑze] *vt* (*trouver de la place pour*) to put (away); to put up; (*fig*) to find a job for; to marry off

caserne [kazɛʁn(ə)] *nf* barracks *pl*

cash [kaʃ] *adv*: **payer ~** to pay cash down
casier [kɑzje] *nm* (*à journaux etc*) rack; (*de bureau*) filing cabinet; (: *à cases*) set of pigeonholes; (*case*) compartment; pigeonhole; (: *à clef*) locker; **~ judiciaire** police record
casino [kazino] *nm* casino
casque [kask(ə)] *nm* helmet; (*chez le coiffeur*) (hair-)drier; (*pour audition*) (head-)phones *pl*, headset
casquette [kaskɛt] *nf* cap
cassant, e [kɑsɑ̃, -ɑ̃t] *adj* brittle; (*fig*) brusque, abrupt
cassation [kɑsɑsjɔ̃] *nf*: **cour de ~** final court of appeal
casse [kɑs] *nf* (*pour voitures*): **mettre à la ~** to scrap; (*dégâts*): **il y a eu de la ~** there were a lot of breakages; **~-cou** *adj inv* daredevil, reckless; **~-croûte** *nm inv* snack; **~-noisette(s)** *nm inv* nutcrackers *pl*; **~-noix** *nm inv* nutcrackers *pl*; **~-pieds** (*fam*) *adj inv*: **il est ~-pieds** he's a pain in the neck
casser [kɑse] *vt* to break; (*ADMIN*: *gradé*) to demote; (*JUR*) to quash; **se ~** *vi* to break
casserole [kasʀɔl] *nf* saucepan
casse-tête [kɑstɛt] *nm inv* (*jeu*) brain teaser; (*difficultés*) headache (*fig*)
cassette [kasɛt] *nf* (*bande magnétique*) cassette; (*coffret*) casket
casseur [kɑsœʀ] *nm* hooligan
cassis [kasis] *nm* blackcurrant
cassoulet [kasulɛ] *nm* bean and sausage hot-pot
cassure [kɑsyʀ] *nf* break, crack
castor [kastɔʀ] *nm* beaver
castrer [kɑstʀe] *vt* (*mâle*) to castrate; (: *cheval*) to geld; (*femelle*) to spay
catalogue [katalɔg] *nm* catalogue
cataloguer [katalɔge] *vt* to catalogue, to list; (*péj*) to put a label on
catalyseur *nm* catalytic convertor
catalyseur [katalizœʀ] *nm* catalyst
cataplasme [kataplasm(ə)] *nm* poultice
cataracte [kataʀakt(ə)] *nf* cataract
catastrophe [katastʀɔf] *nf* catastrophe, disaster; **catastrophé, e** [katastʀɔfe] (*fam*) *adj* deeply saddened
catch [katʃ] *nm* (all-in) wrestling; **catcheur, euse** *nm/f* (all-in) wrestler
catéchisme [kateʃism(ə)] *nm* catechism
catégorie [kategɔʀi] *nf* category
catégorique [kategɔʀik] *adj* categorical
cathédrale [katedʀal] *nf* cathedral
catholique [katɔlik] *adj*, *nm/f* (Roman) Catholic; **pas très ~** *a* bit shady *ou* fishy
catimini [katimini] : **en ~** *adv* on the sly
cauchemar [koʃmaʀ] *nm* nightmare
cause [koz] *nf* cause; (*JUR*) lawsuit, case; **à ~ de** because of, owing to; **pour ~ de** on account of; owing to; (**et) pour ~** and for (a very) good reason; **être en ~** to be at

stake; to be involved; to be in question; **mettre en ~** to implicate; to call into question; **remettre en ~** to challenge; **~r** [koze] *vt* to cause ♦ *vi* to chat, talk; **~rie** [kozʀi] *nf* talk
caution [kosjɔ̃] *nf* guarantee, security; deposit; (*JUR*) bail (bond); (*fig*) backing, support; **payer la ~ de qn** to stand bail for sb; **libéré sous ~** released on bail; **~ner** [kosjɔne] *vt* to guarantee; (*soutenir*) to support
cavalcade [kavalkad] *nf* (*fig*) stampede
cavalier, ière [kavalje, -jɛʀ] *adj* (*désinvolte*) offhand ♦ *nm/f* rider; (*au bal*) partner ♦ *nm* (*ÉCHECS*) knight; **faire ~ seul** to go it alone
cave [kav] *nf* cellar ♦ *adj*: **yeux ~s** sunken eyes
caveau, x [kavo] *nm* vault
caverne [kavɛʀn(ə)] *nf* cave
C.C.P. *sigle m* = **compte chèques postaux**
CD *sigle m* (= *compact disc*) CD
CD-ROM *sigle m* CD-ROM
CE *n abr* (= *Communauté Européenne*) EC

MOT CLÉ

ce, cette [sə, sɛt] (*devant nm* **cet** + *voyelle ou h aspiré*; *pl* **ces**) *dét* (*proximité*) this; these *pl*; (*non-proximité*) that; those *pl*; **cette maison(-ci/là)** this/that house; **cette nuit** (*qui vient*) tonight; (*passée*) last night
♦ *pron* **1**: **c'est** it's *ou* it is; **c'est une peintre** he's *ou* he is a painter; **ce sont des peintres** they're *ou* they are painters; **c'est le facteur** *etc* (*à la porte*) it's the postman; **qui est-ce?** who is it?; (*en désignant*) who is he/she?; **qu'est-ce?** what is it?
2: **~ qui, ~ que, ~ dont** (*chose qui*): **il est bête, ~ qui me chagrine** he's stupid, which saddens me; **tout ~ qui bouge** everything that *ou* which moves; **tout ~ que je sais** all I know; **~ dont j'ai parlé** what I talked about; **~ que c'est grand!** it's so big!; *voir aussi* **-ci**; **est-ce que**; **n'est-ce pas**; **c'est-à-dire**

---

ceci [səsi] *pron* this
cécité [sesite] *nf* blindness
céder [sede] *vt* to give up ♦ *vi* (*pont, barrage*) to give way; (*personne*) to give in; **~ à** to yield to, give in to
CEDEX [sedɛks] *sigle m* (= *courrier d'entreprise à distribution exceptionnelle*) postal service for bulk users
cédille [sedij] *nf* cedilla
cèdre [sɛdʀ(ə)] *nm* cedar
CEI *abr m* (= *Communauté des États Indépendants*) CIS
ceinture [sɛ̃tyʀ] *nf* belt; (*taille*) waist; (*fig*) ring; belt; circle; **~ de sécurité** safety *ou* seat belt; **~r** *vt* (*saisir*) to grasp (round the waist)

cela [səla] *pron* that; *(comme sujet indéfini)* it; **quand/où ~?** when/where (was that)?

célèbre [selɛbʀ(ə)] *adj* famous

célébrer [selebʀe] *vt* to celebrate; *(louer)* to extol

céleri [sɛlʀi] *nm:* **~(-rave)** celeriac; **~ (en branche)** celery

célérité [seleʀite] *nf* speed, swiftness

célibat [seliba] *nm* celibacy; bachelorhood; spinsterhood; **célibataire** [selibatɛʀ] *adj* single, unmarried

celle(s) [sɛl] *pron voir* **celui**

cellier [selje] *nm* storeroom

cellulaire [selylɛʀ] *adj:* **voiture** *ou* **fourgon ~** prison *ou* police van

cellule [selyl] *nf (gén)* cell

cellulite [selylit] *nf* excess fat, cellulite

MOT CLÉ

celui, celle [səlɥi, sɛl] *(mpl* **ceux,** *fpl* **celles)** *pron* **1:** **~-ci/là, celle-ci/là** this one/that one; **ceux-ci, celles-ci** these (ones); **ceux-là, celles-là** those (ones); **~ de mon frère** my brother's; **~ du salon/du dessous** the one in *(ou* from) the lounge/ below

2: **~ qui bouge** the one which *ou* that moves; *(personne)* the one who moves; **~ que je vois** the one (which *ou* that) I see; the one (whom) I see; **~ dont je parle** the one I'm talking about

3 *(valeur indéfinie):* **~ qui veut** whoever wants

---

cendre [sɑ̃dʀ(ə)] *nf* ash; **~s** *nfpl (d'un foyer)* ash(es), cinders; *(volcaniques)* ash *sg;* *(d'un défunt)* ashes; **sous la ~** *(CULIN)* in (the) embers; **cendrier** *nm* ashtray

cène [sɛn] *nf:* **la ~** (Holy) Communion

censé, e [sɑ̃se] *adj:* **être ~ faire** to be supposed to do

censeur [sɑ̃sœʀ] *nm (SCOL)* deputy-head *(BRIT),* vice-principal *(US); (CINÉMA, POL)* censor

censure [sɑ̃syʀ] *nf* censorship; **~r** [sɑ̃syʀe] *vt (CINÉMA, PRESSE)* to censor; *(POL)* to censure

cent [sɑ̃] *num* a hundred, one hundred; **centaine** *nf:* **une centaine (de)** about a hundred, a hundred or so; **plusieurs centaines (de)** several hundred; **des centaines (de)** hundreds (of); **centenaire** *adj* hundred-year-old ♦ *nm (anniversaire)* centenary; **centième** *num* hundredth; **centigrade** *nm* centigrade; **centilitre** *nm* centilitre; **centime** *nm* centime; **centimètre** *nm* centimetre; *(ruban)* tape measure, measuring tape

central, e, aux [sɑ̃tʀal, -o] *adj* central ♦ *nm:* **~ (téléphonique)** (telephone) exchange; **centrale** *nf* power station

centre [sɑ̃tʀ(ə)] *nm* centre; **~ commercial** shopping centre; **~ d'apprentissage** training college; **centre-ville** *nm* town centre, downtown (area) *(US)*

centuple [sɑ̃typl(ə)] *nm:* **le ~ de qch** a hundred times sth; **au ~** a hundredfold

cep [sɛp] *nm* (vine) stock

cèpe [sɛp] *nm* (edible) boletus

cependant [səpɑ̃dɑ̃] *adv* however

céramique [seʀamik] *nf* ceramics *sg*

cercle [sɛʀkl(ə)] *nm* circle; *(objet)* band, hoop; **~ vicieux** vicious circle

cercueil [sɛʀkœj] *nm* coffin

céréale [seʀeal] *nf* cereal

cérémonie [seʀemɔni] *nf* ceremony; **~s** *nfpl (péj)* fuss *sg,* to-do *sg*

cerf [sɛʀ] *nm* stag

cerfeuil [sɛʀfœj] *nm* chervil

cerf-volant [sɛʀvɔlɑ̃] *nm* kite

cerise [səʀiz] *nf* cherry; **cerisier** *nm* cherry (tree)

cerné, e [sɛʀne] *adj:* **les yeux ~s** with dark rings *ou* shadows under the eyes

cerner [sɛʀne] *vt (MIL etc)* to surround; *(fig: problème)* to delimit, define

certain, e [sɛʀtɛ̃, -ɛn] *adj* certain ♦ *dét* certain; **d'un ~ âge** past one's prime, not so young; **un ~ temps** (quite) some time; **~s** some; **certainement** *adv (probablement)* most probably *ou* likely; *(bien sûr)* certainly, of course

certes [sɛʀt(ə)] *adv* admittedly; of course; indeed (yes)

certificat [sɛʀtifika] *nm* certificate

certitude [sɛʀtityd] *nf* certainty

cerveau, x [sɛʀvo] *nm* brain

cervelas [sɛʀvəla] *nm* saveloy

cervelle [sɛʀvɛl] *nf (ANAT)* brain

ces [se] *dét voir* **ce**

C.E.S. *sigle m* (= *Collège d'enseignement secondaire*) ≈ (junior) secondary school *(BRIT)*

cesse [sɛs]: **sans ~** *adv* continually, constantly; continuously; **il n'avait de ~ que** he would not rest until

cesser [sese] *vt* to stop ♦ *vi* to stop, cease; **~ de faire** to stop doing

cessez-le-feu *nm inv* ceasefire

c'est-à-dire [sɛtadiʀ] *adv* that is (to say)

cet, cette [sɛt] *dét voir* **ce**

ceux [sø] *pron voir* **celui**

CFC *abr* (= *chlorofluorocarbon*) CFC

C.F.D.T. *sigle f* = **Confédération française démocratique du travail**

C.G.T. *sigle f* = **Confédération générale du travail**

chacun, e [ʃakœ̃, -yn] *pron* each; *(indéfini)* everyone, everybody

chagrin [ʃagʀɛ̃] *nm* grief, sorrow; **chagriner** *vt* to grieve; to bother

chahut [ʃay] *nm* uproar; **chahuter** *vt* to rag, bait ♦ *vi* to make an uproar

chaîne [ʃɛn] *nf* chain; *(RADIO, TV: stations)*

channel; **travail à la** ~ production line work; ~ **(de montage** ou **de fabrication)** production ou assembly line; ~ **(de montagnes)** (mountain) range; ~ **(haute-fidélité** ou **hi-fi)** hi-fi system; ~ **(stéréo)** stereo (system)

chair [ʃɛʀ] nf flesh ♦ adj: **(couleur)** ~ flesh-coloured; **avoir la** ~ **de poule** to have goosepimples ou gooseflesh; **bien en** ~ plump, well-padded; **en** ~ **et en os** in the flesh

chaire [ʃɛʀ] nf (d'église) pulpit; (d'université) chair

chaise [ʃɛz] nf chair; ~ **longue** deckchair

châle [ʃɑl] nm shawl

chaleur [ʃalœʀ] nf heat; (fig) warmth; fire, fervour; heat

chaleureux, euse [ʃalœʀø, -øz] adj warm

chaloupe [ʃalup] nf launch; (de sauvetage) lifeboat

chalumeau, x [ʃalymo] nm blowlamp, blowtorch

chalutier [ʃalytje] nm trawler

chamailler [ʃamaje]: **se** ~ vi to squabble, bicker

chambouler [ʃɑbule] vt to disrupt, turn upside down

chambre [ʃɑbʀ(ə)] nf bedroom; (TECH) chamber; (POL) chamber, house; (JUR) court; (COMM) chamber; federation; **faire** ~ **à part** to sleep in separate rooms; ~ **à air** (de pneu) (inner) tube; ~ **à coucher** bedroom; ~ **à un lit/deux lits** (à l'hôtel) single-/twin-bedded room; ~ **d'amis** spare ou guest room; ~ **noire** (PHOTO) dark room

chambrer [ʃɑbʀe] vt (vin) to bring to room temperature

chameau, x [ʃamo] nm camel

champ [ʃɑ] nm field; **prendre du** ~ to draw back; ~ **de bataille** battlefield; ~ **de courses** racecourse; ~ **de tir** rifle range

champagne [ʃɑpaɲ] nm champagne

champêtre [ʃɑpɛtʀ(ə)] adj country cpd, rural

champignon [ʃɑpiɲɔ̃] nm mushroom; (terme générique) fungus; ~ **de Paris** button mushroom

champion, ne [ʃɑpjɔ̃, -jɔn] adj, nm/f champion; **championnat** nm championship

chance [ʃɑs] nf: **la** ~ luck; ~s nfpl (probabilités) chances; **une** ~ a stroke ou piece of luck ou good fortune; (occasion) a lucky break; **avoir de la** ~ to be lucky

chanceler [ʃɑsle] vi to totter

chancelier [ʃɑsəlje] nm (allemand) chancellor

chanceux, euse [ʃɑsø, -øz] adj lucky

chandail [ʃɑdaj] nm (thick) sweater

chandelier [ʃɑdəlje] nm candlestick

chandelle [ʃɑdɛl] nf (tallow) candle; **dîner**

aux ~s candlelight dinner

change [ʃɑ̃ʒ] nm (COMM) exchange

changement [ʃɑ̃ʒmɑ̃] nm change; ~ **de vitesses** gears pl; gear change

changer [ʃɑ̃ʒe] vt (modifier) to change, alter; (remplacer, COMM, rhabiller) to change ♦ vi to change, alter; **se** ~ vi to change (o.s.); ~ **de** (remplacer: adresse, nom, voiture etc) to change one's; (échanger, alterner: côté, place, train etc) to change +npl; ~ **de couleur/direction** to change colour/direction; ~ **d'idée** to change one's mind; ~ **de vitesse** to change gear

chanson [ʃɑ̃sɔ̃] nf song

chant [ʃɑ̃] nm song; (art vocal) singing; (d'église) hymn; ~**age** nm blackmail; **faire du** ~ to use blackmail; ~**er** [ʃɑ̃te] vt, vi to sing; **si cela lui chante** (fam) if he feels like it; ~**eur, euse** [ʃɑ̃tœʀ, -øz] nm/f singer

chantier [ʃɑ̃tje] nm (building) site; (sur une route) roadworks pl; **mettre en** ~ to put in hand; ~ **naval** shipyard

chantilly [ʃɑ̃tiji] nf voir **crème**

chantonner [ʃɑ̃tɔne] vi, vt to sing to oneself, hum

chanvre [ʃɑ̃vʀ(ə)] nm hemp

chaparder [ʃapaʀde] vt to pinch

chapeau, x [ʃapo] nm hat; ~ **mou** trilby

chapelet [ʃaplɛ] nm (REL) rosary

chapelle [ʃapɛl] nf chapel; ~ **ardente** chapel of rest

chapelure [ʃaplyʀ] nf (dried) bread-crumbs pl

chapiteau, x [ʃapito] nm (de cirque) marquee, big top

chapitre [ʃapitʀ(ə)] nm chapter; (fig) subject, matter

chaque [ʃak] dét each, every; (indéfini) every

char [ʃaʀ] nm (à foin etc) cart, waggon; (de carnaval) float; ~ **(d'assaut)** tank

charabia [ʃaʀabja] (péj) nm gibberish

charade [ʃaʀad] nf riddle; (mimée) charade

charbon [ʃaʀbɔ̃] nm coal; ~ **de bois** charcoal

charcuterie [ʃaʀkytʀi] nf (magasin) pork butcher's shop and delicatessen; (produits) cooked pork meats pl; **charcutier, ière** nm/f pork butcher

chardon [ʃaʀdɔ̃] nm thistle

charge [ʃaʀʒ(ə)] nf (fardeau) load, burden; (explosif, ÉLEC, MIL, JUR) charge; (rôle, mission) responsibility; ~s nfpl (du loyer) service charges; **à la** ~ **de** (dépendant de) dependent upon; (aux frais de) chargeable to; **j'accepte, à** ~ **de revanche** I accept, provided I can do the same for you one day; **prendre en** ~ to take charge of; (suj: véhicule) to take on; (dépenses) to take care of; ~s **sociales** social security contributions; ~**ment** [ʃaʀʒəmɑ̃] nm (objets) load

charger [ʃaʀʒe] *vt (voiture, fusil, caméra)* to load; *(batterie)* to charge ♦ *vi (MIL etc)* to charge; **se ~ de** *vt* to see to; **~ qn de (faire) qch** to put sb in charge of (doing) sth

chariot [ʃaʀjo] *nm* trolley; *(charrette)* waggon; *(de machine à écrire)* carriage

charité [ʃaʀite] *nf* charity; **faire la ~ à** to give (something) to

charmant, e [ʃaʀmɑ̃, -ɑ̃t] *adj* charming

charme [ʃaʀm(ə)] *nm* charm; **charmer** *vt* to charm

charnel, le [ʃaʀnɛl] *adj* carnal

charnière [ʃaʀnjɛʀ] *nf* hinge; *(fig)* turning-point

charnu, e [ʃaʀny] *adj* fleshy

charpente [ʃaʀpɑ̃t] *nf* frame(work); **charpentier** *nm* carpenter

charpie [ʃaʀpi] *nf*: **en ~** *(fig)* in shreds *ou* ribbons

charrette [ʃaʀɛt] *nf* cart

charrier [ʃaʀje] *vt* to carry (along); to cart, carry

charrue [ʃaʀy] *nf* plough *(BRIT)*, plow *(US)*

chasse [ʃas] *nf* hunting; *(au fusil)* shooting; *(poursuite)* chase; *(aussi:* **~ d'eau)** flush; **la ~ est ouverte** the hunting season is open; **~ gardée** private hunting grounds *pl*; **prendre en ~** to give chase to; **tirer la ~ (d'eau)** to flush the toilet, pull the chain; **~ à courre** hunting

chassé-croisé [ʃasekʀwaze] *nm (fig)* mix-up where people miss each other in turn

chasse-neige [ʃasnɛʒ] *nm inv* snowplough *(BRIT)*, snowplow *(US)*

chasser [ʃase] *vt* to hunt; *(expulser)* to chase away *ou* out, drive away *ou* out; **chasseur, euse** *nm/f* hunter ♦ *nm (avion)* fighter; **chasseur de têtes** *nm (fig)* headhunter

châssis [ʃasi] *nm (AUTO)* chassis; *(cadre)* frame; *(de jardin)* cold frame

chat [ʃa] *nm* cat

châtaigne [ʃatɛɲ] *nf* chestnut; **châtaignier** *nm* chestnut (tree)

châtain [ʃatɛ̃] *adj inv* chestnut (brown); chestnut-haired

château, x [ʃato] *nm* castle; **~ d'eau** water tower; **~ fort** stronghold, fortified castle

châtier [ʃatje] *vt* to punish; *(fig: style)* to polish; **châtiment** *nm* punishment

chaton [ʃatɔ̃] *nm (ZOOL)* kitten

chatouiller [ʃatuje] *vt* to tickle; *(l'odorat, le palais)* to titillate; **chatouilleux, euse** *adj* ticklish; *(fig)* touchy, over-sensitive

chatoyer [ʃatwaje] *vi* to shimmer

châtrer [ʃatʀe] *vt (mâle)* to castrate; (*: cheval)* to geld; *(femelle)* to spay

chatte [ʃat] *nf* (she-)cat

chaud, e [ʃo, -od] *adj (gén)* warm; *(très chaud)* hot; *(fig)* hearty; heated; **il fait ~** it's warm; it's hot; **avoir ~** to be warm; to

be hot; **ça me tient ~** it keeps me warm; **rester au ~** to stay in the warm

chaudière [ʃodjɛʀ] *nf* boiler

chaudron [ʃodʀɔ̃] *nm* cauldron

chauffage [ʃofaʒ] *nm* heating; **~ central** central heating

chauffard [ʃofaʀ] *nm (péj)* reckless driver; hit-and-run driver

chauffe-eau [ʃofo] *nm inv* water-heater

chauffer [ʃofe] *vt* to heat ♦ *vi* to heat up, warm up; *(trop ~: moteur)* to overheat; **se ~** *vi (se mettre en train)* to warm up; *(au soleil)* to warm o.s.

chauffeur [ʃofœʀ] *nm* driver; *(privé)* chauffeur

chaume [ʃom] *nm (du toit)* thatch

chaumière [ʃomjɛʀ] *nf* (thatched) cottage

chaussée [ʃose] *nf* road(way)

chausse-pied [ʃospje] *nm* shoe-horn

chausser [ʃose] *vt (bottes, skis)* to put on; *(enfant)* to put shoes on; **~ du 38/42** to take size 38/42

chaussette [ʃosɛt] *nf* sock

chausson [ʃosɔ̃] *nm* slipper; *(de bébé)* bootee; **~ (aux pommes)** (apple) turnover

chaussure [ʃosyʀ] *nf* shoe; **~s basses** flat shoes; **~s de ski** ski boots

chauve [ʃov] *adj* bald

chauve-souris [ʃovsuʀi] *nf* bat

chauvin, e [ʃovɛ̃, -in] *adj* chauvinistic

chaux [ʃo] *nf* lime; **blanchi à la ~** white-washed

chavirer [ʃaviʀe] *vi* to capsize

chef [ʃɛf] *nm* head, leader; *(de cuisine)* chef; **en ~** *(MIL etc)* in chief; **~ d'accusation** charge; **~ d'entreprise** company head; **~ d'état** head of state; **~ de file** *(de parti etc)* leader; **~ de gare** station master; **~ d'orchestre** conductor *(BRIT)*, director *(US)*; **~-d'œuvre** [ʃɛdœvʀ(ə)] *nm* masterpiece; **~-lieu** [ʃɛfljø] *nm* county town

chemin [ʃəmɛ̃] *nm* path; *(itinéraire, direction, trajet)* way; **en ~** on the way; **~ de fer** railway *(BRIT)*, railroad *(US)*; **par chemin de fer** by rail

cheminée [ʃəmine] *nf* chimney; *(à l'intérieur)* chimney piece, fireplace; *(de bateau)* funnel

cheminement [ʃəminmɑ̃] *nm* progress; course

cheminot [ʃəmino] *nm* railwayman

chemise [ʃəmiz] *nf* shirt; *(dossier)* folder; **~ de nuit** nightdress

chemisier [ʃəmizje] *nm* blouse

chenal, aux [ʃənal, -o] *nm* channel

chêne [ʃɛn] *nm* oak (tree); *(bois)* oak

chenil [ʃənil] *nm* kennels *pl*

chenille [ʃənij] *nf (ZOOL)* caterpillar; *(AUTO)* caterpillar track

chèque [ʃɛk] *nm* cheque *(BRIT)*, check *(US)*; **~ sans provision** bad cheque; **~ de voyage** traveller's cheque; **chéquier** *nm* cheque book

cher, ère [ʃɛʀ] *adj (aimé)* dear; *(coûteux)* expensive, dear ♦ *adv*: **cela coûte ~** it's expensive

chercher [ʃɛʀʃe] *vt* to look for; *(gloire etc)* to seek; **aller ~** to go for, go and fetch; **~ à faire** to try to do; **chercheur, euse** [ʃɛʀʃœʀ, -øz] *nm/f* researcher, research worker

chère [ʃɛʀ] *adj voir* **cher** ♦ *nf*: **la bonne ~** good food

chéri, e [ʃeʀi] *adj* beloved, dear; **(mon) ~** darling

chérir [ʃeʀiʀ] *vt* to cherish

cherté [ʃɛʀte] *nf*: **la ~ de la vie** the high cost of living

chétif, ive [ʃetif, -iv] *adj* puny, stunted

cheval, aux [ʃəval, -o] *nm* horse; *(AUTO)*: **~ (vapeur)** horsepower *no pl*; **faire du ~** to ride; **à ~** on horseback; **à ~ sur** astride; *(fig)* overlapping; **~ de course** racehorse

chevalet [ʃəvalɛ] *nm* easel

chevalier [ʃəvalje] *nm* knight

chevalière [ʃəvaljɛʀ] *nf* signet ring

chevalin, e [ʃəvalɛ̃, -in] *adj*: **boucherie ~e** horse-meat butcher's

chevaucher [ʃəvoʃe] *vi (aussi: se ~)* to overlap (each other) ♦ *vt* to be astride, straddle

chevaux [ʃəvo] *nmpl de* **cheval**

chevelu, e [ʃəvly] *adj* with a good head of hair, hairy *(péj)*

chevelure [ʃəvlyʀ] *nf* hair *no pl*

chevet [ʃəvɛ] *nm*: **au ~ de qn** at sb's bedside; **lampe de ~** bedside lamp

cheveu, x [ʃəvø] *nm* hair; **~x** *nmpl (chevelure) sg*; **avoir les ~x courts** to have short hair

cheville [ʃəvij] *nf (ANAT)* ankle; *(de bois)* peg; *(pour une vis)* plug

chèvre [ʃɛvʀ(ə)] *nf* (she-)goat

chevreau, x [ʃəvʀo] *nm* kid

chèvrefeuille [ʃɛvʀəfœj] *nm* honeysuckle

chevreuil [ʃəvʀœj] *nm* roe deer *inv*; *(CULIN)* venison

chevronné, e [ʃəvʀɔne] *adj* seasoned

                        — MOT CLÉ —

chez [ʃe] *prép* 1 *(à la demeure de)* at; (: *direction)* to; **~ qn** at/to sb's house *ou* place; **~ moi** at home; *(direction)* home

2 *(+profession)* at; (: *direction)* to; **~ le boulanger/dentiste** at or to the baker's/dentist's

3 *(dans le caractère, l'œuvre de)* in; **~ les renards/Racine** in foxes/Racine

---

chez-soi [ʃeswa] *nm inv* home

chic [ʃik] *adj inv* chic, smart; *(généreux)* nice, decent ♦ *nm* stylishness; **~!** great!; **avoir le ~ de** to have the knack of

chicane [ʃikan] *nf (querelle)* squabble

chicaner [ʃikane] *vi (ergoter)*: **~ sur** to quibble about

chiche [ʃiʃ] *adj* niggardly, mean ♦ *excl (à un défi)* you're on!

chichi [ʃiʃi] *(fam) nm* fuss

chicorée [ʃikɔʀe] *nf (café)* chicory; *(salade)* endive

chien [ʃjɛ̃] *nm* dog; **en ~ de fusil** curled up; **~ de garde** guard dog

chiendent [ʃjɛ̃dɑ̃] *nm* couch grass

chienne [ʃjɛn] *nf* dog, bitch

chier [ʃje] *(fam!) vi* to crap *(!)*

chiffon [ʃifɔ̃] *nm (piece of)* rag; **~ner** [ʃifɔne] *vt* to crumple; *(tracasser)* to concern; **~nier** [ʃifɔnje] *nm* rag-and-bone man

chiffre [ʃifʀ(ə)] *nm (représentant un nombre)* figure; numeral; *(montant, total)* total, sum; **en ~s ronds** in round figures; **~ d'affaires** turnover; **chiffrer** *vt (dépense)* to put a figure to, assess; *(message)* to (en)code, cipher

chignon [ʃiɲɔ̃] *nm* chignon, bun

Chili [ʃili] *nm*: **le ~** Chile

chimie [ʃimi] *nf* chemistry; **chimique** *adj* chemical; **produits chimiques** chemicals

Chine [ʃin] *nf*: **la ~** China

chinois, e [ʃinwa, -waz] *adj, nm/f* Chinese ♦ *nm (LING)* Chinese

chiot [ʃjo] *nm* pup(py)

chips [ʃips] *nfpl* crisps *(BRIT)*, (potato) chips *(US)*

chiquenaude [ʃiknod] *nf* flick, flip

chirurgical, e, aux [ʃiʀyʀʒikal, -o] *adj* surgical

chirurgie [ʃiʀyʀʒi] *nf* surgery; **~ esthétique** plastic surgery; **chirurgien, ne** *nm/f* surgeon

choc [ʃɔk] *nm* impact; shock; crash; *(moral)* shock; *(affrontement)* clash

chocolat [ʃɔkɔla] *nm* chocolate; *(boisson)* (hot) chocolate; **~ au lait** milk chocolate

chœur [kœʀ] *nm (chorale)* choir; *(OPÉRA, THÉÂTRE)* chorus; **en ~** in chorus

choisir [ʃwaziʀ] *vt* to choose, select

choix [ʃwa] *nm* choice, selection; **avoir le ~** to have the choice; **premier ~** *(COMM)* class one; **de ~** choice, selected; **au ~** as you wish

chômage [ʃomaʒ] *nm* unemployment; **mettre au ~** to make redundant, put out of work; **être au ~** to be unemployed *ou* out of work; **chômeur, euse** *nm/f* unemployed person

chope [ʃɔp] *nf* tankard

choquer [ʃɔke] *vt (offenser)* to shock; *(commotionner)* to shake (up)

choriste [kɔʀist(ə)] *nm/f* choir member; *(OPÉRA)* chorus member

chorus [kɔʀys] *nm*: **faire ~ (avec)** to voice one's agreement (with)

chose [ʃoz] *nf* thing; **c'est peu de ~** it's nothing (really); it's not much

chou, x [ʃu] *nm* cabbage; **mon petit ~** (my) sweetheart; **~ à la crème** cream bun (*made of choux pastry*)

chouchou, te [ʃuʃu, -ut] *nm/f* (SCOL) teacher's pet

choucroute [ʃukʀut] *nf* sauerkraut

chouette [ʃwɛt] *nf* owl ♦ *adj* (*fam*) great, smashing

chou-fleur [ʃuflœʀ] *nm* cauliflower

choyer [ʃwaje] *vt* to cherish; to pamper

chrétien, ne [kʀetjɛ̃, -ɛn] *adj, nm/f* Christian

Christ [kʀist] *nm*: **le ~** Christ; **christianisme** *nm* Christianity

chrome [kʀom] *nm* chromium; **chromé, e** *adj* chromium-plated

chronique [kʀɔnik] *adj* chronic ♦ *nf* (*de journal*) column, page; (*historique*) chronicle; (RADIO, TV): **la ~ sportive/théâtrale** the sports/theatre review; **la ~ locale** local news and gossip

chronologique [kʀɔnɔlɔʒik] *adj* chronological

chronomètre [kʀɔnɔmɛtʀ(ə)] *nm* stopwatch; **chronométrer** *vt* to time

chrysanthème [kʀizɑ̃tɛm] *nm* chrysanthemum

C.H.U. *sigle m* (= centre hospitalier universitaire) ≈ (teaching) hospital

chuchoter [ʃyʃɔte] *vt, vi* to whisper

chuinter [ʃɥɛ̃te] *vi* to hiss

chut [ʃyt] *excl* sh!

chute [ʃyt] *nf* fall; (*de bois, papier: déchet*) scrap; **faire une ~ (de 10 m)** to fall (10 m); **~ (d'eau)** waterfall; **la ~ des cheveux** hair loss; **~ libre** free fall; **~s de pluie/neige** rain/snowfalls

Chypre [ʃipʀ] *nm/f* Cyprus

-ci [si] *adv voir* par ♦ *dét*: **ce garçon-ci/-là** this/that boy; **ces femmes-ci/-là** these/those women

ci-après [siapʀɛ] *adv* hereafter

cible [sibl(ə)] *nf* target

ciboulette [sibulɛt] *nf* (small) chive

cicatrice [sikatʀis] *nf* scar

cicatriser [sikatʀize] *vt* to heal

ci-contre [sikɔ̃tʀ(ə)] *adv* opposite

ci-dessous [sidəsu] *adv* below

ci-dessus [sidəsy] *adv* above

cidre [sidʀ(ə)] *nm* cider

Cie *abr* (= compagnie) Co.

ciel [sjɛl] *nm* sky; (REL) heaven; **cieux** *nmpl* (*littéraire*) sky *sg*, skies; **à ~ ouvert** open-air; (*mine*) opencast

cierge [sjɛʀʒ(ə)] *nm* candle

cieux [sjø] *nmpl de* **ciel**

cigale [sigal] *nf* cicada

cigare [sigaʀ] *nm* cigar

cigarette [sigaʀɛt] *nf* cigarette

ci-gît [siʒi] *adv +vb* here lies

cigogne [sigɔɲ] *nf* stork

ci-inclus, e [siɛ̃kly, -yz] *adj, adv* enclosed

ci-joint, e [siʒwɛ̃, -ɛ̃t] *adj, adv* enclosed

cil [sil] *nm* (eye)lash

cime [sim] *nf* top; (*montagne*) peak

ciment [simɑ̃] *nm* cement; **~ armé** reinforced concrete

cimetière [simtjɛʀ] *nm* cemetery; (*d'église*) churchyard

cinéaste [sineast(ə)] *nm/f* film-maker

cinéma [sinema] *nm* cinema; **~tographique** *adj* film *cpd*, cinema *cpd*

cinéphile [sinefil] *nm/f* cinema-goer

cinglant, e [sɛ̃glɑ̃, -ɑ̃t] *adj* (*échec*) crushing

cinglé, e [sɛ̃gle] (*fam*) *adj* crazy

cingler [sɛ̃gle] *vt* to lash; (*fig*) to sting

cinq [sɛ̃k] *num* five

cinquantaine [sɛ̃kɑ̃tɛn] *nf*: **une ~ (de)** about fifty; **avoir la ~ (âge)** to be around fifty

cinquante [sɛ̃kɑ̃t] *num* fifty; **cinquantenaire** *adj, nm/f* fifty-year-old

cinquième [sɛ̃kjɛm] *num* fifth

cintre [sɛ̃tʀ(ə)] *nm* coat-hanger

cintré, e [sɛ̃tʀe] *adj* (*chemise*) fitted

cirage [siʀaʒ] *nm* (shoe) polish

circonflexe [siʀkɔ̃flɛks(ə)] *adj*: **accent ~** circumflex accent

circonscription [siʀkɔ̃skʀipsjɔ̃] *nf* district; **~ électorale** (*d'un député*) constituency

circonscrire [siʀkɔ̃skʀiʀ] *vt* to define, delimit; (*incendie*) to contain

circonstance [siʀkɔ̃stɑ̃s] *nf* circumstance; (*occasion*) occasion

circonvenir [siʀkɔ̃vniʀ] *vt* to circumvent

circuit [siʀkɥi] *nm* (*trajet*) tour, (round) trip; (ÉLEC, TECH) circuit

circulaire [siʀkylɛʀ] *adj, nf* circular

circulation [siʀkylasjɔ̃] *nf* circulation; (AUTO): **la ~** (the) traffic

circuler [siʀkyle] *vi* to drive (along); to walk along; (*train etc*) to run; (*sang, devises*) to circulate; **faire ~** (*nouvelle*) to spread (about), circulate; (*badauds*) to move on

cire [siʀ] *nf* wax; **ciré** [siʀe] *nm* oilskin; **cirer** [siʀe] *vt* to wax, polish

cirque [siʀk(ə)] *nm* circus; (GÉO) cirque; (*fig*) chaos, bedlam; carry-on

cisaille(s) [sizaj] *nf(pl)* (gardening) shears *pl*

ciseau, x [sizo] *nm*: **~ (à bois)** chisel; **~x** *nmpl* (*paire de* **~x**) (pair of) scissors

ciseler [sizle] *vt* to chisel, carve

citadin, e [sitadɛ̃, -in] *nm/f* city dweller

citation [sitasjɔ̃] *nf* (*d'auteur*) quotation; (JUR) summons *sg*

cité [site] *nf* town; (*plus grande*) city; **~ universitaire** students' residences *pl*

citer [site] *vt* (*un auteur*) to quote (from); (*nommer*) to name; (JUR) to summon

citerne [sitɛʀn(ə)] *nf* tank

citoyen, ne [sitwajɛ̃, -ɛn] *nm/f* citizen

citron [sitʀɔ̃] *nm* lemon; **~ vert** lime; **citronnade** *nf* lemonade; **citronnier** *nm* lemon tree

citrouille [sitʀuj] nf pumpkin

civet [sivɛ] nm stew

civière [sivjɛʀ] nf stretcher

civil, e [sivil] adj (JUR, ADMIN, poli) civil; (non militaire) civilian; **en ~** in civilian clothes; **dans le ~** in civilian life

civilisation [sivilizɑsjɔ̃] nf civilization

civisme [sivism(ə)] nm public-spiritedness

clair, e [klɛʀ] adj light; (chambre) light, bright; (eau, son, fig) clear ♦ adv: **voir ~** to see clearly; **tirer qch au ~** to clear sth up, clarify sth; **mettre au ~** (notes etc) to tidy up; **le plus ~ de son temps** the better part of his time; **~ de lune** nm moonlight; **clairement** adv clearly

clairière [klɛʀjɛʀ] nf clearing

clairon [klɛʀɔ̃] nm bugle

claironner [klɛʀɔne] vt (fig) to trumpet, shout from the rooftops

clairsemé, e [klɛʀsəme] adj sparse

clairvoyant, e [klɛʀvwajɑ̃, -ɑ̃t] adj perceptive, clear-sighted

clandestin, e [klɑ̃dɛstɛ̃, -in] adj clandestine, covert; **passager ~** stowaway

clapier [klapje] nm (rabbit) hutch

clapoter [klapɔte] vi to lap

claque [klak] nf (gifle) slap

claquer [klake] vi (drapeau) to flap; (porte) to bang, slam; (coup de feu) to ring out ♦ vt (porte) to slam, bang; (doigts) to snap; **se ~ un muscle** to pull ou strain a muscle

claquettes [klakɛt] nfpl tap-dancing sg

clarinette [klaʀinɛt] nf clarinet

clarté [klaʀte] nf lightness; brightness; (d'un son, de l'eau) clearness; (d'une explication) clarity

classe [klas] nf class; (SCOL: local) class(room); (: leçon, élèves) class; **faire la ~** to be a ou the teacher; to teach; **~ment** [klasmɑ̃] nm (rang: SCOL) place; (: SPORT) placing; (liste: SCOL) class list (in order of merit); (: SPORT) placings pl; **~r** [klase] vt (idées, livres) to classify; (papiers) to file; (candidat, concurrent) to grade; (JUR: affaire) to close; **se ~r premier/dernier** to come first/last; (SPORT) to finish first/last

classeur [klasœʀ] nm (cahier) file; (meuble) filing cabinet

classique [klasik] adj classical; (sobre: coupe etc) classic(al); (habituel) standard, classic

clause [kloz] nf clause

claustrer [klostʀe] vt to confine

clavecin [klavsɛ̃] nm harpsichord

clavicule [klavikyl] nf collarbone

clavier [klavje] nm keyboard

clé [kle] nf key; (MUS) clef; (de mécanicien) spanner (BRIT), wrench (US); **prix ~s en main** (d'une voiture) on-the-road price; **~ anglaise** (monkey) wrench; **~ de contact** ignition key

clef [kle] nf = **clé**

clément, e [klemɑ̃, -ɑ̃t] adj (temps) mild; (indulgent) lenient

clerc [klɛʀ] nm: **~ de notaire** solicitor's clerk

clergé [klɛʀʒe] nm clergy

cliché [kliʃe] nm (PHOTO) negative; print; (LING) cliché

client, e [klijɑ̃, -ɑ̃t] nm/f (acheteur) customer, client; (d'hôtel) guest, patron; (du docteur) patient; (de l'avocat) client; **clientèle** nf (du magasin) customers pl, clientèle; (du docteur, de l'avocat) practice

cligner [kliɲe] vi: **~ des yeux** to blink (one's eyes); **~ de l'œil** to wink

clignotant [kliɲɔtɑ̃] nm (AUTO) indicator

clignoter [kliɲɔte] vi (étoiles etc) to twinkle; (lumière) to flash; (: vaciller) to flicker

climat [klima] nm climate

climatisation [klimatizɑsjɔ̃] nf air conditioning; **climatisé, e** adj air-conditioned

clin d'œil [klɛ̃dœj] nm wink; **en un ~** in a flash

clinique [klinik] nf nursing home

clinquant, e [klɛ̃kɑ̃, -ɑ̃t] adj flashy

cliqueter [klikte] vi to clash; to jangle, jingle; to chink

clochard, e [klɔʃaʀ, -aʀd(ə)] nm/f tramp

cloche [klɔʃ] nf (d'église) bell; (fam) clot; **~ à fromage** cheese-cover

cloche-pied [klɔʃpje]: **à ~** adv on one leg, hopping (along)

clocher [klɔʃe] nm church tower; (en pointe) steeple ♦ vi (fam) to be ou go wrong; **de ~** (péj) parochial

cloison [klwazɔ̃] nf partition (wall)

cloître [klwatʀ(ə)] nm cloister

cloîtrer [klwatʀe] vt: **se ~** to shut o.s. up ou away

cloque [klɔk] nf blister

clore [klɔʀ] vt to close; **clos, e** adj voir **maison; huis** ♦ nm (enclosed) field

clôture [klotyʀ] nf closure; (barrière) enclosure; **clôturer** vt (terrain) to enclose; (débats) to close

clou [klu] nm nail; (MÉD) boil; **~s** nmpl (passage clouté) pedestrian crossing; **pneus à ~s** studded tyres; **le ~ du spectacle** the highlight of the show; **~ de girofle** clove; **clouer** vt to nail down ou up

clown [klun] nm clown

club [klœb] nm club

C.N.R.S. sigle m = **Centre nationale de la recherche scientifique**

coasser [kɔase] vi to croak

cobaye [kɔbaj] nm guinea-pig

coca [kɔka] nm Coke (®)

cocaïne [kɔkain] nf cocaine

cocasse [kɔkas] adj comical, funny

coccinelle [kɔksinɛl] nf ladybird (BRIT), ladybug (US)

cocher [kɔʃe] nm coachman ♦ vt to tick

off; (*entailler*) to notch

cochère [kɔʃɛʀ] *adj f*: **porte** ~ carriage entrance

cochon, ne [kɔʃɔ̃, -ɔn] *nm* pig ♦ *adj* (*fam*) dirty, smutty; **cochonnerie** (*fam*) *nf* filth; rubbish, trash

cocktail [kɔktɛl] *nm* cocktail; (*réception*) cocktail party

coco [koko] *nm voir* **noix**; (*fam*) bloke

cocorico [kɔkɔriko] *excl, nm* cock-a-doodle-do

cocotier [kɔkɔtje] *nm* coconut palm

cocotte [kɔkɔt] *nf* (*en fonte*) casserole; ~ (**minute**) pressure cooker; **ma** ~ (*fam*) sweetie (pie)

cocu [kɔky] *nm* cuckold

code [kɔd] *nm* code ♦ *adj*: **phares** ~**s** dipped lights; **se mettre en** ~(**s**) to dip one's (head)lights; ~ **à barres** bar code; ~ **civil** Common Law; ~ **de la route** highway code; ~ **pénal** penal code; ~ **postal** (*numéro*) post (*BRIT*) *ou* zip (*US*) code

cœur [kœʀ] *nm* heart; (*CARTES: couleur*) hearts *pl*; (; *carte*) heart; **avoir bon** ~ to be kind-hearted; **avoir mal au** ~ to feel sick; **en avoir le** ~ **net** to be clear in one's own mind (about it); **par** ~ by heart; **de bon** ~ willingly; **cela lui tient à** ~ that's (very) close to his heart

coffre [kɔfʀ(ə)] *nm* (*meuble*) chest; (*d'auto*) boot (*BRIT*), trunk (*US*); **coffre(-fort)** *nm* safe

coffret [kɔfʀɛ] *nm* casket

cognac [kɔɲak] *nm* brandy, cognac

cogner [kɔɲe] *vi* to knock

cohérent, e [kɔeʀɑ̃, -ɑ̃t] *adj* coherent, consistent

cohorte [kɔɔʀt(ə)] *nf* troop

cohue [kɔy] *nf* crowd

coi, coite [kwa, kwat] *adj*: **rester** ~ to remain silent

coiffe [kwaf] *nf* headdress

coiffé, e [kwafe] *adj*: **bien/mal** ~ with tidy/untidy hair; ~ **en arrière** with one's hair brushed *ou* combed back

coiffer [kwafe] *vt* (*fig*) to cover, top; **se** ~ *vi* to do one's hair; to put on one's hat; ~ **qn** to do sb's hair

coiffeur, euse [kwafœʀ, -øz] *nm/f* hairdresser; **coiffeuse** *nf* (*table*) dressing table

coiffure [kwafyʀ] *nf* (*cheveux*) hairstyle, hairdo; (*chapeau*) hat, headgear *no pl*; (*art*): **la** ~ hairdressing

coin [kwɛ̃] *nm* corner; (*pour coincer*) wedge; **l'épicerie du** ~ the local grocer; **dans le** ~ (*aux alentours*) in the area, around about; locally; **au** ~ **du feu** by the fireside; **regard en** ~ sideways glance

coincé, e [kwɛ̃se] *adj* stuck, jammed; (*fig: inhibé*) inhibited, hung up (*fam*)

coincer [kwɛ̃se] *vt* to jam

coïncidence [kɔɛ̃sidɑ̃s] *nf* coincidence

coïncider [kɔɛ̃side] *vi* to coincide

col [kɔl] *nm* (*de chemise*) collar; (*encolure, cou*) neck; (*de montagne*) pass; ~ **de l'utérus** cervix; ~ **roulé** polo-neck

colère [kɔlɛʀ] *nf* anger; **une** ~ a fit of anger; (**se mettre**) **en** ~ (to get) angry; **coléreux, euse** *adj*; **colérique** *adj* quick-tempered, irascible

colifichet [kɔlifiʃɛ] *nm* trinket

colimaçon [kɔlimasɔ̃] *nm*: **escalier en** ~ spiral staircase

colin [kɔlɛ̃] *nm* hake

colique [kɔlik] *nf* diarrhoea; colic (pains)

colis [kɔli] *nm* parcel

collaborateur, trice [kɔlabɔʀatœʀ, -tʀis] *nm/f* (*aussi POL*) collaborator; (*d'une revue*) contributor

collaborer [kɔlabɔʀe] *vi* to collaborate; ~ **à** to collaborate on; (*revue*) to contribute to

collant, e [kɔlɑ̃, -ɑ̃t] *adj* sticky; (*robe etc*) clinging, skintight; (*péj*) clinging ♦ *nm* (*bas*) tights *pl*

collation [kɔlasjɔ̃] *nf* light meal

colle [kɔl] *nf* glue; (*à papiers peints*) (wallpaper) paste; (*devinette*) teaser, riddle; (*SCOL: fam*) detention

collecte [kɔlɛkt(ə)] *nf* collection

collectif, ive [kɔlɛktif, -iv] *adj* collective; (*visite, billet*) group *cpd*

collection [kɔlɛksjɔ̃] *nf* collection; (*ÉDITION*) series; **collectionner** *vt* (*tableaux, timbres*) to collect; **collectionneur, euse** *nm/f* collector

collectivité [kɔlɛktivite] *nf* group; ~**s locales** (*ADMIN*) local authorities

collège [kɔlɛʒ] *nm* (*école*) (secondary) school; (*assemblée*) body; **collégien** *nm* schoolboy; **collégienne** *nf* schoolgirl

collègue [kɔlɛg] *nm/f* colleague

coller [kɔle] *vt* (*papier, timbre*) to stick (on); (*affiche*) to stick up; (*enveloppe*) to stick down; (*morceaux*) to stick *ou* glue together; (*fam: mettre, fourrer*) to stick, shove; (*SCOL: fam*) to keep in ♦ *vi* (*être collant*) to be sticky; (*adhérer*) to stick; ~ **à** to stick to

collet [kɔlɛ] *nm* (*piège*) snare, noose; (*cou*): **prendre qn au** ~ to grab sb by the throat; ~ **monté** *adj inv* straight-laced

collier [kɔlje] *nm* (*bijou*) necklace; (*de chien, TECH*) collar; ~ (**de barbe**) narrow beard along the line of the jaw

collimateur [kɔlimatœʀ] *nm*: **avoir qn/qch dans le** ~ (*fig*) to have sb/sth in one's sights

colline [kɔlin] *nf* hill

collision [kɔlizjɔ̃] *nf* collision, crash; **entrer en** ~ (**avec**) to collide (with)

colmater [kɔlmate] *vt* (*fuite*) to seal off; (*brèche*) to plug, fill in

colombe [kɔlɔ̃b] *nf* dove

colon [kɔlɔ̃] *nm* settler

colonel [kɔlɔnɛl] *nm* colonel

colonie [kɔlɔni] *nf* colony; ~ **(de vacances)** holiday camp *(for children)*

colonne [kɔlɔn] *nf* column; **se mettre en ~ par deux** to get into twos; ~ **(vertébrale)** spine, spinal column

colorant [kɔlɔrɑ̃] *nm* colouring

colorer [kɔlɔʀe] *vt* to colour

colorier [kɔlɔʀje] *vt* to colour (in)

coloris [kɔlɔʀi] *nm* colour, shade

colporter [kɔlpɔʀte] *vt* to hawk, peddle

colza [kɔlza] *nm* rape (seed)

coma [kɔma] *nm* coma

combat [kɔ̃ba] *nm* fight; fighting *no pl*; ~ **de boxe** boxing match

combattant [kɔ̃batɑ̃] *nm*: **ancien ~** war veteran

combattre [kɔ̃batʀ(ə)] *vt* to fight; *(épidémie, ignorance)* to combat, fight against

combien [kɔ̃bjɛ̃] *adv (quantité)* how much; *(nombre)* how many; *(exclamatif)* how; ~ **de** how much; how many; ~ **de temps** how long; ~ **coûte/pèse ceci?** how much does this cost/weigh?

combinaison [kɔ̃binɛzɔ̃] *nf* combination; *(astuce)* device, scheme; *(de femme)* slip; *(d'aviateur)* flying suit; *(d'homme-grenouille)* wetsuit; *(bleu de travail)* boiler suit *(BRIT)*, coveralls *pl (US)*

combine [kɔ̃bin] *nf* trick; *(péj)* scheme, fiddle *(BRIT)*

combiné [kɔ̃bine] *nm (aussi: ~ téléphonique)* receiver

combiner [kɔ̃bine] *vt* to combine; *(plan, horaire)* to work out, devise

comble [kɔ̃bl(ə)] *adj (salle)* packed (full) ♦ *nm (du bonheur, plaisir)* height; ~**s** *nmpl (CONSTR)* attic *sg*, loft *sg*; **c'est le ~!** that beats everything!

combler [kɔ̃ble] *vt (trou)* to fill in; *(besoin, lacune)* to fill; *(déficit)* to make good; *(satisfaire)* to fulfil

combustible [kɔ̃bystibl(ə)] *nm* fuel

comédie [kɔmedi] *nf* comedy; *(fig)* playacting *no pl*; ~ **musicale** musical; **comédien, ne** *nm/f* actor(tress)

comestible [kɔmɛstibl(ə)] *adj* edible

comique [kɔmik] *adj (drôle)* comical; *(THÉÂTRE)* comic ♦ *nm (artiste)* comic, comedian

comité [kɔmite] *nm* committee; ~ **d'entreprise** works council

commandant [kɔmɑ̃dɑ̃] *nm (gén)* commander, commandant; *(NAVIG, AVIAT)* captain

commande [kɔmɑ̃d] *nf (COMM)* order; ~**s** *nfpl (AVIAT etc)* controls; **sur ~** to order; ~ **à distance** remote control

commandement [kɔmɑ̃dmɑ̃] *nm* command; *(REL)* commandment

commander [kɔmɑ̃de] *vt (COMM)* to order; *(diriger, ordonner)* to command; ~ **à qn de faire** to command *ou* order sb to do

commando [kɔmɑ̃do] *nm* commando (squad)

— MOT CLÉ

comme [kɔm] *prép* **1** *(comparaison)* like; **tout ~ son père** just like his father; **fort ~ un boeuf** as strong as an ox; **joli ~ tout** ever so pretty

2 *(manière)* like; **faites-le ~ ça** do it like this, do it this way; ~ **ci,** ~ **ça** so-so, middling

3 *(en tant que)* as a; **donner ~ prix** to give as a prize; **travailler ~ secrétaire** to work as a secretary

♦ *conj* **1** *(ainsi que)* as; **elle écrit ~ elle parle** she writes as she talks; ~ **si** as if

2 *(au moment où, alors que)* as; **il est parti ~ j'arrivais** he left as I arrived

3 *(parce que, puisque)* as; ~ **il était en retard, il ...** as he was late, he ...

♦ *adv*: ~ **il est fort/c'est bon!** he's so strong/it's so good!

---

commémorer [kɔmemɔʀe] *vt* to commemorate

commencement [kɔmɑ̃smɑ̃] *nm* beginning, start, commencement

commencer [kɔmɑ̃se] *vt, vi* to begin, start, commence; ~ **à** *ou* **de faire** to begin *ou* start doing

comment [kɔmɑ̃] *adv* how ♦ *nm*: **le ~ et le pourquoi** the whys and wherefores; ~**?** *(que dites-vous)* pardon?

commentaire [kɔmɑ̃tɛʀ] *nm* comment; remark

commenter [kɔmɑ̃te] *vt (jugement, événement)* to comment (up)on; *(RADIO, TV: match, manifestation)* to cover

commérages [kɔmeʀaʒ] *nmpl* gossip *sg*

commerçant, e [kɔmɛʀsɑ̃, -ɑ̃t] *nm/f* shopkeeper, trader

commerce [kɔmɛʀs(ə)] *nm (activité)* trade, commerce; *(boutique)* business; **vendu dans le ~** sold in the shops; **commercial, e, aux** *adj* commercial, trading; *(péj)* commercial; **commercialiser** *vt* to market

commère [kɔmɛʀ] *nf* gossip

commettre [kɔmɛtʀ(ə)] *vt* to commit

commis [kɔmi] *nm (de magasin)* (shop) assistant; *(de banque)* clerk; ~ **voyageur** commercial traveller

commissaire [kɔmisɛʀ] *nm (de police)* ≈ (police) superintendent; ~**-priseur** *nm* auctioneer

commissariat [kɔmisaʀja] *nm* police station

commission [kɔmisjɔ̃] *nf (comité, pourcentage)* commission; *(message)* message; *(course)* errand; ~**s** *nfpl (achats)* shopping *sg*

commode [kɔmɔd] *adj (pratique)* convenient, handy; *(facile)* easy; *(air, personne)* easy-going; (*personne*): **pas ~** awkward (to deal with) ♦ *nf* chest of drawers; **commodité** *nf* convenience

commotion [kɔmosjɔ̃] *nf*: **~ (cérébrale)** concussion; **commotionné, e** *adj* shocked, shaken

commun, e [kɔmœ̃, -yn] *adj* common; (*pièce*) communal, shared; (*réunion, effort*) joint; **cela sort du ~** it's out of the ordinary; **le ~ des mortels** the common run of people; **en ~** (*faire*) jointly; **mettre en ~** to pool, share; *voir aussi* **communs**

communauté [kɔmynote] *nf* community; (*JUR*): **régime de la ~** communal estate settlement

commune [kɔmyn] *nf* (*ADMIN*) commune, ≈ district; (: *urbaine*) ≈ borough

communication [kɔmynikasjɔ̃] *nf* communication; **~ (téléphonique)** (telephone) call

communier [kɔmynje] *vi* (*REL*) to receive communion; (*fig*) to be united; **communion** [kɔmynjɔ̃] *nf* communion

communiquer [kɔmynike] *vt* (*nouvelle, dossier*) to pass on, convey; (*maladie*) to pass on; (*peur etc*) to communicate; (*chaleur, mouvement*) to transmit ♦ *vi* to communicate; **se ~ à** (*se propager*) to spread to

communisme [kɔmynism(ə)] *nm* communism; **communiste** *adj, nm/f* communist

communs [kɔmœ̃] *nmpl* (*bâtiments*) outbuildings

commutateur [kɔmytatœʀ] *nm* (*ÉLEC*) (change-over) switch, commutator

compact, e [kɔ̃pakt] *adj* dense; compact

compagne [kɔ̃paɲ] *nf* companion

compagnie [kɔ̃paɲi] *nf* (*firme, MIL*) company; (*groupe*) gathering; **tenir ~ à qn** to keep sb company; **fausser ~ à qn** to give sb the slip, slip *ou* sneak away from sb; **~ aérienne** airline (company)

compagnon [kɔ̃paɲɔ̃] *nm* companion

comparable [kɔ̃paʀabl(ə)] *adj*: **~ (à)** comparable (to)

comparaison [kɔ̃paʀɛzɔ̃] *nf* comparison

comparaître [kɔ̃paʀɛtʀ(ə)] *vi*: **~ (devant)** to appear (before)

comparer [kɔ̃paʀe] *vt* to compare; **~ qch/qn à** *ou* **et** (*pour choisir*) to compare sth/sb with *ou* and; (*pour établir une similitude*) to compare sth/sb to

comparse [kɔ̃paʀs(ə)] (*péj*) *nm/f* associate, stooge

compartiment [kɔ̃paʀtimɑ̃] *nm* compartment

comparution [kɔ̃paʀysjɔ̃] *nf* appearance

compas [kɔ̃pa] *nm* (*GÉOM*) (pair of) compasses *pl*; (*NAVIG*) compass

compatible [kɔ̃patibl(ə)] *adj* compatible

compatir [kɔ̃patiʀ] *vi*: **~ (à)** to sympathize (with)

compatriote [kɔ̃patʀijɔt] *nm/f* compatriot

compenser [kɔ̃pɑ̃se] *vt* to compensate for, make up for

compère [kɔ̃pɛʀ] *nm* accomplice

compétence [kɔ̃petɑ̃s] *nf* competence

compétent, e [kɔ̃petɑ̃, -ɑ̃t] *adj* (*apte*) competent, capable

compétition [kɔ̃petisjɔ̃] *nf* (*gén*) competition; (*SPORT: épreuve*) event; **la ~** competitive sport; **la ~ automobile** motor racing

complainte [kɔ̃plɛ̃t] *nf* lament

complaire [kɔ̃plɛʀ] : **se ~** *vi*: **se ~ dans/parmi** to take pleasure in/in being among

complaisance [kɔ̃plɛzɑ̃s] *nf* kindness; **pavillon de ~** flag of convenience; **complaisant, e** [kɔ̃plɛzɑ̃, -ɑ̃t] *adj* (*aimable*) kind, obliging

complément [kɔ̃plemɑ̃] *nm* complement; remainder; **~ d'information** (*ADMIN*) supplementary *ou* further information; **complémentaire** *adj* complementary; (*additionnel*) supplementary

complet, ète [kɔ̃plɛ, -ɛt] *adj* complete; (*plein: hôtel etc*) full ♦ *nm* (*aussi: ~-veston*) suit; **complètement** *adv* completely; **compléter** *vt* (*porter à la quantité voulue*) to complete; (*augmenter*) to complement, supplement; to add to

complexe [kɔ̃plɛks(ə)] *adj, nm* complex; **complexé, e** *adj* mixed-up, hung-up

complication [kɔ̃plikasjɔ̃] *nf* complexity, intricacy; (*difficulté, ennui*) complication

complice [kɔ̃plis] *nm* accomplice

compliment [kɔ̃plimɑ̃] *nm* (*louange*) compliment; **~s** *nmpl* (*félicitations*) congratulations

compliqué, e [kɔ̃plike] *adj* complicated, complex; (*personne*) complicated

complot [kɔ̃plo] *nm* plot

comportement [kɔ̃pɔʀtəmɑ̃] *nm* behaviour

comporter [kɔ̃pɔʀte] *vt* to consist of, comprise; (*être équipé de*) to have; (*impliquer*) to entail; **se ~** *vi* to behave

composant [kɔ̃pozɑ̃] *nm* component

composante [kɔ̃pozɑ̃t] *nf* component

composé [kɔ̃poze] *nm* compound

composer [kɔ̃poze] *vt* (*musique, texte*) to compose; (*mélange, équipe*) to make up; (*faire partie de*) to make up, form ♦ *vi* (*transiger*) to come to terms; **se ~ de** to be composed of, be made up of; **~ un numéro** to dial a number

compositeur, trice [kɔ̃pozitœʀ, -tʀis] *nm/f* (*MUS*) composer

composition [kɔ̃pozisjɔ̃] *nf* composition; (*SCOL*) test; **de bonne ~** (*accommodant*) easy to deal with

composter [kɔ̃pɔste] *vt* to date-stamp; to punch

compote [kɔ̃pɔt] *nf* stewed fruit *no pl*; **~ de pommes** stewed apples; **compotier** *nm* fruit dish *ou* bowl

compréhensible [kɔ̃preãsibl(ə)] *adj* comprehensible; (*attitude*) understandable
compréhensif, ive [kɔ̃preãsif, -iv] *adj* understanding
comprendre [kɔ̃prãdr(ə)] *vt* to understand; (*se composer de*) to comprise, consist of
compresse [kɔ̃prɛs] *nf* compress
compression [kɔ̃presjɔ̃] *nf* compression; reduction
comprimé [kɔ̃prime] *nm* tablet
comprimer [kɔ̃prime] *vt* to compress; (*fig: crédit etc*) to reduce, cut down
compris, e [kɔ̃pri, -iz] *pp de* **comprendre** ♦ *adj* (*inclus*) included; ~ **entre** (*situé*) contained between; **la maison** ~**e/non** ~**e, y/non** ~ **la maison** including/excluding the house; **100 F tout** ~ 100 F all inclusive *ou* all-in
compromettre [kɔ̃prɔmetr(ə)] *vt* to compromise
compromis [kɔ̃prɔmi] *nm* compromise
comptabilité [kɔ̃tabilite] *nf* (*activité, technique*) accounting, accountancy; (*d'une société: comptes*) accounts *pl*, books *pl*; (: *service*) accounts office
comptable [kɔ̃tabl(ə)] *nm/f* accountant
comptant [kɔ̃tã] *adv*: **payer** ~ to pay cash; **acheter** ~ to buy for cash
compte [kɔ̃t] *nm* count, counting; (*total, montant*) count, (right) number; (*bancaire, facture*) account; ~**s** *nmpl* (*FINANCE*) accounts, books; (*fig*) explanation *sg*; **en fin de** ~ all things considered; **à bon** ~ at a favourable price; (*fig*) lightly; **avoir son** ~ (: *fam*) to have had it; **pour le** ~ **de** on behalf of; **pour son propre** ~ for one's own benefit; **tenir** ~ **de** to take account of; **travailler à son** ~ to work for oneself; **rendre** ~ (**à qn**) **de qch** to give (sb) an account of sth; *voir aussi* **rendre**; ~ **à rebours** countdown; ~ **chèques postaux** Post Office account; ~ **courant** current account
compte-gouttes [kɔ̃tgut] *nm inv* dropper
compter [kɔ̃te] *vt* to count; (*facturer*) to charge for; (*avoir à son actif, comporter*) to have; (*prévoir*) to allow, reckon; (*penser, espérer*): ~ **réussir** to expect to succeed ♦ *vi* to count; (*être économe*) to economize; (*figurer*): ~ **parmi** to be *ou* rank among; ~ **sur** to count (up)on; ~ **avec qch/qn** to reckon with *ou* take account of sth/sb; **sans** ~ **que** besides which
compte rendu [kɔ̃trãdy] *nm* account, report; (*de film, livre*) review
compte-tours [kɔ̃ttur] *nm inv* rev(olution) counter
compteur [kɔ̃tœr] *nm* meter; ~ **de vitesse** speedometer
comptine [kɔ̃tin] *nf* nursery rhyme
comptoir [kɔ̃twar] *nm* (*de magasin*) counter

compulser [kɔ̃pylse] *vt* to consult
comte [kɔ̃t] *nm* count
comtesse [kɔ̃tes] *nf* countess
con, ne [kɔ̃, kɔn] (*fam!*) *adj* damned *ou* bloody (*BRIT*) stupid (*!*)
concéder [kɔ̃sede] *vt* to grant; (*défaite, point*) to concede
concentrer [kɔ̃sãtre] *vt* to concentrate; **se** ~ *vi* to concentrate
concept [kɔ̃sɛpt] *nm* concept
conception [kɔ̃sɛpsjɔ̃] *nf* conception; (*d'une machine etc*) design
concerner [kɔ̃sɛrne] *vt* to concern; **en ce qui me concerne** as far as I am concerned
concert [kɔ̃sɛr] *nm* concert; **de** ~ in unison; together
concerter [kɔ̃sɛrte] *vt* to devise; **se** ~ *vi* (*collaborateurs etc*) to put our (*ou* their *etc*) heads together
concessionnaire [kɔ̃sesjɔnɛr] *nm/f* agent, dealer
concevoir [kɔ̃svwar] *vt* (*idée, projet*) to conceive (of); (*méthode, plan d'appartement, décoration*) to plan, design; (*enfant*) to conceive; **bien/mal conçu** well-/badly-designed
concierge [kɔ̃sjɛrʒ(ə)] *nm/f* caretaker; (*d'hôtel*) head porter
concile [kɔ̃sil] *nm* council
conciliabules [kɔ̃siljabyl] *nmpl* (private) discussions, confabulations
concilier [kɔ̃silje] *vt* to reconcile; **se** ~ *vt* to win over
concitoyen, ne [kɔ̃sitwajɛ̃, -jɛn] *nm/f* fellow citizen
concluant, e [kɔ̃klyã, -ãt] *adj* conclusive
conclure [kɔ̃klyr] *vt* to conclude
conclusion [kɔ̃klyzjɔ̃] *nf* conclusion
conçois *etc vb voir* **concevoir**
concombre [kɔ̃kɔ̃br(ə)] *nm* cucumber
concorder [kɔ̃kɔrde] *vi* to tally, agree
concourir [kɔ̃kurir] *vi* (*SPORT*) to compete; ~ **à** (*effet etc*) to work towards
concours [kɔ̃kur] *nm* competition; (*SCOL*) competitive examination; (*assistance*) aid, help; ~ **de circonstances** combination of circumstances; ~ **hippique** horse show
concret, ète [kɔ̃krɛ, -ɛt] *adj* concrete
concrétiser [kɔ̃kretize] *vt* (*plan, projet*) to put in concrete form; **se** ~ *vi* to materialize
conçu, e [kɔ̃sy] *pp de* **concevoir**
concubinage [kɔ̃kybinaʒ] *nm* (*JUR*) cohabitation
concurrence [kɔ̃kyrãs] *nf* competition; **jusqu'à** ~ **de** up to
concurrent, e [kɔ̃kyrã, -ãt] *nm/f* (*SPORT, ÉCON etc*) competitor; (*SCOL*) candidate
condamner [kɔ̃dane] *vt* (*blâmer*) to condemn; (*JUR*) to sentence; (*porte, ouverture*) to fill in, block up; (*malade*) to give up (hope for); ~ **qn à 2 ans de prison** to sentence sb to 2 years' imprisonment
condensation [kɔ̃dãsasjɔ̃] *nf* condensation

condenser [kɔ̃dɑ̃se] vt to condense; **se ~** vi to condense

condisciple [kɔ̃disipl(ə)] nm/f school fellow, fellow student

condition [kɔ̃disjɔ̃] nf condition; **~s** nfpl (tarif, prix) terms; (circonstances) conditions; **sans ~** unconditional ♦ adv unconditionally; **à ~ de** ou **que** provided that; **conditionnel, le** adj conditional ♦ nm conditional (tense)

conditionnement [kɔ̃disjɔnmɑ̃] nm (emballage) packaging

conditionner [kɔ̃disjɔne] vt (déterminer) to determine; (COMM: produit) to package; (fig: personne) to condition; **air conditionné** air conditioning

condoléances [kɔ̃dɔleɑ̃s] nfpl condolences

conducteur, trice [kɔ̃dyktœr, -tris] nm/f driver ♦ nm (ÉLEC etc) conductor

conduire [kɔ̃dɥir] vt to drive; (délégation, troupeau) to lead; **se ~** vi to behave; **~ vers/à** to lead towards/to; **~ qn quelque part** to take sb somewhere; to drive sb somewhere

conduite [kɔ̃dɥit] nf (comportement) behaviour; (d'eau, de gaz) pipe; **sous la ~ de** led by; **~ à gauche** left-hand drive; **~ intérieure** saloon (car)

cône [kon] nm cone

confection [kɔ̃fɛksjɔ̃] nf (fabrication) making; (COUTURE): **la ~** the clothing industry; **vêtement de ~** ready-to-wear ou off-the-peg garment

confectionner [kɔ̃fɛksjɔne] vt to make

conférence [kɔ̃ferɑ̃s] nf (exposé) lecture; (pourparlers) conference; **~ de presse** press conference

confesser [kɔ̃fese] vt to confess; **se ~** vi (REL) to go to confession

confession [kɔ̃fesjɔ̃] nf confession; (culte: catholique etc) denomination

confiance [kɔ̃fjɑ̃s] nf confidence, trust; faith; **avoir ~ en** to have confidence ou faith in, trust; **mettre qn en ~** to win sb's trust; **~ en soi** self-confidence

confiant, e [kɔ̃fjɑ̃, -ɑ̃t] adj confident; trusting

confidence [kɔ̃fidɑ̃s] nf confidence

confidentiel, le [kɔ̃fidɑ̃sjɛl] adj confidential

confier [kɔ̃fje] vt: **~ à qn** (objet en dépôt, travail etc) to entrust to sb; (secret, pensée) to confide to sb; **se ~ à qn** to confide in sb

confiné, e [kɔ̃fine] adj enclosed; stale

confins [kɔ̃fɛ̃] nmpl: **aux ~ de** on the borders of

confirmation [kɔ̃firmɑsjɔ̃] nf confirmation

confirmer [kɔ̃firme] vt to confirm

confiserie [kɔ̃fizri] nf (magasin) confectioner's ou sweet shop; **~s** nfpl (bonbons) confectionery sg; **confiseur, euse** nm/f

confectioner

confisquer [kɔ̃fiske] vt to confiscate

confit, e [kɔ̃fi, -it] adj: **fruits ~s** crystallized fruits ♦ nm: **~ d'oie** conserve of goose

confiture [kɔ̃fityr] nf jam; **~ d'oranges** (orange) marmalade

conflit [kɔ̃fli] nm conflict

confondre [kɔ̃fɔ̃dr(ə)] vt (jumeaux, faits) to confuse, mix up; (témoin, menteur) to confound; **se ~** vi to merge; **se ~ en excuses** to apologize profusely; **confondu, e** [kɔ̃fɔ̃dy] adj (stupéfait) speechless, overcome

conforme [kɔ̃fɔrm(ə)] adj: **~ à** in accordance with; in keeping with; true to

conformément [kɔ̃fɔrmemɑ̃] adv: **~ à** in accordance with

conformer [kɔ̃fɔrme] vt: **se ~ à** to conform to

conformité [kɔ̃fɔrmite] nf: **en ~ avec** in accordance with, in keeping with

confort [kɔ̃fɔr] nm comfort; **tout ~** (COMM) with all modern conveniences; **confortable** adj comfortable

confrère [kɔ̃frɛr] nm colleague; fellow member; **confrérie** nf brotherhood

confronter [kɔ̃frɔ̃te] vt to confront; (textes) to compare, collate

confus, e [kɔ̃fy, -yz] adj (vague) confused; (embarrassé) embarrassed

confusion [kɔ̃fyzjɔ̃] nf (voir confus) confusion; embarrassment; (voir confondre) confusion, mixing up

congé [kɔ̃ʒe] nm (vacances) holiday; **en ~** on holiday; off (work); **semaine de ~** week off; **prendre ~ de qn** to take one's leave of sb; **donner son ~ à** to give in one's notice to; **~ de maladie** sick leave; **~s payés** paid holiday

congédier [kɔ̃ʒedje] vt to dismiss

congélateur [kɔ̃ʒelatœr] nm freezer, deep freeze

congeler [kɔ̃ʒle] vt to freeze

congestion [kɔ̃ʒɛstjɔ̃] nf congestion; **~ cérébrale** stroke

congestionner [kɔ̃ʒɛstjɔne] vt to congest; (MÉD) to flush

congrès [kɔ̃grɛ] nm congress

congru, e [kɔ̃gry] adj: **la portion ~e** the smallest ou meanest share

conifère [kɔnifɛr] nm conifer

conjecture [kɔ̃ʒɛktyr] nf conjecture

conjoint, e [kɔ̃ʒwɛ̃, -wɛ̃t] adj joint ♦ nm/f spouse

conjonction [kɔ̃ʒɔ̃ksjɔ̃] nf (LING) conjunction

conjonctivite [kɔ̃ʒɔ̃ktivit] nf conjunctivitis

conjoncture [kɔ̃ʒɔ̃ktyr] nf circumstances pl; climate

conjugaison [kɔ̃ʒygɛzɔ̃] nf (LING) conjugation

conjuguer [kɔ̃ʒyge] vt (LING) to conjugate;

(efforts etc) to combine

conjuration [kɔ̃ʒyʀasjɔ̃] *nf* conspiracy

conjurer [kɔ̃ʒyʀe] *vt (sort, maladie)* to avert; *(implorer)* to beseech, entreat

connaissance [kɔnɛsɑ̃s] *nf (savoir)* knowledge *no pl*; *(personne connue)* acquaintance; **être sans ~** to be unconscious; **perdre/reprendre ~** to lose/regain consciousness; **à ma/sa ~** to (the best of) my/his knowledge; **avoir ~ de** to be aware of; **prendre ~ de** *(document etc)* to peruse; **en ~ de cause** with full knowledge of the facts

connaître [kɔnɛtʀ(ə)] *vt* to know; *(éprouver)* to experience; *(avoir)* to have; to enjoy; **~ de nom/vue** to know by name/sight; **ils se sont connus à Genève** they (first) met in Geneva

connecté, e [kɔnɛkte] *adj* on line

connecter [kɔnɛkte] *vt* to connect

connerie [kɔnʀi] *(fam!)* *nf* stupid thing (to do *ou* say)

connu, e [kɔny] *adj (célèbre)* well-known

conquérir [kɔ̃keʀiʀ] *vt* to conquer, win; **conquête** *nf* conquest

consacrer [kɔ̃sakʀe] *vt (REL)* to consecrate; *(fig: usage etc)* to sanction, establish; *(employer)* to devote, dedicate

conscience [kɔ̃sjɑ̃s] *nf* conscience; **avoir/prendre ~ de** to be/become aware of; **perdre ~** to lose consciousness; **avoir bonne/mauvaise ~** to have a clear/guilty conscience; **consciencieux, euse** *adj* conscientious; **conscient, e** *adj* conscious

conscrit [kɔ̃skʀi] *nm* conscript

consécutif, ive [kɔ̃sekytif, -iv] *adj* consecutive; **~ à** following upon

conseil [kɔ̃sɛj] *nm (avis)* piece of advice, advice *no pl*; *(assemblée)* council; **prendre ~ (auprès de qn)** to take advice (from sb); **~ d'administration** board (of directors); **le ~ des ministres** ≈ the Cabinet

conseiller, ère [kɔ̃seje, kɔ̃sɛjɛʀ] *nm/f* adviser ♦ *vt (personne)* to advise; *(méthode, action)* to recommend, advise; **~ à qn de** to advise sb to

consentement [kɔ̃sɑ̃tmɑ̃] *nm* consent

consentir [kɔ̃sɑ̃tiʀ] *vt* to agree, consent

conséquence [kɔ̃sekɑ̃s] *nf* consequence; **en ~** *(donc)* consequently; *(de façon appropriée)* accordingly; **ne pas tirer à ~** to be unlikely to have any repercussions

conséquent, e [kɔ̃sekɑ̃, -ɑ̃t] *adj* logical, rational; *(fam: important)* substantial; **par ~** consequently

conservateur, trice [kɔ̃sɛʀvatœʀ, -tʀis] *nm/f (POL)* conservative; *(de musée)* curator

conservatoire [kɔ̃sɛʀvatwaʀ] *nm* academy; *(ÉCOLOGIE)* conservation area

conserve [kɔ̃sɛʀv(ə)] *nf (gén pl)* canned *ou* tinned *(BRIT)* food; **en ~** canned, tinned *(BRIT)*

conserver [kɔ̃sɛʀve] *vt (faculté)* to retain, keep; *(amis, livres)* to keep; *(préserver, aussi CULIN)* to preserve

considérable [kɔ̃sideʀabl(ə)] *adj* considerable, significant, extensive

considération [kɔ̃sideʀasjɔ̃] *nf* consideration; *(estime)* esteem

considérer [kɔ̃sideʀe] *vt* to consider; **~ qch comme** to regard sth as

consigne [kɔ̃siɲ] *nf (de gare)* left luggage (office) *(BRIT)*, checkroom *(US)*; *(ordre, instruction)* instructions *pl*; **~ automatique** left-luggage locker; **~r** [kɔ̃siɲe] *vt (note, pensée)* to record; *(punir)* to confine to barracks; to put in detention; *(COMM)* to put a deposit on

consistant, e [kɔ̃sistɑ̃, -ɑ̃t] *adj* thick; solid

consister [kɔ̃siste] *vi:* **~ en/dans/à faire** to consist of/in/in doing

consœur [kɔ̃sœʀ] *nf* (lady) colleague; fellow member

consoler [kɔ̃sɔle] *vt* to console

consolider [kɔ̃sɔlide] *vt* to strengthen; *(fig)* to consolidate

consommateur, trice [kɔ̃sɔmatœʀ, -tʀis] *nm/f (ÉCON)* consumer; *(dans un café)* customer

consommation [kɔ̃sɔmasjɔ̃] *nf (boisson)* drink; **~ aux 100 km** *(AUTO)* (fuel) consumption per 100 km

consommer [kɔ̃sɔme] *vt (suj: personne)* to eat *ou* drink, consume; *(: voiture, usine, poêle)* to use, consume ♦ *vi (dans un café)* to (have a) drink

consonne [kɔ̃sɔn] *nf* consonant

conspirer [kɔ̃spiʀe] *vi* to conspire

constamment [kɔ̃stamɑ̃] *adv* constantly

constant, e [kɔ̃stɑ̃, -ɑ̃t] *adj* constant; *(personne)* steadfast

constat [kɔ̃sta] *nm (d'huissier)* certified report; *(de police)* report; *(affirmation)* statement

constatation [kɔ̃statasjɔ̃] *nf (observation)* (observed) fact, observation; *(affirmation)* statement

constater [kɔ̃state] *vt (remarquer)* to note; *(ADMIN, JUR: attester)* to certify; *(dire)* to state

consterner [kɔ̃stɛʀne] *vt* to dismay

constipé, e [kɔ̃stipe] *adj* constipated

constitué, e [kɔ̃stitɥe] *adj:* **~ de** made up *ou* composed of

constituer [kɔ̃stitɥe] *vt (comité, équipe)* to set up; *(dossier, collection)* to put together; *(suj: éléments: composer)* to make up, constitute; *(représenter, être)* to constitute; **se ~ prisonnier** to give o.s. up

constitution [kɔ̃stitysjɔ̃] *nf (composition)* composition, make-up; *(santé, POL)* constitution

constructeur [kɔ̃stʀyktœʀ] *nm* manufacturer, builder

construction [kɔ̃stryksjɔ̃] nf construction, building

construire [kɔ̃strɥir] vt to build, construct

consul [kɔsyl] nm consul; **consulat** nm consulate

consultation [kɔ̃syltasjɔ̃] nf consultation; **~s** nfpl (POL) talks; **heures de ~** (MÉD) surgery (BRIT) ou office (US) hours

consulter [kɔ̃sylte] vt to consult ♦ vi (médecin) to hold surgery (BRIT), be in (the office) (US)

consumer [kɔ̃syme] vt to consume; **se ~** vi to burn

contact [kɔ̃takt] nm contact; **au ~ de** (air, peau) on contact with; (gens) through contact with; **mettre/couper le ~** (AUTO) to switch on/off the ignition; **entrer en** ou **prendre ~ avec** to get in touch ou contact with; **contacter** vt to contact, get in touch with

contagieux, euse [kɔ̃taʒjø, -øz] adj contagious; infectious

contaminer [kɔ̃tamine] vt to contaminate

conte [kɔ̃t] nm tale; **~ de fées** fairy tale

contempler [kɔ̃tɑ̃ple] vt to contemplate, gaze at

contemporain, e [kɔ̃tɑ̃pɔrɛ̃, -ɛn] adj, nm/f, contemporary

contenance [kɔ̃tnɑ̃s] nf (d'un récipient) capacity; (attitude) bearing, attitude; **perdre ~** to lose one's composure

conteneur [kɔ̃tnœr] nm container

contenir [kɔ̃tnir] vt to contain; (avoir une capacité de) to hold

content, e [kɔ̃tɑ̃, -ɑ̃t] adj pleased, glad; **~ de** pleased with; **contenter** vt to satisfy, please; **se ~er de** to content o.s. with

contentieux [kɔ̃tɑ̃sjø] nm (COMM) litigation; litigation department

contenu [kɔ̃tny] nm (d'un bol) contents pl; (d'un texte) content

conter [kɔ̃te] vt to recount, relate

contestable [kɔ̃tɛstabl(ə)] adj questionable

contestation [kɔ̃tɛstasjɔ̃] nf (POL) protest

conteste [kɔ̃tɛst(ə)] : **sans ~** adv unquestionably, indisputably

contester [kɔ̃tɛste] vt to question, contest ♦ vi (POL, gén) to protest, rebel (against established authority)

contexte [kɔ̃tɛkst(ə)] nm context

contigu, ë [kɔ̃tigy] adj: **~ (à)** adjacent (to)

continent [kɔ̃tinɑ̃] nm continent

continu, e [kɔ̃tiny] adj continuous; **(courant) ~** direct current, DC

continuel, le [kɔ̃tinɥɛl] adj (qui se répète) constant, continual; (continu) continuous

continuer [kɔ̃tinɥe] vt (travail, voyage etc) to continue (with), carry on (with), go on (with); (prolonger: alignement, rue) to continue ♦ vi (pluie, vie, bruit) to continue, go on; (voyageur) to go on; **~ à** ou **de faire** to go on ou continue doing

contorsionner [kɔ̃tɔrsjɔne]: **se ~** vi to contort o.s., writhe about

contour [kɔ̃tur] nm outline, contour

contourner [kɔ̃turne] vt to go round

contraceptif, ive [kɔ̃traseptif, -iv] adj, nm contraceptive; **contraception** [kɔ̃trasepsjɔ̃] nf contraception

contracté, e [kɔ̃trakte] adj tense

contracter [kɔ̃trakte] vt (muscle etc) to tense, contract; (maladie, dette, obligation) to contract; (assurance) to take out; **se ~** vi (métal, muscles) to contract

contractuel, le [kɔ̃traktɥɛl] nm/f (agent) traffic warden

contradiction [kɔ̃tradiksjɔ̃] nf contradiction; **contradictoire** adj contradictory, conflicting

contraignant, e [kɔ̃trɛɲɑ̃, -ɑ̃t] adj restricting

contraindre vt: **~ qn à faire** to compel sb to do; **contraint, e** [kɔ̃trɛ̃, -ɛ̃t] adj (mine, air) constrained, forced; **contrainte** nf constraint

contraire [kɔ̃trɛr] adj, nm opposite; **~ à** contrary to; **au ~** on the contrary

contrarier [kɔ̃trarje] vt (personne) to annoy, bother; (fig) to impede; to thwart, frustrate; **contrariété** [kɔ̃trarjete] nf annoyance

contraste [kɔ̃trast(ə)] nm contrast

contrat [kɔ̃tra] nm contract; **~ de travail** employment contract

contravention [kɔ̃travɑ̃sjɔ̃] nf (amende) fine; (P.V. pour stationnement interdit) parking ticket

contre [kɔ̃tr(ə)] prép against; (en échange) (in exchange) for; **par ~** on the other hand

contrebande [kɔ̃trəbɑ̃d] nf (trafic) contraband, smuggling; (marchandise) contraband, smuggled goods pl; **faire la ~ de** to smuggle

contrebas [kɔ̃trəba] : **en ~** adv (down) below

contrebasse [kɔ̃trəbas] nf (double) bass

contre: **~carrer** vt to thwart; **~cœur**: **à ~cœur** adv (be)grudgingly, reluctantly; **~coup** nm repercussions pl; **par ~coup** as an indirect consequence; **~dire** vt (personne) to contradict; (témoignage, assertion, faits) to refute

contrée [kɔ̃tre] nf region; land

contrefaçon [kɔ̃trəfasɔ̃] nf forgery

contrefaire [kɔ̃trəfɛr] vt (document, signature) to forge, counterfeit; (personne, démarche) to mimic; (dénaturer: sa voix etc) to disguise

contre-indication (pl **contre-indications**) nf (MÉD) contra-indication

contre-jour [kɔ̃trəʒur]: **à ~** adv against the sunlight

contremaître [kɔ̃trəmɛtr(ə)] nm foreman

contrepartie [kɔ̃trəparti] nf compensation;

en ~ in return

contre-pied [kɔ̃trəpje] *nm*: **prendre le ~ de** to take the opposing view of; to take the opposite course to

contre-plaqué [kɔ̃trəplake] *nm* plywood

contrepoids [kɔ̃trəpwa] *nm* counterweight, counterbalance

contrer [kɔ̃tre] *vt* to counter

contresens [kɔ̃trəsɑ̃s] *nm* misinterpretation; mistranslation; nonsense *no pl*; **à ~** the wrong way

contretemps [kɔ̃trətɑ̃] *nm* hitch; **à ~** (*MUS*) out of time; (*fig*) at an inopportune moment

contrevenir [kɔ̃trəvnir]: **~ à** *vt* to contravene

contribuable [kɔ̃tribɥabl(ə)] *nm/f* taxpayer

contribuer [kɔ̃tribɥe]: **~ à** *vt* to contribute towards; **contribution** *nf* contribution; **contributions directes/indirectes** direct/indirect taxation; **mettre à contribution** to call upon

contrôle [kɔ̃trol] *nm* checking *no pl*, check; supervision; monitoring; (*test*) test, examination; **perdre le ~ de** (*véhicule*) to lose control of; **~ continu** (*SCOL*) continuous assessment; **~ d'identité** identity check; **~ des naissances** birth control

contrôler [kɔ̃trole] *vt* (*vérifier*) to check; (*surveiller*) to supervise; to monitor, control; (*maîtriser*, *COMM*: *firme*) to control; **contrôleur, euse** *nm/f* (*de train*) (ticket) inspector; (*de bus*) (bus) conductor(tress)

contrordre [kɔ̃trɔrdr(ə)] *nm*: **sauf ~** unless otherwise directed

controversé, e [kɔ̃trɔverse] *adj* (*personnage, question*) controversial

contusion [kɔ̃tyzjɔ̃] *nf* bruise, contusion

convaincre [kɔ̃vɛ̃kr(ə)] *vt*: **~ qn (de qch)** to convince sb (of sth); **~ qn (de faire)** to persuade sb (to do); **~ qn de** (*JUR*: *délit*) to convict sb of

convalescence [kɔ̃valesɑ̃s] *nf* convalescence

convenable [kɔ̃vnabl(ə)] *adj* suitable; (*assez bon, respectable*) decent

convenance [kɔ̃vnɑ̃s] *nf*: **à ma/votre ~** to my/your liking; **~s** *nfpl* (*normes sociales*) proprieties

convenir [kɔ̃vnir] *vi* to be suitable; **~ à** to suit; **il convient de** it is advisable to; (*bienséant*) it is right *ou* proper to; **~ de** (*bienfondé de qch*) to admit (to), acknowledge; (*date, somme etc*) to agree upon; **~ que** (*admettre*) to admit that; **~ de faire** to agree to do

convention [kɔ̃vɑ̃sjɔ̃] *nf* convention; **~s** *nfpl* (*convenances*) convention *sg*; **~ collective** (*ÉCON*) collective agreement; **conventionné, e** *adj* (*ADMIN*) applying charges laid down by the state

convenu, e [kɔ̃vny] *pp de* **convenir** ♦ *adj*

agreed

conversation [kɔ̃vɛrsasjɔ̃] *nf* conversation

convertir [kɔ̃vertir] *vt*: **~ qn (à)** to convert sb (to); **se ~ (à)** to be converted (to); **~ qch en** to convert sth into

conviction [kɔ̃viksjɔ̃] *nf* conviction

convienne *etc vb voir* **convenir**

convier [kɔ̃vje] *vt*: **~ qn à** (*dîner etc*) to (cordially) invite sb to

convive [kɔ̃viv] *nm/f* guest (*at table*)

convivial, e [kɔ̃vivjal] *adj* (*INFORM*) user-friendly

convocation [kɔ̃vɔkasjɔ̃] *nf* (*document*) notification to attend; summons *sg*

convoi [kɔ̃vwa] *nm* (*de voitures, prisonniers*) convoy; (*train*) train

convoiter [kɔ̃vwate] *vt* to covet

convoquer [kɔ̃vɔke] *vt* (*assemblée*) to convene; (*subordonné*) to summon; (*candidat*) to ask to attend; **~ qn (à)** (*réunion*) to invite sb (to attend)

convoyeur [kɔ̃vwajœr] *nm* (*NAVIG*) escort ship; **~ de fonds** security guard

coopération [kɔɔperasjɔ̃] *nf* co-operation; (*ADMIN*): **la C~** ≈ Voluntary Service Overseas (*BRIT*), ≈ Peace Corps (*US*)

coopérer [kɔɔpere] *vi*: **~ (à)** to co-operate (in)

coordonner [kɔɔrdɔne] *vt* to coordinate

copain [kɔpɛ̃] *nm* mate, pal

copeau, x [kɔpo] *nm* shaving

copie [kɔpi] *nf* copy; (*SCOL*) script, paper; exercise

copier [kɔpje] *vt, vi* to copy; **~ sur** to copy from

copieur [kɔpjœr] *nm* (photo)copier

copieux, euse [kɔpjø, -øz] *adj* copious

copine [kɔpin] *nf* = **copain**

copropriété [kɔprɔprijete] *nf* co-ownership, joint ownership

coq [kɔk] *nm* (*MUS*) cock, rooster; **~-à-l'âne** [kɔkalɑn] *nm inv* abrupt change of subject

coque [kɔk] *nf* (*de noix, mollusque*) shell; (*de bateau*) hull; **à la ~** (*CULIN*) (soft-)boiled

coquelicot [kɔkliko] *nm* poppy

coqueluche [kɔklyʃ] *nf* whooping-cough

coquet, te [kɔke, -ɛt] *adj* flirtatious; appearance-conscious; pretty

coquetier [kɔktje] *nm* egg-cup

coquillage [kɔkijaʒ] *nm* (*mollusque*) shellfish *inv*; (*coquille*) shell

coquille [kɔkij] *nf* shell; (*TYPO*) misprint; **~ St Jacques** scallop

coquin, e [kɔkɛ̃, -in] *adj* mischievous, roguish; (*polisson*) naughty

cor [kɔr] *nm* (*MUS*) horn; (*MÉD*): **~ (au pied)** corn; **réclamer à ~ et à cri** to clamour for

corail, aux [kɔraj, -o] *nm* coral *no pl*

Coran [kɔrɑ̃] *nm*: **le ~** the Koran

corbeau, x [kɔrbo] *nm* crow

corbeille [kɔrbɛj] *nf* basket; ~ **à papier** waste paper basket *ou* bin

corbillard [kɔrbijar] *nm* hearse

corde [kɔrd(ə)] *nf* rope; (*de violon, raquette, d'arc*) string; (*ATHLÉTISME, AUTO*): **la** ~ the rails *pl*; **usé jusqu'à la** ~ threadbare; ~ **à linge** washing *ou* clothes line; ~ **à sauter** skipping rope; ~**s vocales** vocal cords; **cordée** [kɔrde] *nf* (*d'alpinistes*) rope, roped party

cordialement [kɔrdjalmɑ̃] *adv* (*formule épistolaire*) (kind) regards

cordon [kɔrdɔ̃] *nm* cord, string; ~ **ombilical** umbilical cord; ~ **sanitaire/de police** sanitary/police cordon

cordonnerie [kɔrdɔnri] *nf* shoe repairer's (shop); **cordonnier** [kɔrdɔnje] *nm* shoe repairer

Corée [kɔre] *nf*: **la** ~ **du Sud/du Nord** South/North Korea

coriace [kɔrjas] *adj* tough

corne [kɔrn(ə)] *nf* horn; (*de cerf*) antler

corneille [kɔrnɛj] *nf* crow

cornemuse [kɔrnəmyz] *nf* bagpipes *pl*

cornet [kɔrnɛ] *nm* (*paper*) cone; (*de glace*) cornet, cone

corniche [kɔrniʃ] *nf* (*de meuble, neigeuse*) cornice; (*route*) coast road

cornichon [kɔrniʃɔ̃] *nm* gherkin

Cornouailles [kɔrnwaj] *nf* Cornwall

corporation [kɔrpɔrasjɔ̃] *nf* corporate body

corporel, le [kɔrpɔrɛl] *adj* bodily; (*punition*) corporal

corps [kɔr] *nm* body; **à son** ~ **défendant** against one's will; **à** ~ **perdu** headlong; **perdu** ~ **et biens** lost with all hands; **prendre** ~ to take shape; ~ **à** ~ *adv* hand-to-hand ♦ *nm* clinch; ~ **de garde** guardroom; **le** ~ **électoral** the electorate; **le** ~ **enseignant** the teaching profession

corpulent, e [kɔrpylɑ̃, -ɑ̃t] *adj* stout

correct, e [kɔrɛkt] *adj* correct; (*passable*) adequate

correction [kɔrɛksjɔ̃] *nf* (*voir corriger*) correction; (*voir correct*) correctness; (*rature, surcharge*) correction, emendation; (*coups*) thrashing

correctionnel, le [kɔrɛksjɔnɛl] *adj* (*JUR*): **tribunal** ~ ≈ criminal court

correspondance [kɔrɛspɔ̃dɑ̃s] *nf* correspondence; (*de train, d'avion*) connection; **cours par** ~ correspondence course; **vente par** ~ mail-order business

correspondant, e [kɔrɛspɔ̃dɑ̃, -ɑ̃t] *nm/f* correspondent; (*TÉL*) person phoning (*ou* being phoned)

correspondre [kɔrɛspɔ̃dr(ə)] *vi* to correspond, tally; ~ **à** to correspond to; ~ **avec qn** to correspond with sb

corrida [kɔrida] *nf* bullfight

corridor [kɔridɔr] *nm* corridor

corriger [kɔriʒe] *vt* (*devoir*) to correct; (*punir*) to thrash; ~ **qn de** (*défaut*) to cure sb of

corrompre [kɔrɔ̃pr(ə)] *vt* to corrupt; (*acheter: témoin etc*) to bribe

corruption [kɔrypsjɔ̃] *nf* corruption; bribery

corsage [kɔrsaʒ] *nm* bodice; blouse

corse [kɔrs(ə)] *adj, nm/f* Corsican ♦ *nf*: **la** **C~** Corsica

corsé, e [kɔrse] *adj* vigorous; (*vin, goût*) full-flavoured; (*fig*) spicy; tricky

corset [kɔrsɛ] *nm* corset; bodice

cortège [kɔrtɛʒ] *nm* procession

corvée [kɔrve] *nf* chore, drudgery *no pl*

cosmétique [kɔsmetik] *nm* beauty care product

cossu, e [kɔsy] *adj* well-to-do

costaud, e [kɔsto, -od] *adj* strong, sturdy

costume [kɔstym] *nm* (*d'homme*) suit; (*de théâtre*) costume; **costumé, e** *adj* dressed up

cote [kɔt] *nf* (*en Bourse etc*) quotation; quoted value; (*d'un cheval*): **la** ~ **de** the odds *pl* on; (*d'un candidat etc*) rating; (*sur un croquis*) dimension; ~ **d'alerte** danger *ou* flood level

côte [kot] *nf* (*rivage*) coast(line); (*pente*) slope; (: *sur une route*) hill; (*d'un tricot, tissu*) rib, ribbing *no pl*; ~ **à** ~ side by side; **la C~** (**d'Azur**) the (French) Riviera

côté [kote] *nm* (*gén*) side; (*direction*) way, direction; **de chaque** ~ (**de**) on each side (of); **de tous les** ~**s** from all directions; **de quel** ~ **est-il parti?** which way did he go?; **de ce/de l'autre** ~ this/the other way; **du** ~ **de** (*provenance*) from; (*direction*) towards; (*proximité*) near; **de** ~ sideways; on one side; to one side; aside; **laisser/mettre de** ~ to leave/put to one side; **à** ~ (right) nearby; beside; next door; (*d'autre part*) besides; **à** ~ **de** beside; next to; **être aux** ~**s de** to be by the side of

coteau, x [kɔto] *nm* hill

côtelette [kotlɛt] *nf* chop

coter [kɔte] *vt* (*en Bourse*) to quote

côtier, ière [kotje, -jɛr] *adj* coastal

cotisation [kɔtizasjɔ̃] *nf* subscription, dues *pl*; (*pour une pension*) contributions *pl*

cotiser [kɔtize] *vi*: ~ (**à**) to pay contributions (to); **se** ~ *vi* to club together

coton [kɔtɔ̃] *nm* cotton; ~ **hydrophile** cotton wool (*BRIT*), absorbent cotton (*US*)

côtoyer [kotwaje] *vt* to be close to; to rub shoulders with; to run alongside

cou [ku] *nm* neck

couchant [kuʃɑ̃] *adj*: **soleil** ~ setting sun

couche [kuʃ] *nf* (*strate: gén, GÉO*) layer; (*de peinture, vernis*) coat; (*de bébé*) nappy (*BRIT*), diaper (*US*); ~**s** *nfpl* (*MÉD*) confinement *sg*; ~ **d'ozone** ozone layer; ~**s socia-**

les social levels *ou* strata

couché, e [kuʃe] *adj* lying down; *(au lit)* in bed

couche-culotte [kuʃkylɔt] *nf* disposable nappy *(BRIT)* *ou* diaper *(US)* and waterproof pants in one

coucher [kuʃe] *nm (du soleil)* setting ♦ *vt (personne)* to put to bed; (: *loger)* to put up; *(objet)* to lay on its side ♦ *vi* to sleep; **se ~** *vi (pour dormir)* to go to bed; *(pour se reposer)* to lie down; *(soleil)* to set; **~ de soleil** sunset

couchette [kuʃɛt] *nf* couchette; *(de marin)* bunk

coucou [kuku] *nm* cuckoo

coude [kud] *nm (ANAT)* elbow; *(de tuyau, de la route)* bend; **~ à ~** shoulder to shoulder, side by side

coudre [kudʀ(ə)] *vt (bouton)* to sew on; *(robe)* to sew (up) ♦ *vi* to sew

couenne [kwan] *nf (de lard)* rind

couette [kwɛt] *nf* duvet, quilt; **~s** *nfpl (cheveux)* bunches

couffin [kufɛ̃] *nm* Moses basket

couler [kule] *vi* to flow, run; *(fuir: stylo, récipient)* to leak; *(sombrer: bateau)* to sink ♦ *vt (cloche, sculpture)* to cast; *(bateau)* to sink; *(fig)* to ruin, bring down

couleur [kulœʀ] *nf* colour *(BRIT)*, color *(US)*; *(CARTES)* suit; **film/télévision en ~s** colo(u)r film/television

couleuvre [kulœvʀ(ə)] *nf* grass snake

coulisse [kulis] *nf*: **~s** *nfpl (THÉÂTRE)* wings; *(fig)*: **dans les ~s** behind the scenes; **coulisser** *vi* to slide, run

couloir [kulwaʀ] *nm* corridor, passage; *(de bus)* gangway; *(d'avion)* aisle; *(sur la route)* bus lane; *(SPORT: de piste)* lane; *(GÉO)* gully; **~ aérien/de navigation** air/shipping lane

coup [ku] *nm (heurt, choc)* knock; *(affectif)* blow, shock; *(agressif)* blow; *(avec arme à feu)* shot; *(de l'horloge)* chime; stroke; *(SPORT)* stroke; shot; blow; *(fam: fois)* time; **~ de coude** nudge (with the elbow); **~ de tonnerre** clap of thunder; **~ de sonnette** ring of the bell; **~ de crayon** stroke of the pencil; **donner un ~ de balai** to give the floor a sweep; **avoir le ~** *(fig)* to have the knack; **boire un ~** to have a drink; **être dans le ~** to be in on it; **du ... so** (you see) ...; **d'un seul ~** *(subitement)* suddenly; *(à la fois)* at one go; in one blow; **du premier ~** first time; **du même ~** at the same time; **à ~ sûr** definitely, without fail; **~ sur ~** in quick succession; **sur le ~** outright; **sous le ~ de** *(surprise etc)* under the influence of; **~ de chance** stroke of luck; **~ de couteau** stab (of a knife); **~ d'envoi** kick-off; **~ d'essai** first attempt; **~ de feu** shot; **~ de filet** *(POLICE)* haul; **~ de frein** (sharp) braking *no pl*; **~ de main:**

donner un ~ de main à qn to give sb a (helping) hand; **~ d'œil** glance; **~ de pied** kick; **~ de poing** punch; **~ de soleil** sunburn *no pl*; **~ de téléphone** phone call; **~ de tête** *(fig)* (sudden) impulse; **~ de théâtre** *(fig)* dramatic turn of events; **~ de vent** gust of wind; **en coup de vent** in a tearing hurry; **~ franc** free kick

coupable [kupabl(ə)] *adj* guilty ♦ *nm/f (gén)* culprit; *(JUR)* guilty party

coupe [kup] *nf (verre)* goblet; *(à fruits)* dish; *(SPORT)* cup; *(de cheveux, de vêtement)* cut; *(graphique, plan)* (cross) section; **être sous la ~ de** to be under the control of

coupe-papier [kuppapje] *nm inv* paper knife

couper [kupe] *vt* to cut; *(retrancher)* to cut (out); *(route, courant)* to cut off; *(appétit)* to take away; *(vin, cidre)* to blend; (: *à table)* to dilute ♦ *vi* to cut; *(prendre un raccourci)* to take a short-cut; **se ~** *vi (se blesser)* to cut o.s.; **~ la parole à qn** to cut sb short

couple [kupl(ə)] *nm* couple

couplet [kuplɛ] *nm* verse

coupole [kupɔl] *nf* dome; cupola

coupon [kupɔ̃] *nm (ticket)* coupon; *(de tissu)* remnant; roll; **~-réponse** *nm* reply coupon

coupure [kupyʀ] *nf* cut; *(billet de banque)* note; *(de journal)* cutting; **~ de courant** power cut

cour [kuʀ] *nf (de ferme, jardin)* (court)yard; *(d'immeuble)* back yard; *(JUR, royale)* court; **faire la ~ à qn** to court sb; **~ d'assises** court of assizes; **~ martiale** court-martial

courage [kuʀaʒ] *nm* courage, bravery; **courageux, euse** *adj* brave, courageous

couramment [kuʀamɑ̃] *adv* commonly; *(parler)* fluently

courant, e [kuʀɑ̃, -ɑ̃t] *adj (fréquent)* common; *(COMM, gén: normal)* standard; *(en cours)* current ♦ *nm* current; *(fig)* movement; trend; **être au ~ (de)** *(fait, nouvelle)* to know (about); **mettre qn au ~ (de)** to tell sb (about); *(nouveau travail etc)* to teach sb the basics (of); **se tenir au ~ (de)** *(techniques etc)* to keep o.s. up-to-date (on); **dans le ~ de** *(pendant)* in the course of; **le 10 ~** *(COMM)* the 10th inst.; **~ d'air** draught; **~ électrique** (electric) current, power

courbature [kuʀbatyʀ] *nf* ache

courbe [kuʀb(ə)] *adj* curved ♦ *nf* curve; **~r** [kuʀbe] *vt* to bend

coureur, euse [kuʀœʀ, -øz] *nm/f (SPORT)* runner *(ou* driver); *(péj)* womanizer; manhunter; **~ automobile** racing driver

courge [kuʀʒ(ə)] *nf (CULIN)* marrow; **courgette** [kuʀʒɛt] *nf* courgette *(BRIT)*, zucchini *(US)*

courir [kuʀiʀ] *vi* to run ♦ *vt (SPORT: épreuve)* to compete in; *(risque)* to run;

(*danger*) to face; ~ **les magasins** to go round the shops; **le bruit court que** the rumour is going round that

couronne [kuʀɔn] *nf* crown; (*de fleurs*) wreath, circlet

courons *etc vb voir* **courir**

courrier [kuʀje] *nm* mail, post; (*lettres à écrire*) letters *pl*; **avion long/moyen ~** long-/medium-haul plane

courroie [kuʀwa] *nf* strap; (*TECH*) belt

courrons *etc vb voir* **courir**

cours [kuʀ] *nm* (*leçon*) lesson; class; (*série de leçons, cheminement*) course; (*écoulement*) flow; (*COMM*) rate; price; **donner libre ~ à** to give free expression to; **avoir ~** (*monnaie*) to be legal tender; (*fig*) to be current; (*SCOL*) to have a class *ou* lecture; **en ~** (*année*) current; (*travaux*) in progress; **en ~ de route** on the way; **au ~ de** in the course of, during; **~ d'eau** waterway; **~ du soir** night school

course [kuʀs(ə)] *nf* running; (*SPORT: épreuve*) race; (*d'un taxi, autocar*) journey, trip; (*petite mission*) errand; **~s** *nfpl* (*achats*) shopping *sg*; **faire des ~s** to do some shopping

court, e [kuʀ, kuʀt(ə)] *adj* short ♦ *adv* short ♦ *nm*: **~ (de tennis)** (tennis) court; **tourner ~** to come to a sudden end; **ça fait ~** that's not very long; **à ~ de** short of; **prendre qn de ~** to catch sb unawares; **tirer à la ~e paille** to draw lots; **~-circuit** *nm* short-circuit

courtier, ère [kuʀtje, -jɛʀ] *nm/f* broker

courtiser [kuʀtize] *vt* to court, woo

courtois, e [kuʀtwa, -waz] *adj* courteous

couru, e [kuʀy] *pp de* **courir** ♦ *adj*: **c'est ~** it's a safe bet

cousais *etc vb voir* **coudre**

couscous [kuskus] *nm* couscous

cousin, e [kuzɛ̃, -in] *nm/f* cousin

coussin [kusɛ̃] *nm* cushion

cousu, e [kuzy] *pp de* **coudre**

coût [ku] *nm* cost; **le ~ de la vie** the cost of living

coûtant [kutɑ̃] *adj m*: **au prix ~** at cost price

couteau, x [kuto] *nm* knife; **~ à cran d'arrêt** flick-knife

coûter [kute] *vt, vi* to cost; **combien ça coûte?** how much is it?, what does it cost?; **coûte que coûte** at all costs; **coûteux, euse** *adj* costly, expensive

coutume [kutym] *nf* custom

couture [kutyʀ] *nf* sewing; dress-making; (*points*) seam; **couturier** [kutyʀje] *nm* fashion designer; **couturière** [kutyʀjɛʀ] *nf* dressmaker

couvée [kuve] *nf* brood, clutch

couvent [kuvɑ̃] *nm* (*de sœurs*) convent; (*de frères*) monastery

couver [kuve] *vt* to hatch; (*maladie*) to be

sickening for ♦ *vi* (*feu*) to smoulder; (*révolte*) to be brewing

couvercle [kuvɛʀkl(ə)] *nm* lid; (*de bombe aérosol etc, qui se visse*) cap, top

couvert, e [kuvɛʀ, -ɛʀt(ə)] *pp de* **couvrir** ♦ *adj* (*ciel*) overcast ♦ *nm* place setting; (*place à table*) place; (*au restaurant*) cover charge; **~s** *nmpl* (*ustensiles*) cutlery *sg*; **~ de** covered with *ou* in; **mettre le ~** to lay the table

couverture [kuvɛʀtyʀ] *nf* blanket; (*de bâtiment*) roofing; (*de livre, assurance, fig*) cover; (*presse*) coverage; **~ chauffante** electric blanket

couveuse [kuvøz] *nf* (*de maternité*) incubator

couvre-feu *nm* curfew

couvre-lit *nm* bedspread

couvrir [kuvʀiʀ] *vt* to cover; **se ~** *vi* (*ciel*) to cloud over; (*s'habiller*) to cover up; (*se coiffer*) to put on one's hat

crabe [kʀab] *nm* crab

cracher [kʀaʃe] *vi, vt* to spit

crachin [kʀaʃɛ̃] *nm* drizzle

craie [kʀɛ] *nf* chalk

craindre [kʀɛ̃dʀ(ə)] *vt* to fear, be afraid of; (*être sensible à: chaleur, froid*) to be easily damaged by

crainte [kʀɛ̃t] *nf* fear; **de ~ de/que** for fear of/that; **craintif, ive** *adj* timid

cramoisi, e [kʀamwazi] *adj* crimson

crampe [kʀɑ̃p] *nf* cramp

cramponner [kʀɑ̃pɔne] : **se ~** *vi*: **se ~ (à)** to hang *ou* cling on (to)

cran [kʀɑ̃] *nm* (*entaille*) notch; (*de courroie*) hole; (*courage*) guts *pl*; **~ d'arrêt** safety catch

crâne [kʀɑn] *nm* skull

crâner [kʀɑne] (*fam*) *vi* to show off

crapaud [kʀapo] *nm* toad

crapule [kʀapyl] *nf* villain

craquement [kʀakmɑ̃] *nm* crack, snap; (*du plancher*) creak, creaking *no pl*

craquer [kʀake] *vi* (*bois, plancher*) to creak; (*fil, branche*) to snap; (*couture*) to come apart; (*fig*) to break down ♦ *vt* (*allumette*) to strike

crasse [kʀas] *nf* grime, filth

cravache [kʀavaʃ] *nf* (riding) crop

cravate [kʀavat] *nf* tie

crawl [kʀol] *nm* crawl; **dos ~é** backstroke

crayeux, euse [kʀɛjø, -øz] *adj* chalky

crayon [kʀɛjɔ̃] *nm* pencil; **~ à bille** ball-point pen; **~ de couleur** crayon, colouring pencil; **~ optique** light pen; **crayon-feutre** [kʀɛjɑ̃føtʀ(ə)] (*pl* **crayons-feutres**) *nm* felt(-tip) pen

créancier, ière [kʀeɑ̃sje, -jɛʀ] *nm/f* creditor

création [kʀeasjɔ̃] *nf* creation

créature [kʀeatyʀ] *nf* creature

crèche [kʀɛʃ] *nf* (*de Noël*) crib; (*garderie*)

crèche, day nursery

crédit [kʀedi] nm (gén) credit; ~s nmpl (fonds) funds; **payer/acheter** à ~ **to pay/buy on credit** ou **on easy terms; faire ~ à qn** to give sb credit; **créditer** vt: **créditer un compte (de)** to credit an account (with)

crédule [kʀedyl] adj credulous, gullible

créer [kʀee] vt to create; (THÉÂTRE) to produce (for the first time)

crémaillère [kʀemajɛʀ] nf (RAIL) rack; **pendre la** ~ to have a house-warming party

crématoire [kʀematwaʀ] adj: **four** ~ crematorium

crème [kʀɛm] nf cream; (entremets) cream dessert ♦ adj inv cream (-coloured); **un (café)** ~ ≈ a white coffee; ~ **à raser** shaving cream; ~ **chantilly** whipped cream; ~ **fouettée** = crème chantilly; **crémerie** nf dairy; **crémeux, euse** adj creamy

créneau, x [kʀeno] nm (de fortification) crenel(le); (fig) gap, slot; (AUTO): **faire un** ~ to reverse into a parking space (alongside the kerb)

crêpe [kʀɛp] nf (galette) pancake ♦ nm (tissu) crêpe; **crêpé, e** adj (cheveux) back-combed; **crêperie** nf pancake shop ou restaurant

crépir [kʀepiʀ] vt to roughcast

crépiter [kʀepite] vi to sputter, splutter; to crackle

crépu, e [kʀepy] adj frizzy, fuzzy

crépuscule [kʀepyskyl] nm twilight, dusk

cresson [kʀesɔ̃] nm watercress

crête [kʀɛt] nf (de coq) comb; (de vague, montagne) crest

creuser [kʀøze] vt (trou, tunnel) to dig; (sol) to dig a hole in; (bois) to hollow out; (fig) to go (deeply) into; **ça creuse** that gives you a real appetite; **se** ~ **(la cervelle)** to rack one's brains

creux, euse [kʀø, -øz] adj hollow ♦ nm hollow; (fig: sur graphique etc) trough; **heures creuses** slack periods; off-peak periods

crevaison [kʀəvɛzɔ̃] nf puncture

crevasse [kʀəvas] nf (dans le sol) crack, fissure; (de glacier) crevasse

crevé, e [kʀəve] adj (fatigué) all in, exhausted

crever [kʀəve] vt (papier) to tear, break; (tambour, ballon) to burst ♦ vi (pneu) to burst; (automobiliste) to have a puncture (BRIT) ou a flat (tire) (US); (fam) to die; **cela lui a crevé un œil** it blinded him in one eye

crevette [kʀəvɛt] nf: ~ **(rose)** prawn; ~ **grise** shrimp

cri [kʀi] nm cry, shout; (d'animal: spécifique) cry, call; **c'est le dernier** ~ (fig) it's the latest fashion

criant, e [kʀijɑ̃, -ɑ̃t] adj (injustice) glaring

criard, e [kʀijaʀ, -aʀd(ə)] adj (couleur) garish, loud; (voix) yelling

crible [kʀibl(ə)] nm riddle; **passer qch au** ~ (fig) to go over sth with a fine-tooth comb

criblé, e [kʀible] adj: ~ **de** riddled with; (de dettes) crippled with

cric [kʀik] nm (AUTO) jack

crier [kʀije] vi (pour appeler) to shout, cry (out); (de peur, de douleur etc) to scream, yell ♦ vt (ordre, injure) to shout (out), yell (out)

crime [kʀim] nm crime; (meurtre) murder; **criminel, le** nm/f criminal; murderer

crin [kʀɛ̃] nm hair no pl; (fibre) horsehair; ~**ière** [kʀinjɛʀ] nf mane

crique [kʀik] nf creek, inlet

criquet [kʀike] nm locust; grasshopper

crise [kʀiz] nf crisis; (MÉD) attack; fit; ~ **cardiaque** heart attack; ~ **de foie** bilious attack; ~ **de nerfs** attack of nerves

crisper [kʀispe] vt to tense; (poings) to clench; **se** ~ vi to tense; to clench; (personne) to get tense

crisser [kʀise] vi (neige) to crunch; (pneu) to screech

cristal, aux [kʀistal, -o] nm crystal; ~**lin, e** adj crystal-clear

critère [kʀitɛʀ] nm criterion

critiquable [kʀitikabl(ə)] adj open to criticism

critique [kʀitik] adj critical ♦ nm/f (de théâtre, musique) critic ♦ nf criticism; (THÉÂTRE etc: article) review; ~**r** [kʀitike] vt (dénigrer) to criticize; (évaluer, juger) to assess, examine (critically)

croasser [kʀoase] vi to caw

Croatie [kʀoasi] nf Croatia

croc [kʀo] nm (dent) fang; (de boucher) hook

croc-en-jambe [kʀokɑ̃ʒɑ̃b] nm: **faire un** ~ **à qn** to trip sb up

croche [kʀoʃ] nf (MUS) quaver (BRIT), eighth note (US); ~**-pied** [kʀoʃpje] nm = croc-en-jambe

crochet [kʀoʃe] nm hook; (détour) detour; (TRICOT: aiguille) crochet hook; (: technique) crochet; **vivre aux** ~**s de qn** to live ou sponge off sb; **crocheter** vt (serrure) to pick

crochu, e [kʀoʃy] adj hooked; claw-like

crocodile [kʀokodil] nm crocodile

crocus [kʀokys] nm crocus

croire [kʀwaʀ] vt to believe; **se** ~ **fort** to think one is strong; ~ **que** to believe ou think that; ~ **à**, ~ **en** to believe in

croîs vb voir **croître**

croisade [kʀwazad] nf crusade

croisé, e [kʀwaze] adj (veston) double-breasted

croisement [kʀwazmɑ̃] nm (carrefour) crossroads sg; (BIO) crossing; crossbreed

croiser [kʀwaze] vt (personne, voiture) to

pass; (*route*) to cross, cut across; (*BIO*) to cross ♦ *vi* (*NAVIG*) to cruise; **se ~** *vi* (*personnes, véhicules*) to pass each other; (*routes, lettres*) to cross; (*regards*) to meet; **~ les jambes/bras** to cross one's legs/fold one's arms

croiseur [kʀwazœʀ] *nm* cruiser (*warship*)

croisière [kʀwazjɛʀ] *nf* cruise; **vitesse de ~** (*AUTO etc*) cruising speed

croissance [kʀwasɑ̃s] *nf* growth

croissant [kʀwasɑ̃] *nm* (*à manger*) croissant; (*motif*) crescent

croître [kʀwatʀ(ə)] *vi* to grow

croix [kʀwa] *nf* cross; **en ~** in the form of a cross; **la C~ Rouge** the Red Cross

croque-monsieur [kʀɔkməsjø] *nm inv* toasted ham and cheese sandwich

croquer [kʀɔke] *vt* (*manger*) to crunch; to munch; (*dessiner*) to sketch ♦ *vi* to be crisp *ou* crunchy; **chocolat à ~** plain dessert chocolate

croquis [kʀɔki] *nm* sketch

crosse [kʀɔs] *nf* (*de fusil*) butt; (*de revolver*) grip

crotte [kʀɔt] *nf* droppings *pl*

crotté, e [kʀɔte] *adj* muddy, mucky

crottin [kʀɔtɛ̃] *nm* dung, manure

crouler [kʀule] *vi* (*s'effondrer*) to collapse; (*être délabré*) to be crumbling

croupe [kʀup] *nf* rump; **en ~** pillion

croupir [kʀupiʀ] *vi* to stagnate

croustillant, e [kʀustijɑ̃, -ɑ̃t] *adj* crisp; (*fig*) spicy

croûte [kʀut] *nf* crust; (*du fromage*) rind; (*MÉD*) scab; **en ~** (*CULIN*) in pastry

croûton [kʀutɔ̃] *nm* (*CULIN*) crouton; (*bout du pain*) crust, heel

croyable [kʀwajabl(ə)] *adj* credible

croyant, e [kʀwajɑ̃, -ɑ̃t] *nm/f* believer

C.R.S. *sigle fpl* (= *Compagnies républicaines de sécurité*) state security police force ♦ *sigle m* member of the C.R.S.

cru, e [kʀy] *adj de* **croire** ♦ *adj* (*non cuit*) raw; (*lumière, couleur*) harsh; (*paroles, description*) crude ♦ *nm* (*vignoble*) vineyard; (*vin*) wine

crû *pp de* **croître**

cruauté [kʀyote] *nf* cruelty

cruche [kʀyʃ] *nf* pitcher, jug

crucifix [kʀysifi] *nm* crucifix

crucifixion [kʀysifiksjɔ̃] *nf* crucifixion

crudités [kʀydite] *nfpl* (*CULIN*) salads

cruel, le [kʀyɛl] *adj* cruel

crus *etc vb voir* **croire**; **croître**

crûs *etc vb voir* **croître**

crustacés [kʀystase] *nmpl* shellfish

Cuba [kyba] *nf* Cuba

cube [kyb] *nm* cube; (*jouet*) brick; **mètre ~** cubic metre; **2 au ~** 2 cubed

cueillette [kœjɛt] *nf* picking; (*quantité*) crop, harvest

cueillir [kœjiʀ] *vt* (*fruits, fleurs*) to pick,

gather; (*fig*) to catch

cuiller [kyijɛʀ] *nf* spoon; **~ à café** coffee spoon; (*CULIN*) ≈ teaspoonful; **~ à soupe** soup-spoon; (*CULIN*) ≈ tablespoonful

cuillère [kyijɛʀ] *nf* = **cuiller**

cuillerée [kyijʀe] *nf* spoonful

cuir [kyiʀ] *nm* leather; **~ chevelu** scalp

cuire [kyiʀ] *vt* (*aliments*) to cook; (*au four*) to bake; (*poterie*) to fire ♦ *vi* to cook; **bien cuit** (*viande*) well done; **trop cuit** overdone

cuisant, e [kyizɑ̃, -ɑ̃t] *adj* (*douleur*) stinging; (*fig: souvenir, échec*) bitter

cuisine [kyizin] *nf* (*pièce*) kitchen; (*art culinaire*) cookery, cooking; (*nourriture*) cooking, food; **faire la ~** to cook

cuisiné, e [kyizine] *adj*: **plat ~** ready-made meal *or* dish; **cuisiner** *vt* to cook; (*fam*) to grill ♦ *vi* to cook; **cuisinier, ière** *nm/f* cook; **cuisinière** *nf* (*poêle*) cooker

cuisse [kyis] *nf* thigh; (*CULIN*) leg

cuisson [kyisɔ̃] *nf* cooking; firing

cuit, e *pp de* **cuire**

cuivre [kyivʀ(ə)] *nm* copper; **les ~s** (*MUS*) the brass

cul [ky] (*fam!*) *nm* arse (*!*)

culasse [kylas] *nf* (*AUTO*) cylinder-head; (*de fusil*) breech

culbute [kylbyt] *nf* somersault; (*accidentelle*) tumble, fall

culminant, e [kylminɑ̃, -ɑ̃t] *adj*: **point ~** highest point

culminer [kylmine] *vi* to reach its highest point; to tower

culot [kylo] *nm* (*effronterie*) cheek

culotte [kylɔt] *nf* (*de femme*) knickers *pl* (*BRIT*), panties *pl*; **~ de cheval** riding breeches *pl*

culpabilité [kylpabilite] *nf* guilt

culte [kylt(ə)] *nm* (*religion*) religion; (*hommage, vénération*) worship; (*protestant*) service

cultivateur, trice [kyltivatœʀ, -tʀis] *nm/f* farmer

cultivé, e [kyltive] *adj* (*personne*) cultured, cultivated

cultiver [kyltive] *vt* to cultivate; (*légumes*) to grow, cultivate

culture [kyltyʀ] *nf* cultivation; growing; (*connaissances etc*) culture; **~ physique** physical training; **culturisme** *nm* body-building

cumin [kymɛ̃] *nm* cumin; (*carvi*) caraway seeds *pl*

cumuler [kymyle] *vt* (*emplois, honneurs*) to hold concurrently; (*salaires*) to draw concurrently; (*JUR: droits*) to accumulate

cupide [kypid] *adj* greedy, grasping

cure [kyʀ] *nf* (*MÉD*) course of treatment; **n'avoir ~ de** to pay no attention to

curé [kyʀe] *nm* parish priest

cure-dent [kyʀdɑ̃] *nm* toothpick

cure-pipe [kyʀpip] *nm* pipe cleaner

curer [kyʀe] *vt* to clean out
curieux, euse [kyʀjø, -øz] *adj* (*étrange*) strange, curious; (*indiscret*) curious, inquisitive ♦ *nmpl* (*badauds*) onlookers; **curiosité** *nf* curiosity; (*site*) unusual feature
curriculum vitae [kyʀikylɔmvite] *nm inv* curriculum vitae
curseur [kyʀsœʀ] *nm* (*INFORM*) cursor
cuti-réaction [kytiʀeaksjɔ̃] *nf* (*MÉD*) skin-test
cuve [kyv] *nf* vat; (*à mazout etc*) tank; **cuvée** [kyve] *nf* vintage
cuvette [kyvɛt] *nf* (*récipient*) bowl, basin; (*GÉO*) basin
C.V. *sigle m* (*AUTO*) = **cheval vapeur**; (*COMM*) = **curriculum vitae**
cyanure [sjanyʀ] *nm* cyanide
cyclable [siklabl(ə)] *adj*: **piste** ~ cycle track
cycle [sikl(ə)] *nm* cycle
cyclisme [siklism(ə)] *nm* cycling
cycliste [siklist(ə)] *nm/f* cyclist ♦ *adj* cycle *cpd*; **coureur** ~ racing cyclist
cyclomoteur [siklɔmɔtœʀ] *nm* moped
cyclone [siklon] *nm* hurricane
cygne [siɲ] *nm* swan
cylindre [silɛ̃dʀ(ə)] *nm* cylinder; **cylindrée** *nf* (*AUTO*) (cubic) capacity
cymbale [sɛ̃bal] *nf* cymbal
cynique [sinik] *adj* cynical
cystite [sistit] *nf* cystitis

D d

d' [d] *prép voir* de
dactylo [daktilo] *nf* (*aussi:* ~*graphe*) typist; (: ~*graphie*) typing; ~**graphier** *vt* to type (out)
dada [dada] *nm* hobby-horse
daigner [deɲe] *vt* to deign
daim [dɛ̃] *nm* (fallow) deer *inv*; (*peau*) buckskin; (*imitation*) suede
dalle [dal] *nf* paving stone; slab
daltonien, ne [daltɔnjɛ̃, -jɛn] *adj* colour-blind
dam [dam] *nm*: **au grand** ~ **de** much to the detriment (*ou* annoyance) of
dame [dam] *nf* lady; (*CARTES, ÉCHECS*) queen; ~**s** *nfpl* (*jeu*) draughts *sg* (*BRIT*), checkers *sg* (*US*)
damner [dɑne] *vt* to damn
dancing [dɑ̃siŋ] *nm* dance hall
Danemark [danmaʀk] *nm* Denmark

danger [dɑ̃ʒe] *nm* danger; **dangereux, euse** [dɑ̃ʒʀø, -øz] *adj* dangerous
danois, e [danwa, -waz] *adj* Danish ♦ *nm/f*: D~, e Dane ♦ *nm* (*LING*) Danish

━━━━━━━━ *MOT CLÉ*

dans [dɑ̃] *prép* **1** (*position*) in; (*à l'intérieur de*) inside; **c'est** ~ **le tiroir/le salon** it's in the drawer/lounge; ~ **la boîte** in *ou* inside the box; **marcher** ~ **la ville** to walk about the town
2 (*direction*) into; **elle a couru** ~ **le salon** she ran into the lounge
3 (*provenance*) out of, from; **je l'ai pris** ~ **le tiroir/salon** I took it out of *ou* from the drawer/lounge; **boire** ~ **un verre** to drink out of *ou* from a glass
4 (*temps*) in; ~ **2 mois** in 2 months, in 2 months' time
5 (*approximation*) about; ~ **les 20F** about 20F

danse [dɑ̃s] *nf*: **la** ~ dancing; **une** ~ **a** dance; **danser** *vi, vt* to dance; **danseur, euse** *nm/f* ballet dancer; (*au bal etc*) dancer; partner
dard [daʀ] *nm* sting (*organ*)
date [dat] *nf* date; **de longue** ~ longstanding; ~ **de naissance** date of birth; ~ **limite** deadline; **dater** *vt, vi* to date; **dater de** to date from; **à dater de** (as) from
datte [dat] *nf* date; **dattier** *nm* date palm
dauphin [dofɛ̃] *nm* (*ZOOL*) dolphin
davantage [davɑ̃taʒ] *adv* more; (*plus longtemps*) longer; ~ **de** more

━━━━━━━━ *MOT CLÉ*

de(d') (*de +le =* **du**, *de +les =* **des**) *prép* **1** (*appartenance*) of; **le toit** ~ **la maison** the roof of the house; **la voiture d'Elisabeth**/~ **mes parents** Elizabeth's/my parents' car
2 (*provenance*) from; **il vient** ~ **Londres** he comes from London; **elle est sortie du cinéma** she came out of the cinema
3 (*caractérisation, mesure*): **un mur** ~ **brique/bureau d'acajou** a brick wall/ mahogany desk; **un billet** ~ **50F** a 50F note; **une pièce** ~ **2m** ~ **large** *ou* **large** = 2m a room 2m wide, a 2m-wide room; **un bébé** ~ **10 mois** a 10-month-old baby; **12 mois** ~ **crédit/travail** 12 months' credit/ work; **augmenter** ~ **10F** to increase by 10F; ~ **14 à 18** from 14 to 18
♦ *dét* **1** (*phrases affirmatives*) some (*souvent omis*); **du vin,** ~ **l'eau, des pommes** (some) wine, (some) water, (some) apples; **des enfants sont venus** some children came; **pendant des mois** for months
2 (*phrases interrogatives et négatives*) any; **a-t-il du vin?** has he got any wine?; **il n'a pas** ~ **pommes/d'enfants** he hasn't (got) any apples/children, he has no apples/

children

dé [de] nm (à jouer) die ou dice; (aussi: ~ à coudre) thimble
déambuler [deɑ̃byle] vi to stroll about
débâcle [debɑkl(ə)] nf rout
déballer [debale] vt to unpack
débandade [debɑ̃dad] nf rout; scattering
débarbouiller [debaʀbuje] vt to wash; se ~ vi to wash (one's face)
débarcadère [debaʀkadɛʀ] nm wharf
débardeur [debaʀdœʀ] nm (maillot) tank top
débarquer [debaʀke] vt to unload, land ♦ vi to disembark; (fig) to turn up
débarras [debaʀa] nm lumber room; junk cupboard; **bon ~!** good riddance!
débarrasser [debaʀase] vt to clear; se ~ de vt to get rid of; ~ qn de (vêtements, paquets) to relieve sb of
débat [deba] nm discussion, debate
débattre [debatʀ(ə)] vt to discuss, debate; se ~ vi to struggle
débaucher [deboʃe] vt (licencier) to lay off, dismiss; (entraîner) to lead astray, debauch
débile [debil] adj weak, feeble; (fam: idiot) dim-witted
débit [debi] nm (d'un liquide, fleuve) flow; (d'un magasin) turnover (of goods); (élocution) delivery; (bancaire) debit; ~ de boissons drinking establishment; ~ de tabac tobacconist's; **~er** vt (compte) to debit; (liquide, gaz) to give out; (couper: bois, viande) to cut up; (péj: paroles etc) to churn out; **~eur, trice** nm/f debtor ♦ adj in debit; (compte) debit cpd
déblayer [debleje] vt to clear
débloquer [debloke] vt (frein) to release; (prix, crédits) to free
déboires [debwaʀ] nmpl setbacks
déboiser [debwaze] vt to deforest
déboîter [debwate] vt (AUTO) to pull out; se ~ **le genou** etc to dislocate one's knee etc
débonnaire [debonɛʀ] adj easy-going, good-natured
débordé, e [debɔʀde] adj: **être ~ (de)** (travail, demandes) to be snowed under (with)
déborder [debɔʀde] vi to overflow; (lait etc) to boil over; ~ **(de) qch** (dépasser) to extend beyond sth
débouché [debuʃe] nm (pour vendre) outlet; (perspective d'emploi) opening
déboucher [debuʃe] vt (évier, tuyau etc) to unblock; (bouteille) to uncork ♦ vi: ~ **de** to emerge from; ~ **sur** to come out onto; to open out onto
débourser [debuʀse] vt to pay out
debout [dəbu] adv: **être ~** (personne) to be standing, stand; (: levé, éveillé) to be up; (chose) to be upright; **être encore ~** (fig: en état) to be still going; **se mettre ~** to

stand up; **se tenir ~** to stand; **~!** stand up!; (du lit) get up!; **cette histoire ne tient pas ~** this story doesn't hold water
déboutonner [debutɔne] vt to undo, unbutton
débraillé, e [debʀaje] adj slovenly, untidy
débrancher [debʀɑ̃ʃe] vt to disconnect; (appareil électrique) to unplug
débrayage [debʀejaʒ] nm (AUTO) clutch; **débrayer** [debʀeje] vi (AUTO) to declutch; (cesser le travail) to stop work
débris [debʀi] nm (fragment) fragment ♦ nmpl rubbish sg; debris sg
débrouillard, e [debʀujaʀ, -aʀd(ə)] adj smart, resourceful
débrouiller [debʀuje] vt to disentangle, untangle; se ~ vi to manage
débusquer [debyske] vt to drive out (from cover)
début [deby] nm beginning, start; **~s** nmpl (dans la vie) beginnings; (de carrière) début sg
débutant, e [debytɑ̃, -ɑ̃t] nm/f beginner, novice
débuter [debyte] vi to begin, start; (faire ses débuts) to start out
deçà [dəsa]: **en ~ de** prép this side of
décacheter [dekaʃte] vt to unseal
décadence [dekadɑ̃s] nf decadence; decline
décaféiné, e [dekafeine] adj decaffeinated
décalage [dekalaʒ] nm gap; discrepancy; ~ **horaire** time difference (between time zones); time-lag
décaler [dekale] vt (dans le temps: avancer) to bring forward; (: retarder) to put back; (changer de position) to shift forward ou back
décalquer [dekalke] vt to trace; (par pression) to transfer
décamper [dekɑ̃pe] vi to clear out ou off
décaper [dekape] vt to strip; (avec abrasif) to scour; (avec papier de verre) to sand
décapiter [dekapite] vt to behead; (par accident) to decapitate
décapotable [dekapotabl(ə)] adj convertible
décapsuler [dekapsyle] vt to take the cap ou top off; **décapsuleur** nm bottle-opener
décédé, e [desede] adj deceased
décéder [desede] vi to die
déceler [desle] vt to discover, detect; to indicate, reveal
décembre [desɑ̃bʀ(ə)] nm December
décemment [desamɑ̃] adv decently
décennie [desni] nf decade
décent, e [desɑ̃, -ɑ̃t] adj decent
déception [desɛpsjɔ̃] nf disappointment
décerner [desɛʀne] vt to award
décès [desɛ] nm death, decease
décevoir [desvwaʀ] vt to disappoint
déchaîner [deʃene] vt to unleash, arouse; se ~ to be unleashed

déchanter [deʃɑ̃te] *vi* to become disillusioned

décharge [deʃaʁʒ(ə)] *nf* (*dépôt d'ordures*) rubbish tip *ou* dump; (*électrique*) electrical discharge; **à la ~ de** in defence of

décharger [deʃaʁʒe] *vt* (*marchandise, véhicule*) to unload; (*ÉLEC, faire feu*) to discharge; **~ qn de** (*responsabilité*) to release sb from

décharné, e [deʃaʁne] *adj* emaciated

déchausser [deʃose] *vt* (*skis*) to take off; **se ~** *vi* to take off one's shoes; (*dent*) to come *ou* work loose

déchéance [deʃeɑ̃s] *nf* degeneration; decay, decline; fall

déchet [deʃɛ] *nm* (*de bois, tissu etc*) scrap; (*perte: gén COMM*) wastage, waste; **~s** *nmpl* (*ordures*) refuse *sg*, rubbish *sg*

déchiffrer [deʃifʁe] *vt* to decipher

déchiqueter [deʃikte] *vt* to tear *ou* pull to pieces

déchirant, e [deʃiʁɑ̃, -ɑ̃t] *adj* heart-rending

déchirement [deʃiʁmɑ̃] *nm* (*chagrin*) wrench, heartbreak; (*gén pl: conflit*) rift, split

déchirer [deʃiʁe] *vt* to tear; (*en morceaux*) to tear up; (*pour ouvrir*) to tear off; (*arracher*) to tear out; (*fig*) to rack; to tear (apart); **se ~** *vi* to tear, rip; **se ~ un muscle** to tear a muscle

déchirure [deʃiʁyʁ] *nf* (*accroc*) tear, rip; **~ musculaire** torn muscle

déchoir [deʃwaʁ] *vi* (*personne*) to lower o.s., demean o.s.

déchu, e [deʃy] *adj* fallen; deposed

décidé, e [deside] *adj* (*personne, air*) determined; **c'est ~** it's decided

décidément [desidemɑ̃] *adv* undoubtedly; really

décider [deside] *vt*: **~ qch** to decide on sth; **se ~ (à faire)** to decide (to do), make up one's mind (to do); **se ~ pour** to decide on *ou* in favour of; **~ de faire/que** to decide to do/that; **~ qn (à faire qch)** to persuade sb (to do sth); **~ de qch** to decide upon sth; (*suj: chose*) to determine sth

décilitre [desilitʁ(ə)] *nm* decilitre

décimal, e, aux [desimal, -o] *adj* decimal; **décimale** *nf* decimal

décimètre [desimɛtʁ(ə)] *nm* decimetre; **double ~** (20 cm) ruler

décisif, ive [desizif, -iv] *adj* decisive

décision [desizjɔ̃] *nf* decision; (*fermeté*) decisiveness, decision

déclaration [deklaʁasjɔ̃] *nf* declaration; registration; (*discours: POL etc*) statement; **~ (d'impôts)** ≈ tax return; **~ (de sinistre)** (insurance) claim

déclarer [deklaʁe] *vt* to declare; (*décès, naissance*) to register; **se ~** *vi* (*feu, maladie*) to break out

déclasser [deklɑse] *vt* to relegate; to downgrade; to lower in status

déclencher [deklɑ̃ʃe] *vt* (*mécanisme etc*) to release; (*sonnerie*) to set off, activate; (*attaque, grève*) to launch; (*provoquer*) to trigger off; **se ~** *vi* to release itself; to go off

déclic [deklik] *nm* trigger mechanism; (*bruit*) click

décliner [dekline] *vi* to decline ♦ *vt* (*invitation*) to decline; (*responsabilité*) to refuse to accept; (*nom, adresse*) to state

déclivité [deklivite] *nf* slope, incline

décocher [dekɔʃe] *vt* to throw; to shoot

décoiffer [dekwafe] *vi*: **se ~** to take off one's hat

déçois *etc vb voir* **décevoir**

décollage [dekɔlaʒ] *nm* (*AVIAT*) takeoff

décoller [dekɔle] *vt* to unstick ♦ *vi* (*avion*) to take off; **se ~** *vi* to come unstuck

décolleté, e [dekɔlte] *adj* low-cut; wearing a low-cut dress ♦ *nm* low neck(line); (*bare*) neck and shoulders; (*plongeant*) cleavage

décolorer [dekɔlɔʁe] *vt* (*tissu*) to fade; (*cheveux*) to bleach, lighten; **se ~** *vi* to fade

décombres [dekɔ̃bʁ(ə)] *nmpl* rubble *sg*, debris *sg*

décommander [dekɔmɑ̃de] *vt* to cancel; (*invités*) to put off; **se ~** *vi* to cancel one's appointment *etc*, cry off

décomposé, e [dekɔ̃poze] *adj* (*pourri*) decomposed; (*visage*) haggard, distorted

décompte [dekɔ̃t] *nm* deduction; (*facture*) detailed account

déconcerter [dekɔ̃sɛʁte] *vt* to disconcert, confound

déconfit, e [dekɔ̃fi, -it] *adj* crestfallen; **~ure** [dekɔ̃fityʁ] *nf* failure, defeat; collapse, ruin

décongeler [dekɔ̃ʒle] *vt* to thaw

déconner [dekɔne] *vi* (*fam*) to talk rubbish

déconseiller [dekɔ̃seje] *vt*: **~ qch (à qn)** to advise (sb) against sth

déconsidérer [dekɔ̃sideʁe] *vt* to discredit

décontracté, e [dekɔ̃tʁakte] *adj* relaxed, laid-back (*fam*)

décontracter [dekɔ̃tʁakte] *vt* to relax; **se ~** *vi* to relax

déconvenue [dekɔ̃vny] *nf* disappointment

décor [dekɔʁ] *nm* décor; (*paysage*) scenery; **~s** *nmpl* (*THÉÂTRE*) scenery *sg*, décor *sg*; (*CINÉMA*) set *sg*; **~ateur** [dekɔʁatœʁ] *nm* (interior) decorator; (*CINÉMA*) set designer; **~ation** [dekɔʁɑsjɔ̃] *nf* decoration; **~er** [dekɔʁe] *vt* to decorate

décortiquer [dekɔʁtike] *vt* to shell; (*riz*) to hull; (*fig*) to dissect

découcher [dekuʃe] *vi* to spend the night away from home

découdre [dekudʁ(ə)] *vt* to unpick; **se ~** *vi* to come unstitched; **en ~** (*fig*) to fight, do battle

découler [dekule] *vi*: **~ de** to ensue *ou* follow from

découper [dekupe] *vt (papier, tissu etc)* to cut up; *(volaille, viande)* to carve; *(détacher: manche, article)* to cut out; **se ~ sur** *(ciel, fond)* to stand out against

décourager [dekuraʒe] *vt* to discourage; **se ~** *vi* to lose heart, become discouraged

décousu, e [dekuzy] *adj* unstitched; *(fig)* disjointed, disconnected

découvert, e [dekuvɛʀ, -ɛʀt(ə)] *adj (tête)* bare, uncovered; *(lieu)* open, exposed ♦ *nm (bancaire)* overdraft; **découverte** *nf* discovery

découvrir [dekuvʀiʀ] *vt* to discover; *(apercevoir)* to see; *(enlever ce qui couvre ou protège)* to uncover; *(montrer, dévoiler)* to reveal; **se ~** *vi* to take off one's hat; to take something off; *(au lit)* to uncover o.s.; *(ciel)* to clear

décret [dekʀɛ] *nm* decree; **décréter** *vt* to decree; to order; to declare

décrié, e [dekʀije] *adj* disparaged

décrire [dekʀiʀ] *vt* to describe

décrocher [dekʀɔʃe] *vt (dépendre)* to take down; *(téléphone)* to take off the hook; (: *pour répondre)*: **~ (le téléphone)** to lift the receiver; *(fig: contrat etc)* to get, land ♦ *vi* to drop out; to switch off

décroître [dekʀwatʀ(ə)] *vi* to decrease, decline

décrypter [dekʀipte] *vt* to decipher

déçu, e [desy] *pp de* **décevoir**

décupler [dekyple] *vt, vi* to increase tenfold

dédaigner [dedɛɲe] *vt* to despise, scorn; *(négliger)* to disregard, spurn

dédaigneux, euse [dedɛɲø, -øz] *adj* scornful, disdainful

dédain [dedɛ̃] *nm* scorn, disdain

dédale [dedal] *nm* maze

dedans [dədɑ̃] *adv* inside; *(pas en plein air)* indoors, inside ♦ *nm* inside; **au ~** on the inside; inside; **en ~** *(vers l'intérieur)* inwards; *voir aussi* **là**

dédicacer [dedikase] *vt*: **~ (à qn)** to sign (for sb), autograph (for sb)

dédier [dedje] *vt* to dedicate

dédire [dediʀ] : **se ~** *vi* to go back on one's word; to retract, recant

dédommager [dedɔmaʒe] *vt*: **~ qn (de)** to compensate sb (for); *(fig)* to repay sb (for)

dédouaner [dedwane] *vt* to clear through customs

dédoubler [dedubLe] *vt (classe, effectifs)* to split (into two); **~ les trains** to run additional trains

déduire [dedɥiʀ] *vt*: **~ qch (de)** *(ôter)* to deduct sth (from); *(conclure)* to deduce *ou* infer sth (from)

déesse [deɛs] *nf* goddess

défaillance [defajɑ̃s] *nf (syncope)* blackout; *(fatigue)* (sudden) weakness *no pl*; *(technique)* fault, failure; *(morale etc)* weak-

ness; **~ cardiaque** heart failure

défaillir [defajiʀ] *vi* to faint; to feel faint; *(mémoire etc)* to fail

défaire [defɛʀ] *vt (installation)* to take down, dismantle; *(paquet etc, nœud, vêtement)* to undo; **se ~** *vi* to come undone; **se ~ de** *(se débarrasser de)* to get rid of; *(se séparer de)* to part with

défait, e [defɛ, -ɛt] *adj (visage)* haggard, ravaged; **défaite** *nf* defeat

défalquer [defalke] *vt* to deduct

défaut [defo] *nm (moral)* fault, failing, defect; *(d'étoffe, métal)* fault, flaw, defect; *(manque, carence)*: **~ de** lack of; shortage of; **en ~** at fault; in the wrong; **faire ~** *(manquer)* to be lacking; **à ~** failing that; **à ~ de** for lack *ou* want of; **par ~** *(JUR)* in his *(ou* her *etc)* absence

défavorable [defavɔʀabl(ə)] *adj (avis, conditions, jury)* unfavourable *(BRIT)*, unfavorable *(US)*

défavoriser [defavɔʀize] *vt* to put at a disadvantage

défection [defɛksjɔ̃] *nf* defection, failure to give support *ou* assistance; failure to appear; **faire ~** *(d'un parti etc)* to withdraw one's support, leave

défectueux, euse [defɛktɥø, -øz] *adj* faulty, defective

défendre [defɑ̃dʀ(ə)] *vt* to defend; *(interdire)* to forbid; **se ~** *vi* to defend o.s.; **~ à qn qch/de faire** to forbid sb sth/to do; **il se défend** *(fig)* he can hold his own; **se ~ de/contre** *(se protéger)* to protect o.s. from/against; **se ~ de** *(se garder de)* to refrain from; *(nier)*: **se ~ de vouloir** to deny wanting

défense [defɑ̃s] *nf* defence; *(d'éléphant etc)* tusk; **"~ de fumer/cracher"** "no smoking/spitting"

déférer [defeʀe] *vt (JUR)* to refer; **~ à** *(requête, décision)* to defer to

déferler [defɛʀle] *vi (vagues)* to break; *(fig)* to surge

défi [defi] *nm (provocation)* challenge; *(bravade)* defiance

défiance [defjɑ̃s] *nf* mistrust, distrust

déficit [defisit] *nm (COMM)* deficit

défier [defje] *vt (provoquer)* to challenge; *(fig)* to defy, brave; **se ~ de** *(se méfier de)* to distrust

défigurer [defigyʀe] *vt* to disfigure

défilé [defile] *nm (GÉO)* (narrow) gorge *ou* pass; *(soldats)* parade; *(manifestants)* procession, march

défiler [defile] *vi (troupes)* to march past; *(sportifs)* to parade; *(manifestants)* to march; *(visiteurs)* to pour, stream; **se ~** *vi (se dérober)* to slip away, sneak off

définir [definiʀ] *vt* to define

définitif, ive [definitif, -iv] *adj (final)* final, definitive; *(pour longtemps)* permanent, definitive; (sans appel) final, definite; **définitive** nf: **en définitive** eventually; (somme toute) when all is said and done

définitivement [definitivmɑ̃] adv definitively; permanently; definitely

déflagration [deflagrɑsjɔ̃] nf explosion

défoncer [defɔ̃se] vt (caisse) to stave in; (porte) to smash in ou down; (lit, fauteuil) to burst (the springs of); (terrain, route) to rip ou plough up

déformation [defɔrmɑsjɔ̃] nf: ~ **professionnelle** conditioning by one's job

déformer [defɔrme] vt to put out of shape; (corps) to deform; (pensée, fait) to distort; **se ~** vi to lose its shape

défouler [defule]: **se ~** vi to unwind, let off steam

défraîchir [defreʃir]: **se ~** vi to fade; to become worn

défrayer [defreje] vt: ~ **qn** to pay sb's expenses; ~ **la chronique** to be in the news

défricher [defriʃe] vt to clear (for cultivation)

défroquer [defrɔke] vi (aussi: se ~) to give up the cloth

défunt, e [defœ̃, -œ̃t] adj: **son ~ père** his late father ♦ nm/f deceased

dégagé, e [degaʒe] adj clear; (ton, air) casual, jaunty

dégagement [degaʒmɑ̃] nm: **voie de ~** slip road; **itinéraire de ~** alternative route (to relieve congestion)

dégager [degaʒe] vt (exhaler) to give off; (délivrer) to free, extricate; (désencombrer) to clear; (isoler: idée, aspect) to bring out; **se ~** vi (odeur) to be given off; (passage, ciel) to clear

dégarnir [degarnir] vt (vider) to empty, clear; **se ~** vi (tempes, crâne) to go bald

dégâts [degɑ] nmpl damage sg

dégel [deʒɛl] nm thaw

dégeler [deʒle] vt to thaw (out); (fig) to unfreeze ♦ vi to thaw (out)

dégénérer [deʒenere] vi to degenerate; (empirer) to go from bad to worse

dégingandé, e [deʒɛ̃gɑ̃de] adj gangling

dégivrer [deʒivre] vt (frigo) to defrost; (vitres) to de-ice

déglutir [deglytir] vt, vi to swallow

dégonflé, e [degɔ̃fle] adj (pneu) flat

dégonfler [degɔ̃fle] vt (pneu, ballon) to let down, deflate; **se ~** vi (fam) to chicken out

dégouliner [deguline] vi to trickle, drip

dégourdi, e [degurdi] adj smart, resourceful

dégourdir [degurdir] vt: **se ~ (les jambes)** to stretch one's legs (fig)

dégoût [degu] nm disgust, distaste

dégoûtant, e [degutɑ̃, -ɑ̃t] adj disgusting

dégoûté, e [degute] adj disgusted; ~ **de** sick of

dégoûter [degute] vt to disgust; ~ **qn de** qch to put sb off sth

dégoutter [degute] vi to drip

dégradé [degrade] nm (PEINTURE) gradation

dégrader [degrade] vt (MIL: officier) to degrade; (abîmer) to damage, deface; **se ~** vi (relations, situation) to deteriorate

dégrafer [degrafe] vt to unclip, unhook

degré [dəgre] nm degree; (d'escalier) step; **alcool à 90 ~s** surgical spirit

dégressif, ive [degresif, -iv] adj on a decreasing scale

dégrèvement [degrɛvmɑ̃] nm tax relief

dégringoler [degrɛ̃gɔle] vi to tumble (down)

dégrossir [degrosir] vt (fig) to work out roughly; to knock the rough edges off

déguenillé, e [degnije] adj ragged, tattered

déguerpir [degɛrpir] vi to clear off

dégueulasse [degœlas] (fam) adj disgusting

déguisement [degizmɑ̃] nm disguise

déguiser [degize] vt to disguise; **se ~** vi (se costumer) to dress up; (pour tromper) to disguise o.s.

déguster [degyste] vt (vins) to taste; (fromages etc) to sample; (savourer) to enjoy, savour

dehors [dəɔr] adv outside; (en plein air) outdoors ♦ nm outside ♦ nmpl (apparences) appearances; **mettre** ou **jeter ~** (expulser) to throw out; **au ~** outside; outwardly; **au ~ de** outside; **en ~** (vers l'extérieur) outside; outwards; **en ~ de** (hormis) apart from

déjà [deʒa] adv already; (auparavant) before, already

déjeuner [deʒœne] vi to (have) lunch; (le matin) to have breakfast ♦ nm lunch; breakfast

déjouer [deʒwe] vt to elude; to foil

delà [dəla] adv: **par ~, en ~ (de), au ~ (de)** beyond

délabrer [delɑbre]: **se ~** vi to fall into decay, become dilapidated

délacer [delase] vt to unlace

délai [delɛ] nm (attente) waiting period; (sursis) extension (of time); (temps accordé) time limit; **à bref ~** shortly, very soon; at short notice; **dans les ~s** within the time limit

délaisser [delese] vt to abandon, desert

délasser [delɑse] vt (reposer) to relax; (divertir) to divert, entertain; **se ~** vi to relax

délateur, trice [delatœr, -tris] nm/f informer

délavé, e [delave] adj faded

délayer [deleje] vt (CULIN) to mix (with water etc); (peinture) to thin down

delco [dɛlko] nm (AUTO) distributor

délecter [delɛkte]: **se ~** vi to revel ou delight in

délégué, e [delege] nm/f delegate; representative

déléguer [delege] vt to delegate

délibéré, e [delibeʀe] adj (conscient) deliberate; (déterminé) determined

délibérer [delibeʀe] vi to deliberate

délicat, e [delika, -at] adj delicate; (plein de tact) tactful; (attentionné) thoughtful; (exigeant) fussy, particular; procédés peu ~s unscrupulous methods; **délicatement** adv delicately; (avec douceur) gently

délice [delis] nm delight

délicieux, euse [delisjø, -jøz] adj (au goût) delicious; (sensation, impression) delightful

délimiter [delimite] vt to delimit, demarcate; to determine; to define

délinquance [delɛ̃kɑ̃s] nf criminality; **délinquant, e** [delɛ̃kɑ̃, -ɑ̃t] adj, nm/f delinquent

délirer [deliʀe] vi to be delirious; (fig) to be raving, be going wild

délit [deli] nm (criminal) offence; ~ **d'initié** (BOURSE) insider dealing ou trading

délivrer [delivʀe] vt (prisonnier) to (set) free, release; (passeport, certificat) to issue; ~ qn de (ennemis) to deliver ou free sb from; (fig) to relieve sb of; to rid sb of

déloger [deloʒe] vt (locataire) to turn out; (objet coincé, ennemi) to dislodge

deltaplane [dɛltaplan] nm hang-glider

déluge [delyʒ] nm (biblique) Flood

déluré, e [delyʀe] adj smart, resourceful; (péj) forward, pert

demain [dəmɛ̃] adv tomorrow

demande [dəmɑ̃d] nf (requête) request; (revendication) demand; (ADMIN, formulaire) application; (ÉCON): la ~ demand; "~s d'emploi" "situations wanted"; ~ de poste job application

demandé, e [dəmɑ̃de] adj (article etc): très ~ (very) much in demand

demander [dəmɑ̃de] vt to ask for; (date, heure etc) to ask; (nécessiter) to require, demand; se ~ to wonder; (sens purement réfléchi) to ask o.s.; ~ qch à qn to ask sb for sth; to ask sb sth; ~ à qn de faire to ask sb to do; **on vous demande au téléphone** you're wanted on the phone

demandeur, euse [dəmɑ̃dœʀ, -øz] nm/f: ~ **d'emploi** job-seeker; (job) applicant

démangeaison [demɑ̃ʒɛzɔ̃] nf itching

démanger [demɑ̃ʒe] vi to itch

démanteler [demɑ̃tle] vt to break up; to demolish

démaquillant [demakijɑ̃] nm make-up remover

démaquiller [demakije] vt: se ~ to remove one's make-up

démarche [demaʀʃ(ə)] nf (allure) gait, walk; (intervention) step; approach; (fig: intellectuelle) thought processes pl; approach; **faire des ~s auprès de qn** to approach sb

démarcheur, euse [demaʀʃœʀ, -øz] nm/f

(COMM) door-to-door salesman(woman)

démarquer [demaʀke] vt (prix) to mark down; (joueur) to stop marking

démarrage [demaʀaʒ] nm start

démarrer [demaʀe] vi (conducteur) to start (up); (véhicule) to move off; (travaux) to get moving; **démarreur** nm (AUTO) starter

démêler [demele] vt to untangle

démêlés [demele] nmpl problems

déménagement [demenaʒmɑ̃] nm move, removal; **camion de** ~ removal van

déménager [demenaʒe] vt (meubles) to (re)move ♦ vi to move (house); **déménageur** nm removal man; (entrepreneur) furniture remover

démener [demne] : **se** ~ vi to thrash about; (fig) to exert o.s.

dément, e [demɑ̃, -ɑ̃t] adj (fou) mad, crazy; (fam) brilliant, fantastic

démentiel, le [demɑ̃sjɛl] adj insane

démentir [demɑ̃tiʀ] vt to refute; ~ **que** to deny that

démerder [demɛʀde] (fam) : **se** ~ vi to sort things out for o.s.

démesuré, e [demzyʀe] adj immoderate

démettre [demɛtʀ(ə)] vt: ~ **qn de** (fonction, poste) to dismiss sb from; **se** ~ **(de ses fonctions)** to resign (from) one's duties; **se** ~ **l'épaule** etc to dislocate one's shoulder etc

demeurant [dəmœʀɑ̃] : **au** ~ adv for all that

demeure [dəmœʀ] nf residence; **mettre qn en** ~ **de faire** to enjoin ou order sb to do; **à** ~ permanently

demeurer [dəmœʀe] vi (habiter) to live; (séjourner) to stay; (rester) to remain

demi, e [dəmi] adj half ♦ nm (bière) ≈ half-pint (0,25 litres) ♦ préfixe: ~... half-, semi-, demi-; **trois heures/bouteilles et** ~**es** three and a half hours/bottles, three hours/bottles and a half; **il est 2 heures/midi et** ~ it's half past 2/12; **à** ~ half-; **à la** ~**e** (heure) on the half-hour; ~**-cercle** nm semicircle; **en** ~**-cercle** adj semicircular ♦ adv in a half circle; ~**-douzaine** nf half-dozen, half a dozen; ~**-finale** nf semifinal; ~**-frère** nm half-brother; ~**-heure** nf half-hour, half an hour; ~**-journée** nf half-day, half a day; ~**-litre** nm half-litre, half a litre; ~**-livre** nf half-pound, half a pound; ~**-mot** adv: **à** ~**-mot** without having to spell things out; ~**-pension** nf (à l'hôtel) half-board; ~**-place** nf half-fare

démis, e [demi, -iz] adj (épaule etc) dislocated

demi: ~**-saison** nf: **vêtements de** ~**saison** spring ou autumn clothing; ~**-sel** adj inv (beurre, fromage) slightly salted; ~**-sœur** nf half-sister

démission [demisjɔ̃] nf resignation; **donner sa** ~ to give ou hand in one's notice; **dé-**

missionner vi (de son poste) to resign
demi-tarif [dəmitaʀif] nm half-price; (TRANSPORTS) half-fare
demi-tour [dəmituʀ] nm about-turn; faire ~ to turn (and go) back; (AUTO) to do a U-turn
démocratie [demɔkʀasi] nf democracy; **démocratique** [demɔkʀatik] adj democratic
démodé, e [demɔde] adj old-fashioned
démographique [demɔgʀafik] adj demographic, population cpd
demoiselle [dəmwazɛl] nf (jeune fille) young lady; (célibataire) single lady, maiden lady; ~ d'honneur bridesmaid
démolir [demɔliʀ] vt to demolish
démon [demɔ̃] nm (enfant turbulent) devil, demon; le D~ the Devil
démonstration [demɔ̃stʀasjɔ̃] nf demonstration; (aérienne, navale) display
démonté, e [demɔ̃te] adj (fig) raging, wild
démonter [demɔ̃te] vt (machine etc) to take down, dismantle; se ~ vi (personne) to lose countenance
démontrer [demɔ̃tʀe] vt to demonstrate
démordre [demɔʀdʀ(ə)] vi: ne pas ~ de to refuse to give up, stick to
démouler [demule] vt (gâteau) to turn out
démuni, e [demyni] adj (sans argent) impoverished
démunir [demyniʀ] vt: ~ qn de to deprive sb of; se ~ de to part with, give up
dénatalité [denatalite] nf fall in the birth rate
dénaturer [denatyʀe] vt (goût) to alter; (pensée, fait) to distort
déniaiser [denjeze] vt: ~ qn to teach sb about life
dénicher [deniʃe] vt to unearth; to track ou hunt down
dénier [denje] vt to deny
dénigrer [denigʀe] vt to denigrate, run down
dénivellation [denivɛlɑsjɔ̃] nf = **dénivellement**
dénivellement [denivɛlmɑ̃] nm ramp; dip; difference in level
dénombrer [denɔ̃bʀe] vt (compter) to count; (énumérer) to enumerate, list
dénomination [denɔminɑsjɔ̃] nf designation, appellation
dénommer [denɔme] vt to name
dénoncer [denɔ̃se] vt to denounce; se ~ vi to give o.s. up, come forward
dénouement [denumɑ̃] nm outcome
dénouer [denwe] vt to unknot, undo
dénoyauter [denwajote] vt to stone
denrée [dɑ̃ʀe] nf: ~s (alimentaires) foodstuffs
dense [dɑ̃s] adj dense
densité [dɑ̃site] nf density
dent [dɑ̃] nf tooth; en ~s de scie serrated; jagged; ~ de lait/sagesse milk/wisdom

tooth; ~aire adj dental
dentelé, e [dɑ̃tle] adj jagged, indented
dentelle [dɑ̃tɛl] nf lace no pl
dentier [dɑ̃tje] nm denture
dentifrice [dɑ̃tifʀis] nm toothpaste
dentiste [dɑ̃tist(ə)] nm/f dentist
dénuder [denyde] vt to bare
dénué, e [denɥe] adj: ~ de devoid of; lacking in; **dénuement** [denɥmɑ̃] nm destitution
déodorant [deɔdɔʀɑ̃] nm deodorant
dépannage [depanaʒ] nm: service de ~ (AUTO) breakdown service
dépanner [depane] vt (voiture, télévision) to fix, repair; (fig) to bail out, help out; **dépanneuse** nf breakdown lorry (BRIT), tow truck (US)
dépareillé, e [depaʀeje] adj (collection, service) incomplete; (objet) odd
déparer [depaʀe] vt to spoil, mar
départ [depaʀ] nm leaving no pl, departure; (SPORT) start; (sur un horaire) departure; au ~ at the start; à son ~ when he left
départager [depaʀtaʒe] vt to decide between
département [depaʀtəmɑ̃] nm department
départir [depaʀtiʀ] : se ~ de vt to abandon, depart from
dépassé, e [depɑse] adj superseded, outmoded; (affolé) panic-stricken
dépasser [depɑse] vt (véhicule, concurrent) to overtake; (endroit) to pass, go past; (somme, limite) to exceed; (fig: en beauté etc) to surpass, outshine; (être en saillie sur) to jut out above (ou in front of) ♦ vi (jupon) to show
dépaysé, e [depeize] adj disoriented
dépecer [depəse] vt to joint, cut up
dépêche [depɛʃ] nf dispatch
dépêcher [depeʃe] vt to dispatch; se ~ vi to hurry
dépeindre [depɛ̃dʀ(ə)] vt to depict
dépendre [depɑ̃dʀ(ə)]: ~ de vt to depend on; (financièrement etc) to be dependent on
dépens [depɑ̃] nmpl: aux ~ de at the expense of
dépense [depɑ̃s] nf spending no pl, expense, expenditure no pl; (fig) consumption; expenditure
dépenser [depɑ̃se] vt to spend; (gaz, eau) to use; (fig) to expend, use up; se ~ vi (se fatiguer) to exert o.s.
dépensier, ière [depɑ̃sje, -jɛʀ] adj: il est ~ he's a spendthrift
déperdition [depɛʀdisjɔ̃] nf loss
dépérir [depeʀiʀ] vi to waste away; to wither
dépêtrer [depetʀe] vt: se ~ de to extricate o.s. from
dépeupler [depœple] vt to depopulate; se ~ vi to be depopulated
dépilatoire [depilatwaʀ] adj depilatory,

hair-removing

dépister [depiste] *vt* to detect; (*voleur*) to track down; (*poursuivants*) to throw off the scent

dépit [depi] *nm* vexation, frustration; **en ~ de** in spite of; **en ~ du bon sens** contrary to all good sense; **dépité, e** *adj* vexed, frustrated

déplacé, e [deplase] *adj* (*propos*) out of place, uncalled-for

déplacement [deplasmã] *nm* (*voyage*) trip, travelling *no pl*

déplacer [deplase] *vt* (*table, voiture*) to move, shift; (*employé*) to transfer, move; (*os, vertèbre etc*) to displace; **se ~** *vi* to move; (*voyager*) to travel

déplaire [deplɛR] *vt*: **ceci me déplaît** I don't like this, I dislike this; **se ~** *vr*: **se quelque part** to be unhappy somewhere; **déplaisant, e** *adj* disagreeable

dépliant [deplijã] *nm* leaflet

déplier [deplije] *vt* to unfold

déplorer [deplɔRe] *vt* (*regretter*) to deplore

déployer [deplwaje] *vt* to open out, spread; to deploy; to display, exhibit

déporter [depɔRte] *vt* (*POL*) to deport; (*dévier*) to carry off course

déposer [depoze] *vt* (*gén: mettre, poser*) to lay *ou* put down; (*à la banque, à la consigne*) to deposit; (*passager*) to drop (off), set down; (*roi*) to depose; (*ADMIN: faire enregistrer*) to file; to register; (*JUR*): **~ (contre)** to testify *ou* give evidence (against); **se ~** *vi* to settle; **dépositaire** *nm/f* (*COMM*) agent

dépôt [depo] *nm* (*à la banque, sédiment*) deposit; (*entrepôt, réserve*) warehouse, store; (*gare*) depot; (*prison*) cells *pl*

dépotoir [depɔtwaR] *nm* dumping ground, rubbish dump

dépouille [depuj] *nf* (*d'animal*) skin, hide; (*humaine*): **~ (mortelle)** mortal remains *pl*

dépouillé, e [depuje] *adj* (*fig*) bare, bald

dépouiller [depuje] *vt* (*animal*) to skin; (*spolier*) to deprive of one's possessions; (*documents*) to go through, peruse; **~ qn/ qch de** to strip sb/sth of; **~ le scrutin** to count the votes

dépourvu, e [depuRvy] *adj*: **~ de** lacking in, without; **au ~** unprepared

déprécier [depResje] *vt* to depreciate; **se ~** *vi* to depreciate

dépression [depResjõ] *nf* depression; **~ (nerveuse)** (nervous) breakdown

déprimer [depRime] *vt* to depress

──────── *MOT CLÉ* ────────

depuis [dəpɥi] *prép* **1** (*point de départ dans le temps*) since; **il habite Paris ~ 1983/l'an dernier** he has been living in Paris since 1983/last year; **~ quand le connaissez-vous?** how long have you known him?

2 (*temps écoulé*) for; **il habite Paris ~ 5 ans** he has been living in Paris for 5 years; **je le connais ~ 3 ans** I've known him for 3 years

3 (*lieu*): **il a plu ~ Metz** it's been raining since Metz; **elle a téléphoné ~ Valence** she rang from Valence

4 (*quantité, rang*) from; **~ les plus petits jusqu'aux plus grands** from the youngest to the oldest

♦ *adv* (*temps*) since (then); **je ne lui ai pas parlé ~** I haven't spoken to him since (then); **~ que** *conj* (ever) since; **~ qu'il m'a dit ça** (ever) since he said that to me

──────────────────────

député, e [depyte] *nm/f* (*POL*) ≈ Member of Parliament (*BRIT*), ≈ Member of Congress (*US*)

députer [depyte] *vt* to delegate

déraciner [deRasine] *vt* to uproot

dérailler [deRaje] *vi* (*train*) to be derailed; **faire ~** to derail

déraisonner [deRɛzɔne] *vi* to talk nonsense, rave

dérangement [deRãʒmã] *nm* (*gêne*) trouble; (*gastrique etc*) disorder; (*mécanique*) breakdown; **en ~** (*téléphone*) out of order

déranger [deRãʒe] *vt* (*personne*) to trouble, bother; to disturb; (*projets*) to disrupt, upset; (*objets, vêtements*) to disarrange; **se ~** *vi* to put o.s. out; to (take the trouble to) come *ou* go out; **est-ce que cela vous dérange si ...?** do you mind if ...?

déraper [deRape] *vi* (*voiture*) to skid; (*personne, semelles, couteau*) to slip

déréglé, e [deRegle] *adj* (*mœurs*) dissolute

dérégler [deRegle] *vt* (*mécanisme*) to put out of order; (*estomac*) to upset

dérider [deRide] *vt* to brighten up; **se ~** *vi* to brighten up

dérision [deRizjõ] *nf*: **tourner en ~** to deride

dérivatif [deRivatif] *nm* distraction

dérive [deRiv] *nf* (*de dériveur*) centre-board; **aller à la ~** (*NAVIG, fig*) to drift

dérivé, e [deRive] *nm* (*TECH*) by-product; **~e** *nf* (*MATH*) derivative

dériver [deRive] *vt* (*MATH*) to derive; (*cours d'eau etc*) to divert ♦ *vi* (*bateau*) to drift; **de** to derive from

dermatologue [dɛRmatɔlɔg] *nm/f* dermatologist

dernier, ière [dɛRnje, -jɛR] *adj* last; (*le plus récent*) latest, last; **lundi/le mois ~** last Monday/month; **du ~ chic** extremely smart; **les ~s honneurs** the last tribute; **en ~** last; **ce ~** the latter; **dernièrement** *adv* recently

dérobé, e [deRɔbe] *adj* (*porte*) secret, hidden; **à la ~e** surreptitiously

dérober [deRɔbe] *vt* to steal; **se ~** *vi* (*s'esquiver*) to slip away; to shy away; **se ~**

sous (*s'effondrer*) to give way beneath; **se ~ à** (*justice, regards*) to hide from; (*obligation*) to shirk; **~ qch à (la vue de) qn** to conceal *ou* hide sth from sb('s view)

dérogation [deRɔgasjɔ̃] *nf* (special) dispensation

déroger [deRɔʒe] : **~ à** *vt* to go against, depart from

dérouiller [deRuje] *vt*: **se ~ les jambes** to stretch one's legs (*fig*)

déroulement [deRulmɑ̃] *nm* (*d'une opération etc*) progress

dérouler [deRule] *vt* (*ficelle*) to unwind; (*papier*) to unroll; **se ~** *vi* (*avoir lieu*) to take place; (*se passer*) to go on; to go (off); to unfold

déroute [deRut] *nf* rout; total collapse; **~r** [deRute] *vt* (*avion, train*) to reroute, divert; (*étonner*) to disconcert, throw (out)

derrière [dɛRjɛR] *adv, prép* behind ♦ *nm* (*d'une maison*) back; (*postérieur*) behind, bottom; **les pattes de ~** the back *ou* hind legs; **par ~** from behind; (*fig*) behind one's back

des [de] *dét voir de* ♦ *prép* +*dét* = **de** +**les**

dès [dɛ] *prép* from; **~ que** as soon as; **~ son retour** as soon as he was (*ou* is) back; **~ lors** from then on; **~ lors que** from the moment (that)

désabusé, e [dezabyze] *adj* disillusioned

désaccord [dezakɔR] *nm* disagreement; **~é, e** [dezakɔRde] *adj* (*MUS*) out of tune

désaffecté, e [dezafɛkte] *adj* disused

désagréable [dezagReable(ə)] *adj* unpleasant

désagréger [dezagReʒe] : **se ~** *vi* to disintegrate, break up

désagrément [dezagRemɑ̃] *nm* annoyance, trouble *no pl*

désaltérer [dezaltere] *vt*: **se ~** to quench one's thirst

désamorcer [dezamɔRse] *vt* to defuse; to forestall

désapprobateur, trice [dezapRɔbatœR, -tRis] *adj* disapproving

désapprouver [dezapRuve] *vt* to disapprove of

désarçonner [dezaRsɔne] *vt* to unseat, throw; (*fig*) to throw, puzzle

désarmant, e [dezaRmɑ̃, -ɑ̃t] *adj* disarming

désarroi [dezaRwa] *nm* disarray

désarticulé, e [dezaRtikyle] *adj* (*pantin, corps*) dislocated

désastre [dezastR(ə)] *nm* disaster

désavantage [dezavɑ̃taʒ] *nm* disadvantage; (*inconvénient*) drawback, disadvantage; **désavantager** *vt* to put at a disadvantage

désavouer [dezavwe] *vt* to disown

désaxé, e [dezakse] *adj* (*fig*) unbalanced

descendre [desɑ̃dR(ə)] *vt* (*escalier, montagne*) to go (*ou* come) down; (*valise, paquet*) to take *ou* get down; (*étagère etc*) to

lower; (*fam: abattre*) to shoot down ♦ *vi* to go (*ou* come) down; (*passager: s'arrêter*) to get out, alight; **~ à pied/en voiture** to walk/drive down; **~ de** (*famille*) to be descended from; **~ du train** to get out of *ou* get off the train; **~ d'un arbre** to climb down from a tree; **~ de cheval** to dismount; **~ à l'hôtel** to stay at a hotel

descente [desɑ̃t] *nf* descent, going down; (*chemin*) way down; (*SKI*) downhill (race); **au milieu de la ~** halfway down; **~ de lit** bedside rug; **~ (de police)** (police) raid

description [dɛskRipsjɔ̃] *nf* description

désemparé, e [dezɑ̃paRe] *adj* bewildered, distraught

désemparer [dezɑ̃paRe] *vi*: **sans ~** without stopping

désemplir [dezɑ̃pliR] *vi*: **ne pas ~** to be always full

déséquilibre [dezekilibR(ə)] *nm* (*position*): **en ~** unsteady; (*fig: des forces, du budget*) imbalance; **déséquilibré, e** [dezekilibRe] *nm/f* (*PSYCH*) unbalanced person; **déséquilibrer** [dezekilibRe] *vt* to throw off balance

désert, e [dezɛR, -ɛRt(ə)] *adj* deserted ♦ *nm* desert

déserter [dezɛRte] *vi, vt* to desert

désertique [dezɛRtik] *adj* desert *cpd*; barren, empty

désespéré, e [dezɛspere] *adj* desperate

désespérer [dezɛspere] *vt* to drive to despair ♦ *vi*: **~ de** to despair of

désespoir [dezɛspwaR] *nm* despair; **en ~ de cause** in desperation

déshabillé [dezabije] *nm* négligée

déshabiller [dezabije] *vt* to undress; **se ~** *vi* to undress (o.s.)

désherbant [dezɛRbɑ̃] *nm* weed-killer

déshériter [dezeRite] *vt* to disinherit

déshérités [dezeRite] *nmpl*: **les ~** the underprivileged

déshonneur [dezɔnœR] *nm* dishonour

déshydraté, e [dezidRate] *adj* dehydrated

desiderata [deziderata] *nmpl* requirements

désigner [dezine] *vt* (*montrer*) to point out, indicate; (*dénommer*) to denote; (*candidat etc*) to name

désinfectant, e [dezɛ̃fɛktɑ̃, -ɑ̃t] *adj, nm* disinfectant; **désinfecter** [dezɛ̃fɛkte] *vt* to disinfect

désintégrer [dezɛ̃tegRe] *vt* to disintegrate; **se ~** *vi* to disintegrate

désintéressé, e [dezɛ̃teRese] *adj* disinterested, unselfish

désintéresser [dezɛ̃teRese] *vt*: **se ~ (de)** to lose interest (in)

désintoxication [dezɛ̃tɔksikasjɔ̃] *nf*: **faire une cure de ~** to undergo treatment for alcoholism (*ou* drug addiction)

désinvolte [dezɛ̃vɔlt(ə)] *adj* casual, offhand; **désinvolture** *nf* casualness

désir [deziʀ] nm wish; (fort, sensuel) desire

désirer [deziʀe] vt to want, wish for; (sexuellement) to desire; **je désire ...** (formule de politesse) I would like ...

désister [deziste]: **se ~** vi to stand down, withdraw

désobéir [dezɔbeiʀ] vi: **~ (à qn/qch)** to disobey (sb/sth); **désobéissant, e** adj disobedient

désobligeant, e [dezɔbliʒɑ̃, -ɑ̃t] adj disagreeable

désodorisant [dezɔdɔʀizɑ̃] nm air freshener, deodorizer

désœuvré, e [dezœvʀe] adj idle

désolé, e [dezɔle] adj (paysage) desolate; **je suis ~** I'm sorry

désoler [dezɔle] vt to distress, grieve

désolidariser [desɔlidaʀize] vt: **se ~ de** ou **d'avec** to dissociate o.s. from

désopilant, e [dezɔpilɑ̃, -ɑ̃t] adj hilarious

désordonné, e [dezɔʀdɔne] adj untidy

désordre [dezɔʀdʀ(ə)] nm disorder(liness), untidiness; (anarchie) disorder; **~s** nmpl (POL) disturbances, disorder sg; **en ~** in a mess, untidy

désorienté, e [dezɔʀjɑ̃te] adj disorientated

désormais [dezɔʀmɛ] adv from now on

désosser [dezɔse] vt to bone

desquelles [dekɛl] prép +pron = **de +lesquelles**

desquels [dekɛl] prép +pron = **de +lesquels**

dessaisir [deseziʀ]: **se ~ de** vt to give up, part with

dessaler [desale] vt (eau de mer) to desalinate; (CULIN) to soak

desséché, e [deseʃe] adj dried up

dessécher [deseʃe] vt to dry out, parch; **se ~** vi to dry out

dessein [desɛ̃] nm design; **à ~** intentionally, deliberately

desserrer [deseʀe] vt to loosen; (frein) to release

dessert [deseʀ] nm dessert, pudding

desserte [deseʀt(ə)] nf (table) side table; (transport): **la ~ du village est assurée par autocar** there is a coach service to the village

desservir [deseʀviʀ] vt (ville, quartier) to serve; (nuire à) to go against, put at a disadvantage; (débarrasser): **~ (la table)** to clear the table

dessin [desɛ̃] nm (œuvre, art) drawing; (motif) pattern, design; (contour) (out)line; **~ animé** cartoon (film); **~ humoristique** cartoon

dessinateur, trice [desinatœʀ, -tʀis] nm/f drawer; (de bandes dessinées) cartoonist; (industriel) draughtsman(woman) (BRIT), draftsman(woman) (US)

dessiner [desine] vt to draw; (concevoir) to design

dessous [dəsu] adv underneath, beneath ♦ nm underside ♦ nmpl (sous-vêtements) underwear sg; **en ~, par ~** underneath; below; **au-dessous (de)** below; (peu digne de) beneath; **avoir le ~** to get the worst of it; **dessous-de-plat** nm inv tablemat

dessus [dəsy] adv on top; (collé, écrit) on it ♦ nm top; **en ~** above; **par ~** adv over it ♦ prép over; **au-dessus (de)** above; **avoir le ~** to get the upper hand; **dessus-de-lit** nm inv bedspread

destin [dɛstɛ̃] nm fate; (avenir) destiny

destinataire [dɛstinatɛʀ] nm/f (POSTES) addressee; (d'un colis) consignee

destination [dɛstinasjɔ̃] nf (lieu) destination; (usage) purpose; **à ~ de** bound for, travelling to

destinée [dɛstine] nf fate; (existence, avenir) destiny

destiner [dɛstine] vt: **~ qn à** (poste, sort) to destine sb for; **~ qn/qch à** (prédestiner) to destine sb/sth to +verbe; **~ qch à qn** (envisager de donner) to intend sth to have sth; (adresser) to intend sth for sb; to aim sth at sb; **être destiné à** (sort) to be destined to +verbe; (usage) to be meant for; (suj: sort) to be in store for

destituer [dɛstitɥe] vt to depose

désuet, ète [desɥɛ, -ɛt] adj outdated, outmoded; **désuétude** nf: **tomber en désuétude** to fall into disuse

détachant [detaʃɑ̃] nm stain remover

détachement [detaʃmɑ̃] nm detachment

détacher [detaʃe] vt (enlever) to detach, remove; (délier) to untie; (ADMIN): **~ qn (auprès de** ou **à)** to post sb (to); **se ~** vi (tomber) to come off; to come out; (se défaire) to come undone; **se ~ sur** to stand out against; **se ~ de** (se désintéresser) to grow away from

détail [detaj] nm detail; (COMM): **le ~** retail; **en ~** in detail; **au ~** (COMM) retail; separately

détaillant [detajɑ̃] nm retailer

détailler [detaje] vt (expliquer) to explain in detail; to detail; (examiner) to look over, examine

détartrant [detaʀtʀɑ̃] nm scale remover

détecter [detɛkte] vt to detect

détective [detɛktiv] nm detective; **~ (privé)** private detective

déteindre [detɛ̃dʀ(ə)] vi (tissu) to fade; (fig): **~ sur** to rub off on

dételer [detle] vt to unharness

détendre [detɑ̃dʀ(ə)] vt: **se ~** to lose its tension; to relax

détenir [detniʀ] vt (fortune, objet, secret) to be in possession of; (prisonnier) to detain, hold; (record, pouvoir) to hold

détente [detɑ̃t] nf relaxation; (d'une arme) trigger

détention [detɑ̃sjɔ̃] nf possession; detention; holding; ~ **préventive** (pre-trial) custody

détenu, e [detny] *nm/f* prisoner

détergent [detɛʀʒɑ̃] *nm* detergent

détériorer [deteʀjɔʀe] *vt* to damage; **se ~** *vi* to deteriorate

déterminé, e [detɛʀmine] *adj* (*résolu*) determined; (*précis*) specific, definite

déterminer [detɛʀmine] *vt* (*fixer*) to determine; (*décider*): ~ **qn à faire** to decide sb to do

déterrer [detɛʀe] *vt* to dig up

détestable [detɛstabl(ə)] *adj* foul, ghastly; detestable, odious

détester [detɛste] *vt* to hate, detest

détonation [detɔnɑsjɔ̃] *nf* detonation, bang, report (of a gun)

détonner [detɔne] *vi* (*MUS*) to go out of tune; (*fig*) to clash

détour [detuʀ] *nm* detour; (*tournant*) bend, curve; **sans ~** (*fig*) plainly

détourné, e [detuʀne] *adj* (*moyen*) roundabout

détournement [detuʀnəmɑ̃] *nm*: ~ **d'avion** hijacking; ~ **de mineur** corruption of a minor

détourner [detuʀne] *vt* to divert; (*par la force*) to hijack; (*yeux, tête*) to turn away; (*de l'argent*) to embezzle; **se ~** *vi* to turn away

détracteur, trice [detʀaktœʀ, -tʀis] *nm/f* disparager, critic

détraquer [detʀake] *vt* to put out of order; (*estomac*) to upset; **se ~** *vi* to go wrong

détrempé, e [detʀɑ̃pe] *adj* (*sol*) sodden, waterlogged

détresse [detʀɛs] *nf* distress

détriment [detʀimɑ̃] *nm*: **au ~ de** to the detriment of

détritus [detʀitys] *nmpl* rubbish *sg*, refuse *sg*

détroit [detʀwa] *nm* strait

détromper [detʀɔ̃pe] *vt* to disabuse

détrôner [detʀone] *vt* to dethrone

détrousser [detʀuse] *vt* to rob

détruire [detʀɥiʀ] *vt* to destroy

dette [dɛt] *nf* debt

D.E.U.G. [døg] *sigle m* = **diplôme d'études universitaires générales**

deuil [dœj] *nm* (*perte*) bereavement; (*période*) mourning; (*chagrin*) grief; **être en ~** to be in mourning

deux [dø] *num* two; **les ~** both; **ses ~ mains** both his hands, his two hands; **deuxième** *num* second; **deuxièmement** *adv* secondly, in the second place; **deux-pièces** *nm inv* (*tailleur*) two-piece suit; (*de bain*) two-piece (swimsuit); (*appartement*) two-roomed flat (*BRIT*) *ou* apartment (*US*); **deux-roues** *nm inv* two-wheeled vehicle

deux points *nm inv* colon *sg*

devais *etc vb voir* **devoir**

dévaler [devale] *vt* to hurtle down

dévaliser [devalize] *vt* to rob, burgle

dévaloriser [devalɔʀize] *vt* to depreciate; **se ~** *vi* to depreciate

dévaluation [devalɥasjɔ̃] *nf* depreciation; (*ÉCON: mesure*) devaluation

devancer [dəvɑ̃se] *vt* to be ahead of; to get ahead of; to arrive before; (*prévenir*) to anticipate

devant [dəvɑ̃] *adv* in front; (*à distance: en avant*) ahead ♦ *prép* in front of; ahead of; (*avec mouvement: passer*) past; (*fig*) before, in front of; faced with; in view of ♦ *nm* front; **prendre les ~s** to make the first move; **les pattes de ~** the front legs, the forelegs; **par ~** (*boutonner*) at the front; (*entrer*) the front way; **aller au-devant de qn** to go out to meet sb; **aller au-devant de** (*désirs de qn*) to anticipate

devanture [dəvɑ̃tyʀ] *nf* (*façade*) (shop) front; (*étalage*) display; (shop) window

déveine [devɛn] *nf* rotten luck *no pl*

développement [devlɔpmɑ̃] *nm* development

développer [devlɔpe] *vt* to develop; **se ~** *vi* to develop

devenir [dəvniʀ] *vb +attrib* to become; ~ **instituteur** to become a teacher; **que sont-ils devenus?** what has become of them?

dévergondé, e [devɛʀgɔ̃de] *adj* wild, shameless

déverser [devɛʀse] *vt* (*liquide*) to pour (out); (*ordures*) to tip (out); **se ~ dans** (*fleuve, mer*) to flow into

dévêtir [devetiʀ] *vt* to undress; **se ~** *vi* to undress

devez *etc vb voir* **devoir**

déviation [devjɑsjɔ̃] *nf* deviation; (*AUTO*) diversion (*BRIT*), detour (*US*)

dévider [devide] *vt* to unwind

devienne *etc vb voir* **devenir**

dévier [devje] *vt* (*fleuve, circulation*) to divert; (*coup*) to deflect ♦ *vi* to veer (off course)

devin [dəvɛ̃] *nm* soothsayer, seer

deviner [dəvine] *vt* to guess; (*prévoir*) to foresee; (*apercevoir*) to distinguish; **devinette** [dəvinɛt] *nf* riddle

devins *etc vb voir* **devenir**

devis [dəvi] *nm* estimate, quotation

dévisager [devizaʒe] *vt* to stare at

devise [dəviz] *nf* (*formule*) motto, watchword; (*ÉCON: monnaie*) currency; ~**s** *nfpl* (*argent*) currency *sg*

deviser [dəvize] *vi* to converse

dévisser [devise] *vt* to unscrew, undo; **se ~** *vi* to come unscrewed

dévoiler [devwale] *vt* to unveil

devoir [dəvwaʀ] *nm* duty; (*SCOL*) homework *no pl*; (: *en classe*) exercise ♦ *vt* (*argent, respect*): ~ **qch (à qn)** to owe (sb) sth; (*suivi de l'infinitif: obligation*): **il doit le faire** he has to do it, he must do it; (: *in-*

tention): **il doit partir demain** he is (due) to leave tomorrow; (: *probabilité*): **il doit être tard** it must be late

dévolu, e [devɔly] *adj*: ~ **à** allotted to ◊ *nm*: **jeter son ~ sur** to fix one's choice on

dévorer [devɔʀe] *vt* to devour; (*suj: feu, soucis*) to consume

dévot, e [devo, -ɔt] *adj* devout, pious

dévotion [devɔsjɔ̃] *nf* devoutness; **être à la ~ de qn** to be totally devoted to sb

dévoué, e [devwe] *adj* devoted

dévouer [devwe]: **se ~** *vi* (*se sacrifier*): **se ~ (pour)** to sacrifice o.s. (for); (*se consacrer*): **se ~ à** to devote *ou* dedicate o.s. to

dévoyé, e [devwaje] *adj* delinquent

devrai *etc vb voir* **devoir**

diabète [djabɛt] *nm* diabetes *sg*; **diabétique** *nm/f* diabetic

diable [djɑbl(ə)] *nm* devil

diabolo [djabɔlo] *nm* (*boisson*) lemonade with fruit cordial

diacre [djakʀ(ə)] *nm* deacon

diagnostic [djagnɔstik] *nm* diagnosis *sg*

diagonal, e, aux [djagɔnal, -o] *adj* diagonal; **~e** *nf* diagonal; **en ~e** diagonally; **lire en ~e** to skim through

diagramme [djagʀam] *nm* chart, graph

dialecte [djalɛkt(ə)] *nm* dialect

dialogue [djalɔg] *nm* dialogue

diamant [djamɑ̃] *nm* diamond; **diamantaire** *nm* diamond dealer

diamètre [djamɛtʀ(ə)] *nm* diameter

diapason [djapazɔ̃] *nm* tuning fork

diaphragme [djafʀagm(ə)] *nm* diaphragm

diaporama [djapɔʀama] *nm* slide show

diapositive [djapɔzitiv] *nf* transparency, slide

diarrhée [djaʀe] *nf* diarrhoea

dictateur [diktatœʀ] *nm* dictator; **dictature** *nf* dictatorship

dictée [dikte] *nf* dictation

dicter [dikte] *vt* to dictate

dictionnaire [diksjɔnɛʀ] *nm* dictionary

dicton [diktɔ̃] *nm* saying, dictum

dièse [djɛz] *nm* sharp

diesel [djezɛl] *nm* diesel ◊ *adj inv* diesel

diète [djɛt] *nf* (*jeûne*) starvation diet; (*régime*) diet

diététique [djetetik] *adj*: **magasin ~** health food shop

dieu, x [djø] *nm* god; **D~** God; **mon D~!** good heavens!

diffamation [difamɑsjɔ̃] *nf* slander; (*écrite*) libel

différé [difeʀe] *nm* (*TV*): **en ~** (pre-)recorded

différence [difeʀɑ̃s] *nf* difference; **à la ~ de** unlike; **différencier** [difeʀɑ̃sje] *vt* to differentiate; **différend** [difeʀɑ̃] *nm* difference (of opinion), disagreement

différent, e [difeʀɑ̃, -ɑ̃t] *adj*: **~ (de)** different (from); **~s objets** different *ou* various

objects

différer [difeʀe] *vt* to postpone, put off ◊ *vi*: **~ (de)** to differ (from)

difficile [difisil] *adj* difficult; (*exigeant*) hard to please; **difficilement** *adv* with difficulty

difficulté [difikylte] *nf* difficulty; **en ~** (*bateau, alpiniste*) in difficulties

difforme [difɔʀm(ə)] *adj* deformed, misshapen

diffuser [difyze] *vt* (*chaleur, bruit*) to diffuse; (*émission, musique*) to broadcast; (*nouvelle, idée*) to circulate; (*COMM*) to distribute

digérer [diʒeʀe] *vt* to digest; (*fig: accepter*) to stomach, put up with; **digestif** *nm* (after-dinner) liqueur

digne [diɲ] *adj* dignified; **~ de** worthy of; **~ de foi** trustworthy

dignité [diɲite] *nf* dignity

digression [digʀesjɔ̃] *nf* digression

digue [dig] *nf* dike, dyke

dilapider [dilapide] *vt* to squander

dilemme [dilɛm] *nm* dilemma

diligence [diliʒɑ̃s] *nf* stagecoach; (*empressement*) despatch

diluer [dilɥe] *vt* to dilute

diluvien, ne [dilyvjɛ̃, -jɛn] *adj*: **pluie ~ne** torrential rain

dimanche [dimɑ̃ʃ] *nm* Sunday

dimension [dimɑ̃sjɔ̃] *nf* (*grandeur*) size; (*cote, de l'espace*) dimension

diminuer [diminɥe] *vt* to reduce, decrease; (*ardeur etc*) to lessen; (*personne: physiquement*) to undermine; (*dénigrer*) to belittle ◊ *vi* to decrease, diminish; **diminutif** *nm* (*surnom*) pet name; **diminution** *nf* decreasing, diminishing

dinde [dɛ̃d] *nf* turkey

dindon [dɛ̃dɔ̃] *nm* turkey

dîner [dine] *nm* dinner ◊ *vi* to have dinner

dingue [dɛ̃g] (*fam*) *adj* crazy

diplomate [diplɔmat] *adj* diplomatic ◊ *nm* diplomat; (*fig*) diplomatist

diplomatie [diplɔmasi] *nf* diplomacy

diplôme [diplom] *nm* diploma; **diplômé, e** *adj* qualified

dire [diʀ] *nm*: **au ~ de** according to ◊ *vt* to say; (*secret, mensonge*) to tell; **leurs ~s** what they say; **~ l'heure/la vérité** to tell the time/the truth; **~ qch à qn** to tell sb sth; **~ à qn qu'il fasse** *ou* **de faire** to tell sb to do; **on dit que** they say that; **ceci dit** that being said; (*à ces mots*) whereupon; **si cela lui dit** (*plaire*) if he fancies it; **que dites-vous de** (*penser*) what do you think of; **on dirait que** it looks (*ou* sounds *etc*) as if; **dis/dites (donc)** I say; (*à propos*) by the way

direct, e [diʀɛkt] *adj* direct ◊ *nm* (*TV*): **en ~** live; **directement** *adv* directly

directeur, trice [diʀɛktœʀ, -tʀis] *nm/f* (*d'entreprise*) director; (*de service*) manager(eress); (*d'école*) head (teacher) (*BRIT*), principal (*US*)

direction [diʀɛksjɔ̃] *nf* management; conducting; supervision; (*AUTO*) steering; (*sens*) direction; "**toutes ~s**" "all routes"

dirent *vb voir* **dire**

dirigeant, e [diʀiʒɑ̃, -ɑ̃t] *adj* managerial; ruling ♦ *nm/f* (*d'un parti etc*) leader; (*d'entreprise*) manager

diriger [diʀiʒe] *vt* (*entreprise*) to manage, run; (*véhicule*) to steer; (*orchestre*) to conduct; (*recherches, travaux*) to supervise; (*braquer: regard, arme*): ~ **sur** to point au level at; **se** ~ *vi* (*s'orienter*) to find one's way; **se** ~ **vers** *ou* **sur** to make *ou* head for

dirigisme [diʀiʒism(ə)] *nm* (*ÉCON*) state intervention, interventionism

dis *etc vb voir* **dire**

discernement [disɛʀnəmɑ̃] *nm* (*bon sens*) discernment, judgement

discerner [disɛʀne] *vt* to discern, make out

discipline [disiplin] *nf* discipline; **discipliner** *vt* to discipline; to control

discontinu, e [diskɔ̃tiny] *adj* intermittent

discontinuer [diskɔ̃tinɥe] *vi*: **sans** ~ without stopping, without a break

disconvenir [diskɔ̃vniʀ] *vi*: **ne pas** ~ **de qch/que** not to deny sth/that

discordant, e [diskɔʀdɑ̃, -ɑ̃t] *adj* discordant; conflicting

discotheque [diskɔtɛk] *nf* (*disques*) record collection; (: *dans une bibliothèque*) record library; (*boîte de nuit*) disco(thèque)

discourir [diskuʀiʀ] *vi* to discourse, hold forth

discours [diskuʀ] *nm* speech

discret, ète [diskʀɛ, -ɛt] *adj* discreet; (*fig*) unobtrusive; quiet

discrétion [diskʀesjɔ̃] *nf* discretion; **être à la** ~ **de qn** to be in sb's hands; **à** ~ unlimited; as much as one wants

discrimination [diskʀiminɑsjɔ̃] *nf* discrimination; **sans** ~ indiscriminately

disculper [diskylpe] *vt* to exonerate

discussion [diskysjɔ̃] *nf* discussion

discutable [diskytabl(ə)] *adj* debatable

discuté, e [diskyte] *adj* controversial

discuter [diskyte] *vt* (*contester*) to question, dispute; (*débattre: prix*) to discuss ♦ *vi* to talk; (*ergoter*) to argue; ~ **de** to discuss

dise *etc vb voir* **dire**

disette [dizɛt] *nf* food shortage

diseuse [dizøz] *nf*: ~ **de bonne aventure** fortuneteller

disgracieux, euse [disgʀasjø, -jøz] *adj* ungainly, awkward

disjoindre [disʒwɛ̃dʀ(ə)] *vt* to take apart; **se** ~ *vi* to come apart

disjoncteur [disʒɔ̃ktœʀ] *nm* (*ÉLEC*) circuit breaker

disloquer [dislɔke] *vt* (*chaise*) to dismantle;

se ~ *vi* (*parti, empire*) to break up; **se** ~ **l'épaule** to dislocate one's shoulder

disons *vb voir* **dire**

disparaître [dispaʀɛtʀ(ə)] *vi* to disappear; (*à la vue*) to vanish, disappear; to be hidden *ou* concealed; (*se perdre: traditions etc*) to die out; **faire** ~ to remove; to get rid of

disparition [dispaʀisjɔ̃] *nf* disappearance

disparu, e [dispaʀy] *nm/f* missing person; (*défunt*) dead person, departed (*littér*)

dispensaire [dispɑ̃sɛʀ] *nm* community clinic

dispenser [dispɑ̃se] *vt* (*donner*) to lavish, bestow; (*exempter*): ~ **qn de** to exempt sb from; **se** ~ **de** *vt* to avoid; to get out of

disperser [dispɛʀse] *vt* to scatter; (*fig: son attention*) to dissipate

disponibilité [dispɔnibilite] *nf* (*ADMIN*): **être en** ~ to be on leave of absence

disponible [dispɔnibl(ə)] *adj* available

dispos [dispo] *adj m*: (**frais et**) ~ fresh (as a daisy)

disposé, e [dispoze] *adj*: **bien/mal** ~ (*humeur*) in a good/bad mood; ~ **à** (*prêt à*) willing *ou* prepared to

disposer [dispoze] *vt* (*arranger, placer*) to arrange ♦ *vi*: **vous pouvez** ~ you may leave; ~ **de** to have (at one's disposal); to use; **se** ~ **à faire** to prepare to do, to be about to do

dispositif [dispozitif] *nm* device; (*fig*) system, plan of action; set-up

disposition [dispozisjɔ̃] *nf* (*arrangement*) arrangement, layout; (*humeur*) mood; (*tendance*) tendency; ~**s** *nfpl* (*mesures*) steps, measures; (*préparatifs*) arrangements; (*loi, testament*) provisions; (*aptitudes*) bent *sg*, aptitude *sg*; **à la** ~ **de qn** at sb's disposal

disproportionné, e [dispʀopɔʀsjɔne] *adj* disproportionate, out of all proportion

dispute [dispyt] *nf* quarrel, argument

disputer [dispyte] *vt* (*match*) to play; (*combat*) to fight; (*course*) to run, fight; **se** ~ *vi* to quarrel; ~ **qch à qn** to fight with sb over sth

disquaire [diskɛʀ] *nm/f* record dealer

disqualifier [diskalifje] *vt* to disqualify

disque [disk(ə)] *nm* (*MUS*) record; (*forme, pièce*) disc; (*SPORT*) discus; ~ **compact** compact disc; ~ **d'embrayage** (*AUTO*) clutch plate

disquette [diskɛt] *nf* floppy disk, diskette

disséminer [disemine] *vt* to scatter

disséquer [diseke] *vt* to dissect

dissertation [disɛʀtɑsjɔ̃] *nf* (*SCOL*) essay

disserter [disɛʀte] *vi*: ~ **sur** to discourse upon

dissimuler [disimyle] *vt* to conceal

dissiper [disipe] *vt* to dissipate; (*fortune*) to squander; **se** ~ *vi* (*brouillard*) to clear, disperse; (*doutes*) to melt away; (*élève*) to become unruly

dissolu, e [disɔly] adj dissolute

dissolvant [disɔlvã] nm solvent; **~ (gras)** nail polish remover

dissonant, e [disɔnã, -ãt] adj discordant

dissoudre [disudʀ(ə)] vt to dissolve; **se ~** vi to dissolve

dissuader [disɥade] vt: **~ qn de faire/de qch** to dissuade sb from doing/from sth

dissuasion [disɥazjõ] nf: **force de ~** deterrent power

distance [distãs] nf distance; (fig: écart) gap; **à ~** at ou from a distance; **distancer** vt to outdistance

distant, e [distã, -ãt] adj (réservé) distant; **~ de** (lieu) far away from

distendre [distãdʀ(ə)] vt to distend; **se ~** vi to distend

distiller [distile] vt to distil; **distillerie** nf distillery

distinct, e [distɛ̃(kt), distɛ̃kt(ə)] adj distinct; **distinctif, ive** adj distinctive

distingué, e [distɛ̃ge] adj distinguished

distinguer [distɛ̃ge] vt to distinguish

distraction [distʀaksjõ] nf (manque d'attention) absent-mindedness; (oubli) lapse (in concentration); (détente) diversion, recreation; (passe-temps) distraction, entertainment

distraire [distʀɛʀ] vt (déranger) to distract; (divertir) to entertain, divert; **se ~** vi to amuse ou enjoy o.s.

distrait, e [distʀɛ, -ɛt] adj absent-minded

distribuer [distʀibɥe] vt to distribute; to hand out; (CARTES) to deal (out); (courrier) to deliver; **distributeur** nm (COMM) distributor; (automatique) (vending) machine; (: de billets) (cash) dispenser; **distribution** nf distribution; (postale) delivery; (choix d'acteurs) casting, cast

dit, e [di, dit] pp de **dire ♦** adj (fixé): **le jour ~** the arranged day; (surnommé): **X, ~ Pierrot** X, known as Pierrot

dites vb voir **dire**

divaguer [divage] vi to ramble; to rave

divan [divã] nm divan

divers, e [divɛʀ, -ɛʀs(ə)] adj (varié) diverse, varied; (différent) different, various ♦ dét (plusieurs) various, several; **(frais) ~** sundries, miscellaneous (expenses)

divertir [divɛʀtiʀ] vt to amuse, entertain; **se ~** vi to amuse ou enjoy o.s.

divin, e [divɛ̃, -in] adj divine

diviser [divize] vt (gén, MATH) to divide; (morceler, subdiviser) to divide (up), split (up); **division** nf division

divorce [divɔʀs(ə)] nm divorce; **divorcé, e** nm/f divorcee; **divorcer** vi to get a divorce, get divorced; **divorcer de** ou **d'avec qn** to divorce sb

divulguer [divylge] vt to divulge, disclose

dix [dis] num ten; **dixième** num tenth

dizaine [dizɛn] nf (10) ten; (environ 10):

une ~ (de) about ten, ten or so

do [do] nm (note) C; (en chantant la gamme) do(h)

dock [dɔk] nm dock

docker [dɔkɛʀ] nm docker

docte [dɔkt(ə)] adj learned

docteur [dɔktœʀ] nm doctor

doctorat [dɔktɔʀa] nm: **~ (d'Université)** doctorate; **~ d'État** ≈ Ph.D.

doctrine [dɔktʀin] nf doctrine

document [dɔkymã] nm document

documentaire [dɔkymãtɛʀ] adj, nm documentary

documentaliste [dɔkymãtalist(ə)] nm/f archivist; researcher

documentation [dɔkymãtasjõ] nf documentation, literature; (PRESSE, TV: service) research

documenter [dɔkymãte] vt: **se ~ (sur)** to gather information (on)

dodeliner [dɔdline] vi: **~ de la tête** to nod one's head gently

dodo [dɔdo] nm: **aller faire ~** to go to beddy-byes

dodu, e [dɔdy] adj plump

dogue [dɔg] nm mastiff

doigt [dwa] nm finger; **à deux ~s de** within an inch of; **un ~ de lait** a drop of milk; **~ de pied** toe

doigté [dwate] nm (MUS) fingering; (fig: habileté) diplomacy, tact

doit etc vb voir **devoir**

doléances [dɔleãs] nfpl complaints; grievances

dollar [dɔlaʀ] nm dollar

D.O.M. [deɔɛm, dɔm] sigle m = **département d'outre-mer**

domaine [dɔmɛn] nm estate, property; (fig) domain, field

domestique [dɔmɛstik] adj domestic ♦ nm/f servant, domestic

domicile [dɔmisil] nm home, place of residence; **à ~** at home; **domicilié, e** adj: **être domicilié à** to have one's home in ou at

dominant, e [dɔminã, -ãt] adj dominant; predominant

dominateur, trice [dɔminatœʀ, -tʀis] adj dominating; domineering

dominer [dɔmine] vt to dominate; (passions etc) to control, master; (surpasser) to outclass, surpass ♦ vi to be in the dominant position; **se ~** vi to control o.s.

domino [dɔmino] nm domino

dommage [dɔmaʒ] nm (préjudice) harm, injury; (dégâts, pertes) damage no pl; **c'est ~ de faire/que** it's a shame ou pity to do/that; **dommages-intérêts** nmpl damages

dompter [dõte] vt to tame; **dompteur, euse** nm/f trainer; liontamer

don [dõ] nm (cadeau) gift; (charité) donation; (aptitude) gift, talent; **avoir des ~s pour** to have a gift ou talent for

donc [dɔ̃k] *conj* therefore, so; *(après une digression)* so, then

donjon [dɔ̃ʒɔ̃] *nm* keep

donné, e [dɔne] *adj (convenu)* given; *(pas cher)*: **c'est** ~ it's a gift; **étant** ~ ... given ...; **donnée** *nf (MATH, gén)* datum

donner [dɔne] *vt* to give; *(vieux habits etc)* to give away; *(spectacle)* to put on; *(film)* to show; ~ **qch à qn** to give sb sth, give sth to sb; ~ **sur** *(suj: fenêtre, chambre)* to look (out) onto; ~ **dans** *(piège etc)* to fall into; **se** ~ **à fond** to give one's all; **s'en** ~ **à cœur joie** *(fam)* to have a great time

── *MOT CLÉ* ─────────

dont [dɔ̃] *pron relatif* **1** *(appartenance: objets)* whose, of which; *(appartenance: êtres animés)* whose; **la maison** ~ **le toit est rouge** the house the roof of which is red; **l'homme** ~ **je connais la sœur** the man whose sister I know

2 *(parmi lesquel(le)s)*: **2 livres,** ~ **l'un est ...** 2 books, one of which is ...; **il y avait plusieurs personnes,** ~ **Gabrielle** there were several people, among them Gabrielle; **10 blessés,** ~ **2 grièvement** 10 injured, 2 of them seriously

3 *(complément d'adjectif, de verbe)*: **le fils** ~ **il est si fier** the son he's so proud of; **ce** ~ **je parle** what I'm talking about

────────────────────

doré, e [dɔʁe] *adj* golden; *(avec dorure)* gilt, gilded

dorénavant [dɔʁenavɑ̃] *adv* henceforth

dorer [dɔʁe] *vt (cadre)* to gild; **(faire)** ~ *(CULIN)* to brown

dorloter [dɔʁlɔte] *vt* to pamper

dormir [dɔʁmiʁ] *vi* to sleep; *(être endormi)* to be asleep

dortoir [dɔʁtwaʁ] *nm* dormitory

dorure [dɔʁyʁ] *nf* gilding

dos [do] *nm* back; *(de livre)* spine; **"voir au** ~**"** "see over"; **de** ~ from the back

dosage [dozaʒ] *nm* mixture

dose [doz] *nf* dose; ~**r** [doze] *vt* to measure out; to mix in the correct proportions; *(fig)* to expend in the right amounts; to strike a balance between

dossard [dosaʁ] *nm* number *(worn by competitor)*

dossier [dosje] *nm (renseignements, fichier)* file; *(de chaise)* back; *(PRESSE)* feature

dot [dɔt] *nf* dowry

doter [dɔte] *vt* to equip

douane [dwan] *nf (poste, bureau)* customs *pl*; *(taxes)* (customs) duty; **douanier, ière** *adj* customs *cpd* ♦ *nm* customs officer

double [dubl(ə)] *adj, adv* double ♦ *nm (2 fois plus)*: **le** ~ **(de)** twice as much (*ou* many) (as); *(autre exemplaire)* duplicate, copy; *(sosie)* double; *(TENNIS)* doubles *sg*;

en ~ **(exemplaire)** in duplicate; **faire** ~ **emploi** to be redundant

doubler [duble] *vt (multiplier par 2)* to double; *(vêtement)* to line; *(dépasser)* to overtake, pass; *(film)* to dub; *(acteur)* to stand in for ♦ *vi* to double

doublure [dublyʁ] *nf* lining; *(CINÉMA)* stand-in

douce [dus] *adj voir* **doux**; **douceâtre** *adj* sickly sweet; **doucement** *adv* gently; slowly; **doucereux, euse** *(péj) adj* sugary; **douceur** *nf* softness; sweetness; mildness; gentleness; **douceurs** *nfpl (friandises)* sweets

douche [duʃ] *nf* shower; ~**s** *nfpl (salle)* shower room *sg*; **doucher: se doucher** *vi* to have *ou* take a shower

doudoune [dudun] *nf* padded jacket; boob *(fam)*

doué, e [dwe] *adj* gifted, talented; ~ **de** endowed with

douille [duj] *nf (ÉLEC)* socket; *(de projectile)* case

douillet, te [duje, -ɛt] *adj* cosy; *(péj)* soft

douleur [dulœʁ] *nf* pain; *(chagrin)* grief, distress; **douloureux, euse** *adj* painful

doute [dut] *nm* doubt; **sans** ~ no doubt; *(probablement)* probably

douter [dute] *vt* to doubt; ~ **de** *(allié)* to doubt, have (one's) doubts about; *(résultat)* to be doubtful of; ~ **de qch/que** to suspect sth/that; **je m'en doutais** I suspected as much

douteux, euse [dutø, -øz] *adj (incertain)* doubtful; *(discutable)* dubious, questionable; *(péj)* dubious-looking

Douvres [duvʁ(ə)] *n* Dover

doux, douce [du, dus] *adj (gén)* soft; *(sucré, agréable)* sweet; *(peu fort: moutarde, clément: climat)* mild; *(pas brusque)* gentle

douzaine [duzɛn] *nf (12)* dozen; *(environ 12)*: **une** ~ **(de)** a dozen or so, twelve or so

douze [duz] *num* twelve; **douzième** *num* twelfth

doyen, ne [dwajɛ̃, -ɛn] *nm/f (en âge, ancienneté)* most senior member; *(de faculté)* dean

dragée [dʁaʒe] *nf* sugared almond; *(MÉD)* (sugar-coated) pill

dragon [dʁagɔ̃] *nm* dragon

draguer [dʁage] *vt (rivière)* to dredge; to drag; *(fam)* to try to pick up

dramatique [dʁamatik] *adj* dramatic; *(tragique)* tragic ♦ *nf (TV)* (television) drama

dramaturge [dʁamatyʁʒ(ə)] *nm* dramatist, playwright

drame [dʁam] *nm (THÉÂTRE)* drama

drap [dʁa] *nm (de lit)* sheet; *(tissu)* woollen fabric

drapeau, x [dʁapo] *nm* flag; **sous les** ~**x** with the colours, in the army

dresser [dʁese] *vt (mettre vertical, monter)*

to put up, erect; (*fig: liste, bilan, contrat*) to draw up; (*animal*) to train; **se ~** *vi* (*falaise, obstacle*) to stand; to tower (up); (*personne*) to draw o.s. up; **~ qn contre qn** to set sb against sb; **~ l'oreille** to prick up one's ears

drogue [dʀɔg] *nf* drug; **la ~** drugs *pl*; **drogué, e** [dʀɔge] *nm/f* drug addict

droguer [dʀɔge] *vt* (*victime*) to drug; (*malade*) to give drugs to; **se ~** *vi* (*aux stupéfiants*) to take drugs; (*péj: de médicaments*) to dose o.s. up

droguerie [dʀɔgʀi] *nf* hardware shop

droguiste [dʀɔgist(ə)] *nm* keeper (*ou* owner) of a hardware shop

droit, e [dʀwa, dʀwat] *adj* (*non courbe*) straight; (*vertical*) upright, straight; (*fig: loyal*) upright, straight(forward); (*opposé à gauche*) right, right-hand ♦ *adv* straight ♦ *nm* (*prérogative*) right; (*taxe*) duty, tax; (: *d'inscription*) fee; (*JUR*): **le ~** law; **avoir le ~ de** to be allowed to; **avoir ~ à** to be entitled to; **être en ~ de** to have a *ou* the right to; **être dans son ~** to be within one's rights; **à ~e** on the right; (*direction*) (to the) right; **~s d'auteur** royalties; **~s d'inscription** *nmpl* enrolment fee; (*competition*) entry fee; **droite** *nf* (*POL*): **la droite** the right (wing)

droitier, ière [dʀwatje, -jɛʀ] *nm/f* right-handed person

droits *nmpl voir* **droit**

droiture [dʀwatyʀ] *nf* uprightness, straightness

drôle [dʀol] *adj* funny; **une ~ d'idée** a funny idea; **drôlement** *adv* (*très*) terribly, awfully

dromadaire [dʀɔmadɛʀ] *nm* dromedary

dru, e [dʀy] *adj* (*cheveux*) thick, bushy; (*pluie*) heavy

du [dy] *dét voir de* ♦ *prép* +*dét* = **de** +**le**

dû, due [dy] *vb voir* **devoir** ♦ *adj* (*somme*) owing, owed; (: *venant à échéance*) due; (*causé par*): **~ à** due to ♦ *nm* due; (*somme*) dues *pl*

dubitatif, ive [dybitatif, -iv] *adj* doubtful, dubious

duc [dyk] *nm* duke; **duchesse** *nf* duchess

dûment [dymã] *adv* duly

Dunkerque [dœkɛʀk] *n* Dunkirk

duo [dɥo] *nm* (*MUS*) duet

dupe [dyp] *nf* dupe ♦ *adj*: (**ne pas**) **être ~ de** (not) to be taken in by

duplex [dyplɛks] *nm* (*appartement*) split-level apartment, duplex

duplicata [dyplikata] *nm* duplicate

duquel [dykɛl] *prép* +*pron* = **de** +**lequel**

dur, e [dyʀ] *adj* (*pierre, siège, travail, problème*) hard; (*lumière, voix, climat*) harsh; (*sévère*) hard, harsh; (*cruel*) hard(-hearted); (*porte, col*) stiff; (*viande*) tough ♦ *adv* hard; **~ d'oreille** hard of hearing

durant [dyʀã] *prép* (*au cours de*) during; (*pendant*) for; **des mois ~** for months

durcir [dyʀsiʀ] *vt, vi* to harden; **se ~** *vi* to harden

durée [dyʀe] *nf* length; (*d'une pile etc*) life; (*déroulement: des opérations etc*) duration

durement [dyʀmã] *adv* harshly

durer [dyʀe] *vi* to last

dureté [dyʀte] *nf* hardness; harshness; stiffness; toughness

durit [dyʀit] (®) *nf* (car radiator) hose

dus *etc vb voir* **devoir**

duvet [dyvɛ] *nm* down; (*sac de couchage*) down-filled sleeping bag

dynamique [dinamik] *adj* dynamic

dynamite [dinamit] *nf* dynamite

dynamiter [dinamite] *vt* to (blow up with) dynamite

dynamo [dinamo] *nf* dynamo

dysenterie [disãtʀi] *nf* dysentery

dyslexie [dislɛksi] *nf* dyslexia, word-blindness

E e

eau, x [o] *nf* water; **~x** *nfpl* (*MED*) waters; **prendre l'~** to leak, let in water; **tomber à l'~** (*fig*) to fall through; **~ courante** running water; **~ de Cologne** Eau de Cologne; **~ de Javel** bleach; **~ de toilette** toilet water; **~ douce** fresh water; **~ minérale** mineral water; **~ plate** still water; **~ salée** salt water; **eau-de-vie** *nf* brandy; **eau-forte** *nf* etching

ébahi, e [ebai] *adj* dumbfounded

ébattre [ebatʀ(ə)] : **s'~** *vi* to frolic

ébaucher [eboʃe] *vt* to sketch out, outline; **s'~** *vi* to take shape

ébène [ebɛn] *nf* ebony

ébéniste [ebenist(ə)] *nm* cabinetmaker

éberlué, e [ebɛʀlɥe] *adj* astounded

éblouir [ebluiʀ] *vt* to dazzle

éblouissement [ebluismã] *nm* (*faiblesse*) dizzy turn

éborgner [ebɔʀɲe] *vt*: **~ qn** to blind sb in one eye

éboueur [ebwœʀ] *nm* dustman (*BRIT*), garbageman (*US*)

ébouillanter [ebujãte] *vt* to scald; (*CULIN*) to blanch

éboulement [ebulmã] *nm* rock fall

ébouler [ebule] : **s'~** *vi* to crumble, collapse

éboulis [ebuli] *nmpl* fallen rocks

ébouriffé, e [eburife] *adj* tousled

ébranler [ebrɑ̃le] *vt* to shake; (*rendre instable: mur*) to weaken; **s'~** *vi* (*partir*) to move off

ébrécher [ebreʃe] *vt* to chip

ébriété [ebrijete] *nf*: **en état d'~** in a state of intoxication

ébrouer [ebrue]: **s'~** *vi* to shake o.s.; (*souffler*) to snort

ébruiter [ebrɥite] *vt* to spread, disclose

ébullition [ebylisjɔ̃] *nf* boiling point; **en ~** boiling; (*fig*) in an uproar

écaille [ekɑj] *nf* (*de poisson*) scale; (*de coquillage*) shell; (*matière*) tortoiseshell; **~r** [ekɑje] *vt* (*poisson*) to scale; (*huître*) to open; **s'~r** *vi* to flake ou peel (off)

écarlate [ekarlat] *adj* scarlet

écarquiller [ekarkije] *vt*: **~ les yeux** to stare wide-eyed

écart [ekar] *nm* gap; (*embardée*) swerve; sideways leap; (*fig*) departure, deviation; **à l'~** out of the way; **à l'~ de** away from

écarté, e [ekarte] *adj* (*lieu*) out-of-the-way, remote; (*ouvert*): **les jambes ~es** legs apart; **les bras ~s** arms outstretched

écarteler [ekartəle] *vt* to quarter; (*fig*) to tear

écarter [ekarte] *vt* (*séparer*) to move apart, separate; (*éloigner*) to push back, move away; (*ouvrir: bras, jambes*) to spread, open; (: *rideau*) to draw (back); (*éliminer: candidat, possibilité*) to dismiss; **s'~** *vi* to part; to move away; **s'~ de** to wander from

écervelé, e [esɛrvəle] *adj* scatterbrained, featherbrained

échafaud [eʃafo] *nm* scaffold

échafaudage [eʃafodaʒ] *nm* scaffolding

échafauder [eʃafode] *vt* (*plan*) to construct

échalote [eʃalɔt] *nf* shallot

échancrure [eʃɑ̃kryr] *nf* (*de robe*) scoop neckline; (*de côte, arête rocheuse*) indentation

échange [eʃɑ̃ʒ] *nm* exchange; **en ~ de** in exchange ou return for

échanger [eʃɑ̃ʒe] *vt*: **~ qch (contre)** to exchange sth (for); **échangeur** *nm* (*AUTO*) interchange

échantillon [eʃɑ̃tijɔ̃] *nm* sample

échappement [eʃapmɑ̃] *nm* (*AUTO*) exhaust

échapper [eʃape]: **~ à** *vt* (*gardien*) to escape (from); (*punition, péril*) to escape; **s'~** *vi* to escape; **~ à qn** (*détail, sens*) to escape sb; (*objet qu'on tient*) to slip out of sb's hands; **laisser ~** (*cri etc*) to let out; **l'~ belle** to have a narrow escape

écharde [eʃard(ə)] *nf* splinter (of wood)

écharpe [eʃarp(ə)] *nf* scarf; (*de maire*) sash; (*MÉD*) sling

échasse [eʃɑs] *nf* stilt

échauffer [eʃofe] *vt* (*métal, moteur*) to overheat; (*fig: exciter*) to fire, excite; **s'~** *vi* (*SPORT*) to warm up; (*dans la discussion*) to become heated

échéance [eʃeɑ̃s] *nf* (*d'un paiement: date*) settlement date; (: *somme due*) financial commitment(s); (*fig*) deadline; **à brève/longue ~** *adj* short-/long-term ♦ *adv* in the short/long run

échéant [eʃeɑ̃] : **le cas ~** *adv* if the case arises

échec [eʃɛk] *nm* failure; (*ÉCHECS*): **~ et mat/au roi** checkmate/check; **~s** *nmpl* (*jeu*) chess *sg*; **tenir en ~** to hold in check; **faire ~ à** to foil ou thwart

échelle [eʃɛl] *nf* ladder; (*fig, d'une carte*) scale

échelon [eʃlɔ̃] *nm* (*d'échelle*) rung; (*ADMIN*) grade

échelonner [eʃlɔne] *vt* to space out

échevelé, e [eʃəvle] *adj* tousled, dishevelled; wild, frenzied

échine [eʃin] *nf* backbone, spine

échiquier [eʃikje] *nm* chessboard

écho [eko] *nm* echo; **~s** *nmpl* (*potins*) gossip *sg*, rumours

échoir [eʃwar] *vi* (*dette*) to fall due; (*délais*) to expire; **~ à** to fall to

échouer [eʃwe] *vi* to fail; **s'~** *vi* to run aground

échu, e [eʃy] *pp* de **échoir**

éclabousser [eklabuse] *vt* to splash

éclair [eklɛr] *nm* (*d'orage*) flash of lightning, lightning no *pl*; (*gâteau*) éclair

éclairage [eklɛraʒ] *nm* lighting

éclaircie [eklɛrsi] *nf* bright interval

éclaircir [eklɛrsir] *vt* to lighten; (*fig*) to clear up; to clarify; (*CULIN*) to thin (down); **s'~** *vi* (*ciel*) to clear; **s'~ la voix** to clear one's throat; **éclaircissement** *nm* clearing up; clarification

éclairer [eklɛre] *vt* (*lieu*) to light (up); (*personne: avec une lampe etc*) to light the way for; (*fig*) to enlighten; to shed light on ♦ *vi*: **~ mal/bien** to give a poor/good light; **s'~ à l'électricité** to have electric lighting

éclaireur, euse [eklɛrœr, -øz] *nm/f* (*scout*) (boy) scout/(girl) guide ♦ *nm* (*MIL*) scout

éclat [ekla] *nm* (*de bombe, de verre*) fragment; (*du soleil, d'une couleur etc*) brightness, brilliance; (*d'une cérémonie*) splendour; (*scandale*): **faire un ~** to cause a commotion; **~s de voix** shouts; **~ de rire** *nm* roar of laughter

éclatant, e [eklatɑ̃, -ɑ̃t] *adj* brilliant

éclater [eklate] *vi* (*pneu*) to burst; (*bombe*) to explode; (*guerre, épidémie*) to break out; (*groupe, parti*) to break up; **~ en sanglots/de rire** to burst out sobbing/laughing

éclipser [eklipse] : **s'~** *vi* to slip away

éclopé, e [eklɔpe] *adj* lame

éclore [eklɔʀ] *vi* (*œuf*) to hatch; (*fleur*) to open (out)

écluse [eklyz] *nf* lock

écœurant, e [ekœʀɑ̃, -ɑ̃t] *adj* (*gâteau etc*) sickly

écœurer [ekœʀe] *vt:* ~ **qn** to make sb feel sick

école [ekɔl] *nf* school; **aller à l'~** to go to school; ~ **normale** teachers' training college; ~ **publique** *nf* state school; **écolier, ière** *nm/f* schoolboy/girl

écologie [ekɔlɔʒi] *nf* ecology; environmental studies *pl*

écologique [ekɔlɔʒik] *adj* environment-friendly

éconduire [ekɔ̃dɥiʀ] *vt* to dismiss

économe [ekɔnɔm] *adj* thrifty ♦ *nm/f* (*de lycée etc*) bursar (*BRIT*), treasurer (*US*)

économie [ekɔnɔmi] *nf* economy; (*gain: d'argent, de temps etc*) saving; (*science*) economics *sg*; ~s *nfpl* (*pécule*) savings; **économique** *adj* (*avantageux*) economical; (*ÉCON*) economic; **économiser** [ekɔnɔmize] *vt, vi* to save

écoper [ekɔpe] *vi* to bale out; (*fig*) to cop it; ~ (**de**) to get

écorce [ekɔʀs(ə)] *nf* bark; (*de fruit*) peel

écorcher [ekɔʀʃe] *vt* (*animal*) to skin; (*égratigner*) to graze; **écorchure** *nf* graze

écossais, e [ekɔsɛ, -ɛz] *adj* Scottish ♦ *nm/f:* **É-, e** Scot

Écosse [ekɔs] *nf:* **l'~** Scotland

écosser [ekɔse] *vt* to shell

écouler [ekule] *vt* to sell; to dispose of; **s'~** *vi* (*eau*) to flow (out); (*jours, temps*) to pass (by)

écourter [ekuʀte] *vt* to curtail, cut short

écoute [ekut] *nf* (*RADIO, TV*): **temps/heure d'~** listening (*ou* viewing) time/hour; **prendre l'~** to tune in; **rester à l'~** (**de**) to stay tuned in (to)

écouter [ekute] *vt* to listen to; **écoutes téléphoniques** phone tapping *sg*; **écouteur** *nm* (*TÉL*) receiver; (*RADIO*) headphones *pl*, headset

écran [ekʀɑ̃] *nm* screen

écrasant, e [ekʀɑzɑ̃, -ɑ̃t] *adj* overwhelming

écraser [ekʀɑze] *vt* to crush; (*piéton*) to run over; **s'~** (**au sol**) to crash; **s'~ contre** to crash into

écrémer [ekʀeme] *vt* to skim

écrevisse [ekʀəvis] *nf* crayfish *inv*

écrier [ekʀije] *vt:* **s'~** *vi* to exclaim

écrin [ekʀɛ̃] *nm* case, box

écrire [ekʀiʀ] *vt* to write; **s'~** to write to each other; **ça s'écrit comment?** how is it spelt?; **écrit** *nm* document; (*examen*) written paper; **par écrit** in writing

écriteau, x [ekʀito] *nm* notice, sign

écriture [ekʀityʀ] *nf* writing; (*COMM*) entry; ~s *nfpl* accounts, books; **l'É~, les É~s** the Scriptures

écrivain [ekʀivɛ̃] *nm* writer

écrou [ekʀu] *nm* nut

écrouer [ekʀue] *vt* to imprison; to remand in custody

écrouler [ekʀule]: **s'~** *vi* to collapse

écru, e [ekʀy] *adj* (*toile*) raw, unbleached; (*couleur*) off-white, écru

ECU *sigle m* ECU

écueil [ekœj] *nm* reef; (*fig*) pitfall; stumbling block

écuelle [ekɥɛl] *nf* bowl

éculé, e [ekyle] *adj* (*chaussure*) down-at-heel; (*fig: péj*) hackneyed

écume [ekym] *nf* foam; (*CULIN*) scum; **écumer** *vt* (*CULIN*) to skim; (*fig*) to plunder

écureuil [ekyʀœj] *nm* squirrel

écurie [ekyʀi] *nf* stable

écusson [ekysɔ̃] *nm* badge

écuyer, ère [ekɥije, -ɛʀ] *nm/f* rider

eczéma [egzema] *nm* eczema

édenté, e [edɑ̃te] *adj* toothless

E.D.F. *sigle f* (= *Électricité de France*) national electricity company

édifice [edifis] *nm* edifice, building

édifier [edifje] *vt* to build, erect; (*fig*) to edify

édit [edi] *nm* edict

éditer [edite] *vt* (*publier*) to publish; (: *disque*) to produce; **éditeur, trice** *nm/f* editor; publisher; **édition** *nf* editing *no pl*; edition; (*industrie du livre*) publishing

édredon [edʀədɔ̃] *nm* eiderdown, comforter (*US*)

éducateur, trice [edykatœʀ, -tʀis] *nm/f* teacher; (*in special school*) instructor

éducatif, ive [edykatif, -iv] *adj* educational

éducation [edykasjɔ̃] *nf* education; (*familiale*) upbringing; (*manières*) (good) manners *pl*; ~ **physique** physical education

édulcorer [edylkɔʀe] *vt* to sweeten; (*fig*) to tone down

éduquer [edyke] *vt* to educate; (*élever*) to bring up; (*faculté*) to train

effacé, e [efase] *adj* unassuming

effacer [efase] *vt* to erase, rub out; **s'~** *vi* (*inscription etc*) to wear off; (*pour laisser passer*) to step aside

effarant, e [efaʀɑ̃, -ɑ̃t] *adj* alarming

effarer [efaʀe] *vt* to alarm

effaroucher [efaʀuʃe] *vt* to frighten *ou* scare away; to alarm

effectif, ive [efɛktif, -iv] *adj* real; effective ♦ *nm* (*MIL*) strength; (*SCOL*) (pupil) numbers *pl*; **effectivement** *adv* effectively; (*réellement*) actually, really; (*en effet*) indeed

effectuer [efɛktɥe] *vt* (*opération*) to carry out; (*déplacement, trajet*) to make; (*mouvement*) to execute

efféminé, e [efemine] *adj* effeminate

effervescent, e [efɛʀvesɑ̃, -ɑ̃t] *adj* effervescent; (fig) agitated

effet [efɛ] nm (résultat, artifice) effect; (impression) impression; ~s nmpl (vêtements etc) things; **faire de l'~** (médicament, menace) to have an effect; **en ~** indeed; ~ **de serre** greenhouse effect; **gaz à ~ de serre** greenhouse gas

efficace [efikas] adj (personne) efficient; (action, médicament) effective

effilé, e [efile] adj slender; sharp; streamlined

effiler [efile] vt (tissu) to fray

effilocher [efilɔʃe] : **s'~** vi to fray

efflanqué, e [eflɑ̃ke] adj emaciated

effleurer [eflœʀe] vt to brush (against); (sujet) to touch upon; (suj: idée, pensée): ~ **qn** to cross sb's mind

effluves [eflyv] nmpl exhalation(s)

effondrer [efɔ̃dʀe]: **s'~** vi to collapse

efforcer [efɔʀse]: **s'~ de** vt: **s'~ de faire** to try hard to do, try hard to

effort [efɔʀ] nm effort

effraction [efʀaksjɔ̃] nf: **s'introduire par ~ dans** to break into

effrayant, e [efʀejɑ̃, -ɑ̃t] adj frightening

effrayer [efʀeje] vt to frighten, scare

effréné, e [efʀene] adj wild

effriter [efʀite]: **s'~** vi to crumble

effroi [efʀwa] nm terror, dread no pl

effronté, e [efʀɔ̃te] adj insolent, brazen

effroyable [efʀwajabl(ə)] adj horrifying, appalling

effusion [efyzjɔ̃] nf effusion; **sans ~ de sang** without bloodshed

égal, e, aux [egal, -o] adj equal; (plan: surface) even, level; (constant: vitesse) steady; (équitable) even ♦ nm/f equal; **être ~ à** (prix, nombre) to be equal to; **ça lui est ~** it's all the same to him; he doesn't mind; **sans ~** matchless, unequalled; **à l'~ de** (comme) just like; **d'~ à ~** as equals; **~ement** adv equally; evenly; steadily; (aussi) too, as well; **~er** vt to equal; **~iser** vt (sol, salaires) to level (out); (chances) to equalize ♦ vi (SPORT) to equalize; **~ité** nf equality; evenness; steadiness; (MATH) identity; **être à ~ité (de points)** to be level

égard [egaʀ] nm: **~s** nmpl consideration sg; **à cet ~** in this respect; **eu ~ à** in view of; **par ~ pour** out of consideration for; **sans ~ pour** without regard for; **à l'~ de** towards; concerning

égarement [egaʀmɑ̃] nm distraction, aberration

égarer [egaʀe] vt to mislay; (moralement) to lead astray; **s'~** vi to get lost, lose one's way; (objet) to go astray; (dans une discussion) to wander

égayer [egeje] vt (personne) to amuse; to cheer up; (récit, endroit) to brighten up, liven up

églantine [eglɑ̃tin] nf wild ou dog rose

église [egliz] nf church; **aller à l'~** to go to church

égoïsme [egɔism(ə)] nm selfishness; **égoïste** adj selfish

égorger [egɔʀʒe] vt to cut the throat of

égosiller [egozije]: **s'~** vi to shout o.s. hoarse

égout [egu] nm sewer

égoutter [egute] vt (linge) to wring out; (vaisselle) to drain ♦ vi to drip; **s'~** vi to drip; **égouttoir** nm draining board; (mobile) draining rack

égratigner [egʀatiɲe] vt to scratch; **égratignure** nf scratch

égrillard, e [egʀijaʀ, -aʀd(ə)] adj ribald

Égypte [eʒipt(ə)] nf: **l'~** Egypt; **égyptien, ne** adj, nm/f Egyptian

eh [e] excl hey!; ~ **bien** well

éhonté, e [eɔ̃te] adj shameless, brazen

éjecter [eʒɛkte] vt (TECH) to eject; (fam) to kick ou chuck out

élaborer [elabɔʀe] vt to elaborate; (projet, stratégie) to work out; (rapport) to draft

élaguer [elage] vt to prune

élan [elɑ̃] nm (ZOOL) elk, moose; (SPORT: avant le saut) run up; (d'objet en mouvement) momentum; (fig: de tendresse etc) surge; **prendre de l'~** to gather speed

élancé, e [elɑ̃se] adj slender

élancement [elɑ̃smɑ̃] nm shooting pain

élancer [elɑ̃se]: **s'~** vi to dash, hurl o.s.; (fig: arbre, clocher) to soar (upwards)

élargir [elaʀʒiʀ] vt to widen; (vêtement) to let out; (JUR) to release; **s'~** vi to widen; (vêtement) to stretch

élastique [elastik] adj elastic ♦ nm (de bureau) rubber band; (pour la couture) elastic no pl

électeur, trice [elɛktœʀ, -tʀis] nm/f elector, voter

élection [elɛksjɔ̃] nf election

électorat [elɛktɔʀa] nm electorate

électricien, ne [elɛktʀisjɛ̃, -jɛn] nm/f electrician

électricité [elɛktʀisite] nf electricity; **allumer/éteindre l'~** to put on/off the light

électrique [elɛktʀik] adj electric(al)

électrochoc [elɛktʀoʃɔk] nm electric shock treatment

électroménager [elɛktʀomenaʒe] adj, nm: **appareils ~s, l'~** domestic (electrical) appliances

électronique [elɛktʀonik] adj electronic ♦ nf electronics sg

électrophone [elɛktʀofɔn] nm record player

élégant, e [elegɑ̃, -ɑ̃t] adj elegant; (solution) neat, elegant; (attitude, procédé) courteous, civilized

élément [elemɑ̃] nm element; (pièce) component, part; **élémentaire** adj elementary

éléphant [elefɑ̃] *nm* elephant

élevage [ɛlvaʒ] *nm* breeding; (*de bovins*) cattle rearing

élévation [elevɑsjɔ̃] *nf* (*gén*) elevation; (*voir élever*) raising; (*voir s'élever*) rise

élevé, e [ɛlve] *adj* (*prix, sommet*) high; (*fig: noble*) elevated; **bien/mal** ~ well-/ill-mannered

élève [elɛv] *nm/f* pupil

élever [ɛlve] *vt* (*enfant*) to bring up, raise; (*bétail, volaille*) to breed; (*abeilles*) to keep; (*hausser: taux, niveau*) to raise; (*fig: âme, esprit*) to elevate; (*édifier: monument*) to put up, erect; **s'~** *vi* (*avion, alpiniste*) to go up; (*niveau, température, aussi: cri etc*) to rise; (*survenir: difficultés*) to arise; **s'~ à** (*suj: frais, dégâts*) to amount to, add up to; **s'~ contre qch** to rise up against sth; ~ **la voix** to raise one's voice; **éleveur, euse** *nm/f* breeder

élimé, e [elime] *adj* threadbare

éliminatoire [eliminatwaʀ] *nf* (*SPORT*) heat

éliminer [elimine] *vt* to eliminate

élire [eliʀ] *vt* to elect

elle [ɛl] *pron* (*sujet*) she; (: *chose*) it; (*complément*) her; it; ~**s** they; them; ~**-même** herself; itself; ~**s-mêmes** themselves; *voir aussi* **il**

élocution [elɔkysjɔ̃] *nf* delivery; **défaut d'~** speech impediment

éloge [elɔʒ] *nm* (*gén no pl*) praise; **élogieux, euse** *adj* laudatory, full of praise

éloigné, e [elwaɲe] *adj* distant, far-off; **éloignement** [elwaɲmɑ̃] *nm* removal; putting off; estrangement; (*fig*) distance

éloigner [elwaɲe] *vt* (*objet*): ~ **qch (de)** to move ou take sth away (from); (*personne*): ~ **qn (de)** to take sb away ou remove sb (from); (*échéance*) to put off, postpone; (*soupçons, danger*) to ward off; **s'~ (de)** (*personne*) to go away (from); (*véhicule*) to move away (from); (*affectivement*) to become estranged (from)

élongation [elɔ̃gɑsjɔ̃] *nf* strained muscle

élu, e [ely] *pp de* **élire** ♦ *nm/f* (*POL*) elected representative

élucubrations [elykybʀɑsjɔ̃] *nfpl* wild imaginings

éluder [elyde] *vt* to evade

Élysée *nm*: (**le palais de) l'~** the Élysée Palace (*the French president's residence*)

émacié, e [emasje] *adj* emaciated

émail, aux [emaj, -o] *nm* enamel

émaillé, e [emaje] *adj* (*fig*): ~ **de** dotted with

émanciper [emɑ̃sipe] *vt* to emancipate; **s'~** *vi* (*fig*) to become emancipated ou liberated

émaner [emane]: ~ **de** *vt* to come from; (*ADMIN*) to proceed from

emballage [ɑ̃balaʒ] *nm* wrapping; packaging

emballer [ɑ̃bale] *vt* to wrap (up); (*dans un*

carton) to pack (up); (*fig: fam*) to thrill (to bits); **s'~** *vi* (*moteur*) to race; (*cheval*) to bolt; (*fig: personne*) to get carried away

embarcadère [ɑ̃baʀkadɛʀ] *nm* wharf, pier

embarcation [ɑ̃baʀkɑsjɔ̃] *nf* (small) boat, (small) craft *inv*

embardée [ɑ̃baʀde] *nf*: **faire une** ~ to swerve

embarquement [ɑ̃baʀkəmɑ̃] *nm* embarkation; loading; boarding

embarquer [ɑ̃baʀke] *vt* (*personne*) to embark; (*marchandise*) to load; (*fam*) to cart off; to nick ♦ *vi* (*passager*) to board; **s'~** *vi* to board; **s'~ dans** (*affaire, aventure*) to embark upon

embarras [ɑ̃baʀa] *nm* (*obstacle*) hindrance; (*confusion*) embarrassment

embarrassant, e [ɑ̃baʀasɑ̃, -ɑ̃t] *adj* embarrassing

embarrasser [ɑ̃baʀase] *vt* (*encombrer*) to clutter (up); (*gêner*) to hinder, hamper; (*fig*) to cause embarrassment to; to put in an awkward position

embauche [ɑ̃boʃ] *nf* hiring; **bureau d'~** labour office; ~**r** [ɑ̃boʃe] *vt* to take on, hire

embaumer [ɑ̃bome] *vt* to embalm; to fill with its fragrance; ~ **la lavande** to be fragrant with (the scent of) lavender

embellie [ɑ̃beli] *nf* brighter period

embellir [ɑ̃beliʀ] *vt* to make more attractive; (*une histoire*) to embellish ♦ *vi* to grow lovelier ou more attractive

embêtements [ɑ̃bɛtmɑ̃] *nmpl* trouble *sg*

embêter [ɑ̃bɛte] *vt* to bother; **s'~** *vi* (*s'ennuyer*) to be bored

emblée [ɑ̃ble]: **d'~** *adv* straightaway

emboîter [ɑ̃bwate] *vt* to fit together; **s'~ (dans)** to fit (into); ~ **le pas à qn** to follow in sb's footsteps

embonpoint [ɑ̃bɔ̃pwɛ̃] *nm* stoutness

embouchure [ɑ̃buʃyʀ] *nf* (*GÉO*) mouth

embourber [ɑ̃buʀbe]: **s'~** *vi* to get stuck in the mud

embourgeoiser [ɑ̃buʀʒwaze]: **s'~** *vi* to adopt a middle-class outlook

embouteillage [ɑ̃butɛjaʒ] *nm* traffic jam

emboutir [ɑ̃butiʀ] *vt* (*heurter*) to crash into, ram

embranchement [ɑ̃bʀɑ̃ʃmɑ̃] *nm* (*routier*) junction; (*classification*) branch

embraser [ɑ̃bʀaze]: **s'~** *vi* to flare up

embrasser [ɑ̃bʀase] *vt* to kiss; (*sujet, période*) to embrace, encompass; (*carrière, métier*) to enter upon

embrasure [ɑ̃bʀazyʀ] *nf*: **dans l'~ de la porte** in the door(way)

embrayage [ɑ̃bʀɛjaʒ] *nm* clutch

embrayer [ɑ̃bʀeje] *vi* (*AUTO*) to let in the clutch

embrigader [ɑ̃bʀigade] *vt* to recruit

embrocher [ɑ̃bʀɔʃe] *vt* to put on a spit

embrouiller [ɑ̃bʀuje] *vt* (*fils*) to tangle

(up); (*fiches, idées, personne*) to muddle up; **s'~** *vi* (*personne*) to get in a muddle

embruns [ɑ̃brœ̃] *nmpl* sea spray *sg*

embûches [ɑ̃byʃ] *nfpl* pitfalls, traps

embué, e [ɑ̃bɥe] *adj* misted up

embuscade [ɑ̃byskad] *nf* ambush

éméché, e [emeʃe] *adj* tipsy, merry

émeraude [ɛmrod] *nf* emerald

émerger [emɛrʒe] *vi* to emerge; (*faire saillie, aussi fig*) to stand out

émeri [ɛmri] *nm*: **toile** *ou* **papier ~** emery paper

émérite [emerit] *adj* highly skilled

émerveiller [emɛrveje] *vt* to fill with wonder; **s'~ de** to marvel at

émetteur, trice [emetœr, -tris] *adj* transmitting; (*poste*) **~ transmitter**

émettre [emɛtr(ə)] *vt* (*son, lumière*) to give out, emit; (*message etc: RADIO*) to transmit; (*billet, timbre, emprunt*) to issue; (*hypothèse, avis*) to voice, put forward ♦ *vi* to broadcast

émeus *etc vb voir* **émouvoir**

émeute [emøt] *nf* riot

émietter [emjete] *vt* to crumble

émigrer [emigre] *vi* to emigrate

éminence [eminɑ̃s] *nf* distinction; (*colline*) knoll, hill; **Son É~** His Eminence; **éminent, e** [eminɑ̃, -ɑ̃t] *adj* distinguished

émission [emisjɔ̃] *nf* emission; transmission; issue; (*RADIO, TV*) programme, broadcast; **~s** *fpl* emissions

emmagasiner [ɑ̃magazine] *vt* to (put into) store; (*fig*) to store up

emmanchure [ɑ̃mɑ̃ʃyr] *nf* armhole

emmêler [ɑ̃mele] *vt* to tangle (up); (*fig*) to muddle up; **s'~** *vi* to get into a tangle

emménager [ɑ̃menaʒe] *vi* to move in; **~ dans** to move into

emmener [ɑ̃mne] *vt* to take (with one); (*comme otage, capture*) to take away; **~ qn au cinéma** to take sb to the cinema

emmerder [ɑ̃mɛrde] (*fam!*) *vt* to bug, bother; **s'~** *vi* to be bored stiff

emmitoufler [ɑ̃mitufle] *vt* to wrap up (warmly)

émoi [emwa] *nm* commotion; (*trouble*) agitation

émonder [emɔ̃de] *vt* to prune

émotif, ive [emɔtif, -iv] *adj* emotional

émotion [emosjɔ̃] *nf* emotion

émousser [emuse] *vt* to blunt; (*fig*) to dull

émouvoir [emuvwar] *vt* (*troubler*) to stir, affect; (*toucher, attendrir*) to move; (*indigner*) to rouse; **s'~** *vi* to be affected; to be moved; to be roused

empailler [ɑ̃paje] *vt* to stuff

empaler [ɑ̃pale] *vt* to impale

emparer [ɑ̃pare]: **s'~ de** *vt* (*objet*) to seize, grab; (*comme otage, MIL*) to seize; (*suj: peur etc*) to take hold of

empâter [ɑ̃pate]: **s'~** *vi* to thicken out

empêchement [ɑ̃pɛʃmɑ̃] *nm* (unexpected) obstacle, hitch

empêcher [ɑ̃peʃe] *vt* to prevent; **~ qn de faire** to prevent *ou* stop sb (from) doing; **il n'empêche que** nevertheless; **il n'a pas pu s'~ de rire** he couldn't help laughing

empereur [ɑ̃prœr] *nm* emperor

empeser [ɑ̃pəze] *vt* to starch

empester [ɑ̃pɛste] *vi* to stink, reek

empêtrer [ɑ̃petre] *vt*: **s'~ dans** (*fils etc*) to get tangled up in

emphase [ɑ̃faz] *nf* pomposity, bombast

empiéter [ɑ̃pjete] *vi*: **~ sur** to encroach upon

empiffrer [ɑ̃pifre]: **s'~** (*péj*) *vi* to stuff o.s.

empiler [ɑ̃pile] *vt* to pile (up)

empire [ɑ̃pir] *nm* empire; (*fig*) influence

empirer [ɑ̃pire] *vi* to worsen, deteriorate

emplacement [ɑ̃plasmɑ̃] *nm* site

emplettes [ɑ̃plɛt] *nfpl* shopping *sg*

emplir [ɑ̃plir] *vt* to fill; **s'~ (de)** to fill (with)

emploi [ɑ̃plwa] *nm* use; (*COMM, ÉCON*) employment; (*poste*) job, situation; **~ du temps** timetable, schedule

employé, e [ɑ̃plwaje] *nm/f* employee; **~ de bureau** office employee *ou* clerk

employer [ɑ̃plwaje] *vt* (*outil, moyen, méthode, mot*) to use; (*ouvrier, main-d'œuvre*) to employ; **s'~ à faire** to apply *ou* devote o.s. to doing; **employeur, euse** *nm/f* employer

empocher [ɑ̃pɔʃe] *vt* to pocket

empoigner [ɑ̃pwaɲe] *vt* to grab

empoisonner [ɑ̃pwazɔne] *vt* to poison; (*empester: air, pièce*) to stink out; (*fam*): **~ qn** to drive sb mad

emporté, e [ɑ̃pɔrte] *adj* quick-tempered

emporter [ɑ̃pɔrte] *vt* to take (with one); (*en dérobant ou enlevant, emmener: blessés, voyageurs*) to take away; (*entraîner*) to carry away; (*arracher*) to tear off; (*avantage, approbation*) to win; **s'~** *vi* (*de colère*) to lose one's temper; **l'~ (sur)** to get the upper hand (of); (*méthode etc*) to prevail (over); **boissons à ~** take-away drinks

empreint, e [ɑ̃prɛ̃, -ɛ̃t] *adj*: **~ de** marked with; tinged with; **empreinte** *nf* (*de pied, main*) print; (*fig*) stamp, mark; **~e (digitale)** fingerprint

empressé, e [ɑ̃prese] *adj* attentive

empressement [ɑ̃prɛsmɑ̃] *nm* (*hâte*) eagerness

empresser [ɑ̃prese]: **s'~** *vi*: **s'~ auprès de qn** to surround sb with attentions; **s'~ de faire** (*se hâter*) to hasten to do

emprise [ɑ̃priz] *nf* hold, ascendancy

emprisonner [ɑ̃prizɔne] *vt* to imprison

emprunt [ɑ̃prœ̃] *nm* borrowing *no pl*, loan

emprunté, e [ɑ̃prœ̃te] *adj* (*fig*) ill-at-ease, awkward

emprunter [ɑ̃prœ̃te] *vt* to borrow; (*itiné-*

raire) to take, follow; (*style, manière*) to adopt, assume

ému, e [emy] *pp de* **émouvoir** ♦ *adj* excited; touched; moved

émulsion [emylsjɔ̃] *nf* (*cosmétique*) (water-based) lotion

MOT CLÉ

en [ɑ̃] *prép* **1** (*endroit, pays*) in; (*direction*) to; **habiter** ~ **France/ville** to live in France/town; **aller** ~ **France/ville** to go to France/town

2 (*moment, temps*) in; ~ **été/juin** in summer/June

3 (*moyen*) by; ~ **avion/taxi** by plane/taxi

4 (*composition*) made of; **c'est** ~ **verre** it is (made of) glass; **un collier** ~ **argent** a silver necklace

5 (*description, état*): **une femme (habillée)** ~ **rouge** a woman (dressed) in red; **peindre qch** ~ **rouge** to paint sth red; ~ **T/étoile** T/star-shaped; ~ **chemise/chaussettes** in one's shirt sleeves/socks: ~ **soldat** as a soldier; **cassé** ~ **plusieurs morceaux** broken into several pieces; ~ **réparation** being repaired, under repair; ~ **vacances** on holiday; ~ **deuil** in mourning; **le même** ~ **plus grand** the same but *ou* only bigger

6 (*avec gérondif*) while; on; by; ~ **dormant** while sleeping, as one sleeps; ~ **sortant** on going out, as he *etc* went out; **sortir** ~ **courant** to run out

♦ *pron* **1** (*indéfini*): **j'**~ **ai/veux** I have/want some; ~ **as-tu?** have you got any?; **je n'**~ **veux pas** I don't want any; **j'**~ **ai 2** I've got 2; **combien y** ~ **a-t-il?** how many (of them) are there?; **j'**~ **ai assez** I've got enough (of it *ou* them); (*j'en ai marre*) I've had enough

2 (*provenance*) from there; **j'**~ **viens** I've come from there

3 (*cause*): **il** ~ **est malade/perd le sommeil** he is ill/can't sleep because of it

4 (*complément de nom, d'adjectif, de verbe*): **j'**~ **connais les dangers** I know its *ou* the dangers; **j'**~ **suis fier/ai besoin** I am proud of it/need it

---

E.N.A. [ɛna] *sigle f* (= *École Nationale d'Administration*) one of the Grandes Écoles

encadrer [ɑ̃kɑdʀe] *vt* (*tableau, image*) to frame; (*fig: entourer*) to surround; (*personnel, soldats etc*) to train

encaissé, e [ɑ̃kese] *adj* steep-sided; with steep banks

encaisser [ɑ̃kese] *vt* (*chèque*) to cash; (*argent*) to collect; (*fig: coup, défaite*) to take

encart [ɑ̃kaʀ] *nm* insert

encastrer [ɑ̃kɑstʀe] *vt*: ~ **qch dans** (*mur*) to embed sth in(to); (*boîtier*) to fit sth into

encaustique [ɑ̃kostik] *nf* polish, wax

enceinte [ɑ̃sɛ̃t] *adj f*: ~ **(de 6 mois)** (6 months) pregnant ♦ *nf* (*mur*) wall; (*espace*) enclosure

encens [ɑ̃sɑ̃] *nm* incense

encercler [ɑ̃sɛʀkle] *vt* to surround

enchaîner [ɑ̃ʃene] *vt* to chain up; (*mouvements, séquences*) to link (together) ♦ *vi* to carry on

enchanté, e [ɑ̃ʃɑ̃te] *adj* delighted; enchanted; ~ **(de faire votre connaissance)** pleased to meet you

enchantement [ɑ̃ʃɑ̃tmɑ̃] *nm* delight; (*magie*) enchantment

enchâsser [ɑ̃ʃɑse] *vt* to set

enchère [ɑ̃ʃɛʀ] *nf* bid; **mettre/vendre aux** ~**s** to put up for (sale by)/sell by auction

enchevêtrer [ɑ̃ʃvetʀe] *vt* to tangle (up)

enclencher [ɑ̃klɑ̃ʃe] *vt* (*mécanisme*) to engage; **s'**~ *vi* to engage

enclin, e [ɑ̃klɛ̃, -ɛ̃n] *adj*: ~ **à** inclined *ou* prone to

enclos [ɑ̃klo] *nm* enclosure

enclume [ɑ̃klym] *nf* anvil

encoche [ɑ̃kɔʃ] *nf* notch

encoignure [ɑ̃kɔɲyʀ] *nf* corner

encolure [ɑ̃kɔlyʀ] *nf* (*tour de cou*) collar size; (*col, cou*) neck

encombrant, e [ɑ̃kɔ̃bʀɑ̃, -ɑ̃t] *adj* cumbersome, bulky

encombre [ɑ̃kɔ̃bʀ(ə)]: **sans** ~ *adv* without mishap *ou* incident

encombrer [ɑ̃kɔ̃bʀe] *vt* to clutter (up); (*gêner*) to hamper; **s'**~ **de** (*bagages etc*) to load *ou* burden o.s. with

encontre [ɑ̃kɔ̃tʀ(ə)]: **à l'**~ **de** *prép* against, counter to

---
MOT CLÉ

encore [ɑ̃kɔʀ] *adv* **1** (*continuation*) still; **il y travaille** ~ he's still working on it; **pas** ~ not yet

2 (*de nouveau*) again; **j'irai** ~ **demain** I'll go again tomorrow; ~ **une fois** (once) again; ~ **deux jours** two more days

3 (*intensif*) even, still; ~ **plus fort/mieux** even louder/better, louder/better still

4 (*restriction*) even so *ou* then, only; ~ **pourrais-je le faire si ...** even so, I might be able to do it if ...; **si** ~ if only

encore que *conj* although

---

encourager [ɑ̃kuʀaʒe] *vt* to encourage

encourir [ɑ̃kuʀiʀ] *vt* to incur

encrasser [ɑ̃kʀase] *vt* to clog up; (*AUTO: bougies*) to soot up

encre [ɑ̃kʀ(ə)] *nf* ink; ~ **de Chine** Indian ink; **encrier** *nm* inkwell

encroûter [ɑ̃kʀute]: **s'**~ *vi* (*fig*) to get into a rut, get set in one's ways

encyclopédie [ɑ̃siklɔpedi] *nf* encyclopaedia

endetter [ɑ̃dete] *vt* to get into debt; **s'**~ *vi* to get into debt

endiablé, e [ādjable] *adj* furious; boisterous

endiguer [ādige] *vt* to dyke (up); *(fig)* to check, hold back

endimancher [ādimāʃe] *vt*: **s'~** to put on one's Sunday best

endive [ādiv] *nf* chicory *no pl*

endoctriner [ādɔktrine] *vt* to indoctrinate

endommager [ādɔmaʒe] *vt* to damage

endormi, e [ādɔrmi] *adj* asleep

endormir [ādɔrmir] *vt* to put to sleep; *(suj: chaleur etc)* to send to sleep; *(MÉD: dent, nerf)* to anaesthetize; *(fig: soupçons)* to allay; **s'~** *vi* to fall asleep, go to sleep

endosser [ādose] *vt* *(responsabilité)* to take, shoulder; *(chèque)* to endorse; *(uniforme, tenue)* to put on, don

endroit [ādrwa] *nm* place; *(opposé à l'envers)* right side; **à l'~** the right way out; the right way up; **à l'~ de** regarding

enduire [āduir] *vt* to coat

enduit [ādui] *nm* coating

endurant, e [ādyrā, -āt] *adj* tough, hardy

endurcir [ādyrsir] *vt* *(physiquement)* to toughen; *(moralement)* to harden; **s'~** *vi* to become tougher; to become hardened

endurer [ādyre] *vt* to endure, bear

énergie [enɛrʒi] *nf* *(PHYSIQUE)* energy; *(TECH)* power; *(morale)* vigour, spirit; **énergique** *adj* energetic; vigorous; *(mesures)* drastic, stringent

énergumène [enɛrgymɛn] *nm* rowdy character *ou* customer

énerver [enɛrve] *vt* to irritate, annoy; **s'~** *vi* to get excited, get worked up

enfance [āfās] *nf* *(âge)* childhood; *(fig)* infancy; *(enfants)* children *pl*

enfant [āfā] *nm/f* child; **~ de chœur** *nm* *(REL)* altar boy; **~er** *vi* to give birth ♦ *vt* to give birth to; **~illage** *(péj)* *nm* childish behaviour *no pl*; **~in, e** *adj* childlike; child *cpd*

enfer [āfɛr] *nm* hell

enfermer [āfɛrme] *vt* to shut up; *(à clef, interner)* to lock up

enfiévré, e [āfjevre] *adj* *(fig)* feverish

enfiler [āfile] *vt* *(vêtement)* to slip on, slip into; *(insérer)*: **~ qch dans** to stick sth into; *(rue, couloir)* to take; *(perles)* to string; *(aiguille)* to thread

enfin [āfɛ̄] *adv* at last; *(en énumérant)* lastly; *(de restriction, résignation)* still; well; *(pour conclure)* in a word

enflammer [āflame] *vt* to set fire to; *(MÉD)* to inflame; **s'~** *vi* to catch fire; to become inflamed

enflé, e [āfle] *adj* swollen

enfler [āfle] *vi* to swell (up)

enfoncer [āfɔ̄se] *vt* *(clou)* to drive in; *(faire pénétrer)*: **~ qch dans** to push *(ou* drive*)* sth into; *(forcer: porte)* to break open; *(: plancher)* to cause to cave in ♦ *vi* *(dans la vase etc)* to sink in; *(sol, surface)* to give way; **s'~** *vi* to sink; **s'~ dans** to sink into; *(forêt, ville)* to disappear into

enfouir [āfwir] *vt* *(dans le sol)* to bury; *(dans un tiroir etc)* to tuck away

enfourcher [āfurʃe] *vt* to mount

enfourner [āfurne] *vt* to put in the oven

enfreindre [āfrɛ̄dr(ə)] *vt* to infringe, break

enfuir [āfuir]: **s'~** *vi* to run away *ou* off

enfumer [āfyme] *vt* to smoke out

engageant, e [āgaʒā, -āt] *adj* attractive, appealing

engagement [āgaʒmā] *nm* *(promesse, contrat, POL)* commitment; *(MIL: combat)* engagement

engager [āgaʒe] *vt* *(embaucher)* to take on, engage; *(commencer)* to start; *(lier)* to bind, commit; *(impliquer, entraîner)* to involve; *(investir)* to invest, lay out; *(faire intervenir)* to engage; *(inciter)* to urge; *(faire pénétrer)* to insert; **s'~** *vi* to hire o.s., get taken on; *(MIL)* to enlist; *(promettre, politiquement)* to commit o.s.; *(débuter)* to start (up); **s'~ à faire** to undertake to do; **s'~ dans** *(rue, passage)* to turn into; *(s'emboîter)* to engage into; *(fig: affaire, discussion)* to enter into, embark on

engelures [āʒlyr] *nfpl* chilblains

engendrer [āʒādre] *vt* to father

engin [āʒɛ̄] *nm* machine; instrument; vehicle; *(AVIAT)* aircraft *inv*; missile

englober [āglobe] *vt* to include

engloutir [āglutir] *vt* to swallow up

engoncé, e [āgɔ̄se] *adj*: **~ dans** cramped in

engorger [āgɔrʒe] *vt* to obstruct, block

engouement [āgumā] *nm* (sudden) passion

engouffrer [āgufre] *vt* to swallow up, devour; **s'~ dans** to rush into

engourdir [āgurdir] *vt* to numb; *(fig)* to dull, blunt; **s'~** *vi* to go numb

engrais [āgrɛ] *nm* manure; **~ (chimique)** (chemical) fertilizer

engraisser [āgrese] *vt* to fatten (up)

engrenage [āgrənaʒ] *nm* gears *pl*, gearing; *(fig)* chain

engueuler [āgœle] *(fam)* *vt* to bawl at

enhardir [āardir]: **s'~** *vi* to grow bolder

énigme [enigm(ə)] *nf* riddle

enivrer [ānivre] *vt*: **s'~** to get drunk; **s'~ de** *(fig)* to become intoxicated with

enjambée [āʒābe] *nf* stride

enjamber [āʒābe] *vt* to stride over; *(suj: pont etc)* to span, straddle

enjeu, x [āʒø] *nm* stakes *pl*

enjoindre [āʒwɛ̄dr(ə)] *vt* to enjoin, order

enjôler [āʒole] *vt* to coax, wheedle

enjoliver [āʒolive] *vt* to embellish; **enjoliveur** *nm* *(AUTO)* hub cap

enjoué, e [āʒwe] *adj* playful

enlacer [ālase] *vt* *(étreindre)* to embrace,

hug

enlaidir [ɑ̃lediʀ] *vt* to make ugly ♦ *vi* to become ugly

enlèvement [ɑ̃lɛvmɑ̃] *nm* (*rapt*) abduction, kidnapping

enlever [ɑ̃lve] *vt* (*ôter: gén*) to remove; (: *vêtement, lunettes*) to take off; (*emporter: ordures etc*) to take away; (*prendre*): ~ **qch à qn** to take sth (away) from sb; (*kidnapper*) to abduct, kidnap; (*obtenir: prix, contrat*) to win

enliser [ɑ̃lize]: **s'~** *vi* to sink, get stuck

enluminure [ɑ̃lyminyʀ] *nf* illumination

enneigé, e [ɑ̃neʒe] *adj* snowy; snowed-up

ennemi, e [ɛnmi] *adj* hostile; (*MIL*) enemy *cpd* ♦ *nm/f* enemy

ennui [ɑ̃nɥi] *nm* (*lassitude*) boredom; (*difficulté*) trouble *no pl*; **avoir des ~s** to have problems; **ennuyer** *vt* to bother; (*lasser*) to bore; **s'ennuyer** *vi* to be bored; **s'ennuyer de** (*regretter*) to miss; **ennuyeux, euse** *adj* boring, tedious; annoying

énoncé [enɔ̃se] *nm* terms *pl*; wording

énoncer [enɔ̃se] *vt* to say, express; (*conditions*) to set out, state

enorgueillir [ɑ̃nɔʀɡœjiʀ]: **s'~ de** *vt* to pride o.s. on; to boast

énorme [enɔʀm(ə)] *adj* enormous, huge; **énormément** *adv* enormously; **énormément de neige/gens** an enormous amount of snow/number of people

enquérir [ɑ̃keʀiʀ]: **s'~ de** *vt* to inquire about

enquête [ɑ̃kɛt] *nf* (*de journaliste, de police*) investigation; (*judiciaire, administrative*) inquiry; (*sondage d'opinion*) survey; **enquêter** *vi* to investigate; to hold an inquiry; to conduct a survey

enquiers *etc vb voir* **enquérir**

enraciné, e [ɑ̃ʀasine] *adj* deep-rooted

enragé, e [ɑ̃ʀaʒe] *adj* (*MÉD*) rabid, with rabies; (*fig*) fanatical

enrageant, e [ɑ̃ʀaʒɑ̃, -ɑ̃t] *adj* infuriating

enrager [ɑ̃ʀaʒe] *vi* to be in a rage

enrayer [ɑ̃ʀeje] *vt* to check, stop; **s'~** *vi* (*arme à feu*) to jam

enregistrement [ɑ̃ʀʒistʀəmɑ̃] *nm* recording; (*ADMIN*) registration; ~ **des bagages** (*à l'aéroport*) baggage check-in; **enregistrer** [ɑ̃ʀʒistʀe] *vt* (*MUS etc, remarquer, noter*) to record; (*fig: mémoriser*) to make a mental note of; (*ADMIN*) to register; (*bagages: par train*) to register; (: *à l'aéroport*) to check in

enrhumer [ɑ̃ʀyme]: **s'~** *vi* to catch a cold

enrichir [ɑ̃ʀiʃiʀ] *vt* to make rich(er); (*fig*) to enrich; **s'~** *vi* to get rich(er)

enrober [ɑ̃ʀɔbe] *vt*: ~ **qch de** to coat sth with; (*fig*) to wrap sth up in

enrôler [ɑ̃ʀole] *vt* to enlist; **s'~ (dans)** to enlist (in)

enrouer [ɑ̃ʀwe]: **s'~** *vi* to go hoarse

enrouler [ɑ̃ʀule] *vt* (*fil, corde*) to wind (up); **s'~** *vi* to coil up; to wind; ~ **qch autour de** to wind sth (a)round

ensanglanté, e [ɑ̃sɑ̃ɡlɑ̃te] *adj* covered with blood

enseignant, e [ɑ̃sɛɲɑ̃, -ɑ̃t] *nm/f* teacher

enseigne [ɑ̃sɛɲ] *nf* sign; **à telle ~ que** so much so that; ~ **lumineuse** neon sign

enseignement [ɑ̃sɛɲmɑ̃] *nm* teaching; (*ADMIN*) education

enseigner [ɑ̃sɛɲe] *vt, vi* to teach; ~ **qch à qn/à qn que** to teach sb sth/sb that

ensemble [ɑ̃sɑ̃bl(ə)]: *adv* together ♦ *nm* (*assemblage, MATH*) set; (*totalité*): **l'~ du/de la** the whole *ou* entire; (*unité, harmonie*) unity; **impression/idée d'~** overall *ou* general impression/idea; **dans l'~** (*en gros*) on the whole

ensemencer [ɑ̃sməse] *vt* to sow

ensevelir [ɑ̃səvliʀ] *vt* to bury

ensoleillé, e [ɑ̃sɔleje] *adj* sunny

ensommeillé, e [ɑ̃sɔmeje] *adj* drowsy

ensorceler [ɑ̃sɔʀsəle] *vt* to enchant, bewitch

ensuite [ɑ̃sɥit] *adv* then, next; (*plus tard*) afterwards, later; ~ **de quoi** after which

ensuivre [ɑ̃sɥivʀ(ə)]: **s'~** *vi* to follow, ensue

entailler [ɑ̃taje] *vt* to notch; to cut

entamer [ɑ̃tame] *vt* (*pain, bouteille*) to start; (*hostilités, pourparlers*) to open; (*fig: altérer*) to make a dent in; to shake; to damage

entasser [ɑ̃tase] *vt* (*empiler*) to pile up, heap up; (*tenir à l'étroit*) to cram together; **s'~** *vi* to pile up; to cram

entendre [ɑ̃tɑ̃dʀ(ə)] *vt* to hear; (*comprendre*) to understand; (*vouloir dire*) to mean; (*vouloir*): ~ **être obéi/que** to mean to be obeyed/that; **s'~** *vi* (*sympathiser*) to get on; (*se mettre d'accord*) to agree; **s'~ à qch/à faire** (*être compétent*) to be good at sth/doing; **j'ai entendu dire que** I've heard (it said) that

entendu, e [ɑ̃tɑ̃dy] *adj* (*réglé*) agreed; (*au courant: air*) knowing; (**c'est**) ~ **all right, agreed**; **c'est** ~ (*concession*) all right, granted; **bien** ~ of course

entente [ɑ̃tɑ̃t] *nf* understanding; (*accord, traité*) agreement; **à double** ~ (*sens*) with a double meaning

entériner [ɑ̃teʀine] *vt* to ratify, confirm

enterrement [ɑ̃tɛʀmɑ̃] *nm* (*cérémonie*) funeral, burial

enterrer [ɑ̃teʀe] *vt* to bury

entêtant, e [ɑ̃tetɑ̃, -ɑ̃t] *adj* heady

entêté, e [ɑ̃tete] *adj* stubborn

en-tête [ɑ̃tɛt] *nm* heading; **papier à ~** headed notepaper

entêter [ɑ̃tete]: **s'~** *vi*: **s'~ (à faire)** to persist (in doing)

enthousiasme [ɑ̃tuzjasm(ə)] *nm* enthusiasm; ~**r** vt to fill with enthusiasm; **s'~r (pour qch)** to get enthusiastic (about sth)

enticher [ɑ̃tiʃe]: **s'~ de** vt to become infatuated with

entier, ère [ɑ̃tje, -jɛʀ] adj (non entamé, en totalité) whole; (total, complet) complete; (fig: caractère) unbending ♦ nm (MATH) whole; **en ~** totally; in its entirety; **lait ~** full-cream milk; **entièrement** adv entirely, wholly

entonner [ɑ̃tɔne] vt (chanson) to strike up

entonnoir [ɑ̃tɔnwaʀ] nm funnel

entorse [ɑ̃tɔʀs(ə)] nf (MÉD) sprain; (fig): ~ **au règlement** infringement of the rule

entortiller [ɑ̃tɔʀtije] vt (envelopper) to wrap; (enrouler) to twist, wind; (duper) to deceive

entourage [ɑ̃tuʀaʒ] nm circle; family (circle); entourage; (ce qui enclôt) surround

entourer [ɑ̃tuʀe] vt to surround; (apporter son soutien à) to rally round; ~ **de** to surround with; (trait) to encircle with

entourloupettes [ɑ̃tuʀlupɛt] nfpl mean tricks

entracte [ɑ̃tʀakt(ə)] nm interval

entraide [ɑ̃tʀɛd] nf mutual aid; **s'~r** vi to help each other

entrain [ɑ̃tʀɛ̃] nm spirit; **avec/sans ~** spiritedly/half-heartedly

entraînement [ɑ̃tʀɛnmɑ̃] nm training; (TECH) drive

entraîner [ɑ̃tʀene] vt (tirer: wagons) to pull; (charrier) to carry ou drag along; (TECH) to drive; (emmener: personne) to take (off); (mener à l'assaut, influencer) to lead; (SPORT) to train; (impliquer) to entail; (causer) to lead to, bring about; **s'~** vi (SPORT) to train; **s'~ à qch/à faire** to train o.s. for sth/to do; ~ **qn à faire** (inciter) to lead sb to do; **entraîneur, euse** nm/f (SPORT) coach, trainer ♦ nm (HIPPISME) trainer; **entraîneuse** nf (de bar) hostess

entraver [ɑ̃tʀave] vt (circulation) to hold up; (action, progrès) to hinder

entre [ɑ̃tʀ(ə)] prép between; (parmi) among(st); **l'un d'~ eux/nous** one of them/us; ~ **eux** among(st) themselves

entre: ~bâillé, e adj half-open, ajar; **~choquer: s'~choquer** vi to knock ou bang together; **~côte** nf entrecôte ou rib steak; **~couper** vt: **~couper qch de** to intersperse sth with; **~croiser: s'~croiser** vi to intertwine

entrée [ɑ̃tʀe] nf entrance; (accès: au cinéma etc) admission; (billet) (admission) ticket; (CULIN) first course; **d'~** from the outset; ~ **en matière** introduction

entrefaites [ɑ̃tʀəfɛt]: **sur ces ~** adv at this juncture

entrefilet [ɑ̃tʀəfilɛ] nm paragraph (short article)

entrejambes [ɑ̃tʀəʒɑ̃b] nm crotch

entrelacer [ɑ̃tʀəlase] vt to intertwine

entrelarder [ɑ̃tʀəlaʀde] vt to lard

entremêler [ɑ̃tʀəmele] vt: ~ **qch de** to (inter)mingle sth with

entremets [ɑ̃tʀəmɛ] nm (cream) dessert

entremetteur, euse [ɑ̃tʀəmɛtœʀ, -øz] nm/f go-between

entremise [ɑ̃tʀəmiz] nf intervention; **par l'~ de** through

entreposer [ɑ̃tʀəpoze] vt to store, put into storage

entrepôt [ɑ̃tʀəpo] nm warehouse

entreprenant, e [ɑ̃tʀəpʀənɑ̃, -ɑ̃t] adj (actif) enterprising; (trop galant) forward

entreprendre [ɑ̃tʀəpʀɑ̃dʀ(ə)] vt (se lancer dans) to undertake; (commencer) to begin ou start (upon); (personne) to buttonhole; to tackle

entrepreneur [ɑ̃tʀəpʀənœʀ] nm: ~ **(en bâtiment)** (building) contractor

entreprise [ɑ̃tʀəpʀiz] nf (société) firm, concern; (action) undertaking, venture

entrer [ɑ̃tʀe] vi to go (ou come) in, enter ♦ vt (INFORM) to enter, input; **(faire) ~ qch dans** to get sth into; ~ **dans** (gén) to enter; (pièce) to go (ou come) into, enter; (club) to join; (heurter) to run into; (être une composante de) to go into; to form part of; ~ **à l'hôpital** to go into hospital; **faire ~** (visiteur) to show in

entresol [ɑ̃tʀəsɔl] nm mezzanine

entre-temps [ɑ̃tʀətɑ̃] adv meanwhile

entretenir [ɑ̃tʀətniʀ] vt to maintain; (famille, maîtresse) to support, keep; **s'~ (de)** to converse (about); ~ **qn (de)** to speak to sb (about)

entretien [ɑ̃tʀətjɛ̃] nm maintenance; (discussion) discussion, talk; (audience) interview

entrevoir [ɑ̃tʀəvwaʀ] vt (à peine) to make out; (brièvement) to catch a glimpse of

entrevue [ɑ̃tʀəvy] nf meeting; (audience) interview

entrouvert, e [ɑ̃tʀuvɛʀ, -ɛʀt(ə)] adj half-open

énumérer [enymeʀe] vt to list, enumerate

envahir [ɑ̃vaiʀ] vt to invade; (suj: inquiétude, peur) to come over; **envahissant, e** (péj) adj (personne) interfering, intrusive

enveloppe [ɑ̃vlɔp] nf (de lettre) envelope; (TECH) casing; outer layer

envelopper [ɑ̃vlɔpe] vt to wrap; (fig) to envelop, shroud

envenimer [ɑ̃vnime] vt to aggravate

envergure [ɑ̃vɛʀgyʀ] nf (fig) scope; calibre

enverrai etc vb voir **envoyer**

envers [ɑ̃vɛʀ] prép towards, to ♦ nm other side; (d'une étoffe) wrong side; **à l'~** upside down; back to front; (vêtement) inside out

envie [ɑ̃vi] nf (sentiment) envy; (souhait) desire, wish; **avoir ~ de (faire)** to feel like (doing); (plus fort) to want (to do); **avoir ~**

que to wish that; **ça lui fait ~** he would like that; **envier** *vt* to envy; **envieux, euse** *adj* envious

environ [ɑ̃viʀɔ̃] *adv*: **~ 3 h/2 km** (around) about 3 o'clock/2 km; *voir aussi* **environs**

environnement [ɑ̃viʀɔnmɑ̃] *nm* environment

environner [ɑ̃viʀɔne] *vt* to surround

environs [ɑ̃viʀɔ̃] *nmpl* surroundings

envisager [ɑ̃vizaʒe] *vt* (*examiner, considérer*) to view, contemplate; (*avoir en vue*) to envisage

envoi [ɑ̃vwa] *nm* (*paquet*) parcel, consignment

envoler [ɑ̃vɔle]: **s'~** *vi* (*oiseau*) to fly away *ou* off; (*avion*) to take off; (*papier, feuille*) to blow away; (*fig*) to vanish (into thin air)

envoûter [ɑ̃vute] *vt* to bewitch

envoyé, e [ɑ̃vwaje] *nm/f* (POL) envoy; (PRESSE) correspondent

envoyer [ɑ̃vwaje] *vt* to send; (*lancer*) to hurl, throw; **~ chercher** to send for

épagneul, e [epaɲœl] *nm/f* spaniel

épais, se [epɛ, -ɛs] *adj* thick; **épaisseur** *nf* thickness

épancher [epɑ̃ʃe]: **s'~** *vi* to open one's heart

épanouir [epanwiʀ]: **s'~** *vi* (*fleur*) to bloom, open out; (*visage*) to light up; (*fig*) to blossom; to open up

épargne [epaʀɲ(ə)] *nf* saving

épargner [epaʀɲe] *vt* to save; (*ne pas tuer ou endommager*) to spare ♦ *vi* to save; **~ qch à qn** to spare sb sth

éparpiller [epaʀpije] *vt* to scatter; (*pour répartir*) to disperse; **s'~** *vi* to scatter; (*fig*) to dissipate one's efforts

épars, e [epaʀ, -aʀs(ə)] *adj* scattered

épatant, e [epatɑ̃, -ɑ̃t] (*fam*) *adj* super

épater [epate] *vt* to amaze; to impress

épaule [epol] *nf* shoulder

épauler [epole] *vt* (*aider*) to back up, support; (*arme*) to raise (to one's shoulder) ♦ *vi* to (take) aim

épaulette [epolɛt] *nf* epaulette; (*rembourrage*) shoulder pad

épave [epav] *nf* wreck

épée [epe] *nf* sword

épeler [eple] *vt* to spell

éperdu, e [epɛʀdy] *adj* distraught, overcome; passionate; frantic

éperon [epʀɔ̃] *nm* spur

épi [epi] *nm* (*de blé, d'orge*) ear

épice [epis] *nf* spice

épicer [epise] *vt* to spice

épicerie [episʀi] *nf* grocer's shop; (*denrées*) groceries *pl*; **~ fine** delicatessen; **épicier, ière** *nm/f* grocer

épidémie [epidemi] *nf* epidemic

épier [epje] *vt* to spy on, watch closely; (*occasion*) to look out for

épilepsie [epilɛpsi] *nf* epilepsy

épiler [epile] *vt* (*jambes*) to remove the hair from; (*sourcils*) to pluck

épilogue [epilɔg] *nm* (*fig*) conclusion, dénouement; **~r** [epilɔge] *vi*: **~r sur** to hold forth on

épinards [epinaʀ] *nmpl* spinach *sg*

épine [epin] *nf* thorn, prickle; (*d'oursin etc*) spine; **~ dorsale** backbone

épingle [epɛ̃gl(ə)] *nf* pin; **~ de nourrice** safety pin; **~ de sûreté** *ou* **double** safety pin

épingler [epɛ̃gle] *vt* (*badge, décoration*): **~ qch sur** to pin sth on(to); (*fam*) to catch, nick

épique [epik] *adj* epic

épisode [epizɔd] *nm* episode; **film/roman à ~s** serial; **épisodique** *adj* occasional

éploré, e [eplɔʀe] *adj* tearful

épluche-légumes [eplyʃlegym] *nm inv* (potato) peeler

éplucher [eplyʃe] *vt* (*fruit, légumes*) to peel; (*fig*) to go over with a fine-tooth comb; **épluchures** *nfpl* peelings

éponge [epɔ̃ʒ] *nf* sponge; **~r** *vt* (*liquide*) to mop up; (*surface*) to sponge; (*fig: déficit*) to soak up; **s'~r le front** to mop one's brow

épopée [epɔpe] *nf* epic

époque [epɔk] *nf* (*de l'histoire*) age, era; (*de l'année, la vie*) time; **d'~** (*meuble*) period *cpd*

époumoner [epumɔne]: **s'~** *vi* to shout o.s. hoarse

épouse [epuz] *nf* wife

épouser [epuze] *vt* to marry; (*fig: idées*) to espouse; (: *forme*) to fit

épousseter [epuste] *vt* to dust

époustouflant, e [epustuflɑ̃, -ɑ̃t] *adj* staggering, mind-boggling

épouvantable [epuvɑ̃tabl(ə)] *adj* appalling, dreadful

épouvantail [epuvɑ̃taj] *nm* (*à oiseaux*) scarecrow

épouvante [epuvɑ̃t] *nf* terror; **film d'~** horror film; **épouvanter** *vt* to terrify

époux [epu] *nm* husband ♦ *nmpl* (married) couple

éprendre [epʀɑ̃dʀ(ə)]: **s'~ de** *vt* to fall in love with

épreuve [epʀœv] *nf* (*d'examen*) test; (*malheur, difficulté*) trial, ordeal; (PHOTO) print; (TYPO) proof; (SPORT) event; **à l'~ des balles** bulletproof; **à toute ~** unfailing; **mettre à l'~** to put to the test

épris, e [epʀi, -iz] *pp de* **éprendre**

éprouver [epʀuve] *vt* (*tester*) to test; (*marquer, faire souffrir*) to afflict, distress; (*ressentir*) to experience

éprouvette [epʀuvɛt] *nf* test tube

épuisé, e [epɥize] *adj* exhausted; (*livre*) out of print; **épuisement** [epɥizmɑ̃] *nm* exhaustion

épuiser [epɥize] *vt* (*fatiguer*) to exhaust,

wear *ou* tire out; (*stock, sujet*) to exhaust; **s'~** *vi* to wear *ou* tire o.s. out, exhaust o.s.; (*stock*) to run out

épurer [epyʀe] *vt* (*liquide*) to purify; (*parti etc*) to purge; (*langue, texte*) to refine

équateur [ekwatœʀ] *nm* equator; **(la république de) l'É~** Ecuador

équation [ekwɑsjɔ̃] *nf* equation

équerre [ekeʀ] *nf* (*à dessin*) (set) square; (*pour fixer*) brace; **en ~** at right angles; **à l'~, d'~** straight

équilibre [ekilibʀ(ə)] *nm* balance; (*d'une balance*) equilibrium; **garder/perdre l'~** to keep/lose one's balance; **être en ~** to be balanced; **équilibré, e** *adj* (*fig*) well-balanced, stable; **équilibrer** *vt* to balance; **s'~r** *vi* (*poids*) to balance; (*fig: défauts etc*) to balance each other out

équipage [ekipaʒ] *nm* crew

équipe [ekip] *nf* team; (*bande: parfois péj*) bunch

équipé, e [ekipe] *adj*: **bien/mal ~** well-/poorly-equipped

équipée [ekipe] *nf* escapade

équipement [ekipmɑ̃] *nm* equipment; **~s** *nmpl* (*installations*) amenities, facilities

équiper [ekipe] *vt* to equip; (*voiture, cuisine*) to equip, fit out; **~ qn/qch de** to equip sb/sth with

équipier, ière [ekipje, -jeʀ] *nm/f* team member

équitable [ekitabl(ə)] *adj* fair

équitation [ekitɑsjɔ̃] *nf* (horse-) riding

équivalent, e [ekivalɑ̃, -ɑ̃t] *adj, nm* equivalent

équivaloir [ekivalwaʀ]: **~ à** *vt* to be equivalent to

équivoque [ekivɔk] *adj* equivocal, ambiguous; (*louche*) dubious

érable [eʀabl(ə)] *nm* maple

érafler [eʀafle] *vt* to scratch; **éraflure** *nf* scratch

éraillé, e [eʀaje] *adj* (*voix*) rasping

ère [eʀ] *nf* era; **en l'an 1050 de notre ~** in the year 1050 A.D.

érection [eʀeksjɔ̃] *nf* erection

éreinter [eʀɛ̃te] *vt* to exhaust, wear out

ériger [eʀiʒe] *vt* (*monument*) to erect

ermite [eʀmit] *nm* hermit

éroder [eʀɔde] *vt* to erode

érotique [eʀɔtik] *adj* erotic

errer [eʀe] *vi* to wander

erreur [eʀœʀ] *nf* mistake, error; (*morale*) error; **faire ~** to be mistaken; **par ~** by mistake; **~ judiciaire** miscarriage of justice

érudit, e [eʀydi, -it] *nm/f* scholar

éruption [eʀypsjɔ̃] *nf* eruption; (*MÉD*) rash

es *vb voir* **être**

ès [es] *prép*: **licencié ~ lettres/sciences ≈** Bachelor of Arts/Science

escabeau, x [eskabo] *nm* (*tabouret*) stool; (*échelle*) stepladder

escadre [eskadʀ(ə)] *nf* (*NAVIG*) squadron; (*AVIAT*) wing

escadron [eskadʀɔ̃] *nm* squadron

escalade [eskalad] *nf* climbing *no pl*; (*POL etc*) escalation

escalader [eskalade] *vt* to climb

escale [eskal] *nf* (*NAVIG*) call; port of call; (*AVIAT*) stop(over); **faire ~ à** to put in at; to stop over at

escalier [eskalje] *nm* stairs *pl*; **dans l'~** *ou* **les ~s** on the stairs; **~ roulant** escalator

escamoter [eskamɔte] *vt* (*esquiver*) to get round, evade; (*faire disparaître*) to conjure away

escapade [eskapad] *nf*: **faire une ~** to go on a jaunt; to run away *ou* off

escargot [eskaʀgo] *nm* snail

escarmouche [eskaʀmuʃ] *nf* skirmish

escarpé, e [eskaʀpe] *adj* steep

escient [esjɑ̃] *nm*: **à bon ~** advisedly

esclaffer [esklafe]: **s'~** *vi* to guffaw

esclandre [esklɑ̃dʀ(ə)] *nm* scene, fracas

esclavage [esklavaʒ] *nm* slavery

esclave [esklav] *nm/f* slave

escompter [eskɔ̃te] *vt* (*COMM*) to discount; (*espérer*) to expect, reckon upon

escorte [eskɔʀt(ə)] *nf* escort

escrime [eskʀim] *nf* fencing

escrimer [eskʀime]: **s'~** *vi*: **s'~ à faire** to wear o.s. out doing

escroc [eskʀo] *nm* swindler, conman

escroquer [eskʀɔke] *vt*: **~ qn (de qch)/qch (à qn)** to swindle sb (out of sth)/sth (out of sb); **escroquerie** *nf* swindle

espace [espas] *nm* space

espacer [espase] *vt* to space out; **s'~** *vi* (*visites etc*) to become less frequent

espadon [espadɔ̃] *nm* swordfish *inv*

espadrille [espadʀij] *nf* rope-soled sandal

Espagne [espaɲ(ə)] *nf*: **l'~** Spain; **espagnol, e** *adj* Spanish ♦ *nm/f*: **Espagnol, e** Spaniard ♦ *nm* (*LING*) Spanish

espèce [espes] *nf* (*BIO, BOT, ZOOL*) species *inv*; (*gén: sorte*) sort, kind, type; (*péj*): **~ de maladroit!** you clumsy oaf!; **~s** *nfpl* (*COMM*) cash *sg*; **en ~** in cash; **en l'~** in the case in point

espérance [espeʀɑ̃s] *nf* hope; **~ de vie** life expectancy

espérer [espeʀe] *vt* to hope for; **j'espère (bien)** I hope so; **~ que/faire** to hope that/to do; **~ en** to trust in

espiègle [espjɛgl(ə)] *adj* mischievous

espion, ne [espjɔ̃, -ɔn] *nm/f* spy

espionnage [espjɔnaʒ] *nm* espionage, spying

espionner [espjɔne] *vt* to spy (up)on

esplanade [esplanad] *nf* esplanade

espoir [espwaʀ] *nm* hope

esprit [espʀi] *nm* (*pensée, intellect*) mind; (*humour, ironie*) wit; (*mentalité, d'une loi etc, fantôme etc*) spirit; **faire de l'~** to try to be witty; **reprendre ses ~s** to come to; **perdre l'~** to lose one's mind

esquimau, de, x [ɛskimo, -od] *adj, nm/f* Eskimo ♦ *nm* ice lolly (*BRIT*), popsicle (*US*)

esquinter [ɛskɛ̃te] (*fam*) *vt* to mess up

esquisse [ɛskis] *nf* sketch

esquisser [ɛskise] *vt* to sketch; **s'~** *vi* (*amélioration*) to begin to be detectable; **~ un sourire** to give a vague smile

esquiver [ɛskive] *vt* to dodge; **s'~** *vi* to slip away

essai [ese] *nm* trying; testing; (*tentative*) attempt, try; (*RUGBY*) try; (*LITTÉRATURE*) essay; **~s** *nmpl* (*AUTO*) trials; **~ gratuit** (*COMM*) free trial; **à l'~** on a trial basis

essaim [esɛ̃] *nm* swarm

essayer [eseje] *vt* (*gén*) to try; (*vêtement, chaussures*) to try (on); (*restaurant, méthode, voiture*) to try (out) ♦ *vi* to try; **~ de faire** to try *ou* attempt to do

essence [esɑ̃s] *nf* (*de voiture*) petrol (*BRIT*), gas(oline) (*US*); (*extrait de plante, PHILOSOPHIE*) essence; (*espèce: d'arbre*) species

essentiel, le [esɑ̃sjɛl] *adj* essential; **c'est l'~** (*ce qui importe*) that's the main thing; **l'~ de** the main part of

essieu, x [esjø] *nm* axle

essor [esɔʀ] *nm* (*de l'économie etc*) rapid expansion

essorer [esɔʀe] *vt* (*en tordant*) to wring (out); (*par la force centrifuge*) to spin-dry; **essoreuse** *nf* mangle, wringer; spin-dryer

essouffler [esufle] *vt* to make breathless; **s'~** *vi* to get out of breath; (*fig*) to run out of steam

essuie-glace [esɥiglas] *nm inv* windscreen (*BRIT*) *ou* windshield (*US*) wiper

essuie-main [esɥimɛ̃] *nm* hand towel

essuyer [esɥije] *vt* to wipe; (*fig: subir*) to suffer; **s'~** *vi* (*après le bain*) to dry o.s.; **~ la vaisselle** to dry up

est[1] [ɛ] *vb voir* **être**

est[2] [ɛst] *nm* east ♦ *adj inv* east; (*région*) east(ern); **à l'est** in the east; (*direction*) to the east, east(wards); **à l'est de** (to the) east of

estampe [ɛstɑ̃p] *nf* print, engraving

est-ce que [ɛskə] *adv*: **~ c'est cher/c'était bon?** is it expensive/was it good?; **quand est-ce qu'il part?** when does he leave?, when is he leaving?; *voir aussi* **que**

esthéticienne [ɛstetisjɛn] *nf* beautician

esthétique [ɛstetik] *adj* attractive; aesthetically pleasing

estimation [ɛstimasjɔ̃] *nf* valuation; assessment

estime [ɛstim] *nf* esteem, regard

estimer [ɛstime] *vt* (*respecter*) to esteem; (*expertiser*) to value; (*évaluer*) to assess, estimate; (*penser*): **~ que/être** to consider that/o.s. to be

estival, e, aux [ɛstival, -o] *adj* summer *cpd*

estivant, e [ɛstivɑ̃, -ɑ̃t] *nm/f* (summer) holiday-maker

estomac [ɛstɔma] *nm* stomach

estomaqué, e [ɛstɔmake] *adj* flabbergasted

estomper [ɛstɔ̃pe] *vt* (*fig*) to blur, dim; **s'~** *vi* to soften; to become blurred

estrade [ɛstʀad] *nf* platform, rostrum

estragon [ɛstʀagɔ̃] *nm* tarragon

estropier [ɛstʀɔpje] *vt* to cripple, maim; (*fig*) to twist, distort

et [e] *conj* and; **~ lui?** what about him?; **~ alors!** so what!

étable [etabl(ə)] *nf* cowshed

établi [etabli] *nm* (work)bench

établir [etabliʀ] *vt* (*papiers d'identité, facture*) to make out; (*liste, programme*) to draw up; (*entreprise, camp, gouvernement, artisan*) to set up; (*réputation, usage, fait, culpabilité*) to establish; **s'~** *vi* (*se faire: entente etc*) to be established; **s'~** (**à son compte**) to set up in business; **s'~ à/près de** to settle in/near

établissement [etablismɑ̃] *nm* making out; drawing up; setting up, establishing; (*entreprise, institution*) establishment; **~ scolaire** school, educational establishment

étage [etaʒ] *nm* (*d'immeuble*) storey, floor; (*de fusée*) stage; (*GÉO: de culture, végétation*) level; **à l'~** upstairs; **au 2ème ~** on the 2nd (*BRIT*) *ou* 3rd (*US*) floor; **de bas ~** low-born

étagère [etaʒɛʀ] *nf* (*rayon*) shelf; (*meuble*) shelves *pl*

étai [etɛ] *nm* stay, prop

étain [etɛ̃] *nm* tin; (*ORFÈVRERIE*) pewter *no pl*

étais *etc vb voir* **être**

étal [etal] *nm* stall

étalage [etalaʒ] *nm* display; display window; **faire ~ de** to show off, parade

étaler [etale] *vt* (*carte, nappe*) to spread (out); (*peinture, liquide*) to spread; (*échelonner: paiements, vacances*) to spread, stagger; (*marchandises*) to display; (*richesses, connaissances*) to parade; **s'~** *vi* (*liquide*) to spread out; (*fam*) to fall flat on one's face; **s'~ sur** (*suj: paiements etc*) to be spread out over

étalon [etalɔ̃] *nm* (*mesure*) standard; (*cheval*) stallion

étamer [etame] *vt* (*casserole*) to tin(plate); (*glace*) to silver

étanche [etɑ̃ʃ] *adj* (*récipient*) watertight; (*montre, vêtement*) waterproof

étancher [etɑ̃ʃe] *vt*: **~ sa soif** to quench one's thirst

étang [etɑ̃] *nm* pond

étant [etɑ̃] *vb voir* **être; donné**

étape [etap] *nf* stage; (*lieu d'arrivée*) stopping place; (: *CYCLISME*) staging point; **faire ~ à** to stop off at

état [eta] *nm* (*POL, condition*) state; (*liste*)

inventory, statement; **en mauvais ~** in poor condition; **en ~ (de marche)** in (working) order; **remettre en ~** to repair; **hors d'~** out of order; **être en ~/hors d'~ de faire** to be in a/in no fit state to do; **en tout ~ de cause** in any event; **être dans tous ses ~s** to be in a state; **faire ~ de** (alléguer) to put forward; **en ~ d'arrestation** under arrest; **~ civil** civil status; **~ des lieux** inventory of fixtures; **étatiser** vt to bring under state control

état-major [etamaʒɔʀ] nm (MIL) staff

États-Unis [etazyni] nmpl: **les ~** the United States

étau, x [eto] nm vice (BRIT), vise (US)

étayer [eteje] vt to prop ou shore up

etc. adv etc

et c(a)etera [ɛtseteʀa] adv et cetera, and so on

été [ete] pp de **être** ♦ nm summer

éteindre [etɛ̃dʀ(ə)] vt (lampe, lumière, radio) to turn ou switch off; (cigarette, incendie, bougie) to put out, extinguish; (JUR: dette) to extinguish; **s'~** vi to go out, to go off; (mourir) to pass away; **éteint, e** adj (fig) lacklustre, dull; (volcan) extinct

étendard [etɑ̃daʀ] nm standard

étendre [etɑ̃dʀ(ə)] vt (pâte, liquide) to spread; (carte etc) to spread out; (linge) to hang up; (bras, jambes, par terre: blessé) to stretch out; (diluer) to dilute, thin; (fig: agrandir) to extend; **s'~** vi (augmenter, se propager) to spread; (terrain, forêt etc) to stretch; (s'allonger) to stretch out; (se coucher) to lie down; (fig: expliquer) to elaborate

étendu, e [etɑ̃dy] adj extensive; **étendue** nf (d'eau, de sable) stretch, expanse; (importance) extent

éternel, le [etɛʀnɛl] adj eternal

éterniser [etɛʀnize]: **s'~** vi to last for ages; to stay for ages

éternité [etɛʀnite] nf eternity

éternuer [etɛʀnɥe] vi to sneeze

êtes vb voir **être**

éthique [etik] adj ethical

ethnie [ɛtni] nf ethnic group

éthylisme [etilism(ə)] nm alcoholism

étiez vb voir **être**

étinceler [etɛ̃sle] vi to sparkle

étincelle [etɛ̃sɛl] nf spark

étioler [etjɔle]: **s'~** vi to wilt

étiqueter [etikte] vt to label

étiquette [etiket] nf label; (protocole): **l'~** etiquette

étirer [etiʀe] vt to stretch; **s'~** vi (personne) to stretch; (convoi, route) **s'~ sur** to stretch out over

étoffe [etɔf] nf material, fabric

étoffer [etɔfe] vt to fill out; **s'~** vi to fill out

étoile [etwal] nf star; **à la belle ~** in the open; **~ de mer** starfish; **~ filante** shooting star; **étoilé, e** adj starry

étole [etɔl] nf stole

étonnant, e [etɔnɑ̃, -ɑ̃t] adj amazing

étonner [etɔne] vt to surprise, amaze; **s'~ que/de** to be amazed that/at; **cela m'~ait (que)** (j'en doute) I'd be very surprised (if)

étouffée [etufe]: **à l'~** adv (CULIN) steamed; braised

étouffer [etufe] vt to suffocate; (bruit) to muffle; (scandale) to hush up ♦ vi to suffocate; **s'~** vi (en mangeant etc) to choke

étourderie [etuʀdəʀi] nf heedlessness no pl; thoughtless blunder

étourdi, e [etuʀdi] adj (distrait) scatterbrained, heedless

étourdir [etuʀdiʀ] vt (assommer) to stun, daze; (griser) to make dizzy ou giddy; **étourdissement** nm dizzy spell

étourneau, x [etuʀno] nm starling

étrange [etʀɑ̃ʒ] adj strange

étranger, ère [etʀɑ̃ʒe, -ɛʀ] adj foreign; (pas de la famille, non familier) strange ♦ nm/f foreigner; stranger ♦ nm: **à l'~** abroad; **de l'~** from abroad; **~ à** (fig) unfamiliar to; irrelevant to

étranglement [etʀɑ̃gləmɑ̃] nm (d'une vallée etc) constriction

étrangler [etʀɑ̃gle] vt to strangle; **s'~** vi (en mangeant etc) to choke

étrave [etʀav] nf stem

─────────────── **MOT CLÉ**

être [ɛtʀ(ə)] nm being; **~ humain** human being

♦ vb +attrib **1** (état, description) to be; **il est instituteur** he is ou he's a teacher; **vous êtes grand/intelligent/fatigué** you are ou you're tall/clever/tired

2 (+à: appartenir) to be; **le livre est à Paul** the book is Paul's ou belongs to Paul; **c'est à moi/eux** it is ou it's mine/theirs

3 (+de: provenance): **il est de Paris** he is from Paris; (: appartenance): **il est des nôtres** he is one of us

4 (date): **nous sommes le 10 janvier** it's the 10th of January (today)

♦ vi to be; **je ne serai pas ici demain** I won't be here tomorrow

♦ vb aux **1** to have; to be; **~ arrivé/allé** to have arrived/gone; **il est parti** he has left, he has gone

2 (forme passive) to be; **~ fait par** to be made by; **il a été promu** he has been promoted

3 (+à: obligation): **c'est à réparer** it needs repairing; **c'est à essayer** it should be tried

♦ vb impers **1**: **il est +adjectif** it is +adjective; **il est impossible de le faire** it's impossible to do it

2 (heure, date): **il est 10 heures** it is ou it's 10 o'clock

3 (*emphatique*): **c'est moi** it's me; **c'est à lui de le faire** it's up to him to do it

étreindre [etʀɛ̃dʀ(ə)] *vt* to clutch, grip; (*amoureusement, amicalement*) to embrace; **s'~** *vi* to embrace

étrenner [etʀene] *vt* to use (*ou* wear) for the first time

étrennes [etʀɛn] *nfpl* Christmas box *sg*

étrier [etʀije] *nm* stirrup

étriller [etʀije] *vt* (*cheval*) to curry; (*fam: battre*) to slaughter (*fig*)

étriqué, e [etʀike] *adj* skimpy

étroit, e [etʀwa, -wat] *adj* narrow; (*vêtement*) tight; (*fig: serré*) close, tight; **à l'~** cramped; **~ d'esprit** narrow-minded

étude [etyd] *nf* studying; (*ouvrage, rapport*) study; (*de notaire: bureau*) office; (: *charge*) practice; (SCOL: *salle de travail*) study room; **~s** *nfpl* (SCOL) studies; **être à l'~** (*projet etc*) to be under consideration; **faire des ~s (de droit/médecine)** to study (law/medicine)

étudiant, e [etydjɑ̃, -ɑ̃t] *nm/f* student

étudié, e [etydje] *adj* (*démarche*) studied; (*système*) carefully designed; (*prix*) keen

étudier [etydje] *vt, vi* to study

étui [etɥi] *nm* case

étuve [etyv] *nf* steamroom

étuvée [etyve] : **à l'~** *adv* braised

eu, eue [y] *pp de* **avoir**

euh [ø] *excl* er

Europe [øʀɔp] *nf*: **l'~** Europe; **européen, ne** *adj, nm/f* European

eus *etc vb voir* **avoir**

eux [ø] *pron* (*sujet*) they; (*objet*) them

évacuer [evakɥe] *vt* to evacuate

évader [evade]: **s'~** *vi* to escape

évangile [evɑ̃ʒil] *nm* gospel

évanouir [evanwiʀ]: **s'~** *vi* to faint; (*disparaître*) to vanish, disappear

évanouissement [evanwismɑ̃] *nm* (*syncope*) fainting fit; (*dans un accident*) loss of consciousness

évaporer [evapɔʀe]: **s'~** *vi* to evaporate

évaser [evaze] *vt* (*tuyau*) to widen, open out; (*jupe, pantalon*) to flare

évasif, ive [evazif, -iv] *adj* evasive

évasion [evazjɔ̃] *nf* escape

évêché [eveʃe] *nm* bishopric; bishop's palace

éveil [evɛj] *nm* awakening; **être en ~** to be alert

éveillé, e [eveje] *adj* awake; (*vif*) alert, sharp

éveiller [eveje] *vt* to (a)waken; **s'~** *vi* to (a)waken; (*fig*) to be aroused

événement [evenmɑ̃] *nm* event

éventail [evɑ̃taj] *nm* fan; (*choix*) range

éventaire [evɑ̃tɛʀ] *nm* stall, stand

éventer [evɑ̃te] *vt* (*secret*) to uncover; **s'~** *vi* (*parfum*) to go stale

éventrer [evɑ̃tʀe] *vt* to disembowel; (*fig*) to tear *ou* rip open

éventualité [evɑ̃tɥalite] *nf* eventuality; possibility; **dans l'~ de** in the event of

éventuel, le [evɑ̃tɥɛl] *adj* possible; **éventuellement** *adv* possibly

évêque [evɛk] *nm* bishop

évertuer [evɛʀtɥe]: **s'~** *vi*: **s'~ à faire** to try very hard to do

éviction [eviksjɔ̃] *nf* ousting; (*de locataire*) eviction

évidemment [evidamɑ̃] *adv* obviously

évidence [evidɑ̃s] *nf* obviousness; obvious fact; **de toute ~** quite obviously *ou* evidently; **en ~** conspicuous; **mettre en ~** to highlight; to bring to the fore; **évident, e** [evidɑ̃, -ɑ̃t] *adj* obvious, evident

évider [evide] *vt* to scoop out

évier [evje] *nm* (kitchen) sink

évincer [evɛ̃se] *vt* to oust

éviter [evite] *vt* to avoid; **~ de faire/que qch ne se passe** to avoid doing/sth happening; **~ qch à qn** to spare sb sth

évolué, e [evolɥe] *adj* advanced

évoluer [evolɥe] *vi* (*enfant, maladie*) to develop; (*situation, moralement*) to evolve, develop; (*aller et venir: danseur etc*) to move about, circle; **évolution** *nf* development; evolution

évoquer [evɔke] *vt* to call to mind, evoke; (*mentionner*) to mention

ex... [ɛks] *préfixe* ex-

exact, e [ɛgzakt] *adj* (*précis*) exact, accurate, precise; (*correct*) correct; (*ponctuel*) punctual; **l'heure ~e** the right *ou* exact time; **exactement** *adv* exactly, accurately, precisely; correctly; (*c'est cela même*) exactly

ex aequo [ɛgzeko] *adj* equally placed

exagéré, e [ɛgzaʒeʀe] *adj* (*prix etc*) excessive

exagérer [ɛgzaʒeʀe] *vt* to exaggerate ♦ *vi* (*abuser*) to go too far; to overstep the mark; (*déformer les faits*) to exaggerate

exalter [ɛgzalte] *vt* (*enthousiasmer*) to excite, elate; (*glorifier*) to exalt

examen [ɛgzamɛ̃] *nm* examination; (SCOL) exam, examination; **à l'~** under consideration; (COMM) on approval

examiner [ɛgzamine] *vt* to examine

exaspérant, e [ɛgzaspeʀɑ̃, -ɑ̃t] *adj* exasperating

exaspérer [ɛgzaspeʀe] *vt* to exasperate; to exacerbate

exaucer [ɛgzose] *vt* (*vœu*) to grant

excédent [ɛksedɑ̃] *nm* surplus; **en ~** surplus; **~ de bagages** excess luggage

excéder [ɛksede] *vt* (*dépasser*) to exceed; (*agacer*) to exasperate

excellence [ɛksɛlɑ̃s] *nf* (*titre*) Excellency

excellent, e [ɛksɛlɑ̃, -ɑ̃t] *adj* excellent

excentrique [ɛksɑ̃tʀik] *adj* eccentric;

(quartier) outlying

excepté, e [ɛksɛpte] *adj, prép*: **les élèves ~s, ~ les élèves** except for the pupils; **~ si** except if

exception [ɛksɛpsjɔ̃] *nf* exception; **à l'~ de** except for, with the exception of; **d'~** *(mesure, loi)* special, exceptional; **exceptionnel, le** *adj* exceptional

excès [ɛksɛ] *nm* surplus ♦ *nmpl* excesses; **à l'~** to excess; **~ de vitesse** speeding *no pl*; **excessif, ive** *adj* excessive

excitant, e [ɛksitɑ̃, -ɑ̃t] *adj* exciting ♦ *nm* stimulant; **excitation** [ɛksitasjɔ̃] *nf (état)* excitement

exciter [ɛksite] *vt* to excite; *(suj: café etc)* to stimulate; **s'~** *vi* to get excited

exclamation [ɛksklamasjɔ̃] *nf* exclamation

exclamer [ɛksklame]: **s'~** *vi* to exclaim

exclure [ɛksklyR] *vt (faire sortir)* to expel; *(ne pas compter)* to exclude, leave out; *(rendre impossible)* to exclude, rule out; **il est exclu que** it's out of the question that ...; **il n'est pas exclu que** ..., it's not impossible that ...; **exclusif, ive** *adj* exclusive; **exclusion** *nf* expulsion; **à l'exclusion de** with the exclusion *ou* exception of; **exclusivité** *nf (COMM)* exclusive rights *pl*; **film passant en exclusivité à** film showing only at

excursion [ɛkskyRsjɔ̃] *nf (en autocar)* excursion, trip; *(à pied)* walk, hike

excuse [ɛkskyz] *nf* excuse; **~s** *nfpl (regret)* apology *sg*, apologies

excuser [ɛkskyze] *vt* to excuse; **s'~ (de)** to apologize (for); **"excusez-moi"** "I'm sorry"; *(pour attirer l'attention)* "excuse me"

exécrable [ɛgzekRabl(ə)] *adj* atrocious

exécrer [ɛgzekRe] *vt* to loathe, abhor

exécuter [ɛgzekyte] *vt (prisonnier)* to execute; *(tâche etc)* to execute, carry out; *(MUS: jouer)* to perform, execute; *(INFORM)* to run; **s'~** *vi* to comply; **exécutif, ive** *adj, nm (POL)* executive; **exécution** *nf* execution; carrying out; **mettre à exécution** to carry out

exemplaire [ɛgzɑ̃plɛR] *nm* copy

exemple [ɛgzɑ̃pl(ə)] *nm* example; **par ~** for instance, for example; **donner l'~** to set an example; **prendre ~ sur** to take as a model; **à l'~ de** just like

exempt, e [ɛgzɑ̃, -ɑ̃t] *adj*: **~ de** *(dispensé de)* exempt from; *(sans)* free from

exercer [ɛgzɛRse] *vt (pratiquer)* to exercise, practise; *(prérogative)* to exercise; *(influence, contrôle)* to exert; *(former)* to exercise, train; **s'~** *vi (sportif, musicien)* to practise; *(se faire sentir: pression etc)* to be exerted

exercice [ɛgzɛRsis] *nm (tâche, travail)* exercise; **l'~** exercise; *(MIL)* drill; **en ~** *(juge)* in office; *(médecin)* practising

exhaustif, ive [ɛgzostif, -iv] *adj* exhaustive

exhiber [ɛgzibe] *vt (montrer: papiers, certificat)* to present, produce; *(péj)* to display, flaunt; **s'~** *vi* to parade; *(suj: exhibitionniste)* to expose o.s.

exhorter [ɛgzɔRte] *vt* to urge

exigeant, e [ɛgziʒɑ̃, -ɑ̃t] *adj* demanding; *(péj)* hard to please

exigence [ɛgziʒɑ̃s] *nf* demand, requirement

exiger [ɛgziʒe] *vt* to demand, require

exigu, ë [ɛgzigy] *adj (lieu)* cramped, tiny

exil [ɛgzil] *nm* exile; **exiler** *vt* to exile; **s'~er** *vi* to go into exile

existence [ɛgzistɑ̃s] *nf* existence

exister [ɛgziste] *vi* to exist; **il existe un/des** there is a/are (some)

exonérer [ɛgzɔneRe] *vt*: **~ de** to exempt from

exorbitant, e [ɛgzɔRbitɑ̃, -ɑ̃t] *adj (somme, nombre)* exorbitant

exorbité, e [ɛgzɔRbite] *adj*: **yeux ~s** bulging eyes

exotique [ɛgzɔtik] *adj* exotic

expatrier [ɛkspatRije] *vt*: **s'~** to leave one's country

expectative [ɛkspɛktativ] *nf*: **être dans l'~** to be still waiting

expédient [ɛkspedjɑ̃] *(péj) nm* expedient; **vivre d'~s** to live by one's wits

expédier [ɛkspedje] *vt (lettre, paquet)* to send; *(troupes)* to dispatch; *(péj: travail etc)* to dispose of, dispatch; **expéditeur, trice** *nm/f* sender

expédition [ɛkspedisjɔ̃] *nf* sending; *(scientifique, sportive, MIL)* expedition

expérience [ɛkspeRjɑ̃s] *nf (de la vie)* experience; *(scientifique)* experiment

expérimenté, e [ɛkspeRimɑ̃te] *adj* experienced

expérimenter [ɛkspeRimɑ̃te] *vt* to test out, experiment with

expert, e [ɛkspɛR, -ɛRt(ə)] *adj, nm* expert; **~ en assurances** insurance valuer; **expert-comptable** *nm* ≈ chartered accountant *(BRIT)*, ≈ certified public accountant *(US)*

expertise [ɛkspɛRtiz] *nf* valuation; assessment; valuer's *(ou* assessor's*)* report; *(JUR)* (forensic) examination

expertiser [ɛkspɛRtize] *vt (objet de valeur)* to value; *(voiture accidentée etc)* to assess damage to

expier [ɛkspje] *vt* to expiate, atone for

expirer [ɛkspiRe] *vi (prendre fin, mourir)* to expire; *(respirer)* to breathe out

explicatif, ive [ɛksplikatif, -iv] *adj* explanatory

explication [ɛksplikasjɔ̃] *nf* explanation; *(discussion)* discussion; argument; **~ de texte** *(SCOL)* critical analysis

explicite [ɛksplisit] *adj* explicit

expliquer [ɛksplike] *vt* to explain; **s'~** to explain (o.s.); *(discuter)* to discuss things; to have it out; **son erreur s'explique** one can understand his mistake

exploit [ɛksplwa] *nm* exploit, feat

exploitation [ɛksplwatasjɔ̃] *nf* exploitation; running; ~ **agricole** farming concern; **exploiter** [ɛksplwate] *vt* (*mine*) to exploit, work; (*entreprise, ferme*) to run, operate; (*clients, ouvriers, erreur, don*) to exploit

explorer [ɛksplɔʀe] *vt* to explore

exploser [ɛksploze] *vi* to explode, blow up; (*engin explosif*) to go off; (*fig: joie, colère*) to burst out, explode; **explosif, ive** *adj, nm* explosive; **explosion** *nf* explosion

exportateur, trice [ɛkspɔʀtatœʀ, -tʀis] *adj* export *cpd*, exporting ♦ *nm* exporter

exportation [ɛkspɔʀtasjɔ̃] *nf* exportation; export

exporter [ɛkspɔʀte] *vt* to export

exposant [ɛkspozɑ̃] *nm* exhibitor

exposé, e [ɛkspoze] *nm* talk ♦ *adj*: ~ **au sud** facing south; **bien** ~ well situated

exposer [ɛkspoze] *vt* (*marchandise*) to display; (*peinture*) to exhibit, show; (*parler de*) to explain, set out; (*mettre en danger, orienter, PHOTO*) to expose; **exposition** *nf* (*manifestation*) exhibition; (*PHOTO*) exposure

exprès[1] [ɛkspʀɛ] *adv* (*délibérément*) on purpose; (*spécialement*) specially

exprès[2], **esse** [ɛkspʀɛs] *adj* (*ordre, défense*) express, formal ♦ *adj inv* (*PTT*) express ♦ *adv* express

express [ɛkspʀɛs] *adj, nm*: (**café**) ~ espresso (coffee); (**train**) ~ fast train

expressément [ɛkspʀɛsemɑ̃] *adv* expressly; specifically

expression [ɛkspʀɛsjɔ̃] *nf* expression

exprimer [ɛkspʀime] *vt* (*sentiment, idée*) to express; (*jus, liquide*) to press out; **s'**~ *vi* (*personne*) to express o.s.

exproprier [ɛkspʀɔpʀije] *vt* to buy up by compulsory purchase, expropriate

expulser [ɛkspylse] *vt* to expel; (*locataire*) to evict; (*SPORT*) to send off

exquis, e [ɛkski, -iz] *adj* exquisite; delightful

exsangue [ɛksɑ̃g] *adj* bloodless, drained of blood

extase [ɛkstaz] *nf* ecstasy; **extasier: s'extasier** *vi* to go into raptures over

extension [ɛkstɑ̃sjɔ̃] *nf* (*d'un muscle, ressort*) stretching; (*fig*) extension; expansion

exténuer [ɛkstenɥe] *vt* to exhaust

extérieur, e [ɛksteʀjœʀ] *adj* (*porte, mur etc*) outer, outside; (*au dehors: escalier, w.- c*) outside; (*commerce*) foreign; (*influences*) external; (*apparent: calme, gaieté etc*) surface *cpd* ♦ *nm* (*d'une maison, d'un récipient etc*) outside, exterior; (*apparence*) exterior; (*d'un groupe social*): **l'**~ the outside world; **à l'**~ outside; (*à l'étranger*) abroad; **extérieurement** *adv* on the outside; (*en apparence*) on the surface

exterminer [ɛkstɛʀmine] *vt* to exterminate, wipe out

externat [ɛkstɛʀna] *nm* day school

externe [ɛkstɛʀn(ə)] *adj* external, outer ♦ *nm/f* (*MÉD*) non-resident medical student (*BRIT*), extern (*US*); (*SCOL*) day pupil

extincteur [ɛkstɛ̃ktœʀ] *nm* (fire) extinguisher

extinction [ɛkstɛ̃ksjɔ̃] *nf*: ~ **de voix** loss of voice

extorquer [ɛkstɔʀke] *vt* to extort

extra [ɛkstʀa] *adj inv* first-rate; top-quality ♦ *nm inv* extra help

extrader [ɛkstʀade] *vt* to extradite

extraire [ɛkstʀɛʀ] *vt* to extract; **extrait** *nm* extract

extraordinaire [ɛkstʀaɔʀdinɛʀ] *adj* extraordinary; (*POL: mesures etc*) special

extravagant, e [ɛkstʀavagɑ̃, -ɑ̃t] *adj* extravagant; wild

extraverti, e [ɛkstʀavɛʀti] *adj* extrovert

extrême [ɛkstʀɛm] *adj, nm* extreme; **extrêmement** *adv* extremely; **extrême-onction** *nf* last rites *pl*; **Extrême-Orient** *nm* Far East

extrémité [ɛkstʀemite] *nf* end; (*situation*) straits *pl*, plight; (*geste désespéré*) extreme action; ~**s** *nfpl* (*pieds et mains*) extremities; **à la dernière** ~ on the point of death

exutoire [ɛgzytwaʀ] *nm* outlet, release

F f

F *abr* = **franc**

fa [fa] *nm inv* (*MUS*) F; (*en chantant la gamme*) fa

fable [fabl(ə)] *nf* fable

fabricant [fabʀikɑ̃] *nm* manufacturer

fabrication [fabʀikasjɔ̃] *nf* manufacture

fabrique [fabʀik] *nf* factory

fabriquer [fabʀike] *vt* to make; (*industriellement*) to manufacture; (*fig*): **qu'est-ce qu'il fabrique?** what is he doing?

fabulation [fabylasjɔ̃] *nf* fantasizing

fac [fak] (*fam*) *abr f* (*SCOL*) = **faculté**

façade [fasad] *nf* front, façade

face [fas] *nf* face; (*fig: aspect*) side ♦ *adj*: **le côté** ~ heads; **perdre la** ~ to lose face; **en** ~ **de** opposite; (*fig*) in front of; **de** ~ from the front; **face on**; ~ **à** facing; (*fig*) faced with, in the face of; **faire** ~ **à** to face; ~ **à** ~ *adv* facing each other ♦ *nm inv* encounter

facétieux, euse [fasesjø, -øz] *adj* mischievous

fâché, e [faʃe] *adj* angry; (*désolé*) sorry

fâcher [faʃe] *vt* to anger; **se ~** *vi* to get angry; **se ~ avec** (*se brouiller*) to fall out with

fâcheux, euse [faʃø, -øz] *adj* unfortunate, regrettable

facile [fasil] *adj* easy; (*accommodant*) easygoing; **~ment** *adv* easily; **facilité** *nf* easiness; (*disposition, don*) aptitude; **facilités** *nfpl* (*possibilités*) facilities; **facilités de paiement** easy terms; **faciliter** *vt* to make easier

façon [fasɔ̃] *nf* (*manière*) way; (*d'une robe etc*) making-up; cut; **~s** *nfpl* (*péj*) fuss *sg*; **de quelle ~?** (in) what way?; **de ~ à/à ce que** so as to/that; **de toute ~** anyway, in any case; **~ner** [fasɔne] *vt* (*fabriquer*) to manufacture; (*travailler: matière*) to shape, fashion; (*fig*) to mould, shape

facteur, trice [faktœʀ, -tʀis] *nm/f* postman(woman) (*BRIT*), mailman(woman) (*US*) ♦ *nm* (*MATH, fig: élément*) factor; **~ de pianos** piano maker

factice [faktis] *adj* artificial

faction [faksjɔ̃] *nf* faction; (*MIL*) guard *ou* sentry (duty); watch

facture [faktyʀ] *nf* (*à payer: gén*) bill; (*: COMM*) invoice; (*d'un artisan, artiste*) technique, workmanship; **facturer** *vt* to invoice

facultatif, ive [fakyltatif, -iv] *adj* optional; (*arrêt de bus*) request *cpd*

faculté [fakylte] *nf* (*intellectuelle, d'université*) faculty; (*pouvoir, possibilité*) power

fade [fad] *adj* insipid

faible [fɛbl(ə)] *adj* weak; (*voix, lumière, vent*) faint; (*rendement, intensité, revenu etc*) low ♦ *nm* weak point; (*pour quelqu'un*) weakness, soft spot; **~ d'esprit** feebleminded; **faiblesse** *nf* weakness; **faiblir** *vi* to weaken; (*lumière*) to dim; (*vent*) to drop

faïence [fajɑ̃s] *nf* earthenware *no pl*; piece of earthenware

faignant, e [fɛɲɑ̃, -ɑ̃t] *nm/f* = **fainéant, e**

faille [faj] *vb voir* **falloir** ♦ *nf* (*GÉO*) fault; (*fig*) flaw, weakness

faillir [fajiʀ] *vi*: **j'ai failli tomber** I almost *ou* very nearly fell

faillite [fajit] *nf* bankruptcy

faim [fɛ̃] *nf* hunger; **avoir ~** to be hungry; **rester sur sa ~** (*aussi fig*) to be left wanting more

fainéant, e [fɛneɑ̃, -ɑ̃t] *nm/f* idler, loafer

<hr>

── MOT CLÉ

faire [fɛʀ] *vt* **1** (*fabriquer, être l'auteur de*) to make; **~ du vin/une offre/un film** to make wine/an offer/a film; **~ du bruit** to make a noise

2 (*effectuer: travail, opération*) to do; **que faites-vous?** (*quel métier etc*) what do you

do?; (*quelle activité: au moment de la question*) what are you doing?; **~ la lessive** to do the washing

3 (*études*) to do; (*sport, musique*) to play; **~ du droit/du français** to do law/French; **~ du rugby/piano** to play rugby/the piano

4 (*simuler*): **~ le malade/l'ignorant** to act the invalid/the fool

5 (*transformer, avoir un effet sur*): **~ de qn un frustré/avocat** to make sb frustrated/a lawyer; **ça ne me fait rien** (*m'est égal*) I don't care *ou* mind; (*me laisse froid*) it has no effect on me; **ça ne fait rien** it doesn't matter; **~ que** (*impliquer*) to mean that

6 (*calculs, prix, mesures*): **2 et 2 font 4** 2 and 2 are *ou* make 4; **ça fait 10 m/15F** it's 10 m/15F; **je vous le fais 10F** I'll let you have it for 10F

7: **qu'a-t-il fait de sa valise?** what has he done with his case?

8: **ne ~ que**: **il ne fait que critiquer** (*sans cesse*) all he (ever) does is criticize; (*seulement*) he's only criticizing

9 (*dire*) to say; **vraiment? fit-il** really? he said

10 (*maladie*) to have; **~ du diabète** to have diabetes *sg*

♦ *vi* **1** (*agir, s'y prendre*) to act, do; **il faut ~ vite** (*ou vous etc*) must act quickly; **comment a-t-il fait pour?** how did he manage to?; **faites comme chez vous** make yourself at home

2 (*paraître*) to look; **~ vieux/démodé** to look old/old-fashioned; **ça fait bien** it looks good

♦ *vb substitut* to do; **ne le casse pas comme je l'ai fait** don't break it as I did; **je peux le voir? - faites!** can I see it? - please do!

♦ *vb impers* **1**: **il fait beau** *etc* the weather is fine *etc*; *voir aussi* **jour froid** *etc*

2 (*temps écoulé, durée*): **ça fait 2 ans qu'il est parti** it's 2 years since he left; **ça fait 2 ans qu'il y est** he's been there for 2 years

♦ *vb semi-aux* **1**: **~ +infinitif** (*action directe*) to make; **~ tomber/bouger qch** to make sth fall/move; **~ démarrer un moteur/ chauffer de l'eau** to start up an engine/ heat some water; **cela fait dormir** it makes you sleep; **~ travailler les enfants** to make the children work *ou* get the children to work

2 (*indirectement, par un intermédiaire*): **~ réparer qch** to get *ou* have sth repaired; **~ punir les enfants** to have the children punished **se ~** *vi* **1** (*vin, fromage*) to mature

2: **cela se fait beaucoup/ne se fait pas** it's done a lot/not done

3: **se ~ +nom ou pron**: **se faire une jupe** to make o.s. a skirt; **se ~ des amis** to make friends; **se ~ du souci** to worry; **il**

ne s'en fait pas he doesn't worry
4: **se ~ +adj** (*devenir*): **se faire vieux** to be
getting old; (*délibérément*): **se ~ beau** to
do o.s. up
5: **se ~ à** (*s'habituer*) to get used to; **je
n'arrive pas à me ~ à la nourriture/au climat** I can't get used to the food/climate
6: **se ~ +infinitif**: **se ~ examiner la vue/
opérer** to have one's eyes tested/have an
operation; **se ~ couper les cheveux** to get
one's hair cut; **il va se ~ tuer/punir** he's
going to get himself killed/get (himself) punished; **il s'est fait aider** he got somebody
to help him; **il s'est fait aider par Simon**
he got Simon to help him; **se ~ ~
un vêtement** to get a garment made for
o.s.
7 (*impersonnel*): **comment se fait-il/
faisait-il que?** how is it/was it that?

faire-part [fɛʀpaʀ] *nm inv* announcement
(of birth, marriage etc)
faisable [fəzabl(ə)] *adj* feasible
faisan, e [fəzɑ̃, -an] *nm/f* pheasant
faisandé, e [fəzɑ̃de] *adj* high (*bad*)
faisceau, x [fɛso] *nm* (*de lumière etc*)
beam; (*de branches etc*) bundle
faisons *vb voir* **faire**
fait, e [fɛ, fɛt] *adj* (*mûr: fromage, melon*)
ripe ♦ *nm* (*événement*) event, occurrence;
(*réalité, donnée*) fact; **c'en est ~ de** that's
the end of; **être le ~ de** (*causé par*) to be
the work of; **être au ~ (de)** to be informed
(of); **au ~** (*à propos*) by the way; **en venir
au ~** to get to the point; **de ~ adj** (*opposé
à: de droit*) de facto ♦ *adv* in fact; **du ~ de
ceci/qu'il a menti** because of ou on account of this/his having lied; **de ce ~** for
this reason; **en ~** in fact; **en ~ de repas**
by way of a meal; **prendre ~ et cause
pour qn** to support sb, side with sb; **prendre qn sur le ~** to catch sb in the act; **~
divers** news item; **~s et gestes: les ~s et
gestes de qn** sb's actions ou doings
faîte [fɛt] *nm* top; (*fig*) pinnacle, height
faites *vb voir* **faire**
faitout [fɛtu] *nm* = **fait-tout**
fait-tout [fɛtu] *nm inv* stewpot
falaise [falɛz] *nf* cliff
fallacieux, euse [falasjø, -øz] *adj* falla-
cious; deceptive; illusory
falloir [falwaʀ] *vb impers*: **il va ~ 100 F**
we'll (ou I'll) need 100 F; **s'en ~**: **il s'en
est fallu de 100 F/5 minutes** we (ou they)
were 100 F short/5 minutes late (ou early);
il s'en faut de beaucoup qu'il soit he is
far from being; **il s'en est fallu de peu que
cela n'arrive** it very nearly happened; **ou
peu s'en faut** or as good as; **il doit ~ du
temps** that must take time; **il me faudrait
100 F** I would need 100 F; **il vous faut
tourner à gauche après l'église** you have

to turn left past the church; **nous avons ce
qu'il (nous) faut** we have what we need; **il
faut qu'il parte/a fallu qu'il parte** (*obligation*) he has to ou must leave/had to leave;
il a fallu le faire it had to be done
falsifier [falsifje] *vt* to falsify; to doctor
famé, e [fame] *adj*: **mal ~** disreputable, of
ill repute
famélique [famelik] *adj* half-starved
fameux, euse [famø, -øz] *adj* (*illustre*) famous; (*bon: repas, plat etc*) first-rate, first-
class; (*valeur intensive*) real, downright
familial, e, aux [familjal, -o] *adj* family
cpd; **familiale** *nf* (*AUTO*) estate car (*BRIT*),
station wagon (*US*)
familiarité [familjaʀite] *nf* informality; fa-
miliarity; **~s** *nfpl* (*privautés*) familiarities
familier, ère [familje, -ɛʀ] *adj* (*connu, impertinent*) familiar; (*dénotant une certaine intimité*) informal, friendly; (*LING*) informal,
colloquial ♦ *nm* regular (visitor)
famille [famij] *nf* family; **il a de la ~ à Paris** he has relatives in Paris
famine [famin] *nf* famine
fanatique [fanatik] *adj* fanatical ♦ *nm/f* fanatic; **fanatisme** *nm* fanaticism
faner [fane]: **se ~** *vi* to fade
fanfare [fɑ̃faʀ] *nf* (*orchestre*) brass band;
(*musique*) fanfare
fanfaron, ne [fɑ̃faʀɔ̃, -ɔn] *nm/f* braggart
fanion [fanjɔ̃] *nm* pennant
fantaisie [fɑ̃tezi] *nf* (*spontanéité*) fancy,
imagination; (*caprice*) whim; extravagance ♦
adj: **bijou/pain (de) ~** costume jewellery/
fancy bread; **fantaisiste** *adj* (*péj*) unorthodox, eccentric ♦ *nm/f* (*de music-hall*) variety
artist ou entertainer
fantasme [fɑ̃tasm(ə)] *nm* fantasy
fantasque [fɑ̃task(ə)] *adj* whimsical, capricious; fantastic
fantastique [fɑ̃tastik] *adj* fantastic
fantôme [fɑ̃tom] *nm* ghost, phantom
faon [fɑ̃] *nm* fawn
farce [faʀs(ə)] *nf* (*viande*) stuffing; (*blague*)
(practical) joke; (*THÉÂTRE*) farce; **farcir** *vt*
(*viande*) to stuff
fard [faʀ] *nm* make-up
fardeau, x [faʀdo] *nm* burden
farder [faʀde] *vt* to make up
farfelu, e [faʀfəly] *adj* hare-brained
farine [faʀin] *nf* flour; **farineux, euse** *adj*
(*sauce, pomme*) floury ♦ *nmpl* (*aliments*)
starchy foods
farouche [faʀuʃ] *adj* shy, timid; savage,
wild; fierce
fart [faʀ(t)] *nm* (ski) wax
fascicule [fasikyl] *nm* volume
fasciner [fasine] *vt* to fascinate
fascisme [faʃism(ə)] *nm* fascism
fasse *etc vb voir* **faire**
faste [fast(ə)] *nm* splendour ♦ *adj*: **c'est un
jour ~** it's his (ou our etc) lucky day

fastidieux, euse [fastidjø, -øz] *adj* tedious, tiresome

fastueux, euse [fastɥø, -øz] *adj* sumptuous, luxurious

fatal, e [fatal] *adj* fatal; (*inévitable*) inevitable; **fatalité** *nf* fate; fateful coincidence; inevitability

fatidique [fatidik] *adj* fateful

fatigant, e [fatigã, -ãt] *adj* tiring; (*agaçant*) tiresome

fatigue [fatig] *nf* tiredness, fatigue

fatigué, e [fatige] *adj* tired

fatiguer [fatige] *vt* to tire, make tired; (*TECH*) to put a strain on, strain; (*fig*: *importuner*) to wear out ♦ *vi* (*moteur*) to labour, strain; **se ~** to get tired; to tire o.s. (out)

fatras [fatʀa] *nm* jumble, hotchpotch

fatuité [fatɥite] *nf* conceitedness, smugness

faubourg [fobuʀ] *nm* suburb

fauché, e [foʃe] (*fam*) *adj* broke

faucher [foʃe] *vt* (*herbe*) to cut; (*champs, blés*) to reap; (*fig*) to cut down; to mow down

faucille [fosij] *nf* sickle

faucon [fokɔ̃] *nm* falcon, hawk

faudra *vb voir* **falloir**

faufiler [fofile] *vt* to tack, baste; **se ~** *vi*: **se ~ dans** to edge one's way into; **se ~ parmi/entre** to thread one's way among/between

faune [fon] *nf* (*ZOOL*) wildlife, fauna

faussaire [fosɛʀ] *nm* forger

fausse [fos] *adj voir* **faux**

faussement [fosmã] *adv* (*accuser*) wrongly, wrongfully; (*croire*) falsely

fausser [fose] *vt* (*objet*) to bend, buckle; (*fig*) to distort

fausseté [foste] *nf* wrongness; falseness

faut *vb voir* **falloir**

faute [fot] *nf* (*erreur*) mistake, error; (*péché, manquement*) misdemeanour; (*FOOTBALL etc*) offence; (*TENNIS*) fault; **c'est de sa/ma ~** it's his/my fault; **être en ~** to be in the wrong; **~ de** (*temps, argent*) for *ou* through lack of; **sans ~** without fail; **~ de frappe** typing error; **~ professionnelle** professional misconduct *no pl*

fauteuil [fotœj] *nm* armchair; **~ d'orchestre** seat in the front stalls; **~ roulant** wheelchair

fauteur [fotœʀ] *nm*: **~ de troubles** trouble-maker

fautif, ive [fotif, -iv] *adj* (*incorrect*) incorrect, inaccurate; (*responsable*) at fault, in the wrong; guilty

fauve [fov] *nm* wildcat ♦ *adj* (*couleur*) fawn

faux¹ [fo] *nf* scythe

faux², fausse [fo, fos] *adj* (*inexact*) wrong; (*piano, voix*) out of tune; (*falsifié*) fake; forged; (*sournois, postiche*) false ♦ *adv* (*MUS*) out of tune ♦ *nm* (*copie*) fake, forgery; (*opposé au vrai*): **le faux** falsehood; **faire faux bond à qn** to stand sb up; **fausse alerte** false alarm; **fausse couche** miscarriage; **faux frais** *nmpl* extras, incidental expenses; **faux pas** tripping *no pl*; (*fig*) faux pas; **faux témoignage** (*délit*) perjury; **faux-filet** *nm* sirloin; **faux-fuyant** *nm* equivocation; **faux-monnayeur** *nm* counterfeiter, forger

faveur [favœʀ] *nf* favour; **traitement de ~** preferential treatment; **à la ~ de** under cover of; thanks to; **en ~ de** in favour of

favorable [favɔʀabl(ə)] *adj* favourable

favori, te [favɔʀi, -it] *adj, nm/f* favourite; **~s** *nmpl* (*barbe*) sideboards (*BRIT*), sideburns

favoriser [favɔʀize] *vt* to favour

fax [faks] *nm* fax

fébrile [febʀil] *adj* feverish, febrile

fécond, e [fekɔ̃, -ɔ̃d] *adj* fertile; **~er** *vt* to fertilize; **~ité** *nf* fertility

fécule [fekyl] *nf* potato flour

féculent [fekylã] *nm* starchy food

fédéral, e, aux [federal, -o] *adj* federal

fée [fe] *nf* fairy; **~rie** *nf* enchantment; **~rique** *adj* magical, fairytale *cpd*

feignant, e [fɛɲã, -ãt] *nm/f* = **fainéant, e**

feindre [fɛ̃dʀ(ə)] *vt* to feign ♦ *vi* to dissemble; **~ de faire** to pretend to do

feinte [fɛ̃t] *nf* (*SPORT*) dummy

fêler [fele] *vt* to crack

félicitations [felisitasjɔ̃] *nfpl* congratulations

féliciter [felisite] *vt*: **~ qn (de)** to congratulate sb (on); **se ~ (de)** to congratulate o.s. (on)

félin, e [felɛ̃, -in] *adj* feline ♦ *nm* (big) cat

fêlure [felyʀ] *nf* crack

femelle [fəmɛl] *adj, nf* female

féminin, e [feminɛ̃, -in] *adj* feminine; (*sexe*) female; (*équipe, vêtements etc*) women's ♦ *nm* (*LING*) feminine; **féministe** *adj* feminist

femme [fam] *nf* woman; (*épouse*) wife; **~ au foyer** *nf* housewife; **~ de chambre** cleaning lady; **~ de ménage = femme de chambre**

fémur [femyʀ] *nm* femur, thighbone

fendre [fãdʀ(ə)] *vt* (*couper en deux*) to split; (*fissurer*) to crack; (*fig: traverser*) to cut through; to cleave through; **se ~** *vi* to crack

fenêtre [fənɛtʀ(ə)] *nf* window

fenouil [fənuj] *nm* fennel

fente [fãt] *nf* (*fissure*) crack; (*de boîte à lettres etc*) slit

féodal, e, aux [feɔdal, -o] *adj* feudal

fer [fɛʀ] *nm* iron; (*de cheval*) shoe; **~ à cheval** horseshoe; **~ (à repasser)** iron; **~ forgé** wrought iron

ferai *etc vb voir* **faire**

fer-blanc [fɛʀblã] *nm* tin(plate)

férié, e [feʀje] adj: **jour ~** public holiday

ferions etc vb voir **faire**

ferme [fɛʀm(ə)] adj firm ♦ adv (travailler etc) hard ♦ nf (exploitation) farm; (maison) farmhouse

fermé, e [fɛʀme] adj closed, shut; (gaz, eau etc) off; (fig: personne) uncommunicative; (: milieu) exclusive

fermenter [fɛʀmɑ̃te] vi to ferment

fermer [fɛʀme] vt to close, shut; (cesser l'exploitation de) to close down, shut down; (eau, lumière, électricité, robinet) to put off, turn off; (aéroport, route) to close ♦ vi to close, shut; to close down, shut down; **se ~** vi (yeux) to close, shut; (fleur, blessure) to close up

fermeté [fɛʀməte] nf firmness

fermeture [fɛʀmətyʀ] nf closing; shutting; closing ou shutting down; putting ou turning off; (dispositif) catch; fastening, fastener; **~ à glissière** = **fermeture éclair**; **~ éclair ®** zip (fastener) (BRIT), zipper (US)

fermier [fɛʀmje] nm farmer; **fermière** nf woman farmer; farmer's wife

fermoir [fɛʀmwaʀ] nm clasp

féroce [feʀɔs] adj ferocious, fierce

ferons vb voir **faire**

ferraille [feʀaj] nf scrap iron; **mettre à la ~** to scrap

ferré, e [fɛʀe] adj hobnailed; steel-tipped; (fam): **~ en** well up on, hot at; **ferrer** [fɛʀe] vt (cheval) to shoe

ferronnerie [fɛʀɔnʀi] nf ironwork

ferroviaire [fɛʀɔvjɛʀ] adj rail(way) cpd (BRIT), rail(road) cpd (US)

ferry(boat) [fɛʀe(bɔt)] nm ferry

fertile [fɛʀtil] adj fertile; **~ en incidents** eventful, packed with incidents

féru, e [feʀy] adj: **~ de** with a keen interest in

férule [feʀyl] nf: **être sous la ~ de qn** to be under sb's (iron) rule

fervent, e [fɛʀvɑ̃, -ɑ̃t] adj fervent

fesse [fɛs] nf buttock; **fessée** nf spanking

festin [fɛstɛ̃] nm feast

festival [fɛstival] nm festival

festoyer [fɛstwaje] vi to feast

fêtard [fɛtaʀ] (péj) nm high liver, merrymaker

fête [fɛt] nf (religieuse) feast; (publique) holiday; (en famille etc) celebration; (kermesse) fête, fair, festival; (du nom) feast day, name day; **faire la ~** to live it up; **faire ~ à qn** to give sb a warm welcome; **les ~s (de fin d'année)** the festive season; **la salle/le comité des ~s** the village hall/festival committee; **~ foraine** (fun)fair; **la F~ Nationale** the national holiday; **fêter** vt to celebrate; (personne) to have a celebration for

fétu [fety] nm: **~ de paille** wisp of straw

feu, x [fø] nm (gén) fire; (signal lumineux) light; (de cuisinière) ring; (sensation de brûlure) burning (sensation) ♦ adj inv: **son père** his late father; **~x** nmpl (éclat, lumière) fire sg; (AUTO) (traffic) lights; **au ~!** (incendie) fire!; **à ~ doux/vif** over a slow/brisk heat; **à petit ~** (CULIN) over a gentle heat; (fig) slowly; **faire ~** to fire; **prendre ~** to catch fire; **mettre le ~ à** to set fire to; **faire du ~** to make a fire; **avez-vous du ~?** (pour cigarette) have you (got) a light?; **~ arrière** rear light; **~ d'artifice** firework; (spectacle) fireworks pl; **~ de joie** bonfire; **~ rouge/vert/orange** red/green/amber (BRIT) ou yellow (US) light; **~x de brouillard** fog-lamps; **~x de croisement** dipped (BRIT) ou dimmed (US) headlights; **~x de position** sidelights; **~x de route** headlights

feuillage [fœjaʒ] nm foliage, leaves pl

feuille [fœj] nf (d'arbre) leaf; (de papier) sheet; **~ d'impôts** tax form; **~ de maladie** medical expenses claim form; **~ de paie** pay slip; **~ de vigne** (BOT) vine leaf; (sur statue) fig leaf; **~ volante** loose sheet

feuillet [fœjɛ] nm leaf

feuilleté, e [fœjte] adj (CULIN) flaky; (verre) laminated

feuilleter [fœjte] vt (livre) to leaf through

feuilleton [fœjtɔ̃] nm serial

feuillu, e [fœjy] adj leafy ♦ nm broadleaved tree

feutre [føtʀ(ə)] nm felt; (chapeau) felt hat; (aussi: stylo-~) felt-tip pen; **feutré, e** adj feltlike; (pas, voix) muffled

fève [fɛv] nf broad bean

février [fevʀije] nm February

fi [fi] excl: **faire ~ de** to snap one's fingers at

fiable [fjabl(ə)] adj reliable

fiacre [fjakʀ(ə)] nm (hackney) cab ou carriage

fiançailles [fjɑ̃saj] nfpl engagement sg

fiancé, e [fjɑ̃se] nm/f fiancé(fiancée) ♦ adj: **être ~ (à)** to be engaged (to)

fiancer [fjɑ̃se]: **se ~** vi to become engaged

fibre [fibʀ(ə)] nf fibre; **~ de verre** fibreglass, glass fibre

ficeler [fisle] vt to tie up

ficelle [fisɛl] nf string no pl; piece ou length of string

fiche [fiʃ] nf (pour fichier) (index) card; (formulaire) form; (ÉLEC) plug

ficher [fiʃe] vt (dans un fichier) to file; (POLICE) to put on file; (planter) to stick, drive; (fam) to do; to give; to stick ou shove; **se ~** (fam) to make fun of; not to care about; **fiche-(moi) le camp** (fam) clear off; **fiche-moi la paix** leave me alone

fichier [fiʃje] nm file; card index

fichu, e [fiʃy] pp de **ficher** (fam) ♦ adj (fam: fini, inutilisable) bust, done for; (: intensif) wretched, darned ♦ nm (foulard) (head)scarf; **mal ~** *(fam)* feeling lousy; useless

fictif, ive [fiktif, -iv] *adj* fictitious

fiction [fiksjɔ̃] *nf* fiction; *(fait imaginé)* invention

fidèle [fidɛl] *adj* faithful ♦ *nm/f (REL)*: **les ~s** the faithful *pl*; *(à l'église)* the congregation *sg*

fief [fjɛf] *nm* fief; *(fig)* preserve; stronghold

fier¹ [fje]: **se fier à** *vt* to trust

fier², fière [fjɛʀ] *adj* proud; **fierté** *nf* pride

fièvre [fjɛvʀ(ə)] *nf* fever; **avoir de la ~/39 de ~** to have a high temperature/a temperature of 39°C; **fiévreux, euse** *adj* feverish

figer [fiʒe] *vt* to congeal; to freeze, root to the spot; **se ~** *vi* to congeal; to freeze; *(institutions etc)* to become set, stop evolving

figue [fig] *nf* fig; **figuier** *nm* fig tree

figurant, e [figyʀɑ̃, -ɑ̃t] *nm/f (THÉÂTRE)* walk-on; *(CINÉMA)* extra

figure [figyʀ] *nf (visage)* face; *(image, tracé, forme, personnage)* figure; *(illustration)* picture, diagram; **faire ~ de** to look like

figuré, e [figyʀe] *adj (sens)* figurative

figurer [figyʀe] *vi* to appear ♦ *vt* to represent; **se ~ que** to imagine that

fil [fil] *nm (brin, fig: d'une histoire)* thread; *(du téléphone)* cable, wire; *(textile de lin)* linen; *(d'un couteau)* edge; **au ~ des années** with the passing of the years; **au ~ de l'eau** with the stream *ou* current; **coup de ~** phone call; **~ à coudre** (sewing) thread; **~ à pêche** fishing line; **~ à plomb** plumbline; **~ de fer** wire; **~ de fer barbelé** barbed wire; **~ électrique** electric wire

filament [filamɑ̃] *nm (ÉLEC)* filament; *(de liquide)* trickle, thread

filandreux, euse [filɑ̃dʀø, -øz] *adj* stringy

filasse [filas] *adj inv* white blond

filature [filatyʀ] *nf (fabrique)* mill; *(policière)* shadowing *no pl*, tailing *no pl*

file [fil] *nf* line; *(AUTO)* lane; **en ~ indienne** in single file; **à la ~** *(d'affilée)* in succession; **~ (d'attente)** queue *(BRIT)*, line *(US)*

filer [file] *vt (tissu, toile)* to spin; *(prendre en filature)* to shadow, tail; *(fam: donner)*: **~ qch à qn** to slip sb sth ♦ *vi (bas, liquide, pâte)* to run; *(aller vite)* to fly past; *(fam: partir)* to make off; **~ doux** to toe the line

filet [filɛ] *nm* net; *(CULIN)* fillet; *(d'eau, de sang)* trickle; *(à provisions)* string bag

filiale [filjal] *nf (COMM)* subsidiary

filière [filjɛʀ] *nf*: **passer par la ~** to go through the (administrative) channels; **suivre la ~** *(dans sa carrière)* to work one's way up (through the hierarchy)

filiforme [filifɔʀm(ə)] *adj* spindly; threadlike

filigrane [filigʀan] *nm (d'un billet, timbre)* watermark; **en ~** *(fig)* showing just beneath the surface

fille [fij] *nf* girl; *(opposé à fils)* daughter; **vieille ~** old maid; **fillette** *nf* (little) girl

filleul, e [fijœl] *nm/f* godchild, godson/daughter

film [film] *nm (pour photo)* (roll of) film; *(œuvre)* film, picture, movie; *(couche)* film; **~ d'animation** animated film; **~ policier** thriller

filon [filɔ̃] *nm* vein, lode; *(fig)* lucrative line, money spinner

fils [fis] *nm* son; **~ à papa** daddy's boy

filtre [filtʀ(ə)] *nm* filter; **~ à air** *(AUTO)* air filter; **filtrer** *vt* to filter; *(fig: candidats, visiteurs)* to screen ♦ *vi* to filter (through)

fin¹ [fɛ̃] *nf* end; **fins** *nfpl (but)* ends; **prendre fin** to come to an end; **mettre fin à** to put an end to; **à la fin** in the end, eventually; **sans fin** *adj* endless ♦ *adv* endlessly

fin², e [fɛ̃, fin] *adj (papier, couche, fil)* thin; *(cheveux, poudre, pointe, visage)* fine; *(taille)* neat, slim; *(esprit, remarque)* subtle; shrewd ♦ *adv (moudre, couper)* finely; **un fin tireur** a crack shot; **avoir la vue/l'ouïe fine** to have sharp *ou* keen eyes/ears; **vin fin** fine wine; **fin gourmet** gourmet; **fin prêt** quite ready; **fines herbes** mixed herbs

final, e [final] *adj* final ♦ *nm (MUS)* finale; **finale** *nf* final; **quarts de finale** quarter finals; **8èmes/16èmes de finale** 2nd/1st round *(in knock-out competition)*; **finalement** *adv* finally, in the end; *(après tout)* after all

finance [finɑ̃s] *nf* finance; **~s** *nfpl (situation)* finances; *(activités)* finance *sg*; **moyennant ~** for a fee; **financer** *vt* to finance; **financier, ière** *adj* financial

finaud, e [fino, -od] *adj* wily

fine [fin] *nf (alcool)* liqueur brandy

finesse [fines] *nf* thinness; fineness; neatness, slimness; subtlety; shrewdness

fini, e [fini] *adj* finished; *(MATH)* finite; *(intensif)*: **un menteur ~** a liar through and through ♦ *nm (d'un objet manufacturé)* finish

finir [finiʀ] *vt* to finish ♦ *vi* to finish, end; **~ quelque part/par faire** to end up *ou* finish up somewhere/doing; **~ de faire** to finish doing; *(cesser)* to stop doing; **il finit par m'agacer** he's beginning to get on my nerves; **~ en pointe/tragédie** to end in a point/in tragedy; **en ~ avec** to be *ou* have done with; **il va mal ~** he will come to a bad end

finition [finisjɔ̃] *nf* finishing; finish

finlandais, e [fɛ̃lɑ̃dɛ, -ɛz] *adj* Finnish ♦ *nm/f*: **F~, e** Finn

Finlande [fɛ̃lɑ̃d] *nf*: **la ~** Finland

fiole [fjɔl] *nf* phial

floriture [flɔʀityʀ] *nf* embellishment, flourish

firme [fiʀm(ə)] *nf* firm

fis vb voir **faire**

fisc [fisk] nm tax authorities pl; ~**al, e, aux** adj tax cpd, fiscal; ~**alité** nf tax system; (charges) taxation

fissure [fisyʀ] nf crack; ~**r** [fisyʀe] vt to crack; **se** ~**r** vi to crack

fiston [fistɔ̃] (fam) nm son, lad

fit vb voir **faire**

fixation [fiksasjɔ̃] nf fixing; fastening; setting; (de ski) binding; (PSYCH) fixation

fixe [fiks(ə)] adj fixed; (emploi) steady, regular ♦ nm (salaire) basic salary; **à heure** ~ at a set time; **menu à prix** ~ set menu

fixé, e [fikse] adj: **être** ~ **(sur)** (savoir à quoi s'en tenir) to have made up one's mind (about); to know for certain (about)

fixer [fikse] vt (attacher): ~ **qch (à/sur)** to fix ou fasten sth (to/onto); (déterminer) to fix, set; (CHIMIE, PHOTO) to fix; (regarder) to stare at; **se** ~ vi (s'établir) to settle down; **se** ~ **sur** (suj: attention) to focus on

flacon [flakɔ̃] nm bottle

flageller [flaʒele] vt to flog, scourge

flageoler [flaʒɔle] vi (jambes) to sag

flageolet [flaʒɔle] nm (MUS) flageolet; (CULIN) dwarf kidney bean

flagrant, e [flagʀɑ̃, -ɑ̃t] adj flagrant, blatant; **en** ~ **délit** in the act

flair [flɛʀ] nm sense of smell; (fig) intuition; **flairer** vt (humer) to sniff (at); (détecter) to scent

flamand, e [flamɑ̃, -ɑ̃d] adj Flemish ♦ nm (LING) Flemish ♦ nm/f: **F**~, **e** Fleming; **les F**~**s** the Flemish

flamant [flamɑ̃] nm flamingo

flambant [flɑ̃bɑ̃] adv: ~ **neuf** brand new

flambé, e [flɑ̃be] adj (CULIN) flambé

flambeau, x [flɑ̃bo] nm (flaming) torch

flambée [flɑ̃be] nf blaze; (fig) flaring-up, explosion

flamber [flɑ̃be] vi to blaze (up)

flamboyer [flɑ̃bwaje] vi to blaze (up); to flame

flamme [flam] nf flame; (fig) fire, fervour; **en** ~**s** on fire, ablaze

flan [flɑ̃] nm (CULIN) custard tart ou pie

flanc [flɑ̃] nm side; (MIL) flank; **prêter le** ~ **à** (fig) to lay o.s. open to

flancher [flɑ̃ʃe] vi to fail, pack up; to quit

flanelle [flanɛl] nf flannel

flâner [flɑne] vi to stroll; **flânerie** nf stroll

flanquer [flɑ̃ke] vt to flank; (fam: mettre) to chuck, shove; (: jeter) to fling; ~ **par terre/à la porte** to fling to the ground/chuck out

flaque [flak] nf (d'eau) puddle; (d'huile, de sang etc) pool

flash [flaʃ] (pl **flashes**) nm (PHOTO) flash; ~ **(d'information)** newsflash

flasque [flask(ə)] adj flabby

flatter [flate] vt to flatter; **se** ~ **de qch** to pride o.s. on sth; **flatterie** nf flattery no pl; **flatteur, euse** adj flattering ♦ nm/f flatterer

fléau, x [fleo] nm scourge

flèche [flɛʃ] nf arrow; (de clocher) spire; (de grue) jib; **monter en** ~ (fig) to soar, rocket; **partir en** ~ to be off like a shot; **fléchette** nf dart; **fléchettes** nfpl (jeu) darts sg

fléchir [fleʃiʀ] vt (corps, genou) to bend; (fig) to sway, weaken ♦ vi (poutre) to sag, bend; (fig) to weaken, flag; to yield

flemmard, e [flemaʀ, -aʀd(ə)] nm/f lazybones sg, loafer

flétrir [fletʀiʀ] vt to wither; **se** ~ vi to wither

fleur [flœʀ] nf flower; (d'un arbre) blossom; **en** ~ (arbre) in blossom; **à** ~ **de terre** just above the ground

fleurer [flœʀe] vt: ~ **la lavande** to have the scent of lavender

fleuri, e [flœʀi] adj in flower ou bloom; surrounded by flowers; (fig) flowery; florid

fleurir [flœʀiʀ] vi (rose) to flower; (arbre) to blossom; (fig) to flourish ♦ vt (tombe) to put flowers on; (chambre) to decorate with flowers

fleuriste [flœʀist(ə)] nm/f florist

fleuron [flœʀɔ̃] nm (fig) jewel

fleuve [flœv] nm river

flexible [flɛksibl(ə)] adj flexible

flexion [flɛksjɔ̃] nf flexing, bending

flic [flik] (fam: péj) nm cop

flipper [flipœʀ] nm pinball (machine)

flirter [flœʀte] vi to flirt

flocon [flɔkɔ̃] nm flake

floraison [flɔʀezɔ̃] nf flowering; blossoming; flourishing

flore [flɔʀ] nf flora

florissant, e [flɔʀisɑ̃] vb voir **fleurir**

flot [flo] nm flood, stream; ~**s** nmpl (de la mer) waves; **être à** ~ (NAVIG) to be afloat; (fig) to be on an even keel; **entrer à** ~**s** to stream ou pour in

flotte [flɔt] nf (NAVIG) fleet; (fam) water; rain

flottement [flɔtmɑ̃] nm (fig) wavering, hesitation

flotter [flɔte] vi to float; (nuage, odeur) to drift; (drapeau) to fly; (vêtements) to hang loose; (monnaie) to float ♦ vt to float; **faire** ~ to float; **flotteur** nm float

flou, e [flu] adj fuzzy, blurred; (fig) woolly, vague

flouer [flue] vt to swindle

fluctuation [flyktɥasjɔ̃] nf fluctuation

fluet, te [flyɛ, -ɛt] adj thin, slight

fluide [flɥid] adj fluid; (circulation etc) flowing freely ♦ nm fluid; (force) (mysterious) power

fluor [flyɔʀ] nm fluorine

fluorescent, e [flyɔʀesɑ̃, -ɑ̃t] adj fluorescent

flûte [flyt] nf flute; (verre) flute glass; (pain) long loaf; ~**!** drat it!; ~ **à bec** recorder

flux [fly] *nm* incoming tide; (*écoulement*) flow; **le ~ et le reflux** the ebb and flow
FM *sigle f* (= *fréquence modulée*) FM
foc [fɔk] *nm* jib
foi [fwa] *nf* faith; **sous la ~ du serment** under *ou* on oath; **ajouter ~ à** to lend credence to; **digne de ~** reliable; **sur la ~ de** on the word *ou* strength of; **être de bonne/mauvaise ~** to be sincere/insincere; **ma ~ ... well ...**
foie [fwa] *nm* liver
foin [fwɛ̃] *nm* hay; **faire du ~** (*fig: fam*) to kick up a row
foire [fwaʀ] *nf* fair; (*fête foraine*) (fun) fair; **faire la ~** (*fig: fam*) to whoop it up; **~ (exposition)** trade fair
fois [fwa] *nf* time; **une/deux ~** once/twice; **2 ~ 2** 2 times 2; **quatre ~ plus grand (que)** four times as big (as); **une ~** (*passé*) once; (*futur*) sometime; **une ~ pour toutes** once and for all; **une ~ que** once; **des ~** (*parfois*) sometimes; **à la ~** (*ensemble*) at once
foison [fwazɔ̃] *nf*: **une ~ de** an abundance of; **à ~** in plenty
foisonner [fwazɔne] *vi* to abound
fol [fɔl] *adj voir* **fou**
folâtrer [fɔlɑtʀe] *vi* to frolic (about)
folie [fɔli] *nf* (*d'une décision, d'un acte*) madness, folly; (*état*) madness, insanity; (*acte*) folly; **la ~ des grandeurs** delusions of grandeur; **faire des ~s** (*en dépenses*) to be extravagant
folklorique [fɔlklɔʀik] *adj* folk *cpd*; (*fam*) weird
folle [fɔl] *adj, nf voir* **fou**; **follement** *adv* (*très*) madly, wildly
foncé, e [fɔ̃se] *adj* dark
foncer [fɔ̃se] *vi* to go darker; (*fam: aller vite*) to tear *ou* belt along; **~ sur** to charge at
foncier, ère [fɔ̃sje, -ɛʀ] *adj* (*honnêteté etc*) basic, fundamental; (*malhonnêteté*) deep-rooted; (*COMM*) real estate *cpd*
fonction [fɔ̃ksjɔ̃] *nf* (*rôle, MATH, LING*) function; (*emploi, poste*) post, position; **~s** *nfpl* (*professionnelles*) duties; **entrer en ~s** to take up one's post *ou* duties; to take up office; **voiture de ~** company car; **être ~ de** (*dépendre de*) to depend on; **en ~ de** (*par rapport à*) according to; **faire ~ de** to serve as; **la ~ publique** the state *ou* civil (*BRIT*) service; **fonctionnaire** [fɔ̃ksjɔnɛʀ] *nm/f* state employee, local authority employee; (*dans l'administration*) ≈ civil servant; **fonctionner** [fɔ̃ksjɔne] *vi* to work, function; (*entreprise*) to operate, function
fond [fɔ̃] *nm* (*d'un récipient, trou*) bottom; (*d'une salle, scène*) back; (*d'un tableau, décor*) background; (*opposé à la forme*) content; (*SPORT*): **le ~** long distance (running); **sans ~** bottomless; **au ~ de** at the

bottom of; at the back of; **à ~** (*connaître, soutenir*) thoroughly; (*appuyer, visser*) right down *ou* home; **à ~ (de train)** (*fam*) full tilt; **dans le ~, au ~** (*en somme*) basically, really; **de ~ en comble** from top to bottom; *voir aussi* **fonds**; **~ de teint** (make-up) foundation; **~ sonore** background noise; background music
fondamental, e, aux [fɔ̃damɑ̃tal, -o] *adj* fundamental
fondant, e [fɔ̃dɑ̃, -ɑ̃t] *adj* (*neige*) melting; (*fruit*) that melts in the mouth
fondateur, trice [fɔ̃datœʀ, -tʀis] *nm/f* founder
fondation [fɔ̃dasjɔ̃] *nf* founding; (*établissement*) foundation; **~s** *nfpl* (*d'une maison*) foundations
fondé, e [fɔ̃de] *adj* (*accusation etc*) well-founded ♦ *nm*: **~ de pouvoir** authorized representative; **être ~ à** to have grounds for *ou* good reason to
fondement [fɔ̃dmɑ̃] *nm* (*derrière*) behind; **~s** *nmpl* (*base*) foundations; **sans ~** (*rumeur etc*) groundless, unfounded
fonder [fɔ̃de] *vt* to found; (*fig*) to base; **se ~ sur** (*suj: personne*) to base o.s. on
fonderie [fɔ̃dʀi] *nf* smelting works *sg*
fondre [fɔ̃dʀ(ə)] *vt* (*aussi: faire ~*) to melt; (*dans l'eau*) to dissolve; (*fig: mélanger*) to merge, blend ♦ *vi* to melt; to dissolve; (*fig*) to melt away; (*se précipiter*): **~ sur** to swoop down on; **~ en larmes** to burst into tears
fonds [fɔ̃] *nm* (*de bibliothèque*) collection; (*COMM*): **~ (de commerce)** business ♦ *nmpl* (*argent*) funds; **à ~ perdus** with little or no hope of getting the money back
fondu, e [fɔ̃dy] *adj* (*beurre, neige*) melted; (*métal*) molten; **fondue** *nf* (*CULIN*) fondue
font *vb voir* **faire**
fontaine [fɔ̃tɛn] *nf* fountain; (*source*) spring
fonte [fɔ̃t] *nf* melting; (*métal*) cast iron; **la ~ des neiges** the (spring) thaw
foot [fut] (*fam*) *nm* football
football [futbol] *nm* football, soccer; **footballeur** *nm* footballer
footing [futiŋ] *nm* jogging; **faire du ~** to go jogging
for [fɔʀ] *nm*: **dans son ~ intérieur** in one's heart of hearts
forain, e [fɔʀɛ̃, -ɛn] *adj* fairground *cpd* ♦ *nm* stallholder; fairground entertainer
forçat [fɔʀsa] *nm* convict
force [fɔʀs(ə)] *nf* strength; (*puissance: surnaturelle etc*) power; (*PHYSIQUE, MÉCANIQUE*) force; **~s** *nfpl* (*physiques*) strength *sg*; (*MIL*) forces; **à ~ d'insister** by dint of insisting; as he (*ou* I *etc*) kept on insisting; **de ~** forcibly; by force; **être de ~ à faire** to be up to doing; **de première ~** first class; **les ~s de l'ordre** the police
forcé, e [fɔʀse] *adj* forced; unintended; in-

evitable

forcément [fɔʀsemɑ̃] *adv* necessarily; inevitably; (*bien sûr*) of course

forcené, e [fɔʀsəne] *nm/f* maniac

forcer [fɔʀse] *vt* (*porte, serrure, plante*) to force; (*moteur, voix*) to strain ♦ *vi* (*SPORT*) to overtax o.s.; **~ la dose** to overdo it; **~ l'allure** to increase the pace; **se ~ (pour faire)** to force o.s. (to do)

forcir [fɔʀsiʀ] *vi* (*grossir*) to broaden out; (*vent*) to freshen

forer [fɔʀe] *vt* to drill, bore

forestier, ère [fɔʀestje, -ɛʀ] *adj* forest *cpd*

forêt [fɔʀe] *nf* forest

forfait [fɔʀfe] *nm* (*COMM*) fixed *ou* set price; all-in deal *ou* price; (*crime*) infamy; **déclarer ~** to withdraw; **travailler à ~** to work for a lump sum; **~aire** *adj* inclusive; set

forge [fɔʀʒ(ə)] *nf* forge, smithy

forger [fɔʀʒe] *vt* to forge; (*fig: personnalité*) to form; (: *prétexte*) to contrive, make up

forgeron [fɔʀʒəʀɔ̃] *nm* (black)smith

formaliser [fɔʀmalize]: **se ~** *vi*: **se ~ (de)** to take offence (at)

formalité [fɔʀmalite] *nf* (*ADMIN, JUR*) formality; (*acte sans importance*): **simple ~** mere formality

format [fɔʀma] *nm* size

formater [fɔʀmate] *vt* (*disque*) to format

formation [fɔʀmɑsjɔ̃] *nf* forming; training; (*MUS*) group; (*MIL, AVIAT, GÉO*) formation; **~ permanente** continuing education; **~ professionnelle** vocational training

forme [fɔʀm(ə)] *nf* (*gén*) form; (*d'un objet*) shape, form; **~s** *nfpl* (*bonnes manières*) proprieties; (*d'une femme*) figure *sg*; **en ~ de poire** pear-shaped; **être en ~** (*SPORT etc*) to be on form; **en bonne et due ~** in due form

formel, le [fɔʀmɛl] *adj* (*preuve, décision*) definite, positive; (*logique*) formal; **formellement** *adv* (*absolument*) positively

former [fɔʀme] *vt* to form; (*éduquer*) to train; **se ~** *vi* to form

formidable [fɔʀmidabl(ə)] *adj* tremendous

formulaire [fɔʀmylɛʀ] *nm* form

formule [fɔʀmyl] *nf* (*gén*) formula; (*formulaire*) form; **~ de politesse** polite phrase; letter ending

formuler [fɔʀmyle] *vt* (*émettre: réponse, vœux*) to formulate; (*expliciter: sa pensée*) to express

fort, e [fɔʀ, fɔʀt(ə)] *adj* strong; (*intensité, rendement*) high, great; (*corpulent*) stout; (*doué*) good, able ♦ *adv* (*serrer, frapper*) hard; (*sonner*) loud(ly); (*beaucoup*) greatly, very much; (*très*) very ♦ *nm* (*édifice*) fort; (*point fort*) strong point, forte; **se faire ~ de ... to** claim one can ...; **au plus ~ de** (*au milieu de*) in the thick of; at the height of; **~e tête** rebel

fortifiant [fɔʀtifjɑ̃] *nm* tonic

fortifier [fɔʀtifje] *vt* to strengthen, fortify; (*MIL*) to fortify

fortiori [fɔʀtjɔʀi] : **à ~** *adv* all the more so

fortuit, e [fɔʀtɥi, -it] *adj* fortuitous, chance *cpd*

fortune [fɔʀtyn] *nf* fortune; **faire ~** to make one's fortune; **de ~** makeshift; chance *cpd*

fortuné, e [fɔʀtyne] *adj* wealthy

fosse [fos] *nf* (*grand trou*) pit; (*tombe*) grave; **~ (d'orchestre)** (orchestra) pit

fossé [fose] *nm* ditch; (*fig*) gulf, gap

fossette [fosɛt] *nf* dimple

fossile [fosil] *nm* fossil

fossoyeur [foswajœʀ] *nm* gravedigger

fou(fol), folle [fu, fɔl] *adj* mad; (*déréglé etc*) wild, erratic; (*fam: extrême, très grand*) terrific, tremendous ♦ *nm/f* madman(woman) ♦ *nm* (*du roi*) jester; **être fou de** to be mad *ou* crazy about; **avoir le fou rire** to have the giggles; **faire le fou** to act the fool

foudre [fudʀ(ə)] *nf*: **la ~** lightning

foudroyant, e [fudʀwajɑ̃, -ɑ̃t] *adj* lightning *cpd*, stunning; (*maladie, poison*) violent

foudroyer [fudʀwaje] *vt* to strike down; **être foudroyé** to be struck by lightning; **~ qn du regard** to glare at sb

fouet [fwe] *nm* whip; (*CULIN*) whisk; **de plein ~** (*se heurter*) head on; **fouetter** *vt* to whip; to whisk

fougère [fuʒɛʀ] *nf* fern

fougue [fug] *nf* ardour, spirit

fouille [fuj] *nf* search; **~s** *nfpl* (*archéologiques*) excavations

fouiller [fuje] *vt* to search; (*creuser*) to dig ♦ *vi* to rummage

fouillis [fuji] *nm* jumble, muddle

fouiner [fwine] (*péj*) *vi*: **~ dans** to nose around *ou* about in

foulard [fulaʀ] *nm* scarf

foule [ful] *nf* crowd; **les ~s** the masses; **la ~ crowds** *pl*; **une ~ de** masses of

foulée [fule] *nf* stride

fouler [fule] *vt* to press; (*sol*) to tread upon; **se ~** *vi* (*fam*) to overexert o.s.; **se ~ la cheville** to sprain one's ankle; **~ aux pieds** to trample underfoot; **foulure** [fulyʀ] *nf* sprain

four [fuʀ] *nm* oven; (*de potier*) kiln; (*THÉÂTRE: échec*) flop

fourbe [fuʀb(ə)] *adj* deceitful

fourbu, e [fuʀby] *adj* exhausted

fourche [fuʀʃ(ə)] *nf* pitchfork; (*de bicyclette*) fork

fourchette [fuʀʃet] *nf* fork; (*STATISTIQUE*) bracket, margin

fourgon [fuʀgɔ̃] *nm* van; (*RAIL*) wag(g)on

fourmi [fuʀmi] *nf* ant; **~s** *nfpl* (*fig*) pins and needles; **fourmilière** *nf* ant-hill

fourmiller [fuʀmije] *vi* to swarm

fournaise [furnɛz] *nf* blaze; (*fig*) furnace, oven

fourneau, x [furno] *nm* stove

fournée [furne] *nf* batch

fourni, e [furni] *adj* (*barbe, cheveux*) thick; (*magasin*): **bien ~ (en)** well stocked (with)

fournir [furnir] *vt* to supply; (*preuve, exemple*) to provide, supply; (*effort*) to put in; **fournisseur, euse** *nm/f* supplier

fourniture [furnityr] *nf* supply(ing); **~s** *nfpl* (*provisions*) supplies

fourrage [fuRaʒ] *nm* fodder

fourrager¹, ère [furaʒe, -ɛr] *adj* fodder *cpd*

fourrager² [furaʒe] *vi*: **fourrager dans/parmi** (*fouiller*) to rummage through /among

fourré, e [fure] *adj* (*bonbon etc*) filled; (*manteau etc*) fur-lined ♦ *nm* thicket

fourreau, x [furo] *nm* sheath

fourrer [fure] (*fam*) *vt* to stick, shove; **se ~ dans/sous** to get into/under

fourre-tout [furtu] *nm inv* (*sac*) holdall; (*péj*) junk room (*ou* cupboard); (*fig*) rag-bag

fourrière [furjɛr] *nf* pound

fourrure [furyr] *nf* fur; (*sur l'animal*) coat

fourvoyer [furvwaje]: **se ~** *vi* to go astray, stray

foutre [futr(ə)] (*fam!*) *vt* = **ficher; foutu, e** (*fam!*) *adj* = **fichu, e**

foyer [fwaje] *nm* (*de cheminée*) hearth; (*famille*) family; (*maison*) home; (*de jeunes etc*) (social) club; hostel; (*salon*) foyer; (*OPTIQUE, PHOTO*) focus *sg*; **lunettes à double ~** bi-focal glasses

fracas [fraka] *nm* din; crash; roar

fracasser [frakase] *vt* to smash

fraction [fraksjɔ̃] *nf* fraction; **fractionner** *vt* to divide (up), split (up)

fracture [fraktyr] *nf* fracture; **~ du crâne** fractured skull; **~r** [fraktyre] *vt* (*coffre, serrure*) to break open; (*os, membre*) to fracture

fragile [fraʒil] *adj* fragile, delicate; (*fig*) frail; **fragilité** *nf* fragility

fragment [fragmɑ̃] *nm* (*d'un objet*) fragment, piece; (*d'un texte*) passage, extract

fraîche [frɛʃ] *adj voir* **frais; fraîcheur** *nf* coolness; freshness; **fraîchir** *vi* to get cooler; (*vent*) to freshen

frais, fraîche [frɛ, frɛʃ] *adj* fresh; (*froid*) cool ♦ *adv* (*récemment*) newly, fresh(ly) ♦ *nm*: **mettre au ~** to put in a cool place ♦ *nmpl* (*débours*) expenses; (*COMM*) costs; (*facturés*) charges; **il fait ~** it's cool; **servir ~** serve chilled; **prendre le ~** to take a breath of cool air; **faire des ~** to spend; to go to a lot of expense; **faire les ~ de** to bear the brunt of; **~ de scolarité** school fees (*BRIT*), tuition (*US*); **~ généraux** overheads

fraise [frɛz] *nf* strawberry; (*TECH*) countersink (bit); (*de dentiste*) drill; **~ des bois** wild strawberry

framboise [frãbwaz] *nf* raspberry

franc, franche [frã, frãʃ] *adj* (*personne*) frank, straightforward; (*visage*) open; (*net: refus, couleur*) clear; (: *coupure*) clean; (*intensif*) downright; (*exempt*): **~ de port** postage paid ♦ *adv*: **parler ~** to be frank ou candid ♦ *nm* franc

français, e [frãsɛ, -ɛz] *adj* French ♦ *nm/f*: **F~, e** Frenchman(woman) ♦ *nm* (*LING*) French; **les F~** the French

France [frãs] *nf*: **la ~** France

franche [frãʃ] *adj voir* **franc; franchement** *adv* frankly; clearly; (*tout à fait*) down- right

franchir [frãʃir] *vt* (*obstacle*) to clear, get over; (*seuil, ligne, rivière*) to cross; (*distance*) to cover

franchise [frãʃiz] *nf* frankness; (*douanière, d'impôt*) exemption; (*ASSURANCES*) excess

franciser [frãsize] *vt* to gallicize, Frenchify

franc-maçon [frãmasɔ̃] *nm* freemason

franco [frãko] *adv* (*COMM*): **~ (de port)** postage paid

francophone [frãkɔfɔn] *adj* French-speaking; **francophonie** *nf* French-speaking communities

franc-parler [frãparle] *nm inv* outspokenness

franc-tireur [frãtirœr] *nm* (*MIL*) irregular; (*fig*) freelance

frange [frãʒ] *nf* fringe

frangipane [frãʒipan] *nf* almond paste

franquette [frãkɛt] *nf*: **à la bonne ~** *adv* without any fuss

frappe [frap] *nf* (*de pianiste, machine à écrire*) touch; (*BOXE*) punch

frappé, e [frape] *adj* iced

frapper [frape] *vt* to hit, strike; (*étonner*) to strike; (*monnaie*) to strike, stamp; **se ~** *vi* (*s'inquiéter*) to get worked up; **~ dans ses mains** to clap one's hands; **~ du poing sur** to bang one's fist on; **frappé de stupeur** dumbfounded

frasques [frask(ə)] *nfpl* escapades

fraternel, le [fraternɛl] *adj* brotherly, fraternal

fraternité [fraternite] *nf* brotherhood

fraude [frod] *nf* fraud; (*SCOL*) cheating; **passer qch en ~** to smuggle sth in (*ou* out); **~ fiscale** tax evasion; **frauder** *vi, vt* to cheat; **frauduleux, euse** *adj* fraudulent

frayer [freje] *vt* to open up, clear ♦ *vi* to spawn; (*fréquenter*): **~ avec** to mix with

frayeur [frejœr] *nf* fright

fredonner [frədɔne] *vt* to hum

freezer [frizœr] *nm* freezing compartment

frein [frɛ̃] *nm* brake; **~ à main** handbrake; **~s à disques/tambour** disc/drum brakes

freiner [frene] *vi* to brake ♦ *vt* (*progrès etc*) to check

frelaté, e [frəlate] *adj* adulterated; (*fig*)

tainted

frêle [fʀɛl] *adj* frail, fragile

frelon [fʀɔlɔ̃] *nm* hornet

frémir [fʀemiʀ] *vi* to tremble, shudder; to shiver; to quiver

frêne [fʀɛn] *nm* ash

frénétique [fʀenetik] *adj* frenzied, frenetic

fréquemment [fʀekamɑ̃] *adv* frequently

fréquent, e [fʀekɑ̃, -ɑ̃t] *adj* frequent

fréquentation [fʀekɑ̃tɑsjɔ̃] *nf* frequenting; seeing; ~**s** *nfpl* (relations) company *sg*

fréquenté, e [fʀekɑ̃te] *adj*: **très** ~ (very) busy; **mal** ~ patronized by disreputable elements

fréquenter [fʀekɑ̃te] *vt* (lieu) to frequent; (personne) to see; **se** ~ to see each other

frère [fʀɛʀ] *nm* brother

fresque [fʀɛsk(ə)] *nf* (ART) fresco

fret [fʀɛ] *nm* freight

frétiller [fʀetije] *vi* to wriggle; to quiver; (chien) to wag its tail

fretin [fʀətɛ̃] *nm*: **menu** ~ small fry

friable [fʀijabl(ə)] *adj* crumbly

friand, e [fʀijɑ̃, -ɑ̃d] *adj*: ~ **de** very fond of

friandise [fʀijɑ̃diz] *nf* sweet

fric [fʀik] (fam) *nm* cash, bread

friche [fʀiʃ] : **en** ~ *adj, adv* (lying) fallow

friction [fʀiksjɔ̃] *nf* (massage) rub, rub-down; (TECH, fig) friction; **frictionner** *vt* to rub (down); to massage

frigidaire [fʀiʒideʀ] (®) *nm* refrigerator

frigide [fʀiʒid] *adj* frigid

frigo [fʀigo] *nm* fridge

frigorifier [fʀigoʀifje] *vt* to refrigerate; **frigorifique** *adj* refrigerating

frileux, euse [fʀilø, -øz] *adj* sensitive to (the) cold

frimer [fʀime] *vi* to put on an act

frimousse [fʀimus] *nf* (sweet) little face

fringale [fʀɛ̃gal] *nf*: **avoir la** ~ to be ravenous

fringant, e [fʀɛ̃gɑ̃, -ɑ̃t] *adj* dashing

fringues [fʀɛ̃g] (fam) *nfpl* clothes

fripé, e [fʀipe] *adj* crumpled

fripon, ne [fʀipɔ̃, -ɔn] *adj* roguish, mischievous ♦ *nm/f* rascal, rogue

fripouille [fʀipuj] *nf* scoundrel

frire [fʀiʀ] *vt, vi*: **faire** ~ to fry

frisé, e [fʀize] *adj* curly; curly-haired

frisson [fʀisɔ̃] *nm* shudder, shiver; quiver; **frissonner** *vi* to shudder, shiver; to quiver

frit, e [fʀi, fʀit] *pp de* **frire**; **frite** *nf*: (pommes) **frites** chips (BRIT), French fries; **friteuse** *nf* chip pan; **friture** *nf* (huile) (deep) fat; (plat): **friture (de poissons)** fried fish; (RADIO) crackle

frivole [fʀivol] *adj* frivolous

froid, e [fʀwa, fʀwad] *adj, nm* cold; **il fait** ~ it's cold; **avoir/prendre** ~ to be/catch cold; **être en** ~ **avec** to be on bad terms with; ~**ement** *adv* (accueillir) coldly; (décider) coolly

froisser [fʀwase] *vt* to crumple (up), crease; (fig) to hurt, offend; **se** ~ *vi* to crumple, crease; to take offence; **se** ~ **un muscle** to strain a muscle

frôler [fʀole] *vt* to brush against; (suj: projectile) to skim past; (fig) to come very close to

fromage [fʀomaʒ] *nm* cheese; ~ **blanc** soft white cheese; **fromager, ère** *nm/f* cheese merchant

froment [fʀomɑ̃] *nm* wheat

froncer [fʀɔ̃se] *vt* to gather; ~ **les sourcils** to frown

frondaisons [fʀɔ̃dɛzɔ̃] *nfpl* foliage *sg*

fronde [fʀɔ̃d] *nf* sling; (fig) rebellion, rebelliousness

front [fʀɔ̃] *nm* forehead, brow; (MIL) front; **de** ~ (se heurter) head-on; (rouler) together (i.e. 2 or 3 abreast); (simultanément) at once; **faire** ~ **à** to face up to; ~ **de mer** (sea) front

frontalier, ère [fʀɔ̃talje, -ɛʀ] *adj* border *cpd*, frontier *cpd* ♦ *nm/f*: (travailleurs) ~**s** commuters from across the border

frontière [fʀɔ̃tjɛʀ] *nf* frontier, border; (fig) frontier, boundary

fronton [fʀɔ̃tɔ̃] *nm* pediment

frotter [fʀote] *vi* to rub, scrape ♦ *vt* to rub; (pour nettoyer) to rub (up); to scrub; ~ **une allumette** to strike a match

fructifier [fʀyktifje] *vi* to yield a profit; **faire** ~ to turn to good account

fructueux, euse [fʀyktɥø, -øz] *adj* fruitful; profitable

fruit [fʀɥi] *nm* fruit *gen no pl*; ~**s de mer** seafood(s); ~**s secs** dried fruit *sg*; ~**é, e** *adj* fruity; ~**ier, ère** *adj*: **arbre** ~**ier** fruit tree ♦ *nm/f* **fruiterer** (BRIT), fruit merchant (US)

fruste [fʀyst(ə)] *adj* unpolished, uncultivated

frustrer [fʀystʀe] *vt* to frustrate

fuel(-oil) [fjul(ɔjl)] *nm* fuel oil; heating oil

fugace [fygas] *adj* fleeting

fugitif, ive [fyʒitif, -iv] *adj* (lueur, amour) fleeting; (prisonnier etc) fugitive, runaway ♦ *nm/f* fugitive

fugue [fyg] *nf*: **faire une** ~ to run away, abscond

fuir [fɥiʀ] *vt* to flee from; (éviter) to shun ♦ *vi* to run away; (gaz, robinet) to leak

fuite [fɥit] *nf* flight; (écoulement, divulgation) leak; **être en** ~ to be on the run; **mettre en** ~ to put to flight

fulgurant, e [fylgyʀɑ̃, -ɑ̃t] *adj* lightning *cpd*, dazzling

fulminer [fylmine] *vi* to thunder forth

fumé, e [fyme] *adj* (CULIN) smoked; (verre) tinted

fume-cigarette [fymsigaʀɛt] *nm inv* cigarette holder

fumée [fyme] *nf* smoke

fumer [fyme] *vi* to smoke; (*soupe*) to steam ♦ *vt* to smoke; (*terre, champ*) to manure

fûmes *etc vb voir* **être**

fumet [fymɛ] *nm* aroma

fumeur, euse [fymœʀ, -øz] *nm/f* smoker

fumeux, euse [fymø, -øz] (*péj*) *adj* woolly, hazy

fumier [fymje] *nm* manure

fumiste [fymist(ə)] *nm/f* (*péj: paresseux*) shirker; (*charlatan*) phoney

fumisterie [fymistəʀi] (*péj*) *nf* fraud, con

funambule [fynãbyl] *nm* tightrope walker

funèbre [fynɛbʀ(ə)] *adj* funeral *cpd*; (*fig*) doleful; funereal

funérailles [fyneʀaj] *nfpl* funeral *sg*

funeste [fynɛst(ə)] *adj* disastrous; deathly

fur [fyʀ] : **au ~ et à mesure** *adv* as one goes along; **au ~ et à mesure que** as

furet [fyʀɛ] *nm* ferret

fureter [fyʀte] *vi* to nose about

fureur [fyʀœʀ] *nf* fury; (*passion*): **~ de** passion for; **faire ~** to be all the rage

furibond, e [fyʀibɔ̃, -ɔ̃d] *adj* furious

furie [fyʀi] *nf* fury; (*femme*) shrew, vixen; **en ~** (*mer*) raging; **furieux, euse** *adj* furious

furoncle [fyʀɔ̃kl(ə)] *nm* boil

furtif, ive [fyʀtif, -iv] *adj* furtive

fus *vb voir* **être**

fusain [fyzɛ̃] *nm* (*ART*) charcoal

fuseau, x [fyzo] *nm* (*pour filer*) spindle; (*pantalon*) (ski) pants; **~ horaire** time zone

fusée [fyze] *nf* rocket; **~ éclairante** flare

fuselé, e [fyzle] *adj* slender; tapering

fuser [fyze] *vi* (*rires etc*) to burst forth

fusible [fyzibl(ə)] *nm* (*ÉLEC: fil*) fuse wire; (: *fiche*) fuse

fusil [fyzi] *nm* (*de guerre, à canon rayé*) rifle, gun; (*de chasse, à canon lisse*) shotgun, gun; **fusillade** *nf* gunfire *no pl*, shooting *no pl*; shooting battle; **fusiller** *vt* to shoot; **fusil-mitrailleur** *nm* machine gun

fusionner [fyzjone] *vi* to merge

fustiger [fystiʒe] *vt* to denounce

fut *vb voir* **être**

fût [fy] *vb voir* **être** ♦ *nm* (*tonneau*) barrel, cask

futaie [fytɛ] *nf* forest, plantation

futé, e [fyte] *adj* crafty

futile [fytil] *adj* futile, frivolous

futur, e [fytyʀ] *adj, nm* future

fuyant, e [fɥijɑ̃, -ɑ̃t] *vb voir* **fuir** ♦ *adj* (*regard etc*) evasive; (*lignes etc*) receding; (*perspective*) vanishing

fuyard, e [fɥijaʀ, -aʀd(ə)] *nm/f* runaway

G g

gabarit [gabaʀi] *nm* (*fig*) size; calibre

gâcher [gɑʃe] *vt* (*gâter*) to spoil, ruin; (*gaspiller*) to waste

gâchette [gɑʃɛt] *nf* trigger

gâchis [gɑʃi] *nm* waste *no pl*

gadoue [gadu] *nf* sludge

gaffe [gaf] *nf* (*instrument*) boat hook; (*erreur*) blunder; **faire ~** (*fam*) to be careful

gage [gaʒ] *nm* (*dans un jeu*) forfeit; (*fig: de fidélité*) token; **~s** *nmpl* (*salaire*) wages; (*garantie*) guarantee *sg*; **mettre en ~** to pawn

gager [gaʒe] *vt* to bet, wager

gageure [gaʒyʀ] *nf*: **c'est une ~** it's attempting the impossible

gagnant, e [gaɲɑ̃, -ɑ̃t] *nm/f* winner

gagne-pain [gaɲpɛ̃] *nm inv* job

gagner [gaɲe] *vt* to win; (*somme d'argent, revenu*) to earn; (*aller vers, atteindre*) to reach; (*envahir*) to overcome; to spread to ♦ *vi* to win; (*fig*) to gain; **~ du temps/de la place** to gain time/save space; **~ sa vie** to earn one's living

gai, e [ge] *adj* gay, cheerful; (*un peu ivre*) merry

gaieté [gete] *nf* cheerfulness; **de ~ de cœur** with a light heart

gaillard, e [gajaʀ, -aʀd(ə)] *adj* (*grivois*) bawdy, ribald ♦ *nm* (*strapping*) fellow

gain [gɛ̃] *nm* (*revenu*) earnings *pl*; (*bénéfice: gén pl*) profits *pl*; (*au jeu*) winnings *pl*; (*fig: de temps, place*) saving; **avoir ~ de cause** to win the case; (*fig*) to be proved right

gaine [gɛn] *nf* (*corset*) girdle; (*fourreau*) sheath

galant, e [galɑ̃, -ɑ̃t] *adj* (*courtois*) courteous, gentlemanly; (*entreprenant*) flirtatious, gallant; (*aventure, poésie*) amorous

galère [galɛʀ] *nf* galley

galérer [galeʀe] (*fam*) *vi* to slog away, work hard

galerie [galʀi] *nf* gallery; (*THÉÂTRE*) circle; (*de voiture*) roof rack; (*fig: spectateurs*) audience; **~ de peinture** (*private*) art gallery; **~ marchande** shopping arcade

galet [galɛ] *nm* pebble; (*TECH*) wheel

galette [galɛt] *nf* flat cake

Galles [gal] *nfpl*: **le pays de ~** Wales

gallois, e [galwa, -waz] *adj* Welsh ♦ *nm* (*LING*) Welsh ♦ *nm/f*: **G~, e** Welshman(woman)

galon [galɔ̃] *nm* (*MIL*) stripe; (*décoratif*) piece of braid

galop [galo] *nm* gallop

galoper [galɔpe] *vi* to gallop

galopin [galɔpɛ̃] *nm* urchin, ragamuffin

galvauder [galvode] *vt* to debase

gambader [gɑ̃bade] *vi* (*animal, enfant*) to leap about

gamelle [gamɛl] *nf* mess tin; billy can

gamin, e [gamɛ̃, -in] *nm/f* kid ♦ *adj* mischievous, playful

gamme [gam] *nf* (*MUS*) scale; (*fig*) range

gammé, e [game] *adj*: **croix ~e** swastika

gant [gɑ̃] *nm* glove; **~ de toilette** face flannel (*BRIT*), face cloth

garage [gaʁaʒ] *nm* garage; **garagiste** *nm/f* garage owner; garage mechanic

garant, e [gaʁɑ̃, -ɑ̃t] *nm/f* guarantor ♦ *nm* guarantee; **se porter ~ de** to vouch for; to be answerable for

garantie [gaʁɑ̃ti] *nf* guarantee; (*gage*) security, surety; **(bon de) ~** guarantee *ou* warranty slip

garantir [gaʁɑ̃tiʁ] *vt* to guarantee; (*protéger*): **~ de** to protect from

garçon [gaʁsɔ̃] *nm* boy; (*célibataire*) bachelor; (*serveur*): **~ (de café)** waiter; **~ de courses** messenger; **garçonnet** *nm* small boy; **garçonnière** *nf* bachelor flat

garde [gaʁd(ə)] *nm* (*de prisonnier*) guard; (*de domaine etc*) warden; (*soldat, sentinelle*) guardsman ♦ *nf* guarding; looking after; (*soldats, BOXE, ESCRIME*) guard; (*faction*) watch; (*TYPO*): **(page de) ~** endpaper; flyleaf; **de ~** on duty; **monter la ~** to stand guard; **mettre en ~** to warn; **prendre ~ (à)** to be careful (of); **~ champêtre** *nm* rural policeman; **~ du corps** *nm* bodyguard; **~ des enfants** *nf* (*après divorce*) custody of the children; **~ des Sceaux** *nm* ≈ Lord Chancellor (*BRIT*), ≈ Attorney General (*US*); **~ à vue** *nf* (*JUR*) ≈ police custody; **~-à-vous** *nm*: **être/se mettre au ~-à-vous** to be at/stand to attention; **~-barrière** *nm/f* level-crossing keeper; **~-boue** *nm inv* mudguard; **~-chasse** *nm* gamekeeper; **~-fou** *nm* railing, parapet; **~-malade** *nm* home nurse; **~-manger** *nm inv* meat safe; pantry, larder

garder [gaʁde] *vt* (*conserver*) to keep; (*surveiller: enfants*) to look after; (: *immeuble, lieu, prisonnier*) to guard; **se ~** *vi* (*aliment: se conserver*) to keep; **se ~ de faire** to be careful not to do; **~ le lit/la chambre** to stay in bed/indoors; **pêche/chasse gardée** private fishing/hunting (ground)

garderie [gaʁdəʁi] *nf* day nursery, crèche

garde-robe [gaʁdəʁɔb] *nf* wardrobe

gardien, ne [gaʁdjɛ̃, -jɛn] *nm/f* (*garde*) guard; (*de prison*) warder; (*de domaine, réserve*) warden; (*de musée etc*) attendant; (*de phare, cimetière*) keeper; (*d'immeuble*) caretaker; (*fig*) guardian; **~ de but** goalkeeper; **~ de la paix** policeman; **~ de nuit** night watchman

gare [gaʁ] *nf* (*railway*) station, train station (*US*) ♦ *excl* watch out!; **~ routière** bus station

garer [gaʁe] *vt* to park; **se ~** *vi* to park; (*pour laisser passer*) to draw into the side

gargariser [gaʁgaʁize]: **se ~** *vi* to gargle; **gargarisme** *nm* gargling *no pl*; gargle

gargote [gaʁgɔt] *nf* cheap restaurant

gargouille [gaʁguj] *nf* gargoyle

gargouiller [gaʁguje] *vi* to gurgle

garnement [gaʁnəmɑ̃] *nm* rascal, scallywag

garni, e [gaʁni] *adj* (*plat*) served with vegetables (*and chips or rice etc*) ♦ *nm* furnished accommodation *no pl*

garnir [gaʁniʁ] *vt* (*orner*) to decorate; to trim; (*approvisionner*) to fill, stock; (*protéger*) to fit

garnison [gaʁnizɔ̃] *nf* garrison

garniture [gaʁnityʁ] *nf* (*CULIN*) vegetables *pl*; filling; (*décoration*) trimming; (*protection*) fittings *pl*; **~ de frein** brake lining

garrot [gaʁo] *nm* (*MÉD*) tourniquet

gars [gɑ] *nm* lad; guy

Gascogne [gaskɔɲ] *nf* Gascony; **le golfe de ~** the Bay of Biscay

gas-oil [gazɔjl] *nm* diesel (oil)

gaspiller [gaspije] *vt* to waste

gastronomique [gastʁɔnɔmik] *adj* gastronomic

gâteau, x [gɑto] *nm* cake; **~ sec** biscuit

gâter [gɑte] *vt* to spoil; **se ~** *vi* (*dent, fruit*) to go bad; (*temps, situation*) to change for the worse

gâterie [gɑtʁi] *nf* little treat

gâteux, euse [gɑtø, -øz] *adj* senile

gauche [goʃ] *adj* left, left-hand; (*maladroit*) awkward, clumsy ♦ *nf* (*POL*) left (wing); **à ~** on the left; (*direction*) (to the) left; **gaucher, ère** *adj* left-handed; **gauchiste** *nm/f* leftist

gaufre [gofʁ(ə)] *nf* waffle

gaufrette [gofʁɛt] *nf* wafer

gaulois, e [golwa, -waz] *adj* Gallic; (*grivois*) bawdy ♦ *nm/f*: **G~, e** Gaul

gausser [gose]: **se ~ de** *vt* to deride

gaver [gave] *vt* to force-feed; (*fig*): **~ de** to cram with, fill up with

gaz [gaz] *nm inv* gas

gaze [gaz] *nf* gauze

gazéifié, e [gazeifje] *adj* aerated

gazette [gazɛt] *nf* news sheet

gazeux, euse [gazø, -øz] *adj* gaseous; (*boisson*) fizzy; (*eau*) sparkling

gazoduc [gazɔdyk] *nm* gas pipeline

gazon [gazɔ̃] *nm* (*herbe*) turf; grass; (*pelouse*) lawn

gazouiller [gazuje] *vi* to chirp; (*enfant*) to

babble

geai [ʒɛ] nm jay

géant, e [ʒeɑ̃, -ɑ̃t] adj gigantic, giant; (COMM) giant-size ♦ nm/f giant

geindre [ʒɛ̃dr(ə)] vi to groan, moan

gel [ʒɛl] nm frost; freezing

gélatine [ʒelatin] nf gelatine

gelée [ʒəle] nf jelly; (gel) frost

geler [ʒəle] vt, vi to freeze; **il gèle** it's freezing

gélule [ʒelyl] nf (MÉD) capsule

Gémeaux [ʒemo] nmpl: **les ~** Gemini

gémir [ʒemir] vi to groan, moan

gemme [ʒɛm] nf gem(stone)

gênant, e [ʒɛnɑ̃, -ɑ̃t] adj annoying; embarrassing

gencive [ʒɑ̃siv] nf gum

gendarme [ʒɑ̃darm(ə)] nm gendarme; **~rie** nf military police force in countryside and small towns; their police station or barracks

gendre [ʒɑ̃dr(ə)] nm son-in-law

gêne [ʒɛn] nf (à respirer, bouger) discomfort, difficulty; (dérangement) bother, trouble; (manque d'argent) financial difficulties pl ou straits pl; (confusion) embarrassment

gêné, e [ʒene] adj embarrassed

gêner [ʒene] vt (incommoder) to bother; (encombrer) to hamper; to be in the way; (embarrasser): **~ qn** to make sb feel ill-at-ease; **se ~** vi to put o.s. out

général, e, aux [ʒeneral, -o] adj, nm general; **en ~** usually, in general; **~e** nf: (répétition) **~e** final dress rehearsal; **~ement** adv generally

généraliser [ʒeneralize] vt, vi to generalize; **se ~** vi to become widespread

généraliste [ʒeneralist(ə)] nm/f general practitioner, G.P.

générateur, trice [ʒeneratœr, -tris] adj: **~ de** which causes

génération [ʒenerasjɔ̃] nf generation

généreux, euse [ʒenerø, -øz] adj generous

générique [ʒenerik] nm (CINÉMA) credits pl, credit titles pl

générosité [ʒenerozite] nf generosity

genêt [ʒəne] nm broom no pl (shrub)

génétique [ʒenetik] adj genetic

Genève [ʒənɛv] n Geneva

génial, e, aux [ʒenjal, -o] adj of genius; (fam: formidable) fantastic, brilliant

génie [ʒeni] nm genius; (MIL): **le ~** the Engineers pl; **~ civil** civil engineering

genièvre [ʒənjɛvr(ə)] nm juniper

génisse [ʒenis] nf heifer

genou, x [ʒnu] nm knee; **à ~x** on one's knees; **se mettre à ~x** to kneel down

genre [ʒɑ̃r] nm kind, type, sort; (allure) manner; (LING) gender

gens [ʒɑ̃] nmpl (f in some phrases) people pl

gentil, le [ʒɑ̃ti, -ij] adj kind; (enfant: sage) good; (endroit etc) nice; **gentillesse** nf kindness; **gentiment** adv kindly

géographie [ʒeɔgrafi] nf geography

geôlier [ʒolje] nm jailer

géologie [ʒeɔlɔʒi] nf geology

géomètre [ʒeɔmɛtr(ə)] nm: (arpenteur-)~ (land) surveyor

géométrie [ʒeɔmetri] nf geometry; **géométrique** adj geometric

gérance [ʒerɑ̃s] nf management; **mettre en ~** to appoint a manager for

géranium [ʒeranjɔm] nm geranium

gérant, e [ʒerɑ̃, -ɑ̃t] nm/f manager(eress)

gerbe [ʒɛrb(ə)] nf (de fleurs) spray; (de blé) sheaf; (fig) shower, burst

gercé, e [ʒɛrse] adj chapped

gerçure [ʒɛrsyr] nf crack

gérer [ʒere] vt to manage

germain, e [ʒɛrmɛ̃, -ɛn] adj: **cousin ~** first cousin

germe [ʒɛrm(ə)] nm germ; **~r** [ʒɛrme] vi to sprout; to germinate

geste [ʒɛst(ə)] nm gesture; move; motion

gestion [ʒɛstjɔ̃] nf management

gibecière [ʒibsjɛr] nf gamebag

gibet [ʒibe] nm gallows pl

gibier [ʒibje] nm (animaux) game; (fig) prey

giboulée [ʒibule] nf sudden shower

gicler [ʒikle] vi to spurt, squirt

gifle [ʒifl(ə)] nf slap (in the face); **gifler** vt to slap (in the face)

gigantesque [ʒigɑ̃tɛsk(ə)] adj gigantic

gigogne [ʒigɔɲ] adj: **lits ~s** truckle (BRIT) ou trundle beds

gigot [ʒigo] nm leg (of mutton ou lamb)

gigoter [ʒigɔte] vi to wriggle (about)

gilet [ʒile] nm waistcoat; (pull) cardigan; (de corps) vest; **~ de sauvetage** life jacket

gingembre [ʒɛ̃ʒɑ̃br(ə)] nm ginger

girafe [ʒiraf] nf giraffe

giratoire [ʒiratwar] adj: **sens ~** roundabout

girofle [ʒirɔfl(ə)] nf: **clou de ~** clove

girouette [ʒirwet] nf weather vane ou cock

gisait etc vb voir **gésir**

gisement [ʒizmɑ̃] nm deposit

gît vb voir **gésir**

gitan, e [ʒitɑ̃, -an] nm/f gipsy

gîte [ʒit] nm home; shelter; **~ (rural)** holiday cottage ou apartment

givre [ʒivr(ə)] nm (hoar) frost

glabre [glabr(ə)] adj hairless; clean-shaven

glace [glas] nf ice; (crème glacée) ice cream; (verre) sheet of glass; (miroir) mirror; (de voiture) window

glacé, e [glase] adj icy; (boisson) iced

glacer [glase] vt to freeze; (boisson) to chill, ice; (gâteau) to ice; (papier, tissu) to glaze; (fig): **~ qn** to chill sb; to make sb's blood run cold

glacial, e [glasjal] *adj* icy
glacier [glasje] *nm* (GÉO) glacier; (*marchand*) ice-cream maker
glacière [glasjɛʀ] *nf* icebox
glaçon [glasɔ̃] *nm* icicle; (*pour boisson*) ice cube
glaise [glɛz] *nf* clay
gland [glɑ̃] *nm* acorn; (*décoration*) tassel
glande [glɑ̃d] *nf* gland
glaner [glane] *vt, vi* to glean
glapir [glapiʀ] *vi* to yelp
glas [glɑ] *nm* knell, toll
glauque [glok] *adj* dull blue-green
glissant, e [glisɑ̃, -ɑ̃t] *adj* slippery
glissement [glismɑ̃] *nm*: ~ **de terrain** landslide
glisser [glise] *vi* (*avancer*) to glide *ou* slide along; (*coulisser, tomber*) to slide; (*déraper*) to slip; (*être glissant*) to be slippery ♦ *vt* to slip; **se ~ dans** to slip into
global, e, aux [glɔbal, -o] *adj* overall
globe [glɔb] *nm* globe
globule [glɔbyl] *nm* (*du sang*) corpuscle
globuleux, euse [glɔbylø, -øz] *adj*: **yeux ~** protruding eyes
gloire [glwaʀ] *nf* glory; (*mérite*) distinction, credit; (*personne*) celebrity; **glorieux, euse** *adj* glorious
glousser [gluse] *vi* to cluck; (*rire*) to chuckle
glouton, ne [glutɔ̃, -ɔn] *adj* gluttonous
gluant, e [glyɑ̃, -ɑ̃t] *adj* sticky, gummy
glycine [glisin] *nf* wisteria
go [go] : **tout de ~** *adv* straight out
G.O. *sigle* = **grandes ondes**
gobelet [gɔblɛ] *nm* tumbler; beaker; (*à dés*) cup
gober [gɔbe] *vt* to swallow
godasse [gɔdas] (*fam*) *nf* shoe
godet [gɔdɛ] *nm* pot
goéland [gɔelɑ̃] *nm* (sea)gull
goélette [gɔelɛt] *nf* schooner
goémon [gɔemɔ̃] *nm* wrack
gogo [gɔgo] : **à ~** *adv* galore
goguenard, e [gɔgnaʀ, -aʀd(ə)] *adj* mocking
goinfre [gwɛ̃fʀ(ə)] *nm* glutton
golf [gɔlf] *nm* golf; golf course
golfe [gɔlf(ə)] *nm* gulf; bay
gomme [gɔm] *nf* (*à effacer*) rubber (BRIT), eraser; **gommer** *vt* to rub out (BRIT), erase
gond [gɔ̃] *nm* hinge; **sortir de ses ~s** (*fig*) to fly off the handle
gondoler [gɔ̃dɔle] : **se ~** *vi* to warp; to buckle
gonflé, e [gɔ̃fle] *adj* swollen; bloated
gonfler [gɔ̃fle] *vt* (*pneu, ballon*) to inflate, blow up; (*nombre, importance*) to inflate ♦ *vi* to swell (up); (CULIN: *pâte*) to rise
gonzesse [gɔ̃zɛs] (*fam*) *nf* chick, bird (BRIT)
goret [gɔʀɛ] *nm* piglet

gorge [gɔʀʒ(ə)] *nf* (ANAT) throat; (*poitrine*) breast
gorgé, e [gɔʀʒe] *adj*: ~ **de** filled with; (*eau*) saturated with; **gorgée** *nf* mouthful; sip; gulp
gorille [gɔʀij] *nm* gorilla; (*fam*) bodyguard
gosier [gozje] *nm* throat
gosse [gɔs] *nm/f* kid
goudron [gudʀɔ̃] *nm* tar; **goudronner** *vt* to tar(mac) (BRIT), asphalt (US)
gouffre [gufʀ(ə)] *nm* abyss, gulf
goujat [guʒa] *nm* boor
goulot [gulo] *nm* neck; **boire au ~** to drink from the bottle
goulu, e [guly] *adj* greedy
gourd, e [guʀ, guʀd(ə)] *adj* numb (with cold)
gourde [guʀd(ə)] *nf* (*récipient*) flask; (*fam*) (clumsy) clot *ou* oaf ♦ *adj* oafish
gourdin [guʀdɛ̃] *nm* club, bludgeon
gourmand, e [guʀmɑ̃, -ɑ̃d] *adj* greedy; **gourmandise** *nf* greed; (*bonbon*) sweet
gousse [gus] *nf*: ~ **d'ail** clove of garlic
goût [gu] *nm* taste; **de bon ~** tasteful; **de mauvais ~** tasteless; **prendre ~ à** to develop a taste *ou* a liking for
goûter [gute] *vt* (*essayer*) to taste; (*apprécier*) to enjoy ♦ *vi* to have (afternoon) tea ♦ *nm* (afternoon) tea
goutte [gut] *nf* drop; (MÉD) gout; (*alcool*) brandy
goutte-à-goutte [gutagut] *nm* (MÉD) drip; **tomber ~** to drip
gouttière [gutjɛʀ] *nf* gutter
gouvernail [guvɛʀnaj] *nm* rudder; (*barre*) helm, tiller
gouvernante [guvɛʀnɑ̃t] *nf* governess
gouverne [guvɛʀn(ə)] *nf*: **pour sa ~** for his guidance
gouvernement [guvɛʀnəmɑ̃] *nm* government; **gouvernemental, e, aux** *adj* government *cpd*; pro-government
gouverner [guvɛʀne] *vt* to govern
grabuge [gʀabyʒ] *nm* mayhem
grâce [gʀɑs] *nf* grace; favour; (JUR) pardon; ~**s** *nfpl* (REL) grace *sg*; **faire ~ à qn de qch** to spare sb sth; **rendre ~(s) à** to give thanks to; **demander ~** to beg for mercy; ~ **à** thanks to; **gracier** *vt* to pardon; **gracieux, euse** *adj* graceful
grade [gʀad] *nm* rank; **monter en ~** to be promoted
gradé [gʀade] *nm* officer
gradin [gʀadɛ̃] *nm* tier; step; ~**s** *nmpl* (*de stade*) terracing *sg*
graduel, le [gʀadɥɛl] *adj* gradual; progressive
graduer [gʀadɥe] *vt* (*effort etc*) to increase gradually; (*règle, verre*) to graduate
grain [gʀɛ̃] *nm* (*gén*) grain; (NAVIG) squall; ~ **de beauté** beauty spot; ~ **de café** coffee bean; ~ **de poivre** peppercorn; ~ **de pous-**

sière speck of dust; **~ de raisin** grape

graine [gʀɛn] *nf* seed

graissage [gʀɛsaʒ] *nm* lubrication, greasing

graisse [gʀɛs] *nf* fat; (*lubrifiant*) grease; **graisser** *vt* to lubricate, grease; (*tacher*) to make greasy

grammaire [gʀamɛʀ] *nf* grammar; **grammatical, e, aux** *adj* grammatical

gramme [gʀam] *nm* gramme

grand, e [gʀɑ̃, gʀɑ̃d] *adj* (*haut*) tall; (*gros, vaste, large*) big, large; (*long*) long; (*sens abstraits*) great ♦ *adv*: **~ ouvert** wide open; **au ~ air** in the open (air); **les ~s blessés** the severely injured; **~ ensemble** housing scheme; **~ magasin** department store; **~e personne** grown-up; **~e surface** hypermarket; **~es écoles** prestige schools of university level; **~es lignes** (*RAIL*) main lines; **~es vacances** summer holidays; **grand-chose** *nm/f inv*: **pas grand-chose** not much; **Grande-Bretagne** *nf* (Great) Britain; **grandeur** *nf* (*dimension*) size; magnitude; (*fig*) greatness; **~eur nature** life-size; **grandir** *vi* to grow ♦ *vt*: **grandir qn** (*suj: vêtement, chaussure*) to make sb look taller; **~-mère** *nf* grandmother; **~-messe** *nf* high mass; **~-peine** *adv*: **à ~-peine** with difficulty; **~-père** *nm* grandfather; **~-route** *nf* main road; **~s-parents** *nmpl* grandparents

grange [gʀɑ̃ʒ] *nf* barn

granit(e) [gʀanit] *nm* granite

graphique [gʀafik] *adj* graphic ♦ *nm* graph

grappe [gʀap] *nf* cluster; **~ de raisin** bunch of grapes

grappiller [gʀapije] *vt* to glean

grappin [gʀapɛ̃] *nm* grapnel; **mettre le ~ sur** (*fig*) to get one's claws on

gras, se [gʀɑ, gʀɑs] *adj* (*viande, soupe*) fatty; (*personne*) fat; (*surface, main*) greasy; (*plaisanterie*) coarse; (*TYPO*) bold ♦ *nm* (*CULIN*) fat; **faire la ~se matinée** to have a lie-in (*BRIT*), sleep late (*US*); **grassement** *adv*: **grassement payé** handsomely paid; **grassouillet, te** *adj* podgy, plump

gratifiant, e [gʀatifjɑ̃, -ɑ̃t] *adj* gratifying, rewarding

gratifier [gʀatifje] *vt*: **~ qn de** to favour sb with; to reward sb with

gratiné, e [gʀatine] *adj* (*CULIN*) au gratin

gratis [gʀatis] *adv* free

gratitude [gʀatityd] *nf* gratitude

gratte-ciel [gʀatsjɛl] *nm inv* skyscraper

gratte-papier [gʀatpapje] (*péj*) *nm inv* pen-pusher

gratter [gʀate] *vt* (*frotter*) to scrape; (*enlever*) to scrape off; (*bras, bouton*) to scratch

gratuit, e [gʀatɥi, -ɥit] *adj* (*entrée, billet*) free; (*fig*) gratuitous

gravats [gʀava] *nmpl* rubble *sg*

grave [gʀav] *adj* (*maladie, accident*) serious, bad; (*sujet, problème*) serious, grave; (*air*)

grave, solemn; (*voix, son*) deep, low-pitched; **gravement** *adv* seriously; gravely

graver [gʀave] *vt* to engrave

gravier [gʀavje] *nm* gravel *no pl*; **gravillons** *nmpl* loose gravel *sg*

gravir [gʀaviʀ] *vt* to climb (up)

gravité [gʀavite] *nf* seriousness; gravity

graviter [gʀavite] *vi* to revolve

gravure [gʀavyʀ] *nf* engraving; (*reproduction*) print; plate

gré [gʀe] *nm*: **à son ~** to his liking; as he pleases; **au ~ de** according to, following; **contre le ~ de qn** against sb's will; **de son (plein) ~** of one's own free will; **bon ~ mal ~** like it or not; **de ~ ou de force** whether one likes it or not; **savoir ~ à qn de qch** to be grateful to sb for sth

grec, grecque [gʀɛk] *adj* Greek; (*classique: vase etc*) Grecian ♦ *nm/f* Greek

Grèce [gʀɛs] *nf*: **la ~** Greece

gréement [gʀemɑ̃] *nm* rigging

greffer [gʀefe] *vt* (*BOT, MÉD: tissu*) to graft; (*MÉD: organe*) to transplant

greffier [gʀefje] *nm* clerk of the court

grêle [gʀɛl] *adj* (*very*) thin ♦ *nf* hail

grêlé, e [gʀele] *adj* pockmarked

grêler [gʀele] *vb impers*: **il grêle** it's hailing; **grêlon** [gʀelɔ̃] *nm* hailstone

grelot [gʀəlo] *nm* little bell

grelotter [gʀəlɔte] *vi* to shiver

grenade [gʀənad] *nf* (*explosive*) grenade; (*BOT*) pomegranate

grenat [gʀəna] *adj inv* dark red

grenier [gʀənje] *nm* attic; (*de ferme*) loft

grenouille [gʀənuj] *nf* frog

grès [gʀɛ] *nm* sandstone; (*poterie*) stoneware

grésiller [gʀezije] *vi* to sizzle; (*RADIO*) to crackle

grève [gʀɛv] *nf* (*d'ouvriers*) strike; (*plage*) shore; **se mettre en/faire ~** to go on/be on strike; **~ de la faim** hunger strike; **~ du zèle** work-to-rule (*BRIT*), slowdown (*US*)

grever [gʀəve] *vt* to put a strain on

gréviste [gʀevist(ə)] *nm/f* striker

gribouiller [gʀibuje] *vt* to scribble, scrawl

grief [gʀijɛf] *nm* grievance; **faire ~ à qn de** to reproach sb for

grièvement [gʀijɛvmɑ̃] *adv* seriously

griffe [gʀif] *nf* claw; (*fig*) signature

griffer [gʀife] *vt* to scratch

griffonner [gʀifɔne] *vt* to scribble

grignoter [gʀiɲɔte] *vt* to nibble *ou* gnaw at

gril [gʀil] *nm* steak *ou* grill pan

grillade [gʀijad] *nf* grill

grillage [gʀijaʒ] *nm* (*treillis*) wire netting; wire fencing

grille [gʀij] *nf* (*clôture*) railings *pl*; (*portail*) (metal) gate; (*d'égout*) (metal) grate; (*fig*) grid

grille-pain [gʀijpɛ̃] *nm inv* toaster

griller [gʀije] *vt (aussi: faire ~: pain)* to toast; (: *viande*) to grill; (*fig: ampoule etc*) to burn out, blow

grillon [gʀijɔ̃] *nm* cricket

grimace [gʀimas] *nf* grimace; (*pour faire rire*): **faire des ~s** to pull *ou* make faces

grimer [gʀime] *vt* to make up

grimper [gʀɛ̃pe] *vi, vt* to climb

grincer [gʀɛ̃se] *vi (porte, roue)* to grate; (*plancher*) to creak; **~ des dents** to grind one's teeth

grincheux, euse [gʀɛ̃ʃø, -øz] *adj* grumpy

grippe [gʀip] *nf* flu, influenza; **grippé, e** *adj*: **être grippé** to have flu

gris, e [gʀi, gʀiz] *adj* grey; (*ivre*) tipsy; **faire ~e mine** to pull a miserable *ou* wry face

grisaille [gʀizaj] *nf* greyness, dullness

griser [gʀize] *vt* to intoxicate

grisonner [gʀizɔne] *vi* to be going grey

grisou [gʀizu] *nm* firedamp

grive [gʀiv] *nf* thrush

grivois, e [gʀivwa, -waz] *adj* saucy

Groenland [gʀɔɛnlɑ̃d] *nm* Greenland

grogner [gʀɔɲe] *vi* to growl; (*fig*) to grumble

groin [gʀwɛ̃] *nm* snout

grommeler [gʀɔmle] *vi* to mutter to o.s.

gronder [gʀɔ̃de] *vi* to rumble; (*fig: révolte*) to be brewing ♦ *vt* to scold

gros, se [gʀo, gʀos] *adj* big, large; (*obèse*) fat; (*travaux, dégâts*) extensive; (*large: trait, fil*) thick, heavy ♦ *adv*: **risquer/gagner ~** to risk/win a lot ♦ *nm* (*COMM*): **le ~ the** wholesale business; **prix de ~** wholesale price; **par ~ temps/grosse mer** in rough weather/heavy seas; **le ~ de** the main body of; the bulk of; **en ~** roughly; (*COMM*) wholesale; **~ lot** jackpot; **~ mot** coarse word; **~ œuvre** *nm* (*CONSTR*) shell (of building); **~ plan** (*PHOTO*) close-up; **~ sel** cooking salt; **~se caisse** big drum

groseille [gʀozɛj] *nf*: **~ (rouge)/(blanche)** red/white currant; **~ à maquereau** gooseberry

grosse [gʀos] *adj voir* gros

grossesse [gʀoses] *nf* pregnancy

grosseur [gʀosœʀ] *nf* size; fatness; (*tumeur*) lump

grossier, ière [gʀosje, -ɛʀ] *adj* coarse; (*travail*) rough; crude; (*évident: erreur*) gross

grossir [gʀosiʀ] *vi (personne)* to put on weight; (*fig*) to grow, get bigger; (*rivière*) to swell ♦ *vt* to increase; to exaggerate; (*au microscope*) to magnify; (*suj: vêtement*): **~ qn** to make sb look fatter

grossiste [gʀosist(ə)] *nm/f* wholesaler

grosso modo [gʀɔsomɔdo] *adv* roughly

grotte [gʀɔt] *nf* cave

grouiller [gʀuje] *vi* to mill about; to swarm about; **~ de** to be swarming with

groupe [gʀup] *nm* group; **le ~ des 7** Group of 7; **~ sanguin** *nm* blood group; **~ment** [gʀupmɑ̃] *nm* grouping; group

grouper [gʀupe] *vt* to group; **se ~** *vi* to get together

grue [gʀy] *nf* crane

grumeaux [gʀymo] *nmpl* lumps

gué [ge] *nm* ford; **passer à ~** to ford

guenilles [gənij] *nfpl* rags

guenon [gənɔ̃] *nf* female monkey

guépard [gepaʀ] *nm* cheetah

guêpe [gɛp] *nf* wasp

guêpier [gepje] *nm* (*fig*) trap

guère [gɛʀ] *adv (avec adjectif, adverbe)*: **ne ... ~** hardly; (*avec verbe*): **ne ... ~** *tournure négative* +much; hardly ever; *tournure négative* +(very) long; **il n'y a ~ que/de** there's hardly anybody (*ou* anything) but/ hardly any

guéridon [geʀidɔ̃] *nm* pedestal table

guérilla [geʀija] *nf* guerrilla warfare

guérir [geʀiʀ] *vt (personne, maladie)* to cure; (*membre, plaie*) to heal ♦ *vi* to recover, be cured; to heal; **guérison** *nf* curing; healing; recovery

guérite [geʀit] *nf* sentry box

guerre [gɛʀ] *nf* war; (*méthode*): **~ atomique** atomic warfare *no pl*; **en ~** at war; **faire la ~ à** to wage war against; **de ~ lasse** finally; **~ d'usure** war of attrition; **guerrier, ière** *adj* warlike ♦ *nm/f* warrior

guet [gɛ] *nm*: **faire le ~** to be on the watch *ou* look-out

guet-apens [gɛtapɑ̃] *nm* ambush

guetter [gete] *vt (épier)* to watch (intently); (*attendre*) to watch (out) for; to be lying in wait for

gueule [gœl] *nf* mouth; (*fam*) face; mouth; **ta ~!** (*fam*) shut up!; **~ de bois** (*fam*) hangover

gueuler [gœle] (*fam*) *vi* to bawl

gui [gi] *nm* mistletoe

guichet [giʃɛ] *nm (de bureau, banque)* counter, window; (*d'une porte*) wicket, hatch; **les ~s** (*à la gare, au théâtre*) the ticket office *sg*

guide [gid] *nm* guide

guider [gide] *vt* to guide

guidon [gidɔ̃] *nm* handlebars *pl*

guignol [giɲɔl] *nm* ≈ Punch and Judy show; (*fig*) clown

guillemets [gijmɛ] *nmpl*: **entre ~** in inverted commas

guillotiner [gijɔtine] *vt* to guillotine

guindé, e [gɛ̃de] *adj* stiff, starchy

guirlande [giʀlɑ̃d] *nf* garland; (*de papier*) paper chain

guise [giz] *nf*: **à votre ~** as you wish *ou* please; **en ~ de** by way of

guitare [gitaʀ] *nf* guitar

gymnase [ʒimnaz] *nm* gym(nasium)

gymnastique [ʒimnastik] *nf* gymnastics *sg*; (*au réveil etc*) keep-fit exercises *pl*

gynécologie [ʒinekɔlɔʒi] *nf* gynaecology; **gynécologue** *nm/f* gynaecologist

H h

habile [abil] *adj* skilful; (*malin*) clever; **habileté** *nf* skill, skilfulness; cleverness

habilité, e [abilite] *adj*: ~ **à faire** entitled to do, empowered to do

habillé, e [abije] *adj* dressed; (*chic*) dressy; (*TECH*): ~ **de** covered with; encased in

habillement [abijmɑ̃] *nm* clothes *pl*

habiller [abije] *vt* to dress; (*fournir en vêtements*) to clothe; **s'~** *vi* to dress (o.s.); (*se déguiser, mettre des vêtements chic*) to dress up

habit [abi] *nm* outfit; ~**s** *nmpl* (*vêtements*) clothes; ~ **(de soirée)** tails *pl*; evening dress

habitant, e [abitɑ̃, -ɑ̃t] *nm/f* inhabitant; (*d'une maison*) occupant

habitation [abitɑsjɔ̃] *nf* living; residence, home; house; ~**s à loyer modéré** low-rent housing *sg*

habiter [abite] *vt* to live in; (*suj: sentiment*) to dwell in ♦ *vi*: ~ **à/dans** to live in *ou* at/in

habitude [abityd] *nf* habit; **avoir l'~ de faire** to be in the habit of doing; (*expérience*) to be used to doing; **d'~** usually; **comme d'~** as usual

habitué, e [abitɥe] *nm/f* regular visitor; regular (customer)

habituel, le [abitɥɛl] *adj* usual

habituer [abitɥe] *vt*: ~ **qn à** to get sb used to; **s'~ à** to get used to

'hache [ˈaʃ] *nf* axe

'hacher [ˈaʃe] *vt* (*viande*) to mince; (*persil*) to chop

'hachis [ˈaʃi] *nm* mince *no pl*

'hachoir [ˈaʃwaʀ] *nm* chopper; (*meat*) mincer; chopping board

'hagard, e [ˈagaʀ, -aʀd(ə)] *adj* wild, distraught

'haie [ˈɛ] *nf* hedge; (*SPORT*) hurdle; (*fig: rang*) line, row

'haillons [ˈajɔ̃] *nmpl* rags

'haine [ˈɛn] *nf* hatred

'haïr [ˈaiʀ] *vt* to detest, hate

'hâlé, e [ˈale] *adj* (sun)tanned, sunburnt

haleine [alɛn] *nf* breath; **hors d'~** out of breath; **tenir en ~** to hold spellbound; to keep in suspense; **de longue ~** long-term

'haler [ˈale] *vt* to haul in; to tow

'haleter [ˈalte] *vt* to pant

'hall [ˈol] *nm* hall

'halle [ˈal] *nf* (covered) market; ~**s** *nfpl* (*d'une grande ville*) central food market *sg*

hallucinant, e [alysinɑ̃, -ɑ̃t] *adj* staggering

hallucination [alysinɑsjɔ̃] *nf* hallucination

'halte [ˈalt(ə)] *nf* stop, break; stopping place; (*RAIL*) halt ♦ *excl* stop!; **faire ~** to stop

haltère [altɛʀ] *nm* dumbbell, barbell; ~**s** *nmpl*: **(poids et) ~s** (*activité*) weight lifting *sg*

'hamac [ˈamak] *nm* hammock

'hameau, x [ˈamo] *nm* hamlet

hameçon [amsɔ̃] *nm* (fish) hook

'hanche [ˈɑ̃ʃ] *nf* hip

'handicapé, e [ˈɑ̃dikape] *nm/f* physically (*ou* mentally) handicapped person; ~ **moteur** spastic

'hangar [ˈɑ̃gaʀ] *nm* shed; (*AVIAT*) hangar

'hanneton [ˈantɔ̃] *nm* cockchafer

'hanter [ˈɑ̃te] *vt* to haunt

'hantise [ˈɑ̃tiz] *nf* obsessive fear

'happer [ˈape] *vt* to snatch; (*suj: train etc*) to hit

'haras [ˈaʀɑ] *nm* stud farm

'harassant, e [ˈaʀasɑ̃, -ɑ̃t] *adj* exhausting

'harceler [ˈaʀsəle] *vt* (*MIL, CHASSE*) to harass, harry; (*importuner*) to plague

'hardi, e [ˈaʀdi] *adj* bold, daring

'hareng [ˈaʀɑ̃] *nm* herring

'hargne [ˈaʀɲ(ə)] *nf* aggressiveness

'haricot [ˈaʀiko] *nm* bean; **haricot blanc** haricot bean; **haricot vert** green bean

harmonica [aʀmɔnika] *nm* mouth organ

harmonie [aʀmɔni] *nf* harmony

'harnacher [ˈaʀnaʃe] *vt* to harness

'harnais [ˈaʀnɛ] *nm* harness

'harpe [ˈaʀp(ə)] *nf* harp

'harponner [ˈaʀpɔne] *vt* to harpoon; (*fam*) to collar

'hasard [ˈazaʀ] *nm*: **le ~** chance, fate; **un ~** a coincidence; a stroke of luck; **au ~** aimlessly; haphazardly; **par ~** by chance; **à tout ~** just in case; on the off chance (*BRIT*); **'hasarder** [ˈazaʀde] *vt* (*mot*) to venture; (*fortune*) to risk

'hâte [ˈɑt] *nf* haste; **à la ~** hurriedly, hastily; **en ~** posthaste, with all possible speed; **avoir ~ de** to be eager *ou* anxious to; ~**r** *vt* to hasten; **se ~r** *vi* to hurry

'hâtif, ive [ˈɑtif, -iv] *adj* hurried; hasty; (*légume*) early

'hausse [ˈos] *nf* rise, increase

'hausser [ˈose] *vt* to raise; ~ **les épaules** to shrug (one's shoulders)

'haut, e [ˈo, ˈot] *adj* high; (*grand*) tall; (*son, voix*) high(-pitched) ♦ *adv* high ♦ *nm* top (part); **de 3 m de ~** 3 m high, 3 m in height; **des ~s et des bas** ups and downs; **en ~ lieu** in high places; **à ~e voix, (tout) ~** aloud, out loud; **du ~ de** from the top of; **de ~ en bas** from top to bottom;

downwards; **plus ~** higher up, further up; (_dans un texte_) above; (_parler_) louder; **en ~** up above; at (_ou_ to) the top; (_dans une maison_) upstairs; **en ~ de** at the top of

'**hautain, e** ['otɛ̃, -ɛn] _adj_ haughty

'**hautbois** ['obwa] _nm_ oboe

'**haut-de-forme** ['odfɔʀm(ə)] _nm_ top hat

'**hauteur** ['otœʀ] _nf_ height; (_fig_) loftiness; haughtiness; **à la ~ de** (_sur la même ligne_) level with; by; (_fig_) equal to; **à la ~** up to it

'**haut-fond** ['ofɔ̃] _nm_ shallow, shoal

'**haut-fourneau** ['ofuʀno] _nm_ blast _ou_ smelting furnace

'**haut-le-cœur** ['olkœʀ] _nm inv_ retch, heave

'**haut-parleur** ['opaʀlœʀ] _nm_ (loud)speaker

'**havre** ['ɑvʀ(ə)] _nm_ haven

'**Haye** ['ɛ] _n_: **la Haye** the Hague

hebdo [ɛbdɔ] (_fam_) _nm_ weekly

hebdomadaire [ɛbdɔmadɛʀ] _adj, nm_ weekly

héberger [ebɛʀʒe] _vt_ to accommodate, lodge; (_réfugiés_) to take in

hébété, e [ebete] _adj_ dazed

hébreu, x [ebʀø] _adj m, nm_ Hebrew

hécatombe [ekatɔ̃b] _nf_ slaughter

hectare [ɛktaʀ] _nm_ hectare

'**hein** ['ɛ̃] _excl_ eh?

'**hélas** ['elas] _excl_ alas! ♦ _adv_ unfortunately

'**héler** [ele] _vt_ to hail

hélice [elis] _nf_ propeller

hélicoptère [elikɔptɛʀ] _nm_ helicopter

helvétique [ɛlvetik] _adj_ Swiss

hémicycle [emisikl(ə)] _nm_ semicircle; (_POL_): **l'~** ≈ the benches (of the Commons) (_BRIT_), ≈ the floor (of the House of Representatives) (_US_)

hémorragie [emɔʀaʒi] _nf_ bleeding _no pl_, haemorrhage

hémorroïdes [emɔʀɔid] _nfpl_ piles, haemorrhoids

'**hennir** ['eniʀ] _vi_ to neigh, whinny

herbe [ɛʀb(ə)] _nf_ grass; (_CULIN, MÉD_) herb; **en ~** unripe; (_fig_) budding; **herbicide** _nm_ weed-killer; **herboriste** _nm/f_ herbalist

'**hère** ['ɛʀ] _nm_: **pauvre hère** poor wretch

héréditaire [eʀeditɛʀ] _adj_ hereditary

'**hérisser** ['eʀise] _vt_: **~ qn** (_fig_) to ruffle sb; **se ~** _vi_ to bristle, bristle up

'**hérisson** ['eʀisɔ̃] _nm_ hedgehog

héritage [eʀitaʒ] _nm_ inheritance; (_fig_) heritage; legacy

hériter [eʀite] _vi_: **~ de qch (de qn)** to inherit sth (from sb); **héritier, ière** _nm/f_ heir(ess)

hermétique [ɛʀmetik] _adj_ airtight; watertight; (_fig_) abstruse; impenetrable

hermine [ɛʀmin] _nf_ ermine

'**hernie** ['ɛʀni] _nf_ hernia

héroïne [eʀɔin] _nf_ heroine; (_drogue_) heroin

'**héron** ['eʀɔ̃] _nm_ heron

'**héros** ['eʀo] _nm_ hero

hésitation [ezitɑsjɔ̃] _nf_ hesitation

hésiter [ezite] _vi_: **~ (à faire)** to hesitate (to do)

hétéroclite [eteʀɔklit] _adj_ heterogeneous; (_objets_) sundry

'**hêtre** ['ɛtʀ(ə)] _nm_ beech

heure [œʀ] _nf_ hour; (_SCOL_) period; (_moment_) time; **c'est l'~** it's time; **quelle ~ est-il?** what time is it?; **2 ~s (du matin)** 2 o'clock (in the morning); **être à l'~** to be on time; (_montre_) to be right; **mettre à l'~** to set right; **à toute ~** at any time; **24 ~s sur 24** round the clock, 24 hours a day; **à l'~ qu'il est** at this time (of day); by now; **sur l'~** at once; **~ de pointe** _nf_ rush hour; **~s supplémentaires** overtime _sg_

heureusement [œʀøzmɑ̃] _adv_ (_par bonheur_) fortunately, luckily

heureux, euse [œʀø, -øz] _adj_ happy; (_chanceux_) lucky, fortunate; (_judicieux_) felicitous, fortunate

'**heurt** ['œʀ] _nm_ (_choc_) collision; **~s** _nmpl_ (_fig_) clashes

'**heurter** ['œʀte] _vt_ (_mur_) to strike, hit; (_personne_) to collide with; (_fig_) to go against, upset; **se ~ à** _vt_ to come up against; '**heurtoir** _nm_ door knocker

hexagone [ɛgzagɔn] _nm_ hexagon; (_la France_) France (_because of its shape_)

'**hiberner** [ibɛʀne] _vi_ to hibernate

'**hibou, x** ['ibu] _nm_ owl

'**hideux, euse** ['idø, -øz] _adj_ hideous

hier [jɛʀ] _adv_ yesterday; **toute la journée d'~** all day yesterday; **toute la matinée d'~** all yesterday morning

'**hiérarchie** ['jeʀaʀʃi] _nf_ hierarchy

hilare [ilaʀ] _adj_ mirthful

hippique [ipik] _adj_ equestrian, horse _cpd_

hippodrome [ipɔdʀom] _nm_ racecourse

hippopotame [ipɔpɔtam] _nm_ hippopotamus

hirondelle [iʀɔ̃dɛl] _nf_ swallow

hirsute [iʀsyt] _adj_ hairy; shaggy; tousled

'**hisser** ['ise] _vt_ to hoist, haul up

histoire [istwaʀ] _nf_ (_science, événements_) history; (_anecdote, récit, mensonge_) story; (_affaire_) business _no pl_; **~s** _nfpl_ (_chichis_) fuss _no pl_; (_ennuis_) trouble _sg_; **historique** _adj_ historical; (_important_) historic

hiver [ivɛʀ] _nm_ winter; **hivernal, e, aux** _adj_ winter _cpd_; wintry; **hiverner** _vi_ to winter

HLM _sigle m/f_ = **habitation(s) à loyer modéré**

'**hobby** ['ɔbi] _nm_ hobby

'**hocher** ['ɔʃe] _vt_: **~ la tête** to nod; (_signe négatif ou dubitatif_) to shake one's head

'**hochet** ['ɔʃɛ] _nm_ rattle

'**hockey** ['ɔkɛ] _nm_: **~ (sur glace/gazon)** (ice/field) hockey

'hold-up ['ɔldœp] *nm inv* hold-up
'hollandais, e ['ɔlɑ̃dɛ, -ez] *adj* Dutch ♦ *nm* (*LING*) Dutch ♦ *nm/f*: **Hollandais, e** Dutchman(woman); **les Hollandais** the Dutch
'Hollande ['ɔlɑ̃d] *nf*: **la ~** Holland
'homard ['ɔmaʀ] *nm* lobster
homéopathique [ɔmeɔpatik] *adj* homoeopathic
homicide [ɔmisid] *nm* murder; **~ involontaire** manslaughter
hommage [ɔmaʒ] *nm* tribute; **~s** *nmpl*: **présenter ses ~s** to pay one's respects; **rendre ~ à** to pay tribute *ou* homage to
homme [ɔm] *nm* man; **~ d'affaires** businessman; **~ d'État** statesman; **~ de main** hired man; **~ de paille** stooge; **~-grenouille** *nm* frogman
homo: **~gène** *adj* homogeneous; **~logue** *nm/f* counterpart, opposite number; **~logué, e** *adj* (*SPORT*) officially recognized, ratified; (*tarif*) authorized; **~nyme** *nm* (*LING*) homonym; (*d'une personne*) namesake; **~sexuel, le** *adj* homosexual
'Hongrie ['ɔ̃gʀi] *nf*: **la Hongrie** Hungary; **'hongrois, e** *adj, nm/f* Hungarian
honnête [ɔnɛt] *adj* (*intègre*) honest; (*juste, satisfaisant*) fair; **~ment** *adv* honestly; **~té** *nf* honesty
honneur [ɔnœʀ] *nm* honour; (*mérite*) credit; **en l'~ de** in honour of; (*événement*) on the occasion of; **faire ~ à** (*engagements*) to honour; (*famille*) to be a credit to; (*fig: repas etc*) to do justice to
honorable [ɔnɔʀabl(ə)] *adj* worthy, honourable; (*suffisant*) decent
honoraire [ɔnɔʀɛʀ] *adj* honorary; **professeur ~** professor emeritus; **honoraires** *nmpl* fees *pl*
honorer [ɔnɔʀe] *vt* to honour; (*estimer*) to hold in high regard; (*faire honneur à*) to do credit to; **s'~ de** *vt* to pride o.s. upon; **honorifique** *adj* honorary
'honte ['ɔ̃t] *nf* shame; **avoir ~ de** to be ashamed of; **faire ~ à qn** to make sb (feel) ashamed; **'honteux, euse** *adj* ashamed; (*conduite, acte*) shameful, disgraceful
hôpital, aux [ɔpital, -o] *nm* hospital
'hoquet ['ɔkɛ] *nm*: **avoir le hoquet** to have (the) hiccoughs; **'hoqueter** *vi* to hiccough
horaire [ɔʀɛʀ] *adj* hourly ♦ *nm* timetable, schedule; **~s** *nmpl* (*d'employé*) hours; **~ souple** flexitime
horizon [ɔʀizɔ̃] *nm* horizon; (*paysage*) landscape, view
horizontal, e, aux [ɔʀizɔ̃tal, -o] *adj* horizontal
horloge [ɔʀlɔʒ] *nf* clock; **horloger, ère** *nm/f* watchmaker; clockmaker; **horlogerie** *nf* watch-making; watchmaker's (shop); clockmaker's (shop)
'hormis ['ɔʀmi] *prép* save
horoscope [ɔʀɔskɔp] *nm* horoscope

horreur [ɔʀœʀ] *nf* horror; **avoir ~ de** to loathe *ou* detest; **horrible** *adj* horrible
horripiler [ɔʀipile] *vt* to exasperate
'hors ['ɔʀ] *prép* except (for); **~ de** out of; **~ pair** outstanding; **~ de propos** inopportune; **être ~ de soi** to be beside o.s.; **~ d'usage** out of service; **~-bord** *nm inv* speedboat (with outboard motor); **~-concours** *adj* ineligible to compete; **~-d'œuvre** *nm inv* hors d'œuvre; **~-jeu** *nm inv* offside; **~-la-loi** *nm inv* outlaw; **~-taxe** *adj* (*boutique, articles*) duty-free
hospice [ɔspis] *nm* (*de vieillards*) home
hospitalier, ière [ɔspitalje, -jɛʀ] *adj* (*accueillant*) hospitable; (*MÉD: service, centre*) hospital *cpd*
hospitalité [ɔspitalite] *nf* hospitality
hostie [ɔsti] *nf* host (*REL*)
hostile [ɔstil] *adj* hostile; **hostilité** *nf* hostility
hôte [ot] *nm* (*maître de maison*) host; (*invité*) guest
hôtel [otɛl] *nm* hotel; **aller à l'~** to stay in a hotel; **~ de ville** town hall; **~ (particulier)** (private) mansion; **hôtelier, ière** *adj* hotel *cpd* ♦ *nm/f* hotelier; **hôtellerie** *nf* hotel business; (*auberge*) inn
hôtesse [otɛs] *nf* hostess; **~ de l'air** air stewardess
'hotte ['ɔt] *nf* (*panier*) basket (carried on the back); (*de cheminée*) hood; **hotte aspirante** cooker hood
'houblon ['ublɔ̃] *nm* (*BOT*) hop; (*pour la bière*) hops *pl*
'houille ['uj] *nf* coal; **houille blanche** hydroelectric power
'houle ['ul] *nf* swell
'houlette ['ulɛt] *nf*: **sous la ~ de** under the guidance of
'houleux, euse ['ulø, -øz] *adj* heavy, swelling; (*fig*) stormy, turbulent
'houspiller ['uspije] *vt* to scold
'housse ['us] *nf* cover; dust cover; loose *ou* stretch cover
'houx ['u] *nm* holly
'hublot ['yblo] *nm* porthole
'huche ['yʃ] *nf*: **~ à pain** bread bin
'huer ['ɥe] *vt* to boo
huile [ɥil] *nf* oil; **huiler** *vt* to oil; **huileux, euse** *adj* oily
huis [ɥi] *nm*: **à ~ clos** in camera
huissier [ɥisje] *nm* usher; (*JUR*) ≈ bailiff
huit ['ɥit] *num* eight; **samedi en huit** a week on Saturday; **'huitaine** *nf*: **une huitaine (de jours)** a week or so; **'huitième** *num* eighth
huître [ɥitʀ(ə)] *nf* oyster
humain, e [ymɛ̃, -ɛn] *adj* human; (*compatissant*) humane ♦ *nm* human (being); **humanité** *nf* humanity
humble [œ̃bl(ə)] *adj* humble
humecter [ymɛkte] *vt* to dampen

'**humer** ['yme] *vt* to smell; to inhale

humeur [ymœʀ] *nf* mood; (*tempérament*) temper; (*irritation*) bad temper; **de bonne/ mauvaise ~** in a good/bad mood

humide [ymid] *adj* damp; (*main, yeux*) moist; (*climat, chaleur*) humid; (*saison, route*) wet

humilier [ymilje] *vt* to humiliate

humilité [ymilite] *nf* humility, humbleness

humoristique [ymɔʀistik] *adj* humorous; humoristic

humour [ymuʀ] *nm* humour; **avoir de l'~** to have a sense of humour; **~ noir** sick humour

'**hurlement** ['yʀləmã] *nm* howling *no pl*, howl, yelling *no pl*, yell

'**hurler** ['yʀle] *vi* to howl, yell

hurluberlu [yʀlybɛʀly] (*péj*) *nm* crank

'**hutte** ['yt] *nf* hut

hydratant, e [idʀatã, -ãt] *adj* (*crème*) moisturizing

hydrate [idʀat] *nm*: **~s de carbone** carbohydrates

hydraulique [idʀolik] *adj* hydraulic

hydravion [idʀavjɔ̃] *nm* seaplane

hydrogène [idʀɔʒɛn] *nm* hydrogen

hydroglisseur [idʀoɡlisœʀ] *nm* hydroplane

hygiénique [iʒjenik] *adj* hygienic

hymne [imn(ə)] *nm* hymn; **~ national** national anthem

hypermarché [ipɛʀmaʀʃe] *nm* hypermarket

hypermétrope [ipɛʀmetʀɔp] *adj* long-sighted

hypnotiser [ipnɔtize] *vt* to hypnotize

hypocrite [ipɔkʀit] *adj* hypocritical

hypothèque [ipɔtɛk] *nf* mortgage

hypothèse [ipɔtɛz] *nf* hypothesis

hystérique [isteʀik] *adj* hysterical

I i

iceberg [isbɛʀɡ] *nm* iceberg

ici [isi] *adv* here; **jusqu'~** as far as this; until now; **d'~ là** by then; in the meantime; **d'~ peu** before long

idéal, e, aux [ideal, -o] *adj* ideal ♦ *nm* ideal; ideals *pl*

idée [ide] *nf* idea; **avoir dans l'~ que** to have an idea that; **~s noires** black *ou* dark thoughts

identifier [idãtifje] *vt* to identify; **s'~ à** (*héros etc*) to identify with

identique [idãtik] *adj*: **~ (à)** identical (to)

identité [idãtite] *nf* identity

idiot, e [idjo, idjɔt] *adj* idiotic ♦ *nm/f* idiot

idole [idɔl] *nf* idol

if [if] *nm* yew

ignare [iɲaʀ] *adj* ignorant

ignoble [iɲɔbl(ə)] *adj* vile

ignorant, e [iɲɔʀã, -ãt] *adj* ignorant

ignorer [iɲɔʀe] *vt* (*ne pas connaître*) not to know, be unaware *ou* ignorant of; (*être sans expérience de*: *plaisir, guerre etc*) not to know about, have no experience of; (*bouder*: *personne*) to ignore

il [il] *pron* he; (*animal, chose, en tournure impersonnelle*) it; **~s** they; *voir aussi* **avoir**

île [il] *nf* island; **les ~s anglo-normandes** the Channel Islands; **les ~s Britanniques** the British Isles

illégal, e, aux [ilegal, -o] *adj* illegal

illégitime [ileʒitim] *adj* illegitimate

illettré, e [iletʀe] *adj*, *nm/f* illiterate

illimité, e [ilimite] *adj* unlimited

illisible [ilizibl(ə)] *adj* illegible; (*roman*) unreadable

illumination [ilyminasjɔ̃] *nf* illumination, floodlighting; (*idée*) flash of inspiration

illuminer [ilymine] *vt* to light up; (*monument, rue*: *pour une fête*) to illuminate, floodlight

illusion [ilyzjɔ̃] *nf* illusion; **se faire des ~s** to delude o.s.; **faire ~** to delude *ou* fool people; **illusionniste** *nm/f* conjuror

illustration [ilystʀasjɔ̃] *nf* illustration

illustre [ilystʀ(ə)] *adj* illustrious

illustré, e [ilystʀe] *adj* illustrated ♦ *nm* illustrated magazine; comic

illustrer [ilystʀe] *vt* to illustrate; **s'~** to become famous, win fame

îlot [ilo] *nm* small island, islet; (*de maisons*) block

ils [il] *pron voir* **il**

image [imaʒ] *nf* (*gén*) picture; (*comparaison, ressemblance, OPTIQUE*) image; **~ de marque** brand image; (*fig*) public image

imagination [imaʒinasjɔ̃] *nf* imagination; (*chimère*) fancy; **avoir de l'~** to be imaginative

imaginer [imaʒine] *vt* to imagine; (*inventer*: *expédient*) to devise, think up; **s'~** *vt* (*se figurer*: *scène etc*) to imagine, picture; **s'~ que** to imagine that

imbécile [ɛ̃besil] *adj* idiotic ♦ *nm/f* idiot

imberbe [ɛ̃bɛʀb(ə)] *adj* beardless

imbiber [ɛ̃bibe] *vt* to moisten, wet; **s'~ de** to become saturated with

imbu, e [ɛ̃by] *adj*: **~ de** full of

imitateur, trice [imitatœʀ, -tʀis] *nm/f* (*gén*) imitator; (*MUSIC-HALL*) impersonator

imitation [imitasjɔ̃] *nf* imitation; (*sketch*) imitation, impression; impersonation

imiter [imite] *vt* to imitate; (*contrefaire*) to forge; (*ressembler à*) to look like

immaculé, e [imakyle] *adj* spotless; immaculate

immatriculation [imatrikylɑsjɔ̃] *nf* registration

immatriculer [imatrikyle] *vt* to register; **faire/se faire ~** to register

immédiat, e [imedja, -at] *adj* immediate ♦ *nm*: **dans l'~** for the time being; **~ement** *adv* immediately

immense [imɑ̃s] *adj* immense

immerger [imɛrʒe] *vt* to immerse, submerge

immeuble [imœbl(ə)] *nm* building; **~ locatif** block of rented flats (*BRIT*), rental building (*US*)

immigration [imigrɑsjɔ̃] *nf* immigration

immigré, e [imigre] *nm/f* immigrant

imminent, e [iminɑ̃, -ɑ̃t] *adj* imminent

immiscer [imise]: **s'~** *vi* to interfere in *ou* with

immobile [imɔbil] *adj* still, motionless; (*fig*) unchanging

immobilier, ière [imɔbilje, -jɛr] *adj* property *cpd* ♦ *nm*: **l'~** the property business

immobiliser [imɔbilize] *vt* (*gén*) to immobilize; (*circulation, véhicule, affaires*) to bring to a standstill; **s'~** (*personne*) to stand still; (*machine, véhicule*) to come to a halt

immonde [imɔ̃d] *adj* foul

immondices [imɔ̃dis] *nmpl* refuse *sg*; filth *sg*

immoral, e, aux [imɔral, -o] *adj* immoral

immuable [imɥabl(ə)] *adj* immutable; unchanging

immunisé, e [imynize] *adj*: **~ contre** immune to

immunité [imynite] *nf* immunity

impact [ɛ̃pakt] *nm* impact

impair, e [ɛ̃pɛr] *adj* odd ♦ *nm* faux pas, blunder

impardonnable [ɛ̃pardɔnabl(ə)] *adj* unpardonable, unforgivable

imparfait, e [ɛ̃parfɛ, -ɛt] *adj* imperfect

impartial, e, aux [ɛ̃parsjal, -o] *adj* impartial, unbiased

impartir [ɛ̃partir] *vt* to assign; to bestow

impasse [ɛ̃pɑs] *nf* dead-end, cul-de-sac; (*fig*) deadlock

impassible [ɛ̃pasibl(ə)] *adj* impassive

impatience [ɛ̃pasjɑ̃s] *nf* impatience

impatient, e [ɛ̃pasjɑ̃, -ɑ̃t] *adj* impatient

impayable [ɛ̃pejabl(ə)] *adj* (*drôle*) priceless

impeccable [ɛ̃pekabl(ə)] *adj* faultless, impeccable; spotlessly clean; impeccably dressed; (*fam*) smashing

impensable [ɛ̃pɑ̃sabl(ə)] *adj* unthinkable; unbelievable

impératif, ive [ɛ̃peratif, -iv] *adj* imperative ♦ *nm* (*LING*) imperative; **~s** *nmpl* (*exigences*) requirements; demands

impératrice [ɛ̃peratris] *nf* empress

impérial, e, aux [ɛ̃perjal, -o] *adj* imperial; **impériale** *nf* top deck

impérieux, euse [ɛ̃perjø, -øz] *adj* (*caractère, ton*) imperious; (*obligation, besoin*) pressing, urgent

impérissable [ɛ̃perisabl(ə)] *adj* undying; imperishable

imperméable [ɛ̃pɛrmeabl(ə)] *adj* waterproof; (*GÉO*) impermeable; (*fig*): **~ à** impervious to ♦ *nm* raincoat

impertinent, e [ɛ̃pɛrtinɑ̃, -ɑ̃t] *adj* impertinent

impétueux, euse [ɛ̃petɥø, -øz] *adj* fiery

impie [ɛ̃pi] *adj* impious, ungodly

impitoyable [ɛ̃pitwajabl(ə)] *adj* pitiless, merciless

implanter [ɛ̃plɑ̃te] *vt* (*usine, industrie, usage*) to establish; (*colons etc*) to settle; (*idée, préjugé*) to implant

impliquer [ɛ̃plike] *vt* to imply; **~ qn (dans)** to implicate sb (in)

impoli, e [ɛ̃pɔli] *adj* impolite, rude

importance [ɛ̃pɔrtɑ̃s] *nf* importance; **sans ~** unimportant

important, e [ɛ̃pɔrtɑ̃, -ɑ̃t] *adj* important; (*en quantité*) considerable, sizeable; extensive; (*péj: airs, ton*) self-important ♦ *nm*: **l'~** the important thing

importateur, trice [ɛ̃pɔrtatœr, -tris] *nm/f* importer

importation [ɛ̃pɔrtɑsjɔ̃] *nf* importation; introduction; (*produit*) import

importer [ɛ̃pɔrte] *vt* (*COMM*) to import; (*maladies, plantes*) to introduce ♦ *vi* (*être important*) to matter; **il importe qu'il fasse** it is important that he should do; **peu m'importe** I don't mind; I don't care; **peu importe (que)** it doesn't matter (if); *voir aussi* **n'importe**

importun, e [ɛ̃pɔrtœ̃, -yn] *adj* irksome, importunate; (*arrivée, visite*) inopportune, ill-timed ♦ *nm* intruder; **importuner** *vt* to bother

imposable [ɛ̃pozabl(e)] *adj* taxable

imposant, e [ɛ̃pozɑ̃, -ɑ̃t] *adj* imposing

imposer [ɛ̃poze] *vt* (*taxer*) to tax; **s'~** (*être nécessaire*) to be imperative; (*montrer sa proéminence*) to stand out, emerge; (*artiste: se faire connaître*) to win recognition; **~ qch à qn** to impose sth on sb; **en ~ à** to impress; **imposition** [ɛ̃pozisjɔ̃] *nf* (*ADMIN*) taxation

impossible [ɛ̃pɔsibl(ə)] *adj* impossible; **il m'est ~ de le faire** it is impossible for me to do it, I can't possibly do it; **faire l'~** to do one's utmost

impôt [ɛ̃po] *nm* tax; (*taxes*) taxation; taxes *pl*; **~s** *nmpl* (*contributions*) (income) tax *sg*; **payer 1000 F d'~s** to pay 1,000 F in tax; **~ foncier** land tax; **~ sur le chiffre d'affaires** corporation (*BRIT*) *ou* corporate (*US*) tax; **~ sur le revenu** income tax

impotent, e [ɛ̃pɔtɑ̃, -ɑ̃t] *adj* disabled

impraticable [ɛ̃pʀatikabl(ə)] *adj* (*projet*) impracticable, unworkable; (*piste*) impassable

imprécis, e [ɛ̃pʀesi, -iz] *adj* imprecise

imprégner [ɛ̃pʀeɲe] *vt* (*tissu, tampon*) to soak, impregnate; (*lieu, air*) to fill; **s'~ de** (*fig*) to absorb

imprenable [ɛ̃pʀənabl(ə)] *adj* (*forteresse*) impregnable; **vue ~** unrestricted view

impression [ɛ̃pʀesjɔ̃] *nf* impression; (*d'un ouvrage, tissu*) printing; **faire bonne ~** to make a good impression

impressionnant, e [ɛ̃pʀesjɔnɑ̃, -ɑ̃t] *adj* impressive; upsetting

impressionner [ɛ̃pʀesjɔne] *vt* (*frapper*) to impress; (*troubler*) to upset

imprévisible [ɛ̃pʀevizibl(ə)] *adj* unforeseeable

imprévoyant, e [ɛ̃pʀevwajɑ̃, -ɑ̃t] *adj* lacking in foresight; (*en matière d'argent*) improvident

imprévu, e [ɛ̃pʀevy] *adj* unforeseen, unexpected ♦ *nm* unexpected incident; **en cas d'~** if anything unexpected happens

imprimante [ɛ̃pʀimɑ̃t] *nf* printer; **~ matricielle** dot-matrix printer

imprimé [ɛ̃pʀime] *nm* (*formulaire*) printed form; (*POSTES*) printed matter *no pl*

imprimer [ɛ̃pʀime] *vt* to print; (*empreinte etc*) to imprint; (*publier*) to publish; (*communiquer: mouvement, impulsion*) to impart, transmit; **imprimerie** *nf* printing; (*établissement*) printing works *sg*; **imprimeur** *nm* printer

impromptu, e [ɛ̃pʀɔ̃pty] *adj* impromptu; sudden

impropre [ɛ̃pʀɔpʀ(ə)] *adj* inappropriate; **~ à** unsuitable for

improviser [ɛ̃pʀɔvize] *vt, vi* to improvise

improviste [ɛ̃pʀɔvist(ə)]: **à l'~** *adv* unexpectedly, without warning

imprudence [ɛ̃pʀydɑ̃s] *nf* carelessness *no pl*; imprudence *no pl*

imprudent, e [ɛ̃pʀydɑ̃, -ɑ̃t] *adj* (*conducteur, geste, action*) careless; (*remarque*) unwise, imprudent; (*projet*) foolhardy

impudent, e [ɛ̃pydɑ̃, -ɑ̃t] *adj* impudent; brazen

impudique [ɛ̃pydik] *adj* shameless

impuissant, e [ɛ̃pɥisɑ̃, -ɑ̃t] *adj* helpless; (*sans effet*) ineffectual; (*sexuellement*) impotent; **~ à faire** powerless to do

impulsif, ive [ɛ̃pylsif, -iv] *adj* impulsive

impulsion [ɛ̃pylsjɔ̃] *nf* (*ÉLEC, instinct*) impulse; (*élan, influence*) impetus

impunément [ɛ̃pynemɑ̃] *adv* with impunity

imputer [ɛ̃pyte] *vt* (*attribuer*) to ascribe, impute; (*COMM*): **~ à ou sur** to charge to

inabordable [inabɔʀdabl(ə)] *adj* (*cher*) prohibitive

inaccessible [inaksesibl(ə)] *adj* inaccessible; unattainable; (*insensible*): **~ à** impervious to

inachevé, e [inaʃve] *adj* unfinished

inadapté, e [inadapte] *adj* (*gén*): **~ à** not adapted to, unsuited to; (*PSYCH*) maladjusted

inadmissible [inadmisibl(ə)] *adj* inadmissible

inadvertance [inadvɛʀtɑ̃s] : **par ~** *adv* inadvertently

inaltérable [inalteʀabl(ə)] *adj* (*matière*) stable; (*fig*) unchanging; **~ à** unaffected by

inamovible [inamɔvibl(ə)] *adj* fixed; (*JUR*) irremovable

inanimé, e [inanime] *adj* (*matière*) inanimate; (*évanoui*) unconscious; (*sans vie*) lifeless

inanition [inanisjɔ̃] *nf*: **tomber d'~** to faint with hunger (and exhaustion)

inaperçu, e [inapɛʀsy] *adj*: **passer ~** to go unnoticed

inappréciable [inapʀesjabl(ə)] *adj* (*service*) invaluable

inapte [inapt(ə)] *adj*: **~ à** incapable of; (*MIL*) unfit for

inattaquable [inatakabl(ə)] *adj* (*texte, preuve*) irrefutable

inattendu, e [inatɑ̃dy] *adj* unexpected

inattentif, ive [inatɑ̃tif, -iv] *adj* inattentive; **~ à** (*dangers, détails*) heedless of; **inattention** *nf*: **faute d'inattention** careless mistake

inaugurer [inɔgyʀe] *vt* (*monument*) to unveil; (*exposition, usine*) to open; (*fig*) to inaugurate

inavouable [inavwabl(ə)] *adj* shameful; undisclosable

inavoué, e [inavwe] *adj* unavowed

incandescence [ɛ̃kɑ̃desɑ̃s] *nf*: **porter à ~** to heat white-hot

incapable [ɛ̃kapabl(ə)] *adj* incapable; **~ de faire** incapable of doing; (*empêché*) unable to do

incapacité [ɛ̃kapasite] *nf* incapability; (*JUR*) incapacity

incarcérer [ɛ̃kaʀseʀe] *vt* to incarcerate, imprison

incarner [ɛ̃kaʀne] *vt* to embody, personify; (*THÉÂTRE*) to play

incartade [ɛ̃kaʀtad] *nf* prank

incassable [ɛ̃kɑsabl(ə)] *adj* unbreakable

incendiaire [ɛ̃sɑ̃djɛʀ] *adj* incendiary; (*fig: discours*) inflammatory ♦ *nmf* fire-raiser, arsonist

incendie [ɛ̃sɑ̃di] *nm* fire; **~ criminel** arson *no pl*; **~ de forêt** forest fire; **~r** [ɛ̃sɑ̃dje] *vt* (*mettre le feu à*) to set fire to, set alight; (*brûler complètement*) to burn down

incertain, e [ɛ̃sɛʀtɛ̃, -ɛn] *adj* uncertain; (*temps*) uncertain, unsettled; (*imprécis: contours*) indistinct, blurred; **incertitude** *nf* uncertainty

incessamment [ɛ̃sɛsamɑ̃] *adv* very shortly

incidemment [ɛ̃sidamɑ̃] *adv* in passing

incident [ɛ̃sidɑ̃] *nm* incident; ~ **de parcours** minor hitch *ou* setback; ~ **technique** technical difficulties *pl*

incinérer [ɛ̃sineʀe] *vt* (*ordures*) to incinerate; (*mort*) to cremate

incisive [ɛ̃siziv] *nf* incisor

inciter [ɛ̃site] *vt*: ~ **qn à (faire) qch** to encourage sb to do sth; (*à la révolte etc*) to incite sb to do sth

inclinable [ɛ̃klinabl(ə)] *adj*: **siège à dossier** ~ reclining seat

inclinaison [ɛ̃klinɛzɔ̃] *nf* (*déclivité: d'une route etc*) incline; (: *d'un toit*) slope; (*état penché*) tilt

inclination [ɛ̃klinɑsjɔ̃] *nf*: ~ **de (la) tête** nod (of the head); ~ **(de buste)** bow

incliner [ɛ̃kline] *vt* (*tête, bouteille*) to tilt ♦ *vi*: ~ **à qch/à faire** to incline towards sth/ doing; **s'~ (devant)** to bow (before); (*céder*) to give in *ou* yield (to); ~ **la tête** *ou* **le front** to give a slight bow

inclure [ɛ̃klyʀ] *vt* to include; (*joindre à un envoi*) to enclose; **jusqu'au 10 mars inclus** until 10th March inclusive

incoercible [ɛ̃kɔɛʀsibl(ə)] *adj* uncontrollable

incohérent, e [ɛ̃kɔeʀɑ̃, -ɑ̃t] *adj* inconsistent; incoherent

incollable [ɛ̃kɔlabl(ə)] *adj*: **il est** ~ he's got all the answers

incolore [ɛ̃kɔlɔʀ] *adj* colourless

incomber [ɛ̃kɔ̃be] : ~ **à** (*suj: devoirs, responsabilité*) to rest upon; (: *frais, travail*) to be the responsibility of

incommensurable [ɛ̃kɔmɑ̃syʀabl(ə)] *adj* immeasurable

incommode [ɛ̃kɔmɔd] *adj* inconvenient; (*posture, siège*) uncomfortable

incommoder [ɛ̃kɔmɔde] *vt*: ~ **qn** to inconvenience sb; (*embarrasser*) to make sb feel uncomfortable

incompétent, e [ɛ̃kɔ̃petɑ̃, -ɑ̃t] *adj* incompetent

incompris, e [ɛ̃kɔ̃pʀi, -iz] *adj* misunderstood

inconcevable [ɛ̃kɔ̃svabl(ə)] *adj* incredible

inconciliable [ɛ̃kɔ̃siljabl(ə)] *adj* irreconcilable

inconditionnel, le [ɛ̃kɔ̃disjɔnɛl] *adj* unconditional; (*partisan*) unquestioning

incongru, e [ɛ̃kɔ̃gʀy] *adj* unseemly

inconnu, e [ɛ̃kɔny] *adj* unknown; new, strange ♦ *nm/f* stranger; unknown person (*ou artist etc*) ♦ *nm*: **l'**~ the unknown; ~**e** *nf* unknown

inconsciemment [ɛ̃kɔ̃sjamɑ̃] *adv* unconsciously

inconscient, e [ɛ̃kɔ̃sjɑ̃, -ɑ̃t] *adj* unconscious; (*irréfléchi*) thoughtless, reckless ♦

nm (*PSYCH*): **l'**~ the unconscious; ~ **de** unaware of

inconsidéré, e [ɛ̃kɔ̃sideʀe] *adj* ill-considered

inconsistant, e [ɛ̃kɔ̃sistɑ̃, -ɑ̃t] *adj* flimsy, weak; runny

incontestable [ɛ̃kɔ̃tɛstabl(ə)] *adj* indisputable

incontournable [ɛ̃kɔ̃tuʀnabl(ə)] *adj* unavoidable

inconvenant, e [ɛ̃kɔ̃vnɑ̃, -ɑ̃t] *adj* unseemly, improper

inconvénient [ɛ̃kɔ̃venjɑ̃] *nm* (*d'une situation, d'un projet*) disadvantage, drawback; (*d'un remède, changement etc*) inconvenience; **si vous n'y voyez pas d'**~ if you have no objections

incorporer [ɛ̃kɔʀpɔʀe] *vt*: ~ **(à)** to mix in (with); (*paragraphe etc*): ~ **(dans)** to incorporate (in); (*MIL: appeler*) to recruit, call up

incorrect, e [ɛ̃kɔʀɛkt] *adj* (*impropre, inconvenant*) improper; (*défectueux*) faulty; (*inexact*) incorrect; (*impoli*) impolite; (*déloyal*) underhand

incrédule [ɛ̃kʀedyl] *adj* incredulous; (*REL*) unbelieving

increvable [ɛ̃kʀəvabl(ə)] (*fam*) *adj* tireless

incriminer [ɛ̃kʀimine] *vt* (*personne*) to incriminate; (*action, conduite*) to bring under attack; (*bonne foi, honnêteté*) to call into question

incroyable [ɛ̃kʀwajabl(ə)] *adj* incredible; unbelievable

incruster [ɛ̃kʀyste] *vt* (*ART*) to inlay; **s'~** *vi* (*invité*) to take root; (*radiateur etc*) to become coated with fur *ou* scale

inculpé, e [ɛ̃kylpe] *nm/f* accused

inculper [ɛ̃kylpe] *vt*: ~ **(de)** to charge (with)

inculquer [ɛ̃kylke] *vt*: ~ **qch à** to inculcate sth in *ou* instil sth into

inculte [ɛ̃kylt] *adj* uncultivated; (*esprit, peuple*) uncultured; (*barbe*) unkempt

Inde [ɛ̃d] *nf*: **l'**~ India

indécis, e [ɛ̃desi, -iz] *adj* indecisive; (*perplexe*) undecided

indéfendable [ɛ̃defɑ̃dabl(ə)] *adj* indefensible

indéfini, e [ɛ̃defini] *adj* (*imprécis, incertain*) undefined; (*illimité, LING*) indefinite; **indéfiniment** *adv* indefinitely; **indéfinissable** *adj* indefinable

indélébile [ɛ̃delebil] *adj* indelible

indélicat, e [ɛ̃delika, -at] *adj* tactless; dishonest

indemne [ɛ̃dɛmn(ə)] *adj* unharmed

indemniser [ɛ̃dɛmnize] *vt*: ~ **qn (de)** to compensate sb (for)

indemnité [ɛ̃dɛmnite] *nf* (*dédommagement*) compensation *no pl*; (*allocation*) allowance; ~ **de licenciement** redundancy payment

indépendamment [ɛ̃depɑ̃damɑ̃] *adv* independently; ~ **de** (*abstraction faite de*) irrespective of; (*en plus de*) over and above

indépendance [ɛ̃depɑ̃dɑ̃s] *nf* independence

indépendant, e [ɛ̃depɑ̃dɑ̃, -ɑ̃t] *adj* independent; ~ **de** independent of

indescriptible [ɛ̃dɛskʀiptibl(ə)] *adj* indescribable

indétermination [ɛ̃detɛʀminasjɔ̃] *nf* indecision; indecisiveness

indéterminé, e [ɛ̃detɛʀmine] *adj* unspecified; indeterminate

index [ɛ̃dɛks] *nm* (*doigt*) index finger; (*d'un livre etc*) index; **mettre à l'~** to blacklist

indexé, e [ɛ̃dɛkse] *adj* (*ÉCON*): ~ (**sur**) index-linked (to)

indicateur [ɛ̃dikatœʀ] *nm* (*POLICE*) informer; (*livre*) guide; directory; (*TECH*) gauge; indicator; ~ **des chemins de fer** railway timetable

indicatif, ive [ɛ̃dikatif, -iv] *adj*: **à titre** ~ for (your) information ♦ *nm* (*LING*) indicative; (*RADIO*) theme *ou* signature tune; (*TÉL*) dialling code

indication [ɛ̃dikasjɔ̃] *nf* indication; (*renseignement*) information *no pl*; ~**s** *nfpl* (*directives*) instructions

indice [ɛ̃dis] *nm* (*marque, signe*) indication, sign; (*POLICE: lors d'une enquête*) clue; (*JUR: présomption*) piece of evidence; (*SCIENCE, ÉCON, TECH*) index

indicible [ɛ̃disibl(ə)] *adj* inexpressible

indien, ne [ɛ̃djɛ̃, -jɛn] *adj, nm/f* Indian

indifféremment [ɛ̃diferamɑ̃] *adv* (*sans distinction*) equally (well); indiscriminately

indifférence [ɛ̃diferɑ̃s] *nf* indifference; **indifférent, e** [ɛ̃diferɑ̃, -ɑ̃t] *adj* (*peu intéressé*) indifferent

indigence [ɛ̃diʒɑ̃s] *nf* poverty

indigène [ɛ̃diʒɛn] *adj* native, indigenous; local ♦ *nm/f* native

indigeste [ɛ̃diʒɛst(ə)] *adj* indigestible

indigestion [ɛ̃diʒɛstjɔ̃] *nf* indigestion *no pl*

indigne [ɛ̃diɲ] *adj* unworthy

indigner [ɛ̃diɲe] *vt*: **s'~** (**de** *ou* **contre**) to be indignant (at)

indiqué, e [ɛ̃dike] *adj* (*date, lieu*) given; (*adéquat, conseillé*) suitable

indiquer [ɛ̃dike] *vt* (*désigner*): ~ **qch/qn à qn** to point sth/sb out to sb; (*suj: pendule, aiguille*) to show; (: *étiquette, plan*) to show, indicate; (*faire connaître: médecin, restaurant*): ~ **qch/qn à qn** to tell sb of sth/sb; (*renseigner sur*) to point out, tell; (*déterminer: date, lieu*) to give, state; (*dénoter*) to indicate, point to

indirect, e [ɛ̃diʀɛkt] *adj* indirect

indiscipline [ɛ̃disiplin] *nf* lack of discipline; **indiscipliné, e** *adj* undisciplined; (*fig*) unmanageable

indiscret, ète [ɛ̃diskʀɛ, -ɛt] *adj* indiscreet

indiscutable [ɛ̃diskytabl(ə)] *adj* indisputable

indispensable [ɛ̃dispɑ̃sabl(ə)] *adj* indispensable; essential

indisposé, e [ɛ̃dispoze] *adj* indisposed

indisposer [ɛ̃dispoze] *vt* (*incommoder*) to upset; (*déplaire à*) to antagonize

indistinct, e [ɛ̃distɛ̃, -ɛ̃kt(ə)] *adj* indistinct; **indistinctement** *adv* (*voir, prononcer*) indistinctly; (*sans distinction*) indiscriminately

individu [ɛ̃dividy] *nm* individual

individuel, le [ɛ̃dividɥɛl] *adj* (*gén*) individual; (*opinion, livret, contrôle, avantages*) personal; **chambre ~le** single room; **maison ~le** detached house

indolore [ɛ̃dɔlɔʀ] *adj* painless

indomptable [ɛ̃dɔ̃tabl(ə)] *adj* untameable; (*fig*) invincible, indomitable

Indonésie [ɛ̃donezi] *nf* Indonesia

indu, e [ɛ̃dy] *adj*: **à des heures ~es** at some ungodly hour

induire [ɛ̃dɥiʀ] *vt*: ~ **qn en erreur** to lead sb astray, mislead sb

indulgent, e [ɛ̃dylʒɑ̃, -ɑ̃t] *adj* (*parent, regard*) indulgent; (*juge, examinateur*) lenient

indûment [ɛ̃dymɑ̃] *adv* wrongly; without due cause

industrie [ɛ̃dystʀi] *nf* industry; **industriel, le** *adj* industrial ♦ *nm* industrialist; manufacturer

inébranlable [inebʀɑ̃labl(ə)] *adj* (*masse, colonne*) solid; (*personne, certitude, foi*) steadfast, unwavering

inédit, e [inedi, -it] *adj* (*correspondance etc*) hitherto unpublished; (*spectacle, moyen*) novel, original

ineffaçable [inefasabl(ə)] *adj* indelible

inefficace [inefikas] *adj* (*remède, moyen*) ineffective; (*machine, employé*) inefficient

inégal, e, aux [inegal, -o] *adj* unequal; uneven; **inégalable** [inegalabl(e)] *adj* matchless; **inégalé, e** [inegale] *adj* unmatched, unequalled

inerte [inɛʀt(ə)] *adj* lifeless; inert

inestimable [inɛstimabl(e)] *adj* priceless; (*fig: bienfait*) invaluable

inévitable [inevitabl(ə)] *adj* unavoidable; (*fatal, habituel*) inevitable

inexact, e [inɛgzakt] *adj* inaccurate, inexact; unpunctual

in extremis [inɛkstʀemis] *adv* at the last minute ♦ *adj* last-minute

infaillible [ɛ̃fajibl(ə)] *adj* infallible

infâme [ɛ̃fɑm] *adj* vile

infanticide [ɛ̃fɑ̃tisid] *nm/f* childmurderer(eress) ♦ *nm* (*meurtre*) infanticide

infarctus [ɛ̃faʀktys] *nm*: ~ (**du myocarde**) coronary (thrombosis)

infatigable [ɛ̃fatigabl(ə)] *adj* tireless

infect, e [ɛ̃fɛkt] *adj* vile; foul; (*repas, vin*) revolting

infecter [ɛ̃fɛkte] *vt* (*atmosphère, eau*) to contaminate; (*MÉD*) to infect; **s'~** to become infected *ou* septic; **infection** *nf* infection

inférieur, e [ɛ̃feʀjœʀ] *adj* lower; (*en qualité, intelligence*) inferior; ~ **à** (*somme, quantité*) less *ou* smaller than; (*moins bon que*) inferior to

infernal, e, aux [ɛ̃fɛʀnal, -o] *adj* (*chaleur, rythme*) infernal; (*méchanceté, complot*) diabolical

infidèle [ɛ̃fidɛl] *adj* unfaithful

infiltrer [ɛ̃filtʀe] : **s'~** *vi* to penetrate into; (*liquide*) to seep into; (*fig: noyauter*) to infiltrate

infime [ɛ̃fim] *adj* minute, tiny; (*inférieur*) lowly

infini, e [ɛ̃fini] *adj* infinite ♦ *nm* infinity; **à l'~** (*MATH*) to infinity; (*agrandir, varier*) infinitely; (*interminablement*) endlessly; **infinité** *nf*: **une infinité de** an infinite number of

infinitif [ɛ̃finitif] *nm* infinitive

infirme [ɛ̃fiʀm(ə)] *adj* disabled ♦ *nm/f* disabled person; ~ **de guerre** war cripple

infirmerie [ɛ̃fiʀməʀi] *nf* sick bay

infirmier, ière [ɛ̃fiʀmje, -jɛʀ] *nm/f* nurse; **infirmière chef** sister; **infirmière visiteuse** ≈ district nurse

infirmité [ɛ̃fiʀmite] *nf* disability

inflammable [ɛ̃flamabl(ə)] *adj* (in)flammable

inflation [ɛ̃flɑsjɔ̃] *nf* inflation

inflexion [ɛ̃flɛksjɔ̃] *nf* inflexion; ~ **de la tête** slight nod (of the head)

infliger [ɛ̃fliʒe] *vt*: ~ **qch (à qn)** to inflict sth (on sb); (*amende, sanction*) to impose sth (on sb)

influence [ɛ̃flyɑ̃s] *nf* influence; (*d'un médicament*) effect; **influencer** *vt* to influence; **influent, e** *adj* influential

influer [ɛ̃flye] : ~ **sur** *vt* to have an influence upon

informaticien, ne [ɛ̃fɔʀmatisjɛ̃, -jɛn] *nm/f* computer scientist

information [ɛ̃fɔʀmɑsjɔ̃] *nf* (*renseignement*) piece of information; (*PRESSE, TV: nouvelle*) item of news; (*diffusion de renseignements, INFORM*) information; (*JUR*) inquiry, investigation; ~**s** *nfpl* (*TV*) news *sg*; **voyage d'~** fact-finding trip

informatique [ɛ̃fɔʀmatik] *nf* (*technique*) data processing; (*science*) computer science ♦ *adj* computer *cpd*; **informatiser** *vt* to computerize

informe [ɛ̃fɔʀm(ə)] *adj* shapeless

informer [ɛ̃fɔʀme] *vt*: ~ **qn (de)** to inform sb (of); **s'~ (de/si)** to inquire *ou* find out (about/whether *ou* if)

infortune [ɛ̃fɔʀtyn] *nf* misfortune

infraction [ɛ̃fʀaksjɔ̃] *nf* offence; ~ **à** violation *ou* breach of; **être en** ~ to be in breach of the law

infranchissable [ɛ̃fʀɑ̃ʃisabl(ə)] *adj* impassable; (*fig*) insuperable

infrastructure [ɛ̃fʀastʀyktyʀ] *nf* (*AVIAT, MIL*) ground installations *pl*; (*ÉCON: touristique etc*) infrastructure

infuser [ɛ̃fyze] *vt, vi* (*thé*) to brew; (*tisane*) to infuse; **infusion** *nf* (*tisane*) herb tea

ingénier [ɛ̃ʒenje] : **s'~** *vi* to strive to do

ingénierie [ɛ̃ʒenjəʀi] *nf* engineering; ~ **génétique** genetic engineering

ingénieur [ɛ̃ʒenjœʀ] *nm* engineer; ~ **du son** sound engineer

ingénieux, euse [ɛ̃ʒenjø, -øz] *adj* ingenious, clever

ingénu, e [ɛ̃ʒeny] *adj* ingenuous, artless

ingérer [ɛ̃ʒeʀe] : **s'~** *vi* to interfere in

ingrat, e [ɛ̃gʀa, -at] *adj* (*personne*) ungrateful; (*sol*) poor; (*travail, sujet*) thankless; (*visage*) unprepossessing

ingrédient [ɛ̃gʀedjɑ̃] *nm* ingredient

ingurgiter [ɛ̃gyʀʒite] *vt* to swallow

inhabitable [inabitabl(ə)] *adj* uninhabitable

inhabituel, le [inabituɛl] *adj* unusual

inhérent, e [ineʀɑ̃, -ɑ̃t] *adj*: ~ **à** inherent in

inhibition [inibisjɔ̃] *nf* inhibition

inhumain, e [inymɛ̃, -ɛn] *adj* inhuman

inhumer [inyme] *vt* to inter, bury

inimitié [inimitje] *nf* enmity

initial, e, aux [inisjal, -o] *adj* initial; **initiale** *nf* initial

initiateur, trice [inisjatœʀ, -tʀis] *nm/f* initiator; (*d'une mode, technique*) innovator, pioneer

initiative [inisjativ] *nf* initiative

initier [inisje] *vt*: ~ **qn à** to initiate sb into; (*faire découvrir: art, jeu*) to introduce sb to

injecté, e [ɛ̃ʒɛkte] *adj*: **yeux ~s de sang** bloodshot eyes

injecter [ɛ̃ʒɛkte] *vt* to inject; **injection** *nf* injection; **à injection** (*AUTO*) fuel injection *cpd*

injure [ɛ̃ʒyʀ] *nf* insult, abuse *no pl*

injurier [ɛ̃ʒyʀje] *vt* to insult, abuse; **injurieux, euse** *adj* abusive, insulting

injuste [ɛ̃ʒyst(ə)] *adj* unjust, unfair; **injustice** *nf* injustice

inlassable [ɛ̃lɑsabl(ə)] *adj* tireless

inné, e [ine] *adj* innate, inborn

innocent, e [inɔsɑ̃, -ɑ̃t] *adj* innocent; **innocenter** *vt* to clear, prove innocent

innombrable [inɔ̃bʀabl(ə)] *adj* innumerable

innommable [inɔmabl(ə)] *adj* unspeakable

innover [inɔve] *vi* to break new ground

inoccupé, e [inɔkype] *adj* unoccupied

inoculer [inɔkyle] *vt* (*volontairement*) to inoculate; (*accidentellement*) to infect

inodore [inɔdɔʀ] *adj* (*gaz*) odourless; (*fleur*) scentless

inoffensif, ive [inɔfɑ̃sif, -iv] *adj* harmless, innocuous

inondation [inɔ̃dɑsjɔ̃] *nf* flooding *no pl*;

flood; **inonder** [inɔ̃de] *vt* to flood; (*fig*) to inundate, overrun

inopérant, e [inɔpeʀɑ̃, -ɑ̃t] *adj* inoperative, ineffective

inopiné, e [inɔpine] *adj* unexpected, sudden

inopportun, e [inɔpɔʀtœ̃, -yn] *adj* illtimed, untimely; inappropriate

inoubliable [inublijabl(ə)] *adj* unforgettable

inouï, e [inwi] *adj* unheard-of, extraordinary

inox(ydable) [inɔks(idabl(ə))] *adj* stainless

inqualifiable [ɛ̃kalifjabl(ə)] *adj* unspeakable

inquiet, ète [ɛ̃kjɛ, -ɛt] *adj* anxious

inquiétant, e [ɛ̃kjetɑ̃, -ɑ̃t] *adj* worrying, disturbing

inquiéter [ɛ̃kjete] *vt* to worry; (*harceler*) to harass; **s'~** to worry; **s'~ de** to worry about; (*s'enquérir de*) to inquire about

inquiétude [ɛ̃kjetyd] *nf* anxiety

insaisissable [ɛ̃sezisabl(ə)] *adj* elusive

insatisfait, e [ɛ̃satisfɛ, -ɛt] *adj* (*non comblé*) unsatisfied; unfulfilled; (*mécontent*) dissatisfied

inscription [ɛ̃skʀipsjɔ̃] *nf* inscription; (*voir s'inscrire*) enrolment; registration

inscrire [ɛ̃skʀiʀ] *vt* (*marquer: sur son calepin etc*) to note ou write down; (: *sur un mur, une affiche etc*) to write; (: *dans la pierre, le métal*) to inscribe; (*mettre: sur une liste, un budget etc*) to put down; **s'~** (*pour une excursion etc*) to put one's name down; **s'~ (à)** (*club, parti*) to join; (*université*) to register or enrol (at); (*examen, concours*) to register (for); **s'~ en faux contre** to challenge; **~ qn à** (*club, parti*) to enrol sb at

insecte [ɛ̃sɛkt(ə)] *nm* insect; **insecticide** *nm* insecticide

insensé, e [ɛ̃sɑ̃se] *adj* mad

insensibiliser [ɛ̃sɑ̃sibilize] *vt* to anaesthetize

insensible [ɛ̃sɑ̃sibl(ə)] *adj* (*nerf, membre*) numb; (*dur, indifférent*) insensitive; (*imperceptible*) imperceptible

insérer [ɛ̃seʀe] *vt* to insert; **s'~ dans** to fit into; to come within

insigne [ɛ̃siɲ] *nm* (*d'un parti, club*) badge ♦ *adj* distinguished

insignifiant, e [ɛ̃siɲifjɑ̃, -ɑ̃t] *adj* insignificant; trivial

insinuer [ɛ̃sinɥe] *vt* to insinuate, imply; **s'~ dans** (*fig*) to creep into

insister [ɛ̃siste] *vi* to insist; (*s'obstiner*) to keep on; **~ sur** (*détail, note*) to stress

insolation [ɛ̃sɔlasjɔ̃] *nf* (*MÉD*) sunstroke *no pl*

insolent, e [ɛ̃sɔlɑ̃, -ɑ̃t] *adj* insolent

insolite [ɛ̃sɔlit] *adj* strange, unusual

insomnie [ɛ̃sɔmni] *nf* insomnia *no pl*, sleeplessness *no pl*

insondable [ɛ̃sɔ̃dabl(ə)] *adj* unfathomable

insonoriser [ɛ̃sɔnɔʀize] *vt* to soundproof

insouciant, e [ɛ̃susjɑ̃, -ɑ̃t] *adj* carefree; (*imprévoyant*) heedless

insoumis, e [ɛ̃sumi, -iz] *adj* (*caractère, enfant*) rebellious, refractory; (*contrée, tribu*) unsubdued

insoupçonnable [ɛ̃supsɔnabl(ə)] *adj* unsuspected; (*personne*) above suspicion

insoupçonné, e [ɛ̃supsɔne] *adj* unsuspected

insoutenable [ɛ̃sutnabl(ə)] *adj* (*argument*) untenable; (*chaleur*) unbearable

inspecter [ɛ̃spɛkte] *vt* to inspect

inspecteur, trice [ɛ̃spɛktœʀ, -tʀis] *nm/f* inspector; **~ d'Académie** (regional) director of education; **~ des finances** ≈ tax inspector (*BRIT*), ≈ Internal Revenue Service agent (*US*)

inspection [ɛ̃spɛksjɔ̃] *nf* inspection

inspirer [ɛ̃spiʀe] *vt* (*gén*) to inspire ♦ *vi* (*aspirer*) to breathe in; **s'~ de** (*suj: artiste*) to draw one's inspiration from

instable [ɛ̃stabl(ə)] *adj* (*meuble, équilibre*) unsteady; (*population, temps*) unsettled; (*régime, caractère*) unstable

installation [ɛ̃stalasjɔ̃] *nf* putting in ou up; fitting out; settling in; (*appareils etc*) fittings *pl*, installations *pl*; **~s** *nfpl* (*appareils*) equipment; (*équipements*) facilities

installer [ɛ̃stale] *vt* (*loger*): **~ qn** to get sb settled; (*placer*) to put, place; (*meuble, gaz, électricité*) to put in; (*rideau, étagère, tente*) to put up; (*appartement*) to fit out; **s'~** (*s'établir: artisan, dentiste etc*) to set o.s. up; (*se loger*) to settle (o.s.); (*emménager*) to settle in; (*sur un siège, à un emplacement*) to settle (down); (*fig: maladie, grève*) to take a firm hold

instamment [ɛ̃stamɑ̃] *adv* urgently

instance [ɛ̃stɑ̃s] *nf* (*ADMIN: autorité*) authority; **~s** *nfpl* (*prières*) entreaties; **affaire en ~** matter pending; **être en ~ de divorce** to be awaiting a divorce

instant [ɛ̃stɑ̃] *nm* moment, instant; **dans un ~** in a moment; **à l'~** this instant; **à tout** ou **chaque ~** at any moment; constantly; **pour l'~** for the moment, for the time being; **par ~s** at times; **de tous les ~s** perpetual

instantané, e [ɛ̃stɑ̃tane] *adj* (*lait, café*) instant; (*explosion, mort*) instantaneous ♦ *nm* snapshot

instar [ɛ̃staʀ]: **à l'~ de** *prép* following the example of, like

instaurer [ɛ̃stɔʀe] *vt* to institute

instinct [ɛ̃stɛ̃] *nm* instinct

instituer [ɛ̃stitɥe] *vt* to set up

institut [ɛ̃stity] *nm* institute; **~ de beauté** beauty salon; **I~ Universitaire de Technologie** ≈ polytechnic

instituteur, trice [ɛ̃stitytœʀ, -tʀis] *nm/f* (primary school) teacher

institution [ɛ̃stitysjɔ̃] nf institution; (collège) private school
instruction [ɛ̃stryksjɔ̃] nf (enseignement, savoir) education; (JUR) (preliminary) investigation and hearing; **~s** nfpl (ordres, mode d'emploi) directions, instructions; **~ civique** civics sg
instruire [ɛ̃strɥir] vt (élèves) to teach; (recrues) to train; (JUR: affaire) to conduct the investigation for; **s'~** to educate o.s.; **instruit, e** adj educated
instrument [ɛ̃strymɑ̃] nm instrument; **~ à cordes/vent** stringed/wind instrument; **~ de mesure** measuring instrument; **~ de musique** musical instrument; **~ de travail** (working) tool
insu [ɛ̃sy] nm: **à l'~ de qn** without sb knowing (it)
insubmersible [ɛ̃sybmɛrsibl(ə)] adj unsinkable
insubordination [ɛ̃sybɔrdinasjɔ̃] nf rebelliousness; (MIL) insubordination
insuccès [ɛ̃syksɛ] nm failure
insuffisant, e [ɛ̃syfizɑ̃, -ɑ̃t] adj insufficient; (élève, travail) inadequate
insuffler [ɛ̃syfle] vt to blow; to inspire
insulaire [ɛ̃sylɛr] adj island cpd; (attitude) insular
insuline [ɛ̃sylin] nf insulin
insulte [ɛ̃sylt(ə)] nf insult; **insulter** vt to insult
insupportable [ɛ̃sypɔrtabl(ə)] adj unbearable
insurger [ɛ̃syrʒe]: **s'~** (contre) vi to rise up ou rebel (against)
insurmontable [ɛ̃syrmɔ̃tabl(ə)] adj (difficulté) insuperable; (aversion) unconquerable
intact, e [ɛ̃takt] adj intact
intangible [ɛ̃tɑ̃ʒibl(ə)] adj intangible; (principe) inviolable
intarissable [ɛ̃tarisabl(ə)] adj inexhaustible
intégral, e, aux [ɛ̃tegral, -o] adj complete
intégrant, e [ɛ̃tegrɑ̃, -ɑ̃t] adj: **faire partie ~e de** to be an integral part of
intègre [ɛ̃tegr(ə)] adj upright
intégrer [ɛ̃tegre] vt to integrate; **s'~ à ou dans** to become integrated into
intégrisme [ɛ̃tegrism(e)] nm fundamentalism
intellectuel, le [ɛ̃telɛktɥɛl] adj intellectual ♦ nm/f intellectual; (péj) highbrow
intelligence [ɛ̃teliʒɑ̃s] nf intelligence; (compréhension): **l'~ de** the understanding of; (complicité): **regard d'~** glance of complicity; (accord): **vivre en bonne ~ avec qn** to be on good terms with sb
intelligent, e [ɛ̃teliʒɑ̃, -ɑ̃t] adj intelligent
intempéries [ɛ̃tɑ̃peri] nfpl bad weather sg
intempestif, ive [ɛ̃tɑ̃pestif, -iv] adj untimely
intenable [ɛ̃tnabl(ə)] adj (chaleur) unbearable

intendant, e [ɛ̃tɑ̃dɑ̃, -ɑ̃t] nm/f (MIL) quartermaster; (SCOL) bursar; (d'une propriété) steward
intense [ɛ̃tɑ̃s] adj intense; **intensif, ive** adj intensive
intenter [ɛ̃tɑ̃te] vt: **~ un procès contre** ou **à** to start proceedings against
intention [ɛ̃tɑ̃sjɔ̃] nf intention; (JUR) intent; **avoir l'~ de faire** to intend to do; **à l'~ de** for; (renseignement) for the benefit of; (film, ouvrage) aimed at; **à cette ~** with this aim in view; **intentionné, e** adj: **bien intentionné** well-meaning ou -intentioned; **mal intentionné** ill-intentioned
interactif, ive [ɛ̃teraktif, -iv] adj (COMPUT) interactive
intercaler [ɛ̃terkale] vt to insert
intercepter [ɛ̃tersɛpte] vt to intercept; (lumière, chaleur) to cut off
interchangeable [ɛ̃terʃɑ̃ʒabl(ə)] adj interchangeable
interclasse [ɛ̃terklɑs] nm (SCOL) break (between classes)
interdiction [ɛ̃terdiksjɔ̃] nf ban
interdire [ɛ̃terdir] vt to forbid; (ADMIN: journal, livre) to ban; **~ à qn de faire** to forbid sb to do, prohibit sb from doing; (suj: empêchement) to prevent sb from doing
interdit, e [ɛ̃terdi, -it] adj (stupéfait) taken aback ♦ nm prohibition
intéressant, e [ɛ̃teresɑ̃, -ɑ̃t] adj interesting
intéressé, e [ɛ̃terese] adj (parties) involved, concerned; (amitié, motifs) self-interested
intéresser [ɛ̃terese] vt (captiver) to interest; (toucher) to be of interest to; (ADMIN: concerner) to affect, concern; **s'~ à** to be interested in
intérêt [ɛ̃terɛ] nm (aussi COMM) interest; (égoïsme) self-interest; **avoir ~ à faire** to do well to do
intérieur, e [ɛ̃terjœr] adj (mur, escalier, poche) inside; (commerce, politique) domestic; (cour, calme, vie) inner; (navigation) inland ♦ nm (d'une maison, d'un récipient etc) inside; (d'un pays, aussi: décor, mobilier) interior; (POL): **l'I~** the Interior; **à l'~ (de)** inside; (fig) within
intérim [ɛ̃terim] nm interim period; **assurer l'~ (de)** to deputize (for); **par ~** interim
intérimaire [ɛ̃terimɛr] nm/f (secrétaire) temporary secretary, temp (BRIT); (suppléant) temporary replacement
intérioriser [ɛ̃terjɔrize] vt to internalize
interlocuteur, trice [ɛ̃terlɔkytœr, -tris] nm/f speaker; **son ~** the person he was speaking to
interloquer [ɛ̃terlɔke] vt to take aback
intermède [ɛ̃termɛd] nm interlude
intermédiaire [ɛ̃termedjɛr] adj intermedi-

ate; middle; half-way ♦ *nm/f* intermediary; (*COMM*) middleman; **sans** ~ directly; **par l'**~ **de** through

intermittence [ɛtɛrmitɑ̃s] *nf*: **par** ~ sporadically, intermittently

internat [ɛtɛrna] *nm* (*SCOL*) boarding school

international, e, aux [ɛtɛrnasjɔnal, -o] *adj*, *nm/f* international

interne [ɛtɛrn(ə)] *adj* internal ♦ *nm/f* (*SCOL*) boarder; (*MÉD*) houseman; ~**r** [ɛtɛrne] *vt* (*POL*) to intern; (*MÉD*) to confine to a mental institution

interpeller [ɛtɛrpele] *vt* (*appeler*) to call out to; (*apostropher*) to shout at; (*POLICE*) to take in for questioning; (*POL*) to question

interphone [ɛtɛrfɔn] *nm* intercom

interposer [ɛtɛrpoze] *vt* to interpose; **s'**~ *vi* to intervene; **par personnes interposées** through a third party

interprète [ɛtɛrprɛt] *nm/f* interpreter; (*porte-parole*) spokesperson

interpréter [ɛtɛrprete] *vt* to interpret

interrogateur, trice [ɛtɛrɔgatœr, -tris] *adj* questioning, inquiring

interrogatif, ive [ɛtɛrɔgatif, -iv] *adj* (*LING*) interrogative

interrogation [ɛtɛrɔgasjɔ̃] *nf* question; (*SCOL*) (written *ou* oral) test

interrogatoire [ɛtɛrɔgatwar] *nm* (*POLICE*) questioning *no pl*; (*JUR*) cross-examination

interroger [ɛtɛrɔʒe] *vt* to question; (*INFORM*) to consult; (*SCOL*) to test

interrompre [ɛtɛrɔ̃pr(ə)] *vt* (*gén*) to interrupt; (*travail, voyage*) to break off, interrupt; **s'**~ to break off

interrupteur [ɛtɛryptœr] *nm* switch

interruption [ɛtɛrypsjɔ̃] *nf* interruption; (*pause*) break

interstice [ɛtɛrstis] *nm* crack; slit

interurbain [ɛtɛryrbɛ̃] *nm* (*TÉL*) long-distance call service ♦ *adj* long-distance

intervalle [ɛtɛrval] *nm* (*espace*) space; (*de temps*) interval; **dans l'**~ in the meantime

intervenir [ɛtɛrvənir] *vi* (*gén*) to intervene; (*survenir*) to take place; ~ **auprès de qn** to intervene with sb

intervention [ɛtɛrvɑ̃sjɔ̃] *nf* intervention; (*discours*) paper; ~ **chirurgicale** (surgical) operation

intervertir [ɛtɛrvɛrtir] *vt* to invert (the order of), reverse

interview [ɛtɛrvju] *nf* interview

intestin, e [ɛtɛstɛ̃, -in] *adj* internal ♦ *nm* intestine

intime [ɛtim] *adj* intimate; (*vie, journal*) private; (*conviction*) inmost; (*dîner, cérémonie*) quiet ♦ *nm/f* close friend

intimer [ɛtime] *vt* (*JUR*) to notify; ~ **à qn l'ordre de faire** to order sb to do

intimider [ɛtimide] *vt* to intimidate

intimité [ɛtimite] *nf*: **dans l'**~ in private; (*sans formalités*) with only a few friends, quietly

intitulé, e [ɛtityle] *adj* entitled

intolérable [ɛtɔlerabl(ə)] *adj* intolerable

intoxication [ɛtɔksikasjɔ̃] *nf*: ~ **alimentaire** food poisoning

intoxiquer [ɛtɔksike] *vt* to poison; (*fig*) to brainwash

intraduisible [ɛtradɥizibl(ə)] *adj* untranslatable; (*fig*) inexpressible

intraitable [ɛtrɛtabl(ə)] *adj* inflexible, uncompromising

intransigeant, e [ɛtrɑ̃ziʒɑ̃, -ɑ̃t] *adj* intransigent; (*morale*) uncompromising

intransitif, ive [ɛtrɑ̃zitif, -iv] *adj* (*LING*) intransitive

intrépide [ɛtrepid] *adj* dauntless

intrigue [ɛtrig] *nf* (*scénario*) plot

intriguer [ɛtrige] *vi* to scheme ♦ *vt* to puzzle, intrigue

intrinsèque [ɛtrɛ̃sɛk] *adj* intrinsic

introduction [ɛtrɔdyksjɔ̃] *nf* introduction

introduire [ɛtrɔdɥir] *vt* to introduce; (*visiteur*) to show in; (*aiguille, clef*): ~ **qch dans** to insert *ou* introduce sth into; **s'**~ **dans** to gain entry into; to get o.s. accepted into; (*eau, fumée*) to get into

introuvable [ɛtruvabl(ə)] *adj* which cannot be found; (*COMM*) unobtainable

introverti, e [ɛtrɔvɛrti] *nm/f* introvert

intrus, e [ɛtry, -yz] *nm/f* intruder

intrusion [ɛtryzjɔ̃] *nf* intrusion; interference

intuition [ɛtɥisjɔ̃] *nf* intuition

inusable [inyzabl(ə)] *adj* hard-wearing

inusité, e [inyzite] *adj* rarely used

inutile [inytil] *adj* useless; (*superflu*) unnecessary; **inutilisable** *adj* unusable

invalide [ɛ̃valid] *adj* disabled ♦ *nm*: ~ **de guerre** disabled ex-serviceman

invasion [ɛ̃vazjɔ̃] *nf* invasion

invectiver [ɛ̃vɛktive] *vt* to hurl abuse at

invendable [ɛ̃vɑ̃dabl(ə)] *adj* unsaleable; unmarketable; **invendus** *nmpl* unsold goods

inventaire [ɛ̃vɑ̃tɛr] *nm* inventory; (*COMM*: *liste*) stocklist; (: *opération*) stocktaking *no pl*; (*fig*) survey

inventer [ɛ̃vɑ̃te] *vt* to invent; (*subterfuge*) to devise, invent; (*histoire, excuse*) to make up, invent; **inventeur** *nm* inventor; **inventif, ive** *adj* inventive; **invention** *nf* invention

inverse [ɛ̃vɛrs(ə)] *adj* reverse; opposite; inverse ♦ *nm* inverse, reverse; **dans l'ordre** ~ in the reverse order; **en sens** ~ in (*ou* from) the opposite direction; **inversement** *adv* conversely; **inverser** *vt* to invert, reverse; (*ÉLEC*) to reverse

investir [ɛ̃vɛstir] *vt* to invest; **investissement** *nm* investment; **investiture** *nf* in-

vestiture; (à une élection) nomination
invétéré, e [ɛ̃vetere] adj (habitude) ingrained; (bavard, buveur) inveterate
invisible [ɛ̃vizibl(ə)] adj invisible
invitation [ɛ̃vitasjɔ̃] nf invitation
invité, e [ɛ̃vite] nm/f guest
inviter [ɛ̃vite] vt to invite; ~ **qn à faire** (suj: chose) to induce ou tempt sb to do
involontaire [ɛ̃vɔlɔ̃tɛʀ] adj (mouvement) involuntary; (insulte) unintentional; (complice) unwitting
invoquer [ɛ̃vɔke] vt (Dieu, muse) to call upon, invoke; (prétexte) to put forward (as an excuse); (loi, texte) to refer to
invraisemblable [ɛ̃vʀɛsɑ̃blabl(ə)] adj unlikely, improbable; incredible
iode [jɔd] nm iodine
irai etc vb voir **aller**
Irak [iʀak] nm Iraq
Iran [iʀɑ̃] nm Iran
irions etc vb voir **aller**
irlandais, e [iʀlɑ̃dɛ, -ɛz] adj Irish ♦ nm/f: **I~, e** Irishman(woman); **les I~** the Irish
Irlande [iʀlɑ̃d] nf Ireland; ~ **du Nord** Northern Ireland
ironie [iʀɔni] nf irony; **ironique** adj ironical; **ironiser** vi to be ironical
irons etc vb voir **aller**
irradier [iʀadje] vi to radiate ♦ vt (aliment) to irradiate
irraisonné, e [iʀɛzɔne] adj irrational, unreasoned
irrationnel, le [iʀasjɔnɛl] adj irrational
irréalisable [iʀealizabl(ə)] adj unrealizable; impracticable
irrécupérable [iʀekypeʀabl(ə)] adj unreclaimable, beyond repair; (personne) beyond redemption
irrécusable [iʀekyzabl(ə)] adj unimpeachable; incontestable
irréductible [iʀedyktibl(ə)] adj indomitable, implacable
irréel, le [iʀeɛl] adj unreal
irréfléchi, e [iʀefleʃi] adj thoughtless
irrégularité [iʀegylaʀite] nf irregularity; unevenness no pl
irrégulier, ière [iʀegylje, -jɛʀ] adj irregular; uneven; (élève, athlète) erratic
irrémédiable [iʀemedjabl(ə)] adj irreparable
irréprochable [iʀepʀoʃabl(ə)] adj irreproachable, beyond reproach; (tenue) impeccable
irrésistible [iʀezistibl(ə)] adj irresistible; (preuve, logique) compelling
irrespectueux, euse [iʀɛspɛktɥø, -øz] adj disrespectful
irriguer [iʀige] vt to irrigate
irritable [iʀitabl(ə)] adj irritable
irriter [iʀite] vt to irritate
irruption [iʀypsjɔ̃] nf irruption no pl; **faire ~ dans** to burst into

islamique [islamik] adj Islamic
Islande [islɑ̃d] nf Iceland
isolant, e [izɔlɑ̃, -ɑ̃t] adj insulating; (insonorisant) soundproofing
isolation [izɔlasjɔ̃] nf insulation
isolé, e [izɔle] adj isolated; insulated
isoler [izɔle] vt to isolate; (prisonnier) to put in solitary confinement; (ville) to cut off, isolate; (ÉLEC) to insulate
isoloir nm polling booth
Israël [isʀaɛl] nm Israel; **israélien, ne** adj, nm/f Israeli; **israélite** adj Jewish ♦ nm/f Jew(Jewess)
issu, e [isy] adj: ~ **de** descended from; (fig) stemming from; ~**e** nf (ouverture, sortie) exit; (solution) way out, solution; (dénouement) outcome; **à l'~e de** at the conclusion ou close of; **rue sans ~e** dead end
Italie [itali] nf Italy; **italien, ne** adj, nm/f Italian ♦ nm (LING) Italian
italique [italik] nm: **en ~** in italics
itinéraire [itineʀɛʀ] nm itinerary, route
IUT sigle m = **Institut universitaire de technologie**
IVG sigle f (= interruption volontaire de grossesse) abortion
ivoire [ivwaʀ] nm ivory
ivre [ivʀ(ə)] adj drunk; ~ **de** (colère, bonheur) wild with; **ivresse** nf drunkenness; **ivrogne** nm/f drunkard

---

J j

j' [ʒ] pron I
jachère [ʒaʃɛʀ] nf: **(être) en ~** (to lie) fallow
jacinthe [ʒasɛ̃t] nf hyacinth
jack [ʒak] nm jack plug
jadis [ʒadis] adv in times past, formerly
jaillir [ʒajiʀ] vi (liquide) to spurt out; (fig) to burst out; to flood out
jais [ʒɛ] nm jet; (d'un noir) **de ~** jet-black
jalon [ʒalɔ̃] nm range pole; (fig) milestone; **jalonner** vt to mark out; (fig) to mark, punctuate
jalousie [ʒaluzi] nf jealousy; (store) (Venetian) blind
jaloux, ouse [ʒalu, -uz] adj jealous
jamais [ʒamɛ] adv never; (sans négation) ever; **ne ... ~** never; **à ~** for ever
jambe [ʒɑ̃b] nf leg
jambon [ʒɑ̃bɔ̃] nm ham
jambonneau, x [ʒɑ̃bɔno] nm knuckle of

ham

jante [ʒɑ̃t] *nf* (wheel) rim

janvier [ʒɑ̃vje] *nm* January

Japon [ʒapɔ̃] *nm* Japan; **japonais, e** *adj, nm/f* Japanese ♦ *nm* (*LING*) Japanese

japper [ʒape] *vi* to yap, yelp

jaquette [ʒaket] *nf* (*de cérémonie*) morning coat; (*de dame*) jacket

jardin [ʒardɛ̃] *nm* garden; ~ **d'enfants** nursery school; **jardinage** *nm* gardening; **jardinier, ière** *nm/f* gardener; **jardinière** *nf* (*de fenêtre*) window box

jarre [ʒaR] *nf* (earthenware) jar

jarret [ʒaRe] *nm* back of knee, ham; (*CULIN*) knuckle, shin

jarretelle [ʒaRtɛl] *nf* suspender (*BRIT*), garter (*US*)

jarretière [ʒaRtjɛR] *nf* garter

jaser [ʒaze] *vi* to chatter, prattle; (*indiscrètement*) to gossip

jatte [ʒat] *nf* basin, bowl

jauge [ʒoʒ] *nf* (*instrument*) gauge; **jauger** *vt* (*fig*) to size up

jaune [ʒon] *adj, nm* yellow ♦ *adv* (*fam*): **rire** ~ to laugh on the other side of one's face; ~ **d'œuf** (egg) yolk; **jaunir** *vi, vt* to turn yellow

jaunisse [ʒonis] *nf* jaundice

Javel [ʒavɛl] *nf voir* **eau**

javelot [ʒavlo] *nm* javelin

J.-C. *sigle* = **Jésus-Christ**

je(j') [ʒ(ə)] *pron* I

jean [dʒin] *nm* jeans *pl*

Jésus-Christ [ʒezykRi(st)] *n* Jesus Christ; **600 avant/après** ~ **ou J.-C.** 600 B.C./A.D.

jet¹ [ʒɛ] *nm* (*lancer*) throwing *no pl*, throw; (*jaillissement*) jet; spurt; (*de tuyau*) nozzle; **du premier** ~ at the first attempt *or* shot; **jet d'eau** fountain; spray

jet² [dʒɛt] *nm* (*avion*) jet

jetable [ʒətabl(ə)] *adj* disposable

jetée [ʒəte] *nf* jetty; pier

jeter [ʒəte] *vt* (*gén*) to throw; (*se défaire de*) to throw away *ou* out; (*son, lueur etc*) to give out; **se** ~ **dans** to flow into; ~ **qch à qn** to throw sth to sb; (*de façon agressive*) to throw sth at sb; ~ **un coup d'œil (à)** to take a look (at); ~ **un sort à qn** to cast a spell on sb

jeton [ʒətɔ̃] *nm* (*au jeu*) counter; (*de téléphone*) token

jette *etc vb voir* **jeter**

jeu, x [ʒø] *nm* (*divertissement, TECH: d'une pièce*) play; (*TENNIS: partie, FOOTBALL etc: façon de jouer*) game; (*THÉÂTRE etc*) acting; (*au casino*): **le** ~ gambling; (*fonctionnement*) working, interplay; (*série d'objets, jouet*) set; (*CARTES*) hand; **en** ~ at stake; at work; **remettre en** ~ to throw in; **entrer/mettre en** ~ to come/bring into play; ~ **de cartes** pack of cards; ~ **d'échecs** chess set; ~ **de hasard** game of

chance; ~ **de mots** pun

jeudi [ʒødi] *nm* Thursday

jeun [ʒœ̃]: **à** ~ *adv* on an empty stomach

jeune [ʒœn] *adj* young; ~ **fille** girl; ~ **homme** young man

jeûne [ʒøn] *nm* fast

jeunesse [ʒœnɛs] *nf* youth; (*aspect*) youthfulness; youngness

joaillerie [ʒɔajRi] *nf* jewel trade; jewellery; **joaillier, ière** *nm/f* jeweller

joie [ʒwa] *nf* joy

joindre [ʒwɛ̃dʀ(ə)] *vt* to join; (*à une lettre*): ~ **qch à** to enclose sth with; (*contacter*) to contact, get in touch with; **se** ~ **à** to join; ~ **les mains** to put one's hands together

joint, e [ʒwɛ̃, ʒwɛ̃t] *adj*: **pièce** ~**e** enclosure ♦ *nm* joint; (*ligne*) join; ~ **de culasse** cylinder head gasket; ~ **de robinet** washer

joli, e [ʒɔli] *adj* pretty, attractive; **c'est du** ~! (*ironique*) that's very nice!; **c'est bien** ~, **mais** ... that's all very well but ...

jonc [ʒɔ̃] *nm* (bul)rush

joncher [ʒɔ̃ʃe] *vt* (*suj: choses*) to be strewed on

jonction [ʒɔ̃ksjɔ̃] *nf* joining; (**point de**) ~ junction

jongleur, euse [ʒɔ̃glœR, -øz] *nm/f* juggler

jonquille [ʒɔ̃kij] *nf* daffodil

Jordanie [ʒɔRdani] *nf*: **la** ~ Jordan

joue [ʒu] *nf* cheek; **mettre en** ~ to take aim at

jouer [ʒwe] *vt* to play; (*somme d'argent, réputation*) to stake, wager; (*pièce, rôle*) to perform; (*film*) to show; (*simuler: sentiment*) to affect, feign ♦ *vi* (*THÉÂTRE, CINÉMA*) to act, perform; (*bois, porte: se voiler*) to warp; (*clef, pièce: avoir du jeu*) to be loose; **se** ~ **de** (*difficultés*) to make light of; to deceive; ~ **sur** (*miser*) to gamble on; ~ **de** (*MUS*) to play; ~ **des coudes** to use one's elbows; ~ **à** (*jeu, sport, roulette*) to play; ~ **avec** (*risquer*) to gamble with; ~ **un tour à qn** to play a trick on sb; ~ **serré** to play a close game; ~ **de malchance** to be dogged with ill-luck

jouet [ʒwe] *nm* toy; **être le** ~ **de** (*illusion etc*) to be the victim of

joueur, euse [ʒwœR, -øz] *nm/f* player; **être beau** ~ to be a good loser

joufflu, e [ʒufly] *adj* chubby-cheeked

joug [ʒu] *nm* yoke

jouir [ʒwiR]: ~ **de** *vt* to enjoy; **jouissance** *nf* pleasure; (*JUR*) use

joujou [ʒuʒu] (*fam*) *nm* toy

jour [ʒuR] *nm* day; (*opposé à la nuit*) day, daytime; (*clarté*) daylight; (*fig: aspect*) light; (*ouverture*) opening; **au** ~ **le** ~ from day to day; **de nos** ~s these days; **il fait** ~ it's daylight; **au grand** ~ (*fig*) in the open; **mettre au** ~ to disclose; **mettre à** ~ to update; **donner le** ~ **à** to give birth to; **voir le** ~ to be born; ~ **férié** *nm* public holiday

journal, aux [ʒuʀnal, -o] nm (news)paper; (personnel) journal, diary; ~ **de bord** log; ~ **parlé/télévisé** radio/television news sg
journalier, ière [ʒuʀnalje, -jɛʀ] adj daily; (banal) everyday
journalisme [ʒuʀnalism(ə)] nm journalism; **journaliste** nm/f journalist
journée [ʒuʀne] nf day; **la** ~ **continue** the 9 to 5 working day
journellement [ʒuʀnɛlmɑ̃] adv daily
joyau, x [ʒwajo] nm gem, jewel
joyeux, euse [ʒwajø, -øz] adj joyful, merry; ~ **Noël** merry Christmas!; ~ **anniversaire!** happy birthday!
jubiler [ʒybile] vi to be jubilant, exult
jucher [ʒyʃe] vt, vi to perch
judas [ʒyda] nm (trou) spy-hole
judiciaire [ʒydisjɛʀ] adj judicial
judicieux, euse [ʒydisjø, -øz] adj judicious
judo [ʒydo] nm judo
juge [ʒyʒ] nm judge; ~ **d'instruction** examining (BRIT) ou committing (US) magistrate; ~ **de paix** justice of the peace
jugé [ʒyʒe] : **au** ~ adv by guesswork
jugement [ʒyʒmɑ̃] nm judgment; (JUR: au pénal) sentence; (: au civil) decision
juger [ʒyʒe] vt to judge; ~ **qn/qch satisfaisant** to consider sb/sth (to be) satisfactory; ~ **bon de faire** to see fit to do; ~ **de** to appreciate
juif, ive [ʒɥif, -iv] adj Jewish ♦ nm/f Jew(Jewess)
juillet [ʒɥijɛ] nm July
juin [ʒɥɛ̃] nm June
jumeau, elle, x [ʒymo, -ɛl] adj, nm/f twin; voir aussi **jumelle**
jumeler [ʒymle] vt to twin
jumelle [ʒymɛl] adj, nf voir **jumeau**; ~s nfpl (appareil) binoculars
jument [ʒymɑ̃] nf mare
jungle [ʒɛ̃gl(ə)] nf jungle
jupe [ʒyp] nf skirt
jupon [ʒypɔ̃] nm waist slip
juré, e [ʒyʀe] nm/f juror
jurer [ʒyʀe] vt (obéissance etc) to swear, vow ♦ vi (dire des jurons) to swear, curse; (dissoner): ~ **(avec)** to clash (with); (s'engager): ~ **de faire/que** to swear ou vow to do/that; (affirmer): ~ **que** to swear ou vouch that; ~ **de qch** (s'en porter garant) to swear to sth
juridique [ʒyʀidik] adj legal
juron [ʒyʀɔ̃] nm curse, swearword
jury [ʒyʀi] nm jury; board
jus [ʒy] nm juice; (de viande) gravy, (meat) juice; ~ **de fruit** fruit juice
jusque [ʒysk(ə)] : **jusqu'à** prép (endroit) as far as, (up) to; (moment) until, till; (limite) up to; ~ **sur/dans** up to; (y compris) even on/in; **jusqu'à ce que** until; **jusqu'à présent** until now
juste [ʒyst(ə)] adj (équitable) just, fair; (légitime) just, justified; (exact, vrai) right; (étroit, insuffisant) tight ♦ adv right; tight; (chanter) in tune; (seulement) just; ~ **assez/au-dessus** just enough/above; **au** ~ exactly; **le** ~ **milieu** the happy medium;
justement adv rightly; justly; (précisément) just, precisely; **justesse** nf (précision) accuracy; (d'une remarque) aptness; (d'une opinion) soundness; **de justesse** just
justice [ʒystis] nf (équité) fairness, justice; (ADMIN) justice; **rendre la** ~ to dispense justice; **rendre** ~ **à qn** to do sb justice; **justicier, ière** [ʒystisje, -jɛʀ] nm/f judge, righter of wrongs
justificatif, ive [ʒystifikatif, -iv] adj (document) supporting; **pièce justificative** written proof
justifier [ʒystifje] vt to justify; ~ **de** to prove
juteux, euse [ʒytø, -øz] adj juicy
juvénile [ʒyvenil] adj young, youthful

K k

K [ka] nm (INFORM) K
kaki [kaki] adj inv khaki
kangourou [kɑ̃guʀu] nm kangaroo
karaté [kaʀate] nm karate
karting [kaʀtiŋ] nm go-carting, karting
kermesse [kɛʀmɛs] nf bazaar, (charity) fête; village fair
kidnapper [kidnape] vt to kidnap
kilo [kilo] nm = **kilogramme**
kilo: ~**gramme** nm kilogramme; ~**métrage** nm number of kilometres travelled, ≈ mileage; ~**mètre** nm kilometre; ~**métrique** adj (distance) in kilometres
kinésithérapeute [kineziteʀapøt] nm/f physiotherapist
kiosque [kjɔsk(ə)] nm kiosk, stall
klaxon [klaksɔn] nm horn; **klaxonner** vi, vt to hoot (BRIT), honk (US)
km. abr = **kilomètre**; **km/h** (= kilomètres/heure) ≈ m.p.h.
Ko [kao] abr (INFORM: kilooctet) K
K.-O. [kao] adj inv (knocked) out
kyste [kist(ə)] nm cyst

L l

l' [l] dét voir **le**

la [la] dét voir **le** ♦ nm (MUS) A; (en chantant la gamme) la

là [la] adv there; (ici) here; (dans le temps) then; **elle n'est pas ~** she isn't here; **c'est ~ que** this is where; **~ où** where; **de ~** (fig) hence; **par ~** by that; **tout est ~** that's what it's all about; voir aussi **-ci**; **celui**; **là-bas** adv there

label [label] nm stamp, seal

labeur [labœʀ] nm toil no pl, toiling no pl

labo [labo] abr m (= **laboratoire**) lab

laboratoire [labɔʀatwaʀ] nm laboratory; **~ de langues** language laboratory

laborieux, euse [labɔʀjø, -øz] adj (tâche) laborious; **classes laborieuses** working classes

labour [labuʀ] nm ploughing no pl; **~s** nmpl (champs) ploughed fields; **cheval de ~** plough- ou cart-horse; **bœuf de ~** ox

labourer [labuʀe] vt to plough; (fig) to make deep gashes ou furrows in

labyrinthe [labiʀɛ̃t] nm labyrinth, maze

lac [lak] nm lake

lacer [lase] vt to lace ou do up

lacérer [laseʀe] vt to tear to shreds

lacet [lasɛ] nm (de chaussure) lace; (de route) sharp bend; (piège) snare

lâche [laʃ] adj (poltron) cowardly; (desserré) loose, slack ♦ nm/f coward

lâcher [laʃe] nm (de ballons, oiseaux) release ♦ vt to let go of; (ce qui tombe, abandonner) to drop; (oiseau, animal: libérer) to release, set free; (fig: mot, remarque) to let slip, come out with; (SPORT: distancer) to leave behind ♦ vi (fil, amarres) to break, give way; (freins) to fail; **~ les amarres** (NAVIG) to cast off (the moorings); **~ les chiens** to unleash the dogs; **~ prise** to let go

lâcheté [laʃte] nf cowardice; lowness

lacrymogène [lakʀimɔʒen] adj: **gaz ~** teargas

lacté, e [lakte] adj (produit, régime) milk cpd

lacune [lakyn] nf gap

là-dedans [ladədɑ̃] adv inside (there), in it; (fig) in that

là-dessous [ladsu] adv underneath, under there; (fig) behind that

là-dessus [ladsy] adv on there; (fig) at that point; about that

ladite [ladit] dét voir **ledit**

lagune [lagyn] nf lagoon

là-haut [la'o] adv up there

laïc [laik] adj, nm/f = **laïque**

laid, e [lɛ, lɛd] adj ugly; **laideur** nf ugliness no pl

lainage [lɛnaʒ] nm woollen garment; woollen material

laine [lɛn] nf wool

laïque [laik] adj lay, civil; (SCOL) state cpd ♦ nm/f layman(woman)

laisse [lɛs] nf (de chien) lead, leash; **tenir en ~** to keep on a lead ou leash

laisser [lɛse] vt to leave ♦ vb aux: **~ qn faire** to let sb do; **se ~ aller** to let o.s. go; **laisse-toi faire** let me (ou him etc) do it; **laisser-aller** nm carelessness, slovenliness; **laissez-passer** nm inv pass

lait [lɛ] nm milk; **frère/sœur de ~** foster brother/sister; **~ condensé/concentré** evaporated/condensed milk; **laiterie** nf dairy; **laitier, ière** adj dairy cpd ♦ nm/f milkman(dairywoman)

laiton [lɛtɔ̃] nm brass

laitue [lety] nf lettuce

laïus [lajys] (péj) nm spiel

lambeau, x [lɑ̃bo] nm scrap; **en ~x** in tatters, tattered

lambris [lɑ̃bʀi] nm panelling no pl

lame [lam] nf blade; (vague) wave; (lamelle) strip; **~ de fond** ground swell no pl; **~ de rasoir** razor blade

lamelle [lamɛl] nf thin strip ou blade

lamentable [lamɑ̃tabl(ə)] adj appalling; pitiful

lamenter [lamɑ̃te]: **se ~** vi to moan (over)

lampadaire [lɑ̃padɛʀ] nm (de salon) standard lamp; (dans la rue) street lamp

lampe [lɑ̃p(ə)] nf lamp; (TECH) valve; **~ à souder** blowlamp; **~ de poche** torch (BRIT), flashlight (US)

lampion [lɑ̃pjɔ̃] nm Chinese lantern

lance [lɑ̃s] nf spear; **~ d'incendie** fire hose

lancée [lɑ̃se] nf: **être/continuer sur sa ~** to be under way/keep going

lancement [lɑ̃smɑ̃] nm launching

lance-pierres [lɑ̃spjɛʀ] nm inv catapult

lancer [lɑ̃se] nm (SPORT) throwing no pl, throw ♦ vt to throw; (émettre, projeter) to throw out, send out; (produit, fusée, bateau, artiste) to launch; (injure) to hurl, fling; (proclamation, mandat d'arrêt) to issue; **se ~** vi (prendre de l'élan) to build up speed; (se précipiter): **se ~ sur** ou **contre** to rush at; **se ~ dans** (discussion) to launch into; (aventure) to embark on; **~ qch à qn** to throw sth to sb; (de façon agressive) to throw sth at sb; **~ du poids** nm putting the shot

lancinant, e [lɑ̃sinɑ̃, -ɑ̃t] adj (regrets etc)

haunting; (douleur) shooting
landau [lɑ̃do] nm pram (BRIT), baby carriage (US)
lande [lɑ̃d] nf moor
langage [lɑ̃gaʒ] nm language
langer [lɑ̃ʒe] vt to change (the nappy (BRIT) ou diaper (US) of)
langouste [lɑ̃gust(ə)] nf crayfish inv; **langoustine** nf Dublin Bay prawn
langue [lɑ̃g] nf (ANAT, CULIN) tongue; (LING) language; **tirer la ~ (à)** to stick out one's tongue (at); **de ~ française** French-speaking; **~ maternelle** native language, mother tongue; **~ verte** slang; **~ vivante** modern language
langueur [lɑ̃gœʀ] nf languidness
languir [lɑ̃giʀ] vi to languish; (conversation) to flag; **faire ~ qn** to keep sb waiting
lanière [lanjɛʀ] nf (de fouet) lash; (de valise, bretelle) strap
lanterne [lɑ̃tɛʀn(ə)] nf (portable) lantern; (électrique) light, lamp; (de voiture) (side)light
laper [lape] vt to lap up
lapidaire [lapidɛʀ] adj stone cpd; (fig) terse
lapin [lapɛ̃] nm rabbit; (peau) rabbitskin; (fourrure) cony
Laponie [laponi] nf Lapland
laps [laps] nm: **~ de temps** space of time, time no pl
laque [lak] nf lacquer; (brute) shellac; (pour cheveux) hair spray
laquelle [lakɛl] pron voir **lequel**
larcin [laʀsɛ̃] nm theft
lard [laʀ] nm (graisse) fat; (bacon) (streaky) bacon
lardon [laʀdɔ̃] nm: **~s** chopped bacon
large [laʀʒ(ə)] adj wide; broad; (fig) generous ♦ adv: **calculer/voir ~** to allow extra/ think big ♦ nm (largeur): **5 m de ~** = 5 m wide ou in width; (mer): **le ~** the open sea; **au ~ de** off; **~ d'esprit** broad-minded; **largement** adv widely; greatly; easily; generously; **largesse** nf generosity; **largesses** nfpl (dons) liberalities; **largeur** nf (qu'on mesure) width; (impression visuelle) wideness, width; breadth; broadness
larguer [laʀge] vt to drop; **~ les amarres** to cast off (the moorings)
larme [laʀm(ə)] nf tear; (fig) drop; **en ~s** in tears; **larmoyer** vi (yeux) to water; (se plaindre) to whimper
larvé, e [laʀve] adj (fig) latent
laryngite [laʀɛ̃ʒit] nf laryngitis
las, lasse [lɑ, lɑs] adj weary
laser [lazɛʀ] nm: (rayon) **~** laser (beam); **chaîne ~** compact disc (player); **disque ~** compact disc
lasse [lɑs] adj voir **las**
lasser [lɑse] vt to weary, tire; **se ~ de** vt to grow weary ou tired of
latéral, e, aux [lateʀal, -o] adj side cpd;

lateral
latin, e [latɛ̃, -in] adj, nm/f Latin ♦ nm (LING) Latin
latitude [latityd] nf latitude
latte [lat] nf lath, slat; (de plancher) board
lauréat, e [lɔʀea, -at] nm/f winner
laurier [lɔʀje] nm (BOT) laurel; (CULIN) bay leaves pl; **~s** nmpl (fig) laurels
lavable [lavabl(ə)] adj washable
lavabo [lavabo] nm washbasin; **~s** nmpl (toilettes) toilet sg
lavage [lavaʒ] nm washing no pl, wash; **~ de cerveau** brainwashing no pl
lavande [lavɑ̃d] nf lavender
lave [lav] nf lava no pl
lave-glace [lavglas] nm windscreen (BRIT) ou windshield (US) washer
lave-linge [lavlɛ̃ʒ] nm inv washing machine
laver [lave] vt to wash; (tache) to wash off; **se ~** vi to have a wash; wash; **se ~ les mains/dents** to wash one's hands/clean one's teeth; **~ qn de** (accusation) to clear sb of; **laverie** nf: **laverie (automatique)** launderette; **lavette** nf dish cloth; (fam) drip; **laveur, euse** nm/f cleaner; **~-vaisselle** nm inv dishwasher; **lavoir** nm wash house
laxatif, ive [laksatif, -iv] adj, nm laxative

MOT CLÉ

le(l'), la [l(ə), l(a)] (pl **les**) art déf **1** the; **~ livre/la pomme/l'arbre** the book/the apple/the tree; **les étudiants** the students
2 (noms abstraits): **~ courage/l'amour/la jeunesse** courage/love/youth
3 (indiquant la possession): **se casser la jambe** etc to break one's leg etc; **levez la main** put your hand up; **avoir les yeux gris/~ nez rouge** to have grey eyes/a red nose
4 (temps): **~ matin/soir** in the morning/ evening; mornings/evenings; **~ jeudi** etc (d'habitude) on Thursdays etc; (ce jeudi-là etc) on (the) Thursday
5 (distribution, évaluation) a, an; **10F ~ mètre/kilo** 10F a ou per metre/kilo; **~ tiers/quart de** a third/quarter of
♦ pron **1** (personne: mâle) him; (: femelle) her; (: pluriel) them; **je ~/la/les vois** I can see him/her/them
2 (animal, chose: singulier) it; (: pluriel) them; **je ~ (ou la) vois** I can see it; **je les vois** I can see them
3 (remplaçant une phrase): **je ne ~ savais pas** I didn't know (about it); **il était riche et ne l'est plus** he was once rich but no longer is

---

lécher [leʃe] vt to lick; (laper: lait, eau) to lick ou lap up; **~ les vitrines** to go window-shopping
leçon [ləsɔ̃] nf lesson; **faire la ~ à** (fig) to

give a lecture to; ~s **de conduite** driving
lessons

lecteur, trice [lɛktœʀ, -tʀis] *nm/f* reader;
(*d'université*) foreign language assistant ♦
nm (*TECH*): ~ **de cassettes** cassette player;
~ **de disque compact** compact disc player;
~ **de disquette** disk drive

lecture [lɛktyʀ] *nf* reading

ledit, ladite [lədi] (*mpl* **lesdits**, *fpl* **lesdites**) *dét* the aforesaid

légal, e, aux [legal, -o] *adj* legal

légende [leʒɑ̃d] *nf* (*mythe*) legend; (*de
carte, image*) key; (*de dessin*) caption

léger, ère [leʒe, -ɛʀ] *adj* light; (*bruit, retard*) slight; (*superficiel*) thoughtless; (*volage*) free and easy; flighty; **à la légère** (*parler, agir*) rashly, thoughtlessly; **légèrement**
adv lightly; thoughtlessly; slightly

législatif, ive [leʒislatif, -iv] *adj* legislative;
législatives *nfpl* general election *sg*; **légis-
lature** [leʒislatyʀ] *nf* legislature; term (of
office)

légitime [leʒitim] *adj* (*JUR*) lawful, legitimate; (*fig*) rightful, legitimate; **en état de ~
défense** in self-defence

legs [lɛg] *nm* legacy

léguer [lege] *vt*: ~ **qch à qn** (*JUR*) to be-
queath sth to sb; (*fig*) to hand sth down *ou*
pass sth on to sb

légume [legym] *nm* vegetable

lendemain [lɑ̃dmɛ̃] *nm*: **le** ~ the next *ou*
following day; **le** ~ **matin/soir** the next *ou*
following morning/evening; **le** ~ **de** the
day after; **sans** ~ short-lived

lent, e [lɑ̃, lɑ̃t] *adj* slow; **lentement** *adv*
slowly; **lenteur** *nf* slowness *no pl*

lentille [lɑ̃tij] *nf* (*OPTIQUE*) lens *sg*; (*CULIN*)
lentil

léopard [leopaʀ] *nm* leopard

lèpre [lɛpʀ(ə)] *nf* leprosy

─────────── *MOT CLÉ*

lequel, laquelle [ləkɛl, lakɛl] (*mpl* **lesquels**, *fpl* **lesquelles**; **à + lequel = auquel,
de + lequel = duquel**) *pron* **1** (*interrogatif*)
which, which one

2 (*relatif: personne: sujet*) who; (: *objet,
après préposition*) whom; (: *chose*) which
♦ *adj*: **auquel cas** in which case

─────────────────────

les [le] *dét voir* **le**

lesbienne [lɛsbjɛn] *nf* lesbian

lesdites [ledit] *dét pl voir* **ledit**

lesdits [ledi] *dét pl voir* **ledit**

léser [leze] *vt* to wrong

lésiner [lezine] *vi*: ~ (**sur**) to skimp (on)

lésion [lezjɔ̃] *nf* lesion, damage *no pl*

lesquelles [lekɛl] *pron pl voir* **lequel**

lesquels [lekɛl] *pron pl voir* **lequel**

lessive [lesiv] *nf* (*poudre*) washing powder;
(*linge*) washing *no pl*, wash

lessiver [lesive] *vt* to wash

lest [lɛst] *nm* ballast

leste [lɛst(ə)] *adj* sprightly, nimble

lettre [lɛtʀ(ə)] *nf* letter; ~s *nfpl* (*littérature*)
literature *sg*; (*SCOL*) arts (subjects); **à la** ~
literally; **en toutes** ~s in full

lettré, e [letʀe] *adj* well-read

leucémie [løsemi] *nf* leukaemia

─────────── *MOT CLÉ*

leur [lœʀ] *adj possessif* their; ~ **maison**
their house; ~s **amis** their friends
♦ *pron* **1** (*objet indirect*) (to) them; **je** ~ **ai
dit la vérité** I told them the truth; **je le** ~
ai donné I gave it to them, I gave them it
2 (*possessif*): **le(la)** ~, **les** ~s theirs

─────────────────────

leurre [lœʀ] *nm* (*appât*) lure; (*fig*) delusion,
snare

leurrer [lœʀe] *vt* to delude, deceive

leurs [lœʀ] *dét voir* **leur**

levain [ləvɛ̃] *nm* leaven

levé, e [ləve] *adj*: **être** ~ to be up

levée [ləve] *nf* (*POSTES*) collection;
(*CARTES*) trick; ~ **de boucliers** general
outcry

lever [ləve] *vt* (*vitre, bras etc*) to raise; (*soulever de terre, supprimer: interdiction, siège*)
to lift; (*séance*) to close; (*impôts, armée*) to
levy ♦ *vi* to rise ♦ *nm*: **au** ~ on getting up;
se ~ *vi* to get up; (*soleil*) to rise; (*jour*) to
break; (*brouillard*) to lift; ~ **de soleil** sun-
rise; ~ **du jour** daybreak

levier [ləvje] *nm* lever

lèvre [lɛvʀ(ə)] *nf* lip

lévrier [levʀije] *nm* greyhound

levure [ləvyʀ] *nf* yeast; ~ **chimique** baking
powder

lexique [lɛksik] *nm* vocabulary; lexicon

lézard [lezaʀ] *nm* lizard

lézarde [lezaʀd(ə)] *nf* crack

liaison [ljezɔ̃] *nf* link; (*amoureuse*) affair;
(*PHONÉTIQUE*) liaison; **entrer/être en** ~
avec to get/be in contact with

liane [ljan] *nf* creeper

liant, e [ljɑ̃, -ɑ̃t] *adj* sociable

liasse [ljas] *nf* wad, bundle

Liban [libɑ̃] *nm*: **le** ~ (the) Lebanon; **liba-
nais, e** *adj, nm/f* Lebanese

libeller [libele] *vt* (*chèque, mandat*): ~
(**au nom de**) to make out (to); (*lettre*) to
word

libellule [libelyl] *nf* dragonfly

libéral, e, aux [liberal, -o] *adj, nm/f* liberal

libérer [libeʀe] *vt* (*délivrer*) to free, liberate;
(: *moralement, PSYCH*) to liberate; (*relâcher,
dégager: gaz*) to release; to discharge; **se** ~
vi (*de rendez-vous*) to get out of previous
engagements

liberté [libɛʀte] *nf* freedom; (*loisir*) free
time; ~s *nfpl* (*privautés*) liberties; **mettre/
être en** ~ to set/be free; **en** ~ **provisoire
surveillée/conditionnelle** on   bai

probation/parole; ~s **individuelles** personal freedom *sg*
libraire [librɛr] *nm/f* bookseller
librairie [librɛri] *nf* bookshop
libre [librə] *adj* free; *(route)* clear; *(place etc)* vacant; empty; not engaged; not taken; *(SCOL)* non-state; **de** ~ *(place)* free; ~ **de qch/de faire** free from sth/to do; ~ **arbitre** free will; ~-**échange** *nm* free trade; ~-**service** *nm* self-service store
Libye [libi] *nf*: **la** ~ Libya
licence [lisãs] *nf (permis)* permit; *(diplôme)* degree; *(liberté)* liberty; licence *(BRIT)*, license *(US)*; licentiousness; **licencié, e** *nm/f (SCOL)*: **licencié ès lettres/en droit** ≈ Bachelor of Arts/Law; *(SPORT)* member of a sports federation
licencier [lisãsje] *vt (renvoyer)* to dismiss; *(débaucher)* to make redundant; to lay off
licite [lisit] *adj* lawful
lie [li] *nf* dregs *pl*, sediment
lié, e [lje] *adj*: **très** ~ **avec** very friendly with *ou* close to; ~ **par** *(serment)* bound by
liège [ljɛʒ] *nm* cork
lien [ljɛ̃] *nm (corde, fig: affectif)* bond; *(rapport)* link, connection; ~ **de parenté** family tie
lier [lje] *vt (attacher)* to tie up; *(joindre)* to link up; *(fig: unir, engager)* to bind; *(CULIN)* to thicken; **se** ~ **avec** to make friends with; ~ **qch à** to tie *ou* link sth to; ~ **conversation avec** to strike up a conversation with
lierre [ljɛr] *nm* ivy
liesse [ljɛs] *nf*: **être en** ~ to be celebrating *ou* jubilant
lieu, x [ljø] *nm* place; ~**x** *nmpl (habitation)* premises; *(endroit: d'un accident etc)* scene *sg*; **en** ~ **sûr** in a safe place; **en premier** ~ in the first place; **en dernier** ~ lastly; **avoir** ~ to take place; **avoir** ~ **de faire** to have grounds for doing; **tenir** ~ **de** to take the place of; to serve as; **donner** ~ **à** to give rise to; **au** ~ **de** instead of
lieu-dit [ljødi] *(pl* **lieux-dits)** *nm* locality
lieutenant [ljøtnã] *nm* lieutenant
lièvre [ljɛvr(ə)] *nm* hare
ligament [ligamã] *nm* ligament
ligne [liɲ] *nf (gén)* line; *(TRANSPORTS: liaison)* service; *(: trajet)* route; *(silhouette)* figure; **entrer en** ~ **de compte** to come into it
lignée [liɲe] *nf* line; lineage; descendants *pl*
ligoter [ligɔte] *vt* to tie up
ligue [lig] *nf* league; **liguer** *vt*: **se liguer contre** *(fig)* to combine against
lilas [lila] *nm* lilac
limace [limas] *nf* slug
limaille [limaj] *nf*: ~ **de fer** iron filings *pl*
limande [limãd] *nf* dab
lime [lim] *nf* file; ~ **à ongles** nail file; **li-mer** *vt* to file
limier [limje] *nm* bloodhound; *(détective)* sleuth
limitation [limitɑsjɔ̃] *nf*: ~ **de vitesse** speed limit
limite [limit] *nf (de terrain)* boundary; *(partie ou point extrême)* limit; **vitesse/charge** ~ maximum speed/load; **cas** ~ borderline case; **date** ~ deadline
limiter [limite] *vt (restreindre)* to limit, restrict; *(délimiter)* to border
limitrophe [limitrɔf] *adj* border *cpd*
limoger [limɔʒe] *vt* to dismiss
limon [limɔ̃] *nm* silt
limonade [limɔnad] *nf* lemonade *(BRIT)*, (lemon) soda *(US)*
lin [lɛ̃] *nm* flax
linceul [lɛ̃sœl] *nm* shroud
linge [lɛ̃ʒ] *nm (serviettes etc)* linen; *(pièce de tissu)* cloth; *(aussi:* ~ **de corps)** underwear; *(:* ~ **de toilette)** towels *pl*; *(lessive)* washing
lingerie [lɛ̃ʒri] *nf* lingerie, underwear
lingot [lɛ̃go] *nm* ingot
linguistique [lɛ̃gɥistik] *adj* linguistic ♦ *nf* linguistics *sg*
lion, ne [ljɔ̃, ljɔn] *nm/f* lion(lioness); *(signe)*: **le L~** Leo; **lionceau, x** *nm* lion cub
liqueur [likœr] *nf* liqueur
liquide [likid] *adj* liquid ♦ *nm* liquid; *(COMM)*: **en** ~ in ready money *ou* cash; **li-quider** [likide] *vt (société, biens, témoin gênant)* to liquidate; *(compte, problème)* to settle; *(COMM: articles)* to clear, sell off; **li-quidités** [likidite] *nfpl (COMM)* liquid assets
lire [lir] *nf (monnaie)* lira ♦ *vt, vi* to read
lis [lis] *nm* = **lys**
lisible [lizibl(ə)] *adj* legible
lisière [lizjɛr] *nf (de forêt)* edge; *(de tissu)* selvage
lisons *vb voir* **lire**
lisse [lis] *adj* smooth
liste [list(ə)] *nf* list; **faire la** ~ **de** to list; ~ **électorale** electoral roll
listing [listiŋ] *nm (INFORM)* printout
lit [li] *nm (gén)* bed; **faire son** ~ to make one's bed; **aller/se mettre au** ~ to go to/get into bed; ~ **de camp** campbed; ~ **d'en-fant** cot *(BRIT)*, crib *(US)*
literie [litri] *nf* bedding, bedclothes *pl*
litière [litjɛr] *nf* litter
litige [litiʒ] *nm* dispute
litre [litr(ə)] *nm* litre; *(récipient)* litre measure
littéraire [literɛr] *adj* literary
littéral, e, aux [literal, -o] *adj* literal
littérature [literatyr] *nf* literature
littoral, aux [litɔral, -o] *nm* coast
liturgie [lityrʒi] *nf* liturgy
livide [livid] *adj* livid, pallid

livraison [livʀɛzɔ̃] *nf* delivery

livre [livʀ(ə)] *nm* book ♦ *nf* (*poids, monnaie*) pound; ~ **de bord** logbook; ~ **de poche** paperback (*pocket size*)

livré, e [livʀe] *adj*: ~ **à soi-même** left to o.s. *ou* one's own devices; **livrée** *nf* livery

livrer [livʀe] *vt* (*COMM*) to deliver; (*otage, coupable*) to hand over; (*secret, information*) to give away; **se** ~ **à** (*se confier*) to confide in; (*se rendre, s'abandonner*) to give o.s. up to; (*faire: pratiques, actes*) to indulge in; (: *travail*) to engage in; (: *sport*) to practise; (*travail: enquête*) to carry out

livret [livʀɛ] *nm* booklet; (*d'opéra*) libretto; ~ **de caisse d'épargne** (savings) bankbook; ~ **de famille** (official) family record book; ~ **scolaire** (school) report book

livreur, euse [livʀœʀ, -øz] *nm/f* delivery boy *ou* man/girl *ou* woman

local, e, aux [lɔkal, -o] *adj* local ♦ *nm* (*salle*) premises *pl*; *voir aussi* **locaux**

localiser [lɔkalize] *vt* (*repérer*) to locate, place; (*limiter*) to confine

localité [lɔkalite] *nf* locality

locataire [lɔkatɛʀ] *nm/f* tenant; (*de chambre*) lodger

location [lɔkasjɔ̃] *nf* (*par le locataire, le loueur*) renting; (*par le propriétaire*) renting out, letting; (*THÉÂTRE*) booking office; "~ **de voitures**" "car rental"

location-vente [lɔkasjɔ̃vɑ̃t] (*pl* ~s-~s) *nf* hire purchase (*BRIT*), instalment plan (*US*)

locaux [lɔko] *nmpl* premises

locomotive [lɔkɔmɔtiv] *nf* locomotive, engine; (*fig*) pacesetter, pacemaker

locution [lɔkysjɔ̃] *nf* phrase

loge [lɔʒ] *nf* (*THÉÂTRE: d'artiste*) dressing room; (: *de spectateurs*) box; (*de concierge, franc-maçon*) lodge

logement [lɔʒmɑ̃] *nm* accommodation *no pl* (*BRIT*), accommodations *pl* (*US*); flat (*BRIT*), apartment (*US*); housing *no pl*

loger [lɔʒe] *vt* to accommodate ♦ *vi* to live; **se** ~ **dans** (*suj: balle, flèche*) to lodge itself in; **trouver à se** ~ to find accommodation; **logeur, euse** *nm/f* landlord(lady)

logiciel [lɔʒisjɛl] *nm* software

logique [lɔʒik] *adj* logical ♦ *nf* logic

logis [lɔʒi] *nm* home; abode, dwelling

loi [lwa] *nf* law; **faire la** ~ to lay down the law

loin [lwɛ̃] *adv* far; (*dans le temps*) a long way off; a long time ago; **plus** ~ further; ~ **de** far from; **au** ~ far off; **de** ~ from a distance; (*fig: de beaucoup*) by far; **il vient de** ~ he's come a long way

lointain, e [lwɛ̃tɛ̃, -ɛn] *adj* faraway, distant; (*dans le futur, passé*) distant, far-off; (*cause, parent*) remote, distant ♦ *nm*: **dans le** ~ in the distance

loir [lwaʀ] *nm* dormouse

loisir [lwaziʀ] *nm*: **heures de** ~ spare time;

~s *nmpl* leisure *sg*; leisure activities; **avoir le** ~ **de faire** to have the time *ou* opportunity to do; **à** ~ at leisure; at one's pleasure

londonien, ne [lɔ̃dɔnjɛ̃, -jɛn] *adj* London *cpd*, of London ♦ *nm/f*: **L~, ne** Londoner

Londres [lɔ̃dʀ(ə)] *n* London

long, longue [lɔ̃, lɔ̃g] *adj* long ♦ *adv*: **en savoir** ~ to know a great deal ♦ *nm*: **de 3 m de** ~ 3 m long, 3 m in length; **ne pas faire** ~ **feu** not to last long; (**tout**) **le** ~ **de** (all) along; **tout au** ~ **de** (*année, vie*) throughout; **de** ~ **en large** (*marcher*) to and fro, up and down; *voir aussi* **longue**

longer [lɔ̃ʒe] *vt* to go (*ou* walk *ou* drive) along(side); (*suj: mur, route*) to border

longiligne [lɔ̃ʒiliɲ] *adj* long-limbed

longitude [lɔ̃ʒityd] *nf* longitude

longitudinal, e, aux [lɔ̃ʒitydinal, -o] *adj* (*running*) lengthways

longtemps [lɔ̃tɑ̃] *adv* (for) a long time, (for) long; **avant** ~ before long; **pour** *ou* **pendant** ~ for a long time; **mettre** ~ **à faire** to take a long time to do

longue [lɔ̃g] *adj voir* **long** ♦ *nf*: **à la** ~ in the end; **longuement** *adv* for a long time

longueur [lɔ̃gœʀ] *nf* length; ~s *nfpl* (*fig: d'un film etc*) tedious parts; **en** ~ lengthwise; **tirer en** ~ to drag on; **à** ~ **de journée** all day long; ~ **d'onde** wavelength

longue-vue [lɔ̃gvy] *nf* telescope

lopin [lɔpɛ̃] *nm*: ~ **de terre** patch of land

loque [lɔk] *nf* (*personne*) wreck; ~s *nfpl* (*habits*) rags

loquet [lɔkɛ] *nm* latch

lorgner [lɔʀɲe] *vt* to eye; (*fig*) to have one's eye on

lors [lɔʀ] : ~ **de** *prép* at the time of; during; ~ **même que** even though

lorsque [lɔʀsk(ə)] *conj* when, as

losange [lɔzɑ̃ʒ] *nm* diamond; (*GÉOM*) lozenge

lot [lo] *nm* (*part*) share; (*de loterie*) prize; (*fig: destin*) fate, lot; (*COMM, INFORM*) batch

loterie [lɔtʀi] *nf* lottery; raffle

loti, e [lɔti] *adj*: **bien/mal** ~ well-/badly off

lotion [lɔsjɔ̃] *nf* lotion

lotir [lɔtiʀ] *vt* (*terrain*) to divide into plots; to sell by lots; **lotissement** *nm* housing development; plot, lot

loto [lɔto] *nm* lotto; numerical lottery

louable [lwabl(ə)] *adj* commendable

louanges [lwɑ̃ʒ] *nfpl* praise *sg*

loubard [lubaʀ] (*fam*) *nm* lout

louche [luʃ] *adj* shady, fishy, dubious ♦ *nf* ladle

loucher [luʃe] *vi* to squint

louer [lwe] *vt* (*maison: suj: propriétaire*) to let, rent (out); (: *locataire*) to rent; (*voiture etc: entreprise*) to hire out (*BRIT*), rent (out); (: *locataire*) to hire, rent; (*réserver*) to

book; (*faire l'éloge de*) to praise; **"à ~"** **"to let"** (*BRIT*), **"for rent"** (*US*)
loup [lu] *nm* wolf
loupe [lup] *nf* magnifying glass
louper [lupe] *vt* (*manquer*) to miss
lourd, e [luʀ, luʀd(ə)] *adj, adv* heavy; **~ de** (*conséquences, menaces*) charged with; **lourdaud, e** (*péj*) *adj* clumsy
loutre [lutʀ(ə)] *nf* otter
louveteau, x [luvto] *nm* wolf-cub; (*scout*) cub (scout)
louvoyer [luvwaje] *vi* (*NAVIG*) to tack; (*fig*) to hedge, evade the issue
lover [lɔve] : **se ~** *vi* to coil up
loyal, e, aux [lwajal, -o] *adj* (*fidèle*) loyal, faithful; (*fair-play*) fair; **loyauté** *nf* loyalty, faithfulness; fairness
loyer [lwaje] *nm* rent
lu, e [ly] *pp de* **lire**
lubie [lybi] *nf* whim, craze
lubrifiant [lybʀifjɑ̃] *nm* lubricant
lubrifier [lybʀifje] *vt* to lubricate
lubrique [lybʀik] *adj* lecherous
lucarne [lykaʀn(ə)] *nf* skylight
lucratif, ive [lykʀatif, -iv] *adj* lucrative, profitable; **à but non ~** non profit-making
lueur [lɥœʀ] *nf* (*chatoyante*) glimmer *no pl*; (*métallique, mouillée*) gleam *no pl*; (*rougeoyante, chaude*) glow *no pl*; (*pâle*) (faint) light; (*fig*) glimmer; gleam
luge [lyʒ] *nf* sledge (*BRIT*), sled (*US*)
lugubre [lygybʀ(ə)] *adj* gloomy; dismal

―――――― *MOT CLÉ* ――――――

lui [lɥi] *pron* **1** (*objet indirect: mâle*) (to) him; (: *femelle*) (to) her; (: *chose, animal*) (to) it; **je ~ ai parlé** I have spoken to him (*ou* to her); **il ~ a offert un cadeau** he gave him (*ou* her) a present
2 (*après préposition, comparatif: personne*) him; (: *chose, animal*) it; **elle est contente de ~** she is pleased with him; **je la connais mieux que ~** I know her better than he does; I know her better than him
3 (*sujet, forme emphatique*) he; **~, il est à Paris** HE is in Paris
4: **~-même** himself; itself

luire [lɥiʀ] *vi* to shine; to glow
lumière [lymjɛʀ] *nf* light; **~s** *nfpl* (*d'une personne*) wisdom *sg*; **mettre en ~** (*fig*) to highlight; **~ du jour** daylight
luminaire [lyminɛʀ] *nm* lamp, light
lumineux, euse [lyminø, -øz] *adj* (*émettant de la lumière*) luminous; (*éclairé*) illuminated; (*ciel, couleur*) bright; (*relatif à la lumière: rayon etc*) of light, light *cpd*; (*fig: regard*) radiant
lunaire [lynɛʀ] *adj* lunar, moon *cpd*
lunatique [lynatik] *adj* whimsical, temperamental
lundi [lœ̃di] *nm* Monday; **~ de Pâques**

Easter Monday
lune [lyn] *nf* moon; **~ de miel** honeymoon
lunette [lynɛt] *nf*: **~s** *nfpl* glasses, spectacles; (*protectrices*) goggles; **~ arrière** (*AUTO*) rear window; **~s de soleil** sun glasses; **~s noires** dark glasses
lus *etc vb voir* **lire**
lustre [lystʀ(ə)] *nm* (*de plafond*) chandelier; (*fig: éclat*) lustre
lustrer [lystʀe] *vt* to shine
lut *vb voir* **lire**
luth [lyt] *nm* lute
lutin [lytɛ̃] *nm* imp, goblin
lutte [lyt] *nf* (*conflit*) struggle; (*sport*) wrestling; **lutter** *vi* to fight, struggle
luxe [lyks(ə)] *nm* luxury; **de ~** luxury *cpd*
Luxembourg [lyksɑ̃buʀ] *nm*: **le ~** Luxembourg
luxer [lykse] *vt*: **se ~ l'épaule** to dislocate one's shoulder
luxueux, euse [lyksɥø, -øz] *adj* luxurious
luxure [lyksyʀ] *nf* lust
lycée [lise] *nm* secondary school; **lycéen, ne** *nm/f* secondary school pupil
lyrique [liʀik] *adj* lyrical; (*OPÉRA*) lyric; **artiste ~** opera singer
lys [lis] *nm* lily

M m

M *abr* = **Monsieur**
m' [m] *pron voir* **me**
ma [ma] *dét voir* **mon**
macaron [makaʀɔ̃] *nm* (*gâteau*) macaroon; (*insigne*) (round) badge
macaronis [makaʀɔni] *nmpl* macaroni *sg*
macédoine [masedwan] *nf*: **~ de fruits** fruit salad; **~ de légumes** *nf* mixed vegetables
macérer [maseʀe] *vi, vt* to macerate; (*dans du vinaigre*) to pickle
mâcher [mɑʃe] *vt* to chew; **ne pas ~ ses mots** not to mince one's words
machin [maʃɛ̃] (*fam*) *nm* thing(umajig)
machinal, e, aux [maʃinal, -o] *adj* mechanical, automatic
machination [maʃinasjɔ̃] *nf* scheming, frame-up
machine [maʃin] *nf* machine; (*locomotive*) engine; (*fig: rouages*) machinery; **~ à écrire** typewriter; **~ à laver/coudre** washing/sewing machine; **~ à sous** fruit machine; **~ à vapeur** steam engine; **machinerie** *nf*

machinery, plant; (*d'un navire*) engine room; **machiniste** *nm* (*de bus, métro*) driver

mâchoire [mɑʃwaʀ] *nf* jaw; ~ **de frein** brake shoe

mâchonner [mɑʃɔne] *vt* to chew (at)

maçon [masɔ̃] *nm* bricklayer; builder; ~**nerie** [masɔnʀi] *nf* (*murs*) brickwork; masonry, stonework; (*activité*) bricklaying; building

maculer [makyle] *vt* to stain

Madame [madam] (*pl* **Mesdames**) *nf*: ~ **X** Mrs X; **occupez-vous de** ~/**Monsieur/ Mademoiselle** please serve this lady/ gentleman/(young) lady; **bonjour** ~/ **Monsieur/Mademoiselle** good morning; (*ton déférent*) good morning Madam/Sir/ Madam; (*le nom est connu*) good morning Mrs/Mr/Miss X; ~/**Monsieur/Mademoiselle!** (*pour appeler*) Madam/Sir/Miss!; ~/ **Monsieur/Mademoiselle** (*sur lettre*) Dear Madam/Sir/Madam; **chère** ~/**cher Monsieur/chère Mademoiselle** Dear Mrs/ Mr/Miss X; **Mesdames** Ladies

Mademoiselle [madmwazɛl] (*pl* **Mesdemoiselles**) *nf* Miss; *voir aussi* **Madame**

madère [madɛʀ] *nm* Madeira (wine)

magasin [magazɛ̃] *nm* (*boutique*) shop; (*entrepôt*) warehouse; (*d'une arme*) magazine; **en** ~ (*COMM*) in stock

magazine [magazin] *nm* magazine

magicien, ne [maʒisjɛ̃, -jɛn] *nm/f* magician

magie [maʒi] *nf* magic; **magique** *adj* magic; (*enchanteur*) magical

magistral, e, aux [maʒistʀal, -o] *adj* (*œuvre, adresse*) masterly; (*ton*) authoritative; (*ex cathedra*): **enseignement** ~ lecturing, lectures *pl*

magistrat [maʒistʀa] *nm* magistrate

magnétique [maɲetik] *adj* magnetic

magnétiser [maɲetize] *vt* to magnetize; (*fig*) to mesmerize, hypnotize

magnétophone [maɲetɔfɔn] *nm* tape recorder; ~ **à cassettes** cassette recorder

magnétoscope [maɲetɔskɔp] *nm* videotape recorder

magnifique [maɲifik] *adj* magnificent

magot [mago] *nm* (*argent*) pile (of money); nest egg

magouille [maguj] *nf* scheming

mai [mɛ] *nm* May

maigre [mɛgʀ(ə)] *adj* (very) thin, skinny; (*viande*) lean; (*fromage*) low-fat; (*végétation*) thin, sparse; (*fig*) poor, meagre, skimpy ♦ *adv*: **faire** ~ not to eat meat; **jours** ~**s** days of abstinence, fish days; **maigreur** *nf* thinness; **maigrir** *vi* to get thinner, lose weight

maille [maj] *nf* stitch; **avoir** ~ **à partir avec qn** to have a brush with sb; ~ **à l'endroit/à l'envers** plain/purl stitch

maillet [majɛ] *nm* mallet

maillon [majɔ̃] *nm* link

maillot [majo] *nm* (*aussi*: ~ **de corps**) vest; (*de danseur*) leotard; (*de sportif*) jersey; ~ **de bain** swimsuit; (*d'homme*) bathing trunks *pl*

main [mɛ̃] *nf* hand; **à la** ~ in one's hand; **se donner la** ~ to hold hands; **donner** *ou* **tendre la** ~ **à qn** to hold out one's hand to sb; **se serrer la** ~ to shake hands; **serrer la** ~ **à qn** to shake hands with sb; **sous la** ~ to *ou* at hand; **attaque à** ~ **armée** armed attack; **à** ~ **droite/gauche** to the right/left; **à** ~ **à remettre en** ~**s propres** to be delivered personally; **de première** ~ (*COMM*: *voiture etc*) second-hand with only one previous owner; **mettre la dernière** ~ **à** to put the finishing touches to; **se faire/ perdre la** ~ to get one's hand in/lose one's touch; **avoir qch bien en** ~ to have (got) the hang of sth

main-d'œuvre [mɛ̃dœvʀ(ə)] *nf* manpower, labour

main-forte [mɛ̃fɔʀt(ə)] *nf*: **prêter** ~ **à qn** to come to sb's assistance

mainmise [mɛ̃miz] *nf* seizure; (*fig*): ~ **sur** complete hold on

maint, e [mɛ̃, mɛ̃t] *adj* many a; ~**s** many; **à** ~**es reprises** time and (time) again

maintenant [mɛ̃tnɑ̃] *adv* now; (*actuellement*) nowadays

maintenir [mɛ̃tniʀ] *vt* (*retenir, soutenir*) to support; (*contenir: foule etc*) to hold back; (*conserver, affirmer*) to maintain; **se** ~ *vi* to hold; to keep steady; to persist

maintien [mɛ̃tjɛ̃] *nm* maintaining; (*attitude*) bearing

maire [mɛʀ] *nm* mayor

mairie [meʀi] *nf* (*bâtiment*) town hall; (*administration*) town council

mais [mɛ] *conj* but; ~ **non!** of course not!; ~ **enfin** but after all; (*indignation*) look here!; ~ **encore?** is that all?

maïs [mais] *nm* maize (*BRIT*), corn (*US*)

maison [mɛzɔ̃] *nf* house; (*chez-soi*) home; (*COMM*) firm ♦ *adj inv* (*CULIN*) home-made; made by the chef; (*fig*) in-house, own; **à la** ~ at home; (*direction*) home; ~ **close** *ou* **de passe** brothel; ~ **de correction** reformatory; ~ **de repos** convalescent home; ~ **de santé** mental home; ~ **des jeunes** ≈ youth club; ~ **mère** parent company; **maisonnée** *nf* household, family; **maisonnette** *nf* small house, cottage

maître, esse [mɛtʀ(ə), mɛtʀɛs] *nm/f* master(mistress); (*SCOL*) teacher, schoolmaster(mistress) ♦ *nm* (*peintre etc*) master; (*titre*): **M**~ Maître, term of address gen for a barrister ♦ *adj* (*principal, essentiel*) main; **être** ~ **de** (*soi-même, situation*) to be in control of; **une** ~**sse femme** a managing woman; ~ **chanteur** blackmailer; ~/ **maîtresse d'école** schoolmaster(mistress);

~ **d'hôtel** (*domestique*) butler; (*d'hôtel*) head waiter; ~ **nageur** lifeguard; **maîtresse** nf (*amante*) mistress; **maîtresse de maison** hostess; housewife

maîtrise [metriz] nf (*aussi:* ~ **de soi**) self-control, self-possession; (*habileté*) skill, mastery; (*suprématie*) mastery, command; (*diplôme*) ≈ master's degree

maîtriser [metrize] vt (*cheval, incendie*) to (bring under) control; (*sujet*) to master; (*émotion*) to control, master; **se** ~ to control o.s.

majestueux, euse [maʒɛstɥø, -øz] adj majestic

majeur, e [maʒœr] adj (*important*) major; (*JUR*) of age; (*fig*) adult ♦ nm (*doigt*) middle finger; **en** ~**e partie** for the most part

majorer [maʒɔre] vt to increase

majoritaire [maʒɔritɛr] adj majority cpd

majorité [maʒɔrite] nf (*gén*) majority; (*parti*) party in power; **en** ~ mainly

majuscule [maʒyskyl] adj, nf: (**lettre**) ~ capital (letter)

mal [mal, mo] (*pl* **maux**) nm (*opposé au bien*) evil; (*tort, dommage*) harm; (*douleur physique*) pain, ache; (*maladie*) illness, sickness no pl ♦ adv badly ♦ adj bad, wrong; **être** ~ to be uncomfortable; **être** ~ **avec qn** to be on bad terms with sb; **être au plus** ~ (*malade*) to be at death's door; (*brouillé*) to be at daggers drawn; **il a** ~ **compris** he misunderstood; **dire/penser du** ~ **de** to speak/think ill of; **ne voir aucun** ~ **à** to see no harm in, see nothing wrong in; **craignant** ~ **faire** fearing he was doing the wrong thing; **faire du** ~ **à qn** to hurt sb; to harm sb; **se faire** ~ to hurt o.s.; **se donner du** ~ **pour faire qch** to go to a lot of trouble to do sth; **ça fait** ~ it hurts; **j'ai** ~ **au dos** my back hurts; **avoir** ~ **à la tête/à la gorge/aux dents** to have a headache/a sore throat/toothache; **avoir le** ~ **du pays** to be homesick; **prendre** ~ to be taken ill, feel unwell; *voir aussi* **cœur**; **maux**; ~ **de mer** seasickness; ~ **en point** adj inv in a bad state

malade [malad] adj ill, sick; (*poitrine, jambe*) bad; (*plante*) diseased ♦ nm/f invalid, sick person; (*à l'hôpital etc*) patient; **tomber** ~ to fall ill; **être** ~ **du cœur** to have heart trouble ou a bad heart; ~ **mental** mentally sick ou ill person

maladie [maladi] nf (*spécifique*) disease, illness; (*mauvaise santé*) illness, sickness; ~ **d'Alzheimer** nf Alzheimer's (disease); **maladif, ive** [maladif, iv] adj (*curiosité, besoin*) pathological

maladresse [maladrɛs] nf clumsiness no pl; (*gaffe*) blunder

maladroit, e [maladrwa, -wat] adj clumsy

malaise [malɛz] nm (*MÉD*) feeling of faintness; feeling of discomfort; (*fig*) uneasiness,

malaise

malaisé, e [maleze] adj difficult

malaria [malarja] nf malaria

malaxer [malakse] vt to knead; to mix

malchance [malʃɑ̃s] nf misfortune, ill luck no pl; **par** ~ unfortunately

mâle [mɑl] adj (*aussi ÉLEC, TECH*) male; (*viril: voix, traits*) manly ♦ nm male

malédiction [malediksjɔ̃] nf curse

mal: ~**encontreux, euse** adj unfortunate, untoward; ~**-en-point** adj inv in a sorry state; ~**entendu** nm misunderstanding; ~**façon** nf fault; ~**faisant, e** adj evil, harmful; ~**faiteur** nm lawbreaker, criminal; burglar, thief; ~**famé, e** adj disreputable

malgache [malgaʃ] adj, nm/f Madagascan, Malagasy ♦ nm (*LING*) Malagasy

malgré [malgre] prép in spite of, despite; ~ **tout** all the same

malheur [malœr] nm (*situation*) adversity, misfortune; (*événement*) misfortune; disaster, tragedy; **faire un** ~ to be a smash hit; **malheureusement** adv unfortunately; **malheureux, euse** adj (*triste*) unhappy, miserable; (*infortuné, regrettable*) unfortunate; (*malchanceux*) unlucky; (*insignifiant*) wretched ♦ nm/f poor soul; unfortunate creature; **les** ~**eux** the destitute

malhonnête [malɔnɛt] adj dishonest

malice [malis] nf mischievousness; (*méchanceté*) **par** ~ out of malice ou spite; **sans** ~ guileless; **malicieux, euse** adj mischievous

malin, igne [malɛ̃, -iɲ] adj (*futé: f gén: maline*) smart, shrewd; (*MÉD*) malignant

malingre [malɛ̃gr(ə)] adj puny

malle [mal] nf trunk

mallette [malɛt] nf (*small*) suitcase; overnight case; attaché case

malmener [malməne] vt to manhandle; (*fig*) to give a rough handling to

malodorant, e [malɔdɔrɑ̃, -ɑ̃t] adj foul- ou ill-smelling

malotru [malɔtry] nm lout, boor

malpropre [malprɔpr(ə)] adj dirty

malsain, e [malsɛ̃, -ɛn] adj unhealthy

malt [malt] nm malt

Malte [malt(ə)] nf Malta

maltraiter [maltrɛte] vt (*brutaliser*) to manhandle, ill-treat

malveillance [malvejɑ̃s] nf (*animosité*) ill will; (*intention de nuire*) malevolence; (*JUR*) malicious intent no pl

malversation [malvɛrsasjɔ̃] nf embezzlement

maman [mamɑ̃] nf mum(my), mother

mamelle [mamɛl] nf teat

mamelon [mamlɔ̃] nm (*ANAT*) nipple; (*colline*) knoll, hillock

mamie [mami] (*fam*) nf granny

mammifère [mamifɛr] nm mammal

manche [mãʃ] nf (de vêtement) sleeve; (d'un jeu, tournoi) round; (GÉO): **la M~** the Channel ♦ nm (d'outil, casserole) handle; (de pelle, pioche etc) shaft; **~ à balai** nm broomstick; (AVIAT, INFORM) joystick

manchette [mãʃɛt] nf (de chemise) cuff; (coup) forearm blow; (titre) headline

manchon [mãʃɔ̃] nm (de fourrure) muff

manchot [mãʃo] nm one-armed man; armless man; (ZOOL) penguin

mandarine [mãdaRin] nf mandarin (orange), tangerine

mandat [mãda] nm (postal) postal ou money order; (d'un député etc) mandate; (procuration) power of attorney, proxy; (PO-LICE) warrant; **~ d'amener** summons sg; **~ d'arrêt** warrant for arrest; **mandataire** nm/f representative; proxy

manège [manɛʒ] nm riding school; (à la foire) roundabout, merry-go-round; (fig) game, ploy

manette [manɛt] nf lever, tap; **~ de jeu** joystick

mangeable [mãʒabl(ə)] adj edible, eatable

mangeoire [mãʒwaR] nf trough, manger

manger [mãʒe] vt to eat; (ronger: suj: rouille etc) to eat into ou away ♦ vi to eat

mangue [mãg] nf mango

maniable [manjabl(ə)] adj (outil) handy; (voiture, voilier) easy to handle

maniaque [manjak] adj finicky, fussy; suffering from a mania ♦ nm/f maniac

manie [mani] nf mania; (tic) odd habit

manier [manje] vt to handle

manière [manjɛR] nf (façon) way, manner; **~s** nfpl (attitude) manners; (chichis) fuss sg; **de ~ à** so as to; **de telle ~ que** in such a way that; **de cette ~** in this way ou manner; **d'une certaine ~** in a way; **d'une ~ générale** generally speaking, as a general rule; **de toute ~** in any case

maniéré, e [manjere] adj affected

manifestant, e [manifɛstã, -ãt] nm/f demonstrator

manifestation [manifɛstasjɔ̃] nf (de joie, mécontentement) expression, demonstration; (symptôme) outward sign; (fête etc) event; (POL) demonstration

manifeste [manifɛst(ə)] adj obvious, evident ♦ nm manifesto

manifester [manifɛste] vt (volonté, intentions) to show, indicate; (joie, peur) to express, show ♦ vi to demonstrate; **se ~** vi (émotion) to show ou express itself; (difficultés) to arise; (symptômes) to appear; (témoin etc) to come forward

manigance [manigãs] nf scheme

manigancer [manigãse] vt to plot

manipuler [manipyle] vt to handle; (fig) to manipulate

manivelle [manivɛl] nf crank

mannequin [manikɛ̃] nm (COUTURE) dummy; (MODE) model

manœuvre [manœvR(ə)] nf (gén) manœuvre (BRIT), maneuver (US) ♦ nm labourer; **~r** [manœvRe] vt to manœuvre (BRIT), maneuver (US); (levier, machine) to operate ♦ vi to manœuvre

manoir [manwaR] nm manor ou country house

manque [mãk] nm (insuffisance): **~ de** lack of; (vide) emptiness, gap; (MÉD) withdrawal; **~s** nmpl (lacunes) faults, defects

manqué, e [mãke] adj failed; **garçon ~** tomboy

manquer [mãke] vi (faire défaut) to be lacking; (être absent) to be missing; (échouer) to fail ♦ vt to miss ♦ vb impers: **il (nous) manque encore 100 F** we are still 100 F short; **il manque des pages (au livre)** there are some pages missing (from the book); **il/cela me manque** I miss him/this; **~ à** (règles etc) to be in breach of, fail to observe; **~ de** to lack; **il a manqué (de) se tuer** he very nearly got killed

mansarde [mãsaRd(ə)] nf attic

mansuétude [mãsɥetyd] nf leniency

manteau, x [mãto] nm coat

manucure [manykyR] nf manicurist

manuel, le [manɥɛl] adj manual ♦ nm (ouvrage) manual, handbook

manufacture [manyfaktyR] nf factory; **manufacturé, e** [manyfaktyRe] adj manufactured

manuscrit, e [manyskRi, -it] adj handwritten ♦ nm manuscript

manutention [manytãsjɔ̃] nf (COMM) handling; (local) storehouse

mappemonde [mapmɔ̃d] nf (plane) map of the world; (sphère) globe

maquereau, x [makRo] nm (ZOOL) mackerel inv; (fam) pimp

maquette [makɛt] nf (d'un décor, bâtiment, véhicule) (scale) model; (d'une page illustrée) paste-up

maquillage [makijaʒ] nm making up; faking; (crème etc) make-up

maquiller [makije] vt (personne, visage) to make up; (truquer: passeport, statistique) to fake; (: voiture volée) to do over (respray etc); **se ~** vi to make up (one's face)

maquis [maki] nm (GÉO) scrub; (MIL) maquis, underground fighting no pl

maraîcher, ère [maReʃe, maReʃɛR] adj: **cultures maraîchères** market gardening sg ♦ nm/f market gardener; **jardin ~** market garden (BRIT), truck farm (US)

marais [maRɛ] nm marsh, swamp

marasme [maRasm(ə)] nm stagnation, slump

marathon [maRatɔ̃] nm marathon

marâtre [maRatR(ə)] nf cruel mother

maraudeur [maRodœR] nm prowler

marbre [maRbR(ə)] nm (pierre, statue) mar-

ble; (d'une table, commode) marble top;
marbrer vt to mottle, blotch
marc [mar] nm (de raisin, pommes) marc;
~ **de café** coffee grounds pl ou dregs pl
marchand, e [marʃɑ̃, -ɑ̃d] nm/f shopkeeper, tradesman(woman); (au marché)
stallholder ♦ adj: **prix/valeur** ~(e) market
price/value; ~/e **de fruits** fruiterer (BRIT),
fruit seller (US); ~/e **de journaux** newsagent (BRIT), newsdealer (US); ~/e **de légumes** greengrocer (BRIT), produce dealer
(US); ~/e **de quatre saisons** costermonger
(BRIT), street vendor (selling fresh fruit and
vegetables) (US)
marchander [marʃɑ̃de] vi to bargain, haggle
marchandise [marʃɑ̃diz] nf goods pl,
merchandise no pl
marche [marʃ(ə)] nf (d'escalier) step; (activité) walking; (promenade, trajet, allure)
walk; (démarche) walk, gait; (MIL etc, MUS)
march; (fonctionnement) running; (progres-
sion) progress; course; **ouvrir/fermer la** ~
to lead the way/bring up the rear; **dans le
sens de la** ~ (RAIL) facing the engine; **en**
~ (monter etc) while the vehicle is moving
ou in motion; **mettre en** ~ to start; **se
mettre en** ~ (personne) to get moving;
(machine) to start; ~ **à suivre** (correct)
procedure; (sur notice) (step by step) instructions pl; ~ **arrière** reverse (gear); **faire**
~ **arrière** to reverse; (fig) to backtrack,
back-pedal
marché [marʃe] nm (lieu, COMM, ÉCON)
market; (ville) trading centre; (transaction)
bargain, deal; **faire du** ~ **noir** to buy and
sell on the black market; ~ **aux puces** flea
market; **M~ commun** Common Market
marchepied [marʃəpje] nm (RAIL) step;
(fig) stepping stone
marcher [marʃe] vi to walk; (MIL) to
march; (aller: voiture, train, affaires) to go;
(prospérer) to go well; (fonctionner) to
work, run; (fam) to go along, agree; to be
taken in; ~ **sur** to walk on; (mettre le pied
sur) to step on ou in; (MIL) to march upon;
~ **dans** (herbe etc) to walk in ou on; (flaque) to step in; **faire** ~ **qn** to pull sb's leg;
to lead sb up the garden path; **marcheur,
euse** nm/f walker
mardi [mardi] nm Tuesday; **M~ gras**
Shrove Tuesday
mare [mar] nf pond
marécage [mareka3] nm marsh, swamp
maréchal, aux [mareʃal, -o] nm marshal
marée [mare] nf tide; (poissons) fresh (sea)
fish; ~ **haute/basse** high/low tide; ~
montante/descendante rising/ebb tide
marémotrice [maremɔtris] adj f tidal
margarine [margarin] nf margarine
marge [mar3(ə)] nf margin; **en** ~ **de** (fig)
on the fringe of; cut off from; ~ **bénéficiai-**

re profit margin
marguerite [margərit] nf marguerite, (ox-
eye) daisy; (d'imprimante) daisy-wheel
mari [mari] nm husband
mariage [marja3] nm (union, état, fig) marriage; (noce) wedding; ~ **civil/religieux** registry office (BRIT) ou civil/church wedding
marié, e [marje] adj married ♦ nm
(bride)groom; **les** ~s the bride and groom;
les (jeunes) ~s the newly-weds; **mariée** nf
bride
marier [marje] vt to marry; (fig) to blend;
se ~ **(avec)** to marry
marin, e [marɛ̃, -in] adj sea cpd, marine ♦
nm sailor
marine [marin] adj voir **marin** ♦ adj inv
navy (blue) ♦ nm (MIL) marine ♦ nf navy;
~ **de guerre** navy; ~ **marchande** merchant
navy
marionnette [marjɔnɛt] nf puppet
maritime [maritim] adj sea cpd, maritime
mark [mark] nm mark
marmelade [marmalad] nf stewed fruit,
compote; ~ **d'oranges** marmalade
marmite [marmit] nf (cooking-)pot
marmonner [marmɔne] vt, vi to mumble,
mutter
marmotter [marmɔte] vt to mumble
Maroc [marɔk] nm: **le** ~ Morocco; **maro-
cain, e** adj, nm/f Moroccan
maroquinerie [marɔkinri] nf leather craft;
fine leather goods pl
marquant, e [markɑ̃, -ɑ̃t] adj outstanding
marque [mark(ə)] nf mark; (SPORT, JEU:
décompte des points) score; (COMM: de produits) brand; make; (de disques) label; **de**
~ (COMM) brand-name cpd; proprietary;
(fig) high-class; distinguished; ~ **de fabrique** trademark; ~ **déposée** registered
trademark
marquer [marke] vt to mark; (inscrire) to
write down; (bétail) to brand; (SPORT: but
etc) to score; (: joueur) to mark; (accentuer:
taille etc) to emphasize; (manifester: refus,
intérêt) to show ♦ vi (événement, personnalité) to stand out, be outstanding; (SPORT)
to score; ~ **les points** (tenir la marque) to
keep the score
marqueterie [markətri] nf inlaid work,
marquetry
marquis [marki] nm marquis ou marquess
marquise [markiz] nf marchioness;
(auvent) glass canopy ou awning
marraine [marɛn] nf godmother
marrant, e [marɑ̃, -ɑ̃t] (fam) adj funny
marre [mar] (fam) adv: **en avoir** ~ **de** to
be fed up with
marrer [mare]: **se** ~ (fam) vi to have a
(good) laugh
marron [marɔ̃] nm (fruit) chestnut ♦ adj inv
brown; **marronnier** nm chestnut (tree)
mars [mars] nm March

marsouin [maʀswɛ̃] *nm* porpoise
marteau, x [maʀto] *nm* hammer; *(de porte)* knocker; **marteau-piqueur** *nm* pneumatic drill
marteler [maʀtəle] *vt* to hammer
martien, ne [maʀsjɛ̃, -jɛn] *adj* Martian, of ou from Mars
martinet [maʀtinɛ] *nm (fouet)* small whip; *(ZOOL)* swift
martyr, e [maʀtiʀ] *nm/f* martyr
martyre [maʀtiʀ] *nm* martyrdom; *(fig: sens affaibli)* agony, torture
martyriser [maʀtiʀize] *vt (REL)* to martyr; *(fig)* to bully; *(enfant)* to batter, beat
marxiste [maʀksist(ə)] *adj, nm/f* Marxist
masculin, e [maskylɛ̃, -in] *adj* masculine; *(sexe, population)* male; *(équipe, vêtements)* men's; *(viril)* manly ♦ *nm* masculine
masque [mask(ə)] *nm* mask; ~**r** [maske] *vt (cacher: paysage, porte)* to hide, conceal; *(dissimuler: vérité, projet)* to mask, obscure
massacre [masakʀ(ə)] *nm* massacre, slaughter; ~**r** [masakʀe] *vt* to massacre, slaughter; *(fig: texte etc)* to murder
massage [masaʒ] *nm* massage
masse [mas] *nf* mass; *(péj)*: **la** ~ the masses *pl*; *(ÉLEC)* earth; *(maillet)* sledgehammer; **une** ~ **de** *(fam)* masses ou loads of; **en** ~ *(en bloc)* in bulk; *(en foule)* en masse ♦ *adj (exécutions, production)* mass *cpd*
masser [mase] *vt (assembler)* to gather; *(pétrir)* to massage; **se** ~ *vi* to gather; **masseur, euse** *nm/f* masseur(euse)
massif, ive [masif, -iv] *adj (porte)* solid, massive; *(visage)* heavy, large; *(bois, or)* solid; *(dose)* massive; *(déportations etc)* mass *cpd* ♦ *nm (montagneux)* massif; *(de fleurs)* clump, bank
massue [masy] *nf* club, bludgeon
mastic [mastik] *nm (pour vitres)* putty; *(pour fentes)* filler
mastiquer [mastike] *vt (aliment)* to chew, masticate; *(fente)* to.fill; *(vitre)* to putty
mat, e [mat] *adj (couleur, métal)* mat(t); *(bruit, son)* dull ♦ *adj inv (ÉCHECS)*: **être** ~ to be checkmate
mât [mɑ] *nm (NAVIG)* mast; *(poteau)* pole, post
match [matʃ] *nm* match; **faire** ~ **nul** to draw; ~ **aller** first leg; ~ **retour** second leg, return match
matelas [matla] *nm* mattress; ~ **pneumatique** air bed ou mattress
matelassé, e [matlase] *adj* padded; quilted
matelot [matlo] *nm* sailor, seaman
mater [mate] *vt (personne)* to bring to heel, subdue; *(révolte)* to put down
matérialiste [mateʀjalist(ə)] *adj* materialistic
matériaux [mateʀjo] *nmpl* material(s)
matériel, le [mateʀjɛl] *adj* material ♦ *nm* equipment *no pl*; *(de camping etc)* gear *no*

pl
maternel, le [matɛʀnɛl] *adj (amour, geste)* motherly, maternal; *(grand-père, oncle)* maternal; **maternelle** *nf (aussi: école maternelle)* (state) nursery school
maternité [matɛʀnite] *nf (établissement)* maternity hospital; *(état de mère)* motherhood, maternity; *(grossesse)* pregnancy
mathématique [matematik] *adj* mathematical; **mathématiques** *nfpl (science)* mathematics *sg*
matière [matjɛʀ] *nf (PHYSIQUE)* matter; *(COMM, TECH)* material, matter *no pl*; *(fig: d'un livre etc)* subject matter, material; *(SCOL)* subject; **en** ~ **de** as regards; ~**s grasses** fat content *sg*; ~**s premières** raw materials
matin [matɛ̃] *nm, adv* morning; **du** ~ **au soir** from morning till night; **de bon** ou **grand** ~ early in the morning; **matinal, e, aux** *adj (toilette, gymnastique)* morning *cpd*; *(de bonne heure)* early; **être matinal** *(personne)* to be up early; to be an early riser
matinée [matine] *nf* morning; *(spectacle)* matinée
matou [matu] *nm* tom(cat)
matraque [matʀak] *nf* club; *(de policier)* truncheon *(BRIT)*, billy *(US)*
matricule [matʀikyl] *nf (aussi: registre* ~*)* roll, register ♦ *nm (: numéro* ~*: MIL)* regimental number; *(: ADMIN)* reference number
matrimonial, e, aux [matʀimɔnjal, -o] *adj* marital, marriage *cpd*
maudire [modiʀ] *vt* to curse
maudit, e [modi, -it] *(fam) adj (satané)* blasted, confounded
maugréer [mogʀee] *vi* to grumble
maussade [mosad] *adj* sullen
mauvais, e [mɔvɛ, -ɛz] *adj* bad; *(faux)*: **le** ~ **numéro/moment** the wrong number/moment; *(méchant, malveillant)* malicious, spiteful; **il fait** ~ the weather is bad; **la mer est** ~**e** the sea is rough; ~ **plaisant** hoaxer; ~**e herbe** weed; ~**e langue** gossip, scandalmonger *(BRIT)*; ~**e passe** difficult situation; bad patch; ~**e tête** rebellious ou headstrong customer
maux [mo] *nmpl* de **mal**; ~ **de ventre** stomachache *sg*
maximum [maksimɔm] *adj, nm* maximum; **au** ~ *(le plus possible)* to the full; as much as one can; *(tout au plus)* at the (very) most ou maximum
mayonnaise [majɔnɛz] *nf* mayonnaise
mazout [mazut] *nm* (fuel) oil
Me *abr* = **Maître**
me(m') [m(ə)] *pron* me; *(réfléchi)* myself
mec [mɛk] *(fam) nm* bloke, guy
mécanicien, ne [mekanisjɛ̃, -jɛn] *nm/f* mechanic; *(RAIL)* (train ou engine) driver
mécanique [mekanik] *adj* mechanical ♦ *nf*

(science) mechanics sg; (technologie) mechanical engineering; (mécanisme) mechanism; engineering; works pl; **ennui** ~ engine trouble no pl

mécanisme [mekanism(ə)] nm mechanism

méchamment [meʃamɑ̃] adv nastily, maliciously, spitefully

méchanceté [meʃɑ̃ste] nf nastiness, maliciousness; nasty ou spiteful ou malicious remark (ou action)

méchant, e [meʃɑ̃, -ɑ̃t] adj nasty, malicious, spiteful; (enfant: pas sage) naughty; (animal) vicious; (avant le nom: valeur péjorative) nasty; miserable; (: intensive) terrific

mèche [mɛʃ] nf (de lampe, bougie) wick; (d'un explosif) fuse; (de vilebrequin, perceuse) bit; (de cheveux) lock; **de** ~ **avec** in league with

mécompte [mekɔ̃t] nm miscalculation; (déception) disappointment

méconnaissable [mekɔnɛsabl(ə)] adj unrecognizable

méconnaître [mekɔnɛtʀ(ə)] vt (ignorer) to be unaware of; (mésestimer) to misjudge

mécontent, e [mekɔ̃tɑ̃, -ɑ̃t] adj: ~ (de) discontented ou dissatisfied ou displeased (with); (contrarié) annoyed (at); **mécontentement** nm dissatisfaction, discontent, displeasure; annoyance

médaille [medaj] nf medal

médaillon [medajɔ̃] nm (portrait) medallion; (bijou) locket

médecin [medsɛ̃] nm doctor; ~ **légiste** forensic surgeon

médecine [medsin] nf medicine; ~ **légale** forensic medicine

média [medja] nmpl: **les** ~ the media

médiatique [medjatik] adj media cpd

médical, e, aux [medikal, -o] adj medical

médicament [medikamɑ̃] nm medicine, drug

médiéval, e, aux [medjeval, -o] adj medieval

médiocre [medjɔkʀ(ə)] adj mediocre, poor

médire [mediʀ] vi: ~ **de** to speak ill of; **médisance** nf scandalmongering (BRIT); piece of scandal ou of malicious gossip

méditer [medite] vt (approfondir) to meditate on, ponder (over); (combiner) to meditate ♦ vi to meditate

Méditerranée [mediteʀane] nf: **la (mer)** ~ the Mediterranean (Sea); **méditerranéen, ne** adj, nm/f Mediterranean

méduse [medyz] nf jellyfish

meeting [mitiŋ] nm (POL, SPORT) rally

méfait [mefɛ] nm (faute) misdemeanour, wrongdoing; ~**s** nmpl (ravages) ravages, damage sg

méfiance [mefjɑ̃s] nf mistrust, distrust; **méfiant, e** [mefjɑ̃, -ɑ̃t] adj mistrustful, distrustful

méfier [mefje] : **se** ~ vi to be wary; to be careful; **se** ~ **de** to mistrust, distrust, be wary of; (faire attention) to be careful about

mégarde [megaʀd(ə)] nf: **par** ~ accidentally; by mistake

mégère [meʒɛʀ] nf shrew

mégot [mego] nm cigarette end

meilleur, e [mejœʀ] adj, adv better; (valeur superlative) best ♦ nm: **le** ~ (celui qui ...) the best (one); (ce qui ...) the best; **le** ~ **des deux** the better of the two; **de** ~**e heure** earlier; ~ **marché** cheaper; **meilleure** nf: **la meilleure** the best (one)

mélancolie [melɑ̃kɔli] nf melancholy, gloom; **mélancolique** adj melancholic, melancholy

mélange [melɑ̃ʒ] nm mixture

mélanger [melɑ̃ʒe] vt (substances) to mix; (vins, couleurs) to blend; (mettre en désordre) to mix up, muddle (up)

mélasse [melas] nf treacle, molasses sg

mêlée [mele] nf mêlée, scramble; (RUGBY) scrum(mage)

mêler [mele] vt (substances, odeurs, races) to mix; (embrouiller) to muddle (up), mix up; **se** ~ vi to mix; to mingle; **se** ~ **à** (suj: personne) to join; to mix with; (suj: odeurs etc) to mingle with; **se** ~ **de** (: personne) to meddle with, interfere in; ~ **qn à** (affaire) to get sb mixed up ou involved in

mélodie [melɔdi] nf melody

melon [məlɔ̃] nm (BOT) (honeydew) melon; (aussi: chapeau ~) bowler (hat)

membre [mɑ̃bʀ(ə)] nm (ANAT) limb; (personne, pays, élément) member ♦ adj member cpd

mémé [meme] (fam) nf granny

MOT CLÉ

même [mɛm] adj **1** (avant le nom) same; **en** ~ **temps** at the same time

2 (après le nom: renforcement): **il est la loyauté** ~ he is loyalty itself; **ce sont ses paroles/celles-là** ~ they are his very words/the very ones

♦ pron: **le(la)** ~ the same one

♦ adv **1** (renforcement): **il n'a** ~ **pas pleuré** he didn't even cry; ~ **lui l'a dit** even HE said it; **ici** ~ at this very place

2: **à** ~: **à** ~ **la bouteille** straight from the bottle; **à** ~ **la peau** next to the skin; **être à** ~ **de faire** to be in a position to do, be able to do

3: **de** ~ to do likewise; **lui de** ~ so does (ou did ou is) he; **de** ~ **que** just as; **il en va de** ~ **pour** the same goes for

---

mémento [memɛ̃to] nm (agenda) appointments diary; (ouvrage) summary

mémoire [memwaʀ] nf memory ♦ nm (ADMIN, JUR) memorandum; (SCOL) dissertation, paper; ~**s** nmpl (souvenirs) memoirs;

à la ~ de to the *ou* in memory of; pour ~ for the record; de ~ from memory; ~ morte/vive (*INFORM*) ROM/RAM

menace [mənas] *nf* threat

menacer [mənase] *vt* to threaten

ménage [menaʒ] *nm* (*travail*) housekeeping, housework; (*couple*) (married) couple; (*famille*, *ADMIN*) household; **faire le ~ to** do the housework

ménagement [menaʒmã] *nm* care and attention; **~s** *nmpl* (*égards*) consideration *sg*, attention *sg*

ménager, ère [menaʒe, -ɛʀ] *adj* household *cpd*, domestic ♦ *vt* (*traiter*) to handle with tact; to treat considerately; (*utiliser*) to use sparingly; to use with care; (*prendre soin de*) to take (great) care of, look after; (*organiser*) to arrange; (*installer*) to put in; to make; **~ qch à qn** (*réserver*) to have sth in store for sb; **ménagère** *nf* housewife

mendiant, e [mãdjã, -ãt] *nm/f* beggar; **mendier** [mãdje] *vi* to beg ♦ *vt* to beg (for)

mener [məne] *vt* to lead; (*enquête*) to conduct; (*affaires*) to manage ♦ *vi*: **~ (à la marque)** to lead, be in the lead; **~ à/dans** (*emmener*) to take to/into; **~ qch à terme** *ou* **à bien** to see sth through (to a successful conclusion), complete sth successfully

meneur, euse [mənœʀ, -øz] *nm/f* leader; (*péj*) agitator; **~ de jeu** host, quizmaster

méningite [menɛ̃ʒit] *nf* meningitis *no pl*

ménopause [menopoz] *nf* menopause

menottes [mənɔt] *nfpl* handcuffs

mensonge [mãsɔ̃ʒ] *nm* lie; lying *no pl*; **mensonger, ère** *adj* false

mensualité [mãsɥalite] *nf* monthly payment; monthly salary

mensuel, le [mãsɥɛl] *adj* monthly

mensurations [mãsyʀasjɔ̃] *nfpl* measurements

mentalité [mãtalite] *nf* mentality

menteur, euse [mãtœʀ, -øz] *nm/f* liar

menthe [mãt] *nf* mint

mention [mãsjɔ̃] *nf* (*note*) note, comment; (*SCOL*): **~ bien** *etc* ≈ grade B *etc* (*ou* upper 2nd class *etc*) pass (*BRIT*), ≈ pass with (high) honors (*US*); **mentionner** *vt* to mention

mentir [mãtiʀ] *vi* to lie; to be lying

menton [mãtɔ̃] *nm* chin

menu, e [məny] *adj* slim, slight; tiny; (*frais*, *difficulté*) minor ♦ *adv* (*couper*, *hacher*) very fine ♦ *nm* menu; **par le ~** (*raconter*) in minute detail; **~e monnaie** small change

menuiserie [mənɥizʀi] *nf* (*travail*) joinery, carpentry; woodwork; (*local*) joiner's workshop; (*ouvrage*) woodwork *no pl*; **menuisier** [mənɥizje] *nm* joiner, carpenter

méprendre [mepʀãdʀ(ə)] : **se ~** *vi* to be mistaken (about)

mépris [mepʀi] *nm* (*dédain*) contempt, scorn; (*indifférence*): **le ~ de** contempt *ou*

disregard for; **au ~ de** regardless of, in defiance of

méprisable [mepʀizabl(ə)] *adj* contemptible, despicable

méprise [mepʀiz] *nf* mistake, error; misunderstanding

mépriser [mepʀize] *vt* to scorn, despise; (*gloire*, *danger*) to scorn, spurn

mer [mɛʀ] *nf* sea; (*marée*) tide; **en ~** at sea; **prendre la ~** to put out to sea; **en haute** *ou* **pleine ~** off shore, on the open sea; **la ~ du Nord/Rouge** the North/Red Sea

mercantile [mɛʀkãtil] (*péj*) *adj* mercenary

mercenaire [mɛʀsənɛʀ] *nm* mercenary, hired soldier

mercerie [mɛʀsəʀi] *nf* haberdashery (*BRIT*), notions (*US*); haberdasher's shop (*BRIT*), notions store (*US*)

merci [mɛʀsi] *excl* thank you ♦ *nf*: **à la ~ de qn/qch** at sb's mercy/the mercy of sth; **~ de** thank you for; **sans ~** merciless(ly)

mercredi [mɛʀkʀədi] *nm* Wednesday

mercure [mɛʀkyʀ] *nm* mercury

merde [mɛʀd(ə)] (*fam!*) *nf* shit (*!*) ♦ *excl* (bloody) hell (*!*)

mère [mɛʀ] *nf* mother; **~ célibataire** unmarried mother

méridional, e, aux [meʀidjɔnal, -o] *adj* southern ♦ *nm/f* Southerner

meringue [məʀɛ̃g] *nf* meringue

mérite [meʀit] *nm* merit; **le ~ (de ceci) lui revient** the credit (for this) is his

mériter [meʀite] *vt* to deserve

merlan [mɛʀlã] *nm* whiting

merle [mɛʀl(ə)] *nm* blackbird

merveille [mɛʀvɛj] *nf* marvel, wonder; **faire ~** to work wonders; **à ~** perfectly, wonderfully

merveilleux, euse [mɛʀvɛjø, -øz] *adj* marvellous, wonderful

mes [me] *dét voir* **mon**

mésange [mezãʒ] *nf* tit(mouse)

mésaventure [mezavãtyʀ] *nf* misadventure, misfortune

Mesdames [medam] *nfpl de* **Madame**

Mesdemoiselles [medmwazɛl] *nfpl de* **Mademoiselle**

mésentente [mezãtãt] *nf* dissension, disagreement

mesquin, e [mɛskɛ̃, -in] *adj* mean, petty

message [mesaʒ] *nm* message; **messager, ère** *nm/f* messenger

messe [mɛs] *nf* mass; **aller à la ~** to go to mass; **~ de minuit** midnight mass

Messieurs [mesjø] *nmpl de* **Monsieur**

mesure [məzyʀ] *nf* (*évaluation*, *dimension*) measurement; (*étalon*, *récipient*, *contenu*) measure; (*MUS*: *cadence*) time, tempo; (: *division*) bar; (*retenue*) moderation; (*disposition*) measure, step; **sur ~** (*costume*) made-to-measure; **à la ~ de** (*fig*) worthy of; on the same scale as; **dans la ~ où** insofar as, inasmuch as; **à ~ que** as; **être en ~ de** to be in a position to

mesurer [məzyre] vt to measure; (*juger*) to weigh up, assess; (*limiter*) to limit, ration; (*modérer*) to moderate; **se ~ avec** to have a confrontation with; to tackle; **il mesure 1 m 80** he's 1 m 80 tall

met vb voir **mettre**

métal, aux [metal, -o] nm metal; **métallique** adj metallic

météo [meteo] nf weather report; ≈ Met Office (*BRIT*), ≈ National Weather Service (*US*)

météorologie [meteɔrɔlɔʒi] nf meteorology

méthode [metɔd] nf method; (*livre, ouvrage*) manual, tutor

métier [metje] nm (*profession: gén*) job; (: *manuel*) trade; (*artisanal*) craft; (*technique, expérience*) (acquired) skill ou technique; (*aussi: ~ à tisser*) (weaving) loom

métis, se [metis] adj, nm/f half-caste, half-breed

métisser [metise] vt to cross

métrage [metraʒ] nm (*de tissu*) length, ≈ yardage; (*CINÉMA*) footage, length; **long/moyen/court ~** full-length/medium-length/short film

mètre [mɛtr(ə)] nm metre; (*règle*) (metre) rule; (*ruban*) tape measure; **métrique** adj metric

métro [metro] nm underground (*BRIT*), subway

métropole [metrɔpɔl] nf (*capitale*) metropolis; (*pays*) home country

mets [mɛ] nm dish

metteur [metœr] nm: **~ en scène** (*THÉÂTRE*) producer; (*CINÉMA*) director; **~ en ondes** producer

─────────────── MOT CLÉ ───────────────

mettre [mɛtr(ə)] vt **1** (*placer*) to put; **~ en bouteille/en sac** to bottle/put in bags ou sacks

2 (*vêtements: revêtir*) to put on; (: *porter*) to wear; **mets ton gilet** put your cardigan on; **je ne mets plus mon manteau** I no longer wear my coat

3 (*faire fonctionner: chauffage, électricité*) to put on; (: *reveil, minuteur*) to set; (*installer: gaz, eau*) to put in, to lay on; **~ en marche** to start up

4 (*consacrer*): **~ du temps à faire qch** to take time to do sth ou over sth

5 (*noter, écrire*) to say, put (down); **qu'est-ce qu'il a mis sur la carte?** what did he say ou write on the card?; **mettez au pluriel ...** put ... into the plural

6 (*supposer*): **mettons que ...** let's suppose ou say that ...

7. **y ~ du sien** to pull one's weight

se ~ vi **1** (*se placer*): **vous pouvez vous ~**

là you can sit (ou stand) there; **où ça se met?** where does it go?; **se ~ au lit** to get into bed; **se ~ au piano** to sit down at the piano; **se ~ de l'encre sur les doigts** to get ink on one's fingers

2 (*s'habiller*): **se ~ en maillot de bain** to get into ou put on a swimsuit; **n'avoir rien à se ~** to have nothing to wear

3: **se ~ à** to begin, start; **se ~ à faire** to begin ou start doing ou to do; **se ~ au piano** to start learning the piano; **se ~ au travail/à l'étude** to get down to work/one's studies

─────────────────────────

meuble [mœbl(ə)] nm piece of furniture; furniture *no pl* ♦ adj (*terre*) loose, friable; **meublé** nm furnished flatlet (*BRIT*) ou room; **meubler** vt to furnish; (*fig*): **meubler qch (de)** to fill sth (with)

meugler [møgle] vi to low, moo

meule [møl] nf (*à broyer*) millstone; (*à aiguiser*) grindstone; (*de foin, blé*) stack; (*de fromage*) round

meunier [n‿mønje] nm miller; **meunière** nf miller's wife

meure etc vb voir **mourir**

meurtre [mœrtr(ə)] nm murder; **meurtrier, ière** adj (*arme etc*) deadly; (*fureur, instincts*) murderous ♦ nm/f murderer (eress); **meurtrière** nf (*ouverture*) loophole

meurtrir [mœrtrir] vt to bruise; (*fig*) to wound; **meurtrissure** nf bruise; (*fig*) scar

meus etc vb voir **mouvoir**

meute [møt] nf pack

Mexico [mɛksiko] n Mexico City

Mexique [mɛksik] nm: **le ~** Mexico

Mgr abr = **Monseigneur**

mi [mi] nm (*MUS*) E; (*en chantant la gamme*) mi ♦ préfixe: **~...** half(-); mid-; **à la ~-janvier** in mid-January; **à ~-jambes/-corps** (up ou down) to the knees/waist; **à ~-hauteur/-pente** halfway up ou down/up ou down the hill

miauler [mijole] vi to mew

miche [miʃ] nf round ou cob loaf

mi-chemin [miʃmɛ̃]: **à ~** adv halfway, midway

mi-clos, e [miklo, -kloz] adj half-closed

micro [mikro] nm mike, microphone; (*INFORM*) micro

microbe [mikrɔb] nm germ, microbe

micro: **~-onde** nf: **four à ~s** microwave oven; **~-ordinateur** nm microcomputer; **~scope** nm microscope

midi [midi] nm midday, noon; (*moment du déjeuner*) lunchtime; (*sud*) south; **à ~** at 12 (o'clock) ou midday ou noon; **en plein ~** (right) in the middle of the day; facing south; **le M~** the South (of France), the Midi

mie [mi] nf crumb (of the loaf)

miel [mjɛl] nm honey

mien, ne [mjɛ̃, mjɛn] *pron*: **le(la) ~(ne), les ~(ne)s** mine; **les ~s** my family

miette [mjɛt] *nf* (*de pain, gâteau*) crumb; (*fig: de la conversation etc*) scrap; **en ~s** in pieces *ou* bits

─────────── MOT CLÉ ───────────

mieux [mjø] *adv* **1** (*d'une meilleure façon*): **~ (que)** better (than); **elle travaille/mange ~** she works/eats better; **elle va ~** she is better

2 (*de la meilleure façon*) best; **ce que je sais le ~** what I know best; **les livres les ~ faits** the best made books

3: **de ~ en ~** better and better

♦ *adj* **1** (*plus à l'aise, en meilleure forme*) better; **se sentir ~** to feel better

2 (*plus satisfaisant*) better; **c'est ~ ainsi** it's better like this; **c'est le ~ des deux** it's the better of the two; **le(la) ~, les ~** the best; **demandez-lui, c'est le ~** ask him, it's the best thing

3 (*plus joli*) better-looking

4: **au ~** at best; **au ~ avec** on the best of terms with; **pour le ~** for the best

♦ *nm* **1** (*progrès*) improvement

2: **de mon/ton ~** as best I/you can (*ou* could); **faire de son ~** to do one's best

─────────────────────────────

mièvre [mjɛvʀ(ə)] *adj* mawkish (*BRIT*), sickly sentimental

mignon, ne [miɲɔ̃, -ɔn] *adj* sweet, cute

migraine [migʀɛn] *nf* headache; migraine

mijoter [miʒɔte] *vt* to simmer; (*préparer avec soin*) to cook lovingly; (*affaire, projet*) to plot, cook up ♦ *vi* to simmer

mil [mil] *num* = **mille**

milieu, x [miljø] *nm* (*centre*) middle; (*fig*) middle course *ou* way; happy medium; (*BIO, GÉO*) environment; (*entourage social*) milieu; background; circle; (*pègre*): **le ~** the underworld; **au ~ de** in the middle of; **au beau** *ou* **en plein ~ (de)** right in the middle (of)

militaire [militɛʀ] *adj* military, army *cpd* ♦ *nm* serviceman

militant, e [militɑ̃, -ɑ̃t] *adj, nm/f* militant

militer [milite] *vi* to be a militant; **~ pour/contre** (*suj: faits, raisons etc*) to militate in favour of/against

mille [mil] *num* a *ou* one thousand ♦ *nm* (*mesure*): **~ (marin)** nautical mile; **mettre dans le ~** to hit the bull's-eye; to be bang on target; **millefeuille** *nm* cream *ou* vanilla slice; **millénaire** *nm* millennium ♦ *adj* thousand-year-old; (*fig*) ancient; **mille-pattes** *nm inv* centipede

millésime [milezim] *nm* year; **millésimé, e** *adj* vintage *cpd*

millet [mijɛ] *nm* millet

milliard [miljaʀ] *nm* milliard, thousand million (*BRIT*), billion (*US*); **milliardaire** *nm/f*

multimillionaire (*BRIT*), billionaire (*US*)

millier [milje] *nm* thousand; **un ~ (de)** a thousand or so, about a thousand; **par ~s** in (their) thousands, by the thousand

milligramme [miligram] *nm* milligramme

millimètre [milimɛtʀ(ə)] *nm* millimetre

million [miljɔ̃] *nm* million; **deux ~s de** two million; **millionnaire** *nm/f* millionaire

mime [mim] *nm/f* (*acteur*) mime(r) ♦ *nm* (*art*) mime, miming

mimer [mime] *vt* to mime; (*singer*) to mimic, take off

mimique [mimik] *nf* (*funny*) face; (*signes*) gesticulations *pl*, sign language *no pl*

minable [minabl(ə)] *adj* shabby(-looking); pathetic

mince [mɛ̃s] *adj* thin; (*personne, taille*) slim, slender; (*fig: profit, connaissances*) slight, small, weak ♦ *excl*: **~ alors!** drat it!, darn it! (*US*); **minceur** *nf* thinness; slimness, slenderness

mine [min] *nf* (*physionomie*) expression, look; (*extérieur*) exterior, appearance; (*de crayon*) lead; (*gisement, exploitation, explosif, fig*) mine; **avoir bonne ~** (*personne*) to look well; (*ironique*) to look an utter idiot; **avoir mauvaise ~** to look unwell *ou* poorly; **faire ~ de faire** to make a pretence of doing; to make as if to do; **~ de rien** with a casual air; although you wouldn't think so

miner [mine] *vt* (*saper*) to undermine, erode; (*MIL*) to mine

minerai [minʀɛ] *nm* ore

minéral, e, aux [mineʀal, -o] *adj, nm* mineral

minéralogique [mineʀalɔʒik] *adj*: **numéro ~** registration number

minet, te [minɛ, -ɛt] *nm/f* (*chat*) pussy-cat; (*péj*) young trendy

mineur, e [minœʀ] *adj* minor ♦ *nm/f* (*JUR*) minor, person under age ♦ *nm* (*travailleur*) miner

miniature [minjatyʀ] *adj, nf* miniature

minibus [minibys] *nm* minibus

mini-cassette [minikasɛt] *nf* cassette (recorder)

minier, ière [minje, -jɛʀ] *adj* mining

mini-jupe [miniʒyp] *nf* mini-skirt

minime [minim] *adj* minor, minimal

minimiser [minimize] *vt* to minimize; (*fig*) to play down

minimum [minimɔm] *adj, nm* minimum; **au ~ (au moins)** at the very least

ministère [ministɛʀ] *nm* (*aussi REL*) ministry; (*cabinet*) government; **~ public** (*JUR*) Prosecution, public prosecutor

ministre [ministʀ(ə)] *nm* (*aussi REL*) minister; **~ d'État** senior minister

Minitel [minitɛl] ® *nm* videotext terminal and service

minorité [minɔʀite] *nf* minority; **être en ~**

to be in the *ou* a minority; **mettre en** ~ (*POL*) to defeat

minoterie [minɔtʀi] *nf* flour-mill

minuit [minɥi] *nm* midnight

minuscule [minyskyl] *adj* minute, tiny ♦ *nf*: (*lettre*) ~ small letter

minute [minyt] *nf* minute; (*JUR: original*) minute, draft; **à la** ~ (just) this instant; there and then; **minuter** *vt* to time; **minuterie** *nf* time switch

minutieux, euse [minysjø, -øz] *adj* meticulous; minutely detailed

mirabelle [miʀabɛl] *nf* (cherry) plum

miracle [miʀakl(ə)] *nm* miracle

mirage [miʀaʒ] *nm* mirage

mire [miʀ] *nf*: **point de** ~ target; (*fig*) focal point; **ligne de** ~ line of sight

miroir [miʀwaʀ] *nm* mirror

miroiter [miʀwate] *vi* to sparkle, shimmer; **faire** ~ **qch à qn** to paint sth in glowing colours for sb, dangle sth in front of sb's eyes

mis, e [mi, miz] *pp de* **mettre** ♦ *adj*: **bien** ~ well-dressed

mise [miz] *nf* (*argent. au jeu*) stake; (*tenue*) clothing; attire; **être de** ~ to be acceptable *ou* in season; ~ **à feu** blast-off; ~ **au point** (*fig*) clarification; ~ **de fonds** capital outlay; ~ **en plis** set; ~ **en scène** production

miser [mize] *vt* (*enjeu*) to stake, bet; ~ **sur** (*cheval, numéro*) to bet on; (*fig*) to bank *ou* count on

misérable [mizeʀabl(ə)] *adj* (*lamentable, malheureux*) pitiful, wretched; (*pauvre*) poverty-stricken; (*insignifiant, mesquin*) miserable ♦ *nm/f* wretch; (*miséreux*) poor wretch

misère [mizɛʀ] *nf* (extreme) poverty, destitution; ~**s** *nfpl* (*malheurs*) woes, miseries; (*ennuis*) little troubles; **salaire de** ~ starvation wage

miséricorde [mizeʀikɔʀd(ə)] *nf* mercy, forgiveness

missile [misil] *nm* missile

mission [misjɔ̃] *nf* mission; **partir en** ~ (*ADMIN, POL*) to go on an assignment; **missionnaire** *nm/f* missionary

mit *vb voir* **mettre**

mité, e [mite] *adj* moth-eaten

mi-temps [mitɑ̃] *nf inv* (*SPORT: période*) half; (: *pause*) half-time; **à** ~ part-time

mitigé, e [mitiʒe] *adj* lukewarm; mixed

mitonner [mitɔne] *vt* to cook with loving care; (*fig*) to cook up quietly

mitoyen, ne [mitwajɛ̃, -ɛn] *adj* common, party *cpd*

mitrailler [mitʀaje] *vt* to machine-gun; (*fig*) to pelt, bombard; (: *photographier*) to take shot after shot of; **mitraillette** *nf* submachine gun; **mitrailleuse** *nf* machine gun

mi-voix [mivwa]: **à** ~ *adv* in a low *ou* hushed voice

mixage [miksaʒ] *nm* (*CINÉMA*) (sound) mixing

mixer [miksœʀ] *nm* (food) mixer

mixte [mikst(ə)] *adj* (*gén*) mixed; (*SCOL*) mixed, coeducational; **à usage** ~ dual-purpose

mixture [mikstyʀ] *nf* mixture; (*fig*) concoction

MLF *sigle m* = Mouvement de Libération de la femme

Mlle (*pl* **Mlles**) *abr* = **Mademoiselle**

MM *abr* = **Messieurs**

Mme (*pl* **Mmes**) *abr* = **Madame**

Mo *abr* = **métro**

mobile [mɔbil] *adj* mobile; (*pièce de machine*) moving; (*élément de meuble etc*) movable ♦ *nm* (*motif*) motive; (*œuvre d'art*) mobile

mobilier, ière [mɔbilje, -jɛʀ] *adj* (*JUR*) personal ♦ *nm* furniture

mobiliser [mɔbilize] *vt* (*MIL, gén*) to mobilize

moche [mɔʃ] (*fam*) *adj* ugly; rotten

modalité [mɔdalite] *nf* form, mode; ~**s** *nfpl* (*d'un accord etc*) clauses, terms

mode [mɔd] *nf* fashion ♦ *nm* (*manière*) form, mode; **à la** ~ fashionable, in fashion; ~ **d'emploi** directions *pl* (for use)

modèle [mɔdɛl] *adj, nm* model; (*qui pose: de peintre*) sitter; ~ **déposé** registered design; ~ **réduit** small-scale model; **modeler** [mɔdle] *vt* (*ART*) to model, mould; (*suj: vêtement, érosion*) to mould, shape

modem [mɔdɛm] *nm* modem

modéré, e [mɔdeʀe] *adj, nm/f* moderate

modérer [mɔdeʀe] *vt* to moderate; **se** ~ *vi* to restrain o.s.

moderne [mɔdɛʀn(ə)] *adj* modern ♦ *nm* modern style; modern furniture; **moderniser** *vt* to modernize

modeste [mɔdɛst(ə)] *adj* modest; **modestie** *nf* modesty

modifier [mɔdifje] *vt* to modify, alter; **se** ~ *vi* to alter

modique [mɔdik] *adj* modest

modiste [mɔdist(ə)] *nf* milliner

modulation [mɔdylasjɔ̃] *nf*: ~ **de fréquence** frequency modulation

module [mɔdyl] *nm* module

moelle [mwal] *nf* marrow

moelleux, euse [mwalø, -øz] *adj* soft; (*au goût, à l'ouïe*) mellow

moellon [mwalɔ̃] *nm* rubble stone

mœurs [mœʀ] *nfpl* (*conduite*) morals; (*manières*) manners; (*pratiques sociales, mode de vie*) habits

mohair [mɔɛʀ] *nm* mohair

moi [mwa] *pron* me; (*emphatique*): ~, **je** ... for my part, I ...; I myself ...

moignon [mwaɲɔ̃] *nm* stump

moi-même [mwamɛm] *pron* myself; (*emphatique*) I myself

moindre [mwɛ̃dʀ(ə)] *adj* lesser; lower; **le(la) ~, les ~s** the least, the slightest
moine [mwan] *nm* monk, friar
moineau, x [mwano] *nm* sparrow

MOT CLÉ
---

moins [mwɛ̃] *adv* **1** (*comparatif*): **~ (que)** less (than); **~ grand que** less tall than, not as tall as; **~ je travaille, mieux je me porte** the less I work, the better I feel
2 (*superlatif*): **le ~** (the) least; **c'est ce que j'aime le ~** it's what I like (the) least; **le(la) ~ doué(e)** the least gifted; **au ~, du ~** at least; **pour le ~** at the very least
3: **~ de** (*quantité*) less (than); (*nombre*) fewer (than); **~ de sable/d'eau** less sand/water; **~ de livres/gens** fewer books/people; **~ de 2 ans** less than 2 years; **~ de midi** not yet midday
4: **de ~, en ~**: **100F/3 jours de ~** 100F/3 days less; **3 livres en ~** 3 books fewer; 3 books too few; **de l'argent en ~** less money; **le soleil en ~** but for the sun, minus the sun; **de ~ en ~** less and less
5: **à ~ de, à ~ que** unless; **à ~ de faire** unless we do (*ou* he does *etc*); **à ~ que tu ne fasses** unless you do; **à ~ d'un accident** barring any accident
♦ *prép*: **4 ~ 2** 4 minus 2; **il est ~ 5** it's 5 to; **il fait ~ 5** it's 5 (degrees) below (freezing), it's minus 5

---

mois [mwa] *nm* month; **~ double** (*COMM*) extra month's salary
moisi [mwazi] *nm* mould, mildew; **odeur de ~** musty smell
moisir [mwaziʀ] *vi* to go mouldy; (*fig*) to rot; to hang about
moisissure [mwazisyʀ] *nf* mould *nopl*
moisson [mwasɔ̃] *nf* harvest; **moissonner** *vt* to harvest, reap; **moissonneuse** *nf* (*machine*) harvester
moite [mwat] *adj* sweaty, sticky
moitié [mwatje] *nf* half; **la ~** half; **la ~ de** half (of); **la ~ du temps/des gens** half the time/the people; **à la ~** halfway through; **à ~** (*avant le verbe*) half; (*avant l'adjectif*) half-; **de ~** by half; **~ ~** half-and-half
mol [mɔl] *adj voir* **mou**
molaire [mɔlɛʀ] *nf* molar
molester [mɔlɛste] *vt* to manhandle, maul (about)
molle [mɔl] *adj voir* **mou**; **mollement** *adv* softly; (*péj*) sluggishly; (*protester*) feebly
mollet [mɔlɛ] *nm* calf ♦ *adj m*: **œuf ~** soft-boiled egg
molletonné, e [mɔltɔne] *adj* fleece-lined
mollir [mɔliʀ] *vi* to give way; to relent; to go soft
môme [mom] (*fam*) *nm/f* (*enfant*) brat ♦ *nf* (*fille*) chick

moment [mɔmɑ̃] *nm* moment; **ce n'est pas le ~** this is not the (right) time; **à un certain ~** at some point; **à un ~ donné** at a certain point; **pour un bon ~** for a good while; **pour le ~** for the moment, for the time being; **au ~ de** at the time of; **au ~ où** as; at a time when; **à tout ~** at any time *ou* moment; constantly, continually; **en ce ~** at the moment; at present; **sur le ~** at the time; **par ~s** now and then, at times; **du ~ où** *ou* **que** seeing that, since; **momentané, e** *adj* temporary, momentary
momie [mɔmi] *nf* mummy
mon, ma [mɔ̃, ma] (*pl* **mes**) *dét* my
Monaco [mɔnako] *nm*: **le ~** Monaco
monarchie [mɔnaʀʃi] *nf* monarchy
monastère [mɔnastɛʀ] *nm* monastery
monceau, x [mɔ̃so] *nm* heap
mondain, e [mɔ̃dɛ̃, -ɛn] *adj* society *cpd*; social; fashionable; **~e** *nf*: **la M~e, la police ~e** ≈ the vice squad
monde [mɔ̃d] *nm* world; (*haute société*): **le ~** (high) society; (*milieu*): **être du même ~** to move in the same circles; (*gens*): **il y a du ~** (*beaucoup de gens*) there are a lot of people; (*quelques personnes*) there are some people; **beaucoup/peu de ~** many/few people; **le meilleur** *etc* **du ~** the best *etc* in the world *ou* on earth; **mettre au ~** to bring into the world; **pas le moins du ~** not in the least; **se faire un ~ de qch** to make a great deal of fuss about sth; **mondial, e, aux** *adj* (*population*) world *cpd*; (*influence*) world-wide; **mondialement** *adv* throughout the world
monégasque [mɔnegask(ə)] *adj* Monegasque, of *ou* from Monaco
monétaire [mɔnetɛʀ] *adj* monetary
moniteur, trice [mɔnitœʀ, -tʀis] *nm/f* (*SPORT*) instructor(tress); (*de colonie de vacances*) supervisor ♦ *nm* (*écran*) monitor
monnaie [mɔnɛ] *nf* (*pièce*) coin; (*ÉCON, gén: moyen d'échange*) currency; (*petites pièces*): **avoir de la ~** to have (some) change; **faire de la ~** to get (some) change; **avoir/faire la ~ de 20 F** to have change of/get change for 20 F; **rendre à qn la ~ (sur 20 F)** to give sb the change (out of *ou* from 20 F); **monnayer** *vt* to convert into cash; (*talent*) to capitalize on
monologue [mɔnɔlɔg] *nm* monologue, soliloquy; **monologuer** *vi* to soliloquize
monopole [mɔnɔpɔl] *nm* monopoly
monotone [mɔnɔtɔn] *adj* monotonous
monseigneur [mɔ̃sɛɲœʀ] *nm* (*archevêque, évêque*) Your (*ou* His) Grace; (*cardinal*) Your (*ou* His) Eminence
Monsieur [məsjø] (*pl* **Messieurs**) *titre* Mr ♦ *nm* (*homme quelconque*): **un/le m~** a/the gentleman; *voir aussi* **Madame**
monstre [mɔ̃stʀ(ə)] *nm* monster ♦ *adj*: **un travail ~** a fantastic amount of work; an

enormous job

mont [mɔ̃] nm: par ~s et par vaux up hill and down dale; **le M~ Blanc** Mont Blanc

montage [mɔ̃taʒ] nm putting up; mounting, setting; assembly; (PHOTO) photomontage; (CINÉMA) editing

montagnard, e [mɔ̃taɲaʀ, -aʀd(ə)] adj mountain cpd ♦ nm/f mountain-dweller

montagne [mɔ̃taɲ] nf (cime) mountain; (région): **la ~** the mountains pl; **~s russes** big dipper sg, switchback sg; **montagneux, euse** [mɔ̃taɲø, -øz] adj mountainous; hilly

montant, e [mɔ̃tɑ̃, -ɑ̃t] adj rising; (robe, corsage) high-necked ♦ nm (somme, total) (sum) total, (total) amount; (de fenêtre) upright; (de lit) post

monte-charge [mɔ̃tʃaʀʒ(ə)] nm inv goods lift, hoist

montée [mɔ̃te] nf rising, rise; ascent, climb; (chemin) way up; (côte) hill; **au milieu de la ~** halfway up

monter [mɔ̃te] vt (escalier, côte) to go (ou come) up; (valise, paquet) to take (ou bring) up; (cheval) to mount; (étagère) to raise; (tente, échafaudage) to put up; (machine) to assemble; (bijou) to mount, set; (COUTURE) to sew on; to sew on; (CINÉMA) to edit; (THÉÂTRE) to put on; stage; (société etc) to set up ♦ vi to go (ou come) up; (avion etc) to climb, go up; (chemin, niveau, température) to go up, rise; (passager) to get on; (à cheval): **~ bien/mal** to ride well/badly; **se ~ à** (frais etc) to add up to, come to; **~ à pied** to walk up, go up on foot; **~ à bicyclette/en voiture** to cycle/drive up, go up by bicycle/by car; **~ dans le train/l'avion** to get into the train/plane, board the train/plane; **~ sur** to climb up onto; **~ à cheval** to get on ou mount a horse

monticule [mɔ̃tikyl] nm mound

montre [mɔ̃tʀ(ə)] nf watch; **faire ~ de** to show, display; **contre la ~** (SPORT) against the clock; **montre-bracelet** nf wristwatch

montrer [mɔ̃tʀe] vt to show; **~ qch à qn** to show sb sth

monture [mɔ̃tyʀ] nf (bête) mount; (d'une bague) setting; (de lunettes) frame

monument [mɔnymɑ̃] nm monument; **~ aux morts** war memorial

moquer [mɔke]: **se ~ de** vt to make fun of, laugh at; (fam: se désintéresser de) not to care about; (tromper): **se ~ de qn** to take sb for a ride

moquette [mɔkɛt] nf fitted carpet

moqueur, euse [mɔkœʀ, -øz] adj mocking

moral, e, aux [mɔʀal, -o] adj moral ♦ nm morale; **avoir le ~ à zéro** to be really down; **morale** nf (conduite) morals pl; (règles) moral code, ethic; (valeurs) moral standards pl, morality; (science) ethics sg,

moral philosophy; (conclusion: d'une fable etc) moral; **faire la morale à** to lecture, preach at; **moralité** nf morality; (conduite) morals pl; (conclusion, enseignement) moral

morceau, x [mɔʀso] nm piece, bit; (d'une œuvre) passage, extract; (MUS) piece; (CULIN: de viande) cut; **mettre en ~x** to pull to pieces ou bits

morceler [mɔʀsəle] vt to break up, divide up

mordant, e [mɔʀdɑ̃, -ɑ̃t] adj scathing, cutting; biting

mordiller [mɔʀdije] vt to nibble at, chew at

mordre [mɔʀdʀ(ə)] vt to bite; (suj: lime, vis) to bite into ♦ vi (poisson) to bite; **~ sur** (fig) to go over into, overlap into; **~ à l'hameçon** to bite, rise to the bait

mordu, e [mɔʀdy] nm/f: **un ~ du jazz** a jazz fanatic

morfondre [mɔʀfɔ̃dʀ(ə)]: **se ~** vi to mope

morgue [mɔʀg(ə)] nf (arrogance) haughtiness; (lieu: de la police) morgue; (: à l'hôpital) mortuary

morne [mɔʀn(ə)] adj dismal, dreary

mors [mɔʀ] nm bit

morse [mɔʀs(ə)] nm (ZOOL) walrus; (TÉL) Morse (code)

morsure [mɔʀsyʀ] nf bite

mort¹ [mɔʀ] nf death

mort², e [mɔʀ, mɔʀt(ə)] pp de **mourir** ♦ adj dead ♦ nm/f (défunt) dead man(woman); (victime): **il y a eu plusieurs ~s** several people were killed, there were several killed ♦ nm (CARTES) dummy; **~ ou vif** dead or alive; **~ de peur/fatigue** frightened to death/dead tired

mortalité [mɔʀtalite] nf mortality, death rate

mortel, le [mɔʀtɛl] adj (poison etc) deadly, lethal; (accident, blessure) fatal; (REL) mortal; (fig) deathly; deadly boring

mortier [mɔʀtje] nm (gén) mortar

mort-né, e [mɔʀne] adj (enfant) stillborn

mortuaire [mɔʀtɥɛʀ] adj funeral cpd

morue [mɔʀy] nf (ZOOL) cod inv

mosaïque [mɔzaik] nf (ART) mosaic; (fig) patchwork

Moscou [mɔsku] n Moscow

mosquée [mɔske] nf mosque

mot [mo] nm word; (message) line, note; (bon mot etc) saying; sally; **~ à ~** word for word; **~ d'ordre** watchword; **~ de passe** password; **~s croisés** crossword (puzzle) sg

motard [mɔtaʀ] nm biker; (policier) motorcycle cop

motel [mɔtɛl] nm motel

moteur, trice [mɔtœʀ, -tʀis] adj (ANAT, PHYSIOL) motor; (TECH) driving; (AUTO): **à 4 roues motrices** 4-wheel drive ♦ nm engine, motor; **à ~** power-driven, motor cpd

motif [mɔtif] nm (cause) motive; (décoratif)

design, pattern, motif; (*d'un tableau*) subject, motif; **~s** *nmpl* (*JUR*) grounds *pl*; **sans ~** groundless

motiver [mɔtive] *vt* (*justifier*) to justify, account for; (*ADMIN, JUR, PSYCH*) to motivate

moto [mɔto] *nf* (motor)bike; **motocycliste** *nm/f* motorcyclist

motorisé, e [mɔtɔrize] *adj* (*troupe*) motorized; (*personne*) having transport *ou* a car

motrice [mɔtris] *adj voir* **moteur**

motte [mɔt] *nf*: **~ de terre** lump of earth, clod (of earth); **~ de beurre** lump of butter; **~ de gazon** turf, sod

mou(mol), molle [mu, mɔl] *adj* soft; (*péj*) flabby; sluggish ♦ *nm* (*abats*) lights *pl*, lungs *pl*; (*de la corde*): **avoir du ~** to be slack

mouche [muʃ] *nf* fly

moucher [muʃe] *vt* (*enfant*) to blow the nose of; (*chandelle*) to snuff (out); **se ~** *vi* to blow one's nose

moucheron [muʃrɔ̃] *nm* midge

moucheté, e [muʃte] *adj* dappled; flecked

mouchoir [muʃwar] *nm* handkerchief, hanky; **~ en papier** tissue, paper hanky

moudre [mudr(ə)] *vt* to grind

moue [mu] *nf* pout; **faire la ~** to pout; (*fig*) to pull a face

mouette [mwɛt] *nf* (sea)gull

moufle [mufl(ə)] *nf* (*gant*) mitt(en)

mouillé, e [muje] *adj* wet

mouiller [muje] *vt* (*humecter*) to wet, moisten; (*tremper*): **~ qn/qch** to make sb/sth wet; (*couper, diluer*) to water down; (*mine etc*) to lay (*NAVIG*) to lie *ou* be at anchor; **se ~** to get wet; (*fam*) to commit o.s. involved

moule [mul] *nf* mussel ♦ *nm* (*creux, CULIN*) mould; (*modèle plein*) cast; **~ à gâteaux** *nm* cake tin (*BRIT*) ou pan (*US*)

moulent *vb voir* **moudre**; **mouler**

mouler [mule] *vt* (*suj: vêtement*) to hug, fit closely round; **~ qch sur** (*fig*) to model sth on

moulin [mulɛ̃] *nm* mill; **~ à café/à poivre** coffee/pepper mill; **~ à légumes** (vegetable) shredder; **~ à paroles** (*fig*) chatterbox; **~ à vent** windmill

moulinet [mulinɛ] *nm* (*de treuil*) winch; (*de canne à pêche*) reel; (*mouvement*): **faire des ~s avec qch** to whirl sth around

moulinette [mulinɛt] *nf* (vegetable) shredder

moulu, e [muly] *pp de* **moudre**

moulure [mulyr] *nf* (*ornement*) moulding

mourant, e [murɑ̃, -ɑ̃t] *adj* dying

mourir [murir] *vi* to die; (*civilisation*) to die out; **~ de froid/faim** to die of exposure/hunger; **~ de faim/d'ennui** (*fig*) to be starving/be bored to death; **~ d'envie de faire** to be dying to do

mousse [mus] *nf* (*BOT*) moss; (*écume: sur eau, bière*) froth, foam; (: *shampooing*) lather; (*CULIN*) mousse ♦ *nm* (*NAVIG*) ship's boy; **bas ~** stretch stockings; **~ à raser** shaving foam; **~ carbonique** (firefighting) foam

mousseline [muslin] *nf* muslin; chiffon

mousser [muse] *vi* to foam; to lather

mousseux, euse [musø, -øz] *adj* frothy ♦ *nm*: (*vin*) **~** sparkling wine

mousson [musɔ̃] *nf* monsoon

moustache [mustaʃ] *nf* moustache; **~s** *nfpl* (*du chat*) whiskers *pl*

moustiquaire [mustikɛr] *nf* mosquito net (*ou* screen)

moustique [mustik] *nm* mosquito

moutarde [mutard(ə)] *nf* mustard

mouton [mutɔ̃] *nm* (*ZOOL, péj*) sheep *inv*; (*peau*) sheepskin; (*CULIN*) mutton

mouvant, e [muvɑ̃, -ɑ̃t] *adj* unsettled; changing; shifting

mouvement [muvmɑ̃] *nm* (*gén, aussi: mécanisme*) movement; (*fig*) activity; impulse; gesture; (*MUS: rythme*) tempo; **en ~** in motion; on the move; **mouvementé, e** *adj* (*vie, poursuite*) eventful; (*réunion*) turbulent

mouvoir [muvwar] *vt* (*levier, membre*) to move; **se ~** *vi* to move

moyen, ne [mwajɛ̃, -ɛn] *adj* average; (*tailles, prix*) medium; (*de grandeur moyenne*) medium-sized ♦ *nm* (*façon*) means *sg*, way; **~s** *nmpl* (*capacités*) means; **au ~ de** by means of; **par tous les ~s** by every possible means, every possible way; **par ses propres ~s** all by oneself; **~ âge** Middle Ages; **~ de transport** means of transport

moyennant [mwajenɑ̃] *prép* (*somme*) for; (*service, conditions*) in return for; (*travail, effort*) with

moyenne [mwajɛn] *nf* average; (*MATH*) mean; (*SCOL: à l'examen*) pass mark; (*AUTO*) average speed; **en ~** on (an) average; **~ d'âge** average age

Moyen-Orient [mwajenɔrjɑ̃] *nm*: **le ~** the Middle East

moyeu, x [mwajø] *nm* hub

MST *sigle f* (= *maladie sexuellement transmissible*) STD

mû, mue [my] *pp de* **mouvoir**

muer [mɥe] *vi* (*oiseau, mammifère*) to moult; (*serpent*) to slough; (*jeune garçon*): **il mue** his voice is breaking; **se ~ en** to transform into

muet, te [mɥɛ, -ɛt] *adj* dumb; (*fig*): **~ d'admiration** *etc* speechless with admiration *etc*; (*joie, douleur, CINÉMA*) silent; (*carte*) blank mute

mufle [myfl(ə)] *nm* muzzle; (*goujat*) boor

mugir [myʒir] *vi* (*taureau*) to bellow; (*vache*) to low; (*fig*) to howl

muguet [mygɛ] *nm* lily of the valley

mule [myl] *nf* (*ZOOL*) (she-)mule

mulet [mylɛ] *nm* (ZOOL) (he-)mule
multiple [myltipl(ə)] *adj* multiple, numerous; (varié) many, manifold ♦ *nm* (MATH) multiple
multiplication [myltiplikɑsjɔ̃] *nf* multiplication
multiplier [myltiplije] *vt* to multiply; **se ~** *vi* to multiply; to increase in number
municipal, e, aux [mynisipal, -o] *adj* municipal; town cpd; ≈ borough cpd
municipalité [mynisipalite] *nf* (corps municipal) town council, corporation
munir [mynir] *vt*: **~ qn/qch de** to equip sb/sth with
munitions [mynisjɔ̃] *nfpl* ammunition *sg*
mur [myr] *nm* wall; **~ du son** sound barrier
mûr, e [myr] *adj* ripe; (personne) mature
muraille [myrɑj] *nf* (high) wall
mural, e, aux [myral, -o] *adj* wall cpd; mural
mûre [myr] *nf* blackberry; mulberry
murer [myre] *vt* (enclos) to wall (in); (porte, issue) to wall up; (personne) to wall up *ou* in
muret [myrɛ] *nm* low wall
mûrir [myrir] *vi* (fruit, blé) to ripen; (abcès, furoncle) to come to a head; (fig: idée, personne) to mature ♦ *vt* to ripen; to (make) mature
murmure [myrmyr] *nm* murmur; **~s** *nmpl* (plaintes) murmurings, mutterings; **murmurer** *vi* to murmur; (se plaindre) to mutter, grumble
muscade [myskad] *nf* (aussi: noix ~) nutmeg
muscat [myska] *nm* muscat grape; muscatel (wine)
muscle [myskl(ə)] *nm* muscle; **musclé, e** *adj* muscular; (fig) strong-arm
museau, x [myzo] *nm* muzzle
musée [myze] *nm* museum; art gallery
museler [myzle] *vt* to muzzle; **muselière** *nf* muzzle
musette [myzɛt] *nf* (sac) lunchbag ♦ *adj* inv (orchestre etc) accordion cpd
musical, e, aux [myzikal, -o] *adj* musical
music-hall [myzikol] *nm* variety theatre; (genre) variety
musicien, ne [myzisjɛ̃, -jɛn] *adj* musical ♦ *nm/f* musician
musique [myzik] *nf* music; (fanfare) band; **~ de chambre** chamber music
musulman, e [myzylmɑ̃, -an] *adj, nm/f* Moslem, Muslim
mutation [mytasjɔ̃] *nf* (ADMIN) transfer
mutilé, e [mytile] *nm/f* disabled person (through loss of limbs)
mutiler [mytile] *vt* to mutilate, maim
mutin, e [mytɛ̃, -in] *adj* (air, ton) mischievous, impish ♦ *nm/f* (MIL, NAVIG) mutineer
mutinerie [mytinri] *nf* mutiny

mutisme [mytism(ə)] *nm* silence
mutuel, le [mytɥɛl] *adj* mutual; **mutuelle** *nf* mutual benefit society
myope [mjɔp] *adj* short-sighted
myosotis [mjozɔtis] *nm* forget-me-not
myrtille [mirtij] *nf* bilberry
mystère [mistɛr] *nm* mystery; **mystérieux, euse** *adj* mysterious
mystifier [mistifje] *vt* to fool; to mystify
mythe [mit] *nm* myth
mythologie [mitɔlɔʒi] *nf* mythology

N n

n' [n] *adv voir* **ne**
nacre [nakr(ə)] *nf* mother-of-pearl
nage [naʒ] *nf* swimming; style of swimming, stroke; **traverser/s'éloigner à la ~** to swim across/away; **en ~** bathed in perspiration
nageoire [naʒwar] *nf* fin
nager [naʒe] *vi* to swim; **nageur, euse** *nm/f* swimmer
naguère [nagɛr] *adv* formerly
naïf, ïve [naif, naiv] *adj* naïve
nain, e [nɛ̃, nɛn] *nm/f* dwarf
naissance [nɛsɑ̃s] *nf* birth; **donner ~ à** to give birth to; (fig) to give rise to
naître [nɛtr(ə)] *vi* to be born; (fig): **~ de** to arise from, be born out of; **il est né en 1960** he was born in 1960; **faire ~** (fig) to give rise to, arouse
naïve [naiv] *adj voir* **naïf**
nana [nana] (fam) *nf* (fille) chick, bird (BRIT)
nantir [nɑ̃tir] *vt*: **~ qn de** to provide sb with; **les nantis** (péj) the well-to-do
nappe [nap] *nf* tablecloth; (fig) sheet; layer; **napperon** *nm* table-mat
naquit etc vb voir **naître**
narguer [narge] *vt* to taunt
narine [narin] *nf* nostril
narquois, e [narkwa, -waz] *adj* derisive, mocking
naseau, x [nazo] *nm* nostril
natal, e [natal] *adj* native
natalité [natalite] *nf* birth rate
natation [natɑsjɔ̃] *nf* swimming
natif, ive [natif, -iv] *adj* native
nation [nɑsjɔ̃] *nf* nation
national, e, aux [nasjonal, -o] *adj* national; **nationale** *nf*: **(route) nationale** ≈ A road (BRIT), ≈ state highway (US); **nationaliser** *vt* to nationalize; **nationalité** *nf*

nationality

natte [nat] *nf* (*tapis*) mat; (*cheveux*) plait

naturaliser [natyʀalize] *vt* to naturalize

nature [natyʀ] *nf* nature ♦ *adj, adv* (*CULIN*) plain, without seasoning or sweetening; (*café, thé*) black, without sugar; **payer en ~** to pay in kind; **~ morte** still-life; **naturel, le** *adj* (*gén, aussi: enfant*) natural ♦ *nm* naturalness; disposition, nature; (*autochtone*) native; **naturellement** *adv* naturally; (*bien sûr*) of course

naufrage [nofʀaʒ] *nm* (ship)wreck; (*fig*) wreck; **faire ~** to be shipwrecked

nauséabond, e [nozeabɔ̃, -ɔ̃d] *adj* foul, nauseous

nausée [noze] *nf* nausea

nautique [notik] *adj* nautical, water *cpd*

nautisme [notism(ə)] *nm* water sports

navet [navɛ] *nm* turnip

navette [navɛt] *nf* shuttle; **faire la ~** (**entre**) to go to and fro *ou* shuttle (between)

navigateur [navigatœʀ] *nm* (*NAVIG*) seafarer, sailor; (*AVIAT*) navigator

navigation [navigasjɔ̃] *nf* navigation, sailing; shipping

naviguer [navige] *vi* to navigate, sail

navire [naviʀ] *nm* ship

navrer [navʀe] *vt* to upset, distress; **je suis navré** I'm so sorry

ne(n') [n(ə)] *adv voir* **pas; plus; jamais** *etc*; (*explétif*) *non traduit*

né, e [ne] *pp* (*voir* **naître**): **~ en 1960** born in 1960; **~e Scott** née Scott

néanmoins [neɑ̃mwɛ̃] *adv* nevertheless

néant [neɑ̃] *nm* nothingness; **réduire à ~** to bring to nought; (*espoir*) to dash

nécessaire [nesesɛʀ] *adj* necessary ♦ *nm* necessary; (*sac*) kit; **~ de couture** sewing kit; **~ de toilette** toilet bag; **nécessité** *nf* necessity; **nécessiter** *vt* to require; **nécessiteux, euse** *adj* needy

nécrologique [nekʀɔlɔʒik] *adj*: **article ~** obituary; **rubrique ~** obituary column

nectar [nɛktaʀ] *nm* (*sucré*) nectar; (*boisson*) sweetened, diluted fruit juice

néerlandais, e [neɛʀlɑ̃dɛ, -ɛz] *adj* Dutch

nef [nɛf] *nf* (*d'église*) nave

néfaste [nefast(ə)] *adj* baneful; ill-fated

négatif, ive [negatif, -iv] *adj* negative ♦ *nm* (*PHOTO*) negative

négligé, e [negliʒe] *adj* (*en désordre*) slovenly ♦ *nm* (*tenue*) negligee

négligent, e [negliʒɑ̃, -ɑ̃t] *adj* careless; negligent

négliger [negliʒe] *vt* (*épouse, jardin*) to neglect; (*tenue*) to be careless about; (*avis, précautions*) to disregard; **~ de faire** to fail to do, not bother to do

négoce [negɔs] *nm* trade

négociant [negɔsjɑ̃] *nm* merchant

négociation [negɔsjasjɔ̃] *nf* negotiation

négocier [negɔsje] *vi, vt* to negotiate

nègre [nɛgʀ(ə)] *nm* Negro; ghost (writer)

négresse [negʀɛs] *nf* Negro woman

neige [nɛʒ] *nf* snow; **neiger** *vi* to snow

nénuphar [nenyfaʀ] *nm* water-lily

néon [neɔ̃] *nm* neon

néophyte [neɔfit] *nm/f* novice

néo-zélandais, e [neɔzelɑ̃dɛ, -ɛz] *adj* New Zealand *cpd* ♦ *nm/f*: **N~, e** New Zealander

nerf [nɛʀ] *nm* nerve; (*fig*) spirit; stamina; **nerveux, euse** *adj* nervous; (*voiture*) nippy, responsive; (*tendineux*) sinewy; **nervosité** *nf* excitability; state of agitation; nervousness

nervure [nɛʀvyʀ] *nf* vein

n'est-ce pas [nɛspa] *adv* isn't it?, won't you? *etc, selon le verbe qui précède*

net, nette [nɛt] *adj* (*sans équivoque, distinct*) clear; (*évident*) definite; (*propre*) neat, clean; (*COMM: prix, salaire*) net ♦ *adv* (*refuser*) flatly ♦ *nm*: **mettre au ~** to copy out; **s'arrêter ~** to stop dead; **nettement** *adv* clearly, distinctly; **netteté** *nf* clearness

nettoyage [nɛtwajaʒ] *nm* cleaning; **~ à sec** dry cleaning

nettoyer [nɛtwaje] *vt* to clean; (*fig*) to clean out

neuf¹ [nœf] *num* nine

neuf², neuve [nœf, nœv] *adj* new ♦ *nm*: **repeindre à ~** to redecorate; **remettre à ~** to do up (as good as new), refurbish

neutre [nøtʀ(ə)] *adj* neutral; (*LING*) neuter ♦ *nm* neuter

neuve [nœv] *adj voir* **neuf²**

neuvième [nœvjɛm] *num* ninth

neveu, x [nəvø] *nm* nephew

névrosé, e [nevʀoze] *adj, nm/f* neurotic

nez [ne] *nm* nose; **~ à ~ avec** face to face with; **avoir du ~** to have flair

ni [ni] *conj*: **~ l'un ~ l'autre ne sont** neither one nor the other are; **il n'a rien dit ~ fait** he hasn't said or done anything

niais, e [njɛ, -ɛz] *adj* silly, thick

niche [niʃ] *nf* (*du chien*) kennel; (*de mur*) recess, niche

nicher [niʃe] *vi* to nest

nid [ni] *nm* nest; **~ de poule** pothole

nièce [njɛs] *nf* niece

nier [nje] *vt* to deny

nigaud, e [nigo, -od] *nm/f* booby, fool

Nil [nil] *nm*: **le ~** the Nile

n'importe [nɛ̃pɔʀt(ə)] *adv*: **~ qui/quoi/où** anybody/anything/anywhere; **~ quand** any time; **~ quel/quelle** any; **~ lequel/laquelle** any (one); **~ comment** (*sans soin*) carelessly

niveau, x [nivo] *nm* level; (*des élèves, études*) standard; **de ~ (avec)** level (with); **le ~ de la mer** sea level; **~ de vie** standard of living

niveler [nivle] *vt* to level

NN *abr* (= *nouvelle norme*) revised standard of hotel classification

noble [nɔbl(ə)] *adj* noble; **noblesse** *nf* nobility; (d'une action etc) nobleness

noce [nɔs] nf wedding; (gens) wedding party (ou guests pl); **faire la ~** (fam) to go on a binge; **~s d'or/d'argent** golden/silver wedding

nocif, ive [nɔsif, -iv] adj harmful, noxious

noctambule [nɔktãbyl] nm night-bird

nocturne [nɔktyʀn(ə)] adj nocturnal ♦ nf late-night opening

Noël [nɔɛl] nm Christmas

nœud [nø] nm (de corde, du bois, NAVIG) knot; (ruban) bow; (fig: liens) bond, tie; **~ papillon** bow tie

noir, e [nwaʀ] adj black; (obscur, sombre) dark ♦ nm/f black man(woman), Negro ♦ nm: **dans le ~** in the dark; **travail au ~** moonlighting; **noirceur** nf blackness; darkness; **noircir** vt, vi to blacken; **noire** nf (MUS) crotchet (BRIT), quarter note (US)

noisette [nwazɛt] nf hazelnut

noix [nwa] nf walnut; (CULIN): **une ~ de beurre** a knob of butter; **~ de cajou** cashew nut; **~ de coco** coconut

nom [nɔ̃] nm name; (LING) noun; **~ d'emprunt** assumed name; **~ de famille** surname; **~ de jeune fille** maiden name; **~ déposé** nm trade name; **~ propre** nm proper noun

nombre [nɔ̃bʀ(ə)] nm number; **venir en ~** to come in large numbers; **depuis ~ d'années** for many years; **ils sont au ~ de 3** there are 3 of them; **au ~ de mes amis** among my friends

nombreux, euse [nɔ̃bʀø, -øz] adj many, numerous; (avec nom sg: foule etc) large; **peu ~** few; small

nombril [nɔ̃bʀi] nm navel

nommer [nɔme] vt (baptiser, mentionner) to name; (qualifier) to call; (élire) to appoint, nominate; **se ~: il se nomme Pascal** his name's Pascal, he's called Pascal

non [nɔ̃] adv (réponse) no; (avec loin, sans, seulement) not; **~ pas que = non que**; **~ que** not that; **moi ~ plus** neither do I, I don't either

non: **~-alcoolisé, e** adj non-alcoholic; **~-fumeur** nm non-smoker; **~-lieu** nm: **il y a eu ~-lieu** the case was dismissed; **~-sens** nm absurdity

nord [nɔʀ] nm North ♦ adj northern; north; **au ~** (situation) in the north; (direction) to the north; **au ~ de** (to the) north of; **nord-est** nm North-East; **nord-ouest** nm North-West

normal, e, aux [nɔʀmal, -o] adj normal; **normale** nf: **la normale** the norm, the average; **normalement** adv (en général) normally; **normaliser** vt (COMM, TECH) to standardize

norme [nɔʀm(ə)] nf norm; (TECH) standard

Norvège [nɔʀvɛʒ] nf Norway; **norvégien, ne** adj, nm/f Norwegian ♦ nm (LING) Norwegian

nos [no] dét voir **notre**

nostalgie [nɔstalʒi] nf nostalgia

notable [nɔtabl(ə)] adj notable, noteworthy; (marqué) noticeable, marked ♦ nm prominent citizen

notaire [nɔtɛʀ] nm notary; solicitor

notamment [nɔtamã] adv in particular, among others

note [nɔt] nf (écrite, MUS) note; (SCOL) mark (BRIT), grade; (facture) bill; **~ de service** memorandum

noté, e [nɔte] adj: **être bien/mal ~** (employé etc) to have a good/bad record

noter [nɔte] vt (écrire) to write down; (remarquer) to note, notice

notice [nɔtis] nf summary, short article; (brochure) leaflet, instruction book

notifier [nɔtifje] vt: **~ qch à qn** to notify sb of sth, notify sth to sb

notion [nɔsjɔ̃] nf notion, idea

notoire [nɔtwaʀ] adj widely known; (en mal) notorious

notre [nɔtʀ(ə), no] (pl nos) dét our

nôtre [notʀ(ə)] pron: **le ~, la ~, les ~s** ours ♦ adj ours; **les ~s** ours; (alliés etc) our own people; **soyez des ~s** join us

nouer [nwe] vt to tie, knot; (fig: alliance etc) to strike up

noueux, euse [nwø, -øz] adj gnarled

nouilles [nuj] nfpl noodles; pasta sg

nourrice [nuʀis] nf wet-nurse

nourrir [nuʀiʀ] vt to feed; (fig: espoir) to harbour, nurse; **logé nourri** with board and lodging; **nourrissant, e** adj nourishing, nutritious

nourrisson [nuʀisɔ̃] nm (unweaned) infant

nourriture [nuʀityʀ] nf food

nous [nu] pron (sujet) we; (objet) us; **nous-mêmes** pron ourselves

nouveau(nouvel), elle, x [nuvo, -ɛl] adj new ♦ nm/f new pupil (ou employee); **de ~, à ~** again; **~ venu, nouvelle venue** newcomer; **~-né, e** nm/f newborn baby; **~té** nf novelty; (COMM) new film (ou book ou creation etc)

nouvel [nuvɛl] adj voir **nouveau**; **N~ An** New Year

nouvelle [nuvɛl] adj voir **nouveau** ♦ nf (piece of) news sg; (LITTÉRATURE) short story; **je suis sans ~s de lui** I haven't heard from him; **N~-Calédonie** nf New Caledonia; **N~-Zélande** nf New Zealand

novembre [nɔvãbʀ(ə)] nm November

novice [nɔvis] adj inexperienced

noyade [nwajad] nf drowning no pl

noyau, x [nwajo] nm (de fruit) stone; (BIO, PHYSIQUE) nucleus; (ÉLEC, GÉO, fig: centre) core; **noyauter** vt (POL) to infiltrate

noyer [nwaje] *nm* walnut (tree); (*bois*) walnut ♦ *vt* to drown; (*fig*) to flood; to submerge; **se ~** *vi* to be drowned, drown; (*suicide*) to drown o.s.

nu, e [ny] *adj* naked; (*membres*) naked, bare; (*chambre, fil, plaine*) bare ♦ *nm* (*ART*) nude; **se mettre ~** to strip; **mettre à ~** to bare

nuage [nɥaʒ] *nm* cloud; **nuageux, euse** *adj* cloudy

nuance [nɥãs] *nf* (*de couleur, sens*) shade; **il y a une ~ (entre)** there's a slight difference (between); **nuancer** *vt* (*opinion*) to bring some reservations *ou* qualifications to

nucléaire [nykleɛʀ] *adj* nuclear

nudiste [nydist(ə)] *nm/f* nudist

nuée [nɥe] *nf*: **une ~ de** a cloud *ou* host *ou* swarm of

nues [ny] *nfpl*: **tomber des ~** to be taken aback; **porter qn aux ~** to praise sb to the skies

nuire [nɥiʀ] *vi* to be harmful; **~ à** to harm, do damage to; **nuisible** *adj* harmful; **animal nuisible** pest

nuit [nɥi] *nf* night; **il fait ~** it's dark; **cette ~** last night; tonight; **~ blanche** sleepless night; **~ de noces** wedding night

nul, nulle [nyl] *adj* (*aucun*) no; (*minime*) nil, non-existent; (*non valable*) null; (*péj*) useless, hopeless ♦ *pron* none, no one; **match ~** draw; **résultat ~ = match nul**; **~le part** nowhere; **nullement** *adv* by no means

numérique [nymeʀik] *adj* numerical

numéro [nymeʀo] *nm* number; (*spectacle*) act, turn; **~ de téléphone** (tele)phone number; **~ vert** *nm* ≈ freefone number (*BRIT*), ≈ toll-free number (*US*); **numéroter** *vt* to number

nu-pieds [nypje] *adj inv* barefoot

nuque [nyk] *nf* nape of the neck

nu-tête [nytɛt] *adj inv* bareheaded

nutritif, ive [nytʀitif, -iv] *adj* nutritional; (*aliment*) nutritious

nylon [nilɔ̃] *nm* nylon

oasis [ɔazis] *nf* oasis

obéir [ɔbeiʀ] *vi* to obey; **~ à** to obey; (*suj: moteur, véhicule*) to respond to; **obéissant, e** *adj* obedient

objecter [ɔbʒɛkte] *vt* (*prétexter*) to plead,

put forward as an excuse; **~ (à qn) que** to object (to sb) that

objecteur [ɔbʒɛktœʀ] *nm*: **~ de conscience** conscientious objector

objectif, ive [ɔbʒɛktif, -iv] *adj* objective ♦ *nm* (*OPTIQUE, PHOTO*) lens *sg*, objective; (*MIL, fig*) objective; **~ à focale variable** zoom lens

objection [ɔbʒɛksjɔ̃] *nf* objection

objet [ɔbʒɛ] *nm* object; (*d'une discussion, recherche*) subject; **être** *ou* **faire l'~ de** (*discussion*) to be the subject of; (*soins*) to be given *ou* shown; **sans ~** purposeless; groundless; **~ d'art** objet d'art; **~s personnels** personal items; **~s trouvés** lost property *sg* (*BRIT*), lost-and-found (*US*)

obligation [ɔbligasjɔ̃] *nf* obligation; (*COMM*) bond, debenture; **obligatoire** *adj* compulsory, obligatory

obligé, e [ɔbliʒe] *adj* (*redevable*): **être très ~ à qn** to be most obliged to sb

obligeance [ɔbliʒɑ̃s] *nf*: **avoir l'~ de ...** to be kind *ou* good enough to ...; **obligeant, e** *adj* obliging; kind

obliger [ɔbliʒe] *vt* (*contraindre*): **~ qn à faire** to force *ou* oblige sb to do; (*JUR: engager*) to bind; (*rendre service à*) to oblige; **je suis bien obligé** I have to

oblique [ɔblik] *adj* oblique; **regard ~** sidelong glance; **en ~** diagonally; **obliquer** *vi*: **obliquer vers** to turn off towards

oblitérer [ɔblitere] *vt* (*timbre-poste*) to cancel

obscène [ɔpsɛn] *adj* obscene

obscur, e [ɔpskyʀ] *adj* dark; (*fig*) obscure; lowly; **~cir** *vt* to darken; (*fig*) to obscure; **s'~cir** *vi* to grow dark; **~ité** *nf* darkness; **dans l'~ité** in the dark, in darkness

obséder [ɔpsede] *vt* to obsess, haunt

obsèques [ɔpsɛk] *nfpl* funeral *sg*

observateur, trice [ɔpsɛʀvatœʀ, -tʀis] *adj* observant, perceptive ♦ *nm/f* observer

observation [ɔpsɛʀvasjɔ̃] *nf* observation; (*d'un règlement etc*) observance; (*reproche*) reproof

observatoire [ɔpsɛʀvatwaʀ] *nm* observatory; (*lieu élevé*) observation post, vantage point

observer [ɔpsɛʀve] *vt* (*regarder*) to observe, watch; (*examiner*) to examine; (*scientifiquement, aussi: règlement, jeûne etc*) to observe; (*surveiller*) to watch; (*remarquer*) to observe, notice; **faire ~ qch à qn** (*dire*) to point out sth to sb

obstacle [ɔpstakl(ə)] *nm* obstacle; (*ÉQUITATION*) jump, hurdle; **faire ~ à** (*lumière*) to block out; (*projet*) to hinder, put obstacles in the path of

obstiné, e [ɔpstine] *adj* obstinate

obstiner [ɔpstine]: **s'~** *vi* to insist, dig one's heels in; **s'~ à faire** to persist (obstinately) in doing; **s'~ sur qch** to keep

working at sth, labour away at sth
obstruer [ɔpstʁye] *vt* to block, obstruct
obtempérer [ɔptɑ̃peʁe] *vi* to obey
obtenir [ɔptəniʁ] *vt* to obtain, get; *(total, résultat)* to arrive at, reach; to achieve, obtain; ~ **de pouvoir faire** to obtain permission to do; ~ **de qn qu'il fasse** to get sb to agree to do; **obtention** *nf* obtaining
obturateur [ɔptyʁatœʁ] *nm* (PHOTO) shutter
obturer [ɔptyʁe] *vt* to close (up); *(dent)* to fill
obus [ɔby] *nm* shell
occasion [ɔkazjɔ̃] *nf* (aubaine, possibilité) opportunity; (circonstance) occasion; (COMM: article non neuf) secondhand buy; (: acquisition avantageuse) bargain; **à plusieurs ~s** on several occasions; **être l'~ de** to occasion, give rise to; **à l'~** sometimes, on occasions; some time; **d'~** secondhand; **occasionnel, le** *adj* (fortuit) chance *cpd*; (non régulier) occasional; casual
occasionner [ɔkazjɔne] *vt* to cause, bring about; ~ **qch à qn** to cause sb sth
occident [ɔksidɑ̃] *nm*: **l'O~** the West; **occidental, e, aux** *adj* western; (POL) Western
occupation [ɔkypasjɔ̃] *nf* occupation
occupé, e [ɔkype] *adj* (MIL, POL) occupied; (personne: affairé, pris) busy; (place, sièges) taken; (toilettes) engaged; (ligne) engaged (BRIT), busy (US)
occuper [ɔkype] *vt* to occupy; (main-d'œuvre) to employ; **s'~ de** (être responsable de) to be in charge of; (se charger de: affaire) to take charge of, deal with; (: clients etc) to attend to; (s'intéresser à, pratiquer) to be involved in; **s'~ (à qch)** to occupy o.s. ou keep o.s. busy (with sth); **ça occupe trop de place** it takes up too much room
occurrence [ɔkyʁɑ̃s] *nf*: **en l'~** in this case
océan [ɔseɑ̃] *nm* ocean; **l'~ Indien** the Indian Ocean
octet [ɔktɛt] *nm* byte
octobre [ɔktɔbʁ(ə)] *nm* October
octroyer [ɔktʁwaje] *vt*: ~ **qch à qn** to grant sth to sb, grant sb sth
oculiste [ɔkylist(ə)] *nm/f* eye specialist
odeur [ɔdœʁ] *nf* smell
odieux, euse [ɔdjø, -øz] *adj* hateful
odorant, e [ɔdɔʁɑ̃, -ɑ̃t] *adj* sweet-smelling, fragrant
odorat [ɔdɔʁa] *nm* (sense of) smell
œil [œj] (pl **yeux**) *nm* eye; **à l'~** (fam) for free; **à l'~ nu** with the naked eye; **tenir qn à l'~** to keep an eye ou a watch on sb; **avoir l'~ à** to keep an eye on; **fermer les yeux (sur)** (fig) to turn a blind eye (to)
œillade [œjad] *nf*: **lancer une ~ à qn** to wink at sb, give sb a wink; **faire des ~s à** to make eyes at
œillères [œjɛʁ] *nfpl* blinkers (BRIT), blin-

ders (US)
œillet [œjɛ] *nm* (BOT) carnation
œuf [œf, pl ø] *nm* egg; ~ **à la coque** *nm* boiled egg; ~ **au plat** fried egg; ~ **de Pâques** Easter egg; ~ **dur** hard-boiled egg; **~s brouillés** scrambled eggs
œuvre [œvʁ(ə)] *nf* (tâche) task, undertaking; (ouvrage achevé, livre, tableau etc) work; (ensemble de la production artistique) works *pl*; (organisation charitable) charity ♦ *nm* (d'un artiste) works *pl*; (CONSTR): **le gros ~** the shell; **être à l'~** to be at work; **mettre en ~** (moyens) to make use of; ~ **d'art** work of art
offense [ɔfɑ̃s] *nf* insult
offenser [ɔfɑ̃se] *vt* to offend, hurt; (principes, Dieu) to offend against; **s'~ de** to take offence at
offert, e [ɔfɛʁ, -ɛʁt(ə)] *pp de* offrir
office [ɔfis] *nm* (charge) office; (agence) bureau, agency; (REL) service ♦ *nm ou nf* (pièce) pantry; **faire ~ de** to act as; to do duty as; **d'~** automatically; ~ **du tourisme** tourist bureau
officiel, le [ɔfisjɛl] *adj, nm/f* official
officier [ɔfisje] *nm* officer ♦ *vi* to officiate; ~ **de l'état-civil** registrar
officieux, euse [ɔfisjø, -øz] *adj* unofficial
officinal, e, aux [ɔfisinal, -o] *adj*: **plantes ~es** medicinal plants
officine [ɔfisin] *nf* (de pharmacie) dispensary; (bureau) agency, office
offrande [ɔfʁɑ̃d] *nf* offering
offre [ɔfʁ(ə)] *nf* offer; (aux enchères) bid; (ADMIN: soumission) tender; (ÉCON): **l'~** supply; **"~s d'emploi"** "situations vacant"; ~ **d'emploi** job advertised; ~ **publique d'achat** takeover bid
offrir [ɔfʁiʁ] *vt*: ~ **(à qn)** to offer (to sb); (faire cadeau de) to give (to sb); **s'~** *vi* (occasion, paysage) to present itself ♦ *vt* (vacances, voiture) to treat o.s. to; ~ **(à qn) de faire qch** to offer to do sth (for sb); ~ **à boire à qn** to offer sb a drink; **s'~ comme guide/en otage** to offer one's services as (a) guide/offer o.s. as hostage
offusquer [ɔfyske] *vt* to offend
ogive [ɔʒiv] *nf*: ~ **nucléaire** nuclear warhead
oie [wa] *nf* (ZOOL) goose
oignon [ɔɲɔ̃] *nm* (BOT, CULIN) onion; (de tulipe etc: bulbe) bulb; (MÉD) bunion
oiseau, x [wazo] *nm* bird; ~ **de proie** bird of prey
oiseux, euse [wazø, -øz] *adj* pointless; trivial
oisif, ive [wazif, -iv] *adj* idle ♦ *nm/f* (péj) man(woman) of leisure
oléoduc [ɔleɔdyk] *nm* (oil) pipeline
olive [ɔliv] *nf* (BOT) olive; **olivier** *nm* olive (tree)
OLP *sigle f* = **Organisation de libération** ♦

de la Palestine

olympique [ɔlɛ̃pik] *adj* Olympic

ombrage [ɔ̃bʀaʒ] *nm* (*ombre*) (leafy) shade; **ombragé, e** *adj* shaded, shady; **ombrageux, euse** *adj* (*cheval*) skittish, nervous; (*personne*) touchy, easily offended

ombre [ɔ̃bʀ(ə)] *nf* (*espace non ensoleillé*) shade; (~ *portée, tache*) shadow; **à l'~** in the shade; **tu me fais de l'~** you're in my light; **ça nous donne de l'~** it gives us (some) shade; **dans l'~** (*fig*) in obscurity; in the dark; ~ **à paupières** eyeshadow; **ombrelle** [ɔ̃bʀɛl] *nf* parasol, sunshade

omelette [ɔmlɛt] *nf* omelette

omettre [ɔmɛtʀ(ə)] *vt* to omit, leave out

omnibus [ɔmnibys] *nm* slow *ou* stopping train

omoplate [ɔmɔplat] *nf* shoulder blade

─────── **MOT CLÉ** ───────

on [ɔ̃] *pron* **1** (*indéterminé*) you, one; ~ **peut le faire ainsi** you *ou* one can do it like this, it can be done like this
2 (*quelqu'un*): ~ **les a attaqués** they were attacked; ~ **vous demande au téléphone** there's a phone call for you, you're wanted on the phone
3 (*nous*) we; ~ **va y aller demain** we're going tomorrow
4 (*les gens*) they; **autrefois,** ~ **croyait ...** they used to believe ...
5: ~ **ne peut plus** *adv*: ~ **ne peut plus stupide** as stupid as can be

oncle [ɔ̃kl(ə)] *nm* uncle

onctueux, euse [ɔ̃ktɥø, -øz] *adj* creamy, smooth; (*fig*) smooth, unctuous

onde [ɔ̃d] *nf* (*PHYSIQUE*) wave; **sur les ~s** on the radio; **mettre en ~s** to produce for the radio; **sur ~s courtes** on short wave *sg*; **moyennes/longues ~s** medium/long wave *sg*

ondée [ɔ̃de] *nf* shower

on-dit [ɔ̃di] *nm inv* rumour

ondoyer [ɔ̃dwaje] *vi* to ripple, wave

onduler [ɔ̃dyle] *vi* to undulate; (*cheveux*) to wave

onéreux, euse [ɔneʀø, -øz] *adj* costly; **à titre** ~ in return for payment

ongle [ɔ̃gl(ə)] *nm* (*ANAT*) nail; **se faire les ~s** to do one's nails

onguent [ɔ̃gɑ̃] *nm* ointment

ont *vb voir* **avoir**

O.N.U. [ɔny] *sigle f* = **Organisation des Nations Unies**

onze [ɔ̃z] *num* eleven; **onzième** *num* eleventh

O.P.A. *sigle f* = **offre publique d'achat**

opaque [ɔpak] *adj* opaque

opéra [ɔpeʀa] *nm* opera; (*édifice*) opera house

opérateur, trice [ɔpeʀatœʀ, -tʀis] *nm/f*

operator; ~ **(de prise de vues)** cameraman

opération [ɔpeʀasjɔ̃] *nf* operation; (*COMM*) dealing

opératoire [ɔpeʀatwaʀ] *adj* operating; (*choc etc*) post-operative

opérer [ɔpeʀe] *vt* (*MÉD*) to operate on; (*faire, exécuter*) to carry out, make ♦ *vi* (*remède: faire effet*) to act, work; (*procéder*) to proceed; (*MÉD*) to operate; **s'~** *vi* (*avoir lieu*) to occur, take place; **se faire** ~ to have an operation

opiner [ɔpine] *vi*: ~ **de la tête** to nod assent

opinion [ɔpinjɔ̃] *nf* opinion; **l'~** (**publique**) public opinion

opportun, e [ɔpɔʀtœ̃, -yn] *adj* timely, opportune; **en temps** ~ at the appropriate time; **~iste** [ɔpɔʀtynist(ə)] *nm/f* opportunist

opposant, e [ɔpozɑ̃, -ɑ̃t] *adj* opposing; **opposants** *nmpl* opponents

opposé, e [ɔpoze] *adj* (*direction, rive*) opposite; (*faction*) opposing; (*couleurs*) contrasting; (*opinions, intérêts*) conflicting; (*contre*): ~ **à** opposed to, against ♦ *nm*: **l'~** the other *ou* opposite side (*ou* direction); (*contraire*) the opposite; **à l'~** (*fig*) on the other hand; **à l'~ de** on the other *ou* opposite side from; (*fig*) contrary to, unlike

opposer [ɔpoze] *vt* (*personnes, armées, équipes*) to oppose; (*couleurs, termes, tons*) to contrast; **s'~** (*sens réciproque*) to conflict; to clash; to contrast; **s'~ à** (*interdire, empêcher*) to oppose; (*tenir tête à*) to rebel against; ~ **qch à** (*comme obstacle, défense*) to set sth against; (*comme objection*) to put sth forward against

opposition [ɔpozisjɔ̃] *nf* opposition; **par** ~ **à** as opposed to, in contrast with; **entrer en** ~ **avec** to come into conflict with; **être en** ~ **avec** (*idées, conduite*) to be at variance with; **faire** ~ **à un chèque** to stop a cheque

oppresser [ɔpʀese] *vt* to oppress; **oppression** *nf* oppression; (*malaise*) feeling of suffocation

opprimer [ɔpʀime] *vt* to oppress; (*liberté, opinion*) to suppress, stifle; (*suj: chaleur etc*) to suffocate, oppress

opter [ɔpte] *vi*: ~ **pour** to opt for; ~ **entre** to choose between

opticien, ne [ɔptisjɛ̃, -ɛn] *nm/f* optician

optimiste [ɔptimist(ə)] *nm/f* optimist ♦ *adj* optimistic

option [ɔpsjɔ̃] *nf* option; **matière à** ~ (*SCOL*) optional subject

optique [ɔptik] *adj* (*nerf*) optic; (*verres*) optical ♦ *nf* (*PHOTO: lentilles etc*) optics *pl*; (*science, industrie*) optics *sg*; (*fig: manière de voir*) perspective

opulent, e [ɔpylɑ̃, -ɑ̃t] *adj* wealthy, opulent; (*formes, poitrine*) ample, generous

or [ɔʀ] *nm* gold ♦ *conj* now, but; **en** ~ gold

cpd; (fig) golden, marvellous

orage [ɔʀaʒ] *nm* (thunder)storm; **orageux, euse** *adj* stormy

oraison [ɔʀɛzɔ̃] *nf* orison, prayer; **~ fu- nèbre** funeral oration

oral, e, aux [ɔʀal, -o] *adj, nm* oral

orange [ɔʀãʒ] *nf* orange ♦ *adj inv* orange; **oranger** *nm* orange tree

orateur [ɔʀatœʀ] *nm* speaker; orator

orbite [ɔʀbit] *nf (ANAT)* (eye-) socket; *(PHYSIQUE)* orbit

orchestre [ɔʀkɛstʀ(ə)] *nm* orchestra; *(de jazz, danse)* band; *(places)* stalls *pl (BRIT)*, orchestra *(US)*; **orchestrer** *vt (MUS)* to orchestrate; *(fig)* to mount, stage-manage

orchidée [ɔʀkide] *nf* orchid

ordinaire [ɔʀdinɛʀ] *adj* ordinary; everyday; standard ♦ *nm* ordinary; *(menus)* everyday fare ♦ *nf (essence)* ≈ two-star (petrol) *(BRIT)*, ≈ regular gas *(US)*; **d'~** usually, normally; **à l'~** usually, ordinarily

ordinateur [ɔʀdinatœʀ] *nm* computer; **~ domestique** home computer; **~ individuel** personal computer

ordonnance [ɔʀdɔnãs] *nf* organization; layout; *(MÉD)* prescription; *(JUR)* order; *(MIL)* orderly, batman *(BRIT)*

ordonné, e [ɔʀdɔne] *adj* tidy, orderly; *(MATH)* ordered

ordonner [ɔʀdɔne] *vt (agencer)* to organize, arrange; *(donner un ordre)*: **~ à qn de faire** to order sb to do; *(REL)* to ordain; *(MÉD)* to prescribe

ordre [ɔʀdʀ(ə)] *nm (gén)* order; *(propreté et soin)* orderliness, tidiness; *(nature)*: **d'~ pratique** of a practical nature; **~s** *nmpl (REL)* holy orders; **mettre en ~** to tidy (up), put in order; **à l'~ de qn** payable to sb; **être aux ~s de qn/sous les ~s de qn** to be at sb's disposal/under sb's command; **jusqu'à nouvel ~** until further notice; **dans le même ~ d'idées** in this connection; **donnez-nous un ~ de grandeur** give us some idea as regards size *(ou* the amount); **de premier ~** first-rate; **~ du jour** *(d'une réunion)* agenda; *(MIL)* order of the day; **à l'~ du jour** *(fig)* topical

ordure [ɔʀdyʀ] *nf* filth *no pl*; **~s** *nfpl (ba- layures, déchets)* rubbish *sg*, refuse *sg*; **~s ménagères** household refuse

oreille [ɔʀɛj] *nf (ANAT)* ear; *(de marmite, tasse)* handle; **avoir de l'~** to have a good ear (for music)

oreiller [ɔʀeje] *nm* pillow

oreillons [ɔʀejɔ̃] *nmpl* mumps *sg*

ores [ɔʀ] : **d'~ et déjà** *adv* already

orfèvrerie [ɔʀfɛvʀəʀi] *nf* goldsmith's *(ou* silversmith's) trade; *(ouvrage)* gold *(ou* sil- ver) plate

organe [ɔʀgan] *nm* organ; *(porte-parole)* representative, mouthpiece

organigramme [ɔʀganigʀam] *nm* organi-

zation chart; flow chart

organique [ɔʀganik] *adj* organic

organisateur, trice [ɔʀganizatœʀ, -tʀis] *nm/f* organizer

organisation [ɔʀganizasjɔ̃] *nf* organization; **O~ des Nations Unies** United Nations (Organization); **O~ du traité de l'Atlanti- que Nord** North Atlantic Treaty Organiza- tion

organiser [ɔʀganize] *vt* to organize; *(mettre sur pied: service etc)* to set up; **s'~** to get organized

organisme [ɔʀganism(ə)] *nm (BIO)* organ- ism; *(corps, ADMIN)* body

organiste [ɔʀganist(ə)] *nm/f* organist

orgasme [ɔʀgasm(ə)] *nm* orgasm, climax

orge [ɔʀʒ(ə)] *nf* barley

orgie [ɔʀʒi] *nf* orgy

orgue [ɔʀg(ə)] *nm* organ; **~s** *nfpl (MUS)* organ *sg*

orgueil [ɔʀgœj] *nm* pride; **orgueilleux, euse** *adj* proud

Orient [ɔʀjã] *nm*: **l'~** the East, the Orient

oriental, e, aux [ɔʀjãtal, -o] *adj* oriental, eastern; *(frontière)* eastern

orientation [ɔʀjãtasjɔ̃] *nf* positioning; orientation; *(d'une maison etc)* aspect; *(d'un journal)* leanings *pl*; **avoir le sens de l'~** to have a (good) sense of direction; **~ pro- fessionnelle** careers advising; careers advi- sory service

orienté, e [ɔʀjãte] *adj (fig: article, journal)* slanted; **bien/mal ~** *(appartement)* well/ badly positioned; **~ au sud** facing south, with a southern aspect

orienter [ɔʀjãte] *vt (placer, disposer: pièce mobile)* to adjust, position; *(tourner)* to di- rect, turn; *(voyageur, touriste, recherches)* to direct; *(fig: élève)* to orientate; **s'~** *(se re- pérer)* to find one's bearings; **s'~ vers** *(fig)* to turn towards

origan [ɔʀigã] *nm (BOT)* oregano

originaire [ɔʀiʒinɛʀ] *adj*: **être ~ de** to be a native of

original, e, aux [ɔʀiʒinal, -o] *adj* original; *(bizarre)* eccentric ♦ *nm/f* eccentric ♦ *nm (document etc, ART)* original; *(dactylogra- phie)* top copy

origine [ɔʀiʒin] *nf* origin; **dès l'~** at *ou* from the outset; **à l'~** originally; **originel, le** *adj* original

O.R.L. *sigle nm/f* = **oto-rhino- laryngologiste**

orme [ɔʀm(ə)] *nm* elm

ornement [ɔʀnəmã] *nm* ornament; *(fig)* embellishment, adornment

orner [ɔʀne] *vt* to decorate, adorn

ornière [ɔʀnjɛʀ] *nf* rut

orphelin, e [ɔʀfəlɛ̃, -in] *adj* orphan(ed) ♦ *nm/f* orphan; **~ de père/mère** fatherless/ motherless; **orphelinat** *nm* orphanage

orteil [ɔʀtɛj] *nm* toe; **gros ~** big toe

orthographe [ɔrtɔgraf] *nf* spelling; **ortho-graphier** *vt* to spell
orthopédiste [ɔrtɔpedist(ə)] *nm/f* orthopaedic specialist
ortie [ɔrti] *nf* (stinging) nettle
os [ɔs, *pl* o] *nm* bone
osciller [ɔsile] *vi* (*pendule*) to swing; (*au vent etc*) to rock; (*TECH*) to oscillate; (*fig*): ~ **entre** to waver *ou* fluctuate between
osé, e [oze] *adj* daring, bold
oseille [ozεj] *nf* sorrel
oser [oze] *vi, vt* to dare; ~ **faire** to dare (to) do
osier [ozje] *nm* willow; **d'**~ wicker(work); **en** ~ = **d'osier**
ossature [ɔsatyr] *nf* (*ANAT*) frame, skeletal structure; (*fig*) framework
osseux, euse [ɔsø, -øz] *adj* bony; (*tissu, maladie, greffe*) bone *cpd*
ostensible [ɔstɑ̃sibl(ə)] *adj* conspicuous
otage [ɔtaʒ] *nm* hostage; **prendre qn comme** ~ to take sb hostage
O.T.A.N. [ɔtɑ̃] *sigle f* = **Organisation du traité de l'Atlantique Nord**
otarie [ɔtari] *nf* sea-lion
ôter [ote] *vt* to remove; (*soustraire*) to take away; ~ **qch à qn** to take sth (away) from sb; ~ **qch de** to remove sth from
otite [ɔtit] *nf* ear infection
oto-rhino(-laryngologiste) [ɔtɔrino(la-rɛ̃gɔlɔʒist(ə))] *nm/f* ear nose and throat specialist
ou [u] *conj* or; ~ ... ~ either ... or; ~ **bien** or (else)

MOT CLÉ

où [u] *pron relatif* **1** (*position, situation*) where, that (*souvent omis*); **la chambre** ~ **il était** the room (that) he was in, the room where he was; **la ville** ~ **je l'ai rencontré** the town where I met him; **la pièce d'**~ **il est sorti** the room he came out of; **le village d'**~ **je viens** the village I come from; **les villes par** ~ **il est passé** the towns he went through

2 (*temps, état*) that (*souvent omis*); **le jour** ~ **il est parti** the day (that) he left; **au prix** ~ **c'est** at the price it is

♦ *adv* **1** (*interrogation*) where; ~ **est-il/va-t-il?** where is he/is he going?; **par** ~? which way?; **d'**~ **vient que ...?** how come ...?

2 (*position*) where; **je sais** ~ **il est** I know where he is; ~ **que l'on aille** wherever you go

---

ouate [wat] *nf* cotton wool (*BRIT*), cotton (*US*); (*bourre*) padding, wadding
oubli [ubli] *nm* (*acte*): **l'**~ **de** forgetting; (*étourderie*) forgetfulness *no pl*; (*négligence*) omission, oversight; (*absence de souvenirs*) oblivion

oublier [ublije] *vt* (*gén*) to forget; (*ne pas voir: erreurs etc*) to miss; (*ne pas mettre: virgule, nom*) to leave out; (*laisser quelque part: chapeau etc*) to leave behind; **s'**~ to forget o.s.
oubliettes [ublijεt] *nfpl* dungeon *sg*
ouest [wεst] *nm* west ♦ *adj inv* west; (*région*) western; **à l'**~ in the west; (*to the*) west, westwards; **à l'**~ **de** (to the) west of
ouf [uf] *excl* phew!
oui [wi] *adv* yes
oui-dire [widir]: **par** ~ *adv* by hearsay
ouïe [wi] *nf* hearing; ~**s** *nfpl* (*de poisson*) gills
ouïr [wir] *vt* to hear; **avoir ouï dire que** to have heard it said that
ouragan [uragɑ̃] *nm* hurricane
ourlet [urlε] *nm* hem
ours [urs] *nm* bear; ~ **brun/blanc** brown/ polar bear; ~ (**en peluche**) teddy (bear)
oursin [ursɛ̃] *nm* sea urchin
ourson [ursɔ̃] *nm* (bear-)cub
ouste [ust(ə)] *excl* hop it!
outil [uti] *nm* tool
outiller [utije] *vt* (*ouvrier, usine*) to equip
outrage [utraʒ] *nm* insult; **faire subir les derniers** ~**s à** (*femme*) to ravish; ~ **à la pudeur** indecent conduct *no pl*; ~**r** [utraʒe] *vt* to offend gravely
outrance [utrɑ̃s]: **à** ~ *adv* excessively, to excess
outre [utr(ə)] *nf* goatskin, water skin ♦ *prép* besides ♦ *adv*: **passer** ~ **à** to disregard, take no notice of; **en** ~ besides, moreover; ~ **que** apart from the fact that; ~ **mesure** immoderately; unduly; ~**-Atlantique** *adv* across the Atlantic; ~**-Manche** *adv* across the Channel; ~**mer** *adj inv* ultramarine; ~**-mer** *adv* overseas; ~**passer** *vt* to go beyond, exceed
ouvert, e [uvεr, -εrt(ə)] *pp de* **ouvrir** ♦ *adj* open; (*robinet, gaz etc*) on; **ouvertement** *adv* openly
ouverture [uvεrtyr] *nf* opening; (*MUS*) overture; (*PHOTO*): ~ (**du diaphragme**) aperture; ~**s** *nfpl* (*propositions*) overtures; ~ **d'esprit** open-mindedness
ouvrable [uvrabl(ə)] *adj*: **jour** ~ working day, weekday
ouvrage [uvraʒ] *nm* (*tâche, de tricot etc, MIL*) work *no pl*; (*texte, livre*) work
ouvragé, e [uvraʒe] *adj* finely embroidered (*ou* worked *ou* carved)
ouvre-boîte(s) [uvrəbwat] *nm inv* tin (*BRIT*) *ou* can opener
ouvre-bouteille(s) [uvrəbutεj] *nm inv* bottle-opener
ouvreuse [uvrøz] *nf* usherette
ouvrier, ière [uvrije, -jεr] *nm/f* worker ♦ *adj* working-class; industrial, labour *cpd*; **classe ouvrière** working class
ouvrir [uvrir] *vt* (*gén*) to open; (*brèche,*

passage, MÉD: abcès) to open up; (commencer l'exploitation de, créer) to open (up); (eau, électricité, chauffage, robinet) to turn on ♦ vi to open; to open up; **s'~** vi to open; **s'~ à qn** to open one's heart to sb; **~ l'appétit à qn** to whet sb's appetite

ovaire [ɔvɛʀ] nm ovary

ovale [ɔval] adj oval

ovni [ɔvni] sigle m (= objet volant non identifié) UFO

oxyder [ɔkside]: **s'~** vi to become oxidized

oxygène [ɔksiʒɛn] nm oxygen; (fig): **cure d'~** fresh air cure

oxygéné, e [ɔksiʒene] adj: **eau ~e** hydrogen peroxide

P p

pacifique [pasifik] adj peaceful ♦ nm: **le P~, l'océan P~** the Pacific (Ocean)

pacte [pakt(ə)] nm pact, treaty

pactiser [paktize] vi: **~ avec** to come to terms with

pagaie [pagɛ] nf paddle

pagaille [pagaj] nf mess, shambles sg

page [paʒ] nf page ♦ nm page (boy); **à la ~** (fig) up-to-date

paiement [pemã] nm payment

païen, ne [pajɛ̃, -jɛn] adj, nm/f pagan, heathen

paillard, e [pajaʀ, -aʀd(ə)] adj bawdy

paillasson [pajasɔ̃] nm doormat

paille [pɑj] nf straw; (défaut) flaw

paillettes [pajɛt] nfpl (décoratives) sequins, spangles; **lessive en ~** soapflakes pl

pain [pɛ̃] nm (substance) bread; (unité) loaf (of bread); (morceau): **~ de cire** etc bar of wax etc; **~ bis/complet** brown/wholemeal (BRIT) ou wholewheat (US) bread; **~ d'épice** gingerbread; **~ de mie** sandwich loaf; **~ de sucre** sugar loaf; **~ grillé** toast

pair, e [pɛʀ] adj (nombre) even ♦ nm peer; **aller de ~** to go hand in hand ou together; **jeune fille au ~** au pair

paire [pɛʀ] nf pair

paisible [pezibl(ə)] adj peaceful, quiet

paître [pɛtʀ(ə)] vi to graze

paix [pe] nf peace; (fig) peacefulness, peace; **faire/avoir la ~** to make/have peace

Pakistan [pakistɑ̃] nm: **le ~** Pakistan

palace [palas] nm luxury hotel

palais [palɛ] nm palace; (ANAT) palate

pale [pal] nf (d'hélice, de rame) blade

pâle [pɑl] adj pale; **bleu ~** pale blue

Palestine [palɛstin] nf: **la ~** Palestine

palet [palɛ] nm disc; (HOCKEY) puck

palette [palɛt] nf (de peintre) palette; (produits) range

pâleur [pɑlœʀ] nf paleness

palier [palje] nm (d'escalier) landing; (fig) level, plateau; (TECH) bearing; **par ~s** in stages

pâlir [pɑliʀ] vi to turn ou go pale; (couleur) to fade

palissade [palisad] nf fence

palliatif [paljatif] nm palliative; (expédient) stopgap measure

pallier [palje]: **~ à** vt to offset, make up for

palmarès [palmaʀɛs] nm record (of achievements); (SCOL) prize list; (SPORT) list of winners

palme [palm(ə)] nf (symbole) palm; (de plongeur) flipper; **palmé, e** adj (pattes) webbed

palmier [palmje] nm palm tree

palombe [palɔ̃b] nf woodpigeon

pâlot, te [pɑlo, -ɔt] adj pale, peaky

palourde [paluʀd(ə)] nf clam

palper [palpe] vt to feel, finger

palpitant, e [palpitɑ̃, -ɑ̃t] adj thrilling

palpiter [palpite] vi (cœur, pouls) to beat; (: plus fort) to pound, throb

paludisme [palydism(ə)] nm malaria

pamphlet [pɑ̃flɛ] nm lampoon, satirical tract

pamplemousse [pɑ̃pləmus] nm grapefruit

pan [pɑ̃] nm section, piece ♦ excl bang!

panachage [panaʃaʒ] nm blend, mix

panache [panaʃ] nm plume; (fig) spirit, panache

panaché, e [panaʃe] adj: **glace ~e** mixed-flavour ice cream; **bière ~e** shandy

pancarte [pɑ̃kaʀt(ə)] nf sign, notice; (dans un défilé) placard

pancréas [pɑ̃kʀeas] nm pancreas

pané, e [pane] adj fried in breadcrumbs

panier [panje] nm basket; **mettre au ~** to chuck away; **~ à provisions** shopping basket

panique [panik] nf, adj panic; **paniquer** vi to panic

panne [pan] nf (d'un mécanisme, moteur) breakdown; **être/tomber en ~** to have broken down/break down; **être en ~ d'essence** ou **sèche** to have run out of petrol (BRIT) ou gas (US); **~ d'électricité** ou **de courant** power ou electrical failure

panneau, x [pano] nm (écriteau) sign, notice; (de boiserie, de tapisserie etc) panel; **~ d'affichage** notice board; **~ de signalisation** roadsign

panonceau, x [panɔ̃so] nm sign

panoplie [panɔpli] nf (jouet) outfit; (d'armes) display; (fig) array

panorama [panɔrama] *nm* panorama
panse [pɑ̃s] *nf* paunch
pansement [pɑ̃smɑ̃] *nm* dressing, bandage;
~ **adhésif** sticking plaster
panser [pɑ̃se] *vt* (*plaie*) to dress, bandage;
(*bras*) to put a dressing on, bandage; (*cheval*) to groom
pantalon [pɑ̃talɔ̃] *nm* (*aussi:* ~*s*, **paire de**
~*s*) trousers *pl*, pair of trousers; ~ **de ski**
ski pants *pl*
pantelant, e [pɑ̃tlɑ̃, -ɑ̃t] *adj* gasping for
breath, panting
panthère [pɑ̃tɛr] *nf* panther
pantin [pɑ̃tɛ̃] *nm* jumping jack; (*péj*) puppet
pantois [pɑ̃twa] *adj m*: **rester** ~ to be flabbergasted
pantomime [pɑ̃tɔmim] *nf* mime; (*pièce*)
mime show
pantoufle [pɑ̃tufl(ə)] *nf* slipper
paon [pɑ̃] *nm* peacock
papa [papa] *nm* dad(dy)
pape [pap] *nm* pope
paperasse [papras] (*péj*) *nf* bumf *no pl*, papers *pl*; **paperasserie** (*péj*) *nf* red tape *no
pl*; paperwork *no pl*
papeterie [papetri] *nf* (*usine*) paper mill;
(*magasin*) stationer's (shop)
papier [papje] *nm* paper; (*article*) article;
~*s nmpl* (*aussi:* ~*s d'identité*) (identity) papers; ~ **à lettres** writing paper, notepaper;
~ **buvard** blotting paper; ~ **carbone** carbon paper; ~ **(d')aluminium** aluminium
(*BRIT*) *ou* aluminum (*US*) foil, tinfoil; ~ **de
verre** sandpaper; ~ **hygiénique** toilet paper; ~ **journal** newsprint; (*pour emballer*)
newspaper; ~ **peint** wallpaper
papillon [papijɔ̃] *nm* butterfly; (*fam: contravention*) (parking) ticket; (*TECH: écrou*)
wing nut; ~ **de nuit** moth
papilloter [papijɔte] *vi* to blink, flicker
paquebot [pakbo] *nm* liner
pâquerette [pakrɛt] *nf* daisy
Pâques [pak] *nm, nfpl* Easter
paquet [pakɛ] *nm* packet; (*colis*) parcel;
(*fig: tas*): ~ **de** pile *ou* heap of; **paquet-
cadeau** *nm* gift-wrapped parcel
par [par] *prép* by; **finir** *etc* ~ to end *etc*
with; ~ **amour** out of love; **passer** ~
Lyon/la côte to go via *ou* through Lyons/
along by the coast; ~ **la fenêtre** (*jeter, regarder*) out of the window; **3** ~ **jour/
personne** 3 a *ou* per day/head; **2** ~ **2** two
at a time; in twos; ~ **ici** this way; (*dans le
coin*) round here; ~**-ci**, ~**-là** here and there
parabole [parabɔl] *nf* (*REL*) parable
parachever [paraʃve] *vt* to perfect
parachute [paraʃyt] *nm* parachute
parachutiste [paraʃytist(ə)] *nm/f* parachutist; (*MIL*) paratrooper
parade [parad] *nf* (*spectacle, défilé*) parade;
(*ESCRIME, BOXE*) parry

paradis [paradi] *nm* heaven, paradise
paradoxe [paradɔks(ə)] *nm* paradox
paraffine [parafin] *nf* paraffin
parages [paraʒ] *nmpl*: **dans les** ~ **(de)** in
the area *ou* vicinity (of)
paragraphe [paragraf] *nm* paragraph
paraître [parɛtr(ə)] *vb* +*attrib* to seem,
look, appear ♦ *vi* to appear; (*être visible*) to
show; (*PRESSE, ÉDITION*) to be published,
come out, appear; (*briller*) to show off ♦ *vb
impers*: **il paraît que** ... it seems *ou* appears that ..., they say that ...; **il me paraît
que** ... it seems to me that ...
parallèle [paralɛl] *adj* parallel; (*police,
marché*) unofficial ♦ *nm* (*comparaison*): **faire un** ~ **entre** to draw a parallel between;
(*GÉO*) parallel ♦ *nf* parallel (line)
paralyser [paralize] *vt* to paralyse
paramédical, e, aux [paramedikal] *adj*:
personnel ~ paramedics *pl*, paramedical
workers *pl*
parapet [parapɛ] *nm* parapet
parapher [parafe] *vt* to initial; to sign
paraphrase [parafrɑz] *nf* paraphrase
parapluie [paraplɥi] *nm* umbrella
parasite [parazit] *nm* parasite; ~*s nmpl*
(*TÉL*) interference *sg*
parasol [parasɔl] *nm* parasol, sunshade
paratonnerre [paratɔnɛr] *nm* lightning
conductor
paravent [paravɑ̃] *nm* folding screen
parc [park] *nm* (*public*) park, gardens *pl*;
(*de château etc*) grounds *pl*; (*pour le bétail*)
pen, enclosure; (*d'enfant*) playpen; (*MIL: entrepôt*) depot; (*ensemble d'unités*) stock; (*de
voitures etc*) fleet; ~ **automobile** (*d'un
pays*) number of cars on the roads; ~
(d'attractions) à thème theme park; ~ **de
stationnement** car park
parcelle [parsɛl] *nf* fragment, scrap; (*de terrain*) plot, parcel
parce que [parsk(ə)] *conj* because
parchemin [parʃəmɛ̃] *nm* parchment
parc(o)mètre [park(ɔ)mɛtr(ə)] *nm* parking
meter
parcourir [parkurir] *vt* (*trajet, distance*) to
cover; (*article, livre*) to skim *ou* glance
through; (*lieu*) to go all over, travel up and
down; (*suj: frisson, vibration*) to run
through
parcours [parkur] *nm* (*trajet*) journey; (*itinéraire*) route; (*SPORT: terrain*) course; (:
tour) round; run; lap
par-dessous [pardəsu] *prép, adv* under(neath)
pardessus [pardəsy] *nm* overcoat
par-dessus [pardəsy] *prép* over (the top
of) ♦ *adv* over (the top); ~ **le marché** on
top of all that
par-devant [pardəvɑ̃] *prép* in the presence
of, before ♦ *adv* at the front; round the
front

pardon → partenaire

pardon [paʀdɔ̃] *nm* forgiveness *no pl* ♦ *excl* sorry!; (*pour interpeller etc*) excuse me!; **demander ~ à qn (de)** to apologize to sb (for); **je vous demande ~** I'm sorry; excuse me

pardonner [paʀdɔne] *vt* to forgive; **~ qch à qn** to forgive sb for sth

pare: **~-balles** *adj inv* bulletproof; **~-boue** *nm inv* mudguard; **~-brise** *nm inv* windscreen (*BRIT*), windshield (*US*); **~-chocs** *nm inv* bumper

pareil, le [paʀɛj] *adj* (*identique*) the same, alike; (*similaire*) similar; (*tel*): **un courage/livre ~** such courage/a book, courage/a book like this; **de ~s livres** such books; **ses ~s** one's fellow men; one's peers; **ne pas avoir son(sa) ~(le)** to be second to none; **~ à** the same as; similar to; **sans ~** unparalleled, unequalled

parent, e [paʀã, -ãt] *nm/f*: **un/une ~/e** a relative *ou* relation ♦ *adj*: **être ~ de** to be related to; **~s** *nmpl* (*père et mère*) parents; **parenté** *nf* (*lien*) relationship

parenthèse [paʀãtɛz] *nf* (*ponctuation*) bracket, parenthesis; (*MATH*) bracket; (*digression*) parenthesis, digression; **ouvrir/fermer la ~** to open/close the brackets; **entre ~s** in brackets; (*fig*) incidentally

parer [paʀe] *vt* to adorn; (*CULIN*) to dress, trim; (*éviter*) to ward off

paresse [paʀɛs] *nf* laziness; **paresseux, euse** *adj* lazy; (*fig*) slow, sluggish

parfaire [paʀfɛʀ] *vt* to perfect

parfait, e [paʀfɛ, -ɛt] *adj* perfect ♦ *nm* (*LING*) perfect (tense); **parfaitement** *adv* perfectly ♦ *excl* (most) certainly

parfois [paʀfwa] *adv* sometimes

parfum [paʀfœ̃] *nm* (*produit*) perfume, scent; (*odeur: de fleur*) scent, fragrance; (: *de tabac, vin*) aroma; (*goût*) flavour; **parfumé, e** *adj* (*fleur, fruit*) fragrant; (*femme*) perfumed; **parfumé au café** coffee-flavoured; **parfumer** *vt* (*suj: odeur, bouquet*) to perfume; (*mouchoir*) to put scent *ou* perfume on; (*crème, gâteau*) to flavour; **parfumerie** *nf* (*commerce*) perfumery; (*produits*) perfumes *pl*; (*boutique*) perfume shop

pari [paʀi] *nm* bet, wager; (*SPORT*) bet

paria [paʀja] *nm* outcast

parier [paʀje] *vt* to bet

Paris [paʀi] *n* Paris; **parisien, ne** *adj* Parisian; (*GÉO, ADMIN*) Paris *cpd* ♦ *nm/f*: **Parisien, ne** Parisian

paritaire [paʀitɛʀ] *adj* joint

parjure [paʀʒyʀ] *nm* perjury

parking [paʀkiŋ] *nm* (*lieu*) car park

parlant, e [paʀlã, -ãt] *adj* (*fig*) graphic, vivid; eloquent; (*CINÉMA*) talking

parlement [paʀləmã] *nm* parliament; **parlementaire** *adj* parliamentary ♦ *nm/f* member of parliament

parlementer [paʀləmãte] *vi* to negotiate, parley

parler [paʀle] *vi* to speak, talk; (*avouer*) to talk; **~ (à qn) de** to talk *ou* speak (to sb) about; **~ le/en français** to speak French/in French; **~ affaires** to talk business; **~ en dormant** to talk in one's sleep; **sans ~ de** (*fig*) not to mention, to say nothing of; **tu parles!** you must be joking!

parloir [paʀlwaʀ] *nm* (*de prison, d'hôpital*) visiting room; (*REL*) parlour

parmi [paʀmi] *prép* among(st)

paroi [paʀwa] *nf* wall; (*cloison*) partition; **~ rocheuse** rock face

paroisse [paʀwas] *nf* parish

parole [paʀɔl] *nf* (*faculté*): **la ~** speech; (*mot, promesse*) word; **~s** *nfpl* (*MUS*) words, lyrics; **tenir ~** to keep one's word; **prendre la ~** to speak; **demander la ~** to ask for permission to speak; **je le crois sur ~** I'll take his word for it

parquer [paʀke] *vt* (*voiture, matériel*) to park; (*bestiaux*) to pen (in *ou* up)

parquet [paʀkɛ] *nm* (*parquet*) floor; (*JUR*): **le ~** the Public Prosecutor's department

parrain [paʀɛ̃] *nm* godfather; (*d'un nouvel adhérent*) sponsor, proposer

parrainer [paʀene] *vt* (*suj: entreprise*) to sponsor

pars *vb voir* **partir**

parsemer [paʀsəme] *vt* (*suj: feuilles, papiers*) to be scattered over; **~ qch de** to scatter sth with

part [paʀ] *nf* (*qui revient à qn*) share; (*fraction, partie*) part; (*FINANCE*) (non-voting) share; **prendre ~ à** (*débat etc*) to take part in; (*soucis, douleur de qn*) to share in; **faire ~ de qch à qn** to announce sth to sb, inform sb of sth; **pour ma ~** as for me, as far as I'm concerned; **à ~ entière** full; **de la ~ de** (*au nom de*) on behalf of; (*donné par*) from; **de toute(s) ~(s)** from all sides *ou* quarters; **de ~ et d'autre** on both sides, on either side; **de ~ en ~** right through; **d'une ~ ... d'autre ~** on the one hand ... on the other hand; **à ~** *adv* separately; (*de côté*) aside ♦ *prép* apart from, except for ♦ *adj* exceptional, special; **faire la ~ des choses** to make allowances

partage [paʀtaʒ] *nm* dividing up; sharing (out) *no pl*, share-out; sharing; **recevoir qch en ~** to receive sth as one's share (*ou* lot)

partager [paʀtaʒe] *vt* to share; (*distribuer, répartir*) to share (out); (*morceler, diviser*) to divide (up); **se ~** *vt* (*héritage etc*) to share between themselves (*ou* ourselves)

partance [paʀtãs] *nf*: **en ~** *adv* outbound, due to leave; **en ~ pour** (bound) for

partant [paʀtã] *vb voir* **partir** ♦ *nm* (*SPORT*) starter; (*HIPPISME*) runner

partenaire [paʀtənɛʀ] *nm/f* partner

parterre [paʀtɛʀ] nm (de fleurs) (flower) bed; (THÉÂTRE) stalls pl

parti [paʀti] nm (POL) party; (décision) course of action; (personne à marier) match; **tirer ~ de** to take advantage of, turn to good account; **prendre le ~ de qn** to stand up for sb, side with sb; **prendre ~ (pour/contre)** to take sides ou a stand (for/against); **prendre son ~ de** to come to terms with; **~ pris** bias

partial, e, aux [paʀsjal, -o] adj biased, partial

participant, e [paʀtisipɑ̃, -ɑ̃t] nm/f participant; (à un concours) entrant

participation [paʀtisipasjɔ̃] nf participation; sharing; (COMM) interest; **la ~ aux bénéfices** profit-sharing

participe [paʀtisip] nm participle

participer [paʀtisipe]: **~ à** vt (course, réunion) to take part in; (profits etc) to share in; (frais etc) to contribute to; (chagrin, succès de qn) to share (in)

particularité [paʀtikylaʀite] nf particularity; (distinctive) characteristic

particule [paʀtikyl] nf particle

particulier, ière [paʀtikylje, -jɛʀ] adj (personnel, privé) private; (spécial) special, particular; (caractéristique) characteristic, distinctive; (spécifique) particular ♦ nm (individu: ADMIN) private individual; **~ à** peculiar to; **en ~** (surtout) in particular, particularly; (en privé) in private; **particulièrement** adv particularly

partie [paʀti] nf (gén) part; (profession, spécialité) field, subject; (JUR etc: protagonistes) party; (de cartes, tennis etc) game; **une ~ de campagne/de pêche** an outing in the country/a fishing party ou trip; **en ~** partly, in part; **faire ~ de** to belong to; (suj: chose) to be part of; **prendre qn à ~** to take sb to task; (malmener) to set on sb; **en grande ~** largely, in the main; **~ civile** (JUR) party claiming damages in a criminal case

partiel, le [paʀsjɛl] adj partial ♦ nm (SCOL) class exam

partir [paʀtiʀ] vi (gén) to go; (quitter) to go, leave; (s'éloigner) to go (ou drive etc) away ou off; (moteur) to start; **~ de** (lieu: quitter) to leave; (: commencer à) to start from; (date) to run ou start from; **à ~ de** from

partisan, e [paʀtizɑ̃, -an] nm/f partisan ♦ adj: **être ~ de qch/de faire** to be in favour of sth/doing

partition [paʀtisjɔ̃] nf (MUS) score

partout [paʀtu] adv everywhere; **~ où il allait** everywhere ou wherever he went; **trente ~** (TENNIS) thirty all

paru pp de paraître

parure [paʀyʀ] nf (bijoux etc) finery no pl; jewellery no pl; (assortiment) set

parution [paʀysjɔ̃] nf publication, appearance

parvenir [paʀvəniʀ]: **~ à** vt (atteindre) to reach; (réussir): **~ à faire** to manage to do, succeed in doing; **faire ~ qch à qn** to have sth sent to sb

parvis [paʀvi] nm square (in front of a church)

pas¹ [pɑ] nm (allure, mesure) pace; (démarche) tread; (enjambée, DANSE) step; (bruit) (foot)step; (trace) footprint; (TECH: de vis, d'écrou) thread; **~ à ~** step by step; **au ~** at walking pace; **à ~ de loup** stealthily; **faire les cent ~** to pace up and down; **faire les premiers ~** to make the first move; **sur le ~ de la porte** on the doorstep

─────── *MOT CLÉ* ───────

pas² [pɑ] adv **1** (en corrélation avec ne, non etc) not; **il ne pleure ~** he does not ou doesn't cry; he's not ou isn't crying; **il n'a ~ pleuré/ne pleurera ~** he did not ou didn't/will not ou won't cry; **ils n'ont ~ de voiture/d'enfants** they haven't got a car/any children, they have no car/children; **il m'a dit de ne ~ le faire** he told me not to do it; **non ~ que ...** not that ...

2 (employé sans ne etc): **~ moi** not me; not I, I don't (ou can't etc); **une pomme ~ mûre** an apple which isn't ripe; **~ plus tard qu'hier** only yesterday; **~ du tout** not at all

3: **~ mal** not bad; not badly; **~ mal de** quite a lot of

──────────────────────

passage [pɑsaʒ] nm (fait de passer) voir passer; (lieu, prix de la traversée, extrait) passage; (chemin) way; **de ~** (touristes) passing through; (amants etc) casual; **~ à niveau** level crossing; **~ clouté** pedestrian crossing; **"~ interdit"** "no entry"; **~ protégé** right of way over secondary road(s) on your right; **~ souterrain** subway (BRIT), underpass

passager, ère [pɑsaʒe, -ɛʀ] adj passing ♦ nm/f passenger; **~ clandestin** stowaway

passant, e [pɑsɑ̃, -ɑ̃t] adj (rue, endroit) busy ♦ nm/f passer-by; **en ~** in passing

passe [pɑs] nf (SPORT, magnétique, NAVIG) pass ♦ nm (passe-partout) master ou skeleton key; **être en ~ de faire** to be on the way to doing

passé, e [pɑse] adj (événement, temps) past; (couleur, tapisserie) faded ♦ prép after ♦ nm past; (LING) past (tense); **~ de mode** out of fashion; **~ composé** perfect (tense); **~ simple** past historic

passe: **~-droit** nm special privilege; **~-montagne** nm balaclava; **~-partout** nm inv master ou skeleton key ♦ adj inv all-purpose; **~-~** nm: **tour de ~-~** trick, sleight of hand no pl

passeport [paspɔʀ] nm passport
passer [pase] vi (se rendre, aller) to go;
(voiture, piétons: défiler) to pass (by), go by;
(faire une halte rapide: facteur, laitier etc) to
come, call; (: pour rendre visite) to call ou
drop in; (air, lumière: franchir un obstacle
etc) to get through; (accusé, projet de loi):
~ **devant** to come before; (film, émission)
to be on; (temps, jours) to pass, go by;
(couleur, papier) to fade; (mode) to die out;
(douleur) to pass, go away; (CARTES) to
pass; (SCOL) to go up (to the next class) ♦
vt (frontière, rivière etc) to cross; (douane)
to go through; (examen) to sit, take; (visite
médicale etc) to have; (journée, temps) to
spend; (donner): ~ **qch à qn** to pass sth to
sb; to give sb sth; (transmettre): ~ **qch à
qn** to pass sth on to sb; (enfiler: vêtement)
to slip on; (faire entrer, mettre): **(faire)** ~
qch dans/par to get sth into/through;
(café) to pour the water on; (thé, soupe) to
strain; (film, pièce) to show, put on; (disque) to play, put on; (marché, accord) to
agree on; (tolérer): ~ **qch à qn** to let sb get
away with sth; **se** ~ vi (avoir lieu: scène,
action) to take place; (se dérouler: entretien
etc) to go; (s'écouler: semaine etc) to pass,
go by; (arriver): **que s'est-il passé?** what
happened?; **se** ~ **de** to go ou do without;
se ~ **les mains sous l'eau/de l'eau sur le
visage** to put one's hands under the tap/
run water over one's face; ~ **par** to go
through; ~ **sur** (faute, détail inutile) to pass
over; ~ **avant qch/qn** (fig) to come before
sth/sb; **laisser** ~ (air, lumière, personne) to
let through; (occasion) to let slip, miss; (erreur) to overlook; ~ **à la radio/télévision**
to be on the radio/on television; ~ **pour
riche** to be taken for a rich man; ~ **en seconde**, ~ **la seconde** (AUTO) to change
into second; ~ **le balai/l'aspirateur** to
sweep up/hoover; **je vous passe M. X** (je
vous mets en communication avec lui) I'm
putting you through to Mr X; (je lui passe
l'appareil) here is Mr X, I'll hand you over
to Mr X
passerelle [pasʀɛl] nf footbridge; (de navire, avion) gangway
passe-temps [pastɑ̃] nm inv pastime
passeur, euse [pasœʀ, -øz] nm/f smuggler
passible [pasibl(ə)] adj: ~ **de** liable to
passif, ive [pasif, -iv] adj passive ♦ nm
(LING) passive; (COMM) liabilities pl
passion [pasjɔ̃] nf passion; **passionnant,
e** adj fascinating; **passionné, e** adj passionate; impassioned; **passionner** vt (personne) to fascinate, grip; **se passionner
pour** to take an avid interest in; to have a
passion for
passoire [paswaʀ] nf sieve; (à légumes)
colander; (à thé) strainer
pastèque [pastɛk] nf watermelon

pasteur [pastœʀ] nm (protestant) minister,
pastor
pastille [pastij] nf (à sucer) lozenge,
pastille; (de papier etc) (small) disc
patate [patat] nf: ~ **douce** sweet potato
patauger [patoʒe] vi (pour s'amuser) to
splash about; (avec effort) to wade about
pâte [pat] nf (à tarte) pastry; (à pain)
dough; (à frire) batter; (substance molle)
paste; cream; ~s nfpl (macaroni etc) pasta
sg; ~ **à modeler** modelling clay, Plasticine
(®: BRIT); ~ **brisée** shortcrust pastry; ~
d'amandes almond paste; ~ **de fruits** crystallized fruit no pl
pâté [pate] nm (charcuterie) pâté; (tache)
ink blot; (de sable) sandpie; ~ **de maisons**
block (of houses); ~ **en croûte** ≈ pork pie
pâtée [pate] nf mash, feed
patente [patɑ̃t] nf (COMM) trading licence
paternel, le [patɛʀnɛl] adj (amour, soins)
fatherly; (ligne, autorité) paternal
pâteux, euse [patø, -øz] adj thick; pasty
pathétique [patetik] adj moving
patience [pasjɑ̃s] nf patience
patient, e [pasjɑ̃, -ɑ̃t] adj, nm/f patient
patienter [pasjɑ̃te] vi to wait
patin [patɛ̃] nm skate; (sport) skating; ~s (à
glace) (ice) skates; ~s **à roulettes** roller
skates
patinage [patinaʒ] nm skating
patiner [patine] vi to skate; (embrayage) to
slip; (roue, voiture) to spin; **se** ~ vi (meuble, cuir) to acquire a sheen; **patineur,
euse** nm/f skater; **patinoire** nf skating
rink, (ice) rink
pâtir [patiʀ]: ~ **de** vt to suffer because of
pâtisserie [patisʀi] nf (boutique) cake
shop; (métier) confectionery; (à la maison)
pastry- ou cake-making, baking; ~s nfpl
(gâteaux) pastries, cakes; **pâtissier, ière**
nm/f pastrycook; confectioner
patois [patwa] nm dialect, patois
patrie [patʀi] nf homeland
patrimoine [patʀimwan] nm inheritance,
patrimony; (culture) heritage
patriotique [patʀijɔtik] adj patriotic
patron, ne [patʀɔ̃, -ɔn] nm/f boss; (REL)
patron saint ♦ nm (COUTURE) pattern
patronat [patʀɔna] nm employers pl
patronner [patʀɔne] vt to sponsor, support
patrouille [patʀuj] nf patrol
patte [pat] nf (jambe) leg; (pied: de chien,
chat) paw; (: d'oiseau) foot; (languette)
strap
pâturage [patyʀaʒ] nm pasture
pâture [patyʀ] nf food
paume [pom] nf palm
paumé, e [pome] (fam) nm/f drop-out
paumer [pome] (fam) vt to lose
paupière [popjɛʀ] nf eyelid
pause [poz] nf (arrêt) break; (en parlant,
MUS) pause

pauvre [povʀ(ə)] *adj* poor; **pauvreté** *nf* (*état*) poverty

pavaner [pavane]: **se ~** *vi* to strut about

pavé, e [pave] *adj* paved; cobbled ♦ *nm* (*bloc*) paving stone; cobblestone; (*pavage*) paving

pavillon [pavijɔ̃] *nm* (*de banlieue*) small (detached) house; (*kiosque*) lodge; pavilion; (*drapeau*) flag

pavoiser [pavwaze] *vi* to put out flags; (*fig*) to rejoice, exult

pavot [pavo] *nm* poppy

payant, e [pɛjɑ̃, -ɑ̃t] *adj* (*spectateurs etc*) paying; (*fig: entreprise*) profitable; **c'est ~** you have to pay, there is a charge

paye [pɛj] *nf* pay, wages *pl*

payer [peje] *vt* (*créancier, employé, loyer*) to pay; (*achat, réparations, fig: faute*) to pay for ♦ *vi* to pay; (*métier*) to be well-paid; (*tactique etc*) to pay off; **il me l'a fait ~ 10 F** he charged me 10 F for it; **~ qch à qn** to buy sth for sb, buy sb sth; **cela ne paie pas de mine** it doesn't look much

pays [pei] *nm* country; land; region; village; **du ~** local

paysage [peizaʒ] *nm* landscape

paysan, ne [peizɑ̃, -an] *nm/f* countryman(woman); farmer; (*péj*) peasant ♦ *adj* country *cpd*, farming; farmers'

Pays-Bas [peiba] *nmpl*: **les ~** the Netherlands

PC *nm* (*INFORM*) PC

PDG *sigle m* = **président directeur général**

péage [peaʒ] *nm* toll; (*endroit*) tollgate; **pont à ~** toll bridge

peau, x [po] *nf* skin; **gants de ~** fine leather gloves; **~ de chamois** (*chiffon*) chamois leather, shammy; **Peau-Rouge** *nm/f* Red Indian, redskin

péché [peʃe] *nm* sin

pêche [pɛʃ] *nf* (*sport, activité*) fishing; (*poissons pêchés*) catch; (*fruit*) peach; **~ à la ligne** (*en rivière*) angling

pécher [peʃe] *vi* (*REL*) to sin; (*fig: personne*) to err; (: *chose*) to be flawed

pêcher [peʃe] *nm* peach tree ♦ *vi* to go fishing ♦ *vt* to catch; to fish for

pécheur, eresse [peʃœʀ, peʃʀɛs] *nm/f* sinner

pêcheur [pɛʃœʀ] *nm* fisherman; angler

pécule [pekyl] *nm* savings *pl*, nest egg

pécuniaire [pekynjɛʀ] *adj* financial

pédagogie [pedagoʒi] *nf* educational methods *pl*, pedagogy; **pédagogique** *adj* educational

pédale [pedal] *nf* pedal

pédalo [pedalo] *nm* pedal-boat

pédant, e [pedɑ̃, -ɑ̃t] (*péj*) *adj* pedantic

pédestre [pedɛstʀ(ə)] *adj*: **tourisme ~** hiking

pédiatre [pedjatʀ(ə)] *nm/f* paediatrician, child specialist

pédicure [pedikyʀ] *nm/f* chiropodist

pègre [pɛgʀ(ə)] *nf* underworld

peignais *etc vb voir* **peindre; peigner**

peigne [pɛɲ] *nm* comb

peigner [peɲe] *vt* to comb (the hair of); **se ~** *vi* to comb one's hair

peignoir [peɲwaʀ] *nm* dressing gown; **~ de bain** bathrobe

peindre [pɛ̃dʀ(ə)] *vt* to paint; (*fig*) to portray, depict

peine [pɛn] *nf* (*affliction*) sorrow, sadness *no pl*; (*mal, effort*) trouble *no pl*, effort; (*difficulté*) difficulty; (*punition, châtiment*) punishment; (*JUR*) sentence; **faire de la ~ à qn** to distress *ou* upset sb; **prendre la ~ de faire** to go to the trouble of doing; **se donner de la ~** to make an effort; **ce n'est pas la ~ de faire** there's no point in doing, it's not worth doing; **à ~** scarcely, hardly, barely; **à ~ ... que** hardly ... than; **défense d'afficher sous ~ d'amende** bill-posters will be fined; **~ capitale** *ou* **de mort** capital punishment; **~ de mort** death sentence; **peiner** *vi* to work hard; to struggle; (*moteur, voiture*) to labour ♦ *vt* to grieve, sadden

peintre [pɛ̃tʀ(ə)] *nm* painter; **~ en bâtiment** house painter

peinture [pɛ̃tyʀ] *nf* painting; (*couche de couleur, couleur*) paint; (*surfaces peintes: aussi:* **~s**) paintwork; **"~ fraîche"** "wet paint"; **~ mate/brillante** matt/gloss paint

péjoratif, ive [peʒɔʀatif, -iv] *adj* pejorative, derogatory

pelage [pəlaʒ] *nm* coat, fur

pêle-mêle [pɛlmɛl] *adv* higgledy-piggledy

peler [pəle] *vt, vi* to peel

pèlerin [pɛlʀɛ̃] *nm* pilgrim

pelle [pɛl] *nf* shovel; (*d'enfant, de terrassier*) spade; **~ mécanique** mechanical digger

pellicule [pelikyl] *nf* film; **~s** *nfpl* (*MÉD*) dandruff *sg*

pelote [pəlɔt] *nf* (*de fil, laine*) ball; (*d'épingles*) pin cushion; **~ basque** pelota

peloton [pəlɔtɔ̃] *nm* group, squad; (*CYCLISME*) pack; **~ d'exécution** firing squad

pelotonner [pəlɔtɔne]: **se ~** *vi* to curl (o.s.) up

pelouse [pəluz] *nf* lawn

peluche [pəlyʃ] *nf*: **animal en ~** fluffy animal, soft toy

pelure [pəlyʀ] *nf* peeling, peel *no pl*

pénal, e, aux [penal, -o] *adj* penal

pénalité [penalite] *nf* penalty

penaud, e [pəno, -od] *adj* sheepish, contrite

penchant [pɑ̃ʃɑ̃] *nm* tendency, propensity; liking, fondness

pencher [pɑ̃ʃe] *vi* to tilt, lean over ♦ *vt* to tilt; **se ~** *vi* to lean over; (*se baisser*) to bend down; **se ~ sur** to bend over; (*fig: problème*) to look into; **se ~ au dehors** to lean out; **~ pour** to be inclined to favour

pendaison [pɑ̃dɛzɔ̃] nf hanging
pendant [pɑ̃dɑ̃] nm: **faire ~ à** to match;
to be the counterpart of ♦ prép during; **~ que** while
pendentif [pɑ̃dɑ̃tif] nm pendant
penderie [pɑ̃dʀi] nf wardrobe
pendre [pɑ̃dʀ(ə)] vt, vi to hang; **se ~ (à)** (se suicider) to hang o.s. (on); **~ à** to hang (down) from; **~ qch à** to hang sth (up) on
pendule [pɑ̃dyl] nf clock ♦ nm pendulum
pénétrer [penetʀe] vi, vt to penetrate; **~ dans** to enter; (suj: projectile) to penetrate (: air, eau) to come into, get into
pénible [penibl(ə)] adj (astreignant) hard; (affligeant) painful; (personne, caractère) tiresome; **~ment** adv with difficulty
péniche [peniʃ] nf barge
pénicilline [penisilin] nf penicillin
péninsule [penɛ̃syl] nf peninsula
pénis [penis] nm penis
pénitence [penitɑ̃s] nf (repentir) penitence; (peine) penance
pénitencier [penitɑ̃sje] nm penitentiary
pénombre [penɔ̃bʀ(ə)] nf half light; darkness
pensée [pɑ̃se] nf thought; (démarche, doctrine) thinking no pl; (BOT) pansy; **en ~** in one's mind
penser [pɑ̃se] vi to think ♦ vt to think; (concevoir: problème, machine) to think out; **~ à** to think of; (songer à: ami, vacances) to think of ou about; (réfléchir à: problème, offre): **~ à qch** to think about sth ou think sth over; **faire ~ à** to remind one of; **~ faire qch** to be thinking of doing sth, intend to do sth
pensif, ive [pɑ̃sif, -iv] adj pensive, thoughtful
pension [pɑ̃sjɔ̃] nf (allocation) pension; (prix du logement) board and lodgings, bed and board; (maison particulière) boarding house; (hôtel) guesthouse, hotel; (école) boarding school; **prendre qn en ~** to take sb (in) as a lodger; **mettre en ~** to send to boarding school; **~ alimentaire** (d'étudiant) living allowance; (de divorcée) maintenance allowance; alimony; **~ complète** full board; **~ de famille** boarding house, guesthouse; **pensionnaire** nm/f boarder; guest; **pensionnat** nm boarding school
pente [pɑ̃t] nf slope; **en ~** sloping
Pentecôte [pɑ̃tkot] nf: **la ~** Whitsun (BRIT), Pentecost
pénurie [penyʀi] nf shortage
pépé [pepe] (fam) nm grandad
pépin [pepɛ̃] nm (BOT: graine) pip; (ennui) snag, hitch
pépinière [pepinjɛʀ] nf nursery
perçant, e [pɛʀsɑ̃, -ɑ̃t] adj sharp, keen; piercing, shrill
percée [pɛʀse] nf (trouée) opening; (MIL, technologique) breakthrough; (SPORT)

break
perce-neige [pɛʀsənɛʒ] nf inv snowdrop
percepteur [pɛʀsɛptœʀ] nm tax collector
perception [pɛʀsɛpsjɔ̃] nf perception; (d'impôts etc) collection; (bureau) tax office
percer [pɛʀse] vt to pierce; (ouverture etc) to make; (mystère, énigme) to penetrate ♦ vi to come through; to break through; **~ une dent** to cut a tooth; **perceuse** nf drill
percevoir [pɛʀsəvwaʀ] vt (distinguer) to perceive, detect; (taxe, impôt) to collect; (revenu, indemnité) to receive
perche [pɛʀʃ(ə)] nf (bâton) pole
percher [pɛʀʃe] vt, vi to perch; **se ~** vi to perch; **perchoir** nm perch
perçois etc vb voir **percevoir**
percolateur [pɛʀkɔlatœʀ] nm percolator
perçu, e pp de **percevoir**
percussion [pɛʀkysjɔ̃] nf percussion
percuter [pɛʀkyte] vt to strike; (suj: véhicule) to crash into
perdant, e [pɛʀdɑ̃, -ɑ̃t] nm/f loser
perdition [pɛʀdisjɔ̃] nf: **en ~** (NAVIG) in distress; **lieu de ~** den of vice
perdre [pɛʀdʀ(ə)] vt to lose; (gaspiller: temps, argent) to waste; (personne: moralement etc) to ruin ♦ vi to lose; (sur une vente) to lose out; **se ~** vi (s'égarer) to get lost, lose one's way; (fig) to go to waste; to disappear, vanish
perdrix [pɛʀdʀi] nf partridge
perdu, e [pɛʀdy] pp de **perdre** ♦ adj (isolé) out-of-the-way; (COMM: emballage) nonreturnable; (malade): **il est ~** there's no hope left for him; **à vos moments ~s in** your spare time
père [pɛʀ] nm father; **~s** nmpl (ancêtres) forefathers; **~ de famille** father; family man; **le ~ Noël** Father Christmas
perfectionné, e [pɛʀfɛksjɔne] adj sophisticated
perfectionner [pɛʀfɛksjɔne] vt to improve, perfect
perforatrice [pɛʀfɔʀatʀis] nf (pour cartes) card-punch; (de bureau) punch
perforer [pɛʀfɔʀe] vt to perforate; to punch a hole (ou holes) in; (ticket, bande, carte) to punch
performant, e [pɛʀfɔʀmɑ̃, -ɑ̃t] adj: **très ~** high-performance cpd
perfusion [pɛʀfyzjɔ̃] nf: **faire une ~ à qn** to put sb on a drip
péril [peʀil] nm peril
périmé, e [peʀime] adj (out)dated; (ADMIN) out-of-date, expired
périmètre [peʀimɛtʀ(ə)] nm perimeter
période [peʀjɔd] nf period; **périodique** adj (phases) periodic; (publication) periodical ♦ nm periodical
péripéties [peʀipesi] nfpl events, episodes
périphérique [peʀifeʀik] adj (quartiers) outlying; (ANAT, TECH) peripheral; (station

de radio) operating from outside France ♦
nm (AUTO) ring road; (INFORM) peripheral
périple [peʀipl(ə)] nm journey
périr [peʀiʀ] vi to die, perish
périssable [peʀisabl(ə)] adj perishable
perle [pɛʀl(ə)] nf pearl; (de plastique, métal,
sueur) bead
perlé, e [pɛʀle] adj: **grève ~e** go-slow
perler [pɛʀle] vi to form in droplets
permanence [pɛʀmanɑ̃s] nf permanence;
(local) (duty) office; emergency service; **assurer une ~** (service public, bureaux) to
operate ou maintain a basic service; **être
de ~** to be on call ou duty; **en ~** permanently; continuously
permanent, e [pɛʀmanɑ̃, -ɑ̃t] adj permanent; (spectacle) continuous; **permanente**
nf perm
perméable [pɛʀmeabl(ə)] adj (terrain) per-
meable; **~ à** (fig) receptive ou open to
permettre [pɛʀmɛtʀ(ə)] vt to allow, permit; **~ à qn de faire/qch** to allow sb to
do/sth; **se ~ de faire** to take the liberty of
doing; **permettez!** excuse me!
permis [pɛʀmi] nm permit, licence; **~ de
chasse** hunting permit; **~ (de conduire)**
(driving) licence (BRIT), (driver's) license
(US); **~ de construire** planning permission
(BRIT), building permit (US); **~ de séjour**
residence permit; **~ de travail** work permit
permission [pɛʀmisjɔ̃] nf permission; (MIL)
leave; **avoir la ~ de faire** to have permission to do; **en ~** on leave
permuter [pɛʀmyte] vt to change around,
permutate ♦ vi to change, swap
Pérou [peʀu] nm Peru
perpétuel, le [pɛʀpetɥɛl] adj perpetual;
(ADMIN etc) permanent; for life
perpétuité [pɛʀpetɥite] nf: **à ~** adj, adv for
life; **être condamné à ~** to receive a life
sentence
perplexe [pɛʀplɛks(ə)] adj perplexed,
puzzled
perquisitionner [pɛʀkizisjɔne] vi to carry
out a search
perron [peʀɔ̃] nm steps pl (in front of mansion etc)
perroquet [peʀɔkɛ] nm parrot
perruche [peʀyʃ] nf budgerigar (BRIT),
budgie (BRIT), parakeet (US)
perruque [peʀyk] nf wig
persan, e [pɛʀsɑ̃, -an] adj Persian
persécuter [pɛʀsekyte] vt to persecute
persévérer [pɛʀsevere] vi to persevere
persiennes [pɛʀsjɛn] nfpl (metal) shutters
persiflage [pɛʀsiflaʒ] nm mockery no pl
persil [pɛʀsi] nm parsley
Persique [pɛʀsik] adj: **le golfe ~** the (Persian) Gulf
persistant, e [pɛʀsistɑ̃, -ɑ̃t] adj persistent;
(feuilles) evergreen
persister [pɛʀsiste] vi to persist; **~ à faire**

qch to persist in doing sth
personnage [pɛʀsɔnaʒ] nm (notable) personality; figure; (individu) character, individual; (THÉÂTRE) character; (PEINTURE)
figure
personnalité [pɛʀsɔnalite] nf personality;
(personnage) prominent figure
personne [pɛʀsɔn] nf person ♦ pron nobody, no one; (quelqu'un) anybody, anyone; **~s** nfpl (gens) people pl; **il n'y a ~**
there's nobody there, there isn't anybody
there; **~ âgée** elderly person; **personnel,
le** adj personal ♦ nm staff, personnel; **personnellement** adv personally
perspective [pɛʀspɛktiv] nf (ART) perspective; (vue, coup d'œil) view; (point de vue)
viewpoint, angle; (chose escomptée, envisa-
gée) prospect; **en ~** in prospect
perspicace [pɛʀspikas] adj clear-sighted,
gifted with (ou showing) insight
persuader [pɛʀsɥade] vt: **~ qn (de/de faire)** to persuade sb (of/to do)
perte [pɛʀt(ə)] nf loss; (de temps) waste;
(fig: morale) ruin; **à ~** (COMM) at a loss; **à
~ de vue** as far as the eye can (ou could)
see; **~ sèche** dead loss; **~s blanches** (vaginal) discharge sg
pertinemment [pɛʀtinamɑ̃] adv to the
point; full well
pertinent, e [pɛʀtinɑ̃, -ɑ̃t] adj apt, relevant
perturbation [pɛʀtyʀbasjɔ̃] nf disruption;
perturbation; **~ (atmosphérique)** at-
mospheric disturbance
perturber [pɛʀtyʀbe] vt to disrupt; (PSYCH)
to perturb, disturb
pervers, e [pɛʀvɛʀ, -ɛʀs(ə)] adj perverted,
depraved; perverse
pervertir [pɛʀvɛʀtiʀ] vt to pervert
pesant, e [pəzɑ̃, -ɑ̃t] adj heavy; (fig) bur-
densome
pesanteur [pəzɑ̃tœʀ] nf gravity
pèse-personne [pɛzpɛʀsɔn] nm (bathroom) scales pl
peser [pəze] vt to weigh ♦ vi to be heavy;
(fig) to carry weight; **~ sur** (fig) to lie
heavy on; to influence
pessimiste [pesimist(ə)] adj pessimistic ♦
nm/f pessimist
peste [pɛst(ə)] nf plague
pester [pɛste] vi: **~ contre** to curse
pétale [petal] nm petal
pétanque [petɑ̃k] nf type of bowls
pétarader [petaʀade] vi to backfire
pétard [petaʀ] nm banger (BRIT), firecrack-
er
péter [pete] vi (fam: casser, sauter) to burst;
to bust; (fam!) to fart (!)
pétillant, e [petijɑ̃, -ɑ̃t] adj (eau etc) sparkling
pétiller [petije] vi (flamme, bois) to crackle;
(mousse, champagne) to bubble; (yeux) to
sparkle

petit, e [pəti, -it] *adj* (*gén*) small; (*main, objet, colline, en âge: enfant*) small, little; (*voyage*) short, little; (*bruit etc*) faint, slight; (*mesquin*) mean; **~s** *nmpl* (*d'un animal*) young *pl*; **faire des ~s** to have kittens (*ou* puppies *etc*); **les tout-petits** the little ones, the tiny tots; **~ à ~** bit by bit, gradually; **~(e) ami(e)** boyfriend/girlfriend; **~ déjeuner** breakfast; **~ pain** (bread) roll; **les ~es annonces** the small ads; **~s pois** garden peas; **~-bourgeois** (*f* **~-bourgeoise**: *péj*) *adj* middle-class; **~-fille** *nf* granddaughter; **~-fils** *nm* grandson

pétition [petisjɔ̃] *nf* petition

petits-enfants [pətizɑ̃fɑ̃] *nmpl* grandchildren

petit-suisse [pətisɥis] (*pl* **petits-suisses**) *nm* small individual pot of cream cheese

pétrin [petrɛ̃] *nm* kneading-trough; (*fig*): **dans le ~** in a jam *ou* fix

pétrir [petriʀ] *vt* to knead

pétrole [petʀɔl] *nm* oil; (*pour lampe, réchaud etc*) paraffin (oil); **pétrolier, ière** *adj* oil *cpd* ♦ *nm* oil tanker

─────────── *MOT CLÉ* ───────────

peu [pø] *adv* **1** (*modifiant verbe, adjectif, adverbe*): **il boit ~** he doesn't drink (very) much; **il est ~ bavard** he's not very talkative; **~ avant/après** shortly before/afterwards

2 (*modifiant nom*): **~ de: ~ de gens/ d'arbres** few *ou* not (very) many people/ trees; **il a ~ d'espoir** he hasn't (got) much hope, he has little hope; **pour ~ de temps** for (only) a short while

3: **~ à ~** little by little; **à ~ près** just about, more or less; **à ~ près 10 kg/10F** approximately 10 kg/10F

♦ *nm* **1**: **le ~ de gens qui** the few people who; **le ~ de sable qui** what little sand, the little sand which

2: **un ~** a little; **un petit ~** a little bit; **un ~ d'espoir** a little hope

♦ *pron*: **le savent** few know (it); **avant** *ou* **sous ~** shortly, before long; **de ~** (only) just

─────────────────────────────

peuple [pœpl(ə)] *nm* people

peupler [pœple] *vt* (*pays, région*) to populate; (*étang*) to stock; (*suj: hommes, poissons*) to inhabit; (*fig: imagination, rêves*) to fill

peuplier [pøplije] *nm* poplar (tree)

peur [pœʀ] *nf* fear; **avoir ~ (de/de faire/ que)** to be frightened *ou* afraid (of/of doing/that); **faire ~ à** to frighten; **de ~ de/que** for fear of/that; **peureux, euse** *adj* fearful, timorous

peut *vb voir* **pouvoir**

peut-être [pøtɛtʀ(ə)] *adv* perhaps, maybe; **~ que** perhaps, maybe; **~ bien qu'il fera/**

est he may well do/be

peux *etc vb voir* **pouvoir**

phare [faʀ] *nm* (*en mer*) lighthouse; (*de véhicule*) headlight; **mettre ses ~s** to put on one's headlights; **~s de recul** reversing lights

pharmacie [faʀmasi] *nf* (*magasin*) chemist's (*BRIT*), pharmacy; (*officine*) pharmacy; (*de salle de bain*) medicine cabinet; **pharmacien, ne** *nm/f* pharmacist, chemist (*BRIT*)

phénomène [fenɔmɛn] *nm* phenomenon; (*monstre*) freak

philanthrope [filɑ̃tʀɔp] *nm/f* philanthropist

philatélie [filateli] *nf* philately, stamp collecting

philosophe [filɔzɔf] *nm/f* philosopher ♦ *adj* philosophical

philosophie [filɔzɔfi] *nf* philosophy

phobie [fɔbi] *nf* phobia

phonétique [fɔnetik] *nf* phonetics *sg*

phoque [fɔk] *nm* seal; (*fourrure*) sealskin

phosphorescent, e [fɔsfɔʀesɑ̃, -ɑ̃t] *adj* luminous

photo [fɔto] *nf* photo(graph); **en ~** in *ou* on a photograph; **prendre en ~** to take a photo of; **aimer la/faire de la ~** to like taking/take photos; **~ d'identité** passport photograph; **~copie** *nf* photocopying; photocopy; **~copier** *vt* to photocopy; **~copieuse** [fɔtokɔpjøz] *nf* photocopier; **~graphe** *nm/f* photographer; **~graphie** *nf* (*procédé, technique*) photography; (*cliché*) photograph; **~graphier** *vt* to photograph

phrase [fʀɑz] *nf* (*LING*) sentence; (*propos, MUS*) phrase

physicien, ne [fizisjɛ̃, -ɛn] *nm/f* physicist

physionomie [fizjɔnɔmi] *nf* face

physique [fizik] *adj* physical ♦ *nm* physique ♦ *nf* physics *sg*; **au ~** physically; **~ment** *adv* physically

piaffer [pjafe] *vi* to stamp

piailler [pjaje] *vi* to squawk

pianiste [pjanist(ə)] *nm/f* pianist

piano [pjano] *nm* piano

pianoter [pjanɔte] *vi* to tinkle away (at the piano); (*tapoter*): **~ sur** to drum one's fingers on

pic [pik] *nm* (*instrument*) pick(axe); (*montagne*) peak; (*ZOOL*) woodpecker; **à ~** vertically; (*fig*) just at the right time

pichet [piʃɛ] *nm* jug

picorer [pikɔʀe] *vt* to peck

picoter [pikɔte] *vt* (*suj: oiseau*) to peck ♦ *vi* (*irriter*) to smart, prickle

pie [pi] *nf* magpie; (*fig*) chatterbox

pièce [pjɛs] *nf* (*d'un logement*) room; (*THÉÂTRE*) play; (*de mécanisme, machine*) part; (*de monnaie*) coin; (*COUTURE*) patch; (*document*) document; (*de drap, fragment, de collection*) piece; **dix francs ~** ten francs each; **vendre à la ~** to sell separately; **travailler/payer à la ~** to do piecework/

pay piece rate; **un maillot une ~** a one-piece swimsuit; **un deux-pièces cuisine** a two-room(ed) flat (*BRIT*) *ou* apartment (*US*) with kitchen; **~ à conviction** exhibit; **~ d'eau** ornamental lake *ou* pond; **~ d'identité: avez-vous une ~ d'identité?** have you got any (means of) identification?; **~ montée** tiered cake; **~s détachées** spares, (spare) parts; **~s justificatives** supporting documents

pied [pje] *nm* foot; (*de verre*) stem; (*de table*) leg; (*de lampe*) base; (*plante*) plant; **à ~ on** foot; **à ~ sec** without getting one's feet wet; **au ~ de la lettre** literally; **de ~ en cap** from head to foot; **en ~** (*portrait*) full-length; **avoir ~** to be able to touch the bottom, not to be out of one's depth; **avoir le ~ marin** to be a good sailor; **sur ~** (*debout, rétabli*) up and about; **mettre sur ~** (*entreprise*) to set up; **mettre à ~** to dismiss; to lay off; **~ de vigne** vine

piédestal, aux [pjedɛstal, -o] *nm* pedestal

pied-noir [pjɛnwaʀ] *nm* Algerian-born Frenchman

piège [pjɛʒ] *nm* trap; **prendre au ~** to trap; **piéger** *vt* (*avec une bombe*) to booby-trap; **lettre/voiture piégée** letter-/car-bomb

pierraille [pjɛʀaj] *nf* loose stones *pl*

pierre [pjɛʀ] *nf* stone; **~ à briquet** flint; **~ fine** semiprecious stone; **~ tombale** tombstone; **pierreries** [pjɛʀʀi] *nfpl* gems, precious stones

piétiner [pjetine] *vi* (*trépigner*) to stamp (one's foot); (*marquer le pas*) to stand about; (*fig*) to be at a standstill ♦ *vt* to trample on

piéton, ne [pjetɔ̃, -ɔn] *nm/f* pedestrian; **piétonnier, ière** *adj:* **rue** *ou* **zone piétonnière** pedestrian precinct

pieu, x [pjø] *nm* post; (*pointu*) stake

pieuvre [pjœvʀ(ə)] *nf* octopus

pieux, euse [pjø, -øz] *adj* pious

piffer [pife] (*fam*) *vt:* **je ne peux pas le ~** I can't stand him

pigeon [piʒɔ̃] *nm* pigeon

piger [piʒe] (*fam*) *vi, vt* to understand

pigiste [piʒist(ə)] *nm/f* freelance(r)

pignon [piɲɔ̃] *nm* (*de mur*) gable; (*d'engrenage*) cog(wheel), gearwheel

pile [pil] *nf* (*tas*) pile; (*ÉLEC*) battery ♦ *adv* (*s'arrêter etc*) dead; **à deux heures ~** at two on the dot; **jouer à ~ ou face** to toss up (for it); **~ ou face?** heads or tails?

piler [pile] *vt* to crush, pound

pileux, euse [pilø, -øz] *adj:* **système ~** (body) hair

pilier [pilje] *nm* pillar

piller [pije] *vt* to pillage, plunder, loot

pilon [pilɔ̃] *nm* pestle

pilote [pilɔt] *nm* pilot; (*de char, voiture*) driver ♦ *adj* pilot *cpd*; **~ de course** racing driver; **~ de ligne/d'essai/de chasse** air-line/test/fighter pilot; **~r** [pilɔte] *vt* to pilot, fly; to drive

pilule [pilyl] *nf* pill; **prendre la ~** to be on the pill

piment [pimɑ̃] *nm* (*BOT*) pepper, capsicum; (*fig*) spice, piquancy

pimpant, e [pɛ̃pɑ̃, -ɑ̃t] *adj* spruce

pin [pɛ̃] *nm* pine (tree); (*bois*) pine(wood)

pinard [pinaʀ] (*fam*) *nm* (cheap) wine, plonk (*BRIT*)

pince [pɛ̃s] *nf* (*outil*) pliers *pl*; (*de homard, crabe*) pincer, claw; (*COUTURE: pli*) dart; **~ à épiler** tweezers *pl*; **~ à linge** clothes peg (*BRIT*) *ou* pin (*US*); **~ à sucre** sugar tongs *pl*

pincé, e [pɛ̃se] *adj* (*air*) stiff

pinceau, x [pɛ̃so] *nm* (paint)brush

pincée [pɛ̃se] *nf:* **une ~ de** a pinch of

pincer [pɛ̃se] *vt* to pinch; (*MUS: cordes*) to pluck; (*fam*) to nab

pincettes [pɛ̃sɛt] *nfpl* (*pour le feu*) (fire) tongs

pinède [pinɛd] *nf* pinewood, pine forest

pingouin [pɛ̃gwɛ̃] *nm* penguin

ping-pong [piŋpɔ̃g] ® *nm* table tennis

pingre [pɛ̃gʀ(ə)] *adj* niggardly

pinson [pɛ̃sɔ̃] *nm* chaffinch

pintade [pɛ̃tad] *nf* guinea-fowl

pioche [pjɔʃ] *nf* pickaxe; **piocher** *vt* to dig up (with a pickaxe)

piolet [pjɔlɛ] *nm* ice axe

pion [pjɔ̃] *nm* (*ÉCHECS*) pawn; (*DAMES*) piece

pionnier [pjɔnje] *nm* pioneer

pipe [pip] *nf* pipe

pipeau, x [pipo] *nm* (reed-)pipe

piquant, e [pikɑ̃, -ɑ̃t] *adj* (*barbe, rosier etc*) prickly; (*saveur, sauce*) hot, pungent; (*fig*) racy; biting ♦ *nm* (*épine*) thorn, prickle; (*fig*) spiciness, spice

pique [pik] *nf* pike; (*fig*) cutting remark ♦ *nm* (*CARTES: couleur*) spades *pl*; (*: carte*) spade

pique-nique [piknik] *nm* picnic

piquer [pike] *vt* (*percer*) to prick; (*planter*): **~ qch dans** to stick sth into; (*MÉD*) to give a jab to; (*: animal blessé etc*) to put to sleep; (*suj: insecte, fumée, ortie*) to sting; (*: poivre*) to burn; (*: froid*) to bite; (*COUTURE*) to machine (stitch); (*intérêt etc*) to arouse; (*fam*) to pick up; (*: voler*) to pinch; (*: arrêter*) to nab ♦ *vi* (*avion*) to go into a dive; **se ~ de faire** to pride o.s. on doing; **~ un galop/un cent mètres** to break into a gallop/put on a sprint

piquet [pikɛ] *nm* (*pieu*) post, stake; (*de tente*) peg; **~ de grève** (strike-) picket; **~ d'incendie** fire-fighting squad

piqûre [pikyʀ] *nf* (*d'épingle*) prick; (*d'ortie*) sting; (*de moustique*) bite; (*MÉD*) injection, shot (*US*); (*COUTURE*) (straight) stitch; straight stitching; **faire une ~ à qn** to give sb an injection

pirate [piʀat] *nm, adj* pirate; **~ de l'air** hijacker

pire [piʀ] *adj* worse; *(superlatif)*: **le(la) ~ ...** the worst ... ♦ *nm*: **le ~ (de)** the worst (of)

pis [pi] *nm (de vache)* udder; *(pire)*: **le ~** the worst ♦ *adj, adv* worse; **~-aller** *nm inv* stopgap

piscine [pisin] *nf* (swimming) pool; **~ couverte** indoor (swimming) pool

pissenlit [pisɑ̃li] *nm* dandelion

pistache [pistaʃ] *nf* pistachio (nut)

piste [pist(ə)] *nf (d'un animal, sentier)* track, trail; *(indice)* lead; *(de stade, de magnétophone)* track; *(de cirque)* ring; *(de danse)* floor; *(de patinage)* rink; *(de ski)* run; *(AVIAT)* runway; **~ cyclable** cycle track

pistolet [pistɔlɛ] *nm (arme)* pistol, gun; *(à peinture)* spray gun; **~ à air comprimé** airgun; **~-mitrailleur** *nm* submachine gun

piston [pistɔ̃] *nm (TECH)* piston; **pistonner** *vt (candidat)* to pull strings for

piteux, euse [pitø, -øz] *adj* pitiful *(avant le nom)*, sorry *(avant le nom)*

pitié [pitje] *nf* pity; **faire ~** to inspire pity; **avoir ~ de** *(compassion)* to pity, feel sorry for; *(merci)* to have pity *ou* mercy on

piton [pitɔ̃] *nm (clou)* peg; **~ rocheux** rocky outcrop

pitoyable [pitwajabl(ə)] *adj* pitiful

pitre [pitʀ(ə)] *nm* clown; **pitrerie** *nf* tomfoolery *no pl*

pittoresque [pitɔʀɛsk(ə)] *adj* picturesque

pivot [pivo] *nm* pivot; **pivoter** *vi* to swivel; to revolve

P.J. *sigle f (= police judiciaire)* ≈ CID *(BRIT)*, ≈ FBI *(US)*

placard [plakaʀ] *nm (armoire)* cupboard; *(affiche)* poster, notice; **~er** *vt (affiche)* to put up

place [plas] *nf (emplacement, situation, classement)* place; *(de ville, village)* square; *(espace libre)* room, space; *(de parking)* space; *(siège: de train, cinéma, voiture)* seat; *(emploi)* job; **en ~** *(mettre)* in its place; **sur ~** on the spot; **faire ~ à** to give way to; **faire de la ~** à to make room for; **ça prend de la ~** it takes up a lot of room *ou* space; **à la ~ de** in place of, instead of; **il y a 20 ~s assises/debout** there are 20 seats/there is standing room for 20

placement [plasmɑ̃] *nm* placing; *(FINANCE)* investment; **bureau de ~** employment agency

placer [plase] *vt* to place; *(convive, spectateur)* to seat; *(capital, argent)* to place, invest; *(dans la conversation)* to put *ou* get in; **se ~ au premier rang** to go and stand *(ou* sit) in the first row

plafond [plafɔ̃] *nm* ceiling

plafonner [plafɔne] *vi* to reach one's *(ou* a) ceiling

plage [plaʒ] *nf* beach; *(fig)* band, bracket; *(de disque)* track, band; **~ arrière** *(AUTO)* parcel *ou* back shelf

plagiat [plaʒja] *nm* plagiarism

plaider [plede] *vi (avocat)* to plead; *(plaignant)* to go to court, litigate ♦ *vt* to plead; **~ pour** *(fig)* to speak for; **plaidoyer** *nm (JUR)* speech for the defence; *(fig)* plea

plaie [plɛ] *nf* wound

plaignant, e [plɛɲɑ̃, -ɑ̃t] *nm/f* plaintiff

plaindre [plɛ̃dʀ(ə)] *vt* to pity, feel sorry for; **se ~** *vi (gémir)* to moan; *(protester, rouspéter)*: **se ~ (à qn) (de)** to complain (to sb) (about); *(souffrir)*: **se ~ de** to complain of

plaine [plɛn] *nf* plain

plain-pied [plɛ̃pje] *adv*: **de ~ (avec)** on the same level (as)

plainte [plɛ̃t] *nf (gémissement)* moan, groan; *(doléance)* complaint; **porter ~** to lodge a complaint

plaire [plɛʀ] *vi* to be a success, be successful; to please; **~ à**: **cela me plaît** I like it; **se ~ quelque part** to like being somewhere *ou* like it somewhere; **s'il vous plaît** please

plaisance [plɛzɑ̃s] *nf (aussi: navigation de ~)* (pleasure) sailing, yachting

plaisant, e [plɛzɑ̃, -ɑ̃t] *adj* pleasant; *(histoire, anecdote)* amusing

plaisanter [plɛzɑ̃te] *vi* to joke; **plaisanterie** *nf* joke; joking *no pl*

plaise *etc vb voir* **plaire**

plaisir [plɛziʀ] *nm* pleasure; **faire ~ à qn** *(délibérément)* to be nice to sb, please sb; *(suj: cadeau, nouvelle etc)*: **ceci me fait ~** I'm delighted *ou* very pleased with this; **pour le** *ou* **par ~** for pleasure

plaît *vb voir* **plaire**

plan, e [plɑ̃, -an] *adj* flat ♦ *nm* plan; *(GÉOM)* plane; *(fig)* level, plane; *(CINÉMA)* shot; **au premier/second ~** in the foreground/middle distance; **à l'arrière ~** in the background; **~ d'eau** lake; pond

planche [plɑ̃ʃ] *nf (pièce de bois)* plank, (wooden) board; *(illustration)* plate; **les ~s** *nfpl (THÉÂTRE)* the stage *sg*, the boards; **~ à repasser** ironing board; **~ à roulettes** skateboard; **~ de salut** *(fig)* sheet anchor

plancher [plɑ̃ʃe] *nm* floor; floorboards *pl*; *(fig)* minimum level ♦ *vi* to work hard

planer [plane] *vi* to glide; **~ sur** *(fig)* to hang over; to hover above

planète [planɛt] *nf* planet

planeur [planœʀ] *nm* glider

planification [planifikasjɔ̃] *nf* (economic) planning

planifier [planifje] *vt* to plan

planning [planiŋ] *nm* programme, schedule; **~ familial** family planning

planque [plɑ̃k] *nf (fam) (emploi peu fatigant)* cushy *(BRIT) ou* easy number; *(cachette)* hiding place

plant [plɑ̃] *nm* seedling, young plant

plante [plɑ̃t] *nf* plant; ~ **d'appartement** house *ou* pot plant; ~ **du pied** sole (of the foot)

planter [plɑ̃te] *vt* (*plante*) to plant; (*enfoncer*) to hammer *ou* drive in; (*tente*) to put up, pitch; (*fam*) to dump; to ditch; **se** ~ (*fam: se tromper*) to get it wrong

plantureux, euse [plɑ̃tyʀø, -øz] *adj* copious, lavish; (*femme*) buxom

plaque [plak] *nf* plate; (*de verglas, d'eczéma*) patch; (*avec inscription*) plaque; ~ **chauffante** hotplate; ~ **de chocolat** bar of chocolate; ~ (**minéralogique** *ou* **d'immatriculation**) number (*BRIT*) *ou* license (*US*) plate; ~ **tournante** (*fig*) centre

plaqué, e [plake] *adj*: ~ **or/argent** gold-/silver-plated; ~ **acajou** veneered in mahogany

plaquer [plake] *vt* (*aplatir*): ~ **qch sur** *ou* **contre** to make sth stick *ou* cling to; (*RUGBY*) to bring down; (*fam: laisser tomber*) to drop

plaquette [plaket] *nf* (*de chocolat*) bar; (*beurre*) pack(et)

plastic [plastik] *nm* plastic explosive

plastique [plastik] *adj, nm* plastic

plastiquer [plastike] *vt* to blow up (*with a plastic bomb*)

plat, e [pla, -at] *adj* flat; (*cheveux*) straight; (*personne, livre*) dull ♦ *nm* (*récipient, CULIN*) dish; (*d'un repas*): **le premier** ~ the first course; **à** ~ **ventre** face down; **à** ~ (*pneu, batterie*) flat; (*personne*) dead beat; ~ **cuisiné** pre-cooked meal; ~ **de résistance** main course; ~ **du jour** dish of the day

platane [platan] *nm* plane tree

plateau, x [plato] *nm* (*support*) tray; (*GÉO*) plateau; (*de tourne-disques*) turntable; (*CINÉMA*) set; ~ **à fromages** cheeseboard

plate-bande [platbɑ̃d] *nf* flower bed

plate-forme [platfɔʀm(ə)] *nf* platform; ~ **de forage/pétrolière** drilling/oil rig

platine [platin] *nm* platinum ♦ *nf* (*d'un tourne-disque*) turntable

plâtras [plɑtʀa] *nm* rubble *no pl*

plâtre [plɑtʀ(ə)] *nm* (*matériau*) plaster; (*statue*) plaster statue; (*MÉD*) (plaster) cast; **avoir un bras dans le** ~ to have an arm in plaster

plein, e [plɛ̃, -ɛn] *adj* full; (*porte, roue*) solid; (*chienne, jument*) big (with young) ♦ *nm*: **faire le** ~ (**d'essence**) to fill up (with petrol); **à** ~**es mains** (*ramasser*) in handfuls; (*empoigner*) firmly; **à** ~ **régime** at maximum revs; (*fig*) full steam; **à** ~ **temps** full-time; **en** ~ **air** in the open air; **en** ~ **soleil** in direct sunlight; **en** ~**e nuit/rue** in the middle of the night/street; **en** ~ **jour** in broad daylight; **en** ~ **sur** right on; **plein-emploi** *nm* full employment

plénitude [plenityd] *nf* fullness

pleurer [plœʀe] *vi* to cry; (*yeux*) to water ♦ *vt* to mourn (for); ~ **sur** to lament (over), to bemoan

pleurnicher [plœʀniʃe] *vi* to snivel, whine

pleurs [plœʀ] *nmpl*: **en** ~ in tears

pleut *vb voir* **pleuvoir**

pleuvoir [pløvwaʀ] *vb impers* to rain ♦ *vi* (*fig*): ~ (**sur**) to shower down (upon); to be showered upon; **il pleut** it's raining

pli [pli] *nm* fold; (*de jupe*) pleat; (*de pantalon*) crease; (*aussi: faux* ~) crease; (*enveloppe*) envelope; (*lettre*) letter; (*CARTES*) trick

pliant, e [plijɑ̃, -ɑ̃t] *adj* folding ♦ *nm* folding stool, campstool

plier [plije] *vt* to fold; (*pour ranger*) to fold up; (*table pliante*) to fold down; (*genou, bras*) to bend ♦ *vi* to bend; (*fig*) to yield; **se** ~ **à** to submit to

plinthe [plɛ̃t] *nf* skirting board

plisser [plise] *vt* (*rider, chiffonner*) to crease; (*jupe*) to put pleats in

plomb [plɔ̃] *nm* (*métal*) lead; (*d'une cartouche*) (lead) shot; (*PÊCHE*) sinker; (*sceau*) (lead) seal; (*ÉLEC*) fuse; **sans** ~ (*essence etc*) unleaded

plombage [plɔ̃baʒ] *nm* (*de dent*) filling

plomber [plɔ̃be] *vt* (*canne, ligne*) to weight (with lead); (*dent*) to fill

plomberie [plɔ̃bʀi] *nf* plumbing

plombier [plɔ̃bje] *nm* plumber

plongeant, e [plɔ̃ʒɑ̃, -ɑ̃t] *adj* (*vue*) from above; (*tir, décolleté*) plunging

plongée [plɔ̃ʒe] *nf* (*SPORT*) diving *no pl*; (: *sans scaphandre*) skin diving

plongeoir [plɔ̃ʒwaʀ] *nm* diving board

plongeon [plɔ̃ʒɔ̃] *nm* dive

plonger [plɔ̃ʒe] *vi* to dive ♦ *vt*: ~ **qch dans** to plunge sth into

ployer [plwaje] *vt* to bend ♦ *vi* to sag; to bend

plu *pp de* **plaire; pleuvoir**

pluie [plɥi] *nf* rain; (*fig*): ~ **de** shower of

plume [plym] *nf* feather; (*pour écrire*) (pen) nib; (*fig*) pen; ~**r** [plyme] *vt* to pluck; **plumier** [plymje] *nm* pencil box

plupart [plypaʀ]: **la** ~ *pron* the majority, most (of them); **la** ~ **des** most, the majority of; **la** ~ **du temps/d'entre nous** most of the time/of us; **pour la** ~ for the most part, mostly

pluriel [plyʀjɛl] *nm* plural

plus¹ [ply] *vb voir* **plaire**

— MOT CLÉ

plus² [ply] *adv* **1** (*forme négative*): **ne ...** ~ no more, no longer; **je n'ai** ~ **d'argent** I've got no more money *ou* no money left; **il ne travaille** ~ he's no longer working, he doesn't work any more

2 [ply, plyz, + *voyelle*] (*comparatif*) more, ...+er; (*superlatif*): **le** ~ the most, the

...+est; ~ **grand/intelligent (que)** bigger/more intelligent (than); **le** ~ **grand/intelligent** the biggest/most intelligent; **tout au** ~ at the very most
3 [plys] (*davantage*) more; **il travaille** ~ **(que)** he works more (than); ~ **il travaille,** ~ **il est heureux** the more he works, the happier he is; ~ **de pain** more bread; ~ **de 10 personnes** more than 10 people, over 10 people; **3 heures de** ~ **que 3 hours** more than; **de** ~ what's more, moreover; **3 kilos en** ~ 3 kilos more; **en** ~ **de** in addition to; **de** ~ **en** ~ more and more; ~ **ou moins** more or less; **ni** ~ **ni moins** no more, no less
♦ *prép* [plys]: **4** ~ **2** 4 plus 2

plusieurs [plyzjœʀ] *dét, pron* several; **ils sont** ~ there are several of them
plus-que-parfait [plyskəpaʀfɛ] *nm* pluperfect, past perfect
plus-value [plyvaly] *nf* appreciation; capital gain; surplus
plut *vb voir* **plaire**
plutôt [plyto] *adv* rather; **je ferais** ~ **ceci** I'd rather *ou* sooner do this; **fais** ~ **comme ça** try this way instead, you'd better try this way; ~ **que (de) faire** rather than *ou* instead of doing
pluvieux, euse [plyvjø, -øz] *adj* rainy, wet
PMU *sigle m* (= *pari mutuel urbain*) system of betting on horses; (*café*) betting agency
pneu [pnø] *nm* tyre (*BRIT*), tire (*US*)
pneumatique [pnømatik] *nm* tyre (*BRIT*), tire (*US*)
pneumonie [pnømɔni] *nf* pneumonia
poche [pɔʃ] *nf* pocket; (*déformation*): **faire une** *ou* **des** ~**(s)** to bag; (*sous les yeux*) bag, pouch; **de** ~ pocket *cpd*
pocher [pɔʃe] *vt* (*CULIN*) to poach
pochette [pɔʃɛt] *nf* (*de timbres*) wallet, envelope; (*d'aiguilles etc*) case; (*mouchoir*) breast pocket handkerchief; ~ **de disque** record sleeve
poêle [pwal] *nm* stove ♦ *nf*: ~ **(à frire)** frying pan
poêlon [pwalɔ̃] *nm* casserole
poème [pɔɛm] *nm* poem
poésie [pɔezi] *nf* (*poème*) poem; (*art*): **la** ~ poetry
poète [pɔɛt] *nm* poet
poids [pwa] *nm* weight; (*SPORT*) shot; **vendre au** ~ to sell by weight; **prendre du** ~ to put on weight; ~ **lourd** (*camion*) lorry (*BRIT*), truck (*US*)
poignard [pwaɲaʀ] *nm* dagger; ~**er** *vt* to stab, knife
poigne [pwaɲ] *nf* grip; (*fig*): **à** ~ firmhanded
poignée [pwaɲe] *nf* (*de sel etc, fig*) handful; (*de couvercle, porte*) handle; ~ **de main** handshake

poignet [pwaɲɛ] *nm* (*ANAT*) wrist; (*de chemise*) cuff
poil [pwal] *nm* (*ANAT*) hair; (*de pinceau, brosse*) bristle; (*de tapis*) strand; (*pelage*) coat; **à** ~ (*fam*) starkers; **au** ~ (*fam*) hunky-dory; **poilu, e** *adj* hairy
poinçon [pwɛ̃sɔ̃] *nm* awl; bodkin; (*marque*) hallmark; **poinçonner** *vt* to stamp; to hallmark; (*billet*) to punch
poing [pwɛ̃] *nm* fist
point [pwɛ̃] *nm* (*marque, signe*) dot; (: *de ponctuation*) full stop, period (*US*); (*moment, de score etc, fig*: *question*) point; (*endroit*) spot; (*COUTURE, TRICOT*) stitch ♦ *adv* = **pas**; **faire le** ~ (*NAVIG*) to take a bearing; (*fig*) to take stock (of the situation); **en tout** ~ in every respect; **sur le** ~ **de faire** (just) about to do; **à tel** ~ **que** so much so that; **mettre au** ~ (*mécanisme, procédé*) to develop; (*appareil-photo*) to focus; (*affaire*) to settle; **à** ~ (*CULIN*) medium; just right; **à** ~ (*nommé*) just at the right time; ~ **(de côté)** stitch (*pain*); ~ **d'eau** spring; water point; ~ **d'exclamation** exclamation mark; ~ **d'interrogation** question mark; ~ **de repère** landmark; (*dans le temps*) point of reference; ~ **de vente** retail outlet; ~ **de vue** viewpoint; (*fig*: *opinion*) point of view; ~ **faible** weak point; ~ **final** full stop, period; ~ **mort** (*AUTO*): **au** ~ **mort** in neutral; ~**s de suspension** suspension points
pointe [pwɛ̃t] *nf* point; (*fig*): **une** ~ **de** a hint of; **être à la** ~ **de** (*fig*) to be in the forefront of; **sur la** ~ **des pieds** on tiptoe; **en** ~ *adv* (*tailler*) into a point ♦ *adj* pointed, tapered; **de** ~ (*technique etc*) leading; **heures/jours de** ~ peak hours/days; ~ **de vitesse** burst of speed
pointer [pwɛ̃te] *vt* (*cocher*) to tick off; (*employés etc*) to check in; (*diriger*: *canon, doigt*): ~ **vers qch** to point at sth ♦ *vi* (*employé*) to clock in
pointillé [pwɛ̃tije] *nm* (*trait*) dotted line
pointilleux, euse [pwɛ̃tijø, -øz] *adj* particular, pernickety
pointu, e [pwɛ̃ty] *adj* pointed; (*clou*) sharp; (*voix*) shrill; (*analyse*) precise
pointure [pwɛ̃tyʀ] *nf* size
point-virgule [pwɛ̃viʀgyl] *nm* semi-colon
poire [pwaʀ] *nf* pear; (*fam*: *péj*) mug
poireau, x [pwaʀo] *nm* leek
poirier [pwaʀje] *nm* pear tree
pois [pwa] *nm* (*BOT*) pea; (*sur une étoffe*) dot, spot; **à** ~ (*cravate etc*) spotted, polka-dot *cpd*
poison [pwazɔ̃] *nm* poison
poisse [pwas] *nf* rotten luck
poisseux, euse [pwasø, -øz] *adj* sticky
poisson [pwasɔ̃] *nm* fish *gén inv*; **les P**~**s** (*signe*) Pisces; ~ **d'avril!** April fool!; ~ **rouge** goldfish; **poissonnerie** *nf* fish-shop;

poissonnier, ière nm/f fishmonger (BRIT), fish merchant (US)

poitrine [pwatʀin] nf chest; (seins) bust, bosom; (CULIN) breast; ~ **de bœuf** brisket

poivre [pwavʀ(ə)] nm pepper; **poivrier** nm (ustensile) pepperpot

poivron [pwavʀɔ̃] nm pepper, capsicum

polar [pɔlaʀ] nm (fam) detective novel

pôle [pol] nm (GÉO, ÉLEC) pole

poli, e [pɔli] adj polite; (lisse) smooth; polished

police [pɔlis] nf police; **peine de simple ~** sentence given by magistrates' or police court; ~ **d'assurance** insurance policy; ~ **des mœurs** ≈ vice squad; ~ **judiciaire** ≈ Criminal Investigation Department (BRIT), ≈ Federal Bureau of Investigation (US); ~ **secours** ≈ emergency services pl (BRIT), ≈ paramedics pl (US)

policier, ière [pɔlisje, -jɛʀ] adj police cpd ♦ nm policeman; (aussi: roman ~) detective novel

polio [pɔljɔ] nf polio

polir [pɔliʀ] vt to polish

polisson, ne [pɔlisɔ̃, -ɔn] adj naughty

politesse [pɔlitɛs] nf politeness

politicien, ne [pɔlitisjɛ̃, -ɛn] nm/f politician

politique [pɔlitik] adj political ♦ nf (science, pratique, activité) politics sg; (mesures, méthode) policies pl; **politiser** vt to politicize

pollen [pɔlɛn] nm pollen

pollution [pɔlysjɔ̃] nf pollution

polo [pɔlo] nm polo shirt

Pologne [pɔlɔɲ] nf: **la ~** Poland; **polonais, e** adj, nm (LING) Polish; **Polonais, e** nm/f Pole

poltron, ne [pɔltʀɔ̃, -ɔn] adj cowardly

polycopier [pɔlikɔpje] vt to duplicate

Polynésie [pɔlinezi] nf: **la ~** Polynesia

polyvalent, e [pɔlivalɑ̃, -ɑ̃t] adj versatile; multi-purpose

pommade [pɔmad] nf ointment, cream

pomme [pɔm] nf (BOT) apple; **tomber dans les ~s** (fam) to pass out; ~ **d'Adam** Adam's apple; ~ **d'arrosoir** (sprinkler) rose; ~ **de pin** pine ou fir cone; ~ **de terre** potato

pommeau, x [pɔmo] nm (boule) knob; (de selle) pommel

pommette [pɔmɛt] nf cheekbone

pommier [pɔmje] nm apple tree

pompe [pɔ̃p] nf pump; (faste) pomp (and ceremony); ~ **à essence** petrol (BRIT) ou gas (US) pump; ~**s funèbres** funeral parlour sg, undertaker's sg

pomper [pɔ̃pe] vt to pump; (évacuer) to pump out; (aspirer) to pump up; (absorber) to soak up

pompeux, euse [pɔ̃pø, -øz] adj pompous

pompier [pɔ̃pje] nm fireman

pompiste [pɔ̃pist(ə)] nm/f petrol (BRIT) ou gas (US) pump attendant

poncer [pɔ̃se] vt to sand (down)

ponctuation [pɔ̃ktɥasjɔ̃] nf punctuation

ponctuel, le [pɔ̃ktɥɛl] adj (à l'heure, aussi TECH) punctual; (fig: opération etc) one-off, single; (scrupuleux) punctilious, meticulous

ponctuer [pɔ̃ktɥe] vt to punctuate

pondéré, e [pɔ̃deʀe] adj level-headed, composed

pondre [pɔ̃dʀ(ə)] vt to lay; (fig) to produce

poney [pɔnɛ] nm pony

pont [pɔ̃] nm bridge; (AUTO) axle; (NAVIG) deck; **faire le ~** to take the extra day off; ~ **de graissage** ramp (in garage); ~ **suspendu** suspension bridge; **P~s et Chaussées** highways department

pont-levis [pɔ̃lvi] nm drawbridge

pop [pɔp] adj inv pop

populace [pɔpylas] (péj) nf rabble

populaire [pɔpylɛʀ] adj popular; (manifestation) mass cpd; (milieux, clientèle) working-class

population [pɔpylasjɔ̃] nf population; ~ **active** nf working population

populeux, euse [pɔpylø, -øz] adj densely populated

porc [pɔʀ] nm (ZOOL) pig; (CULIN) pork; (peau) pigskin

porcelaine [pɔʀsəlɛn] nf porcelain, china; piece of china(ware)

porc-épic [pɔʀkepik] nm porcupine

porche [pɔʀʃ(ə)] nm porch

porcherie [pɔʀʃəʀi] nf pigsty

pore [pɔʀ] nm pore

porno [pɔʀno] adj abr pornographic, porno

port [pɔʀ] nm (NAVIG) harbour, port; (ville) port; (de l'uniforme etc) wearing; (pour lettre) postage; (pour colis, aussi: posture) carriage; ~ **d'arme** (JUR) carrying of a firearm

portable [pɔʀtabl(ə)] nm (COMPUT) laptop (computer)

portail [pɔʀtaj] nm gate; (de cathédrale) portal

portant, e [pɔʀtɑ̃, -ɑ̃t] adj: **bien/mal ~ in** good/poor health

portatif, ive [pɔʀtatif, -iv] adj portable

porte [pɔʀt(ə)] nf door; (de ville, forteresse, SKI) gate; **mettre à la ~** to throw out; ~ **à ~** nm door-to-door selling; ~ **d'entrée** front door; ~**à-faux** nm: **en ~à-faux** cantilevered; (fig) in an awkward position; ~**avions** nm inv aircraft carrier; ~**bagages** nm inv luggage rack; ~**clefs** nm inv key ring; ~**documents** nm inv attaché ou document case

portée [pɔʀte] nf (d'une arme) range; (fig) impact, import; scope, capability; (de chatte etc) litter; (MUS) stave, staff; **à/hors de (de)** within/out of reach (of); **à ~ de (la) main** within (arm's) reach; **à ~ de voix**

within earshot; **à la** ~ **de qn** (*fig*) at sb's level, within sb's capabilities

porte: ~**-fenêtre** *nf* French window; ~**feuille** *nm* wallet; (*POL, BOURSE*) portfolio; ~**-jarretelles** *nm inv* suspender belt; ~**manteau, x** *nm* coat hanger; coat rack; ~**-mine** *nm* propelling (*BRIT*) *ou* mechanical (*US*) pencil; ~**-monnaie** *nm inv* purse; ~**-parole** *nm inv* spokesman

porter [pɔʁte] *vt* to carry; (*sur soi*: *vêtement, barbe, bague*) to wear; (*fig*: *responsabilité etc*) to bear, carry; (*inscription, marque, titre, patronyme*: *suj*: *arbre, fruits, fleurs*) to bear; (*apporter*): ~ **qch quelque part/à qn** to take sth somewhere/to sb ♦ *vi* (*voix, regard, canon*) to carry; (*coup, argument*) to hit home; **se** ~ *vi* (*se sentir*): **se** ~ **bien/mal** to be well/unwell; ~ **sur** (*peser*) to rest on; (*accent*) to fall on; (*conférence etc*) to concern; (*heurter*) to strike; **être porté à faire** to be apt *ou* inclined to do; **se faire** ~ **malade** to report sick; ~ **la main à son chapeau** to raise one's hand to one's hat; ~ **son effort sur** to direct one's efforts towards; ~ **à croire** to lead one to believe

porte-serviettes [pɔʁtsɛʁvjɛt] *nm inv* towel rail

porteur [pɔʁtœʁ] *nm* (*de bagages*) porter; (*de chèque*) bearer

porte-voix [pɔʁtəvwa] *nm inv* megaphone

portier [pɔʁtje] *nm* doorman

portière [pɔʁtjɛʁ] *nf* door

portillon [pɔʁtijɔ̃] *nm* gate

portion [pɔʁsjɔ̃] *nf* (*part*) portion, share; (*partie*) portion, section

portique [pɔʁtik] *nm* (*RAIL*) gantry

porto [pɔʁto] *nm* port (wine)

portrait [pɔʁtʁɛ] *nm* portrait; photograph; **portrait-robot** *nm* Identikit ® *ou* photofit ® picture

portuaire [pɔʁtɥɛʁ] *adj* port *cpd*, harbour *cpd*

portugais, e [pɔʁtygɛ, -ɛz] *adj, nm/f* Portuguese

Portugal [pɔʁtygal] *nm*: **le** ~ Portugal

pose [poz] *nf* laying; hanging; (*attitude, d'un modèle*) pose; (*PHOTO*) exposure

posé, e [poze] *adj* serious

poser [poze] *vt* (*déposer*): ~ **qch (sur)/qn à** to put sth down (on)/drop sb at; (*placer*): ~ **qch sur/quelque part** to put sth on/somewhere; (*installer*: *moquette, carrelage*) to lay; (*rideaux, papier peint*) to hang; (*question*) to ask; (*principe, conditions*) to lay *ou* set down; (*problème*) to formulate; (*difficulté*) to pose ♦ *vi* (*modèle*) to pose; **se** ~ *vi* (*oiseau, avion*) to land; (*question*) to arise

positif, ive [pozitif, -iv] *adj* positive

position [pozisjɔ̃] *nf* position; **prendre** ~ (*fig*) to take a stand

posologie [pozɔlɔʒi] *nf* directions for use, dosage

posséder [posede] *vt* to own, possess; (*qualité, talent*) to have, possess; (*bien connaître*: *métier, langue*) to have mastered, have a thorough knowledge of; (*sexuellement, aussi*: *suj*: *colère etc*) to possess; **possession** *nf* ownership *no pl*; possession

possibilité [posibilite] *nf* possibility; ~**s** *nfpl* (*moyens*) means; (*potentiel*) potential *sg*

possible [posibl(ə)] *adj* possible; (*projet, entreprise*) feasible ♦ *nm*: **faire son** ~ to do all one can, do one's utmost; **le plus/moins de livres** ~ as many/few books as possible; **le plus/moins d'eau** ~ as much/little water as possible; **dès que** ~ as soon as possible

postal, e, aux [postal, -o] *adj* postal

poste [post(ə)] *nf* (*service*) post, postal service; (*administration, bureau*) post office ♦ *nm* (*fonction, MIL*) post; (*TÉL*) extension; (*de radio etc*) set; **mettre à la** ~ to post; **P~s, Télécommunications et Télédiffusion** postal and telecommunications service; ~ **d'essence** *nm* petrol *ou* filling station; ~ **d'incendie** *nm* fire point; ~ **de pilotage** *nm* cockpit; ~ **(de police)** *nm* police station; ~ **de secours** *nm* first-aid post; ~ **de travail** *nm* work station; **poste restante** *nf* poste restante (*BRIT*), general delivery (*US*)

poster¹ [poste] *vt* to post

poster² [pɔstɛʁ] *nm* poster

postérieur, e [pɔsteʁjœʁ] *adj* (*date*) later; (*partie*) back ♦ *nm* (*fam*) behind

posthume [pɔstym] *adj* posthumous

postiche [pɔstiʃ] *nm* hairpiece

postuler [pɔstyle] *vt* (*emploi*) to apply for, put in for

posture [pɔstyʁ] *nf* posture; position

pot [po] *nm* jar, pot; (*en plastique, carton*) carton; (*en métal*) tin; **boire** *ou* **prendre un** ~ (*fam*) to have a drink; ~ **(de chambre)** (chamber)pot; ~ **d'échappement** exhaust pipe; ~ **de fleurs** plant pot, flowerpot; (*plante*) pot plant

potable [pɔtabl(ə)] *adj*: **eau (non)** ~ (non-)drinking water

potage [pɔtaʒ] *nm* soup; soup course

potager, ère [pɔtaʒe, -ɛʁ] *adj* (*plante*) edible, vegetable *cpd*; (*jardin*) ~ kitchen *ou* vegetable garden

pot-au-feu [pɔtofø] *nm inv* (beef) stew

pot-de-vin [pɔdvɛ̃] *nm* bribe

pote [pɔt] (*fam*) *nm* pal

poteau, x [pɔto] *nm* post; ~ **indicateur** signpost

potelé, e [pɔtle] *adj* plump, chubby

potence [pɔtɑ̃s] *nf* gallows *sg*

potentiel, le [pɔtɑ̃sjɛl] *adj, nm* potential

poterie [pɔtʁi] *nf* pottery; piece of pottery

potier [pɔtje] *nm* potter
potins [pɔtɛ̃] *nmpl* gossip *sg*
potiron [pɔtiʀɔ̃] *nm* pumpkin
pou, x [pu] *nm* louse
poubelle [pubɛl] *nf* (dust)bin
pouce [pus] *nm* thumb
poudre [pudʀ(ə)] *nf* powder; *(fard)* (face) powder; *(explosif)* gunpowder; **en ~:** **café en ~** instant coffee; **lait en ~** dried *ou* powdered milk; **poudrier** *nm* (powder) compact
pouffer [pufe] *vi:* **~ (de rire)** to snigger; to giggle
pouilleux, euse [pujø, -øz] *adj* flea-ridden; *(fig)* grubby; seedy
poulailler [pulaje] *nm* henhouse
poulain [pulɛ̃] *nm* foal; *(fig)* protégé
poule [pul] *nf* (ZOOL) hen; (CULIN) (boiling) fowl
poulet [pulɛ] *nm* chicken; *(fam)* cop
poulie [puli] *nf* pulley; block
pouls [pu] *nm* pulse; **prendre le ~ de qn** to feel sb's pulse
poumon [pumɔ̃] *nm* lung
poupe [pup] *nf* stern; **en ~** astern
poupée [pupe] *nf* doll
poupon [pupɔ̃] *nm* babe-in-arms; **pouponnière** *nf* crèche, day nursery
pour [puʀ] *prép* for ♦ *nm:* **le ~ et le contre** the pros and cons; **~ faire** (so as) to do, in order to do; **~ avoir fait** for having done; **~ que** so that, in order that; **~ 100 francs d'essence** 100 francs' worth of petrol; **~ cent** per cent; **~ ce qui est de** as for
pourboire [puʀbwaʀ] *nm* tip
pourcentage [puʀsɑ̃taʒ] *nm* percentage
pourchasser [puʀʃase] *vt* to pursue
pourparlers [puʀpaʀle] *nmpl* talks, negotiations
pourpre [puʀpʀ(ə)] *adj* crimson
pourquoi [puʀkwa] *adv, conj* why ♦ *nm inv:* **le ~ (de)** the reason (for)
pourrai *etc vb voir* **pouvoir**
pourri, e [puʀi] *adj* rotten
pourrir [puʀiʀ] *vi* to rot; *(fruit)* to go rotten *ou* bad ♦ *vt* to rot; *(fig)* to spoil thoroughly; **pourriture** *nf* rot
pourrons *etc vb voir* **pouvoir**
poursuite [puʀsɥit] *nf* pursuit, chase; **~s** *nfpl* (JUR) legal proceedings
poursuivre [puʀsɥivʀ(ə)] *vt* to pursue, chase (after); *(relancer)* to hound, harry; *(obséder)* to haunt; (JUR) to bring proceedings against, prosecute; (: *au civil*) to sue; *(but)* to strive towards; *(voyage, études)* to carry on with, continue ♦ *vi* to carry on, go on; **se ~** *vi* to go on, continue
pourtant [puʀtɑ̃] *adv* yet; **c'est ~ facile** (and) yet it's easy
pourtour [puʀtuʀ] *nm* perimeter
pourvoir [puʀvwaʀ] *vt:* **~ qch/qn de** to equip sth/sb with ♦ *vi:* **~ à** to provide for;

(emploi) to fill; **se ~** *vi* (JUR): **se ~ en cassation** to take one's case to the Court of Appeal
pourvoyeur [puʀvwajœʀ] *nm* supplier
pourvu, e [puʀvy] *adj:* **~ de** equipped with; **~ que** *(si)* provided that, so long as; *(espérons que)* let's hope (that)
pousse [pus] *nf* growth; *(bourgeon)* shoot
poussé, e [puse] *adj* exhaustive
poussée [puse] *nf* thrust; *(coup)* push; (MÉD) eruption; *(fig)* upsurge
pousser [puse] *vt* to push; *(inciter):* **~ qn à** to urge *ou* press sb to +*infin*; *(acculer):* **~ qn à** to drive sb to; *(émettre: cri etc)* to give; *(stimuler)* to urge on; to drive hard; *(poursuivre)* to carry on (further) ♦ *vi* to push; *(croître)* to grow; **se ~** *vi* to move over; **faire ~** *(plante)* to grow
poussette [pusɛt] *nf* (voiture d'enfant) push chair (BRIT), stroller (US)
poussière [pusjɛʀ] *nf* dust; *(grain)* speck of dust; **poussiéreux, euse** *adj* dusty
poussin [pusɛ̃] *nm* chick
poutre [putʀ(ə)] *nf* beam; *(en fer, ciment armé)* girder

MOT CLÉ

pouvoir [puvwaʀ] *nm* power; *(POL: dirigeants):* **le ~** those in power; **les ~s publics** the authorities; **~ d'achat** purchasing power

♦ *vb semi-aux* **1** *(être en état de)* can, be able to; **je ne peux pas le réparer** I can't *ou* I am not able to repair it; **déçu de ne pas ~ le faire** disappointed not to be able to do it

2 *(avoir la permission)* can, may, be allowed to; **vous pouvez aller au cinéma** you can *ou* may go to the pictures

3 *(probabilité, hypothèse)* may, might, could; **il a pu avoir un accident** he may *ou* might *ou* could have had an accident; **il aurait pu le dire!** he might *ou* could have said (so)!

♦ *vb impers* may, might, could; **il peut arriver que** it may *ou* might *ou* could happen that

♦ *vt* can, be able to; **j'ai fait tout ce que j'ai pu** I did all I could; **je n'en peux plus** *(épuisé)* I'm exhausted; *(à bout)* I can't take any more
se ~ *vi:* **il se peut que** it may *ou* might be that; **cela se pourrait** that's quite possible

---

prairie [pʀeʀi] *nf* meadow
praline [pʀalin] *nf* sugared almond
praticable [pʀatikabl(ə)] *adj* passable, practicable
praticien, ne [pʀatisjɛ̃, -jɛn] *nm/f* practitioner
pratique [pʀatik] *nf* practice ♦ *adj* practical
pratiquement [pʀatikmɑ̃] *adv* (pour ainsi

dire) practically, virtually

pratiquer [pʀatike] *vt* to practise; (*SPORT etc*) to go in for; to play; (*intervention, opération*) to carry out; (*ouverture, abri*) to make

pré [pʀe] *nm* meadow

préalable [pʀealabl(ə)] *adj* preliminary; **condition** ~ **(de)** precondition (for), prerequisite (for); **au** ~ beforehand

préambule [pʀeãbyl] *nm* preamble; (*fig*) prelude; **sans** ~ straight away

préavis [pʀeavi] *nm* notice; **communication avec** ~ (*TÉL*) personal *ou* person to person call

précaution [pʀekosjɔ̃] *nf* precaution; **avec** ~ cautiously; **par** ~ as a precaution

précédemment [pʀesedamã] *adv* before, previously

précédent, e [pʀesedã, -ãt] *adj* previous ♦ *nm* precedent; **le jour** ~ the day before, the previous day; **sans** ~ unprecedented

précéder [pʀesede] *vt* to precede; (*marcher ou rouler devant*) to be in front of

précepteur, trice [pʀesɛptœʀ, -tʀis] *nm/f* (private) tutor

prêcher [pʀeʃe] *vt* to preach

précieux, euse [pʀesjø, -øz] *adj* precious; invaluable; (*style, écrivain*) précieux, precious

précipice [pʀesipis] *nm* drop, chasm; (*fig*) abyss

précipitamment [pʀesipitamã] *adv* hurriedly, hastily

précipitation [pʀesipitɑsjɔ̃] *nf* (*hâte*) haste; ~**s** *nfpl* (*pluie*) rain *sg*

précipité, e [pʀesipite] *adj* hurried, hasty

précipiter [pʀesipite] *vt* (*faire tomber*): ~ **qn/qch du haut de** to throw *ou* hurl sb/ sth off *ou* from; (*hâter: marche*) to quicken; (: *départ*) to hasten; **se** ~ *vi* to speed up; **se** ~ **sur/vers** to rush at/towards

précis, e [pʀesi, -iz] *adj* precise; (*tir, mesures*) accurate, precise ♦ *nm* handbook; **précisément** *adv* precisely; **préciser** *vt* (*expliquer*) to be more specific about, clarify; (*spécifier*) to state, specify; **se** ~**er** *vi* to become clear(er); **précision** *nf* precision; accuracy; **point** *ou* **détail** (*being or to be clarified*)

précoce [pʀekɔs] *adj* early; (*enfant*) precocious; (*calvitie*) premature

préconiser [pʀekɔnize] *vt* to advocate

prédécesseur [pʀedesesœʀ] *nm* predecessor

prédilection [pʀedilɛksjɔ̃] *nf*: **avoir une** ~ **pour** to be partial to; **de** ~ favourite

prédire [pʀediʀ] *vt* to predict

prédominer [pʀedɔmine] *vi* to predominate; (*avis*) to prevail

préface [pʀefas] *nf* preface

préfecture [pʀefɛktyʀ] *nf* prefecture; ~ **de police** police headquarters *pl*

préférable [pʀefeʀabl(ə)] *adj* preferable

préféré, e [pʀefeʀe] *adj, nm/f* favourite

préférence [pʀefeʀãs] *nf* preference; **de** ~ preferably

préférer [pʀefeʀe] *vt*: ~ **qn/qch (à)** to prefer sb/sth (to), like sb/sth better (than); ~ **faire** to prefer to do; **je** ~**ais du thé** I would rather have tea, I'd prefer tea

préfet [pʀefɛ] *nm* prefect

préfixe [pʀefiks(ə)] *nm* prefix

préhistorique [pʀeistɔʀik] *adj* prehistoric

préjudice [pʀeʒydis] *nm* (*matériel*) loss; (*moral*) harm *no pl*; **porter** ~ **à** to harm, be detrimental to; **au** ~ **de** at the expense of

préjugé [pʀeʒyʒe] *nm* prejudice; **avoir un** ~ **contre** to be prejudiced *ou* biased against

préjuger [pʀeʒyʒe]: ~ **de** *vt* to prejudge

prélasser [pʀelase]: **se** ~ *vi* to lounge

prélèvement [pʀelɛvmã] *nm*: **faire un** ~ **de sang** to take a blood sample

prélever [pʀelve] *vt* (*échantillon*) to take; (*argent*): ~ **(sur)** to deduct (from); (: *sur son compte*) to withdraw (from)

prématuré, e [pʀematyʀe] *adj* premature; (*retraite*) early ♦ *nm* premature baby

premier, ière [pʀəmje, -jɛʀ] *adj* first; (*branche, marche*) bottom; (*fig*) basic; prime; initial; **le** ~ **venu** the first person to come along; **P~ Ministre** Prime Minister; **première** *nf* (*THÉÂTRE*) first night; (*AUTO*) first (gear); (*AVIAT, RAIL etc*) first class; (*CINÉMA*) première; (*exploit*) first; **premièrement** *adv* firstly

prémonition [pʀemɔnisjɔ̃] *nf* premonition

prémunir [pʀemyniʀ]: **se** ~ *vi*: **se** ~ **contre** to guard against

prenant, e [pʀənã, -ãt] *adj* absorbing, engrossing

prénatal, e [pʀenatal] *adj* (*MÉD*) antenatal

prendre [pʀãdʀ(ə)] *vt* to take; (*ôter*): ~ **qch à** to take sth from; (*aller chercher*) to get, fetch; (*se procurer*) to get; (*malfaiteur, poisson*) to catch; (*passager*) to pick up; (*personnel, aussi: couleur, goût*) to take on; (*locataire*) to take in; (*élève etc: traiter*) to handle; (*voix, ton*) to put on; (*coincer*): **se** ~ **les doigts dans** to get one's fingers caught in ♦ *vi* (*liquide, ciment*) to set; (*greffe, vaccin*) to take; (*feu: foyer*) to go; (: *incendie*) to start; (*allumette*) to light; (*se diriger*): ~ **à gauche** to turn (to the) left; **à tout** ~ on the whole, all in all; **se** ~ **pour** to think one is; **s'en** ~ **à** to attack; **se** ~ **d'amitié/d'affection pour** to befriend/ become fond of; **s'y** ~ (*procéder*) to set about it

preneur [pʀənœʀ] *nm*: **être/trouver** ~ to be willing to buy/find a buyer

preniez *vb voir* **prendre**

prenne *etc vb voir* **prendre**

prénom [pʀenɔ̃] *nm* first *ou* Christian

name

prénuptial, e, aux [pʀenypsjal, -o] *adj* premarital

préoccupation [pʀeɔkypɑsjɔ̃] *nf (souci)* concern; *(idée fixe)* preoccupation

préoccuper [pʀeɔkype] *vt* to concern; to preoccupy

préparatifs [pʀepaʀatif] *nmpl* preparations

préparation [pʀepaʀasjɔ̃] *nf* preparation; *(SCOL)* piece of homework

préparer [pʀepaʀe] *vt* to prepare; *(café)* to make; *(examen)* to prepare for; *(voyage, entreprise)* to plan; **se ~** *vi (orage, tragédie)* to brew, be in the air; **se ~ (à qch/faire)** to prepare (o.s.) *ou* get ready (for sth/to do); **~ qch à qn** *(surprise etc)* to have sth in store for sb

prépondérant, e [pʀepɔ̃deʀɑ̃, -ɑ̃t] *adj* major, dominating

préposé, e [pʀepoze] *adj:* **~ à** in charge of ♦ *nm/f* employee; official; attendant

préposition [pʀepozisjɔ̃] *nf* preposition

près [pʀɛ] *adv* near, close; **~ de** near (to), close to; *(environ)* nearly, almost; **de ~** closely; **à 5 kg ~** to within about 5 kg; **à cela ~ que** apart from the fact that

présage [pʀezaʒ] *nm* omen

présager [pʀezaʒe] *vt* to foresee

presbyte [pʀɛsbit] *adj* long-sighted

presbytère [pʀɛsbitɛʀ] *nm* presbytery

prescription [pʀɛskʀipsjɔ̃] *nf (instruction)* order, instruction; *(MÉD, JUR)* prescription

prescrire [pʀɛskʀiʀ] *vt* to prescribe

préséance [pʀeseɑ̃s] *nf* precedence *no pl*

présence [pʀezɑ̃s] *nf* presence; *(au bureau etc)* attendance; **~ d'esprit** presence of mind

présent, e [pʀezɑ̃, -ɑ̃t] *adj, nm* present; **à ~ (que)** now (that)

présentation [pʀezɑ̃tasjɔ̃] *nf* introduction; presentation; *(allure)* appearance

présenter [pʀezɑ̃te] *vt* to present; *(sympathie, condoléances)* to offer; *(soumettre)* to submit; *(invité, conférencier):* **~ qn (à)** to introduce sb (to) ♦ *vi:* **~ mal/bien** to have an unattractive/a pleasing appearance; **se ~** *vi (sur convocation)* to report, come; *(à une élection)* to stand; *(occasion)* to arise; **se ~ bien/mal** to look good/not too good; **se ~ à** *(examen)* to sit

préservatif [pʀezɛʀvatif] *nm* sheath, condom

préserver [pʀezɛʀve] *vt:* **~ de** to protect from; to save from

président [pʀezidɑ̃] *nm (POL)* president; *(d'une assemblée, COMM)* chairman; **~ directeur général** chairman and managing director

présider [pʀezide] *vt* to preside over; *(dîner)* to be the guest of honour at; **~ à** to direct; to govern

présomptueux, euse [pʀezɔ̃ptɥø, -øz] *adj* presumptuous

presque [pʀɛsk(ə)] *adv* almost, nearly; **~ rien** hardly anything; **~ pas** hardly (at all); **~ pas de** hardly any

presqu'île [pʀɛskil] *nf* peninsula

pressant, e [pʀɛsɑ̃, -ɑ̃t] *adj* urgent; **se faire ~** to become insistent

presse [pʀɛs] *nf* press; *(affluence):* **heures de ~** busy times

pressé, e [pʀese] *adj* in a hurry; *(air)* hurried; *(besogne)* urgent; **orange ~e** fresh orange juice

pressentiment [pʀesɑ̃timɑ̃] *nm* foreboding, premonition

pressentir [pʀesɑ̃tiʀ] *vt* to sense; *(prendre contact avec)* to approach

presse-papiers [pʀɛspapje] *nm inv* paperweight

presser [pʀese] *vt (fruit, éponge)* to squeeze; *(bouton)* to press; *(allure, affaire)* to speed up; *(inciter):* **~ qn de faire** to urge *ou* press sb to do ♦ *vi* to be urgent; **se ~** *vi (se hâter)* to hurry (up); **se ~ contre qn** to squeeze up against sb; **rien ne presse** there's no hurry

pressing [pʀesiŋ] *nm* steam-pressing; *(magasin)* dry-cleaner's

pression [pʀɛsjɔ̃] *nf* pressure; **faire ~ sur** to put pressure on; **~ artérielle** blood pressure

pressoir [pʀeswaʀ] *nm* (wine *ou* oil *etc*) press

prestance [pʀɛstɑ̃s] *nf* presence, imposing bearing

prestataire [pʀɛstatɛʀ] *nm/f* supplier

prestation [pʀɛstasjɔ̃] *nf (allocation)* benefit; *(d'une entreprise)* service provided; *(d'un artiste)* performance

prestidigitateur, trice [pʀɛstidiʒitatœʀ, -tʀis] *nm/f* conjurer

prestigieux, euse [pʀɛstiʒjø, -øz] *adj* prestigious

présumer [pʀezyme] *vt:* **~ que** to presume *ou* assume that; **~ de** to overrate

présupposer [pʀesypoze] *vt* to presuppose

prêt, e [pʀɛ, pʀɛt] *adj* ready ♦ *nm* lending *no pl*; loan; **prêt-à-porter** *nm* ready-to-wear *ou* off-the-peg *(BRIT)* clothes *pl*

prétendant [pʀetɑ̃dɑ̃] *nm* pretender; *(d'une femme)* suitor

prétendre [pʀetɑ̃dʀ(ə)] *vt (affirmer):* **~ que** to claim that; *(avoir l'intention de):* **~ faire qch** to mean *ou* intend to do sth; **~ à** *(droit, titre)* to lay claim to; **prétendu, e** *adj (supposé)* so-called

prête-nom [pʀɛtnɔ̃] *(péj) nm* figurehead

prétentieux, euse [pʀetɑ̃sjø, -øz] *adj* pretentious

prétention [pʀetɑ̃sjɔ̃] *nf* claim; pretentiousness

prêter [pʀete] *vt (livres, argent):* **~ qch (à)** to lend sth (to); *(supposer):* **~ à qn** *(carac-*

tère, propos) to attribute to sb ♦ vi (aussi: se ~: tissu, cuir) to give; **se ~ à** to lend o.s. (ou itself) to; (manigances etc) to go along with; ~ **à** (commentaires etc) to be open to, give rise to; ~ **assistance à** to give help to; ~ **attention à** to pay attention to; ~ **serment** to take the oath; ~ **l'oreille** to listen

prétexte [pʀetɛkst(ə)] nm pretext, excuse; **sous aucun** ~ on no account; **prétexter** vt to give as a pretext ou an excuse

prêtre [pʀɛtʀ(ə)] nm priest

preuve [pʀœv] nf proof; (indice) proof, evidence no pl; **faire** ~ **de** to show; **faire ses** ~**s** to prove o.s. (ou itself)

prévaloir [pʀevalwaʀ] vi to prevail; **se** ~ **de** vt to take advantage of; to pride o.s. on

prévenant, e [pʀevnɑ̃, -ɑ̃t] adj thoughtful, kind

prévenir [pʀevniʀ] vt (avertir): ~ **qn (de)** to warn sb (about); (informer): ~ **qn (de)** to tell ou inform sb (about); (éviter) to avoid, prevent; (anticiper) to forestall; to anticipate

prévention [pʀevɑ̃sjɔ̃] nf prevention; ~ **routière** road safety

prévenu, e [pʀevny] nm/f (JUR) defendant, accused

prévision [pʀevizjɔ̃] nf: ~**s** predictions; forecast sg; **en** ~ **de** in anticipation of; ~**s météorologiques** weather forecast sg

prévoir [pʀevwaʀ] vt (deviner) to foresee; (s'attendre à) to expect, reckon on; (prévenir) to anticipate; (organiser) to plan; (préparer, réserver) to allow; **prévu pour 10h** scheduled for 10 o'clock

prévoyance [pʀevwajɑ̃s] nf: **caisse de** ~ contingency fund

prévoyant, e [pʀevwajɑ̃, -ɑ̃t] adj gifted with (ou showing) foresight

prévu, e [pʀevy] pp de **prévoir**

prier [pʀije] vi to pray ♦ vt (Dieu) to pray to; (implorer) to beg; (demander): ~ **qn de faire** to ask sb to do; **se faire** ~ to need coaxing ou persuading; **je vous en prie** (allez-y) please do; (de rien) don't mention it

prière [pʀijɛʀ] nf prayer; "~ **de faire ...**" "please do ..."

primaire [pʀimɛʀ] adj primary; (péj) simple-minded; simplistic ♦ nm (SCOL) primary education

prime [pʀim] nf (bonification) bonus; (subside) premium, allowance; (COMM: cadeau) free gift; (ASSURANCES, BOURSE) premium ♦ adj: **de** ~ **abord** at first glance

primer [pʀime] vt (l'emporter sur) to prevail over; (récompenser) to award a prize to ♦ vi to dominate; to prevail

primeurs [pʀimœʀ] nfpl early fruits and vegetables

primevère [pʀimvɛʀ] nf primrose

primitif, ive [pʀimitif, -iv] adj primitive; (originel) original

prince [pʀɛ̃s] nm prince; **princesse** nf princess

principal, e, aux [pʀɛ̃sipal, -o] adj principal, main ♦ nm (SCOL) principal, head(master); (essentiel) main thing

principe [pʀɛ̃sip] nm principle; **pour le** ~ on principle; **de** ~ (accord, hostilité) automatic; **par** ~ on principle; **en** ~ (habituellement) as a rule; (théoriquement) in principle

printemps [pʀɛ̃tɑ̃] nm spring

priorité [pʀijɔʀite] nf (AUTO): **avoir la** ~ **(sur)** to have right of way (over); ~ **à droite** right of way to vehicles coming from the right

pris, e [pʀi, pʀiz] pp de **prendre** ♦ adj (place) taken; (journée, mains) full; (billets) sold; (personne) busy; **avoir le nez/la gorge** ~**(e)** to have a stuffy nose/a hoarse throat; **être** ~ **de panique** to be panic-stricken

prise [pʀiz] nf (d'une ville) capture; (PÊCHE, CHASSE) catch; (point d'appui ou pour empoigner) hold; (ELEC: fiche) plug; (: femelle) socket; **être aux** ~**s avec** to be grappling with; ~ **de contact** nf (rencontre) initial meeting, first contact; ~ **de courant** power point; ~ **de sang** blood test; ~ **de terre** earth; ~ **de vue** (photo) shot; ~ **multiple** adaptor

priser [pʀize] vt (tabac, héroïne) to take; (estimer) to prize, value ♦ vi to take snuff

prison [pʀizɔ̃] nf prison; **aller/être en** ~ to go to/be in prison ou jail; **faire de la** ~ to serve time; **prisonnier, ière** nm/f prisoner ♦ adj captive

prit vb voir **prendre**

privé, e [pʀive] adj private; **en** ~ in private

priver [pʀive] vt: ~ **qn de** to deprive sb of; **se** ~ **de** to go ou do without

privilège [pʀivilɛʒ] nm privilege

prix [pʀi] nm (valeur) price; (récompense, SCOL) prize; **hors de** ~ exorbitantly priced; **à aucun** ~ not at any price; **à tout** ~ at all costs; ~ **d'achat/de vente/de revient** purchasing/selling/cost price

probable [pʀɔbabl(ə)] adj likely, probable; ~**ment** adv probably

probant, e [pʀɔbɑ̃, -ɑ̃t] adj convincing

problème [pʀɔblɛm] nm problem

procédé [pʀɔsede] nm (méthode) process; (comportement) behaviour no pl

procéder [pʀɔsede] vi to proceed; to behave; ~ **à** to carry out

procès [pʀɔsɛ] nm trial; (poursuites) proceedings pl; **être en** ~ **avec** to be involved in a lawsuit with

processus [pʀɔsesys] nm process

procès-verbal, aux [pʀɔsɛvɛʀbal, -o] nm (constat) statement; (aussi: P.V.): **avoir un** ~ to get a parking ticket; to be booked; (de réunion) minutes pl

prochain, e [pʀɔʃɛ̃, -ɛn] *adj* next; *(proche)* impending; near ♦ *nm* fellow man; **la ~e fois/semaine** ~e next time/week; **prochainement** *adv* soon, shortly

proche [pʀɔʃ] *adj* nearby; *(dans le temps)* imminent; *(parent, ami)* close; **~s** *nmpl (parents)* close relatives; **être ~ (de)** to be near, be close (to); **de ~ en ~** gradually; **le P~ Orient** the Middle East

proclamer [pʀɔklame] *vt* to proclaim

procuration [pʀɔkyʀasjɔ̃] *nf* proxy; power of attorney

procurer [pʀɔkyʀe] *vt*: **~ qch à qn** *(fournir)* to obtain sth for sb; *(causer: plaisir etc)* to bring sb sth; **se ~** *vt* to get

procureur [pʀɔkyʀœʀ] *nm* public prosecutor

prodige [pʀɔdiʒ] *nm* marvel, wonder; *(personne)* prodigy

prodigue [pʀɔdig] *adj* generous; extravagant; **fils ~** prodigal son

prodiguer [pʀɔdige] *vt (argent, biens)* to be lavish with; *(soins, attentions)*: **~ qch à qn** to give sb sth

producteur, trice [pʀɔdyktœʀ, -tʀis] *nm/f* producer

production [pʀɔdyksjɔ̃] *nf (gén)* production; *(rendement)* output

produire [pʀɔdɥiʀ] *vt* to produce; **se ~** *vi (acteur)* to perform, appear; *(événement)* to happen, occur

produit [pʀɔdɥi] *nm (gén)* product; **~ d'entretien** cleaning product; **~ national brut** gross national product; **~s agricoles** farm produce *sg*; **~s alimentaires** *nmpl* foodstuffs

prof [pʀɔf] *(fam) nm* teacher

profane [pʀɔfan] *adj (REL)* secular ♦ *nm/f* layman(woman)

proférer [pʀɔfeʀe] *vt* to utter

professeur [pʀɔfesœʀ] *nm* teacher; *(titulaire d'une chaire)* professor; **~ (de faculté)** (university) lecturer

profession [pʀɔfesjɔ̃] *nf* profession; **sans ~** unemployed; **professionnel, le** *adj, nm/f* professional

profil [pʀɔfil] *nm* profile; *(d'une voiture)* line, contour; **de ~** in profile; **profiler** *vt* to streamline

profit [pʀɔfi] *nm (avantage)* benefit, advantage; *(COMM, FINANCE)* profit; **au ~ de** in aid of; **tirer ~ de** to profit from

profitable [pʀɔfitabl(ə)] *adj* beneficial; profitable

profiter [pʀɔfite] *vi*: **~ de** to take advantage of; to make the most of; **~ à** to benefit; to be profitable to

profond, e [pʀɔfɔ̃, -ɔ̃d] *adj* deep; *(méditation, mépris)* profound; **profondeur** *nf* depth

progéniture [pʀɔʒenityʀ] *nf* offspring *inv*

programme [pʀɔgʀam] *nm* programme;

(TV, RADIO) programmes *pl*; *(SCOL)* syllabus, curriculum; *(INFORM)* program; **programmer** *vt (TV, RADIO)* to put on, show; *(INFORM)* to program; **programmeur, euse** *nm/f* programmer

progrès [pʀɔgʀɛ] *nm* progress *no pl*; **faire des ~** to make progress

progresser [pʀɔgʀese] *vi* to progress; *(troupes etc)* to make headway *ou* progress; **progressif, ive** *adj* progressive

prohiber [pʀɔibe] *vt* to prohibit, ban

proie [pʀwa] *nf* prey *no pl*

projecteur [pʀɔʒɛktœʀ] *nm* projector; *(de théâtre, cirque)* spotlight

projectile [pʀɔʒɛktil] *nm* missile

projection [pʀɔʒɛksjɔ̃] *nf* projection; showing; **conférence avec ~s** lecture with slides *(ou* a film)

projet [pʀɔʒɛ] *nm* plan; *(ébauche)* draft; **~ de loi** bill

projeter [pʀɔʒte] *vt (envisager)* to plan; *(film, photos)* to project; *(passer)* to show; *(ombre, lueur)* to project; *(jeter)* to throw, cast; *(jeter)* to throw up *(ou* off *ou* out)

prolixe [pʀɔliks(ə)] *adj* verbose

prolongement [pʀɔlɔ̃ʒmɑ̃] *nm* extension; **~s** *nmpl (fig)* repercussions, effects; **dans le ~ de** running on from

prolonger [pʀɔlɔ̃ʒe] *vt (débat, séjour)* to prolong; *(délai, billet, rue)* to extend; *(suj: chose)* to be a continuation *ou* an extension of; **se ~** *vi* to go on

promenade [pʀɔmnad] *nf* walk *(ou* drive *ou* ride); **faire une ~** to go for a walk; **une ~ en voiture/à vélo** a drive/(bicycle) ride

promener [pʀɔmne] *vt (chien)* to take out for a walk; *(doigts, regard)*: **~ qch sur** to run sth over; **se ~** *vi* to go for *(ou* be out for) a walk

promesse [pʀɔmɛs] *nf* promise

promettre [pʀɔmɛtʀ(ə)] *vt* to promise ♦ *vi* to be *ou* look promising; **~ à qn de faire** to promise sb that one will do

promiscuité [pʀɔmiskɥite] *nf* crowding; lack of privacy

promontoire [pʀɔmɔ̃twaʀ] *nm* headland

promoteur, trice [pʀɔmɔtœʀ, -tʀis] *nm/f (instigateur)* instigator, promoter; **~ (immobilier)** property developer *(BRIT)*, real estate promoter *(US)*

promotion [pʀɔmɔsjɔ̃] *nf* promotion

promouvoir [pʀɔmuvwaʀ] *vt* to promote

prompt, e [pʀɔ̃, pʀɔ̃t] *adj* swift, rapid

prôner [pʀone] *vt* to advocate

pronom [pʀɔnɔ̃] *nm* pronoun

prononcer [pʀɔnɔ̃se] *vt (son, mot, jugement)* to pronounce; *(dire)* to utter; *(allocution)* to deliver; **se ~** *vi* to reach a decision, give a verdict; **se ~ sur** to give an opinion on; **se ~ contre** to come down against; **prononciation** *nf* pronunciation

pronostic [pʀɔnɔstik] *nm (MÉD)* prognosis;

(fig: aussi: ~s) forecast
propagande [prɔpagɑ̃d] *nf* propaganda
propager [prɔpaʒe] *vt* to spread; **se ~** *vi* to spread
prophète [prɔfɛt] *nm* prophet
prophétie [prɔfesi] *nf* prophecy
propice [prɔpis] *adj* favourable
proportion [prɔpɔrsjɔ̃] *nf* proportion; **toute(s) ~(s) gardée(s)** making due allowance(s)
propos [prɔpo] *nm (paroles)* talk *no pl*, remark; *(intention)* intention, aim; *(sujet):* **à quel ~?** what about?; **à ~ de** about, regarding; **à tout ~** for no reason at all; **à ~** by the way; *(opportunément)* at the right moment
proposer [prɔpoze] *vt (suggérer):* **~ qch à qn/de faire** to suggest sth (to sb)/doing, propose sth (to sb)/to do; *(offrir):* **~ qch à qn/de faire** to offer sb sth/to do; *(candidat)* to put forward; *(loi, motion)* to propose; **se ~** to offer one's services; **se ~ de faire** to intend *ou* propose to do; **proposition** *nf* suggestion; proposal; offer; *(LING)* clause
propre [prɔpr(ə)] *adj* clean; *(net)* neat, tidy; *(possessif)* own; *(sens)* literal; *(particulier):* **~ à** peculiar to; *(approprié):* **~ à** suitable for; *(de nature à):* **~ à faire** likely to do ♦ *nm:* **recopier au ~** to make a fair copy of; **proprement** *adv* cleanly; neatly, tidily; **le village proprement dit** the village itself; **à proprement parler** strictly speaking; **propreté** *nf* cleanliness; neatness; tidiness
propriétaire [prɔprijetɛr] *nm/f* owner; *(pour le locataire)* landlord(lady)
propriété [prɔprijete] *nf (gén)* property; *(droit)* ownership; *(objet, immeuble, terres)* property *gén no pl*
propulser [prɔpylse] *vt (missile)* to propel; *(projeter)* to hurl, fling
proroger [prɔrɔʒe] *vt* to put back, defer; *(prolonger)* to extend
proscrire [prɔskrir] *vt (bannir)* to banish; *(interdire)* to ban, prohibit
prose [proz] *nf (style)* prose
prospecter [prɔspɛkte] *vt* to prospect; *(COMM)* to canvass
prospectus [prɔspɛktys] *nm* leaflet
prospère [prɔspɛr] *adj* prosperous
prosterner [prɔstɛrne] *: se ~* *vi* to bow low, prostrate o.s.
prostituée [prɔstitɥe] *nf* prostitute
protecteur, trice [prɔtɛktœr, -tris] *adj* protective; *(air, ton: péj)* patronizing ♦ *nm/f* protector
protection [prɔtɛksjɔ̃] *nf* protection; *(d'un personnage influent: aide)* patronage
protéger [prɔteʒe] *vt* to protect; **se ~ de ou contre** to protect o.s. from
protéine [prɔtein] *nf* protein
protestant, e [prɔtɛstɑ̃, -ɑ̃t] *adj, nm/f*
Protestant
protestation [prɔtɛstasjɔ̃] *nf (plainte)* protest
protester [prɔtɛste] *vi:* **~ (contre)** to protest (against *ou* about); **~ de** *(son innocence, sa loyauté)* to protest
prothèse [prɔtɛz] *nf* artificial limb, prosthesis; **~ dentaire** denture
protocole [prɔtɔkɔl] *nm (fig)* etiquette
proue [pru] *nf* bow(s *pl*), prow
prouesse [prues] *nf* feat
prouver [pruve] *vt* to prove
provenance [prɔvnɑ̃s] *nf* origin; *(de mot, coutume)* source; **avion en ~ de** plane (arriving) from
provenir [prɔvnir] : **~ de** *vt* to come from; *(résulter de)* to be the result of
proverbe [prɔvɛrb(ə)] *nm* proverb
province [prɔvɛ̃s] *nf* province
proviseur [prɔvizœr] *nm* ≈ head(teacher) *(BRIT)*, ≈ principal *(US)*
provision [prɔvizjɔ̃] *nf (réserve)* stock, supply; *(avance: à un avocat, avoué)* retainer, retaining fee; *(COMM)* funds *pl* (in account); reserve; **~s** *nfpl (vivres)* provisions, food *no pl*
provisoire [prɔvizwar] *adj* temporary; *(JUR)* provisional
provoquer [prɔvɔke] *vt (inciter):* **~ qn à** to incite sb to; *(défier)* to provoke; *(causer)* to cause, bring about
proxénète [prɔksenɛt] *nm* procurer
proximité [prɔksimite] *nf* nearness, closeness; *(dans le temps)* imminence, closeness; **à ~** near *ou* close by; **à ~ de** near (to), close to
prude [pryd] *adj* prudish
prudemment [prydamɑ̃] *adv* carefully, cautiously; wisely, sensibly
prudence [prydɑ̃s] *nf* carefulness; caution; **avec ~** carefully; cautiously; **par (mesure de) ~** as a precaution
prudent, e [prydɑ̃, -ɑ̃t] *adj (pas téméraire)* careful, cautious; *(: en général)* safety-conscious; *(sage, conseillé)* wise, sensible; *(réservé)* cautious
prune [pryn] *nf* plum
pruneau, x [pryno] *nm* prune
prunelle [prynɛl] *nf* pupil; eye
prunier [prynje] *nm* plum tree
psaume [psom] *nm* psalm
pseudonyme [psødɔnim] *nm (gén)* fictitious name; *(d'écrivain)* pseudonym, pen name; *(de comédien)* stage name
psychiatre [psikjatr(ə)] *nm/f* psychiatrist
psychiatrique [psikjatrik] *adj* psychiatric
psychique [psiʃik] *adj* psychological
psychologie [psikɔlɔʒi] *nf* psychology; **psychologique** *adj* psychological; **psychologue** *nm/f* psychologist
P.T.T. *sigle fpl* = **Postes, Télécommunications et Télédiffusion**

pu *pp de* **pouvoir**
puanteur [pɥɑ̃tœʀ] *nf* stink, stench
pub [pyb] *(fam) abr f* (= *publicité*): **la ~** advertising
public, ique [pyblik] *adj* public; (*école, instruction*) state *cpd* ♦ *nm* public; (*assistance*) audience; **en ~** in public
publicitaire [pyblisitɛʀ] *adj* advertising *cpd*; (*film, voiture*) publicity *cpd*
publicité [pyblisite] *nf* (*méthode, profession*) advertising; (*annonce*) advertisement; (*révélations*) publicity
publier [pyblije] *vt* to publish
publique [pyblik] *adj voir* **public**
puce [pys] *nf* flea; (*INFORM*) chip; **~s** *nfpl* (*marché*) flea market *sg*
pudeur [pydœʀ] *nf* modesty
pudique [pydik] *adj* (*chaste*) modest; (*discret*) discreet
puer [pɥe] *(péj) vi* to stink
puéricultrice [pɥeʀikyltʀis] *nf* p(a)ediatric nurse
puériculture [pɥeʀikyltyʀ] *nf* p(a)ediatric nursing; infant care
puéril, e [pɥeʀil] *adj* childish
puis [pɥi] *vb voir* **pouvoir** ♦ *adv* then
puiser [pɥize] *vt:* **~ (dans)** to draw (from)
puisque [pɥisk(ə)] *conj* since
puissance [pɥisɑ̃s] *nf* power; **en ~** *adj* potential
puissant, e [pɥisɑ̃, -ɑ̃t] *adj* powerful
puisse *etc vb voir* **pouvoir**
puits [pɥi] *nm* well; **~ de mine** mine shaft
pull(-over) [pul(ɔvœʀ)] *nm* sweater
pulluler [pylyle] *vi* to swarm
pulpe [pylp(ə)] *nf* pulp
pulvérisateur [pylveʀizatœʀ] *nm* spray
pulvériser [pylveʀize] *vt* to pulverize; (*liquide*) to spray
punaise [pynɛz] *nf* (*ZOOL*) bug; (*clou*) drawing pin (*BRIT*), thumbtack (*US*)
punch¹ [pɔ̃ʃ] *nm* (*boisson*) punch
punch² [pœnʃ] *nm* (*BOXE, fig*) punch
punir [pyniʀ] *vt* to punish; **punition** *nf* punishment
pupille [pypij] *nf* (*ANAT*) pupil ♦ *nm/f* (*enfant*) ward; **~ de l'État** child in care
pupitre [pypitʀ(ə)] *nm* (*SCOL*) desk; (*REL*) lectern; (*de chef d'orchestre*) rostrum
pur, e [pyʀ] *adj* pure; (*vin*) undiluted; (*whisky*) neat; **en ~e perte** to no avail
purée [pyʀe] *nf:* **~ de pommes de terre** mashed potatoes *pl*; **~ de marrons** chestnut purée
purger [pyʀʒe] *vt* (*radiateur*) to drain; (*circuit hydraulique*) to bleed; (*MÉD, POL*) to purge; (*JUR: peine*) to serve
purin [pyʀɛ̃] *nm* liquid manure
pur-sang [pyʀsɑ̃] *nm inv* thoroughbred
pusillanime [pyzilanim] *adj* fainthearted
putain [pytɛ̃] *(fam!) nf* whore (*!*)
puzzle [pœzl(ə)] *nm* jigsaw (puzzle)

P.V. *sigle m* = **procès-verbal**
pyjama [piʒama] *nm* pyjamas *pl* (*BRIT*), pajamas *pl* (*US*)
pyramide [piʀamid] *nf* pyramid
Pyrénées [piʀene] *nfpl:* **les ~** the Pyrenees

Q q

QG [kyʒe] *sigle m* (= *quartier général*) HQ
QI [kyi] *sigle m* (= *quotient intellectuel*) IQ
quadragénaire [kadʀaʒenɛʀ] *nm/f* man/woman in his/her forties
quadriller [kadʀije] *vt* (*papier*) to mark out in squares; (*POLICE*) to keep under tight control
quadruple [k(w)adʀypl(ə)] *nm:* **le ~ de** four times as much as; **quadruplés, ées** *nm/fpl* quadruplets, quads
quai [ke] *nm* (*de port*) quay; (*de gare*) platform; **être à ~** (*navire*) to be alongside; (*train*) to be in the station
qualifier [kalifje] *vt* to qualify; **se ~** *vi* to qualify; **~ qch/qn de** to describe sth/sb as
qualité [kalite] *nf* quality; (*titre, fonction*) position
quand [kɑ̃] *conj, adv* when; **~ je serai riche** when I'm rich; **~ même** all the same; really; **~ bien même** even though
quant [kɑ̃] *: **~ à** prép* as for, as to; regarding
quant-à-soi [kɑ̃taswa] *nm:* **rester sur son ~** to remain aloof
quantité [kɑ̃tite] *nf* quantity, amount; (*SCIENCE*) quantity; (*grand nombre*): **une ou des ~(s) de** a great deal of
quarantaine [kaʀɑ̃tɛn] *nf* (*MÉD*) quarantine; **avoir la ~** (*âge*) to be around forty; **une ~ (de)** forty or so, about forty
quarante [kaʀɑ̃t] *num* forty
quart [kaʀ] *nm* (*fraction, partie*) quarter; (*surveillance*) watch; **un ~ de beurre** a quarter kilo of butter; **un ~ de vin** a quarter litre of wine; **une livre un ~ ou et ~** one and a quarter pounds; **le ~ de** a quarter of; **~ d'heure** quarter of an hour
quartier [kaʀtje] *nm* (*de ville*) district, area; (*de bœuf*) quarter; (*de fruit, fromage*) piece; **~s** *nmpl* (*MIL, BLASON*) quarters; **cinéma de ~** local cinema; **avoir ~ libre** (*fig*) to be free; **~ général** headquarters *pl*
quartz [kwaʀts] *nm* quartz
quasi [kazi] *adv* almost, nearly; **quasiment** *adv* almost, nearly

quatorze [katɔʀz(ə)] *num* fourteen
quatre [katʀ(ə)] *num* four; **à ~ pattes** on all fours; **tiré à ~ épingles** dressed up to the nines; **faire les ~ cent coups** to get a bit wild; **se mettre en ~ pour qn** to go out of one's way for sb; **~ à ~** (*monter, descendre*) four at a time; **quatre-vingt-dix** *num* ninety; **quatre-vingts** *num* eighty; **quatrième** *num* fourth
quatuor [kwatɥɔʀ] *nm* quartet(te)

MOT CLÉ

que [kə] *conj* **1** (*introduisant complétive*) that; **il sait ~ tu es là** he knows (that) you're here; **je veux ~ tu acceptes** I want you to accept; **il a dit ~ oui** he said he would (*ou* it was *etc*)
2 (*reprise d'autres conjonctions*): **quand il rentrera et qu'il aura mangé** when he gets back and (when) he has eaten; **si vous y allez ou ~ vous ...** if you go there or if you ...
3 (*en tête de phrase: hypothèse, souhait etc*): **qu'il le veuille ou non** whether he likes it or not; **qu'il fasse ce qu'il voudra!** let him do as he pleases!
4 (*après comparatif*) than; as; *voir aussi* **plus; aussi; autant** *etc*
5 (*seulement*): **ne ... ~** only; **il ne boit ~ de l'eau** he only drinks water
♦ *adv* (*exclamation*): **qu'il** *ou* **qu'est-ce qu'il est bête/court vite!** he's so silly!/he runs so fast!; **~ de livres!** what a lot of books!
♦ *pron* **1** (*relatif: personne*) whom; (: *chose*) that, which; **l'homme ~ je vois** the man (whom) I see; **le livre ~ tu vois** the book (that *ou* which) you see; **un jour ~ j'étais ...** a day when I was ...
2 (*interrogatif*) what; **~ fais-tu?, qu'est-ce ~ tu fais?** what are you doing?; **qu'est-ce ~ c'est?** what is it?, what's that?; **~ faire?** what can one do?

MOT CLÉ

quel, quelle [kɛl] *adj* **1** (*interrogatif: personne*) who; (: *chose*) what; which; **~ est cet homme?** who is this man?; **~ est ce livre?** what is this book?; **~ livre/homme?** what book/man?; (*parmi un certain choix*) which book/man?; **~s acteurs préférez-vous?** which actors do you prefer?; **dans ~s pays êtes-vous allé?** which *ou* what countries did you go to?
2 (*exclamatif*): **quelle surprise!** what a surprise!
3: **quel(le) que soit le coupable** whoever is guilty; **~ que soit votre avis** whatever your opinion

quelconque [kɛlkɔ̃k] *adj* (*médiocre*) indifferent, poor; (*sans attrait*) ordinary, plain;

(*indéfini*): **un ami ~** some friend or other

MOT CLÉ

quelque [kɛlkə] *adj* **1** some; a few; (*tournure interrogative*) any; **~ espoir** some hope; **il a ~s amis** he has a few *ou* some friends; **a-t-il ~s amis?** has he any friends?; **les ~s livres qui** the few books which; **20 kg et ~(s)** a bit over 20 kg
2: **~ ... que:** **quelque livre qu'il choisisse** whatever (*ou* whichever) book he chooses
3: **~ chose** something; (*tournure interrogative*) anything; **~ chose d'autre** something else; anything else; **~ part** somewhere; anywhere; **en ~ sorte** as it were
♦ *adv* **1** (*environ*): **~ 100 mètres** some 100 metres
2: **~ peu** rather, somewhat

quelquefois [kɛlkəfwa] *adv* sometimes
quelques-uns, -unes [kɛlkəzœ̃, -yn] *pron* a few, some
quelqu'un [kɛlkœ̃] *pron* someone, somebody; (*+tournure interrogative*) anyone *ou* anybody; **~ d'autre** someone *ou* somebody else; anybody else
quémander [kemɑ̃de] *vt* to beg for
qu'en dira-t-on [kɑ̃diʀatɔ̃] *nm inv*: **le ~** gossip, what people say
querelle [kəʀɛl] *nf* quarrel
quereller [kəʀele]: **se ~** *vi* to quarrel
qu'est-ce que [kɛskə] *voir* **que**
qu'est-ce qui [kɛski] *voir* **qui**
question [kɛstjɔ̃] *nf* (*gén*) question; (*fig*) matter; issue; **il a été ~ de** we (*ou* they) spoke about; **de quoi est-il ~?** what is it about?; **il n'en est pas ~** there's no question of it; **hors de ~** out of the question; **remettre en ~** to question; **~naire** [kɛstjɔnɛʀ] *nm* questionnaire; **~ner** [kɛstjɔne] *vt* to question
quête [kɛt] *nf* collection; (*recherche*) quest, search; **faire la ~** (*à l'église*) to take the collection; (*artiste*) to pass the hat round; **quêter** *vi* (*à l'église*) to take the collection
quetsche [kwɛtʃ(ə)] *nf* damson
queue [kø] *nf* tail; (*fig: du classement*) bottom; (: *de poêle*) handle; (: *de fruit, feuille*) stalk; (: *de train, colonne, file*) rear; **faire la ~** to queue (up) (*BRIT*), line up (*US*); **~ de cheval** ponytail; **queue-de-pie** *nf* (*habit*) tails *pl*, tail coat
qui [ki] *pron* (*personne*) who; (*+prép*) whom; (*chose, animal*) which, that; **qu'est-ce ~ est sur la table?** what is on the table?; **~ est-ce ~?** who?; **~ est-ce que?** who?; whom?; **à ~ est ce sac?** whose bag is this?; **à ~ parlais-tu?** who were you talking to?, to whom were you talking?; **amenez ~ vous voulez** bring who you like; **~ que ce soit** whoever it may be
quiconque [kikɔ̃k] *pron* (*celui qui*) who-

ever, anyone who; (*personne*) anyone, anybody

quiétude [kjetyd] *nf* (*d'un lieu*) quiet, tranquillity; **en toute** ~ in complete peace

quille [kij] *nf*: (**jeu de**) ~**s** skittles *sg* (*BRIT*), bowling (*US*)

quincaillerie [kɛ̃kajʀi] *nf* (*ustensiles*) hardware; (*magasin*) hardware shop; **quincaillier, ière** *nm/f* hardware dealer

quinquagénaire [kɛ̃kaʒenɛʀ] *nm/f* man/woman in his/her fifties

quintal, aux [kɛ̃tal, -o] *nm* quintal (*100 kg*)

quinte [kɛ̃t] *nf*: ~ (**de toux**) coughing fit

quintuple [kɛ̃typl(ə)] *nm*: **le** ~ **de** five times as much as; **quintuplés, ées** *nm/fpl* quintuplets, quins

quinzaine [kɛ̃zɛn] *nf*: **une** ~ (**de**) about fifteen, fifteen or so; **une** ~ (**de jours**) a fortnight

quinze [kɛ̃z] *num* fifteen; **demain en** ~ a fortnight *ou* two weeks tomorrow; **dans** ~ **jours** in a fortnight('s time), in two weeks (' time)

quiproquo [kipʀɔko] *nm* misunderstanding

quittance [kitɑ̃s] *nf* (*reçu*) receipt; (*facture*) bill

quitte [kit] *adj*: **être** ~ **envers qn** to be no longer in sb's debt; (*fig*) to be quits with sb; **être** ~ **de** (*obligation*) to be clear of; **en être** ~ **à bon compte** to have got off lightly; ~ **à faire** even if it means doing

quitter [kite] *vt* to leave; (*espoir, illusion*) to give up; (*vêtement*) to take off; **se** ~ *vi* (*couples, interlocuteurs*) to part; **ne quittez pas** (*au téléphone*) hold the line

qui-vive [kiviv] *nm*: **être sur le** ~ to be on the alert

quoi [kwa] *pron* (*interrogatif*) what; ~ **de neuf?** what's the news?; **as-tu de** ~ **écrire?** have you anything to write with?; **il n'a pas de** ~ **se l'acheter** he can't afford it; ~ **qu'il arrive** whatever happens; ~ **qu'il en soit** be that as it may; ~ **que ce soit** anything at all; "**il n'y a pas de** ~" "(please) don't mention it"; **à** ~ **bon?** what's the use?; **en** ~ **puis-je vous aider?** how can I help you?

quoique [kwak(ə)] *conj* (al)though

quolibet [kɔlibɛ] *nm* gibe, jeer

quote-part [kɔtpaʀ] *nf* share

quotidien, ne [kɔtidjɛ̃, -ɛn] *adj* daily; (*banal*) everyday ♦ *nm* (*journal*) daily (paper)

r. *abr* = **route; rue**

rab [ʀab] (*fam*) *abr m* = **rabiot**

rabâcher [ʀabaʃe] *vt* to keep on repeating

rabais [ʀabɛ] *nm* reduction, discount

rabaisser [ʀabese] *vt* (*rabattre*) to reduce; (*dénigrer*) to belittle

rabattre [ʀabatʀ(ə)] *vt* (*couvercle, siège*) to pull down; (*gibier*) to drive; **se** ~ *vi* (*bords, couvercle*) to fall shut; (*véhicule, coureur*) to cut in; **se** ~ **sur** to fall back on

rabbin [ʀabɛ̃] *nm* rabbi

rabiot [ʀabjo] (*fam*) *nm* extra, more

râblé, e [ʀable] *adj* stocky

rabot [ʀabo] *nm* plane

rabougri, e [ʀabugʀi] *adj* stunted

rabrouer [ʀabʀue] *vt* to snub

racaille [ʀakaj] (*péj*) *nf* rabble, riffraff

raccommoder [ʀakɔmɔde] *vt* to mend, repair; (*chaussette etc*) to darn

raccompagner [ʀakɔ̃paɲe] *vt* to take *ou* see back

raccord [ʀakɔʀ] *nm* link

raccorder [ʀakɔʀde] *vt* to join (up), link up; (*suj: pont etc*) to connect, link

raccourci [ʀakuʀsi] *nm* short cut

raccourcir [ʀakuʀsiʀ] *vt* to shorten

raccrocher [ʀakʀɔʃe] *vt* (*tableau*) to hang back up; (*récepteur*) to put down ♦ *vi* (*TÉL*) to hang up, ring off; **se** ~ **à** *vt* to cling to, hang on to

race [ʀas] *nf* race; (*d'animaux, fig*) breed; (*ascendance*) stock, race; **de** ~ purebred, pedigree

rachat [ʀaʃa] *nm* buying; buying back

racheter [ʀaʃte] *vt* (*article perdu*) to buy another; (*davantage*): ~ **du lait/3 œufs** to buy more milk/another 3 eggs *ou* 3 more eggs; (*après avoir vendu*) to buy back; (*d'occasion*) to buy; (*COMM: part, firme*) to buy up; (: *pension, rente*) to redeem; **se** ~ *vi* (*fig*) to make amends

racial, e, aux [ʀasjal, -o] *adj* racial

racine [ʀasin] *nf* root; ~ **carrée/cubique** square/cube root

raciste [ʀasist(ə)] *adj*, *nm/f* raci(al)ist

racket [ʀakɛt] *nm* racketeering *no pl*

racler [ʀakle] *vt* (*surface*) to scrape; (*tache, boue*) to scrape off

racoler [ʀakɔle] *vt* (*attirer: suj: prostituée*) to solicit; (: *parti, marchand*) to tout for

racontars [Rakɔ̃taR] *nmpl* gossip *sg*

raconter [Rakɔ̃te] *vt*: ~ **(à qn)** (*décrire*) to relate (to sb), tell (sb) about; (*dire*) to tell (sb)

racorni, e [Rakɔrni] *adj* hard(ened)

radar [RadaR] *nm* radar

rade [Rad] *nf* (natural) harbour; **rester en** ~ (*fig*) to be left stranded

radeau, x [Rado] *nm* raft

radiateur [RadjatœR] *nm* radiator, heater; (*AUTO*) radiator; ~ **électrique/à gaz** electric/gas heater *ou* fire

radiation [Radjasjɔ̃] *nf* (*voir radier*) striking off *no pl*; (*PHYSIQUE*) radiation

radical, e, aux [Radikal, -o] *adj* radical

radier [Radje] *vt* to strike off

radieux, euse [Radjø, -øz] *adj* radiant; brilliant, glorious

radin, e [Radɛ̃, -in] (*fam*) *adj* stingy

radio [Radjo] *nf* radio; (*MÉD*) X-ray ♦ *nm* radio operator; **à la** ~ on the radio; **radioactif, ive** *adj* radioactive; **radiodiffuser** *vt* to broadcast; **radiographie** *nf* radiography; (*photo*) X-ray photograph; **radiophonique** *adj* radio *cpd*; **radio-réveil** (*pl* **radios-réveils**) *nm* radio alarm clock; **radiotélévisé, e** *adj* broadcast on radio and television

radis [Radi] *nm* radish

radoter [Radɔte] *vi* to ramble on

radoucir [RadusiR] **se** ~ *vi* (*se réchauffer*) to become milder; (*se calmer*) to calm down; to soften

rafale [Rafal] *nf* (*vent*) gust (of wind); (*tir*) burst of gunfire

raffermir [RafɛRmiR] *vt* to firm up; (*fig*) to strengthen

raffiner [Rafine] *vt* to refine; **raffinerie** *nf* refinery

raffoler [Rafɔle]: ~ **de** *vt* to be very keen on

rafle [Rafl(ə)] *nf* (*de police*) raid

rafler [Rafle] (*fam*) *vt* to swipe, nick

rafraîchir [RafReʃiR] *vt* (*atmosphère, température*) to cool (down); (*aussi: mettre à* ~) to chill; (*fig: rénover*) to brighten up; **se** ~ *vi* to grow cooler; to freshen up; to refresh o.s.; **rafraîchissant, e** *adj* refreshing; **rafraîchissement** *nm* cooling; (*boisson*) cool drink; **rafraîchissements** *nmpl* (*boissons, fruits etc*) refreshments

rage [Raʒ] *nf* (*MÉD*): **la** ~ rabies; (*fureur*) rage, fury; **faire** ~ to rage; ~ **de dents** (raging) toothache

ragot [Rago] (*fam*) *nm* malicious gossip *no pl*

ragoût [Ragu] *nm* (*plat*) stew

raide [Rɛd] *adj* (*tendu*) taut, tight; (*escarpé*) steep; (*droit: cheveux*) straight; (*ankylosé, dur, guindé*) stiff; (*fam*) steep, stiff; flat broke ♦ *adv* (*en pente*) steeply; ~ **mort** stone dead; **raidir** *vt* (*muscles*) to stiffen;

(*câble*) to pull taut; **se raidir** *vi* to stiffen; to become taut; (*personne*) to tense up; to brace o.s.

raie [Rɛ] *nf* (*ZOOL*) skate, ray; (*rayure*) stripe; (*des cheveux*) parting

raifort [RefɔR] *nm* horseradish

rail [Raj] *nm* rail; (*chemins de fer*) railways *pl*; **par** ~ by rail

railler [Raje] *vt* to scoff at, jeer at

rainure [RenyR] *nf* groove; slot

raisin [Rezɛ̃] *nm* (*aussi*: ~**s**) grapes *pl*; ~**s secs** raisins

raison [Rezɔ̃] *nf* reason; **avoir** ~ to be right; **donner** ~ **à qn** to agree with sb; to prove sb right; **se faire une** ~ to learn to live with it; **perdre la** ~ to become insane; to take leave of one's senses; ~ **de plus** all the more reason; **à plus forte** ~ all the more so; **en** ~ **de** because of; according to; in proportion to; **à** ~ **de** at the rate of; ~ **sociale** corporate name; **raisonnable** *adj* reasonable, sensible

raisonnement [Rezɔnmɑ̃] *nm* reasoning; arguing, argument

raisonner [Rezɔne] *vi* (*penser*) to reason; (*argumenter, discuter*) to argue ♦ *vt* (*personne*) to reason with

rajeunir [RaʒœniR] *vt* (*suj: coiffure, robe*): ~ **qn** to make sb look younger; (*: cure etc*) to rejuvenate; (*fig*) to give a new look to; to inject new blood into ♦ *vi* to become (*ou* look) younger

rajouter [Raʒute] *vt*: ~ **du sel/un œuf** to add some more salt/another egg

rajuster [Raʒyste] *vt* (*vêtement*) to straighten, tidy; (*salaires*) to adjust; (*machine*) to readjust

ralenti [Ralɑ̃ti] *nm*: **au** ~ (*AUTO*): **tourner au** ~ to tick over (*AUTO*), idle; **au** ~ (*CINÉMA*) in slow motion; (*fig*) at a slower pace

ralentir [Ralɑ̃tiR] *vt* to slow down

râler [Rɑle] *vi* to groan; (*fam*) to grouse, moan (and groan)

rallier [Ralje] *vt* (*rassembler*) to rally; (*rejoindre*) to rejoin; (*gagner à sa cause*) to win over; **se** ~ **à** (*avis*) to come over *ou* round to

rallonge [Ralɔ̃ʒ] *nf* (*de table*) (extra) leaf; (*argent etc*) extra *no pl*

rallonger [Ralɔ̃ʒe] *vt* to lengthen

rallye [Rali] *nm* rally; (*POL*) march

ramassage [Ramasaʒ] *nm*: ~ **scolaire** school bus service

ramassé, e [Ramase] *adj* (*trapu*) squat

ramasser [Ramase] *vt* (*objet tombé ou par terre, fam*) to pick up; (*recueillir*) to collect; (*récolter*) to gather; **se** ~ *vi* (*sur soi-même*) to huddle up; to crouch; **ramassis** (*péj*) *nm* bunch; jumble

rambarde [Rɑ̃baRd(ə)] *nf* guardrail

rame [Ram] *nf* (*aviron*) oar; (*de métro*)

train; (*de papier*) ream

rameau, x [ʀamo] *nm* (small) branch; **les R~x** (*REL*) Palm Sunday *sg*

ramener [ʀamne] *vt* to bring back; (*reconduire*) to take back; (*rabattre: couverture, visière*): ~ **qch sur** to pull sth back over; ~ **qch à** (*réduire à, aussi MATH*) to reduce sth to

ramer [ʀame] *vi* to row

ramollir [ʀamɔliʀ] *vt* to soften; **se ~** *vi* to go soft

ramoner [ʀamɔne] *vt* to sweep

rampe [ʀɑ̃p] *nf* (*d'escalier*) banister(s *pl*); (*dans un garage, d'un terrain*) ramp; (*THÉÂTRE*): **la ~** the footlights *pl*; ~ **de lancement** launching pad

ramper [ʀɑ̃pe] *vi* to crawl

rancard [ʀɑ̃kaʀ] (*fam*) *nm* date; tip

rancart [ʀɑ̃kaʀ] *nm*: **mettre au ~** to scrap

rance [ʀɑ̃s] *adj* rancid

rancœur [ʀɑ̃kœʀ] *nf* rancour

rançon [ʀɑ̃sɔ̃] *nf* ransom; (*fig*) price

rancune [ʀɑ̃kyn] *nf* grudge, rancour; **garder ~ à qn (de qch)** to bear sb a grudge (for sth); **sans ~!** no hard feelings!; **rancunier, ière** *adj* vindictive, spiteful

randonnée [ʀɑ̃dɔne] *nf* ride; (*à pied*) walk, ramble; hike, hiking *no pl*

rang [ʀɑ̃] *nm* (*rangée*) row; (*grade, classement*) rank; **~s** *nmpl* (*MIL*) ranks; **se mettre en ~s/sur un ~** to get into *ou* form rows/a line; **au premier ~** in the first row; (*fig*) ranking first

rangé, e [ʀɑ̃ʒe] *adj* (*sérieux*) orderly, steady

rangée [ʀɑ̃ʒe] *nf* row

ranger [ʀɑ̃ʒe] *vt* (*classer, grouper*) to order, arrange; (*mettre à sa place*) to put away; (*voiture dans la rue*) to park; (*mettre de l'ordre dans*) to tidy up; (*arranger*) to arrange; (*fig: classer*): ~ **qn/qch parmi** to rank sb/sth among; **se ~** *vi* (*véhicule, conducteur*) to pull over *ou* in; (*piéton*) to step aside; (*s'assagir*) to settle down; **se ~ à** (*avis*) to come round to

ranimer [ʀanime] *vt* (*personne*) to bring round; (*forces, courage*) to restore; (*troupes etc*) to kindle new life in; (*douleur, souvenir*) to revive; (*feu*) to rekindle

rap [ʀap] *nm* rap (music)

rapace [ʀapas] *nm* bird of prey

râpe [ʀɑp] *nf* (*CULIN*) grater

râpé, e [ʀɑpe] *adj* (*tissu*) threadbare

râper [ʀɑpe] *vt* (*CULIN*) to grate

rapetisser [ʀaptise] *vt* to shorten

rapide [ʀapid] *adj* fast; (*prompt*) quick ♦ *nm* express (train); (*de cours d'eau*) rapid; **rapidement** *adv* fast; quickly

rapiécer [ʀapjese] *vt* to patch

rappel [ʀapɛl] *nm* (*THÉÂTRE*) curtain call; (*MÉD: vaccination*) booster; (*ADMIN: de salaire*) back pay *no pl*; (*d'une aventure, d'un nom*) reminder

rappeler [ʀaple] *vt* to call back; (*ambassadeur, MIL*) to recall; (*faire se souvenir*): ~ **qch à qn** to remind sb of sth; **se ~** *vt* (*se souvenir de*) to remember, recall

rapport [ʀapɔʀ] *nm* (*compte rendu*) report; (*profit*) yield, return; revenue; (*lien, analogie*) relationship; (*MATH, TECH*) ratio; **~s** *nmpl* (*entre personnes, pays*) relations; **avoir ~ à** to have something to do with; **être en ~ avec** (*idée de corrélation*) to be related to; **être/se mettre en ~ avec qn** to be/get in touch with sb; **par ~ à** in relation to; ~ **qualité-prix** *nm* value (for money); **~s (sexuels)** (sexual) intercourse *sg*

rapporter [ʀapɔʀte] *vt* (*rendre, ramener*) to bring back; (*apporter davantage*) to bring more; (*suj: investissement*) to yield; (: *activité*) to bring in; (*relater*) to report ♦ *vi* (*investissement*) to give a good return *ou* yield; (: *activité*) to be very profitable; **se ~ à** (*correspondre à*) to relate to; **s'en ~ à** to rely on; ~ **qch à** (*fig: rattacher*) to relate sth to; **rapporteur, euse** *nm/f* (*de procès, commission*) reporter; (*péj*) telltale ♦ *nm* (*GÉOM*) protractor

rapprochement [ʀapʀɔʃmɑ̃] *nm* (*de nations, familles*) reconciliation; (*analogie, rapport*) parallel

rapprocher [ʀapʀɔʃe] *vt* (*chaise d'une table*): ~ **qch (de)** to bring sth closer (to); (*deux objets*) to bring closer together; (*réunir*) to bring together; (*comparer*) to establish a parallel between; **se ~** *vi* to draw closer *ou* nearer; **se ~ de** to come closer to; (*présenter une analogie avec*) to be close to

rapt [ʀapt] *nm* abduction

raquette [ʀakɛt] *nf* (*de tennis*) racket; (*de ping-pong*) bat; (*à neige*) snowshoe

rare [ʀaʀ] *adj* rare; (*main-d'œuvre, denrées*) scarce; (*cheveux, herbe*) sparse

rarement [ʀaʀmɑ̃] *adv* rarely, seldom

ras, e [ʀɑ, ʀɑz] *adj* (*tête, cheveux*) close-cropped; (*poil, herbe*) short ♦ *adv* short; **en ~e campagne** in open country; **à ~ bords** to the brim; **au ~ de** level with; **en avoir ~ le bol** (*fam*) to be fed up; ~ **du cou** *adj* (*pull, robe*) crew-neck

rasade [ʀazad] *nf* glassful

raser [ʀɑze] *vt* (*barbe, cheveux*) to shave off; (*menton, personne*) to shave; (*fam: ennuyer*) to bore; (*démolir*) to raze (to the ground); (*frôler*) to graze, skim; **se ~** *vi* to shave; (*fam*) to be bored (to tears); **rasoir** *nm* razor

rassasier [ʀasazje] *vt* to satisfy

rassemblement [ʀasɑ̃bləmɑ̃] *nm* (*groupe*) gathering; (*POL*) union

rassembler [ʀasɑ̃ble] *vt* (*réunir*) to assemble, gather; (*regrouper, amasser*) to gather together, collect; **se ~** *vi* to gather

rassis, e [Rasi, -iz] *adj (pain)* stale

rassurer [RasyRe] *vt* to reassure; **se ~** *vi* to be reassured; **rassure-toi** don't worry

rat [Ra] *nm* rat

rate [Rat] *nf* spleen

raté, e [Rate] *adj (tentative)* unsuccessful, failed ♦ *nm/f* failure ♦ *nm* misfiring *no pl*

râteau, x [Rato] *nm* rake

râtelier [Ratəlje] *nm* rack; *(fam)* false teeth *pl*

rater [Rate] *vi (affaire, projet etc)* to go wrong, fail ♦ *vt (cible, train, occasion)* to miss; *(démonstration, plat)* to spoil; *(examen)* to fail

ration [Rɑsjɔ̃] *nf* ration; *(fig)* share

ratisser [Ratise] *vt (allée)* to rake; *(feuilles)* to rake up; *(suj: armée, police)* to comb

R.A.T.P. *sigle f* (= Régie autonome des transports parisiens) Paris transport authority

rattacher [Ratafe] *vt (animal, cheveux)* to tie up again; *(incorporer: ADMIN etc)*: **~ qch à** to join sth to; *(fig: relier)*: **~ qch à** to link sth with; *(: lier)*: **~ qn à** to bind *ou* tie sb to

rattraper [RatRape] *vt (fugitif)* to recapture; *(empêcher de tomber)* to catch (hold of); *(atteindre, rejoindre)* to catch up with; *(réparer: imprudence, erreur)* to make up for; **se ~** *vi* to make good one's losses; to make up for it; **se ~ (à)** *(se raccrocher)* to stop o.s. falling (by catching hold of)

rature [RatyR] *nf* deletion, erasure

rauque [Rok] *adj* raucous; hoarse

ravages [Rava3] *nmpl*: **faire des ~** to wreak havoc

ravaler [Ravale] *vt (mur, façade)* to restore; *(déprécier)* to lower

ravi, e [Ravi] *adj*: **être ~ de/que** to be delighted with/that

ravin [Ravɛ̃] *nm* gully, ravine

ravir [RaviR] *vt (enchanter)* to delight; *(enlever)*: **~ qch à qn** to rob sb of sth; **à ~** beautifully

raviser [Ravize] : **se ~** *vi* to change one's mind

ravissant, e [Ravisɑ̃, -ɑ̃t] *adj* delightful

ravisseur, euse [RavisœR, -øz] *nm/f* abductor, kidnapper

ravitailler [Ravitaje] *vt* to resupply; *(véhicule)* to refuel; **se ~** *vi* to get fresh supplies

raviver [Ravive] *vt (feu, douleur)* to revive; *(couleurs)* to brighten up

rayé, e [Reje] *adj (à rayures)* striped

rayer [Reje] *vt (érafler)* to scratch; *(barrer)* to cross out; *(d'une liste)* to cross off

rayon [Rejɔ̃] *nm (de soleil etc)* ray; *(GÉOM)* radius; *(de roue)* spoke; *(étagère)* shelf; *(de grand magasin)* department; **dans un ~ de** within a radius of; **~ d'action** range; **~ de soleil** sunbeam; **~s X** X-rays

rayonnement [Rejɔnmɑ̃] *nm* radiation; *(fig)* radiance; influence

rayonner [Rejɔne] *vi (chaleur, énergie)* to radiate; *(fig)* to shine forth; to be radiant; *(touriste)* to go touring *(from one base)*

rayure [RejyR] *nf (motif)* stripe; *(éraflure)* scratch; *(rainure, d'un fusil)* groove

raz-de-marée [Radmare] *nm inv* tidal wave

ré [Re] *nm (MUS)* D; *(en chantant la gamme)* re

réacteur [Reaktœʀ] *nm* jet engine

réaction [Reaksjɔ̃] *nf* reaction; **moteur à ~** jet engine

réadapter [Readapte] *vt* to readjust; *(MÉD)* to rehabilitate; **se ~ (à)** to readjust (to)

réagir [Rea3iR] *vi* to react

réalisateur, trice [RealizatœR, -tRis] *nm/f* director *(TV, CINÉMA)*

réalisation [Realizɑsjɔ̃] *nf* carrying out; realization; fulfilment; achievement; production; *(œuvre)* production; creation; work

réaliser [Realize] *vt (projet, opération)* to carry out, realize; *(rêve, souhait)* to realize, fulfil; *(exploit)* to achieve; *(achat, vente)* to make; *(film)* to produce; *(se rendre compte de, COMM: bien, capital)* to realize; **se ~** *vi* to be realized

réaliste [Realist(ə)] *adj* realistic

réalité [Realite] *nf* reality; **en ~** in (actual) fact; **dans la ~** in reality; **~ virtuelle** *(COMPUT)* virtual reality

réanimation [Reanimɑsjɔ̃] *nf* resuscitation; **service de ~** intensive care unit

réarmer [RearMe] *vt (arme)* to reload ♦ *vi (état)* to rearm

rébarbatif, ive [RebarBatif, -iv] *adj* forbidding

rebattu, e [Rəbaty] *adj* hackneyed

rebelle [Rəbɛl] *nm/f* rebel ♦ *adj (troupes)* rebel; *(enfant)* rebellious; *(mèche etc)* unruly; **~ à** unamenable to

rebeller [Rəbele]: **se ~** *vi* to rebel

rebondi, e [Rəbɔ̃di] *adj* rounded; chubby

rebondir [Rəbɔ̃diR] *vi (ballon: au sol)* to bounce; *(: contre un mur)* to rebound; *(fig)* to get moving again; **rebondissement** *nm* new development

rebord [RəbɔR] *nm* edge

rebours [RəbuR]: **à ~** *adv* the wrong way

rebrousse-poil [Rəbruspwal] : **à ~** *adv* the wrong way

rebrousser [Rəbruse] *vt*: **~ chemin** to turn back

rebut [Rəby] *nm*: **mettre au ~** to scrap; **~er** [Rəbyte] *vt* to put off

récalcitrant, e [Rekalsitrɑ̃, -ɑ̃t] *adj* refractory

recaler [Rəkale] *vt (SCOL)* to fail

récapituler [Rekapityle] *vt* to recapitulate; to sum up

receler [Rəsəle] *vt (produit d'un vol)* to receive; *(malfaiteur)* to harbour; *(fig)* to conceal; **receleur, euse** *nm/f* receiver

récemment [Resamɑ̃] *adv* recently

recenser [Rəsɑ̃se] *vt* (*population*) to take a census of; (*inventorier*) to list

récent, e [Resɑ̃, -ɑ̃t] *adj* recent

récépissé [Resepise] *nm* receipt

récepteur [Reseptœʀ] *nm* receiver; ~ **(de radio)** radio set *ou* receiver

réception [Resepsjɔ̃] *nf* receiving *no pl*; (*accueil*) reception, welcome; (*bureau*) reception desk; (*réunion mondaine*) reception, party; **réceptionniste** *nm/f* receptionist

recette [Rəsɛt] *nf* (*CULIN*) recipe; (*fig*) formula, recipe; (*COMM*) takings *pl*; ~**s** *nfpl*(: *rentrées*) receipts

receveur, euse [Rəsvœʀ, -øz] *nm/f* (*des contributions*) tax collector; (*des postes*) postmaster(mistress); (*d'autobus*) conductor(tress)

recevoir [Rəsvwaʀ] *vt* to receive; (*client, patient*) to see ♦ *vi* to receive visitors; to give parties; to see patients *etc*; **se ~** *vi* (*athlète*) to land; **être reçu** (*à un examen*) to pass

rechange [Rəʃɑ̃ʒ]: **de ~** *adj* (*pièces, roue*) spare; (*fig: solution*) alternative; **des vêtements de ~** a change of clothes

rechaper [Rəʃape] *vt* to remould, retread

réchapper [Reʃape]: ~ **de** *ou* **à** *vt* (*accident, maladie*) to come through

recharge [Rəʃaʀʒ(ə)] *nf* refill

recharger [Rəʃaʀʒe] *vt* (*camion, fusil, appareil-photo*) to reload; (*briquet, stylo*) to refill; (*batterie*) to recharge

réchaud [Reʃo] *nm* (*portable*) stove; platewarmer

réchauffer [Reʃofe] *vt* (*plat*) to reheat; (*mains, personne*) to warm; **se ~** *vi* (*température*) to get warmer

rêche [Rɛʃ] *adj* rough

recherche [Rəʃɛʀʃ(ə)] *nf* (*action*): **la ~ de** the search for; (*raffinement*) affectedness, studied elegance; (*scientifique etc*): **la ~** research; ~**s** *nfpl* (*de la police*) investigations; (*scientifiques*) research *sg*; **se mettre à la ~ de** to go in search of

recherché, e [Rəʃɛʀʃe] *adj* (*rare, demandé*) much sought-after; (*raffiné*) studied, affected

rechercher [Rəʃɛʀʃe] *vt* (*objet égaré, personne*) to look for; (*causes, nouveau procédé*) to try to find; (*bonheur, amitié*) to seek

rechute [Rəʃyt] *nf* (*MÉD*) relapse

récidiver [Residive] *vi* to commit a subsequent offence; (*fig*) to do it again

récif [Resif] *nm* reef

récipient [Resipjɑ̃] *nm* container

réciproque [Resipʀɔk] *adj* reciprocal

récit [Resi] *nm* story

récital [Resital] *nm* recital

réciter [Resite] *vt* to recite

réclamation [Reklamɑsjɔ̃] *nf* complaint; ~**s**

nfpl (*bureau*) complaints department *sg*

réclame [Reklam] *nf* ad, advert(isement); **article en ~** special offer

réclamer [Reklame] *vt* (*aide, nourriture etc*) to ask for; (*revendiquer*) to claim, demand; (*nécessiter*) to demand, require ♦ *vi* to complain

réclusion [Reklyzjɔ̃] *nf* imprisonment

recoin [Rəkwɛ̃] *nm* nook, corner; (*fig*) hidden recess

reçois *etc vb voir* **recevoir**

récolte [Rekɔlt(ə)] *nf* harvesting; gathering; (*produits*) harvest, crop; (*fig*) crop, collection

récolter [Rekɔlte] *vt* to harvest, gather (in); (*fig*) to collect; to get

recommandé [Rəkɔmɑ̃de] *nm* (*POSTES*): **en ~** by registered mail

recommander [Rəkɔmɑ̃de] *vt* to recommend; (*suj: qualités etc*) to commend; (*POSTES*) to register; **se ~ de qn** to give sb's name as a reference

recommencer [Rəkɔmɑ̃se] *vt* (*reprendre: lutte, séance*) to resume, start again; (*refaire: travail, explications*) to start afresh, start (over) again; (*récidiver: erreur*) to make again ♦ *vi* to start again; (*récidiver*) to do it again

récompense [Rekɔ̃pɑ̃s] *nf* reward; (*prix*) award; **récompenser** *vt*: **récompenser qn (de *ou* pour)** to reward sb (for)

réconcilier [Rekɔ̃silje] *vt* to reconcile; **se ~ (avec)** to be reconciled (with)

reconduire [Rəkɔ̃dɥiʀ] *vt* (*raccompagner*) to take *ou* see back; (*JUR, POL: renouveler*) to renew

réconfort [Rekɔ̃fɔʀ] *nm* comfort

réconforter [Rekɔ̃fɔʀte] *vt* (*consoler*) to comfort; (*revigorer*) to fortify

reconnaissance [Rəkɔnɛsɑ̃s] *nf* recognition; acknowledgement; (*gratitude*) gratitude, gratefulness; (*MIL*) reconnaissance, recce; **reconnaissant, e** [Rəkɔnɛsɑ̃, -ɑ̃t] *adj* grateful

reconnaître [Rəkɔnɛtʀ(ə)] *vt* to recognize; (*MIL: lieu*) to reconnoitre; (*JUR: enfant, dette, droit*) to acknowledge; ~ **que** to admit *ou* acknowledge that; ~ **qn/qch à** to recognize sb/sth by

reconnu, e [R(ə)kɔny] *adj* (*indiscuté, connu*) recognized

reconstituant, e [Rəkɔ̃stitɥɑ̃, -ɑ̃t] *adj* (*aliment, régime*) strength-building

reconstituer [Rəkɔ̃stitɥe] *vt* (*monument ancien*) to recreate; (*fresque, vase brisé*) to piece together, reconstitute; (*événement, accident*) to reconstruct; (*fortune, patrimoine*) to rebuild

reconstruire [Rəkɔ̃stʀɥiʀ] *vt* to rebuild

reconvertir [Rəkɔ̃vɛʀtiʀ]: **se ~** *vr* (*un métier, une branche*) to go into

record [Rəkɔʀ] *nm, adj* record

recoupement [ʀəkupmɑ̃] *nm*: **par ~** by cross-checking

recouper [ʀəkupe]: **se ~** *vi* (*témoignages*) to tie *ou* match up

recourbé, e [ʀəkuʀbe] *adj* curved; hooked; bent

recourir [ʀəkuʀiʀ]: **~ à** *vt* (*ami, agence*) to turn *ou* appeal to; (*force, ruse, emprunt*) to resort to

recours [ʀəkuʀ] *nm* (*JUR*) appeal; **avoir ~ à = recourir à**; **en dernier ~** as a last resort; **~ en grâce** plea for clemency

recouvrer [ʀəkuvʀe] *vt* (*vue, santé etc*) to recover, regain; (*impôts*) to collect; (*créance*) to recover

recouvrir [ʀəkuvʀiʀ] *vt* (*couvrir à nouveau*) to re-cover; (*couvrir entièrement, aussi fig*) to cover; (*cacher, masquer*) to conceal, hide; **se ~** *vi* (*se superposer*) to overlap

récréation [ʀekʀeasjɔ̃] *nf* recreation, entertainment; (*SCOL*) break

récrier [ʀekʀije]: **se ~** *vi* to exclaim

récriminations [ʀekʀiminasjɔ̃] *nfpl* remonstrations, complaints

recroqueviller [ʀəkʀɔkvije]: **se ~** *vi* (*feuilles*) to curl *ou* shrivel up; (*personne*) to huddle up

recrudescence [ʀəkʀydesɑ̃s] *nf* fresh outbreak

recrue [ʀəkʀy] *nf* recruit

recruter [ʀəkʀyte] *vt* to recruit

rectangle [ʀɛktɑ̃gl(ə)] *nm* rectangle; **rectangulaire** *adj* rectangular

recteur [ʀɛktœʀ] *nm* ≈ (regional) director of education (*BRIT*), ≈ state superintendent of education (*US*)

rectificatif, -iv [ʀɛktifikatif, -iv] *nm* correction

rectifier [ʀɛktifje] *vt* (*tracé, virage*) to straighten; (*calcul, adresse*) to correct; (*erreur, faute*) to rectify

rectiligne [ʀɛktiliɲ] *adj* straight; (*GÉOM*) rectilinear

reçu, e [ʀəsy] *pp de* **recevoir** ♦ *adj* (*admis, consacré*) accepted ♦ *nm* (*COMM*) receipt

recueil [ʀəkœj] *nm* collection

recueillir [ʀəkœjiʀ] *vt* to collect; (*voix, suffrages*) to win; (*accueillir: réfugiés, chat*) to take in; **se ~** *vi* to gather one's thoughts; to meditate

recul [ʀəkyl] *nm* retreat; recession; decline; (*d'arme à feu*) recoil, kick; **avoir un mouvement de ~** to recoil; **prendre du ~** to stand back

reculé, e [ʀəkyle] *adj* remote

reculer [ʀəkyle] *vi* to move back, back away; (*AUTO*) to reverse, back (up); (*fig*) to (be on the) decline; to be losing ground; (: *se dérober*) to shrink back ♦ *vt* to move back; to reverse, back (up); (*fig: possibilités, limites*) to extend; (: *date, décision*) to postpone

reculons [ʀəkylɔ̃]: **à ~** *adv* backwards

récupérer [ʀekypeʀe] *vt* to recover, get back; (*heures de travail*) to make up; (*déchets*) to salvage; (*délinquant etc*) to rehabilitate ♦ *vi* to recover

récurer [ʀekyʀe] *vt* to scour

récuser [ʀekyze] *vt* to challenge; **se ~** *vi* to decline to give an opinion

reçut *vb voir* **recevoir**

recycler [ʀəsikle] *vt* (*SCOL*) to reorientate; (*employés*) to retrain; (*TECH*) to recycle

rédacteur, trice [ʀedaktœʀ, -tʀis] *nm/f* (*journaliste*) writer; subeditor; (*d'ouvrage de référence*) editor, compiler; **~ en chef** chief editor; **~ publicitaire** copywriter

rédaction [ʀedaksjɔ̃] *nf* writing; (*rédacteurs*) editorial staff; (*bureau*) editorial office(s); (*SCOL: devoir*) essay, composition

reddition [ʀedisjɔ̃] *nf* surrender

redemander [ʀədmɑ̃de] *vt* to ask again for; to ask for more of

redescendre [ʀədesɑ̃dʀ(ə)] *vi* to go back down ♦ *vt* (*pente etc*) to go back down

redevable [ʀədvabl(ə)] *adj*: **être ~ de qch à qn** (*somme*) to owe sb sth; (*fig*) to be indebted to sb for sth

redevance [ʀədvɑ̃s] *nf* (*TÉL*) rental charge; (*TV*) licence fee

rédiger [ʀediʒe] *vt* to write; (*contrat*) to draw up

redire [ʀədiʀ] *vt* to repeat; **trouver à ~ à** to find fault with

redoublé, e [ʀəduble] *adj*: **à coups ~s** even harder, twice as hard

redoubler [ʀəduble] *vi* (*tempête, violence*) to intensify; (*SCOL*) to repeat a year; **~ de** to be twice as +*adjectif*

redoutable [ʀədutabl(ə)] *adj* formidable, fearsome

redouter [ʀədute] *vt* to fear; (*appréhender*) to dread

redresser [ʀədʀese] *vt* (*arbre, mât*) to set upright; (*pièce tordue*) to straighten out; (*situation, économie*) to put right; **se ~** *vi* (*objet penché*) to right itself; (*personne*) to sit (*ou* stand up) (straight)

réduction [ʀedyksjɔ̃] *nf* reduction

réduire [ʀedɥiʀ] *vt* to reduce; (*prix, dépenses*) to cut, reduce; (*MÉD: fracture*) to set; **se ~ à** (*revenir à*) to boil down to; **se ~ en** (*se transformer en*) to be reduced to

réduit [ʀedɥi] *nm* tiny room; recess

rééducation [ʀeedykasjɔ̃] *nf* (*d'un membre*) re-education; (*de délinquants, d'un blessé*) rehabilitation

réel, le [ʀeɛl] *adj* real

réellement [ʀeɛlmɑ̃] *adv* really

réévaluer [ʀeevalɥe] *vt* to revalue

réexpédier [ʀeɛkspedje] *vt* (*à l'envoyeur*) to return, send back; (*au destinataire*) to send on, forward

refaire [ʀəfɛʀ] *vt* (*faire de nouveau, recommencer*) to do again; (*réparer, restaurer*) to do up

réfection [ʀefɛksjɔ̃] *nf* repair

réfectoire [ʀefɛktwaʀ] *nm* refectory

référence [ʀefeʀɑ̃s] *nf* reference; ~s *nfpl* (*recommandations*) reference *sg*

référer [ʀefeʀe] : **se ~ à** *vt* to refer to; **en ~ à qn** to refer the matter to sb

réfléchi, e [ʀefleʃi] *adj* (*caractère*) thoughtful; (*action*) well-thought-out; (*LING*) reflexive

réfléchir [ʀefleʃiʀ] *vt* to reflect ♦ *vi* to think; **~ à** *ou* **sur** to think about

reflet [ʀəflɛ] *nm* reflection; (*sur l'eau etc*) sheen *no pl*, glint

refléter [ʀəflete] *vt* to reflect; **se ~** *vi* to be reflected

réflexe [ʀeflɛks(ə)] *nm, adj* reflex

réflexion [ʀeflɛksjɔ̃] *nf* (*de la lumière etc, pensée*) reflection; (*fait de penser*) thought; (*remarque*) remark; **~ faite, à la ~** on reflection

refluer [ʀəflye] *vi* to flow back; (*foule*) to surge back

reflux [ʀəfly] *nm* (*de la mer*) ebb

réforme [ʀefɔʀm(ə)] *nf* reform; (*REL*): **la R~** the Reformation

réformer [ʀefɔʀme] *vt* to reform; (*MIL*) to declare unfit for service

refouler [ʀəfule] *vt* (*envahisseurs*) to drive back; (*liquide*) to force back; (*fig*) to suppress; (*PSYCH*) to repress

réfractaire [ʀefʀaktɛʀ] *adj*: **être ~ à** to resist

refrain [ʀəfʀɛ̃] *nm* (*MUS*) refrain, chorus; (*air, fig*) tune

refréner [ʀəfʀene] *vt* to curb, check

réfréner [ʀefʀene] *vt* = **refréner**

réfrigérateur [ʀefʀiʒeʀatœʀ] *nm* refrigerator, fridge

refroidir [ʀəfʀwadiʀ] *vt* to cool ♦ *vi* to cool (down); **se ~** *vi* (*prendre froid*) to catch a chill; (*temps*) to get cooler *ou* colder; (*fig*) to cool (off); **refroidissement** *nm* (*grippe etc*) chill

refuge [ʀəfyʒ] *nm* refuge; (*pour piétons*) (traffic) island

réfugié, e [ʀefyʒje] *adj, nm/f* refugee

réfugier [ʀefyʒje]: **se ~** *vi* to take refuge

refus [ʀəfy] *nm* refusal; **ce n'est pas de ~** I won't say no, it's welcome

refuser [ʀəfyze] *vt* to refuse; (*SCOL: candidat*) to fail; **~ qch à qn** to refuse sb sth; **~ du monde** to have to turn people away; **~ à faire** to refuse to do

réfuter [ʀefyte] *vt* to refute

regagner [ʀəɡaɲe] *vt* (*argent, faveur*) to win back; (*lieu*) to get back to; **~ le temps perdu** to make up (for) lost time

regain [ʀəɡɛ̃] *nm* (*renouveau*): **un ~ de** renewed +*nom*

régal [ʀeɡal] *nm* treat

régaler [ʀeɡale] : **se ~** *vi* to have a delicious meal; (*fig*) to enjoy o.s.

regard [ʀəɡaʀ] *nm* (*coup d'œil*) look, glance; (*expression*) look (in one's eye); **au ~ de** (*loi, morale*) from the point of view of; **en ~** (*vis à vis*) opposite; **en ~ de** in comparison with

regardant, e [ʀəɡaʀdɑ̃, -ɑ̃t] *adj*: **très/peu ~ (sur)** quite fussy/very free (about); (*économe*) very tight-fisted/quite generous (with)

regarder [ʀəɡaʀde] *vt* (*examiner, observer, lire*) to look at; (*film, télévision, match*) to watch; (*envisager: situation, avenir*) to view; (*considérer: son intérêt etc*) to be concerned with; (*être orienté vers*): **~ (vers)** to face; (*concerner*) to concern ♦ *vi* to look; **~ à** (*dépense*) to be fussy with *ou* over; **~ qn/ qch comme** to regard sb/sth as

régie [ʀeʒi] *nf* (*COMM, INDUSTRIE*) state-owned company; (*THÉÂTRE, CINÉMA*) production; (*RADIO, TV*) control room

regimber [ʀəʒɛ̃be] *vi* to balk, jib

régime [ʀeʒim] *nm* (*POL*) régime; (*ADMIN: carcéral, fiscal etc*) system; (*MÉD*) diet; (*TECH*) (engine) speed; (*fig*) rate, pace; (*de bananes, dattes*) bunch; **se mettre au/ suivre un ~** to go on/be on a diet

régiment [ʀeʒimɑ̃] *nm* regiment; (*fig: fam*): **un ~ de** an army of

région [ʀeʒjɔ̃] *nf* region; **régional, e, aux** *adj* regional

régir [ʀeʒiʀ] *vt* to govern

régisseur [ʀeʒisœʀ] *nm* (*d'un domaine*) steward; (*CINÉMA, TV*) assistant director; (*THÉÂTRE*) stage manager

registre [ʀəʒistʀ(ə)] *nm* (*livre*) register; logbook; ledger; (*MUS, LING*) register

réglage [ʀeɡlaʒ] *nm* adjustment; tuning

règle [ʀɛɡl(ə)] *nf* (*instrument*) ruler; (*loi, prescription*) rule; ~s *nfpl* (*PHYSIOL*) period *sg*; **en ~** (*papiers d'identité*) in order; **en ~ générale** as a (general) rule

réglé, e [ʀeɡle] *adj* well-ordered; steady; (*papier*) ruled; (*arrangé*) settled

règlement [ʀɛɡlamɑ̃] *nm* (*paiement*) settlement; (*arrêté*) regulation; (*règles, statuts*) regulations *pl*, rules *pl*; **~ de compte(s)** *nm* settling of old scores; **réglementaire** *adj* conforming to the regulations; (*tenue*) regulation *cpd*; **réglementer** [ʀɛɡlamɑ̃te] *vt* to regulate

régler [ʀeɡle] *vt* (*mécanisme, machine*) to regulate, adjust; (*moteur*) to tune; (*thermostat etc*) to set, adjust; (*conflit, facture*) to settle; (*fournisseur*) to settle up with

réglisse [ʀeɡlis] *nf* liquorice

règne [ʀɛɲ] *nm* (*d'un roi etc, fig*) reign; (*BIO*): **le ~ végétal/animal** the vegetable/ animal kingdom

régner [ʀeɲe] *vi* (*roi*) to rule, reign; (*fig*) to reign

regorger [ʀəɡɔʀʒe] *vi*: **~ de** to overflow

with, be bursting with

regret [ʀəgʀɛ] nm regret; **à ~** with regret; **avec ~** regretfully; **être au ~ de devoir faire** to regret having to do

regrettable [ʀəgʀɛtabl(ə)] adj regrettable

regretter [ʀəgʀɛte] vt to regret; (personne) to miss; **je regrette** I'm sorry

regrouper [ʀəgʀupe] vt (grouper) to group together; (contenir) to include, comprise; **se ~** vi to gather (together)

régulier, ière [ʀegylje, -jɛʀ] adj (gén) regular; (vitesse, qualité) steady; (répartition, pression, paysage) even; (TRANSPORTS: ligne, service) scheduled, regular; (légal, réglementaire) lawful, in order; (fam: correct) straight, on the level; **régulièrement** adv regularly; steadily; evenly; normally

rehausser [ʀəose] vt to heighten, raise

rein [ʀɛ̃] nm kidney; **~s** nmpl (dos) back sg

reine [ʀɛn] nf queen

reine-claude [ʀɛnklod] nf greengage

réintégrer [ʀeɛ̃tegʀe] vt (lieu) to return to; (fonctionnaire) to reinstate

rejaillir [ʀəʒajiʀ] vi to splash up; **~ sur** to splash up onto; (fig) to rebound on; to fall upon

rejet [ʀəʒɛ] nm (action, aussi MÉD) rejection

rejeter [ʀəʒte] vt (relancer) to throw back; (vomir) to bring ou throw up; (écarter) to reject; (déverser) to throw out, discharge; **~ la responsabilité de qch sur qn** to lay the responsibility for sth at sb's door

rejoindre [ʀəʒwɛ̃dʀ(ə)] vt (famille, régiment) to rejoin, return to; (lieu) to get (back) to; (suj: route etc) to meet, join; (rattraper) to catch up (with); **se ~** vi to meet; **je te rejoins au café** I'll see ou meet you at the café

réjouir [ʀeʒwiʀ] vt to delight; **se ~** vi to be delighted; to rejoice; **réjouissances** nfpl (joie) rejoicing sg; (fête) festivities

relâche [ʀəlɑʃ]: **sans ~** without respite ou a break

relâché, e [ʀəlɑʃe] adj loose, lax

relâcher [ʀəlɑʃe] vt to release; (étreinte) to loosen; **se ~** vi to loosen; (discipline) to become slack ou lax; (élève etc) to slacken off

relais [ʀəlɛ] nm (SPORT): **(course de) ~** relay (race); **équipe de ~** shift team; (SPORT) relay team; **prendre le ~ (de)** to take over (from); **~ routier** ≈ transport café (BRIT), ≈ truck stop (US)

relancer [ʀəlɑ̃se] vt (balle) to throw back; (moteur) to restart; (fig) to boost, revive; (personne): **~ qn** to pester sb

relater [ʀəlate] vt to relate, recount

relatif, ive [ʀəlatif, -iv] adj relative

relation [ʀəlasjɔ̃] nf (récit) account, report; (rapport) relation(ship); **~s** nfpl (rapports) relations; relationship sg; (connaissances) connections; **être/entrer en ~(s) avec** to be/get in contact with

relaxer [ʀəlakse] vt to relax; (JUR) to discharge; **se ~** vi to relax

relayer [ʀəleje] vt (collaborateur, coureur etc) to relieve; **se ~** vi (dans une activité) to take it in turns

reléguer [ʀəlege] vt to relegate

relent(s) [ʀəlɑ̃] nm(pl) (foul) smell

relevé, e [ʀəlve] adj (manches) rolled-up; (sauce) highly-seasoned ♦ nm (lecture) reading; (liste) statement; list; (facture) account; **~ de compte** bank statement

relève [ʀəlɛv] nf relief; relief team (ou troops pl); **prendre la ~** to take over

relever [ʀəlve] vt (statue, meuble) to stand up again; (personne tombée) to help up; (vitre, niveau de vie) to raise; (col) to turn up; (style, conversation) to elevate; (plat, sauce) to season; (sentinelle, équipe) to relieve; (fautes, points) to pick up; (constater: traces etc) to find, pick up; (répliquer à: remarque) to react to, reply to; (: défi) to accept, take up; (noter: adresse etc) to take down, note; (: plan) to sketch; (: cotes etc) to plot; (compteur) to read; (ramasser: cahiers) to collect, take in; **se ~** vi (se remettre debout) to get up; **~ de** (maladie) to be recovering from; (être du ressort de) to be a matter for; (ADMIN: dépendre de) to come under; (fig) to pertain to; **~ qn de** (fonctions) to relieve sb of; **~ la tête** to look up; to hold up one's head

relief [ʀəljɛf] nm relief; **~s** nmpl (restes) remains; **mettre en ~** (fig) to bring out, highlight

relier [ʀəlje] vt to link up; (livre) to bind; **~ qch à** to link sth to

religieuse [ʀəliʒjøz] nf nun; (gâteau) cream bun

religieux, euse [ʀəliʒjø, -øz] adj religious ♦ nm monk

religion [ʀəliʒjɔ̃] nf religion; (piété, dévotion) faith

relire [ʀəliʀ] vt (à nouveau) to reread, read again; (vérifier) to read over

reliure [ʀəljyʀ] nf binding

reluire [ʀəlɥiʀ] vi to gleam

remanier [ʀəmanje] vt to reshape, recast; (POL) to reshuffle

remarquable [ʀəmaʀkabl(ə)] adj remarkable

remarque [ʀəmaʀk(ə)] nf remark; (écrite) note

remarquer [ʀəmaʀke] vt (voir) to notice; **se ~** vi to be noticeable; **faire ~ (à qn) que** to point out (to sb) that; **faire ~ qch (à qn)** to point sth out (to sb); **remarquez, ... mind you ...**

remblai [ʀɑ̃blɛ] nm embankment

rembourrer [ʀɑ̃buʀe] vt to stuff; (dossier, vêtement, souliers) to pad

remboursement [ʀɑ̃buʀsəmɑ̃] nm repayment; **envoi contre ~** cash on delivery;

rembourser [ʀɑ̃buʀse] *vt* to pay back, repay

remède [ʀəmɛd] *nm* (*médicament*) medicine; (*traitement, fig*) remedy, cure

remémorer [ʀəmemɔʀe]: **se ~** *vt* to recall, recollect

remerciements [ʀəmɛʀsimɑ̃] *nmpl* thanks

remercier [ʀəmɛʀsje] *vt* to thank; (*congédier*) to dismiss; **~ qn de/d'avoir fait** to thank sb for/for having done

remettre [ʀəmɛtʀ(ə)] *vt* (*vêtement*): **~ qch** to put sth back on; (*replacer*): **~ qch quelque part** to put sth back somewhere; (*ajouter*): **~ du sel/un sucre** to add more salt/another lump of sugar; (*ajourner*): **~ qch (à)** to postpone sth (until); **se ~** *vi* to get better, recover; **se ~ de** to recover from, get over; **s'en ~ à** to leave it (up) to; **~ qch à qn** (*rendre, restituer*) to give sth back to sb; (*donner, confier: paquet, argent*) to hand over sth to sb, deliver sth to sb; (:*prix, décoration*) to present sb with sth

remise [ʀəmiz] *nf* delivery; presentation; (*rabais*) discount; (*local*) shed; **~ de peine** reduction of sentence; **~ en jeu** (*FOOTBALL*) throw-in

remontant [ʀəmɔ̃tɑ̃] *nm* tonic, pick-me-up

remonte-pente [ʀəmɔ̃tpɑ̃t] *nm* ski-lift

remonter [ʀəmɔ̃te] *vi* to go back up; (*jupe*) to ride up ♦ *vt* (*pente*) to go up; (*fleuve*) to sail (*ou* swim *etc*) up; (*manches, pantalon*) to roll up; (*col*) to turn up; (*niveau, limite*) to raise; (*fig: personne*) to buck up; (*moteur, meuble*) to put back together, reassemble; (*montre, mécanisme*) to wind up; **~ le moral à qn** to raise sb's spirits; **~ à** (*dater de*) to date *ou* go back to

remontrance [ʀəmɔ̃tʀɑ̃s] *nf* reproof, reprimand

remontrer [ʀəmɔ̃tʀe] *vt* (*fig*): **en ~ à** to prove one's superiority over

remords [ʀəmɔʀ] *nm* remorse *no pl*; **avoir des ~** to feel remorse

remorque [ʀəmɔʀk(ə)] *nf* trailer; **être en ~** to be on tow; **remorquer** *vt* to tow; **remorqueur** *nm* tug(boat)

remous [ʀəmu] *nm* (*d'un navire*) (back)wash *no pl*; (*de rivière*) swirl, eddy ♦ *nmpl* (*fig*) stir

remparts [ʀɑ̃paʀ] *nmpl* walls, ramparts

remplaçant, e [ʀɑ̃plasɑ̃, -ɑ̃t] *nm/f* replacement, stand-in; (*THÉÂTRE*) understudy; (*SCOL*) supply teacher

remplacement [ʀɑ̃plasmɑ̃] *nm* replacement; (*job*) replacement work *no pl*

remplacer [ʀɑ̃plase] *vt* to replace; (*tenir lieu de*) to take the place of; **~ qch/qn par** to replace sth/sb with

rempli, e [ʀɑ̃pli] *adj* (*emploi du temps*) full, busy; **~ de** full of, filled with

remplir [ʀɑ̃pliʀ] *vt* to fill (up); (*questionnaire*) to fill out *ou* up; (*obligations, fonc-*

tion, condition) to fulfil; **se ~** *vi* to fill up

remporter [ʀɑ̃pɔʀte] *vt* (*marchandise*) to take away; (*fig*) to win, achieve

remuant, e [ʀəmɥɑ̃, -ɑ̃t] *adj* restless

remue-ménage [ʀəmymenaʒ] *nm inv* commotion

remuer [ʀəmɥe] *vt* to move; (*café, sauce*) to stir ♦ *vi* to move; **se ~** *vi* to move

rémunérer [ʀemyneʀe] *vt* to remunerate

renard [ʀənaʀ] *nm* fox

renchérir [ʀɑ̃feʀiʀ] *vi* (*fig*): **~ (sur)** to add something (to)

rencontre [ʀɑ̃kɔ̃tʀ(ə)] *nf* meeting; (*imprévue*) encounter; **aller à la ~ de qn** to go and meet sb

rencontrer [ʀɑ̃kɔ̃tʀe] *vt* to meet; (*mot, expression*) to come across; (*difficultés*) to meet with; **se ~** *vi* to meet; (*véhicules*) to collide

rendement [ʀɑ̃dmɑ̃] *nm* (*d'un travailleur, d'une machine*) output; (*d'une culture*) yield; (*d'un investissement*) return; **à plein ~** at full capacity

rendez-vous [ʀɑ̃devu] *nm* (*rencontre*) appointment; (: *d'amoureux*) date; (*lieu*) meeting place; **donner ~ à qn** to arrange to meet sb; **avoir/prendre ~ (avec)** to have/make an appointment (with)

rendre [ʀɑ̃dʀ(ə)] *vt* (*livre, argent etc*) to give back, return; (*otages, visite etc*) to return; (*sang, aliments*) to bring up; (*exprimer, traduire*) to render; (*faire devenir*): **~ qn célèbre/qch possible** to make sb famous/sth possible; **se ~** *vi* (*capituler*) to surrender, give o.s. up; (*aller*): **se ~ quelque part** to go somewhere; **se ~ compte de qch** to realize sth

rênes [ʀɛn] *nfpl* reins

renfermé, e [ʀɑ̃fɛʀme] *adj* (*fig*) withdrawn ♦ *nm*: **sentir le ~** to smell stuffy

renfermer [ʀɑ̃fɛʀme] *vt* to contain

renflement [ʀɑ̃fləmɑ̃] *nm* bulge

renflouer [ʀɑ̃flue] *vt* to refloat; (*fig*) to set back on its (*ou* his/her *etc*) feet

renfoncement [ʀɑ̃fɔ̃smɑ̃] *nm* recess

renforcer [ʀɑ̃fɔʀse] *vt* to reinforce

renfort [ʀɑ̃fɔʀ]: **~s** *nmpl* reinforcements; **à grand ~ de** with a great deal of

renfrogné, e [ʀɑ̃fʀɔɲe] *adj* sullen

rengaine [ʀɑ̃gɛn] (*péj*) *nf* old tune

renier [ʀənje] *vt* (*parents*) to disown, repudiate; (*foi*) to renounce

renifler [ʀənifle] *vi, vt* to sniff

renne [ʀɛn] *nm* reindeer *inv*

renom [ʀənɔ̃] *nm* reputation; (*célébrité*) renown; **renommé, e** *adj* celebrated, renowned; **renommée** *nf* fame

renoncer [ʀənɔ̃se] *vt*: **~ à** to give up; **~ à faire** to give up the idea of doing

renouer [ʀənwe] *vt*: **~ avec** (*tradition*) to revive; (*habitude*) to take up again; **~ avec qn** to take up with sb again

renouvelable [ʀ(ə)nuvlabl(ə)] *adj (énergie etc)* renewable

renouveler [ʀənuvle] *vt* to renew; *(exploit, méfait)* to repeat; **se ~** *vi (incident)* to recur, happen again; **renouvellement** *nm* renewal; recurrence

rénover [ʀenɔve] *vt (immeuble)* to renovate, do up; *(enseignement)* to reform; *(quartier)* to redevelop

renseignement [ʀɑ̃sɛɲmɑ̃] *nm* information *no pl,* piece of information; **(guichet des) ~s** information desk

renseigner [ʀɑ̃seɲe] *vt:* **~ qn (sur)** to give information to sb (about); **se ~** *vi* to ask for information, make inquiries

rentabilité [ʀɑ̃tabilite] *nf* profitablity

rentable [ʀɑ̃tabl(ə)] *adj* profitable

rente [ʀɑ̃t] *nf* income; pension; government stock *ou* bond; **rentier, ière** *nm/f* person of private means

rentrée [ʀɑ̃tʀe] *nf:* **~ (d'argent)** cash *no pl* coming in; **la ~ (des classes)** the start of the new school year

rentrer [ʀɑ̃tʀe] *vi (entrer de nouveau)* to go *(ou* come) back in; *(entrer)* to go *(ou* come) in; *(revenir chez soi)* to go *(ou* come) (back) home; *(air, clou: pénétrer)* to go in; *(revenu, argent)* to come in ♦ *vt (foins)* to bring in; *(véhicule)* to put away; *(chemise dans pantalon etc)* to tuck in; *(griffes)* to draw in; *(fig: larmes, colère etc)* to hold back; **~ le ventre** to pull in one's stomach; **~ dans** *(heurter)* to crash into; **~ dans l'ordre** to be back to normal; **~ dans ses frais** to recover one's expenses

renversant, e [ʀɑ̃vɛʀsɑ̃, -ɑ̃t] *adj* astounding

renverse [ʀɑ̃vɛʀs(ə)]: **à la ~** *adv* backwards

renverser [ʀɑ̃vɛʀse] *vt (faire tomber: chaise, verre)* to knock over, overturn; *(piéton)* to knock down; *(liquide, contenu)* to spill, upset; *(retourner)* to turn upside down; (: *ordre des mots etc)* to reverse; *(fig: gouvernement etc)* to overthrow; *(stupéfier)* to bowl over; **se ~** *vi* to fall over; to overturn; to spill

renvoi [ʀɑ̃vwa] *nm (référence)* cross-reference; *(éructation)* belch

renvoyer [ʀɑ̃vwaje] *vt* to send back; *(congédier)* to dismiss; *(lumière)* to reflect; *(son)* to echo; *(ajourner):* **~ qch (à)** to put sth off *ou* postpone sth (until); **~ qn à** *(fig)* to refer sb to

repaire [ʀəpɛʀ] *nm* den

répandre [ʀepɑ̃dʀ(ə)] *vt (renverser)* to spill; *(étaler, diffuser)* to spread; *(lumière)* to shed; *(chaleur, odeur)* to give off; **se ~** *vi* to spill; to spread; **répandu, e** *adj (opinion, usage)* widespread

réparation [ʀepaʀɑsjɔ̃] *nf* repair

réparer [ʀepaʀe] *vt* to repair; *(fig: offense)*

to make up for, atone for; (: *oubli, erreur)* to put right

repartie [ʀəpaʀti] *nf* retort; **avoir de la ~** to be quick at repartee

repartir [ʀəpaʀtiʀ] *vi* to set off again; to leave again; *(fig)* to get going again; **~ à zéro** to start from scratch (again)

répartir [ʀepaʀtiʀ] *vt (pour attribuer)* to share out; *(pour disperser, disposer)* to divide up; *(poids, chaleur)* to distribute; **se ~** *vt (travail, rôles)* to share out between themselves; **répartition** *nf* sharing out; dividing up; distribution

repas [ʀəpa] *nm* meal

repasser [ʀəpase] *vi* to come *(ou* go) back ♦ *vt (vêtement, tissu)* to iron; *(examen)* to retake, resit; *(film)* to show again; *(leçon, rôle: revoir)* to go over (again)

repêcher [ʀəpeʃe] *vt (noyé)* to recover the body of; *(candidat)* to pass *(by inflating marks)*

repentir [ʀəpɑ̃tiʀ] *nm* repentance; **se ~** *vi* to repent; **se ~ de** to repent of

répercussions [ʀepɛʀkysjɔ̃] *nfpl (fig)* repercussions

répercuter [ʀepɛʀkyte] *vt (information, hausse des prix)* to pass on; **se ~** *vi (bruit)* to reverberate; *(fig):* **se ~ sur** to have repercussions on

repère [ʀəpɛʀ] *nm* mark; *(monument etc)* landmark

repérer [ʀəpeʀe] *vt (erreur, connaissance)* to spot; *(abri, ennemi)* to locate; **se ~** *vi* to find one's way about

répertoire [ʀepɛʀtwaʀ] *nm (liste)* (alphabetical) list; *(carnet)* index notebook; *(d'un artiste)* repertoire

répéter [ʀepete] *vt* to repeat; *(préparer: leçon: aussi vi)* to learn, go over; *(THÉÂTRE)* to rehearse; **se ~** *vi (redire)* to repeat o.s.; *(se reproduire)* to be repeated, recur

répétition [ʀepetisjɔ̃] *nf* repetition; *(THÉÂTRE)* rehearsal; **~ générale** final dress rehearsal

répit [ʀepi] *nm* respite

replet, ète [ʀəplɛ, -ɛt] *adj* chubby

replier [ʀəplije] *vt (rabattre)* to fold down *ou* over; **se ~** *vi (troupes, armée)* to withdraw, fall back

réplique [ʀeplik] *nf (repartie, fig)* reply; *(THÉÂTRE)* line; *(copie)* replica; **~r** [ʀeplike] *vi* to reply; *(riposter)* to retaliate

répondeur *nm:* **~ automatique** *(TÉL)* answering machine

répondre [ʀepɔ̃dʀ(ə)] *vi* to answer, reply; *(freins, mécanisme)* to respond; **~ à** to reply to, answer; *(affection, salut)* to return; *(provocation, suj: mécanisme etc)* to respond to; *(correspondre à: besoin)* to answer; (: *conditions)* to meet; (: *description)* to match; *(avec impertinence):* **~ à qn** to answer sb back; **~ de** to answer for

réponse [repɔ̃s] *nf* answer, reply; **en ~ à** in reply to

reportage [rəpɔrtaʒ] *nm* (*bref*) report; (*écrit: documentaire*) story; article; (*en direct*) commentary; (*genre, activité*): **le ~** reporting

reporter¹ [rəpɔrtɛr] *nm* reporter

reporter² [rəpɔrte] *vt* (*total*): **~ qch sur** to carry sth forward *ou* over to; (*ajourner*): **~ qch (à)** to postpone sth (until); (*transférer*): **~ qch sur** to transfer sth to; **se ~ à** (*époque*) to think back to; (*document*) to refer to

repos [rəpo] *nm* rest; (*fig*) peace (and quiet); peace of mind; (*MIL*): **~!** stand at ease!; **en ~** at rest; **de tout ~** safe

reposant, e [rəpozɑ̃, -ɑ̃t] *adj* restful

reposer [rəpoze] *vt* (*verre, livre*) to put down; (*délasser*) to rest; (*problème*) to reformulate ♦ *vi* (*liquide, pâte*) to settle, rest; **se ~** *vi* to rest; **se ~ sur qn** to rely on sb; **~ sur** to be built on; (*fig*) to rest on

repoussant, e [rəpusɑ̃, -ɑ̃t] *adj* repulsive

repousser [rəpuse] *vi* to grow again ♦ *vt* to repel, repulse; (*offre*) to turn down, reject; (*tiroir, personne*) to push back; (*différer*) to put back

reprendre [rəprɑ̃dr(ə)] *vt* (*prisonnier, ville*) to recapture; (*objet prêté, donné*) to take back; (*chercher*): **je viendrai te ~ à 4h** I'll come and fetch you at 4; (*se resservir de*): **~ du pain/un œuf** to take (*ou* eat) more bread/another egg; (*firme, entreprise*) to take over; (*travail, promenade*) to resume; (*emprunter: argument, idée*) to take up, use; (*refaire: article etc*) to go over again; (*jupe etc*) to alter; (*émission, pièce*) to put on again; (*réprimander*) to tell off; (*corriger*) to correct ♦ *vi* (*classes, pluie*) to start (up) again; (*activités, travaux, combats*) to resume, start (up) again; (*affaires, industrie*) to pick up; (*dire*): **reprit-il** he went on; **se ~** *vi* (*se ressaisir*) to recover; **s'y ~** to make another attempt; **~ des forces** to recover one's strength; **~ courage** to take new heart; **~ la route** to set off again; **~ haleine** *ou* **son souffle** to get one's breath back

représailles [rəprezaj] *nfpl* reprisals

représentant, e [rəprezɑ̃tɑ̃, -ɑ̃t] *nm/f* representative

représentation [rəprezɑ̃tasjɔ̃] *nf* (*symbole, image*) representation; (*spectacle*) performance

représenter [rəprezɑ̃te] *vt* to represent; (*donner: pièce, opéra*) to perform; **se ~** *vt* (*se figurer*) to imagine; to visualize

répression [represjɔ̃] *nf* (*voir réprimer*) suppression; repression

réprimer [reprime] *vt* (*émotions*) to suppress; (*peuple etc*) to repress

repris [rəpri] *nm*: **~ de justice** ex-prisoner, ex-convict

reprise [rəpriz] *nf* (*recommencement*) resumption; recovery; (*TV*) repeat; (*CINÉMA*) rerun; (*AUTO*) acceleration *no pl*; (*COMM*) trade-in, part exchange; **à plusieurs ~s** on several occasions

repriser [rəprize] *vt* to darn; to mend

reproche [rəprɔʃ] *nm* (*remontrance*) reproach; **faire des ~s à qn** to reproach sb; **sans ~(s)** beyond reproach

reprocher [rəprɔʃe] *vt*: **~ qch à qn** to reproach *ou* blame sb for sth; **~ qch à** (*machine, théorie*) to have sth against

reproduction [rəprɔdyksjɔ̃] *nf* reproduction

reproduire [rəprɔdɥir] *vt* to reproduce; **se ~** *vi* (*BIO*) to reproduce; (*recommencer*) to recur, re-occur

reptile [reptil] *nm* reptile

repu, e [rəpy] *adj* satisfied, sated

républicain, e [repyblikɛ̃, -ɛn] *adj, nm/f* republican

république [repyblik] *nf* republic

répugnant, e [repyɲɑ̃, -ɑ̃t] *adj* repulsive; loathsome

répugner [repyɲe]: **~ à** *vt* to repel *ou* disgust sb; **~ à faire** to be loath *ou* reluctant to do

réputation [repytasjɔ̃] *nf* reputation; **réputé, e** *adj* renowned

requérir [rəkerir] *vt* (*nécessiter*) to require, call for; (*JUR: peine*) to call for, demand

requête [rəkɛt] *nf* request; (*JUR*) petition

requin [rəkɛ̃] *nm* shark

requis, e [rəki, -iz] *adj* required

R.E.R. *sigle m* (= *réseau express régional*) *Greater Paris high-speed train service*

rescapé, e [rɛskape] *nm/f* survivor

rescousse [rɛskus] *nf*: **aller à la ~ de qn** to go to sb's aid *ou* rescue

réseau, x [rezo] *nm* network

réservation [rezɛrvasjɔ̃] *nf* booking, reservation

réserve [rezɛrv(ə)] *nf* (*retenue*) reserve; (*entrepôt*) storeroom; (*restriction, d'Indiens*) reservation; (*de pêche, chasse*) preserve; **sous ~ de** subject to; **sans ~** unreservedly; **de ~** (*provisions etc*) in reserve

réservé, e [rezɛrve] *adj* (*discret*) reserved; (*chasse, pêche*) private

réserver [rezɛrve] *vt* (*gén*) to reserve; (*chambre, billet etc*) to book, reserve; (*garder*): **~ qch pour/à** to keep *ou* save sth for; **~ qch à qn** to reserve (*ou* book) sth for sb

réservoir [rezɛrvwar] *nm* tank

résidence [rezidɑ̃s] *nf* residence; **(en) surveillée** (under) house arrest; **~ secondaire** second home

résidentiel, le [rezidɑ̃sjɛl] *adj* residential

résider [rezide] *vi*: **~ à/dans/en** to reside in; **~ dans** (*fig*) to lie in

résidu [rezidy] *nm* residue *no pl*

résigner [Reziɲe]: **se ~** vi: **se ~ (à qch/à faire)** to resign o.s. (to sth/to doing)

résilier [Rezilje] vt to terminate

résistance [Rezistɑ̃s] nf resistance; (de réchaud, bouilloire: fil) element

résistant, e [Rezistɑ̃, -ɑ̃t] adj (personne) robust, tough; (matériau) strong, hard-wearing

résister [Reziste] vi to resist; ~ à (assaut, tentation) to resist; (effort, souffrance) to withstand; (désobéir à) to stand up to, oppose

résolu, e [Rezɔly] pp de **résoudre** ♦ adj: **être ~ à qch/faire** to be set upon sth/doing

résolution [Rezɔlysjɔ̃] nf solving; (fermeté, décision) resolution

résolve etc vb voir **résoudre**

résonner [Rezɔne] vi (cloche, pas) to reverberate, resound; (salle) to be resonant; ~ **de** to resound with

résorber [RezɔRbe]: **se ~** vi (fig) to be reduced; to be absorbed

résoudre [Rezudʀ(ə)] vt to solve; **se ~ à faire** to bring o.s. to do

respect [Rɛspɛ] nm respect; **tenir en ~ to** keep at bay

respecter [Rɛspɛkte] vt to respect

respectueux, euse [Rɛspɛktɥø, -øz] adj respectful; ~ **de** respectful of

respiration [Rɛspiʀasjɔ̃] nf breathing no pl; ~ **artificielle** artificial respiration

respirer [Rɛspiʀe] vi to breathe; (fig) to get one's breath; to breathe again ♦ vt to breathe (in), inhale; (manifester: santé, calme etc) to exude

resplendir [Rɛsplɑ̃diʀ] vi to shine; (fig): ~ **(de)** to be radiant (with)

responsabilité [Rɛspɔ̃sabilite] nf responsibility; (légale) liability

responsable [Rɛspɔ̃sabl(ə)] adj responsible ♦ nm/f (du ravitaillement etc) person in charge; (de parti, syndicat) official; ~ **de** responsible for; (chargé de) in charge of, responsible for

ressaisir [Rəseziʀ]: **se ~** vi to regain one's self-control

ressasser [Rəsase] vt to keep going over

ressemblance [Rəsɑ̃blɑ̃s] nf resemblance, similarity, likeness

ressemblant, e [Rəsɑ̃blɑ̃, -ɑ̃t] adj (portrait) lifelike, true to life

ressembler [Rəsɑ̃ble]: ~ **à** vt to be like; to resemble; (visuellement) to look like; **se ~** vi to be (ou look) alike

ressemeler [Rəsəmle] vt to (re)sole

ressentiment [Rəsɑ̃timɑ̃] nm resentment

ressentir [Rəsɑ̃tiʀ] vt to feel; **se ~ de** to feel (ou show) the effects of

resserrer [RəseRe] vt (nœud, boulon) to tighten (up); (fig: liens) to strengthen; **se ~** vi (vallée) to narrow

resservir [RəseRviʀ] vi to do ou serve again

♦ vt: ~ **qn (d'un plat)** to give sb a second helping (of a dish)

ressort [RəsɔR] nm (pièce) spring; (force morale) spirit; (recours): **en dernier ~** as a last resort; (compétence): **être du ~ de** to fall within the competence of

ressortir [RəsɔRtiʀ] vi to go (ou come) out (again); (contraster) to stand out; ~ **de** to emerge from; **faire ~** (fig: souligner) to bring out

ressortissant, e [RəsɔRtisɑ̃, -ɑ̃t] nm/f national

ressource [Rəsurs(ə)] nf: **avoir la ~ de** to have the possibility of; ~**s** nfpl (moyens) resources; **leur seule ~ était de** the only course open to them was to

ressusciter [Resysite] vt (fig) to revive, bring back ♦ vi to rise (from the dead)

restant, e [Rɛstɑ̃, -ɑ̃t] adj remaining ♦ nm: **le ~ (de)** the remainder (of); **un ~ de** (de trop) some left-over

restaurant [RɛstoRɑ̃] nm restaurant

restauration [RɛstoRasjɔ̃] nf restoration; (hôtellerie) catering; ~ **rapide** fast food

restaurer [RɛstoRe] vt to restore; **se ~** vi to have something to eat

reste [Rɛst(ə)] nm (restant): **le ~ (de)** the rest (of); (de trop): **un ~ (de)** some left-over; (vestige): **un ~ de** a remnant ou last trace of; (MATH) remainder; ~**s** nmpl (nourriture) left-overs; (d'une cité etc, dépouille mortelle) remains; **du ~, au ~** besides, moreover

rester [Rɛste] vi to stay, remain; (subsister) to remain, be left; (durer) to last, live on ♦ vb impers: **il reste du pain/2 œufs** there's some bread/there are 2 eggs left (over); **il me reste assez de temps** I have enough time left; **ce qui reste à faire** what remains to be done; **restons-en là** let's leave it at that

restituer [Rɛstitɥe] vt (objet, somme): ~ **qch (à qn)** to return sth (to sb); (TECH) to release; (: son) to reproduce

restoroute [RɛstoRut] nm motorway (BRIT) ou highway (US) restaurant

restreindre [RɛstRɛ̃dR(ə)] vt to restrict, limit

restriction [RɛstRiksjɔ̃] nf restriction

résultat [Rezylta] nm result; (d'élection etc) results pl

résulter [Rezylte]: ~ **de** vt to result from, be the result of

résumé [Rezyme] nm summary, résumé

résumer [Rezyme] vt (texte) to summarize; (récapituler) to sum up; **se ~ à** to come down to

résurrection [RezyRɛksjɔ̃] nf resurrection; (fig) revival

rétablir [RetabliR] vt to restore, re-establish; **se ~** vi (guérir) to recover; (silence, calme) to return, be restored; **rétablissement** nm restoring; recovery; (*SPORT*) pull-up

retaper [ʀətape] *vt* (*maison, voiture etc*) to do up; (*fam: revigorer*) to buck up; (*redactylographier*) to retype

retard [ʀətaʀ] *nm* (*d'une personne attendue*) lateness *no pl*; (*sur l'horaire, un programme*) delay; (*fig: scolaire, mental etc*) backwardness; **en ~ (de 2 heures)** (2 hours) late; **avoir du ~** to be late; (*sur un programme*) to be behind (schedule); **prendre du ~** (*train, avion*) to be delayed; (*montre*) to lose (time); **sans ~** without delay

retardement [ʀətaʀdəmɑ̃] : **à ~** *adj* delayed action *cpd*; **bombe à ~** time bomb

retarder [ʀətaʀde] *vt* (*sur un horaire*): **~ qn (d'une heure)** to delay sb (an hour); (*départ, date*): **~ qch (de 2 jours)** to put sth back (2 days), delay sth (for *ou* by 2 days); (*horloge*) to put back ♦ *vi* (*montre*) to be slow; to lose (time)

retenir [ʀətniʀ] *vt* (*garder, retarder*) to keep, detain; (*maintenir: objet qui glisse, fig: colère, larmes*) to hold back; (: *objet suspendu*) to hold; (*fig: empêcher d'agir*): **~ qn (de faire)** to hold sb back (from doing); (*se rappeler*) to retain; (*réserver*) to reserve; (*accepter*) to accept; (*prélever*): **~ qch (sur)** to deduct sth (from); **se ~** *vi* (*se raccrocher*): **se ~ à** to hold onto; (*se contenir*): **se ~ de faire** to restrain o.s. from doing; **~ son souffle** to hold one's breath

retentir [ʀətɑ̃tiʀ] *vi* to ring out; (*salle*): **~ de** to ring *ou* resound with

retentissant, e [ʀətɑ̃tisɑ̃, -ɑ̃t] *adj* resounding; (*fig*) impact-making

retentissement [ʀətɑ̃tismɑ̃] *nm* repercussion; effect, impact; stir

retenu, e [ʀətny] *adj* (*place*) reserved; (*personne: empêché*) held up

retenue [ʀətny] *nf* (*prélèvement*) deduction; (*SCOL*) detention; (*modération*) (self-)restraint; (*réserve*) reserve, reticence

réticence [ʀetisɑ̃s] *nf* hesitation, reluctance *no pl*

rétine [ʀetin] *nf* retina

retiré, e [ʀətiʀe] *adj* secluded; remote

retirer [ʀətiʀe] *vt* to withdraw; (*vêtement, lunettes*) to take off, remove; (*extraire*): **~ qch de** to take sth out of, remove sth from; (*reprendre: bagages, billets*) to collect, pick up

retombées [ʀətɔ̃be] *nfpl* (*radioactives*) fallout *sg*; (*fig*) fallout; spin-offs

retomber [ʀətɔ̃be] *vi* (*à nouveau*) to fall again; (*atterrir: après un saut etc*) to land; (*tomber, redescendre*) to fall back; (*pendre*) to fall, hang (down); (*échoir*): **~ sur qn** to fall on sb

rétorquer [ʀetɔʀke] *vt*: **~ (à qn) que** to retort (to sb) that

retors, e [ʀətɔʀ, -ɔʀs(ə)] *adj* wily

retoucher [ʀətuʃe] *vt* (*photographie*) to touch up; (*texte, vêtement*) to alter

retour [ʀətuʀ] *nm* return; **au ~** when we (*ou* they *etc*) get (*ou* got) back; (*en route*) on the way back; **être de ~ (de)** to be back (from); **par ~ du courrier** by return of post

retourner [ʀətuʀne] *vt* (*dans l'autre sens: matelas, crêpe, foin, terre*) to turn (over); (: *caisse*) to turn upside down; (: *sac, vêtement*) to turn inside out; (*émouvoir: personne*) to shake; (*renvoyer, restituer*): **~ qch à qn** to return sth to sb ♦ *vi* (*aller, revenir*): **~ quelque part/à** to go back *ou* return somewhere/to; **se ~** *vi* to turn over; (*tourner la tête*) to turn round; **~ à** (*état, activité*) to return to, go back to; **se ~ contre** (*fig*) to turn against; **savoir de quoi il retourne** to know what it is all about

retracer [ʀətʀase] *vt* to relate, recount

retrait [ʀətʀɛ] *nm* (*voir retirer*) withdrawal; collection; **en ~** set back; **~ du permis (de conduire)** disqualification from driving (*BRIT*), revocation of driver's license (*US*)

retraite [ʀətʀɛt] *nf* (*d'une armée, REL, refuge*) retreat; (*d'un employé*) retirement; (*revenu*) pension; **prendre sa ~** to retire; **~ anticipée** early retirement; **retraité, e** *adj* retired ♦ *nm/f* pensioner

retrancher [ʀətʀɑ̃ʃe] *vt* (*passage, détails*) to take out, remove; (*nombre, somme*): **~ qch de** to take *ou* deduct sth from; (*couper*) to cut off; **se ~ derrière/dans** to take refuge behind/in

retransmettre [ʀətʀɑ̃smɛtʀ(ə)] *vt* (*RADIO*) to broadcast; (*TV*) to show

rétrécir [ʀetʀesiʀ] *vt* (*vêtement*) to take in ♦ *vi* to shrink; **se ~** *vi* to narrow

rétribution [ʀetʀibysjɔ̃] *nf* payment

rétro [ʀetʀo] *adj inv*: **la mode ~** the nostalgia vogue

rétrograde [ʀetʀogʀad] *adj* reactionary, backward-looking

rétrograder [ʀetʀogʀade] *vi* (*économie*) to regress; (*AUTO*) to change down

rétroprojecteur [ʀetʀopʀoʒɛktœʀ] *nm* overhead projector

rétrospective [ʀetʀospɛktiv] *nf* retrospective exhibition/season; **rétrospectivement** *adv* in retrospect

retrousser [ʀətʀuse] *vt* to roll up

retrouvailles [ʀətʀuvaj] *nfpl* reunion *sg*

retrouver [ʀətʀuve] *vt* (*fugitif, objet perdu*) to find; (*occasion*) to find again; (*calme, santé*) to regain; (*revoir*) to see again; (*rejoindre*) to meet (again), join; **se ~** *vi* to meet; (*s'orienter*) to find one's way; **se ~ quelque part** to find o.s. somewhere; **s'y ~** (*rentrer dans ses frais*) to break even

rétroviseur [ʀetʀovizœʀ] *nm* (rear-view) mirror

réunion [ʀeynjɔ̃] *nf* bringing together; joining; (séance) meeting

réunir [ʀeyniʀ] vt (convoquer) to call together; (rassembler) to gather together; (cumuler) to combine; (rapprocher) to bring together (again), reunite; (rattacher) to join (together); **se ~** vi (se rencontrer) to meet

réussi, e [ʀeysi] adj successful

réussir [ʀeysiʀ] vi to succeed, be successful; (à un examen) to pass; (plante, culture) to thrive, do well ♦ vt to make a success of; **~ à faire** to succeed in doing; **~ à qn** to go right for sb; (aliment) to agree with sb

réussite [ʀeysit] nf success; (CARTES) patience

revaloir [ʀəvalwaʀ] vt: **je vous revaudrai cela** I'll repay you some day; (en mal) I'll pay you back for this

revaloriser [ʀəvalɔʀize] vt (monnaie) to revalue; (salaires) to raise the level of

revanche [ʀəvɑ̃ʃ] nf revenge; **en ~** on the other hand

rêve [ʀɛv] nm dream; (activité psychique): **le ~** dreaming

revêche [ʀəvɛʃ] adj surly, sour-tempered

réveil [ʀevɛj] nm (d'un dormeur) waking up no pl; (fig) awakening; (pendule) alarm (clock); (MIL) reveille; **au ~** on waking (up)

réveille-matin [ʀevɛjmatɛ̃] nm inv alarm clock

réveiller [ʀeveje] vt (personne) to wake up; (fig) to awaken, revive; **se ~** vi to wake up; (fig) to reawaken

réveillon [ʀevɛjɔ̃] nm Christmas Eve; (de la Saint-Sylvestre) New Year's Eve; **réveillonner** vi to celebrate Christmas Eve (ou New Year's Eve)

révélateur, trice [ʀevelatœʀ, -tʀis] adj: **~ (de qch)** revealing (sth) ♦ nm (PHOTO) developer

révéler [ʀevele] vt (gén) to reveal; (faire connaître au public): **~ qn/qch** to make sb/sth widely known, bring sb/sth to the public's notice; **se ~** vi to be revealed, reveal itself ♦ vb +attrib to prove (to be), to be revealed, reveal itself

revenant, e [ʀəvnɑ̃, -ɑ̃t] nm/f ghost

revendeur, euse [ʀəvɑ̃dœʀ, -øz] nm/f (détaillant) retailer; (d'occasions) secondhand dealer

revendication [ʀəvɑ̃dikasjɔ̃] nf claim, demand; **journée de ~** day of action

revendiquer [ʀəvɑ̃dike] vt to claim, demand; (responsabilité) to claim

revendre [ʀəvɑ̃dʀ(ə)] vt (d'occasion) to resell; (détailler) to sell; **à ~** (en abondance) to spare

revenir [ʀəvniʀ] vi to come back; (CULIN): **faire ~** to brown; (coûter): **~ cher/à 100 F (à qn)** to cost (sb) a lot/100 F; **~ à** (études, projet) to return to, go back to; (équivaloir à) to amount to; **~ à qn** (part,

honneur) to go to sb, be sb's; (souvenir, nom) to come back to sb; **~ de** (fig: maladie, étonnement) to recover from; **~ sur** (question, sujet) to go back over; (engagement) to go back on; **~ à la charge** to return to the attack; **~ à soi** to come round; **n'en pas ~**: **je n'en reviens pas** I can't get over it; **~ sur ses pas** to retrace one's steps; **cela revient à dire que/au même** it amounts to saying that/the same thing

revenu [ʀəvny] nm income; (de l'État) revenue; (d'un capital) yield; **~s** nmpl income sg

rêver [ʀeve] vi, vt to dream; **~ de/à** to dream of

réverbère [ʀevɛʀbɛʀ] nm street lamp ou light

réverbérer [ʀevɛʀbeʀe] vt to reflect

révérence [ʀeveʀɑ̃s] nf (salut) bow; (: de femme) curtsey

rêverie [ʀɛvʀi] nf daydreaming no pl, daydream

revers [ʀəvɛʀ] nm (de feuille, main) back; (d'étoffe) wrong side; (de pièce, médaille) back, reverse; (TENNIS, PING-PONG) backhand; (de veston) lapel; (de pantalon) turn-up; (fig: échec) setback

revêtement [ʀəvɛtmɑ̃] nm (de paroi) facing; (des sols) flooring; (de chaussée) surface; (de tuyau etc: enduit) coating

revêtir [ʀəvɛtiʀ] vt (habit) to don, put on; (fig) to take on; **~ qn de** to endow ou invest sb with; **~ qch de** to cover sth with; (fig) to cloak sth in

rêveur, euse [ʀɛvœʀ, -øz] adj dreamy ♦ nm/f dreamer

revient [ʀəvjɛ̃] vb voir **revenir**

revigorer [ʀəvigɔʀe] vt to invigorate, brace up; to revive, buck up

revirement [ʀəviʀmɑ̃] nm change of mind; (d'une situation) reversal

réviser [ʀevize] vt (texte, SCOL: matière) to revise; (machine, installation, moteur) to overhaul, service; (JUR: procès) to review

révision [ʀevizjɔ̃] nf revision; auditing no pl; overhaul; servicing no pl; review; **la ~ des 10000 km** (AUTO) the 10,000 km service

revivre [ʀəvivʀ(ə)] vi (reprendre des forces) to come alive again; (traditions) to be revived ♦ vt (épreuve, moment) to relive

revoir [ʀəvwaʀ] vt to see again; (réviser) to revise ♦ nm: **au ~** goodbye

révoltant, e [ʀevɔltɑ̃, -ɑ̃t] adj revolting; appalling

révolte [ʀevɔlt(ə)] nf rebellion, revolt

révolter [ʀevɔlte] vt to revolt; to outrage, appal; **se ~ (contre)** to rebel (against)

révolu, e [ʀevɔly] adj past; (ADMIN): **âgé de 18 ans ~s** over 18 years of age; **après 3 ans ~s** when 3 full years have passed

révolution [ʀevɔlysjɔ̃] nf revolution; **révo-**

lutionnaire *adj, nm/f* revolutionary
revolver [ʀevɔlvɛʀ] *nm* gun; (*à barillet*) revolver
révoquer [ʀevɔke] *vt* (*fonctionnaire*) to dismiss; (*arrêt, contrat*) to revoke
revue [ʀəvy] *nf* (*inventaire, examen, MIL*) review; (*périodique*) review, magazine; (*de music-hall*) variety show; **passer en ~** to review; to go through
rez-de-chaussée [ʀedʃose] *nm inv* ground floor
RF *sigle* = **République Française**
Rhin [ʀɛ̃] *nm*: **le ~** the Rhine
rhinocéros [ʀinɔseʀɔs] *nm* rhinoceros
Rhône [ʀon] *nm*: **le ~** the Rhone
rhubarbe [ʀybaʀb(ə)] *nf* rhubarb
rhum [ʀɔm] *nm* rum
rhumatisme [ʀymatism(ə)] *nm* rheumatism *no pl*
rhume [ʀym] *nm* cold; **~ de cerveau** head cold; **le ~ des foins** hay fever
ri [ʀi] *pp de* rire
riant, e [ʀjɑ̃, -ɑ̃t] *adj* smiling, cheerful
ricaner [ʀikane] *vi* (*avec méchanceté*) to snigger; (*bêtement*) to giggle
riche [ʀiʃ] *adj* (*gén*) rich; (*personne, pays*) rich, wealthy; **~ en** rich in; **~ de** full of; rich in; **richesse** *nf* wealth; (*fig*) richness; **richesses** *nfpl* (*ressources, argent*) wealth *sg*; (*fig: trésors*) treasures
ricin [ʀisɛ̃] *nm*: **huile de ~** castor oil
ricocher [ʀikɔʃe] *vi*: **~ (sur)** to rebound (off); (*sur l'eau*) to bounce (on *ou* off)
ricochet [ʀikɔʃɛ] *nm*: **faire des ~s** to skip stones; **par ~** on the rebound; (*fig*) as an indirect result
rictus [ʀiktys] *nm* grin; (*snarling*) grimace
ride [ʀid] *nf* wrinkle; (*fig*) ripple
rideau, x [ʀido] *nm* curtain; (*POL*): **le ~ de fer** the Iron Curtain
rider [ʀide] *vt* to wrinkle; (*eau*) to ripple; **se ~** *vi* to become wrinkled
ridicule [ʀidikyl] *adj* ridiculous ♦ *nm*: **le ~** ridicule; **se ridiculiser** *vi* to make a fool of o.s.

───────── **MOT CLÉ** ─────────

rien [ʀjɛ̃] *pron* **1**: **(ne) ... ~** nothing; *tournure negative* + anything; **qu'est-ce que vous avez?** - **~** what have you got? - nothing; **il n'a ~ dit/fait** he said/did nothing; he hasn't said/done anything; **il n'a ~** (*n'est pas blessé*) he's all right; **de ~!** not at all!

2 (*quelque chose*): **a-t-il jamais ~ fait pour nous?** has he ever done anything for us?

3: **~ de**: **~ d'intéressant** nothing interesting; **~ d'autre** nothing else; **~ du tout** nothing at all

4: **~ que** just, only; nothing but; **~ que pour lui faire plaisir** only *ou* just to please him; **~ que la vérité** nothing but the truth;

~ que cela that alone

♦ *nm*: **un petit ~** (*cadeau*) a little something; **des ~s** trivia *pl*; **un ~ de** a hint of; **en un ~ de temps** in no time at all

rieur, euse [ʀjœʀ, -øz] *adj* cheerful
rigide [ʀiʒid] *adj* stiff; (*fig*) rigid; strict
rigole [ʀigɔl] *nf* (*conduit*) channel; (*filet d'eau*) rivulet
rigoler [ʀigɔle] *vi* (*rire*) to laugh; (*s'amuser*) to have (some) fun; (*plaisanter*) to be joking *ou* kidding
rigolo, ote [ʀigɔlo, -ɔt] (*fam*) *adj* funny ♦ *nm/f* comic; (*péj*) fraud, phoney
rigoureux, euse [ʀiguʀø, -øz] *adj* (*morale*) rigorous, strict; (*personne*) stern, strict; (*climat, châtiment*) rigorous, harsh; (*interdiction, neutralité*) strict
rigueur [ʀiguœʀ] *nf* rigour; strictness; harshness; **être de ~** to be the rule; **à la ~** at a pinch; possibly; **tenir ~ à qn de qch** to hold sth against sb
rime [ʀim] *nf* rhyme
rinçage [ʀɛ̃saʒ] *nm* rinsing (out); (*opération*) rinse
rincer [ʀɛ̃se] *vt* to rinse; (*récipient*) to rinse out
ring [ʀiŋ] *nm* (boxing) ring
ringard, e [ʀɛ̃gaʀ, -aʀd(ə)] *adj* old-fashioned
rions *vb voir* rire
riposter [ʀipɔste] *vi* to retaliate ♦ *vt*: **~ que** to retort that; **~ à** to counter; to reply to
rire [ʀiʀ] *vi* to laugh; (*se divertir*) to have fun ♦ *nm* laugh; **le ~** laughter; **~ de** to laugh at; **pour ~** (*pas sérieusement*) for a joke *ou* a laugh
risée [ʀize] *nf*: **être la ~ de** to be the laughing stock of
risible [ʀizibl(ə)] *adj* laughable
risque [ʀisk(ə)] *nm* risk; **le ~** danger; **à ses ~s et périls** at his own risk
risqué, e [ʀiske] *adj* risky; (*plaisanterie*) risqué, daring
risquer [ʀiske] *vt* to risk; (*allusion, question*) to venture, hazard; **ça ne risque rien** it's quite safe; **~ de**: **il risque de se tuer** he could get himself killed; **ce qui risque de se produire** what might *ou* could well happen; **il ne risque pas de recommencer** there's no chance of him doing that again; **se ~ à faire** (*tenter*) to venture *ou* dare to do
rissoler [ʀisɔle] *vi, vt*: **(faire) ~** to brown
ristourne [ʀistuʀn(ə)] *nf* rebate
rite [ʀit] *nm* rite; (*fig*) ritual
rivage [ʀivaʒ] *nm* shore
rival, e, aux [ʀival, -o] *adj, nm/f* rival
rivaliser [ʀivalize] *vi*: **~ avec** to rival, vie with; (*être comparable*) to hold its own against, compare with
rivalité [ʀivalite] *nf* rivalry

rive [ʀiv] *nf* shore; *(de fleuve)* bank
river [ʀive] *vt (clou, pointe)* to clinch; *(plaques)* to rivet together
riverain, e [ʀivʀɛ̃, -ɛn] *nm/f* riverside *(ou* lakeside) resident; local resident
rivet [ʀivɛ] *nm* rivet
rivière [ʀivjɛʀ] *nf* river
rixe [ʀiks(ə)] *nf* brawl, scuffle
riz [ʀi] *nm* rice
R.N. *sigle f* = **route nationale**
robe [ʀɔb] *nf* dress; *(de juge, d'ecclésiastique)* robe; *(de professeur)* gown; *(pelage)* coat; ~ **de chambre** dressing gown; ~ **de grossesse** maternity dress; ~ **de soirée/de mariée** evening/wedding dress
robinet [ʀɔbinɛ] *nm* tap
robot [ʀɔbo] *nm* robot
robuste [ʀɔbyst(ə)] *adj* robust, sturdy
roc [ʀɔk] *nm* rock
rocaille [ʀɔkɑj] *nf* loose stones *pl*; rocky *ou* stony ground; *(jardin)* rockery, rock garden
roche [ʀɔʃ] *nf* rock
rocher [ʀɔʃe] *nm* rock
rocheux, euse [ʀɔʃø, -øz] *adj* rocky
rodage [ʀɔdaʒ] *nm*: **en** ~ = running in
roder [ʀɔde] *vt (AUTO)* to run in
rôder [ʀode] *vi* to roam about; *(de façon suspecte)* to lurk (about *ou* around); **rôdeur, euse** *nm/f* prowler
rogne [ʀɔɲ] *nf*: **être en** ~ to be in a temper
rogner [ʀɔɲe] *vt* to clip; ~ **sur** *(fig)* to cut down *ou* back on
rognons [ʀɔɲɔ̃] *nmpl* kidneys
roi [ʀwa] *nm* king; **le jour** *ou* **la fête des R~s, les R~s** Twelfth Night
roitelet [ʀwatlɛ] *nm* wren
rôle [ʀol] *nm* role; *(contribution)* part
romain, e [ʀɔmɛ̃, -ɛn] *adj, nm/f* Roman
roman, e [ʀɔmɑ̃, -an] *adj (ARCHIT)* Romanesque ♦ *nm* novel; ~ **d'espionnage** spy novel *ou* story; ~ **photo** romantic picture story
romance [ʀɔmɑ̃s] *nf* ballad
romancer [ʀɔmɑ̃se] *vt* to make into a novel; to romanticize
romancier, ière [ʀɔmɑ̃sje, -jɛʀ] *nm/f* novelist
romanesque [ʀɔmanɛsk(ə)] *adj (fantastique)* fantastic; storybook *cpd*; *(sentimental)* romantic
roman-feuilleton [ʀɔmɑ̃fœjtɔ̃] *nm* serialized novel
romanichel, le [ʀɔmaniʃɛl] *nm/f* gipsy
romantique [ʀɔmɑ̃tik] *adj* romantic
romarin [ʀɔmaʀɛ̃] *nm* rosemary
rompre [ʀɔ̃pʀ(ə)] *vt* to break; *(entretien, fiançailles)* to break off ♦ *vi (fiancés)* to break it off; **se** ~ *vi* to break; *(MÉD)* to burst, rupture
rompu, e [ʀɔ̃py] *adj*: ~ **à** with wide ex-

perience of; inured to
ronces [ʀɔ̃s] *nfpl* brambles
ronchonner [ʀɔ̃ʃɔne] *(fam) vi* to grouse, grouch
rond, e [ʀɔ̃, ʀɔ̃d] *adj* round; *(joues, mollets)* well-rounded; *(fam: ivre)* tight ♦ *nm (cercle)* ring; *(fam: sou)*: **je n'ai plus un** ~ I haven't a penny left; **en** ~ *(s'asseoir, danser)* in a ring; **ronde** *nf (gén: de surveillance)* rounds *pl*, patrol; *(danse)* round (dance); *(MUS)* semibreve *(BRIT)*, whole note *(US)*; **à la ronde** *(alentour)*: **à 10 km à la ronde** for 10 km round; **rondelet, te** *adj* plump
rondelle [ʀɔ̃dɛl] *nf (TECH)* washer; *(tranche)* slice, round
rondement [ʀɔ̃dmɑ̃] *adv* briskly; frankly
rondin [ʀɔ̃dɛ̃] *nm* log
rond-point [ʀɔ̃pwɛ̃] *nm* roundabout
ronflant, e [ʀɑ̃flɑ̃, -ɑ̃t] *(péj) adj* high-flown, grand
ronfler [ʀɔ̃fle] *vi* to snore; *(moteur, poêle)* to hum; to roar
ronger [ʀɔ̃ʒe] *vt* to gnaw (at); *(suj: vers, rouille)* to eat into; **se** ~ **les sangs** to worry o.s. sick; **se** ~ **les ongles** to bite one's nails; **rongeur** *nm* rodent
ronronner [ʀɔ̃ʀɔne] *vi* to purr
roquet [ʀɔkɛ] *nm* nasty little lap-dog
rosace [ʀozas] *nf (vitrail)* rose window
rosbif [ʀɔsbif] *nm*: **du** ~ roasting beef; *(cuit)* roast beef; **un** ~ a joint of beef
rose [ʀoz] *nf* rose ♦ *adj* pink
rosé, e [ʀoze] *adj* pinkish; *(vin)* ~ rosé
roseau, x [ʀozo] *nm* reed
rosée [ʀoze] *nf* dew
roseraie [ʀozʀɛ] *nf* rose garden
rosier [ʀozje] *nm* rosebush, rose tree
rosse [ʀɔs] *nf (péj: cheval)* nag ♦ *adj* nasty, vicious
rossignol [ʀɔsiɲɔl] *nm (ZOOL)* nightingale
rot [ʀo] *nm* belch; *(de bébé)* burp
rotatif, ive [ʀɔtatif, -iv] *adj* rotary
rotation [ʀɔtasjɔ̃] *nf* rotation; *(fig)* rotation, swap-around; turnover
roter [ʀɔte] *(fam) vi* to burp, belch
rôti [ʀoti] *nm*: **du** ~ roasting meat; *(cuit)* roast meat; ~ **de bœuf/porc** joint of beef/pork
rotin [ʀɔtɛ̃] *nm* rattan (cane); **fauteuil en** ~ cane (arm)chair
rôtir [ʀotiʀ] *vi, vt (aussi: faire ~)* to roast; **rôtisserie** *nf* steakhouse; roast meat counter *(ou* shop); **rôtissoire** *nf* (roasting) spit
rotule [ʀɔtyl] *nf* kneecap, patella
roturier, ière [ʀɔtyʀje, -jɛʀ] *nm/f* commoner
rouage [ʀwaʒ] *nm* cog(wheel), gearwheel; *(de montre)* part; *(fig)* cog
roucouler [ʀukule] *vi* to coo
roue [ʀu] *nf* wheel; ~ **dentée** cogwheel; ~ **de secours** spare wheel
roué, e [ʀwe] *adj* wily

rouer [Rwe] vt: ~ qn de coups to give sb a thrashing

rouet [Rwe] nm spinning wheel

rouge [Ruʒ] adj, nm/f red ♦ nm red; (fard) rouge; (vin) ~ red wine; **sur la liste** ~ ex-directory (BRIT), unlisted (US); **passer au** ~ (signal) to go red; (automobiliste) to go through a red light; ~ **(à lèvres)** lipstick; **rouge-gorge** nm robin (redbreast)

rougeole [Ruʒɔl] nf measles sg

rougeoyer [Ruʒwaje] vi to glow red

rouget [Ruʒe] nm mullet

rougeur [Ruʒœr] nf redness

rougir [Ruʒiʀ] vi (de honte, timidité) to blush, flush; (de plaisir, colère) to flush; (fraise, tomate) to go ou turn red; (ciel) to redden

rouille [Ruj] nf rust

rouillé, e [Ruje] adj rusty

rouiller [Ruje] vt to rust ♦ vi to rust, go rusty; **se** ~ vi to rust

roulant, e [Rulɑ̃, -ɑ̃t] adj (meuble) on wheels; (surface, trottoir) moving

rouleau, x [Rulo] nm (de papier, tissu, SPORT) roll; (de machine à écrire) roller, platen; (à mise en plis, à peinture, vague) roller; ~ **compresseur** steamroller; ~ **à pâtisserie** rolling pin

roulement [Rulmɑ̃] nm (bruit) rumbling no pl, rumble; (rotation) rotation; turnover; **par** ~ on a rota (BRIT) ou basis (US) basis; ~ **(à billes)** ball bearings pl; ~ **de tambour** drum roll

rouler [Rule] vt to roll; (papier, tapis) to roll up; (CULIN: pâte) to roll out; (fam) to do, con ♦ vi (bille, boule) to roll; (voiture, train) to go, run; (automobiliste) to drive; (cycliste) to ride; (bateau) to roll; (tonnerre) to rumble, roll; **se** ~ **dans** (boue) to roll in; (couverture) to roll o.s. (up) in

roulette [Rulɛt] nf (de table, fauteuil) castor; (de pâtissier) pastry wheel; (jeu): **la** ~ roulette; **à** ~**s** on castors

roulis [Ruli] nm roll(ing)

roulotte [Rulɔt] nf caravan

Roumanie [Rumani] nf Rumania

rouquin, e [Rukɛ̃, -in] (péj) nm/f redhead

rouspéter [Ruspete] (fam) vi to moan

rousse [Rus] adj voir **roux**

roussi [Rusi] nm: **ça sent le** ~ there's a smell of burning; (fig) I can smell trouble

roussir [RusiR] vt to scorch ♦ vi (feuilles) to go ou turn brown; (CULIN): **faire** ~ to brown

route [Rut] nf road; (fig: chemin) way; (iti-néraire, parcours) route; (fig: voie) road, path; **par (la)** ~ by road; **il y a 3h de** ~ it's a 3-hour ride ou journey; **en** ~ on the way; **mettre en** ~ to start up; **se mettre en** ~ to set off; **faire** ~ **vers** to head towards; ~ **nationale** ≈ A road (BRIT), ≈ state high-way (US); **routier, ière** adj road cpd ♦ nm (camionneur) (long-distance) lorry (BRIT) ou truck (US) driver; (restaurant) ≈ transport café (BRIT), ≈ truck stop (US); **routière** nf (voiture) touring car

routine [Rutin] nf routine; **routinier, ière** (péj) adj humdrum; addicted to routine

rouvrir [RuvRiR] vt, vi to reopen, open again; **se** ~ vi to reopen, open again

roux, rousse [Ru, Rus] adj red; (personne) red-haired ♦ nm/f redhead

royal, e, aux [Rwajal, -o] adj royal; (fig) princely

royaume [Rwajom] nm kingdom; (fig) realm; **le R~-Uni** the United Kingdom

royauté [Rwajote] nf (dignité) kingship; (ré-gime) monarchy

ruban [Rybɑ̃] nm (gén) ribbon; (d'acier) strip; ~ **adhésif** adhesive tape

rubéole [Rybeɔl] nf German measles sg, ru-bella

rubis [Rybi] nm ruby

rubrique [RybRik] nf (titre, catégorie) head-ing; (PRESSE: article) column

ruche [Ryʃ] nf hive

rude [Ryd] adj (barbe, toile) rough; (métier, tâche) hard, tough; (climat) severe, harsh; (bourru) harsh, rough; (fruste) rugged, tough; (fam) jolly good

rudement [Rydmɑ̃] (fam) adv (très) terribly; (beaucoup) terribly hard

rudimentaire [Rydimɑ̃tɛR] adj rudimentary, basic

rudoyer [Rydwaje] vt to treat harshly

rue [Ry] nf street

ruée [Rɥe] nf rush

ruelle [Rɥɛl] nf alley(-way)

ruer [Rɥe] vi (cheval) to kick out; **se** ~ vi: **se** ~ **sur** to pounce on; **se** ~ **vers/dans/ hors de** to rush ou dash towards/into/out of

rugby [Rygbi] nm rugby (football)

rugir [RyʒiR] vi to roar

rugueux, euse [Rygø, -øz] adj rough

ruine [Rɥin] nf ruin; ~**s** nfpl (de château etc) ruins

ruiner [Rɥine] vt to ruin

ruineux, euse [Rɥinø, øz] adj ruinous

ruisseau, x [Rɥiso] nm stream, brook

ruisseler [Rɥisle] vi to stream

rumeur [RymœR] nf (bruit confus) rumbling, hubbub no pl; murmur(ing); (nouvelle) ru-mour

ruminer [Rymine] vt (herbe) to ruminate; (fig) to ruminate on ou over, chew over

rupture [RyptyR] nf (de câble, digue) break-ing; (de tendon) rupture, tearing; (de négo-ciations etc) breakdown; (de contrat) breach; (séparation, désunion) break-up, split

rural, e, aux [RyRal, -o] adj rural, country cpd

ruse [Ryz] nf: **la** ~ cunning, craftiness;

trickery; **une ~** a trick, a ruse; **rusé, e** *adj* cunning, crafty

russe [ʀys] *adj, nm/f* Russian ♦ *nm* (*LING*) Russian

Russie [ʀysi] *nf*: **la ~** Russia

rustique [ʀystik] *adj* rustic

rustre [ʀystʀ(ə)] *nm* boor

rutilant, e [ʀytilɑ̃, -ɑ̃t] *adj* gleaming

rythme [ʀitm(ə)] *nm* rhythm; (*vitesse*) rate; (: *de la vie*) pace, tempo

<hr>

S s

s' [s] *pron voir* **se**

sa [sa] *dét voir* **son**[1]

S.A. *sigle* (= *société anonyme*) ≈ Ltd (*BRIT*), ≈ Inc. (*US*)

sable [sabl(ə)] *nm* sand; **~s mouvants** quicksand(s)

sablé [sable] *nm* shortbread biscuit

sabler [sable] *vt* to sand; (*contre le verglas*) to grit; **~ le champagne** to drink champagne

sablier [sablije] *nm* hourglass; (*de cuisine*) egg timer

sablonneux, euse [sablɔnø, -øz] *adj* sandy

saborder [sabɔʀde] *vt* (*navire*) to scuttle; (*fig*) to wind up, shut down

sabot [sabo] *nm* clog; (*de cheval, bœuf*) hoof; **~ de frein** brake shoe

saboter [sabɔte] *vt* to sabotage

sac [sak] *nm* bag; (*à charbon etc*) sack; **mettre à ~** to sack; **~ à dos** rucksack; **~ à main** handbag; **~ à provisions/de voyage** shopping/travelling bag; **~ de couchage** sleeping bag

saccade [sakad] *nf* jerk

saccager [sakaʒe] *vt* (*piller*) to sack; (*dévaster*) to create havoc in

saccharine [sakaʀin] *nf* saccharin

sacerdoce [sasɛʀdɔs] *nm* priesthood; (*fig*) calling, vocation

sache *etc vb voir* **savoir**

sachet [saʃe] *nm* (small) bag; (*de lavande, poudre, shampooing*) sachet; **~ de thé** tea bag

sacoche [sakɔʃ] *nf* (*gén*) bag; (*de bicyclette*) saddlebag

sacre [sakʀ(ə)] *nm* coronation; consecration

sacré, e [sakʀe] *adj* sacred; (*fam: satané*) blasted; (: *fameux*) **un ~ ...** a heck of a ...

sacrement [sakʀəmɑ̃] *nm* sacrament

sacrifice [sakʀifis] *nm* sacrifice

sacrifier [sakʀifje] *vt* to sacrifice; **~ à** to conform to

sacristie [sakʀisti] *nf* sacristy; (*culte protestant*) vestry

sadique [sadik] *adj* sadistic

sage [saʒ] *adj* wise; (*enfant*) good ♦ *nm* wise man; sage

sage-femme [saʒfam] *nf* midwife

sagesse [saʒɛs] *nf* wisdom

Sagittaire [saʒitɛʀ] *nm*: **le ~** Sagittarius

Sahara [saaʀa] *nm*: **le ~** the Sahara (desert)

saignant, e [sɛɲɑ̃, -ɑ̃t] *adj* (*viande*) rare

saignée [seɲe] *nf* (*fig*) heavy losses *pl*

saigner [seɲe] *vi* to bleed ♦ *vt* to bleed; (*animal*) to kill (by bleeding); **~ du nez** to have a nosebleed

saillie [saji] *nf* (*sur un mur etc*) projection; (*trait d'esprit*) witticism

saillir [sajiʀ] *vi* to project, stick out; (*veine, muscle*) to bulge

sain, e [sɛ̃, sɛn] *adj* healthy; (*lectures*) wholesome; **~ d'esprit** sound in mind, sane; **~ et sauf** safe and sound, unharmed

saindoux [sɛ̃du] *nm* lard

saint, e [sɛ̃, sɛ̃t] *adj* holy; (*fig*) saintly ♦ *nm/f* saint; **le S~-Esprit** the Holy Spirit *ou* Ghost; **la S~e Vierge** the Blessed Virgin; **la S~-Sylvestre** New Year's Eve; **sainteté** *nf* holiness

sais *etc vb voir* **savoir**

saisie [sezi] *nf* seizure; **~ (de données)** (data) capture

saisir [seziʀ] *vt* to take hold of, grab; (*fig: occasion*) to seize; (*comprendre*) to grasp; (*entendre*) to get, catch; (*données*) to capture; (*suj: émotions*) to take hold of, come over; (*CULIN*) to fry quickly; (*JUR: biens, publication*) to seize; (: *juridiction*): **~ un tribunal d'une affaire** to submit *ou* refer a case to a court; **se ~ de** *vt* to seize; **saisissant, e** *adj* startling, striking

saison [sezɔ̃] *nf* season; **morte ~** slack season; **saisonnier, ière** *adj* seasonal

sait *vb voir* **savoir**

salade [salad] *nf* (*BOT*) lettuce *etc*; (*CULIN*) (green) salad; (*fam*) tangle, muddle; **~ de fruits** fruit salad; **saladier** *nm* (salad) bowl

salaire [salɛʀ] *nm* (*annuel, mensuel*) salary; (*hebdomadaire, journalier*) pay, wages *pl*; (*fig*) reward; **~ de base** basic salary (*ou* wage); **~ minimum interprofessionnel de croissance** index-linked guaranteed minimum wage

salarié, e [salaʀje] *nm/f* salaried employee; wage-earner

salaud [salo] (*fam!*) *nm* sod (*!*), bastard (*!*)

sale [sal] *adj* dirty, filthy

salé, e [sale] *adj* (*liquide, saveur*) salty; (*CULIN*) salted; (*fig*) spicy; steep

saler [sale] *vt* to salt

saleté [salte] *nf* (*état*) dirtiness; (*crasse*) dirt, filth; (*tache etc*) dirt *no pl*; (*fig*) dirty trick; rubbish *no pl*; filth *no pl*

salière [saljɛʀ] *nf* saltcellar

salin, e [salɛ̃, -in] *adj* saline; **saline** *nf* salt-works *sg*; salt marsh

salir [saliʀ] *vt* to (make) dirty; (*fig*) to soil the reputation of; **se ~** *vi* to get dirty; **salissant, e** *adj* (*tissu*) which shows the dirt; (*métier*) dirty, messy

salle [sal] *nf* room; (*d'hôpital*) ward; (*de restaurant*) dining room; (*d'un cinéma*) auditorium; (: *public*) audience; **faire ~ comble** to have a full house; **~ à manger** dining room; **~ commune** (*d'hôpital*) ward; **~ d'attente** waiting room; **~ de bain(s)** bathroom; **~ de classe** classroom; **~ de concert** concert hall; **~ de consultation** consulting room; **~ d'eau** shower-room; **~ d'embarquement** (*à l'aéroport*) departure lounge; **~ de jeux** games room; playroom; **~ d'opération** (*d'hôpital*) operating theatre; **~ de séjour** living room; **~ de spectacle** theatre; cinema; **~ de thé** tearoom; **des ventes** saleroom

salon [salɔ̃] *nm* lounge, sitting room; (*mobilier*) lounge suite; (*exposition*) exhibition, show; **~ de thé** tearoom

salopard [salɔpaʀ] (*fam!*) *nm* bastard (*!*)

salope [salɔp] (*fam!*) *nf* bitch (*!*)

saloperie [salɔpʀi] (*fam!*) *nf* filth *no pl*; dirty trick; rubbish *no pl*

salopette [salɔpet] *nf* dungarees *pl*; (*d'ouvrier*) overall(s)

salsifis [salsifi] *nm* salsify

salubre [salybʀ(ə)] *adj* healthy, salubrious

saluer [salɥe] *vt* (*pour dire bonjour, fig*) to greet; (*pour dire au revoir*) to take one's leave; (*MIL*) to salute

salut [saly] *nm* (*sauvegarde*) safety; (*REL*) salvation; (*geste*) wave; (*parole*) greeting; (*MIL*) salute ♦ *excl* (*fam*) hi (there)

salutations [salytasjɔ̃] *nfpl* greetings; **recevez mes ~ distinguées** *ou* **respectueuses** yours faithfully

samedi [samdi] *nm* Saturday

SAMU [samy] *sigle m* (= *service d'assistance médicale d'urgence*) ≈ ambulance (service) (*BRIT*), ≈ paramedics *pl* (*US*)

sanction [sɑ̃ksjɔ̃] *nf* sanction; (*fig*) penalty; **sanctionner** *vt* (*loi, usage*) to sanction; (*punir*) to punish

sandale [sɑ̃dal] *nf* sandal

sandwich [sɑ̃dwitʃ] *nm* sandwich

sang [sɑ̃] *nm* blood; **en ~** covered in blood; **se faire du mauvais ~** to fret, get in a state

sang-froid [sɑ̃fʀwa] *nm* calm, sangfroid; **de ~** in cold blood

sanglant, e [sɑ̃glɑ̃, -ɑ̃t] *adj* bloody, covered in blood; (*combat*) bloody

sangle [sɑ̃gl(ə)] *nf* strap

sanglier [sɑ̃glije] *nm* (wild) boar

sanglot [sɑ̃glo] *nm* sob

sangsue [sɑ̃sy] *nf* leech

sanguin, e [sɑ̃gɛ̃, -in] *adj* blood *cpd*; (*fig*) fiery; **sanguinaire** [sɑ̃ginɛʀ] *adj* bloodthirsty; bloody

sanisette [sanizet] *nf* (automatic) public toilet

sanitaire [sanitɛʀ] *adj* health *cpd*; **~s** *nmpl* (*lieu*) bathroom *sg*

sans [sɑ̃] *prép* without; **~ qu'il s'en aperçoive** without him *ou* his noticing; **~-abri** *nmpl* homeless; **~-emploi** [sɑ̃zɑ̃plwa] *n inv* unemployed person; **les ~-emploi** the unemployed; **~-façon** *adj inv* fuss-free; free and easy; **~-gêne** *adj inv* inconsiderate; **~-logis** *nmpl* homeless

santé [sɑ̃te] *nf* health; **en bonne ~** in good health; **boire à la ~ de qn** to drink (to) sb's health; **"à la ~ de"** "here's to"; **à ta/votre ~!** cheers!

saoudien, ne [saudjɛ̃, -jɛn] *adj* Saudi Arabian ♦ *nm/f*: **S~(ne)** Saudi Arabian

saoul, e [su, sul] *adj* = **soûl**

saper [sape] *vt* to undermine, sap

sapeur-pompier [sapœʀpɔ̃pje] *nm* fireman

saphir [safiʀ] *nm* sapphire

sapin [sapɛ̃] *nm* fir (tree); (*bois*) fir; **~ de Noël** Christmas tree

sarcastique [saʀkastik] *adj* sarcastic

sarcler [saʀkle] *vt* to weed

Sardaigne [saʀdɛɲ] *nf*: **la ~** Sardinia

sardine [saʀdin] *nf* sardine

SARL *sigle* (= *société à responsabilité limitée*) ≈ plc (*BRIT*), ≈ Inc. (*US*)

sas [sas] *nm* (*de sous-marin, d'engin spatial*) airlock; (*d'écluse*) lock

satané, e [satane] *adj* confounded

satellite [satelit] *nm* satellite

satin [satɛ̃] *nm* satin

satire [satiʀ] *nf* satire; **satirique** *adj* satirical

satisfaction [satisfaksjɔ̃] *nf* satisfaction

satisfaire [satisfɛʀ] *vt* to satisfy; **~ à** (*engagement*) to fulfil; (*revendications, conditions*) to satisfy, meet; to comply with; **satisfaisant, e** *adj* satisfactory; (*qui fait plaisir*) satisfying; **satisfait, e** *adj* satisfied; **satisfait de** happy *ou* satisfied with

saturer [satyʀe] *vt* to saturate

sauce [sos] *nf* sauce; (*avec un rôti*) gravy; **saucière** *nf* sauceboat

saucisse [sosis] *nf* sausage

saucisson [sosisɔ̃] *nm* (slicing) sausage

sauf, sauve [sof, sov] *adj* unharmed, unhurt; (*fig: honneur*) intact, saved ♦ *prép* except; **laisser la vie sauve à qn** to spare sb's life; **~ si** (*à moins que*) unless; **~ erreur** if I'm not mistaken; **~ avis contraire** unless you hear to the contrary

sauge [soʒ] nf sage
saugrenu, e [sogrəny] adj preposterous
saule [sol] nm willow (tree)
saumon [somɔ̃] nm salmon inv
saumure [somyʀ] nf brine
saupoudrer [supudʀe] vt: ~ qch de to sprinkle sth with
saur [sɔʀ] adj m: hareng ~ smoked ou red herring, kipper
saurai etc vb voir **savoir**
saut [so] nm jump; (discipline sportive) jumping; **faire un ~ chez qn** to pop over to sb's (place); **au ~ du lit** on getting out of bed; **~ à la corde** skipping; **~ à la perche** pole vaulting; **~ en hauteur/longueur** high/long jump; **~ périlleux** somersault
saute [sot] nf sudden change
saute-mouton [sotmutɔ̃] nm: **jouer à ~** to play leapfrog
sauter [sote] vi to jump, leap; (exploser) to blow up, explode; (: fusibles) to blow; (se rompre) to snap, burst; (se détacher) to pop out (ou off) ♦ vt to jump (over), leap (over); (fig: omettre) to skip, miss (out); **faire ~** to blow up, to burst open; (CULIN) to sauté; **~ au cou de qn** to fly into sb's arms
sauterelle [sotʀɛl] nf grasshopper
sautiller [sotije] vi to hop; to skip
sautoir [sotwaʀ] nm: **~ (de perles)** string of pearls
sauvage [sovaʒ] adj (gén) wild; (peuplade) savage; (farouche) unsociable; (barbare) wild, savage; (non officiel) unauthorized, unofficial ♦ nm/f savage; (timide) unsociable type
sauve [sov] adj f voir **sauf**
sauvegarde [sovgaʀd(ə)] nf safeguard; **sauvegarder** vt to safeguard; (INFORM: enregistrer) to save; (: copier) to back up
sauve-qui-peut [sovkipø] excl run for your life!
sauver [sove] vt to save; (porter secours à) to rescue; (récupérer) to salvage, rescue; **se ~** vi (s'enfuir) to run away; (fam: partir) to be off; **sauvetage** nm rescue; **sauveteur** nm rescuer; **sauvette: à la sauvette** adv (vendre) without authorization; (se marier etc) hastily, hurriedly; **sauveur** nm saviour (BRIT), savior (US)
savais etc vb voir **savoir**
savamment [savamɑ̃] adv (avec érudition) learnedly; (habilement) skilfully, cleverly
savant, e [savɑ̃, -ɑ̃t] adj scholarly, learned; (calé) clever ♦ nm scientist
saveur [savœʀ] nf flavour, (fig) savour
savoir [savwaʀ] vt to know; (être capable de): **il sait nager** he can swim ♦ nm knowledge; **se ~** vi (être connu) to be known; **à ~** that is, namely; **faire ~ qch à qn** to let sb know sth; **pas que je sache** not as far as I know
savon [savɔ̃] nm (produit) soap; (morceau)

bar of soap; (fam): **passer un ~ à qn** to give sb a good dressing-down; **savonnette** nf bar of soap; **savonneux, euse** adj soapy
savons vb voir **savoir**
savourer [savure] vt to savour
savoureux, euse [savuʀø, -øz] adj tasty; (fig) spicy, juicy
saxo(phone) [saksɔ(fɔn)] nm sax(ophone)
scabreux, euse [skabʀø, -øz] adj risky; (indécent) improper, shocking
scandale [skɑ̃dal] nm scandal; (tapage): **faire du ~** to make a scene, create a disturbance; **faire ~** to scandalize people; **scandaleux, euse** adj scandalous, outrageous
scandinave [skɑ̃dinav] adj, nm/f Scandinavian
Scandinavie [skɑ̃dinavi] nf Scandinavia
scaphandre [skafɑ̃dʀ(ə)] nm (de plongeur) diving suit; (de cosmonaute) space-suit
scarabée [skaʀabe] nm beetle
sceau, x [so] nm seal; (fig) stamp, mark
scélérat, e [selera, -at] nm/f villain
sceller [sele] vt to seal
scénario [senaʀjo] nm (CINÉMA) scenario; script; (fig) scenario
scène [sɛn] nf (gén) scene; (estrade, fig: théâtre) stage; **entrer en ~** to come on stage; **mettre en ~** (THÉÂTRE) to stage; (CINÉMA) to direct; (fig) to present, introduce; **~ de ménage** nf domestic scene
sceptique [sɛptik] adj sceptical
schéma [ʃema] nm (diagramme) diagram, sketch; (fig) outline; pattern; **~tique** adj diagrammatic(al), schematic; (fig) oversimplified
sciatique [sjatik] nf sciatica
scie [si] nf saw; **~ à découper** fretsaw; **~ à métaux** hacksaw
sciemment [sjamɑ̃] adv knowingly
science [sjɑ̃s] nf science; (savoir) knowledge; (savoir-faire) art, skill; **~s naturelles** (SCOL) natural science sg, biology sg; **~s po** nfpl political science ou studies pl; **scientifique** adj scientific ♦ nm/f scientist; science student
scier [sje] vt to saw; (retrancher) to saw off; **scierie** nf sawmill
scinder [sɛ̃de] vt to split up; **se ~** vi to split up
scintiller [sɛ̃tije] vi to sparkle
scission [sisjɔ̃] nf split
sciure [sjyʀ] nf: **~ (de bois)** sawdust
sclérose [skleʀoz] nf: **~ en plaques** multiple sclerosis
scolaire [skɔlɛʀ] adj school cpd; (péj) schoolish; **scolariser** vt to provide with schooling (ou schools); **scolarité** nf schooling
scooter [skutœʀ] nm (motor) scooter
score [skɔʀ] nm score
scorpion [skɔʀpjɔ̃] nm (signe): **le S~** Scor-

pic
Scotch [skɔtʃ] (®) nm adhesive tape
scout, e [skut] adj, nm scout
script [skript] nm printing; (*CINÉMA*) (shooting) script
script-girl [skriptgœrl] nf continuity girl
scrupule [skrypyl] nm scruple
scruter [skryte] vt to scrutinize; (*l'obscurité*) to peer into
scrutin [skrytɛ̃] nm (*vote*) ballot; (*ensemble des opérations*) poll
sculpter [skylte] vt to sculpt; (*suj: érosion*) to carve; **sculpteur** nm sculptor
sculpture [skyltyr] nf sculpture; ~ **sur bois** wood carving

---

MOT CLÉ

se(s') [s(ə)] pron **1** (*emploi réfléchi*) oneself; (: *masc*) himself; (: *fém*) herself; (: *sujet non humain*) itself; (: *pl*) themselves; **se voir comme l'on est** to see o.s. as one is
2 (*réciproque*) one another, each other; **ils s'aiment** they love one another *ou* each other
3 (*passif*): **cela se répare facilement** it is easily repaired
4 (*possessif*): **se casser la jambe/laver les mains** to break one's leg/wash one's hands

---

séance [seɑ̃s] nf (*d'assemblée, récréative*) meeting, session; (*de tribunal*) sitting, session; (*musicale, CINÉMA, THÉÂTRE*) performance; ~ **tenante** forthwith
seau, x [so] nm bucket, pail
sec, sèche [sɛk, sɛʃ] adj dry; (*raisins, figues*) dried; (*cœur, personne: insensible*) hard, cold ♦ nm: **tenir au** ~ to keep in a dry place ♦ adv hard; **je le bois** ~ I drink it straight *ou* neat; **à** ~ dried up
sécateur [sekatœr] nm secateurs pl (*BRIT*), shears pl
sèche [sɛʃ] adj f voir **sec**
sèche-cheveux [sɛʃʃəvø] nm inv hair-drier
sèche-linge [sɛʃlɛ̃ʒ] nm inv tumble dryer
sécher [seʃe] vt to dry; (*dessécher: peau, blé*) to dry (out); (: *étang*) to dry up ♦ vi to dry; to dry out; to dry up; (*fam: candidat*) to be stumped; **se** ~ (*après le bain*) to dry o.s.
sécheresse [sɛʃrɛs] nf dryness; (*absence de pluie*) drought
séchoir [seʃwar] nm drier
second, e [səgɔ̃, -ɔ̃d] adj second ♦ nm (*assistant*) second in command; (*NAVIG*) first mate; **voyager en** ~e to travel second-class; **de** ~e **main** second-hand; **secondaire** adj secondary; **seconde** nf second; **seconder** vt to assist
secouer [səkwe] vt to shake; (*passagers*) to rock; (*traumatiser*) to shake (up)
secourir [səkurir] vt (*aller sauver*) to (go and) rescue; (*prodiguer des soins à*) to help,

assist; (*venir en aide à*) to assist, aid; **se-courisme** nm first aid; life saving
secours [səkur] nm help, aid, assistance ♦ nmpl aid sg; **au** ~! help!; **appeler au** ~ to shout *ou* call for help; **porter** ~ **à qn** to give sb assistance, help sb; **les premiers** ~ first aid sg
secousse [səkus] nf jolt, bump; (*électrique*) shock; (*fig: psychologique*) jolt, shock; ~ **sismique** *ou* **tellurique** earth tremor
secret, ète [səkrɛ, -ɛt] adj secret; (*fig: renfermé*) reticent, reserved ♦ nm secret; (*discrétion absolue*): **le** ~ secrecy; **au** ~ in solitary confinement
secrétaire [səkreter] nm/f secretary ♦ nm (*meuble*) writing desk; ~ **de direction** private *ou* personal secretary; ~ **d'État** junior minister; ~ **général** nm (*COMM*) company secretary; **secrétariat** nm (*profession*) secretarial work; (*bureau*) office; (: *d'organisation internationale*) secretariat
secteur [sɛktœr] nm sector; (*ADMIN*) district; (*ÉLEC*): **branché sur le** ~ plugged into the mains (supply)
section [sɛksjɔ̃] nf section; (*de parcours d'autobus*) fare stage; (*MIL: unité*) platoon; **sectionner** vt to sever
Sécu [seky] abr f = **sécurité sociale**
séculaire [sekyler] adj secular; (*très vieux*) age-old
sécuriser [sekyrize] vt to give (a feeling of) security to
sécurité [sekyrite] nf safety; security; **système de** ~ safety system; **être en** ~ to be safe; **la** ~ **routière** road safety; **la** ~ **sociale** ≈ (the) Social Security (*BRIT*), ≈ Welfare (*US*)
sédition [sedisjɔ̃] nf insurrection, sedition
séduction [sedyksjɔ̃] nf seduction; (*charme, attrait*) appeal, charm
séduire [seduir] vt to charm; (*femme: abuser de*) to seduce; **séduisant, e** adj (*femme*) seductive; (*homme, offre*) very attractive
ségrégation [segregasjɔ̃] nf segregation
seigle [sɛgl(ə)] nm rye
seigneur [sɛɲœr] nm lord
sein [sɛ̃] nm breast; (*entrailles*) womb; **au** ~ **de** (*équipe, institution*) within; (*flots, bonheur*) in the midst of
séisme [seism(ə)] nm earthquake
seize [sɛz] num sixteen; **seizième** num sixteenth
séjour [seʒur] nm stay; (*pièce*) living room; **séjourner** vi to stay
sel [sɛl] nm salt; (*fig*) wit; spice; ~ **de cuisine/de table** cooking/table salt
sélection [selɛksjɔ̃] nf selection; **sélectionner** vt to select
self-service [sɛlfsɛrvis] adj, nm self-service
selle [sɛl] nf saddle; ~**s** nfpl (*MÉD*) stools; **seller** vt to saddle

sellette [sɛlɛt] *nf*: **être sur la ~** to be on the carpet

selon [səlɔ̃] *prép* according to; (*en se conformant à*) in accordance with; **~ que** according to whether; **~ moi** as I see it

semaine [səmɛn] *nf* week; **en ~** during the week, on weekdays

semblable [sɑ̃blabl(ə)] *adj* similar; (*de ce genre*): **de ~s mésaventures** such mishaps ♦ *nm* fellow creature *ou* man; **~ à** similar to, like

semblant [sɑ̃blɑ̃] *nm*: **un ~ de vérité** a semblance of truth; **faire ~ (de faire)** to pretend (to do)

sembler [sɑ̃ble] *vb* +*attrib* to seem ♦ *vb impers*: **il semble (bien) que/inutile de** it (really) seems *ou* appears that/useless to; **il me semble que** it seems to me that; I think (that); **comme bon lui semble** as he sees fit

semelle [səmɛl] *nf* sole; (*intérieure*) insole, inner sole

semence [səmɑ̃s] *nf* (*graine*) seed

semer [səme] *vt* to sow; (*fig: éparpiller*) to scatter; (: *confusion*) to spread; (: *poursuivants*) to lose, shake off; **semé de** (*difficultés*) riddled with

semestre [səmɛstʀ(ə)] *nm* half-year; (*SCOL*) semester

séminaire [seminɛʀ] *nm* seminar

semi-remorque [səmiʀəmɔʀk(ə)] *nm* articulated lorry (*BRIT*), semi(trailer) (*US*)

semonce [səmɔ̃s] *nf*: **un coup de ~** a shot across the bows

semoule [səmul] *nf* semolina

sempiternel, le [sɛ̃pitɛʀnɛl] *adj* eternal, never-ending

sénat [sena] *nm* Senate; **sénateur** *nm* Senator

sens [sɑ̃s] *nm* (*PHYSIOL, instinct*) sense; (*signification*) meaning, sense; (*direction*) direction; **à mon ~** to my mind; **reprendre ses ~** to regain consciousness; **dans le ~ des aiguilles d'une montre** clockwise; **~ commun** common sense; **~ dessus dessous** upside down; **~ interdit** one-way street; **~ unique** one-way street

sensass [sɑ̃sas] (*fam*) *adj* fantastic

sensation [sɑ̃sasjɔ̃] *nf* sensation; **à ~** (*péj*) sensational

sensé, e [sɑ̃se] *adj* sensible

sensibiliser [sɑ̃sibilize] *vt*: **~ qn à** to make sb sensitive to

sensibilité [sɑ̃sibilite] *nf* sensitivity

sensible [sɑ̃sibl(ə)] *adj* sensitive; (*aux sens*) perceptible; (*appréciable: différence, progrès*) appreciable, noticeable; **sensiblement** *adv* (*notablement*) appreciably, noticeably; (*à peu près*): **ils ont sensiblement le même poids** they weigh approximately the same; **sensiblerie** *nf* sentimentality; squeamishness

sensuel, le [sɑ̃sɥɛl] *adj* sensual; sensuous

sentence [sɑ̃tɑ̃s] *nf* (*jugement*) sentence; (*adage*) maxim

sentier [sɑ̃tje] *nm* path

sentiment [sɑ̃timɑ̃] *nm* feeling; **recevez mes ~s respectueux** yours faithfully; **sentimental, e, aux** *adj* sentimental; (*vie, aventure*) love *cpd*

sentinelle [sɑ̃tinɛl] *nf* sentry

sentir [sɑ̃tiʀ] *vt* (*par l'odorat*) to smell; (*par le goût*) to taste; (*au toucher, fig*) to feel; (*répandre une odeur de*) to smell of; (: *ressemblance*) to smell like; (*avoir la saveur de*) to taste of; to taste like ♦ *vi* to smell; **~ mauvais** to smell bad; **se ~ bien** to feel good; **se ~ mal** (*être indisposé*) to feel unwell *ou* ill; **se ~ le courage/la force de faire** to feel brave/strong enough to do; **il ne peut pas le ~** (*fam*) he can't stand him

séparation [separasjɔ̃] *nf* separation; (*cloison*) division, partition; **~ de corps** legal separation

séparé, e [separe] *adj* (*appartements, pouvoirs*) separate; (*époux*) separated; **~ment** *adv* separately

séparer [separe] *vt* (*gén*) to separate; (*suj: divergences etc*) to divide; to drive apart; (*suj: différences, obstacles*) to stand between; (*détacher*): **~ qch de** to pull sth (off) from; (*diviser*): **~ qch par** to divide sth (up) with; **se ~** *vi* (*époux, amis, adversaires*) to separate, part; (*se diviser: route, tige etc*) to divide; (*se détacher*): **se ~ (de)** to split off (from); to come off; **se ~ de** (*époux*) to separate *ou* part from; (*employé, objet personnel*) to part with; **~ une pièce en deux** to divide a room into two

sept [sɛt] *num* seven

septembre [sɛptɑ̃bʀ(ə)] *nm* September

septennat [sɛptena] *nm* seven year term of office (*of French President*)

septentrional, e, aux [sɛptɑ̃tʀijɔnal, -o] *adj* northern

septicémie [sɛptisemi] *nf* blood poisoning, septicaemia

septième [sɛtjɛm] *num* seventh

septique [sɛptik] *adj*: **fosse ~** septic tank

sépulture [sepyltyʀ] *nf* burial; burial place, grave

séquelles [sekɛl] *nfpl* after-effects; (*fig*) aftermath *sg*; consequences

séquestrer [sekɛstʀe] *vt* (*personne*) to confine illegally; (*biens*) to impound

serai *etc vb voir* **être**

serein, e [səʀɛ̃, -ɛn] *adj* serene; (*jugement*) dispassionate

serez *vb voir* **être**

sergent [sɛʀʒɑ̃] *nm* sergeant

série [seʀi] *nf* (*de questions, d'accidents*) series *inv*; (*de clés, casseroles, outils*) set; (*catégorie: SPORT*) rank; class; **en ~** in quick succession; (*COMM*) mass *cpd*; **de ~**

standard; **hors** ~ (*COMM*) custom-built; (*fig*) outstanding

sérieusement [seʀjøzmɑ̃] *adv* seriously; reliably; responsibly

sérieux, euse [seʀjø, -øz] *adj* serious; (*élève, employé*) reliable, responsible; (*client, maison*) reliable, dependable ♦ *nm* seriousness; reliability; **garder son** ~ to keep a straight face; **prendre qch/qn au** ~ to take sth/sb seriously

serin [səʀɛ̃] *nm* canary

seringue [səʀɛ̃g] *nf* syringe

serions *vb voir* **être**

serment [seʀmɑ̃] *nm* (*juré*) oath; (*promesse*) pledge, vow

sermon [seʀmɔ̃] *nm* sermon

séro-positif, ive [seʀo-] *adj* (*MED*) HIV-positive

serpent [seʀpɑ̃] *nm* snake

serpenter [seʀpɑ̃te] *vi* to wind

serpentin [seʀpɑ̃tɛ̃] *nm* (*tube*) coil; (*ruban*) streamer

serpillière [seʀpijɛʀ] *nf* floorcloth

serre [seʀ] *nf* (*AGR*) greenhouse; ~**s** *nfpl* (*griffes*) claws, talons

serré, e [seʀe] *adj* (*réseau*) dense; (*écriture*) close; (*habits*) tight; (*fig: lutte, match*) tight, close-fought; (*passagers etc*) (tightly) packed

serrer [seʀe] *vt* (*tenir*) to grip *ou* hold tight; (*comprimer, coincer*) to squeeze; (*poings, mâchoires*) to clench; (*suj: vêtement*) to be too tight for; (*fit tightly*) (*rapprocher*) to close up, move closer together; (*ceinture, nœud, frein, vis*) to tighten ♦ *vi*: ~ **à droite** to keep *ou* get over to the right; **se** ~ *vi* (*se rapprocher*) to squeeze up; **se** ~ **contre qn** to huddle up to sb; ~ **la main à qn** to shake sb's hand; ~ **qn dans ses bras** to hug sb, clasp sb in one's arms

serrure [seʀyʀ] *nf* lock

serrurier [seʀyʀje] *nm* locksmith

sert *etc vb voir* **servir**

sertir [seʀtiʀ] *vt* (*pierre*) to set

servante [seʀvɑ̃t] *nf* (maid)servant

serveur, euse [seʀvœʀ, -øz] *nm/f* waiter(waitress)

serviable [seʀvjabl(ə)] *adj* obliging, willing to help

service [seʀvis] *nm* (*gén*) service; (*série de repas*): **premier** ~ first sitting; (*assortiment de vaisselle*) set, service; (*bureau: de la vente etc*) department, section; (*travail*): **pendant le** ~ on duty; ~**s** *nmpl* (*travail, ÉCON*) services; **faire le** ~ to serve; **rendre** ~ **à** to help; **rendre un** ~ **à qn** to do sb a favour; **mettre en** ~ to put into service *ou* operation; **hors** ~ out of order; ~ **après-vente** after-sales service; ~ **d'ordre** police (*ou* stewards) in charge of maintaining order; ~ **militaire** military service; ~**s secrets** secret service *sg*

serviette [seʀvjet] *nf* (*de table*) (table) napkin, serviette; (*de toilette*) towel; (*porte-documents*) briefcase; ~ **hygiénique** sanitary towel

servir [seʀviʀ] *vt* (*gén*) to serve; (*au restaurant*) to wait on; (*au magasin*) to serve, attend to; (*fig: aider*): ~ **qn** to aid sb; to serve sb's interests; (*COMM: rente*) to pay ♦ *vi* (*TENNIS*) to serve; (*CARTES*) to deal; **se** ~ *vi* (*prendre d'un plat*) to help o.s.; **se** ~ **de** (*plat*) to help o.s. to; (*voiture, outil, relations*) to use; **vous êtes servi?** are you being served?; ~ **à qn** (*diplôme, livre*) to be of use to sb; ~ **à qch/faire** (*outil etc*) to be used for sth/doing; **à quoi cela sert-il (de faire)?** what's the use (of doing)?; **cela ne sert à rien** it's no use; ~ (**à qn**) **de** to serve as (for sb); ~ **à dîner** (**à qn**) to serve dinner (to sb)

serviteur [seʀvitœʀ] *nm* servant

servitude [seʀvityd] *nf* servitude; (*fig*) constraint

ses [se] *dét voir* **son**[1]

seuil [sœj] *nm* doorstep; (*fig*) threshold

seul, e [sœl] *adj* (*sans compagnie*) alone; (*avec nuance affective: isolé*) lonely; (*unique*): **un** ~ **livre** only one book, a single book ♦ *adv* (*vivre*) alone, on one's own ♦ *nm, nf*: **il en reste un(e)** ~**(e)** there's only one left; **le** ~ **livre** the only book; ~ **ce livre, ce livre** ~ this book alone, only this book; **parler tout** ~ to talk to oneself; **faire qch (tout)** ~ to do sth (all) on one's own *ou* (all) by oneself; **à lui (tout)** ~ single-handed, on his own

seulement [sœlmɑ̃] *adv* only; **non** ~ ... **mais aussi** *ou* **encore** not only ... but also

sève [sev] *nf* sap

sévère [sevɛʀ] *adj* severe

sévices [sevis] *nmpl* (physical) cruelty *sg*, ill treatment *sg*

sévir [seviʀ] *vi* (*punir*) to use harsh measures, crack down; (*suj: fléau*) to rage, be rampant

sevrer [səvʀe] *vt* (*enfant etc*) to wean

sexe [seks(ə)] *nm* sex; (*organe mâle*) member

sexuel, le [seksɥɛl] *adj* sexual

seyant, e [sejɑ̃, -ɑ̃t] *adj* becoming

shampooing [ʃɑ̃pwɛ̃] *nm* shampoo; **se faire un** ~ to shampoo one's hair

short [ʃɔʀt] *nm* (pair of) shorts *pl*

───────── **MOT CLÉ**

si [si] *nm* (*MUS*) B; (*en chantant la gamme*) ti

♦ *adv* **1** (*oui*) yes

2 (*tellement*) so; ~ **gentil/rapidement** so kind/fast; (*tant et*) ~ **bien que** so much so that; ~ **rapide qu'il soit** however fast he may be

♦ *conj* if; ~ **tu veux** if you want; **je me de-**

mande ~ I wonder if *ou* whether; ~ **seulement** if only

Sicile [sisil] *nf*: **la** ~ Sicily
SIDA [sida] *sigle m* (= *syndrome immuno-déficitaire acquis*) AIDS *sg*
sidéré, e [sidere] *adj* staggered
sidérurgie [sideryRʒi] *nf* steel industry
siècle [sjɛkl(ə)] *nm* century; (*époque*) age
siège [sjɛʒ] *nm* seat; (*d'entreprise*) head office; (*d'organisation*) headquarters *pl*; (*MIL*) siege; ~ **social** registered office
siéger [sjeʒe] *vi* to sit
sien, ne [sjɛ̃, sjɛn] *pron*: **le(la)** ~**(ne)**, **les** ~**(ne)s** his; hers; its; **les** ~**s** (*sa famille*) one's family; **faire des** ~**nes** (*fam*) to be up to one's (usual) tricks
sieste [sjɛst(ə)] *nf* (afternoon) snooze *ou* nap, siesta; **faire la** ~ to have a snooze *ou* nap
sifflement [sifləmã] *nm* whistle, whistling *no pl*; wheezing *no pl*; hissing *no pl*
siffler [sifle] *vi* (*gén*) to whistle; (*en respirant*) to wheeze; (*serpent, vapeur*) to hiss ♦ *vt* (*chanson*) to whistle; (*chien etc*) to whistle for; (*fille*) to whistle at; (*pièce, orateur*) to hiss, boo; (*faute*) to blow one's whistle at; (*fin du match, départ*) to blow one's whistle for; (*fam: verre*) to guzzle
sifflet [sifle] *nm* whistle; **coup de** ~ whistle
siffloter [siflɔte] *vi, vt* to whistle
sigle [sigl(ə)] *nm* acronym
signal, aux [siɲal, -o] *nm* (*signe convenu, appareil*) signal; (*indice, écriteau*) sign; **donner le** ~ **de** to give the signal for; ~ **d'alarme** alarm signal; **signaux (lumineux)** (*AUTO*) traffic signals
signalement [siɲalmã] *nm* description, particulars *pl*
signaler [siɲale] *vt* to indicate; to announce; to report; (*faire remarquer*): ~ **qch à qn/(à qn) que** to point out sth to sb/(to sb) that; **se** ~ **(par)** to distinguish o.s. (by)
signature [siɲatyR] *nf* signature (*action*), signing
signe [siɲ] *nm* sign; (*TYPO*) mark; **faire un** ~ **de la main** to give a sign with one's hand; **faire** ~ **à qn** (*fig*) to get in touch with sb; **faire** ~ **à qn d'entrer** to motion (to) sb to come in; ~**s particuliers** *nmpl* distinguishing marks
signer [siɲe] *vt* to sign; **se** ~ *vi* to cross o.s.
signet [siɲe] *nm* bookmark
significatif, ive [siɲifikatif, -iv] *adj* significant
signification [siɲifikɑsjɔ̃] *nf* meaning
signifier [siɲifje] *vt* (*vouloir dire*) to mean; (*faire connaître*): ~ **qch (à qn)** to make sth known (to sb); (*JUR*): ~ **qch à qn** to serve notice of sth on sb
silence [silɑ̃s] *nm* silence; (*MUS*) rest; **gar-**

der le ~ to keep silent, say nothing; **passer sous** ~ to pass over (in silence); **silencieux, euse** *adj* quiet, silent ♦ *nm* silencer
silex [silɛks] *nm* flint
silhouette [silwɛt] *nf* outline, silhouette; (*lignes, contour*) outline; (*figure*) figure
silicium [silisjɔm] *nm* silicon; **plaquette de** ~ silicon chip
sillage [sijaʒ] *nm* wake; (*fig*) trail
sillon [sijɔ̃] *nm* furrow; (*de disque*) groove; **sillonner** *vt* to criss-cross
simagrées [simagre] *nfpl* fuss *sg*; airs and graces
similaire [similɛR] *adj* similar; **similicuir** *nm* imitation leather; **similitude** *nf* similarity
simple [sɛ̃pl(ə)] *adj* (*gén*) simple; (*non multiple*) single; ~**s** *nmpl* (*MÉD*) medicinal plants; ~ **d'esprit** *nm/f* simpleton; ~ **messieurs** *nm* (*TENNIS*) men's singles *sg*; **un** ~ **particulier** an ordinary citizen; ~ **soldat** private
simulacre [simylakR(ə)] *nm* (*péj*): **un** ~ **de** a pretence of
simuler [simyle] *vt* to sham, simulate
simultané, e [simyltane] *adj* simultaneous
sincère [sɛ̃sɛR] *adj* sincere, genuine; **sincérité** *nf* sincerity
sine qua non [sinekwanɔn] *adj*: **condition** ~ indispensable condition
singe [sɛ̃ʒ] *nm* monkey; (*de grande taille*) ape; ~**r** [sɛ̃ʒe] *vt* to ape, mimic
singeries [sɛ̃ʒRi] *nfpl* antics; (*simagrées*) airs and graces
singulariser [sɛ̃gylaRize] *vt* to mark out; **se** ~ *vi* to call attention to o.s.
singularité [sɛ̃gylaRite] *nf* peculiarity
singulier, ière [sɛ̃gylje, -jɛR] *adj* remarkable, singular ♦ *nm* singular
sinistre [sinistR(ə)] *adj* sinister ♦ *nm* (*incendie*) blaze; (*catastrophe*) disaster; (*ASSURANCES*) damage (*giving rise to a claim*); **sinistré, e** *adj* disaster-stricken ♦ *nm/f* disaster victim
sinon [sinɔ̃] *conj* (*autrement, sans quoi*) otherwise, or else; (*sauf*) except, other than; (*si ce n'est*) if not
sinueux, euse [sinɥø, -øz] *adj* winding; (*fig*) tortuous
sinus [sinys] *nm* (*ANAT*) sinus; (*GÉOM*) sine; **sinusite** *nf* sinusitis
siphon [sifɔ̃] *nm* (*tube, d'eau gazeuse*) siphon; (*d'évier etc*) U-bend
sirène [siRɛn] *nf* siren; ~ **d'alarme** air-raid siren; fire alarm
sirop [siRo] *nm* (*à diluer: de fruit etc*) syrup; (*boisson*) fruit drink; (*pharmaceutique*) syrup, mixture
siroter [siRɔte] *vt* to sip
sismique [sismik] *adj* seismic
site [sit] *nm* (*paysage, environnement*) setting; (*d'une ville etc: emplacement*) site; ~

(pittoresque) beauty spot; **~s touristiques** places of interest

sitôt [sito] *adv*: ~ **parti** as soon as he *etc* had left; ~ **après** straight after; **pas de ~** not for a long time

situation [sitɥasjɔ̃] *nf* (*gén*) situation; (*d'un édifice, d'une ville*) situation, position; location; ~ **de famille** *nf* marital status

situé, e [sitɥe] *adj*: **bien ~** well situated; ~ **à** situated at

situer [sitɥe] *vt* to site, situate; (*en pensée*) to set, place; **se ~** *vi*: **se ~ à/près de** to be situated at/near

six [sis] *num* six; **sixième** *num* sixth

ski [ski] *nm* (*objet*) ski; (*sport*) skiing; **faire du ~** to ski; ~ **de fond** cross-country skiing; ~ **nautique** water-skiing; ~ **de piste** downhill skiing; ~ **de randonnée** cross-country skiing; **skier** *vi* to ski; **skieur, euse** *nm/f* skier

slip [slip] *nm* (*sous-vêtement*) pants *pl*, briefs *pl*; (*de bain*: *d'homme*) trunks *pl*; (: *du bikini*) briefs *pl*

slogan [slɔgɑ̃] *nm* slogan

S.M.I.C. [smik] *sigle m* = **salaire minimum interprofessionnel de croissance**

smicard, e [smikaʀ, -aʀd(ə)] (*fam*) *nm/f* minimum wage earner

smoking [smɔkiŋ] *nm* dinner *ou* evening suit

S.N.C.F. *sigle f* (= *société nationale des chemins de fer français*) French railways

snob [snɔb] *adj* snobbish ♦ *nm/f* snob

sobre [sɔbʀ(ə)] *adj* temperate, abstemious; (*élégance, style*) sober; ~ **de** (*gestes, compliments*) sparing of

sobriquet [sɔbʀikɛ] *nm* nickname

social, e, aux [sɔsjal, -o] *adj* social

socialisme [sɔsjalism(ə)] *nm* socialism; **socialiste** *nm/f* socialist

société [sɔsjete] *nf* society; (*sportive*) club; (*COMM*) company; **la ~ d'abondance/de consommation** the affluent/consumer society; ~ **à responsabilité limitée** type of limited liability company; ~ **anonyme** ≈ limited (*BRIT*) *ou* incorporated (*US*) company

sociologie [sɔsjɔlɔʒi] *nf* sociology

socle [sɔkl(ə)] *nm* (*de colonne, statue*) plinth, pedestal; (*de lampe*) base

socquette [sɔkɛt] *nf* ankle sock

sœur [sœʀ] *nf* sister; (*religieuse*) nun, sister

soi [swa] *pron* oneself; **cela va de ~** that *ou* it goes without saying; **soi-disant** *adj inv* so-called ♦ *adv* supposedly

soie [swa] *nf* silk; (*de porc, sanglier: poil*) bristle; **soierie** *nf* (*tissu*) silk

soif [swaf] *nf* thirst; **avoir ~** to be thirsty; **donner ~ à qn** to make sb thirsty

soigné, e [swaɲe] *adj* (*tenue*) well-groomed, neat; (*travail*) careful, meticulous; (*fam*) whopping; stiff

soigner [swaɲe] *vt* (*malade, maladie: suj:*

docteur) to treat; (*suj: infirmière, mère*) to nurse, look after; (*blessé*) to tend; (*travail, détails*) to take care over; (*jardin, chevelure, invités*) to look after

soigneux, euse [swaɲø, -øz] *adj* (*propre*) tidy, neat; (*méticuleux*) painstaking, careful; ~ **de** careful with

soi-même [swamɛm] *pron* oneself

soin [swɛ̃] *nm* (*application*) care; (*propreté, ordre*) tidiness, neatness; **~s** *nmpl* (*à un malade, blessé*) treatment *sg*, medical attention *sg*; (*attentions, prévenance*) care and attention *sg*; (*hygiène*) care *sg*; **prendre ~ de** to take care of, look after; **prendre ~ de faire** to take care to do; **les premiers ~s** first aid *sg*; **aux bons ~s de** c/o, care of

soir [swaʀ] *nm* evening; **ce ~** this evening, tonight; **demain ~** tomorrow evening, tomorrow night

soirée [swaʀe] *nf* evening; (*réception*) party

soit [swa] *vb voir* **être** ♦ *conj* (*à savoir*) namely; (*ou*): ~ ... ~ either ... or ♦ *adv* so be it, very well; ~ **que** ... ~ **que** *ou* **ou que** whether ... or whether

soixantaine [swasɑ̃tɛn] *nf*: **une ~ (de)** sixty or so, about sixty; **avoir la ~** (*âge*) to be around sixty

soixante [swasɑ̃t] *num* sixty; **soixante-dix** *num* seventy

soja [sɔʒa] *nm* soya; (*graines*) soya beans *pl*

sol [sɔl] *nm* ground; (*de logement*) floor; (*revêtement*) flooring *no pl*; (*territoire, AGR, GÉO*) soil; (*MUS*) G; (: *en chantant la gamme*) so(h)

solaire [sɔlɛʀ] *adj* solar, sun *cpd*

soldat [sɔlda] *nm* soldier

solde [sɔld(ə)] *nf* pay ♦ *nm* (*COMM*) balance; **~s** *nm ou f pl* sale goods; sales; **en ~** at sale price

solder [sɔlde] *vt* (*compte*) to settle; (*marchandise*) to sell at sale price, sell off; **se ~ par** (*fig*) to end in; **article soldé (à) 10 F** item reduced to 10 F

sole [sɔl] *nf* sole *inv* (*fish*)

soleil [sɔlɛj] *nm* sun; (*lumière*) sun(light); (*temps ensoleillé*) sun(shine); (*BOT*) sunflower; **il fait du ~** it's sunny; **au ~** in the sun

solennel, le [sɔlanɛl] *adj* solemn; ceremonial; **solennité** *nf* (*d'une fête*) solemnity

solfège [sɔlfɛʒ] *nm* rudiments *pl* of music; (*exercices*) ear training *no pl*

solidaire [sɔlidɛʀ] *adj* (*personnes*) who stand together, who show solidarity; (*pièces mécaniques*) interdependent; **être ~ de** (*collègues*) to stand by; **solidarité** *nf* solidarity; interdependence; **par solidarité (avec)** in sympathy (with)

solide [sɔlid] *adj* solid; (*mur, maison, meuble*) solid, sturdy; (*connaissances, argument*) sound; (*personne, estomac*) robust, sturdy ♦

nm solid

soliste [sɔlist(ə)] *nm/f* soloist

solitaire [sɔlitɛʀ] *adj* (*sans compagnie*) solitary, lonely; (*lieu*) lonely ♦ *nm/f* recluse; loner

solitude [sɔlityd] *nf* loneliness; (*paix*) solitude

solive [sɔliv] *nf* joist

sollicitations [sɔlisitasjɔ̃] *nfpl* entreaties, appeals; enticements; (*TECH*) stress *sg*

solliciter [sɔlisite] *vt* (*personne*) to appeal to; (*emploi, faveur*) to seek; (*suj: occupations, attractions etc*): ~ **qn** to appeal to sb's curiosity *etc*; to entice sb; to make demands on sb's time

sollicitude [sɔlisityd] *nf* concern

soluble [sɔlybl(ə)] *adj* soluble

solution [sɔlysjɔ̃] *nf* solution; ~ **de facilité** easy way out

solvable [sɔlvabl(ə)] *adj* solvent

sombre [sɔ̃bʀ(ə)] *adj* dark; (*fig*) gloomy

sombrer [sɔ̃bʀe] *vi* (*bateau*) to sink; ~ **dans** (*misère, désespoir*) to sink into

sommaire [sɔmɛʀ] *adj* (*simple*) basic; (*expéditif*) summary ♦ *nm* summary

sommation [sɔmasjɔ̃] *nf* (*JUR*) summons *sg*; (*avant de faire feu*) warning

somme [sɔm] *nf* (*MATH*) sum; (*fig*) amount; (*argent*) sum, amount ♦ *nm*: **faire un** ~ to have a (short) nap; **en** ~ all in all; ~ **toute** all in all

sommeil [sɔmɛj] *nm* sleep; **avoir** ~ to be sleepy; **sommeiller** *vi* to doze; (*fig*) to lie dormant

sommelier [sɔməlje] *nm* wine waiter

sommer [sɔme] *vt*: ~ **qn de faire** to command *ou* order sb to do; (*JUR*) to summon sb to do

sommes *vb voir* **être**

sommet [sɔmɛ] *nm* top; (*d'une montagne*) summit, top; (*fig: de la perfection, gloire*) height

sommier [sɔmje] *nm* (*bed*) base

sommité [sɔmite] *nf* prominent person, leading light

somnambule [sɔmnɑ̃byl] *nm/f* sleepwalker

somnifère [sɔmnifɛʀ] *nm* sleeping drug *no pl* (*ou* pill)

somnoler [sɔmnɔle] *vi* to doze

somptueux, euse [sɔ̃ptɥø, -øz] *adj* sumptuous; lavish

son[1], **sa** [sɔ̃, sa] (*pl* **ses**) *dét* (*antécédent humain: mâle*) his; (: *femelle*) her; (: *valeur indéfinie*) one's, his/her; (*antécédent non humain*) its

son[2] *nm* sound; (*de blé*) bran

sondage [sɔ̃daʒ] *nm*: ~ (**d'opinion**) (opinion) poll

sonde [sɔ̃d] *nf* (*NAVIG*) lead *ou* sounding line; (*MÉD*) probe; catheter; feeding tube; (*TECH*) borer, driller; (*pour fouiller etc*) probe

sonder [sɔ̃de] *vt* (*NAVIG*) to sound; (*atmosphère, plaie, bagages etc*) to probe; (*TECH*) to bore, drill; (*fig*) to sound out; to probe

songe [sɔ̃ʒ] *nm* dream

songer [sɔ̃ʒe] *vi*: ~ **à** (*penser à*) to think of; ~ **que** to consider that; to think that; **songeur, euse** *adj* pensive

sonnant, e [sɔnɑ̃, -ɑ̃t] *adj*: **à 8 heures** ~**es** on the stroke of 8

sonné, e [sɔne] *adj* (*fam*) cracked; **il est midi** ~ it's gone twelve

sonner [sɔne] *vi* to ring ♦ *vt* (*cloche*) to ring; (*glas, tocsin*) to sound; (*portier, infirmière*) to ring for; (*messe*) to ring the bell for; ~ **faux** (*instrument*) to sound out of tune; (*rire*) to ring false; ~ **les heures** to strike the hours

sonnerie [sɔnʀi] *nf* (*son*) ringing; (*sonnette*) bell; (*mécanisme d'horloge*) striking mechanism; ~ **d'alarme** alarm bell

sonnette [sɔnɛt] *nf* bell; ~ **d'alarme** alarm bell

sono [sono] *abr f* = **sonorisation**

sonore [sɔnɔʀ] *adj* (*voix*) sonorous, ringing; (*salle, métal*) resonant; (*ondes, film, signal*) sound *cpd*

sonorisation [sɔnɔʀizasjɔ̃] *nf* (*installations*) public address system, P.A. system

sonorité [sɔnɔʀite] *nf* (*de piano, violon*) tone; (*de voix, mot*) sonority; (*d'une salle*) resonance; acoustics *pl*

sont *vb voir* **être**

sophistiqué, e [sɔfistike] *adj* sophisticated

sorbet [sɔʀbɛ] *nm* water ice, sorbet

sorcellerie [sɔʀsɛlʀi] *nf* witchcraft *no pl*

sorcier [sɔʀsje] *nm* sorcerer; **sorcière** *nf* witch *ou* sorceress

sordide [sɔʀdid] *adj* sordid; squalid

sornettes [sɔʀnɛt] *nfpl* twaddle *sg*

sort [sɔʀ] *nm* (*fortune, destinée*) fate; (*condition, situation*) lot; (*magique*) curse, spell; **tirer au** ~ to draw lots

sorte [sɔʀt(ə)] *nf* sort, kind; **de la** ~ in that way; **de (telle)** ~ **que, en** ~ **que** so that; so much so that; **faire en** ~ **que** to see to it that

sortie [sɔʀti] *nf* (*issue*) way out, exit; (*MIL*) sortie; (*fig: verbale*) outburst; sally; (*promenade*) outing; (*le soir: au restaurant etc*) night out; (*COMM: somme*): ~**s items of** expenditure; outgoings sans *sg*; ~ **de bain** (*vêtement*) bathrobe; ~ **de secours** emergency exit

sortilège [sɔʀtilɛʒ] *nm* (*magic*) spell

sortir [sɔʀtiʀ] *vi* (*gén*) to come out; (*partir, se promener, aller au spectacle*) to go out; (*numéro gagnant*) to come up ♦ *vt* (*gén*) to take out; (*produit, ouvrage, modèle*) to bring out; (*INFORM*) to output; (: *sur papier*) to print out; (*fam: expulser*) to throw out; **se** ~ **de** (*affaire, situation*) to get out of; **s'en** ~ (*malade*) to pull through; (*d'une* *difficulté etc*) to get through; ~ **de** (*gén*) to leave; (*endroit*) to go (*ou* come) out of, leave; (*rainure etc*) to come out of; (*cadre, compétence*) to be outside

sosie [sɔzi] *nm* double

sot, sotte [so, sɔt] *adj* silly, foolish ♦ *nm/f* fool; **sottise** *nf* silliness, foolishness; silly *ou* foolish thing

sou [su] *nm*: **près de ses** ~**s** tight-fisted; **sans le** ~ penniless

soubresaut [subʀəso] *nm* start; jolt

souche [suʃ] *nf* (*d'arbre*) stump; (*de carnet*) counterfoil (*BRIT*), stub; **de vieille** ~ of old stock

souci [susi] *nm* (*inquiétude*) worry; (*préoccupation*) concern; (*BOT*) marigold; **se faire du** ~ to worry

soucier [susje] : **se** ~ **de** *vt* to care about

soucieux, euse [susjø, -øz] *adj* concerned, worried

soucoupe [sukup] *nf* saucer; ~ **volante** flying saucer

soudain, e [sudɛ̃, -ɛn] *adj* (*douleur, mort*) sudden ♦ *adv* suddenly, all of a sudden

soude [sud] *nf* soda

souder [sude] *vt* (*avec fil à souder*) to solder; (*par soudure autogène*) to weld; (*fig*) to bind together

soudoyer [sudwaje] (*péj*) *vt* to bribe

soudure [sudyʀ] *nf* soldering; welding; (*joint*) soldered joint; weld

souffert, e [sufɛʀ, -ɛʀt(ə)] *pp de* **souffrir**

souffle [sufl(ə)] *nm* (*en expirant*) breath; (*en soufflant*) puff, blow; (*respiration*) breathing; (*d'explosion, de ventilateur*) blast; (*du vent*) blowing; **être à bout de** ~ to be out of breath; **un** ~ **d'air** *ou* **de vent** a breath of air, a puff of wind

soufflé, e [sufle] *adj* (*fam: stupéfié*) staggered ♦ *nm* (*CULIN*) soufflé

souffler [sufle] *vi* (*gén*) to blow; (*haleter*) to puff (and blow) ♦ *vt* (*feu, bougie*) to blow out; (*chasser: poussière etc*) to blow away; (*TECH: verre*) to blow; (*suj: explosion*) to destroy (with its blast); (*dire*): ~ **qch à qn** to whisper sth to sb; (*fam: voler*): ~ **qch à qn** to pinch sth from sb

soufflet [sufle] *nm* (*instrument*) bellows *pl*; (*gifle*) slap (in the face)

souffleur [suflœʀ] *nm* (*THÉÂTRE*) prompter

souffrance [sufʀɑ̃s] *nf* suffering; **en** ~ (*marchandise*) awaiting delivery; (*affaire*) pending

souffrant, e [sufʀɑ̃, -ɑ̃t] *adj* unwell

souffre-douleur [sufʀədulœʀ] *nm inv* butt, underdog

souffrir [sufʀiʀ] *vi* to suffer; to be in pain ♦ *vt* to suffer, endure; (*supporter*) to bear, stand; (*admettre: exception etc*) to allow *ou* admit of; ~ **de** (*maladie, froid*) to suffer from

soufre [sufʀ(ə)] *nm* sulphur

souhait [swɛ] *nm* wish; **tous nos** ~**s de** good wishes *ou* our best wishes for; **riche** *etc* **à** ~ as rich *etc* as one could wish; **à vos** ~**s!** bless you!; ~**able** [swɛtabl(ə)] *adj* desirable

souhaiter [swete] *vt* to wish for; ~ **la bonne année à qn** to wish sb a happy New Year

souiller [suje] *vt* to dirty, soil; (*fig*) to sully, tarnish

soûl, e [su, sul] *adj* drunk ♦ *nm*: **tout son** ~ to one's heart's content

soulagement [sulaʒmɑ̃] *nm* relief

soulager [sulaʒe] *vt* to relieve

soûler [sule] *vt*: ~ **qn** to get sb drunk; (*suj: boisson*) to make sb drunk; (*fig*) to make sb's head spin *ou* reel; **se** ~ *vi* to get drunk

soulever [sulve] *vt* to lift; (*vagues, poussière*) to send up; (*peuple*) to stir up (to revolt); (*enthousiasme*) to arouse; (*question, débat*) to raise; **se** ~ *vi* (*peuple*) to rise up; (*personne couchée*) to lift o.s. up; **cela me soulève le cœur** it makes me feel sick

soulier [sulje] *nm* shoe

souligner [suliɲe] *vt* to underline; (*fig*) to emphasize; to stress

soumettre [sumɛtʀ(ə)] *vt* (*pays*) to subject, subjugate; (*rebelle*) to put down, subdue; **se** ~ (**à**) to submit (to); ~ **qn/qch à** to subject sb/sth to; ~ **qch à qn** (*projet etc*) to submit sth to sb

soumis, e [sumi, -iz] *adj* submissive; **revenus** ~ **à l'impôt** taxable income; **soumission** [sumisjɔ̃] *nf* submission; (*docilité*) submissiveness; (*COMM*) tender

soupape [supap] *nf* valve

soupçon [supsɔ̃] *nm* suspicion; (*petite quantité*): **un** ~ **de** a hint *ou* touch of; **soupçonner** *vt* to suspect; **soupçonneux, euse** *adj* suspicious

soupe [sup] *nf* soup; ~ **au lait** *adj inv* quick-tempered

souper [supe] *vi* to have supper ♦ *nm* supper

soupeser [supəze] *vt* to weigh in one's hand(s); (*fig*) to weigh up

soupière [supjɛʀ] *nf* (*soup*) tureen

soupir [supiʀ] *nm* sigh; (*MUS*) crotchet rest

soupirail, aux [supiʀaj, -o] *nm* (small) basement window

soupirer [supiʀe] *vi* to sigh; ~ **après qch** to yearn for sth

souple [supl(ə)] *adj* supple; (*fig: règlement, caractère*) flexible; (: *démarche, taille*) lithe, supple

source [suʀs(ə)] *nf* (*point d'eau*) spring; (*d'un cours d'eau, fig*) source; **de bonne** ~ on good authority

sourcil [suʀsij] *nm* (eye)brow

sourciller [suʀsije] *vi*: **sans** ~ without turning a hair *ou* batting an eyelid

sourcilleux, euse [suʀsijø, -øz] *adj* pernickety

sourd, e [suʀ, suʀd(ə)] adj deaf; (bruit, voix) muffled; (douleur) dull; (lutte) silent, hidden ♦ nm/f deaf person

sourdine [suʀdin] nf (MUS) mute; **en ~** softly, quietly

sourd-muet, sourde-muette [suʀmɥɛ, suʀdmɥɛt] adj deaf-and-dumb ♦ nm/f deaf-mute

souriant, e [suʀjɑ̃, -ɑ̃t] adj cheerful

souricière [suʀisjɛʀ] nf mousetrap; (fig) trap

sourire [suʀiʀ] nm smile ♦ vi to smile; **~ à qn** to smile at sb; (fig) to appeal to sb; to smile on sb; **garder le ~** to keep smiling

souris [suʀi] nf mouse

sournois, e [suʀnwa, -waz] adj deceitful, underhand

sous [su] prép (gén) under; **~ la pluie/le soleil** in the rain/sunshine; **~ terre** underground; **~ peu** shortly, before long

sous-bois [subwa] nm inv undergrowth

souscrire [suskʀiʀ]: **~ à** vt to subscribe to

sous: **~-directeur, trice** nm/f assistant manager(manageress); **~-entendre** vt to imply, infer; **~-entendu, e** adj implied; (LING) understood ♦ nm innuendo, insinuation; **~-estimer** vt to under-estimate; **~-jacent, e** adj underlying; **~-louer** vt to sublet; **~-main** nm inv desk blotter; **en ~-main** secretly; **~-marin, e** adj (flore, volcan) submarine; (navigation, pêche, explosif) underwater ♦ nm submarine; **~-officier** nm ≈ non-commissioned officer (N.C.O.); **~-produit** nm by-product; (fig: péj) pale imitation; **~-signé, e** adj: **je ~signé** I the undersigned; **~-sol** nm basement; **~-titre** nm subtitle

soustraction [sustʀaksjɔ̃] nf subtraction

soustraire [sustʀɛʀ] vt to subtract, take away; (dérober): **~ qch à qn** to remove sth from sb; **se ~ à** (autorité etc) to elude, escape from; **~ qn à** (danger) to shield sb from

sous-traitant [sutʀɛtɑ̃] nm sub-contractor

sous-vêtements [suvɛtmɑ̃] nmpl underwear sg

soutane [sutan] nf cassock, soutane

soute [sut] nf hold

soutènement [sutɛnmɑ̃] nm: **mur de ~** retaining wall

souteneur [sutnœʀ] nm procurer

soutenir [sutniʀ] vt to support; (assaut, choc) to stand up to, withstand; (intérêt, effort) to keep up; (assurer): **~ que** to maintain that; **~ la comparaison avec** to bear ou stand comparison with; **soutenu, e** adj (efforts) sustained, unflagging; (style) elevated

souterrain, e [sutɛʀɛ̃, -ɛn] adj underground ♦ nm underground passage

soutien [sutjɛ̃] nm support; **~ de famille**

breadwinner; **~-gorge** [sutjɛ̃gɔʀʒ(ə)] nm bra

soutirer [sutiʀe] vt: **~ qch à qn** to squeeze ou get sth out of sb

souvenir [suvniʀ] nm (réminiscence) memory; (objet) souvenir ♦ vb: **se ~ de** vt to remember; **se ~ que** to remember that; **en ~ de** in memory ou remembrance of

souvent [suvɑ̃] adv often; **peu ~** seldom, infrequently

souverain, e [suvʀɛ̃, -ɛn] adj sovereign; (fig: mépris) supreme ♦ nm/f sovereign, monarch

soviétique [sɔvjetik] nm/f: **Soviétique** Soviet citizen

soyeux, euse [swajø, øz] adj silky

soyons etc vb voir **être**

spacieux, euse [spasjø, -øz] adj spacious; roomy

spaghettis [spageti] nmpl spaghetti sg

sparadrap [spaʀadʀa] nm sticking plaster (BRIT), Bandaid (®; US)

spatial, e, aux [spasjal, -o] adj (AVIAT) space cpd

speaker, ine [spikœʀ, -kʀin] nm/f announcer

spécial, e, aux [spesjal, -o] adj special; (bizarre) peculiar; **spécialement** adv especially, particularly; (tout exprès) specially

spécialiser [spesjalize]: **se ~** vi to specialize

spécialiste [spesjalist(ə)] nm/f specialist

spécialité [spesjalite] nf speciality; (SCOL) special field

spécifier [spesifje] vt to specify, state

spécimen [spesimɛn] nm specimen; (revue etc) specimen ou sample copy

spectacle [spɛktakl(ə)] nm (tableau, scène) sight; (représentation) show; (industrie) show business; **spectaculaire** adj spectacular

spectateur, trice [spɛktatœʀ, -tʀis] nm/f (CINÉMA etc) member of the audience; (SPORT) spectator; (d'un événement) onlooker, witness

spéculer [spekyle] vi to speculate; **~ sur** (COMM) to speculate in; (réfléchir) to speculate on

spéléologie [speleɔlɔʒi] nf potholing

sperme [spɛʀm(ə)] nm semen, sperm

sphère [sfɛʀ] nf sphere

spirale [spiʀal] nf spiral

spirituel, le [spiʀitɥɛl] adj spiritual; (fin, piquant) witty

spiritueux [spiʀitɥø] nm spirit

splendide [splɑ̃did] adj splendid; magnificent

spontané, e [spɔ̃tane] adj spontaneous

sport [spɔʀ] nm sport ♦ adj inv (vêtement) casual; **faire du ~** to do sport; **sportif, ive** adj (journal, association, épreuve) sports cpd; (allure, démarche) athletic; (attitude, esprit) sporting; ~s d'hiver winter sports

spot [spɔt] nm (lampe) spot(light); (annonce): ~ (publicitaire) commercial (break)

square [skwaʀ] nm public garden(s)

squelette [skəlɛt] nm skeleton; **squelettique** adj scrawny; (fig) skimpy

stabiliser [stabilize] vt to stabilize; (terrain) to consolidate

stable [stabl(ə)] adj stable, steady

stade [stad] nm (SPORT) stadium; (phase, niveau) stage

stage [staʒ] nm training period; training course; **stagiaire** nm/f, adj trainee

stalle [stal] nf stall, box

stand [stɑ̃d] nm (d'exposition) stand; (de foire) stall; ~ de tir (à la foire, SPORT) shooting range

standard [stɑ̃daʀ] adj inv standard ♦ nm switchboard; **standardiste** nm/f switchboard operator

standing [stɑ̃diŋ] nm standing; **immeuble de grand** ~ block of luxury flats (BRIT), condo(minium) (US)

starter [staʀtɛʀ] nm (AUTO) choke

station [stasjɔ̃] nf station; (de bus) stop; (de villégiature) resort; (posture): **la ~ debout** standing, an upright posture; ~ **de ski** ski resort; ~ **de taxis** taxi rank (BRIT) ou stand (US)

stationnement [stasjɔnmɑ̃] nm parking; **stationner** [stasjɔne] vi to park

station-service [stasjɔ̃sɛʀvis] nf service station

statistique [statistik] nf (science) statistics sg; (rapport, étude) statistic ♦ adj statistical

statue [staty] nf statue

statuer [statɥe] vi: ~ **sur** to rule on, give a ruling on

statut [staty] nm status; ~s nmpl (JUR, ADMIN) statutes; **statutaire** adj statutory

Sté abr = société

steak [stɛk] nm steak

sténo(dactylo) [steno(daktilo)] nf shorthand typist (BRIT), stenographer (US)

sténo(graphie) [steno(grafi)] nf shorthand

stéréo(phonique) [stereo(fɔnik)] adj stereo(phonic)

stérile [steʀil] adj sterile; (terre) barren; (fig) fruitless, futile

stérilet [steʀilɛ] nm coil, loop

stériliser [steʀilize] vt to sterilize

stigmates [stigmat] nmpl scars, marks

stimulant [stimylɑ̃] nm (fig) stimulus, incentive

stimuler [stimyle] vt to stimulate

stipuler [stipyle] vt to stipulate

stock [stɔk] nm stock; ~ **d'or** (FINANCE) gold reserves pl; **stocker** vt to stock

stop [stɔp] nm (AUTO: écriteau) stop sign; (: signal) brake-light; ~**per** [stɔpe] vt to stop, halt; (COUTURE) to mend ♦ vi to stop, halt

store [stɔʀ] nm blind; (de magasin) shade, awning

strabisme [stʀabism(ə)] nm squinting

strapontin [stʀapɔ̃tɛ̃] nm jump ou foldaway seat

stratégie [stʀateʒi] nf strategy; **stratégique** adj strategic

stressant, e [stʀesɑ̃, -ɑ̃t] adj stressful

strict, e [stʀikt(ə)] adj strict; (tenue, décor) severe, plain; **son droit le plus** ~ his most basic right; **le** ~ **nécessaire/minimum** the bare essentials/minimum

strie [stʀi] nf streak

strophe [stʀɔf] nf verse, stanza

structure [stʀyktyʀ] nf structure; ~s d'accueil reception facilities

studieux, euse [stydjø, -øz] adj studious; devoted to study

studio [stydjo] nm (logement) (one-roomed) flatlet (BRIT) ou apartment (US); (d'artiste, TV etc) studio

stupéfait, e [stypefɛ, -ɛt] adj astonished

stupéfiant [stypefjɑ̃] nm (MÉD) drug, narcotic

stupéfier [stypefje] vt to stupefy; (étonner) to stun, astonish

stupeur [stypœʀ] nf astonishment

stupide [stypid] adj stupid; **stupidité** nf stupidity; stupid thing (to do ou say)

style [stil] nm style; **meuble de** ~ piece of period furniture

stylé, e [stile] adj well-trained

styliste [stilist(ə)] nm/f designer

stylo [stilo] nm: ~ **(à encre)** (fountain) pen; ~ **(à) bille** ball-point pen

su, e [sy] pp de savoir ♦ nm: **au** ~ **de** with the knowledge of

suave [sɥav] adj sweet; (goût) mellow

subalterne [sybaltɛʀn(ə)] adj (employé, officier) junior; (rôle) subordinate, subsidiary ♦ nm/f subordinate

subconscient [sypkɔ̃sjɑ̃] nm subconscious

subir [sybiʀ] vt (affront, dégâts) to suffer; (influence, charme) to be under; (opération, châtiment) to undergo

subit, e [sybi, -it] adj sudden; **subitement** adv suddenly, all of a sudden

subjectif, ive [sybʒɛktif, -iv] adj subjective

subjonctif [sybʒɔ̃ktif] nm subjunctive

submerger [sybmɛʀʒe] vt to submerge; (fig) to overwhelm

subordonné, e [sybɔʀdɔne] adj, nm/f subordinate; ~ **à** subordinate to; subject to, depending on

subornation [sybɔʀnasjɔ̃] nf bribing

subrepticement [sybʀɛptismɑ̃] adv surreptitiously

subside [sypsid] nm grant

subsidiaire [sypsidjɛʀ] adj: **question** ~ deciding question

subsister [sybziste] vi (rester) to remain, subsist; (vivre) to live; (survivre) to live on

substance [sypstɑ̃s] nf substance

substituer [sypstitɥe] vt: ~ qn/qch à to substitute sb/sth for; **se** ~ à qn (évincer) to substitute o.s. for sb

substitut [sypstity] nm (JUR) deputy public prosecutor; (succédané) substitute

subterfuge [syptɛʀfyʒ] nm subterfuge

subtil, e [syptil] adj subtle

subtiliser [syptilize] vt: ~ qch (à qn) to spirit sth away (from sb)

subvenir [sybvəniʀ]: ~ à vt to meet

subvention [sybvɑ̃sjɔ̃] nf subsidy, grant; **subventionner** vt to subsidize

suc [syk] nm (BOT) sap; (de viande, fruit) juice

succédané [syksedane] nm substitute

succéder [syksede]: ~ à vt (directeur, roi etc) to succeed; (venir après: dans une série) to follow, succeed; **se** ~ vi (accidents, années) to follow one another

succès [syksɛ] nm success; **avoir du** ~ to be a success, be successful; **à** ~ successful; ~ **de librairie** bestseller; ~ **(féminins)** conquests

succession [syksesjɔ̃] nf (série, POL) succession; (JUR: patrimoine) estate, inheritance

succomber [sykɔ̃be] vi to die, succumb; (fig): ~ **à** to give way to, succumb to

succursale [sykyʀsal] nf branch

sucer [syse] vt to suck

sucette [sysɛt] nf (bonbon) lollipop; (de bébé) dummy (BRIT), pacifier (US)

sucre [sykʀ(ə)] nm (substance) sugar; (morceau) lump of sugar, sugar lump ou cube; ~ **d'orge** barley sugar; ~ **en morceaux/ cristallisé/en poudre** lump/granulated/ caster sugar; **sucré, e** adj (produit alimentaire) sweetened; (au goût) sweet; (péj) sugary, honeyed; **sucrer** vt (thé, café) to sweeten, put sugar in; **sucreries** nfpl (bonbons) sweets, sweet things; **sucrier** nm (récipient) sugar bowl

sud [syd] nm: **le** ~ the south ♦ adj inv south; (côte) south, southern; **au** ~ (situation) in the south; (direction) to the south; **au** ~ **de** (to the) south of; **sud-africain, e** adj, nm/f South African; **sud-américain, e** adj, nm/f South American; **sud-est** [sydɛst] nm south-east ♦ adj inv south-east; **sud-ouest** [sydwɛst] nm south-west ♦ adj inv south-west

Suède [sɥɛd] nf: **la** ~ Sweden; **suédois, e** adj Swedish ♦ nm/f: **Suédois, e** Swede ♦ nm (LING) Swedish

suer [sɥe] vi to sweat; (suinter) to ooze

sueur [sɥœʀ] nf sweat; **en** ~ sweating, in a sweat

suffire [syfiʀ] vi (être assez): ~ (à qn/pour qch/pour faire) to be enough ou sufficient (for sb/for sth/to do); **cela suffit pour les irriter/qu'ils se fâchent** it's enough to annoy them/for them to get angry; **il suffit**

d'une négligence ... it only takes one act of carelessness ...; **il suffit qu'on oublie pour que** ... one only needs to forget for ...

suffisamment [syfizamɑ̃] adv sufficiently, enough; ~ **de** sufficient, enough

suffisant, e [syfizɑ̃, -ɑ̃t] adj (temps, ressources) sufficient; (résultats) satisfactory; (vaniteux) self-important, bumptious

suffixe [syfiks(ə)] nm suffix

suffoquer [syfɔke] vt to choke, suffocate; (stupéfier) to stagger, astound ♦ vi to choke, suffocate

suffrage [syfʀaʒ] nm (POL: voix) vote; (du public etc) approval no pl

suggérer [sygʒeʀe] vt to suggest; **suggestion** nf suggestion

suicide [sɥisid] nm suicide

suicider [sɥiside]: **se** ~ vi to commit suicide

suie [sɥi] nf soot

suinter [sɥɛ̃te] vi to ooze

suis vb voir **être**; **suivre**

suisse [sɥis] adj Swiss ♦ nm: **S**~ Swiss pl inv ♦ nf: **la S**~ Switzerland; **la S**~ **romande/allemande** French-speaking/ German-speaking Switzerland; **Suissesse** nf Swiss (woman ou girl)

suite [sɥit] nf (continuation: d'énumération etc) rest, remainder; (: de feuilleton) continuation; (: film etc sur le même thème) sequel; (série: de maisons, succès): **une** ~ **de** a series ou succession of; (MATH) series sg; (conséquence) result; (ordre, liaison logique) coherence; (appartement, MUS) suite; (escorte) retinue, suite; ~**s** nfpl (d'une maladie etc) effects; **prendre la** ~ **de** (directeur etc) to succeed, take over from; **donner** ~ **à** (requête, projet) to follow up; **faire** ~ **à** to follow; **(faisant)** ~ **à votre lettre du** ... further to your letter of the ...; **de** ~ (d'affilée) in succession; (immédiatement) at once; **par la** ~ afterwards, subsequently; **à la** ~ one after the other; **à la** ~ **de** (derrière) behind; (en conséquence de) following; **par** ~ **de** owing to, as a result of

suivant, e [sɥivɑ̃, -ɑ̃t] adj next, following; (ci-après): **l'exercice** ~ the following exercise ♦ prép (selon) according to; **au** ~! next!

suivi, e [sɥivi] adj (régulier) regular; (cohérent) consistent; coherent; **très/peu** ~ (cours) well-/poorly-attended

suivre [sɥivʀ(ə)] vt (gén) to follow; (SCOL: cours) to attend; (: programme) to keep up with; (COMM: article) to continue to stock ♦ vi to follow; (élève) to attend; to keep up; **se** ~ vi (accidents etc) to follow one after the other; (raisonnement) to be coherent; **faire** ~ (lettre) to forward; ~ **son cours** (suj: enquête etc) to run ou take its course; **"à** ~**"** "to be continued"

sujet, te [syʒɛ, -ɛt] adj: **être** ~ **à** (vertige

etc) to be liable *ou* subject to ♦ *nm/f* (*d'un souverain*) subject ♦ *nm* subject; **au ~ de** about; **~ à caution** questionable; **~ de conversation** topic *ou* subject of conversation; **~ d'examen** (*SCOL*) examination question; examination paper

summum [sɔmɔm] *nm*: **le ~ de** the height of

superbe [sypɛʀb(ə)] *adj* magnificent, superb

super(carburant) [sypɛʀ(kaʀbyʀɑ̃)] *nm* ≈ 4-star petrol (*BRIT*), ≈ high-octane gasoline (*US*)

supercherie [sypɛʀʃəʀi] *nf* trick

supérette [sypeʀɛt] *nf* (*COMM*) minimarket, superette (*US*)

superficie [sypɛʀfisi] *nf* (surface) area; (*fig*) surface

superficiel, le [sypɛʀfisjɛl] *adj* superficial

superflu, e [sypɛʀfly] *adj* superfluous

supérieur, e [sypeʀjœʀ] *adj* (*lèvre, étages, classes*) upper; (*plus élevé: température, niveau*): **~ (à)** higher (than); (*meilleur: qualité, produit*): **~ (à)** superior (to); (*excellent, hautain*) superior ♦ *nm, nf* superior; **à l'étage ~** on the next floor up; **supériorité** *nf* superiority

superlatif [sypɛʀlatif] *nm* superlative

supermarché [sypɛʀmaʀʃe] *nm* supermarket

superposer [sypɛʀpoze] *vt* (*faire chevaucher*) to superimpose; **lits superposés** bunk beds

superproduction [sypɛʀpʀɔdyksjɔ̃] *nf* (*film*) spectacular

superpuissance [sypɛʀpɥisɑ̃s] *nf* superpower

superstitieux, euse [sypɛʀstisjø, -øz] *adj* superstitious

superviser [sypɛʀvize] *vt* to supervise

suppléant, e [sypleɑ̃, -ɑ̃t] *adj* (*juge, fonctionnaire*) deputy *cpd*; (*professeur*) supply *cpd* ♦ *nm/f* deputy; supply teacher

suppléer [syplee] *vt* (*ajouter: mot manquant etc*) to supply, provide; (*compenser: lacune*) to fill in; (: *défaut*) to make up for; (*remplacer*) to stand in for; **~ à** to make up for; to substitute for

supplément [syplemɑ̃] *nm* supplement; (*de frites etc*) extra portion; **un ~ de travail** extra *ou* additional work; **ceci est en ~** (*au menu etc*) this is extra, there is an extra charge for this; **~aire** *adj* additional, further; (*train, bus*) relief *cpd*, extra

supplications [syplikɑsjɔ̃] *nfpl* pleas, entreaties

supplice [syplis] *nm* (*peine corporelle*) torture *no pl*; form of torture; (*douleur physique, morale*) torture, agony

supplier [syplije] *vt* to implore, beseech

supplique [syplik] *nf* petition

support [sypɔʀ] *nm* support; (*pour livre,* *outils*) stand

supportable [sypɔʀtabl(ə)] *adj* (*douleur*) bearable

supporter¹ [sypɔʀtɛʀ] *nm* supporter, fan

supporter² [sypɔʀte] *vt* (*poids, poussée*) to support; (*conséquences, épreuve*) to bear, endure; (*défauts, personne*) to put up with; (*suj: chose: chaleur etc*) to withstand; (: *personne: chaleur, vin*) to be able to take

supposé, e [sypoze] *adj* (*nombre*) estimated; (*auteur*) supposed

supposer [sypoze] *vt* to suppose; (*impliquer*) to presuppose; **à ~ que** supposing (that)

suppositoire [sypozitwaʀ] *nm* suppository

suppression [sypʀesjɔ̃] *nf* (*voir supprimer*) removal; deletion; cancellation; suppression

supprimer [sypʀime] *vt* (*cloison, cause, anxiété*) to remove; (*clause, mot*) to delete; (*congés, service d'autobus etc*) to cancel; (*emplois, privilèges, témoin gênant*) to do away with

supputer [sypyte] *vt* to calculate

suprême [sypʀɛm] *adj* supreme

MOT CLÉ

sur *prép* **1** (*position*) on; (*par-dessus*) over; (*au-dessus*) above; **pose-le ~ la table** put it on the table; **je n'ai pas d'argent ~ moi** I haven't any money on me

2 (*direction*) towards; **en allant ~ Paris** going towards Paris; **~ votre droite** on *ou* to your right

3 (*à propos de*) on, about; **un livre/une conférence ~ Balzac** a book/lecture on *ou* about Balzac

4 (*proportion, mesures*) out of; by; **un ~ 10** one in 10; (*SCOL*) one out of 10; **4 m ~ 2** 4 m by 2

sur ce *adv* hereupon

---

sûr, e [syʀ] *adj* sure, certain; (*digne de confiance*) reliable; (*sans danger*) safe; **le plus ~ est de** the safest thing is to; **~ de soi** self-confident; **~ et certain** absolutely certain

suranné, e [syʀane] *adj* outdated, outmoded

surcharge [syʀʃaʀʒ(ə)] *nf* (*de passagers, marchandises*) excess load; (*correction*) alteration

surcharger [syʀʃaʀʒe] *vt* to overload

surchoix [syʀʃwa] *adj inv* top-quality

surclasser [syʀklɑse] *vt* to outclass

surcroît [syʀkʀwa] *nm*: **un ~ de** additional +*nom*; **par ou de ~** moreover; **en ~** in addition

surdité [syʀdite] *nf* deafness

surélever [syʀɛlve] *vt* to raise, heighten

sûrement [syʀmɑ̃] *adv* reliably; safely, securely; (*certainement*) certainly

surenchère [syʀɑ̃ʃɛʀ] *nf* (*aux enchères*)

higher bid; (sur prix fixe) overbid; (fig) overstatement; outbidding tactics pl; **surenchérir** vi to bid higher; (fig) to try and outbid each other

surent vb voir **savoir**

surestimer [syʀɛstime] vt to overestimate

sûreté [syʀte] nf (voir sûr) reliability; safety; (JUR) guaranty; surety; **mettre en** ~ to put in a safe place; **pour plus de** ~ as an extra precaution; to be on the safe side

surf [syʀf] nm surfing

surface [syʀfas] nf surface; (superficie) surface area; **faire** ~ to surface; **en** ~ near the surface; (fig) superficially

surfait, e [syʀfɛ, -ɛt] adj overrated

surfin, e [syʀfɛ̃, -in] adj superfine

surgelé, e [syʀʒəle] adj (deep-) frozen

surgir [syʀʒiʀ] vi to appear suddenly; (jaillir) to shoot up; (fig: problème, conflit) to arise

sur: ~**humain, e** adj superhuman; ~**impression** nf (PHOTO) double exposure; en ~**impression** superimposed; ~**-le-champ** adv immediately; ~**lendemain** nm: **le** ~**lendemain** (soir) two days later (in the evening); **le** ~**lendemain de** two days after; ~**mener** vt to overwork; **se** ~**mener** vi to overwork

surmonter [syʀmɔ̃te] vt (suj: coupole etc) to top; (vaincre) to overcome

surnager [syʀnaʒe] vi to float

surnaturel, le [syʀnatyʀɛl] adj, nm supernatural

surnom [syʀnɔ̃] nm nickname

surnombre [syʀnɔ̃bʀ(ə)] nm: **être en** ~ to be too many (ou one too many)

surpeuplé, e [syʀpœple] adj overpopulated

sur-place [syʀplas] nm: **faire du** ~ to mark time

surplomber [syʀplɔ̃be] vi to be overhanging ♦ vt to overhang; to tower above

surplus [syʀply] nm (COMM) surplus; (reste): ~ **de bois** wood left over

surprenant, e [syʀpʀənɑ̃, -ɑ̃t] adj amazing

surprendre [syʀpʀɑ̃dʀ(ə)] vt (étonner, prendre à l'improviste) to surprise; (tomber sur: intrus etc) to catch; (fig) to detect; to chance upon; to overhear

surpris, e [syʀpʀi, -iz] adj: ~ **de/que** surprised (at/that)

surprise [syʀpʀiz] nf surprise; **faire une** ~ **à qn** to give sb a surprise; ~**-partie** [syʀpʀizpaʀti] nf party

sursaut [syʀso] nm start, jump; ~ **de** (énergie, indignation) sudden fit ou burst of; **en** ~ with a start; **sursauter** vi to (give a) start, jump

surseoir [syʀswaʀ]: ~ **à** vt to defer

sursis [syʀsi] nm (JUR: gén) suspended sentence; (à l'exécution capitale, aussi fig) reprieve; (MIL) deferment

surtaxe [syʀtaks(ə)] nf surcharge

surtout [syʀtu] adv (avant tout, d'abord) above all; (spécialement, particulièrement) especially; ~, **ne dites rien!** whatever you do don't say anything!; ~ **pas!** certainly not ou definitely not!; ~ **que** ... especially as ...

surveillance [syʀvɛjɑ̃s] nf watch; (POLICE, MIL) surveillance; **sous** ~ **médicale** under medical supervision

surveillant, e [syʀvɛjɑ̃, -ɑ̃t] nm/f (de prison) warder; (SCOL) monitor; (de travaux) supervisor, overseer

surveiller [syʀveje] vt (enfant, élèves, bagages) to watch, keep an eye on; (malade) to watch over; (prisonnier, suspect) to keep (a) watch on; (territoire, bâtiment) to (keep) watch over; (travaux, cuisson) to supervise; (SCOL: examen) to invigilate; **se** ~ vi to keep a check ou watch on o.s.; ~ **son langage/sa ligne** to watch one's language/figure

survenir [syʀvəniʀ] vi (incident, retards) to occur, arise; (événement) to take place; (personne) to appear, arrive

survêt(ement) [syʀvɛt(mɑ̃)] nm tracksuit

survie [syʀvi] nf survival; (REL) afterlife

survivant, e [syʀvivɑ̃, -ɑ̃t] nm/f survivor

survivre [syʀvivʀ(ə)] vi to survive; ~ **à** (accident etc) to survive; (personne) to outlive

survoler [syʀvɔle] vt to fly over; (fig: livre) to skim through

survolté, e [syʀvɔlte] adj (fig) worked up

sus [sy(s)]: **en** ~ **de** prép in addition to, over and above; **en** ~ in addition; ~ **à:** ~ **au tyran!** at the tyrant!

susceptible [sysɛptibl(ə)] adj touchy, sensitive; ~ **d'amélioration** that can be improved, open to improvement; ~ **de faire** able to do; liable to do

susciter [sysite] vt (admiration) to arouse; (obstacles, ennuis): ~ **(à qn)** to create (for sb)

suspect, e [syspɛ(kt), -ɛkt(ə)] adj suspicious; (témoignage, opinions) suspect ♦ nm/f suspect

suspecter [syspɛkte] vt to suspect; (honnêteté de qn) to question, have one's suspicions about

suspendre [syspɑ̃dʀ(ə)] vt (accrocher: vêtement): ~ **qch (à)** to hang sth up (on); (fixer: lustre etc): ~ **qch à** to hang sth from; (interrompre, démettre) to suspend; (remettre) to defer; **se** ~ **à** to hang from

suspendu, e [syspɑ̃dy] adj (accroché): ~ **à** hanging on (ou from); (perché): ~ **au-dessus de** suspended over

suspens [syspɑ̃]: **en** ~ adv (affaire) in abeyance; **tenir en** ~ to keep in suspense

suspense [syspɑ̃s] nm suspense

suspension [syspɑ̃sjɔ̃] nf suspension; ~ **d'audience** adjournment

sut vb voir **savoir**

suture [sytyʀ] nf (MÉD): **point de** ~ stitch

svelte [svɛlt(ə)] adj slender, svelte
S.V.P. sigle (= s'il vous plaît) please
syllabe [silab] nf syllable
sylviculture [silvikyltyʀ] nf forestry
symbole [sɛbɔl] nm symbol; **symbolique**
adj symbolic(al); (geste, offrande) token
cpd; (salaire, dommage-intérêts) nominal;
symboliser vt to symbolize
symétrique [simetʀik] adj symmetrical
sympa [sɛpa] adj abr = **sympathique**
sympathie [sɛpati] nf (inclination) liking;
(affinité) fellow feeling; (condoléances) sympathy; **accueillir avec ~** (projet) to receive
favourably; **croyez à toute ma ~** you have
my deepest sympathy
sympathique [sɛpatik] adj nice, friendly;
likeable; pleasant
sympathisant, e [sɛpatizɑ̃, -ɑ̃t] nm/f sym-
pathizer
sympathiser [sɛpatize] vi (voisins etc:
s'entendre) to get on (BRIT) ou along (US)
(well)
symphonie [sɛfɔni] nf symphony
symptôme [sɛptom] nm symptom
synagogue [sinagɔg] nf synagogue
syncope [sɛkɔp] nf (MÉD) blackout; **tomber en ~** to faint, pass out
syndic [sɛdik] nm managing agent
syndical, e, aux [sɛdikal, -o] adj (trade)
union cpd; **syndicaliste** nm/f trade unionist
syndicat [sɛdika] nm (d'ouvriers, employés)
(trade) union; (autre association d'intérêts)
union, association; **~ d'initiative** tourist
office
syndiqué, e [sɛdike] adj belonging to a
(trade) union; **non ~** non-union
syndiquer [sɛdike]: **se ~** vi to form a trade
union; (adhérer) to join a trade union
synonyme [sinɔnim] adj synonymous ♦ nm
synonym; **~ de** synonymous with
syntaxe [sɛtaks(ə)] nf syntax
synthèse [sɛtɛz] nf synthesis
synthétique [sɛtetik] adj synthetic
Syrie [siʀi] nf: **la ~** Syria
systématique [sistematik] adj systematic
système [sistɛm] nm system; **~ D** (fam) re-
sourcefulness

T t

t' [t(ə)] pron voir **te**
ta [ta] dét **ton**[1]
tabac [taba] nm tobacco; tobacconist's
(shop); **~ blond/brun** light/dark tobacco
tabagisme [tabaʒism] nm: **~ passif** passive
smoking
table [tabl(ə)] nf table; **à ~!** dinner etc is
ready!; **se mettre à ~** to sit down to eat;
(fig: fam) to come clean; **mettre la ~** to
lay the table; **faire ~ rase de** to make a
clean sweep of; **~ de cuisson** nf (à
l'électricité) hotplate; (au gaz) gas ring; **~
de nuit** ou **de chevet** bedside table; **~ des
matières** (table of) contents pl
tableau, x [tablo] nm painting; (reproduction, fig) picture; (panneau) board; (schéma)
table, chart; **~ d'affichage** notice board; **~
de bord** dashboard; (AVIAT) instrument
panel; **~ noir** blackboard
tabler [table] vi: **~ sur** to bank on
tablette [tablɛt] nf (planche) shelf; **~ de
chocolat** bar of chocolate
tableur [tablœʀ] nm spreadsheet
tablier [tablije] nm apron
tabouret [tabuʀɛ] nm stool
tac [tak] nm: **du ~ au ~** tit for tat
tache [taʃ] nf (saleté) stain, mark; (ART, de
couleur, lumière) spot; splash, patch; **~ de
rousseur** nf freckle
tâche [taʃ] nf task; **travailler à la ~** to do
piecework
tacher [taʃe] vt to stain, mark; (fig) to
sully, stain
tâcher [taʃe] vi: **~ de faire** to try ou endeavour to do
tacot [tako] (péj) nm banger (BRIT), (old)
heap
tact [takt] nm tact; **avoir du ~** to be tactful
tactique [taktik] adj tactical ♦ nf (technique) tactics sg; (plan) tactic
taie [tɛ] nf: **~ d'oreiller** pillowslip, pillow-
case
taille [taj] nf cutting; pruning; (milieu du
corps) waist; (hauteur) height; (grandeur)
size; **de ~ à faire** capable of doing; **de ~**
sizeable
taille-crayon(s) [tajkʀɛjɔ̃] nm pencil sharpener
tailler [taje] vt (pierre, diamant) to cut;
(arbre, plante) to prune; (vêtement) to cut

out; (*crayon*) to sharpen
tailleur [tɑjœʀ] *nm* (*couturier*) tailor; (*vêtement*) suit; **en ~** (*assis*) cross-legged
taillis [tɑji] *nm* copse
taire [tɛʀ] *vt* to keep to o.s., conceal ♦ *vi*: **faire ~ qn** to make sb be quiet; (*fig*) to silence sb; **se ~** *vi* to be silent *ou* quiet
talc [talk] *nm* talc, talcum powder
talent [talɑ̃] *nm* talent
talon [talɔ̃] *nm* heel; (*de chèque, billet*) stub, counterfoil (*BRIT*); **~s plats/aiguilles** flat/stiletto heels
talonner [talɔne] *vt* to follow hard behind; (*fig*) to hound
talus [taly] *nm* embankment
tambour [tɑ̃buʀ] *nm* (*MUS, aussi TECH*) drum; (*musicien*) drummer; (*porte*) revolving door(s *pl*)
tamis [tami] *nm* sieve
Tamise [tamiz] *nf*: **la ~** the Thames
tamisé, e [tamize] *adj* (*fig*) subdued, soft
tamiser [tamize] *vt* to sieve, sift
tampon [tɑ̃pɔ̃] *nm* (*de coton, d'ouate*) wad, pad; (*amortisseur*) buffer; (*bouchon*) plug, stopper; (*cachet, timbre*) stamp; (*mémoire ~* (*INFORM*) buffer; (*hygiénique*) tampon; **tamponner** *vt* (*timbres*) to stamp; (*heurter*) to crash *ou* ram into; **tamponneuse** *adj*: **autos tamponneuses** dodgems
tandis [tɑ̃di] : **~ que** *conj* while
tanguer [tɑ̃ge] *vi* to pitch (and toss)
tanière [tanjɛʀ] *nf* lair, den
tanné, e [tane] *adj* weather-beaten
tanner [tane] *vt* to tan
tant [tɑ̃] *adv* so much; **~ de** (*sable, eau*) so much; (*gens, livres*) so many; **~ que** as long as; (*comparatif*) as much as; **~ mieux** that's great; so much the better; **~ pis** never mind; too bad
tante [tɑ̃t] *nf* aunt
tantôt [tɑ̃to] *adv* (*parfois*): **~ ... ~** now ... now; (*cet après-midi*) this afternoon
tapage [tapaʒ] *nm* uproar, din
tapageur, euse [tapaʒœʀ, -øz] *adj* loud, flashy; noisy
tape [tap] *nf* slap
tape-à-l'œil [tapalœj] *adj inv* flashy, showy
taper [tape] *vt* (*porte*) to bang, slam; (*dactylographier*) to type (out); (*fam: emprunter*): **~ qn de 10 F** to touch sb for 10 F ♦ *vi* (*soleil*) to beat down; **~ sur qn** to thump sb; (*fig*) to run sb down; **~ sur qch** to hit sth; **~ à** (*porte etc*) to knock on; **~ dans** (*se servir*) to dig into; **~ des mains/pieds** to clap one's hands/stamp one's feet; **~ (à la machine)** to type; **se ~ un travail** (*fam*) to land o.s. a job
tapi, e [tapi] *adj* crouching, cowering; hidden away
tapis [tapi] *nm* carpet; (*de table*) cloth; **mettre sur le ~** (*fig*) to bring up for discussion; **~ de sol** (*de tente*) groundsheet;

~ roulant conveyor belt
tapisser [tapise] *vt* (*avec du papier peint*) to paper; (*recouvrir*): **~ qch (de)** to cover sth (with)
tapisserie [tapisʀi] *nf* (*tenture, broderie*) tapestry; (*papier peint*) wallpaper
tapissier, ière [tapisje, -jɛʀ] *nm/f*: **~(-décorateur)** upholsterer (and decorator)
tapoter [tapɔte] *vt* to pat, tap
taquiner [takine] *vt* to tease
tarabiscoté, e [taʀabiskɔte] *adj* overornate, fussy
tard [taʀ] *adv* late; **plus ~** later (on); **au plus ~** at the latest; **sur le ~** late in life
tarder [taʀde] *vi* (*chose*) to be a long time coming; (*personne*): **~ à faire** to delay doing; **il me tarde d'être** I am longing to be; **sans (plus) ~** without (further) delay
tardif, ive [taʀdif, -iv] *adj* late
targuer [taʀge] : **se ~ de** *vt* to boast about
tarif [taʀif] *nm* (*liste*) price list; tariff; (*barème*) rates *pl*; fares *pl*; tariff; (*prix*) rate; fare
tarir [taʀiʀ] *vi* to dry up, run dry
tarte [taʀt(ə)] *nf* tart
tartine [taʀtin] *nf* slice of bread; **~ de miel** slice of bread and honey; **tartiner** *vt* to spread; **fromage à tartiner** cheese spread
tartre [taʀtʀ(ə)] *nm* (*des dents*) tartar; (*de chaudière*) fur, scale
tas [tɑ] *nm* heap, pile; (*fig*): **un ~ de** heaps of, lots of; **en ~** in a heap *ou* pile; **formé sur le ~** trained on the job
tasse [tɑs] *nf* cup; **~ à café** coffee cup
tassé, e [tɑse] *adj*: **bien ~** (*café etc*) strong
tasser [tɑse] *vt* (*terre, neige*) to pack down; (*entasser*): **~ qch dans** to cram sth into; **se ~** *vi* (*terrain*) to settle; (*fig*) to sort itself out, settle down
tâter [tɑte] *vt* to feel; (*fig*) to try out; **se ~** (*hésiter*) to be in two minds; **~ de** (*prison etc*) to have a taste of
tatillon, ne [tatijɔ̃, -ɔn] *adj* pernickety
tâtonnement [tɑtɔnmɑ̃] *nm*: **par ~s** (*fig*) by trial and error
tâtonner [tɑtɔne] *vi* to grope one's way along
tâtons [tɑtɔ̃] : **à ~: chercher/avancer à tâtons** *adv* to grope around for/grope one's way forward
tatouer [tatwe] *vt* to tattoo
taudis [todi] *nm* hovel, slum
taule [tol] (*fam*) *nf* nick (*fam*), prison
taupe [top] *nf* mole
taureau, x [tɔʀo] *nm* bull; (*signe*): **le T~** Taurus
tauromachie [tɔʀɔmaʃi] *nf* bullfighting
taux [to] *nm* rate; (*d'alcool*) level; **~ d'intérêt** interest rate
taxe [taks] *nf* tax; (*douanière*) duty; **~ à la valeur ajoutée** value added tax (*BRIT*); **~ de séjour** tourist tax

taxer [takse] vt (personne) to tax; (produit) to put a tax on, tax; (fig): ~ qn de to call sb +attrib; to accuse sb of, tax sb with

taxi [taksi] nm taxi

Tchécoslovaquie [tʃekɔslɔvaki] nf Czechoslovakia; **tchèque** adj, nm/f Czech ♦ nm (LING) Czech

te(t') [t(ə)] pron you; (réfléchi) yourself

technicien, ne [tɛknisjɛ̃, -jɛn] nm/f technician

technique [tɛknik] adj technical ♦ nf technique; **techniquement** adv technically

technologie [tɛknɔlɔʒi] nf technology; **technologique** adj technological

teck [tɛk] nm teak

teignais etc vb voir teindre

teindre [tɛ̃dʀ(ə)] vt to dye

teint, e [tɛ̃, tɛ̃t] adj dyed ♦ nm (du visage) complexion; colour ♦ nf shade; **grand ~** colourfast

teinté, e [tɛ̃te] adj: ~ de (fig) tinged with

teinter [tɛ̃te] vt to tint; (bois) to stain; **teinture** nf dyeing; (substance) dye; (MÉD) tincture

teinturerie [tɛ̃tyʀʀi] nf dry cleaner's

teinturier [tɛ̃tyʀje] nm dry cleaner

tel, telle [tɛl] adj (pareil) such; (comme): ~ un/des ... like a/like ...; (indéfini) such-and-such a, a given; (intensif): **un ~/de ~s** ... such (a)/such ...; **rien de ~** nothing like it, no such thing; ~ **que** like, such as; ~ **quel** as it is ou stands (ou was etc)

télé: [tele] abr f (= télévision) TV, telly (BRIT); (poste) TV (set), telly; **à la ~** on TV, on telly

télécabine [telekabin] nf (benne) cable car

télécarte [telekaʀt(ə)] nf phonecard

télé: ~**commande** nf remote control; ~**copie** nf fax; **envoyer qch par ~copie** to fax sth; ~**distribution** nf cable TV; ~**férique** nm = téléphérique; ~**gramme** nm telegram; ~**graphier** vt to telegraph, cable; ~**guider** vt to operate by remote control, radio-control; ~**journal** nm TV news magazine programme; ~**matique** nf telematics sg; ~**objectif** nm telephoto lens

téléphérique [teleferik] nm cable car

téléphone [telefɔn] nm telephone; **avoir le ~** to be on the (tele)phone; **au ~** on the phone; ~ **de voiture** car phone; **téléphoner** vi to telephone, ring; to make a phone call; **téléphoner à** to phone, call up (BRIT); **téléphonique** adj (tele)phone cpd

télescope [telɛskɔp] nm telescope

télescoper [telɛskɔpe] vt to smash up; **se ~** (véhicules) to concertina

télé: ~**scripteur** nm teleprinter; ~**siège** nm chairlift; ~**ski** nm ski-tow; ~**spectateur, trice** nm/f (television) viewer; ~**viseur** nm television set; ~**vision** nf television; **à la ~vision** on television

télex [telɛks] nm telex

telle [tɛl] adj voir tel

tellement [tɛlmɑ̃] adv (tant) so much; (si) so; ~ **de** (sable, eau) so much; (gens, livres) so many; **il s'est endormi ~ il était fatigué** he was so tired (that) he fell asleep; **pas ~** not (all) that much; not (all) that +adjectif

téméraire [temeʀɛʀ] adj reckless, rash; **témérité** nf recklessness, rashness

témoignage [temwaɲaʒ] nm (JUR: déclaration) testimony no pl, evidence no pl; (: faits) evidence no pl; (rapport, récit) account; (fig: d'affection etc) token, mark; expression

témoigner [temwaɲe] vt (intérêt, gratitude) to show ♦ vi (JUR) to testify, give evidence; ~ **de** to bear witness to, testify to

témoin [temwɛ̃] nm witness; (fig) testimony ♦ adj control cpd, test cpd; **appartement ~** show flat (BRIT); **être ~ de** to witness; ~ **oculaire** eyewitness

tempe [tɑ̃p] nf temple

tempérament [tɑ̃peʀamɑ̃] nm temperament, disposition; **à ~** (vente) on deferred (payment) terms; (achat) by instalments, hire purchase cpd

température [tɑ̃peʀatyʀ] nf temperature; **avoir ou faire de la ~** to be running ou have a temperature

tempéré, e [tɑ̃peʀe] adj temperate

tempête [tɑ̃pɛt] nf storm; ~ **de sable/ neige** sand/snowstorm

temple [tɑ̃pl(ə)] nm temple; (protestant) church

temporaire [tɑ̃pɔʀɛʀ] adj temporary

temps [tɑ̃] nm (atmosphérique) weather; (durée) time; (époque) time, times pl; (LING) tense; (MUS) beat; (TECH) stroke; **il fait beau/mauvais ~** the weather is fine/ bad; **avoir le ~/tout le ~** to have time/ plenty of time; **en ~ de paix/guerre** in peacetime/wartime; **en ~ utile ou voulu** in due time ou course; **de ~ en ~, de ~ à autre** from time to time; **à ~** (partir, arriver) in time; **à ~ partiel** part-time; **dans le ~** at one time; **de tout ~** always; ~ **d'arrêt** pause, halt; ~ **mort** (COMM) slack period

tenable [tənabl(ə)] adj bearable

tenace [tənas] adj tenacious, persistent

tenailler [tənaje] vt (fig) to torment

tenailles [tənaj] nfpl pincers

tenais etc vb voir tenir

tenancier, ière [tənɑ̃sje, -jɛʀ] nm/f manager/manageress

tenant, e [tənɑ̃, -ɑ̃t] nm/f (SPORT): ~ **du titre** title-holder

tendance [tɑ̃dɑ̃s] nf (opinions) leanings pl, sympathies pl; (inclination) tendency; (évolution) trend; **avoir ~ à** to have a tendency to, tend to

tendeur [tɑ̃dœʀ] nm (attache) elastic strap

tendre [tɑ̃dʀ(ə)] adj tender; (bois, roche,

couleur) soft ♦ *vt (élastique, peau)* to stretch, draw tight; *(muscle)* to tense; *(donner)*: ~ **qch à qn** to hold sth out to sb; to offer sb sth; *(fig: piège)* to set, lay; **se ~** *vi (corde)* to tighten; *(relations)* to become strained; ~ **à qch/à faire** to tend towards sth/to do; ~ **l'oreille** to prick up one's ears; ~ **la main/le bras** to hold out one's hand/stretch out one's arm; **tendrement** *adv* tenderly; **tendresse** *nf* tenderness

tendu, e [tɑ̃dy] *pp de* **tendre** ♦ *adj* tight; tensed; strained

ténèbres [tenɛbʀ(ə)] *nfpl* darkness *sg*

teneur [tənœʀ] *nf* content; *(d'une lettre)* terms *pl*, content

tenir [təniʀ] *vt* to hold; *(magasin, hôtel)* to run; *(promesse)* to keep ♦ *vi* to hold; *(neige, gel)* to last; **se ~** *vi (avoir lieu)* to be held, take place; *(être: personne)* to stand; **se ~ droit** to stand *(ou* sit) up straight; **bien se ~** to behave well; **se ~ à qch** to hold on to sth; **s'en ~ à qch** to confine o.s. to sth; to stick to sth; ~ **à** to be attached to; to care about; to depend on; to stem from; ~ **à faire** to want to do; ~ **de** to partake of; to take after; **ça ne tient qu'à lui** it is entirely up to him; ~ **qn pour** to take sb for; ~ **qch de qn** *(histoire)* to have heard *ou* learnt sth from sb; *(qualité, défaut)* to have inherited *ou* got sth from sb; ~ **les comptes** to keep the books; ~ **le coup** to hold out; ~ **au chaud** to keep hot; **tiens/tenez, voilà le stylo** there's the pen!; **tiens, Alain!** look, here's Alain!; **tiens?** *(surprise)* really?

tennis [tenis] *nm* tennis; *(court)* tennis court ♦ *nm ou f pl (aussi:* **chaussures de ~)** tennis *ou* gym shoes; ~ **de table** table tennis; **tennisman** *nm* tennis player

tension [tɑ̃sjɔ̃] *nf* tension; *(fig)* tension; strain; *(MÉD)* blood pressure; **faire** *ou* **avoir de la ~** to have high blood pressure

tentation [tɑ̃tasjɔ̃] *nf* temptation

tentative [tɑ̃tativ] *nf* attempt, bid

tente [tɑ̃t] *nf* tent

tenter [tɑ̃te] *vt (éprouver, attirer)* to tempt; *(essayer)*: ~ **qch/de faire** to attempt *ou* try sth/to do; ~ **sa chance** to try one's luck

tenture [tɑ̃tyʀ] *nf* hanging

tenu, e [təny] *pp de* **tenir** ♦ *adj (maison, comptes)*: **bien ~** well-kept; *(obligé)*: ~ **de faire** under an obligation to do ♦ *nf (action de tenir)* running; keeping; holding; *(vêtements)* clothes *pl*, gear; *(allure)* dress *no pl*, appearance; *(comportement)* manners *pl*, behaviour; **en petite tenue** scantily dressed *ou* clad; **~e de route** *(AUTO)* road-holding; **~e de soirée** evening dress

ter [tɛʀ] *adj:* **16** ~ **16b** *ou* **B**

térébenthine [teʀebɑ̃tin] *nf:* **(essence de) ~** (oil of) turpentine

terme [tɛʀm(ə)] *nm* term; *(fin)* end; **à**

court/long ~ short-/long-term *ou* -range ♦ *adv* in the short/long term; **avant ~** *(MÉD)* prematurely; **mettre un ~ à** to put an end *ou* a stop to

terminaison [tɛʀminɛzɔ̃] *nf (LING)* ending

terminal, e, aux [tɛʀminal, -o] *adj* final ♦ *nm* terminal; **terminale** *nf (SCOL)* ≈ sixth form *ou* year *(BRIT)*, ≈ twelfth grade *(US)*

terminer [tɛʀmine] *vt* to end; *(travail, repas)* to finish; **se ~** *vi* to end

terne [tɛʀn(ə)] *adj* dull

ternir [tɛʀniʀ] *vt* to dull; *(fig)* to sully, tarnish; **se ~** *vi* to become dull

terrain [tɛʀɛ̃] *nm (sol, fig)* ground; *(COMM)* land *no pl*, plot (of land); site; **sur le ~** *(fig)* on the field; ~ **d'aviation** airfield; ~ **de camping** campsite; ~ **de football/rugby** football/rugby pitch *(BRIT)* ou field *(US)*; ~ **de golf** golf course; ~ **de jeu** games field; playground; ~ **de sport** sports ground; ~ **vague** waste ground *no pl*

terrasse [tɛʀas] *nf* terrace; **à la ~** *(café)* outside; **~ment** [tɛʀasmɑ̃] *nm* earthmoving, earthworks *pl*; embankment; **~r** [tɛʀase] *vt (adversaire)* to floor; *(suj: maladie etc)* to lay low

terre [tɛʀ] *nf (gén, aussi ÉLEC)* earth; *(substance)* soil, earth; *(opposé à mer)* land *no pl*; *(contrée)* land; **~s** *nfpl (terrains)* lands, land *sg*; **en ~** *(pipe, poterie)* clay *cpd*; **à** *ou* **par ~** *(mettre, être)* on the ground *(ou* floor); *(jeter, tomber)* to the ground, down; ~ **à** ~ *adj inv* down-to-earth; ~ **cuite** earthenware; terracotta; **la ~ ferme** dry land; ~ **glaise** clay

terreau [tɛʀo] *nm* compost

terre-plein [tɛʀplɛ̃] *nm* platform

terrer [tɛʀe]: **se ~** *vi* to hide away; to go to ground

terrestre [tɛʀɛstʀ(ə)] *adj (surface)* earth's, of the earth; *(BOT, ZOOL, MIL)* land *cpd*; *(REL)* earthly, worldly

terreur [tɛʀœʀ] *nf* terror *no pl*

terrible [tɛʀibl(ə)] *adj* terrible, dreadful; *(fam)* terrific

terrien, ne [tɛʀjɛ̃, -jɛn] *adj:* **propriétaire ~** landowner ♦ *nm/f (non martien etc)* earthling

terrier [tɛʀje] *nm* burrow, hole; *(chien)* terrier

terril [tɛʀil] *nm* slag heap

terrine [tɛʀin] *nf (récipient)* terrine; *(CULIN)* pâté

territoire [tɛʀitwaʀ] *nm* territory

terroir [tɛʀwaʀ] *nm (AGR)* soil; region

terrorisme [tɛʀɔʀism(ə)] *nm* terrorism; **terroriste** *nm/f* terrorist

tertiaire [tɛʀsjɛʀ] *adj* tertiary ♦ *nm (ÉCON)* service industries *pl*

tertre [tɛʀtʀ(ə)] *nm* hillock, mound

tes [te] *dét voir* **ton**[1]

tesson [tesɔ̃] *nm:* ~ **de bouteille** piece of

broken bottle

test [tɛst] *nm* test

testament [tɛstamɑ̃] *nm* (*JUR*) will; (*REL*) Testament; (*fig*) legacy

tester [tɛste] *vt* to test

testicule [tɛstikyl] *nm* testicle

tétanos [tetanos] *nm* tetanus

têtard [tɛtaʀ] *nm* tadpole

tête [tɛt] *nf* head; (*cheveux*) hair *no pl*; (*visage*) face; **de ~** (*wagon etc*) front *cpd* ♦ *adv* (*calculer*) in one's head, mentally; **tenir ~ à qn** to stand up to sb; **la ~ en bas** with one's head down; **la ~ la première** (*tomber*) headfirst; **la ~** (*FOOTBALL*) to head the ball; **faire la ~** (*fig*) to sulk; **en ~** (*SPORT*) in the lead; at the front; **en ~ à ~** in private, alone together; **de la ~ aux pieds** from head to toe; **~ de lecture** (playback) head; **~ de liste** (*POL*) chief candidate; **~ de série** (*TENNIS*) seeded player, seed

tête-à-queue [tɛtakø] *nm inv*: **faire un ~** to spin round

téter [tete] *vt*: **~ (sa mère)** to suck at one's mother's breast, feed

tétine [tetin] *nf* teat; (*sucette*) dummy (*BRIT*), pacifier (*US*)

têtu, e [tety] *adj* stubborn, pigheaded

texte [tɛkst(ə)] *nm* text

textile [tɛkstil] *adj* textile *cpd* ♦ *nm* textile; textile industry

texture [tɛkstyʀ] *nf* texture

TGV *sigle m* (= *train à grande vitesse*) high-speed train

thé [te] *nm* tea; **prendre le ~** to have tea; **faire le ~** to make the tea

théâtral, e, aux [teatʀal, -o] *adj* theatrical

théâtre [teatʀ(ə)] *nm* theatre; (*œuvres*) plays *pl*, dramatic works *pl*; (*fig: lieu*): **le ~ de** the scene of; (*péj*) histrionics *pl*, playacting; **faire du ~** to be on the stage; to do some acting

théière [tejɛʀ] *nf* teapot

thème [tɛm] *nm* theme; (*SCOL: traduction*) prose (composition)

théologie [teɔlɔʒi] *nf* theology

théorie [teɔʀi] *nf* theory; **théorique** *adj* theoretical

thérapie [teʀapi] *nf* therapy

thermal, e, aux [tɛʀmal, -o] *adj*: **station ~e** spa; **cure ~e** water cure

thermes [tɛʀm(ə)] *nmpl* thermal baths

thermomètre [tɛʀmɔmɛtʀ(ə)] *nm* thermometer

thermos [tɛʀmos] ® *nm ou nf*: **(bouteille) ~** vacuum *ou* Thermos ® flask

thermostat [tɛʀmɔsta] *nm* thermostat

thèse [tɛz] *nf* thesis

thon [tɔ̃] *nm* tuna (fish)

thym [tɛ̃] *nm* thyme

tibia [tibja] *nm* shinbone, tibia; shin

tic [tik] *nm* tic, (nervous) twitch; (*de lan-*

gage etc) mannerism

ticket [tikɛ] *nm* ticket; **~ de caisse** *nm* receipt; **~ de quai** platform ticket

tiède [tjɛd] *adj* lukewarm; tepid; (*vent, air*) mild, warm; **tiédir** *vi* to cool; to grow warmer

tien, ne [tjɛ̃, tjɛn] *pron*: **le(la) ~(ne)**, **les ~(ne)s** yours; **à la ~ne!** cheers!

tiens [tjɛ̃] *vb, excl voir* **tenir**

tierce [tjɛʀs(ə)] *adj voir* **tiers**

tiercé [tjɛʀse] *nm* system of forecast betting giving first 3 horses

tiers, tierce [tjɛʀ, tjɛʀs(ə)] *adj* third ♦ *nm* (*JUR*) third party; (*fraction*) third; **le ~ monde** the Third World

tige [tiʒ] *nf* stem; (*baguette*) rod

tignasse [tiɲas] (*péj*) *nf* mop of hair

tigre [tigʀ(ə)] *nm* tiger

tigré, e [tigʀe] *adj* striped; spotted

tilleul [tijœl] *nm* lime (tree), linden (tree); (*boisson*) lime(-blossom) tea

timbale [tɛ̃bal] *nf* (metal) tumbler; **~s** *nfpl* (*MUS*) timpani, kettledrums

timbre [tɛ̃bʀ(ə)] *nm* (*tampon*) stamp; (*aussi: ~-poste*) (postage) stamp; (*MUS: de voix, instrument*) timbre, tone

timbré, e [tɛ̃bʀe] (*fam*) *adj* daft

timide [timid] *adj* shy; timid; (*timoré*) timid, timorous; **timidement** *adv* shyly; timidly; **timidité** *nf* shyness; timidity

tins *etc vb voir* **tenir**

tintamarre [tɛ̃tamaʀ] *nm* din, uproar

tinter [tɛ̃te] *vi* to ring, chime; (*argent, clefs*) to jingle

tir [tiʀ] *nm* (*sport*) shooting; (*fait ou manière de tirer*) firing *no pl*; (*stand*) shooting gallery; **~ à l'arc** archery; **~ au pigeon** clay pigeon shooting

tirage [tiʀaʒ] *nm* (*action*) printing; (*PHOTO*) print; (*de journal*) circulation; (*de livre*) (print-)run; edition; (*de loterie*) draw; **~ au sort** drawing lots

tirailler [tiʀaje] *vt* to pull at, tug at ♦ *vi* to fire at random

tirant [tiʀɑ̃] *nm*: **~ d'eau** draught

tire [tiʀ] *nf*: **vol à la ~** pickpocketing

tiré, e [tiʀe] *adj* (*traits*) drawn ♦ *nm* (*COMM*) drawee; **~ par les cheveux** farfetched

tire-au-flanc [tiʀoflɑ̃] (*péj*) *nm inv* skiver

tire-bouchon [tiʀbuʃɔ̃] *nm* corkscrew

tirelire [tiʀliʀ] *nf* moneybox

tirer [tiʀe] *vt* (*gén*) to pull; (*extraire*): **~ qch de** to take *ou* pull sth out of; to get sth out of; to extract sth from; (*tracer: ligne, trait*) to draw, trace; (*fermer: rideau*) to draw, close; (*choisir: carte, conclusion, aussi COMM: chèque*) to draw; (*en faisant feu: balle, coup*) to fire; (: *animal*) to shoot; (*journal, livre, photo*) to print; (*FOOTBALL: corner etc*) to take ♦ *vi* (*faire feu*) to fire; (*faire du tir, FOOTBALL*) to shoot; (*chemi-*

née) to draw; **se ~** *vi (fam)* to push off; **s'en ~** to pull through, get off; **~ sur** to pull on *ou* at; to shoot *ou* fire at; *(pipe)* to draw on; *(fig: avoisiner)* to verge *ou* border on; **~ qn de** *(embarras etc)* to help *ou* get sb out of; **~ à l'arc/la carabine** to shoot with a bow and arrow/with a rifle

tiret [tiʀɛ] *nm* dash

tireur, euse [tiʀœʀ, -øz] *nm/f (COMM)* drawer ♦ *nm* gunman; **~ d'élite** marksman

tiroir [tiʀwaʀ] *nm* drawer; **tiroir-caisse** *nm* till

tisane [tizan] *nf* herb tea

tisonnier [tizɔnje] *nm* poker

tisser [tise] *vt* to weave; **tisserand** *nm* weaver

tissu [tisy] *nm* fabric, material, cloth *no pl; (ANAT, BIO)* tissue

tissu-éponge [tisyepɔ̃ʒ] *nm* (terry) towelling *no pl*

titre [titʀ(ə)] *nm (gén)* title; *(de journal)* headline; *(diplôme)* qualification; *(COMM)* security; **en ~** *(champion)* official; **à juste ~** with just cause, rightly; **à quel ~?** on what grounds?; **à aucun ~** on no account; **au même ~ (que)** in the same way (as); **à ~ d'information** for (your) information; **à ~ gracieux** free of charge; **à ~ d'essai** on a trial basis; **à ~ privé** in a private capacity; **~ de propriété** title deed; **~ de transport** ticket

tituber [titybe] *vi* to stagger (along)

titulaire [titylɛʀ] *adj (ADMIN)* appointed, with tenure ♦ *nm/f* incumbent; **être ~ de** *(poste)* to hold; *(permis)* to be the holder of

toast [tost] *nm* slice *ou* piece of toast; *(de bienvenue)* (welcoming) toast; **porter un ~ à qn** to propose *ou* drink a toast to sb

toboggan [tɔbɔɡɑ̃] *nm* toboggan; *(jeu)* slide

tocsin [tɔksɛ̃] *nm* alarm (bell)

toge [tɔʒ] *nf* toga; *(de juge)* gown

toi [twa] *pron* you

toile [twal] *nf (matériau)* cloth *no pl; (bâche)* piece of canvas; *(tableau)* canvas; **~ cirée** oilcloth; **~ d'araignée** cobweb; **~ de fond** *(fig)* backdrop

toilette [twalɛt] *nf* wash; *(habits)* outfit; dress *no pl;* **~s** *nfpl (w.-c.)* toilet *sg;* **faire sa ~** to have a wash, get washed; **articles de ~** toiletries

toi-même [twamɛm] *pron* yourself

toiser [twaze] *vt* to eye up and down

toison [twazɔ̃] *nf (de mouton)* fleece; *(cheveux)* mane

toit [twa] *nm* roof; **~ ouvrant** sunroof

toiture [twatyʀ] *nf* roof

tôle [tol] *nf (plaque)* steel *ou* iron sheet; **~ ondulée** corrugated iron

tolérable [tɔleʀabl(ə)] *adj* tolerable, bearable

tolérant, e [tɔleʀɑ̃, -ɑ̃t] *adj* tolerant

tolérer [tɔleʀe] *vt* to tolerate; *(ADMIN: hors taxe etc)* to allow

tollé [tɔle] *nm* outcry

tomate [tɔmat] *nf* tomato

tombe [tɔ̃b] *nf (sépulture)* grave; *(avec monument)* tomb

tombeau, x [tɔ̃bo] *nm* tomb

tombée [tɔ̃be] *nf:* **à la ~ de la nuit** at the close of day, at nightfall

tomber [tɔ̃be] *vi* to fall; **laisser ~** to drop; **~ sur** *(rencontrer)* to come across; *(attaquer)* to set about; **~ de fatigue/sommeil** to drop from exhaustion/be falling asleep on one's feet; **ça tombe bien** that's come at the right time; **il est bien tombé** he's been lucky

tome [tɔm] *nm* volume

ton¹, ta [tɔ̃, ta] *(pl* **tes)** *dét* your

ton² [tɔ̃] *nm (gén)* tone; *(MUS)* key; *(couleur)* shade, tone; **de bon ton** in good taste

tonalité [tɔnalite] *nf (au téléphone)* dialling tone; *(MUS)* key; *(fig)* tone

tondeuse [tɔ̃døz] *nf (à gazon)* (lawn)mower; *(du coiffeur)* clippers *pl; (pour la tonte)* shears *pl*

tondre [tɔ̃dʀ(ə)] *vt (pelouse, herbe)* to mow; *(haie)* to cut, clip; *(mouton, toison)* to shear; *(cheveux)* to crop

tonifier [tɔnifje] *vt (peau, organisme)* to tone up

tonique [tɔnik] *adj* fortifying ♦ *nm* tonic

tonne [tɔn] *nf* metric ton, tonne

tonneau, x [tɔno] *nm (à vin, cidre)* barrel; *(NAVIG)* ton; **faire des ~x** *(voiture, avion)* to roll over

tonnelle [tɔnɛl] *nf* bower, arbour

tonner [tɔne] *vi* to thunder; **il tonne** it is thundering, there's some thunder

tonnerre [tɔnɛʀ] *nm* thunder

tonus [tɔnys] *nm* dynamism

top [tɔp] *nm:* **au 3ème ~** at the 3rd stroke

topinambour [tɔpinɑ̃buʀ] *nm* Jerusalem artichoke

toque [tɔk] *nf (de fourrure)* fur hat; **~ de cuisinier** chef's hat; **~ de jockey/juge** jockey's/judge's cap

toqué, e [tɔke] *(fam) adj* cracked

torche [tɔʀʃ(ə)] *nf* torch

torchon [tɔʀʃɔ̃] *nm* cloth, duster; *(à vaisselle)* tea towel *ou* cloth

tordre [tɔʀdʀ(ə)] *vt (chiffon)* to wring; *(barre, fig: visage)* to twist; **se ~** *vi (barre)* to bend; *(roue)* to twist, buckle; *(ver, serpent)* to writhe; **se ~ le pied/bras** to twist one's foot/arm; **tordu, e** [tɔʀdy] *adj (fig)* warped, twisted

tornade [tɔʀnad] *nf* tornado

torpille [tɔʀpij] *nf* torpedo

torréfier [tɔʀefje] *vt* to roast

torrent [tɔʀɑ̃] *nm* torrent

torse [tɔʀs(ə)] *nm (ANAT)* torso; chest

torsion [tɔʀsjɔ̃] nf twisting; torsion

tort [tɔʀ] nm (défaut) fault; (préjudice) wrong no pl; **~s** nmpl (JUR) fault sg; **avoir ~** to be wrong; **être dans son ~** to be in the wrong; **donner ~ à qn** to lay the blame on sb; (fig) to prove sb wrong; **causer du ~ à** to harm; to be harmful ou detrimental to; **à ~** wrongly; **à ~ et à travers** wildly

torticolis [tɔʀtikɔli] nm stiff neck

tortiller [tɔʀtije] vt to twist; to twiddle; **se ~** vi to wriggle, squirm

tortionnaire [tɔʀsjɔnɛʀ] nm torturer

tortue [tɔʀty] nf tortoise

tortueux, euse [tɔʀtɥø, -øz] adj (rue) twisting; (fig) tortuous

torture [tɔʀtyʀ] nf torture; **torturer** vt to torture; (fig) to torment

tôt [to] adv early; **~ ou tard** sooner or later; **si ~** so early; (déjà) so soon; **au plus ~** at the earliest; **il eut ~ fait de faire** he soon did

total, e, aux [tɔtal, -o] adj, nm total; **au ~** in total ou all; **faire le ~** to work out the total, add up; **totalement** adv totally, completely; **totaliser** vt to total (up)

totalité [tɔtalite] nf: **la ~ de** all of, the total amount (ou number) of; the whole **+sg; en ~** entirely

toubib [tubib] (fam) nm doctor

touchant, e [tuʃɑ̃, -ɑ̃t] adj touching

touche [tuʃ] nf (de piano, de machine à écrire) key; (PEINTURE etc) stroke, touch; (fig: de nostalgie) touch, hint; (FOOTBALL: aussi: **remise en ~**) throw-in; (aussi: **ligne de ~**) touch-line

toucher [tuʃe] nm touch ♦ vt to touch; (palper) to feel; (atteindre: d'un coup de feu etc) to hit; (concerner) to concern, affect; (contacter) to reach, contact; (recevoir: récompense) to receive, get; (: salaire) to draw, get; (: chèque) to cash; **se ~** (être en contact) to touch; **au ~** to the touch; **~ à** to touch; (concerner) to have to do with, concern; **je vais lui en ~ un mot** I'll have a word with him about it; **~ à sa fin** to be drawing to a close

touffe [tuf] nf tuft

touffu, e [tufy] adj thick, dense

toujours [tuʒuʀ] adv always; (encore) still; (constamment) forever; **~ plus** more and more; **pour ~** forever; **~ est-il que** the fact remains that; **essaie ~** (you can) try anyway

toupet [tupɛ] (fam) nm cheek

toupie [tupi] nf (spinning) top

tour [tuʀ] nf tower; (immeuble) high-rise block (BRIT) ou building (US); (ÉCHECS) castle, rook ♦ nm (excursion) stroll, walk; run, ride; trip; (SPORT: aussi: **~ de piste**) lap; (d'être servi ou de jouer etc) turn; (de roue etc) revolution; (circonférence): **de 3 m**

de **~** 3 m round, with a circumference ou girth of 3 m; (POL: aussi: **~ de scrutin**) ballot; (ruse, de prestidigitation) trick; (de potier) wheel; (à bois, métaux) lathe; **faire le ~ de** to go round; (à pied) to walk round; **c'est au ~ de Renée** it's Renée's turn; **à ~ de rôle, ~ à ~** in turn; **~ de chant** song recital; **~ de contrôle** nf control tower; **~ de garde** spell of duty; **~ d'horizon** (fig) general survey; **~ de taille/tête** waist/head measurement

tourbe [tuʀb(ə)] nf peat

tourbillon [tuʀbijɔ̃] nm whirlwind; (d'eau) whirlpool; (fig) whirl, swirl; **tourbillonner** vi to whirl (round)

tourelle [tuʀɛl] nf turret

tourisme [tuʀism(ə)] nm tourism; **agence de ~** tourist agency; **faire du ~** to go sightseeing; to go touring; **touriste** nm/f tourist; **touristique** adj tourist cpd; (région) touristic

tourment [tuʀmɑ̃] nm torment

tourmenter [tuʀmɑ̃te] vt to torment; **se ~** vi to fret, worry o.s.

tournant [tuʀnɑ̃] nm (de route) bend; (fig) turning point

tournebroche [tuʀnəbʀɔʃ] nm roasting spit

tourne-disque [tuʀnədisk(ə)] nm record player

tournée [tuʀne] nf (du facteur etc) round; (d'artiste, politicien) tour; (au café) round (of drinks)

tournemain [tuʀnəmɛ̃] : **en un ~** adv (as) quick as a flash

tourner [tuʀne] vt to turn; (sauce, mélange) to stir; (contourner) to get round; (CINÉMA) to shoot; to make ♦ vi to turn; (moteur) to run; (compteur) to tick away; (lait etc) to turn (sour); **se ~** vi to turn round; **se ~ vers** to turn to; to turn towards; **bien ~** to turn out well; **~ autour de** to go round; (péj) to hang round; **~ à/en** to turn into; **~ le dos à** to turn one's back on; to have one's back to; **~ de l'œil** to pass out

tournesol [tuʀnəsɔl] nm sunflower

tournevis [tuʀnəvis] nm screwdriver

tourniquet [tuʀnike] nm (pour arroser) sprinkler; (portillon) turnstile; (présentoir) revolving stand, spinner

tournoi [tuʀnwa] nm tournament

tournoyer [tuʀnwaje] vi to whirl round; to swirl round

tournure [tuʀnyʀ] nf (LING) turn of phrase; form; phrasing; (évolution): **la ~ de qch** the way sth is developing; (aspect): **la ~ de** the look of; **~ d'esprit** turn ou cast of mind; **la ~ des événements** the turn of events

tourte [tuʀt(ə)] nf pie

tous [adj tu, pron tus] adj, pron voir **tout**

Toussaint [tusɛ̃] nf: **la ~** All Saints' Day

tousser [tuse] vi to cough

─────────── MOT CLÉ ───────────

tout, e [tu, tut] (*mpl* **tous**, *fpl* **toutes**) *adj* **1** (*avec article singulier*) all; ~ **le lait** all the milk; ~**e la nuit** all night, the whole night; ~ **le livre** the whole book; ~ **un pain** a whole loaf; ~ **le temps** all the time; the whole time; **c'est** ~ **le contraire** it's quite the opposite
2 (*avec article pluriel*) every; all; **tous les livres** all the books; ~**es les nuits** every night; ~**es les fois** every time; ~**es les trois/deux semaines** every third/other *ou* second week, every three/two weeks; **tous les deux** both *ou* each of us (*ou* them *ou* you); ~**es les trois** all three of us (*ou* them *ou* you)
3 (*sans article*): **à** ~ **âge** at any age; **pour** ~**e nourriture, il avait ...** his only food was ...
♦ *pron* everything, all; **il a** ~ **fait** he's done everything; **je les vois tous** I can see them all *ou* all of them; **nous y sommes tous allés** all of us went, we all went; **en** ~ in all; ~ **ce qu'il sait** all he knows
♦ *nm* whole; **le** ~ all of it (*ou* them); **le** ~ **est de ...** the main thing is to ...; **pas du** ~ not at all
♦ *adv* **1** (*très, complètement*) very; ~ **près** very near; **le** ~ **premier** the very first; ~ **seul** all alone; **le livre** ~ **entier** the whole book; ~ **en haut** right at the top; ~ **droit** straight ahead
2: ~ **en** while; ~ **en travaillant** while working, as he *etc* works
3 ~ **d'abord** first of all; ~ **à coup** suddenly; ~ **à fait** absolutely; ~ **à l'heure** a short while ago; (*futur*) in a short while, shortly; **à** ~ **à l'heure!** see you later!; ~ **de même** all the same; ~ **le monde** everybody; ~ **de suite** immediately, straight away; ~ **terrain** *ou* **tous terrains** all-terrain

toutefois [tutfwa] *adv* however
toutes [tut] *adj, pron voir* **tout**
toux [tu] *nf* cough
toxicomane [tɔksikɔman] *nm/f* drug addict
trac [tʀak] *nm* nerves *pl*
tracasser [tʀakase] *vt* to worry, bother; to harass; **tracasseries** [tʀakasʀi] *nfpl* (*chicanes*) annoyances
trace [tʀas] *nf* (*empreintes*) tracks *pl*; (*marques, aussi fig*) mark; (*restes, vestige*) trace; (*indice*) sign; ~**s de pas** footprints
tracé [tʀase] *nm* line; layout
tracer [tʀase] *vt* to draw; (*mot*) to trace; (*piste*) to open up
tract [tʀakt] *nm* tract, pamphlet
tractations [tʀaktɔsjɔ̃] *nfpl* dealings, bargaining *sg*
tracteur [tʀaktœʀ] *nm* tractor
traction [tʀaksjɔ̃] *nf*: ~ **avant/arrière** front-wheel/rear-wheel drive
tradition [tʀadisjɔ̃] *nf* tradition; **traditionnel, le** *adj* traditional
traducteur, trice [tʀadyktœʀ, -tʀis] *nm/f* translator
traduction [tʀadyksjɔ̃] *nf* translation
traduire [tʀadɥiʀ] *vt* to translate; (*exprimer*) to render, convey
trafic [tʀafik] *nm* traffic; ~ **d'armes** arms dealing; **trafiquant, e** *nm/f* trafficker; dealer; **trafiquer** (*péj*) *vt* to doctor, tamper with
tragédie [tʀaʒedi] *nf* tragedy
tragique [tʀaʒik] *adj* tragic
trahir [tʀaiʀ] *vt* to betray; (*fig*) to give away, reveal; **trahison** *nf* betrayal; (*JUR*) treason
train [tʀɛ̃] *nm* (*RAIL*) train; (*allure*) pace; (*fig: ensemble*) set; **mettre qch en** ~ to get sth under way; **mettre qn en** ~ to put sb in good spirits; **se mettre en** ~ to get started; to warm up; **se sentir en** ~ to feel in good form; ~ **d'atterrissage** undercarriage; ~ **de vie** style of living; ~ **électrique** (*jouet*) (electric) train set; ~-**autos-couchettes** car-sleeper train
traîne [tʀɛn] *nf* (*de robe*) train; **être à la** ~ to be in tow; to lag behind
traîneau, x [tʀɛno] *nm* sleigh, sledge
traînée [tʀene] *nf* streak, trail; (*péj*) slut
traîner [tʀene] *vt* (*remorque*) to pull; (*enfant, chien*) to drag *ou* trail along ♦ *vi* (*être en désordre*) to lie around; (*marcher*) to dawdle (along); (*vagabonder*) to hang about; (*agir lentement*) to idle about; (*durer*) to drag on; **se** ~ *vi* to drag o.s. along; ~ **les pieds** to drag one's feet
train-train [tʀɛ̃tʀɛ̃] *nm* humdrum routine
traire [tʀɛʀ] *vt* to milk
trait [tʀɛ] *nm* (*ligne*) line; (*de dessin*) stroke; (*caractéristique*) feature, trait; ~**s** *nmpl* (*du visage*) features; **d'un** ~ (*boire*) in one gulp; **de** ~ (*animal*) draught; **avoir** ~ **à** to concern; ~ **d'union** hyphen; (*fig*) link
traitant, e [tʀetɑ̃, -ɑ̃t] *adj*: **votre médecin** ~ your usual *ou* family doctor; **crème** ~**e** conditioning cream
traite [tʀet] *nf* (*COMM*) draft; (*AGR*) milking; **d'une** ~ without stopping; **la** ~ **des noirs** the slave trade
traité [tʀete] *nm* treaty
traitement [tʀetmɑ̃] *nm* treatment; processing; (*salaire*) salary; ~ **de données/texte** data/word processing
traiter [tʀete] *vt* (*gén*) to treat; (*TECH, INFORM*) to process; (*affaire*) to deal with, handle; (*qualifier*): ~ **qn d'idiot** to call sb a fool ♦ *vi* to deal; ~ **de** to deal with
traiteur [tʀetœʀ] *nm* caterer
traître, esse [tʀetʀ(ə), -tʀes] *adj* (*dangereux*) treacherous ♦ *nm* traitor
trajectoire [tʀaʒɛktwaʀ] *nf* path

trajet [tʀaʒɛ] nm journey; (itinéraire) route; (fig) path, course

trame [tʀam] nf (de tissu) weft; (fig) framework; texture

tramer [tʀame] vt to plot, hatch

tramway [tʀamwɛ] nm tram(way); tram(car) (BRIT), streetcar (US)

tranchant, e [tʀɑ̃ʃɑ̃, -ɑ̃t] adj sharp; (fig) peremptory ♦ nm (d'un couteau) cutting edge; (de la main) edge

tranche [tʀɑ̃ʃ] nf (morceau) slice; (arête) edge; (partie) section; (série) block; issue; bracket

tranché, e [tʀɑ̃ʃe] adj (couleurs) distinct, sharply contrasted; (opinions) clear-cut, definite; **tranchée** nf trench

trancher [tʀɑ̃ʃe] vt to cut, sever; (fig: résoudre) to settle ♦ vi to take a decision; ~ **avec** to contrast sharply with

tranquille [tʀɑ̃kil] adj calm, quiet; (enfant, élève) quiet; (rassuré) easy in one's mind, with one's mind at rest; **se tenir** ~ (enfant) to be quiet; **laisse-moi/laisse-ça** ~ leave me/it alone; **tranquillité** nf quietness; peace (and quiet)

transat [tʀɑ̃zat] nm deckchair

transborder [tʀɑ̃sbɔʀde] vt to tran(s)ship

trans: ~férer vt to transfer; **~fert** nm transfer; **~figurer** vt to transform; **~formation** nf transformation; (RUGBY) conversion

transformer [tʀɑ̃sfɔʀme] vt to transform, alter; (matière première, appartement, RUGBY) to convert; **~ en** to transform into; to turn into; to convert into

transfusion [tʀɑ̃sfyzjɔ̃] nf: ~ **sanguine** blood transfusion

transgresser [tʀɑ̃sgʀese] vt to contravene, disobey

transi, e [tʀɑ̃zi] adj numb (with cold), chilled to the bone

transiger [tʀɑ̃ziʒe] vi to compromise

transit [tʀɑ̃zit] nm transit; **transiter** vi to pass in transit

transitif, ive [tʀɑ̃zitif, -iv] adj transitive

transition [tʀɑ̃zisjɔ̃] nf transition; **transitoire** adj transitional; transient

translucide [tʀɑ̃slysid] adj translucent

transmetteur [tʀɑ̃smetœʀ] nm transmitter

transmettre [tʀɑ̃smɛtʀ(ə)] vt (passer): ~ **qch à qn** to pass sth on to sb; (TECH, TÉL, MÉD) to transmit; (TV, RADIO: re~) to broadcast

trans: ~mission nf transmission; **~paraître** vi to show (through); **~parence** nf transparence; **par ~parence** (regarder) against the light; (voir) showing through; **~parent, e** adj transparent; **~percer** vt to go through, pierce; **~piration** nf perspiration; **~pirer** vi to perspire; **~planter** vt (MÉD, BOT) to transplant; (personne) to uproot; **~port** nm transport; **~ports en**

commun public transport sg

transporter [tʀɑ̃spɔʀte] vt to carry, move; (COMM) to transport, convey; **transporteur** nm haulage contractor (BRIT), trucker (US)

transversal, e, aux [tʀɑ̃svɛʀsal, -o] adj transverse, cross(-); cross-country; running at right angles

trapèze [tʀapɛz] nm (au cirque) trapeze

trappe [tʀap] nf trap door

trapu, e [tʀapy] adj squat, stocky

traquenard [tʀaknaʀ] nm trap

traquer [tʀake] vt to track down; (harceler) to hound

traumatiser [tʀomatize] vt to traumatize

travail, aux [tʀavaj, -o] nm (gén) work; (tâche, métier) work no pl, job; (ÉCON, MÉD) labour; **être sans** ~ (employé) to be out of work ou unemployed; voir aussi **travaux**; ~ **(au) noir** moonlighting

travailler [tʀavaje] vi to work; (bois) to warp ♦ vt (bois, métal) to work; (objet d'art, discipline, fig: influencer) to work on; **cela le travaille** it is on his mind; ~ **à** to work on; (fig: contribuer à) to work towards; **travailleur, euse** adj hard-working ♦ nm/f worker; **travailliste** adj ≈ Labour (BRIT) cpd

travaux [tʀavo] nmpl (de réparation, agricoles etc) work sg; (sur route) roadworks pl; (de construction) building (work); ~ **des champs** farmwork sg; ~ **dirigés** (SCOL) supervised practical work sg; ~ **forcés** hard labour sg; ~ **manuels** (SCOL) handicrafts; ~ **ménagers** housework sg

travée [tʀave] nf row; (ARCHIT) bay; span

travers [tʀavɛʀ] nm fault, failing; **en** ~ **(de)** across; **au** ~ **(de)** through; **de** ~ askew ♦ adv sideways; (fig) the wrong way; **à** ~ through; **regarder de** ~ (fig) to look askance at

traverse [tʀavɛʀs(ə)] nf (de voie ferrée) sleeper; **chemin de** ~ shortcut

traversée [tʀavɛʀse] nf crossing

traverser [tʀavɛʀse] vt (gén) to cross; (ville, tunnel, aussi: percer, fig) to go through; (suj: ligne, trait) to run across

traversin [tʀavɛʀsɛ̃] nm bolster

travestir [tʀavɛstiʀ] vt (vérité) to misrepresent; **se** ~ vi to dress up; to dress as a woman

trébucher [tʀebyʃe] vi: ~ **(sur)** to stumble (over), trip (against)

trèfle [tʀɛfl(ə)] nm (BOT) clover; (CARTES: couleur) clubs pl; (: carte) club

treille [tʀɛj] nf vine arbour; climbing vine

treillis [tʀeji] nm (métallique) wire-mesh

treize [tʀɛz] num thirteen; **treizième** num thirteenth

tréma [tʀema] nm diaeresis

tremblement [tʀɑ̃bləmɑ̃] nm: ~ **de terre** earthquake

trembler [tʀãble] *vi* to tremble, shake; ~ **de** (*froid, fièvre*) to shiver ou tremble with; (*peur*) to shake ou tremble with; ~ **pour qn** to fear for sb

trémousser [tʀemuse] : **se** ~ *vi* to jig about, wriggle about

trempe [tʀãp] *nf* (*fig*): **de cette/sa** ~ of this/his calibre

trempé, e [tʀãpe] *adj* soaking (wet), drenched; (*TECH*) tempered

tremper [tʀãpe] *vt* to soak, drench; (*aussi*: **faire** ~, **mettre à** ~) to soak; (*plonger*): ~ **qch dans** to dip sth in(to) ♦ *vi* to soak; (*fig*): ~ **dans** to be involved ou have a hand in; **se** ~ *vi* to have a quick dip; **trempette** *nf*: **faire trempette** to go paddling

tremplin [tʀãplɛ̃] *nm* springboard; (*SKI*) ski-jump

trentaine [tʀãtɛn] *nf*: **une** ~ (**de**) thirty or so, about thirty; **avoir la** ~ (*âge*) to be around thirty

trente [tʀãt] *num* thirty; **trentième** *num* thirtieth

trépidant, e [tʀepidã, -ãt] *adj* (*fig*: *rythme*) pulsating; (: *vie*) hectic

trépied [tʀepje] *nm* tripod

trépigner [tʀepiɲe] *vi* to stamp (one's feet)

très [tʀɛ] *adv* very; much +*pp*, highly +*pp*

trésor [tʀezɔʀ] *nm* treasure; (*ADMIN*) finances *pl*; funds *pl*; **T~ (public)** public revenue

trésorerie [tʀezɔʀʀi] *nf* (*gestion*) accounts *pl*; (*bureaux*) accounts department; **difficultés de** ~ cash problems, shortage of cash ou funds

trésorier, ière [tʀezɔʀje, -jɛʀ] *nm/f* treasurer

tressaillir [tʀesajiʀ] *vi* to shiver, shudder; to quiver

tressauter [tʀesote] *vi* to start, jump

tresse [tʀɛs] *nf* braid, plait

tresser [tʀese] *vt* (*cheveux*) to braid, plait; (*fil, jonc*) to plait; (*corbeille*) to weave; (*corde*) to twist

tréteau, x [tʀeto] *nm* trestle

treuil [tʀœj] *nm* winch

trêve [tʀɛv] *nf* (*MIL, POL*) truce; (*fig*) respite; ~ **de ...** enough of this ...

tri [tʀi] *nm* sorting out *no pl*; selection; (*POSTES*) sorting; sorting office

triangle [tʀijãgl(ə)] *nm* triangle

tribord [tʀibɔʀ] *nm*: **à** ~ to starboard, on the starboard side

tribu [tʀiby] *nf* tribe

tribunal, aux [tʀibynal, -o] *nm* (*JUR*) court; (*MIL*) tribunal

tribune [tʀibyn] *nf* (*estrade*) platform, rostrum; (*débat*) forum; (*d'église, de tribunal*) gallery; (*de stade*) stand

tribut [tʀiby] *nm* tribute

tributaire [tʀibytɛʀ] *adj*: **être** ~ **de** to be dependent on

tricher [tʀiʃe] *vi* to cheat

tricolore [tʀikɔlɔʀ] *adj* three-coloured; (*français*) red, white and blue

tricot [tʀiko] *nm* (*technique, ouvrage*) knitting *no pl*; (*tissu*) knitted fabric; (*vêtement*) jersey, sweater

tricoter [tʀikɔte] *vt* to knit

trictrac [tʀiktʀak] *nm* backgammon

tricycle [tʀisikl(ə)] *nm* tricycle

triennal, e, aux [tʀiɛnal, -o] *adj* three-yearly; three-year

trier [tʀije] *vt* to sort out; (*POSTES, fruits*) to sort

trimestre [tʀimɛstʀ(ə)] *nm* (*SCOL*) term; (*COMM*) quarter; **trimestriel, le** *adj* quarterly; (*SCOL*) end-of-term

tringle [tʀɛ̃gl(ə)] *nf* rod

trinquer [tʀɛ̃ke] *vi* to clink glasses

triomphe [tʀijɔ̃f] *nm* triumph

triompher [tʀijɔ̃fe] *vi* to triumph, win; ~ **de** to triumph over, overcome

tripes [tʀip] *nfpl* (*CULIN*) tripe *sg*

triple [tʀipl(ə)] *adj* triple; treble ♦ *nm*: **le** ~ (**de**) (*comparaison*) three times as much (as); **en** ~ **exemplaire** in triplicate; **tripler** *vi, vt* to triple, treble

triplés, ées [tʀiple] *nm/fpl* triplets

tripoter [tʀipote] *vt* to fiddle with

trique [tʀik] *nf* cudgel

triste [tʀist(ə)] *adj* sad; (*péj*): ~ **personnage/affaire** sorry individual/affair; **tristesse** *nf* sadness

trivial, e, aux [tʀivjal, -o] *adj* coarse, crude; (*commun*) mundane

troc [tʀɔk] *nm* barter

trognon [tʀɔɲɔ̃] *nm* (*de fruit*) core; (*de légume*) stalk

trois [tʀwa] *num* three; **troisième** *num* third; **trois quarts** *nmpl*: **les trois quarts de** three-quarters of

trombe [tʀɔ̃b] *nf*: **des** ~s **d'eau** a downpour; **en** ~ like a whirlwind

trombone [tʀɔ̃bɔn] *nm* (*MUS*) trombone; (*de bureau*) paper clip

trompe [tʀɔ̃p] *nf* (*d'éléphant*) trunk; (*MUS*) trumpet, horn

tromper [tʀɔ̃pe] *vt* to deceive; (*vigilance, poursuivants*) to elude; **se** ~ *vi* to make a mistake, be mistaken; **se** ~ **de voiture/jour** to take the wrong car/get the day wrong; **se** ~ **de 3 cm/20 F** to be out by 3 cm/20 F; ~**ie** *nf* deception, trickery *no pl*

trompette [tʀɔ̃pɛt] *nf* trumpet; **en** ~ (*nez*) turned-up

tronc [tʀɔ̃] *nm* (*BOT, ANAT*) trunk; (*d'église*) collection box

tronçon [tʀɔ̃sɔ̃] *nm* section

tronçonner [tʀɔ̃sɔne] *vt* to saw up

trône [tʀon] *nm* throne

trop [tʀo] *adv* (+*vb*) too much; (+*adjectif, adverbe*) too; ~ (**nombreux**) too many; ~

peu (nombreux) too few; ~ **(souvent)** too often; ~ **(longtemps)** (for) too long; ~ **de** (*nombre*) too many; (*quantité*) too much; **de** ~, **en** ~: **des livres en** ~ a few books too many; **du lait en** ~ too much milk; **3 livres/3 F de** ~ 3 books too many/3 F too much

tropical, e, aux [tʀɔpikal, -o] *adj* tropical

tropique [tʀɔpik] *nm* tropic

trop-plein [tʀɔplɛ̃] *nm* (*tuyau*) overflow *ou* outlet (pipe); (*liquide*) overflow

troquer [tʀɔke] *vt*: ~ **qch contre** to barter *ou* trade sth for; (*fig*) to swap sth for

trot [tʀo] *nm* trot; ~**ter** [tʀɔte] *vi* to trot; (*fig*) to scamper along (*ou* about)

trottiner [tʀɔtine] *vi* (*fig*) to scamper along (*ou* about); **trottinette** [tʀɔtinet] *nf* (child's) scooter

trottoir [tʀɔtwaʀ] *nm* pavement; **faire le** ~ (*péj*) to walk the streets; ~ **roulant** moving walkway, travellator

trou [tʀu] *nm* hole; (*fig*) gap; (*COMM*) deficit; ~ **d'air** air pocket; ~ **d'ozone** ozone hole; **le** ~ **de la serrure** the keyhole; ~ **de mémoire** blank, lapse of memory

trouble [tʀubl(ə)] *adj* (*liquide*) cloudy; (*image, mémoire*) indistinct, hazy; (*affaire*) shady, murky ♦ *nm* (*désarroi*) agitation; (*embarras*) confusion; (*zizanie*) unrest, discord; ~**s** *nmpl* (*POL*) disturbances, troubles, unrest *sg*; (*MÉD*) trouble *sg*, disorders

troubler [tʀuble] *vt* (*embarrasser*) to confuse, disconcert; (*émouvoir*) to agitate; to disturb; (*perturber: ordre etc*) to disrupt; (*liquide*) to make cloudy; **se** ~ *vi* (*personne*) to become flustered *ou* confused

trouée [tʀue] *nf* gap; (*MIL*) breach

trouer [tʀue] *vt* to make a hole (*ou* holes) in; (*fig*) to pierce

trouille [tʀuj] (*fam*) *nf*: **avoir la** ~ to be scared to death

troupe [tʀup] *nf* troop; ~ **(de théâtre)** (theatrical) company

troupeau, x [tʀupo] *nm* (*de moutons*) flock; (*de vaches*) herd

trousse [tʀus] *nf* case, kit; (*d'écolier*) pencil case; (*de docteur*) instrument case; **aux** ~**s de** (*fig*) on the heels *ou* tail of; ~ **à outils** toolkit; ~ **de toilette** toilet bag

trousseau, x [tʀuso] *nm* (*de mariée*) trousseau; ~ **de clefs** bunch of keys

trouvaille [tʀuvaj] *nf* find

trouver [tʀuve] *vt* to find; (*rendre visite*): **aller/venir** ~ **qn** to go/come and see sb; **se** ~ *vi* (*être*) to be; (*être soudain*) to be suddenly; **il se trouve que** it happens that, it turns out that; **se** ~ **bien** to feel well; **se** ~ **mal** to pass out; **je trouve que** I find *ou* think that; ~ **à boire/critiquer** to find something to drink/criticize

truand [tʀyɑ̃] *nm* villain, crook

truander [tʀyɑ̃de] *vt* to cheat

truc [tʀyk] *nm* (*astuce*) way, device; (*de cinéma, prestidigitateur*) trick effect; (*chose*) thing, thingumajig; **avoir le** ~ to have the knack

truchement [tʀyʃmɑ̃] *nm*: **par le** ~ **de qn** through (the intervention of) sb

truelle [tʀyɛl] *nf* trowel

truffe [tʀyf] *nf* truffle; (*nez*) nose

truffé, e [tʀyfe] *adj*: ~ **de** (*fig*) peppered with; bristling with

truie [tʀɥi] *nf* sow

truite [tʀɥit] *nf* trout *inv*

truquer [tʀyke] *vt* (*élections, serrure, dés*) to fix; (*CINÉMA*) to use special effects in

T.S.V.P. *sigle* (= *tournez s.v.p.*) P.T.O.

T.T.C. *sigle* = **toutes taxes comprises**

tu[1] [ty] *pron* you

tu[2]**, e** [ty] *pp de* **taire**

tuba [tyba] *nm* (*MUS*) tuba; (*SPORT*) snorkel

tube [tyb] *nm* tube; pipe; (*chanson, disque*) hit song *ou* record

tuer [tɥe] *vt* to kill; **se** ~ *vi* to be killed; (*suicide*) to kill o.s.; **tuerie** *nf* slaughter *no pl*

tue-tête [tytɛt] : **à** ~ *adv* at the top of one's voice

tueur [tɥœʀ] *nm* killer; ~ **à gages** hired killer

tuile [tɥil] *nf* tile; (*fam*) spot of bad luck, blow

tulipe [tylip] *nf* tulip

tuméfié, e [tymefje] *adj* puffy, swollen

tumeur [tymœʀ] *nf* growth, tumour

tumulte [tymylt(ə)] *nm* commotion

tumultueux, euse [tymyltɥø, -øz] *adj* stormy, turbulent

tunique [tynik] *nf* tunic

Tunisie [tynizi] *nf*: **la** ~ Tunisia; **tunisien, ne** *adj, nm/f* Tunisian

tunnel [tynɛl] *nm* tunnel

turbulences [tyʀbylɑ̃s] *nfpl* (*AVIAT*) turbulence *sg*

turbulent, e [tyʀbylɑ̃, -ɑ̃t] *adj* boisterous, unruly

turc, turque [tyʀk(ə)] *adj* Turkish ♦ *nm/f*: **T**~, **Turque** Turk/Turkish woman ♦ *nm* (*LING*) Turkish

turf [tyʀf] *nm* racing; **turfiste** *nm/f* racegoer

Turquie [tyʀki] *nf*: **la** ~ Turkey

turquoise [tyʀkwaz] *nf* turquoise ♦ *adj inv* turquoise

tus etc *vb voir* **taire**

tutelle [tytɛl] *nf* (*JUR*) guardianship; (*POL*) trusteeship; **sous la** ~ **de** (*fig*) under the supervision of

tuteur [tytœʀ] *nm* (*JUR*) guardian; (*de plante*) stake, support

tutoyer [tytwaje] *vt*: ~ **qn** to address sb as "tu"

tuyau, x [tɥijo] *nm* pipe; (*flexible*) tube; (*fam*) tip; *gen no pl*; ~ **d'arrosage** hosepipe; ~ **d'échappement** exhaust pipe; **~te-rie** nf piping no pl

T.V.A. sigle f (= taxe à la valeur ajoutée) VAT

tympan [tɛ̃pɑ̃] nm (ANAT) eardrum

type [tip] nm type; (fam) chap, guy ♦ adj typical, standard

typé, e [tipe] adj ethnic

typhoïde [tifɔid] nf typhoid

typique [tipik] adj typical

tyran [tiʀɑ̃] nm tyrant

tzigane [dzigan] adj gypsy ♦ nm/f gypsy

U u

ulcère [ylsɛʀ] nm ulcer; **ulcérer** [ylseʀe] vt (fig) to sicken, appal

ultérieur, e [ylteʀjœʀ] adj later, subsequent; **remis à une date ~e** postponed to a later date

ultime [yltim] adj final

ultra... [yltʀa] préfixe: **ultramoderne/-rapide** ultra-modern/-fast

───── MOT CLÉ ─────

un, une [œ̃, yn] art indéf a; (devant voyelle) an; ~ **garçon/vieillard** a boy/an old man; **une fille** a girl
♦ pron one; **l'~ des meilleurs** one of the best; **l'~ ..., l'autre** (the) one ..., the other; **les ~s ..., les autres** some ..., others; **l'~ et l'autre** both (of them); **l'~ ou l'autre** either (of them); **l'~ l'autre, les ~s les autres** each other, one another; **pas ~ seul** not a single one; ~ **par ~** one by one
♦ num one; **une pomme seulement** one apple only

─────────────────

unanime [ynanim] adj unanimous; **unanimité** nf: **à l'unanimité** unanimously

uni, e [yni] adj (ton, tissu) plain; (surface) smooth, even; (famille) close(-knit); (pays) united

unifier [ynifje] vt to unite, unify

uniforme [ynifɔʀm(ə)] adj (mouvement) regular, uniform; (surface, ton) even; (objets, maisons) uniform ♦ nm uniform; **uniformiser** vt to make uniform; (systèmes) to standardize

union [ynjɔ̃] nf union; ~ **de consommateurs** consumers' association; **l'U~ soviétique** the Soviet Union

unique [ynik] adj (seul) only; (le même): **un**

prix/système ~ a single price/system; (exceptionnel) unique; **fils/fille** ~ only son/daughter, only child; **uniquement** adv only, solely; (juste) only, merely

unir [yniʀ] vt (nations) to unite; (éléments, couleurs) to combine; (en mariage) to unite, join together; **s'~** to unite; (en mariage) to be joined together; ~ **qch à** to unite sth with; to combine sth with

unité [ynite] nf (harmonie, cohésion) unity; (COMM, MIL, de mesure, MATH) unit

univers [ynivɛʀ] nm universe

universel, le [ynivɛʀsɛl] adj universal; (esprit) all-embracing

universitaire [ynivɛʀsitɛʀ] adj university cpd; (diplôme, études) academic, university cpd ♦ nm/f academic

université [ynivɛʀsite] nf university

urbain, e [yʀbɛ̃, -ɛn] adj urban, city cpd, town cpd; (poli) urbane; **urbanisme** nm town planning

urgence [yʀʒɑ̃s] nf urgency; (MÉD etc) emergency; **d'~** emergency cpd ♦ adv as a matter of urgency

urgent, e [yʀʒɑ̃, -ɑ̃t] adj urgent

urine [yʀin] nf urine; **urinoir** [yʀinwaʀ] nm (public) urinal

urne [yʀn(ə)] nf (électorale) ballot box; (vase) urn

urticaire [yʀtikɛʀ] nf nettle rash

us [ys] nmpl: ~ **et coutumes** (habits and) customs

USA sigle mpl: **les** ~ the USA

usage [yzaʒ] nm (emploi, utilisation) use; (coutume) custom; (LING): **l'~** usage; **à l'~ de** (pour) for (use of); **en** ~ in use; **hors d'~** out of service; wrecked; **à ~ interne** to be taken; **à ~ externe** for external use only; **usagé, e** [yzaʒe] adj (usé) worn; (d'occasion) used; **usager, ère** [yzaʒe, -ɛʀ] nm/f user

usé, e [yze] adj worn; (banal) hackneyed

user [yze] vt (outil) to wear down; (vêtement) to wear out; (matière) to wear away; (consommer: charbon etc) to use; **s'~** vi to wear; to wear out; (fig) to decline; ~ **de** (moyen, procédé) to use, employ; (droit) to exercise

usine [yzin] nf factory; ~ **marémotrice** tidal power station

usité, e [yzite] adj common

ustensile [ystɑ̃sil] nm implement; ~ **de cuisine** kitchen utensil

usuel, le [yzɥɛl] adj everyday, common

usure [yzyʀ] nf wear; worn state

ut [yt] nm (MUS) C

utérus [yteʀys] nm uterus, womb

utile [ytil] adj useful

utilisation [ytilizasjɔ̃] nf use

utiliser [ytilize] vt to use

utilitaire [ytilitɛʀ] adj utilitarian; (objets) practical

utilité [ytilite] *nf* usefulness *no pl*; use; **re-connu d'~ publique** state-approved

va *vb voir* **aller**

vacance [vakɑ̃s] *nf* (ADMIN) vacancy; **~s** *nfpl* holiday(s *pl*), vacation *sg*; **prendre des/ses ~s** to take a holiday/one's holiday(s); **aller en ~s** to go on holiday; **vacancier, ière** *nm/f* holiday-maker

vacant, e [vakɑ̃, -ɑ̃t] *adj* vacant

vacarme [vakaʀm(ə)] *nm* row, din

vaccin [vaksɛ̃] *nm* vaccine; (*opération*) vaccination; **vaccination** *nf* vaccination; **vacciner** *vt* to vaccinate; (*fig*) to make immune

vache [vaʃ] *nf* (ZOOL) cow; (*cuir*) cowhide ♦ *adj* (*fam*) rotten, mean; **~ment** (*fam*) *adv* damned, hellish

vaciller [vasije] *vi* to sway, wobble; (*bougie, lumière*) to flicker; (*fig*) to be failing, falter

va-et-vient [vaevjɛ̃] *nm inv* (*de personnes, véhicules*) comings and goings *pl*, to-ings and fro-ings *pl*

vagabond [vagabɔ̃] *nm* (*rôdeur*) tramp, vagrant; (*voyageur*) wanderer; **~er** [vagabɔ̃de] *vi* to roam, wander

vagin [vaʒɛ̃] *nm* vagina

vague [vag] *nf* wave ♦ *adj* vague; (*regard*) faraway; (*manteau, robe*) loose(-fitting); (*quelconque*): **un ~ bureau/cousin** some office/cousin or other; **~ de fond** ground swell

vaillant, e [vajɑ̃, -ɑ̃t] *adj* (*courageux*) gallant; (*robuste*) hale and hearty

vaille *vb voir* **valoir**

vain, e [vɛ̃, vɛn] *adj* vain; **en ~** in vain

vaincre [vɛ̃kʀ(ə)] *vt* to defeat; (*fig*) to conquer, overcome; **vaincu, e** *nm/f* defeated party; **vainqueur** *nm* victor; (SPORT) winner

vais *vb voir* **aller**

vaisseau, x [vɛso] *nm* (ANAT) vessel; (NAVIG) ship, vessel; **~ spatial** spaceship

vaisselier [vɛselje] *nm* dresser

vaisselle [vɛsɛl] *nf* (*service*) crockery; (*plats etc à laver*) (dirty) dishes *pl*; (*lavage*) washing-up; **faire la ~** to do the dishes *pl*

val [val] (*pl* **vaux** *ou* **~s**) *nm* valley

valable [valabl(ə)] *adj* valid; (*acceptable*) decent, worthwhile

valent *etc vb voir* **valoir**

valet [valɛ] *nm* valet; (CARTES) jack

valeur [valœʀ] *nf* (*gén*) value; (*mérite*) worth, merit; (COMM: *titre*) security; **mettre en ~** (*terrain, région*) to develop; (*fig*) to highlight; to show off to advantage; **avoir de la ~** to be valuable; **sans ~** worthless; **prendre de la ~** to go up *ou* gain in value

valide [valid] *adj* (*en bonne santé*) fit; (*valable*) valid; **valider** *vt* to validate

valions *vb voir* **valoir**

valise [valiz] *nf* (*suit*)case

vallée [vale] *nf* valley

vallon [valɔ̃] *nm* small valley

valoir [valwaʀ] *vi* (*être valable*) to hold, apply ♦ *vt* (*prix, valeur, effort*) to be worth; (*causer*): **~ qch à qn** to earn sb sth; **se ~** *vi* to be of equal merit; (*péj*) to be two of a kind; **faire ~** (*droits, prérogatives*) to assert; **faire ~ que** to point out that; **à ~ sur** to be deducted from; **vaille que vaille** somehow or other; **cela ne me dit rien qui vaille** I don't like the look of it at all; **ce climat ne me vaut rien** this climate doesn't suit me; **~ la peine** to be worth the trouble *ou* worth it; **~ mieux: il vaut mieux se taire** it's better to say nothing; **ça ne vaut rien** it's worthless; **que vaut ce candidat?** how good is this applicant?

valoriser [valɔʀize] *vt* (ÉCON) to develop (the economy of); (PSYCH) to increase the standing of

valse [vals(ə)] *nf* waltz

valu, e [valy] *pp de* **valoir**

vandalisme [vɑ̃dalism(ə)] *nm* vandalism

vanille [vanij] *nf* vanilla

vanité [vanite] *nf* vanity; **vaniteux, euse** *adj* vain, conceited

vanne [van] *nf* gate; (*fig*) joke

vannerie [vanʀi] *nf* basketwork

vantard, e [vɑ̃taʀ, -aʀd(ə)] *adj* boastful

vanter [vɑ̃te] *vt* to speak highly of, vaunt; **se ~** *vi* to boast, brag; **se ~ de** to pride o.s. on; (*péj*) to boast of

vapeur [vapœʀ] *nf* steam; (*émanation*) vapour, fumes *pl*; **~s** *nfpl* (*bouffées*) vapours; **à ~** steam-powered, steam *cpd*; **cuit à la ~** steamed

vaporeux, euse [vapɔʀø, -øz] *adj* (*flou*) hazy, misty; (*léger*) filmy

vaporisateur [vapɔʀizatœʀ] *nm* spray; **vaporiser** [vapɔʀize] *vt* (*parfum etc*) to spray

varappe [vaʀap] *nf* rock climbing

vareuse [vaʀøz] *nf* (*blouson*) pea jacket; (*d'uniforme*) tunic

variable [vaʀjabl(ə)] *adj* variable; (*temps, humeur*) changeable; (*divers: résultats*) varied, various

varice [vaʀis] *nf* varicose vein

varicelle [vaʀisɛl] *nf* chickenpox

varié, e [vaʀje] *adj* varied; (*divers*) various

varier [vaʀje] *vi* to vary; (*temps, humeur*) to change ♦ *vt* to vary

variété [vaʀjete] *nf* variety; **~s** *nfpl*: **spectacle/émission de ~s** variety show
variole [vaʀjɔl] *nf* smallpox
vas *vb voir* **aller**
vase [vaz] *nm* vase ♦ *nf* silt, mud
vaseux, euse [vazø, -øz] *adj* silty, muddy; *(fig: confus)* woolly, hazy; *(: fatigué)* peaky; woozy
vasistas [vazistas] *nm* fanlight
vaste [vast(ə)] *adj* vast, immense
vaudrai *etc vb voir* **valoir**
vaurien, ne [voʀjɛ̃, -ɛn] *nm/f* good-for-nothing, guttersnipe
vaut *vb voir* **valoir**
vautour [votuʀ] *nm* vulture
vautrer [votʀe]: **se ~** *vi*: **se ~ dans/sur** to wallow in/sprawl on
vaux [vo] *nmpl de* **val** ♦ *vb voir* **valoir**
va-vite [vavit]: **à la ~** *adv* in a rush *ou* hurry
veau, x [vo] *nm (ZOOL)* calf; *(CULIN)* veal; *(peau)* calfskin
vécu, e [veky] *pp de* **vivre**
vedette [vədɛt] *nf (artiste etc)* star; *(canot)* patrol boat; launch
végétal, e, aux [veʒetal, -o] *adj* vegetable ♦ *nm* vegetable, plant
végétarien, ne [veʒetaʀjɛ̃, -ɛn] *adj, nm/f* vegetarian
végétation [veʒetasjɔ̃] *nf* vegetation; **~s** *nfpl (MÉD)* adenoids
véhicule [veikyl] *nm* vehicle; **~ utilitaire** commercial vehicle
veille [vɛj] *nf (garde)* watch; *(PSYCH)* wakefulness; *(jour)*: **la ~ (de)** the day before; **la ~ au soir** the previous evening; **à la ~ de** on the eve of
veillée [veje] *nf (soirée)* evening; *(réunion)* evening gathering; **~ (mortuaire)** watch
veiller [veje] *vi* to stay up; to be awake; to be on watch ♦ *vt (malade, mort)* to watch over, sit up with; **~ à** to attend to, to see to; **~ à ce que** to make sure that; **~ sur** to keep a watch on
veilleur [vɛjœʀ] *nm*: **~de nuit** night watchman
veilleuse [vɛjøz] *nf (lampe)* night light; *(AUTO)* sidelight; *(flamme)* pilot light; **en ~** *(lampe)* dimmed
veine [vɛn] *nf (ANAT, du bois etc)* vein; *(filon)* vein, seam; *(fam: chance)*: **avoir de la ~** to be lucky
véliplanchiste [veliplɑ̃ʃist(ə)] *nm/f* windsurfer
velléités [veleite] *nfpl* vague impulses
vélo [velo] *nm* bike, cycle; **faire du ~** to go cycling; **~ tout-terrain** mountain bike
vélomoteur [velɔmɔtœʀ] *nm* moped
velours [vəluʀ] *nm* velvet; **~ côtelé** corduroy
velouté, e [vəlute] *adj (au toucher)* velvety; *(à la vue)* soft, mellow; *(au goût)* smooth,

mellow
velu, e [vəly] *adj* hairy
venais *etc vb voir* **venir**
venaison [vənɛzɔ̃] *nf* venison
vendange [vɑ̃dɑ̃ʒ] *nf (opération, période: aussi: ~s)* grape harvest; *(raisins)* grape crop, grapes *pl*; **~r** [vɑ̃dɑ̃ʒe] *vi* to harvest the grapes
vendeur, euse [vɑ̃dœʀ, -øz] *nm/f (de magasin)* shop assistant; *(COMM)* salesman(woman) ♦ *nm (JUR)* vendor, seller; **~ de journaux** newspaper seller
vendre [vɑ̃dʀ(ə)] *vt* to sell; **~ qch à qn** to sell sb sth; **"à ~"** "for sale"
vendredi [vɑ̃dʀədi] *nm* Friday; **V~ saint** Good Friday
vendu, e [vɑ̃dy] *adj (péj: corrompu)* corrupt
vénéneux, euse [venenø, -øz] *adj* poisonous
vénérien, ne [veneʀjɛ̃, -ɛn] *adj* venereal
vengeance [vɑ̃ʒɑ̃s] *nf* vengeance *no pl*, revenge *no pl*
venger [vɑ̃ʒe] *vt* to avenge; **se ~** *vi* to avenge o.s., **se ~ de qch** to avenge o.s. for sth; to take one's revenge for sth; **se ~ de qn** to take revenge on sb; **se ~ sur** to take revenge on; to take it out on
venimeux, euse [vənimø, -øz] *adj* poisonous, venomous; *(fig: haineux)* venomous, vicious
venin [vənɛ̃] *nm* venom, poison
venir [vəniʀ] *vi* to come; **~ de** to come from; **~ de faire: je viens d'y aller/de le voir** I've just been there/seen him; **s'il vient à pleuvoir** if it should rain; **j'en viens à croire que** I have come to believe that; **faire ~** *(docteur, plombier)* to call (out)
vent [vɑ̃] *nm* wind; **il y a du ~** it's windy; **c'est du ~** it's all hot air; **au ~** to windward; **sous le ~** to leeward; **avoir le ~ debout/arrière** to head into the wind/have the wind astern; **dans le ~** *(fam)* trendy
vente [vɑ̃t] *nf* sale; **la ~** *(activité)* selling; *(secteur)* sales *pl*; **mettre en ~** to put on sale; *(objets personnels)* to put up for sale; **~ aux enchères** auction sale; **~ de charité** jumble sale
venteux, euse [vɑ̃tø, -øz] *adj* windy
ventilateur [vɑ̃tilatœʀ] *nm* fan
ventiler [vɑ̃tile] *vt* to ventilate; *(total, statistiques)* to break down
ventouse [vɑ̃tuz] *nf (de caoutchouc)* suction pad; *(ZOOL)* sucker
ventre [vɑ̃tʀ(ə)] *nm (ANAT)* stomach; *(fig)* belly; **avoir mal au ~** to have stomach ache *(BRIT) ou* a stomach ache *(US)*
ventriloque [vɑ̃tʀilɔk] *nm/f* ventriloquist
venu, e [vəny] *pp de* **venir** ♦ *adj*: **être mal ~ à ou de faire** to have no grounds for doing, be in no position to do
ver [vɛʀ] *nm* worm; *(des fruits etc)* maggot; *(du bois)* woodworm *no pl*; *voir aussi* **vers**;

~ **à soie** silkworm; ~ **de terre** earthworm; ~ **luisant** glow-worm; ~ **solitaire** tapeworm

verbaliser [vɛʀbalize] vi (POLICE) to book ou report an offender

verbe [vɛʀb(ə)] nm verb

verdeur [vɛʀdœʀ] nf (vigueur) vigour, vitality; (crudité) forthrightness

verdict [vɛʀdik(t)] nm verdict

verdir [vɛʀdiʀ] vi, vt to turn green

verdure [vɛʀdyʀ] nf greenery

véreux, euse [veʀø, -øz] adj worm-eaten; (malhonnête) shady, corrupt

verge [vɛʀʒ(ə)] nf (ANAT) penis; (baguette) stick, cane

verger [vɛʀʒe] nm orchard

verglacé, e [vɛʀglase] adj icy, iced-over

verglas [vɛʀgla] nm (black) ice

vergogne [vɛʀgɔɲ]: **sans** ~ adv shamelessly

véridique [veʀidik] adj truthful

vérification [veʀifikɑsjɔ̃] nf checking no pl, check

vérifier [veʀifje] vt to check; (corroborer) to confirm, bear out

véritable [veʀitabl(ə)] adj real; (ami, amour) true

vérité [veʀite] nf truth; (d'un portrait romanesque) lifelikeness; (sincérité) truthfulness, sincerity

vermeil, le [vɛʀmɛj] adj ruby red

vermine [vɛʀmin] nf vermin pl

vermoulu, e [vɛʀmuly] adj worm-eaten, with woodworm

verni, e [vɛʀni] adj (fam) lucky; **cuir** ~ patent leather

vernir [vɛʀniʀ] vt (bois, tableau, ongles) to varnish; (poterie) to glaze

vernis [vɛʀni] nm (enduit) varnish; glaze; (fig) veneer; ~ **à ongles** nail polish ou varnish; ~**sage** [vɛʀnisaʒ] nm varnishing; glazing; (d'une exposition) preview

vérole [veʀɔl] nf (variole) smallpox

verrai etc vb voir **voir**

verre [vɛʀ] nm glass; (de lunettes) lens sg; **boire** ou **prendre un** ~ to have a drink; ~**s de contact** contact lenses; **verrerie** [vɛʀi] nf (fabrique) glassworks sg; (activité) glass-making; (objets) glassware; **verrière** [vɛʀjɛʀ] nf (grand vitrage) window; (toit vitré) glass roof

verrons etc vb voir **voir**

verrou [veʀu] nm (targette) bolt; (fig) constriction; **mettre qn sous les** ~**s** to put sb behind bars; **verrouillage** nm locking; **verrouiller** vt to bolt; to lock

verrue [veʀy] nf wart

vers [vɛʀ] nm line ♦ nmpl (poésie) verse sg ♦ prép (en direction de) toward(s); (près de) around (about); (temporel) about, around

versant [vɛʀsɑ̃] nm slopes pl, side

versatile [vɛʀsatil] adj fickle, changeable

verse [vɛʀs(ə)]: **à** ~ adv: **il pleut à** ~ it's pouring (with rain)

Verseau [vɛʀso] nm: **le** ~ Aquarius

versement [vɛʀsəmɑ̃] nm payment; **en 3** ~**s** in 3 instalments

verser [vɛʀse] vt (liquide, grains) to pour; (larmes, sang) to shed; (argent) to pay ♦ vi (véhicule) to overturn; (fig): ~ **dans** to lapse into

verset [vɛʀse] nm verse

version [vɛʀsjɔ̃] nf version; (SCOL) translation (into the mother tongue)

verso [vɛʀso] nm back; **voir au** ~ see over(leaf)

vert, e [vɛʀ, vɛʀt(ə)] adj green; (vin) young; (vigoureux) sprightly; (cru) forthright ♦ nm green

vertèbre [vɛʀtɛbʀ(ə)] nf vertebra

vertement [vɛʀtəmɑ̃] adv (réprimander) sharply

vertical, e, aux [vɛʀtikal, -o] adj vertical; ~**e** nf vertical; **à la** ~**e** vertically; ~**ement** adv vertically

vertige [vɛʀtiʒ] nm (peur du vide) vertigo; (étourdissement) dizzy spell; (fig) fever; **vertigineux, euse** adj breathtaking

vertu [vɛʀty] nf virtue; **en** ~ **de** in accordance with; **vertueux, euse** adj virtuous

verve [vɛʀv(ə)] nf witty eloquence; **être en** ~ to be in brilliant form

verveine [vɛʀvɛn] nf (BOT) verbena, vervain; (infusion) verbena tea

vésicule [vezikyl] nf vesicle; ~ **biliaire** gall-bladder

vessie [vesi] nf bladder

veste [vɛst(ə)] nf jacket; ~ **droite/croisée** single-/double-breasted jacket

vestiaire [vɛstjɛʀ] nm (au théâtre etc) cloakroom; (de stade etc) changing-room (BRIT), locker-room (US)

vestibule [vɛstibyl] nm hall

vestige [vɛstiʒ] nm relic; (fig) vestige; ~**s** nmpl remains

vestimentaire [vɛstimɑ̃tɛʀ] adj (détail) of dress; (élégance) sartorial; **dépenses** ~**s** spending on clothes

veston [vɛstɔ̃] nm jacket

vêtement [vɛtmɑ̃] nm garment, item of clothing; ~**s** nmpl clothes

vétérinaire [veteʀinɛʀ] nm/f vet, veterinary surgeon

vêtir [vetiʀ] vt to clothe, dress

veto [veto] nm veto; **opposer un** ~ **à** to veto

vêtu, e [vety] pp de **vêtir**

vétuste [vetyst(ə)] adj ancient, timeworn

veuf, veuve [vœf, vœv] adj widowed ♦ nm widower

veuille etc vb voir **vouloir**

veuillez vb voir **vouloir**

veule [vøl] adj spineless

veuve [vœv] nf widow

veux vb voir **vouloir**
vexations [vɛksɑsjɔ̃] nfpl humiliations
vexer [vɛkse] vt to hurt, upset; **se ~** vi to be hurt, get upset
viabiliser [vjabilize] vt to provide with services (water etc)
viable [vjabl(ə)] adj viable; (économie, industrie etc) sustainable
viager, ère [vjaʒe, -ɛʀ] adj: **rente viagère** life annuity
viande [vjɑ̃d] nf meat
vibrer [vibʀe] vi to vibrate; (son, voix) to be vibrant; (fig) to be stirred; **faire ~** to (cause to) vibrate; to stir, thrill
vice [vis] nm vice; (défaut) fault ♦ préfixe: **~ ...** vice-; **~ de forme** legal flaw ou irregularity
vichy [viʃi] nm (toile) gingham
vicié, e [visje] adj (air) polluted, tainted; (JUR) invalidated
vicieux, euse [visjø, -øz] adj (pervers) dirty(-minded); nasty; (fautif) incorrect, wrong
vicinal, e, aux [visinal, -o] adj: **chemin ~** by-road, byway
victime [viktim] nf victim; (d'accident) casualty
victoire [viktwaʀ] nf victory
victuailles [viktɥaj] nfpl provisions
vidange [vidɑ̃ʒ] nf (d'un fossé, réservoir) emptying; (AUTO) oil change; (de lavabo: bonde) waste outlet; **~s** nfpl (matières) sewage sg; **vidanger** vt to empty
vide [vid] adj empty ♦ nm (PHYSIQUE) vacuum; (espace) (empty) space, gap; (futilité, néant) void; **avoir peur du ~** to be afraid of heights; **emballé sous ~** vacuum packed; **à ~** (sans occupants) empty; (sans charge) unladen
vidéo [video] nf video ♦ adj: **cassette ~** video cassette
vide-ordures [vidɔʀdyʀ] nm inv (rubbish) chute
vide-poches [vidpɔʃ] nm inv tidy; (AUTO) glove compartment
vider [vide] vt to empty; (CULIN: volaille, poisson) to gut, clean out; **se ~** vi to empty; **~ les lieux** to quit ou vacate the premises; **videur** nm (de boîte de nuit) bouncer
vie [vi] nf life; **être en ~** to be alive; **sans ~** lifeless; **à ~** for life
vieil [vjɛj] adj m voir **vieux**
vieillard [vjɛjaʀ] nm old man; **les ~s** old people, the elderly
vieille [vjɛj] adj, nf voir **vieux**
vieilleries [vjɛjʀi] nfpl old things
vieillesse [vjɛjɛs] nf old age
vieillir [vjejiʀ] vi (prendre de l'âge) to grow old; (population, vin) to age; (doctrine, auteur) to become dated ♦ vt to age; **vieillissement** nm growing old; ageing

Vienne [vjɛn] nf Vienna
viens vb voir **venir**
vierge [vjɛʀʒ(ə)] adj virgin; (page) clean, blank ♦ nf virgin; (signe): **la V~** Virgo; **~ de** (sans) free from, unsullied by
Vietnam [vjetnam] nm = **Viêt-nam**
Viêt-nam [vjetnam] nm Vietnam
vietnamien, ne [vjetnamjɛ̃, -jɛn] adj, nm/f Vietnamese
vieux(vieil), vieille [vjø, vjɛj] adj old ♦ nm/f old man(woman) ♦ nmpl: **mon vieux/ma vieille** (fam) old man/girl; **prendre un coup de vieux** to put years on; **vieux garçon** bachelor; **vieux jeu** adj inv old-fashioned
vif, vive [vif, viv] adj (animé) lively; (alerte, brusque, aigu) sharp; (lumière, couleur) brilliant; (air) crisp; (vent, émotion) keen; (fort: regret, déception) great, deep; (vivant): **brûlé ~** burnt alive; **de vive voix** personally; **piquer qn au ~** to cut sb to the quick; **à ~** (plaie) open; **avoir les nerfs à ~** to be on edge
vigie [viʒi] nf look-out; look-out post
vigne [viɲ] nf (plante) vine; (plantation) vineyard
vigneron [viɲʀɔ̃] nm wine grower
vignette [viɲɛt] nf (motif) vignette; (de marque) manufacturer's label ou seal; (ADMIN) ≈ (road) tax disc (BRIT), ≈ license plate sticker (US); price label (used for reimbursement)
vignoble [viɲɔbl(ə)] nm (plantation) vineyard; (vignes d'une région) vineyards pl
vigoureux, euse [viguʀø, -øz] adj vigorous, robust
vigueur [vigœʀ] nf vigour; **entrer en ~** to come into force; **en ~** current
vil, e [vil] adj vile, base; **à ~ prix** at a very low price
vilain, e [vilɛ̃, -ɛn] adj (laid) ugly; (affaire, blessure) nasty; (pas sage: enfant) naughty
villa [vila] nf (detached) house; **~ en multipropriété** time-share villa
village [vilaʒ] nm village; **villageois, e** adj village cpd ♦ nm/f villager
ville [vil] nf town; (importante) city; (administration): **la ~** ≈ the Corporation; ≈ the (town) council
villégiature [vileʒjatyʀ] nf holiday; (holiday) resort
vin [vɛ̃] nm wine; **avoir le ~ gai** to get happy after a few drinks; **~ d'honneur** reception (with wine and snacks); **~ de pays** local wine; **~ ordinaire** table wine
vinaigre [vinɛgʀ(ə)] nm vinegar; **vinaigrette** nf vinaigrette, French dressing
vindicatif, ive [vɛ̃dikatif, -iv] adj vindictive
vineux, euse [vinø, -øz] adj win(e)y
vingt [vɛ̃, vɛ̃t] num twenty; **~aine** nf: **une ~aine (de)** about twenty, twenty or so; **~ième** num twentieth

vinicole [vinikɔl] *adj* wine *cpd*, wine-growing

vins *etc vb voir* **venir**

vinyle [vinil] *nm* vinyl

viol [vjɔl] *nm* (*d'une femme*) rape; (*d'un lieu sacré*) violation

violacé, e [vjɔlase] *adj* purplish, mauvish

violemment [vjɔlamã] *adv* violently

violence [vjɔlɑ̃s] *nf* violence

violent, e [vjɔlɑ̃, -ɑ̃t] *adj* violent; (*remède*) drastic

violer [vjɔle] *vt* (*femme*) to rape; (*sépulture, loi, traité*) to violate

violet, te [vjɔlɛ, -ɛt] *adj, nm* purple, mauve; **violette** *nf* (*fleur*) violet

violon [vjɔlɔ̃] *nm* violin; (*fam: prison*) lock-up

violoncelle [vjɔlɔ̃sɛl] *nm* cello

violoniste [vjɔlɔnist(ə)] *nm/f* violinist

vipère [vipɛʀ] *nf* viper, adder

virage [viʀaʒ] *nm* (*d'un véhicule*) turn; (*d'une route, piste*) bend; (*fig: POL*) about-turn

virée [viʀe] *nf* (*courte*) run; (: *à pied*) walk; (*longue*) trip; hike, walking tour

virement [viʀmã] *nm* (*COMM*) transfer

virent *vb voir* **voir**

virer [viʀe] *vt* (*COMM*): ~ **qch (sur)** to transfer sth (into) ♦ *vi* to turn; (*CHIMIE*) to change colour; ~ **de bord** to tack

virevolter [viʀvɔlte] *vi* to twirl around

virgule [viʀgyl] *nf* comma; (*MATH*) point

viril, e [viʀil] *adj* (*propre à l'homme*) masculine; (*énergique, courageux*) manly, virile

virtuel, le [viʀtɥɛl] *adj* potential; (*théorique*) virtual

virtuose [viʀtɥoz] *nm/f* (*MUS*) virtuoso; (*gén*) master

virus [viʀys] *nm* (*aussi: COMPUT*) virus

vis¹ [vi] *vb voir* **voir; vivre**

vis² [vis] *nf* screw

visa [viza] *nm* (*sceau*) stamp; (*validation de passeport*) visa

visage [vizaʒ] *nm* face

vis-à-vis [vizavi] *adv* face to face ♦ *nm* person opposite; house *etc* opposite; ~ **de** opposite; (*fig*) vis-à-vis; **en** ~ facing each other

viscéral, e, aux [viseʀal, -o] *adj* (*fig*) deep-seated, deep-rooted

visée [vize] : ~**s** *nfpl* (*intentions*) designs

viser [vize] *vi* to aim ♦ *vt* to aim at; (*concerner*) to be aimed *ou* directed at; (*apposer un visa sur*) to stamp, visa; ~ **à qch/faire** to aim at sth/at doing *ou* to do; **viseur** [vizœʀ] *nm* (*d'arme*) sights *pl*; (*PHOTO*) viewfinder

visibilité [vizibilite] *nf* visibility

visible [vizibl(ə)] *adj* visible; (*disponible*): **est-il ~?** can he see me?, will he see visitors?

visière [vizjɛʀ] *nf* (*de casquette*) peak; (*qui s'attache*) eyeshade

vision [vizjɔ̃] *nf* vision; (*sens*) (eye)sight, vision; (*fait de voir*): **la ~ de** the sight of

visionneuse [vizjɔnøz] *nf* viewer

visite [vizit] *nf* visit; (*visiteur*) visitor; (*médicale, à domicile*) visit, call; **la ~** (*MÉD*) medical examination; **faire une ~ à qn** to call on sb, pay sb a visit; **rendre ~ à qn** to visit sb, pay sb a visit; **être en ~ (chez qn)** to be visiting (sb); **heures de ~** (*hôpital, prison*) visiting hours

visiter [vizite] *vt* to visit; (*musée, ville*) to visit, go round; **visiteur, euse** *nm/f* visitor

vison [vizɔ̃] *nm* mink

visser [vise] *vt*: ~ **qch** (*fixer, serrer*) to screw sth on

visuel, le [vizɥɛl] *adj* visual

vit *vb voir* **voir; vivre**

vital, e, aux [vital, -o] *adj* vital

vitamine [vitamin] *nf* vitamin

vite [vit] *adv* (*rapidement*) quickly, fast; (*sans délai*) quickly; soon; **faire ~** to act quickly; to be quick

vitesse [vites] *nf* speed; (*AUTO: dispositif*) gear; **prendre qn de ~** to outstrip sb; get ahead of sb; **prendre de la ~** to pick up *ou* gather speed; **à toute ~** at full *ou* top speed

viticole [vitikɔl] *adj* wine *cpd*, wine-growing

viticulteur [vitikyltœʀ] *nm* wine grower

vitrage [vitʀaʒ] *nm* glass *no pl*; (*rideau*) net curtain

vitrail, aux [vitʀaj, -o] *nm* stained-glass window

vitre [vitʀ(ə)] *nf* (window) pane; (*de portière, voiture*) window

vitré, e [vitʀe] *adj* glass *cpd*

vitrer [vitʀe] *vt* to glaze

vitreux, euse [vitʀø, -øz] *adj* (*terne*) glassy

vitrine [vitʀin] *nf* (*devanture*) (shop) window; (*étalage*) display; (*petite armoire*) display cabinet; ~ **publicitaire** display case, showcase

vitupérer [vitypeʀe] *vi* to rant and rave

vivace [vivas] *adj* (*arbre, plante*) hardy; (*fig*) indestructible, inveterate

vivacité [vivasite] *nf* liveliness, vivacity; sharpness; brilliance

vivant, e [vivɑ̃, -ɑ̃t] *adj* (*qui vit*) living, alive; (*animé*) lively; (*preuve, exemple*) living ♦ *nm*: **du ~ de qn** in sb's lifetime

vivats [viva] *nmpl* cheers

vive [viv] *adj/ voir* **vif** ♦ *vb voir* **vivre** ♦ *excl*: ~ **le roi!** long live the king!; **vivement** *adv* vivaciously; sharply ♦ *excl*: **vivement les vacances!** roll on the holidays!

viveur [vivœʀ] (*péj*) *nm* high liver, pleasure-seeker

vivier [vivje] *nm* fish tank; fishpond

vivifiant, e [vivifjɑ̃, -ɑ̃t] *adj* invigorating

vivions *vb voir* **vivre**

vivoter [vivɔte] *vi* (*personne*) to scrape a

living, get by; (*fig: affaire etc*) to struggle along

vivre [vivʀ(ə)] *vi, vt* to live; **il vit encore** he is still alive; **se laisser** ~ to take life as it comes; **ne plus** ~ (*être anxieux*) to live on one's nerves; **il a vécu** (*eu une vie aventureuse*) he has seen life; **être facile à** ~ to be easy to get on with; **faire** ~ **qn** (*pourvoir à sa subsistance*) to provide (a living) for sb; **vivres** *nmpl* provisions, food supplies

vlan [vlɑ̃] *excl* wham!, bang!

vocable [vɔkabl(ə)] *nm* term

vocabulaire [vɔkabylɛʀ] *nm* vocabulary

vocation [vɔkasjɔ̃] *nf* vocation, calling

vociférer [vɔsifeʀe] *vi, vt* to scream

vœu, x [vø] *nm* wish; (*à Dieu*) vow; **faire** ~ **de** to take a vow of; ~**x de bonne année** best wishes for the New Year

vogue [vɔg] *nf* fashion, vogue

voguer [vɔge] *vi* to sail

voici [vwasi] *prép* (*pour introduire, désigner*) here is +*sg*, here are +*pl*; **et** ~ **que ... and** now it (*ou* he) ...; *voir aussi* **voilà**

voie [vwa] *nf* way; (*RAIL*) track, line; (*AUTO*) lane; **être en bonne** ~ to be going well; **mettre qn sur la** ~ to put sb on the right track; **être en** ~ **d'achèvement/de renovation** to be nearing completion/in the process of renovation; **par** ~ **buccale** *ou* **orale** orally; **à** ~ **étroite** narrow-gauge; ~ **d'eau** (*NAVIG*) leak; ~ **de garage** (*RAIL*) siding; ~ **ferrée** track; railway line

voilà [vwala] *prép* (*en désignant*) there is +*sg*, there are +*pl*; **les** ~ *ou* **voici** here *ou* there they are; ~ *ou* **voici un** here's one, there's one; ~ *ou* **voici deux ans** two years ago; ~ *ou* **voici deux ans que** it's two years since; **et** ~**!** there we are!; ~ **tout** that's all; "~ *ou* **voici**" (*en offrant etc*) "there *ou* here you are"

voile [vwal] *nm* veil; (*tissu léger*) net ♦ *nf* sail; (*sport*) sailing

voiler [vwale] *vt* to veil; (*fausser: roue*) to buckle; (: *bois*) to warp; **se** ~ *vi* (*lune, regard*) to mist over; (*voix*) to become husky; (*roue, disque*) to buckle; (*planche*) to warp

voilier [vwalje] *nm* sailing ship; (*de plaisance*) sailing boat

voilure [vwalyʀ] *nf* (*de voilier*) sails *pl*

voir [vwaʀ] *vi, vt* to see; **se** ~ *vt*: **se** ~ **critiquer/transformer** to be criticized/transformed; **cela se voit** (*cela arrive*) it happens; (*c'est visible*) that's obvious, it shows; ~ **venir** (*fig*) to wait and see; **faire** ~ **qch à qn** to show sb sth; **en faire** ~ **à qn** (*fig*) to give sb a hard time; **ne pas pouvoir** ~ **qn** not to be able to stand sb; **voyons!** let's see now; (*indignation etc*) come (along) now; **avoir quelque chose à** ~ **avec** to have something to do with

voire [vwaʀ] *adv* indeed; nay; or even

voisin, e [vwazɛ̃, -in] *adj* (*proche*) neighbouring; (*contigu*) next; (*ressemblant*) connected ♦ *nm/f* neighbour; **voisinage** *nm* (*proximité*) proximity; (*environs*) vicinity; (*quartier, voisins*) neighbourhood

voiture [vwatyʀ] *nf* car; (*wagon*) coach, carriage; ~ **d'enfant** pram (*BRIT*), baby carriage (*US*); ~ **de sport** sports car; ~**-lit** *nf* sleeper

voix [vwa] *nf* voice; (*POL*) vote; **à haute** ~ aloud; **à** ~ **basse** in a low voice; **à 2/4** ~ (*MUS*) in 2/4 parts; **avoir** ~ **au chapitre** to have a say in the matter

vol [vɔl] *nm* (*mode de locomotion*) flying; (*trajet, voyage, groupe d'oiseaux*) flight; (*larcin*) theft; **à** ~ **d'oiseau** as the crow flies; **au** ~: **attraper qch au** ~ to catch sth as it flies past; **en** ~ in flight; ~ **à main armée** armed robbery; ~ **à voile** gliding; ~ **libre** hang-gliding

volage [vɔlaʒ] *adj* fickle

volaille [vɔlaj] *nf* (*oiseaux*) poultry *pl*; (*viande*) poultry *no pl*; (*oiseau*) fowl

volant, e [vɔlɑ̃, -ɑ̃t] *adj voir* **feuille** *etc* ♦ *nm* (*d'automobile*) (steering) wheel; (*de commande*) wheel; (*objet lancé*) shuttlecock; (*bande de tissu*) flounce

volcan [vɔlkɑ̃] *nm* volcano

volée [vɔle] *nf* (*TENNIS*) volley; **à la** ~: **rattraper à la** ~ to catch in mid-air; **à toute** ~ (*sonner les cloches*) vigorously; (*lancer un projectile*) with full force; ~ **de coups/de flèches** volley of blows/arrows

voler [vɔle] *vi* (*avion, oiseau, fig*) to fly; (*voleur*) to steal ♦ *vt* (*objet*) to steal; (*personne*) to rob; ~ **qch à qn** to steal sth from sb

volet [vɔlɛ] *nm* (*de fenêtre*) shutter; (*de feuillet, document*) section

voleur, euse [vɔlœʀ, -øz] *nm/f* thief ♦ *adj* thieving

volontaire [vɔlɔ̃tɛʀ] *adj* voluntary; (*caractère, personne: décidé*) self-willed ♦ *nm/f* volunteer

volonté [vɔlɔ̃te] *nf* (*faculté de vouloir*) will; (*énergie, fermeté*) will(power); (*souhait, désir*) wish; **à** ~ as much as one likes; **bonne** ~ goodwill, willingness; **mauvaise** ~ lack of goodwill, unwillingness

volontiers [vɔlɔ̃tje] *adv* (*de bonne grâce*) willingly; (*avec plaisir*) willingly, gladly; (*habituellement, souvent*) readily, willingly

volt [vɔlt] *nm* volt

volte-face [vɔltəfas] *nf inv* about-turn

voltige [vɔltiʒ] *nf* (*ÉQUITATION*) trick riding; (*au cirque*) acrobatics *sg*; ~**r** [vɔltiʒe] *vi* to flutter (about)

volume [vɔlym] *nm* volume; (*GÉOM: solide*) solid; **volumineux, euse** *adj* voluminous, bulky

volupté [vɔlypte] *nf* sensual delight *ou* pleasure

vomir [vɔmiʀ] *vi* to vomit, be sick ♦ *vt* to vomit, bring up; (*fig*) to belch out, spew out; (*exécrer*) to loathe, abhor

vont [vɔ̃] *vb voir* **aller**

vos [vo] *dét voir* **votre**

vote [vɔt] *nm* vote; ~ **par correspondance/procuration** postal/proxy vote

voter [vɔte] *vi* to vote ♦ *vt* (*loi, décision*) to vote for

votre [vɔtʀ(ə)] (*pl* **vos**) *dét* your

vôtre [votʀ(ə)] *pron*: **le** ~, **la** ~, **les** ~**s** yours; **les** ~**s** (*fig*) your family *ou* folks; **à la** ~ (*toast*) your (good) health!

voudrai *etc vb voir* **vouloir**

voué, e [vwe] *adj*: ~ **à** doomed to

vouer [vwe] *vt*: ~ **qch à** (*Dieu/un saint*) to dedicate sth to; ~ **sa vie à** (*étude, cause etc*) to devote one's life to; ~ **une amitié éternelle à qn** to vow undying friendship to sb

---
MOT CLÉ
---

vouloir [vulwaʀ] *nm*: **le bon** ~ **de qn** sb's goodwill; sb's pleasure

♦ *vt* **1** (*exiger, désirer*) to want; ~ **faire/que qn fasse** to want to do/sb to do; **voulez-vous du thé?** would you like *ou* do you want some tea?; **que me veut-il?** what does he want with me?; **sans le** ~ (*involontairement*) without meaning to, unintentionally; **je voudrais ceci/faire** I would *ou* I'd like this/to do

2 (*consentir*): **je veux bien** (*bonne volonté*) I'll be happy to; (*concession*) fair enough, that's fine; **oui, si on veut** (*en quelque sorte*) yes, if you like; **veuillez attendre** please wait; **veuillez agréer ...** (*formule épistolaire*) yours faithfully

3: **en** ~ **à qn** to bear sb a grudge; **s'en** ~ (**de**) to be annoyed with o.s. (for); **il en veut à mon argent** he's after my money

4: ~ **de**: **l'entreprise ne veut plus de lui** the firm doesn't want him any more; **elle ne veut pas de son aide** she doesn't want his help

5: ~ **dire** to mean

---

voulu, e [vuly] *adj* (*requis*) required, requisite; (*délibéré*) deliberate, intentional; *voir aussi* **vouloir**

vous [vu] *pron* you; (*objet indirect*) (to) you; (*réfléchi: sg*) yourself; (: *pl*) yourselves; (*réciproque*) each other; ~**-même** yourself; ~**-mêmes** yourselves

voûte [vut] *nf* vault

voûter [vute] *vt*: **se** ~ *vi* (*dos, personne*) to become stooped

vouvoyer [vuvwaje] *vt*: ~ **qn** to address sb as "vous"

voyage [vwajaʒ] *nm* journey, trip; (*fait de voyager*): **le** ~ travel(ling); **partir/être en** ~ to go off/be away on a journey *ou* trip; **faire bon** ~ to have a good journey; ~ **d'agrément/d'affaires** pleasure/business trip; ~ **de noces** honeymoon; ~ **organisé** package tour

voyager [vwajaʒe] *vi* to travel; **voyageur, euse** *nm/f* traveller; (*passager*) passenger

voyant, e [vwajɑ̃, -ɑ̃t] *adj* (*couleur*) loud, gaudy ♦ *nm* (*signal*) (warning) light.

voyante [vwajɑ̃t] *nf* clairvoyant

voyelle [vwajɛl] *nf* vowel

voyons *etc vb voir* **voir**

voyou [vwaju] *nm* lout, hoodlum; (*enfant*) guttersnipe

vrac [vʀak] : **en** ~ *adv* higgledy-piggledy; (*COMM*) in bulk

vrai, e [vʀɛ] *adj* (*véridique: récit, faits*) true; (*non factice, authentique*) real; **à** ~ **dire** to tell the truth

vraiment [vʀɛmɑ̃] *adv* really

vraisemblable [vʀɛsɑ̃blablə(ə)] *adj* likely, probable

vraisemblance [vʀɛsɑ̃blɑ̃s] *nf* likelihood; (*romanesque*) verisimilitude

vrille [vʀij] *nf* (*de plante*) tendril; (*outil*) gimlet; (*spirale*) spiral; (*AVIAT*) spin

vrombir [vʀɔ̃biʀ] *vi* to hum

vu, e [vy] *pp de* **voir** ♦ *adj*: **bien/mal** ~ (*fig*) well/poorly thought of; good/bad form ♦ *prép* (*en raison de*) in view of; ~ **que** in view of the fact that

vue [vy] *nf* (*fait de voir*): **la** ~ **de** the sight of; (*sens, faculté*) (eye)sight; (*panorama, image, photo*) view; ~**s** *nfpl* (*idées*) views; (*dessein*) designs; **hors de** ~ out of sight; **tirer à** ~ to shoot on sight; **à** ~ **d'œil** visibly; at a quick glance; **en** ~ (*visible*) in sight; (*COMM*) in the public eye; **en** ~ **de faire** with a view to doing

vulgaire [vylgɛʀ] *adj* (*grossier*) vulgar, coarse; (*trivial*) commonplace, mundane; (*péj: quelconque*): **de** ~**s touristes** common tourists; (*BOT, ZOOL: non latin*) common; **vulgariser** *vt* to popularize

vulnérable [vylneʀabl(ə)] *adj* vulnerable

W w
---

wagon [vagɔ̃] *nm* (*de voyageurs*) carriage; (*de marchandises*) truck, wagon; **wagon-lit** *nm* sleeper, sleeping car; **wagon-restaurant** *nm* restaurant *ou* dining car

wallon, ne [valɔ̃, -ɔn] *adj* Walloon

waters [watɛʀ] *nmpl* toilet *sg*
watt [wat] *nm* watt
w.-c. [vese] *nmpl* toilet *sg*, lavatory *sg*
week-end [wikɛnd] *nm* weekend
western [wɛstɛʀn] *nm* western
whisky [wiski] (*pl* **whiskies**) *nm* whisky

yoghourt [jɔguʀt] *nm* = **yaourt**
yougoslave [jugɔslav] *nm/f* Yugo-slav(ian)
Yougoslavie [jugɔslavi] *nf* Yugoslavia

xérès [gzeʀɛs] *nm* sherry
xylophone [ksilɔfɔn] *nm* xylophone

y [i] *adv* (*à cet endroit*) there; (*dessus*) on it (*ou* them); (*dedans*) in it (*ou* them) ♦ *pron* (about *ou* on *ou* of) it (*d'après le verbe employé*); **j'~ pense** I'm thinking about it; *voir aussi* **aller; avoir**
yacht [jɔt] *nm* yacht
yaourt [jauʀt] *nm* yoghurt
yeux [jø] *nmpl de* **œil**

zèbre [zɛbʀ(ə)] *nm* (*ZOOL*) zebra
zébré, e [zebʀe] *adj* striped, streaked
zèle [zɛl] *nm* zeal; **faire du ~** (*péj*) to be over-zealous
zéro [zeʀo] *nm* zero, nought (*BRIT*); **au-dessous de ~** below zero (Centigrade) *ou* freezing; **partir de ~** to start from scratch; **trois (buts) à ~** 3 (goals to) nil
zeste [zɛst(ə)] *nm* peel, zest
zézayer [zezeje] *vi* to have a lisp
zigzag [zigzag] *nm* zigzag
zinc [zɛ̃g] *nm* (*CHIMIE*) zinc; (*comptoir*) bar, counter
zizanie [zizani] *nf*: **semer la ~** to stir up ill-feeling
zodiaque [zɔdjak] *nm* zodiac
zona [zona] *nm* shingles *sg*
zone [zon] *nf* zone, area; (*quartiers*): **la ~** the slum belt; **~ bleue** ≈ restricted parking area; **~ industrielle** *nf* industrial estate
zoo [zoo] *nm* zoo
zoologie [zɔɔlɔʒi] *nf* zoology; **zoologique** *adj* zoological
zut [zyt] *excl* dash (it)! (*BRIT*), nuts! (*US*)

ENGLISH - FRENCH
ANGLAIS - FRANÇAIS

A a

A [eɪ] *n* (*MUS*) la *m*

─────────── *KEYWORD* ───────────

a [eɪ, ə] (*before vowel or silent h: an*) *indef art* **1** un(e); ~ **book** un livre; **an apple** une pomme; **she's** ~ **doctor** elle est médecin
2 (*instead of the number 'one'*) un(e); ~ **year ago** il y a un an; ~ **hundred/ thousand etc pounds** cent/mille *etc* livres
3 (*in expressing ratios, prices etc*): **3** ~ **day/week** 3 par jour/semaine; **10 km** ~**n hour** 10 km à l'heure; **30p** ~ **kilo** 30p le kilo

──────────────────────────────

A.A. *n abbr* = **Alcoholics Anonymous**; (*BRIT*: = *Automobile Association*) ≈ TCF *m*
A.A.A. (*US*) *n abbr* (= *American Automobile Association*) ≈ TCF *m*
aback [ə'bæk] *adv*: **to be taken** ~ être stupéfait(e), être décontenancé(e)
abandon [ə'bændən] *vt* abandonner ♦ *n*: **with** ~ avec désinvolture
abate [ə'beɪt] *vi* s'apaiser, se calmer
abbey ['æbɪ] *n* abbaye *f*
abbot ['æbət] *n* père supérieur
abbreviation [əbriːvɪ'eɪʃən] *n* abréviation *f*
abdicate ['æbdɪkeɪt] *vt, vi* abdiquer
abdomen ['æbdəmən] *n* abdomen *m*
abduct [æb'dʌkt] *vt* enlever
aberration [æbə'reɪʃən] *n* anomalie *f*
abet [ə'bet] *vt see* **aid**
abeyance [ə'beɪəns] *n*: **in** ~ (*law*) tombé(e) en désuétude; (*matter*) en suspens
abide [ə'baɪd] *vt*: **I can't** ~ **it/him** je ne peux pas le souffrir *or* supporter; ~ **by** *vt fus* observer, respecter
ability [ə'bɪlɪtɪ] *n* compétence *f*; capacité *f*; (*skill*) talent *m*
abject ['æbdʒekt] *adj* (*poverty*) sordide; (*apology*) plat(e)
ablaze [ə'bleɪz] *adj* en feu, en flammes
able ['eɪbl] *adj* capable, compétent(e); **to be** ~ **to do sth** être capable de faire qch, pouvoir faire qch; ~**-bodied** *adj* robuste; **ably** ['eɪblɪ] *adv* avec compétence *or* talent, habilement
abnormal [æb'nɔːməl] *adj* anormal(e)
aboard [ə'bɔːd] *adv* à bord ♦ *prep* à bord de
abode [ə'bəud] *n* (*LAW*): **of no fixed** ~ sans domicile fixe
abolish [ə'bɒlɪʃ] *vt* abolir
aborigine [æbə'rɪdʒɪniː] *n* aborigène *m/f*
abort [ə'bɔːt] *vt* faire avorter; ~**ion** [ə'bɔːʃən] *n* avortement *m*; **to have an** ~**ion** se faire avorter; ~**ive** *adj* manqué(e)
abound [ə'baund] *vi* abonder; **to** ~ **in** *or* **with** abonder en, regorger de

─────────── *KEYWORD* ───────────

about [ə'baut] *adv* **1** (*approximately*) environ, à peu près; ~ **a hundred/thousand etc** environ cent/mille *etc*, une centaine (de)/un millier (de) *etc*; **it takes** ~ **10 hours** ça prend environ *or* à peu près 10 heures; **at** ~ **2 o'clock** vers 2 heures; **I've just** ~ **finished** j'ai presque fini
2 (*referring to place*) çà et là, deci delà; **to run** ~ courir çà et là; **to walk** ~ se promener, aller et venir
3: **to be** ~ **to do sth** être sur le point de faire qch
♦ *prep* **1** (*relating to*) au sujet de, à propos de; **a book** ~ **London** un livre sur Londres; **what is it** ~? de quoi s'agit-il?; **we talked** ~ **it** nous en avons parlé; **what** *or* **how** ~ **doing this?** et si nous faisions ceci?
2 (*referring to place*) dans; **to walk** ~ **the town** se promener dans la ville

──────────────────────────────

about-face [ə'baut'feɪs] *n* demi-tour *m*
about-turn [ə'baut'tɜːn] *n* (*MIL*) demi-tour *m*; (*fig*) volte-face *f*

above [ə'bʌv] *adv* au-dessus ♦ *prep* au-dessus de; (*more*) plus de; **mentioned ~** mentionné ci-dessus; **~ all** par-dessus tout, surtout; **~board** *adj* franc(franche); honnête

abrasive [ə'breɪzɪv] *adj* abrasif(ive); (*fig*) caustique, agressif(ive)

abreast [ə'brest] *adv* de front; **to keep ~ of** se tenir au courant de

abridge [ə'brɪdʒ] *vt* abréger

abroad [ə'brɔːd] *adv* à l'étranger

abrupt [ə'brʌpt] *adj* (*steep, blunt*) abrupt(e); (*sudden, gruff*) brusque; **~ly** *adv* (*speak, end*) brusquement

abscess ['æbsɪs] *n* abcès *m*

abscond [əb'skɒnd] *vi* disparaître, s'enfuir

absence ['æbsəns] *n* absence *f*

absent ['æbsənt] *adj* absent(e); **~ee** [æbsən'tiː] *n* absent(e); (*habitual*) absentéiste *m/f*; **~-minded** *adj* distrait(e)

absolute ['æbsəluːt] *adj* absolu(e); **~ly** [æbsə'luːtlɪ] *adv* absolument

absolve [əb'zɒlv] *vt*: **to ~ sb (from)** (*blame, responsibility, sin*) absoudre qn (de)

absorb [əb'zɔːb] *vt* absorber; **to be ~ed in a book** être plongé(e) dans un livre; **~ent cotton** (*US*) *n* coton *m* hydrophile; **absorption** [əb'zɔːpʃən] *n* absorption *f*; (*fig*) concentration *f*

abstain [əb'steɪn] *vi*: **to ~ (from)** s'abstenir (de)

abstract ['æbstrækt] *adj* abstrait(e)

absurd [əb'sɜːd] *adj* absurde

abuse [*n* ə'bjuːs, *vb* ə'bjuːz] *n* abus *m*; (*insults*) insultes *fpl*, injures *fpl* ♦ *vt* abuser de; (*insult*) insulter; **abusive** [ə'bjuːsɪv] *adj* grossier(ère), injurieux(euse)

abysmal [ə'bɪzməl] *adj* exécrable; (*ignorance etc*) sans bornes

abyss [ə'bɪs] *n* abîme *m*, gouffre *m*

AC *abbr* (= *alternating current*) courant alternatif

academic [ækə'demɪk] *adj* universitaire; (*person: scholarly*) intellectuel(le); (*pej: issue*) oiseux(euse), purement théorique ♦ *n* universitaire *m/f*; **~ year** *n* année *f* universitaire

academy [ə'kædəmɪ] *n* (*learned body*) académie *f*; (*school*) collège *m*; **~ of music** conservatoire *m*

accelerate [æk'seləreɪt] *vt, vi* accélérer; **accelerator** [æk'seləreɪtə*] *n* accélérateur *m*

accent ['æksent] *n* accent *m*

accept [ək'sept] *vt* accepter; **~able** *adj* acceptable; **~ance** *n* acceptation *f*

access ['ækses] *n* accès *m*; (*JUR: in divorce*) droit *m* de visite; **~ible** [æk'sesɪbl] *adj* accessible

accessory [æk'sesərɪ] *n* accessoire *m*; (*LAW*): **~ to** complice de

accident ['æksɪdənt] *n* accident *m*; (*chance*) hasard *m*; **by ~** accidentellement; par ha-sard; **~al** [æksɪ'dentl] *adj* accidentel(le); **~ally** [æksɪ'dentəlɪ] *adv* accidentellement; **~-prone** *adj* sujet(te) aux accidents

acclaim [ə'kleɪm] *n* acclamations *fpl* ♦ *vt* acclamer

accommodate [ə'kɒmədeɪt] *vt* loger, recevoir; (*oblige, help*) obliger; (*car etc*) contenir; **accommodating** [ə'kɒmədeɪtɪŋ] *adj* obligeant(e), arrangeant(e); **accommodation** [əkɒmə'deɪʃən] (*US* ~**s**) *n* logement *m*

accompany [ə'kʌmpənɪ] *vt* accompagner

accomplice [ə'kʌmplɪs] *n* complice *m/f*

accomplish [ə'kʌmplɪʃ] *vt* accomplir; **~ment** *n* accomplissement *m*; réussite *f*; (*skill: gen pl*) talent *m*

accord [ə'kɔːd] *n* accord *m* ♦ *vt* accorder; **of his own ~** de son plein gré; **~ance** *n*: **in ~ance with** conformément à; **~ing**: **~ing to** *prep* selon; **~ingly** *adv* en conséquence

accordion [ə'kɔːdɪən] *n* accordéon *m*

accost [ə'kɒst] *vt* aborder

account [ə'kaʊnt] *n* (*COMM*) compte *m*; (*report*) compte rendu; récit *m*; **~s** *npl* (*COMM*) comptabilité *f*, comptes; **of no ~** sans importance; **on ~** en acompte; **on no ~** en aucun cas; **on ~ of** à cause de; **to take into ~, take ~ of** tenir compte de; **~ for** *vt fus* expliquer, rendre compte de; **~able** *adj*: **~able (to)** responsable (devant); **~ancy** [ə'kaʊntənsɪ] *n* comptabilité *f*; **~ant** [ə'kaʊntənt] *n* comptable *m/f*; **~ number** *n* (*at bank etc*) numéro *m* de compte

accrued interest [əkruːd-] *n* intérêt *m* cumulé

accumulate [ə'kjuːmjʊleɪt] *vt* accumuler, amasser ♦ *vi* s'accumuler, s'amasser

accuracy ['ækjʊrəsɪ] *n* exactitude *f*, précision *f*

accurate ['ækjʊrɪt] *adj* exact(e), précis(e); **~ly** *adv* avec précision

accusation [ækjuː'zeɪʃən] *n* accusation *f*

accuse [ə'kjuːz] *vt*: **to ~ sb (of sth)** accuser qn (de qch); **~d** *n*: **the ~d** l'accusé(e)

accustom [ə'kʌstəm] *vt* accoutumer, habituer; **~ed** *adj* (*usual*) habituel(le); (*in the habit*): **~ed to** habitué(e) *or* accoutumé(e) à

ace [eɪs] *n* as *m*

ache [eɪk] *n* mal *m*, douleur *f* ♦ *vi* (*yearn*): **to ~ to do sth** mourir d'envie de faire qch; **my head ~s** j'ai mal à la tête

achieve [ə'tʃiːv] *vt* (*aim*) atteindre; (*victory, success*) remporter, obtenir; **~ment** *n* exploit *m*, réussite *f*

acid ['æsɪd] *adj* acide ♦ *n* acide *m*; **~ rain** *n* pluies *fpl* acides

acknowledge [ək'nɒlɪdʒ] *vt* (*letter: also: ~ receipt of*) accuser réception de; (*fact*) reconnaître; **~ment** *n* (*of letter*) accusé *m* de réception

acne ['æknɪ] *n* acné *m*

acorn ['eɪkɔːn] *n* gland *m*

acoustic [ə'kuːstɪk] *adj* acoustique; **~s** *n, npl* acoustique *f*

acquaint [ə'kweɪnt] *vt:* **to ~ sb with sth** mettre qn au courant de qch; **to be ~ed with** connaître; **~ance** *n* connaissance *f*

acquiesce [ækwɪ'es] *vi:* **to ~ to** acquiescer *or* consentir à

acquire [ə'kwaɪə*] *vt* acquérir

acquit [ə'kwɪt] *vt* acquitter; **to ~ o.s. well** bien se comporter, s'en tirer très honorablement

acre ['eɪkə*] *n* acre *f* (= *4047 m²*)

acrid ['ækrɪd] *adj* âcre

acrobat ['ækrəbæt] *n* acrobate *m/f*

across [ə'krɒs] *prep (on the other side)* de l'autre côté de; *(crosswise)* en travers de ♦ *adv* de l'autre côté; en travers; **to run/ swim ~** traverser en courant/à la nage; **~ from** en face de

acrylic [ə'krɪlɪk] *adj* acrylique

act [ækt] *n* acte *m*, action *f; (of play)* acte; *(in music-hall etc)* numéro *m; (LAW)* loi *f* ♦ *vi* agir; *(THEATRE)* jouer; *(pretend)* jouer la comédie ♦ *vt (part)* jouer, tenir; **in the ~ of** en train de; **to ~ as** servir de; **~ing** *adj* suppléant(e), par intérim ♦ *n (activity):* **to do some ~ing** faire du théâtre (*or* du cinéma)

action ['ækʃən] *n* action *f; (MIL)* combat(s) *m(pl); (LAW)* procès *m*, action en justice; **out of ~** hors de combat; *(machine)* hors d'usage; **to take ~** agir, prendre des mesures; **~ replay** *n (TV)* ralenti *m*

activate ['æktɪveɪt] *vt (mechanism)* actionner, faire fonctionner

active ['æktɪv] *adj* actif(ive); *(volcano)* en activité; **~ly** *adv* activement

activity [æk'tɪvɪtɪ] *n* activité *f*

actor ['æktə*] *n* acteur *m*

actress ['æktrɪs] *n* actrice *f*

actual ['æktjuəl] *adj* réel(le), véritable; **~ly** *adv (really)* réellement, véritablement; *(in fact)* en fait

acumen ['ækjumen] *n* perspicacité *f*

acute [ə'kjuːt] *adj* aigu(ë); *(mind, observer)* pénétrant(e), perspicace

ad [æd] *n abbr* = **advertisement**

A.D. *adv abbr* (= *anno Domini*) ap. J.-C.

adamant ['ædəmənt] *adj* inflexible

adapt [ə'dæpt] *vt* adapter ♦ *vi:* **to ~ (to)** s'adapter (à); **~able** *adj (device)* adaptable; *(person)* qui s'adapte facilement; **~er, ~or** *n (ELEC)* adaptateur *m*, adaptateur *m*

add [æd] *vt* ajouter; *(figures: also:* **to ~ up***)* additionner ♦ *vi:* **to ~ to** *(increase)* ajouter à, accroître

adder ['ædə*] *n* vipère *f*

addict ['ædɪkt] *n* intoxiqué(e); *(fig)* fanatique *m/f*; **~ed** [ə'dɪktɪd] *adj:* **to be ~ed to**

(drugs, drink etc) être adonné(e) à; *(fig: football etc)* être un(e) fanatique de; **~ion** [ə'dɪkʃən] *n (MED)* dépendance *f*; **~ive** *adj* qui crée une dépendance

addition [ə'dɪʃən] *n* addition *f*; *(thing added)* ajout *m*; **in ~** de plus; de surcroît; **in ~ to** en plus de; **~al** *adj* supplémentaire

additive ['ædɪtɪv] *n* additif *m*

address [ə'dres] *n* adresse *f*; *(talk)* discours *m*, allocution *f* ♦ *vt* adresser; *(speak to)* s'adresser à; **to ~ (o.s. to) a problem** s'attaquer à un problème

adept ['ædept] *adj:* **~ at** expert(e) à *or* en

adequate ['ædɪkwɪt] *adj* adéquat(e); suffisant(e)

adhere [əd'hɪə*] *vi:* **to ~ to** adhérer à; *(fig: rule, decision)* se tenir à

adhesive [əd'hiːzɪv] *n* adhésif *m*; **~ tape** *n (BRIT)* ruban adhésif; *(US: MED)* sparadrap *m*

ad hoc [æd'hɔk] *adj* improvisé(e), ad hoc

adjective ['ædʒəktɪv] *n* adjectif *m*

adjoining [ə'dʒɔɪnɪŋ] *adj* voisin(e), adjacent(e), attenant(e)

adjourn [ə'dʒɜːn] *vt* ajourner ♦ *vi* suspendre la séance; lever la séance; clore la session

adjust [ə'dʒʌst] *vt* ajuster, régler; rajuster ♦ *vi:* **to ~ (to)** s'adapter (à); **~able** *adj* réglable; **~ment** *n (PSYCH)* adaptation *f; (to machine)* ajustage *m*, réglage *m; (of prices, wages)* rajustement *m*

ad-lib [æd'lɪb] *vt, vi* improviser; **ad lib** *adv* à volonté, à loisir

administer [æd'mɪnɪstə*] *vt* administrer; *(justice)* rendre

administration [ədmɪnɪs'treɪʃən] *n* administration *f*

administrative [əd'mɪnɪstrətɪv] *adj* administratif(ive)

admiral ['ædmərəl] *n* amiral *m*; **A~ty** ['ædmərəltɪ] *(BRIT)* *n (also:* **A~ty Board***):* **the A~ty** ministère *m* de la Marine

admire [əd'maɪə*] *vt* admirer

admission [əd'mɪʃən] *n* admission *f*; *(to exhibition, night club etc)* entrée *f*; *(confession)* aveu *m*

admit [əd'mɪt] *vt* laisser entrer; admettre; *(agree)* reconnaître, admettre; **~ to** *vt fus* reconnaître, avouer; **~tance** *n* admission *f*, (droit *m* d')entrée *f*; **~tedly** *adv* il faut en convenir

admonish [əd'mɒnɪʃ] *vt* donner un avertissement à; réprimander

ad nauseam [æd'nɔːsɪæm] *adv (repeat, talk)* à n'en plus finir

ado [ə'duː] *n:* **without (any) more ~** sans plus de cérémonies

adolescence [ædə'lesns] *n* adolescence *f*; **adolescent** [ædə'lesnt] *adj, n* adolescent(e)

adopt [ə'dɒpt] *vt* adopter; **~ed** *adj* adoptif(ive), adopté(e); **~ion** [ə'dɒpʃən] *n* adoption f

adore [ə'dɔ:*] vt adorer

adorn [ə'dɔ:n] vt orner

Adriatic (Sea) [eɪdrɪ'ætɪk-] n Adriatique f

adrift [ə'drɪft] adv à la dérive

adult ['ædʌlt] n adulte m/f ♦ adj adulte; (literature, education) pour adultes

adultery [ə'dʌltərɪ] n adultère m

advance [əd'vɑ:ns] n avance f ♦ adj: ~ booking réservation f ♦ vt avancer ♦ vi avancer, s'avancer; ~ notice avertissement m; to make ~s (to sb) faire des propositions (à qn); (amorously) faire des avances (à qn); in ~ à l'avance, d'avance; ~d adj avancé(e); (SCOL: studies) supérieur(e)

advantage [əd'vɑ:ntɪdʒ] n (also TENNIS) avantage m; to take ~ of (person) exploiter

advent ['ædvent] n avènement m, venue f; A~ Avent m

adventure [əd'ventʃə*] n aventure f

adverb ['ædvɜ:b] n adverbe m

adverse ['ædvɜ:s] adj défavorable, contraire

advert ['ædvɜ:t] (BRIT) n abbr = **advertisement**

advertise ['ædvətaɪz] vi(vt) faire de la publicité (pour); mettre une annonce (pour vendre); to ~ for (staff, accommodation) faire paraître une annonce pour trouver; ~ment [əd'vɜ:tɪsmənt] n (COMM) réclame f, publicité f; (in classified ads) annonce f; ~r ['ædvətaɪzə*] n (in newspaper etc) annonceur m; **advertising** ['ædvətaɪzɪŋ] n publicité f

advice [əd'vaɪs] n conseils mpl; (notification) avis m; **piece of ~** conseil; to take legal ~ consulter un avocat

advisable [əd'vaɪzəbl] adj conseillé(e), indiqué(e)

advise [əd'vaɪz] vt conseiller; to ~ sb of sth aviser or informer qn de qch; to ~ against sth/doing sth déconseiller qch/conseiller de ne pas faire qch; ~dly [əd'vaɪzədlɪ] adv (deliberately) délibérément; ~r n conseiller(ère); **advisor** n = ~r; **advisory** [əd'vaɪzərɪ] adj consultatif(ive)

advocate [vb 'ædvəkeɪt, n 'ædvəkət] n (upholder) défenseur m, avocat(e), partisan(e); (LAW) avocat(e) ♦ vt recommander, prôner

aerial ['eərɪəl] n antenne f ♦ adj aérien(ne)

aerobics [eər'əubɪks] n aérobic f

aeroplane ['eərəpleɪn] (BRIT) n avion m

aerosol ['eərəsɒl] n aérosol m

aesthetic [ɪs'θetɪk] adj esthétique

afar [ə'fɑ:*] adv: **from ~** de loin

affair [ə'feə*] n affaire f; (also: love ~) liaison f; aventure f

affect [ə'fekt] vt affecter; (disease) atteindre; ~**ed** adj affecté(e)

affection [ə'fekʃən] n affection f; ~**ate** [ə'fekʃənɪt] adj affectueux(euse)

affinity [ə'fɪnɪtɪ] n (bond, rapport): **to have**

an ~ **with/for** avoir une affinité avec/pour; (resemblance): **to have an ~ with** avoir une ressemblance avec

afflict [ə'flɪkt] vt affliger

affluence ['æfluəns] n abondance f, opulence f

affluent ['æfluənt] adj (person, family, surroundings) aisé(e), riche; **the ~ society** la société d'abondance

afford [ə'fɔ:d] vt se permettre; avoir les moyens d'acheter or d'entretenir; (provide) fournir, procurer

afield [ə'fi:ld] adv: **(from) far ~** (de) loin

afloat [ə'fləut] adj, adv à flot; **to stay ~** surnager

afoot [ə'fut] adv: **there is something ~** il se prépare quelque chose

afraid [ə'freɪd] adj effrayé(e); **to be ~ of** or **to** avoir peur de; **I am ~ that ...** je suis désolé(e), mais ...; **I am ~ so/not** hélas oui/non

afresh [ə'freʃ] adv de nouveau

Africa ['æfrɪkə] n Afrique f; ~**n** adj africain(e) ♦ n Africain(e)

aft [ɑ:ft] adv à l'arrière, vers l'arrière

after ['ɑ:ftə*] prep, adv après ♦ conj après que, après avoir or être +pp; **what/who are you ~?** que cql/qui cherchez-vous?; ~ **he left/having done** après qu'il fut parti/après avoir fait; **ask ~ him** demandez de ses nouvelles; **to name sb ~ sb** donner à qn le nom de qn; **twenty ~ eight** (US) huit heures vingt; ~ **all** après tout; ~ **you!** après vous, Monsieur (or Madame etc); ~**-effects** npl (of disaster, radiation, drink etc) répercussions fpl; (of illness) séquelles fpl, suites fpl; ~**math** n conséquences fpl, suites fpl; ~**noon** n après-midi m or f; ~**s** (inf) n (dessert) dessert m; ~**-sales service** (BRIT) n (for car, washing machine etc) service m après-vente; ~**-shave (lotion)** n after-shave m; ~**thought** n: **I had an ~thought** il m'est venu une idée après coup; ~**wards** (US ~**ward**) adv après

again [ə'gen] adv de nouveau, encore (une fois); **to do sth** ~ refaire qch; **not ... ~** ne ... plus; ~ **and** ~ à plusieurs reprises

against [ə'genst] prep contre; (compared to) par rapport à

age [eɪdʒ] n âge m ♦ vt, vi vieillir; **it's been ~s since** ça fait une éternité que ... ne; **he is 20 years of ~** il a 20 ans; **to come of ~** atteindre sa majorité; ~**d**[1] adj: ~**d 10** âgé(e) de 10 ans; ~**d**[2] ['eɪdʒɪd] npl: **the ~d** les personnes âgées; ~ **group** n tranche f d'âge; ~ **limit** n limite f d'âge

agency ['eɪdʒənsɪ] n agence f; (government body) organisme m, office m

agenda [ə'dʒendə] n ordre m du jour

agent ['eɪdʒənt] n agent m, représentant m; (firm) concessionnaire m

aggravate ['ægrəveɪt] vt aggraver; (annoy)

exaspérer

aggregate ['ægrɪgɪt] *n* ensemble *m*, total *m*

aggressive [ə'gresɪv] *adj* agressif(ive)

aggrieved [ə'griːvd] *adj* chagriné(e), affligé(e)

aghast [ə'gɑːst] *adj* consterné(e), atterré(e)

agitate ['ædʒɪteɪt] *vt* (*person*) agiter, émouvoir, troubler ♦ *vi*: **to ~ for/against** faire campagne pour/contre

AGM *n abbr* (= *annual general meeting*) AG *f*, assemblée générale

ago [ə'gəʊ] *adv*: **2 days ~** il y a deux jours; **not long ~** il n'y a pas longtemps; **how long ~?** il y a combien de temps (de cela)?

agog [ə'gɒg] *adj* en émoi

agonizing ['ægənaɪzɪŋ] *adj* angoissant(e); déchirant(e)

agony ['ægənɪ] *n* (*pain*) douleur *f* atroce; **to be in ~** souffrir le martyre

agree [ə'griː] *vt* (*price*) convenir de ♦ *vi*: **to ~ with** (*person*) être d'accord avec; (*statements etc*) concorder avec; (*LING*) s'accorder avec; **to ~ to do** accepter de *or* consentir à faire; **to ~ to sth** consentir à qch; **to ~ that** (*admit*) convenir *or* reconnaître que; **garlic doesn't ~ with me** je ne supporte pas l'ail; **~able** *adj* agréable; (*willing*) consentant(e), d'accord; **~d** *adj* (*time, place*) convenu(e); **~ment** *n* accord *m*; **in ~ment** d'accord

agricultural [ægrɪ'kʌltʃərəl] *adj* agricole

agriculture ['ægrɪkʌltʃə*] *n* agriculture *f*

aground [ə'graʊnd] *adv*: **to run ~** échouer, s'échouer

ahead [ə'hed] *adv* (*in front: of position, place*) devant; (*: at the head*) en avant; (*look, plan, think*) en avant; **~ of** devant; (*fig: schedule etc*) en avance sur; **~ of time** en avance; **go right** *or* **straight ~** allez tout droit; **go ~!** (*fig: permission*) allez-y!

aid [eɪd] *n* aide *f*; (*device*) appareil *m* ♦ *vt* aider; **in ~ of** en faveur de; **to ~ and abet** (*LAW*) se faire le complice de; *see also* **hearing**

aide [eɪd] *n* (*person*) aide *mf*, assistant(e)

AIDS [eɪdz] *n abbr* (= *acquired immune deficiency syndrome*) SIDA *m*

ailing ['eɪlɪŋ] *adj* malade

ailment ['eɪlmənt] *n* affection *f*

aim [eɪm] *vt*: **to ~ sth (at)** (*gun, camera*) braquer *or* pointer qch (sur); (*missile*) lancer qch (à *or* contre *or* en direction de); (*blow*) allonger qch (à); (*remark*) destiner *or* adresser qch (à) ♦ *vi* (*also: to take ~*) viser ♦ *n* but *m*; (*skill*): **his ~ is bad** il vise mal; **to ~ at** viser; (*fig*) viser (à); **to ~ to do** avoir l'intention de faire; **~less** *adj* sans but

ain't [eɪnt] (*inf*) = **am not**; **aren't**; **isn't**

air [ɛə*] *n* air *m* ♦ *vt* (*room, bed, clothes*) aérer; (*grievances, views, ideas*) exposer, faire connaître ♦ *cpd* (*currents, attack etc*) aérien(ne); (*attack*) aérien(ne) en l'air; **by ~** (*travel*) par avion; **to be on the ~** (*RADIO, TV: programme*) être diffusé(e); (*: station*) diffuser; **~bed** *n* matelas *m* pneumatique; **~borne** *adj* en vol; **~-conditioned** *adj* climatisé(e); **~ conditioning** *n* climatisation *f*; **~craft** *n inv* avion *m*; **~craft carrier** *n* porte-avions *m inv*; **~field** *n* terrain *m* d'aviation; **A~ Force** *n* armée *f* de l'air; **~ freshener** *n* désodorisant *m*; **~gun** *n* fusil *m* à air comprimé; **~ hostess** *n* (*BRIT*) hôtesse *f* de l'air; **~ letter** *n* (*BRIT*) aérogramme *m*; **~lift** *n* pont aérien; **~line** *n* ligne aérienne, compagnie *f* d'aviation; **~liner** *n* avion *m* de ligne; **~mail** *n*: **by ~mail** par avion; **~plane** *n* (*US*) avion *m*; **~port** *n* aéroport *m*; **~ raid** *n* attaque *or* raid aérien(ne); **~sick** *adj*: **to be ~sick** avoir le mal de l'air; **air space** espace aérien; **~ terminal** *n* aérogare *f*; **~tight** *adj* hermétique; **~- traffic controller** *n* aiguilleur *m* du ciel; **~y** *adj* bien aéré(e); (*manners*) dégagé(e)

aisle [aɪl] *n* (*of church*) allée centrale; nef latérale; (*of theatre etc*) couloir *m*, passage *m*, allée

ajar [ə'dʒɑː*] *adj* entrouvert(e)

akin [ə'kɪn] *adj*: **~ to** (*similar*) qui tient de *or* ressemble à

alarm [ə'lɑːm] *n* alarme *f* ♦ *vt* alarmer; **~ call** *n* coup de fil *m* pour réveiller; **~ clock** *n* réveille-matin *m inv*, réveil *m*

alas [ə'læs] *excl* hélas!

albeit [ɔːl'biːɪt] *conj* (*although*) bien que +*sub*, encore que +*sub*

album ['ælbəm] *n* album *m*

alcohol ['ælkəhɒl] *n* alcool *m*; **~ic** [ælkə'hɒlɪk] *adj* alcoolique ♦ *n* alcoolique *m/f*; **A~ics Anonymous** Alcooliques anonymes

ale [eɪl] *n* bière *f*

alert [ə'lɜːt] *adj* alerte, vif(vive); vigilant(e) ♦ *n* alerte *f* ♦ *vt* alerter; **on the ~** sur le qui-vive; (*MIL*) en état d'alerte

algebra ['ældʒɪbrə] *n* algèbre *m*

Algeria [æl'dʒɪərɪə] *n* Algérie *f*

alias ['eɪlɪəs] *adv* alias ♦ *n* faux nom, nom d'emprunt; (*writer*) pseudonyme *m*

alibi ['ælɪbaɪ] *n* alibi *m*

alien ['eɪlɪən] *n* étranger(ère); (*from outer space*) extraterrestre *mf* ♦ *adj*: **~ (to)** étranger(ère) (à); **~ate** *vt* aliéner; s'aliéner

alight [ə'laɪt] *adj, adv* en feu ♦ *vi* mettre pied à terre; (*passenger*) descendre; (*bird*) se poser

alike [ə'laɪk] *adj* semblable, pareil(le) ♦ *adv* de même; **to look ~** se ressembler

alimony ['ælɪmənɪ] *n* (*payment*) pension *f* alimentaire

alive [ə'laɪv] *adj* vivant(e); (*lively*) plein(e) de vie

─────────── KEYWORD ───────────

all [ɔːl] *adj* (*singular*) tout(e); (*plural*) tous(toutes); ~ **day** toute la journée; ~ **night** toute la nuit; ~ **men** tous les hommes; ~ **five** tous les cinq; ~ **the food** toute la nourriture; ~ **the books** tous les livres; ~ **the time** tout le temps; ~ **his life** toute sa vie
♦ *pron* **1** tout; **I ate it** ~, **I ate** ~ **of it** j'ai tout mangé; ~ **of us went** nous y sommes tous allés; ~ **of the boys went** tous les garçons y sont allés
2 (*in phrases*): **above** ~ surtout, par-dessus tout; **after** ~ après tout; **at** ~: **not at** ~ (*in answer to question*) pas du tout; (*in answer to thanks*) je vous en prie!; **I'm not at** ~ **tired** je ne suis pas du tout fatigué(e); **anything at** ~ **will do** n'importe quoi fera l'affaire; ~ **in** ~ tout bien considéré, en fin de compte
♦ *adv*: ~ **alone** tout(e) seul(e); **it's not as hard as** ~ **that** ce n'est pas si difficile que ça; ~ **the more/the better** d'autant plus/mieux; ~ **but** presque, pratiquement; **the score is 2** ~ le score est de 2 partout

allay [ə'leɪ] *vt* (*fears*) apaiser, calmer
allege [ə'ledʒ] *vt* alléguer, prétendre; ~**dly** [ə'ledʒɪdlɪ] *adv* à ce que l'on prétend, paraît-il
allegiance [ə'liːdʒəns] *n* allégeance *f*, fidélité *f*, obéissance *f*
allergic [ə'lɜːdʒɪk] *adj*: ~ **to** allergique à; **allergy** ['ælədʒɪ] *n* allergie *f*
alleviate [ə'liːvɪeɪt] *vt* soulager, adoucir
alley ['ælɪ] *n* ruelle *f*
alliance [ə'laɪəns] *n* alliance *f*
allied ['ælaɪd] *adj* allié(e)
all-in ['ɔːlɪn] (*BRIT*) *adj* (*also adv: charge*) tout compris; ~ **wrestling** *n* lutte *f* libre
all-night ['ɔːl'naɪt] *adj* ouvert(e) *or* qui dure toute la nuit
allocate ['æləkeɪt] *vt* (*share out*) répartir, distribuer; (*duties*): **to** ~ **sth to** assigner *or* attribuer qch à; (*sum, time*): **to** ~ **sth to** allouer qch à
allot [ə'lɒt] *vt*: **to** ~ (**to**) (*money*) répartir (entre), distribuer (à); (*time*) allouer (à); ~**ment** *n* (*share*) part *f*; (*garden*) lopin *m* de terre (*loué à la municipalité*)
all-out ['ɔːl'aʊt] *adj* (*effort etc*) total(e) ♦ *adv*: **all out** à fond
allow [ə'laʊ] *vt* (*practice, behaviour*) permettre, autoriser; (*sum to spend etc*) accorder; allouer; (*sum, time estimated*) compter, prévoir; (*claim, goal*) admettre; (*concede*): **to** ~ **that** convenir que; **to** ~ **sb to do** permettre à qn de faire, autoriser qn à faire; **he is** ~**ed to** ... on lui permet de ...; ~ **for** *vt fus* tenir compte de; ~**ance** *n* (*money received*) allocation *f*; subside *m*; indemnité *f*,

(*TAX*) somme *f* déductible du revenu imposable, abattement *m*; **to make** ~**ances for** tenir compte de
alloy ['ælɔɪ] *n* alliage *m*
all: ~ **right** *adv* (*feel, work*) bien; (*as answer*) d'accord; ~-**rounder** *n*: **to be a good** ~-**rounder** être doué(e) en tout; ~-**time** *adj* (*record*) sans précédent, absolu(e)
allude [ə'luːd] *vi*: **to** ~ **to** faire allusion à
alluring [ə'ljʊərɪŋ] *adj* séduisant(e)
ally [*n* 'ælaɪ, *vb* ə'laɪ] *n* allié *m* ♦ *vt*: **to** ~ **o.s. with** s'allier avec
almighty [ɔːl'maɪtɪ] *adj* tout-puissant; (*tremendous*) énorme
almond ['ɑːmənd] *n* amande *f*
almost ['ɔːlməʊst] *adv* presque
alms [ɑːmz] *npl* aumône *f*
aloft [ə'lɒft] *adv* en l'air
alone [ə'ləʊn] *adj, adv* seul(e); **to leave sb** ~ laisser qn tranquille; **to leave sth** ~ ne pas toucher à qch; **let** ~ ... sans parler de ...; encore moins ...
along [ə'lɒŋ] *prep* le long de ♦ *adv*: **is he coming** ~ **with us?** vient-il avec nous?; **he was hopping/limping** ~ il avançait en sautillant/boitant; ~ **with** (*together with: person*) en compagnie de; (: *thing*) avec, en plus de; **all** ~ (*all the time*) depuis le début; ~**side** *prep* le long de; à côté de ♦ *adv* bord à bord
aloof [ə'luːf] *adj* distant(e) ♦ *adv*: **to stand** ~ se tenir à distance *or* à l'écart
aloud [ə'laʊd] *adv* à haute voix
alphabet ['ælfəbet] *n* alphabet *m*; ~**ical** [ælfə'betɪkl] *adj* alphabétique
alpine ['ælpaɪn] *adj* alpin(e), alpestre
Alps [ælps] *npl*: **the** ~ les Alpes *fpl*
already [ɔːl'redɪ] *adv* déjà
alright ['ɔːl'raɪt] (*BRIT*) *adv* = **all right**
Alsatian [æl'seɪʃən] (*BRIT*) *n* (*dog*) berger allemand
also ['ɔːlsəʊ] *adv* aussi
altar ['ɔːltə*] *n* autel *m*
alter ['ɔːltə*] *vt, vi* changer
alternate [*adj* ɒl'tɜːnɪt, *vb* 'ɒltɜːneɪt] *adj* alterné(e), alternant(e), alternatif(ive) ♦ *vi* alterner; **on** ~ **days** un jour sur deux, tous les deux jours; **alternating current** *n* courant alternatif
alternative [ɒl'tɜːnətɪv] *adj* (*solutions*) possible, au choix; (*plan*) autre, de rechange; (*lifestyle, medicine*) parallèle ♦ *n* (*choice*) alternative *f*; (*other possibility*) solution *f* de remplacement *or* de rechange, autre possibilité *f*; **an** ~ **comedian** un nouveau comique; ~**ly** *adv*: ~**ly one could** one autre *or* l'autre solution serait de, on pourrait aussi
alternator ['ɒltɜːneɪtə*] *n* (*AUT*) alternateur *m*
although [ɔːl'ðəʊ] *conj* bien que +*sub*
altitude ['æltɪtjuːd] *n* altitude *f*
alto ['æltəʊ] *n* (*female*) contralto *m*; (*male*)

haute-contre f
altogether [ɔːltəˈgeðə*] adv entièrement,
tout à fait; (on the whole) tout compte fait;
(in all) en tout
aluminium [æljuˈmɪnɪəm] (BRIT), **aluminum** [əˈluːmɪnəm] (US) n aluminium m
always [ˈɔːlweɪz] adv toujours
Alzheimer's (disease) [ælts'haɪməz] n
maladie f d'Alzheimer
am [æm] vb see **be**
a.m. adv abbr (= ante meridiem) du matin
amalgamate [əˈmælgəmeɪt] vt, vi fusionner
amateur [ˈæmətə:*] n amateur m; ~**ish**
(pej) adj d'amateur
amaze [əˈmeɪz] vt stupéfier; **to be ~d (at)**
être stupéfait(e) (de); ~**ment** n stupéfac-
tion f, stupeur f; **amazing** [əˈmeɪzɪŋ] adj
étonnant(e); exceptionnel(le)
ambassador [æmˈbæsədə*] n ambassadeur
m
amber [ˈæmbə*] n ambre m; **at** ~ (BRIT:
AUT) à l'orange
ambiguous [æmˈbɪgjuəs] adj ambigu(ë)
ambition [æmˈbɪʃən] n ambition f
ambitious [æmˈbɪʃəs] adj ambitieux(euse)
amble [ˈæmbl] vi (also: to ~ along) aller
d'un pas tranquille
ambulance [ˈæmbjuləns] n ambulance f
ambush [ˈæmbʊʃ] n embuscade f ♦ vt tendre une embuscade à
amenable [əˈmiːnəbl] adj: ~ **to** (advice etc)
disposé(e) à écouter
amend [əˈmend] vt (law) amender; (text)
corriger; **to make ~s** réparer ses torts, faire
amende honorable
amenities [əˈmiːnɪtɪz] npl aménagements
mpl, équipements mpl
America [əˈmerɪkə] n Amérique f; ~**n** adj
américain(e) ♦ n Américain(e)
amiable [ˈeɪmɪəbl] adj aimable, affable
amicable [ˈæmɪkəbl] adj amical(e); (JUR) à
l'amiable
amid(st) [əˈmɪd(st)] prep parmi, au milieu
de
amiss [əˈmɪs] adj, adv: **there's something**
~ il y a quelque chose qui ne va pas or
qui cloche; **to take sth** ~ prendre qch mal
or de travers
ammonia [əˈməʊnɪə] n (gas) ammoniac m;
(liquid) ammoniaque f
ammunition [æmjuˈnɪʃən] n munitions fpl
amok [əˈmɒk] adv: **to run** ~ être pris(e)
d'un accès de folie furieuse
among(st) [əˈmʌŋ(st)] prep parmi, entre
amorous [ˈæmərəs] adj amoureux(euse)
amount [əˈmaʊnt] n (sum) somme f, montant m; (quantity) quantité f, nombre m ♦
vi: **to** ~ **to** (total) s'élever à; (be same as)
équivaloir à, revenir à
amp(ere) [ˈæmp(eə*)] n ampère m
ample [ˈæmpl] adj ample; spacieux(euse);
(enough): **this is** ~ c'est largement suffi-

sant; **to have** ~ **time/room** avoir bien assez de temps/place
amplifier [ˈæmplɪfaɪə*] n amplificateur m
amuse [əˈmjuːz] vt amuser, divertir;
~**ment** n amusement m; ~**ment arcade**
n salle f de jeu
an [æn] indef art see **a**
anaemic [əˈniːmɪk] (US **anemic**) adj anémique
anaesthetic [ænɪsˈθetɪk] n anesthésique m
analog(ue) [ˈænəlɒg] adj (watch, computer)
analogique
analyse [ˈænəlaɪz] (US **analyze**) vt analyser;
analysis [əˈnælɪsɪs] (pl **analyses**) n analyse
f; **analyst** [ˈænəlɪst] n (POL etc) spécialiste
m/f; (US) psychanalyste m/f
analyze [ˈænəlaɪz] (US) vt = **analyse**
anarchist [ˈænəkɪst] n anarchiste m/f
anarchy [ˈænəkɪ] n anarchie f
anatomy [əˈnætəmɪ] n anatomie f
ancestor [ˈænsɪstə*] n ancêtre m, aïeul m
anchor [ˈæŋkə*] n ancre f ♦ vi (also: to
drop ~) jeter l'ancre, mouiller ♦ vt mettre à
l'ancre; (fig): **to** ~ **sth to** fixer qch à; **to
weigh** ~ lever l'ancre
anchovy [ˈæntʃəvɪ] n anchois m
ancient [ˈeɪnʃənt] adj ancien(ne), antique;
(person) d'un âge vénérable; (car) antédilu-
vien(ne)
ancillary [ænˈsɪlərɪ] adj auxiliaire
and [ænd] conj et; ~ **so on** et ainsi de suite; **try** ~ **come** tâchez de venir; **he talked**
~ **talked** il n'a pas arrêté de parler; **better**
~ **better** de mieux en mieux
anew [əˈnjuː] adv à nouveau
angel [ˈeɪndʒəl] n ange m
anger [ˈæŋgə*] n colère f
angina [ænˈdʒaɪnə] n angine f de poitrine
angle [ˈæŋgl] n angle m; **from their** ~ de
leur point de vue
angler [ˈæŋglə*] n pêcheur(euse) à la ligne
Anglican [ˈæŋglɪkən] adj, n anglican(e)
angling [ˈæŋglɪŋ] n pêche f à la ligne
angrily [ˈæŋgrɪlɪ] adv avec colère
angry [ˈæŋgrɪ] adj en colère, furieux(euse);
(wound) enflammé(e); **to be** ~ **with sb/at
sth** être furieux contre qn/de qch; **to get**
~ se fâcher, se mettre en colère
anguish [ˈæŋgwɪʃ] n (physical) supplice m;
(mental) angoisse f
angular [ˈæŋgjulə*] adj anguleux(euse)
animal [ˈænɪməl] n animal m ♦ adj ani-
mal(e)
animate [vb ˈænɪmeɪt, adj ˈænɪmət] vt animer ♦ adj animé(e), vivant(e); ~**d** adj ani-
mé(e)
aniseed [ˈænɪsiːd] n anis m
ankle [ˈæŋkl] n cheville f; ~ **sock** n socquette f
annex [n ˈæneks, vb əˈneks] n (also: BRIT:
~**e**) annexe f ♦ vt annexer
anniversary [ænɪˈvɜːsərɪ] n anniversaire m

announce [ə'naʊns] vt annoncer; (*birth, death*) faire part de; **~ment** n annonce f; (*for births etc: in newspaper*) avis m de faire-part; (: *letter, card*) faire-part m; **~r** n (*RADIO, TV: between programmes*) speaker(ine)

annoy [ə'nɔɪ] vt agacer, ennuyer, contrarier; **don't get ~ed!** ne vous fâchez pas!; **~ance** n mécontentement m, contrariété f; **~ing** adj agaçant(e), contrariant(e)

annual ['ænjʊəl] adj annuel(le) ♦ n (*BOT*) plante annuelle; (*children's book*) album m

annul [ə'nʌl] vt annuler

annum ['ænəm] n see **per**

anonymous [ə'nɒnɪməs] adj anonyme

anorak ['ænəræk] n anorak m

another [ə'nʌðə*] adj: **~ book** (*one more*) un autre livre, encore un livre, un livre de plus; (*a different one*) un autre livre ♦ pron un(e) autre, encore un(e), un(e) de plus; *see also* **one**

answer ['ɑ:nsə*] n réponse f; (*to problem*) solution f ♦ vi répondre ♦ vt (*reply to*) répondre à; (*problem*) résoudre; (*prayer*) exaucer; **in ~ to your letter** en réponse à votre lettre; **to ~ the phone** répondre (au téléphone); **to ~ the bell** or **the door** aller or venir ouvrir (la porte); **~ back** vi répondre, répliquer; **~ for** vt fus (*person*) répondre de, se porter garant de; (*crime, one's actions*) être responsable de; **~ to** vt fus (*description*) répondre or correspondre à; **~able** adj: **~able (to sb/for sth)** responsable (devant qn/de qch); **~ing machine** n répondeur m automatique

ant [ænt] n fourmi f

antagonism [æn'tægənɪzəm] n antagonisme m

antagonize [æn'tægənaɪz] vt éveiller l'hostilité de, contrarier

Antarctic [ænt'ɑ:ktɪk] n: **the ~** l'Antarctique m

antenatal [ænti'neɪtl] adj prénatal(e); **~ clinic** n service m de consultation prénatale

anthem ['ænθəm] n: **national ~** hymne national

anti: **~-aircraft** [ænti'ɛəkrɑ:ft] adj (*missile*) anti-aérien(ne); **~biotic** ['æntɪbaɪ'ɒtɪk] n antibiotique m; **~body** ['æntɪbɒdɪ] n anticorps m

anticipate [æn'tɪsɪpeɪt] vt s'attendre à; prévoir; (*wishes, request*) aller au devant de, devancer

anticipation [æntɪsɪ'peɪʃən] n attente f, **with ~** impatiemment

anticlimax ['æntɪ'klaɪmæks] n déception f, douche froide (col)

anticlockwise ['æntɪ'klɒkwaɪz] adj, adv dans le sens inverse des aiguilles d'une montre

antics ['æntɪks] npl singeries fpl

antifreeze ['æntɪfri:z] n antigel m

antihistamine [ænti'hɪstəmi:n] n antihistaminique m

antiquated ['æntɪkweɪtɪd] adj vieilli(e), suranné(e), vieillot(te)

antique [æn'ti:k] n objet m d'art ancien, meuble ancien or d'époque, antiquité f ♦ adj ancien(ne); **~ dealer** n antiquaire m; **~ shop** n magasin m d'antiquités

anti: **~Semitism** [æntɪ'semɪtɪzəm] n antisémitisme m; **~septic** [æntɪ'septɪk] n antiseptique m; **~social** [æntɪ'səʊʃl] adj peu liant(e), sauvage, insociable; (*against society*) antisocial(e)

antlers ['æntləz] npl bois mpl, ramure f

anvil ['ænvɪl] n enclume f

anxiety [æŋ'zaɪətɪ] n anxiété f; (*keenness*): **~ to do** grand désir or impatience f de faire

anxious ['æŋkʃəs] adj anxieux(euse), angoissé(e); (*worrying: time, situation*) inquiétant(e); (*keen*): **~ to do/that** qui tient beaucoup à faire/à ce que; impatient(e) de faire/que

─────────────── **KEYWORD**

any ['enɪ] adj **1** (*in questions etc: singular*) du, de l', de la; (*in questions etc: plural*) des; **have you ~ butter/children/ink?** avez-vous du beurre/des enfants/de l'encre?

2 (*with negative*) de, d'; **I haven't ~ money/books** je n'ai pas d'argent/de livres

3 (*no matter which*) n'importe quel(le); **choose ~ book you like** vous pouvez choisir n'importe quel livre

4 (*in phrases*): **in ~ case** de toute façon; **~ day now** d'un jour à l'autre; **at ~ moment** à tout moment, d'un instant à l'autre; **at ~ rate** en tout cas

♦ pron **1** (*in questions etc*) en; **have you got ~?** est-ce que vous en avez?; **can ~ of you sing?** est-ce que parmi vous il y en a qui chantent?

2 (*with negative*) en; **I haven't ~ (of them)** je n'en ai pas, je n'en ai aucun

3 (*no matter which one(s)*) n'importe lequel (or laquelle); **take ~ of those books (you like)** vous pouvez prendre n'importe lequel de ces livres

♦ adv **1** (*in questions etc*): **do you want ~ more soup/sandwiches?** voulez-vous encore de la soupe/des sandwichs?; **are you feeling ~ better?** est-ce que vous vous sentez mieux?

2 (*with negative*): **I can't hear him ~ more** je ne l'entends plus; **don't wait ~ longer** n'attendez pas plus longtemps

─────────────

any: **~body** ['enɪbɒdɪ] pron n'importe qui; (*in interrogative sentences*) quelqu'un; (*in negative sentences*): **I don't see ~** je ne vois personne; ~**how** adv (at any rate) de toute façon, quand même; (haphazard) n'importe comment; ~**one** [-wʌn] pron = anybody; ~**thing** pron n'importe quoi, quelque chose, ne ... rien; ~**way** adv de toute façon; ~**where** adv n'importe où, quelque part; **I don't see him** ~ je ne le vois nulle part

apart [ə'pɑːt] adv (to one side) à part; de côté; à l'écart; (separately) séparément; **10 miles** ~ à 10 miles l'un de l'autre; **to take** ~ démonter; ~ **from** à part, excepté

apartheid [ə'pɑːteɪt] n apartheid m

apartment [ə'pɑːtmənt] n (US) appartement m, logement m; (room) chambre f; ~ **building** (US) n immeuble m; maison divisée en appartements

ape [eɪp] n (grand) singe ♦ vt singer

apéritif [ə'perɪtiːf] n apéritif m

aperture ['æpətjʊə*] n orifice m, ouverture f; (PHOT) ouverture (du diaphragme)

apex ['eɪpeks] n sommet m

apiece [ə'piːs] adv chacun(e)

apologetic [əpɒlə'dʒetɪk] adj (tone, letter) d'excuse; (person): **to be** ~ s'excuser

apologize [ə'pɒlədʒaɪz] vi: **to** ~ **(for sth to sb)** s'excuser (de qch auprès de qn), présenter des excuses (à qn pour qch)

apology [ə'pɒlədʒɪ] n excuses fpl

apostrophe [ə'pɒstrəfɪ] n apostrophe f

appal [ə'pɔːl] vt consterner; ~**ling** [ə'pɔːlɪŋ] adj épouvantable; (stupidity) consternant(e)

apparatus [æpə'reɪtəs] n appareil m, dispositif m; (in gymnasium) agrès mpl; (of government) dispositif m

apparel [ə'pærəl] (US) n habillement m

apparent [ə'pærənt] adj apparent(e); ~**ly** adv apparemment

appeal [ə'piːl] vi (LAW) faire or interjeter appel ♦ n appel m; (request) prière f; appel m; (charm) attrait m, charme m; **to** ~ **for** lancer un appel pour; **to** ~ **to** (beg) faire appel à; (be attractive) plaire à; **it doesn't** ~ **to me** cela ne m'attire pas; ~**ing** adj (attractive) attrayant(e)

appear [ə'pɪə*] vi apparaître, se montrer; (LAW) comparaître; (publication) paraître, sortir, être publié(e); (seem) paraître, sembler; **it would** ~ **that** il semble que; **to** ~ **in Hamlet** jouer dans Hamlet; **to** ~ **on TV** passer à la télé; ~**ance** n apparition f; parution f; (look, aspect) apparence f, aspect m

appease [ə'piːz] vt apaiser, calmer

appendicitis [əpendɪ'saɪtɪs] n appendicite f

appendix [ə'pendɪks] (pl **appendices**) n appendice m

appetite ['æpɪtaɪt] n appétit m

appetizer ['æpɪtaɪzə*] n amuse-gueule m; (drink) apéritif m

applaud [ə'plɔːd] vt, vi applaudir

applause [ə'plɔːz] n applaudissements mpl

apple ['æpl] n pomme f; ~ **tree** n pommier m

appliance [ə'plaɪəns] n appareil m

applicable [ə'plɪkəbl] adj (relevant): **to be** ~ **to** valoir pour

applicant ['æplɪkənt] n: ~ **(for)** candidat(e) (à)

application [æplɪ'keɪʃən] n application f; (for a job, a grant etc) demande f; candidature f; ~ **form** n formulaire m de demande

applied [ə'plaɪd] adj appliqué(e)

apply [ə'plaɪ] vt (paint, ointment): **to** ~ **(to)** appliquer (sur); (law etc): **to** ~ **(to)** appliquer (à) ♦ vi: **to** ~ **to** (be suitable for, relevant to) s'appliquer à; (ask) s'adresser à; **to** ~ **(for)** (permit, grant) faire une demande (en vue d'obtenir); (job) poser sa candidature (pour), faire une demande d'emploi (concernant); **to** ~ **o.s. to** s'appliquer à

appoint [ə'pɔɪnt] vt nommer, engager; ~**ed** adj: **at the** ~**ed time** à l'heure dite; ~**ment** n nomination f; (meeting) rendez-vous m; **to make an** ~**ment (with)** prendre rendez-vous (avec)

appraisal [ə'preɪzl] n évaluation f

appreciate [ə'priːʃɪeɪt] vt (like) apprécier; (be grateful for) être reconnaissant(e) de; (understand) comprendre; se rendre compte de ♦ vi (FINANCE) prendre de la valeur

appreciation [əpriːʃɪ'eɪʃən] n appréciation f; (gratitude) reconnaissance f; (COMM) hausse f, valorisation f

appreciative [ə'priːʃɪətɪv] adj (person) sensible; (comment) élogieux(euse)

apprehensive [æprɪ'hensɪv] adj inquiet(ète), appréhensif(ive)

apprentice [ə'prentɪs] n apprenti m; ~**ship** n apprentissage m

approach [ə'prəʊtʃ] vi approcher ♦ vt (come near) approcher de; (ask, apply to) s'adresser à; (situation, problem) aborder ♦ n approche f; (access) accès m; ~**able** adj accessible

appropriate [adj ə'prəʊprɪət, vb ə'prəʊprɪeɪt] adj (moment, remark) opportun(e); (tool etc) approprié(e) ♦ vt (take) s'approprier

approval [ə'pruːvəl] n approbation f; **on** ~ (COMM) à l'examen

approve [ə'pruːv] vt approuver; ~ **of** vt fus approuver

approximate [adj ə'prɒksɪmɪt, vb ə'prɒksɪmeɪt] adj approximatif(ive) ♦ vt se rapprocher de, être proche de; ~**ly** adv approximativement

apricot ['eɪprɪkɒt] n abricot m

April ['eɪprəl] n avril m; ~ **Fool's Day** le premier avril

apron ['eɪprən] n tablier m

apt [æpt] adj (suitable) approprié(e); (likely): ~ **to do** susceptible de faire; qui a tendance à faire

Aquarius [ə'kwɛərɪəs] *n* le Verseau
Arab ['ærəb] *adj* arabe ♦ *n* Arabe *m/f*; ~**ian** [ə'reɪbɪən] *adj* arabe; ~**ic** ['ærəbɪk] *adj* arabe ♦ *n* arabe *m*
arbitrary ['ɑːbɪtrərɪ] *adj* arbitraire
arbitration [ɑːbɪ'treɪʃən] *n* arbitrage *m*
arcade [ɑː'keɪd] *n* arcade *f*; (*passage with shops*) passage *m*, galerie marchande
arch [ɑːtʃ] *n* arc *m*; (*of foot*) cambrure *f*, voûte *f* plantaire ♦ *vt* arquer, cambrer
archaeologist [ɑːkɪ'ɒlədʒɪst] *n* archéologue *m/f*; **archaeology** [ɑːkɪ'ɒlədʒɪ] *n* archéologie *f*
archbishop ['ɑːtʃ'bɪʃəp] *n* archevêque *m*
archenemy ['ɑːtʃ'enɪmɪ] *n* ennemi *m* de toujours *or* juré
archeology *etc* (*US*) = **archaeology** *etc*
archery [ɑːtʃərɪ] *n* tir *m* à l'arc
architect ['ɑːkɪtekt] *n* architecte *m*; ~**ure** *n* architecture *f*
archives ['ɑːkaɪvz] *npl* archives *fpl*
Arctic ['ɑːktɪk] *adj* arctique ♦ *n*: **the ~** l'Arctique *m*
ardent ['ɑːdənt] *adj* fervent(e)
are [ɑː*] *vb see* **be**
area ['ɛərɪə] *n* (*GEOM*) superficie *f*; (*zone*) région *f*; (: *smaller*) secteur *m*, partie *f*; (*in room*) coin *m*; (*knowledge, research*) domaine *m*
aren't [ɑːnt] = **are not**
Argentina [ɑːdʒən'tiːnə] *n* Argentine *f*; **Argentinian** [ɑːdʒən'tɪnɪən] *adj* argentin(e) ♦ *n* Argentin(e)
arguably ['ɑːɡjuəblɪ] *adv*: **it is ~** ... on peut soutenir que c'est ...
argue ['ɑːɡjuː] *vi* (*quarrel*) se disputer; (*reason*) argumenter; **to ~ that** objecter *or* alléguer que
argument ['ɑːɡjumənt] *n* (*reasons*) argument *m*; (*quarrel*) dispute *f*; ~**ative** [ɑːɡjuʹmentətɪv] *adj* ergoteur(euse), raisonneur(euse)
Aries ['ɛəriːz] *n* le Bélier
arise [ə'raɪz] (*pt* **arose**, *pp* **arisen**) *vi* survenir, se présenter
aristocrat ['ærɪstəkræt] *n* aristocrate *m/f*
arithmetic [ə'rɪθmətɪk] *n* arithmétique *f*
ark [ɑːk] *n*: **Noah's A~** l'Arche *f* de Noé
arm [ɑːm] *n* bras *m* ♦ *vt* armer; ~**s** *npl* (*weapons, HERALDRY*) armes *fpl*; ~ **in** ~ bras dessus bras dessous
armaments ['ɑːməmənts] *npl* armement *m*
arm: ~**chair** *n* fauteuil *m*; ~**ed** *adj* armé(e); ~**ed robbery** *n* vol *m* à main armée
armour ['ɑːmə*] (*US* **armor**) *n* armure *f*; (*MIL*: *tanks*) blindés *mpl*; ~**ed car** *n* véhicule blindé
armpit ['ɑːmpɪt] *n* aisselle *f*
armrest ['ɑːmrest] *n* accoudoir *m*
army ['ɑːmɪ] *n* armée *f*
aroma [ə'rəumə] *n* arôme *m*

arose [ə'rəuz] *pt of* **arise**
around [ə'raund] *adv* autour; (*nearby*) dans les parages ♦ *prep* autour de; (*near*) près de; (*fig: about*) environ; (: *date, time*) vers
arouse [ə'rauz] *vt* (*sleeper*) éveiller; (*curiosity, passions*) éveiller, susciter; (*anger*) exciter
arrange [ə'reɪndʒ] *vt* arranger; **to ~ to do sth** prévoir de faire qch; ~**ment** *n* arrangement *m*; ~**ments** *npl* (*plans etc*) arrangements *mpl*, dispositions *fpl*
array [ə'reɪ] *n*: ~ **of** déploiement *m or* étalage *m* de
arrears [ə'rɪəz] *npl* arriéré *m*; **to be in ~ with one's rent** devoir un arriéré de loyer
arrest [ə'rest] *vt* arrêter; (*sb's attention*) retenir, attirer ♦ *n* arrestation *f*; **under ~** en état d'arrestation
arrival [ə'raɪvəl] *n* arrivée *f*; **new ~** nouveau venu, nouvelle venue; (*baby*) nouveau-né(e)
arrive [ə'raɪv] *vi* arriver
arrogant ['ærəgənt] *adj* arrogant(e)
arrow ['ærəu] *n* flèche *f*
arse [ɑːs] (*BRIT: infl*) *n* cul *m* (*!*)
arson ['ɑːsn] *n* incendie criminel
art [ɑːt] *n* art *m*; **A~s** *npl* (*SCOL*) les lettres *fpl*
artery ['ɑːtərɪ] *n* artère *f*
artful ['ɑːtful] *adj* astucieux(euse), rusé(e)
art gallery *n* musée *m* d'art; (*small and private*) galerie *f* de peinture
arthritis [ɑː'θraɪtɪs] *n* arthrite *f*
artichoke ['ɑːtɪtʃəuk] *n* (*also: globe ~*) artichaut *m*; (: *Jerusalem ~*) topinambour *m*
article ['ɑːtɪkl] *n* article *m*; ~**s** *npl* (*BRIT: LAW: training*) ≈ stage *m*; ~ **of clothing** vêtement *m*
articulate [*adj* ɑː'tɪkjulɪt, *vb* ɑː'tɪkjuleɪt] *adj* (*person*) qui s'exprime bien; (*speech*) bien articulé(e), prononcé(e) clairement ♦ *vt* exprimer; ~**d lorry** (*BRIT*) *n* (camion *m*) semi-remorque *m*
artificial [ɑːtɪ'fɪʃəl] *adj* artificiel(le)
artist ['ɑːtɪst] *n* artiste *m/f*; ~**ic** [ɑː'tɪstɪk] *adj* artistique; ~**ry** *n* art *m*, talent *m*
art school *n* ≈ école *f* des beaux-arts

────────────── KEYWORD

as [æz] *conj* **1** (*referring to time*) comme, alors que; à mesure que; **he came in ~ I was leaving** il est arrivé comme je partais; ~ **the years went by** à mesure que les années passaient; ~ **from tomorrow** à partir de demain
2 (*in comparisons*): ~ **big** ~ aussi grand que; **twice ~ big** ~ deux fois plus grand que; ~ **much** *or* **many** ~ autant que; ~ **much money/many books** autant d'argent/de livres que; ~ **soon** ~ dès que
3 (*since, because*) comme, puisque; ~ **he had to be home by 10** ... comme il *or*

puisqu'il devait être de retour avant 10h ...
4 (referring to manner, way) comme; **do ~ you wish** faites comme vous voudrez
5 (concerning): **~ for** or **to that** quant à cela, pour ce qui est de cela
6: **~ if** or **though** comme si; **he looked ~ if he was ill** il avait l'air d'être malade; see also **long; such; well**
♦ prep: **he works ~ a driver** il travaille comme chauffeur; **~ chairman of the company, he ...** en tant que président de la compagnie, il ...; **dressed up ~ a cowboy** déguisé en cowboy; **he gave me it ~ a present** il me l'a offert, il m'en a fait cadeau

a.s.a.p. abbr (= as soon as possible) dès que possible
asbestos [æz'bɛstəs] n amiante f
ascend [ə'sɛnd] vt gravir; (throne) monter sur
ascent [ə'sɛnt] n ascension f
ascertain [æsə'teɪn] vt vérifier
ascribe [ə'skraɪb] vt: **to ~ sth to** attribuer qch à
ash [æʃ] n (dust) cendre f; (also: ~ tree) frêne m
ashamed [ə'ʃeɪmd] adj honteux(euse), confus(e); **to be ~ of** avoir honte de
ashen ['æʃən] adj (pale) cendreux(euse), blême
ashore [ə'ʃɔː*] adv à terre
ashtray ['æʃtreɪ] n cendrier m
Ash Wednesday n mercredi m des cendres
Asia ['eɪʃə] n Asie f; **~n** n Asiatique m/f ♦ adj asiatique
aside [ə'saɪd] adv de côté; à l'écart ♦ n aparté m
ask [ɑːsk] vt demander; (invite) inviter; **to ~ sb sth/to do sth** demander qch à qn/à qn de faire qch; **to ~ sb about sth** questionner qn sur qch; se renseigner auprès de qn sur qch; **to ~ (sb) a question** poser une question (à qn); **to ~ sb out to dinner** inviter qn au restaurant; **~ after** vt fus demander des nouvelles de; **~ for** vt fus demander; (trouble) chercher
askance [ə'kɑːns] adv: **to look ~ at sb** regarder qn de travers or d'un œil désapprobateur
asking price ['ɑːskɪŋ] n: **the ~** le prix de départ
asleep [ə'sliːp] adj endormi(e); **to fall ~** s'endormir
asparagus [əs'pærəgəs] n asperges fpl
aspect ['æspɛkt] n aspect m; (direction in which a building etc faces) orientation f, exposition f
aspersions [əs'pɜːʃənz] npl: **to cast ~ on** dénigrer
aspire [əs'paɪə*] vi: **to ~ to** aspirer à

aspirin ['æsprɪn] n aspirine f
ass [æs] n âne m; (inf) imbécile m/f; (US: inf!) cul m (!)
assailant [ə'seɪlənt] n agresseur m; assaillant m
assassinate [ə'sæsɪneɪt] vt assassiner; **assassination** [əsæsɪ'neɪʃən] n assassinat m
assault [ə'sɔːlt] n (MIL) assaut m; (gen: attack) agression f ♦ vt attaquer; (sexually) violenter
assemble [ə'sɛmbl] vt assembler ♦ vi s'assembler, se rassembler
assembly [ə'sɛmblɪ] n assemblée f, réunion f; (institution) assemblée; (construction) assemblage m; **~ line** n chaîne f de montage
assent [ə'sɛnt] n assentiment m, consentement m
assert [ə'sɜːt] vt affirmer, déclarer; (one's authority) faire valoir; (one's innocence) protester de
assess [ə'sɛs] vt évaluer; (tax, payment) établir or fixer le montant de; (property etc: for tax) calculer la valeur imposable de; (person) juger la valeur de; **~ment** n évaluation f, fixation f, calcul m de la valeur imposable de, jugement m; **~or** n expert m (impôt et assurance)
asset ['æsɛt] n avantage m, atout m; **~s** npl (FINANCE) capital m; avoir(s) m(pl); actif m
assign [ə'saɪn] vt (date) fixer; (task) assigner à; (resources) affecter à; **~ment** [ə'saɪnmənt] n tâche f, mission f
assist [ə'sɪst] vt aider, assister; **~ance** n aide f, assistance f; **~ant** n assistant(e), adjoint(e); (BRIT: also: **shop ~ant**) vendeur(euse)
associate [adj, n ə'səʊʃɪɪt, vb ə'səʊʃɪeɪt] adj, n associé(e) ♦ vt associer ♦ vi: **to ~ with sb** fréquenter qn; **association** [əsəʊsɪ'eɪʃən] n association f
assorted [ə'sɔːtɪd] adj assorti(e)
assortment [ə'sɔːtmənt] n assortiment m
assume [ə'sjuːm] vt supposer; (responsibilities etc) assumer; (attitude, name) prendre, adopter; **~d name** n nom m d'emprunt; **assumption** [ə'sʌmpʃən] n supposition f, hypothèse f; (of power) assomption f, prise f
assurance [ə'ʃʊərəns] n assurance f
assure [ə'ʃʊə*] vt assurer
asthma ['æsmə] n asthme m
astonish [əs'tɒnɪʃ] vt étonner, stupéfier; **~ment** n étonnement m
astound [əs'taʊnd] vt stupéfier, sidérer
astray [əs'treɪ] adv: **to go ~** s'égarer; (fig) quitter le droit chemin; **to lead ~** détourner du droit chemin
astride [əs'traɪd] prep à cheval sur
astrology [əs'trɒlədʒɪ] n astrologie f
astronaut ['æstrənɔːt] n astronaute m/f
astronomy [əs'trɒnəmɪ] n astronomie f
astute [əs'tjuːt] adj astucieux(euse)

asylum [ə'saɪləm] *n* asile *m*

KEYWORD

at [æt] *prep* **1** (*referring to position, direction*) à; ~ **the top** au sommet; ~ **home/school** à la maison *or* chez soi/à l'école; ~ **the baker's** à la boulangerie, chez le boulanger; **to look** ~ **sth** regarder qch
2 (*referring to time*): ~ **4 o'clock** à 4 heures; ~ **Christmas** à Noël; ~ **night** la nuit; ~ **times** par moments, parfois
3 (*referring to rates, speed etc*) à; ~ **£1 a kilo** une livre le kilo; **two** ~ **a time** deux à la fois; ~ **50 km/h** à 50 km/h
4 (*referring to manner*): ~ **a stroke** d'un seul coup; ~ **peace** en paix
5 (*referring to activity*): **to be** ~ **work** être à l'œuvre, travailler; **to play** ~ **cowboys** jouer aux cowboys; **to be good** ~ **sth** être bon en qch
6 (*referring to cause*): **shocked/surprised/annoyed** ~ **sth** choqué par/étonné de/agacé par qch; **I went** ~ **his suggestion** j'y suis allé sur son conseil

ate [et, eɪt] *pt of* **eat**
atheist ['eɪθɪɪst] *n* athée *m/f*
Athens ['æθɪnz] *n* Athènes
athlete ['æθliːt] *n* athlète *m/f*
athletic [æθ'letɪk] *adj* athlétique; ~**s** *n* athlétisme *m*
Atlantic [ət'læntɪk] *adj* atlantique ♦ *n*: **the** ~ **(Ocean)** l'Atlantique *m*, l'océan *m* Atlantique
atlas ['ætləs] *n* atlas *m*
atmosphere ['ætməsfɪə*] *n* atmosphère *f*
atom ['ætəm] *n* atome *m*; ~**ic** [ə'tɒmɪk] *adj* atomique; ~**(ic) bomb** *n* bombe *f* atomique; ~**izer** ['ætəmaɪzə*] *n* atomiseur *m*
atone [ə'təʊn] *vi*: **to** ~ **for** expier, racheter
atrocious [ə'trəʊʃəs] *adj* (*very bad*) atroce, exécrable
attach [ə'tætʃ] *vt* attacher; (*document, letter*) joindre; **to be** ~**ed to sb/sth** être attaché à qn/qch
attaché case [ə'tæʃeɪ-] *n* mallette *f*, attaché-case *m*
attachment [ə'tætʃmənt] *n* (*tool*) accessoire *m*; (*love*): ~ **(to)** affection *f* (pour), attachement *m* (à)
attack [ə'tæk] *vt* attaquer; (*task etc*) s'attaquer à ♦ *n* attaque *f*; (*also: heart* ~) crise *f* cardiaque
attain [ə'teɪn] *vt* (*also: to* ~ *to*) parvenir à, atteindre; (: *knowledge*) acquérir; ~**ments** *npl* connaissances *fpl*, résultats *mpl*
attempt [ə'tempt] *n* tentative *f* ♦ *vt* essayer, tenter; **to make an** ~ **on sb's life** attenter à la vie de qn; ~**ed** *adj*: ~**ed murder/suicide** tentative *f* de meurtre/suicide
attend [ə'tend] *vt* (*course*) suivre; (*meeting, talk*) assister à; (*school, church*) aller à, fréquenter; (*patient*) soigner, s'occuper de; ~ **to** *vt fus* (*needs, affairs etc*) s'occuper de; (*customer, patient*) s'occuper de; ~**ance** *n* (*being present*) présence *f*; (*people present*) assistance *f*; ~**ant** *n* employé(e) ♦ *adj* (*dangers*) inhérent(e), concomitant(e)
attention [ə'tenʃən] *n* attention *f*; ~**!** (*MIL*) garde-à-vous!; **for the** ~ **of** (*ADMIN*) à l'attention de
attentive [ə'tentɪv] *adj* attentif(ive); (*kind*) prévenant(e)
attest [ə'test] *vi*: **to** ~ **to** (*demonstrate*) démontrer; (*confirm*) témoigner
attic ['ætɪk] *n* grenier *m*
attitude ['ætɪtjuːd] *n* attitude *f*; pose *f*, maintien *m*
attorney [ə'tɜːnɪ] *n* (*US: lawyer*) avoué *m*; **A~ General** *n* (*BRIT*) ≈ procureur général; (*US*) ≈ garde *m* des Sceaux, ministre *m* de la Justice
attract [ə'trækt] *vt* attirer; ~**ion** [ə'trækʃən] *n* (*gen pl: pleasant things*) attraction *f*, attrait *m*; (*PHYSICS*) attraction *f*; (*fig: towards sb or sth*) attirance *f*; ~**ive** *adj* attrayant(e); (*person*) séduisant(e)
attribute [*n* 'ætrɪbjuːt, *vb* ə'trɪbjuːt] *n* attribut *m* ♦ *vt*: **to** ~ **sth to** attribuer qch à
attrition [ə'trɪʃən] *n*: **war of** ~ guerre *f* d'usure
aubergine ['əʊbəʒiːn] *n* aubergine *f*
auction ['ɔːkʃən] *n* (*also: sale by* ~) vente *f* aux enchères ♦ *vt* (: *to sell by* ~) vendre aux enchères; (: *to put up for* ~) mettre aux enchères; ~**eer** [ɔːkʃə'nɪə*] *n* commissaire-priseur *m*
audience ['ɔːdɪəns] *n* (*people*) assistance *f*; public *m*; spectateurs *mpl*; (*interview*) audience *f*
audiovisual ['ɔːdɪəʊ'vɪʒʊəl] *adj* audiovisuel(le); ~ **aids** *npl* supports *or* moyens audiovisuels
audit ['ɔːdɪt] *vt* vérifier
audition [ɔː'dɪʃən] *n* audition *f*
auditor ['ɔːdɪtə*] *n* vérificateur *m* des comptes
augur ['ɔːɡə*] *vi*: **it** ~**s well** c'est bon signe *or* de bon augure
August ['ɔːɡəst] *n* août *m*
aunt [ɑːnt] *n* tante *f*; ~**ie** *n dimin of* **aunt**; ~**y** *n dimin of* **aunt**
au pair ['əʊ'peə*] *n* (*also*: ~ *girl*) jeune fille *f* au pair
auspicious [ɔːs'pɪʃəs] *adj* de bon augure, propice
Australia [ɒs'treɪlɪə] *n* Australie *f*; ~**n** *adj* australien(ne) ♦ *n* Australien(ne)
Austria ['ɒstrɪə] *n* Autriche *f*; ~**n** *adj* autrichien(ne) ♦ *n* Autrichien(ne)
authentic [ɔː'θentɪk] *adj* authentique
author ['ɔːθə*] *n* auteur *m*
authoritarian [ɔːθɒrɪ'teərɪən] *adj* autoritaire)

authoritative [ɔː'θɒrɪtətɪv] *adj* (*account*) digne de foi; (*study, treatise*) qui fait autorité; (*person, manner*) autoritaire

authority [ɔː'θɒrɪtɪ] *n* autorité f, (*permission*) autorisation (formelle); **the authorities** *npl* (*ruling body*) les autorités *fpl*, l'administration f

authorize ['ɔːθəraɪz] *vt* autoriser

auto ['ɔːtəu] (*US*) *n* auto f, voiture f

auto: **~biography** [ɔːtəubaɪ'ɒgrəfɪ] *n* autobiographie f; **~graph** ['ɔːtəgrɑːf] *n* autographe m ♦ *vt* signer, dédicacer; **~mated** ['ɔːtəmeɪtɪd] *adj* automatisé(e), automatique; **~matic** [ɔːtə'mætɪk] *adj* automatique ♦ *n* (*gun*) automatique m; (*washing machine*) machine f à laver automatique; (*BRIT: AUT*) voiture f à transmission automatique; **~matically** *adv* automatiquement; **~mation** [ɔːtə'meɪʃən] *n* automatisation f (électronique); **~mobile** ['ɔːtəməbiːl] (*US*) *n* automobile f, **~nomy** [ɔː'tɒnəmɪ] *n* autonomie f

autumn ['ɔːtəm] *n* automne m; **in ~** en automne

auxiliary [ɔːg'zɪlɪərɪ] *adj* auxiliaire ♦ *n* auxiliaire *m/f*

avail [ə'veɪl] *vt*: **to ~ o.s. of** profiter de ♦ *n*: **to no ~** sans résultat, en vain, en pure perte

availability [əveɪlə'bɪlɪtɪ] *n* disponibilité f

available [ə'veɪləbl] *adj* disponible

avalanche ['ævəlɑːnʃ] *n* avalanche f

Ave *abbr* = **avenue**

avenge [ə'vendʒ] *vt* venger

avenue ['ævənjuː] *n* avenue f; (*fig*) moyen m

average ['ævərɪdʒ] *n* moyenne f, (*fig*) moyen m ♦ *adj* moyen(ne) ♦ *vt* (*a certain figure*) atteindre or faire etc en moyenne; **on ~** en moyenne; **~ out** *vi*: **to ~ out at** représenter en moyenne, donner une moyenne de

averse [ə'vɜːs] *adj*: **to be ~ to sth/doing sth** éprouver une forte répugnance envers qch/à faire qch

avert [ə'vɜːt] *vt* prévenir, écarter; (*one's eyes*) détourner

aviary ['eɪvɪərɪ] *n* volière f

avocado [ævə'kɑːdəu] *n* (*also: BRIT: ~ pear*) avocat m

avoid [ə'vɔɪd] *vt* éviter

await [ə'weɪt] *vt* attendre

awake [ə'weɪk] (*pt* **awoke**, *pp* **awoken**) *adj* éveillé(e) ♦ *vt* éveiller ♦ *vi* s'éveiller; **~ to** (*dangers, possibilities*) conscient(e) de; **to be ~** être réveillé(e); **he was still ~** il ne dormait pas encore; **~ning** n réveil m

award [ə'wɔːd] *n* récompense f, prix m; (*LAW: damages*) dommages-intérêts *mpl* ♦ *vt* (*prize*) décerner; (*LAW: damages*) accorder

aware [ə'wɛə*] *adj*: **~ (of)** (*conscious*)

conscient(e) (de); (*informed*) au courant (de); **to become ~ of/that** prendre conscience de/que; se rendre compte de/ que; **~ness** *n* conscience f, connaissance f

awash [ə'wɒʃ] *adj*: **~ (with)** inondé(e) (de)

away [ə'weɪ] *adj, adv* au loin; absent(e); **two kilometres ~** à (une distance de) deux kilomètres, à deux kilomètres de distance; **two hours ~ by car** à deux heures de voiture *or* de route; **the holiday was two weeks ~** il restait deux semaines jusqu'aux vacances; **~ from** loin de; **he's ~ for a week** il est parti (pour) une semaine; **to pedal/work/laugh ~** être en train de pédaler/travailler/rire; **to fade ~** (*sound*) s'affaiblir; (*colour*) s'estomper; **to wither ~** (*plant*) se dessécher; **to take ~** emporter; (*subtract*) enlever; **~ game** *n* (*SPORT*) match m à l'extérieur

awe [ɔː] *n* respect mêlé de crainte; **~-inspiring** *adj* impressionnant(e); **~some** *adj* impressionnant(e)

awful ['ɔːfʊl] *adj* affreux(euse); **an ~ lot (of)** un nombre incroyable (de); **~ly** *adv* (*very*) terriblement, vraiment

awhile [ə'waɪl] *adv* un moment, quelque temps

awkward ['ɔːkwəd] *adj* (*clumsy*) gauche, maladroit(e); (*inconvenient*) peu pratique; (*embarrassing*) gênant(e), délicat(e)

awning ['ɔːnɪŋ] *n* (*of tent*) auvent m; (*of shop*) store m; (*of hotel etc*) marquise f

awoke [ə'wəuk] *pt* of **awake**; **~n** [ə'wəukən] *pp* of **awake**

awry [ə'raɪ] *adj, adv* de travers; **to go ~** mal tourner

axe [æks] (*US* **ax**) *n* hache f ♦ *vt* (*project etc*) abandonner; (*jobs*) supprimer; **axes** ['æksɪz] *npl* of **axe**

axis ['æksɪs, pl -siːz] (*pl* **axes**) *n* axe m

axle ['æksl] *n* (*also: ~-tree: AUT*) essieu m

ay(e) [aɪ] *excl* (*yes*) oui

B b

B [biː] *n* (*MUS*) si m

B.A. *abbr* = **Bachelor of Arts**

babble ['bæbl] *vi* bredouiller; (*baby, stream*) gazouiller

baby ['beɪbɪ] *n* bébé m; (*US: inf: darling*): **come on, ~!** viens ma belle/mon gars!; **~ carriage** (*US*) *n* voiture f d'enfant; **~-sit** *vi* garder les enfants; **~-sitter** *n* babysitter *m/f*

bachelor ['bætʃələ*] *n* célibataire *m*; **B~ of Arts/Science** ≈ licencié(e) ès *or* en lettres/sciences

back [bæk] *n* (*of person, horse, book*) dos *m*; (*of hand*) dos, revers *m*; (*of house*) derrière *m*; (*of car, train*) arrière *m*; (*of chair*) dossier *m*; (*of page*) verso *m*; (*of room, audience*) fond *m*; (*SPORT*) arrière *m* ♦ *vt* (*candidate: also:* ~ **up**) soutenir, appuyer; (*horse: at races*) parier *or* miser sur; (*car*) (faire) reculer ♦ *vi* (*also:* ~ **up**) reculer; (*car etc*) faire marche arrière ♦ *adj* (*in compounds*) de derrière, à l'arrière ♦ *adv* (*not forward*) en arrière; (*returned*): **he's** ~ il est rentré, il est de retour; (*restitution*): **throw the ball** ~ renvoie la balle; (*again*): **he called** ~ il a rappelé; ~ **seat/wheels** (*AUT*) sièges *mpl*/roues *fpl* arrières; ~ **payments/rent** arriéré *m* de paiements/ loyer; **he ran** ~ il est revenu en courant; ~ **down** *vi* rabattre de ses prétentions; ~ **out** *vi* (*of promise*) se dédire; ~ **up** *vt* (*candidate etc*) soutenir, appuyer; (*COMPUT*) sauvegarder; ~**bencher** (*BRIT*) *n* membre du parlement sans portefeuille; ~**bone** *n* colonne vertébrale, épine dorsale; ~**cloth** (*BRIT*) *n* toile *f* de fond; ~**date** *vt* (*letter*) antidater; ~**dated pay rise** augmentation *f* avec effet rétroactif; ~**drop** *n* = backcloth; ~**fire** *vi* (*AUT*) pétarader; (*plans*) mal tourner; ~**ground** *n* arrière-plan *m*; (*of events*) situation *f*, conjoncture *f*; (*basic knowledge*) éléments *mpl* de base; (*experience*) formation *f*; **family** ~**ground** milieu familial; ~**hand** *n* (*TENNIS: also:* ~**hand stroke**) revers *m*; ~**hander** (*BRIT*) *n* (*bribe*) pot-de-vin *m*; ~**ing** *n* (*fig*) soutien *m*, appui *m*; ~**lash** *n* contre-coup *m*, répercussion *f*; ~**log** *n*: ~**log of work** travail *m* en retard; ~ **number** *n* (*of magazine etc*) vieux numéro; ~**pack** *n* sac *m* à dos; ~ **pay** *n* rappel *m* de salaire; ~**side** (*inf*) *n* derrière *m*, postérieur *m*; ~**stage** *adv* derrière la scène, dans la coulisse; ~**stroke** *n* dos crawlé; ~**up** *adj* (*train, plane*) supplémentaire, de réserve; (*COMPUT*) de sauvegarde ♦ *n* (*support*) appui *m*, soutien *m*; (*also:* ~**up disk/file**) sauvegarde *f*; ~**ward** *adj* (*movement*) en arrière; (*person, country*) arriéré(e); attardé(e); ~**wards** *adv* (*move, go*) en arrière; (*read a list*) à l'envers, à rebours; (*fall*) à la renverse; (*walk*) à reculons; ~**water** *n* (*fig*) coin reculé; bled perdu (*péj*); ~**yard** *n* arrière-cour *f*

bacon ['beɪkən] *n* bacon *m*, lard *m*

bacteria [bæk'tɪərɪə] *npl* bactéries *fpl*

bad [bæd] *adj* mauvais(e); (*child*) vilain(e); (*mistake, accident etc*) grave; (*meat, food*) gâté(e), avarié(e); attardé(e); **his** ~ **leg** sa jambe malade; **to go** ~ (*meat, food*) se gâter

bade [bæd] *pt of* bid

badge [bædʒ] *n* insigne *m*; (*of policeman*) plaque *f*

badger ['bædʒə*] *n* blaireau *m*

badly ['bædlɪ] *adv* (*work, dress etc*) mal; ~ **wounded** grièvement blessé; **he needs it** ~ il en a absolument besoin; ~ **off** *adj, adv* dans la gêne

badminton ['bædmɪntən] *n* badminton *m*

bad-tempered ['bæd'tempəd] *adj* (*person: by nature*) ayant mauvais caractère; (: *on one occasion*) de mauvaise humeur

baffle ['bæfl] *vt* (*puzzle*) déconcerter

bag [bæg] *n* sac *m* ♦ *vt* (*inf: take*) empocher; s'approprier; ~**s of** (*inf: lots of*) des masses de; ~**gage** *n* bagages *mpl*; ~**gy** *adj* avachi(e), qui fait des poches; ~**pipes** *npl* cornemuse *f*

bail [beɪl] *n* (*payment*) caution *f*; (*release*) mise *f* en liberté sous caution ♦ *vt* (*prisoner: also: grant* ~ *to*) mettre en liberté sous caution; (*boat: also:* ~ *out*) écoper; **on** ~ (*prisoner*) sous caution; *see also* **bale**; ~ **out** *vt* (*prisoner*) payer la caution de

bailiff ['beɪlɪf] *n* (*BRIT*) ≈ huissier *m*; (*US*) ≈ huissier-audiencier *m*

bait [beɪt] *n* appât *m* ♦ *vt* appâter; (*fig: tease*) tourmenter

bake [beɪk] *vt* (faire) cuire au four ♦ *vi* (*bread etc*) cuire (au four); (*make cakes etc*) faire de la pâtisserie; ~**d beans** *npl* haricots blancs à la sauce tomate; ~**r** *n* boulanger *m*; ~**ry** *n* boulangerie *f*; boulangerie industrielle; **baking** *n* cuisson *f*; **baking powder** *n* levure *f* (chimique)

balance ['bæləns] *n* équilibre *m*; (*COMM: sum*) solde *m*; (*remainder*) reste *m*; (*scales*) balance *f* ♦ *vt* mettre *or* faire tenir en équilibre; (*pros and cons*) peser; (*budget*) équilibrer; (*account*) balancer; ~ **of trade/ payments** balance commerciale/des comptes *or* paiements; ~**d** *adj* (*personality, diet*) équilibré(e); (*report*) objectif(ive); ~ **sheet** *n* bilan *m*

balcony ['bælkənɪ] *n* balcon *m*; (*in theatre*) deuxième balcon

bald [bɔːld] *adj* chauve; (*tyre*) lisse

bale [beɪl] *n* balle *f*, ballot *m*; ~ **out** *vi* (*of a plane*) sauter en parachute

ball [bɔːl] *n* boule *f*; (*football*) ballon *m*; (*for tennis, golf*) balle *f*; (*of wool*) pelote *f*; (*of string*) bobine *f*; (*dance*) bal *m*; **to play** ~ (**with sb**) (*fig*) coopérer (avec qn)

ballast ['bæləst] *n* lest *m*

ball bearings *npl* roulement *m* à billes

ballerina [bælə'riːnə] *n* ballerine *f*

ballet ['bæleɪ] *n* ballet *m*; (*art*) danse *f* (classique); ~ **dancer** *n* danseur(euse) *m/f* de ballet

balloon [bə'luːn] *n* ballon *m*; (*in comic strip*) bulle *f*

ballot ['bælət] *n* scrutin *m*; ~ **paper** *n* bulletin *m* de vote

ballpoint (pen) ['bɔːlpɔɪnt-] *n* stylo *m* à bille

ballroom ['bɔːlrʊm] *n* salle *f* de bal

balm [bɑːm] *n* baume *m*

ban [bæn] *n* interdiction *f* ♦ *vt* interdire

banana [bə'nɑːnə] *n* banane *f*

band [bænd] *n* bande *f*; (*at a dance*) orchestre *m*; (*MIL*) musique *f*, fanfare *f*; ~ **together** *vi* se liguer

bandage ['bændɪdʒ] *n* bandage *m*, pansement *m* ♦ *vt* bander

Bandaid ['bændeɪd] *n* (*US* ®) *n* pansement adhésif

bandwagon ['bændwægən] *n*: **to jump on the** ~ (*fig*) monter dans *or* prendre le train en marche

bandy ['bændɪ] *vt* (*jokes, insults, ideas*) échanger

bandy-legged ['bændɪ'legɪd] *adj* aux jambes arquées

bang [bæŋ] *n* détonation *f*; (*of door*) claquement *m*; (*blow*) coup (violent) ♦ *vt* frapper (violemment); (*door*) claquer ♦ *vi* détoner; claquer ♦ *excl* pan!

bangs [bæŋz] (*US*) *npl* (*fringe*) frange *f*

banish ['bænɪʃ] *vt* bannir

banister(s) ['bænɪstə(z)] *n(pl)* rampe *f* (d'escalier)

bank [bæŋk] *n* banque *f*; (*of river, lake*) bord *m*, rive *f*; (*of earth*) talus *m*, remblai *m* ♦ *vi* (*AVIAT*) virer sur l'aile; ~ **on** *vt fus* miser *or* tabler sur; ~ **account** *n* compte *m* en banque; ~ **card** *n* carte *f* d'identité bancaire; ~**er** *n* banquier *m*; ~**er's card** (*BRIT*) *n* = **bank card**; ~ **holiday** (*BRIT*) *n* jour férié (*les banques sont fermées*); ~**ing** *n* opérations *fpl* bancaires; profession *f* de banquier; ~**note** *n* billet *m* de banque; ~ **rate** *n* taux *m* de l'escompte

bankrupt ['bæŋkrʌpt] *adj* en faillite; **to go** ~ faire faillite; ~**cy** *n* faillite *f*

bank statement *n* relevé *m* de compte

banner ['bænə*] *n* bannière *f*

bannister(s) ['bænɪstə(z)] *n(pl)* = **banister(s)**

banns [bænz] *npl* bans *mpl*

baptism ['bæptɪzəm] *n* baptême *m*

bar [bɑː*] *n* (*pub*) bar *m*; (*counter: in pub*) comptoir *m*, bar; (*rod: of metal etc*) barre *f*; (*on window etc*) barreau *m*; (*of chocolate*) tablette *f*, plaque *f*; (*fig*) obstacle *m*; (*prohibition*) mesure *f* d'exclusion; (*MUS*) mesure *f* ♦ *vt* (*road*) barrer; (*window*) munir de barreaux; (*person*) exclure; (*activity*) interdire; ~ **of soap** savonnette *f*; **the B~** (*LAW*) le barreau; **behind** ~**s** (*prisoner*) sous les verrous; ~ **none** sans exception

barbaric [bɑː'bærɪk] *adj* barbare

barbecue ['bɑːbɪkjuː] *n* barbecue *m*

barbed wire ['bɑːbd-] *n* fil *m* de fer barbelé

barber ['bɑːbə*] *n* coiffeur *m* (pour hommes)

bar code *n* (*on goods*) code *m* à barres

bare [bɛə*] *adj* nu(e) ♦ *vt* mettre à nu, dénuder; (*teeth*) montrer; **the** ~ **necessities** le strict nécessaire; ~**back** *adv* à cru, sans selle; ~**faced** *adj* impudent(e), effronté(e); ~**foot** *adj, adv* nu-pieds, (les) pieds nus; ~**ly** *adv* à peine

bargain ['bɑːgɪn] *n* (*transaction*) marché *m*; (*good buy*) affaire *f*, occasion *f* ♦ *vi* (*haggle*) marchander; (*negotiate*): **to** ~ (**with sb**) négocier (avec qn), traiter (avec qn); **into the** ~ par-dessus le marché; ~ **for** *vt fus*: **he got more than he** ~**ed for** il ne s'attendait pas à un coup pareil

barge [bɑːdʒ] *n* péniche *f*; ~ **in** *vi* (*walk in*) faire irruption; (*interrupt talk*) intervenir mal à propos

bark [bɑːk] *n* (*of tree*) écorce *f*; (*of dog*) aboiement *m* ♦ *vi* aboyer

barley ['bɑːlɪ] *n* orge *f*; ~ **sugar** *n* sucre *m* d'orge

barmaid ['bɑːmeɪd] *n* serveuse *f* (de bar), barmaid *f*

barman ['bɑːmən] (*irreg*) *n* serveur *m* (de bar), barman *m*

barn [bɑːn] *n* grange *f*

barometer [bə'rɒmɪtə*] *n* baromètre *m*

baron ['bærən] *n* baron *m*; ~**ess** *n* baronne *f*

barracks ['bærəks] *npl* caserne *f*

barrage ['bærɑːʒ] *n* (*MIL*) tir *m* de barrage; (*dam*) barrage *m*; (*fig*) pluie *f*

barrel ['bærəl] *n* tonneau *m*; (*of oil*) baril *m*; (*of gun*) canon *m*

barren ['bærən] *adj* stérile

barricade [bærɪ'keɪd] *n* barricade *f*

barrier ['bærɪə*] *n* barrière *f*; (*fig: to progress etc*) obstacle *m*

barring ['bɑːrɪŋ] *prep* sauf

barrister ['bærɪstə*] (*BRIT*) *n* avocat (plaidant)

barrow ['bærəʊ] *n* (*wheel*~) charrette *f* à bras

bartender ['bɑːtendə*] (*US*) *n* barman *m*

barter ['bɑːtə*] *vt*: **to** ~ **sth for** échanger qch contre

base [beɪs] *n* base *f*; (*of tree, post*) pied *m* ♦ *vt*: **to** ~ **sth on** baser *or* fonder qch sur ♦ *adj* vil(e), bas(se)

baseball ['beɪsbɔːl] *n* base-ball *m*

basement ['beɪsmənt] *n* sous-sol *m*

bases¹ ['beɪsɪz] *npl* of **base**

bases² ['beɪsiːz] *npl* of **basis**

bash [bæʃ] (*inf*) *vt* frapper, cogner

bashful ['bæʃful] *adj* timide; modeste

basic ['beɪsɪk] *adj* fondamental(e), de base; (*minimal*) rudimentaire; ~**ally** *adv* fondamentalement, à la base; (*in fact*) en fait, au fond; ~**s** *npl*: **the** ~**s** l'essentiel *m*

basil ['bæzl] *n* basilic *m*

basin ['beɪsn] *n* (*vessel, also GEO*) cuvette *f*,

bassin m; (*also:* wash~) lavabo m

basis ['beɪsɪs] (*pl* **bases**) n base f; **on a trial ~** à titre d'essai; **on a part-time ~** à temps partiel

bask [bɑːsk] vi: **to ~ in the sun** se chauffer au soleil

basket ['bɑːskɪt] n corbeille f; (*with handle*) panier m; **~ball** n basket-ball m

bass [beɪs] n (*MUS*) basse f

bassoon [bə'suːn] n (*MUS*) basson m

bastard ['bɑːstəd] n enfant naturel(le), bâtard(e); (*inf!*) salaud m (!)

bat [bæt] n chauve-souris f; (*for baseball etc*) batte f; (*BRIT: for table tennis*) raquette f ♦ vt: **he didn't ~ an eyelid** il n'a pas sourcillé *or* bronché

batch [bætʃ] n (*of bread*) fournée f; (*of papers*) liasse f

bated ['beɪtɪd] adj: **with ~ breath** en retenant son souffle

bath [bɑːθ, pl bɑːðz] n bain m; (~tub) baignoire f ♦ vt baigner, donner un bain à; **to have a ~** prendre un bain; *see also* **baths**

bathe [beɪð] vi se baigner ♦ vt (*wound*) laver

bathing ['beɪðɪŋ] n baignade f; **~ cap** n bonnet m de bain; **~ costume** (*US* **~ suit**) n maillot m (de bain)

bath: ~robe n peignoir m de bain; **~room** n salle f de bains; **~s** [bɑːðz] npl (*also: swimming ~*) piscine f; **~ towel** n serviette f de bain

baton ['bætən] n bâton m; (*MUS*) baguette f; (*club*) matraque f

batter ['bætə*] vt battre ♦ n pâte f à frire; **~ed** adj (*hat, pan*) cabossé(e)

battery ['bætərɪ] n batterie f; (*of torch*) pile f

battle ['bætl] n bataille f, combat m ♦ vi se battre, lutter; **~field** n champ m de bataille; **~ship** n cuirassé m

bawdy ['bɔːdɪ] adj paillard(e)

bawl [bɔːl] vi hurler; (*child*) brailler

bay [beɪ] n (*of sea*) baie f; **to hold sb at ~** tenir qn à distance or en échec; **~ leaf** n laurier m; **~ window** n baie vitrée

bazaar [bə'zɑː*] n bazar m; vente f de charité

B & B n abbr = **bed and breakfast**

BBC n abbr (= *British Broadcasting Corporation*) office de la radiodiffusion et télévision britannique

B.C. adv abbr (= *before Christ*) av. J.-C.

─────── KEYWORD ───────

be [biː] (*pt* **was, were**, *pp* **been**) aux vb **1** (*with present participle: forming continuous tenses*): **what are you doing?** que faites-vous?; **they're coming tomorrow** ils viennent demain; **I've been waiting for you for 2 hours** je t'attends depuis 2 heures

2 (*with pp: forming passives*) être; **to ~ killed** être tué(e); **he was nowhere to ~ seen** on ne le voyait nulle part

3 (*in tag questions*): **it was fun, wasn't it?** c'était drôle, n'est-ce pas?; **she's back, is she?** elle est rentrée, n'est-ce pas or alors?

4 (+*to* +*infinitive*): **the house is to ~ sold** la maison doit être vendue; **he's not to open it** il ne doit pas l'ouvrir

♦ vb + complement **1** (*gen*) être; **I'm English** je suis anglais(e); **I'm tired** je suis fatigué(e); **I'm hot/cold** j'ai chaud/froid; **he's a doctor** il est médecin; **2 and 2 are 4** 2 et 2 font 4

2 (*of health*) aller; **how are you?** comment allez-vous?; **he's fine now** il va bien maintenant; **he's very ill** il est très malade

3 (*of age*) avoir; **how old are you?** quel âge avez-vous?; **I'm sixteen (years old)** j'ai seize ans

4 (*cost*) coûter; **how much was the meal?** combien a coûté le repas?; **that'll ~ £5, please** ça fera 5 livres, s'il vous plaît

♦ vi **1** (*exist, occur etc*) être, exister; **the prettiest girl that ever was** la fille la plus jolie qui ait jamais existé; **~ that as it may** quoi qu'il en soit; **so ~ it** soit

2 (*referring to place*) être, se trouver; **I won't ~ here tomorrow** je ne serai pas là demain; **Edinburgh is in Scotland** Édimbourg est or se trouve en Écosse

3 (*referring to movement*) aller; **where have you been?** où êtes-vous allé(s)?

♦ impers vb **1** (*referring to time, distance*) être; **it's 5 o'clock** il est 5 heures; **it's the 28th of April** c'est le 28 avril; **it's 10 km to the village** le village est à 10 km

2 (*referring to the weather*) faire; **it's too hot/cold** il fait trop chaud/froid; **it's windy** il y a du vent

3 (*emphatic*): **it's me/the postman** c'est moi/le facteur

beach [biːtʃ] n plage f ♦ vt échouer

beacon ['biːkən] n (*lighthouse*) fanal m; (*marker*) balise f

bead [biːd] n perle f

beak [biːk] n bec m

beaker ['biːkə*] n gobelet m

beam [biːm] n poutre f; (*of light*) rayon m ♦ vi rayonner

bean [biːn] n haricot m; (*of coffee*) grain m; **runner ~** haricot m (à rames); **broad ~** fève f; **~sprouts** npl germes mpl de soja

bear [bɛə*] (*pt* **bore**, *pp* **borne**) n ours m ♦ vt porter; (*endure*) supporter ♦ vi: **to ~ right/left** obliger à droite/gauche, se diriger vers la droite/gauche; **~ out** vt corroborer, confirmer; **~ up** vi (*person*) tenir le coup

beard [bɪəd] n barbe f; **~ed** adj barbu(e)

bearer ['bɛərə*] n porteur m; (*of passport*) titulaire m/f

bearing ['bɛərɪŋ] *n* maintien *m*, allure *f*; (*connection*) rapport *m*; **~s** *npl* (*also*: **ball ~s**) roulement *m* (à billes); **to take a ~** faire le point

beast [biːst] *n* bête *f*; (*inf: person*) brute *f*; **~ly** *adj* infect(e)

beat [biːt] (*pt* **beat**, *pp* **beaten**) *n* battement *m*; (*MUS*) temps *m*, mesure *f*; (*of policeman*) ronde *f* ♦ *vt, vi* battre; **off the ~en track** hors des chemins *or* sentiers battus; **~ it!** (*inf*) fiche(-moi) le camp!; **~ off** *vt* repousser; **~ up** *vt* (*inf: person*) tabasser; (*eggs*) battre; **~ing** *n* raclée *f*

beautiful ['bjuːtɪful] *adj* beau(belle); **~ly** *adv* admirablement

beauty ['bjuːtɪ] *n* beauté *f*; **~ salon** *n* institut *m* de beauté; **~ spot** (*BRIT*) *n* (*TOURISM*) site naturel (d'une grande beauté)

beaver ['biːvə*] *n* castor *m*

became [bɪ'keɪm] *pt of* **become**

because [bɪ'kɒz] *conj* parce que; **~ of** *prep* à cause de

beck [bek] *n*: **to be at sb's ~ and call** être à l'entière disposition de qn

beckon ['bekən] *vt* (*also*: **~ to**) faire signe (de venir) à

become [bɪ'kʌm] (*irreg: like* **come**) *vi* devenir; **to ~ fat/thin** grossir/maigrir

becoming [bɪ'kʌmɪŋ] *adj* (*behaviour*) convenable, bienséant(e); (*clothes*) seyant(e)

bed [bed] *n* lit *m*; (*of flowers*) parterre *m*; (*of coal, clay*) couche *f*; (*of sea*) fond *m*; **to go to ~** aller se coucher; **~ and breakfast** *n* (*terms*) chambre et petit déjeuner; (*place*) ≈ chambre *f* d'hôte; **~clothes** *npl* couvertures *fpl* et draps *mpl*; **~ding** *n* literie *f*

bedraggled [bɪ'drægld] *adj* (*person, clothes*) débraillé(e); (*hair: wet*) trempé(e)

bed: **~ridden** *adj* cloué(e) au lit; **~room** *n* chambre *f* (à coucher); **~side** *n*: **at sb's ~side** au chevet de qn; **~sit(ter)** (*BRIT*) *n* chambre meublée, studio *m*; **~spread** *n* couvre-lit *m*, dessus-de-lit *m inv*; **~time** *n* heure *f* du coucher

bee [biː] *n* abeille *f*

beech [biːtʃ] *n* hêtre *m*

beef [biːf] *n* bœuf *m*; **roast ~** rosbif *m*; **~burger** *n* hamburger *m*; **~eater** *n* hallebardier de la Tour de Londres

beehive ['biːhaɪv] *n* ruche *f*

beeline ['biːlaɪn] *n*: **to make a ~ for** se diriger tout droit vers

been [biːn] *pp of* **be**

beer [bɪə*] *n* bière *f*

beet [biːt] *n* (*vegetable*) betterave *f*; (*US: also*: **red ~**) betterave (potagère)

beetle ['biːtl] *n* scarabée *m*

beetroot ['biːtruːt] (*BRIT*) *n* betterave *f*

before [bɪ'fɔː*] *prep* (*in time*) avant; (*in space*) devant ♦ *conj* avant que +*sub*; avant

de ♦ *adv* avant; devant; **~ going** avant de partir; **~ she goes** avant qu'elle ne parte; **the week ~** la semaine précédente *or* d'avant; **I've seen it ~** je l'ai déjà vu; **~hand** *adv* au préalable, à l'avance

beg [beg] *vi* mendier ♦ *vt* mendier; (*forgiveness, mercy etc*) demander; (*entreat*) supplier; *see also* **pardon**

began [bɪ'gæn] *pt of* **begin**

beggar ['begə*] *n* mendiant(e)

begin [bɪ'gɪn] (*pt* **began**, *pp* **begun**) *vt, vi* commencer; **to ~ doing** *or* **to do sth** commencer à *or* de faire qch; **~ner** *n* débutant(e); **~ning** *n* commencement *m*, début *m*

behalf [bɪ'hɑːf] *n*: **on ~ of**, (*US*) **in ~ of** (*representing*) de la part de; (*for benefit of*) pour le compte de; **on my/his ~** pour moi/lui

behave [bɪ'heɪv] *vi* se conduire, se comporter; (*well: also*: **~ o.s.**) se conduire bien *or* comme il faut

behaviour [bɪ'heɪvjə*] (*US* **behavior**) *n* comportement *m*, conduite *f*

behead [bɪ'hed] *vt* décapiter

beheld [bɪ'held] *pt, pp of* **behold**

behind [bɪ'haɪnd] *prep* derrière; (*time, progress*) en retard sur; (*work, studies*) en retard dans ♦ *adv* derrière ♦ *n* derrière *m*; **to be ~ (schedule)** avoir du retard; **~ the scenes** dans les coulisses

behold [bɪ'həʊld] (*irreg: like* **hold**) *vt* apercevoir, voir

beige [beɪʒ] *adj* beige

Beijing ['beɪ'dʒɪŋ] *n* Bei-jing, Pékin

being ['biːɪŋ] *n* être *m*

Beirut [beɪ'ruːt] *n* Beyrouth

belated [bɪ'leɪtɪd] *adj* tardif(ive)

belch [beltʃ] *vi* avoir un renvoi, roter ♦ *vt* (*also*: **~ out: smoke etc**) vomir, cracher

belfry ['belfrɪ] *n* beffroi *m*

Belgian ['beldʒən] *adj* belge, de Belgique ♦ *n* Belge *m/f*

Belgium ['beldʒəm] *n* Belgique *f*

belie [bɪ'laɪ] *vt* démentir

belief [bɪ'liːf] *n* (*opinion*) conviction *f*; (*trust, faith*) foi *f*

believe [bɪ'liːv] *vt, vi* croire; **to ~ in** (*God*) croire en; (*method, ghosts*) croire à; **~r** *n* (*in idea, activity*): **~r in** partisan(e) de; (*REL*) croyant(e)

belittle [bɪ'lɪtl] *vt* déprécier, rabaisser

bell [bel] *n* cloche *f*; (*small*) clochette *f*, grelot *m*; (*on door*) sonnette *f*; (*electric*) sonnerie *f*

belligerent [bɪ'lɪdʒərənt] *adj* (*person, attitude*) agressif(ive)

bellow ['beləʊ] *vi* (*bull*) meugler; (*person*) brailler

belly ['belɪ] *n* ventre *m*

belong [bɪ'lɒŋ] *vi*: **to ~ to** appartenir à; (*club etc*) faire partie de; **this book ~s**

here ce livre va ici; **~ings** *npl* affaires *fpl*, possessions *fpl*

beloved [bɪˈlʌvɪd] *adj* (bien-)aimé(e)

below [bɪˈləʊ] *prep* sous, au-dessous de ♦ *adv* en dessous; **see ~** voir plus bas *or* plus loin *or* ci-dessous

belt [belt] *n* ceinture *f*; (*of land*) région *f*; (*TECH*) courroie *f* ♦ *vt* (*thrash*) donner une raclée à; **~way** (*US*) *n* (*AUT*) route *f* de ceinture; (: *motorway*) périphérique *m*

bemused [bɪˈmjuːzd] *adj* stupéfié(e)

bench [bentʃ] *n* (*gen, also BRIT: POL*) banc *m*; (*in workshop*) établi *m*; **the B~** (*LAW: judge*) le juge; (: *judges collectively*) la magistrature, la Cour

bend [bend] (*pt, pp* **bent**) *vt* courber; (*leg, arm*) plier ♦ *vi* se courber ♦ *n* (*BRIT: in road*) virage *m*, tournant *m*; (*in pipe, river*) coude *m*; **~ down** *vi* se baisser; **~ over** *vi* se pencher

beneath [bɪˈniːθ] *prep* sous, au-dessous de; (*unworthy of*) indigne de ♦ *adv* dessous, au-dessous, en bas

benefactor [ˈbenɪfæktə*] *n* bienfaiteur *m*

beneficial [benɪˈfɪʃl] *adj* salutaire; avantageux(euse); **~ to the health** bon(ne) pour la santé

benefit [ˈbenɪfɪt] *n* avantage *m*, profit *m*; (*allowance of money*) allocation *f* ♦ *vt* faire du bien à, profiter à ♦ *vi*: **he'll ~ from it** cela lui fera du bien, il y gagnera *or* s'en trouvera bien

Benelux [ˈbenɪlʌks] *n* Bénélux *m*

benevolent [bɪˈnevələnt] *adj* bienveillant(e); (*organization*) bénévole

benign [bɪˈnaɪn] *adj* (*person, smile*) bienveillant(e), affable; (*MED*) bénin(igne)

bent [bent] *pt, pp of* **bend** ♦ *n* inclination *f*, penchant *m*; **to be ~ on** être résolu(e) à

bequest [bɪˈkwest] *n* legs *m*

bereaved [bɪˈriːvd] *n*: **the ~** la famille du disparu

beret [ˈbereɪ] *n* béret *m*

Berlin [bəːˈlɪn] *n* Berlin

berm [bɜːm] (*US*) *n* (*AUT*) accotement *m*

berry [ˈberɪ] *n* baie *f*

berserk [bəˈsɜːk] *adj*: **to go ~** (*madman, crowd*) se déchaîner

berth [bɜːθ] *n* (*bed*) couchette *f*; (*for ship*) poste *m* d'amarrage, mouillage *m* ♦ *vi* (*in harbour*) venir à quai; (*at anchor*) mouiller

beseech [bɪˈsiːtʃ] (*pt, pp* **besought**) *vt* implorer, supplier

beset [bɪˈset] (*pt, pp* **beset**) *vt* assaillir

beside [bɪˈsaɪd] *prep* à côté de; **to be ~ o.s. (with anger)** être hors de soi; **that's ~ the point** cela n'a rien à voir; **~s** [-z] *adv* en outre, de plus; (*in any case*) d'ailleurs ♦ *prep* (*as well as*) en plus de

besiege [bɪˈsiːdʒ] *vt* (*town*) assiéger; (*fig*) assaillir

besought [bɪˈsɔːt] *pt, pp of* **beseech**

best [best] *adj* meilleur(e) ♦ *adv* le mieux; **the ~ part of** (*quantity*) le plus clair de, la plus grande partie de; **at ~** au mieux; **to make the ~ of sth** s'accommoder de qch (du mieux que l'on peut); **to do one's ~** faire de son mieux; **to the ~ of my knowledge** pour autant que je sache; **to the ~ of my ability** du mieux que je pourrai; **~ man** *n* garçon *m* d'honneur

bestow [bɪˈstəʊ] *vt*: **to ~ sth on sb** accorder qch à qn; (*title*) conférer qch à qn

bet [bet] (*pt, pp* **bet** *or* **betted**) *n* pari *m* ♦ *vt, vi* parier

betray [bɪˈtreɪ] *vt* trahir; **~al** *n* trahison *f*

better [ˈbetə*] *adj* meilleur(e) ♦ *adv* mieux ♦ *vt* améliorer ♦ *n*: **to get the ~ of** triompher de, l'emporter sur; **you had ~ do it** vous feriez mieux de le faire; **he thought ~ of it** il s'est ravisé; **to get ~** aller mieux; s'améliorer; **~ off** *adj* plus à l'aise financièrement; (*fig*): **you'd be ~ off this way** vous vous en trouveriez mieux ainsi

betting [ˈbetɪŋ] *n* paris *mpl*; **~ shop** (*BRIT*) *n* bureau *m* de paris

between [bɪˈtwiːn] *prep* entre ♦ *adv*: (**in**) **~** au milieu; dans l'intervalle; (*in time*) dans l'intervalle

beverage [ˈbevərɪdʒ] *n* boisson *f* (*gén sans alcool*)

beware [bɪˈwɛə*] *vi*: **to ~ (of)** prendre garde (à); "**~ of the dog**" "(attention) chien méchant"

bewildered [bɪˈwɪldəd] *adj* dérouté(e), ahuri(e)

beyond [bɪˈjɒnd] *prep* (*in space, time*) au-delà de; (*exceeding*) au-dessus de ♦ *adv* au-delà; **~ doubt** hors de doute; **~ repair** irréparable

bias [ˈbaɪəs] *n* (*prejudice*) préjugé *m*, parti pris; **~(s)ed** *adj* partial(e), montrant un parti pris

bib [bɪb] *n* bavoir *m*, bavette *f*

Bible [ˈbaɪbl] *n* Bible *f*

bicarbonate of soda [baɪˈkɑːbənɪt-] *n* bicarbonate *m* de soude

bicker [ˈbɪkə*] *vi* se chamailler

bicycle [ˈbaɪsɪkl] *n* bicyclette *f*

bid [bɪd] (*pt* **bid** *or* **bade**, *pp* **bid(den)**) *n* offre *f*; (*at auction*) enchère *f*; (*attempt*) tentative *f* ♦ *vi* faire une enchère *or* offre ♦ *vt* faire une enchère *or* offre de; **to ~ sb good day** souhaiter le bonjour à qn; **~der** *n*: **the highest ~der** le plus offrant; **~ding** *n* enchères *fpl*

bide [baɪd] *vt*: **to ~ one's time** attendre son heure

bifocals [baɪˈfəʊkəlz] *npl* verres *mpl* à double foyer, lunettes bifocales

big [bɪg] *adj* grand(e); gros(se)

bigheaded [ˈbɪgˈhedɪd] *adj* prétentieux(euse)

bigot [ˈbɪgət] *n* fanatique *m/f*, sectaire *m/f*;

~ed *adj* fanatique, sectaire; **~ry** *n* fanatisme *m*, sectarisme *m*
big top *n* grand chapiteau
bike [baɪk] *n* vélo *m*, bécane *f*
bikini [bɪˈkiːnɪ] *n* bikini *m*
bilingual [baɪˈlɪŋgwəl] *adj* bilingue
bill [bɪl] *n* note *f*, facture *f*; (*POL*) projet *m* de loi; (*US: banknote*) billet *m* (de banque); (*of bird*) bec *m*; (*THEATRE*): **on the ~** à l'affiche; **"post no ~s"** "défense d'afficher"; **to fit** *or* **fill the ~** (*fig*) faire l'affaire; **~board** *n* panneau *m* d'affichage
billet [ˈbɪlɪt] *n* cantonnement *m* (chez l'habitant)
billfold [ˈbɪlfəʊld] (*US*) *n* portefeuille *m*
billiards [ˈbɪljədz] *n* (jeu *m* de) billard *m*
billion [ˈbɪljən] *n* (*BRIT*) billion *m* (*million de millions*); (*US*) milliard *m*
bin [bɪn] *n* boîte *f*; (*also: dust~*) poubelle *f*; (*for coal*) coffre *m*
bind [baɪnd] (*pt, pp* **bound**) *vt* attacher; (*book*) relier; (*oblige*) obliger, contraindre ♦ *n* (*inf: nuisance*) scie *f*; **~ing** *adj* (*contract*) constituant une obligation
binge [bɪndʒ] (*inf*) *n*: **to go on a/the ~** (*inf*) aller faire la bringue
bingo [ˈbɪŋgəʊ] *n* jeu de loto pratiqué dans des établissements publics
binoculars [bɪˈnɒkjʊləz] *npl* jumelles *fpl*
bio... *prefix*: **~chemistry** *n* biochimie *f*, **~graphy** *n* biographie *f*; **~logical** *adj* biologique; **~logy** *n* biologie *f*
birch [bɜːtʃ] *n* bouleau *m*
bird [bɜːd] *n* oiseau *m*; (*BRIT: inf: girl*) nana *f*, **~'s-eye view** *n* vue *f* à vol d'oiseau; (*fig*) vue d'ensemble *or* générale; **~watcher** *n* ornithologue *m/f* amateur
Biro [ˈbaɪrəʊ] *n* (®) stylo *m* à bille
birth [bɜːθ] *n* naissance *f*; **to give ~ to** (*subj: woman*) donner naissance à; (*: animal*) mettre bas; **~ certificate** *n* acte *m* de naissance; **~ control** *n* (*policy*) limitation *f* des naissances; (*method*) méthode(s) contraceptive(s); **~day** *n* anniversaire *m* ♦ *cpd* d'anniversaire; **~place** *n* lieu *m* de naissance; (*fig*) berceau *m*; **~ rate** *n* (taux *m* de) natalité *f*
biscuit [ˈbɪskɪt] *n* (*BRIT*) biscuit *m*; (*US*) petit pain au lait
bisect [baɪˈsekt] *vt* couper *or* diviser en deux
bishop [ˈbɪʃəp] *n* évêque *m*; (*CHESS*) fou *m*
bit [bɪt] *pt of* **bite** ♦ *n* morceau *m*; (*of tool*) mèche *f*; (*of horse*) mors *m*; (*COMPUT*) élément *m* binaire; **a ~ of** un peu de; **a ~ mad** un peu fou; **~ by ~** petit à petit
bitch [bɪtʃ] *n* (*dog*) chienne *f*, (*inf!*) salope *f* (*!*), garce *f*
bite [baɪt] (*pt* **bit**, *pp* **bitten**) *vt, vi* mordre; (*insect*) piquer ♦ *n* (*insect ~*) piqûre *f*; (*mouthful*) bouchée *f*; **let's have a ~ (to eat)** (*inf*) mangeons un morceau; **to ~**

one's nails se ronger les ongles
bitter [ˈbɪtə*] *adj* amer(ère); (*weather, wind*) glacial(e); (*criticism*) cinglant(e); (*struggle*) acharné(e) ♦ *n* (*BRIT: beer*) bière *f* (forte); **~ness** *n* amertume *f*; (*taste*) goût amer
blab [blæb] *vi* jaser, trop parler
black [blæk] *adj* noir(e) ♦ *n* (*colour*) noir *m*; (*person*): **B~** noir(e) ♦ *vt* (*BRIT: INDUSTRY*) boycotter; **to give sb a ~ eye** pocher l'œil à qn, faire un œil au beurre noir à qn; **~ and blue** couvert(e) de bleus; **to be in the ~** (*in credit*) être créditeur(trice); **~berry** *n* mûre *f*; **~bird** *n* merle *m*; **~board** *n* tableau noir; **~ coffee** *n* café noir; **~currant** *n* cassis *m*; **~en** *vt* noircir; **~ ice** *n* verglas *m*; **~leg** (*BRIT*) *n* briseur *m* de grève, jaune *m*; **~list** *n* liste noire; **~mail** *n* chantage *m* ♦ *vt* faire chanter, soumettre au chantage; **~ market** *n* marché noir; **~out** *n* panne *f* d'électricité; (*TV etc*) interruption *f* d'émission; (*fainting*) syncope *f*; **B~ Sea** *n*: **the B~ Sea** la mer Noire; **~ sheep** *n* brebis galeuse; **~smith** *n* forgeron *m*; **~ spot** *n* (*AUT*) point noir
bladder [ˈblædə*] *n* vessie *f*
blade [bleɪd] *n* lame *f*, (*of propeller*) pale *f*; **~ of grass** brin *m* d'herbe
blame [bleɪm] *n* faute *f*, blâme *m* ♦ *vt*: **to ~ sb/sth for sth** attribuer à qn/qch la responsabilité de qch; reprocher qch à qn/qch; **who's to ~?** qui est le fautif *or* coupable *or* responsable?; **~less** *adj* irréprochable
bland [blænd] *adj* (*taste, food*) doux(douce), fade
blank [blæŋk] *adj* blanc(blanche); (*look*) sans expression, dénué(e) d'expression ♦ *n* espace *m* vide, blanc *m*; (*cartridge*) cartouche *f* à blanc; **his mind was a ~** il avait la tête vide; **~ cheque** *n* chèque *m* en blanc
blanket [ˈblæŋkɪt] *n* couverture *f*; (*of snow, cloud*) couche *f*
blare [blɛə*] *vi* beugler
blast [blɑːst] *n* souffle *m*; (*of explosive*) explosion *f* ♦ *vt* faire sauter *or* exploser; **~-off** *n* (*SPACE*) lancement *m*
blatant [ˈbleɪtənt] *adj* flagrant(e), criant(e)
blaze [bleɪz] *n* (*fire*) incendie *m*; (*fig*) flamboiement *m* ♦ *vi* (*fire*) flamber; (*fig: eyes*) flamboyer; (*: guns*) crépiter ♦ *vt*: **to ~ a trail** (*fig*) montrer la voie
blazer [ˈbleɪzə*] *n* blazer *m*
bleach [bliːtʃ] *n* (*also: household ~*) eau *f* de Javel ♦ *vt* (*linen etc*) blanchir; **~ed** *adj* (*hair*) oxygéné(e), décoloré(e); **~ers** [ˈbliːtʃəz] (*US*) *npl* (*SPORT*) gradins *mpl* (en plein soleil)
bleak [bliːk] *adj* morne; (*countryside*) désolé(e)
bleary-eyed [ˈblɪərɪˈaɪd] *adj* aux yeux pleins de sommeil
bleat [bliːt] *vi* bêler

bleed [bliːd] (*pt, pp* **bled**) *vt, vi* saigner; **my nose is** ~**ing** je saigne du nez

bleeper ['bliːpə*] *n* (*device*) bip *m*

blemish ['blemɪʃ] *n* défaut *m*; (*on fruit, reputation*) tache *f*

blend [blend] *n* mélange *m* ♦ *vt* mélanger ♦ *vi* (*colours etc: also:* ~ **in**) se mélanger, se fondre

bless [bles] (*pt, pp* **blessed** *or* **blest**) *vt* bénir; ~ **you!** (*after sneeze*) à vos souhaits!; ~**ing** *n* bénédiction *f*; (*godsend*) bienfait *m*

blew [bluː] *pt of* **blow**

blight [blaɪt] *vt* (*hopes etc*) anéantir; (*life*) briser

blimey ['blaɪmɪ] (*BRIT: inf*) *excl* mince alors!

blind [blaɪnd] *adj* aveugle ♦ *n* (*for window*) store *m* ♦ *vt* aveugler; ~ **alley** *n* impasse *f*; ~ **corner** (*BRIT*) *n* virage *m* sans visibilité; ~**fold** *n* bandeau *m* ♦ *adj, adv* les yeux bandés ♦ *vt* bander les yeux à; ~**ly** *adv* aveuglément; ~**ness** *n* cécité *f*; ~ **spot** *n* (*AUT etc*) angle mort; **that is her** ~ **spot** (*fig*) elle refuse d'y voir clair sur ce point

blink [blɪŋk] *vi* cligner des yeux; (*light*) clignoter; ~**ers** *npl* œillères *fpl*

bliss [blɪs] *n* félicité *f*, bonheur *m* sans mélange

blister ['blɪstə*] *n* (*on skin*) ampoule *f*, cloque *f*; (*on paintwork, rubber*) boursouflure *f* ♦ *vi* (*paint*) se boursoufler, se cloquer

blithely ['blaɪðlɪ] *adv* (*unconcernedly*) tranquillement

blizzard ['blɪzəd] *n* blizzard *m*, tempête *f* de neige

bloated ['bləʊtɪd] *adj* (*face*) bouffi(e); (*stomach, person*) gonflé(e)

blob [blɒb] *n* (*drop*) goutte *f*; (*stain, spot*) tache *f*

block [blɒk] *n* bloc *m*; (*in pipes*) obstruction *f*; (*toy*) cube *m*; (*of buildings*) pâté *m* (de maisons) ♦ *vt* bloquer; (*fig*) faire obstacle à; ~ **of flats** (*BRIT*) *n* immeuble (locatif); **mental** ~ trou *m* de mémoire; ~**ade** *n* blocus *m*; ~**age** *n* obstruction *f*; ~**buster** *n* (*film, book*) grand succès; ~ **letters** *npl* majuscules *fpl*

bloke [bləʊk] (*BRIT: inf*) *n* type *m*

blond(e) [blɒnd] *adj, n* blond(e)

blood [blʌd] *n* sang *m*; ~ **donor** *n* donneur(euse) de sang; ~ **group** *n* groupe sanguin; ~**hound** *n* limier *m*; ~ **poisoning** *n* empoisonnement *m* du sang; ~ **pressure** *n* tension *f* (artérielle); ~**shed** *n* effusion *f* de sang, carnage *m*; ~**shot** *adj*: ~**shot eyes** yeux injectés de sang; ~**stream** *n* sang *m*, système sanguin; ~ **test** *n* prise *f* de sang; ~**thirsty** *adj* sanguinaire; ~ **vessel** *n* vaisseau sanguin; ~**y** *adj* sanglant(e); (*nose*) en sang; (*BRIT: inf!*): **this** ~**y** ... ce foutu ... (*!*), ce putain de ... (*!*); ~**y strong/good** vachement *or* sacré-

ment fort/bon; ~**y-minded** (*BRIT: inf*) *adj* contrariant(e), obstiné(e)

bloom [bluːm] *n* fleur *f* ♦ *vi* être en fleur

blossom ['blɒsəm] *n* fleur(s) *f(pl)* ♦ *vi* être en fleurs; (*fig*) s'épanouir; **to** ~ **into** devenir

blot [blɒt] *n* tache *f* ♦ *vt* tacher; ~ **out** *vt* (*memories*) effacer; (*view*) cacher, masquer

blotchy ['blɒtʃɪ] *adj* (*complexion*) couvert(e) de marbrures

blotting paper ['blɒtɪŋ-] *n* buvard *m*

blouse [blauz] *n* chemisier *m*, corsage *m*

blow [bləʊ] (*pt* **blew**, *pp* **blown**) *n* coup *m* ♦ *vi* souffler ♦ *vt* souffler; (*fuse*) faire sauter; (*instrument*) jouer de; **to** ~ **one's nose** se moucher; **to** ~ **a whistle** siffler; ~ **away** *vt* chasser, faire s'envoler; ~ **down** *vt* faire tomber, renverser; ~ **off** *vt* emporter; ~ **out** *vi* (*fire, flame*) s'éteindre; ~ **over** *vi* s'apaiser; ~ **up** *vt* faire sauter; (*tyre*) gonfler; (*PHOT*) agrandir ♦ *vi* exploser, sauter; ~**dry** *n* brushing *m*; ~**lamp** (*BRIT*) *n* chalumeau *m*; ~**out** *n* (*of tyre*) éclatement *m*; ~**torch** *n* = **blowlamp**

blue [bluː] *adj* bleu(e); (*fig*) triste; ~**s** *n* (*MUS*): **the** ~**s** le blues; ~ **film/joke** film *m*/histoire *f* pornographique; **to come out of the** ~ (*fig*) être complètement inattendu; ~**bell** *n* jacinthe *f* des bois; ~**bottle** *n* mouche *f* à viande; ~**print** *n* (*fig*) projet *m*, plan directeur

bluff [blʌf] *vi* bluffer ♦ *n* bluff *m*; **to call sb's** ~ mettre qn au défi d'exécuter ses menaces

blunder ['blʌndə*] *n* gaffe *f*, bévue *f* ♦ *vi* faire une gaffe *or* une bévue

blunt [blʌnt] *adj* (*person*) brusque, ne mâchant pas ses mots; (*knife*) émoussé(e), peu tranchant(e); (*pencil*) mal taillé

blur [blɜː*] *n* tache *or* masse floue *or* confuse ♦ *vt* brouiller

blurb [blɜːb] *n* notice *f* publicitaire; (*for book*) texte *m* de présentation

blurt out [blɜːt] *vt* (*reveal*) lâcher

blush [blʌʃ] *vi* rougir ♦ *n* rougeur *f*

blustery ['blʌstərɪ] *adj* (*weather*) à bourrasques

boar [bɔː*] *n* sanglier *m*

board [bɔːd] *n* planche *f*; (*on wall*) panneau *m*; (*for chess*) échiquier *m*; (*cardboard*) carton *m*; (*committee*) conseil *m*, comité *m*; (*in firm*) conseil d'administration; (*NAUT, AVIAT*): **on** ~ à bord ♦ *vt* (*ship*) monter à bord de; (*train*) monter dans; **full** ~ (*BRIT*) pension complète; **half** ~ demi-pension *f*; ~ **and lodging** chambre *f* avec pension; **which goes by the** ~ (*fig*) qu'on laisse tomber, qu'on abandonne; ~ **up** *vt* (*door, window*) boucher; ~**er** *n* (*SCOL*) interne *m/f*, pensionnaire; ~**ing card** *n* = **boarding pass**; ~**ing house** *n* pension *f*; ~**ing pass** *n* (*AVIAT, NAUT*) carte *f* d'embarquement; ~**ing school** n internat m, pensionnat m; ~ **room** n salle f du conseil d'administration

boast [bəʊst] vi: **to** ~ **(about** or **of)** se vanter (de)

boat [bəʊt] n bateau m; (small) canot m; barque f; ~**er** n (hat) canotier m

bob [bɒb] vi (boat, cork on water: also: ~ up and down) danser, se balancer

bobby ['bɒbɪ] (BRIT: inf) n ≈ agent m (de police)

bobsleigh ['bɒbsleɪ] n bob m

bode [bəʊd] vi: **to** ~ **well/ill (for)** être de bon/mauvais augure (pour)

bodily ['bɒdɪlɪ] adj corporel(le) ♦ adv dans ses bras

body ['bɒdɪ] n corps m; (of car) carrosserie f; (of plane) fuselage m; (fig: society) organe m, organisme m; (: quantity) ensemble m, masse f; (of wine) corps m; ~**building** n culturisme m; ~**guard** n garde m du corps; ~**work** n carrosserie f

bog [bɒg] n tourbière f ♦ vt: **to get** ~**ged down** (fig) s'enliser

boggle ['bɒgl] vi: **the mind** ~**s** c'est incroyable, on en reste sidéré

bogus ['bəʊgəs] adj bidon inv; fantôme

boil [bɔɪl] vt (faire) bouillir ♦ vi bouillir ♦ n (MED) furoncle m; **to come to the** (BRIT) ~ or **a** (US) ~ bouillir; ~ **down to** vt fus (fig) se réduire or ramener à; ~ **over** vi déborder; ~**ed egg** n œuf m à la coque; ~**ed potatoes** npl pommes fpl à l'anglaise or à l'eau; ~**er** n chaudière f; ~**ing point** n point m d'ébullition

boisterous ['bɔɪstərəs] adj bruyant(e), tapageur(euse)

bold [bəʊld] adj hardi(e), audacieux(euse); (pej) effronté(e); (outline, colour) franc(franche), tranché(e), marqué(e); (pattern) grand(e)

bollard ['bɒləd] (BRIT) n (AUT) borne lumineuse or de signalisation

bolster ['bəʊlstə*]: ~ **up** vt soutenir

bolt [bəʊlt] n (lock) verrou m; (with nut) boulon m ♦ adv: ~ **upright** droit(e) comme un piquet ♦ vt verrouiller; (TECH: also: ~ on, ~ together) boulonner; (food) engloutir ♦ vi (horse) s'emballer

bomb [bɒm] n bombe f ♦ vt bombarder

bombastic [bɒm'bæstɪk] adj pompeux(euse)

bomb: ~ **disposal unit** n section f de déminage; ~**er** n (AVIAT) bombardier m; ~**shell** n (fig) bombe f

bona fide ['bəʊnə'faɪdɪ] adj (traveller) véritable

bond [bɒnd] n lien m; (binding promise) engagement m, obligation f; (COMM) obligation; **in** ~ (of goods) en douane

bondage ['bɒndɪdʒ] n esclavage m

bone [bəʊn] n os m; (of fish) arête f ♦ vt désosser, ôter les arêtes de; ~ **idle** adj fainéant(e)

bonfire ['bɒnfaɪə*] n feu m (de joie); (for rubbish) feu

bonnet ['bɒnɪt] n bonnet m; (BRIT: of car) capot m

bonus ['bəʊnəs] n prime f, gratification f

bony ['bəʊnɪ] adj (arm, face, MED: tissue) osseux(euse); (meat) plein(e) d'os; (fish) plein d'arêtes

boo [buː] excl hou!, peuh! ♦ vt huer

booby trap ['buːbɪ-] n engin piégé

book [bʊk] n livre m; (of stamps, tickets) carnet m ♦ vt (ticket) prendre; (seat, room) réserver; (driver) dresser un procès-verbal à; (football player) prendre le nom de; ~**s** npl (accounts) comptes mpl, comptabilité f; ~**case** n bibliothèque f (meuble); ~**ing office** (BRIT) n bureau m de location; ~**keeping** n comptabilité f; ~**let** n brochure f; ~**maker** n bookmaker m; ~**seller** n libraire m/f; ~**shop** n librairie f; ~**store** n librairie f

boom [buːm] n (noise) grondement m; (in prices, population) forte augmentation f ♦ vi gronder; prospérer

boon [buːn] n bénédiction f, grand avantage

boost [buːst] n stimulant m, remontant m ♦ vt stimuler; ~**er** n (MED) rappel m

boot [buːt] n botte f; (for hiking) chaussure f (de marche); (for football etc) soulier m; (BRIT: of car) coffre m ♦ vt (COMPUT) amorcer, initialiser; **to** ~ (in addition) pardessus le marché

booth [buːð] n (at fair) baraque (foraine); (telephone etc) cabine f; (also: voting ~) isoloir m

booty ['buːtɪ] n butin m

booze [buːz] (inf) n boissons fpl alcooliques, alcool m

border ['bɔːdə*] n bordure f; bord m; (of a country) frontière f ♦ vt border; (also: ~ on: country) être limitrophe de; **B~s** n (GEO): **the B~s** la région frontière entre l'Écosse et l'Angleterre; ~ **on** vt fus être voisin(e) de, toucher à; ~**line** n (fig) ligne f de démarcation; ~**line case** n cas m limite

bore [bɔː*] pt of **bear** ♦ vt (hole) percer; (oil well, tunnel) creuser; (person) ennuyer, raser ♦ n raseur(euse); (of gun) calibre m; **to be** ~**d** s'ennuyer; ~**dom** n ennui m; **boring** adj ennuyeux(euse)

born [bɔːn] adj: **to be** ~ naître; **I was** ~ **in 1960** je suis né en 1960

borne [bɔːn] pp of **bear**

borough ['bʌrə] n municipalité f

borrow ['bɒrəʊ] vt: **to** ~ **sth (from sb)** emprunter qch (à qn)

Bosnia (and) Herzegovina [bɒsnɪə (ənd) hɜːzəgəʊviːnə] n Bosnie-Herzégovine f

bosom ['bʊzəm] n poitrine f; (fig) sein m; ~ **friend** n ami(e) intime

boss [bɒs] n patron(ne) ♦ vt (also: ~ around/about) commander; ~**y** adj autoritaire

bosun ['bəʊsn] n maître m d'équipage

botany ['bɒtənɪ] n botanique f

botch [bɒtʃ] vt (also: ~ up) saboter, bâcler

both [bəʊθ] adj les deux, l'un(e) et l'autre ♦ pron: ~ (of them) les deux, tous(toutes) (les) deux, l'un(e) et l'autre: **they sell ~ the fabric and the finished curtains** ils vendent (et) le tissu et les rideaux (finis), ils vendent à la fois le tissu et les rideaux (finis); ~ **of us went, we ~ went** nous y sommes allés (tous) les deux

bother ['bɒðə*] vt (worry) tracasser; (disturb) déranger ♦ vi (also: ~ o.s.) se tracasser, se faire du souci ♦ n: **it is a ~ to have to do** c'est vraiment ennuyeux d'avoir à faire; **it's no ~** aucun problème; **to ~ doing** prendre la peine de faire

bottle ['bɒtl] n bouteille f; (baby's) biberon m ♦ vt mettre en bouteille(s); ~ **up** vt refouler, contenir; ~ **bank** n conteneur m à verre; ~**neck** n étranglement m; ~**opener** n ouvre-bouteille m

bottom ['bɒtəm] n (of container, sea etc) fond m; (buttocks) derrière m; (of page, list) bas m ♦ adj du fond; du bas; **the ~ of the class** le dernier de la classe; ~**less** adj (funds) inépuisable

bough [baʊ] n branche f, rameau m

bought [bɔːt] pt, pp of **buy**

boulder ['bəʊldə*] n gros rocher

bounce [baʊns] vi (ball) rebondir; (cheque) être refusé(sans provision) ♦ vt faire rebondir ♦ n (rebound) rebond m; ~**r** (inf) n (at dance, club) videur m

bound [baʊnd] pt, pp of **bind** ♦ n (gen pl) limite f; (leap) bond m ♦ vi (leap) bondir ♦ vt (limit) borner ♦ adj: **to be ~ to do sth** (obliged) être obligé(e) or avoir obligation de faire qch; **he's ~ to fail** (likely) il est sûr d'échouer, son échec est inévitable or assuré; ~ **by** (law, regulation) engagé(e) par; ~ **for** à destination de; **out of ~s** dont l'accès est interdit

boundary ['baʊndərɪ] n frontière f

boundless ['baʊndlɪs] adj sans bornes

bout [baʊt] n période f; (of malaria etc) accès m, crise f, attaque f; (BOXING etc) combat m, match m

bow[1] [bəʊ] n nœud m; (weapon) arc m; (MUS) archet m

bow[2] [baʊ] n (with body) révérence f, inclination f (du buste or corps); (NAUT: also: ~s) proue f ♦ vi faire une révérence, s'incliner; (yield): **to ~ to** or **before** s'incliner devant, se soumettre à

bowels ['baʊəlz] npl intestins mpl; (fig) entrailles fpl

bowl [bəʊl] n (for eating) bol m; (ball) boule f ♦ vi (CRICKET, BASEBALL) lancer (la balle)

bow-legged ['bəʊ'legɪd] adj aux jambes arquées

bowler ['bəʊlə*] n (CRICKET, BASEBALL) lanceur m (de la balle); (BRIT: also: ~ hat) (chapeau m) melon m

bowling ['bəʊlɪŋ] n (game) jeu m de boules; jeu m de quilles; ~ **alley** n bowling m; ~ **green** n terrain m de boules (gazonné et carré)

bowls [bəʊlz] n (game) (jeu m de) boules fpl

bow tie ['bəʊ-] n nœud m papillon

box [bɒks] n (also: cardboard ~) carton m; (THEATRE) loge f ♦ vt mettre en boîte; (SPORT) boxer avec ♦ vi boxer, faire de la boxe; ~**er** n (person) boxeur m; ~**ing** n (SPORT) boxe f; **B~ing Day** (BRIT) n le lendemain de Noël; ~**ing gloves** npl gants mpl de boxe; ~**ing ring** n ring m; ~ **office** n bureau m de location; ~**room** n débarras m; chambrette f

boy [bɔɪ] n garçon m

boycott ['bɔɪkɒt] n boycottage m ♦ vt boycotter

boyfriend ['bɔɪfrend] n (petit) ami

boyish ['bɔɪʃ] adj (behaviour) de garçon; (girl) garçonnier(ière)

BR abbr = **British Rail**

bra [brɑː] n soutien-gorge m

brace [breɪs] n (on teeth) appareil m (dentaire); (tool) vilbrequin m ♦ vt (knees, shoulders) appuyer; ~**s** npl (BRIT: for trousers) bretelles fpl; **to ~ o.s.** (lit) s'arcbouter; (fig) se préparer mentalement

bracelet ['breɪslɪt] n bracelet m

bracing ['breɪsɪŋ] adj tonifiant(e), tonique

bracket ['brækɪt] n (TECH) tasseau m, support m; (group) classe f, tranche f; (also: brace ~) accolade f; (: round ~) parenthèse f; (: square ~) crochet m ♦ vt mettre entre parenthèse(s); (fig: also: ~ together) regrouper

brag [bræg] vi se vanter

braid [breɪd] n (trimming) galon m; (of hair) tresse f

brain [breɪn] n cerveau m; ~**s** npl (intellect, CULIN) cervelle f; **he's got ~s** il est intelligent; ~**child** n invention personnelle; ~**wash** vt faire subir un lavage de cerveau à; ~**wave** n idée géniale; ~**y** adj intelligent(e), doué(e)

braise [breɪz] vt braiser

brake [breɪk] n (on vehicle, also fig) frein m ♦ vi freiner; ~ **fluid** n liquide m de freins; ~ **light** n feu m de stop

bran [bræn] n son m

branch [brɑːntʃ] n branche f; (COMM) succursale f ♦ vi bifurquer; ~ **out** vi (fig): **to ~ out into** étendre ses activités à

brand [brænd] n marque (commerciale) ♦ vt (cattle) marquer (au fer rouge); ~**-new** adj tout(e) neuf(neuve), flambant neuf(neuve)

brandy ['brændɪ] n cognac m, fine f

brash [bræʃ] adj effronté(e)

brass [brɑːs] n cuivre m (jaune), laiton m; **the ~** (MUS) les cuivres; **~ band** n fanfare f

brassière ['bræsɪə*] n soutien-gorge m

brat [bræt] (pej) n miocche m/f, môme m/f

brave [breɪv] adj courageux(euse), brave ♦ n guerrier indien ♦ vt braver, affronter; **~ry** n bravoure f, courage m

brawl [brɔːl] n rixe f, bagarre f

bray [breɪ] vi braire

brazen ['breɪzn] adj impudent(e), effronté(e) ♦ vt: **to ~ it out** payer d'effronterie, crâner

brazier ['breɪzɪə*] n brasero m

Brazil [brə'zɪl] n Brésil m

breach [briːtʃ] vt ouvrir une brèche dans ♦ n (gap) brèche f; (breaking): **~ of contract** rupture f de contrat; **~ of the peace** attentat m à l'ordre public

bread [bred] n pain m; **~ and butter** n tartines (beurrées); (fig) subsistance f; **~ bin** (BRIT) n boîte f à pain; (bigger) huche f à pain; **~box** (US) n = ~bin; **~crumbs** npl miettes fpl de pain; (CULIN) chapelure f, panure f; **~line** n: **to be on the ~line** être sans le sou or dans l'indigence

breadth [bretθ] n largeur f; (fig) ampleur f

breadwinner ['bredwɪnə*] n soutien m de famille

break [breɪk] (pt **broke**, pp **broken**) vt casser, briser; (promise) rompre; (law) violer ♦ vi (se) casser, se briser; (weather) tourner; (story, news) se répandre; (day) se lever ♦ n (gap) brèche f; (fracture) cassure f; (pause, interval) interruption f, arrêt m; (: short) pause f; (: at school) récréation f; (chance) chance f, occasion f favorable; **to ~ one's leg** etc se casser la jambe etc; **to ~ a record** battre un record; **to ~ the news to sb** annoncer la nouvelle à qn; **~ even** rentrer dans ses frais; **~ free** or **loose** se dégager, s'échapper; **~ open** (door etc) forcer, fracturer; **~ down** vt (figures, data) décomposer, analyser ♦ vi s'effondrer; (MED) faire une dépression (nerveuse); (AUT) tomber en panne; **~ in** vt (horse etc) dresser ♦ vi (burglar) entrer par effraction; (interrupt) interrompre; **~ into** vt fus (house) s'introduire or pénétrer par effraction dans; **~ off** vi (speaker) s'interrompre; (branch) se rompre; **~ out** vi éclater, se déclarer; (prisoner) s'évader; **to ~ out in spots** or **a rash** avoir une éruption de boutons; **~ up** vi (ship) se disloquer; (crowd, meeting) se disperser, se séparer; (marriage) se briser; (SCOL) entrer en vacances ♦ vt casser; (fight etc) interrompre, faire cesser; **~age** n casse f; **~down** n (AUT) panne f; (in communications, marriage) rupture f; (MED: also: ner-

vous ~) dépression (nerveuse); (of statistics) ventilation f; **~down van** (BRIT) n dépanneuse f; **~er** n brisant m

breakfast ['brekfəst] n petit déjeuner

break: **~-in** n cambriolage m; **~ing and entering** n (LAW) effraction f; **~through** n percée f; **~water** n brise-lames m inv, digue f

breast [brest] n (of woman) sein m; (chest, of meat) poitrine f; **~-feed** (irreg: like **feed**) vt, vi allaiter; **~stroke** n brasse f

breath [breθ] n haleine f; **out of ~** à bout de souffle, essoufflé(e)

Breathalyser ['breθəlaɪzə*] (®) n Alcootest m (®)

breathe [briːð] vt, vi respirer; **~ in** vt, vi aspirer, inspirer; **~ out** vt, vi expirer; **~r** n moment de repos or de répit; **breathing** ['briːðɪŋ] n respiration f; **breathing space** n (fig) (moment m de) répit m

breathless ['breθlɪs] adj essoufflé(e), haletant(e); oppressé(e)

breathtaking ['breθteɪkɪŋ] adj stupéfiant(e), à vous couper le souffle

breed [briːd] (pt, pp **bred**) vt élever, faire l'élevage de ♦ vi se reproduire ♦ n race f, variété f; **~ing** n (upbringing) éducation f

breeze [briːz] n brise f, **breezy** ['briːzɪ] adj frais(fraîche); aéré(e); (manner etc) désinvolte, jovial(e)

brevity ['brevɪtɪ] n brièveté f

brew [bruː] vt (tea) faire infuser; (beer) brasser ♦ vi (fig) se préparer, couver; **~ery** n brasserie f (fabrique)

bribe [braɪb] n pot-de-vin m ♦ vt acheter; soudoyer; **~ry** n corruption f

brick [brɪk] n brique f; **~layer** n maçon m

bridal ['braɪdl] adj nuptial(e)

bride [braɪd] n mariée f, épouse f; **~groom** n marié m, époux m; **~smaid** n demoiselle f d'honneur

bridge [brɪdʒ] n pont m; (NAUT) passerelle f (de commandement); (of nose) arête f; (CARDS, DENTISTRY) bridge m ♦ vt (fig: gap, gulf) combler

bridle ['braɪdl] n bride f; **~ path** n piste or allée cavalière

brief [briːf] adj bref(brève) ♦ n (LAW) dossier m, cause f; (gen) tâche f ♦ vt mettre au courant; **~s** npl (undergarment) slip m; **~case** n serviette f, porte-documents m inv; **~ly** adv brièvement

bright [braɪt] adj brillant(e); (room, weather) clair(e); (clever: person, idea) intelligent(e); (cheerful: colour, person) vif(vive)

brighten (also **~ up**) vt (room) éclaircir, égayer; (event) égayer ♦ vi s'éclaircir; (person) retrouver un peu de sa gaieté; (face) s'éclairer; (prospects) s'améliorer

brilliance ['brɪljəns] n éclat m

brilliant ['brɪljənt] adj brillant(e); (sunshine, light) éclatant(e); (inf: holiday etc) super

brim [brɪm] *n* bord *m*

brine [braɪn] *n* (*CULIN*) saumure *f*

bring [brɪŋ] (*pt, pp* **brought**) *vt* apporter; (*person*) amener; ~ **about** *vt* provoquer, entraîner; ~ **back** *vt* rapporter; ramener; (*restore: hanging*) réinstaurer; ~ **down** *vt* (*price*) faire baisser; (*enemy plane*) descendre; (*government*) faire tomber; ~ **forward** *vt* avancer; ~ **off** *vt* (*task, plan*) réussir, mener à bien; ~ **out** *vt* (*meaning*) faire ressortir; (*book*) publier; (*object*) sortir; ~ **round** *vt* (*unconscious person*) ranimer; ~ **to** *vt* = ~ **round**; ~ **up** *vt* (*child*) élever; (*carry up*) monter; (*question*) soulever; (*food: vomit*) vomir, rendre

brink [brɪŋk] *n* bord *m*

brisk [brɪsk] *adj* vif(vive)

bristle [ˈbrɪsl] *n* poil *m* ♦ *vi* se hérisser

Britain [ˈbrɪtən] *n* (*also: Great* ~) Grande-Bretagne *f*

British [ˈbrɪtɪʃ] *adj* britannique ♦ *npl*: **the** ~ les Britanniques *mpl*; ~ **Isles** *npl*: **the** ~ **Isles** les Iles *fpl* Britanniques; ~ **Rail** *n* compagnie ferroviaire britannique

Briton [ˈbrɪtən] *n* Britannique *m/f*

Brittany [ˈbrɪtənɪ] *n* Bretagne *f*

brittle [ˈbrɪtl] *adj* cassant(e), fragile

broach [brəʊtʃ] *vt* (*subject*) aborder

broad [brɔːd] *adj* large; (*general: outlines*) grand(e); (*: distinction*) général(e); (*accent*) prononcé(e); **in** ~ **daylight** en plein jour; ~**cast** (*pt, pp* ~**cast**) *n* émission *f* ♦ *vt* radiodiffuser; téléviser ♦ *vi* émettre; ~**en** *vt* élargir ♦ *vi* s'élargir; **to** ~**en one's mind** élargir ses horizons; ~**ly** *adv* en gros, généralement; ~**-minded** *adj* large d'esprit

broccoli [ˈbrɒkəlɪ] *n* brocoli *m*

brochure [ˈbrəʊʃʊə*] *n* prospectus *m*, dépliant *m*

broil [brɔɪl] *vt* griller

broke [brəʊk] *pt of* **break** ♦ *adj* (*inf*) fauché(e)

broken [ˈbrəʊkən] *pp of* **break** ♦ *adj* cassé(e); (*machine: also:* ~ **down**) fichu(e); **in** ~ **English/French** dans un anglais/français approximatif *or* hésitant; ~ **leg** *etc* jambe *etc* cassée; ~**-hearted** *adj* (ayant) le cœur brisé

broker [ˈbrəʊkə*] *n* courtier *m*

brolly [ˈbrɒlɪ] (*BRIT: inf*) *n* pépin *m*, parapluie *m*

bronchitis [brɒŋˈkaɪtɪs] *n* bronchite *f*

bronze [brɒnz] *n* bronze *m*

brooch [brəʊtʃ] *n* broche *f*

brood [bruːd] *n* couvée *f* ♦ *vi* (*person*) méditer (sombrement), ruminer

broom [bruːm] *n* balai *m*; (*BOT*) genêt *m*; ~**stick** *n* manche *m* à balai

Bros. *abbr* = **Brothers**

broth [brɒθ] *n* bouillon *m* de viande et de légumes

brothel [ˈbrɒθl] *n* maison close, bordel *m*

brother [ˈbrʌðə*] *n* frère *m*; ~**-in-law** *n* beau-frère *m*

brought [brɔːt] *pt, pp of* **bring**

brow [braʊ] *n* front *m*; (*eye*~) sourcil *m*; (*of hill*) sommet *m*

brown [braʊn] *adj* brun(e), marron *inv*; (*hair*) châtain *inv*; brun; (*eyes*) marron *inv*; (*tanned*) bronzé(e) ♦ *n* (*colour*) brun *m* ♦ *vt* (*CULIN*) faire dorer; ~ **bread** *n* pain *m* bis; **B~ie** [ˈbraʊnɪ] *n* (*also:* ~ **Guide**) jeannette *f*, éclaireuse (cadette); ~**ie** [ˈbraʊnɪ] (*US*) *n* (*cake*) gâteau *m* au chocolat et aux noix; ~ **paper** *n* papier *m* d'emballage; ~ **sugar** *n* cassonade *f*

browse [braʊz] *vi* (*among books*) bouquiner, feuilleter les livres; **to** ~ **through a book** feuilleter un livre

bruise [bruːz] *n* bleu *m*, contusion *f* ♦ *vt* contusionner, meurtrir

brunette [bruːˈnet] *n* (femme) brune

brunt [brʌnt] *n*: **the** ~ **of** (*attack, criticism etc*) le plus gros de

brush [brʌʃ] *n* brosse *f*; (*painting*) pinceau *m*; (*shaving*) blaireau *m*; (*quarrel*) accrochage *m*, prise *f* de bec ♦ *vt* brosser; (*also:* ~ **against**) effleurer, frôler; ~ **aside** *vt* écarter, balayer; ~ **up** *vt* (*knowledge*) rafraîchir, réviser; ~**wood** *n* broussailles *fpl*, taillis *m*

Brussels [ˈbrʌslz] *n* Bruxelles; ~ **sprout** *n* chou *m* de Bruxelles

brutal [ˈbruːtl] *adj* brutal(e)

brute [bruːt] *n* brute *f* ♦ *adj*: **by** ~ **force** par la force

BSc *abbr* = **Bachelor of Science**

bubble [ˈbʌbl] *n* bulle *f* ♦ *vi* bouillonner, faire des bulles; (*sparkle*) pétiller; ~ **bath** *n* bain moussant; ~ **gum** *n* bubblegum *m*

buck [bʌk] *n* mâle *m* (*d'un lapin, daim etc*); (*US: inf*) dollar *m* ♦ *vi* ruer, lancer une ruade; **to pass the** ~ **(to sb)** se décharger de la responsabilité (sur qn); ~ **up** *vi* (*cheer up*) reprendre du poil de la bête, se remonter

bucket [ˈbʌkɪt] *n* seau *m*

buckle [ˈbʌkl] *n* boucle *f* ♦ *vt* (*belt etc*) boucler, attacher ♦ *vi* (*warp*) tordre, gauchir; (*: wheel*) se voiler; se déformer

bud [bʌd] *n* bourgeon *m*; (*of flower*) bouton *m* ♦ *vi* bourgeonner; (*flower*) éclore

Buddhism [ˈbʊdɪzəm] *n* bouddhisme *m*

budding [ˈbʌdɪŋ] *adj* (*poet etc*) en herbe; (*passion etc*) naissant(e)

buddy [ˈbʌdɪ] (*US*) *n* copain *m*

budge [bʌdʒ] *vt* faire bouger; (*fig: person*) faire changer d'avis ♦ *vi* bouger; changer d'avis

budgerigar [ˈbʌdʒərɪɡɑː*] (*BRIT*) *n* perruche *f*

budget [ˈbʌdʒɪt] *n* budget *m* ♦ *vi*: **to** ~ **for sth** inscrire qch au budget

budgie [ˈbʌdʒɪ] (*BRIT*) *n* = **budgerigar**

buff [bʌf] *adj* (couleur *f*) chamois *m* ♦ *n* (*inf: enthusiast*) mordu(e); **he's a ... ~** c'est un mordu de ...

buffalo ['bʌfələu] (*pl* ~ *or* ~**es**) *n* buffle *m*; (*US*) bison *m*

buffer ['bʌfə*] *n* tampon *m*; (*COMPUT*) mémoire *f* tampon

buffet¹ ['bʌfɪt] *vt* secouer, ébranler

buffet² ['bufeɪ] *n* (*food, BRIT: bar*) buffet *m*; ~ **car** (*BRIT*) *n* (*RAIL*) voiture-buffet *f*

bug [bʌg] *n* (*insect*) punaise *f*; (*: gen*) insecte *m*, bestiole *f*; (*fig: germ*) virus *m*, microbe *m*; (*COMPUT*) erreur *f*; (*fig: spy device*) dispositif *m* d'écoute (électronique) ♦ *vt* garnir de dispositifs d'écoute; (*inf: annoy*) embêter

bugle ['bju:gl] *n* clairon *m*

build [bɪld] (*pt, pp* **built**) *n* (*of person*) carrure *f*, charpente *f* ♦ *vt* construire, bâtir; ~ **up** *vt* accumuler, amasser; accroître; ~**er** *n* entrepreneur *m*; ~**ing** *n* (*trade*) construction *f*; (*house, structure*) bâtiment *m*, construction; (*offices, flats*) immeuble *m*; ~**ing society** (*BRIT*) *n* société *f* de crédit immobilier

built [bɪlt] *pt, pp of* **build**; ~-**in** *adj* (*cupboard, oven*) encastré(e); (*device*) incorporé(e); intégré(e); ~-**up area** *n* zone urbanisée

bulb [bʌlb] *n* (*BOT*) bulbe *m*, oignon *m*; (*ELEC*) ampoule *f*

bulge [bʌldʒ] *n* renflement *m*, gonflement *m* ♦ *vi* (*pocket, file etc*) être plein(e) à craquer; (*cheeks*) être gonflé(e)

bulk [bʌlk] *n* masse *f*, volume *m*; (*of person*) corpulence *f*; **in** ~ (*COMM*) en vrac; **the** ~ **of** la plus grande *or* grosse partie de; ~**y** *adj* volumineux(euse), encombrant(e)

bull [bul] *n* taureau *m*; (*male elephant/whale*) mâle *m*; ~**dog** *n* bouledogue *m*

bulldozer ['buldəuzə*] *n* bulldozer *m*

bullet ['bulɪt] *n* balle *f* (*de fusil etc*)

bulletin ['bulɪtɪn] *n* bulletin *m*, communiqué *m*; (*news* ~) (bulletin d')informations *fpl*

bulletproof ['bulɪtpru:f] *adj* (*car*) blindé(e); (*vest etc*) pare-balles *inv*

bullfight ['bulfaɪt] *n* corrida *f*, course *f* de taureaux; ~**er** *n* torero *m*; ~**ing** *n* tauromachie *f*

bullion ['buljən] *n* or *m or* argent *m* en lingots

bull: ~**ock** ['bulək] *n* bœuf *m*; ~**ring** ['bulrɪŋ] *n* arènes *fpl*; ~'**s-eye** ['bulzaɪ] *n* centre *m* (*de la cible*)

bully ['bulɪ] *n* brute *f*, tyran *m* ♦ *vt* tyranniser, rudoyer

bum [bʌm] *n* (*inf: backside*) derrière *m*; (*esp US: tramp*) vagabond(e), traîne-savates *m/f inv*

bumblebee ['bʌmblbi:] *n* bourdon *m*

bump [bʌmp] *n* (*in car: minor accident*) accrochage *m*; (*jolt*) cahot *m*; (*on road etc, on head*) bosse *f* ♦ *vt* heurter, cogner; ~ **into** *vt fus* rentrer dans, tamponner; (*meet*) tomber sur; ~**er** *n* pare-chocs *m inv* ♦ *adj*: ~**er crop/harvest** récolte/moisson exceptionnelle; ~**er cars** *npl* autos tamponneuses

bumpy ['bʌmpɪ] *adj* cahoteux(euse)

bun [bʌn] *n* petit pain au lait; (*of hair*) chignon *m*

bunch [bʌntʃ] *n* (*of flowers*) bouquet *m*; (*of keys*) trousseau *m*; (*of bananas*) régime *m*; (*of people*) groupe *m*; ~**es** *npl* (*in hair*) couettes *fpl*; ~ **of grapes** grappe *f* de raisin

bundle ['bʌndl] *n* paquet *m* ♦ *vt* (*also:* ~ *up*) faire un paquet de; (*put*): **to** ~ **sth/sb into** fourrer *or* enfourner qch/qn dans

bungalow ['bʌŋgələu] *n* bungalow *m*

bungle ['bʌŋgl] *vt* bâcler, gâcher

bunion ['bʌnjən] *n* oignon *m* (*au pied*)

bunk [bʌŋk] *n* couchette *f*; ~ **beds** *npl* lits superposés

bunker ['bʌŋkə*] *n* (*coal store*) soute *f* à charbon; (*MIL, GOLF*) bunker *m*

bunny ['bʌnɪ] *n* (*also:* ~ *rabbit*) Jeannot *m* lapin

bunting ['bʌntɪŋ] *n* pavoisement *m*, drapeaux *mpl*

buoy [bɔɪ] *n* bouée *f*; ~ **up** *vt* faire flotter; (*fig*) soutenir, épauler; ~**ant** *adj* capable de flotter; (*carefree*) gai(e), plein(e) d'entrain; (*economy*) ferme, actif

burden ['bɜ:dn] *n* fardeau *m* ♦ *vt* (*trouble*) accabler, surcharger

bureau ['bjuərəu] (*pl* ~**x**) *n* (*BRIT: writing desk*) bureau *m*, secrétaire *m*; (*US: chest of drawers*) commode *f*; (*office*) bureau, office *m*; ~**cracy** [bju'rɒkrəsɪ] *n* bureaucratie *f*

burglar ['bɜ:glə*] *n* cambrioleur *m*; ~ **alarm** *n* sonnerie *f* d'alarme; ~**y** *n* cambriolage *m*

Burgundy ['bɜ:gəndɪ] *n* Bourgogne *f*

burial ['berɪəl] *n* enterrement *m*

burly ['bɜ:lɪ] *adj* de forte carrure, costaud(e)

Burma ['bɜ:mə] *n* Birmanie *f*

burn [bɜ:n] (*pt, pp* **burned** *or* **burnt**) *vt, vi* brûler ♦ *n* brûlure *f*; ~ **down** *vt* incendier, détruire par le feu; ~**er** *n* brûleur *m*; ~**ing** *adj* brûlant(e); (*house*) en flammes; (*ambition*) dévorant(e)

burrow ['bʌrəu] *n* terrier *m* ♦ *vt* creuser

bursary ['bɜ:sərɪ] (*BRIT*) *n* bourse *f* (d'études)

burst [bɜ:st] (*pt, pp* **burst**) *vt* crever; faire éclater; (*subj: river: banks etc*) rompre ♦ *vi* éclater; (*tyre*) crever ♦ *n* (*of gunfire*) rafale *f* (*de tir*); (*also:* ~ *pipe*) rupture *f*; fuite *f*; **a** ~ **of enthusiasm/energy** un accès d'enthousiasme/d'énergie; **to** ~ **into flames** s'enflammer soudainement; **to** ~ **out laughing** éclater de rire; **to** ~ **into tears** fondre en larmes; **to be** ~**ing with** être plein (à craquer) de; (*fig*) être débordant(e) de; ~ **into** *vt fus* (*room etc*) faire irruption dans

bury ['bɛrɪ] *vt* enterrer

bus [bʌs, *pl* '-ɪz] (*pl* ~**es**) *n* autobus *m*

bush [buʃ] *n* buisson *m*; (*scrubland*) brousse *f*; **to beat about the** ~ tourner autour du pot; ~**y** ['buʃɪ] *adj* broussailleux(euse), touffu(e)

busily ['bɪzɪlɪ] *adv* activement

business ['bɪznɪs] *n* (*matter, firm*) affaire *f*; (*trading*) affaires *fpl*; (*job, duty*) travail *m*; **to be away on** ~ être en déplacement d'affaires; **it's none of my** ~ cela ne me regarde pas, ce ne sont pas mes affaires; **he means** ~ il ne plaisante pas, il est sérieux; ~**like** *adj* sérieux(euse), efficace; ~**man** (*irreg*) *n* homme *m* d'affaires; ~ **trip** *n* voyage *m* d'affaires; ~**woman** (*irreg*) *n* femme *f* d'affaires

busker ['bʌskə*] (*BRIT*) *n* musicien ambulant

bus stop *n* arrêt *m* d'autobus

bust [bʌst] *n* buste *m*; (*measurement*) tour *m* de poitrine ♦ *adj* (*inf: broken*) fichu(e), fini(e); **to go** ~ faire faillite

bustle ['bʌsl] *n* remue-ménage *m*, affairement *m* ♦ *vi* s'affairer, se démener; **bustling** *adj* (*town*) bruyant(e), affairé(e)

busy ['bɪzɪ] *adj* occupé(e); (*shop, street*) très fréquenté(e) ♦ *vt*: **to** ~ **o.s.** s'occuper; ~**body** *n* mouche *f* du coche, âme *f* charitable; ~ **signal** (*US*) *n* (*TEL*) tonalité *f* occupé *inv*

but [bʌt] *conj* mais; **I'd love to come,** ~ **I'm busy** j'aimerais venir mais je suis occupé ♦ *prep* (*apart from, except*) sauf, excepté; **we've had nothing** ~ **trouble** nous n'avons eu que des ennuis; **no-one** ~ **him can do it** lui seul peut le faire; ~ **for you/your help** sans toi/ton aide; **anything** ~ **that** tout sauf *or* excepté ça, tout mais pas ça ♦ *adv* (*just, only*) ne ... que; **she's** ~ **a child** elle n'est qu'une enfant; **had I** ~ **known** si seulement j'avais su; **all** ~ **finished** pratiquement terminé

butcher ['butʃə*] *n* boucher *m* ♦ *vt* massacrer; (*cattle etc for meat*) tuer; ~'**s (shop)** *n* boucherie *f*

butler ['bʌtlə*] *n* maître *m* d'hôtel

butt [bʌt] *n* (*large barrel*) gros tonneau; (*of gun*) crosse *f*; (*of cigarette*) mégot *m*; (*BRIT: fig: target*) cible *f* ♦ *vt* donner un coup de tête à; ~ **in** *vi* (*interrupt*) s'immiscer dans la conversation

butter ['bʌtə*] *n* beurre *m* ♦ *vt* beurrer; ~**cup** *n* bouton *m* d'or; ~**fly** *n* papillon *m*; (*SWIMMING: also*: ~**fly stroke**) brasse *f* papillon

buttocks ['bʌtəks] *npl* fesses *fpl*

button ['bʌtn] *n* bouton *m*; (*US: badge*) pin

m ♦ *vt* (*also*: ~ **up**) boutonner ♦ *vi* se boutonner

buttress ['bʌtrɪs] *n* contrefort *m*

buxom ['bʌksəm] *adj* aux formes avantageuses *or* épanouies

buy [baɪ] (*pt, pp* **bought**) *vt* acheter ♦ *n* achat *m*; **to** ~ **sb sth/sth from sb** acheter qch à qn; **to** ~ **sb a drink** offrir un verre *or* à boire à qn; ~**er** *n* acheteur(euse)

buzz [bʌz] *n* bourdonnement *m*; (*inf: phone call*) **to give sb a** ~ passer un coup *m* de fil à qn ♦ *vi* bourdonner; ~**er** ['bʌzə*] *n* timbre *m* électrique; ~ **word** (*inf*) *n* mot *m* à la mode

by [baɪ] *prep* **1** (*referring to cause, agent*) par, de; **killed** ~ **lightning** tué par la foudre; **surrounded** ~ **a fence** entouré d'une barrière; **a painting** ~ **Picasso** un tableau de Picasso

2 (*referring to method, manner, means*): ~ **bus/car** en autobus/voiture; ~ **train** par le *or* en train; **to pay** ~ **cheque** payer par chèque; ~ **saving hard, he ...** à force d'économiser, il ...

3 (*via, through*) par; **we came** ~ **Dover** nous sommes venus par Douvres

4 (*close to, past*) à côté de; **the house** ~ **the school** la maison à côté de l'école; **a holiday** ~ **the sea** des vacances au bord de la mer; **she sat** ~ **his bed** elle était assise à son chevet; **she went** ~ **me** elle est passée à côté de moi; **I go** ~ **the post office every day** je passe devant la poste tous les jours

5 (*with time: not later than*) avant; (: *during*): ~ **daylight** à la lumière du jour; ~ **night** la nuit, de nuit; ~ **4 o'clock** avant 4 heures; ~ **this time tomorrow** d'ici demain à la même heure; ~ **the time I got here it was too late** lorsque je suis arrivé il était déjà trop tard

6 (*amount*) à; ~ **the kilo/metre** au kilo/au mètre; **paid** ~ **the hour** payé à l'heure

7 (*MATH, measure*): **to divide/multiply** ~ **3** diviser/multiplier par 3; **a room 3 metres** ~ **4** une pièce de 3 mètres sur 4; **it's broader** ~ **a metre** c'est plus large d'un mètre; **one** ~ **one** un à un; **little** ~ **little** petit à petit, peu à peu

8 (*according to*) d'après, selon; **it's 3 o'clock** ~ **my watch** il est 3 heures à ma montre; **it's all right** ~ **me** je n'ai rien contre

9: (**all**) ~ **oneself** *etc* tout(e) seul(e)

10: ~ **the way** au fait, à propos

♦ *adv* **1** *see* **go**; **pass** *etc*

2: ~ **and** ~ un peu plus tard, bientôt; ~ **and large** dans l'ensemble

bye(-bye) ['baɪ('baɪ)] *excl* au revoir!, salut!

by(e)-law ['baɪlɔː] n arrêté municipal
by: ~**-election** (BRIT) n élection (législative) partielle; ~**gone** adj passé(e) ♦ n: **let ~gones be ~gones** passons l'éponge, oublions le passé; ~**pass** n (route f de) contournement m; (MED) pontage m ♦ vt éviter; ~**-product** n sous-produit m, dérivé m; (fig) conséquence f secondaire, retombée f; ~**stander** ['baɪstændə*] n spectateur(trice), badaud(e)
byte [baɪt] n (COMPUT) octet m
byword ['baɪwɜːd] n: **to be a ~ for** être synonyme de (fig)
by-your-leave ['baɪjɔː'liːv] n: **without so much as a ~** sans même demander la permission

---

C c

C [siː] n (MUS) do m
CA abbr = **chartered accountant**
cab [kæb] n taxi m; (of train, truck) cabine f
cabaret ['kæbəreɪ] n (show) spectacle m de cabaret
cabbage ['kæbɪdʒ] n chou m
cabin ['kæbɪn] n (house) cabane f, hutte f; (on ship) cabine f; (on plane) compartiment m; ~ **cruiser** n cruiser m
cabinet ['kæbɪnɪt] n (POL) cabinet m; (furniture) petit meuble à tiroirs et rayons; (also: display ~) vitrine f, petite armoire vitrée
cable ['keɪbl] n câble m ♦ vt câbler, télégraphier; ~**-car** n téléphérique m; ~ **television** n télévision f par câble
cache [kæʃ] n stock m
cackle ['kækl] vi caqueter
cactus ['kæktəs, pl -taɪ] (pl **cacti**) n cactus m
cadet [kə'det] n (MIL) élève m officier
cadge [kædʒ] (inf) vt: **to ~ (from or off)** se faire donner (par)
café ['kæfɪ] n ≈ café(-restaurant) m (sans alcool)
cage [keɪdʒ] n cage f
cagey ['keɪdʒɪ] (inf) adj réticent(e); méfiant(e)
cagoule [kə'guːl] n K-way m (®)
cajole [kə'dʒəʊl] vt couvrir de flatteries or de gentillesses
cake [keɪk] n gâteau m; ~ **of soap** savonnette f; ~**d** adj: ~**d with** raidi(e) par, couvert(e) d'une croûte de
calculate ['kælkjʊleɪt] vt calculer; (estimate:

chances, effect) évaluer; **calculation** [kælkjʊ'leɪʃən] n calcul m; **calculator** n machine f à calculer, calculatrice f; (pocket) calculette f
calendar ['kælɪndə*] n calendrier m; ~ **year** n année civile
calf [kɑːf] (pl **calves**) n (of cow) veau m; (of other animals) petit m; (also: ~skin) veau m, vachette f; (ANAT) mollet m
calibre ['kælɪbə*] (US **caliber**) n calibre m
call [kɔːl] vt appeler; (meeting) convoquer ♦ vi appeler; (visit: also: ~ **in**, ~ **round**) passer ♦ n (shout) appel m, cri m; (also: telephone ~) coup m de téléphone; (visit) visite f; **she's ~ed Suzanne** elle s'appelle Suzanne; **to be on ~** être de permanence; ~ **back** vi (return) repasser; (TEL) rappeler; ~ **for** vt fus (demand) demander; (fetch) passer prendre; ~ **off** vt annuler; ~ **on** vt fus (visit) rendre visite à, passer voir; (request): **to ~ on sb to do** inviter qn à faire; ~ **out** vi pousser un cri or des cris; ~ **up** vt (MIL) appeler, mobiliser; (TEL) appeler; ~**box** (BRIT) n (TEL) cabine f téléphonique; ~**er** n (TEL) personne f qui appelle; (visitor) visiteur m; ~ **girl** n call-girl n; ~**-in** (US) n (RADIO, TV: phone-in) programme m à ligne ouverte; ~**ing** n vocation f; (trade, occupation) état m; ~**ing card** (US) n carte f de visite
callous ['kæləs] adj dur(e), insensible
calm [kɑːm] adj calme ♦ n calme m ♦ vt calmer, apaiser; ~ **down** vi se calmer ♦ vt calmer, apaiser
Calor gas ['kælə-] (®) n butane m, butagaz m (®)
calorie ['kælərɪ] n calorie f
calves [kɑːvz] npl of **calf**
camber ['kæmbə*] n (of road) bombement m
Cambodia [kæm'bəʊdjə] n Cambodge m
camcorder ['kæmkɔːdə*] n camescope m
came [keɪm] pt of **come**
camel ['kæməl] n chameau m
camera ['kæmərə] n (PHOT) appareil-photo m; (also: cine~, movie ~) caméra f; **in ~** à huis clos; ~**man** (irreg) n caméraman m
camouflage ['kæməflɑːʒ] n camouflage m ♦ vt camoufler
camp [kæmp] n camp m ♦ vi camper ♦ adj (man) efféminé(e)
campaign [kæm'peɪn] n (MIL, POL etc) campagne f ♦ vi faire campagne
camp: ~**bed** (BRIT) n lit m de camp; ~**er** n campeur(euse); (vehicle) camping-car m; ~**ing** n camping m; **to go ~ing** faire du camping; ~**site** ['kæmpsaɪt] n campement m, (terrain m de) camping m
campus ['kæmpəs] n campus m
can¹ [kæn] n (of milk, oil, water) bidon m; (tin) boîte f de conserve ♦ vt mettre en conserve

———— KEYWORD ————

can² [kæn] (*negative* **cannot**, **can't**; *conditional and pt* **could**) *aux vb* **1** (*be able to*) pouvoir; **you ~ do it if you try** vous pouvez le faire si vous essayez; **I ~'t hear you** je ne t'entends pas
2 (*know how to*) savoir; **I ~ swim/play tennis/drive** je sais nager/jouer au tennis/conduire; **~ you speak French?** parlez-vous français?
3 (*may*) pouvoir; **~ I use your phone?** puis-je me servir de votre téléphone?
4 (*expressing disbelief, puzzlement etc*): **it ~'t be true!** ce n'est pas possible!; **what CAN he want?** qu'est-ce qu'il peut bien vouloir?
5 (*expressing possibility, suggestion etc*): **he could be in the library** il est peut-être dans la bibliothèque; **she could have been delayed** il se peut qu'elle ait été retardée

Canada ['kænədə] *n* Canada *m*; **Canadian** [kə'neɪdɪən] *adj* canadien(ne) ♦ *n* Canadien(ne)
canal [kə'næl] *n* canal *m*
canary [kə'nɛərɪ] *n* canari *m*, serin *m*
cancel ['kænsəl] *vt* annuler; (*train*) supprimer; (*party, appointment*) décommander; (*cross out*) barrer, rayer; **~lation** [kænsə'leɪʃən] *n* annulation *f*, suppression *f*
cancer ['kænsə*] *n* (MED) cancer *m*; **C~** (ASTROLOGY) le Cancer
candid ['kændɪd] *adj* (très) franc(franche), sincère
candidate ['kændɪdeɪt] *n* candidat(e)
candle ['kændl] *n* bougie *f*; (*of tallow*) chandelle *f*; (*in church*) cierge *m*; **~light** *n*: **by ~light** à la lumière d'une bougie; (*dinner*) aux chandelles; **~stick** *n* (*also: ~ holder*) bougeoir *m*; (*bigger, ornate*) chandelier *m*
candour ['kændə*] (US **candor**) *n* (grande) franchise *or* sincérité
candy ['kændɪ] *n* sucre candi; (US) bonbon *m*; **~-floss** (BRIT) *n* barbe *f* à papa
cane [keɪn] *n* canne *f*; (*for furniture, baskets etc*) rotin *m* ♦ *vt* (BRIT: SCOL) administrer des coups de bâton à
canister ['kænɪstə*] *n* boîte *f*; (*of gas, pressurized substance*) bombe *f*
cannabis ['kænəbɪs] *n* (*drug*) cannabis *m*
canned [kænd] *adj* (*food*) en boîte, en conserve
cannon ['kænən] (*pl* ~ *or* ~**s**) *n* (*gun*) canon *m*
cannot ['kænɒt] = **can not**
canoe [kə'nuː] *n* pirogue *f*; (SPORT) canoë *m*
canon ['kænən] *n* (*clergyman*) chanoine *m*; (*standard*) canon *m*
can-opener [-'əupnə*] *n* ouvre-boîte *m*
canopy ['kænəpɪ] *n* baldaquin *m*; dais *m*

can't [kɑːnt] = **can not**
cantankerous [kæn'tæŋkərəs] *adj* querelleur(euse), acariâtre
canteen [kæn'tiːn] *n* cantine *f*; (BRIT: *of cutlery*) ménagère *f*
canter ['kæntə*] *vi* (*horse*) aller au petit galop
canvas ['kænvəs] *n* toile *f*
canvass ['kænvəs] *vi* (POL): **to ~ for** faire campagne pour ♦ *vt* (*investigate: opinions etc*) sonder
canyon ['kænjən] *n* cañon *m*, gorge (profonde)
cap [kæp] *n* casquette *f*; (*of pen*) capuchon *m*; (*of bottle*) capsule *f*; (*contraceptive: also: Dutch ~*) diaphragme *m*; (*for toy gun*) amorce *f* ♦ *vt* (*outdo*) surpasser; (*put limit on*) plafonner
capability [keɪpə'bɪlɪtɪ] *n* aptitude *f*, capacité *f*
capable ['keɪpəbl] *adj* capable
capacity [kə'pæsɪtɪ] *n* capacité *f*; (*capability*) aptitude *f*; (*of factory*) rendement *m*
cape [keɪp] *n* (*garment*) cape *f*; (GEO) cap *m*
caper ['keɪpə*] *n* (CULIN: *gen*: ~**s**) câpre *f*; (*prank*) farce *f*
capital ['kæpɪtl] *n* (*also: ~ city*) capitale *f*; (*money*) capital *m*; (*also: ~ letter*) majuscule *f*; **~ gains tax** *n* (COMM) impôt *m* sur les plus-values; **~ism** *n* capitalisme *m*; **~ist** *adj* capitaliste ♦ *n* capitaliste *m/f*; **~ize** *vi*: **to ~ize on** tirer parti de; **~ punishment** *n* peine capitale
Capricorn ['kæprɪkɔːn] *n* (ASTROLOGY) le Capricorne
capsize [kæp'saɪz] *vt* faire chavirer ♦ *vi* chavirer
capsule ['kæpsjuːl] *n* capsule *f*
captain ['kæptɪn] *n* capitaine *m*
caption ['kæpʃən] *n* légende *f*
captive ['kæptɪv] *adj, n* captif(ive)
capture ['kæptʃə*] *vt* capturer, prendre; (*attention*) capter; (COMPUT) saisir ♦ *n* capture *f*; (*data ~*) saisie *f* de données
car [kɑː*] *n* voiture *f*, auto *f*; (RAIL) wagon *m*, voiture
caramel ['kærəməl] *n* caramel *m*
caravan ['kærəvæn] *n* caravane *f*; **~ site** (BRIT) *n* camping *m* pour caravanes
carbohydrate [kɑːbəu'haɪdreɪt] *n* hydrate *m* de carbone; (*food*) féculent *m*
carbon ['kɑːbən] *n* carbone *m*; **~ dioxide** *n* gaz *m* carbonique; **~ monoxide** *n* oxyde *m* de carbone; **~ paper** *n* papier *m* carbone
carburettor ['kɑːbjurɛtə*] (US **carburetor**) *n* carburateur *m*
card [kɑːd] *n* carte *f*; (*material*) carton *m*; **~board** *n* carton *m*; **~ game** *n* jeu *m* de cartes
cardiac ['kɑːdɪæk] *adj* cardiaque

cardigan ['kɑːdɪgən] *n* cardigan *m*
cardinal ['kɑːdɪnl] *adj* cardinal(e) ♦ *n* cardinal *m*
card index *n* fichier *m*
care [kɛə*] *n* soin *m*, attention *f*; (*worry*) souci *m*; (*charge*) charge *f*, garde *f* ♦ *vi*: to ~ **about** se soucier de, s'intéresser à; (*person*) être attaché(e) à; ~ **of** chez, aux bons soins de; **in sb's** ~ à la garde de qn, confié(e) à qn; **to take** ~ **(to do)** faire attention (à faire); **to take** ~ **of** s'occuper de; **I don't** ~ ça m'est bien égal; **I couldn't** ~ **less** je m'en fiche complètement (*inf*); ~ **for** *vt fus* s'occuper de; (*like*) aimer
career [kə'rɪə*] *n* carrière *f* ♦ *vi* (*also*: ~ **along**) aller à toute allure; ~ **woman** (*irreg*) *n* femme ambitieuse
care: ~**free** ['kɛəfriː] *adj* sans souci, insouciant(e); ~**ful** ['kɛəful] *adj* (*thorough*) soigneux(euse); (*cautious*) prudent(e); **(be)** ~**ful!** (fais) attention!; ~**fully** *adv* avec soin, soigneusement; prudemment; ~**less** ['kɛəlɪs] *adj* négligent(e); (*heedless*) insouciant(e); ~**r** [kɛərə*] *n* (*MED*) aide *f*
caress [kə'rɛs] *n* caresse *f* ♦ *vt* caresser
caretaker ['kɛəteɪkə*] *n* gardien(ne), concierge *m/f*
car-ferry ['kɑːferɪ] *n* (*on sea*) ferry(-boat) *m*
cargo ['kɑːgəʊ] (*pl* ~**es**) *n* cargaison *f*, chargement *m*
car hire *n* location *f* de voitures
Caribbean [kærɪ'biːən] *adj*: **the** ~ **(Sea)** la mer des Antilles *or* Caraïbes
caring ['kɛərɪŋ] *adj* (*person*) bienveillant(e); (*society, organization*) humanitaire
carnal ['kɑːnl] *adj* charnel(le)
carnation [kɑː'neɪʃən] *n* œillet *m*
carnival ['kɑːnɪvəl] *n* (*public celebration*) carnaval *m*; (*US: funfair*) fête foraine
carol ['kærl] *n*: **(Christmas)** ~ chant *m* de Noël
carp [kɑːp] *n* (*fish*) carpe *f*; ~ **at** *vt fus* critiquer
car park (*BRIT*) *n* parking *m*, parc *m* de stationnement
carpenter ['kɑːpɪntə*] *n* charpentier *m*;
carpentry ['kɑːpɪntrɪ] *n* menuiserie *f*
carpet ['kɑːpɪt] *n* tapis *m* ♦ *vt* recouvrir d'un tapis; ~ **slippers** *npl* pantoufles *fpl*; ~ **sweeper** *n* balai *m* mécanique
car phone *n* (*TEL*) téléphone *m* de voiture
carriage ['kærɪdʒ] *n* voiture *f*; (*of goods*) transport *m*; (: *cost*) port *m*; ~**way** (*BRIT*) *n* (*part of road*) chaussée *f*
carrier ['kærɪə*] *n* transporteur *m*, camionneur *m*; (*company*) entreprise *f* de transport; (*MED*) porteur(euse); ~ **bag** (*BRIT*) *n* sac *m* (en papier ou en plastique)
carrot ['kærət] *n* carotte *f*
carry ['kærɪ] *vt* (*subj: person*) porter; (: *vehicle*) transporter; (*involve: responsibilities etc*) comporter, impliquer ♦ *vi* (*sound*) porter;

to get carried away (*fig*) s'emballer, s'enthousiasmer; ~ **on** *vi*: **to** ~ **on with sth/doing** continuer qch/de faire ♦ *vt* poursuivre; ~ **out** *vt* (*orders*) exécuter; (*investigation*) mener; ~**cot** (*BRIT*) *n* porte-bébé *m*; ~**-on** (*inf*) *n* (*fuss*) histoires *fpl*
cart [kɑːt] *n* charrette *f* ♦ *vt* (*inf*) transporter, trimballer (*inf*)
carton ['kɑːtən] *n* (*box*) carton *m*; (*of yogurt*) pot *m*; (*of cigarettes*) cartouche *f*
cartoon [kɑː'tuːn] *n* (*PRESS*) dessin *m* (humoristique), caricature *f*; (*BRIT: comic strip*) bande dessinée; (*CINEMA*) dessin animé
cartridge ['kɑːtrɪdʒ] *n* cartouche *f*
carve [kɑːv] *vt* (*meat*) découper; (*wood, stone*) tailler, sculpter; ~ **up** *vt* découper; (*fig: country*) morceler; **carving** ['kɑːvɪŋ] *n* sculpture *f*; **carving knife** *n* couteau *m* à découper
car wash *n* station *f* de lavage (de voitures)
case [keɪs] *n* cas *m*; (*LAW*) affaire *f*, procès *m*; (*box*) caisse *f*, boîte *f*, étui *m*; (*BRIT: also: suit~*) valise *f*; **in** ~ **of** en cas de; **in** ~ **he ...** au cas où il ...; **just in** ~ à tout hasard; **in any** ~ en tout cas, de toute façon
cash [kæʃ] *n* argent *m*; (*COMM*) argent liquide, espèces *fpl* ♦ *vt* encaisser; **to pay (in)** ~ payer comptant; ~ **on delivery** payable *or* paiement à la livraison; ~**-book** *n* livre *m* de caisse; ~ **card** (*BRIT*) *n* carte *f* de retrait; ~ **desk** (*BRIT*) *n* caisse *f*; ~ **dispenser** (*BRIT*) *n* distributeur *m* automatique de billets, billeterie *f*
cashew [kæ'ʃuː] *n* (*also:* ~ **nut**) noix *f* de cajou
cashier [kæ'ʃɪə*] *n* caissier(ère)
cashmere ['kæʃmɪə*] *n* cachemire *m*
cash register *n* caisse (enregistreuse)
casing ['keɪsɪŋ] *n* revêtement (protecteur), enveloppe (protectrice)
casino [kə'siːnəʊ] *n* casino *m*
casket ['kɑːskɪt] *n* coffret *m*; (*US: coffin*) cercueil *m*
casserole ['kæsərəʊl] *n* (*container*) cocotte *f*; (*food*) ragoût *m* (en cocotte)
cassette [kæ'set] *n* cassette *f*, musicassette *f*; ~ **player** *n* lecteur *m* de cassettes; ~ **recorder** *n* magnétophone *m* à cassettes
cast [kɑːst] (*pt, pp* **cast**) *vt* (*throw*) jeter; (*shed*) perdre; se dépouiller de; (*statue*) mouler; (*THEATRE*): **to** ~ **sb as Hamlet** attribuer à qn le rôle de Hamlet ♦ *n* (*THEATRE*) distribution *f*; (*also: plaster* ~) plâtre *m*; **to** ~ **one's vote** voter; ~ **off** *vi* (*NAUT*) larguer les amarres; (*KNITTING*) arrêter les mailles; ~ **on** *vi* (*KNITTING*) monter les mailles
castaway ['kɑːstəweɪ] *n* naufragé(e)
caster sugar ['kɑːstə-] (*BRIT*) *n* sucre *m* semoule

casting vote ['kɑːstɪŋ-] (*BRIT*) *n* voix prépondérante (*pour départager*)

cast iron *n* fonte *f*

castle ['kɑːsl] *n* château (fort); (*CHESS*) tour *f*

castor ['kɑːstə*] *n* (*wheel*) roulette *f*; ~ **oil** *n* huile *f* de ricin

castrate [kæs'treɪt] *vt* châtrer

casual ['kæʒjul] *adj* (*by chance*) de hasard, fait(e) au hasard, fortuit(e); (*irregular: work etc*) temporaire; (*unconcerned*) désinvolte; ~**ly** *adv* avec désinvolture, négligemment; (*dress*) de façon décontractée

casualty ['kæʒjultɪ] *n* accidenté(e), blessé(e); (*dead*) victime *f*, mort(e); (*MED: department*) urgences *fpl*

casual wear *n* vêtements *mpl* décontractés

cat [kæt] *n* chat *m*

catalogue ['kætəlɔg] (*US* **catalog**) *n* catalogue *m* ♦ *vt* cataloguer

catalyst ['kætəlɪst] *n* catalyseur *m*

catalytic converter [kætə'lɪtɪk kən'vɜːtə*] *n* pot *m* catalytique

catapult ['kætəpʌlt] (*BRIT*) *n* (*sling*) lance-pierres *m inv*, fronde *m*

catarrh [kə'tɑː*] *n* rhume *m* chronique, catarrhe *m*

catastrophe [kə'tæstrəfɪ] *n* catastrophe *f*

catch [kætʃ] (*pt, pp* **caught**) *vt* attraper; (*person: by surprise*) prendre, surprendre; (*understand, hear*) saisir ♦ *vi* (*fire*) prendre; (*become trapped*) se prendre, s'accrocher ♦ *n* prise *f*; (*trick*) attrape *f*; (*of lock*) loquet *m*; **to ~ sb's attention** *or* **eye** attirer l'attention de qn; **to ~ one's breath** retenir son souffle; **to ~ fire** prendre feu; **to ~ sight of** apercevoir; ~ **on** *vi* saisir; (*grow popular*) prendre; ~ **up** *vi* se rattraper, combler son retard ♦ *vt* (*also:* ~ **up with**) rattraper; ~**ing** *adj* (*MED*) contagieux(euse); ~**ment area** ['kætʃmənt-] (*BRIT*) *n* (*SCOL*) secteur *m* de recrutement; (*of hospital*) circonscription hospitalière; ~ **phrase** *n* slogan *m*; expression *f* (à la mode); ~**y** *adj* (*tune*) facile à retenir

category ['kætɪgərɪ] *n* catégorie *f*

cater ['keɪtə*] *vi* (*provide food*) **to ~** (*for*) préparer des repas (pour), se charger de la restauration (pour); ~ **for** (*BRIT*) *vt fus* (*needs*) satisfaire, pourvoir à; (*readers, consumers*) s'adresser à, pourvoir aux besoins de; ~**er** *n* traiteur *m*; fournisseur *m*; ~**ing** *n* restauration *f*; approvisionnement *m*, ravitaillement *m*

caterpillar ['kætəpɪlə*] *n* chenille *f*; ~ **track** ® *n* chenille *f*

cathedral [kə'θiːdrəl] *n* cathédrale *f*

catholic ['kæθəlɪk] *adj* (*tastes*) éclectique, varié(e); **C~** *adj* catholique ♦ *n* catholique *m/f*

Catseye ['kætsaɪ] (®: *BRIT*) *n* (*AUT*) catadioptre *m*

cattle ['kætl] *npl* bétail *m*

catty ['kætɪ] *adj* méchant(e)

caucus ['kɔːkəs] *n* (*POL: group*) comité local d'un parti politique; (*US: POL*) comité électoral (pour désigner des candidats)

caught [kɔːt] *pt, pp of* **catch**

cauliflower ['kɒlɪflauə*] *n* chou-fleur *m*

cause [kɔːz] *n* cause *f* ♦ *vt* causer

caution ['kɔːʃən] *n* prudence *f*; (*warning*) avertissement *m* ♦ *vt* avertir, donner un avertissement à

cautious ['kɔːʃəs] *adj* prudent(e)

cavalry ['kævəlrɪ] *n* cavalerie *f*

cave [keɪv] *n* caverne, grotte *f*; ~ **in** *vi* (*roof etc*) s'effondrer; ~**man** (*irreg*) *n* homme *m* des cavernes

caviar(e) ['kævɪɑː*] *n* caviar *m*

cavort [kə'vɔːt] *vi* cabrioler, faire des cabrioles

CB *n abbr* (= *Citizens' Band (Radio)*) CB *f*

CBI *n abbr* (= *Confederation of British Industries*) groupement du patronat

cc *abbr* = **carbon copy; cubic centimetres**

CD *n abbr* (= *compact disc (player)*) CD *m*; ~**-ROM** *n abbr* (= *compact disc read-only memory*) CD-ROM *m*

cease [siːs] *vt, vi* cesser; ~**fire** *n* cessez-le-feu *m*; ~**less** *adj* incessant(e), continuel(le)

cedar ['siːdə*] *n* cèdre *m*

ceiling ['siːlɪŋ] *n* plafond *m*

celebrate ['selɪbreɪt] *vt, vi* célébrer; ~**d** *adj* célèbre; **celebration** [selɪ'breɪʃən] *n* célébration *f*

celery ['selərɪ] *n* céleri *m* (à côtes)

cell [sel] *n* cellule *f*; (*ELEC*) élément *m* (*de pile*)

cellar ['selə*] *n* cave *f*

cello *n* violoncelle *m*

cellphone [sel'fəun] *n* téléphone *m* cellulaire

Celt [kelt, selt] *n* Celte *m/f*; ~**ic** ['keltɪk, 'seltɪk] *adj* celte

cement [sɪ'ment] *n* ciment *m*; ~ **mixer** *n* bétonnière *f*

cemetery ['semɪtrɪ] *n* cimetière *m*

censor ['sensə*] *n* censeur *m* ♦ *vt* censurer; ~**ship** *n* censure *f*

censure ['senʃə*] *vt* blâmer, critiquer

census ['sensəs] *n* recensement *m*

cent [sent] *n* (*US etc: coin*) cent *m* (= *un centième du dollar*); *see also* **per**

centenary [sen'tiːnərɪ] *n* centenaire *m*

center ['sentə*] (*US*) *n* = **centre**

centigrade ['sentɪgreɪd] *adj* centigrade

centimetre ['sentɪmiːtə*] (*US* **centimeter**) *n* centimètre *m*

centipede ['sentɪpiːd] *n* mille-pattes *m inv*

central ['sentrəl] *adj* central(e); **C~ America** *n* Amérique centrale; ~ **heating** *n* chauffage central; ~ **reservation** (*BRIT*) *n* (*AUT*) terre-plein central

centre ['sentə*] (*US* **center**) *n* centre *m* ♦ *vt* centrer; ~-**forward** n (SPORT) avant-centre m; ~-**half** n (SPORT) demi-centre m

century ['sentjʊrɪ] n siècle m; **20th** ~ XXe siècle

ceramic [sɪ'ræmɪk] adj céramique

cereal ['sɪərɪəl] n céréale f

ceremony ['serɪmənɪ] n cérémonie f; **to stand on** ~ faire des façons

certain ['sɜːtən] adj certain(e); **for** ~ certainement, sûrement; ~**ly** adv certainement; ~**ty** n certitude f

certificate [sə'tɪfɪkɪt] n certificat m

certified mail ['sɜːtɪfaɪd-] (US) n: **by** ~ en recommandé, avec avis de réception

certified public accountant (US) n expert-comptable m

certify ['sɜːtɪfaɪ] vt certifier; (award diploma to) conférer un diplôme etc à; (declare insane) déclarer malade mental(e)

cervical ['sɜːvɪkl] adj: ~ **cancer** cancer m du col de l'utérus; ~ **smear** frottis vaginal

cervix ['sɜːvɪks] n col m de l'utérus

cf. abbr (= compare) cf., voir

CFC n abbr (= chlorofluorocarbon) CFC m (gen pl)

ch. abbr (= chapter) chap.

chafe [tʃeɪf] vt irriter, frotter contre

chain [tʃeɪn] n chaîne f ♦ vt (also: ~ up) enchaîner, attacher (avec une chaîne); ~ **reaction** n réaction f en chaîne; ~-**smoke** vi fumer cigarette sur cigarette; ~ **store** n magasin m à succursales multiples

chair [tʃeə*] n chaise f; (arm~) fauteuil m; (of university) chaire f; (of meeting, committee) présidence f ♦ vt (meeting) présider; ~**lift** n télésiège m; ~**man** (irreg) n président m

chalet ['ʃæleɪ] n chalet m

chalice ['tʃælɪs] n calice m

chalk [tʃɔːk] n craie f

challenge ['tʃælɪndʒ] n défi m ♦ vt défier; (statement, right) mettre en question, contester; **to** ~ **sb to do** mettre qn au défi de faire; **challenging** ['tʃælɪndʒɪŋ] adj (tone, look) de défi, provocateur(trice); (task, career) qui représente un défi or une gageure

chamber ['tʃeɪmbə*] n chambre f; ~ **of commerce** chambre de commerce; ~**maid** n femme f de chambre; ~ **music** n musique f de chambre

champagne [ʃæm'peɪn] n champagne m

champion ['tʃæmpɪən] n champion(ne); ~**ship** n championnat m

chance [tʃɑːns] n (opportunity) occasion f, possibilité f; (hope, likelihood) chance f; (risk) risque m ♦ vt: **to** ~ **it** risquer (le coup), essayer ♦ adj fortuit(e), de hasard; **to take a** ~ prendre un risque; **by** ~ par hasard

chancellor ['tʃɑːnsələ*] n chancelier m; **C**~ **of the Exchequer** (BRIT) n chancelier

m de l'Échiquier, ≈ ministre m des Finances

chandelier [ʃændɪ'lɪə*] n lustre m

change [tʃeɪndʒ] vt (alter, replace, COMM: money) changer; (hands, trains, clothes, one's name) changer de; (transform): **to** ~ **sb into** changer or transformer qn en ♦ vi (gen) changer; (one's clothes) se changer; (be transformed): **to** ~ **into** se changer or transformer en ♦ n changement m; (money) monnaie f; **to** ~ **gear** (AUT) changer de vitesse; **to** ~ **one's mind** changer d'avis; **a** ~ **of clothes** des vêtements de rechange; **for a** ~ pour changer; ~**able** adj (weather) variable; ~ **machine** n distributeur m de monnaie; ~**over** n (to new system) changement m, passage m

changing ['tʃeɪndʒɪŋ] adj changeant(e); ~ **room** (BRIT) n (in shop) salon m d'essayage; (SPORT) vestiaire m

channel ['tʃænl] n (TV) chaîne f; (navigable passage) chenal m; (irrigation) canal m ♦ vt canaliser; **the (English) C**~ la Manche; **the C**~ **Islands** les îles de la Manche, les îles Anglo-Normandes

chant [tʃɑːnt] n chant m; (REL) psalmodie f ♦ vt chanter, scander

chaos ['keɪɒs] n chaos m

chap [tʃæp] (BRIT: inf) n (man) type m

chapel ['tʃæpəl] n chapelle f; (BRIT: non-conformist ~) église f

chaplain ['tʃæplɪn] n aumônier m

chapped ['tʃæpt] adj (skin, lips) gercé(e)

chapter ['tʃæptə*] n chapitre m

char [tʃɑː*] vt (burn) carboniser

character ['kærɪktə*] n caractère m; (in novel, film) personnage m; (eccentric) numéro m, phénomène m; ~**istic** [kærɪktə'rɪstɪk] adj caractéristique ♦ n caractéristique f

charcoal ['tʃɑːkəʊl] n charbon m de bois; (for drawing) charbon m

charge [tʃɑːdʒ] n (cost) prix (demandé); (accusation) accusation f; (LAW) inculpation f ♦ vt: **to** ~ **sb (with)** inculper qn (de); (battery, enemy) charger; (customer, sum) faire payer ♦ vi foncer; ~**s** npl (costs) frais mpl; **to reverse the** ~**s** (TEL) téléphoner en P.C.V.; **to take** ~ **of** se charger de; **to be in** ~ **of** être responsable de, s'occuper de; **how much do you** ~? combien prenez-vous?; **to** ~ **an expense (up) to sb** mettre une dépense sur le compte de qn; ~ **card** n carte f de client

charity ['tʃærɪtɪ] n charité f; (organization) institution f charitable or de bienfaisance, œuvre f (de charité)

charm [tʃɑːm] n charme m; (on bracelet) breloque f ♦ vt charmer, enchanter; ~**ing** adj charmant(e)

chart [tʃɑːt] n tableau m, diagramme m; graphique m; (map) carte marine ♦ vt dresser or établir la carte de; ~**s** npl (hit pa-

rade) hit-parade *m*

charter ['tʃɑːtə*] *vt* (*plane*) affréter ♦ *n* (*document*) charte *f*; ~**ed accountant** (*BRIT*) *n* expert-comptable *m*; ~ **flight** *n* charter *m*

chase [tʃeɪs] *vt* poursuivre, pourchasser; (*also*: ~ *away*) chasser ♦ *n* poursuite *f*, chasse *f*

chasm ['kæzəm] *n* gouffre *m*, abîme *m*

chat [tʃæt] *vi* (*also*: *have a* ~) bavarder, causer ♦ *n* conversation *f*; ~ **show** (*BRIT*) *n* causerie télévisée

chatter ['tʃætə*] *vi* (*person*) bavarder; (*animal*) jacasser ♦ *n* bavardage *m*; jacassement *m*; **my teeth are** ~**ing** je claque des dents; ~**box** (*inf*) *n* moulin *m* à paroles

chatty ['tʃætɪ] *adj* (*style*) familier(ère); (*person*) bavard(e)

chauffeur ['ʃəufə*] *n* chauffeur *m* (de maître)

chauvinist ['ʃəuvɪnɪst] *n* (*male* ~) phallocrate *m*; (*nationalist*) chauvin(e)

cheap [tʃiːp] *adj* bon marché *inv*, pas cher(chère); (*joke*) facile, d'un goût douteux; (*poor quality*) à bon marché, de qualité médiocre ♦ *adv* à bon marché, pour pas cher; ~**er** *adj* moins cher(chère); ~**ly** *adv* à bon marché, à bon compte

cheat [tʃiːt] *vi* tricher ♦ *vt* tromper, duper; (*rob*): **to** ~ **sb out of sth** escroquer qch à qn ♦ *n* tricheur(euse); escroc *m*

check [tʃek] *vt* vérifier; (*passport, ticket*) contrôler; (*halt*) arrêter; (*restrain*) maîtriser ♦ *n* vérification *f*, contrôle *m*; (*curb*) frein *m*; (*US*: *bill*) addition *f*; (*pattern*: *gen pl*) carreaux *mpl*; (*US*) = **cheque** ♦ *adj* (*pattern, cloth*) à carreaux; ~ **in** *vi* (*in hotel*) remplir sa fiche (d'hôtel); (*at airport*) se présenter à l'enregistrement ♦ *vt* (*luggage*) (faire) enregistrer; ~ **out** *vi* (*in hotel*) régler sa note; ~ **up** *vi*: **to** ~ **up (on sth)** vérifier (qch); **to** ~ **up on sb** se renseigner sur le compte de qn; ~**ered** (*US*) *adj* = **chequered**; ~**ers** (*US*) *npl* jeu *m* de dames; ~**-in (desk)** *n* enregistrement *m*; ~**ing account** (*US*) *n* (*current account*) compte courant; ~**mate** *n* échec et mat *m*; ~**out** *n* (*in shop*) caisse *f*; ~**point** *n* contrôle *m*; ~**room** (*US*) *n* (*left-luggage office*) consigne *f*; ~**up** (*MED*) *n* examen médical, check-up *m*

cheek [tʃiːk] *n* joue *f*; (*impudence*) toupet *m*, culot *m*; ~**bone** *n* pommette *f*; ~**y** *adj* effronté(e), culotté(e)

cheep [tʃiːp] *vi* piauler

cheer [tʃɪə*] *vt* acclamer, applaudir; (*gladden*) réjouir, réconforter ♦ *vi* applaudir ♦ *n* (*gen pl*) acclamations *fpl*, applaudissements *mpl*; bravos *mpl*, hourras *mpl*; ~**s!** à la vôtre!; ~ **up** *vi* se dérider, reprendre courage ♦ *vt* remonter le moral à *or* de, dérider; ~**ful** *adj* gai(e), joyeux(euse)

cheerio ['tʃɪərɪ'əu] (*BRIT*) *excl* salut!, au revoir!

cheese [tʃiːz] *n* fromage *m*; ~**board** *n* plateau *m* de fromages

cheetah ['tʃiːtə] *n* guépard *m*

chef [ʃef] *n* chef (cuisinier)

chemical ['kemɪkəl] *adj* chimique ♦ *n* produit *m* chimique

chemist ['kemɪst] *n* (*BRIT*: *pharmacist*) pharmacien(ne); (*scientist*) chimiste *m/f*; ~**ry** *n* chimie *f*; ~**'s (shop)** (*BRIT*) *n* pharmacie *f*

cheque [tʃek] (*BRIT*) *n* chèque *m*; ~**book** *n* chéquier *m*, carnet *m* de chèques; ~ **card** *n* carte *f* (d'identité) bancaire

chequered ['tʃekəd] (*US* **checkered**) *adj* (*fig*) varié(e)

cherish ['tʃerɪʃ] *vt* chérir; ~**ed** *adj* (*dream, memory*) cher(chère)

cherry ['tʃerɪ] *n* cerise *f*; (*also*: ~ *tree*) cerisier *m*

chess [tʃes] *n* échecs *mpl*; ~**board** *n* échiquier *m*

chest [tʃest] *n* poitrine *f*; (*box*) coffre *m*, caisse *f*; ~ **of drawers** *n* commode *f*

chestnut ['tʃesnʌt] *n* châtaigne *f*; (*also*: ~ *tree*) châtaignier *m*

chew [tʃuː] *vt* mâcher; ~**ing gum** *n* chewing-gum *m*

chic [ʃiːk] *adj* chic *inv*, élégant(e)

chick [tʃɪk] *n* poussin *m*; (*inf*) nana *f*

chicken ['tʃɪkɪn] *n* poulet *m*; (*inf*: *coward*) poule mouillée; ~ **out** (*inf*) *vi* se dégonfler; ~**pox** ['tʃɪkɪnpɒks] *n* varicelle *f*

chicory ['tʃɪkərɪ] *n* (*for coffee*) chicorée *f*; (*salad*) endive

chief [tʃiːf] *n* chef ♦ *adj* principal(e); ~ **executive** (*US* **chief executive officer**) *n* directeur(trice) général(e); ~**ly** *adv* principalement, surtout

chiffon ['ʃɪfɒn] *n* mousseline *f* de soie

chilblain ['tʃɪlbleɪn] *n* engelure *f*

child [tʃaɪld] (*pl* ~**ren**) *n* enfant *m/f*; ~**birth** *n* accouchement *m*; ~**hood** *n* enfance *f*; ~**ish** *adj* puéril(e), enfantin(e); ~**like** *adj* d'enfant, innocent(e); ~ **minder** (*BRIT*) *n* garde *f* d'enfants

Chile ['tʃɪlɪ] *n* Chili *m*

chill [tʃɪl] *n* (*of water*) froid *m*; (*of air*) fraîcheur *f*; (*MED*) refroidissement *m*, coup *m* de froid ♦ *vt* (*person*) faire frissonner; (*CULIN*) mettre au frais, rafraîchir

chil(l)i ['tʃɪlɪ] *n* piment *m* (rouge)

chilly ['tʃɪlɪ] *adj* froid(e), glacé(e); (*sensitive to cold*) frileux(euse); **to feel** ~ avoir froid

chime [tʃaɪm] *n* carillon *m* ♦ *vi* carillonner, sonner

chimney ['tʃɪmnɪ] *n* cheminée *f*; ~ **sweep** *n* ramoneur *m*

chimpanzee [tʃɪmpæn'zi:] *n* chimpanzé *m*

chin [tʃɪn] *n* menton *m*

China ['tʃaɪnə] *n* Chine *f*

china ['tʃaɪnə] n porcelaine f; (crockery) (vaisselle f en) porcelaine
Chinese [tʃaɪ'niːz] adj chinois(e) ♦ n inv (person) Chinois(e); (LING) chinois m
chink [tʃɪŋk] n (opening) fente f, fissure f; (noise) tintement m
chip [tʃɪp] n (gen pl: CULIN: BRIT) frite f; (: US: potato ~) chip m; (of wood) copeau m; (of glass, stone) éclat m; (also: micro~) puce f ♦ vt (cup, plate) ébrécher; ~ **in** vi mettre son grain de sel; (contribute) contribuer
chiropodist [kɪ'rɒpədɪst] (BRIT) n pédicure m/f
chirp [tʃɜːp] vi pépier, gazouiller
chisel ['tʃɪzl] n ciseau m
chit [tʃɪt] n mot m, note f
chitchat ['tʃɪttʃæt] n bavardage m
chivalry ['ʃɪvəlrɪ] n esprit m chevaleresque, galanterie f
chives [tʃaɪvz] npl ciboulette f, civette f
chock-a-block ['tʃɒkə'blɒk], **chock-full** [tʃɒk'ful] adj plein(e) à craquer
chocolate ['tʃɒklɪt] n chocolat m
choice [tʃɔɪs] n choix m ♦ adj de choix
choir ['kwaɪə*] n chœur m, chorale f; **~boy** n jeune choriste m
choke [tʃəuk] vi étouffer ♦ vt étrangler; étouffer ♦ n (AUT) starter m; **street ~d with traffic** rue engorgée or embouteillée
cholesterol [kə'lɛstərɒl] n cholestérol m
choose [tʃuːz] (pt **chose**, pp **chosen**) vt choisir; **to ~ to do** décider de faire, juger bon de faire
choosy ['tʃuːzɪ] adj: **(to be) ~** (faire le/la) difficile
chop [tʃɒp] vt (wood) couper (à la hache); (CULIN: also: ~ up) couper (fin), émincer, hacher (en morceaux) ♦ n (CULIN) côtelette f; **~s** npl (jaws) mâchoires fpl
chopper ['tʃɒpə*] n (helicopter) hélicoptère m, hélico m
choppy ['tʃɒpɪ] adj (sea) un peu agité(e)
chopsticks ['tʃɒpstɪks] npl baguettes fpl
chord [kɔːd] n (MUS) accord m
chore [tʃɔː*] n travail m de routine; **household ~s** npl travaux mpl du ménage
chortle ['tʃɔːtl] vi glousser
chorus ['kɔːrəs] n chœur m; (repeated part of song: also: fig) refrain m
chose [tʃəuz] pt of **choose**
chosen ['tʃəuzn] pp of **choose**
Christ [kraɪst] n Christ m
christen ['krɪsn] vt baptiser
Christian ['krɪstɪən] adj, n chrétien(ne); **~ity** [krɪstɪ'ænɪtɪ] n christianisme m; **~ name** n prénom m
Christmas ['krɪsməs] n Noël m or f; **Happy or Merry ~!** joyeux Noël!; **~ card** n carte f de Noël; **~ Day** n le jour de Noël; **~ Eve** n la veille de Noël; la nuit de Noël; **~ tree** n arbre m de Noël

chrome [krəum] n chrome m
chromium ['krəumɪəm] n chrome m
chronic ['krɒnɪk] adj chronique
chronicle ['krɒnɪkl] n chronique f
chronological [krɒnə'lɒdʒɪkəl] adj chronologique
chrysanthemum [krɪ'sænθəməm] n chrysanthème m
chubby ['tʃʌbɪ] adj potelé(e), rondelet(te)
chuck [tʃʌk] (inf) vt (throw) lancer, jeter; (BRIT: also: ~ up: job) lâcher; (: person) plaquer; **~ out** vt flanquer dehors or à la porte; (rubbish) jeter
chuckle ['tʃʌkl] vi glousser
chug [tʃʌg] vi faire teuf-teuf; (also: ~ along) avancer en faisant teuf-teuf
chum [tʃʌm] n copain(copine)
chunk [tʃʌŋk] n gros morceau
church [tʃɜːtʃ] n église f; **~yard** n cimetière m
churn [tʃɜːn] n (for butter) baratte f; (also: milk ~) (grand) bidon à lait; **~ out** vt débiter
chute [ʃuːt] n glissoire f; (also: rubbish ~) vide-ordures m inv
chutney ['tʃʌtnɪ] n condiment m à base de fruits au vinaigre
CIA (US) n abbr (= Central Intelligence Agency) CIA f
CID (BRIT) n abbr (= Criminal Investigation Department) ≈ P.J. f
cider ['saɪdə*] n cidre m
cigar [sɪ'gɑː*] n cigare m
cigarette [sɪgə'rɛt] n cigarette f; **~ case** n étui m à cigarettes; **~ end** n mégot m
Cinderella [sɪndə'rɛlə] n Cendrillon
cinders ['sɪndəz] npl cendres fpl
cine-camera ['sɪnɪ'kæmərə] (BRIT) n caméra f
cinema ['sɪnəmə] n cinéma m
cinnamon ['sɪnəmən] n cannelle f
circle ['sɜːkl] n cercle m; (in cinema, theatre) balcon m ♦ vi faire or décrire des cercles ♦ vt (move round) faire le tour de, tourner autour de; (surround) entourer, encercler
circuit ['sɜːkɪt] n circuit m; **~ous** [sɜː'kjuːɪtəs] adj indirect(e), qui fait un détour
circular ['sɜːkjulə*] adj circulaire ♦ n circulaire f
circulate ['sɜːkjuleɪt] vi circuler ♦ vt faire circuler; **circulation** [sɜːkju'leɪʃən] n circulation f; (of newspaper) tirage m
circumflex ['sɜːkəmflɛks] n (also: ~ accent) accent m circonflexe
circumstances ['sɜːkəmstənsəz] npl circonstances fpl; (financial condition) moyens mpl, situation financière
circumvent [sɜːkəm'vɛnt] vt (rule, difficulty) tourner
circus ['sɜːkəs] n cirque m
CIS n abbr (= Commonwealth of Indepen-

dent States) CEI *f*

cistern ['sɪstən] *n* réservoir *m* (d'eau); (*in toilet*) réservoir de la chasse d'eau

citizen ['sɪtɪzn] *n* citoyen(ne); (*resident*): **the ~s of this town** les habitants de cette ville; **~ship** *n* citoyenneté *f*

citrus fruit ['sɪtrəs-] *n* agrume *m*

city ['sɪtɪ] *n* ville *f*, cité *f*; **the C~** la Cité de Londres (*centre des affaires*)

civic ['sɪvɪk] *adj* civique; (*authorities*) municipal(e); **~ centre** (*BRIT*) *n* centre administratif (municipal)

civil ['sɪvɪl] *adj* civil(e); (*polite*) poli(e), courtois(e); (*disobedience, defence*) passif(ive); **~ engineer** *n* ingénieur *m* des travaux publics; **~ian** [sɪ'vɪlɪən] *adj*, *n* civil(e)

civilization [sɪvɪlaɪ'zeɪʃən] *n* civilisation *f*

civilized ['sɪvɪlaɪzd] *adj* civilisé(e); (*fig*) où règnent les bonnes manières

civil: **~ law** *n* code civil; (*study*) droit civil; **~ servant** *n* fonctionnaire *m/f*; **C~ Service** *n* fonction publique, administration *f*; **~ war** *n* guerre civile

clad [klæd] *adj:* **~ (in)** habillé(e) (de)

claim [kleɪm] *vt* revendiquer; (*rights, inheritance*) demander, prétendre à; (*assert*) déclarer, prétendre ♦ *vi* (*for insurance*) faire une déclaration de sinistre ♦ *n* revendication *f*; demande *f*; prétention *f*, déclaration *f*; (*right*) droit *m*, titre *m*; **~ant** *n* (*ADMIN, LAW*) requérant(e)

clairvoyant [kleə'vɔɪənt] *n* voyant(e), extra-lucide *m/f*

clam [klæm] *n* palourde *f*

clamber ['klæmbə*] *vi* grimper, se hisser

clammy ['klæmɪ] *adj* humide (et froid(e)), moite

clamour ['klæmə*] (*US* **clamor**) *vi:* **to ~ for** réclamer à grands cris

clamp [klæmp] *n* agrafe *f*, crampon *m* ♦ *vt* serrer; (*sth to sth*) fixer; **~ down on** *vt fus* sévir or prendre des mesures draconiennes contre

clan [klæn] *n* clan *m*

clang [klæŋ] *vi* émettre un bruit or fracas métallique

clap [klæp] *vi* applaudir; **~ping** *n* applaudissements *mpl*

claret ['klærɪt] *n* (vin *m* de) bordeaux *m* (rouge)

clarinet [klærɪ'net] *n* clarinette *f*

clarity ['klærɪtɪ] *n* clarté *f*

clash [klæʃ] *n* choc *m*; (*fig*) conflit *m* ♦ *vi* se heurter; être or entrer en conflit; (*colours*) jurer; (*two events*) tomber en même temps

clasp [klɑːsp] *n* (*of necklace, bag*) fermoir *m*; (*hold, embrace*) étreinte *f* ♦ *vt* serrer, étreindre

class [klɑːs] *n* classe *f* ♦ *vt* classer, classifier

classic ['klæsɪk] *adj* classique ♦ *n* (*author, work*) classique *m*; **~al** *adj* classique

classified ['klæsɪfaɪd] *adj* (*information*) secret(ète); **~ advertisement** *n* petite annonce

classmate ['klɑːsmeɪt] *n* camarade *m/f* de classe

classroom ['klɑːsrʊm] *n* (salle *f* de) classe *f*

clatter ['klætə*] *n* cliquetis *m* ♦ *vi* cliqueter

clause [klɔːz] *n* clause *f*; (*LING*) proposition *f*

claw [klɔː] *n* griffe *f*; (*of bird of prey*) serre *f*; (*of lobster*) pince *f*; **~ at** *vt fus* essayer de s'agripper à or griffer

clay [kleɪ] *n* argile *f*

clean [kliːn] *adj* propre; (*clear, smooth*) net(te); (*record, reputation*) sans tache; (*joke, story*) correct(e) ♦ *vt* nettoyer; **~ out** *vt* nettoyer (à fond); **~ up** *vt* nettoyer; (*fig*) remettre de l'ordre dans; **~-cut** *adj* (*person*) net(te), soigné(e); **~er** *n* (*person*) nettoyeur(euse), femme *f* de ménage; (*product*) détachant *m*; **~er's** *n* (*also:* dry **~er's**) teinturier *m*; **~ing** *n* nettoyage *m*; **~liness** ['klenlɪnɪs] *n* propreté *f*

cleanse [klenz] *vt* nettoyer; (*purify*) purifier; **~r** *n* (*for face*) démaquillant *m*

clean-shaven ['kliːn'ʃeɪvn] *adj* rasé(e) de près

cleansing department ['klenzɪŋ-] (*BRIT*) *n* service *m* de voirie

clear ['klɪə*] *adj* clair(e); (*glass, plastic*) transparent(e); (*road, way*) libre, dégagé(e); (*conscience*) net(te) ♦ *vt* (*room*) débarrasser; (*of people*) faire évacuer; (*cheque*) compenser; (*LAW: suspect*) innocenter; (*obstacle*) franchir or sauter sans heurter ♦ *vi* (*weather*) s'éclaircir; (*fog*) se dissiper ♦ *adv:* **~ of** à distance de, à l'écart de; **to ~ the table** débarrasser la table, desservir; **~ up** *vt* ranger, mettre en ordre; (*mystery*) éclaircir, résoudre; **~ance** ['klɪərəns] *n* (*removal*) déblaiement *m*; (*permission*) autorisation *f*; **~-cut** *adj* clair(e), nettement défini(e); **~ing** *n* (*in forest*) clairière *f*; **~ing bank** (*BRIT*) *n* banque qui appartient à une chambre de compensation; **~ly** *adv* clairement; (*evidently*) de toute évidence; **~way** (*BRIT*) *n* route *f* à stationnement interdit

clef [klef] *n* (*MUS*) clé *f*

cleft [kleft] *n* (*in rock*) crevasse *f*, fissure *f*

clench [klentʃ] *vt* serrer

clergy ['klɜːdʒɪ] *n* clergé *m*; **~man** (*irreg*) *n* ecclésiastique *m*

clerical ['klerɪkəl] *adj* de bureau, d'employé de bureau; (*REL*) clérical(e), du clergé

clerk [klɑːk, (*US*) klɜːk] *n* employé(e) de bureau; (*US: salesperson*) vendeur(euse)

clever ['klevə*] *adj* (*mentally*) intelligent(e); (*deft, crafty*) habile, adroit(e); (*device, arrangement*) ingénieux(euse), astucieux(euse)

clew [kluː] (*US*) *n* = **clue**

click [klɪk] *vi* faire un bruit sec or un déclic ♦ *vt:* **to ~ one's tongue** faire claquer sa

langue; **to ~ one's heels** claquer des talons
client ['klaɪənt] n client(e)
cliff [klɪf] n falaise f
climate ['klaɪmɪt] n climat m
climax ['klaɪmæks] n apogée m, point culminant; (sexual) orgasme m
climb [klaɪm] vi grimper, monter ♦ vt gravir, escalader, monter sur ♦ n montée f, escalade f; **~-down** n reculade f, dérobade f; **~er** n (mountaineer) grimpeur(euse), varappeur(euse); (plant) plante grimpante; **~ing** n (mountaineering) escalade f, varappe f
clinch [klɪntʃ] vt (deal) conclure, sceller
cling [klɪŋ] (pt, pp **clung**) vi: **to ~ (to)** se cramponner (à), s'accrocher (à); (of clothes) coller (à)
clinic ['klɪnɪk] n centre médical; **~al** adj clinique; (attitude) froid(e), détaché(e)
clink [klɪŋk] vi tinter, cliqueter
clip [klɪp] n (for hair) barrette f; (also: paper ~) trombone m ♦ vt (fasten) attacher; (hair, nails) couper; (hedge) tailler; **~pers** npl (for hedge) sécateur m; (also: nail ~pers) coupe-ongles m inv; **~ping** n (from newspaper) coupure f de journal
cloak [kləuk] n grande cape ♦ vt (fig) masquer, cacher; **~room** n (for coats etc) vestiaire m; (BRIT: WC) toilettes fpl
clock [klɒk] n (large) horloge f; (small) pendule f; **~ in** (BRIT) vi pointer (en arrivant); **~ off** (BRIT) vi pointer (en partant); **~ on** (BRIT) vi = **clock in**; **~ out** (BRIT) vi = **clock off**; **~wise** adv dans le sens des aiguilles d'une montre; **~work** n rouages mpl, mécanisme m; (of clock) mouvement m (d'horlogerie) ♦ adj mécanique
clog [klɒg] n sabot m ♦ vt boucher ♦ vi (also: ~ up) se boucher
cloister ['klɔɪstə*] n cloître m
close¹ [kləus] adj (near): **~(to)** près (de), proche (de); (contact, link) étroit(e); (contest) très serré(e); (watch) étroit(e), strict(e); (examination) attentif(ive), minutieux(euse); (weather) lourd(e), étouffant(e) ♦ adv près, à proximité; **~ to** près de; **~ by** adj proche ♦ adv tout(e) près; **~ at hand** = **by**; **a ~ friend** un ami intime; **to have a ~ shave** (fig) l'échapper belle
close² [kləuz] vt fermer ♦ vi (shop etc) fermer; (lid, door etc) se fermer; (end) se terminer, se conclure ♦ n (end) conclusion f, fin f; **~ down** vt, vi fermer (définitivement)
closed [kləuzd] adj fermé(e); **~ shop** n organisation f qui n'admet que des travailleurs syndiqués
close-knit [kləus'nɪt] adj (family, community) très uni(e)
closely ['kləuslɪ] adv (examine, watch) de près
closet ['klɒzɪt] n (cupboard) placard m, réduit m

close-up ['kləusʌp] n gros plan
closure ['kləuʒə*] n fermeture f
clot [klɒt] n (gen: blood ~) caillot m; (inf: person) ballot m ♦ vi (blood) se coaguler
cloth [klɒθ] n (material) tissu m, étoffe f, (also: tea~) torchon m; lavette f
clothe [kləuð] vt habiller, vêtir; **~s** npl vêtements mpl, habits mpl; **~s brush** n brosse f à habits; **~s line** n corde f (à linge); **~s peg** (US **~s pin**) n pince f à linge
clothing ['kləuðɪŋ] n = **clothes**
cloud [klaud] n nuage m; **~burst** n grosse averse; **~y** adj nuageux(euse), couvert(e); (liquid) trouble
clout [klaut] vt flanquer une taloche à
clove [kləuv] n (CULIN: spice) clou m de girofle; **~ of garlic** gousse f d'ail
clover ['kləuvə*] n trèfle m
clown [klaun] n clown m ♦ vi (also: ~ about, ~ around) faire le clown
cloying ['klɔɪɪŋ] adj (taste, smell) écœurant(e)
club [klʌb] n (society, place; also: golf ~) club m; (weapon) massue f, matraque f ♦ vt matraquer ♦ vi: **to ~ together** s'associer; **~s** npl (CARDS) trèfle m; **~ car** (US) n (RAIL) wagon-restaurant m; **~house** n club m
cluck [klʌk] vi glousser
clue [klu:] n indice m; (in crosswords) définition f; **I haven't a ~** je n'en ai pas la moindre idée
clump [klʌmp] n: **~ of trees** bouquet m d'arbres; **a ~ of buildings** un ensemble de bâtiments
clumsy ['klʌmzɪ] adj gauche, maladroit(e)
clung [klʌŋ] pt, pp of **cling**
cluster ['klʌstə*] n (of people) (petit) groupe; (of flowers) grappe f; (of stars) amas m ♦ vi se rassembler
clutch [klʌtʃ] n (grip, grasp) étreinte f, prise f; (AUT) embrayage m ♦ vt (grasp) agripper; (hold tightly) serrer fort; (hold on to) se cramponner à
clutter ['klʌtə*] vt (also: ~ up) encombrer
CND n abbr (= Campaign for Nuclear Disarmament) mouvement pour le désarmement nucléaire
Co. abbr = **county; company**
c/o abbr (= care of) c/o, aux bons soins de
coach [kəutʃ] n (bus) autocar m; (horse-drawn) diligence f; (of train) voiture f, wagon m; (SPORT: trainer) entraîneur(euse); (SCOL: tutor) répétiteur(trice) ♦ vt entraîner; (student) faire travailler; **~ trip** n excursion f en car
coal [kəul] n charbon m; **~ face** n front m de taille; **~field** n bassin houiller
coalition [kəuə'lɪʃən] n coalition f
coal: ~man ['kəulmən] (irreg) n charbonnier m, marchand m de charbon; **~ merchant** n = **~man**; **~mine** ['kəulmaɪn]

n mine *f* de charbon

coarse [kɔːs] *adj* grossier(ère), rude

coast [kəust] *n* côte *f* ♦ *vi* (*car, cycle etc*) descendre en roue libre; **~al** *adj* côtier(ère); **~guard** *n* garde-côte *m*; (*service*) gendarmerie *f* maritime; **~line** *n* côte *f*, littoral *m*

coat [kəut] *n* manteau *m*; (*of animal*) pelage *m*, poil *m*; (*of paint*) couche *f* ♦ *vt* couvrir; **~ hanger** *n* cintre *m*; **~ing** *n* couche *f*, revêtement *m*; **~ of arms** *n* blason *m*, armoiries *fpl*

coax [kəuks] *vt* persuader par des cajoleries

cob [kɔb] *n* see **corn**

cobbler ['kɔblə*] *n* cordonnier *m*

cobbles ['kɔblz] (*also:* **cobblestones**) *npl* pavés (ronds)

cobweb ['kɔbweb] *n* toile *f* d'araignée

cocaine [kə'keɪn] *n* cocaïne *f*

cock [kɔk] *n* (*rooster*) coq *m*; (*male bird*) mâle *m* ♦ *vt* (*gun*) armer; **~erel** *n* jeune coq *m*; **~-eyed** *adj* (*idea, method*) absurde, qui ne tient pas debout

cockle ['kɔkl] *n* coque *f*

cockney ['kɔknɪ] *n* cockney *m, habitant des quartiers populaires de l'East End de Londres*, ≈ faubourien(ne)

cockpit ['kɔkpɪt] *n* (*in aircraft*) poste *m* de pilotage, cockpit *m*

cockroach ['kɔkrəutʃ] *n* cafard *m*

cocktail ['kɔkteɪl] *n* cocktail *m* (*fruit ~ etc*) salade *f*; **~ cabinet** *n* (meuble-)bar *m*; **~ party** *n* cocktail *m*

cocoa ['kəukəu] *n* cacao *m*

coconut ['kəukənʌt] *n* noix *f* de coco

COD *abbr* = **cash on delivery**

cod [kɔd] *n* morue fraîche, cabillaud *m*

code [kəud] *n* code *m*

cod-liver oil ['kɔdlɪvər-] *n* huile *f* de foie de morue

coercion [kəu'ɜːʃən] *n* contrainte *f*

coffee ['kɔfɪ] *n* café *m*; **~ bar** (*BRIT*) *n* café *m*; **~ bean** *n* grain *m* de café; **~ break** *n* pause-café *f*; **~pot** *n* cafetière *f*; **~ table** *n* (petite) table basse

coffin ['kɔfɪn] *n* cercueil *m*

cog [kɔg] *n* dent *f* (d'engrenage); (*wheel*) roue dentée

cogent ['kəudʒənt] *adj* puissant(e), convaincant(e)

coil [kɔɪl] *n* rouleau *m*, bobine *f*; (*contraceptive*) stérilet *m* ♦ *vt* enrouler

coin [kɔɪn] *n* pièce *f* de monnaie ♦ *vt* (*word*) inventer; **~age** *n* monnaie *f*, système *m* monétaire; **~ box** (*BRIT*) *n* cabine *f* téléphonique

coincide [kəuɪn'saɪd] *vi* coïncider; **~nce** [kəu'ɪnsɪdəns] *n* coïncidence *f*

Coke [kəuk] (®) *n* coca *m*

coke [kəuk] *n* coke *m*

colander ['kʌləndə*] *n* passoire *f*

cold [kəuld] *adj* froid(e) ♦ *n* froid *m*; (*MED*) rhume *m*; **it's ~** il fait froid; **to be** or **feel ~** (*person*) avoir froid; **to catch ~** prendre or attraper froid; **to catch a ~** attraper un rhume; **in ~ blood** de sang-froid; **~-shoulder** *vt* se montrer froid(e) envers, snober; **~ sore** *n* bouton *m* de fièvre

coleslaw ['kəulslɔː] *n* sorte de salade de chou cru

colic ['kɔlɪk] *n* colique(s) *f(pl)*

collapse [kə'læps] *vi* s'effondrer, s'écrouler ♦ *n* effondrement *m*, écroulement *m*; **collapsible** [kə'læpsəbl] *adj* pliant(e); télescopique

collar ['kɔlə*] *n* (*of coat, shirt*) col *m*; (*for animal*) collier *m*; **~bone** *n* clavicule *f*

collateral [kɔ'lætərəl] *n* nantissement *m*

colleague ['kɔliːg] *n* collègue *m/f*

collect [kə'lekt] *vt* rassembler; ramasser; (*as a hobby*) collectionner; (*BRIT: call and pick up*) (passer) prendre; (*mail*) faire la levée de, ramasser; (*money owed*) encaisser; (*donations, subscriptions*) recueillir ♦ *vi* (*people*) se rassembler; (*things*) s'amasser; **to call ~** (*US: TEL*) téléphoner en P.C.V.; **~ion** [kə'lekʃən] *n* collection *f*; (*of mail*) levée *f*; (*for money*) collecte *f*, quête *f*; **~or** [kə'lektə*] *n* collectionneur *m*

college ['kɔlɪdʒ] *n* collège *m*

collide [kə'laɪd] *vi* entrer en collision

collie ['kɔlɪ] *n* (*dog*) colley *m*

colliery ['kɔlɪərɪ] (*BRIT*) *n* mine *f* de charbon, houillère *f*

collision [kə'lɪʒən] *n* collision *f*

colloquial [kə'ləukwɪəl] *adj* familier(ère)

colon ['kəulən] *n* (*sign*) deux-points *m inv*; (*MED*) côlon *m*

colonel ['kɜːnl] *n* colonel *m*

colony ['kɔlənɪ] *n* colonie *f*

colour ['kʌlə*] (*US* **color**) *n* couleur *f* ♦ *vt* (*paint*) peindre; (*dye*) teindre; (*news*) fausser, exagérer ♦ *vi* (*blush*) rougir; **~s** *npl* (*of party, club*) couleurs *fpl*; **~ in** *vt* colorier; **~ bar** *n* discrimination raciale (*dans un établissement*); **~-blind** *adj* daltonien(ne); **~ed** *adj* (*person*) de couleur; (*illustration*) en couleur; **~ film** *n* (*for camera*) pellicule *f* (en) couleur; **~ful** *adj* coloré(e), vif(vive); (*personality*) pittoresque, haut(e) en couleurs; **~ing** *n* colorant *m*; (*complexion*) teint *m*; **~ scheme** *n* combinaison *f* de(s) couleurs; **~ television** *n* télévision *f* (en) couleur

colt [kəult] *n* poulain *m*

column ['kɔləm] *n* colonne *f*; **~ist** ['kɔləmnɪst] *n* chroniqueur(euse)

coma ['kəumə] *n* coma *m*

comb [kəum] *n* peigne *m* ♦ *vt* (*hair*) peigner; (*area*) ratisser, passer au peigne fin

combat ['kɔmbæt] *n* combat *m* ♦ *vt* combattre, lutter contre

combination [kɔmbɪ'neɪʃən] *n* combinaison *f*

combine [*vb* kəm'baın, *n* 'kɒmbaın] *vt*: to ~ sth with sth combiner qch avec qch; (*one quality with another*) joindre *or* allier qch à qch ♦ *vi* s'associer; (*CHEM*) se combiner ♦ *n* (*ECON*) trust *m*; ~ (**harvester**) *n* moissonneuse-batteuse(-lieuse) *f*

come [kʌm] (*pt* **came**, *pp* **come**) *vi* venir, arriver; **to** ~ **to** (*decision etc*) parvenir *or* arriver à; **to** ~ **undone/loose** se défaire/ desserrer; ~ **about** *vi* se produire, arriver; ~ **across** *vt fus* rencontrer par hasard, tomber sur; ~ **along** *vi* = **to come on**; ~ **away** *vi* partir, s'en aller, se détacher; ~ **back** *vi* revenir; ~ **by** *vt fus* (*acquire*) obtenir, se procurer; ~ **down** *vi* descendre; (*prices*) baisser; (*buildings*) s'écrouler, être démoli(e); ~ **forward** *vi* s'avancer, se présenter, s'annoncer; ~ **from** *vt fus* être originaire de, venir de; ~ **in** *vi* entrer; ~ **in for** *vt* (*criticism etc*) être l'objet de; ~ **into** *vt fus* (*money*) hériter de; ~ **off** *vi* (*button*) se détacher; (*stain*) s'enlever; (*attempt*) réussir; ~ **on** *vi* (*pupil, work, project*) faire des progrès, s'avancer; (*lights, electricity*) s'allumer; (*central heating*) se mettre en marche; ~ **on!** viens!, allons!, allez!; ~ **out** *vi* sortir; (*book*) paraître; (*strike*) cesser le travail, se mettre en grève; ~ **round** *vi* (*after faint, operation*) revenir à soi, reprendre connaissance; ~ **to** *vi* revenir à soi; ~ **up** *vi* monter; ~ **up against** *vt fus* (*resistance, difficulties*) rencontrer; ~ **up with** *vt fus*: **he came up with an idea** il a eu une idée, il a proposé quelque chose; ~ **upon** *vt fus* tomber sur; ~**back** [ˈkʌmbæk] *n* (*THEATRE etc*) rentrée *f*

comedian [kəˈmiːdıən] *n* (*in music hall etc*) comique *m*; (*THEATRE*) comédien *m*

comedy [ˈkɒmədı] *n* comédie *f*

comeuppance [kʌmˈʌpəns] *n*: **to get one's** ~ recevoir ce qu'on mérite

comfort [ˈkʌmfət] *n* confort *m*, bien-être *m*; (*relief*) soulagement *m*, réconfort *m* ♦ *vt* consoler, réconforter; **the** ~**s of home** les commodités *fpl* de la maison; ~**able** *adj* confortable; (*person*) à l'aise; (*patient*) dont l'état est stationnaire; (*walk etc*) facile; ~**ably** *adv* (*sit*) confortablement; (*live*) à l'aise; ~ **station** (*US*) *n* toilettes *fpl*

comic [ˈkɒmık] *adj* (*also*: ~**al**) comique ♦ *n* comique *m*; (*BRIT*: *magazine*) illustré *m*; ~ **strip** *n* bande dessinée

coming [ˈkʌmıŋ] *n* arrivée *f* ♦ *adj* prochain(e), à venir; ~**(s) and going(s)** *n(pl)* va-et-vient *m inv*

comma [ˈkɒmə] *n* virgule *f*

command [kəˈmɑːnd] *n* ordre *m*, commandement *m*; (*MIL*: *authority*) commandement; (*mastery*) maîtrise *f* ♦ *vt* (*troops*) commander; **to** ~ **sb to do** ordonner à qn de faire; ~**eer** [kɒmənˈdıə*] *vt* réquisitionner; ~**er** *n* (*MIL*) commandant *m*

commando [kəˈmɑːndəʊ] *n* commando *m*; membre *m* d'un commando

commemorate [kəˈmeməreıt] *vt* commémorer

commence [kəˈmens] *vt*, *vi* commencer

commend [kəˈmend] *vt* louer; (*recommend*) recommander

commensurate [kəˈmensjʊrıt] *adj*: ~ **with** *or* **to** en proportion de, proportionné(e) à

comment [ˈkɒment] *n* commentaire *m* ♦ *vi*: **to** ~ **(on)** faire des remarques (sur); "**no** ~" "je n'ai rien à dire"; ~**ary** [ˈkɒməntrı] *n* commentaire *m*; (*SPORT*) reportage *m* (en direct); ~**ator** [ˈkɒmənteıtə*] *n* commentateur *m*; reporter *m*

commerce [ˈkɒmɜːs] *n* commerce *m*

commercial [kəˈmɜːʃəl] *adj* commercial(e) ♦ *n* (*TV*, *RADIO*) annonce *f* publicitaire, spot *m* (publicitaire); ~ **radio** *n* radio privée; ~ **television** *n* télévision privée

commiserate [kəˈmızəreıt] *vi*: **to** ~ **with sb** témoigner de la sympathie pour qn

commission [kəˈmıʃən] *n* (*order for work*) commande *f*, (*committee, fee*) commission *f* ♦ *vt* (*work of art*) commander, charger un artiste de l'exécution de; **out of** ~ (*not working*) hors service; ~**aire** [kəmıʃəˈnɛə*] (*BRIT*) *n* (*at shop, cinema etc*) portier *m* (en uniforme); ~**er** *n* (*POLICE*) préfet *m* (de police)

commit [kəˈmıt] *vt* (*act*) commettre; (*resources*) consacrer; (*to sb's care*) confier (à); **to** ~ **o.s.** (**to do**) s'engager (à faire); **to** ~ **suicide** se suicider; ~**ment** *n* engagement *m*; (*obligation*) responsabilité(s) *f(pl)*

committee [kəˈmıtı] *n* comité *m*

commodity [kəˈmɒdıtı] *n* produit *m*, marchandise *f*, article *m*

common [ˈkɒmən] *adj* commun(e); (*usual*) courant(e) ♦ *n* terrain communal; **the** **C**~**s** *npl* la chambre des Communes; **in** ~ en commun; ~**er** *n* roturier(ière); ~ **law** *n* droit coutumier; ~**ly** *adv* communément, généralement; couramment; **C**~ **Market** *n*: **the** **C**~ **Market** le Marché commun; ~**place** *adj* banal(e), ordinaire; ~ **room** *n* salle commune; ~ **sense** *n* bon sens; **C**~**wealth** (*BRIT*) *n*: **the** **C**~**wealth** le Commonwealth

commotion [kəˈməʊʃən] *n* désordre *m*, tumulte *m*

communal [ˈkɒmjuːnl] *adj* (*life*) communautaire; (*for common use*) commun(e)

commune [*n* ˈkɒmjuːn, *vb* kəˈmjuːn] *n* (*group*) communauté *f* ♦ *vi*: **to** ~ **with** communier avec

communicate [kəˈmjuːnıkeıt] *vt*, *vi* communiquer

communication [kəmjuːnıˈkeıʃən] *n* communication *f*; ~ **cord** (*BRIT*) *n* sonnette *f* d'alarme

communion [kəˈmjuːnıən] *n* (*also*: *Holy*

C~) communion f

communism ['kɒmjunɪzəm] n communisme m; **communist** ['kɒmjunɪst] adj communiste ♦ n communiste m/f

community [kə'mjuːnɪtɪ] n communauté f; ~ **centre** n centre m de loisirs; ~ **chest** (US) n fonds commun; ~ **home** n (school) centre m d'éducation surveillée

commutation ticket [kɒmjuː'teɪʃən-] (US) n carte f d'abonnement

commute [kə'mjuːt] vi faire un trajet journalier (de son domicile à son bureau) ♦ vt (LAW) commuer; ~**r** n banlieusard(e) (qui ... see vi)

compact [adj kəm'pækt, n 'kɒmpækt] adj compact(e) ♦ n (also: powder ~) poudrier m; ~ **disc** n disque compact; ~ **disc player** n lecteur m de disque compact

companion [kəm'pænɪən] n compagnon(compagne); ~**ship** n camaraderie f

company ['kʌmpənɪ] n compagnie f; to keep sb ~ tenir compagnie à qn; ~ **secretary** (BRIT) n (COMM) secrétaire général (d'une société)

comparative [kəm'pærətɪv] adj (study) comparatif(ive); (relative) relatif(ive); ~**ly** adv (relatively) relativement

compare [kəm'pɛə*] vt: to ~ sth/sb with/to comparer qch/qn avec or et/à ♦ vi: to ~ (with) se comparer (à); être comparable (à); **comparison** [kəm'pærɪsn] n comparaison f

compartment [kəm'pɑːtmənt] n compartiment m

compass ['kʌmpəs] n boussole f; ~**es** npl (GEOM: also: pair of ~es) compas m

compassion [kəm'pæʃən] n compassion f; ~**ate** adj compatissant(e)

compatible [kəm'pætɪbl] adj compatible

compel [kəm'pel] vt contraindre, obliger; ~**ling** adj (fig: argument) irrésistible

compensate ['kɒmpenseɪt] vt indemniser, dédommager ♦ vi: to ~ for compenser; **compensation** [kɒmpen'seɪʃn] n compensation f; (money) dédommagement m, indemnité f

compère ['kɒmpɛə*] n (TV) animateur(trice)

compete [kəm'piːt] vi: to ~ (with) rivaliser (avec), faire concurrence (à)

competent ['kɒmpɪtənt] adj compétent(e), capable

competition [kɒmpɪ'tɪʃən] n (contest) compétition f, concours m; (ECON) concurrence f

competitive [kəm'petɪtɪv] adj (ECON) concurrentiel(le); (sport) de compétition; (person) qui a l'esprit de compétition

competitor [kəm'petɪtə*] n concurrent(e)

complacency [kəm'pleɪsnsɪ] n suffisance f, vaine complaisance

complain [kəm'pleɪn] vi: to ~ (about) se plaindre (de); (in shop etc) réclamer (au sujet de); to ~ of (pain) se plaindre de; ~**t** n plainte f; réclamation f; (MED) affection f

complement [n 'kɒmplɪmənt, vb 'kɒmplɪment] n complément m; (especially of ship's crew etc) effectif complet ♦ vt (enhance) compléter; ~**ary** [kɒmplɪ'mentərɪ] adj complémentaire

complete [kəm'pliːt] adj complet(ète) ♦ vt achever, parachever; (set, group) compléter; (a form) remplir; ~**ly** adv complètement; **completion** [kəm'pliːʃən] n achèvement m; (of contract) exécution f

complex ['kɒmpleks] adj complexe ♦ n complexe m

complexion [kəm'plekʃən] n (of face) teint m

compliance [kəm'plaɪəns] n (submission) docilité f; (agreement): ~ **with** le fait de se conformer à; **in** ~ **with** en accord avec

complicate ['kɒmplɪkeɪt] vt compliquer; ~**d** adj compliqué(e); **complication** [kɒmplɪ'keɪʃn] n complication f

compliment [n 'kɒmplɪmənt, vb 'kɒmplɪment] n compliment m ♦ vt complimenter; ~**s** npl (respects) compliments mpl, hommages mpl; **to pay sb a** ~ faire or adresser un compliment à qn; ~**ary** [kɒmplɪ'mentərɪ] adj flatteur(euse); (free) (offert(e)) à titre gracieux; ~**ary ticket** n billet m de faveur

comply [kəm'plaɪ] vi: to ~ **with** se soumettre à, se conformer à

component [kəm'pəunənt] n composant m, élément m

compose [kəm'pəuz] vt composer; (form): **to be** ~**d of** se composer de; **to** ~ **o.s.** se calmer, se maîtriser; prendre une contenance; ~**d** adj calme, posé(e); ~**r** n (MUS) compositeur m; **composition** [kɒmpə'zɪʃən] n composition f; **composure** [kəm'pəuʒə*] n calme m, maîtrise f de soi

compound ['kɒmpaund] n composé m; (enclosure) enclos m, enceinte f; ~ **fracture** n fracture compliquée; ~ **interest** n intérêt composé

comprehend [kɒmprɪ'hend] vt comprendre; **comprehension** [kɒmprɪ'henʃən] n compréhension f

comprehensive [kɒmprɪ'hensɪv] adj (très) complet(ète); ~ **policy** n (INSURANCE) assurance f tous risques; ~ **(school)** (BRIT) n école secondaire polyvalente, ≈ C.E.S. m

compress [vb kəm'pres, n 'kɒmpres] vt comprimer; (text, information) condenser ♦ n (MED) compresse f

comprise [kəm'praɪz] vt (also: be ~d of) comprendre; (constitute) constituer, représenter

compromise ['kɒmprəmaɪz] n compromis m ♦ vt compromettre ♦ vi transiger, accepter un compromis

compulsion [kəm'pʌlʃən] *n* contrainte *f*, force *f*

compulsive [kəm'pʌlsɪv] *adj* (PSYCH) compulsif(ive); (book, film etc) captivant(e)

compulsory [kəm'pʌlsərɪ] *adj* obligatoire

computer [kəm'pjuːtə*] *n* ordinateur *m*; ~ **game** *n* jeu *m* vidéo; ~**ize** *vt* informatiser; ~ **programmer** *n* programmeur(euse); ~ **programming** *n* programmation *f*; ~ **science** *n* informatique *f*; **computing** *n* = ~ **science**

comrade ['kɒmrɪd] *n* camarade *m/f*

con [kɒn] *vt* duper; (cheat) escroquer ♦ *n* escroquerie *f*

conceal [kən'siːl] *vt* cacher, dissimuler

conceit [kən'siːt] *n* vanité *f*, suffisance *f*, prétention *f*; ~**ed** *adj* vaniteux(euse), suffisant(e)

conceive [kən'siːv] *vt, vi* concevoir

concentrate ['kɒnsəntreɪt] *vi* se concentrer ♦ *vt* concentrer

concentration [kɒnsən'treɪʃən] *n* concentration *f*; ~ **camp** *n* camp *m* de concentration

concept ['kɒnsept] *n* concept *m*

concern [kən'sɜːn] *n* affaire *f*, (COMM) entreprise *f*, firme *f*, (anxiety) inquiétude *f*, souci *m* ♦ *vt* concerner; **to be** ~**ed (about)** s'inquiéter (de), être inquiet(e) (au sujet de); ~**ing** *prep* en ce qui concerne, à propos de

concert ['kɒnsət] *n* concert *m*; ~**ed** *adj* concerté(e); ~ **hall** *n* salle *f* de concert

concerto [kən'tʃɜːtəʊ] *n* concerto *m*

concession [kən'seʃən] *n* concession *f*; **tax** ~ dégrèvement fiscal

conclude [kən'kluːd] *vt* conclure; **conclusion** [kən'kluːʒən] *n* conclusion *f*; **conclusive** [kən'kluːsɪv] *adj* concluant(e), définitif(ive)

concoct [kən'kɒkt] *vt* confectionner, composer; (fig) inventer; ~**ion** [kən'kɒkʃən] *n* mélange *m*

concourse ['kɒŋkɔːs] *n* (hall) hall *m*, salle *f* des pas perdus

concrete ['kɒŋkriːt] *n* béton *m* ♦ *adj* concret(ète); (floor etc) en béton

concur [kən'kɜː*] *vi* (agree) être d'accord

concurrently [kən'kʌrəntlɪ] *adv* simultanément

concussion [kən'kʌʃən] *n* (MED) commotion (cérébrale)

condemn [kən'dem] *vt* condamner

condensation [kɒnden'seɪʃən] *n* condensation *f*

condense [kən'dens] *vi* se condenser ♦ *vt* condenser; ~**d milk** *n* lait concentré (sucré)

condition [kən'dɪʃən] *n* condition *f*; (MED) état *m* ♦ *vt* déterminer, conditionner; **on** ~ **that** à condition que +sub, à condition de; ~**al** *adj* conditionnel(le); ~**er** *n* (for hair)

baume après-shampooing *m*; (for fabrics) assouplissant *m*

condolences [kən'dəʊlənsɪz] *npl* condoléances *fpl*

condom ['kɒndəm] *n* préservatif *m*

condominium [kɒndə'mɪnɪəm] (US) *n* (building) immeuble *m* (en copropriété)

condone [kən'dəʊn] *vt* fermer les yeux sur, approuver (tacitement)

conducive [kən'djuːsɪv] *adj*: ~ **to** favorable à, qui contribue à

conduct [*n* 'kɒndʌkt, *vb* kən'dʌkt] *n* conduite *f* ♦ *vt* conduire; (MUS) diriger; **to** ~ **o.s.** se conduire, se comporter; ~**ed tour** *n* voyage organisé; (of building) visite guidée; ~**or** [kən'dʌktə*] *n* (of orchestra) chef *m* d'orchestre; (on bus) receveur *m*; (US: on train) chef *m* de train; (ELEC) conducteur *m*; ~**ress** [kən'dʌktrɪs] *n* (on bus) receveuse *f*

cone [kəʊn] *n* cône *m*; (for ice-cream) cornet *m*; (BOT) pomme *f* de pin, cône

confectioner [kən'fekʃənə*] *n* confiseur(cuse); ~**'s (shop)** *n* confiserie *f*, ~**y** *n* confiserie *f*

confer [kən'fɜː*] *vt*: **to** ~ **sth on** conférer qch à ♦ *vi* conférer, s'entretenir

conference ['kɒnfərəns] *n* conférence *f*

confess [kən'fes] *vt* confesser, avouer ♦ *vi* se confesser; ~**ion** [kən'feʃən] *n* confession *f*

confetti [kən'fetɪ] *n* confettis *mpl*

confide [kən'faɪd] *vi*: **to** ~ **in** se confier à

confidence ['kɒnfɪdəns] *n* confiance *f*; (also: self-~) assurance *f*, confiance en soi; (secret) confidence *f*; **in** ~ (speak, write) en confidence, confidentiellement; ~ **trick** *n* escroquerie *f*; **confident** ['kɒnfɪdənt] *adj* sûr(e), assuré(e); **confidential** [kɒnfɪ'denʃəl] *adj* confidentiel(le)

confine [kən'faɪn] *vt* limiter, borner; (shut up) confiner, enfermer; ~**d** *adj* (space) restreint(e), réduit(e); ~**ment** *n* emprisonnement *m*, détention *f*; ~**s** ['kɒnfaɪnz] *npl* confins *mpl*, bornes *fpl*

confirm [kən'fɜːm] *vt* confirmer; (appointment) ratifier; ~**ation** [kɒnfə'meɪʃən] *n* confirmation *f*; ~**ed** *adj* invétéré(e), incorrigible

confiscate ['kɒnfɪskeɪt] *vt* confisquer

conflict [*n* 'kɒnflɪkt, *vb* kən'flɪkt] *n* conflit *m*, lutte *f* ♦ *vi* être *or* entrer en conflit; (opinions) s'opposer, se heurter; ~**ing** [kən'flɪktɪŋ] *adj* contradictoire

conform [kən'fɔːm] *vi*: **to** ~ **(to)** se conformer (à)

confound [kən'faʊnd] *vt* confondre

confront [kən'frʌnt] *vt* confronter, mettre en présence; (enemy, danger) affronter, faire face à; ~**ation** [kɒnfrən'teɪʃən] *n* confrontation *f*

confuse [kən'fjuːz] *vt* (person) troubler; (si-

tuation) embrouiller; (*one thing with another*) confondre; **~d** *adj* (*person*) dérouté(e), désorienté(e); **confusing** *adj* peu clair(e), déroutant(e); **confusion** [kən'fjuːʒən] *n* confusion *f*

congeal [kən'dʒiːl] *vi* (*blood*) se coaguler; (*oil etc*) se figer

congenial [kən'dʒiːnɪəl] *adj* sympathique, agréable

congested [kən'dʒestɪd] *adj* (*MED*) congestionné(e); (*area*) surpeuplé(e); (*road*) bloqué(e)

congestion [kən'dʒestʃən] *n* congestion *f*, (*fig*) encombrement *m*

congratulate [kən'grætjuleɪt] *vt*: **to ~ sb (on)** féliciter qn (de); **congratulations** [kəngrætju'leɪʃənz] *npl* félicitations *fpl*

congregate ['kɒŋgrɪgeɪt] *vi* se rassembler, se réunir

congregation [kɒŋgrɪ'geɪʃən] *n* assemblée *f* (des fidèles)

congress ['kɒŋgres] *n* congrès *m*; **~man** (*irreg: US*) *n* membre *m* du Congrès

conjunction [kən'dʒʌŋkʃən] *n* (*LING*) conjonction *f*

conjunctivitis [kəndʒʌŋktɪ'vaɪtɪs] *n* conjonctivite *f*

conjure ['kʌndʒə*] *vi* faire des tours de passe-passe; **~ up** *vt* (*ghost, spirit*) faire apparaître; (*memories*) évoquer; **~r** *n* prestidigitateur *m*, illusionniste *m/f*

conk out [kɒŋk-] (*inf*) *vi* tomber *or* rester en panne

con man (*irreg*) *n* escroc *m*

connect [kə'nekt] *vt* joindre, relier; (*ELEC*) connecter; (*TEL: caller*) mettre en connection (*with* avec); (: *new subscriber*) brancher; (*fig*) établir un rapport entre, faire un rapprochement entre ♦ *vi* (*train*): **to ~ with** assurer la correspondance avec; **to be ~ed with** (*fig*) avoir un rapport avec; avoir des rapports avec, être en relation avec; **~ion** [kə'nekʃə] *n* relation *f*, lien *m*; (*ELEC*) connexion *f*; (*train, plane etc*) correspondance *f*; (*TEL*) branchement *m*, communication *f*

connive [kə'naɪv] *vi*: **to ~ at** se faire le complice de

conquer ['kɒŋkə*] *vt* conquérir; (*feelings*) vaincre, surmonter

conquest ['kɒŋkwest] *n* conquête *f*

cons [kɒnz] *npl see* **convenience; pro**

conscience ['kɒnʃəns] *n* conscience *f*; **conscientious** [kɒnʃɪ'enʃəs] *adj* consciencieux(euse)

conscious ['kɒnʃəs] *adj* conscient(e); **~ness** *n* conscience *f*; (*MED*) connaissance *f*

conscript ['kɒnskrɪpt] *n* conscrit *m*

consent [kən'sent] *n* consentement *m* ♦ *vi*: **to ~ (to)** consentir (à)

consequence ['kɒnsɪkwəns] *n* conséquence

f, suites *fpl*; (*significance*) importance *f*

consequently ['kɒnsɪkwəntlɪ] *adv* par conséquent, donc

conservation [kɒnsə'veɪʃən] *n* préservation *f*, protection *f*

conservative [kən'sɜːvətɪv] *adj* conservateur(trice); **at a ~ estimate** au bas mot; **C~** (*BRIT*) *adj, n* (*POL*) conservateur(trice)

conservatory [kən'sɜːvətrɪ] *n* (*greenhouse*) serre *f*

conserve [kən'sɜːv] *vt* conserver, préserver; (*supplies, energy*) économiser ♦ *n* confiture *f*

consider [kən'sɪdə*] *vt* (*study*) considérer, réfléchir à; (*take into account*) penser à, prendre en considération; (*regard, judge*) considérer, estimer; **to ~ doing sth** envisager de faire qch; **~able** [kən'sɪdərəbl] *adj* considérable; **~ably** *adv* nettement; **~ate** [kən'sɪdərɪt] *adj* prévenant(e), plein(e) d'égards; **~ation** [kənsɪdə'reɪʃən] *n* considération *f*; **~ing** [kən'sɪdərɪŋ] *prep* étant donné

consign [kən'saɪn] *vt* expédier; (*to sb's care*) confier; (*fig*) livrer; **~ment** *n* arrivage *m*, envoi *m*

consist [kən'sɪst] *vi*: **to ~ of** consister en, se composer de

consistency [kən'sɪstənsɪ] *n* consistance *f*, (*fig*) cohérence *f*

consistent [kən'sɪstənt] *adj* logique, cohérent(e)

consolation [kɒnsə'leɪʃən] *n* consolation *f*

console ['kɒnsəul] *n* (*COMPUT*) console *f*

consonant ['kɒnsənənt] *n* consonne *f*

conspicuous [kən'spɪkjuəs] *adj* voyant(e), qui attire l'attention

conspiracy [kən'spɪrəsɪ] *n* conspiration *f*, complot *m*

constable ['kʌnstəbl] (*BRIT*) *n* ≈ agent *m* de police, gendarme *m*; **chief ~** ≈ préfet *m* de police

constabulary [kən'stæbjulərɪ] (*BRIT*) *n* ≈ police *f*, gendarmerie *f*

constant ['kɒnstənt] *adj* constant(e); incessant(e); **~ly** *adv* constamment, sans cesse

constipated ['kɒnstɪpeɪtəd] *adj* constipé(e); **constipation** [kɒnstɪ'peɪʃən] *n* constipation *f*

constituency [kən'stɪtjuənsɪ] *n* circonscription électorale

constituent [kən'stɪtjuənt] *n* (*POL*) électeur(trice); (*part*) élément constitutif, composant *m*

constitution [kɒnstɪ'tjuːʃən] *n* constitution *f*; **~al** *adj* constitutionnel(le)

constraint [kən'streint] *n* contrainte *f*

construct [kən'strʌkt] *vt* construire; **~ion** [kən'strʌkʃən] *n* construction *f*; **~ive** *adj* constructif(ive)

construe [kən'struː] *vt* interpréter, expliquer

consul ['kɒnsl] *n* consul *m*; **~ate** ['kɒnsjʊlət] *n* consulat *m*

consult [kən'sʌlt] *vt* consulter; **~ant** *n* (*MED*) médecin consultant; (*other specialist*) consultant *m*, (expert-) conseil *m*; **~ing room** (*BRIT*) *n* cabinet *m* de consultation

consume [kən'sju:m] *vt* consommer; **~r** *n* consommateur(trice); **~r goods** *npl* biens *mpl* de consommation; **~r society** *n* société *f* de consommation

consummate ['kɒnsʌmeɪt] *vt* consommer

consumption [kən'sʌmpʃən] *n* consommation *f*

cont. *abbr* (= **continued**) suite

contact ['kɒntækt] *n* contact *m*; (*person*) connaissance *f*, relation *f* ♦ *vt* contacter, se mettre en contact or en rapport avec; **~ lenses** *npl* verres *mpl* de contact, lentilles *fpl*

contagious [kən'teɪdʒəs] *adj* contagieux(euse)

contain [kən'teɪn] *vt* contenir; **to ~ o.s.** se contenir, se maîtriser; **~er** *n* récipient *m*; (*for shipping etc*) container *m*

contaminate [kən'tæmɪneɪt] *vt* contaminer

cont'd *abbr* (= **continued**) suite

contemplate ['kɒntəmpleɪt] *vt* contempler; (*consider*) envisager

contemporary [kən'tempərəri] *adj* contemporain(e); (*design, wallpaper*) moderne ♦ *n* contemporain(e)

contempt [kən'tempt] *n* mépris *m*, dédain *m*; **~ of court** (*LAW*) outrage *m* à l'autorité de la justice; **~uous** *adj* dédaigneux(euse), méprisant(e)

contend [kən'tend] *vt*: **to ~ that** soutenir or prétendre que ♦ *vi*: **to ~ with** (*compete*) rivaliser avec; (*struggle*) lutter avec; **~er** *n* concurrent(e); (*POL*) candidat(e)

content [*adj, vb* kən'tent, *n* 'kɒntent] *adj* content(e), satisfait(e) ♦ *vt* contenter, satisfaire ♦ *n* contenu *m*; (*of fat, moisture*) teneur *f*; **~s** *npl* (*of container etc*) contenu *m*; (**table of**) **~s** table *f* des matières; **~ed** *adj* content(e), satisfait(e)

contention [kən'tenʃən] *n* dispute *f*, contestation *f*, (*argument*) assertion *f*, affirmation *f*

contest [*n* 'kɒntest, *vb* kən'test] *n* combat *m*, lutte *f*; (*competition*) concours *m* ♦ *vt* (*decision, statement*) contester, discuter; (*compete for*) disputer; **~ant** [kən'testənt] *n* concurrent(e); (*in fight*) adversaire *m/f*

context ['kɒntekst] *n* contexte *m*

continent ['kɒntɪnənt] *n* continent *m*; **the C~** (*BRIT*) l'Europe continentale; **~al** [kɒntɪ'nentl] *adj* continental(e); **~al quilt** (*BRIT*) *n* couette *f*

contingency [kən'tɪndʒənsɪ] *n* éventualité *f*, événement imprévu

continual [kən'tɪnjʊəl] *adj* continuel(le)

continuation [kəntɪnju'eɪʃən] *n* continua-

tion *f*, (*after interruption*) reprise *f*; (*of story*) suite *f*

continue [kən'tɪnju:] *vi, vt* continuer; (*after interruption*) reprendre, poursuivre

continuity [kɒntɪ'nju:ɪtɪ] *n* continuité *f*; (*TV etc*) enchaînement *m*

continuous [kən'tɪnjʊəs] *adj* continu(e); (*LING*) progressif(ive); **~ stationery** *n* papier *m* en continu

contort [kən'tɔ:t] *vt* tordre, crisper

contour ['kɒntʊə*] *n* contour *m*, profil *m*; (*on map: also:* **~ line**) courbe *f* de niveau

contraband ['kɒntrəbænd] *n* contrebande *f*

contraceptive [kɒntrə'septɪv] *adj* contraceptif(ive), anticonceptionnel(le) ♦ *n* contraceptif *m*

contract [*n* 'kɒntrækt, *vb* kən'trækt] *n* contrat *m* ♦ *vi* (*become smaller*) se contracter, se resserrer; (*COMM*): **to ~ to do sth** s'engager (par contrat) à faire qch; **~ion** [kən'trækʃən] *n* contraction *f*; **~or** [kən'træktə*] *n* entrepreneur *m*

contradict [kɒntrə'dɪkt] *vt* contredire

contraption [kən'træpʃən] (*pej*) *n* machin *m*, truc *m*

contrary¹ ['kɒntrərɪ] *adj* contraire, opposé(e) ♦ *n* contraire *m*; **on the ~** au contraire; **unless you hear to the ~** sauf avis contraire

contrary² [kən'treərɪ] *adj* (*perverse*) contrariant(e), entêté(e)

contrast [*n* 'kɒntrɑːst, *vb* kən'trɑːst] *n* contraste *m* ♦ *vt* mettre en contraste, contraster; **in ~ to** *or* **with** contrairement à

contravene [kɒntrə'vi:n] *vt* enfreindre, violer, contrevenir à

contribute [kən'trɪbju:t] *vi* contribuer ♦ *vt*: **to ~ £10/an article to** donner 10 livres/un article à; **to ~ to** contribuer à; (*newspaper*) collaborer à; **contribution** [kɒntrɪ'bju:ʃən] *n* contribution *f*; **contributor** [kən'trɪbjʊtə*] *n* (*to newspaper*) collaborateur(trice)

contrive [kən'traɪv] *vi*: **to ~ to do** s'arranger pour faire, trouver le moyen de faire;

control [kən'trəʊl] *vt* maîtriser, commander; (*check*) contrôler ♦ *n* contrôle *m*, autorité *f*; maîtrise *f*; **~s** *npl* (*of machine etc*) commandes *fpl*; (*on radio, TV*) boutons *mpl* de réglage; **everything is under ~** tout va bien, j'ai (*or* il a *etc*) la situation en main; **to be in ~ of** être maître de, maîtriser; **the car went out of ~** j'ai (*or* il a *etc*) perdu le contrôle du véhicule; **~ panel** *n* tableau *m* de commande; **~ room** *n* salle *f* des commandes; **~ tower** *n* (*AVIAT*) tour *f* de contrôle

controversial [kɒntrə'vɜ:ʃəl] *adj* (*topic*) discutable, controversé(e); (*person*) qui fait beaucoup parler de lui; **controversy** ['kɒntrəvɜːsɪ] *n* controverse *f*, polémique *f*

convalesce [kɒnvə'les] *vi* relever de maladie, se remettre (d'une maladie)

convector [kən'vɛktə*] n (*heater*) radiateur m (à convexion)

convene [kən'vi:n] vt convoquer, assembler ♦ vi se réunir, s'assembler

convenience [kən'vi:nɪəns] n commodité f; **at your ~** quand or comme cela vous convient; **all modern ~s,** (*BRIT*) **all mod cons** avec tout le confort moderne, tout confort

convenient [kən'vi:nɪənt] adj commode

convent ['kɒnvənt] n couvent m

convention [kən'vɛnʃən] n convention f; **~al** adj conventionnel(le)

conversant [kən'vɜ:sənt] adj: **to be ~ with** s'y connaître en; être au courant de

conversation [kɒnvə'seɪʃən] n conversation f

converse [n 'kɒnvɜ:s, vb kən'vɜ:s] n contraire m, inverse m ♦ vi s'entretenir; **~ly** [kɒn'vɜ:slɪ] adv inversement, réciproquement

convert [vb kən'vɜ:t, n 'kɒnvɜ:t] vt (*REL, COMM*) convertir; (*alter*) transformer; (*house*) aménager ♦ n converti(e); **~ible** n (voiture f) décapotable f

convey [kən'veɪ] vt transporter; (*thanks*) transmettre; (*idea*) communiquer; **~or belt** n convoyeur m, tapis roulant

convict [vb kən'vɪkt, n 'kɒnvɪkt] vt déclarer (or reconnaître) coupable ♦ n forçat m, détenu m; **~ion** [kən'vɪkʃən] n (*LAW*) condamnation f; (*belief*) conviction f

convince [kən'vɪns] vt convaincre, persuader; **convincing** adj persuasif(ive), convaincant(e)

convoluted [kɒnvə'lu:tɪd] adj (*argument*) compliqué(e)

convulse [kən'vʌls] vt: **to be ~d with laughter/pain** se tordre de rire/douleur

coo [ku:] vi roucouler

cook [kʊk] vt (*faire*) cuire ♦ vi cuire; (*person*) faire la cuisine ♦ n cuisinier(ière); **~book** n livre m de cuisine; **~er** n cuisinière f; **~ery** n cuisine f; **~ery book** (*BRIT*) n = **cookbook**; **~ie** (*US*) n biscuit m, petit gâteau sec; **~ing** n cuisine f

cool [ku:l] adj frais(fraîche); (*calm, unemotional*) calme; (*unfriendly*) froid(e) ♦ vt, vi rafraîchir, refroidir

coop [ku:p] n poulailler m; (*for rabbits*) clapier m ♦ vt: **to ~ up** (*fig*) cloîtrer, enfermer

cooperate [kəʊ'ɒpəreɪt] vi coopérer, collaborer; **cooperation** [kəʊɒpə'reɪʃən] n coopération f, collaboration f; **cooperative** [kəʊ'ɒpərətɪv] adj coopératif(ive) ♦ n coopérative f

coordinate [vb kəʊ'ɔ:dɪneɪt, n kəʊ'ɔ:dɪnət] vt coordonner ♦ n (*MATH*) coordonnée f; **~s** npl (*clothes*) ensemble m, coordonnés mpl

co-ownership ['kəʊ'əʊnəʃɪp] n copropriété f

cop [kɒp] (*inf*) n flic m

cope [kəʊp] vi: **to ~ with** faire face à; (*solve*) venir à bout de

copper ['kɒpə*] n cuivre m; (*BRIT: inf: policeman*) flic m; **~s** npl (*coins*) petite monnaie; **~ sulphate** n sulfate m de cuivre

copy ['kɒpɪ] n copie f; (*of book etc*) exemplaire m ♦ vt copier; **~right** n droit m d'auteur, copyright m

coral ['kɒrəl] n corail m; **~ reef** n récif m de corail

cord [kɔ:d] n corde f; (*fabric*) velours côtelé; (*ELEC*) cordon m, fil m

cordial ['kɔ:dɪəl] adj cordial(e), chaleureux(euse) ♦ n cordial m

cordon ['kɔ:dn] n cordon m; **~ off** vt boucler (*par cordon de police*)

corduroy ['kɔ:dərɔɪ] n velours côtelé

core [kɔ:*] n noyau m; (*of fruit*) trognon m, cœur m; (*of building, problem*) cœur ♦ vt enlever le trognon or le cœur de

cork [kɔ:k] n liège m; (*of bottle*) bouchon m; **~screw** n tire-bouchon m

corn [kɔ:n] n (*BRIT: wheat*) blé m; (*US: maize*) maïs m; (*on foot*) cor m; **~ on the cob** (*CULIN*) épi m de maïs; **~ed beef** ['kɔ:nd-] n corned-beef m

corner ['kɔ:nə*] n coin m; (*AUT*) tournant m, virage m; (*FOOTBALL: also:* ~ **kick**) corner m ♦ vt acculer, mettre au pied du mur; coincer; (*COMM: market*) accaparer ♦ vi prendre un virage; **~stone** n pierre f angulaire

cornet ['kɔ:nɪt] n (*MUS*) cornet m à pistons; (*BRIT: of ice-cream*) cornet (de glace)

cornflakes ['kɔ:nfleɪks] npl corn-flakes mpl

cornflour ['kɔ:nflaʊə*] (*BRIT*), **cornstarch** ['kɔ:nstɑːtʃ] (*US*) n farine f de maïs, maïzena f (®)

Cornwall ['kɔ:nwəl] n Cornouailles f

corny ['kɔ:nɪ] (*inf*) adj rebattu(e)

coronary ['kɒrənərɪ] n (*also:* ~ **thrombosis**) infarctus m (du myocarde), thrombose f coronarienne

coronation [kɒrə'neɪʃən] n couronnement m

coroner ['kɒrənə*] n officier chargé de déterminer les causes d'un décès

corporal ['kɔ:pərəl] n caporal m, brigadier m ♦ adj: ~ **punishment** châtiment corporel

corporate ['kɔ:pərɪt] adj en commun, collectif(ive); (*COMM*) de l'entreprise

corporation [kɔ:pə'reɪʃən] n (*of town*) municipalité f, conseil municipal; (*COMM*) société f

corps [kɔ:*, pl kɔ:z] (*pl* **corps**) n corps m

corpse [kɔ:ps] n cadavre m

correct [kə'rɛkt] adj (*accurate*) correct(e), exact(e); (*proper*) correct, convenable ♦ vt corriger; **~ion** [kə'rɛkʃən] n correction f

correspond [kɒrɪs'pɒnd] vi correspondre;

~**ence** *n* correspondance *f*; ~**ence course** *n* cours *m* par correspondance; ~**ent** *n* correspondant(e)

corridor ['kɒrɪdɔ:*] *n* couloir *m*, corridor *m*

corrode [kə'rəʊd] *vt* corroder, ronger ♦ *vi* se corroder

corrugated ['kɒrəgeɪtɪd] *adj* plissé(e); ondulé(e); ~ **iron** *n* tôle ondulée

corrupt [kə'rʌpt] *adj* corrompu(e) ♦ *vt* corrompre; ~**ion** [kə'rʌpʃən] *n* corruption *f*

Corsica ['kɔ:sɪkə] *n* Corse *f*

cosmetic [kɒz'metɪk] *n* produit *m* de beauté, cosmétique *m*

cosset ['kɒsɪt] *vt* choyer, dorloter

cost [kɒst] (*pt, pp* cost) *n* coût *m* ♦ *vi* coûter ♦ *vt* établir or calculer le prix de revient de; ~**s** *npl* (*COMM*) frais *mpl*; (*LAW*) dépens *mpl*; **it** ~**s £5/too much** cela coûte cinq livres/c'est trop cher; **at all** ~**s** coûte que coûte, à tout prix

co-star ['kəʊstɑ:*] *n* partenaire *m/f*

cost-effective ['kɒstɪ'fektɪv] *adj* rentable

costly ['kɒstlɪ] *adj* coûteux(euse)

cost-of-living ['kɒstəv'lɪvɪŋ] *adj*: ~ **allowance** indemnité *f* de vie chère; ~ **index** index *m* du coût de la vie

cost price (*BRIT*) *n* prix coûtant or de revient

costume ['kɒstju:m] *n* costume *m*; (*lady's suit*) tailleur *m*; (*BRIT: also: swimming* ~) maillot *m* (de bain); ~ **jewellery** *n* bijoux *mpl* fantaisie

cosy ['kəʊzɪ] (*US* **cozy**) *adj* douillet(te); (*person*) à l'aise, au chaud

cot [kɒt] *n* (*BRIT: child's*) lit *m* d'enfant, petit lit; (*US: campbed*) lit de camp

cottage ['kɒtɪdʒ] *n* petite maison (à la campagne), cottage *m*; ~ **cheese** *n* fromage blanc (*maigre*)

cotton ['kɒtn] *n* coton *m*; ~ **on** (*inf*) *vi*: **to** ~ **on to** piger; ~ **candy** (*US*) *n* barbe *f* à papa; ~ **wool** (*BRIT*) *n* ouate *f*, coton *m* hydrophile

couch [kaʊtʃ] *n* canapé *m*; divan *m*

couchette [ku:'ʃet] *n* couchette *f*

cough [kɒf] *vi* tousser ♦ *n* toux *f*; ~ **drop** *n* pastille *f* pour or contre la toux

could [kʊd] *pt of* **can²**; ~**n't** = **could not**

council ['kaʊnsl] *n* conseil *m*; **city** or **town** ~ conseil municipal; ~ **estate** (*BRIT*) *n* (zone *f* de) logements loués à/par la municipalité; ~ **house** (*BRIT*) *n* maison *f* (à loyer modéré) louée par la municipalité; ~**lor** ['kaʊnsɪlə*] *n* conseiller(ère)

counsel ['kaʊnsl] *n* (*lawyer*) avocat(e); (*advice*) conseil *m*, consultation *f*; ~**lor** *n* conseiller(ère); (*US: lawyer*) avocat(e)

count [kaʊnt] *vt, vi* compter ♦ *n* compte *m*; (*nobleman*) comte *m*; ~ **on** *vt fus* compter sur; ~**down** *n* compte *m* à rebours

countenance ['kaʊntɪnəns] *n* expression *f* ♦ *vt* approuver

counter ['kaʊntə*] *n* comptoir *m*; (*in post office, bank*) guichet *m*; (*in game*) jeton *m* ♦ *vt* aller à l'encontre de, opposer ♦ *adv*: ~ **to** contrairement à; ~**act** [kaʊntə'rækt] *vt* neutraliser, contrebalancer; ~**feit** ['kaʊntəfi:t] *n* faux *m*, contrefaçon *f* ♦ *vt* contrefaire ♦ *adj* faux(fausse); ~**foil** ['kaʊntəfɔɪl] *n* talon *m*, souche *f*; ~**mand** ['kaʊntəmɑ:nd] *vt* annuler; ~**part** ['kaʊntəpɑ:t] *n* (*of person etc*) homologue *m/f*

countess ['kaʊntɪs] *n* comtesse *f*

countless ['kaʊntlɪs] *adj* innombrable

country ['kʌntrɪ] *n* pays *m*; (*native land*) patrie *f*; (*as opposed to town*) campagne *f*; (*region*) région *f*, pays; ~ **dancing** (*BRIT*) *n* danse *f* folklorique; ~ **house** *n* manoir *m*, (petit) château; ~**man** (*irreg*) *n* (*compatriot*) compatriote *m*; (*country dweller*) habitant *m* de la campagne, campagnard *m*; ~**side** *n* campagne *f*

county ['kaʊntɪ] *n* comté *m*

coup [ku:] (*pl* ~**s**) *n* beau coup; (*also*: ~ *d'état*) coup d'État

couple ['kʌpl] *n* couple *m*; **a** ~ **of** deux; (*a few*) quelques

coupon ['ku:pɒn] *n* coupon *m*, bon-prime *m*, bon-réclame *m*; (*COMM*) coupon

courage ['kʌrɪdʒ] *n* courage *m*

courier ['kʊrɪə*] *n* messager *m*, courrier *m*; (*for tourists*) accompagnateur(trice), guide *m/f*

course [kɔ:s] *n* cours *m*; (*of ship*) route *f*; (*for golf*) terrain *m*; (*part of meal*) plat *m*; **first** ~ entrée *f*; **of** ~ bien sûr; ~ **of action** parti *m*, ligne *f* de conduite; ~ **of treatment** (*MED*) traitement *m*

court [kɔ:t] *n* cour *f*; (*LAW*) cour, tribunal *m*; (*TENNIS*) court *m* ♦ *vt* (*woman*) courtiser, faire la cour à; **to take to** ~ actionner or poursuivre en justice

courteous ['kɜ:tɪəs] *adj* courtois(e), poli(e)

courtesy ['kɜ:təsɪ] *n* courtoisie *f*, politesse *f*; (**by**) ~ **of** avec l'aimable autorisation de

court: ~**-house** ['kɔ:thaʊs] (*US*) *n* palais *m* de justice; ~**ier** ['kɔ:tɪə*] *n* courtisan *m*, dame *f* de la cour; ~ **martial** (*pl* ~**s martial**) *n* cour martiale, conseil *m* de guerre; ~**room** ['kɔ:trʊm] *n* salle *f* de tribunal; ~**yard** ['kɔ:tjɑ:d] *n* cour *f*

cousin ['kʌzn] *n* cousin(e); **first** ~ cousin(e) germain(e)

cove [kəʊv] *n* petite baie, anse *f*

covenant ['kʌvənənt] *n* engagement *m*

cover ['kʌvə*] *vt* couvrir ♦ *n* couverture *f*; (*of pan*) couvercle *m*; (*over furniture*) housse *f*; (*shelter*) abri *m*; **to take** ~ se mettre à l'abri; **under** ~ à l'abri; **under** ~ **of darkness** à la faveur de la nuit; **under separate** ~ (*COMM*) sous pli séparé; **to** ~ **up for sb** couvrir qn; ~**age** *n* (*TV, PRESS*) reportage *m*; ~ **charge** *n* couvert *m* (*supplément à* payer); ~**ing** n couche f; ~**ing letter** (US ~ **letter**) n lettre explicative; ~ **note** n (INSURANCE) police f provisoire

covert ['kʌvət] adj (threat) voilé(e), caché(e); (glance) furtif(ive)

cover-up ['kʌvərʌp] n tentative f pour étouffer une affaire

covet ['kʌvɪt] vt convoiter

cow [kau] n vache f ♦ vt effrayer, intimider

coward ['kauəd] n lâche m/f; ~**ice** ['kauədɪs] n lâcheté f; ~**ly** adj lâche

cowboy ['kaubɔɪ] n cow-boy m

cower ['kauə*] vi se recroqueviller

coy [kɔɪ] adj faussement effarouché(e) or timide

cozy ['kəuzɪ] (US) adj = **cosy**

CPA (US) n abbr = **certified public accountant**

crab [kræb] n crabe m; ~ **apple** n pomme f sauvage

crack [kræk] n fente f, fissure f; fêlure f; lézarde f; (noise) craquement m, coup (sec); (drug) crack m ♦ vt fendre, fissurer; fêler; lézarder; (whip) faire claquer; (nut) casser; (code) déchiffrer; (problem) résoudre ♦ adj (athlete) de première classe, d'élite; ~ **down on** vt fus mettre un frein à; ~ **up** vi être au bout du rouleau, s'effondrer; ~**er** n (Christmas ~er) pétard m; (biscuit) biscuit m (salé)

crackle ['krækl] vi crépiter, grésiller

cradle ['kreɪdl] n berceau m

craft [krɑːft] n métier (artisanal); (pl inv: boat) embarcation f, barque f; (: plane) appareil m; ~**sman** (irreg) n artisan m, ouvrier (qualifié); ~**smanship** n travail m; ~**y** adj rusé(e), malin(igne)

crag [kræg] n rocher escarpé

cram [kræm] vt (fill): **to ~ sth with** bourrer qch de; (put): **to ~ sth into** fourrer qch dans ♦ vi (for exams) bachoter

cramp [kræmp] n crampe f ♦ vt gêner, entraver; ~**ed** adj à l'étroit, très serré(e)

cranberry ['krænbərɪ] n canneberge f

crane [kreɪn] n grue f

crank [kræŋk] n manivelle f; (person) excentrique m/f; ~**shaft** n vilebrequin m

cranny ['krænɪ] n see **nook**

crash [kræʃ] n fracas m; (of car) collision f, (of plane) accident m ♦ vt avoir un accident avec ♦ vi (plane) s'écraser; (two cars) se percuter, s'emboutir; (COMM) s'effondrer; **to ~ into** se jeter or se fracasser contre; ~ **course** n cours intensif; ~ **helmet** n casque (protecteur); ~ **landing** n atterrissage forcé or en catastrophe

crate [kreɪt] n cageot m; (for bottles) caisse f

cravat(e) [krə'væt] n foulard (noué autour du cou)

crave [kreɪv] vt, vi: **to ~ (for)** avoir une envie irrésistible de

crawl [krɔːl] vi ramper; (vehicle) avancer au pas ♦ n (SWIMMING) crawl m

crayfish ['kreɪfɪʃ] n inv (freshwater) écrevisse f; (saltwater) langoustine f

crayon ['kreɪən] n crayon m (de couleur)

craze [kreɪz] n engouement m

crazy ['kreɪzɪ] adj fou(folle)

creak [kriːk] vi grincer; craquer

cream [kriːm] n crème f ♦ adj (colour) crème inv; ~ **cake** n (petit) gâteau à la crème; ~ **cheese** n fromage m à la crème, fromage blanc; ~**y** adj crémeux(euse)

crease [kriːs] n pli m ♦ vt froisser, chiffonner ♦ vi se froisser, se chiffonner

create [krɪ'eɪt] vt créer; **creation** [krɪ'eɪʃən] n création f; **creative** [krɪ'eɪtɪv] adj (artistic) créatif(ive); (ingenious) ingénieux(euse)

creature ['kriːtʃə*] n créature f

crèche [krɛʃ] n garderie f, crèche f

credence ['kriːdəns] n: **to lend** or **give ~ to** ajouter foi à

credentials [krɪ'denʃəlz] npl (references) références fpl; (papers of identity) pièce f d'identité

credit ['kredɪt] n crédit m; (recognition) honneur m ♦ vt (COMM) créditer; (believe: also: **give ~ to**) ajouter foi à, croire; ~**s** npl (CINEMA, TV) générique m; **to be in ~** (person, bank account) être créditeur(trice); **to ~ sb with** (fig) prêter or attribuer à qn; ~ **card** n carte f de crédit; ~**or** n créancier(ière)

creed [kriːd] n croyance f; credo m

creek [kriːk] n crique f, anse f; (US: stream) ruisseau m, petit cours d'eau

creep [kriːp] (pt, pp **crept**) vi ramper; ~**er** n plante grimpante; ~**y** adj (frightening) qui fait frissonner, qui donne la chair de poule

cremate [krɪ'meɪt] vt incinérer

crematorium [kremə'tɔːrɪəm] (pl ~**ia**) n four m crématoire

crêpe [kreɪp] n crêpe m; ~ **bandage** (BRIT) n bande f Velpeau (®)

crept [krept] pt, pp of **creep**

crescent ['kresnt] n croissant m; (street) rue f (en arc de cercle)

cress [kres] n cresson m

crest [krest] n crête f; ~**fallen** adj déconfit(e), découragé(e)

crevice ['krevɪs] n fissure f, lézarde f, fente f

crew [kruː] n équipage m; (CINEMA) équipe f; ~**-cut** n: **to have a ~-cut** avoir les cheveux en brosse; ~**-neck** n col ras du cou

crib [krɪb] n lit m d'enfant; (for baby) berceau m ♦ vt (inf) copier

crick [krɪk] n: ~ **in the neck** torticolis m; ~ **in the back** tour m de reins

cricket ['krɪkɪt] n (insect) grillon m, cri-cri m inv; (game) cricket m

crime [kraɪm] n crime m; **criminal** ['krɪmɪnl] adj, n criminel(le)

crimson ['krɪmzn] *adj* cramoisi(e)
cringe [krɪndʒ] *vi* avoir un mouvement de recul
crinkle ['krɪŋkl] *vt* froisser, chiffonner
cripple ['krɪpl] *n* boiteux(euse), infirme *m/f* ♦ *vt* estropier
crisis ['kraɪsɪs] (*pl* **crises**) *n* crise *f*
crisp [krɪsp] *adj* croquant(e); (*weather*) vif(vive); (*manner etc*) brusque; **~s** (*BRIT*) *npl* (pommes) chips *fpl*
crisscross ['krɪskrɒs] *adj* entrecroisé(e)
criterion [kraɪ'tɪərɪən] (*pl* **~ia**) *n* critère *m*
critic ['krɪtɪk] *n* critique *m*; **~al** *adj* critique; **~ally** *adv* (*examine*) d'un œil critique; (*speak etc*) sévèrement; **~ally ill** gravement malade; **~ism** ['krɪtɪsɪzəm] *n* critique *f*; **~ize** ['krɪtɪsaɪz] *vt* critiquer
croak [krəʊk] *vi* (*frog*) coasser; (*raven*) croasser; (*person*) parler d'une voix rauque
Croatia [krəʊ'eɪʃə] *n* Croatie *f*
crochet ['krəʊʃeɪ] *n* travail *m* au crochet
crockery ['krɒkərɪ] *n* vaisselle *f*
crocodile ['krɒkədaɪl] *n* crocodile *m*
crocus ['krəʊkəs] *n* crocus *m*
croft [krɒft] (*BRIT*) *n* petite ferme
crony ['krəʊnɪ] (*inf: pej*) *n* copain(copine)
crook [krʊk] *n* escroc *m*; (*of shepherd*) houlette *f*; **~ed** ['krʊkɪd] *adj* courbé(e), tordu(e); (*action*) malhonnête
crop [krɒp] *n* (*produce*) culture *f*; (*amount produced*) récolte *f*; (*riding ~*) cravache *f* ♦ *vt* (*hair*) tondre; **~ up** *vi* surgir, se présenter, survenir
cross [krɒs] *n* croix *f*; (*BIO etc*) croisement *m* ♦ *vt* (*street etc*) traverser; (*arms, legs, BIO*) croiser; (*cheque*) barrer ♦ *adj* en colère, fâché(e); **~ out** *vt* barrer, biffer; **~ over** *vi* traverser; **~bar** *n* barre (transversale); **~-country** (*race*) *n* cross(-country) *m*; **~-examine** *vt* (*LAW*) faire subir un examen contradictoire à; **~-eyed** *adj* qui louche; **~fire** *n* feux croisés; **~ing** *n* (*see passage*) traversée *f*; (*also: pedestrian ~ing*) passage clouté; **~ing guard** (*US*) *n* contractuel(le) qui fait traverser la rue aux enfants; **~ purposes** *npl*: **to be at ~ purposes with sb** comprendre qn de travers; **~-reference** *n* renvoi *m*, référence *f*; **~roads** *n* carrefour *m*; **~ section** *n* (*of object*) coupe transversale; (*in population*) échantillon *m*; **~walk** (*US*) *n* passage clouté; **~wind** *n* vent *m* de travers; **~word** *n* mots *mpl* croisés
crotch [krɒtʃ] *n* (*ANAT, of garment*) entrejambes *m inv*
crouch [kraʊtʃ] *vi* s'accroupir; se tapir
crow [krəʊ] *n* (*bird*) corneille *f*; (*of cock*) chant *m* du coq, cocorico *m* ♦ *vi* (*cock*) chanter
crowbar ['krəʊbɑː*] *n* levier *m*
crowd [kraʊd] *n* foule *f* ♦ *vt* remplir ♦ *vi* affluer, s'attrouper, s'entasser; **to ~ in** entrer

en foule; **~ed** *adj* bondé(e), plein(e)
crown [kraʊn] *n* couronne *f*; (*of head*) sommet *m* de la tête; (*of hill*) sommet ♦ *vt* couronner; **~ jewels** *npl* joyaux *mpl* de la Couronne; **~ prince** *n* prince héritier
crow's-feet ['krəʊzfiːt] *npl* pattes *fpl* d'oie
crucial ['kruːʃəl] *adj* crucial(e), décisif(ive)
crucifix ['kruːsɪfɪks] *n* (*REL*) crucifix *m*; **~ion** [kruːsɪ'fɪkʃən] *n* (*REL*) crucifixion *f*
crude [kruːd] *adj* (*materials*) brut(e); non raffiné(e); (*fig: basic*) rudimentaire, sommaire; (*: vulgar*) cru(e), grossier(ère); **~ (oil)** *n* (pétrole) brut *m*
cruel ['krʊəl] *adj* cruel(le); **~ty** *n* cruauté *f*
cruise [kruːz] *n* croisière *f* ♦ *vi* (*ship*) croiser; (*car*) rouler; **~r** *n* croiseur *m*; (*motorboat*) yacht *m* de croisière
crumb [krʌm] *n* miette *f*
crumble ['krʌmbl] *vt* émietter ♦ *vi* (*plaster etc*) s'effriter; (*land, earth*) s'ébouler; (*building*) s'écrouler, crouler; (*fig*) s'effondrer; **crumbly** ['krʌmblɪ] *adj* friable
crumpet ['krʌmpɪt] *n* petite crêpe (épaisse)
crumple ['krʌmpl] *vt* froisser, friper
crunch [krʌntʃ] *vt* croquer; (*underfoot*) faire craquer *or* crisser, écraser ♦ *n* (*fig*) instant *m or* moment *m* critique, moment de vérité; **~y** *adj* croquant(e), croustillant(e)
crusade [kruː'seɪd] *n* croisade *f*
crush [krʌʃ] *n* foule *f*, cohue *f*; (*love*): **to have a ~ on sb** avoir le béguin pour qn (*inf*); (*drink*): **lemon ~** citron pressé ♦ *vt* écraser; (*crumple*) froisser; (*fig: hopes*) anéantir
crust [krʌst] *n* croûte *f*
crutch [krʌtʃ] *n* béquille *f*
crux [krʌks] *n* point crucial
cry [kraɪ] *vi* pleurer; (*shout: also: ~ out*) crier ♦ *n* cri *m*; **~ off** (*inf*) *vi* se dédire; se décommander
cryptic ['krɪptɪk] *adj* énigmatique
crystal ['krɪstl] *n* cristal *m*; **~-clear** *adj* clair(e) comme de l'eau de roche
cub [kʌb] *n* petit *m* (*d'un animal*); (*also: C~ scout*) louveteau *m*
Cuba ['kjuːbə] *n* Cuba *m*
cubbyhole ['kʌbɪhəʊl] *n* cagibi *m*
cube [kjuːb] *n* cube *m* ♦ *vt* (*MATH*) élever au cube; **cubic** ['kjuːbɪk] *adj* cubique; **cubic metre** *etc* mètre *m etc* cube; **cubic capacity** *n* cylindrée *f*
cubicle ['kjuːbɪkl] *n* (*in hospital*) box *m*; (*at pool*) cabine *f*
cuckoo ['kʊkuː] *n* coucou *m*; **~ clock** *n* (pendule *f* à) coucou *m*
cucumber ['kjuːkʌmbə*] *n* concombre *m*
cuddle ['kʌdl] *vt* câliner, caresser ♦ *vi* se blottir l'un contre l'autre
cue [kjuː] *n* (*snooker ~*) queue *f* de billard; (*THEATRE etc*) signal *m*
cuff [kʌf] *n* (*BRIT: of shirt, coat etc*) poignet *m*, manchette *f*; (*US: of trousers*) revers *m*;

(blow) tape f; **off the ~** à l'improviste; **~ links** npl boutons mpl de manchette

cul-de-sac ['kʌldəsæk] n cul-de-sac m, impasse f

cull [kʌl] vt sélectionner ♦ n *(of animals)* massacre m

culminate ['kʌlmɪneɪt] vi: **to ~ in** finir or se terminer par; *(end in)* mener à; **culmination** [kʌlmɪ'neɪʃən] n point culminant

culottes [kjuː'lɒts] npl jupe-culotte f

culprit ['kʌlprɪt] n coupable m/f

cult [kʌlt] n culte m

cultivate ['kʌltɪveɪt] vt cultiver; **cultivation** [kʌltɪ'veɪʃən] n culture f

cultural ['kʌltʃərəl] adj culturel(le)

culture ['kʌltʃə*] n culture f; **~d** adj *(person)* cultivé(e)

cumbersome ['kʌmbəsəm] adj encombrant(e), embarrassant(e)

cunning ['kʌnɪŋ] n ruse f, astuce f ♦ adj rusé(e), malin(igne); *(device, idea)* astucieux(euse)

cup [kʌp] n tasse f; *(as prize)* coupe f; *(of bra)* bonnet m

cupboard ['kʌbəd] n armoire f; *(built-in)* placard m

cup tie *(BRIT)* n match m de coupe

curate ['kjuərɪt] n vicaire m

curator [kju'reɪtə*] n conservateur m *(d'un musée etc)*

curb [kɜːb] vt refréner, mettre un frein à ♦ n *(fig)* frein m, restriction f; *(US: kerb)* bord m du trottoir

curdle ['kɜːdl] vi se cailler

cure [kjuə*] vt guérir; *(CULIN: salt)* saler; *(: smoke)* fumer; *(: dry)* sécher ♦ n remède m

curfew ['kɜːfjuː] n couvre-feu m

curio ['kjuərɪəu] n bibelot m, curiosité f

curiosity [kjuərɪ'ɒsɪtɪ] n curiosité f

curious ['kjuərɪəs] adj curieux(euse)

curl [kɜːl] n boucle f (de cheveux) ♦ vt, vi boucler; *(tightly)* friser; **~ up** vi s'enrouler; se pelotonner; **~er** n bigoudi m, rouleau m; **~y** adj bouclé(e); frisé(e)

currant ['kʌrənt] n *(dried)* raisin m de Corinthe, raisin sec; *(bush)* groseiller m; *(fruit)* groseille f

currency ['kʌrənsɪ] n monnaie f; **to gain ~** *(fig)* s'accréditer

current ['kʌrənt] n courant m ♦ adj courant(e); **~ account** *(BRIT)* n compte courant; **~ affairs** npl *(questions fpl d')*actualité f; **~ly** adv actuellement

curriculum [kə'rɪkjuləm] *(pl* **~s** *or* **curricula)** n programme m d'études; **~ vitae** n curriculum vitae m

curry ['kʌrɪ] n curry m ♦ vt: **to ~ favour with** chercher à s'attirer les bonnes grâces de

curse [kɜːs] vi jurer, blasphémer ♦ vt maudire ♦ n *(spell)* malédiction f; *(problem, scourge)* fléau m; *(swearword)* juron m

cursor ['kɜːsə*] n *(COMPUT)* curseur m

cursory ['kɜːsərɪ] adj superficiel(le), hâtif(ive)

curt [kɜːt] adj brusque, sec(sèche)

curtail [kɜː'teɪl] vt *(visit etc)* écourter; *(expenses, freedom etc)* réduire

curtain ['kɜːtn] n rideau m

curts(e)y ['kɜːtsɪ] vi faire une révérence

curve [kɜːv] n courbe f; *(in the road)* tournant m, virage m ♦ vi se courber; *(road)* faire une courbe

cushion ['kuʃən] n coussin m ♦ vt *(fall, shock)* amortir

custard ['kʌstəd] n *(for pouring)* crème anglaise

custody ['kʌstədɪ] n *(of child)* garde f; **to take sb into ~** *(suspect)* placer qn en détention préventive

custom ['kʌstəm] n coutume f, usage m; *(COMM)* clientèle f; **~ary** adj habituel(le)

customer ['kʌstəmə*] n client(e)

customized ['kʌstəmaɪzd] adj *(car etc)* construit(e) sur commande

custom-made ['kʌstəm'meɪd] adj *(clothes)* fait(e) sur mesure; *(other goods)* hors série, fait(e) sur commande

customs ['kʌstəmz] npl douane f; **~ officer** n douanier(ière)

cut [kʌt] *(pt, pp* **cut)** vt couper; *(meat)* découper; *(reduce)* réduire ♦ vi couper ♦ n coupure f; *(of clothes)* coupe f; *(in salary etc)* réduction f; *(of meat)* morceau m; **to ~ one's hand** se couper la main; **to ~ a tooth** percer une dent; **~ down** vt fus *(tree etc)* couper, abattre; *(consumption)* réduire; **~ off** vt couper; *(fig)* isoler; **~ out** vt découper; *(stop)* arrêter; *(remove)* ôter; **~ up** vt *(paper, meat)* découper; **~back** n réduction f

cute [kjuːt] adj mignon(ne), adorable

cuticle remover ['kjuːtɪkl-] n *(on nail)* repousse-peaux m inv

cutlery ['kʌtlərɪ] n couverts mpl

cutlet ['kʌtlɪt] n côtelette f

cut: ~out n *(switch)* coupe-circuit m inv; *(cardboard ~out)* découpage m; **~-price** *(US* **~-rate)** adj au rabais, à prix réduit; **~throat** n assassin m ♦ adj acharné(e)

cutting ['kʌtɪŋ] adj tranchant(e), coupant(e); *(fig)* cinglant(e), mordant(e) ♦ n *(BRIT: from newspaper)* coupure f (de journal); *(from plant)* bouture f

CV n abbr = **curriculum vitae**

cwt abbr = **hundredweight(s)**

cyanide ['saɪənaɪd] n cyanure m

cycle ['saɪkl] n cycle m; *(bicycle)* bicyclette f, vélo m ♦ vi faire de la bicyclette; **cycling** ['saɪklɪŋ] n cyclisme m; **cyclist** ['saɪklɪst] n cycliste m/f

cygnet ['sɪgnɪt] n jeune cygne m

cylinder ['sɪlɪndə*] n cylindre m; **~-head gasket** n joint m de culasse

cymbals ['sɪmbəlz] npl cymbales fpl
cynic ['sɪnɪk] n cynique m/f; **~al** adj cynique; **~ism** ['sɪnɪsɪzəm] n cynisme m
Cypriot ['sɪprɪət] adj cypriote, chypriote ♦ n Cypriote m/f, Chypriote m/f
Cyprus ['saɪprəs] n Chypre f
cyst [sɪst] n kyste m
cystitis [sɪs'taɪtɪs] n cystite f
czar [zɑ:*] n tsar m
Czech [tʃek] adj tchèque ♦ n Tchèque m/f; (LING) tchèque m
Czechoslovak [tʃekə'sləuvæk] adj, n = **Czechoslovakian**
Czechoslovakia [tʃekəslə'vækɪə] n Tchécoslovaquie f; **~n** adj tchécoslovaque ♦ n Tchécoslovaque m/f

—————— _D d_

D [di:] n (MUS) ré m
dab [dæb] vt (eyes, wound) tamponner; (paint, cream) appliquer (par petites touches or rapidement)
dabble ['dæbl] vi: **to ~ in** faire or se mêler or s'occuper un peu de
dad [dæd] n papa m
daddy ['dædɪ] n papa m
daffodil ['dæfədɪl] n jonquille f
daft [dɑ:ft] adj idiot(e), stupide
dagger ['dægə*] n poignard m
daily ['deɪlɪ] adj quotidien(ne), journalier(ère) ♦ n quotidien m ♦ adv tous les jours
dainty ['deɪntɪ] adj délicat(e), mignon(ne)
dairy ['dɛərɪ] n (BRIT: shop) crémerie f, laiterie f; (on farm) laiterie f; **~ products** npl produits laitiers; **~ store** (US) n crémerie f, laiterie f
dais ['deɪɪs] n estrade f
daisy ['deɪzɪ] n pâquerette f; **~ wheel** (on printer) n marguerite f
dale [deɪl] n vallon m
dam [dæm] n barrage m ♦ vt endiguer
damage ['dæmɪdʒ] n dégâts mpl, dommages mpl; (fig) tort m ♦ vt endommager, abîmer; (fig) faire du tort à; **~s** npl (LAW) dommages-intérêts mpl
damn [dæm] vt condamner; (curse) maudire ♦ n (inf): **I don't give a ~** je m'en fous ♦ adj (inf: also: **~ed**): **this ~ ...** ce sacré or foutu ...; **~ (it)!** zut!; **~ing** adj accablant(e)
damp [dæmp] adj humide ♦ n humidité f ♦ vt (also: **~en**: cloth, rag) humecter; (: enthu-

siasm) refroidir
damson ['dæmzən] n prune f de Damas
dance [dɑ:ns] n danse f; (social event) bal m ♦ vi danser; **~ hall** n salle f de bal, dancing m; **~r** n danseur(euse); **dancing** ['dɑ:nsɪŋ] n danse f
dandelion ['dændɪlaɪən] n pissenlit m
dandruff ['dændrəf] n pellicules fpl
Dane [deɪn] n Danois(e)
danger ['deɪndʒə*] n danger m; **there is a ~ of fire** il y a (un) risque d'incendie; **in ~** en danger; **he was in ~ of falling** il risquait de tomber; **~ous** adj dangereux(euse)
dangle ['dæŋgl] vt balancer ♦ vi pendre
Danish ['deɪnɪʃ] adj danois(e) ♦ n (LING) danois m
dapper ['dæpə*] adj pimpant(e)
dare [dɛə*] vt: **to ~ sb to do** défier qn de faire ♦ vi: **to ~ (to) do sth** oser faire qch; **I ~ say** (I suppose) il est probable (que); **~devil** n casse-cou m inv; **daring** ['dɛərɪŋ] adj hardi(e), audacieux(euse); (dress) osé(e) ♦ n audace f, hardiesse f
dark [dɑ:k] adj (night, room) obscur(e), sombre; (colour, complexion) foncé(e), sombre ♦ n: **in the ~** dans le noir; **in the ~ about** (fig) ignorant tout de; **after ~** après la tombée de la nuit; **~en** vt obscurcir, assombrir ♦ vi s'obscurcir, s'assombrir; **~ glasses** npl lunettes noires; **~ness** n obscurité f; **~room** n chambre noire
darling ['dɑ:lɪŋ] adj chéri(e) ♦ n chéri(e); (favourite): **to be the ~ of** être la coqueluche de
darn [dɑ:n] vt repriser, raccommoder
dart [dɑ:t] n fléchette f; (sewing) pince f ♦ vi: **to ~ towards** (also: **make a ~ towards**) se précipiter or s'élancer vers; **~s** n (jeu m de) fléchettes fpl; **to ~ away/along** partir/passer comme une flèche; **~board** n cible f (de jeu de fléchettes)
dash [dæʃ] n (sign) tiret m; (small quantity) goutte f, larme f ♦ vt (missile) jeter or lancer violemment; (hopes) anéantir ♦ vi: **to ~ towards** (also: **make a ~ towards**) se précipiter or se ruer vers; **~ away** vi partir à toute allure, filer; **~ off** vi = **~ away**
dashboard ['dæʃbɔ:d] n (AUT) tableau m de bord
dashing ['dæʃɪŋ] adj fringant(e)
data ['deɪtə] npl données fpl; **~base** n (COMPUT) base f de données; **~ processing** n traitement m de données
date [deɪt] n date f; (with sb) rendez-vous m; (fruit) datte f ♦ vt dater; (person) sortir avec; **~ of birth** date de naissance; **to ~** (until now) à ce jour; **out of ~** (passport) périmé; (theory etc) dépassé(e); (clothes etc) démodé(e); **up to ~** moderne; (news) très récent; **~d** adj démodé(e)
daub [dɔ:b] vt barbouiller
daughter ['dɔ:tə*] n fille f; **~-in-law** n

belle-fille *f*, bru *f*

daunting ['dɔ:ntɪŋ] *adj* décourageant(e)

dawdle ['dɔ:dl] *vi* traîner, lambiner

dawn [dɔ:n] *n* aube *f*, aurore *f* ♦ *vi* (*day*) se lever, poindre; (*fig*): **it ~ed on him that ...** il lui vint à l'esprit que ...

day [deɪ] *n* jour *m*; (*as duration*) journée *f*; (*period of time, age*) époque *f*, temps *m*; **the ~ before** la veille, le jour précédent; **the ~ after, the following ~** le lendemain, le jour suivant; **the ~ after tomorrow** après-demain; **the ~ before yesterday** avant-hier; **by ~** de jour; **~break** *n* point *m* du jour; **~dream** *vi* rêver (tout éveillé); **~light** *n* (lumière *f* du) jour *m*; **~ return** (*BRIT*) *n* billet *m* d'aller-retour (valable pour la journée); **~time** *n* jour *m*, journée *f*; **~-to-day** *adj* quotidien(ne); (*event*) journalier(ère)

daze [deɪz] *vt* (*stun*) étourdir ♦ *n*: **in a ~** étourdi(e), hébété(e)

dazzle ['dæzl] *vt* éblouir, aveugler

DC *abbr* (= *direct current*) courant continu

D-day ['di:deɪ] *n* le jour J

dead [ded] *adj* mort(e); (*numb*) engourdi(e), insensible; (*battery*) à plat; (*telephone*): **the line is ~** la ligne est coupée ♦ *adv* absolument, complètement ♦ *npl*: **the ~** les morts; **he was shot ~** il a été tué d'un coup de revolver; **~ on time** à l'heure pile; **~ tired** éreinté(e), complètement fourbu(e); **to stop ~** s'arrêter pile *or* net; **~en** *vt* (*blow, sound*) amortir; (*pain*) calmer; **~ end** *n* impasse *f*; **~ heat** *n* (*SPORT*): **to finish in a ~ heat** terminer ex æquo; **~line** *n* date *f or* heure *f* limite; **~lock** *n* (*fig*) impasse *f*; **~ loss** *n*: **to be a ~ loss** (*inf: person*) être bon(ne) à rien; **~ly** *adj* mortel(le); (*weapon*) meurtrier(ère); (*accuracy*) extrême; **~pan** *adj* impassible; **D~ Sea** *n*: **the D~ Sea** la mer Morte

deaf [def] *adj* sourd(e); **~en** *vt* rendre sourd; **~-mute** *n* sourd(e)-muet(te); **~ness** *n* surdité *f*

deal [di:l] (*pt, pp* **dealt**) *n* affaire *f*, marché *m* ♦ *vt* (*blow*) porter; (*cards*) donner, distribuer; **a great ~ (of)** beaucoup (de); **~ in** *vt fus* faire le commerce de; **~ with** *vt fus* (*person, problem*) s'occuper *or* se charger de; (*be about: book etc*) traiter de; **~er** *n* marchand *m*; **~ings** *npl* (*COMM*) transactions *fpl*; (*relations*) relations *fpl*, rapports *mpl*

dean [di:n] *n* (*REL, BRIT: SCOL*) doyen *m*; (*US*) conseiller(ère) (principal(e)) d'éducation

dear [dɪə*] *adj* cher(chère); (*expensive*) cher, coûteux(euse) ♦ *n*: **my ~** mon cher/ ma chère; **~ me!** mon Dieu!; **D~ Sir/ Madam** (*in letter*) Monsieur/Madame; **D~ Mr/Mrs X** Cher Monsieur/Chère Madame; **~ly** *adv* (*love*) tendrement; (*pay*) cher

death [deθ] *n* mort *f*; (*fatality*) mort *m*; (*ADMIN*) décès *m*; **~ certificate** *n* acte *m* de décès; **~ly** *adj* de mort; **~ penalty** *n* peine *f* de mort; **~ rate** *n* (taux *m* de) mortalité *f*, **~ toll** *n* nombre *m* de morts

debar [dɪ'bɑ:*] *vt*: **to ~ sb from doing** interdire à qn de faire

debase [dɪ'beɪs] *vt* (*value*) déprécier, dévaloriser

debatable [dɪ'beɪtəbl] *adj* discutable

debate [dɪ'beɪt] *n* discussion *f*, débat *m* ♦ *vt* discuter, débattre

debit ['debɪt] *n* débit *m* ♦ *vt*: **to ~ a sum to sb** *or* **to sb's account** porter une somme au débit de qn, débiter qn d'une somme; *see also* **direct**

debt [det] *n* dette *f*; **to be in ~** avoir des dettes, être endetté(e); **~or** *n* débiteur(trice)

debunk [di:'bʌŋk] *vt* (*theory, claim*) montrer le ridicule de

decade ['dekeɪd] *n* décennie *f*, décade *f*

decadence ['dekədəns] *n* décadence *f*

decaffeinated [di:'kæfɪneɪtɪd] *adj* décaféiné(e)

decanter [dɪ'kæntə*] *n* carafe *f*

decay [dɪ'keɪ] *n* (*of building*) délabrement *m*; (*also: tooth ~*) carie *f* (dentaire) ♦ *vi* (*rot*) se décomposer, pourrir; (: *teeth*) se carier

deceased [dɪ'si:st] *n* défunt *m*

deceit [dɪ'si:t] *n* tromperie *f*, supercherie *f*; **~ful** *adj* trompeur(euse); **deceive** [dɪ'si:v] *vt* tromper

December [dɪ'sembə*] *n* décembre *m*

decent ['di:sənt] *adj* décent(e), convenable; **they were very ~ about it** ils se sont montrés très chic

deception [dɪ'sepʃən] *n* tromperie *f*

deceptive [dɪ'septɪv] *adj* trompeur(euse)

decide [dɪ'saɪd] *vt* (*person*) décider; (*question, argument*) trancher, régler ♦ *vi* se décider, décider; **to ~ to do/that** décider de faire/que; **to ~ on** décider, se décider pour; **~d** *adj* (*resolute*) résolu(e), décidé(e); (*clear, definite*) net(te), marqué(e); **~dly** [dɪ'saɪdɪdlɪ] *adv* résolument; (*distinctly*) incontestablement, nettement

deciduous [dɪ'sɪdjuəs] *adj* à feuilles caduques

decimal ['desɪməl] *adj* décimal(e) ♦ *n* décimale *f*; **~ point** *n* ≈ virgule *f*

decipher [dɪ'saɪfə*] *vt* déchiffrer

decision [dɪ'sɪʒən] *n* décision *f*

decisive [dɪ'saɪsɪv] *adj* décisif(ive); (*person*) décidé(e)

deck [dek] *n* (*NAUT*) pont *m*; (*of bus*): **top ~** impériale *f*; (*of cards*) jeu *m*; (*record ~*) platine *f*; **~chair** *n* chaise longue

declare [dɪ'klɛə*] *vt* déclarer

decline [dɪ'klaɪn] *n* (*decay*) déclin *m*; (*lessening*) baisse *f* ♦ *vt* refuser, décliner ♦ *vi*

décliner; (*business*) baisser
decoder [diːˈkəʊdə*] *n* (*TV*) décodeur *m*
decorate [ˈdekəreɪt] *vt* (*adorn, give a medal to*) décorer; (*paint and paper*) peindre et tapisser; **decoration** [dekəˈreɪʃən] *n* (*medal etc, adornment*) décoration *f*; **decorator** [ˈdekəreɪtə*] *n* peintre-décorateur *m*
decoy [ˈdiːkɔɪ] *n* piège *m*; (*person*) compère *m*
decrease [*n* ˈdiːkriːs, *vb* diːˈkriːs] *n*: ~ (**in**) diminution *f* (de) ♦ *vt, vi* diminuer
decree [dɪˈkriː] *n* (*POL, REL*) décret *m*; (*LAW*) arrêt *m*, jugement *m*; ~ **nisi** [-ˈnaɪsaɪ] *n* jugement *m* provisoire de divorce
dedicate [ˈdedɪkeɪt] *vt* consacrer; (*book etc*) dédier; **dedication** [dedɪˈkeɪʃən] *n* (*devotion*) dévouement *m*; (*in book*) dédicace *f*
deduce [dɪˈdjuːs] *vt* déduire, conclure
deduct [dɪˈdʌkt] *vt*: **to** ~ **sth** (**from**) déduire qch (de), retrancher qch (de); ~**ion** [dɪˈdʌkʃən] *n* (*deducting, deducing*) déduction *f*; (*from wage etc*) prélèvement *m*, retenue *f*
deed [diːd] *n* action *f*, acte *m*; (*LAW*) acte notarié, contrat *m*
deem [diːm] *vt* (*formal*) juger
deep [diːp] *adj* profond(e); (*voice*) grave ♦ *adv*: **spectators stood 20** ~ il y avait 20 rangs de spectateurs; **4 metres** ~ de 4 mètres de profondeur; ~**en** *vt* approfondir ♦ *vi* (*fig*) s'épaissir; ~**freeze** *n* congélateur *m*; ~**fry** *vt* faire frire (en friteuse); ~**ly** *adv* profondément; (*interested*) vivement; ~**-sea diver** *n* sous-marin(e); ~**-sea diving** *n* plongée sous-marine; ~**-sea fishing** *n* grande pêche; ~**-seated** *adj* profond(e), profondément enraciné(e)
deer [dɪə*] *n inv*: (**red**) ~ cerf *m*, biche *f*; (**fallow**) ~ daim *m*; (**roe**) ~ chevreuil *m*; ~**skin** *n* daim
deface [dɪˈfeɪs] *vt* dégrader; (*notice, poster*) barbouiller
default [dɪˈfɔːlt] *n* (*COMPUT: also*: ~ **value**) valeur *f* par défaut; **by** ~ (*LAW*) par défaut, par contumace; (*SPORT*) par forfait
defeat [dɪˈfiːt] *n* défaite *f* ♦ *vt* (*team, opponents*) battre
defect [*n* ˈdiːfekt, *vb* dɪˈfekt] *n* défaut *m* ♦ *vi*: **to** ~ **to the enemy/the West** passer à l'ennemi/à l'Ouest; ~**ive** [dɪˈfektɪv] *adj* défectueux(euse)
defence [dɪˈfens] (*US* **defense**) *n* défense *f*; ~**less** *adj* sans défense
defend [dɪˈfend] *vt* défendre; ~**ant** *n* défendeur(deresse); (*in criminal case*) accusé(e), prévenu(e); ~**er** *n* défenseur *m*
defer [dɪˈfɜː*] *vt* (*postpone*) différer, ajourner
defiance [dɪˈfaɪəns] *n* défi *m*; **in** ~ **of** au mépris de; **defiant** [dɪˈfaɪənt] *adj* provocant(e), de défi; (*person*) rebelle, intraitable
deficiency [dɪˈfɪʃənsɪ] *n* insuffisance *f*, défi-

cience *f*; **deficient** *adj* (*inadequate*) insuffisant(e); **to be deficient in** manquer de
deficit [ˈdefɪsɪt] *n* déficit *m*
defile [*vb* dɪˈfaɪl, *n* ˈdiːfaɪl] *vt* souiller, profaner
define [dɪˈfaɪn] *vt* définir
definite [ˈdefɪnɪt] *adj* (*fixed*) défini(e), (bien) déterminé(e); (*clear, obvious*) net(te), manifeste; (*certain*) sûr(e); **he was** ~ **about it** il a été catégorique; ~**ly** *adv* sans aucun doute
definition [defɪˈnɪʃən] *n* définition *f*; (*clearness*) netteté *f*
deflate [diːˈfleɪt] *vt* dégonfler
deflect [dɪˈflekt] *vt* détourner, faire dévier
deformed [dɪˈfɔːmd] *adj* difforme
defraud [dɪˈfrɔːd] *vt* frauder; **to** ~ **sb of sth** escroquer qch à qn
defrost [diːˈfrɒst] *vt* dégivrer; (*food*) décongeler; ~**er** (*US*) *n* (*demister*) dispositif *m* anti-buée *inv*
deft [deft] *adj* adroit(e), preste
defunct [dɪˈfʌŋkt] *adj* défunt(e)
defuse [diːˈfjuːz] *vt* désamorcer
defy [dɪˈfaɪ] *vt* défier; (*efforts etc*) résister à
degenerate [*vb* dɪˈdʒenəreɪt, *adj* dɪˈdʒenərɪt] *vi* dégénérer ♦ *adj* dégénéré(e)
degree [dɪˈɡriː] *n* degré *m*; (*SCOL*) diplôme *m* (universitaire); **a** (**first**) ~ **in maths** une licence en maths; **by** ~**s** (*gradually*) par degrés; **to some** ~, **to a certain** ~ jusqu'à un certain point, dans une certaine mesure
dehydrated [diːhaɪˈdreɪtɪd] *adj* déshydraté(e); (*milk, eggs*) en poudre
de-ice [diːˈaɪs] *vt* (*windscreen*) dégivrer
deign [deɪn] *vi*: **to** ~ **to do** daigner faire
dejected [dɪˈdʒektɪd] *adj* abattu(e), déprimé(e)
delay [dɪˈleɪ] *vt* retarder ♦ *vi* s'attarder ♦ *n* délai *m*, retard *m*; **to be** ~**ed** être en retard
delectable [dɪˈlektəbl] *adj* délicieux(euse)
delegate [*n* ˈdelɪɡɪt, *vb* ˈdelɪɡeɪt] *n* délégué(e) ♦ *vt* déléguer
delete [dɪˈliːt] *vt* rayer, supprimer
deliberate [*adj* dɪˈlɪbərɪt, *vb* dɪˈlɪbəreɪt] *adj* (*intentional*) délibéré(e); (*slow*) mesuré(e) ♦ *vi* délibérer, réfléchir; ~**ly** *adv* (*on purpose*) exprès, délibérément
delicacy [ˈdelɪkəsɪ] *n* délicatesse *f*; (*food*) mets fin *or* délicat, friandise *f*
delicate [ˈdelɪkɪt] *adj* délicat(e)
delicatessen [delɪkəˈtesn] *n* épicerie fine
delicious [dɪˈlɪʃəs] *adj* délicieux(euse)
delight [dɪˈlaɪt] *n* (grande) joie, grand plaisir ♦ *vt* enchanter; **to take (a)** ~ **in** prendre grand plaisir à; ~**ed** *adj*: ~**ed** (**at** *or* **with/to do**) ravi(e) (de/de faire); ~**ful** *adj* (*person*) adorable; (*meal, evening*) merveilleux(euse)
delinquent [dɪˈlɪŋkwənt] *adj, n* délinquant(e)
delirious [dɪˈlɪrɪəs] *adj*: **to be** ~ délirer

deliver [dɪ'lɪvə*] vt (mail) distribuer; (goods) livrer; (message) remettre; (speech) prononcer; (MED: baby) mettre au monde; ~**y** n distribution f; livraison f; (of speaker) élocution f; (MED) accouchement m; **to take** ~**y of** prendre livraison de

delude [dɪ'luːd] vt tromper, leurrer

delusion [dɪ'luːʒən] n illusion f

delve [delv] vi: **to** ~ **into** fouiller dans; (subject) approfondir

demand [dɪ'mɑːnd] vt réclamer, exiger ♦ n exigence f; (claim) revendication f; (ECON) demande f; **in** ~ demandé(e), recherché(e); **on** ~ sur demande; ~**ing** adj (person) exigeant(e); (work) astreignant(e)

demean [dɪ'miːn] vt: **to** ~ **o.s.** s'abaisser

demeanour [dɪ'miːnə*] (US **demeanor**) n comportement m; maintien m

demented [dɪ'mentɪd] adj dément(e), fou(folle)

demise [dɪ'maɪz] n mort f

demister [diː'mɪstə*] (BRIT) n (AUT) dispositif m anti-buée inv

demo ['deməʊ] (inf) n abbr (= demonstration) manif f

democracy [dɪ'mɒkrəsɪ] n démocratie f; **democrat** ['deməkræt] n démocrate m/f; **democratic** [demə'krætɪk] adj démocratique

demolish [dɪ'mɒlɪʃ] vt démolir

demonstrate ['demənstreɪt] vt démontrer, prouver; (show) faire une démonstration de ♦ vi: **to** ~ **(for/against)** manifester (en faveur de/contre); **demonstration** [demən'streɪʃən] n démonstration f, manifestation f; **demonstrator** ['demənstreɪtə*] n (POL) manifestant(e)

demote [dɪ'məʊt] vt rétrograder

demure [dɪ'mjʊə*] adj sage, réservé(e)

den [den] n tanière f, antre m

denatured alcohol [diː'neɪtʃəd-] (US) n alcool m à brûler

denial [dɪ'naɪəl] n démenti m; (refusal) dénégation f

denim ['denɪm] n jean m; ~**s** npl (jeans) (blue-)jean(s) m(pl)

Denmark ['denmɑːk] n Danemark m

denomination [dɪnɒmɪ'neɪʃən] n (of money) valeur f; (REL) confession f

denounce [dɪ'naʊns] vt dénoncer

dense [dens] adj dense; (stupid) obtus(e), bouché(e); ~**ly** adv: ~**ly populated** à forte densité de population

density ['densɪtɪ] n densité f; **double/high-**~ **diskette** disquette f double densité/haute densité

dent [dent] n bosse f ♦ vt (also: **make a** ~ **in**) cabosser

dental ['dentl] adj dentaire; ~ **surgeon** n (chirurgien(ne)) dentiste

dentist ['dentɪst] n dentiste m/f

dentures ['dentʃəz] npl dentier m sg

deny [dɪ'naɪ] vt nier; (refuse) refuser

deodorant [diː'əʊdərənt] n déodorant m, désodorisant m

depart [dɪ'pɑːt] vi partir; **to** ~ **from** (fig: differ from) s'écarter de

department [dɪ'pɑːtmənt] n (COMM) rayon m; (SCOL) section f; (POL) ministère m, département m; ~ **store** n grand magasin

departure [dɪ'pɑːtʃə*] n départ m; **a new** ~ une nouvelle voie; ~ **lounge** n (at airport) salle f d'embarquement

depend [dɪ'pend] vi: **to** ~ **on** dépendre de; (rely on) compter sur; **it** ~**s** cela dépend; ~**ing on the result** selon le résultat; ~**able** adj (person) sérieux(euse), sûr(e); (car, watch) solide, fiable; ~**ant** n personne f à charge; ~**ent** adj: **to be** ~**ent (on)** dépendre (de) ♦ n = **dependant**

depict [dɪ'pɪkt] vt (in picture) représenter; (in words) (dé)peindre, décrire

depleted [dɪ'pliːtɪd] adj (considérablement) réduit(e) or diminué(e)

deport [dɪ'pɔːt] vt expulser

deposit [dɪ'pɒzɪt] n (CHEM, COMM, GEO) dépôt m; (of ore, oil) gisement m; (part payment) arrhes fpl, acompte m; (on bottle etc) consigne f; (for hired goods etc) cautionnement m, garantie f ♦ vt déposer; ~ **account** n compte m sur livret

depot ['depəʊ] n dépôt m; (US: RAIL) gare f

depress [dɪ'pres] vt déprimer; (press down) appuyer sur, abaisser; (prices, wages) faire baisser; ~**ed** adj (person) déprimé(e); (area) en déclin, touché(e) par le sous-emploi; ~**ing** adj déprimant(e); ~**ion** [dɪ'preʃən] n dépression f; (hollow) creux m

deprivation [deprɪ'veɪʃən] n privation f; (loss) perte f

deprive [dɪ'praɪv] vt: **to** ~ **sb of** priver qn de; ~**d** adj déshérité(e)

depth [depθ] n profondeur f; **in the** ~**s of despair** au plus profond du désespoir; **to be out of one's** ~ avoir perdu pied, nager

deputize ['depjutaɪz] vi: **to** ~ **for** assurer l'intérim de

deputy ['depjutɪ] adj adjoint(e) ♦ n (second in command) adjoint(e); (US: also ~ **sheriff**) shérif adjoint; ~ **head** n directeur adjoint, sous-directeur m

derail [dɪ'reɪl] vt: **to be** ~**ed** dérailler

deranged [dɪ'reɪndʒd] adj: **to be (mentally)** ~ avoir le cerveau dérangé

derby ['dɑːbɪ] (US) n (bowler hat) (chapeau m) melon m

derelict ['derɪlɪkt] adj abandonné(e), à l'abandon

derisory [dɪ'raɪsərɪ] adj (sum) dérisoire; (smile, person) moqueur(euse)

derive [dɪ'raɪv] vt: **to** ~ **sth from** tirer qch de; trouver qch dans; **to** ~ **from** provenir de, dériver de

derogatory [dɪ'rɒgətərɪ] adj désobligeant(e); péjoratif(ive)

descend [dɪˈsend] *vt, vi* descendre; **to ~ from** descendre de, être issu(e) de; **to ~ to (doing) sth** s'abaisser à (faire) qch; **descent** [dɪˈsent] *n* descente *f*; (*origin*) origine *f*

describe [dɪsˈkraɪb] *vt* décrire; **description** [dɪsˈkrɪpʃən] *n* description *f*; (*sort*) sorte *f*, espèce *f*

desecrate [ˈdesɪkreɪt] *vt* profaner

desert [*n* ˈdezət, *vb* dɪˈzəːt] *n* désert *m* ♦ *vt* déserter, abandonner ♦ *vi* (*MIL*) déserter; **~s** *npl*: **to get one's just ~** ce qu'on mérite; **~er** *n* déserteur *m*; **~ion** [dɪˈzəːʃən] *n* (*MIL*) désertion *f*; (*LAW: of spouse*) abandon *m* du domicile conjugal; **~ island** *n* île déserte

deserve [dɪˈzəːv] *vt* mériter; **deserving** [dɪˈzəːvɪŋ] *adj* (*person*) méritant(e); (*action, cause*) méritoire

design [dɪˈzaɪn] *n* (*sketch*) plan *m*, dessin *m*; (*layout, shape*) conception *f*, ligne *f*; (*pattern*) dessin *m*, motif(s) *m(pl)*; (*COMM, art*) design *m*, stylisme *m*; (*intention*) dessein *m* ♦ *vt* dessiner; élaborer; **~er** [dɪˈzaɪnə*] *n* (*TECH*) concepteur-projeteur *m*; (*ART*) dessinateur(trice), designer *m*; (*fashion*) styliste *m/f*

desire [dɪˈzaɪə*] *n* désir *m* ♦ *vt* désirer

desk [desk] *n* (*in office*) bureau *m*; (*for pupil*) pupitre *m*; (*BRIT: in shop, restaurant*) caisse *f*; (*in hotel, at airport*) réception *f*

desolate [ˈdesəlɪt] *adj* désolé(e); (*person*) affligé(e)

despair [dɪsˈpeə*] *n* désespoir *m* ♦ *vi*: **to ~ of** désespérer de

despatch [dɪsˈpætʃ] *n, vt* = **dispatch**

desperate [ˈdespərɪt] *adj* désespéré(e); (*criminal*) prêt(e) à tout; **to be ~ for sth/ to do sth** avoir désespérément besoin de qch/de faire qch; **~ly** [ˈdespərɪtlɪ] *adv* désespérément; (*very*) terriblement, extrêmement

desperation [despəˈreɪʃən] *n* désespoir *m*; **in (sheer) ~** en désespoir de cause

despicable [dɪsˈpɪkəbl] *adj* méprisable

despise [dɪsˈpaɪz] *vt* mépriser

despite [dɪsˈpaɪt] *prep* malgré, en dépit de

despondent [dɪsˈpɔndənt] *adj* découragé(e), abattu(e)

dessert [dɪˈzəːt] *n* dessert *m*; **~spoon** *n* cuiller *f* à dessert

destination [destɪˈneɪʃən] *n* destination *f*

destined [ˈdestɪnd] *adj*: **to be ~ to do/for sth** être destiné(e) à faire/à qch

destiny [ˈdestɪnɪ] *n* destinée *f*, destin *m*

destitute [ˈdestɪtjuːt] *adj* indigent(e)

destroy [dɪsˈtrɔɪ] *vt* détruire; (*injured horse*) abattre; (*dog*) faire piquer; **~er** *n* (*NAUT*) contre-torpilleur *m*

destruction [dɪsˈtrʌkʃən] *n* destruction *f*

detach [dɪˈtætʃ] *vt* détacher; **~ed** *adj* (*attitude, person*) détaché(e); **~ed house** *n* pa-

villon *m*, maison(nette) (individuelle); **~ment** *n* (*MIL*) détachement *m*; (*fig*) détachement, indifférence *f*

detail [ˈdiːteɪl] *n* détail *m* ♦ *vt* raconter en détail, énumérer; **in ~** en détail; **~ed** *adj* détaillé(e)

detain [dɪˈteɪn] *vt* retenir; (*in captivity*) détenir; (*in hospital*) hospitaliser

detect [dɪˈtekt] *vt* déceler, percevoir; (*MED, POLICE*) dépister; (*MIL, RADAR, TECH*) détecter; **~ion** [dɪˈtekʃən] *n* découverte *f*; **~ive** *n* agent *m* de la sûreté, policier *m*; **private ~ive** détective privé; **~ive story** *n* roman policier

detention [dɪˈtenʃən] *n* détention *f*; (*SCOL*) retenue *f*, consigne *f*

deter [dɪˈtəː*] *vt* dissuader

detergent [dɪˈtəːdʒənt] *n* détergent *m*, détersif *m*

deteriorate [dɪˈtɪərɪəreɪt] *vi* se détériorer, se dégrader

determine [dɪˈtəːmɪn] *vt* déterminer; **to ~ to do** résoudre de faire, se déterminer à faire; **~d** *adj* (*person*) déterminé(e), décidé(e)

deterrent [dɪˈterənt] *n* effet *m* de dissuasion; **force** *f* **de dissuasion**

detonate [ˈdetəneɪt] *vt* faire détoner *or* exploser

detour [ˈdiːtuə*] *n* détour *m*; (*US: AUT: diversion*) déviation *f*

detract [dɪˈtrækt] *vt*: **to ~ from** (*quality, pleasure*) diminuer; (*reputation*) porter atteinte à

detriment [ˈdetrɪmənt] *n*: **to the ~ of** au détriment de, au préjudice de; **~al** [detrɪˈmentl] *adj*: **~al to** préjudiciable *or* nuisible à

devaluation [dɪvæljuˈeɪʃən] *n* dévaluation *f*

devastate [ˈdevəsteɪt] *vt* (*also fig*) dévaster; **devastating** *adj* dévastateur(trice); (*news*) accablant(e)

develop [dɪˈveləp] *vt* (*gen*) développer; (*disease*) commencer à souffrir de; (*resources*) mettre en valeur, exploiter ♦ *vi* se développer; (*situation, disease: evolve*) évoluer; (*facts, symptoms: appear*) se manifester, se produire; **~ing country** *n* pays *m* en voie de développement; **the machine has ~ed a fault** un problème s'est manifesté dans cette machine; **~er** *n* (*also: property ~er*) promoteur *m*; **~ment** *n* développement *m*; (*of affair, case*) rebondissement *m*, fait(s) nouveau(x)

device [dɪˈvaɪs] *n* (*apparatus*) engin *m*, dispositif *m*

devil [ˈdevl] *n* diable *m*; démon *m*

devious [ˈdiːvɪəs] *adj* (*person*) sournois(e), dissimulé(e)

devise [dɪˈvaɪz] *vt* imaginer, concevoir

devoid [dɪˈvɔɪd] *adj*: **~ of** dépourvu(e) de, dénué(e) de

devolution [diːvə'luːʃən] n (POL) décentralisation f

devote [dɪ'vəʊt] vt: **to ~ sth to** consacrer qch à; **~d** adj dévoué(e); **to be ~d to** (book etc) être consacré(e) à; (person) être très attaché(e) à; **~e** [devəʊ'tiː] n (REL) adepte m/f; (MUS, SPORT) fervent(e)

devotion [dɪ'vəʊʃən] n dévouement m, attachement m; (REL) dévotion f, piété f

devour [dɪ'vaʊə*] vt dévorer

devout [dɪ'vaʊt] adj pieux(euse), dévot(e)

dew [djuː] n rosée f

diabetes [daɪə'biːtiːz] n diabète m; **diabetic** [daɪə'betɪk] adj diabétique ♦ n diabétique m/f

diabolical [daɪə'bɒlɪkl] (inf) adj (weather) atroce; (behaviour) infernal(e)

diagnosis [daɪəg'nəʊsɪs, pl daɪəg'nəʊsiːz] (pl **diagnoses**) n diagnostic m

diagonal [daɪ'ægənl] adj diagonal(e) ♦ n diagonale f

diagram ['daɪəgræm] n diagramme m, schéma m

dial ['daɪəl] n cadran m ♦ vt (number) faire, composer; **~ code** (US) n = **dialling code**

dialect ['daɪəlekt] n dialecte m

dialling code ['daɪəlɪŋ-] (BRIT) n indicatif m (téléphonique)

dialling tone ['daɪəlɪŋ-] (BRIT) n tonalité f

dialogue ['daɪəlɒg] n dialogue m

dial tone (US) n = **dialling tone**

diameter [daɪ'æmɪtə*] n diamètre m

diamond ['daɪəmənd] n diamant m; (shape) losange m; **~s** npl (CARDS) carreau m

diaper ['daɪəpə*] (US) n couche f

diaphragm ['daɪəfræm] n diaphragme m

diarrhoea [daɪə'riːə] (US **diarrhea**) n diarrhée f

diary ['daɪərɪ] n (daily account) journal m; (book) agenda m

dice [daɪs] n inv dé m ♦ vt (CULIN) couper en dés or en cubes

dictate [vb dɪk'teɪt] vt dicter

dictation [dɪk'teɪʃən] n dictée f

dictator [dɪk'teɪtə*] n dictateur m; **~ship** n dictature f

dictionary ['dɪkʃənrɪ] n dictionnaire m

did [dɪd] pt of do; **~n't** = did not

die [daɪ] vi mourir; **to be dying for sth** avoir une envie folle de qch; **to be dying to do sth** mourir d'envie de faire qch; **~ away** vi s'éteindre; **~ down** vi se calmer, s'apaiser; **~ out** vi disparaître

die-hard ['daɪhɑːd] n réactionnaire m/f, jusqu'au-boutiste m/f

diesel ['diːzəl] n (vehicle) diesel m; (also: **~ oil**) carburant m diesel, gas-oil m; **~ engine** n moteur m diesel

diet ['daɪət] n alimentation f; (restricted food) régime m ♦ vi (also: be on a ~) suivre un régime

differ ['dɪfə*] vi (be different): **to ~ (from)**

être différent (de); différer (de); (disagree): **to ~ (from sb over sth)** ne pas être d'accord (avec qn au sujet de qch); **~ence** n différence f; (quarrel) différend m, désaccord m; **~ent** adj différent(e); **~entiate** [dɪfə'renʃɪeɪt] vi: **to ~entiate (between)** faire une différence (entre)

difficult ['dɪfɪkəlt] adj difficile; **~y** n difficulté f

diffident ['dɪfɪdənt] adj qui manque de confiance or d'assurance

dig [dɪg] (pt, pp dug) vt (hole) creuser; (garden) bêcher ♦ n (prod) coup m de coude; (fig) coup de griffe or de patte; (archeological) fouilles fpl; **~ in** vi (MIL: also: ~ o.s. in) se retrancher; **~ into** vt fus (savings) puiser dans; **to ~ one's nails into sth** enfoncer ses ongles dans qch; **~ up** vt déterrer

digest [vb daɪ'dʒest, n 'daɪdʒest] vt digérer ♦ n sommaire m, résumé m; **~ion** n digestion f

digit ['dɪdʒɪt] n (number) chiffre m; (finger) doigt m; **~al** adj digital(e), à affichage numérique or digital; **~al computer** calculateur m numérique

dignified ['dɪgnɪfaɪd] adj digne

dignity ['dɪgnɪtɪ] n dignité f

digress [daɪ'gres] vi: **to ~ from** s'écarter de, s'éloigner de

digs [dɪgz] (BRIT: inf) npl piaule f, chambre meublée

dilapidated [dɪ'læpɪdeɪtɪd] adj délabré(e)

dilemma [daɪ'lemə] n dilemme m

diligent ['dɪlɪdʒənt] adj appliqué(e), assidu(e)

dilute [daɪ'luːt] vt diluer

dim [dɪm] adj (light) faible; (memory, outline) vague, indécis(e); (figure) vague, indistinct(e); (room) sombre; (stupid) borné(e), obtus(e) ♦ vt (light) réduire, baisser; (US: AUT) mettre en code

dime [daɪm] (US) n = **10 cents**

dimension [dɪ'menʃən] n dimension f

diminish [dɪ'mɪnɪʃ] vt, vi diminuer

diminutive [dɪ'mɪnjutɪv] adj minuscule, tout(e) petit(e)

dimmers ['dɪməz] (US) npl (AUT) phares mpl code inv; feux mpl de position

dimple ['dɪmpl] n fossette f

din [dɪn] n vacarme m

dine [daɪn] vi dîner; **~r** n (person) dîneur(euse); (US: restaurant) petit restaurant

dinghy ['dɪŋgɪ] n youyou m; (also: rubber ~) canot m pneumatique; (: sailing ~) voilier m, dériveur m

dingy ['dɪndʒɪ] adj miteux(euse), minable

dining car ['daɪnɪŋ-] (BRIT) n wagon-restaurant m

dining room ['daɪnɪŋ-] n salle f à manger

dinner ['dɪnə*] n dîner m; (lunch) déjeuner

m; *(public)* banquet *m*; ~ **jacket** *n* smoking *m*; ~ **party** *n* dîner *m*; ~ **time** *n* heure *f* du dîner; *(midday)* heure du déjeuner

dint [dɪnt] *n*: **by ~ of (doing)** à force de (faire)

dip [dɪp] *n* déclivité *f*; *(in sea)* baignade *f*, bain *m*; *(CULIN)* ≈ sauce *f* ♦ *vt* tremper, plonger; *(BRIT: AUT: lights)* mettre en code, baisser ♦ *vi* plonger

diploma [dɪˈpləʊmə] *n* diplôme *m*

diplomacy [dɪˈpləʊməsɪ] *n* diplomatie *f*

diplomat [ˈdɪpləmæt] *n* diplomate *m*; ~**ic** [dɪpləˈmætɪk] *adj* diplomatique

dipstick [ˈdɪpstɪk] *n* *(AUT)* jauge *f* de niveau d'huile

dipswitch [ˈdɪpswɪtʃ] *(BRIT)* *n* *(AUT)* interrupteur *m* de lumière réduite

dire [daɪə*] *adj* terrible, extrême, affreux(euse)

direct [daɪˈrɛkt] *adj* direct(e) ♦ *vt* diriger, orienter *(letter, remark)* adresser; *(film, programme)* réaliser; *(play)* mettre en scène; *(order)*: **to ~ sb to do sth** ordonner à qn de faire qch ♦ *adv* directement; **can you ~ me to ...?** pouvez-vous m'indiquer le chemin de ...?; ~ **debit** *(BRIT)* *n* prélèvement *m* automatique

direction [dɪˈrɛkʃən] *n* direction *f*; ~**s** *npl* *(advice)* indications *fpl*; **sense of ~** sens *m* de l'orientation; ~**s for use** mode *m* d'emploi

directly [dɪˈrɛktlɪ] *adv* *(in a straight line)* directement, tout droit; *(at once)* tout de suite, immédiatement

director [dɪˈrɛktə*] *n* directeur *m*; *(THEATRE)* metteur *m* en scène; *(CINEMA, TV)* réalisateur(trice)

directory [dɪˈrɛktərɪ] *n* annuaire *m*; *(COMPUT)* répertoire *m*

dirt [dɜːt] *n* saleté *f*; crasse *f*; *(earth)* terre *f*, boue *f*; ~**-cheap** *adj* très bon marché *inv*; ~**y** *adj* sale ♦ *vt* salir; ~ **trick** coup tordu

disability [dɪsəˈbɪlɪtɪ] *n* invalidité *f*, infirmité *f*

disabled [dɪsˈeɪbld] *adj* infirme, invalide ♦ *npl*: **the ~** les handicapés

disadvantage [dɪsədˈvɑːntɪdʒ] *n* désavantage *m*, inconvénient *m*

disagree [dɪsəˈɡriː] *vi* *(be different)* ne pas concorder; *(be against, think otherwise)*: **to ~ (with)** être en désaccord (avec); ~**able** *adj* désagréable; ~**ment** *n* désaccord *m*, différend *m*

disallow [ˈdɪsəˈlaʊ] *vt* rejeter

disappear [dɪsəˈpɪə*] *vi* disparaître; ~**ance** *n* disparition *f*

disappoint [dɪsəˈpɔɪnt] *vt* décevoir; ~**ed** *adj* déçu(e); ~**ing** *adj* décevant(e); ~**ment** *n* déception *f*

disapproval [dɪsəˈpruːvəl] *n* désapprobation *f*

disapprove [dɪsəˈpruːv] *vi*: **to ~ (of)** désapprouver

disarmament [dɪsˈɑːməmənt] *n* désarmement *m*

disarray [ˈdɪsəˈreɪ] *n*: **in ~** *(army)* en déroute; *(organization)* en désarroi; *(hair, clothes)* en désordre

disaster [dɪˈzɑːstə*] *n* catastrophe *f*, désastre *m*

disband [dɪsˈbænd] *vt* démobiliser; disperser ♦ *vi* se séparer; se disperser

disbelief [ˈdɪsbəˈliːf] *n* incrédulité *f*

disc [dɪsk] *n* disque *m*; *(COMPUT)* = **disk**

discard [ˈdɪskɑːd] *vt* *(old things)* se débarrasser de; *(fig)* écarter, renoncer à

discern [dɪˈsɜːn] *vt* discerner, distinguer; ~**ing** *adj* perspicace

discharge [*vb* dɪsˈtʃɑːdʒ, *n* ˈdɪstʃɑːdʒ] *vt* décharger; *(duties)* s'acquitter de; *(patient)* renvoyer (chez lui); *(employee)* congédier, licencier; *(soldier)* rendre à la vie civile, réformer; *(defendant)* relaxer, élargir ♦ *n* décharge *f*; *(dismissal)* renvoi *m*; licenciement *m*; élargissement *m*; *(MED)* écoulement *m*

discipline [ˈdɪsɪplɪn] *n* discipline *f*

disc jockey *n* disc-jockey *m*

disclaim [dɪsˈkleɪm] *vt* nier

disclose [dɪsˈkləʊz] *vt* révéler, divulguer; **disclosure** [dɪsˈkləʊʒə*] *n* révélation *f*

disco [ˈdɪskəʊ] *n abbr* = **discothèque**

discomfort [dɪsˈkʌmfət] *n* malaise *m*, gêne *f*; *(lack of comfort)* manque *m* de confort

disconcert [dɪskənˈsɜːt] *vt* déconcerter

disconnect [ˈdɪskəˈnɛkt] *vt* *(ELEC, RADIO, pipe)* débrancher; *(TEL, water)* couper

discontent [dɪskənˈtɛnt] *n* mécontentement *m*; ~**ed** *adj* mécontent(e)

discontinue [ˈdɪskənˈtɪnjuː] *vt* cesser, interrompre; "~**d**" *(COMM)* "fin de série"

discord [ˈdɪskɔːd] *n* discorde *f*, dissension *f*; *(MUS)* dissonance *f*

discotheque [ˈdɪskəʊtɛk] *n* discothèque *f*

discount [*n* ˈdɪskaʊnt, *vb* dɪsˈkaʊnt] *n* remise *f*, rabais *m* ♦ *vt* *(sum)* faire une remise de; *(fig)* ne pas tenir compte de

discourage [dɪsˈkʌrɪdʒ] *vt* décourager

discover [dɪsˈkʌvə*] *vt* découvrir; ~**y** *n* découverte *f*

discredit [dɪsˈkrɛdɪt] *vt* *(idea)* mettre en doute; *(person)* discréditer

discreet [dɪsˈkriːt] *adj* discret(ète)

discrepancy [dɪsˈkrɛpənsɪ] *n* divergence *f*, contradiction *f*

discretion [dɪsˈkrɛʃən] *n* discrétion *f*; **use your own ~** à vous de juger

discriminate [dɪsˈkrɪmɪneɪt] *vi*: **to ~ between** établir une distinction entre, faire la différence entre; **to ~ against** pratiquer une discrimination contre; **discriminating** *adj* qui a du discernement; **discrimination** [dɪskrɪmɪˈneɪʃən] *n* discrimination *f*; *(judgment)* discernement *m*

discuss [dɪs'kʌs] *vt* discuter de; (*debate*) discuter; **~ion** [dɪs'kʌʃən] *n* discussion *f*

disdain [dɪs'deɪn] *n* dédain *m*

disease [dɪ'ziːz] *n* maladie *f*

disembark [dɪsɪm'bɑːk] *vt, vi* débarquer

disengage [dɪsɪn'geɪdʒ] *vt*: **to ~ the clutch** (*AUT*) débrayer

disentangle [dɪsɪn'tæŋgl] *vt* (*wool, wire*) démêler, débrouiller; (*from wreckage*) dégager

disfigure [dɪs'fɪgə*] *vt* défigurer

disgrace [dɪs'greɪs] *n* honte *f*; (*disfavour*) disgrâce *f* ♦ *vt* déshonorer, couvrir de honte; **~ful** *adj* scandaleux(euse), honteux(euse)

disgruntled [dɪs'grʌntld] *adj* mécontent(e)

disguise [dɪs'gaɪz] *n* déguisement *m* ♦ *vt* déguiser; **in ~** déguisé(e)

disgust [dɪs'gʌst] *n* dégoût *m*, aversion *f* ♦ *vt* dégoûter, écœurer; **~ing** *adj* dégoûtant(e); révoltant(e)

dish [dɪʃ] *n* plat *m*; **to do** *or* **wash the ~es** faire la vaisselle; **~ out** *vt* servir, distribuer; **~ up** *vt* servir; **~cloth** *n* (*for washing*) lavette *f*

dishearten [dɪs'hɑːtn] *vt* décourager

dishevelled [dɪ'ʃevəld] (*US* **disheveled**) *adj* ébouriffé(e); décoiffé(e); débraillé(e)

dishonest [dɪs'ɒnɪst] *adj* malhonnête

dishonour [dɪs'ɒnə*] (*US* **dishonor**) *n* déshonneur *m*; **~able** *adj* (*behaviour*) déshonorant(e); (*person*) peu honorable

dishtowel ['dɪʃtaʊəl] (*US*) *n* torchon *m*

dishwasher ['dɪʃwɒʃə*] *n* lave-vaisselle *m*

disillusion [dɪsɪ'luːʒən] *vt* désabuser, désillusionner

disincentive ['dɪsɪn'sentɪv] *n*: **to be a ~** être démotivant(e)

disinfect [dɪsɪn'fekt] *vt* désinfecter; **~ant** *n* désinfectant *m*

disintegrate [dɪs'ɪntɪgreɪt] *vi* se désintégrer

disinterested [dɪs'ɪntrɪstɪd] *adj* désintéressé(e)

disjointed [dɪs'dʒɔɪntɪd] *adj* décousu(e), incohérent(e)

disk [dɪsk] *n* (*COMPUT*) disque *m*; (: *floppy ~*) disquette *f*; **single-/double-sided ~** disquette simple/double face; **~ drive** *n* lecteur *m* de disquettes; **~ette** [dɪs'ket] *n* disquette *f*, disque *m* souple

dislike [dɪs'laɪk] *n* aversion *f*, antipathie *f* ♦ *vt* ne pas aimer

dislocate ['dɪsləʊkeɪt] *vt* disloquer; déboiter

dislodge [dɪs'lɒdʒ] *vt* déplacer, faire bouger

disloyal ['dɪs'lɔɪəl] *adj* déloyal(e)

dismal ['dɪzməl] *adj* lugubre, maussade

dismantle [dɪs'mæntl] *vt* démonter

dismay [dɪs'meɪ] *n* consternation *f*

dismiss [dɪs'mɪs] *vt* congédier, renvoyer; (*soldiers*) faire rompre les rangs à; (*idea*) écarter; (*LAW*): **to ~ a case** rendre une fin de non-recevoir; **~al** *n* renvoi *m*

dismount [dɪs'maʊnt] *vi* mettre pied à terre, descendre

disobedient [dɪsə'biːdɪənt] *adj* désobéissant(e)

disobey ['dɪsə'beɪ] *vt* désobéir à

disorder [dɪs'ɔːdə*] *n* désordre *m*; (*rioting*) désordres *mpl*; (*MED*) troubles *mpl*; **~ly** [dɪs'ɔːdəlɪ] *adj* en désordre; désordonné(e)

disorientated [dɪs'ɔːrɪenteɪtɪd] *adj* désorienté(e)

disown [dɪs'əʊn] *vt* renier

disparaging [dɪs'pærɪdʒɪŋ] *adj* désobligeant(e)

dispassionate [dɪs'pæʃnɪt] *adj* calme, froid(e); impartial(e), objectif(ive)

dispatch [dɪs'pætʃ] *vt* expédier, envoyer ♦ *n* envoi *m*, expédition *f*; (*MIL, PRESS*) dépêche *f*

dispel [dɪs'pel] *vt* dissiper, chasser

dispense [dɪs'pens] *vt* distribuer, administrer; **~ with** *vt fus* se passer de; **~r** *n* (*machine*) distributeur *m*; **dispensing chemist** (*BRIT*) *n* pharmacie *f*

disperse [dɪs'pɜːs] *vt* disperser ♦ *vi* se disperser

dispirited [dɪs'pɪrɪtɪd] *adj* découragé(e), déprimé(e)

displace [dɪs'pleɪs] *vt* déplacer

display [dɪs'pleɪ] *n* étalage *m*; déploiement *m*; affichage *m*; (*screen*) écran *m*, visuel *m*; (*of feeling*) manifestation *f* ♦ *vt* montrer; (*goods*) mettre à l'étalage, exposer; (*results, departure times*) afficher; (*pej*) faire étalage de

displease [dɪs'pliːz] *vt* mécontenter, contrarier; **~d** *adj*: **~d with** mécontent(e) de; **displeasure** [dɪs'pleʒə*] *n* mécontentement *m*

disposable [dɪs'pəʊzəbl] *adj* (*pack etc*) jetable, à jeter; (*income*) disponible; **~ nappy** (*BRIT*) *n* couche *f* à jeter, couche-culotte *f*

disposal [dɪs'pəʊzəl] *n* (*of goods for sale*) vente *f*; (*of property*) disposition *f*, cession *f*; (*of rubbish*) enlèvement *m*; destruction *f*; **at one's ~** à sa disposition

dispose [dɪs'pəʊz] *vt* disposer; **~ of** *vt fus* (*unwanted goods etc*) se débarrasser de, se défaire de; (*problem*) expédier; **~d** [dɪs'pəʊzd] *adj*: **to be ~d to do sth** être disposé(e) à faire qch; **disposition** [dɪspə'zɪʃən] *n* disposition *f*; (*temperament*) naturel *m*

disprove [dɪs'pruːv] *vt* réfuter

dispute [dɪs'pjuːt] *n* discussion *f*; (*also: industrial ~*) conflit *m* ♦ *vt* contester; (*matter*) discuter; (*victory*) disputer

disqualify [dɪs'kwɒlɪfaɪ] *vt* (*SPORT*) disqualifier; **to ~ sb for sth/from doing** rendre qn inapte à qch/à faire

disquiet [dɪs'kwaɪət] *n* inquiétude *f*, trouble *m*

disregard [dɪsrɪ'gɑːd] *vt* ne pas tenir compte de

disrepair ['dɪsrɪ'peə*] n: **to fall into ~**
(building) tomber en ruine

disreputable [dɪs'repjutəbl] adj (person) de
mauvaise réputation; (behaviour) déshono-
rant(e)

disrespectful [dɪsrɪ'spektful] adj irrespec-
tueux(euse)

disrupt [dɪs'rʌpt] vt (plans) déranger;
(conversation) interrompre

dissatisfied [dɪs'sætɪsfaɪd] adj: **~ (with)** in-
satisfait(e) (de)

dissect [dɪ'sekt] vt disséquer

dissent [dɪ'sent] n dissentiment m, différence f d'opinion

dissertation [dɪsə'teɪʃən] n mémoire m

disservice [dɪs'sɜːvɪs] n: **to do sb a ~** rendre un mauvais service à qn

dissimilar ['dɪ'sɪmɪlə*] adj: **~ (to)** dissemblable (à), différent(e) (de)

dissipate ['dɪsɪpeɪt] vt dissiper; (money, efforts) disperser

dissolute ['dɪsəluːt] adj débauché(e), disso-
lu(e)

dissolve [dɪ'zɒlv] vt dissoudre ♦ vi se dissoudre, fondre; **to ~ in(to) tears** fondre en
larmes

distance ['dɪstəns] n distance f; **in the ~**
au loin

distant ['dɪstənt] adj lointain(e), éloigné(e);
(manner) distant(e), froid(e)

distaste [dɪs'teɪst] n dégoût m; **~ful** adj
déplaisant(e), désagréable

distended [dɪs'tendɪd] adj (stomach) dila-
té(e)

distil, (US) **distill** [dɪs'tɪl] vt distiller; **~lery**
n distillerie f

distinct [dɪs'tɪŋkt] adj distinct(e); (clear)
marqué(e); **as ~ from** par opposition à;
~ion [dɪs'tɪŋkʃən] n distinction f; (in exam)
mention f très bien; **~ive** adj distinctif(ive)

distinguish [dɪs'tɪŋgwɪʃ] vt distinguer; **~ed**
adj (eminent) distingué(e); **~ing** adj (feature) distinctif(ive), caractéristique

distort [dɪs'tɔːt] vt déformer

distract [dɪs'trækt] vt distraire, déranger;
~ed adj distrait(e); (anxious) éperdu(e), éga-
ré(e); **~ion** [dɪs'trækʃən] n distraction f, égarement m

distraught [dɪs'trɔːt] adj éperdu(e)

distress [dɪs'tres] n détresse f ♦ vt affliger;
~ing adj douloureux(euse), pénible

distribute [dɪs'trɪbjuːt] vt distribuer; **distribution** [dɪstrɪ'bjuːʃən] n distribution f; **distributor** [dɪs'trɪbjutə*] n distributeur m

district ['dɪstrɪkt] n (of country) région f; (of
town) quartier m; (ADMIN) district m; **~
attorney** (US) n ≈ procureur m de la République; **~ nurse** (BRIT) n infirmière visiteuse

distrust [dɪs'trʌst] n méfiance f ♦ vt se méfier de

disturb [dɪs'tɜːb] vt troubler; (inconvenience) déranger; **~ance** n dérangement m;
(violent event, political etc) troubles mpl;
~ed adj (worried, upset) agité(e), trou-
blé(e); **to be emotionally ~ed** avoir des
problèmes affectifs; **~ing** adj troublant(e),
inquiétant(e)

disuse ['dɪs'juːs] n: **to fall into ~** tomber
en désuétude

disused ['dɪs'juːzd] adj désaffecté(e)

ditch [dɪtʃ] n fossé m; (irrigation) rigole f ♦
vt (inf) abandonner; (person) plaquer

dither ['dɪðə*] vi hésiter

ditto ['dɪtəu] adv idem

dive [daɪv] n plongeon m; (of submarine)
plongée f ♦ vi plonger; **to ~ into** (bag, drawer etc) plonger la main dans; (shop, car etc)
se précipiter dans; **~r** n plongeur m

diversion [daɪ'vɜːʃən] n (BRIT: AUT) déviation f; (distraction, MIL) diversion f

divert [daɪ'vɜːt] vt (funds, BRIT: traffic) dévier; (river, attention) détourner

divide [dɪ'vaɪd] vt diviser; (separate) séparer
♦ vi se diviser; **~d highway** (US) n route f
à quatre voies

dividend ['dɪvɪdend] n dividende m

divine [dɪ'vaɪn] adj divin(e)

diving ['daɪvɪŋ] n plongée (sous-marine); **~
board** n plongeoir m

divinity [dɪ'vɪnɪtɪ] n divinité f; (SCOL) théologie f

division [dɪ'vɪʒən] n division f

divorce [dɪ'vɔːs] n divorce m ♦ vt divorcer
d'avec; (dissociate) séparer; **~d** adj divor-
cé(e); **~e** [dɪvɔː'siː] n divorcé(e)

D.I.Y. (BRIT) n abbr = **do-it-yourself**

dizzy ['dɪzɪ] adj: **to make sb ~** donner le
vertige à qn; **to feel ~** avoir la tête qui
tourne

DJ n abbr = **disc jockey**

─────────────── *KEYWORD*

do [duː] (pt **did**, pp **done**) n (inf: party etc)
soirée f, fête f

♦ vb **1** (in negative constructions) non traduit; **I ~n't understand** je ne comprends
pas

2 (to form questions) non traduit; **didn't
you know?** vous ne le saviez pas?; **why
didn't you come?** pourquoi n'êtes-vous pas
venu?

3 (for emphasis, in polite expressions): **she
does seem rather late** je trouve qu'elle est
bien en retard; **~ sit down/help yourself**
asseyez-vous/servez-vous je vous en prie

4 (used to avoid repeating vb): **she swims
better than I ~** elle nage mieux que moi;
~ you agree? - yes, I ~/no, I ~n't vous
êtes d'accord? - oui/non; **she lives in
Glasgow - so ~ I** elle habite Glasgow -
moi aussi; **who broke it? - I did** qui l'a
cassé? - c'est moi

5 (in question tags): **he laughed, didn't he?** il a ri, n'est-ce pas?; **I ~n't know him, ~ I?** je ne le connais pas, je crois
♦ vt (gen: carry out, perform etc) faire; **what are you ~ing tonight?** qu'est-ce que vous faites ce soir?; **to ~ the cooking/washing-up** faire la cuisine/la vaisselle; **to ~ one's teeth/hair/nails** se brosser les dents/se coiffer/se faire les ongles; **the car was ~ing 100** la voiture faisait du 100 (à l'heure)
♦ vi **1** (act, behave) faire; **~ as I ~** faites comme moi
2 (get on, fare) marcher; **the firm is ~ing well** l'entreprise marche bien; **how ~ you ~?** comment allez-vous?; (on being introduced) enchanté(e)!
3 (suit) aller; **will it ~?** est-ce que ça ira?
4 (be sufficient) suffire, aller; **will £10 ~?** est-ce que 10 livres suffiront?; **that'll ~** ça suffit, ça ira; **that'll ~!** (in annoyance) ça va ou suffit comme ça!; **to make ~ (with)** se contenter (de)
do away with vt fus supprimer
do up vt (laces, dress) attacher; (buttons) boutonner; (zip) fermer; (renovate: room) refaire; (: house) remettre à neuf
do with vt fus (need): **I could do with a drink/some help** quelque chose à boire/un peu d'aide ne serait pas de refus; (be connected): **that has nothing to ~ with you** cela ne vous concerne pas; **I won't have anything to ~ with it** je ne veux pas m'en mêler
do without vi s'en passer ♦ vt fus se passer de

dock [dɔk] n dock m; (LAW) banc m des accusés ♦ vi se mettre à quai; (SPACE) s'arrimer; **~er** n docker m; **~yard** n chantier m de construction navale
doctor ['dɔktə*] n médecin m, docteur m; (PhD etc) docteur ♦ vt (drink) frelater; **D~ of Philosophy** n (degree) doctorat m; (person) Docteur m en Droit or Lettres etc, titulaire m/f d'un doctorat
document ['dɔkjumənt] n document m; **~ary** [dɔkju'mentəri] adj documentaire ♦ n documentaire m
dodge [dɔdʒ] n truc m; combine f ♦ vt esquiver, éviter
dodgems ['dɔdʒəmz] (BRIT) npl autos tamponneuses
doe [dəu] n (deer) biche f; (rabbit) lapine f
does [dʌz] vb see do; **~n't** = does not
dog [dɔg] n chien(ne) m ♦ vt suivre de près; poursuivre, harceler; **~ collar** n collier m de chien; (fig) faux-col m d'ecclésiastique; **~-eared** adj corné(e)
dogged ['dɔgɪd] adj obstiné(e), opiniâtre
dogsbody ['dɔgzbɔdɪ] n bonne f à tout faire, tâcheron m

doings ['duːɪŋz] npl activités fpl
do-it-yourself ['duːɪtjə'self] n bricolage m
doldrums ['dɔldrəmz] npl: **to be in the ~** avoir le cafard; (business) être dans le marasme
dole [dəul] n (BRIT: payment) allocation f de chômage; **on the ~** au chômage; **~ out** vt donner au compte-goutte
doleful ['dəulful] adj plaintif(ive), lugubre
doll [dɔl] n poupée f
dollar ['dɔlə*] n dollar m
dolled up ['dɔld-] (inf) adj: **(all) ~** sur son trente et un
dolphin ['dɔlfɪn] n dauphin m
dome [dəum] n dôme m
domestic [də'mestɪk] adj (task, appliances) ménager(ère); (of country: trade, situation etc) intérieur(e); (animal) domestique; **~ated** adj (animal) domestiqué(e); (husband) pantouflard(e)
dominate ['dɔmɪneɪt] vt dominer
domineering [dɔmɪ'nɪərɪŋ] adj dominateur(trice), autoritaire
dominion [də'mɪnɪən] n (territory) territoire m; **to have ~ over** contrôler
domino ['dɔmɪnəu] (pl **~es**) n domino m; **~es** n (game) dominos mpl
don [dɔn] (BRIT) n professeur m d'université
donate [dəu'neɪt] vt faire don de, donner
done [dʌn] pp of do
donkey ['dɔŋkɪ] n âne m
donor ['dəunə*] n (of blood etc) donneur(euse); (to charity) donateur(trice)
don't [dəunt] vb = do not
donut (US) n = doughnut
doodle ['duːdl] vi griffonner, gribouiller
doom [duːm] n destin m ♦ vt: **to be ~ed (to failure)** être voué(e) à l'échec; **~sday** n le Jugement dernier
door [dɔː*] n porte f; (RAIL, car) portière f; **~bell** n sonnette f; **~handle** n poignée f de la porte; (car) poignée de portière; **~man** (irreg) n (in hotel) portier m; **~mat** n paillasson m; **~step** n pas m de (la) porte, seuil m; **~way** n (embrasure f de la) porte f
dope [dəup] n (inf: drug) drogue f; (: person) andouille f ♦ vt (horse etc) doper
dopey ['dəupɪ] (inf) adj à moitié endormi(e)
dormant ['dɔːmənt] adj assoupi(e), en veilleuse
dormitory ['dɔːmɪtrɪ] n dortoir m; (US: building) résidence f universitaire
dormouse ['dɔːmaus, pl 'dɔːmaɪs] (pl **dormice**) n loir m
dose [dəus] n dose f
doss house ['dɔs-] (BRIT) n asile m de nuit
dot [dɔt] n point m; (on material) pois m ♦ vt: **~ted with** parsemé(e) de; **on the ~** à l'heure tapante or pile
dote [dəut]: **to ~ on** vt fus être fou(folle)

de
dot-matrix printer [dɒt'meɪtrɪks-] n imprimante matricielle
dotted line n pointillé(s) m(pl)
double ['dʌbl] adj double ♦ adv (twice): **to cost ~ (sth)** coûter le double (de qch) or deux fois plus (que qch) ♦ n double m ♦ vt doubler; (fold) plier en deux ♦ vi doubler; **~s** n (TENNIS) double m; **on** or (BRIT) **at the ~** au pas de course; **~ bass** (BRIT) n contrebasse f; **~ bed** n grand lit; **~ bend** (BRIT) n virage m en S; **~-breasted** adj croisé(e); **~cross** vt doubler, trahir; **~decker** n autobus m à impériale; **~ glazing** (BRIT) n double vitrage m; **~ room** n chambre f pour deux personnes; **doubly** ['dʌblɪ] adv doublement, deux fois plus
doubt [daut] n doute m ♦ vt douter de; **to ~ that** douter que; **~ful** adj douteux(euse); (person) incertain(e); **~less** adv sans doute, sûrement
dough [dəu] n pâte f; **~nut** (US **donut**) n beignet m
douse [dauz] vt (drench) tremper, inonder; (extinguish) éteindre
dove [dʌv] n colombe f
Dover ['dəuvə*] n Douvres
dovetail ['dʌvteɪl] vi (fig) concorder
dowdy ['daudɪ] adj démodé(e); mal fagoté(e) (inf)
down [daun] n (soft feathers) duvet m ♦ adv en bas, vers le bas; (on the ground) par terre ♦ prep en bas de; (along) le long de ♦ vt (inf: drink, food) s'envoyer; **~ with X!** à bas X!; **~-and-out** n clochard(e); **~-at-heel** adj éculé(e); (fig) miteux(euse); **~cast** adj démoralisé(e); **~fall** n chute f, ruine f; **~hearted** adj découragé(e); **~hill** adv: **to go ~hill** descendre; (fig) péricliter; **~ payment** n acompte m; **~pour** n pluie torrentielle, déluge m; **~right** adj (lie etc) effronté(e); (refusal) catégorique
Down's syndrome [daunz-] n (MED) trisomie f
down: **~stairs** adv au rez-de-chaussée; à l'étage inférieur; **~stream** adv en aval; **~-to-earth** adj terre à terre inv; **~town** adv en ville; **~ under** adv en Australie (or Nouvelle-Zélande); **~ward** adj, adv vers le bas; **~wards** adv vers le bas
dowry ['daurɪ] n dot f
doz. abbr = **dozen**
doze [dəuz] vi sommeiller; **~ off** vi s'assoupir
dozen ['dʌzn] n douzaine f; **a ~ books** une douzaine de livres; **~s of** des centaines de
Dr. abbr = **doctor; drive**
drab [dræb] adj terne, morne
draft [drɑːft] n ébauche f; (of letter, essay etc) brouillon m; (COMM) traite f; (US: call-up) conscription f ♦ vt faire le brouillon

or un projet de; (MIL: send) détacher; see also **draught**
draftsman ['drɑːftsmən] (irreg: US) n = **draughtsman**
drag [dræg] vt traîner; (river) draguer ♦ vi traîner ♦ n (inf) casse-pieds m/f; (women's clothing): **in ~** (en) travesti; **~ on** vi s'éterniser
dragon ['drægən] n dragon m
dragonfly ['drægənflaɪ] n libellule f
drain [dreɪn] n égout m, canalisation f; (on resources) saignée f ♦ vt (land, marshes etc) drainer, assécher; (vegetables) égoutter; (glass) vider ♦ vi (water) s'écouler; **~age** n drainage m; système m d'égouts or de canalisations; **~ing board** (US **~board**) n égouttoir m; **~pipe** n tuyau m d'écoulement
drama ['drɑːmə] n (art) théâtre m, art m dramatique; (play) pièce f (de théâtre); (event) drame m; **~tic** [drə'mætɪk] adj dramatique; spectaculaire; **~tist** ['dræmətɪst] n auteur m dramatique; **~tize** vt (events) dramatiser; (adapt: for TV/cinema) adapter pour la télévision/pour l'écran
drank [dræŋk] pt of **drink**
drape [dreɪp] vt draper; **~s** (US) npl rideaux mpl
drastic ['dræstɪk] adj sévère; énergique; (change) radical(e)
draught [drɑːft] (US **draft**) n courant m d'air; (NAUT) tirant m d'eau; **on ~** (beer) à la pression; **~board** (BRIT) n damier m; **~s** (BRIT) n (jeu m de) dames fpl
draughtsman ['drɑːftsmən] (irreg) n dessinateur(trice) (industriel(le))
draw [drɔː] (pt **drew**, pp **drawn**) vt tirer; (tooth) arracher, extraire; (attract) attirer; (picture) dessiner; (line, circle) tracer; (money) retirer; (wages) toucher ♦ vi (SPORT) faire match nul ♦ n match nul; (lottery) tirage m au sort; loterie f; **to ~ near** s'approcher; **~ out** vi (lengthen) s'allonger ♦ vt (money) retirer; **~ up** vi (stop) s'arrêter ♦ vt (chair) approcher; (document) établir, dresser; **~back** n inconvénient m, désavantage m; **~bridge** n pont-levis m; **~er** [drɔː*] n tiroir m
drawing ['drɔːɪŋ] n dessin m; **~ board** n planche f à dessin; **~ pin** (BRIT) n punaise f; **~ room** n salon m
drawl [drɔːl] n accent traînant
drawn [drɔːn] pp of **draw**
dread [dred] n terreur f, effroi m ♦ vt redouter, appréhender; **~ful** adj affreux(euse)
dream [driːm] (pt, pp **dreamed** or **dreamt**) n rêve m ♦ vt, vi rêver; **~y** adj rêveur(euse); (music) langoureux(euse)
dreary ['drɪərɪ] adj morne; monotone
dredge [dredʒ] vt draguer
dregs [dregz] npl lie f
drench [drentʃ] vt tremper

dress [dres] *n* robe *f*; (*no pl*: *clothing*) habillement *m*, tenue *f* ♦ *vi* s'habiller ♦ *vt* habiller; (*wound*) panser; **to get ~ed** s'habiller; **~ up** *vi* s'habiller; (*in fancy ~*) se déguiser; **~ circle** *n* (*BRIT*) *n* (*THEATRE*) premier balcon; **~er** *n* (*furniture*) vaisselier *m*; (: *US*) coiffeuse *f*, commode *f*; **~ing** *n* (*MED*) pansement *m*; (*CULIN*) sauce *f*, assaisonnement *m*; **~ing gown** (*BRIT*) *n* robe *f* de chambre; **~ing room** (*THEATRE*) loge *f*; (*SPORT*) vestiaire *m*; **~ing table** *n* coiffeuse *f*; **~maker** *n* couturière *f*; **~ rehearsal** *n* (répétition) générale *f*

drew [druː] *pt* of **draw**

dribble ['drɪbl] *vi* (*baby*) baver ♦ *vt* (*ball*) dribbler

dried [draɪd] *adj* (*fruit, beans*) sec(sèche); (*eggs, milk*) en poudre

drier ['draɪə*] *n* = **dryer**

drift [drɪft] *n* (*of current etc*) force *f*; direction *f*, mouvement *m*; (*of snow*) rafale *f*; (: *on ground*) congère *f*; (*general meaning*) sens (général) ♦ *vi* (*boat*) aller à la dérive, dériver; (*sand, snow*) s'amonceler, s'entasser; **~wood** *n* bois flotté

drill [drɪl] *n* perceuse *f*; (~ *bit*) foret *m*, mèche *f*; (*of dentist*) roulette *f*, fraise *f*; (*MIL*) exercice *m* ♦ *vt* percer; (*troops*) entraîner ♦ *vi* (*for oil*) faire un *or* des forage(s)

drink [drɪŋk] (*pt* **drank**, *pp* **drunk**) *n* boisson *f*; (*alcoholic*) verre *m* ♦ *vt, vi* boire; **to have a ~** boire quelque chose, boire un verre; prendre l'apéritif; **a ~ of water** un verre d'eau; **~er** *n* buveur(euse); **~ing water** *n* eau *f* potable

drip [drɪp] *n* goutte *f*; (*MED*) goutte-à-goutte *m inv*; perfusion *f* ♦ *vi* tomber goutte à goutte; (*tap*) goutter; **~-dry** *adj* (*shirt*) sans repassage; **~ping** *n* graisse *f* (de rôti)

drive [draɪv] (*pt* **drove**, *pp* **driven**) *n* promenade *f or* trajet *m* en voiture; (*also: ~way*) allée *f*; (*energy*) dynamisme *m*, énergie *f*; (*push*) effort (concerté), campagne *f* (*push*); (*disk ~*) lecteur *m* de disquettes ♦ *vt* conduire; (*push*) chasser, pousser; (*TECH: motor, wheel*) faire fonctionner; entraîner; (*nail, stake etc*): **to ~ sth into sth** enfoncer qch dans qch ♦ *vi* (*AUT: at controls*) conduire; (: *travel*) aller en voiture; **left-/right-hand ~** conduite *f* à gauche/droite; **to ~ sb mad** rendre qn fou(folle); **to ~ sb home/ to the airport** reconduire qn chez lui/ conduire qn à l'aéroport

drivel ['drɪvl] (*inf*) *n* idioties *fpl*

driver ['draɪvə*] *n* conducteur(trice); (*of taxi, bus*) chauffeur *m*; **~'s license** (*US*) *n* permis *m* de conduire

driveway ['draɪvweɪ] *n* allée *f*

driving ['draɪvɪŋ] *n* conduite *f*; **~ instructor** *n* moniteur *m* d'auto-école; **~ lesson** *n* leçon *f* de conduite; **~ licence** (*BRIT*) *n* permis *m* de conduire; **~ school** *n* auto-école *f*; **~ test** *n* examen *m* du permis de conduire

drizzle ['drɪzl] *n* bruine *f*, crachin *m*

drone [drəʊn] *n* bourdonnement *m*; (*male bee*) faux bourdon

drool [druːl] *vi* baver

droop [druːp] *vi* (*shoulders*) tomber; (*head*) pencher; (*flower*) pencher la tête

drop [drɒp] *n* goutte *f*; (*fall*) baisse *f*; (*also: parachute ~*) saut *m* ♦ *vt* laisser tomber; (*voice, eyes, price*) baisser; (*set down from car*) déposer ♦ *vi* tomber; **~s** *npl* (*MED*) gouttes; **~ off** *vi* (*sleep*) s'assoupir ♦ *vt* (*passenger*) déposer; **~ out** *vi* (*withdraw*) se retirer; (*student etc*) abandonner, décrocher; **~out** *n* marginal(e); **~per** *n* compte-gouttes *m inv*; **~pings** *npl* crottes *fpl*

drought [draut] *n* sécheresse *f*

drove [drəʊv] *pt* of **drive**

drown [draun] *vt* noyer ♦ *vi* se noyer

drowsy ['drauzɪ] *adj* somnolent(e)

drudgery ['drʌdʒərɪ] *n* corvée *f*

drug [drʌg] *n* médicament *m*; (*narcotic*) drogue *f* ♦ *vt* droguer; **to be on ~s** se droguer; **~ addict** *n* toxicomane *m/f*; **~gist** (*US*) *n* pharmacien(ne)-droguiste; **~store** (*US*) *n* pharmacie-droguerie, drugstore *m*

drum [drʌm] *n* tambour *m*; (*for oil, petrol*) bidon *m*; **~s** *npl* (*kit*) batterie *f*; **~mer** *n* (joueur *m* de) tambour *m*

drunk [drʌŋk] *pp* of **drink** ♦ *adj* ivre, soûl(e) ♦ *n* (*also: ~ard*) ivrogne *m/f*; **~en** *adj* (*person*) ivre, soûl(e); (*rage, stupor*) ivrogne, d'ivrogne

dry [draɪ] *adj* sec(sèche); (*day*) sans pluie; (*humour*) pince-sans-rire *inv*; (*lake, riverbed, well*) à sec ♦ *vt* sécher; (*clothes*) faire sécher ♦ *vi* sécher; **~ up** *vi* tarir; **~-cleaner's** *n* teinturerie *f*; **~er** *n* séchoir *m*; (*spin-~er*) essoreuse *f*; **~ness** *n* sécheresse *f*; **~ rot** *n* pourriture sèche (*du bois*)

dual ['djuəl] *adj* double; **~ carriageway** (*BRIT*) *n* route *f* à quatre voies *or* à chaussées séparées; **~ purpose** *adj* à double usage

dubbed [dʌbd] *adj* (*CINEMA*) doublé(e)

dubious ['djuːbɪəs] *adj* hésitant(e), incertain(e); (*reputation, company*) douteux(euse)

duchess ['dʌtʃɪs] *n* duchesse *f*

duck [dʌk] *n* canard *m* ♦ *vi* se baisser vivement, baisser subitement la tête; **~ling** *n* caneton *m*

duct [dʌkt] *n* conduite *f*, canalisation *f*; (*ANAT*) conduit *m*

dud [dʌd] *n* (*object, tool*): **it's a ~** c'est de la camelote, ça ne marche pas ♦ *adj*: **~ cheque** (*BRIT*) chèque sans provision

due [djuː] *adj* dû(due); (*expected*) attendu(e); (*fitting*) qui convient ♦ *n*: **to give sb his** (*or* **her**) **~** être juste envers qn ♦ *adv*: **~ north** droit vers le nord; **~s** *npl* (*for club,* *union*) cotisation *f*; (*in harbour*) droits *mpl* (de port); **in ~ course** en temps utile *or* voulu; finalement; **~ to** dû(due) à; causé(e) par; **he's ~ to finish tomorrow** normalement il doit finir demain

duet [dju:'et] *n* duo *m*

duffel bag [dʌfl] *n* sac *m* marin

duffel coat *n* duffel-coat *m*

dug [dʌg] *pt, pp of* **dig**

duke [dju:k] *n* duc *m*

dull [dʌl] *adj* terne, morne; (*boring*) ennuyeux(euse); (*sound, pain*) sourd(e); (*weather, day*) gris(e), maussade ♦ *vt* (*pain, grief*) atténuer; (*mind, senses*) engourdir

duly ['dju:lɪ] *adv* (*on time*) en temps voulu; (*as expected*) comme il se doit

dumb [dʌm] *adj* muet(te); (*stupid*) bête; **~founded** [dʌm'faundɪd] *adj* sidéré(e)

dummy ['dʌmɪ] *n* (*tailor's model*) mannequin *m*; (*mock-up*) factice *m*, maquette *f*; (*BRIT: for baby*) tétine *f* ♦ *adj* faux(fausse), factice

dump [dʌmp] *n* (*also: rubbish dump*) décharge (publique); (*pej*) trou *m* ♦ *vt* (*put down*) déposer; déverser; (*get rid of*) se débarrasser de; (*COMPUT: data*) vider, transférer

dumpling ['dʌmplɪŋ] *n* boulette *f* (de pâte)

dumpy ['dʌmpɪ] *adj* boulot(te)

dunce [dʌns] *n* âne *m*, cancre *m*

dune [dju:n] *n* dune *f*

dung [dʌŋ] *n* fumier *m*

dungarees [dʌŋgə'ri:z] *npl* salopette *f*; bleu(s) *m(pl)*

dungeon ['dʌndʒən] *n* cachot *m*

duplex ['dju:pleks] (*US*) *n* maison jumelée; (*apartment*) duplex *m*

duplicate [*n* 'dju:plɪkɪt, *vb* 'dju:plɪkeɪt] *n* double *m* ♦ *vt* faire un double de; (*on machine*) polycopier; photocopier; **in ~** en deux exemplaires

durable ['djuərəbl] *adj* durable; (*clothes, metal*) résistant(e), solide

duration [djuə'reɪʃən] *n* durée *f*

duress [djuə'res] *n*: **under ~** sous la contrainte

during ['djuərɪŋ] *prep* pendant, au cours de

dusk [dʌsk] *n* crépuscule *m*

dust [dʌst] *n* poussière *f* ♦ *vt* (*furniture*) épousseter, essuyer; (*cake etc*) **to ~ with** saupoudrer de; **~bin** (*BRIT*) *n* poubelle *f*; **~er** *n* chiffon *m*; **~man** (*BRIT irreg*) *n* boueux *m*, éboueur *m*; **~y** *adj* poussiéreux(euse)

Dutch [dʌtʃ] *adj* hollandais(e), néerlandais(e) ♦ *n* (*LING*) hollandais *m* ♦ *adv* (*inf*): **to go ~** partager les frais; **the ~** *npl* (*people*) les Hollandais; **~man** (*irreg*) *n* Hollandais; **~woman** (*irreg*) *n* Hollandaise *f*

dutiful ['dju:tɪful] *adj* (*child*) respectueux(euse)

duty ['dju:tɪ] *n* devoir *m*; (*tax*) droit *m*, taxe

f; **on ~** de service; (*at night etc*) de garde; **off ~** libre, pas de service *or* de garde; **~-free** *adj* exempté(e) de douane, hors taxe *inv*

duvet ['du:veɪ] (*BRIT*) *n* couette *f*

dwarf [dwɔ:f] (*pl* **dwarves**) *n* nain(e) ♦ *vt* écraser

dwell [dwel] (*pt, pp* **dwelt**) *vi* demeurer; **~ on** *vt fus* s'appesantir sur; **~ing** *n* habitation *f*, demeure *f*

dwindle ['dwɪndl] *vi* diminuer, décroître

dye [daɪ] *n* teinture *f* ♦ *vt* teindre

dying ['daɪɪŋ] *adj* mourant(e), agonisant(e)

dyke [daɪk] (*BRIT*) *n* digue *f*

dynamic [daɪ'næmɪk] *adj* dynamique

dynamite ['daɪnəmaɪt] *n* dynamite *f*

dynamo ['daɪnəməu] *n* dynamo *f*

dyslexia [dɪs'leksɪə] *n* dyslexie *f*

E e

E [i:] *n* (*MUS*) mi *m*

each [i:tʃ] *adj* chaque ♦ *pron* chacun(e); **~ other** l'un(e) l'autre; **they hate ~ other** ils se détestent (mutuellement); **you are jealous of ~ other** vous êtes jaloux l'un de l'autre; **they have 2 books ~** ils ont 2 livres chacun

eager ['i:gə*] *adj* (*keen*) avide; **to be ~ to do sth** avoir très envie de faire qch; **to be ~ for** désirer vivement, être avide de

eagle ['i:gl] *n* aigle *m*

ear [ɪə*] *n* oreille *f*; (*of corn*) épi *m*; **~ache** *n* mal *m* aux oreilles; **~drum** *n* tympan *m*

earl [ɜ:l] (*BRIT*) *n* comte *m*

earlier ['ɜ:lɪə*] *adj* (*date etc*) plus rapproché(e); (*edition, fashion etc*) plus ancien(ne), antérieur(e) ♦ *adv* plus tôt

early ['ɜ:lɪ] *adv* tôt, de bonne heure; (*ahead of time*) en avance; (*near the beginning*) au début ♦ *adj* qui se manifeste (*or* se fait) tôt *or* de bonne heure; (*work*) de jeunesse; (*settler, Christian*) premier(ère); (*reply*) rapide; (*death*) prématuré(e); **to have an ~ night** se coucher tôt *or* de bonne heure; **in the ~ or ~ in the spring/19th century** au début du printemps/19ème siècle; **~ retirement** *n*: **to take ~ retirement** prendre sa retraite anticipée

earmark ['ɪəmɑ:k] *vt*: **to ~ sth for** réserver *or* destiner qch à

earn [ɜ:n] *vt* gagner; (*COMM: yield*) rapporter

earnest ['ɜːnɪst] *adj* sérieux(euse); **in ~** *adv* sérieusement

earnings ['ɜːnɪŋz] *npl* salaire *m*; *(of company)* bénéfices *mpl*

earphones ['ɪəfəʊnz] *npl* écouteurs *mpl*

earring ['ɪərɪŋ] *n* boucle *f* d'oreille

earshot ['ɪəʃɒt] *n*: **within ~** à portée de voix

earth [ɜːθ] *n (gen, also BRIT: ELEC)* terre *f* ♦ *vt* relier à la terre; **~enware** *n* poterie *f*, faïence *f*; **~quake** *n* tremblement *m* de terre, séisme *m*; **~y** ['ɜːθɪ] *adj (vulgar: humour)* truculent(e)

ease [iːz] *n* facilité *f*, aisance *f*; *(comfort)* bien-être *m* ♦ *vt (soothe)* calmer; *(loosen)* relâcher, détendre; **to ~ sth in/out** faire pénétrer/sortir qch délicatement or avec douceur; faciliter la pénétration/la sortie de qch; **at ~!** *(MIL)* repos!; **~ off**, **~ up** *vi* diminuer; *(slow down)* ralentir; **~ up** *vi* = **ease off**

easel ['iːzl] *n* chevalet *m*

easily ['iːzɪlɪ] *adv* facilement

east [iːst] *n* est *m* ♦ *adj (wind)* d'est; *(side)* est *inv* ♦ *adv* à l'est, vers l'est; **the E~** l'Orient *m*; *(POL)* les pays *mpl* de l'Est

Easter ['iːstə*] *n* Pâques *fpl*; **~ egg** *n* œuf *m* de Pâques

east: **~erly** ['iːstəlɪ] *adj (wind)* d'est; *(direction)* est *inv*; *(point)* à l'est; **~ern** ['iːstən] *adj* de l'est, oriental(e); **~ward(s)** ['iːstwəd(z)] *adv* vers l'est, à l'est

easy ['iːzɪ] *adj* facile; *(manner)* aisé(e) ♦ *adv*: **to take it** or **things ~** ne pas se fatiguer; *(not worry)* ne pas se faire; **~ chair** *n* fauteuil *m*; **~-going** *adj* accommodant(e), facile à vivre

eat [iːt] *(pt ate, pp eaten) vt, vi* manger; **~ away** *vt* ronger, attaquer; *(savings)* entamer; **~ into** *vt fus* = **eat away at**

eaves [iːvz] *npl* avant-toit *m*

eavesdrop ['iːvzdrɒp] *vi*: **to ~ (on a conversation)** écouter (une conversation) de façon indiscrète

ebb [eb] *n* reflux *m* ♦ *vi* refluer; *(fig: also:* **~ away**) décliner

ebony ['ebənɪ] *n* ébène *f*

EC *n abbr (= European Community)* C.E. *f*

eccentric [ɪk'sentrɪk] *adj* excentrique ♦ *n* excentrique *m/f*

echo ['ekəʊ] *(pl* **~es**) *n* écho *m* ♦ *vt* répéter ♦ *vi* résonner, faire écho

eclipse [ɪ'klɪps] *n* éclipse *f*

ecology [ɪ'kɒlədʒɪ] *n* écologie *f*

economic [iːkə'nɒmɪk] *adj* économique; *(business etc)* rentable; **~al** *adj* économique; *(person)* économe; **~s** *n* économie *f* politique ♦ *npl (of project, situation)* aspect *m* financier

economize [ɪ'kɒnəmaɪz] *vi* économiser, faire des économies

economy [ɪ'kɒnəmɪ] *n* économie *f*; **~ class** *n* classe *f* touriste; **~ size** *n* format *m* économique

ecstasy ['ekstəsɪ] *n* extase *f*; **ecstatic** *adj* extatique

ECU [eiːkjuː] *n abbr (= European Currency Unit)* ECU *m*

eczema ['eksɪmə] *n* eczéma *m*

edge [edʒ] *n* bord *m*; *(of knife etc)* tranchant *m*, fil *m* ♦ *vt* border; **on ~** *(fig)* crispé(e), tendu(e); **to ~ away from** s'éloigner furtivement de; **~ways** *adv*: **he couldn't get a word in ~ways** il ne pouvait pas placer un mot

edgy ['edʒɪ] *adj* crispé(e), tendu(e)

edible ['edɪbl] *adj* comestible

edict ['iːdɪkt] *n* décret *m*

Edinburgh ['edɪnbərə] *n* Édimbourg

edit ['edɪt] *vt (text, book)* éditer; *(report)* préparer; *(film)* monter; *(broadcast)* réaliser; **~ion** [ɪ'dɪʃən] *n* édition *f*; **~or** *n (of column)* rédacteur(trice); *(of newspaper)* rédacteur(trice) en chef; *(of sb's work)* éditeur(trice); **~orial** [edɪ'tɔːrɪəl] *adj* de la rédaction, éditorial(e) ♦ *n* éditorial *m*

educate ['edjʊkeɪt] *vt (teach)* instruire; *(instruct)* éduquer

education [edjʊ'keɪʃən] *n* éducation *f*; *(studies)* études *fpl*; *(teaching)* enseignement *m*, instruction *f*; **~al** *adj (experience, toy)* pédagogique; *(institution)* scolaire; *(policy)* d'éducation

eel [iːl] *n* anguille *f*

eerie ['ɪərɪ] *adj* inquiétant(e)

effect [ɪ'fekt] *n* effet *m* ♦ *vt* effectuer; **to take ~** *(law)* entrer en vigueur, prendre effet; *(drug)* agir, faire son effet; **in ~** en fait; **~ive** *adj* efficace; *(actual)* véritable; **~ively** *adv* efficacement; *(in reality)* effectivement; **~iveness** *n* efficacité *f*

effeminate [ɪ'femɪnɪt] *adj* efféminé(e)

effervescent [efə'vesnt] *adj (drink)* gazeux(euse)

efficiency [ɪ'fɪʃənsɪ] *n* efficacité *f*; *(of machine)* rendement *m*

efficient [ɪ'fɪʃənt] *adj* efficace; *(machine)* qui a un bon rendement

effort ['efət] *n* effort *m*; **~less** *adj (style)* aisé(e); *(achievement)* facile

effusive [ɪ'fjuːsɪv] *adj* chaleureux(euse)

e.g. *adv abbr (= exempli gratia)* par exemple, p. ex.

egg [eg] *n* œuf *m*; **hard-boiled/soft-boiled ~** œuf dur/à la coque; **~ on** *vt* pousser; **~cup** *n* coquetier *m*; **~plant** *n (esp US)* aubergine *f*; **~shell** *n* coquille *f* d'œuf

ego ['iːgəʊ] *n (self-esteem)* amour-propre *m*

egotism ['egəʊtɪzəm] *n* égotisme *m*

egotist ['egəʊtɪst] *n* égocentrique *m/f*

Egypt ['iːdʒɪpt] *n* Égypte *f*; **~ian** [ɪ'dʒɪpʃən] *adj* égyptien(ne) ♦ *n* Égyptien(ne)

eiderdown ['aɪdədaʊn] *n* édredon *m*

eight [eɪt] *num* huit; **~een** *num* dix-huit; **~h** [eɪtθ] *num* huitième; **~y** *num* quatre-vingt(s)

Eire ['ɛərə] n République f d'Irlande

either ['aɪðə*] adj l'un ou l'autre; (both, each) chaque ♦ pron: ~ (of them) l'un ou l'autre ♦ adv non plus ♦ conj: ~ good or bad ou bon ou mauvais, soit bon soit mauvais; on ~ side de chaque côté; I don't like ~ je n'aime ni l'un ni l'autre; no, I don't ~ moi non plus

eject [ɪ'dʒekt] vt (tenant etc) expulser; (object) éjecter

eke [iːk] : to ~ out vt faire durer

elaborate [adj ɪ'læbərɪt, vb ɪ'læbəreɪt] adj compliqué(e), recherché(e) ♦ vt élaborer ♦ vi: to ~ (on) entrer dans les détails (de)

elapse [ɪ'læps] vi s'écouler, passer

elastic [ɪ'læstɪk] adj élastique ♦ n élastique m; ~ band n élastique m

elated [ɪ'leɪtɪd] adj transporté(e) de joie

elation [ɪ'leɪʃən] n allégresse f

elbow ['elbəʊ] n coude m

elder ['eldə*] adj aîné(e) ♦ n (tree) sureau m; one's ~s ses aînés; ~ly adj âgé(e) ♦ npl: the ~ly les personnes âgées

eldest ['eldɪst] adj, n: the ~ (child) l'aîné(e) (des enfants)

elect [ɪ'lekt] vt élire ♦ adj: the president ~ le président désigné; to ~ to do choisir de faire; ~ion [ɪ'lekʃən] n élection f; ~ioneering [ɪlekʃə'nɪərɪŋ] n propagande électorale, manœuvres électorales; ~or n électeur(trice); ~orate n électorat m

electric [ɪ'lektrɪk] adj électrique; ~al adj électrique; ~ blanket n couverture chauffante; ~ fire (BRIT) n radiateur m électrique; ~ian [ɪlek'trɪʃən] n électricien m

electricity [ɪlek'trɪsɪtɪ] n électricité f

electrify [ɪ'lektrɪfaɪ] vt (RAIL, fence) électrifier; (audience) électriser

electronic [ɪlek'trɒnɪk] adj électronique; ~s n électronique f

elegant ['elɪɡənt] adj élégant(e)

element ['elɪmənt] n (gen) élément m; (of heater, kettle etc) résistance f; ~ary [elɪ'mentərɪ] adj élémentaire; (school, education) primaire

elephant ['elɪfənt] n éléphant m

elevation [elɪ'veɪʃən] n (raising, promotion) avancement m, promotion f; (height) hauteur f

elevator ['elɪveɪtə*] n (in warehouse etc) élévateur m, monte-charge m inv; (US: lift) ascenseur m

eleven [ɪ'levn] num onze; ~ses npl ≈ pause-café f; ~th num onzième

elicit [ɪ'lɪsɪt] vt: to ~ (from) obtenir (de), arracher (à)

eligible ['elɪdʒəbl] adj: to be ~ for remplir les conditions requises pour; an ~ young man/woman un beau parti

elm [elm] n orme m

elongated ['iːlɒŋɡeɪtɪd] adj allongé(e)

elope [ɪ'ləʊp] vi (lovers) s'enfuir (ensemble); ~ment [ɪ'ləʊpmənt] n fugue amoureuse

eloquent ['eləkwənt] adj éloquent(e)

else [els] adv d'autre; something ~ quelque chose d'autre, autre chose; somewhere ~ ailleurs, autre part; everywhere ~ partout ailleurs; nobody ~ personne d'autre; where ~? à quel autre endroit?; little ~ pas grand-chose d'autre; ~where adv ailleurs, autre part

elude [ɪ'luːd] vt échapper à

elusive [ɪ'luːsɪv] adj insaisissable

emaciated [ɪ'meɪsɪeɪtɪd] adj émacié(e), décharné(e)

emancipate [ɪ'mænsɪpeɪt] vt émanciper

embankment [ɪm'bæŋkmənt] n (of road, railway) remblai m, talus m; (of river) berge f, quai m

embark [ɪm'bɑːk] vi embarquer; to ~ on (journey) entreprendre; (fig) se lancer or s'embarquer dans; ~ation [embɑː'keɪʃən] n embarquement m

embarrass [ɪm'bærəs] vt embarrasser, gêner; ~ed adj gêné(e); ~ing adj gênant(e), embarrassant(e); ~ment n embarras m, gêne f

embassy ['embəsɪ] n ambassade f

embedded [ɪm'bedɪd] adj enfoncé(e)

embellish [ɪm'belɪʃ] vt orner, décorer; (fig: account) enjoliver

embers ['embəz] npl braise f

embezzle [ɪm'bezl] vt détourner

embezzlement [ɪm'bezlmənt] n détournement m de fonds

embitter [ɪm'bɪtə*] vt (person) aigrir; (relations) envenimer

embody [ɪm'bɒdɪ] vt (features) réunir, comprendre; (ideas) formuler, exprimer

embossed [ɪm'bɒst] adj (metal) estampé(e); (leather) frappé(e); ~ wallpaper papier gaufré

embrace [ɪm'breɪs] vt embrasser, étreindre; (include) embrasser ♦ vi s'étreindre, s'embrasser ♦ n étreinte f

embroider [ɪm'brɔɪdə*] vt broder; ~y n broderie f

emerald ['emərəld] n émeraude f

emerge [ɪ'mɜːdʒ] vi apparaître; (from room, car) surgir; (from sleep, imprisonment) sortir

emergency [ɪ'mɜːdʒənsɪ] n urgence f; in an ~ en cas d'urgence; ~ cord n sonnette f d'alarme; ~ exit n sortie f de secours; ~ landing n atterrissage forcé; ~ services npl: the ~ services (fire, police, ambulance) les services mpl d'urgence

emergent [ɪ'mɜːdʒənt] adj (nation) en voie de développement; (group) en développement

emery board ['emərɪ-] n lime f à ongles (en carton émerisé)

emigrate ['emɪɡreɪt] vi émigrer

eminent ['emɪnənt] adj éminent(e)

emissions [ɪ'mɪʃənz] *npl* émissions *fpl*

emit [ɪ'mɪt] *vt* émettre

emotion [ɪ'məʊʃən] *n* émotion *f*; ~**al** *adj* (*person*) émotif(ive), très sensible; (*needs, exhaustion*) affectif(ive); (*scene*) émouvant(e); (*tone, speech*) qui fait appel aux sentiments

emotive [ɪ'məʊtɪv] *adj* chargé(e) d'émotion; (*subject*) sensible

emperor ['empərə*] *n* empereur *m*

emphasis ['emfəsɪs] (*pl* **-ases**) *n* (*stress*) accent *m*; (*importance*) insistance *f*

emphasize ['emfəsaɪz] *vt* (*syllable, word, point*) appuyer *or* insister sur; (*feature*) souligner, accentuer

emphatic [ɪm'fætɪk] *adj* (*strong*) énergique, vigoureux(euse); (*unambiguous, clear*) catégorique; ~**ally** [ɪm'fætɪkəlɪ] *adv* avec vigueur *or* énergie; catégoriquement

empire ['empaɪə*] *n* empire *m*

employ [ɪm'plɔɪ] *vt* employer; ~**ee** *n* employé(e); ~**er** *n* employeur(euse); ~**ment** *n* emploi *m*; ~**ment agency** *n* agence *f or* bureau *m* de placement

empower [ɪm'paʊə*] *vt*: **to ~ sb to do** autoriser *or* habiliter qn à faire

empress ['emprɪs] *n* impératrice *f*

emptiness ['emptɪnəs] *n* (*of area, region*) aspect *m* désertique; (*of life*) vide *m*, vacuité *f*

empty ['emptɪ] *adj* vide; (*threat, promise*) en l'air, vain(e) ♦ *vt* vider ♦ *vi* se vider; (*liquid*) s'écouler; ~**-handed** *adj* les mains vides

emulate ['emjʊleɪt] *vt* rivaliser avec, imiter

emulsion [ɪ'mʌlʃən] *n* émulsion *f*; ~ (**paint**) *n* peinture mate

enable [ɪ'neɪbl] *vt*: **to ~ sb to do** permettre à qn de faire

enact [ɪn'ækt] *vt* (*law*) promulguer; (*play*) jouer

enamel [ɪ'næməl] *n* émail *m*; (*also*: ~ **paint**) peinture laquée

enamoured [ɪn'æməd] *adj*: **to be ~ of** être entiché(e) de

encased [ɪn'keɪst] *adj*: ~ **in** enfermé(e) *or* enchâssé(e) dans

enchant [ɪn'tʃɑːnt] *vt* enchanter; ~**ing** *adj* ravissant(e), enchanteur(teresse)

encl. *abbr* = **enclosed**

enclose [ɪn'kləʊz] *vt* (*land*) clôturer; (*space, object*) entourer; (*letter etc*): **to ~ (with)** joindre (à); **please find ~d** veuillez trouver ci-joint

enclosure [ɪn'kləʊʒə*] *n* enceinte *f*

encompass [ɪn'kʌmpəs] *vt* (*include*) contenir, inclure

encore ['ɒŋkɔː*] *excl* bis ♦ *n* bis *m*

encounter [ɪn'kaʊntə*] *n* rencontre *f* ♦ *vt* rencontrer

encourage [ɪn'kʌrɪdʒ] *vt* encourager; ~**ment** *n* encouragement *m*

encroach [ɪn'krəʊtʃ] *vi*: **to ~ (up)on** empiéter sur

encyclop(a)edia [ensaɪkləʊ'piːdɪə] *n* encyclopédie *f*

end [end] *n* (*gen, also*: *aim*) fin *f*; (*of table, street, rope etc*) bout *m*, extrémité *f* ♦ *vt* terminer; (*also*: **bring to an ~, put an ~ to**) mettre fin à ♦ *vi* se terminer, finir; **in the ~** finalement; **on ~** (*object*) debout, dressé(e); **to stand on ~** (*hair*) se dresser sur la tête; **for hours on ~** pendant des heures et des heures; ~ **up** *vi*: **to ~ up in** (*condition*) finir *or* se terminer par; (*place*) finir *or* aboutir à

endanger [ɪn'deɪndʒə*] *vt* mettre en danger

endearing [ɪn'dɪərɪŋ] *adj* attachant(e)

endeavour [ɪn'devə*] (*US* **endeavor**) *n* tentative *f*, effort *m* ♦ *vi*: **to ~ to do** tenter *or* s'efforcer de faire

ending ['endɪŋ] *n* dénouement *m*, fin *f*; (*LING*) terminaison *f*

endive ['endaɪv] *n* chicorée *f*; (*smooth*) endive *f*

endless ['endlɪs] *adj* sans fin, interminable

endorse [ɪn'dɔːs] *vt* (*cheque*) endosser; (*approve*) appuyer, approuver, sanctionner; ~**ment** *n* (*approval*) appui *m*, aval *m*; (*BRIT: on driving licence*) contravention portée au permis de conduire

endow [ɪn'dau] *vt*: **to ~ (with)** doter (de)

endure [ɪn'djʊə*] *vt* supporter, endurer ♦ *vi* durer

enemy ['enɪmɪ] *adj, n* ennemi(e)

energetic [enə'dʒetɪk] *adj* énergique; (*activity*) qui fait se dépenser (physiquement)

energy ['enədʒɪ] *n* énergie *f*

enforce [ɪn'fɔːs] *vt* (*LAW*) appliquer, faire respecter

engage [ɪn'ɡeɪdʒ] *vt* engager; (*attention etc*) retenir ♦ *vi* (*TECH*) s'enclencher, s'engrener; **to ~ in** se lancer dans; ~**d** *adj* (*BRIT: busy, in use*) occupé(e); (*betrothed*) fiancé(e); **to get ~d** se fiancer; ~**d tone** *n* (*TEL*) tonalité *f* occupé *inv or* pas libre; ~**ment** *n* obligation *f*, engagement *m*; rendez-vous *m inv*; (*to marry*) fiançailles *fpl*; ~**ment ring** *n* bague *f* de fiançailles

engaging [ɪn'ɡeɪdʒɪŋ] *adj* engageant(e), attirant(e)

engender [ɪn'dʒendə*] *vt* produire, causer

engine ['endʒɪn] *n* (*AUT*) moteur *m*; (*RAIL*) locomotive *f*; ~ **driver** *n* mécanicien *m*

engineer [endʒɪ'nɪə*] *n* ingénieur *m*; (*BRIT: repairer*) dépanneur *m*; (*NAVY, US RAIL*) mécanicien *m*; ~**ing** [-'nɪərɪŋ] *n* engineering *m*, ingénierie *f*; (*of bridges, ships*) génie *m*; (*of machine*) mécanique *f*

England ['ɪŋɡlənd] *n* Angleterre *f*

English ['ɪŋɡlɪʃ] *adj* anglais(e) ♦ *n* (*LING*) anglais *m*; **the ~** *npl* (*people*) les Anglais; **the ~ Channel** la Manche; ~**man** (*irreg*) *n* Anglais; ~**woman** (*irreg*) *n* Anglaise *f*

engraving [ɪnˈgreɪvɪŋ] *n* gravure *f*

engrossed [ɪnˈgrəust] *adj*: ~ **in** absorbé(e) par, plongé(e) dans

engulf [ɪnˈgʌlf] *vt* engloutir

enhance [ɪnˈhɑːns] *vt* rehausser, mettre en valeur

enjoy [ɪnˈdʒɔɪ] *vt* aimer, prendre plaisir à; (*have: health, fortune*) jouir de; (: *success*) connaître; **to ~ o.s.** s'amuser; **~able** *adj* agréable; **~ment** *n* plaisir *m*

enlarge [ɪnˈlɑːdʒ] *vt* accroître, (*PHOT*) agrandir ♦ *vi*: **to ~ on** (*subject*) s'étendre sur; **~ment** *n* (*PHOT*) agrandissement *m*

enlighten [ɪnˈlaɪtn] *vt* éclairer; **~ed** *adj* éclairé(e); **~ment** *n*: **the E~ment** (*HISTORY*) ≈ le Siècle des lumières

enlist [ɪnˈlɪst] *vt* recruter; (*support*) s'assurer ♦ *vi* s'engager

enmity [ˈenmɪtɪ] *n* inimitié *f*

enormous [ɪˈnɔːməs] *adj* énorme

enough [ɪˈnʌf] *adj, pron*: ~ **time/books** assez *or* suffisamment de temps/livres ♦ *adv*: **big** ~ assez *or* suffisamment grand; **have you got** ~? en avez-vous assez?; **he has not worked** ~ il n'a pas assez *or* suffisamment travaillé; ~ **to eat** assez à manger; ~**!** assez!, ça suffit!; **that's** ~, **thanks** cela suffit *or* c'est assez, merci; **I've had** ~ **of him** j'en ai assez de lui; ... **which, funnily** *or* **oddly** ~ ... qui, chose curieuse

enquire [ɪnˈkwaɪə*] *vt, vi* = **inquire**

enrage [ɪnˈreɪdʒ] *vt* mettre en fureur *or* en rage, rendre furieux(euse)

enrol [ɪnˈrəul] (*US* ~**l**) *vt* inscrire ♦ *vi* s'inscrire; **~ment** (*US* **~lment**) *n* inscription *f*

ensue [ɪnˈsjuː] *vi* s'ensuivre, résulter

ensure [ɪnˈʃuə*] *vt* assurer; garantir; **to ~ that** s'assurer que

entail [ɪnˈteɪl] *vt* entraîner, occasionner

entangled [ɪnˈtæŋgld] *adj*: **to become ~** (**in**) s'empêtrer (dans)

enter [ˈentə*] *vt* (*room*) entrer dans, pénétrer dans; (*club, army*) entrer à; (*competition*) s'inscrire à *or* pour; (*sb for a competition*) (faire) inscrire; (*write down*) inscrire, noter; (*COMPUT*) entrer, introduire ♦ *vi* entrer; ~ **for** *vt fus* s'inscrire à, se présenter pour *or* à; ~ **into** *vt fus* (*explanation*) se lancer dans; (*discussion, negotiations*) entamer; (*agreement*) conclure

enterprise [ˈentəpraɪz] *n* entreprise *f*; (*initiative*) (esprit *m* d')initiative *f*; **free ~** libre entreprise; **private ~** entreprise privée

enterprising [ˈentəpraɪzɪŋ] *adj* entreprenant(e), dynamique; (*scheme*) audacieux(euse)

entertain [entəˈteɪn] *vt* amuser, distraire; (*invite*) recevoir (à dîner); (*idea, plan*) envisager; **~er** *n* artiste *m/f* de variétés; **~ing** *adj* amusant(e), distrayant(e); **~ment** *n* (*amusement*) divertissement *m*, amusement *m*; (*show*) spectacle *m*

enthralled [ɪnˈθrɔːld] *adj* captivé(e)

enthusiasm [ɪnˈθuːzɪæzəm] *n* enthousiasme *m*

enthusiast [ɪnˈθuːzɪæst] *n* enthousiaste *m/f*; **~ic** [ɪnθuːzɪˈæstɪk] *adj* enthousiaste; **to be ~ic about** être enthousiasmé(e) par

entice [ɪnˈtaɪs] *vt* attirer, séduire

entire [ɪnˈtaɪə*] *adj* (tout) entier(ère); **~ly** *adv* entièrement, complètement; **~ty** [ɪnˈtaɪərətɪ] *n*: **in its ~ty** dans sa totalité

entitle [ɪnˈtaɪtl] *vt*: **to ~ sb to sth** donner droit à qch à qn; **~d** *adj* (*book*) intitulé(e); **to be ~d to do** avoir le droit de *or* être habilité à faire

entrance [*n* ˈentrəns, *vb* ɪnˈtrɑːns] *n* entrée *f* ♦ *vt* enchanter, ravir; **to gain ~ to** (*university etc*) être admis à; ~ **examination** *n* examen *m* d'entrée; ~ **fee** *n* (*to museum etc*) prix *m* d'entrée; (*to join club etc*) droit *m* d'inscription; ~ **ramp** (*US*) *n* (*AUT*) bretelle *f* d'accès

entrant [ˈentrənt] *n* participant(e); concurrent(e); (*BRIT: in exam*) candidat(e)

entrenched [ɪnˈtrentʃt] *adj* retranché(e); (*ideas*) arrêté(e)

entrepreneur [ɒntrəprəˈnɜː*] *n* entrepreneur *m*

entrust [ɪnˈtrʌst] *vt*: **to ~ sth to** confier qch à

entry [ˈentrɪ] *n* entrée *f*; (*in register*) inscription *f*; **no ~** défense d'entrer, entrée interdite; (*AUT*) sens interdit; ~ **form** feuille *f* d'inscription; ~ **phone** (*BRIT*) *n* interphone *m*

enunciate [ɪˈnʌnsɪeɪt] *vt* énoncer; (*word*) articuler, prononcer

envelop [ɪnˈveləp] *vt* envelopper

envelope [ˈenvələup] *n* enveloppe *f*

envious [ˈenvɪəs] *adj* envieux(euse)

environment [ɪnˈvaɪərənmənt] *n* environnement *m*; (*social, moral*) milieu *m*; **~al** [ɪnvaɪərənˈmentl] *adj* écologique; du milieu; **~-friendly** *adj* écologique

envisage [ɪnˈvɪzɪdʒ] *vt* (*foresee*) prévoir

envoy [ˈenvɔɪ] *n* (*diplomat*) ministre *m* plénipotentiaire

envy [ˈenvɪ] *n* envie *f* ♦ *vt* envier; **to ~ sb sth** envier qch à qn

epic [ˈepɪk] *n* épopée *f* ♦ *adj* épique

epidemic [epɪˈdemɪk] *n* épidémie *f*

epilepsy [ˈepɪlepsɪ] *n* épilepsie *f*

episode [ˈepɪsəud] *n* épisode *m*

epitome [ɪˈpɪtəmɪ] *n* modèle *m*; **epitomize** [ɪˈpɪtəmaɪz] *vt* incarner

equable [ˈekwəbl] *adj* égal(e); de tempérament égal

equal [ˈiːkwl] *adj* égal(e) ♦ *n* égal(e) ♦ *vt* égaler; ~ **to** (*task*) à la hauteur de; **~ity** [ɪˈkwɒlɪtɪ] *n* égalité *f*; **~ize** *vi* (*SPORT*) égaliser; **~ly** *adv* également; (*just as*) tout aussi

equanimity [ekwəˈnɪmɪtɪ] *n* égalité *f* d'humeur

equate [ɪ'kweɪt] *vt*: **to ~ sth with** comparer qch à; assimiler qch à; **equation** [ɪ'kweɪʒən] *n* (*MATH*) équation *f*

equator [ɪ'kweɪtə*] *n* équateur *m*

equilibrium [iːkwɪ'lɪbrɪəm] *n* équilibre *m*

equip [ɪ'kwɪp] *vt*: **to ~ (with)** équiper (de); **to be well ~ped** (*office etc*) être bien équipé(e); **he is well ~ped for the job** il a les compétences requises pour ce travail; **~ment** *n* équipement *m*; (*electrical etc*) appareillage *m*, installation *f*

equities ['ekwɪtɪz] (*BRIT*) *npl* (*COMM*) actions cotées en Bourse

equivalent [ɪ'kwɪvələnt] *adj*: **~ (to)** équivalent(e) (à) ♦ *n* équivalent *m*

equivocal [ɪ'kwɪvəkəl] *adj* équivoque; (*open to suspicion*) douteux (euse)

era ['ɪərə] *n* ère *f*, époque *f*

eradicate [ɪ'rædɪkeɪt] *vt* éliminer

erase [ɪ'reɪz] *vt* effacer; **~r** *n* gomme *f*

erect [ɪ'rekt] *adj* droit(e) ♦ *vt* construire; (*monument*) ériger; élever; (*tent etc*) dresser; **~ion** [ɪ'rekʃən] *n* érection *f*

ERM *n abbr* (= *Exchange Rate Mechanism*) SME *m*

erode [ɪ'rəud] *vt* éroder; (*metal*) ronger

erotic [ɪ'rɒtɪk] *adj* érotique

err [ɜː*] *vi* (*formal: make a mistake*) se tromper

errand ['erənd] *n* course *f*, commission *f*

erratic [ɪ'rætɪk] *adj* irrégulier(ère); inconstant(e)

error ['erə*] *n* erreur *f*

erupt [ɪ'rʌpt] *vi* entrer en éruption; (*fig*) éclater; **~ion** [ɪ'rʌpʃən] *n* éruption *f*

escalate ['eskəleɪt] *vi* s'intensifier

escalator ['eskəleɪtə*] *n* escalier roulant

escapade [eskə'peɪd] *n* fredaine *f*, équipée *f*

escape [ɪs'keɪp] *n* fuite *f*; (*from prison*) évasion *f* ♦ *vi* s'échapper, fuir; (*from jail*) s'évader; (*fig*) s'en tirer; (*leak*) s'échapper ♦ *vt* échapper à; **to ~ from** (*person*) échapper à; (*place*) s'échapper de; (*fig*) fuir; **escapism** [-ɪzəm] *n* (*fig*) évasion *f*

escort [*n* 'eskɔːt, *vb* ɪs'kɔːt] *n* escorte *f* ♦ *vt* escorter

Eskimo ['eskɪməu] *n* Esquimau(de)

esophagus [iː'sɒfəgəs] (*US*) *n* = **oesophagus**

especially [ɪs'peʃəlɪ] *adv* (*particularly*) particulièrement; (*above all*) surtout

espionage ['espɪənɑːʒ] *n* espionnage *m*

Esquire [ɪs'kwaɪə*] *n*: **J Brown, ~** Monsieur J. Brown

essay ['eseɪ] *n* (*SCOL*) dissertation *f*; (*LITERATURE*) essai *m*

essence ['esəns] *n* essence *f*

essential [ɪ'senʃəl] *adj* essentiel(le); (*basic*) fondamental(e) ♦ *n*: **~s** éléments essentiels; **~ly** *adv* essentiellement

establish [ɪs'tæblɪʃ] *vt* établir; (*business*) fonder, créer; (*one's power etc*) asseoir, affermir; **~ed** *adj* bien établi(e); **~ment** *n* établissement *m*; (*founding*) création *f*; **the E~ment** les pouvoirs établis; l'ordre établi; les milieux dirigeants

estate [ɪs'teɪt] *n* (*land*) domaine *m*, propriété *f*; (*LAW*) biens *mpl*, succession *f*; (*BRIT: also: housing ~*) lotissement *m*, cité *f*; **~ agent** *n* agent immobilier; **~ car** (*BRIT*) *n* break *m*

esteem [ɪs'tiːm] *n* estime *f*

esthetic [ɪs'θetɪk] (*US*) *adj* = **aesthetic**

estimate [*n* 'estɪmət, *vb* 'estɪmeɪt] *n* estimation *f*; (*COMM*) devis *m* ♦ *vt* estimer; **estimation** [estɪ'meɪʃən] *n* opinion *f*; (*calculation*) estimation *f*

estranged [ɪ'streɪndʒd] *adj* séparé(e); dont on s'est séparé(e)

etc. *abbr* (= *et cetera*) etc

etching ['etʃɪŋ] *n* eau-forte *f*

eternal [ɪ'tɜːnl] *adj* éternel(le)

eternity [ɪ'tɜːnɪtɪ] *n* éternité *f*

ethical ['eθɪkəl] *adj* moral(e); **ethics** ['eθɪks] *n* éthique *f* ♦ *npl* moralité *f*

Ethiopia [iːθɪ'əupɪə] *n* Éthiopie *f*

ethnic ['eθnɪk] *adj* ethnique; (*music etc*) folklorique

ethos ['iːθɒs] *n* génie *m*

etiquette ['etɪket] *n* convenances *fpl*, étiquette *f*

Eurocheque ['juərəu'tʃek] *n* eurochèque *m*

Europe ['juərəp] *n* Europe *f*; **~an** [juərə'piːən] *adj* européen(ne) ♦ *n* Européen(ne)

evacuate [ɪ'vækjueɪt] *vt* évacuer

evade [ɪ'veɪd] *vt* échapper à; (*question etc*) éluder; (*duties*) se dérober à; **to ~ tax** frauder le fisc

evaporate [ɪ'væpəreɪt] *vi* s'évaporer; **~d milk** *n* lait condensé non sucré

evasion [ɪ'veɪʒən] *n* dérobade *f*, **tax ~** fraude fiscale

eve [iːv] *n*: **on the ~ of** à la veille de

even ['iːvən] *adj* (*level, smooth*) régulier(ère); (*equal*) égal(e); (*number*) pair(e) ♦ *adv* même; **~ if** même si +*indic*; **~ though** alors même que +*cond*; **~ more** encore plus; **~ so** quand même; **not ~** pas même; **to get ~ with sb** prendre sa revanche sur qn; **~ out** *vi* s'égaliser

evening ['iːvnɪŋ] *n* soir *m*; (*as duration, event*) soirée *f*; **in the ~** le soir; **~ class** *n* cours *m* du soir; **~ dress** *n* tenue *f* de soirée

event [ɪ'vent] *n* événement *m*; (*SPORT*) épreuve *f*; **in the ~ of** en cas de; **~ful** *adj* mouvementé(e)

eventual [ɪ'ventʃuəl] *adj* final(e); **~ity** [ɪventʃu'ælɪtɪ] *n* possibilité *f*, éventualité *f*; **~ly** *adv* finalement

ever ['evə*] *adv* jamais; (*at all times*) toujours; **the best** ~ le meilleur qu'on ait jamais vu; **have you** ~ **seen it?** l'as-tu déjà vu?, as-tu eu l'occasion *or* t'est-il arrivé de le voir?; **why** ~ **not?** mais enfin, pourquoi pas?; ~ **since** *adv* depuis ♦ *conj* depuis que; ~**green** *n* arbre *m* à feuilles persistantes; ~**lasting** *adj* éternel(le)

every ['evrɪ] *adj* chaque; ~ **day** tous les jours, chaque jour; ~ **other/third day** tous les deux/trois jours; ~ **other car** une voiture sur deux; ~ **now and then** de temps en temps; ~**body** *pron* tout le monde, tous *pl*; ~**day** *adj* quotidien(ne); de tous les jours; ~**one** *pron* = **everybody**; ~**thing** *pron* tout; ~**where** *adv* partout

evict [ɪ'vɪkt] *vt* expulser; ~**ion** [ɪ'vɪkʃən] *n* expulsion *f*

evidence ['evɪdəns] *n* (*proof*) preuve(s) *f(pl)*; (*of witness*) témoignage *m*; (*sign*): **to show** ~ **of** présenter des signes de; **to give** ~ témoigner, déposer

evident ['evɪdənt] *adj* évident(e); ~**ly** *adv* de toute évidence; (*apparently*) apparemment

evil ['iːvl] *adj* mauvais(e) ♦ *n* mal *m*

evoke [ɪ'vəuk] *vt* évoquer

evolution [iːvə'luːʃən] *n* évolution *f*

evolve [ɪ'vɔlv] *vt* élaborer ♦ *vi* évoluer

ewe [juː] *n* brebis *f*

ex- [eks] *prefix* ex-

exact [ɪg'zækt] *adj* exact(e) ♦ *vt*: **to** ~ **sth (from)** extorquer qch (à); exiger qch (de); ~**ing** *adj* exigeant(e); (*work*) astreignant(e); ~**ly** *adv* exactement

exaggerate [ɪg'zædʒəreɪt] *vt, vi* exagérer; **exaggeration** [ɪgzædʒə'reɪʃən] *n* exagération *f*

exalted [ɪg'zɔːltɪd] *adj* (*prominent*) élevé(e); (: *person*) haut placé(e)

exam [ɪg'zæm] *n abbr* (*SCOL*) = **examination**

examination [ɪgzæmɪ'neɪʃən] *n* (*SCOL, MED*) examen *m*

examine [ɪg'zæmɪn] *vt* (*gen*) examiner; (*SCOL: person*) interroger; ~**r** *n* examinateur(trice)

example [ɪg'zɑːmpl] *n* exemple *m*; **for** ~ par exemple

exasperate [ɪg'zɑːspəreɪt] *vt* exaspérer; **exasperation** [ɪgzɑːspə'reɪʃən] *n* exaspération *f*, irritation *f*

excavate ['ekskəveɪt] *vt* excaver; **excavation** [ekskə'veɪʃən] *n* fouilles *fpl*

exceed [ɪk'siːd] *vt* dépasser; (*one's powers*) outrepasser; ~**ingly** *adv* extrêmement

excellent ['eksələnt] *adj* excellent(e)

except [ɪk'sept] *prep* (*also:* ~ **for,** ~**ing**) sauf, excepté ♦ *vt* excepter; ~ **if/when** sauf si/quand; ~ **that** sauf que, si ce n'est que; ~**ion** [ɪk'sepʃən] *n* exception *f*; **to take** ~**ion to** s'offusquer de; ~**ional** [ɪk'sepʃənl] *adj* exceptionnel(le)

excerpt ['eksɜːpt] *n* extrait *m*

excess [ek'ses] *n* excès *m*; ~ **baggage** *n* excédent *m* de bagages; ~ **fare** (*BRIT*) *n* supplément *m*; ~**ive** *adj* excessif(ive)

exchange [ɪks'tʃeɪndʒ] *n* échange *m*; (*also:* **telephone** ~) central *m* ♦ *vt*: **to** ~ **(for)** échanger (contre); ~ **rate** *n* taux *m* de change

Exchequer [ɪks'tʃekə*] (*BRIT*) *n*: **the** ~ l'Échiquier *m*, ≈ le ministère des Finances

excise [*n* 'eksaɪz, *vb* ek'saɪz] *n* taxe *f* ♦ *vt* exciser

excite [ɪk'saɪt] *vt* exciter; **to get** ~**d** s'exciter; ~**ment** *n* excitation *f*; **exciting** *adj* passionnant(e)

exclaim [ɪks'kleɪm] *vi* s'exclamer; **exclamation** [eksklə'meɪʃən] *n* exclamation *f*; **exclamation mark** *n* point *m* d'exclamation

exclude [ɪks'kluːd] *vt* exclure

exclusive [ɪks'kluːsɪv] *adj* exclusif(ive); (*club, district*) sélect(e); (*item of news*) en exclusivité; ~ **of VAT** TVA non comprise; **mutually** ~ qui s'excluent l'un(e) l'autre

excruciating [ɪks'kruːʃɪeɪtɪŋ] *adj* atroce

excursion [ɪks'kɜːʃən] *n* excursion *f*

excuse [*n* ɪks'kjuːs, *vb* ɪks'kjuːz] *n* excuse *f* ♦ *vt* excuser; **to** ~ **sb from** (*activity*) dispenser qn de; ~ **me!** excusez-moi!, pardon!; **now if you will** ~ **me,** ... maintenant, si vous (le) permettez ...

ex-directory ['eksdaɪ'rektərɪ] (*BRIT*) *adj* sur la liste rouge

execute ['eksɪkjuːt] *vt* exécuter

execution [eksɪ'kjuːʃən] *n* exécution *f*; ~**er** *n* bourreau *m*

executive [ɪg'zekjutɪv] *n* (*COMM*) cadre *m*; (*of organization, political party*) bureau *m* ♦ *adj* exécutif(ive)

exemplify [ɪg'zemplɪfaɪ] *vt* illustrer; (*typify*) incarner

exempt [ɪg'zempt] *adj*: ~ **from** exempté(e) *or* dispensé(e) de ♦ *vt*: **to** ~ **sb from** exempter *or* dispenser qn de

exercise ['eksəsaɪz] *n* exercice *m* ♦ *vt* exercer; (*patience etc*) faire preuve de; (*dog*) promener ♦ *vi* prendre de l'exercice; ~ **bike** *n* vélo *m* d'appartement; ~ **book** *n* cahier *m*

exert [ɪg'zɜːt] *vt* exercer, employer; **to** ~ **o.s.** se dépenser; ~**ion** [ɪg'zɜːʃən] *n* effort *m*

exhale [eks'heɪl] *vt* exhaler ♦ *vi* expirer

exhaust [ɪg'zɔːst] *n* (*also:* ~ **fumes**) gaz *mpl* d'échappement; (: ~ **pipe**) tuyau *m* d'échappement ♦ *vt* épuiser; ~**ed** *adj* épuisé(e); ~**ion** [ɪg'zɔːstʃən] *n* épuisement *m*; **nervous** ~**ion** fatigue nerveuse; surmenage mental; ~**ive** *adj* très complet(ète)

exhibit [ɪg'zɪbɪt] *n* (*ART*) pièce exposée, objet exposé; (*LAW*) pièce à conviction ♦ *vt* exposer; (*courage, skill*) faire preuve de;

~ion [eksɪ'bɪʃən] n exposition f; (of ill-temper, talent etc) démonstration f

exhilarating [ɪg'zɪləreɪtɪŋ] adj grisant(e); stimulant(e)

exile ['eksaɪl] n exil m; (person) exilé(e) ♦ vt exiler

exist [ɪg'zɪst] vi exister; **~ence** n existence f; **~ing** adj actuel(le)

exit ['eksɪt] n sortie f ♦ vi (COMPUT, THEATRE) sortir; **~ ramp** n (AUT) bretelle f d'accès

exodus ['eksədəs] n exode m

exonerate [ɪg'zɒnəreɪt] vt: **to ~ from** disculper de

exotic [ɪg'zɒtɪk] adj exotique

expand [ɪks'pænd] vt agrandir; accroître ♦ vi (trade etc) se développer, s'accroître; (gas, metal) se dilater

expanse [ɪks'pæns] n étendue f

expansion [ɪks'pænʃən] n développement m, accroissement m

expect [ɪks'pekt] vt (anticipate) s'attendre à, s'attendre à ce que +sub; (count on) compter sur, escompter; (require) demander, exiger; (suppose) supposer; (await, also baby) attendre ♦ vi: **to be ~ing** être enceinte; **~ancy** n (anticipation) attente f; **life ~ancy** espérance f de vie; **~ant mother** n future maman; **~ation** n [ekspek'teɪʃən] n attente f, espérance(s) f(pl)

expedient [ɪks'piːdɪənt] adj indiqué(e), opportun(e) ♦ n expédient m

expedition [ekspɪ'dɪʃən] n expédition f

expel [ɪks'pel] vt chasser, expulser; (SCOL) renvoyer

expend [ɪks'pend] vt consacrer; (money) dépenser; **~able** adj remplaçable; **~iture** [ɪk'spendɪtʃə*] n dépense f; dépenses fpl

expense [ɪks'pens] n dépense f, frais mpl; (high cost) coût m; **~s** npl (COMM) frais mpl; **at the ~ of** aux dépens de; **~ account** n (note f de) frais mpl

expensive [ɪks'pensɪv] adj cher(chère), coûteux(euse); **to be ~** coûter cher

experience [ɪks'pɪərɪəns] n expérience f ♦ vt connaître, faire l'expérience de; (feeling) éprouver; **~d** adj expérimenté(e)

experiment [n ɪks'perɪmənt, vb ɪks'perɪment] n expérience f ♦ vi faire une expérience; **to ~ with** expérimenter

expert ['ekspɜːt] adj expert(e) ♦ n expert m; **~ise** [ekspə'tiːz] n (grande) compétence f

expire [ɪks'paɪə*] vi expirer; **expiry** n expiration f

explain [ɪks'pleɪn] vt expliquer; **explanation** [eksplə'neɪʃən] n explication f; **explanatory** [ɪks'plænətərɪ] adj explicatif(ive)

explicit [ɪks'plɪsɪt] adj explicite; (definite) formel(le)

explode [ɪks'pləʊd] vi exploser

exploit [n 'eksplɔɪt, vb ɪks'plɔɪt] n exploit m ♦ vt exploiter; **~ation** [eksplɔɪ'teɪʃən] n exploitation f

exploratory [eks'plɒrətərɪ] adj (expedition) d'exploration; (fig: talks) préliminaire; **~ operation** n (MED) sondage m

explore [ɪks'plɔː*] vt explorer; (possibilities) étudier, examiner; **~r** n explorateur(trice)

explosion [ɪks'pləʊʒən] n explosion f; **explosive** [ɪks'pləʊzɪv] adj explosif(ive) ♦ n explosif m

exponent [eks'pəʊnənt] n (of school of thought etc) interprète m, représentant m

export [vb eks'pɔːt, n 'ekspɔːt] vt exporter ♦ n exportation f ♦ cpd d'exportation; **~er** n exportateur m

expose [ɪks'pəʊz] vt exposer; (unmask) démasquer, dévoiler; **~d** [ɪks'pəʊzd] adj (position, house) exposé(e)

exposure [ɪks'pəʊʒə*] n exposition f; (publicity) couverture f; (PHOT) (temps m de) pose f; (: shot) pose; **to die from ~** (MED) mourir de froid; **~ meter** n posemètre m

express [ɪks'pres] adj (definite) formel(le), exprès(esse); (BRIT: letter etc) exprès inv ♦ n (train) rapide m; (bus) car m express ♦ vt exprimer; **~ion** [ɪks'preʃən] n expression f; **~ly** adv expressément, formellement; **~way** (US) n (urban motorway) voie f express (à plusieurs files)

exquisite [eks'kwɪzɪt] adj exquis(e)

extend [ɪks'tend] vt (visit, street) prolonger; (building) agrandir; (offer) présenter, offrir; (hand, arm) tendre ♦ vi s'étendre

extension [ɪks'tenʃən] n prolongation f; agrandissement m; (building) annexe f; (to wire, table) rallonge f; (telephone: in offices) poste m; (: in private house) téléphone m supplémentaire

extensive [ɪks'tensɪv] adj étendu(e), vaste; (damage, alterations) considérable: (inquiries) approfondi(e); **~ly** adv: **he's travelled ~ly** il a beaucoup voyagé

extent [ɪks'tent] n étendue f; **to some ~** dans une certaine mesure; **to what ~?** dans quelle mesure?, jusqu'à quel point?; **to the ~ of ...** au point de ...; **to such an ~ that ...** à tel point que ...

extenuating [eks'tenjʊeɪtɪŋ] adj: **~ circumstances** circonstances atténuantes

exterior [eks'tɪərɪə*] adj extérieur(e) ♦ n extérieur m; dehors m

external [eks'tɜːnl] adj externe

extinct [ɪks'tɪŋkt] adj éteint(e)

extinguish [ɪks'tɪŋgwɪʃ] vt éteindre; **~er** n (also: fire ~er) extincteur m

extort [ɪks'tɔːt] vt: **to ~ sth (from)** extorquer qch (à); **~ionate** [ɪks'tɔːʃənɪt] adj exorbitant(e)

extra ['ekstrə] adj supplémentaire, de plus ♦ adv (in addition) en plus ♦ n supplément m; (perk) à-côté m; (THEATRE) figurant(e) ♦ prefix extra...

extract [vb ɪks'trækt, n 'ekstrækt] vt extrai

re; (*tooth*) arracher; (*money, promise*) soutirer ♦ *n* extrait *m*

extracurricular ['ekstrəkə'rɪkjʊlə*] *adj* parascolaire

extradite ['ekstrədaɪt] *vt* extrader

extra: ~**marital** [ekstrə'mærɪtl] *adj* extraconjugal(e); ~**mural** [ekstrə'mjʊərl] *adj* hors faculté *inv*; (*lecture*) public(que); ~**ordinary** [ɪks'trɔːdnrɪ] *adj* extraordinaire

extravagance [ɪks'trævəgəns] *n* prodigalités *fpl*, dépense *f*; (*single act*) folie *f*, dépense excessive; **extravagant** [ɪks'trævəgənt] *adj* extravagant(e); (*in spending: person*) prodigue, dépensier(ère); (*: tastes*) dispendieux(euse)

extreme [ɪks'triːm] *adj* extrême ♦ *n* extrême *m*; ~**ly** *adv* extrêmement

extricate ['ekstrɪkeɪt] *vt*: **to ~ sth (from)** dégager qch (de)

extrovert ['ekstrəvvɜːt] *n* extraverti(e)

eye [aɪ] *n* œil *m* (*pl* yeux); (*of needle*) trou *m*, chas *m* ♦ *vt* examiner; **to keep an ~ on** surveiller; ~**ball** *n* globe *m* oculaire; ~**bath** (*BRIT*) *n* œillère *f* (*pour bains d'œil*); ~**brow** *n* sourcil *m*; ~**brow pencil** *n* crayon *m* à sourcils; ~**drops** *npl* gouttes *fpl* pour les yeux; ~**lash** *n* cil *m*; ~**lid** *n* paupière *f*, ~**liner** *n* eye-liner *m*; ~**opener** *n* révélation *f*; ~**shadow** *n* ombre *f* à paupières; ~**sight** *n* vue *f*; ~**sore** *n* horreur *f*; ~ **witness** *n* témoin *m* oculaire

---

F f

F [ef] *n* (*MUS*) fa *m* ♦ *abbr* = Fahrenheit

fable ['feɪbl] *n* fable *f*

fabric ['fæbrɪk] *n* tissu *m*

fabrication [fæbrɪ'keɪʃən] *n* (*lies*) invention(s) *f(pl)*, fabulation *f*; (*making*) fabrication *f*

fabulous ['fæbjʊləs] *adj* fabuleux(euse); (*inf: super*) formidable

face [feɪs] *n* visage *m*, figure *f*; (*expression*) expression *f*; (*of clock*) cadran *m*; (*of cliff*) paroi *f*; (*of mountain*) face *f*; (*of building*) façade *f* ♦ *vt* faire face à; ~ **down** (*person*) à plat ventre; (*card*) face en dessous; **to lose/save** ~ perdre/sauver la face; **to make** *or* **pull a** ~ faire une grimace; **in the** ~ **of** (*difficulties etc*) face à, devant; **on the** ~ **of it** à première vue; ~ **to** ~ face à face; ~ **up to** *vt fus* faire face à, affronter; ~ **cloth** (*BRIT*) *n* gant *m* de toilette; ~ **cream** *n* crème *f* pour le visage; ~ **lift** *n*

lifting *m*; (*of building etc*) ravalement *m*, retapage *m*; ~ **value** *n* (*of coin*) valeur nominale; **to take sth at** ~ **value** (*fig*) prendre qch pour argent comptant

facilities [fə'sɪlɪtɪz] *npl* installations *fpl*, équipement *m*; **credit** ~ facilités *fpl* de paiement

facing ['feɪsɪŋ] *prep* face à, en face de

facsimile [fæk'sɪmɪlɪ] *n* (*exact replica*) facsimilé *m*; (*fax*) télécopie *f*

fact [fækt] *n* fait *m*; **in** ~ en fait

factor ['fæktə*] *n* facteur *m*

factory ['fæktərɪ] *n* usine *f*, fabrique *f*

factual ['fæktjʊəl] *adj* basé(e) sur les faits

faculty ['fækəltɪ] *n* faculté *f*; (*US: teaching staff*) corps enseignant

fad [fæd] *n* (*craze*) engouement *m*

fade [feɪd] *vi* se décolorer, passer; (*light, sound*) s'affaiblir; (*flower*) se faner

fag [fæg] (*BRIT: inf*) *n* (*cigarette*) sèche *f*

fail [feɪl] *vt* (*exam*) échouer à; (*candidate*) recaler; (*subj: courage, memory*) faire défaut à ♦ *vi* échouer; (*brakes*) lâcher; (*eyesight, health, light*) baisser, s'affaiblir; **to ~ to do sth** (*neglect*) négliger de faire qch; (*be unable*) ne pas arriver *or* parvenir à faire qch; **without** ~ à coup sûr; sans faute; ~**ing** *n* défaut *m* ♦ *prep* faute de; ~**ure** *n* échec *m*; (*person*) raté(e); (*mechanical etc*) défaillance *f*

faint [feɪnt] *adj* faible; (*recollection*) vague; (*mark*) à peine visible ♦ *n* évanouissement *m* ♦ *vi* s'évanouir; **to feel** ~ défaillir

fair [feə*] *adj* équitable, juste, impartial(e); (*hair*) blond(e); (*skin, complexion*) pâle, blanc(blanche); (*weather*) beau(belle); (*good enough*) assez bon(ne); (*sizeable*) considérable ♦ *adv*: **to play** ~ jouer franc-jeu ♦ *n* foire *f*; (*BRIT: fun*~) fête (foraine); ~**ly** *adv* équitablement; (*quite*) assez; ~**ness** *n* justice *f*, équité *f*, impartialité *f*

fairy ['feərɪ] *n* fée *f*; ~ **tale** *n* conte *m* de fées

faith [feɪθ] *n* foi *f*; (*trust*) confiance *f*; (*specific religion*) religion *f*; ~**ful** *adj* fidèle; ~**fully** *adv* see **yours**

fake [feɪk] *n* (*painting etc*) faux *m*; (*person*) imposteur *m* ♦ *adj* faux(fausse) ♦ *vt* simuler; (*painting*) faire un faux de

falcon ['fɔːlkən] *n* faucon *m*

fall [fɔːl] (*pt* fell, *pp* fallen) *n* chute *f*; (*US: autumn*) automne *m* ♦ *vi* tomber; (*price, temperature, dollar*) baisser; ~**s** *npl* (*waterfall*) chute *f* d'eau, cascade *f*; **to** ~ **flat** (*on one's face*) tomber de tout son long, s'étaler; (*joke*) tomber à plat; (*plan*) échouer; ~ **back** *vi* reculer, se retirer; ~ **back on** *vt fus* se rabattre sur; ~ **behind** *vi* prendre du retard; ~ **down** *vi* (*person*) tomber; (*building*) s'effondrer, s'écrouler; ~ **for** *vt fus* (*trick, story etc*) se laisser prendre à;

(*person*) tomber amoureux de; ~ **in** *vi* s'effondrer; (*MIL*) se mettre en rangs; ~ **off** *vi* tomber; (*diminish*) baisser, diminuer; ~ **out** *vi* (*hair, teeth*) tomber; (*MIL*) rompre les rangs; (*friends etc*) se brouiller; ~ **through** *vi* (*plan, project*) tomber à l'eau

fallacy ['fæləsɪ] *n* erreur *f*, illusion *f*

fallout ['fɔːlaʊt] *n* retombées (radioactives); ~ **shelter** *n* abri *m* antiatomique

fallow ['fæləʊ] *adj* en jachère; en friche

false [fɔːls] *adj* faux(fausse); ~ **alarm** *n* fausse alerte; ~ **pretences** *npl*: **under** ~ **pretences** sous un faux prétexte; ~ **teeth** (*BRIT*) *npl* fausses dents

falter ['fɔːltə*] *vi* chanceler, vaciller

fame [feɪm] *n* renommée *f*, renom *m*

familiar [fə'mɪlɪə*] *adj* familier(ère); **to be** ~ **with** (*subject*) connaître

family ['fæmɪlɪ] *n* famille *f* ♦ *cpd* (*business, doctor etc*) de famille; **has he any** ~? (*children*) a-t-il des enfants?

famine ['fæmɪn] *n* famine *f*

famished ['fæmɪʃt] (*inf*) *adj* affamé(e)

famous ['feɪməs] *adj* célèbre; ~**ly** *adv* (*get on*) fameusement, à merveille

fan [fæn] *n* (*folding*) éventail *m*; (*ELEC*) ventilateur *m*; (*of person*) fan *m*, admirateur(trice); (*of team, sport etc*) supporter *m*/*f* ♦ *vt* éventer; (*fire, quarrel*) attiser; ~ **out** *vi* se déployer (en éventail)

fanatic [fə'nætɪk] *n* fanatique *m*/*f*

fan belt *n* courroie *f* de ventilateur

fanciful ['fænsɪful] *adj* fantaisiste

fancy ['fænsɪ] *n* fantaisie *f*, envie *f*; imagination *f* ♦ *adj* (de) fantaisie *inv* ♦ *vt* (*feel like, want*) avoir envie de; (*imagine, think*) imaginer; **to take a** ~ **to** se prendre d'affection pour; s'enticher de; **he fancies her** (*inf*) elle lui plaît; ~ **dress** *n* déguisement *m*, travesti *m*; ~-**dress ball** *n* bal masqué *or* costumé

fang [fæŋ] *n* croc *m*; (*of snake*) crochet *m*

fantastic [fæn'tæstɪk] *adj* fantastique

fantasy ['fæntəzɪ] *n* imagination *f*, fantaisie *f*; (*dream*) chimère *f*

far [fɑː*] *adj* lointain(e), éloigné(e) ♦ *adv* loin; ~ **away** *or* **off** au loin, dans le lointain; **at the** ~ **side/end** à l'autre côté/bout; ~ **better** beaucoup mieux; ~ **from** loin de; **by** ~ de loin, de beaucoup; **go as** ~ **as the farm** allez jusqu'à la ferme; **as** ~ **as I know** pour autant que je sache; **how** ~ **is it to ...?** combien y a-t-il jusqu'à ...?; **how** ~ **have you got?** où en êtes-vous?; ~**away** *adj* lointain(e); (*look*) distrait(e)

farce [fɑːs] *n* farce *f*

farcical ['fɑːsɪkəl] *adj* grotesque

fare [fɛə*] *n* (*on trains, buses*) prix *m* du billet; (*in taxi*) prix de la course; (*food*) table *f*, chère *f*; **half** ~ demi-tarif; **full** ~ plein tarif

Far East *n*: **the** ~ l'Extrême-Orient *m*

farewell [fɛə'wel] *excl* adieu ♦ *n* adieu

farm [fɑːm] *n* ferme *f* ♦ *vt* cultiver; ~**er** *n* fermier(ère); cultivateur(trice); ~**hand** *n* ouvrier(ère) agricole; ~**house** *n* (maison *f* de) ferme *f*; ~**ing** *n* agriculture *f*; (*of animals*) élevage *m*; ~**land** *n* terres cultivées; ~ **worker** *n* = farmhand; ~**yard** *n* cour *f* de ferme

far-reaching ['fɑː'riːtʃɪŋ] *adj* d'une grande portée

fart [fɑːt] (*inf*!) *vi* péter

farther ['fɑːðə*] *adv* plus loin ♦ *adj* plus éloigné(e), plus lointain(e)

farthest ['fɑːðɪst] *superl* of **far**

fascinate ['fæsɪneɪt] *vt* fasciner; **fascinating** *adj* fascinant(e)

fascism ['fæʃɪzəm] *n* fascisme *m*

fashion ['fæʃən] *n* mode *f*; (*manner*) façon *f*, manière *f* ♦ *vt* façonner; **in** ~ à la mode; **out of** ~ démodé(e); ~**able** *adj* à la mode; ~ **show** *n* défilé *m* de mannequins *or* de mode

fast [fɑːst] *adj* rapide; (*clock*): **to be** ~ avancer; (*dye, colour*) grand *or* bon teint *inv* ♦ *adv* vite, rapidement; (*stuck, held*) solidement ♦ *n* jeûne *m* ♦ *vi* jeûner; ~ **asleep** profondément endormi

fasten ['fɑːsn] *vt* attacher, fixer; (*coat*) attacher, fermer ♦ *vi* se fermer, s'attacher; ~**er** *n* attache *f*; ~**ing** *n* = **fastener**

fast food *n* fast food *m*, restauration *f* rapide

fastidious [fæs'tɪdɪəs] *adj* exigeant(e), difficile

fat [fæt] *adj* gros(se) ♦ *n* graisse *f*; (*on meat*) gras *m*; (*for cooking*) matière grasse

fatal ['feɪtl] *adj* (*injury etc*) mortel(le); (*mistake*) fatal(e); ~**ity** [fə'tælɪtɪ] *n* (*road death etc*) victime *f*, décès *m*

fate [feɪt] *n* destin *m*; (*of person*) sort *m*; ~**ful** *adj* fatidique

father ['fɑːðə*] *n* père *m*; ~-**in-law** *n* beau-père *m*; ~**ly** *adj* paternel(le)

fathom ['fæðəm] *n* brasse *f* (= 1828 mm) ♦ *vt* (*mystery*) sonder, pénétrer

fatigue [fə'tiːg] *n* fatigue *f*

fatten ['fætn] *vt, vi* engraisser

fatty ['fætɪ] *adj* (*food*) gras(se) ♦ *n* (*inf*) gros(se)

fatuous ['fætjʊəs] *adj* stupide

faucet ['fɔːsɪt] (*US*) *n* robinet *m*

fault [fɔːlt] *n* faute *f*; (*defect*) défaut *m*; (*GEO*) faille *f* ♦ *vt* trouver des défauts à; **it's my** ~ c'est de ma faute; **to find** ~ **with** trouver à redire *or* à critiquer à; **at** ~ fautif(ive), coupable; ~**y** *adj* défectueux(euse)

fauna ['fɔːnə] *n* faune *f*

faux pas ['fəʊ'pɑː] *n inv* impair *m*, bévue *f*, gaffe *f*

favour ['feɪvə*] (*US* **favor**) *n* faveur *f*; (*help*) service *m* ♦ *vt* (*proposition*) être en faveur de; (*pupil etc*) favoriser; (*team, horse*) donner gagnant; **to do sb a ~** rendre un service à qn; **to find ~ with** trouver grâce aux yeux de; **in ~ of** en faveur de; **~able** *adj* favorable; **~ite** ['feɪvərɪt] *adj, n* favori(te)

fawn [fɔ:n] *n* faon *m* ♦ *adj* (*also:* ~-**coloured**) fauve ♦ *vi:* **to ~ (up)on** flatter servilement

fax [fæks] *n* (*document*) télécopie *f*; (*machine*) télécopieur *m* ♦ *vt* envoyer par télécopie

FBI ['efbi:'aɪ] *n abbr* (*US:* = *Federal Bureau of Investigation*) F.B.I. *m*

fear [fɪə*] *n* crainte *f*, peur *f* ♦ *vt* craindre; **for ~ of** de peur que +*sub*, de peur de +*infin*; **~ful** *adj* craintif(ive); (*sight, noise*) affreux(euse), épouvantable; **~less** *adj* intrépide

feasible ['fi:zəbl] *adj* faisable, réalisable

feast [fi:st] *n* festin *m*, banquet *m*; (*REL: also:* ~ *day*) fête *f* ♦ *vi* festoyer

feat [fi:t] *n* exploit *m*, prouesse *f*

feather ['feðə*] *n* plume *f*

feature ['fi:tʃə*] *n* caractéristique *f*; (*article*) chronique *f*, rubrique *f* ♦ *vt* (*subj: film*) avoir pour vedette(s) ♦ *vi:* **to ~ in** figurer (en bonne place) dans; (*in film*) jouer dans; **~s** *npl* (*of face*) traits *mpl*; ~ **film** *n* long métrage

February ['februərɪ] *n* février *m*

fed [fed] *pt, pp* of **feed**

federal ['fedərəl] *adj* fédéral(e)

fed up *adj:* **to be ~** en avoir marre, en avoir plein le dos

fee [fi:] *n* rémunération *f*; (*of doctor, lawyer*) honoraires *mpl*; (*for examination*) droits *mpl*; **school ~s** frais *mpl* de scolarité

feeble ['fi:bl] *adj* faible; (*pathetic: attempt, excuse*) pauvre; (:*joke*) piteux(euse)

feed [fi:d] (*pt, pp* **fed**) *n* (*of baby*) tétée *f*; (*of animal*) fourrage *m*; pâture *f*; (*on printer*) mécanisme *m* d'alimentation ♦ *vt* (*person*) nourrir; (*BRIT: baby*) donner le sein à; (: *with bottle*) donner le biberon à; (*horse etc*) donner à manger à; (*machine*) alimenter; (*data, information*): **to ~ sth into** fournir qch à; ~ **on** *vt fus* se nourrir de; **~back** *n* feed-back *m inv*; **~ing bottle** (*BRIT*) *n* biberon *m*

feel [fi:l] (*pt, pp* **felt**) *n* sensation *f*; (*impression*) impression *f* ♦ *vt* toucher; (*explore*) tâter, palper; (*cold, pain*) sentir; (*grief, anger*) ressentir, éprouver; (*think, believe*) trouver; **to ~ hungry/cold** avoir faim/froid; **to ~ lonely/better** se sentir seul/mieux; **I don't ~ well** je ne me sens pas bien; **it ~s soft** c'est doux(douce) au toucher; **to ~ like** (*want*) avoir envie de; ~ **about** *vi* fouiller, tâtonner; ~**er** *n* (*of insect*) antenne *f*; **to put out ~ers** *or* **a ~er** tâter le terrain; **~ing** *n* (*physical*) sensation *f*; (*emotional*) sentiment *m*

feet [fi:t] *npl of* **foot**

feign [feɪn] *vt* feindre, simuler

fell [fel] *pt of* **fall** ♦ *vt* (*tree, person*) abattre

fellow ['feləʊ] *n* type *m*; (*comrade*) compagnon *m*; (*of learned society*) membre *m* ♦ *cpd:* **their ~ prisoners/students** leurs camarades prisonniers/d'étude; ~ **citizen** *n* concitoyen(ne) *m/f*; ~ **countryman** (*irreg*) *n* compatriote *m*; ~ **men** *npl* semblables *mpl*; **~ship** *n* (*society*) association *f*; (*comradeship*) amitié *f*, camaraderie *f*; (*grant*) sorte de bourse universitaire

felony ['felənɪ] *n* crime *m*, forfait *m*

felt [felt] *pt, pp of* **feel** ♦ *n* feutre *m*; **~-tip pen** *n* stylo-feutre *m*

female ['fi:meɪl] *n* (*ZOOL*) femelle *f*; (*pej: woman*) bonne femme ♦ *adj* (*BIO*) femelle; (*sex, character*) féminin(e); (*vote etc*) des femmes

feminine ['femɪnɪn] *adj* féminin(e)

feminist ['femɪnɪst] *n* féministe *m/f*

fence [fens] *n* barrière *f* ♦ *vt* (*also:* ~ **in**) clôturer ♦ *vi* faire de l'escrime; **fencing** ['fensɪŋ] *n* escrime *m*

fend [fend] *vi:* **to ~ for o.s.** se débrouiller (tout seul); ~ **off** *vt* (*attack etc*) parer

fender ['fendə*] *n* garde-feu *m inv*; (*on boat*) défense *f*; (*US: of car*) aile *f*

ferment [*vb* fə'ment, *n* 'f3:ment] *vi* fermenter ♦ *n* agitation *f*, effervescence *f*

fern [f3:n] *n* fougère *f*

ferocious [fə'rəʊʃəs] *adj* féroce

ferret ['ferɪt] *n* furet *m*

ferry ['ferɪ] *n* (*small*) bac *m*; (*large: also:* ~**boat**) ferry(-boat) *m* ♦ *vt* transporter

fertile ['f3:taɪl] *adj* fertile; (*BIO*) fécond(e); **fertilizer** ['f3:tɪlaɪzə*] *n* engrais *m*

fester ['festə*] *vi* suppurer

festival ['festɪvəl] *n* (*REL*) fête *f*; (*ART, MUS*) festival *m*

festive ['festɪv] *adj* de fête; **the ~ season** (*BRIT: Christmas*) la période des fêtes; **festivities** [fes'tɪvɪtɪz] *npl* réjouissances *fpl*

festoon [fes'tu:n] *vt:* **to ~ with** orner de

fetch [fetʃ] *vt* aller chercher; (*sell for*) rapporter

fetching ['fetʃɪŋ] *adj* charmant(e)

fête [feɪt] *n* fête *f*, kermesse *f*

fetish ['fetɪʃ] *n:* **to make a ~ of** être obsédé(e) par

feud [fju:d] *n* dispute *f*, dissension *f*

fever ['fi:və*] *n* fièvre *f*; **~ish** *adj* fiévreux(euse), fébrile

few [fju:] *adj* (*not many*) peu de; **a ~** *adj* quelques ♦ *pron* quelques-uns(unes); **~er** *adj* moins de; moins (nombreux); **~est** *adj* le moins (de)

fiancé, e [fɪ'ɑ:nseɪ] *n* fiancé(e) *m/f*

fib [fɪb] *n* bobard *m*

fibre ['faɪbə*] (*US* **fiber**) *n* fibre *f*; **~-glass** (®) *n* fibre de verre

fickle ['fɪkl] *adj* inconstant(e), volage, capricieux(euse)

fiction ['fɪkʃən] *n* romans *mpl*, littérature *f*

romanesque; (*invention*) fiction *f*; ~**al** *adj* fictif(ive)

fictitious [fɪk'tɪʃəs] *adj* fictif(ive), imaginaire

fiddle ['fɪdl] *n* (*MUS*) violon *m*; (*cheating*) combine *f*; escroquerie *f* ♦ *vt* (*BRIT: accounts*) falsifier, maquiller; ~ **with** *vt fus* tripoter

fidget ['fɪdʒɪt] *vi* se trémousser, remuer

field [fiːld] *n* champ *m*; (*fig*) domaine *m*, champ; (*SPORT: ground*) terrain *m*; ~ **marshal** *n* maréchal *m*; ~**work** *n* travaux *mpl* pratiques (sur le terrain)

fiend [fiːnd] *n* démon *m*; ~**ish** *adj* diabolique, abominable

fierce [fɪəs] *adj* (*look, animal*) féroce, sauvage; (*wind, attack, person*) (très) violent(e); (*fighting, enemy*) acharné(e)

fiery ['faɪərɪ] *adj* ardent(e), brûlant(e); (*temperament*) fougueux(euse)

fifteen [fɪf'tiːn] *num* quinze

fifth [fɪfθ] *num* cinquième

fifty ['fɪftɪ] *num* cinquante; ~-**fifty** *adj*: a ~-**fifty chance** *etc* une chance *etc* sur deux ♦ *adv* moitié-moitié

fig [fɪg] *n* figue *f*

fight [faɪt] (*pt, pp* **fought**) *n* (*MIL*) combat *m*; (*between persons*) bagarre *f*; (*against cancer etc*) lutte *f* ♦ *vt* se battre contre; (*cancer, alcoholism, emotion*) combattre, lutter contre; (*election*) se présenter à ♦ *vi* se battre; ~**er** *n* (*fig*) lutteur *m*; (*plane*) chasseur *m*; ~**ing** *n* combats *mpl* (*brawl*) bagarres *fpl*

figment ['fɪgmənt] *n*: a ~ **of the imagination** une invention

figurative ['fɪgərətɪv] *adj* figuré(e)

figure ['fɪgə*] *n* figure *f*; (*number, cipher*) chiffre *m*; (*body, outline*) silhouette *f*; (*shape*) ligne *f*, formes *fpl* ♦ *vt* (*think: esp US*) supposer ♦ *vi* (*appear*) figurer; ~ **out** *vt* (*work out*) calculer; ~**head** *n* (*NAUT*) figure *f* de proue; (*pej*) prête-nom *m*; ~ **of speech** *n* figure *f* de rhétorique

file [faɪl] *n* (*dossier*) dossier *m*; (*folder*) dossier, chemise *f*; (: *with hinges*) classeur *m*; (*COMPUT*) fichier *m*; (*row*) file *f*; (*tool*) lime *f* ♦ *vt* (*nails, wood*) limer; (*papers*) classer; (*LAW: claim*) faire enregistrer; déposer ♦ *vi*: to ~ **in/out** entrer/sortir l'un derrière l'autre; to ~ **for divorce** faire une demande en divorce; **filing cabinet** *n* classeur *m* (*meuble*)

fill [fɪl] *vt* remplir; (*need*) répondre à ♦ *n*: to **eat one's** ~ manger à sa faim; to ~ **with** remplir de; ~ **in** *vt* (*hole*) boucher; (*form*) remplir; ~ **up** *vt* remplir; ~ **it up, please** (*AUT*) le plein, s'il vous plaît

fillet ['fɪlɪt] *n* filet *m*; ~ **steak** *n* filet *m* de bœuf, tournedos *m*

filling ['fɪlɪŋ] *n* (*CULIN*) garniture *f*, farce *f*; (*for tooth*) plombage *m*; ~ **station** *n*

station-service *f*

film [fɪlm] *n* film *m*; (*PHOT*) pellicule *f*, film; (*of powder, liquid*) couche *f*, pellicule ♦ *vt* (*scene*) filmer ♦ *vi* tourner; ~ **star** *n* vedette *f* de cinéma

filter ['fɪltə*] *n* filtre *m* ♦ *vt* filtrer; ~ **lane** *n* (*AUT*) voie *f* de sortie; ~-**tipped** *adj* à bout filtre

filth [fɪlθ] *n* saleté *f*; ~**y** *adj* sale, dégoûtant(e); (*language*) ordurier(ère)

fin [fɪn] *n* (*of fish*) nageoire *f*

final ['faɪnl] *adj* final(e); (*definitive*) définitif(ive) ♦ *n* (*SPORT*) finale *f*; ~**s** *npl* (*SCOL*) examens *mpl* de dernière année; ~**e** [fɪ'nɑːlɪ] *n* finale *m*; ~**ize** *vt* mettre au point; ~**ly** *adv* (*eventually*) enfin, finalement; (*lastly*) en dernier lieu

finance [faɪ'næns] *n* finance *f* ♦ *vt* financer; ~**s** *npl* (*financial position*) finances *fpl*; **financial** [faɪ'nænʃəl] *adj* financier(ère)

find [faɪnd] (*pt, pp* **found**) *vt* trouver; (*lost object*) retrouver ♦ *n* trouvaille *f*, découverte *f*; to ~ **sb guilty** (*LAW*) déclarer qn coupable; ~ **out** *vt* (*truth, secret*) découvrir; (*person*) démasquer ♦ *vi*: to ~ **out about** (*make enquiries*) se renseigner; (*by chance*) apprendre; ~**ings** *npl* (*LAW*) conclusions *fpl*, verdict *m*; (*of report*) conclusions

fine [faɪn] *adj* (*excellent*) excellent(e); (*thin, not coarse, subtle*) fin(e); (*weather*) beau(belle) ♦ *adv* (*well*) très bien ♦ *n* (*LAW*) amende *f*; contravention *f* ♦ *vt* (*LAW*) condamner à une amende; donner une contravention à; to **be** ~ (*person*) aller bien; (*weather*) être beau; ~ **arts** *npl* beaux-arts *mpl*

finery ['faɪnərɪ] *n* parure *f*

finger ['fɪŋgə*] *n* doigt *m* ♦ *vt* palper, toucher; **little** ~ auriculaire *m*, petit doigt; **index** ~ index *m*; ~**nail** *n* ongle *m* (de la main); ~**print** *n* empreinte digitale; ~**tip** *n* bout *m* du doigt

finicky ['fɪnɪkɪ] *adj* tatillon(ne), méticuleux(euse); minutieux(euse)

finish ['fɪnɪʃ] *n* fin *f*; (*SPORT*) arrivée *f*; (*polish etc*) finition *f* ♦ *vt* finir, terminer ♦ *vi* finir, se terminer; to ~ **doing sth** finir de faire qch; to ~ **third** arriver *or* terminer troisième; ~ **off** *vt* finir, terminer; (*kill*) achever; ~ **up** *vi*, *vt* finir; ~**ing line** *n* ligne *f* d'arrivée; ~**ing school** *n* institution privée (*pour jeunes filles*)

finite ['faɪnaɪt] *adj* fini(e); (*verb*) conjugué(e)

Finland ['fɪnlənd] *n* Finlande *f*

Finn [fɪn] *n* Finnois(e); Finlandais(e); ~**ish** *adj* finnois(e); finlandais(e) ♦ *n* (*LING*) finnois *m*

fir [fɜː*] *n* sapin *m*

fire [faɪə*] *n* feu *m*; (*accidental*) incendie *m*; (*heater*) radiateur *m* ♦ *vt* (*discharge*): to ~ **a gun** tirer un coup de feu; (*fig*) enflammer, animer; (*inf: dismiss*) mettre à la porte, renvoyer ♦ *vi* (*shoot*) tirer, faire feu; **on ~** en feu; **~ alarm** *n* avertisseur *m* d'incendie; **~arm** *n* arme *f* à feu; **~ brigade** *n* (sapeurs-)pompiers *mpl*; **~ department** (*US*) *n* = **fire brigade**; **~ engine** *n* (*vehicle*) voiture *f* des pompiers; **~ escape** *n* escalier *m* de secours; **~ extinguisher** *n* extincteur *m*; **~man** *n* pompier *m*; **~place** *n* cheminée *f*; **~side** *n* foyer *m*, coin *m* du feu; **~ station** *n* caserne *f* de pompiers; **~wood** *n* bois *m* de chauffage; **~works** *npl* feux *mpl* d'artifice; (*display*) feu(x) d'artifice

firing squad ['faɪərɪŋ-] *n* peloton *m* d'exécution

firm [fɜːm] *adj* ferme ♦ *n* compagnie *f*, firme *f*

first [fɜːst] *adj* premier(ère) ♦ *adv* (*before all others*) le premier, la première; (*before all other things*) en premier, d'abord; (*when listing reasons etc*) en premier lieu, premièrement ♦ *n* (*person: in race*) premier(ère); (*BRIT: SCOL*) mention *f* très bien; (*AUT*) première *f*; **at ~** au commencement, au début; **~ of all** tout d'abord, pour commencer; **~ aid** *n* premiers secours *or* soins; **~-aid kit** *n* trousse *f* à pharmacie; **~-class** *adj* de première classe; (*excellent*) excellent(e), exceptionnel(le); **~-hand** *adj* de première main; **~ lady** (*US*) *n* femme *f* du président; **~ly** *adv* premièrement, en premier lieu; **~ name** *n* prénom *m*; **~-rate** *adj* excellent(e)

fish [fɪʃ] *n inv* poisson *m* ♦ *vt*, *vi* pêcher; **to go ~ing** aller à la pêche; **~erman** *n* pêcheur *m*; **~ farm** *n* établissement *m* piscicole; **~ fingers** (*BRIT*) *npl* bâtonnets de poisson (congelés); **~ing boat** *n* barque *f* *or* bateau *m* de pêche; **~ing line** *n* ligne *f* (de pêche); **~ing rod** *n* canne *f* à pêche; **~monger's (shop)** *n* poissonnerie *f*; **~ sticks** (*US*) *npl* = **fish fingers**; **~y** (*inf*) *adj* suspect(e), louche

fist [fɪst] *n* poing *m*

fit [fɪt] *adj* (*healthy*) en (bonne) forme; (*proper*) convenable; approprié(e) ♦ *vt* (*subj: clothes*) aller à; (*put in, attach*) installer, poser; adapter; (*equip*) équiper, garnir, munir; (*suit*) convenir à ♦ *vi* (*clothes*) aller; (*parts*) s'adapter; (*in space, gap*) entrer, s'adapter ♦ *n* (*MED*) accès *m*, crise *f*; (*of anger*) accès; (*of hysterics, jealousy*) crise; **~ to** en état de; **~ for** digne de; apte à; **~ of coughing** quinte *f* de toux; **a ~ of giggles** le fou rire; **this dress is a good ~** cette robe (me) va très bien; **by ~s and starts** par à-coups; **~ in** *vi* s'accorder; s'adapter; **~ful** *adj* (*sleep*) agité(e); **~ment** *n* meuble encastré, élément *m*; **~ness** *n* (*MED*) forme *f* physique; **~ted carpet** *n* moquette *f*; **~ted kitchen** (*BRIT*) *n* cuisine équipée; **~ter** *n* monteur

m; **~ting** *adj* approprié(e) ♦ *n* (*of dress*) essayage *m*; (*of piece of equipment*) pose *f*, installation *f*; **~tings** *npl* (*in building*) installations *fpl*; **~ting room** *n* cabine *f* d'essayage

five [faɪv] *num* cinq; **~r** (*BRIT*) *n* billet *m* de cinq livres; (*US*) billet *m* de cinq dollars

fix [fɪks] *vt* (*date, amount etc*) fixer; (*organize*) arranger; (*mend*) réparer; (*meal, drink*) préparer ♦ *n*: **to be in a ~** être dans le pétrin; **~ up** *vt* (*meeting*) arranger; **to ~ sb up with sth** faire avoir qch à qn; **~ation** [fɪkˈseɪʃən] *n* (*PSYCH*) fixation *f*; (*fig*) obsession *f*; **~ed** [fɪkst] *adj* (*prices etc*) fixe; (*smile*) figé(e); **~ture** [ˈfɪkstʃə*] *n* installation *f* (fixe); (*SPORT*) rencontre *f* (au programme)

fizzle [ˈfɪzl] *vi*: **~ out** *vi* (*interest*) s'estomper; (*strike, film*) se terminer en queue de poisson

fizzy [ˈfɪzɪ] *adj* pétillant(e); gazeux(euse)

flabbergasted [ˈflæbəɡɑːstɪd] *adj* sidéré(e), ahuri(e)

flabby [ˈflæbɪ] *adj* mou(molle)

flag [flæɡ] *n* drapeau *m*; (*also: ~stone*) dalle *f* ♦ *vi* faiblir; fléchir; **~ down** *vt* héler, faire signe (de s'arrêter) à; **~pole** [ˈflæɡpəul] *n* mât *m*; **~ship** *n* vaisseau *m* amiral; (*fig*) produit *m* vedette

flair [flɛə*] *n* flair *m*

flak [flæk] *n* (*MIL*) tir antiaérien; (*inf: criticism*) critiques *fpl*

flake [fleɪk] *n* (*of rust, paint*) écaille *f*; (*of snow, soap powder*) flocon *m* ♦ *vi* (*also: ~ off*) s'écailler

flamboyant [flæmˈbɔɪənt] *adj* flamboyant(e), éclatant(e); (*person*) haut(e) en couleur

flame [fleɪm] *n* flamme *f*

flamingo [fləˈmɪŋɡəu] *n* flamant *m* (rose)

flammable [ˈflæməbl] *adj* inflammable

flan [flæn] (*BRIT*) *n* tarte *f*

flank [flæŋk] *n* flanc *m* ♦ *vt* flanquer

flannel [ˈflænl] *n* (*fabric*) flanelle *f*; (*BRIT: also: face ~*) gant *m* de toilette; **~s** *npl* (*trousers*) pantalon *m* de flanelle

flap [flæp] *n* (*of pocket, envelope*) rabat *m* ♦ *vt* (*wings*) battre (de) ♦ *vi* (*sail, flag*) claquer; (*inf: also: be in a ~*) paniquer

flare [flɛə*] *n* (*signal*) signal lumineux; (*in skirt etc*) évasement *m*; **~ up** *vi* s'embraser; (*fig: person*) se mettre en colère, s'emporter; (: *revolt etc*) éclater

flash [flæʃ] *n* éclair *m*; (*also: news ~*) flash *m* (d'information); (*PHOT*) flash *m* ♦ *vt* (*light*) projeter; (*send: message*) câbler; (*look*) jeter; (*smile*) lancer ♦ *vi* (*light*) clignoter; **a ~ of lightning** un éclair; **in a ~** en un clin d'œil; **to ~ one's headlights** faire un appel de phares; **to ~ by** *or* **past** (*person*) passer comme un éclair (devant); **~bulb** *n* ampoule *f* de flash; **~cube** *n* cube-flash *m*; **~light** *n* lampe *f* de poche

flashy ['flæʃɪ] (*pej*) *adj* tape-à-l'œil *inv*, tapageur(euse)

flask [flɑːsk] *n* flacon *m*, bouteille *f*; (**vacuum**) ~ **thermos** *m* or *f* ®

flat [flæt] *adj* plat(e); (*tyre*) dégonflé(e), à plat; (*beer*) éventé(e); (*denial*) catégorique; (*MUS*) bémol *inv*; (: *voice*) faux(fausse); (*fee, rate*) fixe ♦ *n* (*BRIT: apartment*) appartement *m*; (*AUT*) crevaison *f*; (*MUS*) bémol *m*; **to work ~ out** travailler d'arrache-pied; ~**ly** *adv* catégoriquement; ~**ten** *vt* (*also*: ~**ten out**) aplatir; (*crop*) coucher; (*building(s)*) raser

flatter ['flætə*] *vt* flatter; ~**ing** *adj* flatteur(euse); ~**y** *n* flatterie *f*

flaunt [flɔːnt] *vt* faire étalage de

flavour ['fleɪvə*] (*US* **flavor**) *n* goût *m*, saveur *f*; (*of ice cream etc*) parfum *m* ♦ *vt* parfumer; **vanilla-flavoured** à l'arôme de vanille, à la vanille; ~**ing** *n* arôme *m*

flaw [flɔː] *n* défaut *m*; ~**less** *adj* sans défaut

flax [flæks] *n* lin *m*; ~**en** *adj* blond(e)

flea [fliː] *n* puce *f*

fleck [flɛk] *n* tacheture *f*; moucheture *f*

flee [fliː] (*pt, pp* **fled**) *vt* fuir ♦ *vi* fuir, s'enfuir

fleece [fliːs] *n* toison *f* ♦ *vt* (*inf*) voler, filouter

fleet [fliːt] *n* flotte *f*; (*of lorries etc*) parc *m*, convoi *m*

fleeting ['fliːtɪŋ] *adj* fugace, fugitif(ive); (*visit*) très bref(brève)

Flemish ['flɛmɪʃ] *adj* flamand(e)

flesh [flɛʃ] *n* chair *f*; ~ **wound** *n* blessure superficielle

flew [fluː] *pt of* **fly**

flex [flɛks] *n* fil *m* or câble *m* électrique ♦ *vt* (*knee*) fléchir; (*muscles*) tendre

flexible *adj* flexible

flick [flɪk] *n* petite tape; chiquenaude *f*; (*of duster*) petit coup ♦ *vt* donner un petit coup à; (*switch*) appuyer sur; ~ **through** *vt fus* feuilleter

flicker ['flɪkə*] *vi* (*light*) vaciller; **his eyelids** ~**ed** il a cillé

flier ['flaɪə*] *n* aviateur *m*

flight [flaɪt] *n* vol *m*; (*escape*) fuite *f*; (*also*: ~ **of steps**) escalier *m*; ~ **attendant** (*US*) *n* steward *m*, hôtesse *f* de l'air; ~ **deck** *n* (*AVIAT*) poste *m* de pilotage; (*NAUT*) pont *m* d'envol

flimsy ['flɪmzɪ] *adj* peu solide; (*clothes*) trop léger(ère); (*excuse*) pauvre, mince

flinch [flɪntʃ] *vi* tressaillir; **to ~ from** se dérober à, reculer devant

fling [flɪŋ] (*pt, pp* **flung**) *vt* jeter, lancer

flint [flɪnt] *n* silex *m*; (*in lighter*) pierre *f* (à briquet)

flip [flɪp] *vt* (*throw*) lancer (d'une chiquenaude); **to ~ a coin** jouer à pile ou face; **to ~ sth over** retourner qch

flippant ['flɪpənt] *adj* désinvolte, irrévérencieux(euse)

flipper ['flɪpə*] *n* (*of seal etc*) nageoire *f*; (*for swimming*) palme *f*

flirt [flɜːt] *vi* flirter ♦ *n* flirteur(euse) *m/f*

flit [flɪt] *vi* voleter

float [fləʊt] *n* flotteur *m*; (*in procession*) char *m*; (*money*) réserve *f* ♦ *vi* flotter

flock [flɒk] *n* troupeau *m*; (*of birds*) vol *m*; (*REL*) ouailles *fpl* ♦ *vi*: **to ~ to** se rendre en masse à

flog [flɒg] *vt* fouetter

flood [flʌd] *n* inondation *f*; (*of letters, refugees etc*) flot *m* ♦ *vt* inonder ♦ *vi* (*people*): **to ~ into** envahir; ~**ing** *n* inondation *f*; ~**light** *n* projecteur *m*

floor [flɔː*] *n* sol *m*; (*storey*) étage *m*; (*of sea, valley*) fond *m* ♦ *vt* (*subj: question*) décontenancer; (: *blow*) terrasser; **on the ~** par terre; **ground ~**, (*US*) **first ~** rez-de-chaussée *m inv*; **first ~**, (*US*) **second ~** premier étage; ~**board** *n* planche *f* (du plancher); ~ **show** *n* spectacle *m* de variétés

flop [flɒp] *n* fiasco *m* ♦ *vi* être un fiasco; (*fall: into chair*) s'affaler, s'effondrer

floppy ['flɒpɪ] *adj* lâche, flottant(e); ~ (**disk**) *n* (*COMPUT*) disquette *f*

flora ['flɔːrə] *n* flore *f*

floral ['flɔːrəl] *adj* (*dress*) à fleurs

florid ['flɒrɪd] *adj* (*complexion*) coloré(e); (*style*) plein(e) de fioritures

florist ['flɒrɪst] *n* fleuriste *m/f*

flounce [flaʊns] **to ~ out** *vi* sortir dans un mouvement d'humeur

flounder ['flaʊndə*] *vi* patauger ♦ *n* (*ZOOL*) flet *m*

flour ['flaʊə*] *n* farine *f*

flourish ['flʌrɪʃ] *vi* prospérer ♦ *n* (*gesture*) moulinet *m*

flout [flaʊt] *vt* se moquer de, faire fi de

flow [fləʊ] *n* (*ELEC, of river*) courant *m*; (*of blood in veins*) circulation *f*; (*of tide*) flux *m*; (*of orders, data*) flot *m* ♦ *vi* couler; (*traffic*) s'écouler; (*robes, hair*) flotter; **the ~ of traffic** l'écoulement *m* de la circulation; ~ **chart** *n* organigramme *m*

flower ['flaʊə*] *n* fleur *f* ♦ *vi* fleurir; ~ **bed** *n* plate-bande *f*; ~**pot** *n* pot *m* (de fleurs); ~**y** *adj* fleuri(e)

flown [fləʊn] *pp of* **fly**

flu [fluː] *n* grippe *f*

fluctuate ['flʌktjʊeɪt] *vi* varier, fluctuer

fluent ['fluːənt] *adj* (*speech*) coulant(e), aisé(e); **he speaks ~ French, he's ~ in French** il parle couramment le français

fluff [flʌf] *n* duvet *m*; (*on jacket, carpet*) peluche *f*; ~**y** *adj* duveteux(euse); (*toy*) en peluche

fluid ['fluːɪd] *adj* fluide ♦ *n* fluide *m*

fluke [fluːk] (*inf*) *n* (*luck*) coup *m* de veine

flung [flʌŋ] *pt, pp of* **fling**

fluoride ['fluəraɪd] n fluorure f; ~ **tooth-paste** n dentifrice m au fluor

flurry ['flʌrɪ] n (of snow) rafale f, bourrasque f; ~ **of activity/excitement** affairement m/excitation f soudain(e)

flush [flʌʃ] n (on face) rougeur f, (fig: of youth, beauty etc) éclat m ♦ vt nettoyer à grande eau ♦ vi rougir ♦ adj: ~ **with** au ras de, de niveau avec; **to** ~ **the toilet** tirer la chasse (d'eau); ~ **out** vt (game, birds) débusquer; ~**ed** adj (tout(e)) rouge

flustered ['flʌstəd] adj énervé(e)

flute [flu:t] n flûte f

flutter ['flʌtə*] n (of panic, excitement) agitation f, (of wings) battement m ♦ vi (bird) battre des ailes, voleter

flux [flʌks] n: **in a state of** ~ fluctuant sans cesse

fly [flaɪ] (pt **flew**, pp **flown**) n (insect) mouche f; (on trousers: also: **flies**) braguette f ♦ vt piloter; (passengers, cargo) transporter (par avion); (distances) parcourir ♦ vi voler; (passengers) aller en avion; (escape) s'enfuir, fuir, (flag) se déployer; ~ **away** vi (bird, insect) s'envoler; ~ **off** vi = **fly away**; ~**ing** n (activity) aviation f; (action) vol m ♦ adj: **a** ~**ing visit** une visite éclair; **with** ~**ing colours** haut la main; ~**ing saucer** n soucoupe volante; ~**ing start** n: **to get off to a** ~**ing start** prendre un excellent départ; ~**over** (BRIT) n (bridge) saut-de-mouton m; ~**sheet** n (for tent) double toit m

foal [fəul] n poulain m

foam [fəum] n écume f; (on beer) mousse f; (also: ~ **rubber**) caoutchouc m mousse ♦ vi (liquid) écumer; (soapy water) mousser

fob [fɔb] vt: **to** ~ **sb off** se débarrasser de qn

focal point ['fəukəl-] n (fig) point central

focus ['fəukəs] (pl ~**es**) n foyer m; (of interest) centre m ♦ vt (field glasses etc) mettre au point ♦ vi: **to** ~ **(on)** (with camera) régler la mise au point (sur); (person) fixer son regard (sur); **out of/in** ~ (picture) flou(e)/net(te); (camera) pas au point/au point

fodder ['fɔdə*] n fourrage m

foe [fəu] n ennemi m

fog [fɔg] n brouillard m; ~**gy** adj: **it's** ~**gy** il y a du brouillard; ~ **lamp** n (AUT) phare m antibrouillard; ~ **light** (US) n = **fog lamp**

foil [fɔɪl] vt déjouer, contrecarrer ♦ n feuille f de métal; (kitchen ~) papier m d'alu(minium); (complement) repoussoir m; (FENCING) fleuret m

fold [fəuld] n (bend, crease) pli m; (AGR) parc m à moutons; (fig) bercail m ♦ vt plier; (arms) croiser; ~ **up** vi (map, table etc) se plier; (business) fermer boutique ♦ vt (map, clothes) plier; ~**er** n (for papers)

chemise f; (: with hinges) classeur m; ~**ing** adj (chair, bed) pliant(e)

foliage ['fəulɪɪdʒ] n feuillage m

folk [fəuk] npl gens mpl ♦ cpd folklorique; ~**s** npl (parents) parents mpl; ~**lore** ['fəuklɔ:*] n folklore m; ~ **song** n chanson f folklorique

follow ['fɔləu] vt suivre ♦ vi suivre; (result) s'ensuivre; **to** ~ **suit** (fig) faire de même; ~ **up** vt (letter, offer) donner suite à; (case) suivre; ~**er** n disciple m/f, partisan(e); ~**ing** adj suivant(e) ♦ n partisans mpl, disciples mpl

folly ['fɔlɪ] n inconscience f, folie f

fond [fɔnd] adj (memory, look) tendre; (hopes, dreams) un peu fou(folle); **to be** ~ **of** aimer beaucoup

fondle ['fɔndl] vt caresser

font [fɔnt] n (in church: for baptism) fonts baptismaux; (TYP) fonte f

food [fu:d] n nourriture f; ~ **mixer** n mixer m; ~ **poisoning** n intoxication f alimentaire; ~ **processor** n robot m de cuisine; ~**stuffs** npl denrées fpl alimentaires

fool [fu:l] n idiot(e); (CULIN) mousse f de fruits ♦ vt berner, duper ♦ vi faire l'idiot or l'imbécile; ~**hardy** adj téméraire, imprudent(e); ~**ish** adj idiot(e), stupide; (rash) imprudent(e), insensé; ~**proof** adj (plan etc) infaillible

foot [fut] (pl **feet**) n pied m; (of animal) patte f; (measure) pied (= 30,48 cm; 12 inches) ♦ vt (bill) payer; **on** ~ à pied; ~**age** n (CINEMA: length) ≈ métrage m; (: material) séquences fpl; ~**ball** n ballon m (de football); (sport: BRIT) football m, foot m; (: US) football américain; ~**ball player** (BRIT) n (also: **footballer**) joueur m de football; ~**brake** n frein m à pédale; ~**bridge** n passerelle f; ~**hills** npl contreforts mpl; ~**hold** n prise f (de pied); ~**ing** n (fig) position f; **to lose one's** ~**ing** perdre pied; ~**lights** npl rampe f; ~**man** (irreg) n valet m de pied; ~**note** n note f (en bas de page); ~**path** n sentier m; (in street) trottoir m; ~**print** n trace f (de pas); ~**step** n pas m; ~**wear** n chaussure(s) f(pl)

for [fɔ:*] prep **1** (indicating destination, intention, purpose) pour; **the train** ~ **London** le train pour or (à destination) de Londres; **he went** ~ **the paper** il est allé chercher le journal; **it's time** ~ **lunch** c'est l'heure du déjeuner; **what's it** ~? ça sert à quoi?; **what** ~? (why) pourquoi?

2 (on behalf of, representing) pour; **the MP** ~ **Hove** le député de Hove; **to work** ~ **sb/sth** travailler pour qn/qch; **G** ~ **George** G comme Georges

3 (because of) pour; ~ **this reason** pour cette raison; ~ **fear of being criticized** de

peur d'être critiqué
4 (with regard to) pour; **it's cold ~ July** il fait froid pour juillet; **a gift ~ languages** un don pour les langues
5 (in exchange for): **I sold it ~ £5** je l'ai vendu 5 livres; **to pay 50 pence ~ a ticket** payer un billet 50 pence
6 (in favour of) pour; **are you ~ or against us?** êtes-vous pour ou contre nous?
7 (referring to distance) pendant, sur; **there are roadworks ~ 5 km** il y a des travaux sur 5 km; **we walked ~ miles** nous avons marché pendant des kilomètres
8 (referring to time) pendant; depuis; pour; **he was away ~ 2 years** il a été absent pendant 2 ans; **she will be away ~ a month** elle sera absente (pendant) un mois; **I have known her ~ years** je la connais depuis des années; **can you do it ~ tomorrow?** est-ce que tu peux le faire pour demain?
9 (with infinitive clauses): **it is not ~ me to decide** ce n'est pas à moi de décider; **it would be best ~ you to leave** le mieux serait que vous partiez; **there is still time ~ you to do it** vous avez encore le temps de le faire; **~ this to be possible ...** pour que cela soit possible ...
10 (in spite of): **~ all his work/efforts** malgré tout son travail/tous ses efforts; **~ all his complaints, he's very fond of her** il a beau se plaindre, il l'aime beaucoup
♦ conj (since, as: rather formal) car

forage ['fɒrɪdʒ] vi fourrager
foray ['fɒreɪ] n incursion f
forbid [fə'bɪd] (pt **forbad(e)**, pp **forbidden**) vt défendre, interdire; **to ~ sb to do sth** défendre or interdire à qn de faire; **~ding** adj sévère, sombre
force [fɔːs] n force f ♦ vt forcer; (push) pousser (de force); **the F~s** npl (MIL) l'armée f; **in ~** en vigueur; **~-feed** vt nourrir de force; **~ful** adj énergique, volontaire
forcibly ['fɔːsəblɪ] adv par la force, de force; (express) énergiquement
ford [fɔːd] n gué m
fore [fɔː*] n: **to come to the ~** se faire remarquer
fore: **~arm** ['fɔːrɑːm] n avant-bras m inv; **~boding** [fɔː'bəʊdɪŋ] n pressentiment m (néfaste); **~cast** ['fɔːkɑːst] (irreg: like **cast**) n prévision f ♦ vt prévoir; **~court** ['fɔːkɔːt] n (of garage) devant m; **~fathers** ['fɔːfɑːðəz] npl ancêtres mpl; **~finger** ['fɔːfɪŋgə*] n index m
forefront ['fɔːfrʌnt] n: **in the ~ of** au premier rang or plan de
forego [fɔː'gəʊ] (irreg: like **go**) vt renoncer à; **~ne** ['fɔːgɒn] adj: **it's a ~ne conclusion** c'est couru d'avance
foreground ['fɔːgraʊnd] n premier plan

forehead ['fɒrɪd] n front m
foreign ['fɒrɪn] adj étranger(ère); (trade) extérieur(e); **~er** n étranger(ère); **~ exchange** n change m; **F~ Office** (BRIT) n ministère m des affaires étrangères; **F~ Secretary** (BRIT) n ministre m des affaires étrangères
foreleg ['fɔːleg] n (cat, dog) patte f de devant; (horse) jambe antérieure
foreman ['fɔːmən] (irreg) n (factory, building site) contremaître m, chef m d'équipe
foremost ['fɔːməʊst] adj le(la) plus en vue; premier(ère) ♦ adv: **first and ~** avant tout, tout d'abord
forensic [fə'rensɪk] adj: **~ medicine** médecine légale; **~ scientist** n médecin m légiste
forerunner ['fɔːrʌnə*] n précurseur m
foresee [fɔː'siː] (irreg: like **see**) vt prévoir; **~able** adj prévisible
foreshadow [fɔː'ʃædəʊ] vt présager, annoncer, laisser prévoir
foresight ['fɔːsaɪt] n prévoyance f
forest ['fɒrɪst] n forêt f
forestall [fɔː'stɔːl] vt devancer
forestry ['fɒrɪstrɪ] n sylviculture f
foretaste ['fɔːteɪst] n avant-goût m
foretell [fɔː'tel] (irreg: like **tell**) vt prédire
foretold [fɔː'təʊld] pt, pp of **foretell**
forever [fə'revə*] adv pour toujours; (fig) continuellement
forewent [fɔː'went] pt of **forego**
foreword ['fɔːwɜːd] n avant-propos m inv
forfeit ['fɔːfɪt] vt (lose) perdre
forgave [fə'geɪv] pt of **forgive**
forge [fɔːdʒ] n forge f ♦ vt (signature) contrefaire; (wrought iron) forger; **to ~ money** (BRIT) fabriquer de la fausse monnaie; **~ ahead** vi pousser de l'avant, prendre de l'avance; **~r** n faussaire m; **~ry** n faux m, contrefaçon f
forget [fə'get] (pt **forgot**, pp **forgotten**) vt, vi oublier; **~ful** adj distrait(e), étourdi(e); **~-me-not** n myosotis m
forgive [fə'gɪv] (pt **forgave**, pp **forgiven**) vt pardonner; **to ~ sb for sth/for doing sth** pardonner qch à qn/à qn de faire qch; **~ness** n pardon m
forgo [fɔː'gəʊ] (pt **forwent**, pp **forgone**) vt = **forego**
fork [fɔːk] n (for eating) fourchette f; (for gardening) fourche f; (of roads) bifurcation f; (of railways) embranchement m ♦ vi (road) bifurquer; **~ out** vt (inf) allonger; **~-lift truck** n chariot élévateur
forlorn [fə'lɔːn] adj (deserted) abandonné(e); (attempt, hope) désespéré(e)
form [fɔːm] n forme f; (SCOL) classe f; (questionnaire) formulaire m ♦ vt former; (habit) contracter; **in top ~** en pleine forme
formal ['fɔːməl] adj (offer, receipt) en bonne et due forme; (person) cérémonieux(euse);

(*dinner*) officiel(le); (*clothes*) de soirée; (*garden*) à la française; (*education*) à proprement parler; **~ly** *adv* officiellement; cérémonieusement

format ['fɔːmæt] *n* format *m* ♦ *vt* (*COMPUT*) formater

formative ['fɔːmətɪv] *adj*: **~ years** années *fpl* d'apprentissage *or* de formation

former ['fɔːmə*] *adj* ancien(ne) (*before n*), précédent(e); **the ~ ... the latter** le premier ... le second, celui-là ... celui-ci; **~ly** *adv* autrefois

formidable ['fɔːmɪdəbl] *adj* redoutable

formula ['fɔːmjulə] (*pl* **~s** *or* **formulae**) *n* formule *f*

forsake [fə'seɪk] (*pt* **forsook**, *pp* **forsaken**) *vt* abandonner

fort [fɔːt] *n* fort *m*

forte ['fɔːtɪ] *n* (point) fort *m*

forth [fɔːθ] *adv* en avant; **to go back and ~** aller et venir; **and so ~** et ainsi de suite; **~coming** *adj* (*event*) qui va avoir lieu prochainement; (*character*) ouvert(e), communicatif(ive); (*available*) disponible; **~right** *adj* franc(franche), direct(e); **~with** *adv* sur-le-champ

fortify ['fɔːtɪfaɪ] *vt* fortifier

fortitude ['fɔːtɪtjuːd] *n* courage *m*

fortnight ['fɔːtnaɪt] (*BRIT*) *n* quinzaine *f*, quinze jours *mpl*; **~ly** (*BRIT*) *adj* bimensuel(le) ♦ *adv* tous les quinze jours

fortunate ['fɔːtʃənɪt] *adj* heureux(euse); (*person*) chanceux (euse); **it is ~ that** c'est une chance que; **~ly** *adv* heureusement

fortune ['fɔːtʃən] *n* chance *f*; (*wealth*) fortune *f*; **~-teller** *n* diseuse *f* de bonne aventure

forty ['fɔːtɪ] *num* quarante

forward ['fɔːwəd] *adj* (*ahead of schedule*) en avance; (*movement, position*) en avant, vers l'avant; (*not shy*) direct(e); effronté(e) ♦ *n* (*SPORT*) avant *m* ♦ *vt* (*letter*) faire suivre; (*parcel, goods*) expédier; (*fig*) promouvoir, favoriser; **~(s)** *adv* en avant; **to move ~** avancer

fossil ['fɔsl] *n* fossile *m*

foster ['fɔstə*] *vt* encourager, favoriser; (*child*) élever (*sans obligation d'adopter*); **~ child** *n* enfant adoptif(ive)

fought [fɔːt] *pt, pp of* **fight**

foul [faul] *adj* (*weather, smell, food*) infect(e); (*language*) ordurier(ère) ♦ *n* (*SPORT*) faute *f* ♦ *vt* (*dirty*) salir, encrasser; **he's got a ~ temper** il a un caractère de chien; **~ play** *n* (*LAW*) acte criminel

found [faund] *pt, pp of* **find** ♦ *vt* (*establish*) fonder; **~ation** [faun'deɪʃən] *n* (*act*) fondation *f*; (*base*) fondement *m*; (*also:* **~ation cream**) fond *m* de teint; **~ations** *npl* (*of building*) fondations *fpl*

founder ['faundə*] *n* fondateur *m* ♦ *vi* couler, sombrer

foundry ['faundrɪ] *n* fonderie *f*

fountain ['fauntɪn] *n* fontaine *f*; **~ pen** *n* stylo *m* (à encre)

four [fɔː*] *num* quatre; **on all ~s** à quatre pattes; **~-poster** *n* (*also:* **~-poster bed**) lit *m* à baldaquin; **~some** *n* (*game*) partie *f* à quatre; (*outing*) sortie *f* à quatre

fourteen [fɔː'tiːn] *num* quatorze

fourth [fɔːθ] *num* quatrième

fowl [faul] *n* volaille *f*

fox [fɔks] *n* renard *m* ♦ *vt* mystifier

foyer ['fɔɪeɪ] *n* (*hotel*) hall *m*; (*THEATRE*) foyer *m*

fraction ['frækʃən] *n* fraction *f*

fracture ['fræktʃə*] *n* fracture *f*

fragile ['frædʒaɪl] *adj* fragile

fragment ['frægmənt] *n* fragment *m*

fragrant ['freɪgrənt] *adj* parfumé(e), odorant(e)

frail [freɪl] *adj* fragile, délicat(e)

frame [freɪm] *n* charpente *f*; (*of picture, bicycle*) cadre *m*; (*of door, window*) encadrement *m*, chambranle *m*; (*of spectacles: also:* **~s**) monture *f* ♦ *vt* encadrer; **~ of mind** disposition *f* d'esprit; **~work** *n* structure *f*

France [frɑːns] *n* France *f*

franchise ['fræntʃaɪz] *n* (*POL*) droit *m* de vote; (*COMM*) franchise *f*

frank [fræŋk] *adj* franc(franche) ♦ *vt* (*letter*) affranchir; **~ly** *adv* franchement

frantic ['fræntɪk] *adj* (*hectic*) frénétique; (*distraught*) hors de soi

fraternity [frə'tɜːnɪtɪ] *n* (*spirit*) fraternité *f*; (*club*) communauté *f*, confrérie *f*

fraud [frɔːd] *n* supercherie *f*, fraude *f*, tromperie *f*; (*person*) imposteur *m*

fraught [frɔːt] *adj*: **~ with** chargé(e) de, plein(e) de

fray [freɪ] *n* bagarre *f* ♦ *vi* s'effilocher; **tempers were ~ed** les gens commençaient à s'énerver

freak [friːk] *n* (*also cpd*) phénomène *m*, créature *or* événement exceptionnel(le) par sa rareté

freckle ['frekl] *n* tache *f* de rousseur

free [friː] *adj* libre; (*gratis*) gratuit(e) ♦ *vt* (*prisoner etc*) libérer; (*jammed object or person*) dégager; **~ (of charge), for ~** gratuitement; **~dom** ['friːdəm] *n* liberté *f*; **~-for-all** *n* mêlée générale; **~ gift** *n* prime *f*; **~hold** *n* propriété foncière libre; **~ kick** *n* coup franc; **~lance** *adj* indépendant(e); **~ly** *adv* librement, (*liberally*) libéralement; **F~mason** *n* franc-maçon *m*; **F~post** (®) *n* port payé; **~-range** *adj* (*hen, eggs*) de ferme; **~ trade** *n* libre-échange *m*; **~way** (*US*) *n* autoroute *f*; **~ will** *n* libre arbitre *m*; **of one's own ~ will** de son plein gré

freeze [friːz] (*pt* **froze**, *pp* **frozen**) *vi* geler ♦ *vt* geler; (*food*) congeler; (*prices, salaries*) bloquer, geler ♦ *n* gel *m*; (*fig*) blocage *m*; **~-dried** *adj* lyophilisé(e); **~r** *n* congélateur *m*

freezing ['friːzɪŋ] *adj*: ~ (**cold**) (*weather, water*) glacial(e) ♦ *n* **3 degrees below** ~ 3 degrés au-dessous de zéro; ~ **point** *n* point *m* de congélation

freight [freɪt] *n* (*goods*) fret *m*, cargaison *f*; (*money charged*) fret, prix *m* du transport; ~ **train** *n* train *m* de marchandises

French [frentʃ] *adj* français(e) ♦ *n* (*LING*) français *m*; **the** ~ *npl* (*people*) les Français; ~ **bean** *n* haricot vert; ~ **fried** (**potatoes**), ~ **fries** (*US*) *npl* (pommes de terre *fpl*) frites *fpl*; ~**man** (*irreg*) *n* Français *m*; ~ **window** *n* porte-fenêtre *f*, ~**woman** (*irreg*) *n* Française *f*

frenzy ['frenzɪ] *n* frénésie *f*

frequency ['friːkwənsɪ] *n* fréquence *f*

frequent [*adj* 'friːkwənt, *vb* frɪ'kwent] *adj* fréquent(e) ♦ *vt* fréquenter; ~**ly** *adv* fréquemment

fresh [freʃ] *adj* frais(fraîche); (*new*) nouveau(nouvelle); (*cheeky*) familier(ère), culotté(e); ~**en** *vi* (*wind, air*) fraîchir; ~**en up** *vi* faire un brin de toilette; ~**er** (*BRIT: inf*) *n* (*SCOL*) bizuth *m*, étudiant(e) de 1ère année; ~**ly** *adv* nouvellement, récemment; ~**man** (*US: irreg*) *n* = fresher; ~**ness** *n* fraîcheur *f*, ~**water** *adj* (*fish*) d'eau douce

fret [fret] *vi* s'agiter, se tracasser

friar ['fraɪə*] *n* moine *m*, frère *m*

friction ['frɪkʃən] *n* friction *f*

Friday ['fraɪdeɪ] *n* vendredi *m*

fridge [frɪdʒ] (*BRIT*) *n* frigo *m*, frigidaire *m* (®)

fried [fraɪd] *adj* frit(e); ~ **egg** œuf *m* sur le plat

friend [frend] *n* ami(e); ~**ly** *adj* amical(e); gentil(le); (*place*) accueillant(e); ~**ship** *n* amitié *f*

frieze [friːz] *n* frise *f*

fright [fraɪt] *n* peur *f*, effroi *m*; **to take** ~ prendre peur, s'effrayer; ~**en** *vt* effrayer, faire peur à; ~**ened** *adj*: **to be** ~**ened** (**of**) avoir peur (de); ~**ening** *adj* effrayant(e); ~**ful** *adj* affreux(euse)

frigid ['frɪdʒɪd] *adj* (*woman*) frigide

frill [frɪl] *n* (*of dress*) volant *m*; (*of shirt*) jabot *m*

fringe [frɪndʒ] *n* (*BRIT: of hair*) frange *f*; (*edge: of forest etc*) bordure *f*, ~ **benefits** *npl* avantages sociaux *or* en nature

frisk [frɪsk] *vt* fouiller

fritter ['frɪtə*] *n* beignet *m*; ~ **away** *vt* gaspiller

frivolous ['frɪvələs] *adj* frivole

frizzy ['frɪzɪ] *adj* crépu(e)

fro [frəʊ] *adv*: **to go to and** ~ aller et venir

frock [frɒk] *n* robe *f*

frog [frɒg] *n* grenouille *f*, ~**man** *n* homme-grenouille *m*

frolic ['frɒlɪk] *vi* folâtrer, batifoler

── KEYWORD

from [frɒm] *prep* **1** (*indicating starting place, origin etc*) de; **where do you come** ~?, **where are you** ~? d'où venez-vous?; **London to Paris** de Londres à Paris; **a letter** ~ **my sister** une lettre de ma sœur; **to drink** ~ **the bottle** boire à (même) la bouteille

2 (*indicating time*) (à partir) de; ~ **one o'clock to** *or* **until** *or* **till two** d'une heure à deux heures; ~ **January (on)** à partir de janvier

3 (*indicating distance*) de; **the hotel is one kilometre** ~ **the beach** l'hôtel est à un kilomètre de la plage

4 (*indicating price, number etc*) de; **the interest rate was increased** ~ **9% to 10%** le taux d'intérêt a augmenté de 9 à 10%

5 (*indicating difference*) de; **he can't tell red** ~ **green** il ne peut pas distinguer le rouge du vert

6 (*because of, on the basis of*): ~ **what he says** d'après ce qu'il dit; **weak** ~ **hunger** affaibli par la faim

---

front [frʌnt] *n* (*of house, dress*) devant *m*; (*of coach, train*) avant *m*; (*promenade: also:* **sea** ~) bord *m* de mer; (*MIL, METEOROLOGY*) front *m*; (*fig: appearances*) contenance *f*, façade *f* ♦ *adj* de devant; (*seat*) avant *inv*; **in** ~ (**of**) devant; ~**age** ['frʌntɪdʒ] *n* (*of building*) façade *f*; ~ **door** *n* porte *f* d'entrée; (*of car*) portière *f* avant; ~**ier** ['frʌntɪə*] *n* frontière *f*; ~ **page** *n* première page; ~ **room** (*BRIT*) *n* pièce *f* de devant, salon *m*; ~**-wheel drive** *n* traction *f* avant

frost [frɒst] *n* gel *m*, gelée *f*; (*also: hoar~*) givre *m*; ~**bite** *n* gelures *fpl*; ~**ed** (*glass*) dépoli(e); ~**y** *adj* (*weather, welcome*) glacial(e)

froth [frɒθ] *n* mousse *f*; écume *f*

frown [fraʊn] *vi* froncer les sourcils

froze [frəʊz] *pt of* **freeze**

frozen ['frəʊzn] *pp of* **freeze**

fruit [fruːt] *n inv* fruit *m*; ~**erer** *n* fruitier *m*, marchand(e) de fruits; ~**ful** *adj* (*fig*) fructueux(euse); ~**ion** [fruː'ɪʃən] *n*: **to come to** ~**ion** se réaliser; ~ **juice** *n* jus *m* de fruit; ~ **machine** (*BRIT*) *n* machine *f* à sous; ~ **salad** *n* salade *f* de fruits

frustrate [frʌs'treɪt] *vt* frustrer

fry [fraɪ] (*pt, pp* **fried**) *vt* (faire) frire; *see also* **small**; ~**ing pan** *n* poêle *f* (à frire)

ft. *abbr* = **foot; feet**

fuddy-duddy ['fʌdɪdʌdɪ] (*pej*) *n* vieux schnock

fudge [fʌdʒ] *n* (*CULIN*) caramel *m*

fuel [fjʊəl] *n* (*for heating*) combustible *m*; (*for propelling*) carburant *m*; ~ **oil** *n* mazout *m*; ~ **tank** *n* (*in vehicle*) réservoir *m*

fugitive ['fjuːdʒɪtɪv] *n* fugitif(ive)

fulfil [ful'fɪl] (US ~l) vt (function, condition) remplir; (order) exécuter; (wish, desire) satisfaire, réaliser; (wish, desire etc) réalisation f; (feeling) contentement m

full [ful] adj plein(e); (details, information) complet(ète); (skirt) ample, large ♦ adv: **to know ~ well** that savoir fort bien que; **I'm ~ (up)** j'ai bien mangé; **a ~ two hours** deux bonnes heures; **at ~ speed** à toute vitesse; **in ~** (reproduce, quote) intégralement; (write) en toutes lettres; **~ employment** plein emploi; **to pay in ~** tout payer; **~-length** adj (film) long métrage; (portrait, mirror) en pied; (coat) long(ue); **~ moon** n pleine lune; **~-scale** adj (attack, war) complet(ète), total(e); (model) grandeur nature inv; **~ stop** n point m; **~-time** adj, adv (work) à plein temps; **~y** adv entièrement, complètement; (at least) au moins; **~y-fledged** adj (teacher, barrister) diplômé(e); (citizen, member) à part entière

fumble ['fʌmbl] vi: **~ with** tripoter

fume [fjuːm] vi rager; **~s** npl vapeurs fpl, émanations fpl, gaz mpl

fun [fʌn] n amusement m, divertissement m; **to have ~** s'amuser; **for ~** pour rire; **to make ~ of** se moquer de

function ['fʌŋkʃən] n fonction f; (social occasion) cérémonie f, soirée officielle ♦ vi fonctionner; **~al** adj fonctionnel(le)

fund [fʌnd] n caisse f, fonds m; (source, store) source f, mine f; **~s** npl (money) fonds mpl

fundamental [fʌndə'mentl] adj fondamental(e)

funeral ['fjuːnərəl] n enterrement m, obsèques fpl; **~ parlour** n entreprise f de pompes funèbres; **~ service** n service m funèbre

funfair ['fʌnfɛə*] (BRIT) n fête (foraine)

fungus ['fʌŋgəs] (pl **fungi**) n champignon m; (mould) moisissure f

funnel ['fʌnl] n entonnoir m; (of ship) cheminée f

funny ['fʌnɪ] adj amusant(e), drôle; (strange) curieux(euse), bizarre

fur [fɜː*] n fourrure f; (BRIT: in kettle etc) (dépôt m de) tartre m; **~ coat** n manteau m de fourrure

furious ['fjuərɪəs] adj furieux(euse); (effort) acharné(e)

furlong ['fɜːlɒŋ] n = 201,17 m

furlough ['fɜːləu] n permission f, congé m

furnace ['fɜːnɪs] n fourneau m

furnish ['fɜːnɪʃ] vt meubler; (supply): **to ~ sb with sth** fournir qch à qn; **~ings** npl mobilier m, ameublement m

furniture ['fɜːnɪtʃə*] n meubles mpl, mobilier m; **piece of ~** meuble m

furrow ['fʌrəu] n sillon m

furry ['fɜːrɪ] adj (animal) à fourrure; (toy) en peluche

further ['fɜːðə*] adj (additional) supplémentaire, autre; nouveau (nouvelle) ♦ adv plus loin; (more) davantage; (moreover) de plus ♦ vt faire avancer or progresser, promouvoir; **~ education** n enseignement m postscolaire; **~more** adv de plus, en outre

furthest ['fɜːðɪst] superl of **far**

fury ['fjuərɪ] n fureur f

fuse [fjuːz] (US **fuze**) n fusible m; (for bomb etc) amorce f, détonateur m ♦ vt, vi (metal) fondre; **to ~ the lights** (BRIT) faire sauter les plombs; **~ box** n boîte f à fusibles

fuss [fʌs] n (excitement) agitation f, (complaining) histoire(s) f(pl); **to make a ~** faire des histoires; **to make a ~ of sb** être aux petits soins pour qn; **~y** adj (person) tatillon(ne), difficile; (dress, style) tarabiscoté(e)

future ['fjuːtʃə*] adj futur(e) ♦ n avenir m; (LING) futur m; **in ~** à l'avenir

fuze [fjuːz] (US) n, vt, vi = **fuse**

fuzzy ['fʌzɪ] adj (PHOT) flou(e); (hair) crépu(e)

G g

G [dʒiː] n (MUS) sol m

G7 n abbr (= Group of 7) le groupe des 7

gabble ['gæbl] vi bredouiller

gable ['geɪbl] n pignon m

gadget ['gædʒɪt] n gadget m

Gaelic ['geɪlɪk] adj gaélique ♦ n (LING) gaélique m

gag [gæg] n (on mouth) bâillon m; (joke) gag m ♦ vt bâillonner

gaiety ['geɪətɪ] n gaieté f

gain [geɪn] n (improvement) gain m; (profit) gain, profit m; (increase): **~ (in)** augmentation f (de) ♦ vt gagner ♦ vi (watch) avancer; **to ~ 3 lbs (in weight)** prendre 3 livres; **to ~ on sb** (catch up) rattraper qn; **to ~ from/by** gagner de/à

gait [geɪt] n démarche f

gal. abbr = **gallon**

gale [geɪl] n rafale f de vent; coup m de vent

gallant ['gælənt] adj vaillant(e), brave; (towards ladies) galant

gall bladder ['gɔːl-] n vésicule f biliaire

gallery ['gælərɪ] n galerie f; (also: art ~) musée m; (: private) galerie

galley ['gælɪ] n (ship's kitchen) cambuse f

gallon ['gælən] n gallon m (BRIT = 4,5 l; US

= 3,8 l)

gallop ['gæləp] n galop m ♦ vi galoper

gallows ['gæləʊz] n potence f

gallstone ['gɔːlstəʊn] n calcul m biliaire

galore [gə'lɔː*] adv en abondance, à gogo

Gambia n: **(The)** ~ la Gambie

gambit ['gæmbɪt] n (fig): **(opening)** ~ manœuvre f stratégique

gamble ['gæmbl] n pari m, risque calculé ♦ vt, vi jouer; **to** ~ **on** (fig) miser sur; ~**r** n joueur m; **gambling** ['gæmblɪŋ] n jeu m

game [geɪm] n jeu m; (match) match m; (strategy, scheme) plan m; projet m; (HUNTING) gibier m ♦ adj (willing): **to be** ~ **(for)** être prêt(e) (à or pour); **big** ~ gros gibier; ~**keeper** n garde-chasse m

gammon ['gæmən] n (bacon) quartier m de lard fumé; (ham) jambon fumé

gamut ['gæmət] n gamme f

gang [gæŋ] n bande f; (of workmen) équipe f; ~ **up** vi: **to** ~ **up on sb** se liguer contre qn; ~**ster** ['gæŋstə*] n gangster m; ~**way** n passerelle f; (BRIT: of bus, plane) couloir central; (: in cinema) allée centrale

gaol [dʒeɪl] (BRIT) n = **jail**

gap [gæp] n trou m; (in time) intervalle m; (difference): ~ **between** écart m entre

gape [geɪp] vi (person) être or rester bouche bée; (hole, shirt) être ouvert(e); **gaping** ['geɪpɪŋ] adj (hole) béant(e)

garage ['gærɑːʒ] n garage m

garbage ['gɑːbɪdʒ] n (US: rubbish) ordures fpl, détritus mpl; (inf: nonsense) foutaises fpl; ~ **can** (US) n poubelle f, boîte f à ordures

garbled ['gɑːbld] adj (account, message) embrouillé(e)

garden ['gɑːdn] n jardin m; ~**s** npl jardin public; ~**er** n jardinier m; ~**ing** n jardinage m

gargle ['gɑːgl] vi se gargariser

garish ['gɛərɪʃ] adj criard(e), voyant(e); (light) cru(e)

garland ['gɑːlənd] n guirlande f; couronne f

garlic ['gɑːlɪk] n ail m

garment ['gɑːmənt] n vêtement m

garrison ['gærɪsən] n garnison f

garrulous ['gærʊləs] adj volubile, loquace

garter ['gɑːtə*] n jarretière f; (US) jarretelle f

gas [gæs] n gaz m; (US: ~oline) essence f ♦ vt asphyxier; ~ **cooker** (BRIT) n cuisinière f à gaz; ~ **cylinder** n bouteille f de gaz; ~ **fire** (BRIT) n radiateur m à gaz

gash [gæʃ] n entaille f; (on face) balafre f

gasket ['gæskɪt] n (AUT) joint m de culasse

gas mask n masque m à gaz

gas meter n compteur m à gaz

gasoline ['gæsəliːn] (US) n essence f

gasp [gɑːsp] vi haleter; ~ **out** vt (say) dire dans un souffle or d'une voix entrecoupée

gas station (US) n station-service f

gas tap n bouton m (de cuisinière à gaz); (on pipe) robinet m à gaz

gastric adj gastrique; ~ **flu** grippe f intestinale

gate [geɪt] n (of garden) portail m; (of field) barrière f; (of building, at airport) porte f; ~**crash** vt s'introduire sans invitation dans; ~**way** n porte f

gather ['gæðə*] vt (flowers, fruit) cueillir; (pick up) ramasser; (assemble) rassembler, réunir; recueillir; (understand) comprendre; (SEWING) froncer ♦ vi (assemble) se rassembler; **to** ~ **speed** prendre de la vitesse; ~**ing** n rassemblement m

gaudy ['gɔːdɪ] adj voyant(e)

gauge [geɪdʒ] n (instrument) jauge f ♦ vt jauger

gaunt [gɔːnt] adj (thin) décharné(e); (grim, desolate) désolé(e)

gauntlet ['gɔːntlɪt] n (glove) gant m; (fig): **to run the** ~ **through an angry crowd** se frayer un passage à travers une foule hostile; **to throw down the** ~ jeter le gant

gauze [gɔːz] n gaze f

gave [geɪv] pt of **give**

gay [geɪ] adj (homosexual) homosexuel(le); (cheerful) gai(e), réjoui(e); (colour etc) gai, vif(vive)

gaze [geɪz] n regard m fixe ♦ vi: **to** ~ **at** fixer du regard

gazump (BRIT) vi revenir sur une promesse de vente (pour accepter une offre plus intéressante)

GB abbr = **Great Britain**

GCE n abbr (BRIT) = **General Certificate of Education**

GCSE n abbr (BRIT) = **General Certificate of Secondary Education**

gear [gɪə*] n matériel m, équipement m; attirail m; (TECH) engrenage m; (AUT) vitesse f ♦ vt (fig: adapt): **to** ~ **sth to** adapter qch à; **top** (or US **high**) ~ quatrième (or cinquième) vitesse; **low** ~ première vitesse; **in** ~ en prise; ~ **box** n boîte f de vitesses; ~ **lever** (US ~ **shift**) n levier m de vitesse

geese [giːs] npl of **goose**

gel [dʒel] n gel m

gelignite ['dʒelɪgnaɪt] n plastic m

gem [dʒem] n pierre précieuse

Gemini ['dʒemɪniː] n les Gémeaux mpl

gender ['dʒendə*] n genre m

general ['dʒenərəl] n général m ♦ adj général(e); **in** ~ en général; ~ **delivery** n poste restante; ~ **election** n élection(s) législative(s); ~**ly** adv généralement; ~ **practitioner** n généraliste m/f

generate ['dʒenəreɪt] vt engendrer; (electricity etc) produire

generation [dʒenə'reɪʃən] n génération f; (of electricity etc) production f

generator ['dʒenəreɪtə*] n générateur m

generosity [dʒenə'rɒsɪtɪ] n générosité f;

generous ['dʒenərəs] *adj* généreux(euse); *(copious)* copieux(euse)
genetic engineering [dʒɪ'netɪk-] *n* ingénierie *f* génétique
genetics [dʒɪ'netɪks] *n* génétique *f*
Geneva [dʒɪ'niːvə] *n* Genève
genial ['dʒiːnɪəl] *adj* cordial(e), chaleureux(euse)
genitals ['dʒenɪtlz] *npl* organes génitaux
genius ['dʒiːnɪəs] *n* génie *m*
genteel [dʒen'tiːl] *adj* de bon ton, distingué(e)
gentle ['dʒentl] *adj* doux(douce)
gentleman ['dʒentlmən] *n* monsieur *m*; *(well-bred man)* gentleman *m*
gently ['dʒentlɪ] *adv* doucement
gentry ['dʒentrɪ] *n inv*: **the ~** la petite noblesse
gents [dʒents] *n* W.-C. *mpl* (pour hommes)
genuine ['dʒenjuɪn] *adj* véritable, authentique; *(person)* sincère
geography [dʒɪ'ɒgrəfɪ] *n* géographie *f*
geology [dʒɪ'ɒlədʒɪ] *n* géologie *f*
geometric(al) [dʒɪə'metrɪk(l)] *adj* géométrique
geometry [dʒɪ'ɒmɪtrɪ] *n* géométrie *f*
geranium [dʒɪ'reɪnɪəm] *n* géranium *m*
geriatric [dʒerɪ'ætrɪk] *adj* gériatrique
germ [dʒɜːm] *n* (MED) microbe *m*
German ['dʒɜːmən] *adj* allemand(e) ♦ *n* Allemand(e); (LING) allemand *m*; **~ measles** (BRIT) *n* rubéole *f*
Germany ['dʒɜːmənɪ] *n* Allemagne *f*
gesture ['dʒestʃə*] *n* geste *m*

KEYWORD

get [get] *(pt, pp* got, *pp* gotten *(US)) vi* **1** *(become, be)* devenir; **to ~ old/tired** devenir vieux/fatigué, vieillir/se fatiguer; **to ~ drunk** s'enivrer; **to ~ killed** se faire tuer; **when do I ~ paid?** quand est-ce que je serai payé?; **it's ~ting late** il se fait tard
2 *(go)*: **to ~ to/from** aller à/de; **to ~ home** rentrer chez soi; **how did you ~ here?** comment es-tu arrivé ici?
3 *(begin)* commencer *or* se mettre à; **I'm ~ting to like him** je commence à l'apprécier; **let's ~ going** *or* **started** allons-y
4 *(modal aux vb)*: **you've got to do it** il faut que vous le fassiez; **I've got to tell the police** je dois le dire à la police
♦ *vt* **1**: **to ~ sth done** *(do)* faire qch; *(have done)* faire faire qch; **to ~ one's hair cut** se faire couper les cheveux; **to ~ sb to do sth** faire faire qch à qn; **to ~ sb drunk** enivrer qn
2 *(obtain: money, permission, results)* obtenir, avoir; *(find: job, flat)* trouver; *(fetch: person, doctor, object)* aller chercher; **to ~ sth for sb** procurer qch à qn; **~ me Mr Jones, please** *(on phone)* passez-moi Mr Jones, s'il vous plaît; **can I ~ you a drink?**

est-ce que je peux vous servir à boire?
3 *(receive: present, letter)* recevoir, avoir; *(acquire: reputation)* avoir; *(: prize)* obtenir; **what did you ~ for your birthday?** qu'est-ce que tu as eu pour ton anniversaire?
4 *(catch)* prendre, saisir, attraper; *(hit: target etc)* atteindre; **to ~ sb by the arm/throat** prendre *or* saisir *or* attraper qn par le bras/à la gorge; **~ him!** arrête-le!
5 *(take, move)* faire parvenir; **do you think we'll ~ it through the door?** on arrivera à le faire passer par la porte?; **I'll ~ you there somehow** je me débrouillerai pour t'y emmener
6 *(catch, take: plane, bus etc)* prendre
7 *(understand)* comprendre, saisir; *(hear)* entendre; **I've got it!** j'ai compris!; **I didn't ~ your name** je n'ai pas entendu votre nom
8 *(have, possess)*: **to have got** avoir; **how many have you got?** vous en avez combien?
get about *vi* se déplacer; *(news)* se répandre
get along *vi (agree)* s'entendre; *(depart)* s'en aller; *(manage)* = **get by**
get at *vt fus (attack)* s'en prendre à; *(reach)* attraper, atteindre
get away *vi* partir, s'en aller; *(escape)* s'échapper
get away with *vt fus* en être quitte pour; se faire passer *or* pardonner
get back *vi (return)* rentrer ♦ *vt* récupérer, recouvrer
get by *vi (pass)* passer; *(manage)* se débrouiller
get down *vi, vt fus* descendre ♦ *vt* descendre; *(depress)* déprimer
get down to *vt fus (work)* se mettre à (faire)
get in *vi* rentrer; *(train)* arriver; **get into** *vt fus* entrer dans; *(car, train etc)* monter dans; *(clothes)* mettre, enfiler, endosser; **to get into bed/a rage** se mettre au lit/en colère
get off *vi (from train etc)* descendre; *(depart: person, car)* s'en aller; *(escape)* s'en tirer ♦ *vt (remove: clothes, stain)* enlever ♦ *vt fus (train, bus)* descendre de
get on *vi (at exam etc)* se débrouiller; *(agree)*: **to get on (with)** s'entendre (avec) ♦ *vt fus* monter dans; *(horse)* monter sur
get out *vi* sortir; *(of vehicle)* descendre ♦ *vt* sortir
get out of *vt fus* sortir de; *(duty etc)* échapper à, se soustraire à
get over *vt fus (illness)* se remettre de
get round *vt fus* contourner; *(fig: person)* entortiller
get through *vi (TEL)* avoir la communication; **to get through to sb** atteindre qn

get together *vi* se réunir ♦ *vt* assembler
get up *vi* (*rise*) se lever ♦ *vt fus* monter
get up to *vt fus* (*reach*) arriver à; (*prank etc*) faire

getaway ['getǝweɪ] *n*: **to make one's ~** filer

geyser ['giːzǝ*] *n* (GEO) geyser *m*; (BRIT: *water heater*) chauffe-eau *m inv*

Ghana ['gɑːnǝ] *n* Ghana *m*

ghastly ['gɑːstlɪ] *adj* atroce, horrible; (*pale*) livide, blême

gherkin ['gɜːkɪn] *n* cornichon *m*

ghetto blaster ['getǝʊ-] *n* stéréo *f* portable

ghost [gǝʊst] *n* fantôme *m*, revenant *m*

giant ['dʒaɪǝnt] *n* géant(e) ♦ *adj* géant(e), énorme

gibberish ['dʒɪbǝrɪʃ] *n* charabia *m*

giblets ['dʒɪblɪts] *npl* abats *mpl*

Gibraltar [dʒɪ'brɔːltǝ*] *n* Gibraltar *m*

giddy ['gɪdɪ] *adj* (*dizzy*): **to be** or **feel ~** avoir le vertige

gift [gɪft] *n* cadeau *m*; (*donation, ability*) don *m*; ~**ed** *adj* doué(e); ~ **token** *n* chèque-cadeau *m*

gigantic [dʒaɪ'gæntɪk] *adj* gigantesque

giggle ['gɪgl] *vi* pouffer (de rire), rire sottement

gill [dʒɪl] *n* (*measure*) = 0.25 pints (BRIT = 0.15 l, US = 0.12 l)

gills [gɪlz] *npl* (*of fish*) ouïes *fpl*, branchies *fpl*

gilt [gɪlt] *adj* doré(e) ♦ *n* dorure *f*; ~**-edged** *adj* (COMM) de premier ordre

gimmick ['gɪmɪk] *n* truc *m*

gin [dʒɪn] *n* (*liquor*) gin *m*

ginger ['dʒɪndʒǝ*] *n* gingembre *m*; ~ **ale** *n* boisson gazeuse au gingembre; ~ **beer** *n* = ginger ale; ~**bread** *n* pain *m* d'épices

gingerly ['dʒɪndʒǝlɪ] *adv* avec précaution

gipsy ['dʒɪpsɪ] *n* = **gypsy**

giraffe [dʒɪ'rɑːf] *n* girafe *f*

girder ['gɜːdǝ*] *n* poutrelle *f*

girdle ['gɜːdl] *n* (*corset*) gaine *f*

girl [gɜːl] *n* fille *f*, fillette *f*; (*young unmarried woman*) jeune fille; (*daughter*) fille; **an English ~** une jeune Anglaise; ~**friend** *n* (*of girl*) amie *f*; (*of boy*) petite amie; ~**ish** *adj* de petite or de jeune fille; (*for a boy*) efféminé(e)

giro ['dʒaɪrǝʊ] *n* (*bank* ~) virement *m* bancaire; (*post office* ~) mandat *m*; (BRIT: *welfare cheque*) mandat d'allocation chômage

girth [gɜːθ] *n* circonférence *f*; (*of horse*) sangle *f*

gist [dʒɪst] *n* essentiel *m*

give [gɪv] (*pt* gave, *pp* given) *vt* donner ♦ *vi* (*break*) céder; (*stretch: fabric*) se prêter; **to ~ sb sth**, ~ **sth to sb** donner qch à qn; **to ~ a cry/sigh** pousser un cri/un soupir; ~ **away** *vt* donner; (~ *free*) faire cadeau de; (*betray*) donner, trahir; (*disclose*) révé-

ler; (*bride*) conduire à l'autel; ~ **back** *vt* rendre; ~ **in** *vi* céder ♦ *vt* donner; ~ **off** *vt* dégager; ~ **out** *vt* distribuer; annoncer; ~ **up** *vi* renoncer ♦ *vt* renoncer à; **to ~ up smoking** arrêter de fumer; **to ~ o.s. up** se rendre; ~ **way** (BRIT) *vi* céder; (AUT) céder la priorité

glacier ['glæsɪǝ*] *n* glacier *m*

glad [glæd] *adj* content(e); ~**ly** *adv* volontiers

glamorous ['glæmǝrǝs] *adj* (*person*) séduisant(e); (*job*) prestigieux (euse)

glamour ['glæmǝ*] *n* éclat *m*, prestige *m*

glance [glɑːns] *n* coup *m* d'œil ♦ *vi*: **to ~ at** jeter un coup d'œil à; ~ **off** *vt fus* (*bullet*) ricocher sur; **glancing** ['glɑːnsɪŋ] *adj* (*blow*) oblique

gland [glænd] *n* glande *f*

glare [glɛǝ*] *n* (*of anger*) regard furieux; (*of light*) lumière éblouissante; (*of publicity*) feux *mpl* ♦ *vi* briller d'un éclat aveuglant; **to ~ at** lancer un regard furieux à; **glaring** ['glɛǝrɪŋ] *adj* (*mistake*) criant(e), qui saute aux yeux

glass [glɑːs] *n* verre *m*; ~**es** *npl* (*spectacles*) lunettes *fpl*; ~**house** (BRIT) *n* (*for plants*) serre *f*; ~**ware** *n* verrerie *f*

glaze [gleɪz] *vt* (*door, window*) vitrer; (*pottery*) vernir ♦ *n* (*on pottery*) vernis *m*; ~**d** *adj* (*pottery*) verni(e); (*eyes*) vitreux(euse)

glazier ['gleɪzɪǝ*] *n* vitrier *m*

gleam [gliːm] *vi* luire, briller

glean [gliːn] *vt* (*information*) glaner

glee [gliː] *n* joie *f*

glib [glɪb] *adj* (*person*) qui a du bagou; (*response*) désinvolte, facile

glide [glaɪd] *vi* glisser; (AVIAT, *birds*) planer; ~**r** *n* (AVIAT) planeur *m*; **gliding** ['glaɪdɪŋ] *n* (SPORT) vol *m* à voile

glimmer ['glɪmǝ*] *n* lueur *f*

glimpse [glɪmps] *n* vision passagère, aperçu *m* ♦ *vt* entrevoir, apercevoir

glint [glɪnt] *vi* étinceler

glisten ['glɪsn] *vi* briller, luire

glitter ['glɪtǝ*] *vi* scintiller, briller

gloat [glǝʊt] *vi*: **to ~ (over)** jubiler (à propos de)

global ['glǝʊbl] *adj* mondial(e)

globe [glǝʊb] *n* globe *m*

gloom [gluːm] *n* obscurité *f*; (*sadness*) tristesse *f*, mélancolie *f*; ~**y** *adj* sombre, triste, lugubre

glorious ['glɔːrɪǝs] *adj* glorieux(euse); splendide

glory ['glɔːrɪ] *n* gloire *f*; (*splendour*) splendeur *f*

gloss [glɒs] *n* (*shine*) brillant *m*, vernis *m*; (*also*: ~ *paint*) peinture brillante or laquée; ~ **over** *vt fus* glisser sur

glossary ['glɒsǝrɪ] *n* glossaire *m*

glossy ['glɒsɪ] *adj* brillant(e); ~ **magazine** magazine *m* de luxe

glove [glʌv] n gant m; ~ **compartment** n (AUT) boîte f à gants, vide-poches m inv

glow [gləʊ] vi rougeoyer; (face) rayonner; (eyes) briller

glower ['glaʊə*] vi: **to ~ (at)** lancer des regards mauvais (à)

glucose ['gluːkəʊz] n glucose m

glue [gluː] n colle f ♦ vt coller

glum [glʌm] adj sombre, morne

glut [glʌt] n surabondance f

glutton ['glʌtn] n glouton(ne); **a ~ for work** un bourreau de travail; **a ~ for punishment** un masochiste (fig)

gnarled [nɑːld] adj noueux(euse)

gnat [næt] n moucheron m

gnaw [nɔː] vt ronger

go [gəʊ] (pt **went**, pp **gone**; pl **~es**) vi aller; (depart) partir, s'en aller; (work) marcher; (be sold): **to ~ for £10** se vendre 10 livres; (fit, suit): **to ~ with** aller avec; (become): **to ~ pale/mouldy** pâlir/moisir; (break etc) céder ♦ n: **to have a ~ (at)** essayer (de faire); **to be on the ~** être en mouvement; **whose ~ is it?** à qui est-ce de jouer?; **he's ~ing to do il** va faire, il est sur le point de faire; **to ~ for a walk** aller se promener; **to ~ dancing** aller danser; **how did it ~?** comment est-ce que ça s'est passé?; **to ~ round the back/by the shop** passer par derrière/devant le magasin; ~ **about** vi (rumour) se répandre ♦ vt fus: **how do I ~ about this?** comment dois-je m'y prendre (pour faire ceci)?; ~ **ahead** vi (make progress) avancer; (get going) y aller; ~ **along** vi aller, avancer ♦ vt fus longer, parcourir; (like) aimer; (attack) s'en prendre à, attaquer; ~ **in** vi entrer; ~ **in for** vt fus (competition) se présenter à; (like) aimer; ~ **into** vt fus entrer dans; (investigate) étudier, examiner; (embark on) se lancer dans; ~ **off** vi partir, s'en aller; (food) se gâter; (explode) sauter; (event) se dérouler ♦ vt fus ne plus aimer; **the gun went off** le coup est parti; ~ **on** vi continuer; (happen) se passer; **to ~ on doing** continuer à faire; ~ **out** vi sortir; (fire, light) s'éteindre; ~ **over** vt fus (check) revoir, vérifier; ~ **through** vt fus (town etc) traverser; ~ **up** vi monter; (price) augmenter ♦ vt fus gravir; ~ **without** vt fus se passer de

goad [gəʊd] vt aiguillonner

go-ahead ['gəʊəhed] adj dynamique, entreprenant(e) ♦ n feu vert

goal [gəʊl] n but m; ~**keeper** n gardien m de but; ~**post** n poteau m de but

goat [gəʊt] n chèvre f

gobble ['gɔbl] vt (also: ~ **down**, ~ **up**) engloutir

go-between ['gəʊ-] n intermédiaire m/f

god [gɔd] n dieu m; **G~** n Dieu m; ~**child** n filleul(e); ~**daughter** n filleule f; ~**dess** n déesse f; ~**father** n parrain m; ~**forsaken** adj maudit(e); ~**mother** n marraine f; ~**send** n aubaine f; ~**son** n filleul m

goggles ['gɔglz] npl (for skiing etc) lunettes protectrices

going ['gəʊɪŋ] n (conditions) état m du terrain ♦ adj: **the ~ rate** le tarif (en vigueur)

gold [gəʊld] n or m ♦ adj en or; (reserves) d'or; ~**en** adj (made of gold) en or; (gold in colour) doré(e); ~**fish** n poisson m rouge; ~**-plated** adj plaqué(e or inv); ~**smith** n orfèvre m

golf [gɔlf] n golf m; ~ **ball** n balle f de golf; (on typewriter) boule m; ~ **club** n club m de golf; (stick) club m, crosse f de golf; ~ **course** n (terrain m de) golf m; ~**er** n joueur(euse) de golf

gone [gɔn] pp of **go**

gong [gɔŋ] n gong m

good [gʊd] adj bon(ne); (kind) gentil(le); (child) sage ♦ n bien m; ~**s** npl (COMM) marchandises fpl, articles mpl; **~! bon!, très bien!; to be ~ at** être bon en; **to be ~ for** être bon pour; **would you be ~ enough to ...?** auriez-vous la bonté or l'amabilité de ...?; **a ~ deal (of)** beaucoup (de); **a ~ many** beaucoup (de); **to make ~** vi (succeed) faire son chemin, réussir ♦ vt (deficit) combler; (losses) compenser; **it's no ~ complaining** cela ne sert à rien de se plaindre; **for ~** pour de bon, une fois pour toutes; ~ **morning/afternoon!** bonjour!; ~ **evening!** bonsoir!; ~ **night!** bonsoir!; (on going to bed) bonne nuit!; ~**bye!** excl au revoir!; **G~ Friday** n Vendredi m Saint; ~**looking** adj beau(belle), bien inv; ~**natured** adj (person) qui a un bon naturel; ~**ness** n (of person) bonté f; **for ~ness sake!** je vous en prie!; ~**ness gracious!** mon Dieu!; ~**s train** n (BRIT) train m de marchandises; ~**will** n bonne volonté

goose [guːs] (pl **geese**) n oie f

gooseberry ['gʊzbərɪ] n groseille f à maquereau; **to play ~** (BRIT) tenir la chandelle

gooseflesh ['guːsfleʃ] n, **goose pimples** npl chair f de poule

gore [gɔː*] vt encorner ♦ n sang m

gorge [gɔːdʒ] n gorge f ♦ vt: **to ~ o.s. (on)** se gorger (de)

gorgeous ['gɔːdʒəs] adj splendide, superbe

gorilla [gə'rɪlə] n gorille m

gorse [gɔːs] n ajoncs mpl

gory ['gɔːrɪ] adj sanglant(e); (details) horrible

go-slow ['gəu'sləu] (BRIT) n grève perlée

gospel ['gɔspəl] n évangile m

gossip ['gɔsɪp] n (chat) bavardages mpl; commérage m, cancans mpl; (person) commère f ♦ vi bavarder; (maliciously) cancaner, faire des commérages

got [gɔt] pt, pp of **get**

gotten ['gɔtn] (US) pp of **get**

gout [gaut] n goutte f

govern ['gʌvən] vt gouverner; **~ess** ['gʌvənɪs] n gouvernante f; **~ment** ['gʌvnmənt] n gouvernement m; (BRIT: ministers) ministère m; **~or** ['gʌvənə*] n (of state, bank) gouverneur m; (of school, hospital) ≈ membre m/f du conseil d'établissement; (BRIT: of prison) directeur(trice)

gown [gaun] n robe f; (of teacher, BRIT: of judge) toge f

GP n abbr = **general practitioner**

grab [græb] vt saisir, empoigner ♦ vi: **to ~ at** essayer de saisir

grace [greɪs] n grâce f ♦ vt honorer; (adorn) orner; **5 days' ~** cinq jours de répit; **~ful** adj gracieux(euse), élégant(e); **gracious** ['greɪʃəs] adj bienveillant(e)

grade [greɪd] n (COMM) qualité; f (in hierarchy) catégorie f, grade m, échelon m; (SCOL) note f; (US: school class) classe f ♦ vt classer; **~ crossing** (US) n passage m à niveau; **~ school** (US) n école f primaire

gradient ['greɪdɪənt] n inclinaison f, pente f

gradual ['grædjuəl] adj graduel(le), progressif(ive); **~ly** adv peu à peu, graduellement

graduate [n 'grædjuɪt, vb 'grædjueɪt] n diplômé(e), licencié(e); (US: of high school) bachelier(ère) ♦ vi obtenir son diplôme; (US) obtenir son baccalauréat; **graduation** [grædju'eɪʃən] n (cérémonie f de) remise f des diplômes

graffiti [grə'fiːtɪ] npl graffiti mpl

graft [grɑːft] n (AGR, MED) greffe f; (bribery) corruption f ♦ vt greffer; **hard ~** (BRIT: inf) boulot acharné

grain [greɪn] n grain m

gram [græm] n gramme m

grammar ['græmə*] n grammaire f; **~ school** (BRIT) n ≈ lycée m; **grammatical** [grə'mætɪkl] adj grammatical(e)

gramme [græm] n = **gram**

grand [grænd] adj magnifique, splendide; (gesture etc) noble; **~children** npl petits-enfants mpl; **~dad** (inf) n grand-papa m; **~daughter** n petite-fille f; **~father** n grand-père m; **~ma** (inf) n grand-maman f; **~mother** n grand-mère f; **~pa** (inf) n = **~dad**; **~parents** npl grands-parents mpl; **~ piano** n piano m à queue; **~son** n petit-fils m; **~stand** n (SPORT) tribune f

granite ['grænɪt] n granit m

granny ['grænɪ] (inf) n grand-maman f

grant [grɑːnt] vt accorder; (a request) accéder à; (admit) concéder ♦ n (SCOL) bourse

f; (ADMIN) subside m, subvention f; **to take it for ~ed** trouver tout naturel que +sub; **to take sb for ~ed** considérer qn comme faisant partie du décor

granulated sugar ['grænjuleɪtɪd-] n sucre m en poudre

grape [greɪp] n raisin m; **~fruit** ['greɪpfruːt] n pamplemousse m

graph [grɑːf] n graphique m; **~ic** ['græfɪk] adj graphique; (account, description) vivant(e); **~ics** n arts mpl graphiques, graphisme m ♦ npl représentations fpl graphiques

grapple ['græpl] vi: **to ~ with** être aux prises avec

grasp [grɑːsp] vt saisir ♦ n (grip) prise f; (understanding) compréhension f, connaissance f, **~ing** adj cupide

grass [grɑːs] n herbe f; (lawn) gazon m; **~hopper** n sauterelle f; **~-roots** adj de la base, du peuple

grate [greɪt] n grille f de cheminée ♦ vi grincer ♦ vt (CULIN) râper

grateful ['greɪtful] adj reconnaissant(e)

grater ['greɪtə*] n râpe f

gratifying ['grætɪfaɪɪŋ] adj agréable

grating ['greɪtɪŋ] n (iron bars) grille f ♦ adj (noise) grinçant(e)

gratitude ['grætɪtjuːd] n gratitude f

gratuity [grə'tjuːɪtɪ] n pourboire m

grave [greɪv] n tombe f ♦ adj grave, sérieux(euse)

gravel ['grævəl] n gravier m

gravestone ['greɪvstəun] n pierre tombale

graveyard ['greɪvjɑːd] n cimetière m

gravity ['grævɪtɪ] n (PHYSICS) gravité f; pesanteur f; (seriousness) gravité

gravy ['greɪvɪ] n jus m (de viande); sauce f

gray [greɪ] (US) adj = **grey**

graze [greɪz] vi paître, brouter ♦ vt (touch lightly) frôler, effleurer; (scrape) écorcher ♦ n écorchure f

grease [griːs] n (fat) graisse f; (lubricant) lubrifiant m ♦ vt graisser; lubrifier; **~proof paper** (BRIT) n papier sulfurisé; **greasy** ['griːsɪ] adj gras(se), graisseux(euse)

great [greɪt] adj grand(e); (inf) formidable; **G~ Britain** n Grande-Bretagne f; **~-grandfather** n arrière-grand-père m; **~-grandmother** n arrière-grand-mère f; **~ly** adv très, grandement; (with verbs) beaucoup; **~ness** n grandeur f

Greece [griːs] n Grèce f

greed [griːd] n (also: **~iness**) avidité f; (for food) gourmandise f, gloutonnerie f; **~y** adj avide; gourmand(e), glouton(ne)

Greek [griːk] adj grec(grecque) ♦ n Grec(Grecque); (LING) grec m

green [griːn] adj vert(e); (inexperienced) (bien) jeune, naïf(naïve); (POL) vert(e), écologiste; (ecological) écologique ♦ n vert m; (stretch of grass) pelouse f; **~s** npl (vegeta-

bles) légumes verts; (*POL*): **the G~s** les Verts *mpl*; **The G~ Party** (*BRIT*: *POL*) le parti écologiste; **~ belt** *n* (*round town*) ceinture verte; **~ card** *n* (*AUT*) carte verte; (*US*) permis *m* de travail; **~ery** *n* verdure *f*; **~grocer** (*BRIT*) *n* marchand *m* de fruits et légumes; **~house** *n* serre *f*; **~house effect** *n* effet *m* de serre; **~house gas** *n* gas *m* à effet de serre; **~ish** *adj* verdâtre

Greenland ['griːnlənd] *n* Groenland *m*

greet [griːt] *vt* accueillir; **~ing** *n* salutation *f*; **~ing(s) card** *n* carte *f* de vœux

gregarious [grɪ'gɛərɪəs] *adj* (*person*) sociable

grenade [grɪ'neɪd] *n* grenade *f*

grew [gruː] *pt of* grow

grey [greɪ] (*US* **gray**) *adj* gris(e); (*dismal*) sombre; **~-haired** *adj* grisonnant(e); **~hound** *n* lévrier *m*

grid [grɪd] *n* grille *f*; (*ELEC*) réseau *m*

grief [griːf] *n* chagrin *m*, douleur *f*

grievance ['griːvəns] *n* doléance *f*, grief *m*

grieve [griːv] *vi* avoir du chagrin; se désoler ♦ *vt* faire de la peine à, affliger; **to ~ for sb** (*dead person*) pleurer qn

grievous ['griːvəs] *adj* (*LAW*): **~ bodily harm** coups *mpl* et blessures *fpl*

grill [grɪl] *n* (*on cooker*) gril *m*; (*food: also mixed ~*) grillade(s) f(*pl*) ♦ *vt* (*BRIT*) griller; (*inf: question*) cuisiner

grille [grɪl] *n* grille *f*, grillage *m*; (*AUT*) calandre *f*

grim [grɪm] *adj* sinistre, lugubre; (*serious, stern*) sévère

grimace [grɪ'meɪs] *n* grimace *f* ♦ *vi* grimacer, faire une grimace

grime [graɪm] *n* crasse *f*, saleté *f*

grin [grɪn] *n* large sourire *m* ♦ *vi* sourire

grind [graɪnd] (*pt, pp* **ground**) *vt* écraser; (*coffee, pepper etc*) moudre; (*US: meat*) hacher; (*make sharp*) aiguiser ♦ *n* (*work*) corvée *f*

grip [grɪp] *n* (*hold*) prise *f*, étreinte *f*; (*control*) emprise *f*; (*grasp*) connaissance *f*; (*handle*) poignée *f*; (*holdall*) sac *m* de voyage ♦ *vt* saisir, empoigner; **to come to ~s with** en venir aux prises avec; **~ping** *adj* prenant(e), palpitant(e)

grisly ['grɪzlɪ] *adj* sinistre, macabre

gristle ['grɪsl] *n* cartilage *m*

grit [grɪt] *n* gravillon *m*; (*courage*) cran *m* ♦ *vt* (*road*) sabler; **to ~ one's teeth** serrer les dents

groan [grəun] *n* (*of pain*) gémissement *m* ♦ *vi* gémir

grocer ['grəusə*] *n* épicier *m*; **~ies** *npl* provisions *fpl*; **~'s (shop)** *n* épicerie *f*

groin [grɔɪn] *n* aine *f*

groom [gruːm] *n* palefrenier *m*; (*also: bride~*) marié *m* ♦ *vt* (*horse*) panser; (*fig*): **to ~ sb for** former qn pour; **well-groomed** très soigné(e)

groove [gruːv] *n* rainure *f*

grope [grəup] *vi*: **to ~ for** chercher à tâtons

gross [grəus] *adj* grossier(ère); (*COMM*) brut(e); **~ly** *adv* (*greatly*) très, grandement

grotto ['grɒtəu] *n* grotte *f*

grotty ['grɒtɪ] (*inf*) *adj* minable, affreux(euse)

ground [graund] *pt, pp of* grind ♦ *n* sol *m*, terre *f*; (*land*) terrain *m*, terres *fpl*; (*SPORT*) terrain; (*US: also: ~ wire*) terre; (*reason: gen pl*) raison *f* ♦ *vt* (*plane*) empêcher de décoller, retenir au sol; (*US: ELEC*) équiper d'une prise de terre; **~s** *npl* (*of coffee etc*) marc *m*; (*gardens etc*) parc *m*, domaine *m*; **on the ~, to the ~** par terre; **to gain/lose ~** gagner/perdre du terrain; **~ cloth** (*US*) *n* = **groundsheet**; **~ing** *n* (*in education*) connaissances *fpl* de base; **~less** *adj* sans fondement; **~sheet** (*BRIT*) *n* tapis *m* de sol; **~ staff** *n* personnel *m* au sol; **~swell** *n* lame *f* or vague *f* de fond; **~work** *n* préparation *f*

group [gruːp] *n* groupe *m* ♦ *vt* (*also: ~ together*) grouper ♦ *vi* se grouper

grouse [graus] *n inv* (*bird*) grouse *f* ♦ *vi* (*complain*) rouspéter, râler

grove [grəuv] *n* bosquet *m*

grovel ['grɒvl] *vi* (*fig*) ramper

grow [grəu] (*pt* **grew**, *pp* **grown**) *vi* pousser, croître; (*person*) grandir; (*increase*) augmenter, se développer; (*become*): **to ~ rich/weak** s'enrichir/s'affaiblir; (*develop*): **he's ~n out of his jacket** sa veste est (devenue) trop petite pour lui; **he'll ~ out of it!** ça lui passera! ♦ *vt* cultiver, faire pousser; (*beard*) laisser pousser; **~ up** *vi* grandir; **~er** *n* producteur *m*; **~ing** *adj* (*fear, amount*) croissant(e), grandissant(e)

growl [graul] *vi* grogner

grown [grəun] *pp of* grow; **~-up** *n* adulte *m/f*, grande personne

growth [grəuθ] *n* croissance *f*, développement *m*; (*what has grown*) pousse *f*; poussée *f*; (*MED*) grosseur *f*, tumeur *f*

grub [grʌb] *n* larve *f*; (*inf: food*) bouffe *f*

grubby ['grʌbɪ] *adj* crasseux(euse)

grudge [grʌdʒ] *n* rancune *f* ♦ *vt*: **to ~ sb sth** (*in giving*) donner qch à qn à contrecœur; (*resent*) reprocher qch à qn; **to bear sb a ~ (for)** garder rancune *or* en vouloir à qn (de)

gruelling ['gruəlɪŋ] (*US* **grueling**) *adj* exténuant(e)

gruesome ['gruːsəm] *adj* horrible

gruff [grʌf] *adj* bourru(e)

grumble ['grʌmbl] *vi* rouspéter, ronchonner

grumpy ['grʌmpɪ] *adj* grincheux(euse)

grunt [grʌnt] *vi* grogner

G-string ['dʒiː-] *n* (*garment*) cache-sexe *m inv*

guarantee [gærən'tiː] *n* garantie *f* ♦ *vt* garantir

guard [gɑːd] *n* garde *f*; (*one man*) garde *m*; (*BRIT: RAIL*) chef *m* de train; (*on machine*) dispositif *m* de sûreté; (*also: fire~*) garde-feu *m* ♦ *vt* garder, surveiller; (*protect*): **to ~ (against** *or* **from)** protéger (contre); **~ against** *vt* (*prevent*) empêcher, se protéger de; **~ed** *adj* (*fig*) prudent(e); **~ian** *n* gardien(ne); (*of minor*) tuteur(trice); **~'s van** (*BRIT*) (*RAIL*) fourgon *m*

guerrilla [gə'rɪlə] *n* guérillero *m*

guess [ges] *vt* deviner; (*estimate*) évaluer; (*US*) croire, penser ♦ *vi* deviner ♦ *n* supposition *f*, hypothèse *f*; **to take** *or* **have a ~** essayer de deviner; **~work** *n* hypothèse *f*

guest [gest] *n* invité(e); (*in hotel*) client(e); **~-house** *n* pension *f*; **~ room** *n* chambre *f* d'amis

guffaw [gʌ'fɔː] *vi* pouffer de rire

guidance ['gaɪdəns] *n* conseils *mpl*

guide [gaɪd] *n* (*person, book etc*) guide *m*; (*BRIT: also: girl ~*) guide *f* ♦ *vt* guider; **~book** *n* guide *m*; **~ dog** *n* chien *m* d'aveugle; **~lines** *npl* (*fig*) instructions (générales), conseils *mpl*

guild [gɪld] *n* corporation *f*; cercle *m*, association *f*

guile [gaɪl] *n* astuce *f*

guillotine [gɪlə'tiːn] *n* guillotine *f*

guilt [gɪlt] *n* culpabilité *f*; **~y** *adj* coupable

guinea pig ['gɪnɪ~] *n* cobaye *m*

guise [gaɪz] *n* aspect *m*, apparence *f*

guitar [gɪ'tɑː] *n* guitare *f*

gulf [gʌlf] *n* golfe *m*; (*abyss*) gouffre *m*

gull [gʌl] *n* mouette *f*; (*larger*) goéland *m*

gullet ['gʌlɪt] *n* gosier *m*

gullible ['gʌlɪbl] *adj* crédule

gully ['gʌlɪ] *n* ravin *m*; ravine *f*; couloir *m*

gulp [gʌlp] *vi* avaler sa salive ♦ *vt* (*also: ~ down*) avaler

gum [gʌm] *n* (*ANAT*) gencive *f*; (*glue*) colle *f*; (*sweet: also ~drop*) boule *f* de gomme; (*also: chewing ~*) chewing-gum *m* ♦ *vt* coller; **~boots** (*BRIT*) *npl* bottes *fpl* en caoutchouc

gun [gʌn] *n* (*small*) revolver *m*, pistolet *m*; (*rifle*) fusil *m*, carabine *f*; (*cannon*) canon *m*; **~boat** *n* canonnière *f*; **~fire** *n* fusillade *f*; **~man** *n* bandit armé; **~point** *n*: **at ~point** sous la menace du pistolet (*or* fusil); **~powder** *n* poudre *f* à canon; **~shot** *n* coup *m* de feu

gurgle ['gɜːgl] *vi* gargouiller; (*baby*) gazouiller

gush [gʌʃ] *vi* jaillir; (*fig*) se répandre en effusions

gust [gʌst] *n* (*of wind*) rafale *f*; (*of smoke*) bouffée *f*

gusto ['gʌstəu] *n* enthousiasme *m*

gut [gʌt] *n* intestin *m*, boyau *m*; **~s** *npl* (*inf: courage*) cran *m*

gutter ['gʌtə*] *n* (*in street*) caniveau *m*; (*of roof*) gouttière *f*

guy [gaɪ] *n* (*inf: man*) type *m*; (*also: ~rope*) corde *f*; (*BRIT: figure*) effigie de Guy Fawkes (*brûlée en plein air le 5 novembre*)

guzzle ['gʌzl] *vt* avaler gloutonnement

gym [dʒɪm] *n* (*also: ~nasium*) gymnase *m*; (*also: ~nastics*) gym *f*; **~nast** ['dʒɪmnæst] *n* gymnaste *m/f*; **~nastics** [dʒɪm'næstɪks] *n, npl* gymnastique *f*; **~ shoes** *npl* chaussures *fpl* de gym; **~slip** (*BRIT*) *n* tunique *f* (d'écolière)

gynaecologist [gaɪnɪ'kɔlədʒɪst] (*US* **gynecologist**) *n* gynécologue *m/f*

gypsy ['dʒɪpsɪ] *n* gitan(e), bohémien(ne)

—— *H h*

haberdashery [hæbə'dæʃərɪ] (*BRIT*) *n* mercerie *f*

habit ['hæbɪt] *n* habitude *f*; (*REL: costume*) habit *m*

habitual [hə'bɪtjuəl] *adj* habituel(le); (*drinker, liar*) invétéré(e)

hack [hæk] *vt* hacher, tailler ♦ *n* (*pej: writer*) nègre *m*; **~er** *n* (*COMPUT*) pirate *m* (informatique); (*: enthusiast*) passionné(e) *m/f* des ordinateurs

hackneyed ['hæknɪd] *adj* usé(e), rebattu(e)

had [hæd] *pt, pp of* **have**

haddock ['hædək] (*pl* ~ *or* ~**s**) *n* églefin *m*; **smoked ~** haddock *m*

hadn't ['hædnt] = **had not**

haemorrhage ['hemərɪdʒ] (*US* **hemorrhage**) *n* hémorragie *f*

haemorrhoids ['hemərɔɪdz] (*US* **hemorroids**) *npl* hémorroïdes *fpl*

haggle ['hægl] *vi* marchander

Hague [heɪg] *n*: **The ~** La Haye

hail [heɪl] *n* grêle *f* ♦ *vt* (*call*) héler; (*acclaim*) acclamer ♦ *vi* grêler; **~stone** *n* grêlon *m*

hair [heə*] *n* cheveux *mpl*; (*of animal*) pelage *m*; (*single hair: on head*) cheveu *m*; (*on body; of animal*) poil *m*; **to do one's ~** se coiffer; **~brush** *n* brosse *f* à cheveux; **~cut** *n* coupe *f* (de cheveux); **~do** *n* coiffure *f*; **~dresser** *n* coiffeur(euse); **~dresser's** *n* salon *m* de coiffure, coiffeur *m*; **~ dryer** *n* sèche-cheveux *m*; **~grip** *n* pince *f* à cheveux; **~net** *n* filet *m* à cheveux; **~piece** *n* perruque *f*; **~pin** *n* épingle *f* à cheveux; **~pin bend** (*US* **~pin curve**) *n* virage *m* en épingle à cheveux; **~-raising** *adj* à (vous) faire dresser les cheveux sur la tête; **~ removing cream** *n* crème *f* dépilatoire; **~ spray** *n* laque *f* (pour les cheveux); **~style** *n* coiffure *f*; **~y** *adj* poilu(e); *(inf: fig)* effrayant(e)

hake [heɪk] *(pl ~ or ~s)* *n* colin *m*, merlu *m*

half [hɑːf] *(pl halves)* *n* moitié *f*, *(of beer: also: ~ pint)* ≈ demi *m*; *(RAIL, bus also: ~ fare)* demi-tarif *m* ♦ *adj* demi(e) ♦ *adv* (à) moitié, à demi; **~ a dozen** une demi-douzaine; **~ a pound** une demi-livre, ≈ 250 g; **two** and **a ~** deux et demi; **to cut sth in ~** couper qch en deux; **~-baked** *adj (plan)* qui ne tient pas debout; **~-caste** *n* métis(se); **~-hearted** *adj* tiède, sans enthousiasme; **~-hour** *n* demi-heure *f*, **half-mast: at ~-mast** *adv (flag)* en berne; **~penny** ['heɪpnɪ] *(BRIT)* *n* demi-penny *m*; **~-price** *adj, adv:* **(at)** **~-price** à moitié prix; **~ term** *(BRIT)* *n (SCOL)* congé *m* de demi-trimestre; **~-time** *n* mi-temps *f*; **~way** *adv* à mi-chemin

hall [hɔːl] *n* salle *f*, *(entrance way)* hall *m*, entrée *f*

hallmark ['hɔːlmɑːk] *n* poinçon *m*; *(fig)* marque *f*

hallo [hʌˈləʊ] *excl* = **hello**

hall of residence *(BRIT: pl **halls of residence**) *n* résidence *f* universitaire

Hallowe'en ['hæləʊˈiːn] *n* veille *f* de la Toussaint

hallucination [həluːsɪˈneɪʃən] *n* hallucination *f*

hallway ['hɔːlweɪ] *n* vestibule *m*

halo ['heɪləʊ] *n (of saint etc)* auréole *f*

halt [hɔːlt] *n* halte *f*, arrêt *m* ♦ *vt* *(progress etc)* interrompre ♦ *vi* faire halte, s'arrêter

halve [hɑːv] *vt (apple etc)* partager *or* diviser en deux; *(expense)* réduire de moitié; **~s** [hɑːvz] *npl* of **half**

ham [hæm] *n* jambon *m*

hamburger ['hæmbɜːgə*] *n* hamburger *m*

hamlet ['hæmlɪt] *n* hameau *m*

hammer ['hæmə*] *n* marteau *m* ♦ *vt (nail)* enfoncer; *(fig)* démolir ♦ *vi (on door)* frapper à coups redoublés; **to ~ an idea into sb** faire entrer de force une idée dans la tête de qn

hammock ['hæmək] *n* hamac *m*

hamper ['hæmpə*] *vt* gêner ♦ *n* panier *m* (d'osier)

hamster ['hæmstə*] *n* hamster *m*

hand [hænd] *n* main *f*, *(of clock)* aiguille *f*; *(handwriting)* écriture *f*; *(worker)* ouvrier(ère); *(at cards)* jeu *m* ♦ *vt* passer, donner; **to give** *or* **lend sb a ~** donner un coup de main à qn; **at ~** à portée de la main; **in ~** *(time)* à disposition; *(job, situation)* en main; **to be on ~** *(person)* être disponible; *(emergency services)* se tenir

prêt(e) (à intervenir); **to ~** *(information etc)* sous la main, à portée de la main; **on the one ~ ..., on the other ~** d'une part ..., d'autre part; **~ in** *vt* remettre; **~ out** *vt* distribuer; **~ over** *vt* transmettre; céder; **~bag** *n* sac *m* à main; **~book** *n* manuel *m*; **~brake** *n* frein *m* à main; **~cuffs** *npl* menottes *fpl*; **~ful** *n* poignée *f*

handicap ['hændɪkæp] *n* handicap *m* ♦ *vt* handicaper; **mentally/physically ~ped** handicapé(e) mentalement/physiquement

handicraft ['hændɪkrɑːft] *n (travail m d')*artisanat *m*, technique artisanale; *(object)* objet artisanal

handiwork ['hændɪwɜːk] *n* ouvrage *m*

handkerchief ['hæŋkətʃɪf] *n* mouchoir *m*

handle ['hændl] *n (of door etc)* poignée *f*; *(of cup etc)* anse *f*; *(of knife etc)* manche *m*; *(of saucepan)* queue *f*; *(for winding)* manivelle *f* ♦ *vt* toucher, manier; *(deal with)* s'occuper de; *(treat: people)* prendre; **"~ with care"** "fragile"; **to fly off the ~** s'énerver; **~bar(s)** *n(pl)* guidon *m*

hand: **~-luggage** *n* bagages *mpl* à main; **~made** *adj* fait(e) à la main; **~out** *n (from government, parents)* aide *f*, don *m*; *(leaflet)* documentation *f*, prospectus *m*; *(summary of lecture)* polycopié *m*; **~rail** *n* rampe *f*, main courante *f*; **~shake** *n* poignée *f* de main

handsome ['hænsəm] *adj* beau (belle); *(profit, return)* considérable

handwriting ['hændraɪtɪŋ] *n* écriture *f*

handy ['hændɪ] *adj (person)* adroit(e); *(close at hand)* sous la main; *(convenient)* pratique; **~man** ['hændɪmən] *(irreg)* *n* bricoleur *m*; *(servant)* homme *m* à tout faire

hang [hæŋ] *(pt, pp hung)* *vt* accrocher; *(criminal: pt, pp: hanged)* pendre ♦ *vi* pendre; *(hair, drapery)* tomber; **to get the ~ of (doing) sth** *(inf)* attraper le coup pour faire qch; **~ about** *vi* traîner; **~ around** *vi* = **hang about**; **~ on** *vi (wait)* attendre; **~ up** *vi (TEL):* **to ~ up (on sb)** raccrocher (au nez de qn) ♦ *vt (coat, painting)* accrocher, suspendre

hangar ['hæŋə*] *n* hangar *m*

hanger ['hæŋə*] *n* cintre *m*, portemanteau *m*; **~-on** ['hæŋər'ɒn] *n* parasite *m*

hang: **~-gliding** ['hæŋglaɪdɪŋ] *n* deltaplane *m*, vol *m* libre; **~over** ['hæŋəʊvə*] *n (after drinking)* gueule *f* de bois; **~-up** ['hæŋʌp] *n* complexe *m*

hanker ['hæŋkə*] *vi:* **to ~ after** avoir envie de

hankie, hanky ['hæŋkɪ] *n abbr* = **handkerchief**

haphazard ['hæp'hæzəd] *adj* fait(e) au hasard, fait(e) au petit bonheur

happen ['hæpən] *vi* arriver; se passer, se produire; **it so ~s that** il se trouve que; **as it ~s** justement; **~ing** *n* événement *m*

happily ['hæpɪlɪ] *adv* heureusement; *(cheerfully)* joyeusement
happiness ['hæpɪnɪs] *n* bonheur *m*
happy ['hæpɪ] *adj* heureux(euse); ~ **with** *(arrangements etc)* satisfait(e) de; **to be ~ to do** faire volontiers; ~ **birthday!** bon anniversaire!; ~**-go-lucky** *adj* insouciant(e)
harass ['hærəs] *vt* accabler, tourmenter; ~**ment** *n* tracasseries *fpl*
harbour ['hɑːbə*] *(US* **harbor)** *n* port *m* ♦ *vt* héberger, abriter; *(hope, fear etc)* entretenir
hard [hɑːd] *adj* dur(e); *(question, problem)* difficile, dur(e); *(facts, evidence)* concret(ète) ♦ *adv (work)* dur; *(think, try)* sérieusement; **to look ~ at** regarder fixement; *(thing)* regarder de près; **no ~ feelings!** sans rancune!; **to be ~ of hearing** être dur(e) d'oreille; **to be ~ done by** être traité(e) injustement; ~**back** *n* livre relié; ~ **cash** *n* espèces *fpl*; ~ **disk** *n (COMPUT)* disque dur; ~**en** *vt* durcir; *(fig)* endurcir ♦ *vi* durcir; ~**-headed** *adj* réaliste; décidé(e); ~ **labour** *n* travaux forcés
hardly ['hɑːdlɪ] *adv (scarcely, no sooner)* à peine; ~ **anywhere/ever** presque nulle part/jamais
hard: ~**ship** *n* épreuves *fpl*; ~ **up** *(inf) adj* fauché(e); ~**ware** *n* quincaillerie *f*, *(COMPUT, MIL)* matériel *m*; ~**ware shop** *n* quincaillerie *f*; ~**-wearing** *adj* solide; ~**-working** *adj* travailleur(euse)
hardy ['hɑːdɪ] *adj* robuste; *(plant)* résistant(e) au gel
hare [hɛə*] *n* lièvre *m*; ~**-brained** *adj* farfelu(e)
harm [hɑːm] *n* mal *m*; *(wrong)* tort *m* ♦ *vt (person)* faire du mal or du tort à; *(thing)* endommager; **out of ~'s way** à l'abri du danger, en lieu sûr; ~**ful** *adj* nuisible; ~**less** *adj* inoffensif(ive); sans méchanceté
harmony ['hɑːmənɪ] *n* harmonie *f*
harness ['hɑːnɪs] *n* harnais *m*; *(safety ~)* harnais de sécurité ♦ *vt (horse)* harnacher; *(resources)* exploiter
harp [hɑːp] *n* harpe *f* ♦ *vi*: **to ~ on about** rabâcher
harrowing ['hærəʊɪŋ] *adj* déchirant(e), très pénible
harsh [hɑːʃ] *adj (hard)* dur(e); *(severe)* sévère; *(unpleasant: sound)* discordant(e); *(: light)* cru(e)
harvest ['hɑːvɪst] *n (of corn)* moisson *f*; *(of fruit)* récolte *f*; *(of grapes)* vendange *f* ♦ *vt* moissonner; récolter; vendanger
has [hæz] *vb see* **have**
hash [hæʃ] *n (CULIN)* hachis *m*; *(fig: mess)* gâchis *m*
hasn't ['hæznt] = **has not**
hassle ['hæsl] *n (inf: bother)* histoires *fpl*, tracas *mpl*
haste [heɪst] *n* hâte *f*, précipitation *f*; ~**n** ['heɪsn] *vt* hâter, accélérer ♦ *vi* se hâter, s'empresser; **hastily** *adv* à la hâte; précipitamment; **hasty** ['heɪstɪ] *adj* hâtif(ive); précipité(e)
hat [hæt] *n* chapeau *m*
hatch [hætʃ] *n (NAUT: also: ~way)* écoutille *f*; *(also: service ~)* passe-plats *m inv* ♦ *vi* éclore
hatchback ['hætʃbæk] *n (AUT)* modèle *m* avec hayon arrière
hatchet ['hætʃɪt] *n* hachette *f*
hate [heɪt] *vt* haïr, détester ♦ *n* haine *f*; ~**ful** *adj* odieux(euse), détestable; **hatred** ['heɪtrɪd] *n* haine *f*
haughty ['hɔːtɪ] *adj* hautain(e), arrogant(e)
haul [hɔːl] *vt* traîner, tirer ♦ *n (of fish)* prise *f*; *(of stolen goods etc)* butin *m*; ~**age** *n* transport routier; *(costs)* frais *mpl* de transport; ~**ier** *(US* **hauler)** *n (company)* transporteur (routier); *(driver)* camionneur *m*
haunch [hɔːntʃ] *n* hanche *f*; *(of meat)* cuissot *m*
haunt [hɔːnt] *vt* hanter ♦ *n* repaire *m*

─────────── **KEYWORD**

have [hæv] *(pt, pp* **had)** *aux vb* **1** *(gen)* avoir; être; **to ~ arrived/gone** être arrivé(e)/allé(e); **to ~ eaten/slept** avoir mangé/dormi; **he has been promoted** il a eu une promotion
2 *(in tag questions)*: **you've done it, ~n't you?** vous l'avez fait, n'est-ce pas?
3 *(in short answers and questions)*: **no I ~n't/yes we have!** mais non!/mais si!; **so I ~!** ah oui!, oui c'est vrai!; **I've been there before,** ~ **you?** j'y suis déjà allé, et vous?
♦ *modal aux vb (be obliged)*: **to ~ (got) to do sth** devoir faire qch; être obligé(e) de faire qch; **she has (got) to do it** elle doit le faire, il faut qu'elle le fasse; **you ~n't to tell her** vous ne devez pas le lui dire
♦ *vt* **1** *(possess, obtain)* avoir; **he has (got) blue eyes/dark hair** il a les yeux bleus/les cheveux bruns; **may I ~ your address?** puis-je avoir votre adresse?
2 *(+noun: take, hold etc)*: **to ~ breakfast/a bath/a shower** prendre le petit déjeuner/un bain/une douche; **to ~ dinner/lunch** dîner/déjeuner; **to ~ a swim** nager; **to ~ a meeting** se réunir; **to ~ a party** organiser une fête
3: **to ~ sth done** faire faire qch; **to ~ one's hair cut** se faire couper les cheveux; **to ~ sb do sth** faire faire qch à qn
4 *(experience, suffer)* avoir; **to ~ a cold/flu** avoir un rhume/la grippe; **to ~ an operation** se faire opérer
5 *(inf: dupe)* avoir; **he's been had** il s'est fait avoir or rouler
have out *vt*: **to have it out with sb** *(settle a problem etc)* s'expliquer (franchement)

avec qn

haven ['heɪvn] *n* port *m*; (*fig*) havre *m*

haven't ['hævnt] = **have not**

havoc ['hævək] *n* ravages *mpl*

hawk [hɔːk] *n* faucon *m*

hay [heɪ] *n* foin *m*; ~ **fever** *n* rhume *m* des foins; ~**stack** *n* meule *f* de foin

haywire ['heɪwaɪə*] (*inf*) *adj*: **to go** ~ (*machine*) se détraquer; (*plans*) mal tourner

hazard ['hæzəd] *n* (*danger*) danger *m*, risque *m* ♦ *vt* risquer, hasarder; ~ (**warning**) **lights** *npl* (*AUT*) feux *mpl* de détresse

haze [heɪz] *n* brume *f*

hazelnut ['heɪzlnʌt] *n* noisette *f*

hazy ['heɪzɪ] *adj* brumeux(euse); (*idea*) vague

he [hiː] *pron* il; **it is** ~ **who** ... c'est lui qui ...

head [hed] *n* tête *f*; (*leader*) chef *m*; (*of school*) directeur(trice) ♦ *vt* (*list*) être en tête de; (*group*) être à la tête de; ~**s** (**or tails**) pile (ou face); ~ **first** la tête la première; ~ **over heels in love** follement *or* éperdument amoureux(euse); **to** ~ **a ball** faire une tête; ~ **for** *vt fus* se diriger vers; ~**ache** *n* mal *m* de tête; ~**dress** (*BRIT*) *n* (*of Red Indian etc*) coiffure *f*; ~**ing** *n* titre *m*; ~**lamp** (*BRIT*) *n* = **headlight**; ~**land** *n* promontoire *m*, cap *m*; ~**light** *n* phare *m*; ~**line** *n* titre *m*; ~**long** *adv* (*fall*) la tête la première; (*rush*) tête baissée; ~**master** *n* directeur *m*; ~**mistress** *n* directrice *f*; ~ **office** *n* bureau central, siège *m*; ~-**on** *adj* (*collision*) de plein fouet; (*confrontation*) en face à face; ~**phones** *npl* casque *m* (à écouteurs); ~**quarters** *npl* bureau *or* siège central; (*MIL*) quartier général; ~**rest** *n* appui-tête *m*; ~**room** *n* (*in car*) hauteur *f* de plafond; (*under bridge*) hauteur limite; ~**scarf** *n* foulard *m*; ~**strong** *adj* têtu(e), entêté(e); ~ **waiter** *n* maître *m* d'hôtel; ~**way** *n*: **to make** ~**way** avancer, faire des progrès; ~**wind** *n* vent *m* contraire; (*NAUT*) vent debout; ~**y** *adj* capiteux(euse); enivrant(e); (*experience*) grisant(e)

heal [hiːl] *vt*, *vi* guérir

health [helθ] *n* santé *f*; ~ **food** *n* aliment(s) naturel(s); ~ **food shop** *n* magasin *m* diététique; **H**~ **Service** (*BRIT*) *n*: **the H**~ **Service** ≈ la Sécurité sociale; ~**y** *adj* (*person*) en bonne santé; (*climate, food, attitude etc*) sain(e), bon(ne) pour la santé

heap [hiːp] *n* tas *m* ♦ *vt*: **to** ~ (**up**) entasser, amonceler; **she** ~**ed her plate with cakes** elle a chargé son assiette de gâteaux

hear [hɪə*] (*pt*, *pp* **heard**) *vt* entendre; (*news*) apprendre ♦ *vi* entendre; **to** ~ **about** entendre parler de; avoir des nouvelles de; **to** ~ **from sb** recevoir *or* avoir des nouvelles de qn; ~**ing** ['hɪərɪŋ] *n* (*sense*) ouïe *f*; (*of witnesses*) audition *f*; (*of a case*)

audience *f*; ~**ing aid** *n* appareil *m* acoustique; ~**say** ['hɪəseɪ]: **by** ~**say** *adv* par ouï-dire *m*

hearse [hɜːs] *n* corbillard *m*

heart [hɑːt] *n* cœur *m*; ~**s** *npl* (*CARDS*) cœur; **to lose/take** ~ perdre/prendre courage; **at** ~ au fond; **by** ~ (*learn, know*) par cœur; ~ **attack** *n* crise *f* cardiaque; ~**beat** *n* battement *m* du cœur; ~**breaking** *adj* déchirant(e), qui fend le cœur; ~**broken** *adj*: **to be** ~**broken** avoir beaucoup de chagrin *or* le cœur brisé; ~**burn** *n* brûlures *fpl* d'estomac; ~ **failure** *n* arrêt *m* du cœur; ~**felt** *adj* sincère

hearth [hɑːθ] *n* foyer *m*, cheminée *f*

heartily ['hɑːtɪlɪ] *adv* chaleureusement; (*laugh*) de bon cœur; (*eat*) de bon appétit; **to agree** ~ être entièrement d'accord

heartland ['hɑːtlænd] *n* (*of country, region*) centre *m*

hearty ['hɑːtɪ] *adj* chaleureux(euse); (*appetite*) robuste; (*dislike*) cordial(e)

heat [hiːt] *n* chaleur *f*; (*fig*) feu *m*, agitation *f*; (*SPORT: also:* qualifying ~) éliminatoire *f* ♦ *vt* chauffer; ~ **up** *vi* (*water*) chauffer; (*room*) se réchauffer ♦ *vt* réchauffer; ~**ed** *adj* chauffé(e); (*fig*) passionné(e), échauffé(e); ~**er** *n* appareil *m* de chauffage; radiateur *m*; (*in car*) chauffage *m*; (*water* ~) chauffe-eau *m*

heath [hiːθ] (*BRIT*) *n* lande *f*

heather ['heðə*] *n* bruyère *f*

heating ['hiːtɪŋ] *n* chauffage *m*

heatstroke ['hiːtstrəʊk] *n* (*MED*) coup *m* de chaleur

heatwave *n* vague *f* de chaleur

heave [hiːv] *vt* soulever (avec effort); (*drag*) traîner ♦ *vi* se soulever; (*retch*) avoir un haut-le-cœur; **to** ~ **a sigh** pousser un soupir

heaven ['hevn] *n* ciel *m*, paradis *m*; (*fig*) paradis; ~**ly** *adj* céleste, divin(e)

heavily ['hevɪlɪ] *adv* lourdement; (*drink, smoke*) beaucoup; (*sleep, sigh*) profondément

heavy ['hevɪ] *adj* lourd(e); (*work, sea, rain, eater*) gros(se); (*snow*) beaucoup de; (*drinker, smoker*) grand(e); (*breathing*) bruyant(e); (*schedule, week*) chargé(e); ~ **goods vehicle** *n* poids lourd; ~**weight** *n* (*SPORT*) poids lourd

Hebrew ['hiːbruː] *adj* hébraïque ♦ *n* (*LING*) hébreu *m*

Hebrides ['hebrɪdiːz] *npl*: **the** ~ les Hébrides *fpl*

heckle ['hekl] *vt* interpeller (*un orateur*)

hectic ['hektɪk] *adj* agité(e), trépidant(e)

he'd [hiːd] = **he would**; **he had**

hedge [hedʒ] *n* haie *f* ♦ *vi* se dérober; **to** ~ **one's bets** (*fig*) se couvrir

hedgehog ['hedʒhɒg] *n* hérisson *m*

heed [hiːd] *vt* (*also:* **take** ~ **of**) tenir compte

de; ~**less** *adj* insouciant(e)
heel [hi:l] *n* talon *m* ♦ *vt* (*shoe*) retalonner
hefty ['heftɪ] *adj* (*person*) costaud(e); (*parcel*) lourd(e); (*profit*) gros(se)
heifer ['hefə*] *n* génisse *f*
height [haɪt] *n* (*of person*) taille *f*, grandeur *f*; (*of object*) hauteur *f*; (*of plane, mountain*) altitude *f*; (*high ground*) hauteur, éminence *f*; (*fig: of glory*) sommet *m*; (: *of luxury, stupidity*) comble *m*; ~**en** *vt* (*fig*) augmenter
heir [ɛə*] *n* héritier *m*; ~**ess** ['ɛərɪs] *n* héritière *f*; ~**loom** *n* héritage *m*, meuble *m* (*or* bijou *m or* tableau *m*) de famille
held [held] *pt, pp of* **hold**
helicopter ['helɪkɒptə*] *n* hélicoptère *m*
hell [hel] *n* enfer *m*; ~**!** (*inf!*) merde!
he'll [hi:l] = **he will; he shall**
hellish ['helɪʃ] (*inf*) *adj* infernal(e)
hello [hʌ'ləu] *excl* bonjour!; (*to attract attention*) hé!; (*surprise*) tiens!
helm [helm] *n* (NAUT) barre *f*
helmet ['helmɪt] *n* casque *m*
help [help] *n* aide *f*; (*cleaner*) femme *f* de ménage ♦ *vt* aider; ~**!** au secours!; ~ *yourself* servez-vous; **he can't** ~ **it** il n'y peut rien; ~**er** *n* aide *m/f*, assistant(e); ~**ful** *adj* serviable, obligeant(e); (*useful*) utile; ~**ing** *n* portion *f*; ~**less** *adj* impuissant(e); (*defenceless*) faible
hem [hem] *n* ourlet *m* ♦ *vt* ourler; ~ **in** *vt* cerner
hemorrhage ['hemərɪdʒ] (US) *n* = **haemorrhage**
hemorrhoids ['hemərɔɪdz] (US) *npl* = **haemorrhoids**
hen [hen] *n* poule *f*
hence [hens] *adv* (*therefore*) d'où, de là; **2 years** ~ d'ici 2 ans, dans 2 ans; ~**forth** *adv* dorénavant
henchman ['hentʃmən] (*pej: irreg*) *n* acolyte *m*
her [hɜː*] *pron* (*direct*) la, l'; (*indirect*) lui; (*stressed, after prep*) elle ♦ *adj* son(sa), ses *pl*; *see also* **me; my**
herald ['herəld] *n* héraut *m* ♦ *vt* annoncer; ~**ry** ['herəldrɪ] *n* (*study*) héraldique *f*; (*coat of arms*) blason *m*
herb [hɜːb] *n* herbe *f*
herd [hɜːd] *n* troupeau *m*
here [hɪə*] *adv* ici; (*time*) alors ♦ *excl* tiens!, tenez!; ~**!** présent!; ~ **is,** ~ **are** voici; ~ **he/she is!** le/la voici!; ~**after** *adv* après, plus tard; ~**by** *adv* (*formal: in letter*) par la présente
hereditary [hɪ'redɪtərɪ] *adj* héréditaire
heresy ['herəsɪ] *n* hérésie *f*
heritage ['herɪtɪdʒ] *n* (*of country*) patrimoine *m*
hermit ['hɜːmɪt] *n* ermite *m*
hernia ['hɜːnɪə] *n* hernie *f*
hero ['hɪərəu] (*pl* ~**es**) *n* héros *m*
heroin ['herəuɪn] *n* héroïne *f*

heroine ['herəuɪn] *n* héroïne *f*
heron ['herən] *n* héron *m*
herring ['herɪŋ] *n* hareng *m*
hers [hɜːz] *pron* le(la) sien(ne), les siens(siennes); *see also* **mine**[1]
herself [hɜː'self] *pron* (*reflexive*) se; (*emphatic*) elle-même; (*after prep*) elle; *see also* **oneself**
he's [hi:z] = **he is; he has**
hesitant ['hezɪtənt] *adj* hésitant(e), indécis(e)
hesitate ['hezɪteɪt] *vi* hésiter; **hesitation** [hezɪ'teɪʃən] *n* hésitation *f*
hew [hju:] (*pp* **hewed** *or* **hewn**) *vt* (*stone*) tailler; (*wood*) couper
heyday ['heɪdeɪ] *n*: **the** ~ **of** l'âge *m* d'or de, les beaux jours de
HGV *n abbr* = **heavy goods vehicle**
hi [haɪ] *excl* salut!; (*to attract attention*) hé!
hiatus [haɪ'eɪtəs] *n* (*gap*) lacune *f*; (*interruption*) pause *f*
hibernate ['haɪbəneɪt] *vi* hiberner
hiccough, hiccup ['hɪkʌp] *vi* hoqueter; ~**s** *npl* hoquet *m*
hide [haɪd] (*pt* **hid,** *pp* **hidden**) *n* (*skin*) peau *f* ♦ *vt* cacher ♦ *vi*: **to** ~ (**from sb**) se cacher (de qn); ~**-and-seek** *n* cache-cache *m*; ~**away** *n* cachette *f*
hideous ['hɪdɪəs] *adj* hideux(euse)
hiding ['haɪdɪŋ] *n* (*beating*) correction *f*, volée *f* de coups; **to be in** ~ (*concealed*) se tenir caché(e)
hierarchy ['haɪəra:kɪ] *n* hiérarchie *f*
hi-fi ['haɪfaɪ] *n* hi-fi *f inv* ♦ *adj* hi-fi *inv*
high [haɪ] *adj* haut(e); (*speed, respect, number*) grand(e); (*price*) élevé(e); (*wind*) fort(e), violent(e); (*voice*) aigu(aiguë) ♦ *adv* haut; **20 m** ~ haut(e de 20 m; ~**brow** *adj, n* intellectuel(le); ~**chair** *n* (*child's*) chaise haute; ~**er education** *n* études supérieures; ~**handed** *adj* très autoritaire; très cavalier(ère); ~ **jump** *n* (SPORT) saut *m* en hauteur; ~**lands** *npl*: **the H~lands** les Highlands *mpl*; ~**light** *n* (*fig: of event*) point culminant ♦ *vt* faire ressortir, souligner; ~**lights** *npl* (*in hair*) reflets *mpl*; ~**ly** *adv* très, fort, hautement; **to speak/think** ~**ly of sb** dire/penser beaucoup de bien de qn; ~**ly paid** *adj* très bien payé(e); ~**ly strung** *adj* nerveux(euse), toujours très tendu(e); ~**ness** *n*: **Her** (*or* **His**) **H~ness** Son Altesse *f*; ~**-pitched** *adj* aigu(aiguë); ~**rise** *adj*: ~**rise block,** ~**rise flats** tour *f* (d'habitation); ~ **school** *n* lycée *m*; (US) établissement *m* d'enseignement supérieur; ~ **season** (BRIT) *n* haute saison; ~ **street** (BRIT) *n* grand-rue *f*; ~**way** *n* route nationale; **H~way Code** (BRIT) *n* code *m* de la route
hijack ['haɪdʒæk] *vt* (*plane*) détourner; ~**er** *n* pirate *m* de l'air
hike [haɪk] *vi* aller *or* faire des excursions à

pied ♦ *n* excursion *f* à pied, randonnée *f*; ~**r** *n* promeneur(euse), excursionniste *m/f*

hilarious [hɪˈlɛərɪəs] *adj* (*account, event*) désopilant(e)

hill [hɪl] *n* colline *f*; (*fairly high*) montagne *f*; (*on road*) côte *f*; ~**side** *n* (flanc *m* de) coteau *m*; ~**y** *adj* vallonné(e); montagneux(euse)

hilt [hɪlt] *n* (*of sword*) garde *f*; **to the ~** (*fig: support*) à fond

him [hɪm] *pron* (*direct*) le, l'; (*stressed, indirect, after prep*) lui; *see also* **me**; ~**self** [hɪmˈsɛlf] *pron* (*reflexive*) se; (*emphatic*) lui-même; (*after prep*) lui; *see also* **oneself**

hind [haɪnd] *adj* de derrière

hinder [ˈhɪndə*] *vt* gêner; (*delay*) retarder; **hindrance** [ˈhɪndrəns] *n* gêne *f*, obstacle *m*

hindsight [ˈhaɪndsaɪt] *n*: **with ~** avec du recul, rétrospectivement

Hindu [ˈhɪnduː] *adj* hindou(e)

hinge [hɪndʒ] *n* charnière *f* ♦ *vi* (*fig*): **to ~ on** dépendre de

hint [hɪnt] *n* allusion *f*; (*advice*) conseil *m* ♦ *vt*: **to ~ that** insinuer que ♦ *vi*: **to ~ at** faire une allusion à

hip [hɪp] *n* hanche *f*

hippopotamus [hɪpəˈpɒtəməs] (*pl* ~**es** *or* **hippopotami**) *n* hippopotame *m*

hire [ˈhaɪə*] *vt* (*BRIT: car, equipment*) louer; (*worker*) embaucher, engager ♦ *n* location *f*; **for ~** à louer; (*taxi*) libre; ~ **purchase** (*BRIT*) *n* achat *m* (*or* vente *f*) à tempérament *or* crédit

his [hɪz] *pron* le(la) sien(ne), les siens(siennes) ♦ *adj* son(sa), ses *pl*; *see also* **my**; **mine**¹

hiss [hɪs] *vi* siffler

historic [hɪsˈtɒrɪk] *adj* historique

historical [hɪsˈtɒrɪkəl] *adj* historique

history [ˈhɪstərɪ] *n* histoire *f*

hit [hɪt] (*pt, pp* **hit**) *vt* frapper; (*reach: target*) atteindre, toucher; (*collide with: car*) entrer en collision avec, heurter; (*fig: affect*) toucher ♦ *n* coup *m*; (*success*) succès *m*; (: *song*) tube *m*; **to ~ it off with sb** bien s'entendre avec qn; ~**-and-run driver** *n* chauffard *m* (coupable du délit de fuite)

hitch [hɪtʃ] *vt* (*fasten*) accrocher, attacher; (*also:* ~ **up**) remonter d'une saccade ♦ *n* (*difficulty*) anicroche *f*, contretemps *m*; **to ~ a lift** faire du stop

hitchhike [ˈhɪtʃhaɪk] *vi* faire de l'auto-stop; ~**r** *n* auto-stoppeur(euse)

hi-tech [ˈhaɪˈtɛk] *adj* de pointe

hitherto [ˈhɪðəˈtuː] *adv* jusqu'ici

HIV: ~**-negative/-positive** *adj* séro-négatif(ive)/-positif(ive)

hive [haɪv] *n* ruche *f*; ~ **off** (*inf*) *vt* mettre à part, séparer

HMS *abbr* = **Her (His) Majesty's Ship**

hoard [hɔːd] *n* (*of food*) provisions *fpl*, réserves *fpl*; (*of money*) trésor *m* ♦ *vt* amasser; ~**ing** [ˈhɔːdɪŋ] (*BRIT*) *n* (*for posters*) panneau *m* d'affichage *or* publicitaire

hoarse [hɔːs] *adj* enroué(e)

hoax [həʊks] *n* canular *m*

hob [hɒb] *n* plaque (chauffante)

hobble [ˈhɒbl] *vi* boitiller

hobby [ˈhɒbɪ] *n* passe-temps favori; ~**horse** *n* (*fig*) dada *m*

hobo [ˈhəʊbəʊ] (*US*) *n* vagabond *m*

hockey [ˈhɒkɪ] *n* hockey *m*

hog [hɒg] *n* porc (châtré) ♦ *vt* (*fig*) accaparer; **to go the whole ~** aller jusqu'au bout

hoist [hɔɪst] *n* (*apparatus*) palan *m* ♦ *vt* hisser

hold [həʊld] (*pt, pp* **held**) *vt* tenir; (*contain*) contenir; (*believe*) considérer; (*possess*) avoir; (*detain*) détenir ♦ *vi* (*withstand pressure*) tenir (bon); (*be valid*) valoir ♦ *n* (*also fig*) prise *f*; (*NAUT*) cale *f*; ~ **the line!** (*TEL*) ne quittez pas!; **to ~ one's own** (*fig*) (bien) se défendre; **to catch** *or* **get (a) ~ of** saisir; **to get ~ of** (*fig*) trouver; ~ **back** *vt* retenir; (*secret*) taire; ~ **down** *vt* (*person*) maintenir à terre; (*job*) occuper; ~ **off** *vt* tenir à distance; ~ **on** *vi* tenir bon; (*wait*) attendre; ~ **on!** (*TEL*) ne quittez pas!; ~ **on to** *vt fus* se cramponner à; (*keep*) conserver, garder; ~ **out** *vt* offrir ♦ *vi* (*resist*) tenir bon; ~ **up** *vt* (*raise*) lever; (*support*) soutenir; (*delay*) retarder; (*rob*) braquer; ~**all** (*BRIT*) *n* fourre-tout *m inv*; ~**er** *n* (*of ticket, record*) détenteur(trice); (*of office, title etc*) titulaire *m/f*; (*container*) support *m*; ~**ing** *n* (*share*) intérêts *mpl*; (*farm*) ferme *f*; ~**-up** *n* (*robbery*) hold-up *m*; (*delay*) retard *m*; (*BRIT: in traffic*) bouchon *m*

hole [həʊl] *n* trou *m*

holiday [ˈhɒlədɪ] *n* vacances *fpl*; (*day off*) jour *m* de congé; (*public*) jour férié; **on ~** en congé; ~ **camp** *n* (*also:* ~ *centre*) camp *m* de vacances; ~**-maker** (*BRIT*) *n* vacancier(ère); ~ **resort** *n* centre *m* de villégiature *or* de vacances

Holland [ˈhɒlənd] *n* Hollande *f*

hollow [ˈhɒləʊ] *adj* creux(euse) ♦ *n* creux *m* ♦ *vt*: **to ~ out** creuser, évider

holly [ˈhɒlɪ] *n* houx *m*

holocaust [ˈhɒləkɔːst] *n* holocauste *m*

holster [ˈhəʊlstə*] *n* étui *m* de revolver

holy [ˈhəʊlɪ] *adj* saint(e); (*bread, water*) bénit(e); (*ground*) sacré(e); **H~ Ghost** *n* Saint-Esprit *m*

homage [ˈhɒmɪdʒ] *n* hommage *m*; **to pay ~ to** rendre hommage à

home [həʊm] *n* foyer *m*, maison *f*; (*country*) pays natal, patrie *f*; (*institution*) maison ♦ *adj* de famille; (*ECON, POL*) national(e), intérieur(e); (*SPORT: game*) sur leur (*or* notre) terrain; (*team*) qui reçoit ♦ *adv* chez soi, à la maison; au pays natal; (*right in: nail etc*) à fond; **at ~** chez soi, à la maison; **make yourself at ~** faites comme chez

vous; ~ **address** n domicile permanent;
~**land** n patrie f; ~**less** adj sans foyer;
sans abri; ~**ly** adj (plain) simple, sans prétention; ~**-made** adj fait(e) à la maison;
H~ Office (BRIT) n ministère m de l'Intérieur; ~ **rule** n autonomie f; **H~ Secre-**
tary (BRIT) n ministre m de l'Intérieur;
~**sick** adj: **to be ~sick** avoir le mal du
pays; s'ennuyer de sa famille; ~ **town** n
ville natale; ~**ward** adj (journey) du retour;
~**work** n devoirs mpl

homogeneous [hɒmə'dʒiːnɪəs] adj homo-
gène

homosexual ['hɒməu'seksjuəl] adj, n ho-
mosexuel(le)

honest ['ɒnɪst] adj honnête; (sincere)
franc(franche); ~**ly** adv honnêtement; franchement; ~**y** n honnêteté f

honey ['hʌnɪ] n miel m; ~**comb** n rayon m
de miel; ~**moon** n lune f de miel, voyage
m de noces; ~**suckle** n ['hʌnɪsʌkl] (BOT) n
chèvrefeuille m

honk [hɒŋk] vi (AUT) klaxonner

honorary ['ɒnərərɪ] adj honoraire; (duty,
title) honorifique

honour ['ɒnə*] (US **honor**) vt honorer ♦ n
honneur m; **hono(u)rable** adj honorable;
hono(u)rs degree n (SCOL) licence avec
mention

hood [hud] n capuchon m; (of cooker) hotte
f; (AUT: BRIT) capote f; (: US) capot m

hoof [huːf] (pl **hooves**) n sabot m

hook [huk] n crochet m; (on dress) agrafe f;
(for fishing) hameçon m ♦ vt accrocher;
(fish) prendre

hooligan ['huːlɪgən] n voyou m

hoop [huːp] n cerceau m

hooray [huː'reɪ] excl hourra

hoot [huːt] vi (AUT) klaxonner; (siren) mugir; (owl) hululer; ~**er** n (BRIT: AUT)
klaxon m; (NAUT, factory) sirène f

Hoover ['huːvə*] (®:BRIT) n aspirateur m ♦
vt: **h~** passer l'aspirateur dans or sur

hooves [huːvz] npl of **hoof**

hop [hɒp] vi (on one foot) sauter à cloche-
pied; (bird) sautiller

hope [həup] vt, vi espérer ♦ n espoir m; **I ~**
so je l'espère; **I ~ not** j'espère que non;
~**ful** adj (person) plein(e) d'espoir; (situation) prometteur(euse), encourageant(e);
~**fully** adv (expectantly) avec espoir, avec
optimisme; (one hopes) avec un peu de
chance; ~**less** adj désespéré(e); (useless)
nul(le)

hops [hɒps] npl houblon m

horizon [hə'raɪzn] n horizon m; ~**tal**
[hɒrɪ'zɒntl] adj horizontal(e)

horn [hɔːn] n corne f; (MUS: also: French
~) cor m; (AUT) klaxon m

hornet ['hɔːnɪt] n frelon m

horny ['hɔːnɪ] (inf) adj (aroused) en rut, ex-
cité(e)

horoscope ['hɒrəskəup] n horoscope m

horrendous [hə'rendəs] adj horrible, af-
freux(euse)

horrible ['hɒrɪbl] adj horrible, affreux(euse)

horrid ['hɒrɪd] adj épouvantable

horrify ['hɒrɪfaɪ] vt horrifier

horror ['hɒrə*] n horreur f; ~ **film** n film
m d'épouvante

hors d'œuvre [ɔː'dəːvrə] n (CULIN) hors-
d'œuvre m inv

horse [hɔːs] n cheval m; ~**back** n: **on**
~**back** à cheval; ~ **chestnut** n marron m
(d'Inde); ~**man** (irreg) n cavalier m;
~**power** n puissance f (en chevaux); ~**-**
racing n courses fpl de chevaux; ~**radish**
n raifort m; ~**shoe** n fer m à cheval

hose [həuz] n (also: ~**pipe**) tuyau m; (: garden ~) tuyau d'arrosage

hospitable [hɒs'pɪtəbl] adj hospitalier(ère)

hospital ['hɒspɪtl] n hôpital m; **in ~** à
l'hôpital

hospitality [hɒspɪ'tælɪtɪ] n hospitalité f

host [həust] n hôte m; (TV, RADIO) anima-
teur(trice); (REL) hostie f; (large number): **a**
~ **of** une foule de

hostage ['hɒstɪdʒ] n otage m

hostel ['hɒstəl] n foyer m; (also: youth ~)
auberge f de jeunesse

hostess ['həustes] n hôtesse f; (TV, RADIO)
animatrice f

hostile ['hɒstaɪl] adj hostile; **hostility**
[hɒs'tɪlɪtɪ] n hostilité f

hot [hɒt] adj chaud(e); (as opposed to only
warm) très chaud; (spicy) fort(e); (contest
etc) acharné(e); (temper) passionné(e); **to**
be ~ (person) avoir chaud; (object) être
(très) chaud; **it is ~** (weather) il fait chaud;
~**bed** n (fig) foyer m, pépinière f; ~ **dog**
n hot-dog m

hotel [həu'tel] n hôtel m

hot: ~**-headed** adj impétueux(euse);
~**house** n serre (chaude); ~**line** n (POL)
téléphone m rouge, ligne directe; ~**ly** adv
passionnément, violemment; ~**plate** n (on
cooker) plaque chauffante; ~**-water bottle**
n bouillotte f

hound [haund] vt poursuivre avec acharne-
ment ♦ n chien courant

hour ['auə*] n heure f; ~**ly** adj, adv toutes
les heures; (rate) horaire

house [n haus, pl 'hauzɪz, vb hauz] n maison f; (POL) chambre f; (THEATRE) salle f;
auditoire m ♦ vt (person) loger, héberger;
(objects) abriter; **on the ~** (fig) aux frais de
la maison; ~ **arrest** n assignation f à résidence; ~**boat** n bateau m (aménagé en habitation); ~**bound** adj confiné(e) chez soi;
~**breaking** n cambriolage m (avec effraction); ~**coat** n peignoir m; ~**hold** n (persons) famille f, maisonnée f; (ADMIN etc)
ménage m; ~**keeper** n gouvernante f;
~**keeping** n (work) ménage m; ~**keeping**

(money) argent *m* du ménage; **~-warming (party)** *n* pendaison *f* de crémaillère; **~wife** (*irreg*) *n* ménagère *f*; femme *f* au foyer; **~work** *n* (travaux *mpl* du) ménage *m*

housing ['hauzɪŋ] *n* logement *m*; **~ development,** **~ estate** *n* lotissement *m*

hovel ['hɒvəl] *n* taudis *m*

hover ['hɒvə*] *vi* planer; **~craft** *n* aéroglisseur *m*

how [hau] *adv* comment; **~ are you?** comment allez-vous?; **~ do you do?** bonjour; enchanté(e); **~ far is it to?** combien y a-t-il jusqu'à ...?; **~ long have you been here?** depuis combien de temps êtes-vous là?; **~ lovely!** que or comme c'est joli!; **~ many/much?** combien?; **~ many people/ much milk?** combien de gens/lait?; **~ old are you?** quel âge avez-vous?

however [hau'evə*] *adv* de quelque façon *or* manière que +*subj*; (+*adj*) quelque *or* si ... que +*subj*; (*in questions*) comment ♦ *conj* pourtant, cependant

howl [haul] *vi* hurler

H.P. *abbr* = **hire purchase**

h.p. *abbr* = **horsepower**

HQ *abbr* = **headquarters**

hub [hʌb] *n* (*of wheel*) moyeu *m*; (*fig*) centre *m*, foyer *m*

hubbub ['hʌbʌb] *n* brouhaha *m*

hubcap ['hʌbkæp] *n* enjoliveur *m*

huddle ['hʌdl] *vi*: **to ~ together** se blottir les uns contre les autres

hue [hju:] *n* teinte *f*, nuance *f*; **~ and cry** *n* tollé (général), clameur *f*

huff [hʌf] *n*: **in a ~** fâché(e)

hug [hʌg] *vt* serrer dans ses bras; (*shore, kerb*) serrer

huge [hju:dʒ] *adj* énorme, immense

hulk [hʌlk] *n* (*ship*) épave *f*; (*car, building*) carcasse *f*; (*person*) mastodonte *m*

hull [hʌl] *n* coque *f*

hullo [hʌ'ləu] *excl* = **hello**

hum [hʌm] *vt* (*tune*) fredonner ♦ *vi* fredonner; (*insect*) bourdonner; (*plane, tool*) vrombir

human ['hju:mən] *adj* humain(e) ♦ *n* = **(being)** être humain; **~e** [hju:'meɪn] *adj* humain(e), humanitaire; **~itarian** [hju:mænɪ'tɛərɪən] *adj* humanitaire; **~ity** [hju:'mænɪtɪ] *n* humanité *f*

humble ['hʌmbl] *adj* humble, modeste ♦ *vt* humilier

humbug ['hʌmbʌg] *n* fumisterie *f*; (*BRIT*) bonbon *m* à la menthe

humdrum ['hʌmdrʌm] *adj* monotone, banal(e)

humid ['hju:mɪd] *adj* humide

humiliate [hju:'mɪlɪeɪt] *vt* humilier; **humiliation** *n* humiliation *f*

humorous ['hju:mərəs] *adj* humoristique; (*person*) plein(e) d'humour

humour ['hju:mə*] (*US* **humor**) *n* humour *m*; (*mood*) humeur *f* ♦ *vt* (*person*) faire plaisir à; se prêter aux caprices de

hump [hʌmp] *n* bosse *f*

humpbacked ['hʌmpbækt] *adj*: **~ bridge** pont *m* en dos d'âne

hunch [hʌntʃ] *n* (*premonition*) intuition *f*; **~back** *n* bossu(e); **~ed** *adj* voûté(e)

hundred ['hʌndrɪd] *num* cent; **~s of** des centaines de; **~weight** *n* (*BRIT*) = 50.8 *kg*; (*US*) = 45.3 *kg*

hung [hʌŋ] *pt, pp of* **hang**

Hungary ['hʌŋgərɪ] *n* Hongrie *f*

hunger ['hʌŋgə*] *n* faim *f* ♦ *vi*: **to ~ for** avoir faim de, désirer ardemment

hungry ['hʌŋgrɪ] *adj* affamé(e); (*keen*): **~ for** avide de; **to be ~** avoir faim

hunk [hʌŋk] *n* (*of bread etc*) gros morceau

hunt [hʌnt] *vt* chasser; (*criminal*) pourchasser ♦ *vi* chasser; (*search*): **to ~ for** chercher (partout) ♦ *n* chasse *f*; **~er** *n* chasseur *m*; **~ing** *n* chasse *f*

hurdle ['hɜ:dl] *n* (*SPORT*) haie *f*; (*fig*) obstacle *m*

hurl [hɜ:l] *vt* lancer (avec violence); (*abuse, insults*) lancer

hurrah [hu'rɑ:] *excl* = **hooray**

hurray [hu'reɪ] *excl* = **hooray**

hurricane ['hʌrɪkən] *n* ouragan *m*

hurried ['hʌrɪd] *adj* pressé(e), précipité(e); (*work*) fait(e) à la hâte; **~ly** *adv* précipitamment, à la hâte

hurry ['hʌrɪ] (*vb: also:* **~ up**) *n* hâte *f*, précipitation *f* ♦ *vi* se presser, se dépêcher ♦ *vt* (*person*) faire presser, faire se dépêcher; (*work*) presser; **to be in a ~** être pressé(e); **to do sth in a ~** faire qch en vitesse; **to ~ in/out** entrer/sortir précipitamment

hurt [hɜ:t] (*pt, pp* **hurt**) *vt* (*cause pain to*) faire mal à; (*injure, fig*) blesser ♦ *vi* faire mal ♦ *adj* blessé(e); **~ful** *adj* (*remark*) blessant(e)

hurtle ['hɜ:tl] *vi*: **to ~ past** passer en trombe; **to ~ down** dégringoler

husband ['hʌzbənd] *n* mari *m*

hush [hʌʃ] *n* calme *m*, silence *m* ♦ *vt* faire taire; **~! chut!**; **~ up** *vt* (*scandal*) étouffer

husk [hʌsk] *n* (*of wheat*) balle *f*; (*of rice, maize*) enveloppe *f*

husky ['hʌskɪ] *adj* rauque ♦ *n* chien *m* esquimau *or* de traîneau

hustle ['hʌsl] *vt* pousser, bousculer ♦ *n*: **~ and bustle** tourbillon *m* (d'activité)

hut [hʌt] *n* hutte *f*; (*shed*) cabane *f*

hutch [hʌtʃ] *n* clapier *m*

hyacinth ['haɪəsɪnθ] *n* jacinthe *f*

hydrant ['haɪdrənt] *n* (*also:* **fire ~**) bouche *f* d'incendie

hydraulic [haɪ'drɒlɪk] *adj* hydraulique

hydroelectric [haɪdrəuɪ'lektrɪk] *adj* hydroélectrique

hydrofoil ['haɪdrəufɔɪl] *n* hydrofoil *m*

hydrogen ['haɪdrɪdʒən] n hydrogène m
hyena [haɪ'iːnə] n hyène f
hygiene ['haɪdʒiːn] n hygiène f
hymn [hɪm] n hymne m; cantique m
hype [haɪp] (*inf*) n battage m publicitaire
hypermarket ['haɪpəˈmɑːkɪt] (*BRIT*) n hypermarché m
hyphen ['haɪfən] n trait m d'union
hypnotize ['hɪpnətaɪz] vt hypnotiser
hypocrisy [hɪ'pɔkrɪsɪ] n hypocrisie f; **hypocrite** ['hɪpəkrɪt] n hypocrite m/f; **hypocritical** adj hypocrite
hypothesis [haɪ'pɔθɪsɪs] (*pl* **~es**) n hypothèse f
hysterical [hɪs'terɪkəl] adj hystérique; (*funny*) hilarant(e); ~ **laughter** fou rire m
hysterics [hɪs'terɪks] npl: **to be in/have ~** (*anger, panic*) avoir une crise de nerfs; (*laughter*) attraper un fou rire

I i

I [aɪ] pron je; (*before vowel*) j'; (*stressed*) moi
ice [aɪs] n glace f; (*on road*) verglas m ♦ vt (*cake*) glacer ♦ vi (*also: ~ over, ~ up*) geler; (: *window*) se givrer; ~**berg** n iceberg m; ~**box** n (*US*) réfrigérateur m; (*BRIT*) compartiment m à glace; (*insulated box*) glacière f; ~ **cream** n glace f; ~ **cube** n glaçon m; ~**d** adj glacé(e); ~ **hockey** n hockey m sur glace; **I~land** ['aɪslənd] n Islande f; ~ **lolly** n (*BRIT*) esquimau m (glace); ~ **rink** n patinoire f; ~**skating** n patinage m (sur glace)
icicle ['aɪsɪkl] n glaçon m (*naturel*)
icing ['aɪsɪŋ] n (*CULIN*) glace f; ~ **sugar** (*BRIT*) n sucre m glace
icy ['aɪsɪ] adj glacé(e); (*road*) verglacé(e); (*weather, temperature*) glacial(e)
I'd [aɪd] = **I would; I had**
idea [aɪ'dɪə] n idée f
ideal [aɪ'dɪəl] n idéal m ♦ adj idéal(e)
identical [aɪ'dentɪkəl] adj identique
identification [aɪdentɪfɪ'keɪʃən] n identification f; **means of ~** pièce f d'identité
identify [aɪ'dentɪfaɪ] vt identifier
Identikit picture [aɪ'dentɪkɪt-] ® n portrait-robot m
identity [aɪ'dentɪtɪ] n identité f; ~ **card** n carte f d'identité
ideology [aɪdɪ'ɔlədʒɪ] n idéologie f
idiom ['ɪdɪəm] n expression f idiomatique; (*style*) style m

idiosyncrasy [ɪdɪə'sɪŋkrəsɪ] n (*of person*) particularité f, petite manie
idiot ['ɪdɪət] n idiot(e), imbécile m/f; ~**ic** [ɪdɪ'ɔtɪk] adj idiot(e), bête, stupide
idle ['aɪdl] adj sans occupation, désœuvré(e); (*lazy*) oisif(ive), paresseux(euse); (*unemployed*) au chômage; (*question, pleasures*) vain(e), futile ♦ vi (*engine*) tourner au ralenti; **to lie ~** être arrêté(e), ne pas fonctionner; ~ **away** vt: **to ~ away the time** passer son temps à ne rien faire
idol ['aɪdl] n idole f; ~**ize** vt idolâtrer, adorer
i.e. adv abbr (= *id est*) c'est-à-dire
if [ɪf] conj si; ~ **so** si c'est le cas; ~ **not** sinon; ~ **only** si seulement
ignite [ɪg'naɪt] vt mettre le feu à, enflammer ♦ vi s'enflammer
ignition [ɪg'nɪʃən] n (*AUT*) allumage m; **to switch on/off the ~** mettre/couper le contact; ~ **key** n clé f de contact
ignorant ['ɪgnərənt] adj ignorant(e); **to be ~ of** (*subject*) ne rien connaître à; (*events*) ne pas être au courant de
ignore [ɪg'nɔː*] vt ne tenir aucun compte de; (*person*) faire semblant de ne pas reconnaître, ignorer; (*fact*) méconnaître
ill [ɪl] adj (*sick*) malade; (*bad*) mauvais(e) ♦ n mal m ♦ adv: **to speak/think ~ of** dire/penser du mal de; ~**s** npl (*misfortunes*) maux mpl, malheurs mpl; **to be taken ~** tomber malade; ~**-advised** adj (*decision*) peu judicieux(euse); (*person*) malavisé(e); ~**-at-ease** adj mal à l'aise
I'll [aɪl] = **I will; I shall**
illegal [ɪ'liːgəl] adj illégal(e)
illegible [ɪ'ledʒəbl] adj illisible
illegitimate [ɪlɪ'dʒɪtɪmət] adj illégitime
ill: ~-fated [ɪl'feɪtɪd] adj malheureux(euse); (*day*) néfaste; ~ **feeling** n ressentiment m, rancune f
illiterate [ɪ'lɪtərət] adj illettré(e); (*letter*) plein(e) de fautes
ill: ~-mannered [ɪl'mænəd] adj (*child*) mal élevé(e); ~**ness** ['ɪlnəs] n maladie f; ~**treat** [ɪl'triːt] vt maltraiter
illuminate [ɪ'luːmɪneɪt] vt (*room, street*) éclairer; (*for special effect*) illuminer; **illumination** [ɪluːmɪ'neɪʃən] n éclairage m; illumination f
illusion [ɪ'luːʒən] n illusion f
illustrate ['ɪləstreɪt] vt illustrer; **illustration** [ɪləs'treɪʃən] n illustration f
ill will n malveillance f
I'm [aɪm] = **I am**
image ['ɪmɪdʒ] n image f; (*public face*) image de marque; ~**ry** n images fpl
imaginary [ɪ'mædʒɪnərɪ] adj imaginaire
imagination [ɪmædʒɪ'neɪʃən] n imagination f
imaginative [ɪ'mædʒɪnətɪv] adj imaginatif(ive); (*person*) plein(e) d'imagination

imagine [ɪ'mædʒɪn] vt imaginer, s'imaginer; (*suppose*) imaginer, supposer

imbalance [ɪm'bæləns] n déséquilibre m

imbue [ɪm'bjuː] vt: **to ~ sb/sth with** imprégner qn/qch de

imitate ['ɪmɪteɪt] vt imiter; **imitation** [ɪmɪ'teɪʃən] n imitation f

immaculate [ɪ'mækjulɪt] adj impeccable; (REL) immaculé(e)

immaterial [ɪmə'tɪərɪəl] adj sans importance, insignifiant(e)

immature [ɪmə'tjuə*] adj (*fruit*) (qui n'est) pas mûr(e); (*person*) qui manque de maturité

immediate [ɪ'miːdɪət] adj immédiat(e); **~ly** adv (*at once*) immédiatement; **~ly next to** juste à côté de

immense [ɪ'mens] adj immense; énorme

immerse [ɪ'mɜːs] vt immerger, plonger; **immersion heater** [ɪ'mɜːʃən-] (BRIT) n chauffe-eau m électrique

immigrant ['ɪmɪɡrənt] n immigrant(e); immigré(e); **immigration** [ɪmɪ'ɡreɪʃən] n immigration f

imminent ['ɪmɪnənt] adj imminent(e)

immoral [ɪ'mɔrəl] adj immoral(e)

immortal [ɪ'mɔːtl] adj, n immortel(le)

immune [ɪ'mjuːn] adj: **~ (to)** immunisé(e) (contre); (*fig*) à l'abri de; **immunity** [ɪ'mjuːnɪtɪ] n immunité f

imp [ɪmp] n lutin m; (*child*) petit diable

impact ['ɪmpækt] n choc m, impact m; (*fig*) impact

impair [ɪm'peə*] vt détériorer, diminuer

impart [ɪm'pɑːt] vt communiquer, transmettre; (*flavour*) donner

impartial [ɪm'pɑːʃəl] adj impartial(e)

impassable [ɪm'pɑːsəbl] adj infranchissable; (*road*) impraticable

impassive [ɪm'pæsɪv] adj impassible

impatience [ɪm'peɪʃəns] n impatience f

impatient [ɪm'peɪʃənt] adj impatient(e); **to get** or **grow ~** s'impatienter

impeccable [ɪm'pekəbl] adj impeccable, parfait(e)

impede [ɪm'piːd] vt gêner

impediment [ɪm'pedɪmənt] n obstacle m; (*also: speech ~*) défaut m d'élocution

impending [ɪm'pendɪŋ] adj imminent(e)

imperative [ɪm'perətɪv] adj (*need*) urgent(e), pressant(e); (*tone*) impérieux(euse) ♦ n (LING) impératif m

imperfect [ɪm'pɜːfɪkt] adj imparfait(e); (*goods etc*) défectueux(euse)

imperial [ɪm'pɪərɪəl] adj impérial(e); (BRIT: *measure*) légal(e)

impersonal [ɪm'pɜːsnl] adj impersonnel(le)

impersonate [ɪm'pɜːsəneɪt] vt se faire passer pour; (THEATRE) imiter

impertinent [ɪm'pɜːtɪnənt] adj impertinent(e), insolent(e)

impervious [ɪm'pɜːvɪəs] adj (*fig*): **~ to** insensible à

impetuous [ɪm'petjuəs] adj impétueux(euse), fougueux(euse)

impetus ['ɪmpɪtəs] n impulsion f; (*of runner*) élan m

impinge [ɪm'pɪndʒ]: **to ~ on** vt fus (*person*) affecter, toucher; (*rights*) empiéter sur

implement [n 'ɪmplɪmənt, vb 'ɪmplɪment] n outil m, instrument m; (*for cooking*) ustensile m ♦ vt exécuter

implicit [ɪm'plɪsɪt] adj implicite; (*complete*) absolu(e), sans réserve

imply [ɪm'plaɪ] vt suggérer, laisser entendre; indiquer, supposer

impolite [ɪmpə'laɪt] adj impoli(e)

import [vb ɪm'pɔːt, n 'ɪmpɔːt] vt importer ♦ n (COMM) importation f

importance [ɪm'pɔːtəns] n importance f

important [ɪm'pɔːtənt] adj important(e)

importer [ɪm'pɔːtə*] n importateur(trice)

impose [ɪm'pəuz] vt imposer ♦ vi: **to ~ on sb** abuser de la gentillesse de qn; **imposing** [ɪm'pəuzɪŋ] adj imposant(e), impressionnant(e); **imposition** [ɪmpə'zɪʃən] n (*of tax etc*) imposition f; **to be an imposition on** (*person*) abuser de la gentillesse or la bonté de

impossible [ɪm'pɒsəbl] adj impossible

impotent ['ɪmpətənt] adj impuissant(e)

impound [ɪm'paund] vt confisquer, saisir

impoverished [ɪm'pɒvərɪʃt] adj appauvri(e), pauvre

impractical [ɪm'præktɪkəl] adj pas pratique; (*person*) qui manque d'esprit pratique

impregnable [ɪm'preɡnəbl] adj (*fortress*) imprenable

impress [ɪm'pres] vt impressionner, faire impression sur; (*mark*) imprimer, marquer; **to ~ sth on sb** faire bien comprendre qch à qn

impression [ɪm'preʃən] n impression f; (*of stamp, seal*) empreinte f; (*imitation*) imitation f; **to be under the ~ that** avoir l'impression que; **~ist** n (ART) impressionniste m/f; (*entertainer*) imitateur(trice) m/f

impressive [ɪm'presɪv] adj impressionnant(e)

imprint ['ɪmprɪnt] n (*outline*) marque f, empreinte f

imprison [ɪm'prɪzn] vt emprisonner, mettre en prison

improbable [ɪm'prɒbəbl] adj improbable; (*excuse*) peu plausible

improper [ɪm'prɒpə*] adj (*unsuitable*) déplacé(e), de mauvais goût; indécent(e); (*dishonest*) malhonnête

improve [ɪm'pruːv] vt améliorer ♦ vi s'améliorer; (*pupil etc*) faire des progrès; **~ment** n amélioration f (*in* de); progrès m

improvise ['ɪmprəvaɪz] vt, vi improviser

impudent ['ɪmpjudənt] adj impudent(e)

impulse ['ɪmpʌls] n impulsion f; **on ~** impulsivement, sur un coup de tête; **impulsive** [ɪmˈpʌlsɪv] *adj* impulsif(ive)

KEYWORD
---

in [ɪn] *prep* **1** (*indicating place, position*) dans; ~ **the house/the fridge** dans la maison/le frigo; ~ **the garden** dans le *or* au jardin; ~ **town** en ville; ~ **the country** à la campagne; ~ **school** à l'école; ~ **here/there** ici/là

2 (*with place names: of town, region, country*): ~ **London** à Londres; ~ **England** en Angleterre; ~ **Japan** au Japon; ~ **the United States** aux États-Unis

3 (*indicating time: during*): ~ **spring** au printemps; ~ **summer** en été; ~ **May/1992** en mai/1992; ~ **the afternoon** (dans) l'après-midi; **at 4 o'clock** ~ **the afternoon** à 4 heures de l'après-midi

4 (*indicating time: in the space of*) en; (: *future*) dans; **I did it** ~ **3 hours/days** je l'ai fait en 3 heures/jours; **I'll see you** ~ **2 weeks** *or* ~ **2 weeks' time** je te verrai dans 2 semaines

5 (*indicating manner etc*) à; ~ **a loud/soft voice** à voix haute/basse; ~ **pencil** au crayon; ~ **French** en français; **the boy** ~ **the blue shirt** le garçon à *or* avec la chemise bleue

6 (*indicating circumstances*): ~ **the sun** au soleil; ~ **the shade** à l'ombre; ~ **the rain** sous la pluie

7 (*indicating mood, state*): ~ **tears** en larmes; ~ **anger** sous le coup de la colère; ~ **despair** au désespoir; ~ **good condition** en bon état; **to live** ~ **luxury** vivre dans le luxe

8 (*with ratios, numbers*): **1** ~ **10 (households)**, **1 (household)** ~ **10** 1 (ménage) sur 10; **20 pence** ~ **the pound** 20 pence par livre sterling; **they lined up** ~ **twos** ils se mirent en rangs (deux) par deux; ~ **hundreds** par centaines

9 (*referring to people, works*) chez; **the disease is common** ~ **children** c'est une maladie courante chez les enfants; ~ **(the works of) Dickens** chez Dickens, dans (l'œuvre de) Dickens

10 (*indicating profession etc*) dans; **to be** ~ **teaching** être dans l'enseignement

11 (*after superlative*) de; **the best pupil** ~ **the class** le meilleur élève de la classe

12 (*with present participle*): ~ **saying this** en disant ceci

♦ *adv*: **to be** ~ (*person: at home, work*) être là; (*train, ship, plane*) être arrivé(e); (*in fashion*) être à la mode; **to ask sb** ~ inviter qn à entrer; **to run/limp** *etc* ~ entrer en courant/clopinant

♦ *n*: **the** ~**s and outs (of)** (*of proposal, situation etc*) les tenants et aboutissants (de)

in. *abbr* = **inch**

inability [ɪnəˈbɪlɪtɪ] *n* incapacité *f*

inaccurate [ɪnˈækjʊrɪt] *adj* inexact(e); (*person*) qui manque de précision

inadequate [ɪnˈædɪkwət] *adj* insuffisant(e), inadéquat(e)

inadvertently [ɪnədˈvɜːtəntlɪ] *adv* par mégarde

inadvisable [ɪnədˈvaɪzəbl] *adj* (*action*) à déconseiller

inane [ɪˈneɪn] *adj* inepte, stupide

inanimate [ɪnˈænɪmət] *adj* inanimé(e)

inappropriate [ɪnəˈprəʊprɪət] *adj* inopportun(e), mal à propos; (*word, expression*) impropre

inarticulate [ɪnɑːˈtɪkjʊlət] *adj* (*person*) qui s'exprime mal; (*speech*) indistinct(e)

inasmuch as [ɪnəzˈmʌtʃəz] *adv* (*insofar as*) dans la mesure où; (*seeing that*) attendu que

inauguration [ɪnɔːgjʊˈreɪʃən] *n* inauguration *f*; (*of president*) investiture *f*

inborn [ɪnˈbɔːn] *adj* (*quality*) inné(e)

inbred [ˈɪnbred] *adj* inné(e), naturel(le); (*family*) consanguin(e)

Inc. *abbr* = **incorporated**

incapable [ɪnˈkeɪpəbl] *adj* incapable

incapacitate [ɪnkəˈpæsɪteɪt] *vt*: **to** ~ **sb from doing** rendre qn incapable de faire

incense [*n* ˈɪnsens, *vb* ɪnˈsens] *n* encens *m* ♦ *vt* (*anger*) mettre en colère

incentive [ɪnˈsentɪv] *n* encouragement *m*, raison *f* de se donner de la peine

incessant [ɪnˈsesnt] *adj* incessant(e); ~**ly** *adv* sans cesse, constamment

inch [ɪntʃ] *n* pouce *m* (= 25 mm; 12 in a foot); **within an** ~ **of** à deux doigts de; **he didn't give an** ~ (*fig*) il n'a pas voulu céder d'un pouce; ~ **forward** *vi* avancer petit à petit

incident [ˈɪnsɪdənt] *n* incident *m*

incidental [ɪnsɪˈdentl] *adj* (*additional*) accessoire; ~ **to** qui accompagne; ~**ly** *adv* (*by the way*) à propos

inclination [ɪnklɪˈneɪʃən] *n* (*fig*) inclination *f*

incline [*n* ˈɪnklaɪn, *vb* ɪnˈklaɪn] *n* pente *f* ♦ *vt* incliner ♦ *vi* (*surface*) s'incliner; **to be** ~**d to do** avoir tendance à faire

include [ɪnˈkluːd] *vt* inclure, comprendre; **including** [ɪnˈkluːdɪŋ] *prep* y compris

inclusive [ɪnˈkluːsɪv] *adj* inclus(e), compris(e); ~ **of tax** *etc* taxes *etc* comprises

income [ˈɪnkʌm] *n* revenu *m*; ~ **tax** *n* impôt *m* sur le revenu

incoming [ˈɪnkʌmɪŋ] *adj* qui arrive; (*president*) entrant(e); ~ **mail** courrier *m* du jour; ~ **tide** marée montante

incompetent [ɪnˈkɒmpɪtənt] *adj* incompétent(e), incapable

incomplete [ˌɪnkəm'pliːt] *adj* incomplet(ète)
incongruous [ɪn'kɒŋgruəs] *adj* incongru(e)
inconsiderate [ˌɪnkən'sɪdərɪt] *adj* (*person*) qui manque d'égards; (*action*) inconsidéré(e)
inconsistency [ˌɪnkən'sɪstənsɪ] *n* (*of actions etc*) inconséquence *f*; (*of work*) irrégularité *f*; (*of statement etc*) incohérence *f*
inconsistent [ˌɪnkən'sɪstənt] *adj* inconséquent(e); irrégulier(ère); peu cohérent(e); ~ **with** incompatible avec
inconspicuous [ˌɪnkən'spɪkjuəs] *adj* qui passe inaperçu(e); (*colour, dress*) discret(ète)
inconvenience [ˌɪnkən'viːnɪəns] *n* inconvénient *m*; (*trouble*) dérangement *m* ♦ *vt* déranger
inconvenient [ˌɪnkən'viːnɪənt] *adj* (*house*) malcommode; (*time, place*) mal choisi(e), qui ne convient pas; (*visitor*) importun(e)
incorporate [ɪn'kɔːpəreɪt] *vt* incorporer; (*contain*) contenir; ~**d company** (*US*) *n* ≈ société *f* anonyme
incorrect [ˌɪnkə'rekt] *adj* incorrect(e)
increase [*n* 'ɪnkriːs, *vb* ɪn'kriːs] *n* augmentation *f* ♦ *vi, vt* augmenter; **increasing** [ɪn'kriːsɪŋ] *adj* (*number*) croissant(e); **increasingly** [ɪn'kriːsɪŋlɪ] *adv* de plus en plus
incredible [ɪn'kredəbl] *adj* incroyable
incredulous [ɪn'kredjuləs] *adj* incrédule
incubator ['ɪnkjubeɪtə*] *n* (*for babies*) couveuse *f*
incumbent [ɪn'kʌmbənt] *n* (*president*) président *m* en exercice; (*REL*) titulaire *m/f* ♦ *adj*: **it is ~ on him to ...** il lui incombe or appartient de ...
incur [ɪn'kɜː*] *vt* (*expenses*) encourir; (*anger, risk*) s'exposer à; (*debt*) contracter; (*loss*) subir
indebted [ɪn'detɪd] *adj*: **to be ~ to sb (for)** être redevable à qn (de)
indecent [ɪn'diːsnt] *adj* indécent(e), inconvenant(e); ~ **assault** (*BRIT*) *n* attentat *m* à la pudeur; ~ **exposure** *n* outrage *m* (public) à la pudeur
indecisive [ˌɪndɪ'saɪsɪv] *adj* (*person*) indécis(e)
indeed [ɪn'diːd] *adv* vraiment; en effet; (*furthermore*) d'ailleurs; **yes ~!** certainement!
indefinitely [ɪn'defɪnɪtlɪ] *adv* (*wait*) indéfiniment
indemnity [ɪn'demnɪtɪ] *n* (*safeguard*) assurance *f*, garantie *f*; (*compensation*) indemnité *f*
independence [ˌɪndɪ'pendəns] *n* indépendance *f*; **independent** [ˌɪndɪ'pendənt] *adj* indépendant(e); (*school*) privé(e); (*radio*) libre
index ['ɪndeks] *n* (*pl*: ~**es**: *in book*) index *m*; (: *in library etc*) catalogue *m*; (*pl*: *indices*: *ratio, sign*) indice *m*; ~ **card** *n* fiche *f*; ~-**linked** *adj* indexé(e)

(sur le coût de la vie *etc*)
India ['ɪndɪə] *n* Inde *f*; ~**n** *adj* indien(ne) ♦ *n* Indien(ne); (**American**) ~**n** Indien(ne) (d'Amérique)
indicate ['ɪndɪkeɪt] *vt* indiquer; **indication** [ˌɪndɪ'keɪʃən] *n* indication *f*, signe *m*; **indicative** [ɪn'dɪkətɪv] *adj*: **indicative of** symptomatique de ♦ *n* (*LING*) indicatif *m*; **indicator** ['ɪndɪkeɪtə*] *n* (*sign*) indicateur *m*; (*AUT*) clignotant *m*
indices ['ɪndɪsiːz] *npl of* **index**
indictment [ɪn'daɪtmənt] *n* accusation *f*
indifferent [ɪn'dɪfrənt] *adj* indifférent(e); (*poor*) médiocre, quelconque
indigenous [ɪn'dɪdʒɪnəs] *adj* indigène
indigestion [ˌɪndɪ'dʒestʃən] *n* indigestion *f*, mauvaise digestion
indignant [ɪn'dɪgnənt] *adj*: ~ **(at sth/with sb)** indigné(e) (de qch/contre qn)
indignity [ɪn'dɪgnɪtɪ] *n* indignité *f*, affront *m*
indirect [ˌɪndɪ'rekt] *adj* indirect(e)
indiscreet [ˌɪndɪs'kriːt] *adj* indiscret(ète); (*rash*) imprudent(e)
indiscriminate [ˌɪndɪs'krɪmɪnət] *adj* (*person*) qui manque de discernement; (*killings*) commis(e) au hasard
indisputable [ˌɪndɪs'pjuːtəbl] *adj* incontestable, indiscutable
individual [ˌɪndɪ'vɪdjuəl] *n* individu *m* ♦ *adj* individuel(le); (*characteristic*) particulier(ère), original(e)
indoctrination [ɪndɒktrɪ'neɪʃən] *n* endoctrinement *m*
Indonesia [ˌɪndəʊ'niːzɪə] *n* Indonésie *f*
indoor ['ɪndɔː*] *adj* (*plant*) d'appartement; (*swimming pool*) couvert(e); (*sport, games*) pratiqué(e) en salle; ~**s** [ɪn'dɔːz] *adv* à l'intérieur
induce [ɪn'djuːs] *vt* (*persuade*) persuader; (*bring about*) provoquer; ~**ment** *n* (*incentive*) récompense *f*; (*pej*: *bribe*) pot-de-vin *m*
indulge [ɪn'dʌldʒ] *vt* (*whim*) céder à, satisfaire; (*child*) gâter ♦ *vi*: **to ~ in sth** (*luxury*) se permettre qch; (*fantasies etc*) se livrer à qch; ~**nce** *n* fantaisie *f* (que l'on s'offre); (*leniency*) indulgence *f*; ~**nt** *adj* indulgent(e)
industrial [ɪn'dʌstrɪəl] *adj* industriel(le); (*injury*) du travail; ~ **action** *n* action revendicative; ~ **estate** (*BRIT*) *n* zone industrielle; ~**ist** *n* industriel *m*; ~ **park** (*US*) *n* = **industrial estate**
industrious [ɪn'dʌstrɪəs] *adj* travailleur(euse)
industry ['ɪndəstrɪ] *n* industrie *f*; (*diligence*) zèle *m*, application *f*
inebriated [ɪ'niːbrɪeɪtɪd] *adj* ivre
inedible [ɪn'edɪbl] *adj* immangeable; (*plant etc*) non comestible
ineffective [ˌɪnɪ'fektɪv], **ineffectual** [ˌɪnɪ'fektjuəl] *adj* inefficace

inefficient [ɪnɪˈfɪʃənt] *adj* inefficace

inequality [ɪnɪˈkwɒlɪtɪ] *n* inégalité *f*

inescapable [ɪnɪsˈkeɪpəbl] *adj* inéluctable, inévitable

inevitable [ɪnˈevɪtəbl] *adj* inévitable; **inevitably** *adv* inévitablement

inexhaustible [ɪnɪgˈzɔːstəbl] *adj* inépuisable

inexpensive [ɪnɪksˈpensɪv] *adj* bon marché *inv*

inexperienced [ɪnɪksˈpɪərɪənst] *adj* inexpérimenté(e)

infallible [ɪnˈfæləbl] *adj* infaillible

infamous [ˈɪnfəməs] *adj* infâme, abominable

infancy [ˈɪnfənsɪ] *n* petite enfance, bas âge

infant [ˈɪnfənt] *n* (*baby*) nourrisson *m*; (*young child*) petit(e) *n* enfant; ~ **school** (*BRIT*) *n* classes *fpl* préparatoires (*entre 5 et 7 ans*)

infatuated [ɪnˈfætjʊeɪtɪd] *adj*: ~ **with** entiché(e) de; **infatuation** [ɪnfætjuˈeɪʃən] *n* engouement *m*

infect [ɪnˈfekt] *vt* infecter, contaminer; ~**ion** [ɪnˈfekʃən] *n* infection *f*, (*contagion*) contagion *f*; ~**ious** [ɪnˈfekʃəs] *adj* infectieux(euse); (*also fig*) contagieux(euse)

infer [ɪnˈfɜː*] *vt* conclure, déduire; (*imply*) suggérer

inferior [ɪnˈfɪərɪə*] *adj* inférieur(e); (*goods*) de qualité inférieure *n* inférieur(e); (*in rank*) subalterne *m/f*; ~**ity** [ɪnfɪərɪˈɒrɪtɪ] *n* infériorité *f*; ~**ity complex** *n* complexe *m* d'infériorité

inferno [ɪnˈfɜːnəʊ] *n* (*blaze*) brasier *m*

infertile [ɪnˈfɜːtaɪl] *adj* stérile

infighting [ˈɪnfaɪtɪŋ] *n* querelles *fpl* internes

infinite [ˈɪnfɪnɪt] *adj* infini(e)

infinitive [ɪnˈfɪnɪtɪv] *n* infinitif *m*

infinity [ɪnˈfɪnɪtɪ] *n* infinité *f*, (*also MATH*) infini *m*

infirmary [ɪnˈfɜːmərɪ] *n* (*hospital*) hôpital *m*

inflamed [ɪnˈfleɪmd] *adj* enflammé(e)

inflammable [ɪnˈflæməbl] (*BRIT*) *adj* inflammable

inflammation [ɪnfləˈmeɪʃən] *n* inflammation *f*

inflatable [ɪnˈfleɪtəbl] *adj* gonflable

inflate [ɪnˈfleɪt] *vt* (*tyre, balloon*) gonfler; (*price*) faire monter; **inflation** [ɪnˈfleɪʃən] *n* (*ECON*) inflation *f*; **inflationary** [ɪnˈfleɪʃnərɪ] *adj* inflationniste

inflict [ɪnˈflɪkt] *vt*: **to** ~ **on** infliger à

influence [ˈɪnfluəns] *n* influence *f* ♦ *vt* influencer; **under the** ~ **of alcohol** en état d'ébriété; **influential** [ɪnflʊˈenʃəl] *adj* influent(e)

influenza [ɪnflʊˈenzə] *n* grippe *f*

influx [ˈɪnflʌks] *n* afflux *m*

inform [ɪnˈfɔːm] *vt*: **to** ~ **sb (of)** informer *or* avertir qn (de) ♦ *vi*: **to** ~ **on sb** dénoncer qn

informal [ɪnˈfɔːməl] *adj* (*person, manner, party*) simple; (*visit, discussion*) dénué(e) de formalités; (*announcement, invitation*) non officiel(le); (*colloquial*) familier(ère); ~**ity** [ɪnfɔːˈmælɪtɪ] *n* simplicité *f*, absence *f* de cérémonie; caractère non officiel

informant [ɪnˈfɔːmənt] *n* informateur(trice)

information [ɪnfəˈmeɪʃən] *n* information *f*, renseignements *mpl*; (*knowledge*) connaissances *fpl*; **a piece of** ~ un renseignement; ~ **office** *n* bureau *m* de renseignements

informative [ɪnˈfɔːmətɪv] *adj* instructif(ive)

informer [ɪnˈfɔːmə*] *n* (*also: police* ~) indicateur(trice)

infringe [ɪnˈfrɪndʒ] *vt* enfreindre ♦ *vi*: **to** ~ **on** empiéter sur; ~**ment** *n*: ~**ment (of)** infraction *f* (à)

infuriating [ɪnˈfjʊərɪeɪtɪŋ] *adj* exaspérant(e)

ingenious [ɪnˈdʒiːnɪəs] *adj* ingénieux(euse); **ingenuity** [ɪndʒɪˈnjuːɪtɪ] *n* ingéniosité *f*

ingenuous [ɪnˈdʒenjuəs] *adj* naïf(naïve), ingénu(e)

ingot [ˈɪŋgət] *n* lingot *m*

ingrained [ɪnˈgreɪnd] *adj* enraciné(e)

ingratiate [ɪnˈgreɪʃɪeɪt] *vt*: **to** ~ **o.s. with** s'insinuer dans les bonnes grâces de, se faire bien voir de

ingredient [ɪnˈgriːdɪənt] *n* ingrédient *m*; (*fig*) élément *m*

inhabit [ɪnˈhæbɪt] *vt* habiter; ~**ant** [ɪnˈhæbɪtnt] *n* habitant(e)

inhale [ɪnˈheɪl] *vt* respirer; (*smoke*) avaler ♦ *vi* aspirer; (*in smoking*) avaler la fumée

inherent [ɪnˈhɪərənt] *adj*: ~ (**in** *or* **to**) inhérent(e) (à)

inherit [ɪnˈherɪt] *vt* hériter (de); ~**ance** *n* héritage *m*

inhibit [ɪnˈhɪbɪt] *vt* (*PSYCH*) inhiber; (*growth*) freiner; ~**ion** [ɪnhɪˈbɪʃən] *n* inhibition *f*

inhuman [ɪnˈhjuːmən] *adj* inhumain(e)

initial [ɪˈnɪʃəl] *adj* initial(e) ♦ *n* initiale *f* ♦ *vt* parafer; ~**s** *npl* (*letters*) initiales *fpl*; (*as signature*) parafe *m*; ~**ly** *adv* initialement, au début

initiate [ɪˈnɪʃɪeɪt] *vt* (*start*) entreprendre; amorcer; lancer; (*person*) initier; **to** ~ **proceedings against sb** intenter une action à qn

initiative [ɪˈnɪʃətɪv] *n* initiative *f*

inject [ɪnˈdʒekt] *vt* injecter; (*person*): **to** ~ **sb with sth** faire une piqûre de qch à qn; ~**ion** [ɪnˈdʒekʃən] *n* injection *f*, piqûre *f*

injure [ˈɪndʒə*] *vt* blesser; (*reputation etc*) compromettre; ~**d** *adj* blessé(e); **injury** [ˈɪndʒərɪ] *n* blessure *f*; **injury time** *n* (*SPORT*) arrêts *mpl* de jeu

injustice [ɪnˈdʒʌstɪs] *n* injustice *f*

ink [ɪŋk] *n* encre *f*

inkling [ˈɪŋklɪŋ] *n*: **to have an/no** ~ **of** avoir une (vague) idée de/n'avoir aucune idée de

inlaid ['ɪn'leɪd] adj incrusté(e); (table etc) marqueté(e)

inland [adj 'ɪnlənd, adv 'ɪnlænd] adj intérieur(e) ♦ adv à l'intérieur, dans les terres; **I~ Revenue** (BRIT) n fisc m

in-laws ['ɪnlɔːz] npl beaux-parents mpl; belle famille

inlet ['ɪnlet] n (GEO) crique f

inmate ['ɪnmeɪt] n (in prison) détenu(e); (in asylum) interné(e)

inn [ɪn] n auberge f

innate [ɪ'neɪt] adj inné(e)

inner ['ɪnə*] adj intérieur(e); ~ **city** n centre m de zone urbaine; ~ **tube** n (of tyre) chambre f à air

innings ['ɪnɪŋz] n (CRICKET) tour m de batte

innocent ['ɪnəsnt] adj innocent(e)

innocuous [ɪ'nɒkjʊəs] adj inoffensif(ive)

innuendo [ɪnjʊ'endəʊ] (pl ~es) n insinuation f, allusion (malveillante)

innumerable [ɪ'njuːmərəbl] adj innombrable

inordinately [ɪ'nɔːdɪnɪtlɪ] adv démesurément

inpatient ['ɪnpeɪʃənt] n malade hospitalisé(e)

input ['ɪnpʊt] n (resources) ressources fpl; (COMPUT) entrée f (de données); (: data) données fpl

inquest ['ɪnkwest] n enquête f; (coroner's) ~ enquête judiciaire

inquire [ɪn'kwaɪə*] vi demander ♦ vt demander; to ~ **about** se renseigner sur; ~ **into** vt fus faire une enquête sur; **inquiry** [ɪn'kwaɪərɪ] n demande f de renseignements; (investigation) enquête f, investigation f; **inquiry office** (BRIT) n bureau m de renseignements

inquisitive [ɪn'kwɪzɪtɪv] adj curieux(euse)

inroads ['ɪnrəʊdz] npl: **to make** ~ **into** (savings etc) entamer

ins abbr = **inches**

insane [ɪn'seɪn] adj fou(folle); (MED) aliéné(e); **insanity** [ɪn'sænɪtɪ] n folie f; (MED) aliénation (mentale)

inscription [ɪn'skrɪpʃən] n inscription f; (in book) dédicace f

inscrutable [ɪn'skruːtəbl] adj impénétrable; (comment) obscur(e)

insect ['ɪnsekt] n insecte m; ~**icide** [ɪn'sektɪsaɪd] n insecticide m

insecure [ɪnsɪ'kjʊə*] adj peu solide; peu sûr(e); (person) anxieux(euse)

insensitive [ɪn'sensɪtɪv] adj insensible

insert [ɪn'sɜːt] vt insérer; ~**ion** [ɪn'sɜːʃən] n insertion f

in-service ['ɪn'sɜːvɪs] adj (training) continu(e), en cours d'emploi; (course) de perfectionnement; de recyclage

inshore ['ɪn'ʃɔː*] adj côtier(ère) ♦ adv près de la côte; (move) vers la côte

inside ['ɪn'saɪd] n intérieur m ♦ adj intérieur(e) ♦ adv à l'intérieur, dedans ♦ prep à l'intérieur de; (of time): ~ **10 minutes** en moins de 10 minutes; ~**s** npl (inf) intestins mpl; ~ **information** n renseignements obtenus à la source; ~ **lane** n (AUT: BRIT) voie f de gauche; (: US, Europe etc) voie de droite; ~ **out** adv à l'envers; (know) à fond

insider dealing, insider trading n (St Ex) délit m d'initié

insight ['ɪnsaɪt] n perspicacité f; (glimpse, idea) aperçu m

insignificant [ɪnsɪg'nɪfɪkənt] adj insignifiant(e)

insincere [ɪnsɪn'sɪə*] adj hypocrite

insinuate [ɪn'sɪnjʊeɪt] vt insinuer

insist [ɪn'sɪst] vi insister; to ~ **on doing** insister pour faire; to ~ **on sth** exiger qch; to ~ **that** insister pour que; (claim) maintenir or soutenir que; ~**ent** adj insistant(e), pressant(e); (noise, action) ininterrompu(e)

insole ['ɪnsəʊl] n (removable) semelle intérieure

insolent ['ɪnsələnt] adj insolent(e)

insolvent [ɪn'sɒlvənt] adj insolvable

insomnia [ɪn'sɒmnɪə] n insomnie f

inspect [ɪn'spekt] vt inspecter; (ticket) contrôler; ~**ion** [ɪn'spekʃən] n inspection f; contrôle m; ~**or** n inspecteur(trice); (BRIT: on buses, trains) contrôleur(euse)

inspire [ɪn'spaɪə*] vt inspirer

install [ɪn'stɔːl] vt installer; ~**ation** [ɪnstə'leɪʃən] n installation f

instalment [ɪn'stɔːlmənt] (US **installment**) n acompte m, versement partiel; (of TV serial etc) épisode m; **in** ~**s** (pay) à tempérament; (receive) en plusieurs fois

instance ['ɪnstəns] n exemple m; **for** ~ par exemple; **in the first** ~ tout d'abord, en premier lieu

instant ['ɪnstənt] n instant m ♦ adj immédiat(e); (coffee, food) instantané(e), en poudre; ~**ly** adv immédiatement, tout de suite

instead [ɪn'sted] adv au lieu de cela; ~ **of** au lieu de; ~ **of sb** à la place de qn

instep ['ɪnstep] n cou-de-pied m; (of shoe) cambrure f

instigate ['ɪnstɪgeɪt] vt (rebellion) fomenter, provoquer; (talks etc) promouvoir

instil [ɪn'stɪl] vt: **to** ~ **(into)** inculquer (à); (courage) insuffler (à)

instinct ['ɪnstɪŋkt] n instinct m

institute ['ɪnstɪtjuːt] n institut m ♦ vt instituer, établir; (inquiry) ouvrir; (proceedings) entamer

institution [ɪnstɪ'tjuːʃən] n institution f; (educational) établissement m (scolaire); (mental home) établissement (psychiatrique)

instruct [ɪn'strʌkt] vt: **to** ~ **sb in sth** enseigner qch à qn; to ~ **sb to do** charger qn or ordonner à qn de faire; ~**ion** [ɪn'strʌkʃən] n instruction f; ~**ions** npl (orders) directives *fpl*; ~**ions (for use)** mode *m* d'emploi; ~**or** *n* professeur *m*; (*for skiing, driving*) moniteur *m*

instrument ['ɪnstrʊmənt] *n* instrument *m*; ~**al** [ɪnstrʊ'mentl] *adj*: **to be** ~**al in** contribuer à; ~ **panel** *n* tableau *m* de bord

insufficient [ɪnsə'fɪʃənt] *adj* insuffisant(e)

insular ['ɪnsjʊlə*] *adj* (*outlook*) borné(e); (*person*) aux vues étroites

insulate ['ɪnsjʊleɪt] *vt* isoler; (*against sound*) insonoriser; **insulating tape** *n* ruban isolant; **insulation** [ɪnsjʊ'leɪʃən] *n* isolation *f*; insonorisation *f*

insulin ['ɪnsjʊlɪn] *n* insuline *f*

insult [*n* 'ɪnsʌlt, *vb* ɪn'sʌlt] *n* insulte *f*, affront *m* ♦ *vt* insulter, faire affront à

insurance [ɪn'ʃʊərəns] *n* assurance *f*; **fire/ life** ~ assurance-incendie/-vie; ~ **policy** *n* police *f* d'assurance

insure [ɪn'ʃʊə*] *vt* assurer; **to** ~ **(o.s.) against** (*fig*) parer à

intact [ɪn'tækt] *adj* intact(e)

intake ['ɪnteɪk] *n* (*of food, oxygen*) consommation *f*, (*BRIT: SCOL*): **an** ~ **of 200 a year** 200 admissions *fpl* par an

integral ['ɪntɪɡrəl] *adj* (*part*) intégrant(e)

integrate ['ɪntɪɡreɪt] *vt* intégrer ♦ *vi* s'intégrer

intellect ['ɪntɪlekt] *n* intelligence *f*; ~**ual** [ɪntɪ'lektjʊəl] *adj, n* intellectuel(le)

intelligence [ɪn'telɪdʒəns] *n* intelligence *f*, (*MIL etc*) informations *fpl*, renseignements *mpl*; ~ **service** *n* services secrets; **intelligent** [ɪn'telɪdʒənt] *adj* intelligent(e)

intend [ɪn'tend] *vt* (*gift etc*): **to** ~ **sth for** destiner qch à; **to** ~ **to do** avoir l'intention de faire; ~**ed** *adj* (*journey*) projeté(e); (*effect*) voulu(e); (*insult*) intentionnel(le)

intense [ɪn'tens] *adj* intense; (*person*) véhément(e); ~**ly** *adv* intensément; profondément

intensive [ɪn'tensɪv] *adj* intensif(ive); ~ **care unit** *n* service *m* de réanimation

intent [ɪn'tent] *n* intention *f* ♦ *adj* attentif(ive); (*absorbed*): ~ **(on)** absorbé(e) (par); **to all** ~**s and purposes** en fait, pratiquement; **to be** ~ **on doing sth** être (bien) décidé à faire qch

intention [ɪn'tenʃən] *n* intention *f*; ~**al** *adj* intentionnel(le), délibéré(e)

intently [ɪn'tentlɪ] *adv* attentivement

interact [ɪntər'ækt] *vi* avoir une action réciproque; (*people*) communiquer; ~**ive** *adj* (*COMPUT*) interactif(ive)

interchange [*n* 'ɪntətʃeɪndʒ, *vb* ɪntə'tʃeɪndʒ] *n* (*exchange*) échange *m*; (*on motorway*) échangeur *m*; ~**able** [ɪntə'tʃeɪndʒəbl] *adj* interchangeable

intercom ['ɪntəkɔm] *n* interphone *m*

intercourse ['ɪntəkɔːs] *n* (*sexual*) rapports *mpl*

interest ['ɪntrest] *n* intérêt *m*; (*pastime*):

my main ~ ce qui m'intéresse le plus; (*COMM*) intérêts *mpl* ♦ *vt* intéresser; **to be** ~**ed in sth** s'intéresser à qch; **i am** ~**ed in going** ça m'intéresse d'y aller; ~**ing** *adj* intéressant(e); ~ **rate** *n* taux *m* d'intérêt

interface ['ɪntəfeɪs] *n* (*COMPUT*) interface *f*

interfere [ɪntə'fɪə*] *vi*: **to** ~ **in** (*quarrel*) s'immiscer dans; (*other people's business*) se mêler de; **to** ~ **with** (*object*) toucher à; (*plans*) contrecarrer; (*duty*) être en conflit avec; ~**nce** [ɪntə'fɪərəns] *n* (*in affairs*) ingérance *f*, (*RADIO, TV*) parasites *mpl*

interim ['ɪntərɪm] *adj* provisoire ♦ *n*: **in the** ~ dans l'intérim, entre-temps

interior [ɪn'tɪərɪə*] *n* intérieur *m* ♦ *adj* intérieur(e); (*minister, department*) de l'Intérieur; ~ **designer** *n* styliste *m/f*, designer *m/f*

interjection [ɪntə'dʒekʃən] *n* (*interruption*) interruption *f*; (*LING*) interjection *f*

interlock [ɪntə'lɔk] *vi* s'enclencher

interlude ['ɪntəluːd] *n* intervalle *m*; (*THEATRE*) intermède *m*

intermediate [ɪntə'miːdɪət] *adj* intermédiaire; (*SCOL: course, level*) moyen(ne)

intermission [ɪntə'mɪʃən] *n* pause *f*, (*THEATRE, CINEMA*) entracte *m*

intern [*vb* ɪn'tɜːn, *n* 'ɪntɜːn] *vt* interner ♦ *n* (*US*) interne *m/f*

internal [ɪn'tɜːnl] *adj* interne; (*politics*) intérieur(e); ~**ly** *adv*: "**not to be taken** ~**ly**" "pour usage externe"; **I**~ **Revenue Service** (*US*) *n* fisc *m*

international [ɪntə'næʃnəl] *adj* international(e)

interplay ['ɪntəpleɪ] *n* effet *m* réciproque, interaction *f*

interpret [ɪn'tɜːprɪt] *vt* interpréter ♦ *vi* servir d'interprète; ~**er** *n* interprète *m/f*

interrelated [ɪntərɪ'leɪtɪd] *adj* en corrélation, en rapport étroit

interrogate [ɪn'terəɡeɪt] *vt* interroger; (*suspect etc*) soumettre à un interrogatoire; **interrogation** [ɪntərə'ɡeɪʃən] *n* interrogation *f*, interrogatoire *m*

interrupt [ɪntə'rʌpt] *vt, vi* interrompre; ~**ion** *n* interruption *f*

intersect [ɪntə'sekt] *vi* (*roads*) se croiser, se couper; ~**ion** [ɪntə'sekʃən] *n* (*of roads*) croisement *m*

intersperse [ɪntə'spɜːs] *vt*: **to** ~ **with** parsemer de

intertwine [ɪntə'twaɪn] *vi* s'entrelacer

interval ['ɪntəvəl] *n* intervalle *m*; (*BRIT: THEATRE*) entracte *m*; (*: SPORT*) mi-temps *f*; **at** ~**s** par intervalles

intervene [ɪntə'viːn] *vi* (*person*) intervenir; (*event*) survenir; (*time*) s'écouler (entretemps); **intervention** [ɪntə'venʃən] *n* intervention *f*

interview ['ɪntəvjuː] *n* (*RADIO, TV etc*) interview *f*; (*for job*) entrevue *f* ♦ *vt* interviewer; avoir une entrevue avec; **~er** n (RA-DIO, TV) interviewer m

intestine [ɪnˈtestɪn] n intestin m

intimacy [ˈɪntɪməsɪ] n intimité f

intimate [adj ˈɪntɪmət, vb ˈɪntɪmeɪt] adj intime; (friendship) profond(e); (knowledge) approfondi(e) ♦ vt (hint) suggérer, laisser entendre

into [ˈɪntʊ] prep dans; **~ pieces/French** en morceaux/français

intolerant [ɪnˈtɒlərənt] adj: **~ (of)** intolérant(e) (de)

intoxicated [ɪnˈtɒksɪkeɪtɪd] adj (drunk) ivre; **intoxication** [ɪntɒksɪˈkeɪʃən] n ivresse f

intractable [ɪnˈtræktəbl] adj (child) indocile, insoumis(e); (problem) insoluble

intransitive [ɪnˈtrænsɪtɪv] adj intransitif(ive)

intravenous [ɪntrəˈviːnəs] adj intraveineux(euse)

in-tray [ˈɪntreɪ] n courrier m "arrivée"

intricate [ˈɪntrɪkət] adj complexe, compliqué(e)

intrigue [ɪnˈtriːg] n intrigue f ♦ vt intriguer; **intriguing** [ɪnˈtriːgɪŋ] adj fascinant(e)

intrinsic [ɪnˈtrɪnsɪk] adj intrinsèque

introduce [ɪntrəˈdjuːs] vt introduire; (TV show, people to each other) présenter; **to ~ sb to** (pastime, technique) initier qn à; **introduction** [ɪntrəˈdʌkʃən] n introduction f; (of person) présentation f; (to new experience) initiation f; **introductory** [ɪntrəˈdʌktərɪ] adj préliminaire, d'introduction; **introductory offer** n (COMM) offre f de lancement

intrude [ɪnˈtruːd] vi (person) être importun(e); **to ~ on** (conversation etc) s'immiscer dans; **~r** n intrus(e)

intuition [ɪntjuːˈɪʃən] n intuition f

inundate [ˈɪnʌndeɪt] vt: **to ~ with** inonder de

invade [ɪnˈveɪd] vt envahir

invalid [n ˈɪnvəlɪd, adj ɪnˈvælɪd] n malade m/f; (with disability) invalide m/f ♦ adj (not valid) non valide or valable

invaluable [ɪnˈvæljʊəbl] adj inestimable, inappréciable

invariably [ɪnˈvɛərɪəblɪ] adv invariablement; toujours

invent [ɪnˈvent] vt inventer; **~ion** [ɪnˈvenʃən] n invention f, **~ive** adj inventif(ive); **~or** n inventeur(trice)

inventory [ˈɪnvəntrɪ] n inventaire m

invert [ɪnˈvɜːt] vt intervertir; (cup, object) retourner; **~ed commas** (BRIT) npl guillemets mpl

invest [ɪnˈvest] vt investir ♦ vi: **to ~ in** sth placer son argent dans qch; (fig) s'offrir qch

investigate [ɪnˈvestɪgeɪt] vt (crime etc) faire une enquête sur; **investigation** [ɪnvestɪˈgeɪʃən] n (of crime) enquête f

investment [ɪnˈvestmənt] n investissement m, placement m

investor [ɪnˈvestə*] n investisseur m; actionnaire m/f

invigilator [ɪnˈvɪdʒɪleɪtə*] n surveillant(e)

invigorating [ɪnˈvɪgəreɪtɪŋ] adj vivifiant(e); (fig) stimulant(e)

invisible [ɪnˈvɪzəbl] adj invisible

invitation [ɪnvɪˈteɪʃən] n invitation f

invite [ɪnˈvaɪt] vt inviter; (opinions etc) demander; **inviting** [ɪnˈvaɪtɪŋ] adj engageant(e), attrayant(e)

invoice [ˈɪnvɔɪs] n facture f

involuntary [ɪnˈvɒləntərɪ] adj involontaire

involve [ɪnˈvɒlv] vt (entail) entraîner, nécessiter; (concern) concerner; (associate): **to ~ sb (in)** impliquer qn (dans), mêler qn (à); faire participer qn (à); **~d** adj (complicated) complexe; **to be ~d in** participer à; (engrossed) être absorbé(e) par; **~ment** n: **~ment (in)** participation f (à); rôle m (dans); (enthusiasm) enthousiasme m (pour)

inward [ˈɪnwəd] adj (thought, feeling) profond(e), intime; (movement) vers l'intérieur; **~(s)** adv vers l'intérieur

I/O abbr (COMPUT: = input/output) E/S

iodine [ˈaɪədiːn] n iode m

iota [aɪˈəʊtə] n (fig) brin m, grain m

IOU n abbr (= I owe you) reconnaissance f de dette

IQ n abbr (= intelligence quotient) Q.I. m

IRA n abbr (= Irish Republican Army) IRA f

Iran [ɪˈrɑːn] n Iran m

Iraq [ɪˈrɑːk] n Irak m

irate [aɪˈreɪt] adj courroucé(e)

Ireland [ˈaɪələnd] n Irlande f

iris [ˈaɪrɪs] (pl **~es**) n iris m

Irish [ˈaɪrɪʃ] adj irlandais(e) ♦ npl: **the ~** les Irlandais; **~man** (irreg) n Irlandais m; **~ Sea** n mer f d'Irlande; **~woman** (irreg) n Irlandaise f

iron [ˈaɪən] n fer m; (for clothes) fer m à repasser ♦ cpd de or en fer; (fig) de fer ♦ vt (clothes) repasser; **~ out** vt (fig) aplanir; faire disparaître; **the I~ Curtain** n le rideau de fer

ironic(al) [aɪˈrɒnɪk(əl)] adj ironique

ironing [ˈaɪənɪŋ] n repassage m; **~ board** n planche f à repasser

ironmonger's (shop) [ˈaɪənmʌŋgəz-] n quincaillerie f

irony [ˈaɪərənɪ] n ironie f

irrational [ɪˈræʃənl] adj irrationnel(le)

irregular [ɪˈregjʊlə*] adj irrégulier(ère); (surface) inégal(e)

irrelevant [ɪˈreləvənt] adj sans rapport, hors de propos

irresistible [ɪrɪˈzɪstəbl] adj irrésistible

irrespective [ɪrɪˈspektɪv]: **~ of** prep sans tenir compte de

irresponsible [ɪrɪˈspɒnsəbl] adj (act) irréfléchi(e); (person) irresponsable, inconscient(e)

irrigate ['ɪrɪgeɪt] *vt* irriguer; **irrigation** [ɪrɪ'geɪʃən] *n* irrigation *f*

irritate ['ɪrɪteɪt] *vt* irriter; **irritating** *adj* irritant(e); **irritation** [ɪrɪ'teɪʃən] *n* irritation *f*

IRS *n abbr* = **Internal Revenue Service**

is [ɪz] *vb see* **be**

Islam ['ɪzlɑːm] *n* Islam *m*

island ['aɪlənd] *n* île *f*; ~**er** *n* habitant(e) d'une île, insulaire *m/f*

isle [aɪl] *n* île *f*

isn't ['ɪznt] = **is not**

isolate ['aɪsəʊleɪt] *vt* isoler; ~**d** *adj* isolé(e); **isolation** [aɪsəʊ'leɪʃən] *n* isolation *f*

Israel ['ɪzreɪəl] *n* Israël *m*; ~**i** [ɪz'reɪlɪ] *adj* israélien(ne) ♦ *n* Israélien(ne)

issue ['ɪʃuː] *n* question *f*, problème *m*; (*of book*) publication *f*, parution *f*; (*of banknotes etc*) émission *f*; (*of newspaper etc*) numéro *m* ♦ *vt* (*rations, equipment*) distribuer; (*statement*) publier, faire; (*banknotes etc*) émettre, mettre en circulation; **at** ~ en jeu, en cause; **to take** ~ **with sb (over)** exprimer son désaccord avec qn (sur); **to make an** ~ **of sth** faire une montagne de qch

─────── **KEYWORD**

it [ɪt] *pron* **1** (*specific: subject*) il(elle); (: *direct object*) le(la, l'); (: *indirect object*) lui; ~**'s on the table** c'est or il (or elle) est sur la table; **about/from/of** ~ en; **I spoke to him about** ~ je lui en ai parlé; **what did you learn from** ~? qu'est-ce que vous en avez retiré?; **I'm proud of** ~ j'en suis fier; **in/to** ~ y; **put the book in** ~ mettez-y le livre; **he agreed to** ~ il y a consenti; **did you go to** ~? (*party, concert etc*) est-ce que vous y êtes allé(s)?

2 (*impersonal*) il; ce; ~**'s raining** il pleut; ~**'s Friday tomorrow** demain c'est vendredi *or* nous sommes vendredi; ~**'s 6 o'clock** il est 6 heures; **who is** ~? - ~**'s me** qui est-ce? - c'est moi

Italian [ɪ'tæljən] *adj* italien(ne) ♦ *n* Italien(ne); (*LING*) italien *m*

italics [ɪ'tælɪks] *npl* italiques *fpl*

Italy ['ɪtəlɪ] *n* Italie *f*

itch [ɪtʃ] *n* démangeaison *f* ♦ *vi* (*person*) éprouver des démangeaisons; (*part of body*) démanger; **I'm** ~**ing to do** l'envie me démange de faire; ~**y** *adj* qui démange; **to be** ~**y** avoir des démangeaisons

it'd ['ɪtd] = **it would; it had**

item ['aɪtəm] *n* article *m*; (*on agenda*) question *f*, point *m*; (*also: news* ~) nouvelle *f*; ~**ize** *vt* détailler, faire une liste de

itinerary [aɪ'tɪnərərɪ] *n* itinéraire *m*

it: ~**'ll** ['ɪtl] = **it will; it shall**; ~**s** [ɪts] *adj* son(sa), ses *pl*; ~**'s** [ɪts] = **it is; it has**; ~**self** [ɪt'self] *pron* (*reflexive*) se; (*emphatic*) lui-même(elle-même)

ITV *n abbr* (*BRIT:* = *Independent Television*)

chaîne privée

IUD *n abbr* (= *intra-uterine device*) DIU *m*, stérilet *m*

I've [aɪv] = **I have**

ivory ['aɪvərɪ] *n* ivoire *m*

ivy ['aɪvɪ] *n* lierre *m*

─────── *J j*

jab [dʒæb] *vt:* **to** ~ **sth into** enfoncer *or* planter qch dans ♦ *n* (*inf: injection*) piqûre *f*

jack [dʒæk] *n* (*AUT*) cric *m*; (*CARDS*) valet *m*; ~ **up** *vt* soulever (au cric)

jackal ['dʒækəl] *n* chacal *m*

jackdaw ['dʒækdɔː] *n* choucas *m*

jacket ['dʒækɪt] *n* veste *f*, veston *m*; (*of book*) jaquette *f*, couverture *f*

jackknife ['dʒæknaɪf] *vi:* **the lorry** ~**d** la remorque (du camion) s'est mise en travers

jack plug *n* (*ELEC*) prise jack mâle *f*

jackpot ['dʒækpɒt] *n* gros lot

jaded ['dʒeɪdɪd] *adj* éreinté(e), fatigué(e)

jagged ['dʒægɪd] *adj* dentelé(e)

jail [dʒeɪl] *n* prison *f* ♦ *vt* emprisonner, mettre en prison

jam [dʒæm] *n* confiture *f*; (*also: traffic* ~) embouteillage *m* ♦ *vt* (*passage etc*) encombrer, obstruer; (*mechanism, drawer etc*) bloquer, coincer; (*RADIO*) brouiller ♦ *vi* se coincer, se bloquer; (*gun*) s'enrayer; **to be in a** ~ (*inf*) être dans le pétrin; **to** ~ **sth into** entasser qch dans; enfoncer qch dans

jangle ['dʒæŋgl] *vi* cliqueter

janitor ['dʒænɪtə*] *n* concierge *m*

January ['dʒænjʊərɪ] *n* janvier *m*

Japan [dʒə'pæn] *n* Japon *m*; ~**ese** *adj* [dʒæpə'niːz] japonais(e) ♦ *n inv* Japonais(e); (*LING*) japonais *m*

jar [dʒɑː*] *n* (*stone, earthenware*) pot *m*; (*glass*) bocal *m* ♦ *vi* (*sound discordant*) produire un son grinçant *or* discordant; (*colours etc*) jurer

jargon ['dʒɑːgən] *n* jargon *m*

jaundice ['dʒɔːndɪs] *n* jaunisse *f*; ~**d** *adj* (*fig*) envieux(euse), désapprobateur(trice)

javelin ['dʒævlɪn] *n* javelot *m*

jaw [dʒɔː] *n* mâchoire *f*

jay [dʒeɪ] *n* geai *m*; ~**walker** ['dʒeɪwɔːkə*] *n* piéton indiscipliné

jazz [dʒæz] *n* jazz *m*; ~ **up** *vt* animer, égayer

jealous ['dʒeləs] *adj* jaloux(ouse); ~**y** *n* jalousie *f*

jeans [dʒiːnz] npl jean m
jeer [dʒɪə*] vi: **to ~ (at)** se moquer cruelle-ment (de), railler
jelly ['dʒelɪ] n gelée f; **~fish** n méduse f
jeopardy ['dʒepədɪ] n: **to be in ~** être en danger or péril
jerk [dʒɜːk] n secousse f; saccade f; sursaut m, spasme m; (inf: idiot) pauvre type m ♦ vt (pull) tirer brusquement ♦ vi (vehicles) ca-hoter
jersey ['dʒɜːzɪ] n (pullover) tricot m; (fabric) jersey m
Jesus ['dʒiːzəs] n Jésus
jet [dʒet] n (gas, liquid) jet m; (AVIAT) avion m à réaction, jet m; **~-black** adj (d'un noir) de jais; **~ engine** n moteur m à réaction; **~ lag** n (fatigue due au) décalage m horaire
jettison ['dʒetɪsn] vt jeter par-dessus bord
jetty ['dʒetɪ] n jetée f, digue f
Jew [dʒuː] n Juif m
jewel ['dʒuːəl] n bijou m, joyau m; (in watch) rubis m; **~ler** (US **~er**) n bijou-tier(ère), joaillier m; **~ler's (shop)** n bijou-terie f, joaillerie f; **~lery** (US **~ry**) n bijoux mpl
Jewess ['dʒuːɪs] n Juive f
Jewish ['dʒuːɪʃ] adj juif(juive)
jibe [dʒaɪb] n sarcasme m
jiffy ['dʒɪfɪ] (inf) n: **in a ~** en un clin d'œil
jigsaw ['dʒɪgsɔː] n (also: **~ puzzle**) puzzle m
jilt [dʒɪlt] vt laisser tomber, plaquer
jingle ['dʒɪŋgl] n (for advert) couplet m pu-blicitaire ♦ vi cliqueter, tinter
jinx [dʒɪŋks] (inf) n (mauvais) sort
jitters ['dʒɪtəz] (inf) npl: **to get the ~** (inf) avoir la trouille or la frousse
job [dʒɒb] n (chore, task) travail m, tâche f; (employment) emploi m, poste m, place f; **it's a good ~ that ...** c'est heureux or c'est une chance que ...; **just the ~!** (c'est) juste or exactement ce qu'il faut!; **~ centre** (BRIT) n agence f pour l'emploi; **~less** adj sans travail, au chômage
jockey ['dʒɒkɪ] n jockey m ♦ vi: **to ~ for position** manœuvrer pour être bien placé
jocular ['dʒɒkjʊlə*] adj jovial(e), enjoué(e); facétieux(euse)
jog [dʒɒg] vt secouer ♦ vi (SPORT) faire du jogging; **to ~ sb's memory** rafraîchir la mémoire de qn; **~ along** vi cheminer; trot-ter; **~ging** n jogging m
join [dʒɔɪn] vt (put together) unir, assem-bler; (become member of) s'inscrire à; (meet) rejoindre, retrouver; (queue) se join-dre à ♦ vi (roads, rivers) se rejoindre, se rencontrer ♦ n raccord m; **~ in** vi se met-tre de la partie, participer ♦ vt fus partici-per à, se mêler à; **~ up** vi (meet) se rejoin-dre; (MIL) s'engager; **~er** ['dʒɔɪnə*] (BRIT) n menuisier m

joint [dʒɔɪnt] n (TECH) jointure f; joint m; (ANAT) articulation f, jointure; (BRIT: CULIN) rôti m; (inf: place) boîte f; (: of can-nabis) joint m ♦ adj commun(e); **~ ac-count** n (with bank etc) compte joint
joke [dʒəʊk] n plaisanterie f; (also: practical ~) farce f ♦ vi plaisanter; **to play a ~ on** jouer un tour à, faire une farce à; **~r** n (CARDS) joker m
jolly ['dʒɒlɪ] adj gai(e), enjoué(e); (enjoya-ble) amusant(e), plaisant(e) ♦ adv (BRIT: inf) rudement, drôlement
jolt [dʒəʊlt] n cahot m, secousse f; (shock) choc m ♦ vt cahoter, secouer
Jordan ['dʒɔːdən] n (country) Jordanie f
jostle ['dʒɒsl] vt bousculer, pousser
jot [dʒɒt] n: **not one ~** pas un brin; **~ down** vt noter; **~ter** (BRIT) n cahier m (de brouillon); (pad) bloc-notes m
journal ['dʒɜːnl] n journal m; **~ism** n jour-nalisme m; **~ist** n journaliste m/f
journey ['dʒɜːnɪ] n voyage m; (distance covered) trajet m
joy [dʒɔɪ] n joie f; **~ful** adj joyeux(euse); **~rider** n personne qui fait une virée dans une voiture volée; **~stick** n (AVIAT, COMPUT) manche m à balai
JP n abbr = **Justice of the Peace**
Jr abbr = **junior**
jubilant ['dʒuːbɪlənt] adj triomphant(e); ré-joui(e)
judge [dʒʌdʒ] n juge m ♦ vt juger; **judg(e)ment** n jugement m
judicial [dʒuː'dɪʃəl] adj judiciaire
judiciary [dʒuː'dɪʃɪərɪ] n (pouvoir m) judi-ciaire m
judo ['dʒuːdəʊ] n judo m
jug [dʒʌg] n pot m, cruche f
juggernaut ['dʒʌgənɔːt] (BRIT) n (huge truck) énorme poids lourd
juggle ['dʒʌgl] vi jongler; **~r** n jongleur m
Jugoslav etc = **Yugoslav** etc
juice [dʒuːs] n jus m; **juicy** ['dʒuːsɪ] adj ju-teux(euse)
jukebox ['dʒuːkbɒks] n juke-box m
July [dʒuː'laɪ] n juillet m
jumble ['dʒʌmbl] n fouillis m ♦ vt (also: ~ up) mélanger, brouiller; **~ sale** (BRIT) n vente f de charité
jumbo (jet) ['dʒʌmbəʊ-] n jumbo-jet m, gros porteur
jump [dʒʌmp] vi sauter, bondir; (start) sur-sauter; (increase) monter en flèche ♦ vt sauter, franchir ♦ n saut m, bond m; sursaut m; **to ~ the queue** (BRIT) passer avant son tour
jumper ['dʒʌmpə*] n (BRIT: pullover) pull-over m; (US: dress) robe-chasuble f
jumper cables (US), **jump leads** (BRIT) npl câbles mpl de démarrage
jumpy ['dʒʌmpɪ] adj nerveux(euse), agité(e)
Jun. abbr = **junior**

junction ['dʒʌŋkʃən] (*BRIT*) *n* (*of roads*) carrefour *m*; (*of rails*) embranchement *m*
juncture ['dʒʌŋktʃə*] *n*: **at this ~** à ce moment-là, sur ces entrefaites
June [dʒuːn] *n* juin *m*
jungle ['dʒʌŋgl] *n* jungle *f*
junior ['dʒuːnɪə*] *adj, n*: **he's ~ to me (by 2 years), he's my ~ (by 2 years)** il est mon cadet (de 2 ans), il est plus jeune que moi (de 2 ans); **he's ~ to me** (*seniority*) il est en dessous de moi (dans la hiérarchie), j'ai plus d'ancienneté que lui; **~ school** (*BRIT*) *n* ≈ école *f* primaire
junk [dʒʌŋk] *n* (*rubbish*) camelote *f*; (*cheap goods*) bric-à-brac *m inv*; **~ food** *n* aliments *mpl* sans grande valeur nutritive; **~ mail** *n* prospectus *mpl* (*non sollicités*); **~ shop** *n* (boutique *f* de) brocanteur *m*
Junr *abbr* = **junior**
juror ['dʒuərə*] *n* juré *m*
jury ['dʒuərɪ] *n* jury *m*
just [dʒʌst] *adj* juste ♦ *adv*: **he's ~ done it/left** il vient de le faire/partir; **~ right/ two o'clock** exactement *or* juste ce qu'il faut/deux heures; **she's ~ as clever as you** elle est tout aussi intelligente que vous; **it's ~ as well (that)** ... heureusement que ...; **~ as he was leaving** au moment *or* à l'instant précis où il partait; **~ before/ enough/here** juste avant/assez/ici; **it's ~ me/a mistake** ce n'est que moi/(rien) qu'une erreur; **~ missed/caught** manqué/ attrapé de justesse; **~ listen to this!** écoutez un peu ça!
justice ['dʒʌstɪs] *n* justice *f*; (*US: judge*) juge *m* de la Cour suprême; **J~ of the Peace** *n* juge *m* de paix
justify ['dʒʌstɪfaɪ] *vt* justifier
jut [dʒʌt] *vi* (*also*: **~ out**) dépasser, faire saillie
juvenile ['dʒuːvənaɪl] *adj* juvénile; (*court, books*) pour enfants ♦ *n* adolescent(e)

K k

K *abbr* (= *one thousand*) K; (= *kilobyte*) Ko
kangaroo [kæŋgə'ruː] *n* kangourou *m*
karate [kə'rɑːtɪ] *n* karaté *m*
kebab [kə'bæb] *n* kébab *m*
keel [kiːl] *n* quille *f*
keen [kiːn] *adj* (*eager*) plein(e) d'enthousiasme; (*interest, desire, competition*) vif(vive); (*eye, intelligence*) pénétrant(e);

(*edge*) effilé(e); **to be ~ to do** *or* **on doing sth** désirer vivement faire qch, tenir beaucoup à faire qch; **to be ~ on sth/sb** aimer beaucoup qch/qn
keep [kiːp] (*pt, pp* **kept**) *vt* (*retain, preserve*) garder; (*detain*) retenir; (*shop, accounts, diary, promise*) tenir; (*house*) avoir; (*support*) entretenir; (*chickens, bees etc*) élever ♦ *vi* (*remain*) rester; (*food*) se conserver ♦ *n* (*of castle*) donjon *m*; (*food etc*): **enough for his ~** assez pour (assurer) sa subsistance; (*inf*): **for ~s** pour de bon, pour toujours; **to ~ doing sth** ne pas arrêter de faire qch; **to ~ sb from doing** empêcher qn de faire *or* que qn ne fasse; **to ~ sb happy/a place tidy** faire que qn soit content/qu'un endroit reste propre; **to ~ sth to o.s.** garder qch pour soi, tenir qch secret; **to ~ sth (back) from sb** cacher qch à qn; **to ~ time** (*clock*) être à l'heure, ne pas retarder; **well kept** bien entretenu(e); **~ on** *vi*: **to ~ on doing** continuer à faire; **don't ~ on about it!** arrête (d'en parler)!; **~ out** *vt* empêcher d'entrer; **"~ out"** "défense d'entrer"; **~ up** *vt* continuer, maintenir ♦ *vi*: **to ~ up with sb** (*in race etc*) aller aussi vite que qn; (*in work etc*) se maintenir au niveau de qn; **~er** *n* gardien(ne); **~-fit** *n* gymnastique *f* d'entretien; **~ing** *n* (*care*) garde *f*; **in ~ing with** en accord avec; **~sake** *n* souvenir *m*
kennel ['kenl] *n* niche *f*; **~s** *npl* (*boarding ~s*) chenil *m*
kerb [kɜːb] (*BRIT*) *n* bordure *f* du trottoir
kernel ['kɜːnl] *n* (*of nut*) amande *f*; (*fig*) noyau *m*
kettle ['ketl] *n* bouilloire *f*; **~drum** *n* timbale *f*
key [kiː] *n* (*gen, MUS*) clé *f*; (*of piano, typewriter*) touche *f* ♦ *cpd* clé ♦ *vt* (*also*: **~ in**) introduire (au clavier), saisir; **~board** *n* clavier *m*; **~ed up** *adj* (*person*) surexcité(e); **~hole** *n* trou *m* de la serrure; **~note** *n* (*of speech*) note dominante; (*MUS*) tonique *f*; **~ ring** *n* porte-clés *m*
khaki ['kɑːkɪ] *n* kaki *m*
kick [kɪk] *vt* donner un coup de pied à ♦ *vi* (*horse*) ruer ♦ *n* coup *m* de pied; (*thrill*): **he does it for ~s** il le fait parce que ça l'excite, il le fait pour le plaisir; **to ~ the habit** (*inf*) arrêter; **~ off** *vi* (*SPORT*) donner le coup d'envoi
kid [kɪd] *n* (*inf: child*) gamin(e), gosse *m/f*; (*animal, leather*) chevreau *m* ♦ *vi* (*inf*) plaisanter, blaguer
kidnap ['kɪdnæp] *vt* enlever, kidnapper; **~per** *n* ravisseur(euse); **~ping** *n* enlèvement *m*
kidney ['kɪdnɪ] *n* (*ANAT*) rein *m*; (*CULIN*) rognon *m*
kill [kɪl] *vt* tuer ♦ *n* mise *f* à mort; **~er** *n* tueur(euse); meurtrier(ère); **~ing** *n* meurtre *m*; (*of group of people*) tuerie *f*, massacre

m; **to make a ~ing** (*inf*) réussir un beau coup (de filet); **~joy** *n* rabat-joie *m/f*
kiln [kɪln] *n* four *m*
kilo ['kiːləʊ] *n* kilo *m*; **~byte** *n* (COMPUT) kilo-octet *m*; **~gram(me)** ['kɪləʊgræm] *n* kilogramme *m*; **~metre** ['kɪləmiːtə*] (US **~meter**) *n* kilomètre *m*; **~watt** *n* kilowatt *m*
kilt [kɪlt] *n* kilt *m*
kin [kɪn] *n see* next; kith
kind [kaɪnd] *adj* gentil(le), aimable ♦ *n* sorte *f*, espèce *f*, genre *m*; **to be two of a ~** se ressembler; **in ~** (COMM) en nature
kindergarten ['kɪndəgɑːtn] *n* jardin *m* d'enfants
kind-hearted ['kaɪnd'hɑːtɪd] *adj* bon(bonne)
kindle ['kɪndl] *vt* allumer, enflammer
kindly ['kaɪndlɪ] *adj* bienveillant(e), plein(e) de gentillesse ♦ *adv* avec bonté; **will you ~** ...! auriez-vous la bonté *or* l'obligeance de ...?
kindness ['kaɪndnəs] *n* bonté *f*, gentillesse *f*
kindred ['kɪndrɪd] *adj*: **~ spirit** âme *f* sœur
kinetic [kɪ'netɪk] *adj* cinétique
king [kɪŋ] *n* roi *m*; **~dom** *n* royaume *m*; **~fisher** *n* martin-pêcheur *m*; **~-size bed** *n* grand lit (*de 1,95 m de large*); **~-size(d)** *adj* format géant *inv*; (*cigarettes*) long(longue)
kinky ['kɪŋkɪ] (*pej*) *adj* (*person*) excentrique; (*sexually*) aux goûts spéciaux
kiosk ['kiːɒsk] *n* kiosque *m*; (BRIT: TEL) cabine *f* (téléphonique)
kipper ['kɪpə*] *n* hareng fumé et salé
kiss [kɪs] *n* baiser *m* ♦ *vt* embrasser; **to ~ (each other)** s'embrasser; **~ of life** (BRIT) *n* bouche à bouche *m*
kit [kɪt] *n* équipement *m*, matériel *m*; (*set of tools etc*) trousse *f*, (*for assembly*) kit *m*
kitchen ['kɪtʃɪn] *n* cuisine *f*; **~ sink** *n* évier *m*
kite [kaɪt] *n* (*toy*) cerf-volant *m*
kith [kɪθ] *n*: **~ and kin** parents et amis *mpl*
kitten ['kɪtn] *n* chaton *m*, petit chat *m*
kitty ['kɪtɪ] *n* (*money*) cagnotte *f*
knack [næk] *n*: **to have the ~ of doing** avoir le coup pour faire
knapsack ['næpsæk] *n* musette *f*
knead [niːd] *vt* pétrir
knee [niː] *n* genou *m*; **~cap** *n* rotule *f*
kneel [niːl] (*pt, pp* **knelt**) *vi* (*also*: **~ down**) s'agenouiller
knew [njuː] *pt of* know
knickers ['nɪkəz] (BRIT) *npl* culotte *f* (de femme)
knife [naɪf] (*pl* **knives**) *n* couteau *m* ♦ *vt* poignarder, frapper d'un coup de couteau
knight [naɪt] *n* chevalier *m*; (CHESS) cavalier *m*; **~hood** (BRIT) *n* (*title*): **to get a ~hood** être fait chevalier
knit [nɪt] *vt* tricoter ♦ *vi* tricoter; (*broken*

bones) se ressouder; **to ~ one's brows** froncer les sourcils; **~ting** *n* tricot *m*; **~ting needle** *n* aiguille *f* à tricoter; **~wear** *n* tricots *mpl*, lainages *mpl*
knives [naɪvz] *npl of* knife
knob [nɒb] *n* bouton *m*
knock [nɒk] *vt* frapper; (*bump into*) heurter; (*inf*) dénigrer ♦ *vi* (*at door etc*): **to ~ at** *or* **on** frapper à ♦ *n* coup *m*; **~ down** *vt* renverser; **~ off** *vi* (*inf: finish*) s'arrêter (de travailler) ♦ *vt* (*from price*) faire un rabais de; (*inf: steal*) piquer; **~ out** *vt* assommer; (BOXING) mettre k.-o.; (*defeat*) éliminer; **~ over** *vt* renverser, faire tomber; **~er** *n* (*on door*) heurtoir *m*; **~out** *n* (BOXING) knock-out *m*, K.-O. *m*; **~out competition** *n* compétition *f* avec épreuves éliminatoires
knot [nɒt] *n* (*gen*) nœud *m* ♦ *vt* nouer; **~ty** *adj* (*fig*) épineux(euse)
know [nəʊ] (*pt* **knew**, *pp* **known**) *vt* savoir; (*person, place*) connaître; **to ~ how to do** savoir (comment) faire; **to ~ how to swim** savoir nager; **to ~ about** *or* **of sth** être au courant de qch; **to ~ about** *or* **of sb** avoir entendu parler de qn; **~-all** (*pej*) *n* je-sais-tout *m/f*; **~-how** *n* savoir-faire *m*; **~ing** *adj* (*look etc*) entendu(e); **~ingly** *adv* sciemment; (*smile, look*) d'un air entendu
knowledge ['nɒlɪdʒ] *n* connaissance *f*; (*learning*) connaissances, savoir *m*; **~able** *adj* bien informé(e)
knuckle ['nʌkl] *n* articulation *f* (des doigts), jointure *f*
Koran [kɔː'rɑːn] *n* Coran *m*
Korea [kə'rɪə] *n* Corée *f*
kosher ['kəʊʃə*] *adj* kascher *inv*

L l

L *abbr* (= *lake, large*) L; (= *left*) g; (= BRIT: AUT: = *learner*) signale un conducteur débutant
lab [læb] *n abbr* (= *laboratory*) labo *m*
label ['leɪbl] *n* étiquette *f* ♦ *vt* étiqueter
labor *etc* (US) = **labour** *etc*
laboratory [lə'bɒrətərɪ] *n* laboratoire *m*
labour ['leɪbə*] (US **labor**) *n* (*work*) travail *m*; (*workforce*) main-d'œuvre *f*; **(at)** travailler dur (à), peiner (sur) ♦ *vt*: **to ~ a point** insister sur un point; **in ~** (MED) en travail, en train d'accoucher; **L~, the L~ party** (BRIT) le parti travailliste, les travaillistes *mpl*; **~ed** *adj* (*breathing*) péni-

ble, difficile; **~er** *n* manœuvre *m*; **farm ~er** *n* ouvrier *m* agricole

lace [leɪs] *n* dentelle *f*; (*of shoe etc*) lacet *m* ♦ *vt* (*shoe: also: ~ up*) lacer

lack [læk] *n* manque *m* ♦ *vt* manquer de; **through** *or* **for ~ of** faute de, par manque de; **to be ~ing** manquer, faire défaut; **to be ~ing in** manquer de

lacquer ['lækə*] *n* laque *f*

lad [læd] *n* garçon *m*, gars *m*

ladder ['lædə*] *n* échelle *f*; (*BRIT*: *in tights*) maille filée

laden ['leɪdn] *adj*: **~ (with)** chargé(e) (de)

ladle ['leɪdl] *n* louche *f*

lady ['leɪdɪ] *n* dame *f*; (*in address*): **ladies and gentlemen** Mesdames (et) Messieurs; **young ~** jeune fille *f*; (*married*) jeune femme *f*; **the ladies' (room)** les toilettes *fpl* (pour dames); **~bird** *n* coccinelle *f*; **~bug** (*US*) *n* = **ladybird**; **~like** *adj* distingué(e); **~ship** *n*: **your ~ship** Madame la comtesse (*or* la baronne *etc*)

lag [læg] *n* retard *m* ♦ *vi* (*also: ~ behind*) rester en arrière, traîner; (*fig*) rester en traîne ♦ *vt* (*pipes*) calorifuger

lager ['lɑːgə*] *n* bière blonde

lagoon [lə'guːn] *n* lagune *f*

laid [leɪd] *pt, pp of* **lay**; **~-back** (*inf*) *adj* relaxe, décontracté(e); **~ up** *adj* alité(e)

lain [leɪn] *pp of* **lie**

lake [leɪk] *n* lac *m*

lamb [læm] *n* agneau *m*; **~ chop** *n* côtelette *f* d'agneau

lame [leɪm] *adj* boiteux(euse)

lament [lə'ment] *n* lamentation *f* ♦ *vt* pleurer, se lamenter sur

laminated ['læmɪneɪtɪd] *adj* laminé(e); (*windscreen*) (en verre) feuilleté

lamp [læmp] *n* lampe *f*; **~post** (*BRIT*) *n* réverbère *m*; **~shade** *n* abat-jour *m inv*

lance [lɑːns] *vt* (*MED*) inciser

land [lænd] *n* (*as opposed to sea*) terre *f* (ferme); (*soil*) terre; terrain *m*; (*estate*) terre(s), domaine(s) *m(pl)*; (*country*) pays *m* ♦ *vi* (*AVIAT*) atterrir; (*fig*) (re)tomber ♦ *vt* (*passengers, goods*) débarquer; **to ~ sb with sth** (*inf*) coller qch à qn; **~ up** *vi* atterrir, (finir par) se retrouver; **~fill site** *n* décharge *f*; **~ing** *n* (*AVIAT*) atterrissage *m*; (*of staircase*) palier *m*; (*of troops*) débarquement *m*; **~ing gear** *n* train *m* d'atterrissage; **~ing strip** *n* piste *f* d'atterrissage; **~lady** *n* propriétaire *f*, logeuse *f*; (*of pub*) patronne *f*; **~locked** *adj* sans littoral; **~lord** *n* propriétaire *m*, logeur *m*; (*of pub etc*) patron *m*; **~mark** *n* (point *m* de) repère *m*; **to be a ~mark** (*fig*) faire date *or* époque; **~owner** *n* propriétaire foncier *or* terrien; **~scape** ['lændskeɪp] *n* paysage *m*; **~scape gardener** *n* jardinier(ère) paysagiste; **~slide** ['lændslaɪd] *n* (*GEO*) glissement *m* (de terrain); (*fig*: *POL*) raz-de-

marée (électoral)

lane [leɪn] *n* (*in country*) chemin *m*; (*AUT*) voie *f*; file *f*; (*in race*) couloir *m*

language ['læŋgwɪdʒ] *n* langue *f*; (*way one speaks*) langage *m*; **bad ~** grossièretés *fpl*, langage grossier; **~ laboratory** *n* laboratoire *m* de langues

lank [læŋk] *adj* (*hair*) raide et terne

lanky ['læŋkɪ] *adj* grand(e) et maigre, efflanqué(e)

lantern ['læntən] *n* lanterne *f*

lap [læp] *n* (*of track*) tour *m* (de piste); (*of body*): **in** *or* **on one's ~** sur les genoux ♦ *vt* (*also: ~ up*) laper ♦ *vi* (*waves*) clapoter; **~ up** *vt* (*fig*) accepter béatement, gober

lapel [lə'pel] *n* revers *m*

Lapland ['læplænd] *n* Laponie *f*

lapse [læps] *n* défaillance *f*; (*in behaviour*) écart *m* de conduite ♦ *vi* (*LAW*) cesser d'être en vigueur; (*contract*) expirer; **to ~ into bad habits** prendre de mauvaises habitudes; **~ of time** laps *m* de temps, intervalle *m*

laptop (computer) ['læptɒp-] *n* portable *m*

larceny ['lɑːsənɪ] *n* vol *m*

larch [lɑːtʃ] *n* mélèze *m*

lard [lɑːd] *n* saindoux *m*

larder ['lɑːdə*] *n* garde-manger *m inv*

large [lɑːdʒ] *adj* grand(e); (*person, animal*) gros(se); **at ~** (*free*) en liberté; (*generally*) en général; *see also* **by**; **~ly** *adv* en grande partie; (*principally*) surtout; **~-scale** *adj* (*action*) d'envergure; (*map*) à grande échelle

lark [lɑːk] *n* (*bird*) alouette *f*; (*joke*) blague *f*, farce *f*; **~ about** *vi* faire l'idiot, rigoler

laryngitis [lærɪn'dʒaɪtɪs] *n* laryngite *f*

laser ['leɪzə*] *n* laser *m*; **~ printer** *n* imprimante *f* laser

lash [læʃ] *n* coup *m* de fouet; (*also: eye~*) cil *m* ♦ *vt* fouetter; (*tie*) attacher; **~ out** *vi*: **to ~ out at** *or* **against** attaquer violemment

lass [læs] (*BRIT*) *n* (jeune) fille *f*

lasso [læ'suː] *n* lasso *m*

last [lɑːst] *adj* dernier(ère) ♦ *adv* en dernier; (*finally*) finalement ♦ *vi* durer; **~ week** la semaine dernière; **~ night** (*evening*) hier soir; (*night*) la nuit dernière; **at ~** enfin; **~ but one** avant-dernier(ère); **~-ditch** *adj* (*attempt*) ultime, désespéré(e); **~ing** *adj* durable; **~ly** *adv* en dernier lieu, pour finir; **~-minute** *adj* de dernière minute

latch [lætʃ] *n* loquet *m*

late [leɪt] *adj* (*not on time*) en retard; (*far on in day etc*) tardif(ive); (*edition, delivery*) dernier(ère); (*former*) ancien(ne) ♦ *adv* tard; (*behind time, schedule*) en retard; **of ~** dernièrement; **in ~ May** vers la fin (du mois) de mai, fin mai; **the ~ Mr X** feu M. X; **~comer** *n* retardataire *m/f*; **~ly** *adv* ré-

cemment; ~**r** ['leɪtə*] *adj* (*date etc*) ulté-
rieur(e); (*version etc*) plus récent(e) ♦ *adv*
plus tard; ~**r on** plus tard; ~**st** ['leɪtɪst] *adj*
tout(e) dernier(ère); **at the** ~**st** au plus
tard
lathe [leɪð] *n* tour *m*
lather ['lɑːðə*] *n* mousse *f* (de savon) ♦ *vt*
savonner
Latin ['lætɪn] *n* latin *m* ♦ *adj* latin(e); ~
America *n* Amérique latine; ~ **American**
adj latino-américain(e)
latitude ['lætɪtjuːd] *n* latitude *f*
latter ['lætə*] *adj* deuxième, dernier(ère) ♦
n: **the** ~ ce dernier, celui-ci; ~**ly** *adv* dernièrement, récemment
laudable ['lɔːdəbl] *adj* louable
laugh [lɑːf] *n* rire *m* ♦ *vi* rire; ~ **at** *vt fus*
se moquer de; rire de; ~ **off** *vt* écarter par
une plaisanterie *or* par une boutade; ~**able**
adj risible, ridicule; ~**ing stock** *n*: **the**
~**ing stock of** la risée de; ~**ter** *n* rire *m*;
rires *mpl*
launch [lɔːntʃ] *n* lancement *m*; (*motorboat*)
vedette *f* ♦ *vt* lancer; ~ **into** *vt fus* se lancer dans
Launderette [lɔːn'dret] (*BRIT*: ®), **Laun-
dromat** ['lɔːndrəmæt] (*US*: ®) *n* laverie *f*
(automatique)
laundry ['lɔːndrɪ] *n* (*clothes*) linge *m*; (*business*) blanchisserie *f*, (*room*) buanderie *f*
laureate ['lɔːrɪət] *adj see* **poet**
laurel ['lɔrəl] *n* laurier *m*
lava ['lɑːvə] *n* lave *f*
lavatory ['lævətrɪ] *n* toilettes *fpl*
lavender ['lævɪndə*] *n* lavande *f*
lavish ['lævɪʃ] *adj* (*amount*) copieux(euse);
(*person*): ~ **with** prodigue de ♦ *vt*: **to** ~
sth on sb prodiguer qch à qn; (*money*) dépenser qch sans compter pour qn/qch
law [lɔː] *n* loi *f*; (*science*) droit *m*; ~-
abiding *adj* respectueux(euse) des lois; ~
and order *n* l'ordre public; ~ **court** *n* tribunal *m*, cour *f* de justice; ~**ful** *adj* lé-
gal(e); ~**less** *adj* (*action*) illégal(e)
lawn [lɔːn] *n* pelouse *f*; ~**mower** *n* tondeuse *f* à gazon; ~ **tennis** *n* tennis *m*
law school (*US*) *n* faculté *f* de droit
lawsuit ['lɔːsuːt] *n* procès *m*
lawyer ['lɔːjə*] *n* (*consultant, with company*)
juriste *m*; (*for sales, wills etc*) notaire *m*;
(*partner, in court*) avocat *m*
lax [læks] *adj* relâché(e)
laxative ['læksətɪv] *n* laxatif *m*
lay [leɪ] (*pt, pp* laid) *pt of* **lie** ♦ *adj* laïque;
(*not expert*) profane ♦ *vt* poser, mettre;
(*eggs*) pondre; **to** ~ **the table** mettre la table; ~ **aside** *vt* mettre de côté; ~ **by** *vt* =
lay aside; ~ **down** *vt* poser; **to** ~ **down**
the law faire la loi; **to** ~ **down one's life**
sacrifier sa vie; ~ **off** *vt* (*workers*) licencier;
~ **on** *vt* (*provide*) fournir; ~ **out** *vt* (*display*) disposer, étaler; ~**about** (*inf*) *n* fai-

néant(e); ~-**by** (*BRIT*) *n* aire *f* de stationnement (sur le bas-côté)
layer ['leɪə*] *n* couche *f*
layman ['leɪmən] (*irreg*) *n* profane *m*
layout ['leɪaʊt] *n* disposition *f*, plan *m*,
agencement *m*; (*PRESS*) mise *f* en page
laze [leɪz] *vi* (*also*: ~ **about**) paresser
lazy ['leɪzɪ] *adj* paresseux(euse)
lb *abbr* = **pound** (*weight*)
lead[1] [liːd] (*pt, pp* led) *n* (*distance, time
ahead*) avance *f*; (*clue*) piste *f*; (*THEATRE*)
rôle principal; (*ELEC*) fil *m*; (*for dog*) laisse
f ♦ *vt* mener, conduire; (*be leader of*) être à
la tête de ♦ *vi* (*street etc*) mener, conduire;
(*SPORT*) mener, être en tête; **in the** ~ en
tête; **to** ~ **the way** montrer le chemin; ~
away *vt* emmener; ~ **back** *vt*: **to** ~ **back
to** ramener à; ~ **on** *vt* (*tease*) faire marcher; ~ **to** *vt fus* mener à; conduire à; ~
up to *vt fus* conduire à
lead[2] [led] *n* (*metal*) plomb *m*; (*in pencil*)
mine *f*; ~**en** ['ledn] *adj* (*sky, sea*) de plomb
leader ['liːdə*] *n* chef *m*; dirigeant(e), leader *m*; (*SPORT: in league*) leader; (: *in race*)
coureur *m* de tête; ~**ship** *n* direction *f*;
(*quality*) qualités *fpl* de chef
lead-free ['led'friː] *adj* (*petrol*) sans plomb
leading ['liːdɪŋ] *adj* principal(e); de premier
plan; (*in race*) de tête; ~ **lady** *n* (*THEATRE*)
vedette (féminine); ~ **light** *n* (*person*) vedette *f*, sommité *f*; ~ **man** (*irreg*) *n* vedette
(masculine)
lead singer [liːd-] *n* (*in pop group*) (chanteur *m*) vedette *f*
leaf [liːf] (*pl* **leaves**) *n* feuille *f* ♦ *vi*: **to** ~
through feuilleter; **to turn over a new** ~
changer de conduite *or* d'existence
leaflet ['liːflɪt] *n* prospectus *m*, brochure *f*;
(*POL, REL*) tract *m*
league [liːg] *n* ligue *f*, (*FOOTBALL*) championnat *m*; **to be in** ~ **with** avoir partie
liée avec, être de mèche avec
leak [liːk] *n* fuite *f* ♦ *vi* (*pipe, liquid etc*) fuir;
(*shoes*) prendre l'eau; (*ship*) faire eau ♦ *vt*
(*information*) divulguer
lean [liːn] (*pt, pp* **leaned** *or* **leant**) *adj* maigre ♦ *vt*: **to** ~ **sth on sth** appuyer qch sur
qch ♦ *vi* (*slope*) pencher; (*rest*): **to** ~
against s'appuyer contre; être appuyé(e)
contre; **to** ~ **on** s'appuyer sur; **to** ~ **back/
forward** se pencher en arrière/avant; ~
out *vi* se pencher au dehors; ~ **over** *vi* se
pencher; ~**ing** *n*: ~**ing (towards)** tendance
f (à), penchant *m* (pour)
leap [liːp] (*pt, pp* **leaped** *or* **leapt**) *n* bond
m, saut *m* ♦ *vi* bondir, sauter; ~**frog** *n*
saute-mouton *m*; ~ **year** *n* année *f* bissextile
learn [lɜːn] (*pt, pp* ~**ed** *or* **learnt**) *vt, vi* apprendre; **to** ~ **to do sth** apprendre à faire
qch; **to** ~ **about** *or* **of sth** (*hear, read*) apprendre qch; ~**ed** ['lɜːnɪd] *adj* érudit(e), sa-

vant(e); **~er** (*BRIT*) *n* (*also*: ~er driver)
(conducteur(trice)) débutant(e); **~ing** *n*
(*knowledge*) savoir *m*

lease [li:s] *n* bail *m* ♦ *vt* louer à bail

leash [li:ʃ] *n* laisse *f*

least [li:st] *adj*: **the** ~ (+*noun*) le(la) plus
petit(e), le(la) moindre; (: *smallest amount
of*) le moins de ♦ *adv* (+*verb*) le moins;
(+*adj*): **the** ~ le(la) moins; **at** ~ au moins;
(*or rather*) du moins; **not in the** ~ pas le
moins du monde

leather ['leðə*] *n* cuir *m*

leave [li:v] (*pt, pp* **left**) *vt* laisser; (*go away
from*) quitter; (*forget*) oublier ♦ *vi* partir,
s'en aller ♦ *n* (*time off*) congé *m*; (*MIL also*:
consent) permission *f*; **to be left** rester;
there's some milk left over il reste du lait;
on ~ en permission; ~ **behind** *vt* (*person,
object*) laisser; (*forget*) oublier; ~ **out** *vt*
oublier, omettre; **~ of absence** *n* congé
exceptionnel, (*MIL*) permission spéciale

leaves [li:vz] *npl of* **leaf**

Lebanon ['lebənən] *n* Liban *m*

lecherous ['letʃərəs] (*pej*) *adj* lubrique

lecture ['lektʃə*] *n* conférence *f*; (*SCOL*)
cours *m* ♦ *vi* donner des cours; enseigner ♦
vt (*scold*) sermonner, réprimander; **to give
a** ~ **on** faire une conférence sur; donner
un cours sur; **~r** ['lektʃərə*] (*BRIT*) *n* (*at
university*) professeur *m* (d'université)

led [led] *pt, pp of* **lead**

ledge [ledʒ] *n* (*of window, on wall*) rebord
m; (*of mountain*) saillie *f*, corniche *f*

ledger ['ledʒə*] *n* (*COMM*) registre *m*,
grand livre

leech [li:tʃ] *n* (*also fig*) sangsue *f*

leek [li:k] *n* poireau *m*

leer [lɪə*] *vi*: **to** ~ **at sb** regarder qn d'un
air mauvais *or* concupiscent

leeway ['li:weɪ] *n* (*fig*): **to have some** ~
avoir une certaine liberté d'action

left [left] *pt, pp of* **leave** ♦ *adj* (*not right*)
gauche ♦ *n* gauche *f* ♦ *adv* à gauche; **on
the** ~, **to the** ~ à gauche; **the L~** (*POL*)
la gauche; **~-handed** *adj* gaucher(ère); **~-
hand side** *n* gauche *f*, côté *m* gauche; **~-
luggage (office)** (*BRIT*) *n* consigne *f*;
~overs *npl* restes *mpl*; **~-wing** *adj* (*POL*)
de gauche

leg [leg] *n* jambe *f*; (*of animal*) patte *f*; (*of
furniture*) pied *m*; (*CULIN: of chicken, pork*)
cuisse *f*; (: *of lamb*) gigot *m*; (*of journey*)
étape *f*; **1st/2nd** ~ (*SPORT*) match *m*
aller/retour

legacy ['legəsɪ] *n* héritage *m*, legs *m*

legal ['li:gəl] *adj* légal(e); ~ **holiday** (*US*) *n*
jour férié; ~ **tender** *n* monnaie légale

legend ['ledʒənd] *n* légende *f*

legible ['ledʒəbl] *adj* lisible

legislation [ledʒɪs'leɪʃən] *n* législation *f*; **legislature** ['ledʒɪsleɪtʃə*] *n* (*corps*) *m* législatif

legitimate [lɪ'dʒɪtɪmət] *adj* légitime

leg-room ['legrʊm] *n* place *f* pour les jambes

leisure ['leʒə*] *n* loisir *m*, temps *m* libre;
loisirs *mpl*; **at** ~ (tout) à loisir; à tête repo-
sée; ~ **centre** *n* centre *m* de loisirs; **~ly**
adj tranquille; fait(e) sans se presser

lemon ['lemən] *n* citron *m*; **~ade** *n* limonade *f*; ~ **tea** *n* thé *m* au citron

lend [lend] (*pt, pp* **lent**) *vt*: **to** ~ **sth (to sb)**
prêter qch (à qn)

length [leŋθ] *n* longueur *f*; (*section: of road,
pipe etc*) morceau *m*, bout *m*; (*of time*) durée *f*; **at** ~ (*at last*) enfin, à la fin; (*lengthi-
ly*) longuement; **~en** *vt* allonger, prolonger
♦ *vi* s'allonger; **~ways** *adv* dans le sens de
la longueur, en long; **~y** *adj* (très)
long(longue)

lenient ['li:nɪənt] *adj* indulgent(e), clé-
ment(e)

lens [lenz] *n* lentille *f*; (*of spectacles*) verre
m; (*of camera*) objectif *m*

Lent [lent] *n* Carême *m*

lent [lent] *pt, pp of* **lend**

lentil ['lentl] *n* lentille *f*

Leo ['li:əʊ] *n* le Lion

leotard ['li:ətɑ:d] *n* maillot *m* (*de danseur
etc*), collant *m*

leprosy ['leprəsɪ] *n* lèpre *f*

lesbian ['lezbɪən] *n* lesbienne *f*

less [les] *adj* moins de ♦ *pron, adv* moins ♦
prep moins; ~ **than that/you** moins que
cela/vous; ~ **than half** moins de la moitié;
~ **than ever** moins que jamais; ~ **and** ~
de moins en moins; **the** ~ **he works** ...
moins il travaille ...

lessen ['lesn] *vi* diminuer, s'atténuer ♦ *vt*
diminuer, réduire, atténuer

lesser ['lesə*] *adj* moindre; **to a** ~ **extent** à
un degré moindre

lesson ['lesn] *n* leçon *f*; **to teach sb a** ~
(*fig*) donner une bonne leçon à qn

lest [lest] *conj* de peur que +*sub*

let [let] (*pt, pp* **let**) *vt* laisser; (*BRIT: lease*)
louer; **to** ~ **sb do sth** laisser qn faire qch;
to ~ **sb know sth** faire savoir qch à qn,
prévenir qn de qch; **~'s go** allons-y; ~
him come qu'il vienne; **"to** ~**"** "à louer";
~ **down** *vt* (*tyre*) dégonfler; (*person*) décevoir, faire faux bond à; ~ **go** *vi* lâcher prise ♦ *vt* lâcher; ~ **in** *vt* laisser entrer; (*visitor etc*) faire entrer; ~ **off** *vt* (*culprit*) ne
pas punir; (*firework etc*) faire partir; ~ **on**
(*inf*) *vi* dire; ~ **out** *vt* laisser sortir;
(*scream*) laisser échapper; ~ **up** *vi* diminuer; (*cease*) s'arrêter

lethal ['li:θəl] *adj* mortel(le), fatal(e)

letter ['letə*] *n* lettre *f*; ~ **bomb** *n* lettre
piégée; **~-box** (*BRIT*) *n* boîte *f* aux *or* à lettres; **~ing** *n* lettres *fpl*; caractères *mpl*

lettuce ['letɪs] *n* laitue *f*, salade *f*

let-up ['letʌp] *n* répit *m*, arrêt *m*

leukaemia [luːˈkiːmɪə] (*US* **leukemia**) *n* leucémie *f*

level [ˈlevl] *adj* plat(e), plan(e), uni(e); horizontal(e) ♦ *n* niveau *m* ♦ *vt* niveler, aplanir; **to be ~ with** être au même niveau que; **to draw ~ with** (*person, vehicle*) arriver à la hauteur de; **"A" ~s** (*BRIT*) ≈ baccalauréat *m*; **"O" ~s** (*BRIT*) ≈ B.E.P.C.; **on the ~** (*fig: honest*) régulier(ère); **~ off** *vi* (*prices etc*) se stabiliser; **~ out** *vi* = **level off**; **~ crossing** (*BRIT*) *n* passage *m* à niveau; **~-headed** *adj* équilibré(e)

lever [ˈliːvə*] *n* levier *m*; **~age** *n:* **~age** (**on** *or* **with**) prise *f* (sur)

levity [ˈlevɪtɪ] *n* légéreté *f*

levy [ˈlevɪ] *n* taxe *f*, impôt *m* ♦ *vt* prélever, imposer; percevoir

lewd [luːd] *adj* obscène, lubrique

liability [laɪəˈbɪlɪtɪ] *n* responsabilité *f*; (*handicap*) handicap *m*; **liabilities** *npl* (*on balance sheet*) passif *m*

liable [ˈlaɪəbl] *adj* (*subject*): **~ to** sujet(te) à; passible de; (*responsible*): **~ (for)** responsable (de); (*likely*): **~ to do** susceptible de faire

liaise [lɪˈeɪz] *vi:* **to ~ with** assurer la liaison avec; **liaison** [liːˈeɪzɒn] *n* liaison *f*

liar [ˈlaɪə*] *n* menteur(euse)

libel [ˈlaɪbəl] *n* diffamation *f*; (*document*) écrit *m* diffamatoire ♦ *vt* diffamer

liberal [ˈlɪbərəl] *adj* libéral(e); (*generous*): **~ with** prodigue de, généreux(euse) avec; **the L~ Democrats** (*BRIT*) le parti libéral-démocrate

liberation [lɪbəˈreɪʃən] *n* libération *f*

liberty [ˈlɪbətɪ] *n* liberté *f*; **to be at ~ to do** être libre de faire

Libra [ˈliːbrə] *n* la Balance

librarian [laɪˈbrɛərɪən] *n* bibliothécaire *m/f*

library [ˈlaɪbrərɪ] *n* bibliothèque *f*

libretto [lɪˈbretəʊ] *n* livret *m*

Libya [ˈlɪbɪə] *n* Libye *f*

lice [laɪs] *npl of* **louse**

licence [ˈlaɪsəns] (*US* **license**) *n* autorisation *f*, permis *m*; (*RADIO, TV*) redevance *f*; **driving ~, (***US***) driver's license** permis *m* (de conduire); **~ number** *n* numéro *m* d'immatriculation; **~ plate** *n* plaque *f* minéralogique

license [ˈlaɪsəns] *n* (*US*) = **licence** ♦ *vt* donner une licence à; **~d** *adj* (*car*) muni(e) de la vignette; (*to sell alcohol*) patenté(e) pour la vente des spiritueux, qui a une licence de débit de boissons

lick [lɪk] *vt* lécher; (*inf: defeat*) écraser; **to ~ one's lips** (*fig*) se frotter les mains

licorice [ˈlɪkərɪs] (*US*) *n* = **liquorice**

lid [lɪd] *n* couvercle *m*; (*eye~*) paupière *f*

lie [laɪ] (*pt* **lay**, *pp* **lain**) *vi* (*rest*) être étendu(e) *or* allongé(e) *or* couché(e); (*in grave*) être enterré(e), reposer; (*be situated*) se trouver, être; (*be untruthful: pt, pp* **lied**) mentir ♦ *n* mensonge *m*; **to ~ low** (*fig*) se cacher; **~ about** *vi* traîner; **~ around** *vi* = **lie about**; **~-down** (*BRIT*) *n:* **to have a ~-down** s'allonger, se reposer; **~-in** (*BRIT*) *n:* **to have a ~-in** faire la grasse matinée

lieutenant [lefˈtenənt, (*US*) luːˈtenənt] *n* lieutenant *m*

life [laɪf] (*pl* **lives**) *n* vie *f*; **to come to ~** (*fig*) s'animer; **~ assurance** (*BRIT*) *n* = **life insurance**; **~belt** (*BRIT*) *n* bouée *f* de sauvetage; **~boat** *n* canot *m* *or* chaloupe *f* de sauvetage; **~buoy** *n* bouée *f* de sauvetage; **~guard** *n* surveillant *m* de baignade; **~ insurance** *n* assurance-vie *f*; **~ jacket** *n* gilet *m* *or* ceinture *f* de sauvetage; **~less** *adj* sans vie, inanimé(e); (*dull*) qui manque de vie *or* de vigueur; **~like** *adj* qui semble vrai(e) *or* vivant(e); (*painting*) réaliste; **~line** *n:* **it was his ~line** ça l'a sauvé; **~long** *adj* de toute une vie, de toujours; **~ preserver** (*US*) *n* = **lifebelt** *or* **life jacket**; **~ sentence** *n* condamnation *f* à perpétuité; **~-size(d)** *adj* grandeur nature *inv*; **~ span** *n* (durée *f* de) vie *f*; **~ style** *n* style *m* *or* mode *m* de vie; **~-support system** *n* (*MED*) respirateur artificiel; **~time** *n* vie *f*; **in his ~time** de son vivant

lift [lɪft] *vt* soulever, lever; (*end*) supprimer, lever ♦ *vi* (*fog*) se lever ♦ *n* (*BRIT: elevator*) ascenseur *m*; **to give sb a ~** (:*AUT*) emmener *or* prendre qn en voiture; **~-off** *n* décollage *m*

light [laɪt] (*pt, pp* **lit**) *n* lumière *f*; (*lamp*) lampe *f*; (*AUT: rear ~*) feu *m*; (: *head~*) phare *m*; (*for cigarette etc*): **have you got a ~?** avez-vous du feu? ♦ *vt* (*candle, cigarette, fire*) allumer; (*room*) éclairer ♦ *adj* (*room, colour*) clair(e); (*not heavy*) léger(ère); (*not strenuous*) peu fatigant(e); **~s** *npl* (*AUT: traffic ~s*) feux *mpl*; **to come to ~** être dévoilé(e) *or* découvert(e); **~ up** *vi* (*face*) s'éclairer ♦ *vt* (*illuminate*) éclairer, illuminer; **~ bulb** *n* ampoule *f*; **~en** *vt* (*make less heavy*) alléger; **~er** *n* (*also: cigarette ~er*) briquet *m*; **~-headed** *adj* étourdi(e); (*excited*) grisé(e); **~-hearted** *adj* gai(e), joyeux(euse), enjoué(e); **~house** *n* phare *m*; **~ing** *n* (*on road*) éclairage *m*; (*in theatre*) éclairages; **~ly** *adv* légèrement; **to get off ~ly** s'en tirer à bon compte; **~ness** *n* (*in weight*) légèreté *f*

lightning [ˈlaɪtnɪŋ] *n* éclair *m*, foudre *f*; **~ conductor** *n* paratonnerre *m*; **~ rod** (*US*) *n* = **lightning conductor**

light pen *n* crayon *m* optique

lightweight [ˈlaɪtweɪt] *adj* (*suit*) léger(ère) ♦ *n* (*BOXING*) poids léger

like [laɪk] *vt* aimer (bien) ♦ *prep* comme ♦ *adj* semblable, pareil(le) ♦ *n:* **and the ~** et d'autres du même genre; **his ~s and dislikes** ses goûts *mpl* *or* préférences *fpl*; **I would ~, I'd ~** je voudrais, j'aimerais;

would you ~ a coffee? voulez-vous du café?; **to be/look ~ sb/sth** ressembler à qn/qch; **what does it look ~?** de quoi est-ce que ça a l'air?; **what does it taste ~?** quel goût est-ce que ça a?; **that's just ~ him** c'est bien de lui, ça lui ressemble; **do it ~ this** fais-le comme ceci; **it's nothing ~ ...** ce n'est pas du tout comme ...; **~able** *adj* sympathique, agréable

likelihood ['laɪklɪhʊd] *n* probabilité *f*

likely ['laɪklɪ] *adj* probable; plausible; **he's ~ to leave** il va sûrement partir, il risque fort de partir; **not ~!** (*inf*) pas de danger!

likeness ['laɪknɪs] *n* ressemblance *f*; **that's a good ~** c'est très ressemblant

likewise ['laɪkwaɪz] *adv* de même, pareillement

liking ['laɪkɪŋ] *n* (*for person*) affection *f*; (*for thing*) penchant *m*, goût *m*

lilac ['laɪlək] *n* lilas *m*

lily ['lɪlɪ] *n* lis *m*; **~ of the valley** *n* muguet *m*

limb [lɪm] *n* membre *m*

limber up ['lɪmbə*-] *vi* se dégourdir, faire des exercices d'assouplissement

limbo ['lɪmbəu] *n*: **to be in ~** (*fig*) être tombé(e) dans l'oubli

lime [laɪm] *n* (*tree*) tilleul *m*; (*fruit*) lime *f*, citron vert; (*GEO*) chaux *f*

limelight ['laɪmlaɪt] *n*: **in the ~** (*fig*) en vedette, au premier plan

limerick ['lɪmərɪk] *n* poème *m* humoristique (de 5 vers)

limestone ['laɪmstəun] *n* pierre *f* à chaux; (*GEO*) calcaire *m*

limit ['lɪmɪt] *n* limite *f* ♦ *vt* limiter; **~ed** *adj* limité(e), restreint(e); **to be ~ed to** se limiter à, ne concerner que; **~ed (liability) company** (*BRIT*) *n* ≈ société *f* anonyme

limp [lɪmp] *n*: **to have a ~** boiter ♦ *vi* boiter ♦ *adj* mou(molle)

limpet ['lɪmpɪt] *n* patelle *f*

line [laɪn] *n* ligne *f*; (*stroke*) trait *m*; (*wrinkle*) ride *f*; (*rope*) corde *f*; (*wire*) fil *m*; (*of poem*) vers *m*; (*row, series*) rangée *f*; (*of people*) file *f*, queue *f*; (*railway track*) voie *f*; (*COMM: series of goods*) article(s) *m(pl)*; (*work*) métier *m*, type *m* d'activité; (*attitude, policy*) position *f* ♦ *vt*: **to ~ (with)** (*clothes*) doubler (de); (*box*) garnir or tapisser (de); (*subj: trees, crowd*) border; **in a ~** aligné(e); **in his ~ of business** dans sa partie, dans son rayon; **in ~ with** en accord avec; **~ up** *vi* s'aligner, se mettre en rang(s) ♦ *vt* aligner; (*event*) prévoir, préparer

lined [laɪnd] *adj* (*face*) ridé(e), marqué(e); (*paper*) réglé(e)

linen ['lɪnɪn] *n* linge *m* (de maison); (*cloth*) lin *m*

liner ['laɪnə*] *n* paquebot *m* (de ligne); (*for bin*) sac *m* à poubelle

linesman ['laɪnzmən] (*irreg*) *n* juge *m* de touche; (*TENNIS*) juge *m* de ligne

line-up ['laɪnʌp] *n* (*US: queue*) file *f*; (*SPORT*) (composition *f* de l')équipe *f*

linger ['lɪŋgə*] *vi* s'attarder; traîner; (*smell, tradition*) persister

lingo ['lɪŋgəu] (*inf: pl ~es*) *n pej* jargon *m*

linguist ['lɪŋgwɪst] *n*: **to be a good ~** être doué(e) par les langues

linguistics [lɪŋ'gwɪstɪks] *n* linguistique *f*

lining ['laɪnɪŋ] *n* doublure *f*

link [lɪŋk] *n* lien *m*, rapport *m*; (*of a chain*) maillon *m* ♦ *vt* relier, lier, unir; **~s** *npl* (*GOLF*) (terrain *m* de) golf *m*; **~ up** *vt* relier ♦ *vi* se rejoindre; s'associer

lino ['laɪnəu] *n* = **linoleum**

linoleum [lɪ'nəulɪəm] *n* linoléum *m*

lion ['laɪən] *n* lion *m*; **~ess** *n* lionne *f*

lip [lɪp] *n* lèvre *f*; **~-read** *vi* lire sur les lèvres; **~ salve** *n* pommade *f* rosat *or* pour les lèvres; **~ service** *n*: **to pay ~ service to sth** ne reconnaître le mérite de qch que pour la forme; **~stick** *n* rouge *m* à lèvres

liqueur [lɪ'kjuə*] *n* liqueur *f*

liquid ['lɪkwɪd] *adj* liquide ♦ *n* liquide *m*; **~ize** ['lɪkwɪdaɪz] *vt* (*CULIN*) passer au mixer; **~izer** *n* mixer *m*

liquor ['lɪkə*] (*US*) *n* spiritueux *m*, alcool *m*

liquorice ['lɪkərɪs] (*BRIT*) *n* réglisse *f*

liquor store (*US*) *n* magasin *m* de vins et spiritueux

lisp [lɪsp] *vi* zézayer

list [lɪst] *n* liste *f* ♦ *vt* (*write down*) faire une or la liste de; (*mention*) énumérer; **~ed building** (*BRIT*) *n* monument classé

listen ['lɪsn] *vi* écouter; **to ~ to** écouter; **~er** *n* auditeur(trice)

listless ['lɪstləs] *adj* indolent(e), apathique

lit [lɪt] *pt, pp of* **light**

liter ['li:tə*] (*US*) *n* = **litre**

literacy ['lɪtərəsɪ] *n* degré *m* d'alphabétisation, fait *m* de savoir lire et écrire

literal ['lɪtərəl] *adj* littéral(e); **~ly** *adv* littéralement; (*really*) réellement

literary ['lɪtərərɪ] *adj* littéraire

literate ['lɪtərət] *adj* qui sait lire et écrire, instruit(e)

literature ['lɪtrətʃə*] *n* littérature *f*; (*brochures etc*) documentation *f*

lithe [laɪð] *adj* agile, souple

litigation [lɪtɪ'geɪʃən] *n* litige *m*; contentieux *m*

litre ['li:tə*] (*US litre*) *n* litre *m*

litter ['lɪtə*] *n* (*rubbish*) détritus *mpl*, ordures *fpl*; (*young animals*) portée *f*; **~ bin** (*BRIT*) *n* boîte *f* à ordures, poubelle *f*; **~ed** *adj*: **~ed with** jonché(e) de, couvert(e) de

little ['lɪtl] *adj* (*small*) petit(e) ♦ *adv* peu; **~ milk/time** peu de lait/temps; **a ~** un peu (de); **a ~ bit** un peu; **~ by ~** petit à petit, peu à peu

live¹ [laɪv] *adj* (*animal*) vivant(e), en vie;

(wire) sous tension; *(bullet, bomb)* non explosé(e); *(broadcast)* en direct; *(performance)* en public

live² [lɪv] *vi* vivre; *(reside)* vivre, habiter; ~ **down** *vt* faire oublier (avec le temps); ~ **on** *vt fus (food, salary)* vivre de; ~ **together** *vi* vivre ensemble, cohabiter; ~ **up to** *vt fus* se montrer à la hauteur de

livelihood ['laɪvlɪhʊd] *n* moyens *mpl* d'existence

lively ['laɪvlɪ] *adj* vif(vive), plein(e) d'entrain; *(place, book)* vivant(e)

liven up ['laɪvn-] *vt* animer ♦ *vi* s'animer

liver ['lɪvə*] *n* foie *m*

lives [laɪvz] *npl of* **life**

livestock ['laɪvstɒk] *n* bétail *m*, cheptel *m*

livid ['lɪvɪd] *adj* livide, blafard(e); *(inf: furious)* furieux(euse), furibond(e)

living ['lɪvɪŋ] *adj* vivant(e), en vie ♦ *n*: **to earn** *or* **make a** ~ gagner sa vie; ~ **conditions** *npl* conditions *fpl* de vie; ~ **room** *n* salle *f* de séjour; ~ **standards** *npl* niveau *m* de vie; ~ **wage** *n* salaire *m* permettant de vivre (décemment)

lizard ['lɪzəd] *n* lézard *m*

load [ləʊd] *n (weight)* poids *m*; *(thing carried)* chargement *m*, charge *f* ♦ *vt (also:* ~ *up)*: **to** ~ **(with)** charger (de); *(gun, camera)* charger (avec); *(COMPUT)* charger; **a** ~ **of**, ~**s of** *(fig)* un *or* des tas de, des masses de; **to talk a** ~ **of rubbish** dire des bêtises; ~**ed** *adj (question)* insidieux(euse); *(inf: rich)* bourré(e) de fric

loaf [ləʊf] *(pl* **loaves***) n* pain *m*, miche *f*

loan [ləʊn] *n* prêt *m* ♦ *vt* prêter; **on** ~ prêté(e), en prêt

loath [ləʊθ] *adj*: **to be** ~ **to do** répugner à faire

loathe [ləʊð] *vt* détester, avoir en horreur

loaves [ləʊvz] *npl of* **loaf**

lobby ['lɒbɪ] *n* hall *m*, entrée *f*; *(POL)* groupe *m* de pression, lobby *m* ♦ *vt* faire pression sur

lobster ['lɒbstə*] *n* homard *m*

local ['ləʊkəl] *adj* local(e) ♦ *n (BRIT: pub)* pub *m or* café *m* du coin; **the** ~**s** *npl (inhabitants)* les gens *mpl* du pays *or* du coin; ~ **anaesthetic** *n* anesthésie locale; ~ **call** *n* communication urbaine; ~ **government** *n* administration locale *or* municipale; ~**ity** [ləʊ'kælɪtɪ] *n* région *f*, environs *mpl*; *(position)* lieu *m*

locate [ləʊ'keɪt] *vt (find)* trouver, repérer; *(situate)*: **to be** ~**d in** être situé(e) à *or* en

location [ləʊ'keɪʃən] *n* emplacement *m*; **on** ~ *(CINEMA)* en extérieur

loch [lɒx] *n* lac *m*, loch *m*

lock [lɒk] *n (of door, box)* serrure *f*; *(of canal)* écluse *f*; *(of hair)* mèche *f*, boucle *f* ♦ *vt (with key)* fermer à clé ♦ *vi (door etc)* fermer à clé; *(wheels)* se bloquer; ~ **in** *vt* enfermer; ~ **out** *vt* enfermer dehors; *(delibe-*

rately) mettre à la porte; ~ **up** *vt (person)* enfermer; *(house)* fermer à clé ♦ *vi* tout fermer (à clé)

locker ['lɒkə*] *n* casier *m*; *(in station)* consigne *f* automatique

locket ['lɒkɪt] *n* médaillon *m*

locksmith ['lɒksmɪθ] *n* serrurier *m*

lockup ['lɒkʌp] *n (prison)* prison *f*

locum ['ləʊkəm] *n (MED)* suppléant(e) (de médecin)

lodge [lɒdʒ] *n* pavillon *m* (de gardien); *(hunting)* ~ pavillon de chasse ♦ *vi (person)*: **to** ~ **(with)** être logé(e) (chez), être en pension (chez); *(bullet)* se loger ♦ *vt*: **to** ~ **a complaint** porter plainte; ~**r** *n* locataire *m/f*; *(with meals)* pensionnaire *m/f*; **lodgings** ['lɒdʒɪŋz] *npl* chambre *f*; meublé *m*

loft [lɒft] *n* grenier *m*

lofty ['lɒftɪ] *adj (noble)* noble, élevé(e); *(haughty)* hautain(e)

log [lɒg] *n (of wood)* bûche *f*; *(book)* = **logbook** ♦ *vt (record)* noter

logbook ['lɒgbʊk] *n (NAUT)* livre *m or* journal *m* de bord; *(AVIAT)* carnet *m* de vol; *(of car)* ≈ carte grise

loggerheads ['lɒgəhedz] *npl*: **at** ~ **(with)** à couteaux tirés (avec)

logic ['lɒdʒɪk] *n* logique *f*, ~**al** *adj* logique

loin [lɔɪn] *n (CULIN)* filet *m*, longe *f*

loiter ['lɔɪtə*] *vi* traîner

loll [lɒl] *vi (also:* ~ *about)* se prélasser, fainéanter

lollipop ['lɒlɪpɒp] *n* sucette *f*, ~ **man/lady** *(BRIT: irreg) n* contractuel(le) qui fait traverser la rue aux enfants

London ['lʌndən] *n* Londres *m*; ~**er** *n* Londonien(ne)

lone [ləʊn] *adj* solitaire

loneliness ['ləʊnlɪnəs] *n* solitude *f*, isolement *m*; **lonely** ['ləʊnlɪ] *adj* seul(e); solitaire, isolé(e)

long [lɒŋ] *adj* long(longue) ♦ *adv* longtemps ♦ *vi*: **to** ~ **for sth** avoir très envie de qch; attendre qch avec impatience; **so** *or* **as** ~ **as** pourvu que; **don't be** ~! dépêchez-vous!; **how** ~ **is this river/course?** quelle est la longueur de ce fleuve/la durée de ce cours?; **6 metres** ~ *(long)* de 6 mètres; **6 months** ~ qui dure 6 mois, de 6 mois; **all night** ~ toute la nuit; **he no** ~**er comes** il ne vient plus; ~ **before/after** longtemps avant/après; **before** ~ *(+future)* avant peu, dans peu de temps; *(+past)* peu de temps) après; **at** ~ **last** enfin; ~-**distance** *adj (call)* interurbain(e); ~**hand** *n* écriture normale *or* courante; ~**ing** *n* désir *m*, envie *f*, nostalgie *f*

longitude ['lɒŋgɪtjuːd] *n* longitude *f*

long: ~ **jump** *n* saut *m* en longueur; ~-**life** *adj* longue durée *inv*; *(milk)* upérisé(e); ~-**lost** *adj (person)* perdu(e) de vue depuis longtemps; ~-**playing record** *n* (disque *m*)

33 tours *inv*; ~**-range** *adj* à longue portée; ~**-sighted** *adj* (*MED*) presbyte; ~**standing** *adj* de longue date; ~**-suffering** *adj* empreint(e) d'une patience résignée; extrêmement patient(e); ~**-term** *adj* à long terme; ~ **wave** *n* grandes ondes; ~**-winded** *adj* intarissable, interminable

loo [luː] (*BRIT: inf*) *n* W.-C. *mpl*, petit coin

look [luk] *vi* regarder; (*seem*) sembler, paraître, avoir l'air; (*building etc*): **to ~ south/(out) onto the sea** donner au sud/sur la mer ♦ *n* regard *m*; (*appearance*) air *m*, allure *f*, aspect *m*; ~**s** *npl* (*good ~s*) physique *m*, beauté *f*; **to have a ~** regarder; ~**!** regardez!; ~ (**here**)! (*annoyance*) écoutez!; ~ **after** *vt fus* (*care for, deal with*) s'occuper de; ~ **at** *vt fus*, regarder (*problem etc*) examiner; ~ **back** *vi*: **to ~ back on** (*event etc*) évoquer, repenser à; ~ **down on** *vt fus* (*fig*) regarder de haut, dédaigner; ~ **for** *vt fus* chercher; ~ **forward to** *vt fus* attendre avec impatience; **we ~ forward to hearing from you** (*in letter*) dans l'attente de vous lire; ~ **into** *vt fus* examiner, étudier; ~ **on** *vi* regarder (en spectateur); ~ **out** *vi* (*beware*): **to ~ out (for)** prendre garde (à), faire attention (à); ~ **out for** *vt fus* être à la recherche de; guetter; ~ **round** *vi* regarder derrière soi, se retourner; ~ **to** *vt fus* (*rely on*) compter sur; ~ **up** *vi* lever les yeux; (*improve*) s'améliorer ♦ *vt* (*word, name*) chercher; ~ **up to** *vt fus* avoir du respect pour; ~**out** *n* poste *m* de guet; (*person*) guetteur *m*; **to be on the ~out (for)** guetter

loom [luːm] *vi* (*also*: ~ **up**) surgir; (*approach: event etc*) être imminent(e); (*threaten*) menacer ♦ *n* (*for weaving*) métier *m* à tisser

loony ['luːnɪ] (*inf*) *adj, n* timbré(e), cinglé(e)

loop [luːp] *n* boucle *f*; ~**hole** *n* (*fig*) porte *f* de sortie; échappatoire *f*

loose [luːs] *adj* (*knot, screw*) desserré(e); (*clothes*) ample, lâche; (*hair*) dénoué(e), épars(e); (*not firmly fixed*) pas solide; (*morals, discipline*) relâché(e) ♦ *n*: **on the ~** en liberté; ~ **change** *n* petite monnaie; ~ **chippings** *npl* (*on road*) gravillons *mpl*; ~ **end** *n*: **to be at a ~ end** *or* (*US*) **at ~ ends** ne pas trop savoir quoi faire; ~**ly** *adv* sans serrer; (*imprecisely*) approximativement; ~**n** *vt* desserrer

loot [luːt] *n* (*inf: money*) pognon *m*, fric *m* ♦ *vt* piller

lopsided ['lop'saɪdɪd] *adj* de travers, asymétrique

lord [lɔːd] *n* seigneur *m*; **L~ Smith** lord Smith; **the L~** le Seigneur; **good L~!** mon Dieu!; **the (House of) L~s** (*BRIT*) la Chambre des lords; **my L~** = **your lordship**; **L~ship** *n*: **your L~ship** Monsieur le comte (*or* le baron *or* le juge); (*to bishop*) Monsei-

gneur

lore [lɔː*] *n* tradition(s) *f(pl)*

lorry ['lorɪ] (*BRIT*) *n* camion *m*; ~ **driver** (*BRIT*) *n* camionneur *m*, routier *m*

lose [luːz] (*pt, pp* **lost**) *vt, vi* perdre; **to ~ (time)** (*clock*) retarder; **to get lost** *vi* se perdre; ~**r** *n* perdant(e)

loss [lɒs] *n* perte *f*; **to be at a ~** être perplexe *or* embarrassé(e)

lost [lɒst] *pt, pp of* **lose** ♦ *adj* perdu(e); ~ **and found** (*US*), ~ **property** *n* objets trouvés

lot [lɒt] *n* (*set*) lot *m*; **the ~** le tout; **a ~ (of)** beaucoup (de); ~**s of** des tas de; **to draw ~s (for sth)** tirer (qch) au sort

lotion ['ləuʃən] *n* lotion *f*

lottery ['lotərɪ] *n* loterie *f*

loud [laud] *adj* bruyant(e), sonore; (*voice*) fort(e); (*support, condemnation*) vigoureux(euse); (*gaudy*) voyant(e), tapageur(euse) ♦ *adv* (*speak etc*) fort; **out ~** tout haut; ~**-hailer** (*BRIT*) *n* porte-voix *m inv*; ~**ly** *adv* fort, bruyamment; ~ **speaker** *n* haut-parleur *m*

lounge [laundʒ] *n* salon *m*; (*at airport*) salle *f*; (*BRIT: also*: ~ **bar**) (salle de) café *m or* bar *m* ♦ *vi* (*also*: ~ **about** *or* **around**) se prélasser, paresser; ~ **suit** (*BRIT*) *n* complet *m*; (*on invitation*) "tenue de ville"

louse [laus] *n* (*pl* **lice**) *n* pou *m*

lousy ['lauzɪ] (*inf*) *adj* infect(e), moche; **I feel ~** je suis mal fichu(e)

lout [laut] *n* rustre *m*, butor *m*

lovable ['lʌvəbl] *adj* adorable; très sympathique

love [lʌv] *n* amour *m* ♦ *vt* aimer; (*caringly, kindly*) aimer beaucoup; "~ (**from) Anne**" "affectueusement, Anne"; **I ~ chocolate** j'adore le chocolat; **to be/fall in ~ with** être/tomber amoureux(euse) de; **to make ~** faire l'amour; **"15 ~"** (*TENNIS*) "15 à rien *or* zéro"; ~ **affair** *n* liaison (amoureuse); ~ **life** *n* vie sentimentale

lovely ['lʌvlɪ] *adj* (très) joli(e), ravissant(e); (*delightful: person*) charmant(e); (*holiday etc*) (très) agréable

lover ['lʌvə*] *n* amant *m*; (*person in love*) amoureux(euse); (*amateur*): **a ~ of** un amateur de; un(e) amoureux(euse) de

loving ['lʌvɪŋ] *adj* affectueux(euse), tendre

low [ləu] *adj* bas(basse); (*quality*) mauvais(e), inférieur(e); (*person: depressed*) déprimé(e); (: *ill*) bas(basse), affaibli(e) ♦ *adv* bas ♦ *n* (*METEOROLOGY*) dépression *f*; **to be ~ on** être à court de; **to feel ~** se sentir déprimé(e); **to reach an all-time ~** être au plus bas; ~**-alcohol** *adj* peu alcoolisé(e); ~**-cut** *adj* (*dress*) décolleté(e)

lower ['ləuə*] *adj* inférieur(e) ♦ *vt* abaisser, baisser

low: ~**-fat** *adj* maigre; ~**lands** *npl* (*GEO*) plaines *fpl*; ~**ly** *adj* humble, modeste

loyalty ['lɔɪəltɪ] n loyauté f, fidélité f
lozenge ['lɒzɪndʒ] n (*MED*) pastille f
LP n abbr = **long-playing record**
L-plates ['elpleɪts] (*BRIT*) npl plaques fpl d'apprenti conducteur
Ltd abbr (= *limited*) ≈ S.A.
lubricant ['lu:brɪkənt] n lubrifiant m
lubricate ['lu:brɪkeɪt] vt lubrifier, graisser
luck [lʌk] n chance f; **bad** ~ malchance f, malheur m; **bad** or **hard** or **tough** ~! pas de chance!; **good** ~! bonne chance!; ~**ily** adv heureusement, par bonheur; ~**y** adj (*person*) qui a de la chance; (*coincidence, event*) heureux(euse); (*object*) porte-bonheur inv
ludicrous ['lu:dɪkrəs] adj ridicule, absurde
lug [lʌg] (*inf*) vt traîner, tirer
luggage ['lʌgɪdʒ] n bagages mpl; ~ **rack** n (*on car*) galerie f
lukewarm ['lu:kwɔ:m] adj tiède
lull [lʌl] n accalmie f; (*in conversation*) pause f ♦ vt: **to** ~ **sb to sleep** bercer qn pour qu'il s'endorme; **to be** ~**ed into a false sense of security** s'endormir dans une fausse sécurité
lullaby ['lʌləbaɪ] n berceuse f
lumbago [lʌm'beɪgəu] n lumbago m
lumber ['lʌmbə*] n (*wood*) bois m de charpente; (*junk*) bric-à-brac m inv ♦ vt: **to be** ~**ed with** (*inf*) se farcir; ~**jack** n bûcheron m
luminous ['lu:mɪnəs] adj lumineux(euse)
lump [lʌmp] n morceau m; (*swelling*) grosseur f ♦ vt: **to** ~ **together** réunir, mettre en tas; ~ **sum** n somme globale or forfaitaire; ~**y** adj (*sauce*) avec des grumeaux; (*bed*) défoncé(e), peu confortable
lunar ['lu:nə*] adj lunaire
lunatic ['lu:nətɪk] adj fou(folle), cinglé(e) (*inf*)
lunch [lʌntʃ] n déjeuner m
luncheon ['lʌntʃən] n déjeuner m (chic); ~ **meat** n sorte de mortadelle; ~ **voucher** (*BRIT*) n chèque-repas m
lung [lʌŋ] n poumon m
lunge [lʌndʒ] vi (*also*: ~ **forward**) faire un mouvement brusque en avant; **to** ~ **at** envoyer or assener un coup à
lurch [lɜ:tʃ] vi vaciller, tituber ♦ n écart m brusque; **to leave sb in the** ~ laisser qn se débrouiller tout(e) seul(e)
lure [ljuə*] n (*attraction*) attrait m, charme m ♦ vt attirer or persuader par la ruse
lurid ['ljuərɪd] adj affreux(euse), atroce; (*pej: colour, dress*) criard(e)
lurk [lɜ:k] vi se tapir, se cacher
luscious ['lʌʃəs] adj succulent(e); appétissant(e)
lush [lʌʃ] adj luxuriant(e)
lust [lʌst] n (*sexual*) luxure f; lubricité f; désir m; (*fig*): ~ **for** soif f de; ~ **after**, ~ **for** vt fus (*sexually*) convoiter, désirer; ~**y**

['lʌstɪ] adj vigoureux(euse), robuste
Luxembourg ['lʌksəmbɜ:g] n Luxembourg m
luxurious [lʌg'zjuərɪəs] adj luxueux(euse);
luxury ['lʌkʃərɪ] n luxe m ♦ cpd de luxe
lying ['laɪɪŋ] n mensonge(s) m(pl) ♦ vb see **lie**
lyrical adj lyrique
lyrics ['lɪrɪks] npl (*of song*) paroles fpl

── *M m*

m. abbr = **metre**; **mile**; **million**
M.A. abbr = **Master of Arts**
mac [mæk] (*BRIT*) n imper(méable) m
macaroni [mækə'rəunɪ] n macaroni mpl
machine [mə'ʃi:n] n machine f ♦ vt (*TECH*) façonner à la machine; (*dress etc*) coudre à la machine; ~ **gun** n mitrailleuse f; ~ **language** n (*COMPUT*) langage-machine m; ~**ry** n machinerie f, machines fpl; (*fig*) mécanisme(s) m(pl)
mackerel ['mækrəl] n inv maquereau m
mackintosh ['mækɪntɒʃ] (*BRIT*) n imperméable m
mad [mæd] adj fou(folle); (*foolish*) insensé(e); (*angry*) furieux(euse); (*keen*): **to be** ~ **about** être fou(folle) de
madam ['mædəm] n madame f
madden ['mædn] vt exaspérer
made [meɪd] pt, pp of **make**
Madeira [mə'dɪərə] n (*GEO*) Madère f; (*wine*) madère m
made-to-measure ['meɪdtə'meʒə*] (*BRIT*) adj fait(e) sur mesure
madly ['mædlɪ] adv follement; ~ **in love** éperdument amoureux(euse)
madman ['mædmən] (*irreg*) n fou m
madness ['mædnəs] n folie f
magazine ['mægəzi:n] n (*PRESS*) magazine m, revue f; (*RADIO, TV: also*: ~ **programme**) magazine
maggot ['mægət] n ver m, asticot m
magic ['mædʒɪk] n magie f ♦ adj magique; ~**al** adj magique; (*experience, evening*) merveilleux (euse); ~**ian** [mə'dʒɪʃən] n magicien (ne); (*conjurer*) prestidigitateur m
magistrate ['mædʒɪstreɪt] n magistrat m; juge m
magnet ['mægnɪt] n aimant m; ~**ic** [mæg'netɪk] adj magnétique
magnificent [mæg'nɪfɪsənt] adj superbe, magnifique; (*splendid: robe, building*) somp-

tueux(euse), magnifique

magnify ['mægnɪfaɪ] *vt* grossir; *(sound)* amplifier; **~ing glass** *n* loupe *f*

magnitude ['mægnɪtjuːd] *n* ampleur *f*

magpie ['mægpaɪ] *n* pie *f*

mahogany [mə'hɒgənɪ] *n* acajou *m*

maid [meɪd] *n* bonne *f*; **old ~** *(pej)* vieille fille

maiden ['meɪdn] *n* jeune fille *f* ♦ *adj (aunt etc)* non mariée; *(speech, voyage)* inaugural(e); **~ name** *n* nom *m* de jeune fille

mail [meɪl] *n* poste *f*; *(letters)* courrier *m* ♦ *vt* envoyer (par la poste); **~box** *(US)* *n* boîte *f* aux lettres; **~ing list** *n* liste *f* d'adresses; **~-order** *n* vente *f* or achat *m* par correspondance

maim [meɪm] *vt* mutiler

main [meɪn] *adj* principal(e) ♦ *n*: **the ~(s)** *n(pl) (gas, water)* conduite principale, canalisation *f*; **the ~s** *npl (ELEC)* le secteur; **in the ~** dans l'ensemble; **~frame** *n (COMPUT)* (gros) ordinateur, unité centrale; **~land** *n* continent *m*; **~ly** *adv* principalement, surtout; **~ road** *n* grand-route *f*; **~stay** *n (fig)* pilier *m*; **~stream** *n* courant principal

maintain [meɪn'teɪn] *vt* entretenir; *(continue)* maintenir; *(affirm)* soutenir; **maintenance** ['meɪntənəns] *n* entretien *m*; *(alimony)* pension *f* alimentaire

maize [meɪz] *n* maïs *m*

majestic [mə'dʒestɪk] *adj* majestueux(euse)

majesty ['mædʒɪstɪ] *n* majesté *f*

major ['meɪdʒə*] *n (MIL)* commandant *m* ♦ *adj (important)* important(e); *(most important)* principal(e); *(MUS)* majeur(e)

Majorca [mə'jɔːkə] *n* Majorque *f*

majority [mə'dʒɒrɪtɪ] *n* majorité *f*

make [meɪk] *(pt, pp made)* *vt* faire; *(manufacture)* faire, fabriquer; *(earn)* gagner; *(cause to be)* **to ~ sb sad** *etc* rendre qn triste *etc*; *(force)* **to ~ sb do sth** obliger qn à faire qch, faire faire qch à qn; *(equal)*: **2 and 2 ~ 4** 2 et 2 font 4 ♦ *n* fabrication *f*; *(brand)* marque *f*; **to ~ a fool of sb** *(ridicule)* ridiculiser qn; *(trick)* avoir or duper qn; **to ~ a profit** faire un or des bénéfice(s); **to ~ a loss** essuyer une perte; **to ~ it** *(arrive)* arriver; *(achieve sth)* parvenir à qch, réussir; **what time do you ~ it?** quelle heure avez-vous?; **to ~ do with** se contenter de; se débrouiller avec; **~ for** *vt fus (place)* se diriger vers; **~ out** *vt (write out: cheque)* faire; *(decipher)* déchiffrer; *(understand)* comprendre; *(see)* distinguer; **~ up** *vt (constitute)* constituer; *(invent)* inventer, imaginer; *(parcel, bed)* faire ♦ *vi* se réconcilier; *(with cosmetics)* se maquiller; **~ up for** *vt fus* compenser; **~-believe** *n*: **it's just** *(game)* c'est pour faire semblant; *(invention)* c'est de l'invention pure; **~r** *n* fabricant *m*; **~shift** *adj* provisoire,

improvisé(e); **~-up** *n* maquillage *m*; **~-up remover** *n* démaquillant *m*

making ['meɪkɪŋ] *n (fig)*: **in the ~** en formation *or* gestation; **to have the ~s of** *(actor, athlete etc)* avoir l'étoffe de

malaria [mə'lɛərɪə] *n* malaria *f*

Malaysia [mə'leɪzɪə] *n* Malaisie *f*

male [meɪl] *n (BIO)* mâle *m* ♦ *adj* mâle; *(sex, attitude)* masculin(e); *(child etc)* du sexe masculin

malevolent [mə'levələnt] *adj* malveillant(e)

malfunction [mæl'fʌŋkʃən] *n* fonctionnement défectueux

malice ['mælɪs] *n* méchanceté *f*, malveillance *f*; **malicious** [mə'lɪʃəs] *adj* méchant(e), malveillant(e)

malign [mə'laɪn] *vt* diffamer, calomnier

malignant [mə'lɪgnənt] *adj (MED)* malin(igne)

mall [mɔːl] *n (also: shopping ~)* centre commercial

mallet ['mælɪt] *n* maillet *m*

malpractice [mæl'præktɪs] *n* faute professionnelle; négligence *f*

malt [mɔːlt] *n* malt *m* ♦ *cpd (also: ~ whisky)* pur malt

Malta ['mɔːltə] *n* Malte *f*

mammal ['mæməl] *n* mammifère *m*

mammoth ['mæməθ] *n* mammouth *m* ♦ *adj* géant(e), monstre

man [mæn] *(pl men)* *n* homme *m* ♦ *vt (NAUT: ship)* garnir d'hommes; *(MIL: gun)* servir; *(: post)* être de service à; *(machine)* assurer le fonctionnement de; **an old ~** un vieillard; **~ and wife** mari et femme

manage ['mænɪdʒ] *vi* se débrouiller ♦ *vt (be in charge of)* s'occuper de; *(: business etc)* gérer; *(control: ship)* manier, manœuvrer; *(: person)* savoir s'y prendre avec; **to ~ to do** réussir à faire; **~able** *adj (task)* faisable; *(number)* raisonnable; **~ment** *n* gestion *f*, administration *f*, direction *f*; **~r** *n* directeur *m*; administrateur *m*; *(SPORT)* manager *m*; *(of artist)* impresario *m*; **~ress** [mænɪdʒə'res] *n* directrice *f*, gérante *f*; **~rial** [mænə'dʒɪərɪəl] *adj* directorial(e); *(skills)* de cadre, de gestion; **managing director** ['mænɪdʒɪŋ] *n* directeur général

mandarin ['mændərɪn] *n (also: ~ orange)* mandarine *f*; *(person)* mandarin *m*

mandatory ['mændətərɪ] *adj* obligatoire

mane [meɪn] *n* crinière *f*

maneuver *(US) vt, vi, n* = **manoeuvre**

manfully ['mænfʊlɪ] *adv* vaillamment

mangle ['mæŋgl] *vt* déchiqueter; mutiler

mango ['mæŋgəʊ] *(pl ~es)* *n* mangue *f*

mangy ['meɪndʒɪ] *adj* galeux(euse)

manhandle ['mænhændl] *vt* malmener

man: ~hole ['mænhəʊl] *n* trou *m* d'homme; **~hood** ['mænhʊd] *n* âge *m* d'homme; virilité *f*; **~-hour** ['mæn'aʊə*] *n* heure *f* de main-d'œuvre; **~hunt** ['mænhʌnt] *n (POLI-*

CE) chasse *f* à l'homme

mania ['meɪnɪə] *n* manie *f*; **~c** ['meɪnɪæk] *n* maniaque *m/f*; (*fig*) fou(folle) *m/f*; **manic** ['mænɪk] *adj* maniaque

manicure ['mænɪkjʊə*] *n* manucure *f*; **~ set** *n* trousse *f* à ongles

manifest ['mænɪfest] *vt* manifester ♦ *adj* manifeste, évident(e)

manifesto [mænɪ'festəʊ] *n* manifeste *m*

manipulate [mə'nɪpjʊleɪt] *vt* manipuler; (*system, situation*) exploiter

man: **~kind** [mæn'kaɪnd] *n* humanité *f*, genre humain; **~ly** ['mænlɪ] *adj* viril(e); **~made** ['mæn'meɪd] *adj* artificiel(le); (*fibre*) synthétique

manner ['mænə*] *n* manière *f*, façon *f*; (*behaviour*) attitude *f*, comportement *m*; (*sort*) **all ~ of** toutes sortes de; **~s** *npl* (*behaviour*) manières *f*; **~ism** *n* particularité *f* de langage (*or de comportement*), tic *m*

manoeuvre [mə'nu:və*] (*US* **maneuver**) *vt* (*move*) manœuvrer; (*manipulate: person*) manipuler; (*: situation*) exploiter ♦ *vi* manœuvrer ♦ *n* manœuvre *f*

manor ['mænə*] *n* (*also:* ~ **house**) manoir *m*

manpower ['mænpaʊə*] *n* main-d'œuvre *f*

mansion ['mænʃən] *n* château *m*, manoir *m*

manslaughter ['mænslɔːtə*] *n* homicide *m* involontaire

mantelpiece ['mæntlpiːs] *n* cheminée *f*

manual ['mænjʊəl] *adj* manuel(le) ♦ *n* manuel *m*

manufacture [mænjʊ'fæktʃə*] *vt* fabriquer ♦ *n* fabrication *f*; **~r** *n* fabricant *m*

manure [mə'njʊə*] *n* fumier *m*

manuscript ['mænjʊskrɪpt] *n* manuscrit *m*

many ['menɪ] *adj* beaucoup de, de nombreux(euses) ♦ *pron* beaucoup, un grand nombre; **a great ~** un grand nombre (de); **~ a ...** bien des ..., plus d'un(e) ...

map [mæp] *n* carte *f*; (*of town*) plan *m*; **~ out** *vt* tracer; (*task*) planifier

maple ['meɪpl] *n* érable *m*

mar [mɑː*] *vt* gâcher, gâter

marathon ['mærəθən] *n* marathon *m*

marble ['mɑːbl] *n* marbre *m*; (*toy*) bille *f*

March [mɑːtʃ] *n* mars *m*

march [mɑːtʃ] *vi* marcher au pas; (*fig: protesters*) défiler ♦ *n* marche *f*; (*demonstration*) manifestation *f*

mare [meə*] *n* jument *f*

margarine [mɑːdʒə'riːn] *n* margarine *f*

margin ['mɑːdʒɪn] *n* marge *f*; **~al** (**seat**) *n* (*POL*) siège disputé

marigold ['mærɪgəʊld] *n* souci *m*

marijuana [mærɪ'wɑːnə] *n* marijuana *f*

marina [mə'riːnə] *n* (*harbour*) marina *f*

marine [mə'riːn] *adj* marin(e) ♦ *n* fusilier marin; (*US*) marine *m*; **~ engineer** *n* ingénieur *m* en génie maritime

marital ['mærɪtl] *adj* matrimonial(e); **~ status** *n* situation *f* de famille

marjoram ['mɑːdʒərəm] *n* marjolaine *f*

mark [mɑːk] *n* marque *f*; (*of skid etc*) trace *f*; (*BRIT: SCOL*) note *f*; (*currency*) mark *m* ♦ *vt* marquer; (*stain*) tacher; (*BRIT: SCOL*) noter; corriger; **to ~ time** marquer le pas; **~er** *n* (*sign*) jalon *m*; (*bookmark*) signet *m*

market ['mɑːkɪt] *n* marché *m* ♦ *vt* (*COMM*) commercialiser; **~ garden** (*BRIT*) *n* jardin maraîcher; **~ing** *n* marketing *m*; **~place** *n* place *f* du marché; (*COMM*) marché *m*; **~ research** *n* étude *f* de marché

marksman ['mɑːksmən] (*irreg*) *n* tireur *m* d'élite

marmalade ['mɑːməleɪd] *n* confiture *f* d'oranges

maroon [mə'ruːn] *vt*: **to be ~ed** être abandonné(e); (*fig*) être bloqué(e) ♦ *adj* bordeaux *inv*

marquee [mɑː'kiː] *n* chapiteau *m*

marriage ['mærɪdʒ] *n* mariage *m*; **~ bureau** *n* agence matrimoniale; **~ certificate** *n* extrait *m* d'acte de mariage

married ['mærɪd] *adj* marié(e); (*life, love*) conjugal(e)

marrow ['mærəʊ] *n* moelle *f*; (*vegetable*) courge *f*

marry ['mærɪ] *vt* épouser, se marier avec; (*subj: father, priest etc*) marier ♦ *vi* (*also: get married*) se marier

Mars [mɑːz] *n* (*planet*) Mars *f*

marsh [mɑːʃ] *n* marais *m*, marécage *m*

marshal ['mɑːʃəl] *n* maréchal *m*; (*US: fire, police*) ≈ capitaine *m*; (*SPORT*) membre *m* du service d'ordre ♦ *vt* rassembler

marshy ['mɑːʃɪ] *adj* marécageux(euse)

martyr ['mɑːtə*] *n* martyr(e); **~dom** *n* martyre *m*

marvel ['mɑːvəl] *n* merveille *f* ♦ *vi*: **to ~ (at)** s'émerveiller (de); **~lous** (*US* **~ous**) *adj* merveilleux(euse)

Marxist ['mɑːksɪst] *adj* marxiste ♦ *n* marxiste *m/f*

marzipan [mɑːzɪ'pæn] *n* pâte *f* d'amandes

mascara [mæs'kɑːrə] *n* mascara *m*

masculine ['mæskjʊlɪn] *adj* masculin(e)

mash [mæʃ] *vt* écraser, réduire en purée; **~ed potatoes** *npl* purée *f* de pommes de terre

mask [mɑːsk] *n* masque *m* ♦ *vt* masquer

mason ['meɪsn] *n* (*also: stone~*) maçon *m*; (*: free~*) franc-maçon *m*; **~ry** *n* maçonnerie *f*

masquerade [mæskə'reɪd] *vi*: **to ~ as** se faire passer pour

mass [mæs] *n* multitude *f*, masse *f*; (*PHYSICS*) masse; (*REL*) messe *f* ♦ *cpd* (*communication*) de masse; (*unemployment*) massif(ive) ♦ *vi* se masser; **the ~es** les masses; **~es of** des tas de

massacre ['mæsəkə*] *n* massacre *m*

massage ['mæsɑːʒ] n massage m ♦ vt masser

massive ['mæsɪv] adj énorme, massif(ive)

mass media n inv mass-media mpl

mass production n fabrication f en série

mast [mɑːst] n mât m; (RADIO) pylône m

master ['mɑːstə*] n maître m; (in secondary school) professeur m; (title for boys): M~ X Monsieur X ♦ vt maîtriser; (learn) apprendre à fond; ~ly adj magistral(e); ~mind n esprit supérieur ♦ vt diriger, être le cerveau de; M~ of Arts/Science n ≈ maîtrise f (en lettres/sciences); ~piece n chef-d'œuvre m; ~plan n stratégie f d'ensemble; ~y n maîtrise f; connaissance parfaite

mat [mæt] n petit tapis; (also: door~) paillasson m; (: table~) napperon m ♦ adj = matt

match [mætʃ] n allumette f; (game) match m, partie f; (fig) égal(e) ♦ vt (also: ~ up) assortir; (go well with) aller bien avec, s'assortir à; (equal) égaler, valoir ♦ vi être assorti(e); to be a good ~ être bien assorti(e); ~box n boîte f d'allumettes; ~ing adj assorti(e)

mate [meɪt] n (inf) copain(copine); (animal) partenaire m/f, mâle/femelle; (in merchant navy) second m ♦ vi s'accoupler

material [mə'tɪərɪəl] n (substance) matière f, matériau m; (cloth) tissu m, étoffe f; (information, data) données fpl ♦ adj matériel(le); (relevant: evidence) pertinent(e); ~s npl (equipment) matériaux mpl

maternal [mə'tɜːnl] adj maternel(le)

maternity [mə'tɜːnɪtɪ] n maternité f; ~ dress n robe f de grossesse; ~ hospital n maternité f

mathematical [mæθə'mætɪkl] adj mathématique; **mathematics** [mæθə'mætɪks] n mathématiques fpl

maths [mæθs] (US **math**) n math(s) fpl

matinée ['mætɪneɪ] n matinée f

mating call ['meɪtɪŋ-] n appel m du mâle

matrices ['meɪtrɪsiːz] npl of **matrix**

matriculation [mətrɪkju'leɪʃən] n inscription f

matrimonial [mætrɪ'məʊnɪəl] adj matrimonial(e), conjugal(e)

matrimony ['mætrɪmənɪ] n mariage m

matrix ['meɪtrɪks] (pl **matrices**) n matrice f

matron ['meɪtrən] n (in hospital) infirmière-chef f; (in school) infirmière

mat(t) [mæt] adj mat(e)

matted ['mætɪd] adj emmêlé(e)

matter ['mætə*] n question f; (PHYSICS) matière f; (content) contenu m, fond m; (MED: pus) pus m ♦ vi importer; ~s npl (affairs, situation) la situation; it doesn't ~ cela n'a pas d'importance; (I don't mind) cela ne fait rien; what's the ~? qu'est-ce qu'il y a?, qu'est-ce qui ne va pas?; no ~ what quoiqu'il arrive; as a ~ of course

tout naturellement; as a ~ of fact en fait; ~-of-fact adj terre à terre; (voice) neutre

mattress ['mætrəs] n matelas m

mature [mə'tjʊə*] adj mûr(e); (cheese) fait(e); (wine) arrivé(e) à maturité ♦ vi (person) mûrir; (wine, cheese) se faire

maul [mɔːl] vt lacérer

mausoleum [mɔːsə'lɪəm] n mausolée m

mauve [məʊv] adj mauve

maverick ['mævərɪk] n (fig) non-conformiste m/f

maximum ['mæksɪməm] (pl **maxima**) adj maximum ♦ n maximum m

May [meɪ] n mai m; ~ Day n le Premier Mai; see also **mayday**

may [meɪ] (conditional **might**) vi (indicating possibility): he ~ come il se peut qu'il vienne; (be allowed to): ~ I smoke? puis-je fumer?; (wishes): ~ God bless you! (que) Dieu vous bénisse!; you ~ as well go à votre place, je partirais

maybe ['meɪbiː] adv peut-être; ~ he'll ... peut-être qu'il ...

mayday ['meɪdeɪ] n SOS m

mayhem ['meɪhem] n grabuge m

mayonnaise [meɪə'neɪz] n mayonnaise f

mayor [mɛə*] n maire m; ~ess n épouse f du maire

maze [meɪz] n labyrinthe m, dédale m

MD n abbr (= Doctor of Medicine) titre universitaire; = **managing director**

me [miː] pron me, m' +vowel; (stressed, after prep) moi; he heard ~ il m'a entendu(e); give ~ a book donnez-moi un livre; after ~ après moi

meadow ['medəʊ] n prairie f, pré m

meagre ['miːgə*] (US **meager**) adj maigre

meal [miːl] n repas m; (flour) farine f; ~time n l'heure f du repas

mean [miːn] (pt, pp **meant**) adj (with money) avare, radin(e); (unkind) méchant(e); (shabby) misérable; (average) moyen(ne) ♦ vt signifier, vouloir dire; (refer to) faire allusion à, parler de; (intend): to ~ to do avoir l'intention de faire ♦ n moyenne f, ~s npl (way, money) moyens mpl; by ~s of par l'intermédiaire de; au moyen de; by all ~s! je vous en prie!; to be ~t for sb/sth être destiné(e) à qn/qch; do you ~ it? vous êtes sérieux?; what do you ~? que voulez-vous dire?

meander [mɪ'ændə*] vi faire des méandres

meaning ['miːnɪŋ] n signification f, sens m; ~ful adj significatif(ive); (relationship, occasion) important(e); ~less adj dénué(e) de sens

meanness ['miːnnɪs] n (with money) avarice f; (unkindness) méchanceté f; (shabbiness) médiocrité f

meant [ment] pt, pp of **mean**

meantime ['miːntaɪm] adv (also: in the ~) pendant ce temps

meanwhile ['mi:nwaɪl] *adv* = **meantime**
measles ['mi:zlz] *n* rougeole *f*
measly ['mi:zlɪ] (*inf*) *adj* minable
measure ['meʒə*] *vt, vi* mesurer ♦ *n* mesure *f*; (*ruler*) règle (graduée); ~**ments** *npl* mesures *fpl*; **chest/hip** ~**ment** tour *m* de poitrine/hanches
meat [mi:t] *n* viande *f*; ~**ball** *n* boulette *f* de viande
Mecca ['mekə] *n* la Mecque
mechanic [mɪ'kænɪk] *n* mécanicien *m*; ~**al** *adj* mécanique; ~**s** *n* (*PHYSICS*) mécanique *f* ♦ *npl* (*of reading, government etc*) mécanisme *m*
mechanism ['mekənɪzəm] *n* mécanisme *m*
medal ['medl] *n* médaille *f*; ~**lion** *n* médaillon *m*; ~**list** (*US* ~**ist**) *n* (*SPORT*) médaillé(e)
meddle ['medl] *vi*: **to** ~ **in** se mêler de, s'occuper de; **to** ~ **with** toucher à
media ['mi:dɪə] *npl* media *mpl*
mediaeval [medɪ'i:vəl] *adj* = **medieval**
median ['mi:dɪən] (*US*) *n* (*also*: ~ **strip**) bande médiane
mediate ['mi:dɪeɪt] *vi* servir d'intermédiaire
Medicaid ['medɪkeɪd] (®:*US*) *n* assistance médicale aux indigents
medical ['medɪkəl] *adj* médical(e) ♦ *n* visite médicale
Medicare ['medɪkɛə*] (®:*US*) *n* assistance médicale aux personnes âgées
medication [medɪ'keɪʃən] *n* (*drugs*) médicaments *mpl*
medicine ['medsɪn] *n* médecine *f*; (*drug*) médicament *m*
medieval [medɪ'i:vəl] *adj* médiéval(e)
mediocre [mi:dɪ'əukə*] *adj* médiocre
meditate ['medɪteɪt] *vi* méditer
Mediterranean [medɪtə'reɪnɪən] *adj* méditerranéen(ne); **the** ~ (**Sea**) la (mer) Méditerranée
medium ['mi:dɪəm] (*pl* **media**) *adj* moyen(ne) ♦ *n* (*means*) moyen *m*; (*pl mediums: person*) médium *m*; **the happy** ~ le juste milieu; ~ **wave** *n* ondes moyennes
medley ['medlɪ] *n* mélange *m*; (*MUS*) potpourri *m*
meek [mi:k] *adj* doux(douce), humble
meet [mi:t] (*pt, pp* **met**) *vt* rencontrer; (*by arrangement*) retrouver, rejoindre; (*for the first time*) faire la connaissance de; (*go and fetch*): **I'll** ~ **you at the station** j'irai te chercher à la gare; (*opponent, danger*) faire face à; (*obligations*) satisfaire à ♦ *vi* (*friends*) se rencontrer, se retrouver; (*in session*) se réunir; (*join: lines, roads*) se rejoindre; ~ **with** *vt fus* rencontrer; ~**ing** *n* rencontre *f*; (*session: of club etc*) réunion *f*; (*POL*) meeting *m*; **she's at a** ~**ing** (*COMM*) elle est en conférence
megabyte ['megəbaɪt] *n* (*COMPUT*) mégaoctet *m*

megaphone ['megəfəun] *n* porte-voix *m inv*
melancholy ['melənkəlɪ] *n* mélancolie *f* ♦ *adj* mélancolique
mellow ['meləu] *adj* velouté(e); doux(douce); (*sound*) mélodieux(euse) ♦ *vi* (*person*) s'adoucir
melody ['melədɪ] *n* mélodie *f*
melon ['melən] *n* melon *m*
melt [melt] *vi* fondre ♦ *vt* faire fondre; (*metal*) fondre; ~ **away** *vi* fondre complètement; ~ **down** *vt* fondre; ~**down** *n* fusion *f* (du cœur d'un réacteur nucléaire); ~**ing pot** *n* (*fig*) creuset *m*
member ['membə*] *n* membre *m*; **M~ of Parliament** (*BRIT*) député *m*; **M~ of the European Parliament** Eurodéputé *m*; ~**ship** *n* adhésion *f*; statut *m* de membre; (*members*) membres *mpl*, adhérents *mpl*; ~**ship card** *n* carte *f* de membre
memento [mə'mentəu] *n* souvenir *m*
memo ['meməu] *n* note *f* (de service)
memoirs ['memwɑːz] *npl* mémoires *mpl*
memorandum [memə'rændəm] (*pl* **memoranda**) *n* note *f* (de service)
memorial [mɪ'mɔ:rɪəl] *n* mémorial *m* ♦ *adj* commémoratif(ive)
memorize ['meməraɪz] *vt* apprendre par cœur; retenir
memory ['memərɪ] *n* mémoire *f*, (*recollection*) souvenir *m*
men [men] *npl of* **man**
menace ['menɪs] *n* menace *f*; (*nuisance*) plaie *f* ♦ *vt* menacer; **menacing** *adj* menaçant(e)
mend [mend] *vt* réparer; (*darn*) raccommoder, repriser ♦ *n*: **on the** ~ en voie de guérison; **to** ~ **one's ways** s'amender; ~**ing** *n* réparation *f*; (*clothes*) raccommodage *m*
menial ['mi:nɪəl] *adj* subalterne
meningitis [menɪn'dʒaɪtɪs] *n* méningite *f*
menopause ['menəupɔːz] *n* ménopause *f*
menstruation [menstru'eɪʃən] *n* menstruation *f*
mental ['mentl] *adj* mental(e); ~**ity** [men'tælɪtɪ] *n* mentalité *f*
mention ['menʃən] *n* mention *f* ♦ *vt* mentionner, faire mention de; **don't** ~ **it!** je vous en prie, il n'y a pas de quoi!
menu ['menju:] *n* (*set* ~, *COMPUT*) menu *m*; (*list of dishes*) carte *f*
MEP *n abbr* = **Member of the European Parliament**
mercenary ['mɜːsɪnərɪ] *adj* intéressé(e), mercenaire ♦ *n* mercenaire *m*
merchandise ['mɜːtʃəndaɪz] *n* marchandises *fpl*
merchant ['mɜːtʃənt] *n* négociant *m*, marchand *m*; ~ **bank** (*BRIT*) *n* banque *f* d'affaires; ~ **navy** (*US* ~ **marine**) *n* marine marchande
merciful ['mɜːsɪful] *adj* miséricor-

dieux(euse), clément(e); **a ~ release** une délivrance

merciless ['mɜːsɪləs] *adj* impitoyable, sans pitié

mercury ['mɜːkjʊrɪ] *n* mercure *m*

mercy ['mɜːsɪ] *n* pitié *f*, indulgence *f*; (*REL*) miséricorde *f*; **at the ~ of** à la merci de

mere [mɪə*] *adj* simple; (*chance*) pur(e); **a ~ two hours** seulement deux heures; **~ly** *adv* simplement, purement

merge [mɜːdʒ] *vt* unir ♦ *vi* (*colours, shapes, sounds*) se mêler; (*roads*) se joindre; (*COMM*) fusionner; **~r** *n* (*COMM*) fusion *f*

meringue [məˈræŋ] *n* meringue *f*

merit ['merɪt] *n* mérite *m*, valeur *f*

mermaid ['mɜːmeɪd] *n* sirène *f*

merry ['merɪ] *adj* gai(e); **M~ Christmas!** Joyeux Noël!; **~-go-round** *n* manège *m*

mesh [meʃ] *n* maille *f*

mesmerize ['mezməraɪz] *vt* hypnotiser; fasciner

mess [mes] *n* désordre *m*, fouillis *m*, pagaille *f*; (*muddle: of situation*) gâchis *m*; (*dirt*) saleté *f*; (*MIL*) mess *m*, cantine *f*; **~ about** (*inf*) *vi* perdre son temps; **~ about with** (*inf*) *vt fus* tripoter; **~ around** (*inf*) *vi* = **mess about**; **~ around with** *vt fus* = **mess about with**; **~ up** *vt* (*dirty*) salir; (*spoil*) gâcher

message ['mesɪdʒ] *n* message *m*

messenger ['mesɪndʒə*] *n* messager *m*

Messrs ['mesəz] *abbr* (*on letters*) MM

messy ['mesɪ] *adj* sale; en désordre

met [met] *pt, pp of* **meet**

metal ['metl] *n* métal *m*; **~lic** *adj* métallique

meteorology [miːtɪəˈrɒlədʒɪ] *n* météorologie *f*

mete out [miːt-] *vt* infliger; (*justice*) rendre

meter ['miːtə*] *n* (*instrument*) compteur *m*; (*also: parking ~*) parcomètre *m*; (*US: unit*) = **metre**

method ['meθəd] *n* méthode *f*; **~ical** *adj* méthodique; **M~ist** ['meθədɪst] *n* méthodiste *m/f*

meths [meθs] (*BRIT*), **methylated spirit** ['meθɪleɪtɪd-] (*BRIT*) *n* alcool *m* à brûler

metre ['miːtə*] (*US* **meter**) *n* mètre *m*

metric ['metrɪk] *adj* métrique

metropolitan [metrəˈpɒlɪtən] *adj* métropolitain(e); **the M~ Police** (*BRIT*) la police londonienne

mettle ['metl] *n*: **to be on one's ~** être d'attaque

mew [mjuː] *vi* (*cat*) miauler

mews [mjuːz] (*BRIT*) *n*: **~ cottage** cottage aménagé dans une ancienne écurie

Mexico ['meksɪkəʊ] *n* Mexique *m*

miaow [miːˈaʊ] *vi* miauler

mice [maɪs] *npl of* **mouse**

micro ['maɪkrəʊ] *n* (*also: ~computer*) micro-ordinateur *m*

microchip ['maɪkrəʊtʃɪp] *n* puce *f*

microphone ['maɪkrəfəʊn] *n* microphone *m*

microscope ['maɪkrəskəʊp] *n* microscope *m*

microwave ['maɪkrəʊweɪv] *n* (*also: ~ oven*) four *m* à micro-ondes

mid [mɪd] *adj*: **in ~ May** à la mi-mai; **~ afternoon** le milieu de l'après-midi; **in ~ air** en plein ciel; **~day** *n* midi *m*

middle ['mɪdl] *n* milieu *m*; (*waist*) taille *f* ♦ *adj* du milieu; (*average*) moyen(ne); **in the ~ of the night** au milieu de la nuit; **~-aged** *adj* d'un certain âge; **M~ Ages** *npl*: **the M~ Ages** le moyen âge; **~-class** *adj* ≈ bourgeois(e); **~ class(es)** *n(pl)*: **the ~ class(es)** ≈ les classes moyennes; **M~ East** *n* Proche-Orient *m*, Moyen-Orient *m*; **~man** (*irreg*) *n* intermédiaire *m*; **~ name** *n* deuxième nom *m*; **~-of-the-road** *adj* (*politician*) modéré(e); (*music*) neutre; **~weight** *n* (*BOXING*) poids moyen; **middling** ['mɪdlɪŋ] *adj* moyen(ne)

midge [mɪdʒ] *n* moucheron *m*

midget ['mɪdʒɪt] *n* nain(e)

Midlands ['mɪdləndz] *npl* comtés du centre de l'Angleterre

midnight ['mɪdnaɪt] *n* minuit *m*

midriff ['mɪdrɪf] *n* estomac *m*, taille *f*

midst [mɪdst] *n*: **in the ~ of** au milieu de

midsummer ['mɪdˈsʌmə*] *n* milieu *m* de l'été

midway ['mɪdˈweɪ] *adj, adv*: **~ (between)** à mi-chemin (entre); **~ through ...** au milieu de ..., en plein(e) ...

midweek ['mɪdˈwiːk] *n* milieu *m* de la semaine

midwife ['mɪdwaɪf] (*pl* **midwives**) *n* sage-femme *f*

midwinter ['mɪdˈwɪntə*] *n*: **in ~** en plein hiver

might [maɪt] *vb see* **may** ♦ *n* puissance *f*, force *f*; **~y** *adj* puissant(e)

migraine ['miːgreɪn] *n* migraine *f*

migrant ['maɪgrənt] *adj* (*bird*) migrateur(trice); (*worker*) saisonnier(ère)

migrate [maɪˈgreɪt] *vi* émigrer

mike [maɪk] *n* *abbr* (= *microphone*) micro *m*

mild [maɪld] *adj* doux(douce); (*reproach, infection*) léger(ère); (*illness*) bénin(igne); (*interest*) modéré(e); (*taste*) peu relevé(e)

mildly ['maɪldlɪ] *adv* doucement; légèrement; **to put it ~** c'est le moins qu'on puisse dire

mile [maɪl] *n* mi(l)le *m* (= 1609 *m*); **~age** *n* distance *f* en milles, ≈ kilométrage *m*; **~ometer** [maɪˈlɒmɪtə*] *n* compteur *m* (kilométrique); **~stone** *n* borne *f*; (*fig*) jalon *m*

militant ['mɪlɪtnt] *adj* militant(e)

military ['mɪlɪtərɪ] *adj* militaire

militate ['mɪlɪteɪt] *vi*: to ~ **against** (*prevent*) empêcher

militia [mɪ'lɪʃə] *n* milice(s) *f(pl)*

milk [mɪlk] *n* lait *m* ♦ *vt* (*cow*) traire; (*fig: person*) dépouiller, plumer; (: *situation*) exploiter à fond; ~ **chocolate** *n* chocolat *m* au lait; ~**man** (*irreg*) *n* laitier *m*; ~ **shake** *n* milk-shake *m*; ~**y** *adj* (*drink*) au lait; (*colour*) laiteux(euse); **M~y Way** *n* voie lactée

mill [mɪl] *n* moulin *m*; (*steel* ~) aciérie *f*; (*spinning* ~) filature *f*; (*flour* ~) minoterie *f* ♦ *vt* moudre, broyer ♦ *vi* (*also*: ~ *about*) grouiller; ~**er** *n* meunier *m*

milligram(me) ['mɪlɪɡræm] *n* milligramme *m*

millimetre ['mɪlɪmiːtə*] (*US* **millimeter**) *n* millimètre *m*

millinery ['mɪlɪnərɪ] *n* chapellerie *f*

million ['mɪljən] *n* million *m*; ~**aire** [mɪljə'neə*] *n* millionnaire *m*

milometer [maɪ'lɒmɪtə*] *n* ≈ compteur *m* kilométrique

mime [maɪm] *n* mime *m* ♦ *vt, vi* mimer

mimic ['mɪmɪk] *n* imitateur(trice) ♦ *vt* imiter, contrefaire

min. *abbr* = **minute(s); minimum**

mince [mɪns] *vt* hacher ♦ *vi* (*in walking*) marcher à petits pas maniérés ♦ *n* (*BRIT: CULIN*) viande hachée, hachis *m*; ~**meat** *n* (*fruit*) hachis de fruits secs utilisé en pâtisserie; (*US: meat*) viande hachée, hachis; ~ **pie** *n* (*sweet*) sorte de tarte aux fruits secs; ~**r** *n* hachoir *m*

mind [maɪnd] *n* esprit *m* ♦ *vt* (*attend to, look after*) s'occuper de; (*be careful*) faire attention à; (*object to*): **I don't ~ the noise** le bruit ne me dérange pas; **I don't ~ cela** ne me dérange pas; **it is on my ~** cela me préoccupe; **to my ~** à mon avis *or* sens; **to be out of one's ~** ne plus avoir toute sa raison; **to keep** *or* **bear sth in ~** tenir compte de qch; **to make up one's ~** se décider; **~ you, ...** remarquez ...; **never ~** ça ne fait rien; (*don't worry*) ne vous en faites pas; **"~ the step"** "attention à la marche"; ~**er** *n* (*child~er*) gardienne *f*; (*inf: bodyguard*) ange gardien (*fig*); ~**ful** *adj*: ~**ful of** attentif(ive) à, soucieux(euse) de; ~**less** *adj* irréfléchi(e); (*boring: job*) idiot(e)

mine[1] [maɪn] *pron* le(la) mien(ne), les miens(miennes) ♦ *adj*: **this book is mine** ce livre est à moi

mine[2] [maɪn] *n* mine *f* ♦ *vt* (*coal*) extraire; (*ship, beach*) miner; ~**field** *n* champ *m* de mines; (*fig*) situation (très délicate); ~**r** *n* mineur *m*

mineral ['mɪnərəl] *adj* minéral(e) ♦ *n* minéral *m*; ~**s** *npl* (*BRIT: soft drinks*) boissons gazeuses; ~ **water** *n* eau minérale

mingle ['mɪŋɡl] *vi*: **to ~ with** se mêler à

miniature ['mɪnɪtʃə*] *adj* (en) miniature ♦ *n* miniature *f*

minibus ['mɪnɪbʌs] *n* minibus *m*

minim ['mɪnɪm] *n* (*MUS*) blanche *f*

minimal ['mɪnɪməl] *adj* minime

minimize ['mɪnɪmaɪz] *vt* (*reduce*) réduire au minimum; (*play down*) minimiser

minimum ['mɪnɪməm] (*pl* **minima**) *adj, n* minimum *m*

mining ['maɪnɪŋ] *n* exploitation minière

miniskirt ['mɪnɪskɜːt] *n* mini-jupe *f*

minister ['mɪnɪstə*] *n* (*BRIT: POL*) ministre *m*; (*REL*) pasteur *m* ♦ *vi*: **to ~ to sb('s needs)** pourvoir aux besoins de qn; ~**ial** [mɪnɪs'tɪərɪəl] (*BRIT*) *adj* (*POL*) ministériel(le)

ministry ['mɪnɪstrɪ] *n* (*BRIT: POL*) ministère *m*; (*REL*): **to go into the ~** devenir pasteur

mink [mɪŋk] *n* vison *m*

minor ['maɪnə*] *adj* petit(e), de peu d'importance; (*MUS, poet, problem*) mineur(e) ♦ *n* (*LAW*) mineur(e)

minority [maɪ'nɒrɪtɪ] *n* minorité *f*

mint [mɪnt] *n* (*plant*) menthe *f*; (*sweet*) bonbon *m* à la menthe ♦ *vt* (*coins*) battre; **the (Royal) M~,** (*US*) **the (US) M~** ≈ l'Hôtel *m* de la Monnaie; **in ~ condition** à l'état de neuf

minus ['maɪnəs] *n* (*also*: ~ **sign**) signe *m* moins ♦ *prep* moins

minute[1] [maɪ'njuːt] *adj* minuscule; (*detail, search*) minutieux(euse)

minute[2] ['mɪnɪt] *n* minute *f*; ~**s** *npl* (*official record*) procès-verbal, compte rendu

miracle ['mɪrəkl] *n* miracle *m*

mirage ['mɪrɑːʒ] *n* mirage *m*

mirror ['mɪrə*] *n* miroir *m*, glace *f*; (*in car*) rétroviseur *m*

mirth [mɜːθ] *n* gaieté *f*

misadventure [mɪsəd'ventʃə*] *n* mésaventure *f*

misapprehension ['mɪsæprɪ'henʃən] *n* malentendu *m*, méprise *f*

misappropriate [mɪsə'prəuprɪeɪt] *vt* détourner

misbehave ['mɪsbɪ'heɪv] *vi* se conduire mal

miscalculate [mɪs'kælkjuleɪt] *vt* mal calculer

miscarriage ['mɪskærɪdʒ] *n* (*MED*) fausse couche *f*; ~ **of justice** erreur *f* judiciaire

miscellaneous [mɪsɪ'leɪnɪəs] *adj* (*items*) divers(es); (*selection*) varié(e)

mischief ['mɪstʃɪf] *n* (*naughtiness*) sottises *fpl*; (*fun*) farce *f*; (*playfulness*) espièglerie *f*; (*maliciousness*) méchanceté *f*; **mischievous** ['mɪstʃɪvəs] *adj* (*playful, naughty*) coquin(e), espiègle

misconception ['mɪskən'sepʃən] *n* idée fausse

misconduct [mɪs'kɒndʌkt] *n* inconduite *f*; **professional ~** faute professionnelle

misdemeanour [mɪsdɪ'miːnə*] (*US* **misdemeanor**) *n* écart *m* de conduite; infraction *f*

miser ['maɪzə*] *n* avare *m/f*

miserable ['mɪzərəbl] *adj* (*person, expression*) malheureux(euse); (*conditions*) misérable; (*weather*) maussade; (*offer, donation*) minable; (*failure*) pitoyable

miserly ['maɪzəlɪ] *adj* avare

misery ['mɪzərɪ] *n* (*unhappiness*) tristesse *f*; (*pain*) souffrances *fpl*; (*wretchedness*) misère *f*

misfire ['mɪs'faɪə*] *vi* rater

misfit ['mɪsfɪt] *n* (*person*) inadapté(e)

misfortune [mɪs'fɔːtʃən] *n* malchance *f*, malheur *m*

misgiving [mɪs'gɪvɪŋ] *n* (*apprehension*) craintes *fpl*; **to have ~s about** avoir des doutes quant à

misguided ['mɪs'gaɪdɪd] *adj* malavisé(e)

mishandle ['mɪs'hændl] *vt* (*mismanage*) mal s'y prendre pour faire *or* résoudre *etc*

mishap ['mɪshæp] *n* mésaventure *f*

misinform [mɪsɪn'fɔːm] *vt* mal renseigner

misinterpret ['mɪsɪn'tɜːprɪt] *vt* mal interpréter

misjudge ['mɪs'dʒʌdʒ] *vt* méjuger

mislay [mɪs'leɪ] (*irreg: like* lay) *vt* égarer

mislead [mɪs'liːd] (*irreg: like* lead) *vt* induire en erreur; **~ing** *adj* trompeur(euse)

mismanage [mɪs'mænɪdʒ] *vt* mal gérer

misnomer ['mɪs'nəʊmə*] *n* terme *or* qualificatif trompeur *or* peu approprié

misplace ['mɪs'pleɪs] *vt* égarer

misprint ['mɪsprɪnt] *n* faute *f* d'impression

Miss [mɪs] *n* Mademoiselle

miss [mɪs] *vt* (*fail to get, attend or see*) manquer, rater; (*regret the absence of*) **I ~ him/it** il/cela me manque ♦ *vi* manquer ♦ *n* (*shot*) coup manqué; **~ out** (*BRIT*) *vt* oublier

misshapen ['mɪs'ʃeɪpən] *adj* difforme

missile ['mɪsaɪl] *n* (*MIL*) missile *m*; (*object thrown*) projectile *m*

missing ['mɪsɪŋ] *adj* manquant(e); (*after escape, disaster: person*) disparu(e); **to go ~** disparaître; **to be ~** avoir disparu

mission ['mɪʃən] *n* mission *f*; **~ary** *n* missionnaire *m/f*

misspent ['mɪs'spent] *adj*: **his ~ youth** sa folle jeunesse

mist [mɪst] *n* (*light*) brume *f*; (*heavy*) brouillard *m* ♦ *vi* (*also*: ~ **over**: *eyes*) s'embuer; **~ over** *vi* (*windows etc*) s'embuer; **~ up** *vi* = **mist over**

mistake [mɪs'teɪk] (*irreg: like* take) *n* erreur *f*, faute *f* ♦ *vt* (*meaning, remark*) mal comprendre; se méprendre sur; **to make a ~** se tromper, faire une erreur; **by ~** par erreur, par inadvertance; **to ~ for** prendre pour; **~n** *pp of* **mistake** ♦ *adj* (*idea etc*) erroné(e); **to be ~n** faire erreur, se tromper

mister ['mɪstə*] *n* (*inf*) Monsieur *m*; *see also* **Mr**

mistletoe ['mɪsltəʊ] *n* gui *m*

mistook [mɪs'tʊk] *pt of* **mistake**

mistress ['mɪstrɪs] *n* maîtresse *f*; (*BRIT: in primary school*) institutrice *f*; (: *in secondary school*) professeur *m*

mistrust ['mɪs'trʌst] *vt* se méfier de

misty ['mɪstɪ] *adj* brumeux(euse); (*glasses, window*) embué(e)

misunderstand ['mɪsʌndə'stænd] (*irreg*) *vt, vi* mal comprendre; **~ing** *n* méprise *f*, malentendu *m*

misuse [*n* 'mɪs'juːs, *vb* 'mɪs'juːz] *n* mauvais emploi; (*of power*) abus *m* ♦ *vt* mal employer; abuser de; **~ of funds** détournement *m* de fonds

mitigate ['mɪtɪgeɪt] *vt* atténuer

mitt(en) ['mɪt(n)] *n* mitaine *f*; moufle *f*

mix [mɪks] *vt* mélanger; (*sauce, drink etc*) préparer ♦ *vi* se mélanger; (*socialize*): **he doesn't ~ well** il est peu sociable ♦ *n* mélange *m*; **to ~ with** (*people*) fréquenter; **~ up** *vt* mélanger; (*confuse*) confondre; **~ed** *adj* (*feelings, reactions*) contradictoire; (*salad*) mélangé(e); (*school, marriage*) mixte; **~ed grill** *n* assortiment *m* de grillades; **~ed-up** *adj* (*confused*) désorienté(e), embrouillé(e); **~er** *n* (*for food*) batteur *m*, mixer *m*; (*person*): **he is a good ~er** il est très liant; **~ture** *n* assortiment *m*, mélange *m*; (*MED*) préparation *f*; **~-up** *n* confusion *f*

mm *abbr* (= *millimeter*) mm

moan [məʊn] *n* gémissement *m* ♦ *vi* gémir; (*inf: complain*): **to ~ (about)** se plaindre (de)

moat [məʊt] *n* fossé *m*, douves *fpl*

mob [mɒb] *n* foule *f*; (*disorderly*) cohue *f* ♦ *vt* assaillir

mobile ['məʊbaɪl] *adj* mobile ♦ *n* mobile *m*; **~ home** *n* (grande) caravane; **~ phone** *n* téléphone portatif

mock [mɒk] *vt* ridiculiser; (*laugh at*) se moquer de ♦ *adj* faux(fausse); **~ exam** examen blanc; **~ery** *n* moquerie *f*, raillerie *f*; **to make a ~ery of** tourner en dérision; **~-up** *n* maquette *f*

mod [mɒd] *adj see* **convenience**

mode [məʊd] *n* mode *m*

model ['mɒdl] *n* modèle *m*; (*person: for fashion*) mannequin *m*; (: *for artist*) modèle ♦ *vt* (*with clay etc*) modeler ♦ *vi* travailler comme mannequin ♦ *adj* (*railway: toy*) modèle réduit *inv*; (*child, factory*) modèle; **to ~ clothes** présenter des vêtements; **to ~ o.s. on** imiter

modem ['məʊdem] (*COMPUT*) *n* modem *m*

moderate [*adj, n* 'mɒdərət, *vb* 'mɒdəreɪt] *adj* modéré(e); (*amount, change*) peu important(e) ♦ *vi* se calmer ♦ *vt* modérer

modern ['mɒdən] *adj* moderne; **~ize** *vt* moderniser

modest ['mɒdɪst] *adj* modeste; **~y** *n* modestie f

modicum ['mɒdɪkəm] *n*: **a ~ of** un minimum de

modify ['mɒdɪfaɪ] *vt* modifier

mogul ['məʊgəl] *n* (*fig*) nabab *m*

mohair ['məʊheə*] *n* mohair *m*

moist [mɔɪst] *adj* humide, moite; **~en** ['mɔɪsən] *vt* humecter, mouiller légèrement; **~ure** ['mɔɪstʃə*] *n* humidité *f*, **~urizer** ['mɔɪstʃəraɪzə*] *n* produit hydratant

molar ['məʊlə*] *n* molaire *f*

molasses [mə'læsɪz] *n* mélasse *f*

mold [məʊld] (*US*) *n, vt* = **mould**

mole [məʊl] *n* (*animal, fig: spy*) taupe *f*; (*spot*) grain *m* de beauté

molest [məʊ'lest] *vt* (*harass*) molester; (*JUR: sexually*) attenter à la pudeur de

mollycoddle ['mɒlɪkɒdl] *vt* chouchouter, couver

molt [məʊlt] (*US*) *vi* = **moult**

molten ['məʊltən] *adj* fondu(e); (*rock*) en fusion

mom [mɒm] (*US*) *n* = **mum**

moment ['məʊmənt] *n* moment *m*, instant *m*; **at the ~** en ce moment; **at that ~** à ce moment-là; **~ary** *adj* momentané(e), passager(ère); **~ous** [məʊ'mentəs] *adj* important(e), capital(e)

momentum [məʊ'mentəm] *n* élan *m*, vitesse acquise; (*fig*) dynamique *f*; **to gather ~** prendre de la vitesse

mommy ['mɒmɪ] (*US*) *n* = **mummy**

Monaco ['mɒnəkəʊ] *n* Monaco *m*

monarch ['mɒnək] *n* monarque *m*; **~y** *n* monarchie *f*

monastery ['mɒnəstrɪ] *n* monastère *m*

Monday ['mʌndeɪ] *n* lundi *m*

monetary ['mʌnɪtɔrɪ] *adj* monétaire

money ['mʌnɪ] *n* argent *m*; **to make ~** gagner de l'argent; **~ order** *n* mandat *m*; **~-spinner** (*inf*) *n* mine *f* d'or (*fig*)

mongrel ['mʌŋgrəl] *n* (*dog*) bâtard *m*

monitor ['mɒnɪtə*] *n* (*TV, COMPUT*) moniteur *m* ♦ *vt* contrôler; (*broadcast*) être à l'écoute de; (*progress*) suivre (de près)

monk [mʌŋk] *n* moine *m*

monkey ['mʌŋkɪ] *n* singe *m*; **~ nut** (*BRIT*) *n* cacahuète *f*; **~ wrench** *n* clé *f* à molette

monopoly [mə'nɒpəlɪ] *n* monopole *m*

monotone ['mɒnətəʊn] *n* ton *m* (*or* voix *f*) monocorde

monotonous [mə'nɒtənəs] *adj* monotone

monsoon [mɒn'suːn] *n* mousson *f*

monster ['mɒnstə*] *n* monstre *m*

monstrous ['mɒnstrəs] *adj* monstrueux(euse); (*huge*) gigantesque

month [mʌnθ] *n* mois *m*; **~ly** *adj* mensuel(le) ♦ *adv* mensuellement

monument ['mɒnjʊmənt] *n* monument *m*

moo [muː] *vi* meugler, beugler

mood [muːd] *n* humeur *f*, disposition *f*; **to be in a good/bad ~** être de bonne/

mauvaise humeur; **~y** *adj* (*variable*) d'humeur changeante, lunatique; (*sullen*) morose, maussade

moon [muːn] *n* lune *f*; **~light** *n* clair *m* de lune; **~lighting** *n* travail *m* au noir; **~lit** *adj*: **a ~lit night** une nuit de lune

moor [mʊə*] *n* lande *f* ♦ *vt* (*ship*) amarrer ♦ *vi* mouiller; **~land** ['mʊələnd] *n* lande *f*

moose [muːs] *n inv* élan *m*

mop [mɒp] *n* balai *m* à laver; (*for dishes*) lavette *f* (à vaisselle) ♦ *vt* essuyer; **~ of hair** tignasse *f*; **~ up** *vt* éponger

mope [məʊp] *vi* avoir le cafard, se morfondre

moped ['məʊped] *n* cyclomoteur *m*

moral ['mɒrəl] *adj* moral(e) ♦ *n* morale *f*; **~s** *npl* (*attitude, behaviour*) moralité *f*

morale [mɒ'rɑːl] *n* moral *m*

morality [mə'rælɪtɪ] *n* moralité *f*

morass [mə'ræs] *n* marais *m*, marécage *m*

--- *KEYWORD*

more [mɔː*] *adj* **1** (*greater in number etc*) plus (de), davantage; **~ people/work (than)** plus de gens/de travail (que)
2 (*additional*) encore (de); **do you want (some) ~ tea?** voulez-vous encore du thé?; **I have no** *or* **I don't have any ~ money** je n'ai plus d'argent; **it'll take a few ~ weeks** ça prendra encore quelques semaines
♦ *pron* plus, davantage; **~ than 10** plus de 10; **it cost ~ than we expected** cela a coûté plus que prévu; **I want ~** j'en veux plus *or* davantage; **is there any ~?** est-ce qu'il en reste?; **there's no ~** il n'y en a plus; **a little ~** un peu plus; **many/much ~** beaucoup plus, bien davantage
♦ *adv*: **~ dangerous/easily (than)** plus dangereux/facilement (que); **~ and ~ expensive** de plus en plus cher; **~ or less** plus ou moins; **~ than ever** plus que jamais

moreover [mɔː'rəʊvə*] *adv* de plus

morning ['mɔːnɪŋ] *n* matin *m*; matinée *f* ♦ *cpd* matinal(e); (*paper*) du matin; **in the ~** le matin; **7 o'clock in the ~** 7 heures du matin; **~ sickness** *n* nausées matinales

Morocco [mə'rɒkəʊ] *n* Maroc *m*

moron ['mɔːrɒn] (*inf*) *n* idiot(e)

Morse [mɔːs] *n*: **~ (code)** morse *m*

morsel ['mɔːsl] *n* bouchée *f*

mortar ['mɔːtə*] *n* mortier *m*

mortgage ['mɔːgɪdʒ] *n* hypothèque *f*; (*loan*) prêt *m* (*or* crédit *m*) hypothécaire ♦ *vt* hypothéquer; **~ company** (*US*) *n* société *f* de crédit immobilier

mortuary ['mɔːtjʊərɪ] *n* morgue *f*

mosaic [məʊ'zeɪɪk] *n* mosaïque *f*

Moscow ['mɒskəʊ] *n* Moscou *m*

Moslem ['mɒzləm] *adj, n* = **Muslim**

mosque [mɒsk] *n* mosquée *f*

mosquito [mɒsˈkiːtəʊ] (*pl* ~es) *n* moustique *m*

moss [mɒs] *n* mousse *f*

most [məʊst] *adj* la plupart de; le plus de ♦ *pron* la plupart ♦ *adv* le plus; (*very*) très, extrêmement; **the ~** (*also*: + *adjective*) le plus; ~ **of** la plus grande partie de; ~ **of them** la plupart d'entre eux; **I saw (the) ~** j'en ai vu la plupart; c'est moi qui en ai vu le plus; **at the (very)** ~ au plus; **to make the ~ of** profiter au maximum de; ~**ly** *adv* (*chiefly*) surtout; (*usually*) généralement

MOT *n abbr* (*BRIT*: = *Ministry of Transport*): **the ~** (**test**) *la visite technique (annuelle) obligatoire des véhicules à moteur*

motel [məʊˈtɛl] *n* motel *m*

moth [mɒθ] *n* papillon *m* de nuit; (*in clothes*) mite *f*; ~**ball** *n* boule *f* de naphtaline

mother [ˈmʌðə*] *n* mère *f* ♦ *vt* (*act as mother to*) servir de mère à; (*pamper, protect*) materner; ~ **country** mère patrie; ~**hood** *n* maternité *f*; ~**-in-law** *n* belle-mère *f*; ~**ly** *adj* maternel(le); ~**-of-pearl** *n* nacre *f*; ~**-to-be** *n* future maman; ~ **tongue** *n* langue maternelle

motion [ˈməʊʃən] *n* mouvement *m*; (*gesture*) geste *m*; (*at meeting*) motion *f* ♦ *vt, vi*: **to ~ (to) sb to do** faire signe à qn de faire; ~**less** *adj* immobile, sans mouvement; ~ **picture** *n* film *m*

motivated [ˈməʊtɪveɪtɪd] *adj* motivé(e)

motive [ˈməʊtɪv] *n* motif *m*, mobile *m*

motley [ˈmɒtlɪ] *adj* hétéroclite

motor [ˈməʊtə*] *n* moteur *m*; (*BRIT: inf: vehicle*) auto *f* ♦ *cpd* (*industry, vehicle*) automobile; ~**bike** *n* moto *f*; ~**boat** *n* bateau *m* à moteur; ~**car** (*BRIT*) *n* automobile *f*; ~**cycle** *n* vélomoteur *m*; ~**cycle racing** *n* course *f* de motos; ~**cyclist** *n* motocycliste *m/f*; ~**ing** (*BRIT*) *n* tourisme *m* automobile; ~**ist** [ˈməʊtərɪst] *n* automobiliste *m/f*; ~ **mechanic** *n* mécanicien *m* garagiste; ~ **racing** (*BRIT*) *n* course *f* automobile; ~ **trade** *n* secteur *m* de l'automobile; ~**way** (*BRIT*) *n* autoroute *f*

mottled [ˈmɒtld] *adj* tacheté(e), marbré(e)

motto [ˈmɒtəʊ] (*pl* ~es) *n* devise *f*

mould [məʊld] (*US* **mold**) *n* moule *m*; (*mildew*) moisissure *f* ♦ *vt* mouler, modeler; (*fig*) façonner; **mo(u)ldy** *adj* moisi(e); (*smell*) de moisi

moult [məʊlt] (*US* **molt**) *vi* muer

mound [maʊnd] *n* monticule *m*, tertre *m*; (*heap*) monceau *m*, tas *m*

mount [maʊnt] *n* mont *m*, montagne *f* ♦ *vt* monter ♦ *vi* (*inflation, tension*) augmenter; (*also*: ~ **up**: *problems etc*) s'accumuler; ~ **up** *vi* (*bills, costs, savings*) s'accumuler

mountain [ˈmaʊntɪn] *n* montagne *f* ♦ *cpd* de montagne; ~ **bike** *n* VTT *m*, vélo tout-terrain; ~**eer** [maʊntɪˈnɪə*] *n* alpiniste *m/f*; ~**eering** *n* alpinisme *m*; ~**ous** *adj* montagneux(euse); ~ **rescue team** *n* équipe *f* de secours en montagne; ~**side** *n* flanc *m* or versant *m* de la montagne

mourn [mɔːn] *vt* pleurer ♦ *vi*: **to ~ (for)** (*person*) pleurer (la mort de); ~**er** *n* parent(e) or ami(e) du défunt; personne *f* en deuil; ~**ful** *adj* triste, lugubre; ~**ing** *n* deuil *m*; **in ~ing** en deuil

mouse [maʊs] (*pl* **mice**) *n* (*also* COMPUT) souris *f*; ~**trap** *n* souricière *f*

mousse [muːs] *n* mousse *f*

moustache [məsˈtɑːʃ] (*US* **mustache**) *n* moustache(s) *f(pl)*

mousy [ˈmaʊsɪ] *adj* (*hair*) d'un châtain terne

mouth [maʊθ, *pl* maʊðz] (*pl* ~s) *n* bouche *f*; (*of dog, cat*) gueule *f*; (*of river*) embouchure *f*; (*of hole, cave*) ouverture *f*; ~**ful** *n* bouchée *f*; ~ **organ** *n* harmonica *m*; ~**piece** *n* (*of musical instrument*) embouchure *f*; (*spokesman*) porte-parole *m inv*; ~**wash** *n* eau *f* dentifrice; ~**watering** *adj* qui met l'eau à la bouche

movable [ˈmuːvəbl] *adj* mobile

move [muːv] *n* (*movement*) mouvement *m*; (*in game*) coup *m*; (*: turn to play*) tour *m*; (*change: of house*) déménagement *m*; (*: of job*) changement *m* d'emploi ♦ *vt* déplacer, bouger; (*emotionally*) émouvoir; (*POL: resolution etc*) proposer; (*in game*) jouer ♦ *vi* (*gen*) bouger, remuer; (*traffic*) circuler; (*also*: ~ **house**) déménager; (*situation*) progresser; **that was a good ~** bien joué!; **to ~ sb to do sth** pousser or inciter qn à faire qch; **to get a ~ on** se dépêcher, se remuer; ~ **about** *vi* (*fidget*) remuer; (*travel*) voyager, se déplacer; (*change residence, job*) ne pas rester au même endroit; ~ **along** *vi* se pousser; ~ **around** *vi* = **move about**; ~ **away** *vi* s'en aller; ~ **back** *vi* revenir, retourner; ~ **forward** *vi* avancer; ~ **in** *vi* (*to a house*) emménager; (*police, soldiers*) intervenir; ~ **on** *vi* se remettre en route; ~ **out** *vi* (*of house*) déménager; ~ **over** *vi* se pousser, se déplacer; ~ **up** *vi* (*pupil*) passer dans la classe supérieure; (*employee*) avoir de l'avancement; ~**able** *adj* = **movable**

movement [ˈmuːvmənt] *n* mouvement *m*

movie [ˈmuːvɪ] *n* film *m*; **the ~s** le cinéma; ~ **camera** *n* caméra *f*

moving [ˈmuːvɪŋ] *adj* en mouvement; (*emotional*) émouvant(e)

mow [məʊ] (*pt* **mowed**, *pp* **mowed** or **mown**) *vt* faucher; (*lawn*) tondre; ~ **down** *vt* faucher; ~**er** *n* (*also*: *lawnmower*) tondeuse *f* à gazon

MP *n abbr* = **Member of Parliament**

mph *abbr* = **miles per hour**

Mr [ˈmɪstə*] (*US* **Mr.**) *n*: ~ **Smith** Monsieur Smith, M. Smith

Mrs [ˈmɪsɪz] (*US* **Mrs.**) *n*: ~ **Smith** Madame

Smith, Mme Smith
Ms [mɪz] n (US **Ms.**) n (= *Miss or Mrs*): ~ **Smith** ≈ Madame Smith, Mme Smith
MSc *abbr* = **Master of Science**
much [mʌtʃ] *adj* beaucoup de ♦ *adv, n, pron* beaucoup; **how** ~ **is it?** combien est-ce que ça coûte?; **too** ~ trop (de); **as** ~ **as** autant de
muck [mʌk] n (*dirt*) saleté f; ~ **about** (*or*) **around** (*inf*) *vi* faire l'imbécile; ~ **up** (*inf*) *vt* (*exam, interview*) se planter à (*fam*); ~**y** *adj* (très) sale; (*book, film*) cochon(ne)
mud [mʌd] n boue f
muddle [ˈmʌdl] n (*mess*) pagaille f, désordre m; (*mix-up*) confusion f ♦ *vt* (*also*: ~ **up**) embrouiller; ~ **through** *vi* se débrouiller
muddy [ˈmʌdɪ] *adj* boueux(euse); **mudguard** [ˈmʌdgɑːd] n garde-boue m *inv*
muffin [ˈmʌfɪn] n muffin m
muffle [ˈmʌfl] *vt* (*sound*) assourdir, étouffer; (*against cold*) emmitoufler; ~**d** *adj* (*sound*) étouffé(e); (*person*) emmitouflé(e); ~**r** (US) n (AUT) silencieux m
mug [mʌg] n (*cup*) grande tasse (*sans soucoupe*); (: *for beer*) chope f; (*inf*: *face*) bouille f; (: *fool*) poire f ♦ *vt* (*assault*) agresser; ~**ging** n agression f
muggy [ˈmʌgɪ] *adj* lourd(e), moite
mule [mjuːl] n mule f
mull over [mʌl-] *vt* réfléchir à
multi-level [ˈmʌltɪlevl] (US) *adj* = **multistorey**
multiple [ˈmʌltɪpl] *adj* multiple ♦ n multiple m; ~ **sclerosis** n sclérose f en plaques
multiplication [mʌltɪplɪˈkeɪʃən] n multiplication f; **multiply** [ˈmʌltɪplaɪ] *vt* multiplier ♦ *vi* se multiplier
multistorey [ˈmʌltɪˈstɔːrɪ] (BRIT) *adj* (*building*) à étages; (*car park*) à étages *or* niveaux multiples
mum [mʌm] (BRIT: *inf*) n maman f ♦ *adj*: **to keep** ~ ne pas souffler mot
mumble [ˈmʌmbl] *vt, vi* marmotter, marmonner
mummy [ˈmʌmɪ] n (BRIT: *mother*) maman f; (*embalmed*) momie f
mumps [mʌmps] n oreillons mpl
munch [mʌntʃ] *vt, vi* mâcher
mundane [mʌnˈdeɪn] *adj* banal(e), terre à terre *inv*
municipal [mjuːˈnɪsɪpəl] *adj* municipal(e)
murder [ˈmɜːdə*] n meurtre m, assassinat m ♦ *vt* assassiner; ~**er** n meurtrier m, assassin m; ~**ous** *adj* meurtrier(ère)
murky [ˈmɜːkɪ] *adj* sombre, ténébreux(euse); (*water*) trouble
murmur [ˈmɜːmə*] n murmure m ♦ *vt, vi* murmurer
muscle [ˈmʌsl] n muscle m; (*fig*) force f; ~ **in** *vi* (*on territory*) envahir; (*on success*) exploiter

muscular [ˈmʌskjʊlə*] *adj* musculaire; (*person, arm*) musclé(e)
muse [mjuːz] *vi* méditer, songer
museum [mjuːˈzɪəm] n musée m
mushroom [ˈmʌʃruːm] n champignon m ♦ *vi* pousser comme un champignon
music [ˈmjuːzɪk] n musique f; ~**al** *adj* musical(e); (*person*) musicien(ne) ♦ n (*show*) comédie musicale; ~**al instrument** n instrument m de musique; ~**ian** [mjuːˈzɪʃən] n musicien(ne)
Muslim [ˈmʌzlɪm] *adj, n* musulman(e)
muslin [ˈmʌzlɪn] n mousseline f
mussel [ˈmʌsl] n moule f
must [mʌst] *aux vb* (*obligation*): **I** ~ **do it** je dois le faire, il faut que je le fasse; (*probability*): **he** ~ **be there by now** il doit y être maintenant, il y est probablement maintenant; (*suggestion, invitation*): **you** ~ **come and see me** il faut que vous veniez me voir; (*indicating sth unwelcome*): **why** ~ **he behave so badly?** qu'est-ce qui le pousse à se conduire si mal? ♦ n nécessité f, impératif m; **it's a** ~ c'est indispensable
mustache (US) n = **moustache**
mustard [ˈmʌstəd] n moutarde f
muster [ˈmʌstə*] *vt* rassembler
mustn't [ˈmʌsnt] = **must not**
mute [mjuːt] *adj* muet(te)
muted [ˈmjuːtɪd] *adj* (*colour*) sourd(e); (*reaction*) voilé(e)
mutiny [ˈmjuːtɪnɪ] n mutinerie f ♦ *vi* se mutiner
mutter [ˈmʌtə*] *vt, vi* marmonner, marmotter
mutton [ˈmʌtn] n mouton m
mutual [ˈmjuːtjʊəl] *adj* mutuel(le), réciproque; (*benefit, interest*) commun(e); ~**ly** *adv* mutuellement
muzzle [ˈmʌzl] n museau m; (*protective device*) muselière f; (*of gun*) gueule f ♦ *vt* museler
my [maɪ] *adj* mon(ma), mes *pl*; ~ **house/car/gloves** ma maison/mon auto/mes gants; **I've washed** ~ **hair/cut** ~ **finger** je me suis lavé les cheveux/coupé le doigt; ~**self** [maɪˈself] *pron* (*reflexive*) me; (*emphatic*) moi-même; (*after prep*) moi; *see also* **oneself**
mysterious [mɪsˈtɪərɪəs] *adj* mystérieux(euse)
mystery [ˈmɪstərɪ] n mystère m
mystify [ˈmɪstɪfaɪ] *vt* mystifier; (*puzzle*) ébahir
myth [mɪθ] n mythe m; ~**ology** [mɪˈθɒlədʒɪ] n mythologie f

N n

n/a *abbr* = **not applicable**

nag [næg] *vt* (*scold*) être toujours après, reprendre sans arrêt; **~ging** *adj* (*doubt, pain*) persistant(e)

nail [neɪl] *n* (*human*) ongle *m*; (*metal*) clou *m* ♦ *vt* clouer; **to ~ sb down to a date/ price** contraindre qn à accepter *or* donner une date/un prix; **~brush** *n* brosse *f* à ongles; **~file** *n* lime *f* à ongles; **~ polish** vernis *m* à ongles; **~ polish remover** *n* dissolvant *m*; **~ scissors** *npl* ciseaux *mpl* à ongles; **~ varnish** (*BRIT*) *n* = **nail polish**

naïve [naɪˈiːv] *adj* naïf(ïve)

naked [ˈneɪkɪd] *adj* nu(e)

name [neɪm] *n* nom *m*; (*reputation*) réputation *f* ♦ *vt* nommer; (*identify: accomplice etc*) citer; (*price, date*) fixer, donner; **by ~** par son nom; **in the ~ of** au nom de; **what's your ~?** comment vous appelezvous?; **~less** *adj* sans nom; (*witness, contributor*) anonyme; **~ly** *adv* à savoir; **~sake** *n* homonyme *m*

nanny [ˈnænɪ] *n* bonne *f* d'enfants

nap [næp] *n* (*sleep*) (petit) somme ♦ *vi*: **to be caught ~ping** être pris à l'improviste *or* en défaut

nape [neɪp] *n*: **~ of the neck** nuque *f*

napkin [ˈnæpkɪn] *n* serviette *f* (de table)

nappy [ˈnæpɪ] (*BRIT*) *n* couche *f* (*gen pl*); **~ rash** *n*: **to have a ~ rash** avoir les fesses rouges

narcissus [nɑːˈsɪsəs, *pl* nɑːˈsɪsaɪ] (*pl* **narcissi**) *n* narcisse *m*

narcotic [nɑːˈkɒtɪk] *n* (*drug*) stupéfiant *m*; (*MED*) narcotique *m*

narrative [ˈnærətɪv] *n* récit *m*

narrow [ˈnærəʊ] *adj* étroit(e); (*fig*) restreint(e), limité(e) ♦ *vi* (*road*) devenir plus étroit, se rétrécir; (*gap, difference*) se réduire; **to have a ~ escape** l'échapper belle; **to ~ sth down to** réduire qch à; **~ly** *adv*: **he ~ly missed injury/the tree** il a failli se blesser/rentrer dans l'arbre; **~-minded** *adj* à l'esprit étroit, borné(e); (*attitude*) borné(e)

nasty [ˈnɑːstɪ] *adj* (*person: malicious*) méchant(e); (*: rude*) très désagréable; (*smell*) dégoûtant(e); (*wound, situation, disease*) mauvais(e)

nation [ˈneɪʃən] *n* nation *f*

national [ˈnæʃənl] *adj* national(e) ♦ *n* (*abroad*) ressortissant(e); (*when home*) national(e); **~ dress** *n* costume national; **N~ Health Service** (*BRIT*) *n* service national de santé, ≈ Sécurité Sociale; **N~ Insurance** (*BRIT*) *n* ≈ Sécurité Sociale; **~ism** [ˈnæʃnəlɪzəm] *n* nationalisme *m*; **~ist** [ˈnæʃnəlɪst] *adj* nationaliste ♦ *n* nationaliste *m/f*; **~ity** [næʃəˈnælɪtɪ] *n* nationalité *f*; **~ize** *vt* nationaliser; **~ly** *adv* (*as a nation*) du point de vue national; (*nationwide*) dans le pays entier

nationwide [ˈneɪʃənwaɪd] *adj* s'étendant à l'ensemble du pays; (*problem*) à l'échelle du pays entier ♦ *adv* à travers *or* dans tout le pays

native [ˈneɪtɪv] *n* autochtone *m/f*, habitant(e) du pays ♦ *adj* du pays, indigène; (*country*) natal(e); (*ability*) inné(e); **a ~ of Russia** une personne originaire de Russie; **a ~ speaker of French** une personne de langue maternelle française; **~ language** *n* langue maternelle

NATO [ˈneɪtəʊ] *n abbr* (= *North Atlantic Treaty Organization*) OTAN *f*

natural [ˈnætʃrəl] *adj* naturel(le); **~ gas** *n* gaz naturel; **~ize** *vt* naturaliser; (*plant*) acclimater; **to become ~ized** (*person*) se faire naturaliser; **~ly** *adv* naturellement

nature [ˈneɪtʃə*] *n* nature *f*; **by ~** par tempérament, de nature

naught [nɔːt] *n* = **nought**

naughty [ˈnɔːtɪ] *adj* (*child*) vilain(e), pas sage

nausea [ˈnɔːsɪə] *n* nausée *f*; **nauseate** [ˈnɔːsɪeɪt] *vt* écœurer, donner la nausée à

naval [ˈneɪvəl] *adj* naval(e); **~ officer** *n* officier *m* de marine

nave [neɪv] *n* nef *f*

navel [ˈneɪvəl] *n* nombril *m*

navigate [ˈnævɪgeɪt] *vt* (*steer*) diriger; (*plot course*) naviguer ♦ *vi* naviguer; **navigation** [nævɪˈgeɪʃən] *n* navigation *f*

navvy [ˈnævɪ] (*BRIT*) *n* terrassier *m*

navy [ˈneɪvɪ] *n* marine *f*; **~(-blue)** *adj* bleu marine *inv*

Nazi [ˈnɑːtsɪ] *n* Nazi(e)

NB *abbr* (= *nota bene*) NB

near [nɪə*] *adj* proche ♦ *adv* près ♦ *prep* (*also: ~ to*) près de ♦ *vt* approcher de; **~by** *adj* proche ♦ *adv* tout près, à proximité; **~ly** *adv* presque; **I ~ly fell** j'ai failli tomber; **~ miss** *n* (*AVIAT*) quasi-collision *f*; **that was a ~ miss** (*gen*) il s'en est fallu de peu; (*of shot*) c'est passé très près; **~side** *n* (*AUT: BRIT*) côté *m* gauche; (*: in US, Europe*) côté droit; **~-sighted** *adj* myope

neat [niːt] *adj* (*person, work*) soigné(e); (*room etc*) bien tenu(e) *or* rangé(e); (*skilful*) habile; (*spirits*) pur(e); **~ly** *adv* avec soin *or* ordre; habilement

necessarily [ˈnesɪsərɪlɪ] *adv* nécessairement

necessary ['nesɪsərɪ] *adj* nécessaire

necessity [nɪ'sesɪtɪ] *n* nécessité *f*; (*thing needed*) chose nécessaire *or* essentielle; **necessities** *npl* nécessaire *m*

neck [nek] *n* cou *m*; (*of animal, garment*) encolure *f*; (*of bottle*) goulot *m* ♦ *vi* (*inf*) se peloter; ~ **and** ~ à égalité; ~**lace** ['neklɪs] *n* collier *m*; ~**line** *n* encolure *f*; ~**tie** *n* cravate *f*

need [niːd] *n* besoin *m* ♦ *vt* avoir besoin de; **to** ~ **to do** devoir faire; avoir besoin de faire; **you don't** ~ **to go** vous n'avez pas besoin *or* vous n'êtes pas obligé de partir

needle ['niːdl] *n* aiguille *f* ♦ *vt* asticoter, tourmenter

needless ['niːdlɪs] *adj* inutile

needlework ['niːdlwɜːk] *n* (*activity*) travaux *mpl* d'aiguille; (*object(s)*) ouvrage *m*

needn't ['niːdnt] = need not

needy ['niːdɪ] *adj* nécessiteux(euse)

negative ['negətɪv] *n* (PHOT, ELEC) négatif *m*; (LING) terme *m* de négation ♦ *adj* négatif(ive)

neglect [nɪ'glekt] *vt* négliger ♦ *n* (*of person, duty, garden*) le fait de négliger; (*state*) abandon *m*

negligee ['neglɪʒeɪ] *n* déshabillé *m*

negotiate [nɪ'gəʊʃɪeɪt] *vi, vt* négocier; **negotiation** [nɪgəʊʃɪ'eɪʃən] *n* négociation *f*, pourparlers *mpl*

Negro ['niːgrəʊ] (!; *pl* ~**es**) *n* Noir(e)

neigh [neɪ] *vi* hennir

neighbour ['neɪbə*] (US **neighbor**) *n* voisin(e); ~**hood** *n* (*place*) quartier *m*; (*people*) voisinage *m*; ~**ing** *adj* voisin(e), avoisinant(e); ~**ly** *adj* obligeant(e); (*action etc*) amical(e)

neither ['naɪðə*] *adj, pron* aucun(e) (des deux), ni l'un(e) ni l'autre ♦ *conj*: **I didn't move and** ~ **did Claude** je n'ai pas bougé, (et) Claude non plus; ..., ~ **did I refuse** ..., (et *or* mais) je n'ai pas non plus refusé ... ♦ *adv*: ~ **good nor bad** ni bon ni mauvais

neon ['niːɒn] *n* néon *m*; ~ **light** *n* lampe *f* au néon

nephew ['nefjuː] *n* neveu *m*

nerve [nɜːv] *n* nerf *m*; (*fig: courage*) sang-froid *m*, courage *m*; (: *impudence*) aplomb *m*, toupet *m*; **to have a fit of the** ~**s** avoir le trac; ~-**racking** *adj* angoissant(e)

nervous ['nɜːvəs] *adj* nerveux(euse); (*anxious*) inquiet(ète), plein(e) d'appréhension; (*timid*) intimidé(e); ~ **breakdown** *n* dépression nerveuse

nest [nest] *n* nid *m* ♦ *vi* (se) nicher, faire son nid; ~ **egg** *n* (*fig*) bas *m* de laine, magot *m*

nestle ['nesl] *vi* se blottir

net [net] *n* filet *m* ♦ *adj* net(te) ♦ *vt* (*fish etc*) prendre au filet; (*profit*) rapporter; ~**ball** *n* netball *m*; ~ **curtains** *npl* voilages *mpl*

Netherlands ['neðələndz] *npl*: **the** ~ les Pays-Bas *mpl*

nett [net] *adj* = net

netting ['netɪŋ] *n* (*for fence etc*) treillis *m*, grillage *m*

nettle ['netl] *n* ortie *f*

network ['netwɜːk] *n* réseau *m*

neurotic [njʊə'rɒtɪk] *adj, n* névrosé(e)

neuter ['njuːtə*] *adj* neutre ♦ *vt* (*cat etc*) châtrer, couper

neutral ['njuːtrəl] *adj* neutre ♦ *n* (AUT) point mort; ~**ize** *vt* neutraliser

never ['nevə*] *adv* (ne ...) jamais; ~ **again** plus jamais; ~ **in my life** jamais de ma vie; *see also* **mind**; ~-**ending** *adj* interminable; ~**theless** [nevəðə'les] *adv* néanmoins, malgré tout

new [njuː] *adj* nouveau(nouvelle); (*brand new*) neuf(neuve); ~-**born** *adj* nouveau-né(e); ~**comer** ['njuːkʌmə*] *n* nouveau venu/nouvelle venue; ~-**fangled** (*pej*) *adj* ultramoderne (et farfelu(e)); ~-**found** *adj* (*enthusiasm*) de fraîche date; (*friend*) nouveau(nouvelle); ~**ly** *adv* nouvellement, récemment; ~**ly-weds** *npl* jeunes mariés *mpl*

news [njuːz] *n* nouvelle(s) *f(pl)*; (RADIO, TV) informations *fpl*, actualités *fpl*; **a piece of** ~ une nouvelle; ~ **agency** *n* agence *f* de presse; ~**agent** (BRIT) *n* marchand *m* de journaux; ~**caster** *n* présentateur(trice); ~**dealer** (US) *n* = **newsagent**; ~ **flash** *n* flash *m* d'information; ~**letter** *n* bulletin *m*; ~**paper** *n* journal *m*; ~**print** *n* papier *m* (de) journal; ~**reader** *n* = **newscaster**; ~**reel** *n* actualités (filmées); ~ **stand** *n* kiosque *m* à journaux

newt [njuːt] *n* triton *m*

New Year *n* Nouvel An; ~'**s Day** *n* le jour de l'An; ~'**s Eve** *n* la Saint-Sylvestre

New Zealand [-'ziːlənd] *n* la Nouvelle-Zélande; ~**er** *n* Néo-zélandais(e)

next [nekst] *adj* (*seat, room*) voisin(e), d'à côté; (*meeting, bus stop*) suivant(e); (*in time*) prochain(e) ♦ *adv* (*place*) à côté; (*time*) la fois suivante, la prochaine fois; (*afterwards*) ensuite; **the** ~ **day** le lendemain, le jour suivant *or* d'après; ~ **year** l'année prochaine; ~ **time** la prochaine fois; ~ **to** à côté de; ~ **to nothing** presque rien; ~, **please!** (*at doctor's*) au suivant!; ~ **door** *adv* à côté ♦ *adj* d'à côté; ~-**of-kin** *n* parent *m* le plus proche

NHS *n abbr* = **National Health Service**

nib [nɪb] *n* (bec *m* de) plume *f*

nibble ['nɪbl] *vt* grignoter

nice [naɪs] *adj* (*pleasant, likeable*) agréable; (*pretty*) joli(e); (*kind*) gentil(le); ~**ly** *adv* agréablement; joliment; gentiment

niceties ['naɪsɪtɪz] *npl* subtilités *fpl*

nick [nɪk] *n* (*indentation*) encoche *f*; (*wound*) entaille *f* ♦ *vt* (BRIT: *inf*) faucher,

piquer; **in the ~ of time** juste à temps
nickel ['nɪkl] *n* nickel *m*; (*US*) pièce *f* de 5
cents
nickname ['nɪkneɪm] *n* surnom *m* ♦ *vt* surnommer
niece [niːs] *n* nièce *f*
Nigeria [naɪ'dʒɪərɪə] *n* Nigéria *m* or *f*
niggling ['nɪglɪŋ] *adj* (*person*) tatillon(ne);
(*detail*) insignifiant(e); (*doubts, injury*) persistant(e)
night [naɪt] *n* nuit *f*; (*evening*) soir *m*; **at ~**
la nuit; **by ~** de nuit; **the ~ before last**
avant-hier soir; **~cap** *n* boisson prise avant
le coucher; **~ club** *n* boîte *f* de nuit;
~dress *n* chemise *f* de nuit; **~fall** *n* tombée *f* de la nuit; **~gown** *n* chemise *f* de
nuit; **~ie** ['naɪtɪ] *n* chemise *f* de nuit; **~ingale** ['naɪtɪŋgeɪl] *n* rossignol *m*; **~life**
['naɪtlaɪf] *n* vie *f* nocturne; **~ly** ['naɪtlɪ] *adj*
de chaque nuit or soir; (*by night*) nocturne
♦ *adv* chaque nuit or soir; **~mare**
['naɪtmeə*] *n* cauchemar *m*; **~ porter** *n*
gardien *m* de nuit, concierge *m* de service
la nuit; **~ school** *n* cours *mpl* du soir; **~
shift** *n* équipe *f* de nuit; **~-time** *n* nuit *f*;
~ watchman *n* veilleur *m* or gardien *m*
de nuit
nil [nɪl] *n* rien *m*; (*BRIT: SPORT*) zéro *m*
Nile [naɪl] *n*: **the ~** le Nil
nimble ['nɪmbl] *adj* agile
nine [naɪn] *num* neuf *m*; **~teen** *num* dix-neuf;
~ty *num* quatre-vingt-dix
ninth [naɪnθ] *num* neuvième
nip [nɪp] *vt* pincer
nipple ['nɪpl] *n* (*ANAT*) mamelon *m*, bout
m du sein
nitrogen ['naɪtrədʒən] *n* azote *m*

―――――――――― *KEYWORD* ――――――――――

no [nəu] (*pl* **~es**) *adv* (*opposite of "yes"*)
non; **are you coming? - ~** (**I'm not**) est-ce
que vous venez? - non; **would you like
some more? - ~ thank you** vous en voulez encore? - non merci
♦ *adj* (*not any*) pas de, aucun(e) (*used with
"ne"*); **I have ~ money/books** je n'ai pas
d'argent/de livres; **~ student would have
done it** aucun étudiant ne l'aurait fait; **"~
smoking"** "défense de fumer"; **"~ dogs"**
"les chiens ne sont pas admis"
♦ *n* non *m*

nobility [nəu'bɪlɪtɪ] *n* noblesse *f*
noble ['nəubl] *adj* noble
nobody ['nəubədɪ] *pron* personne
nod [nɒd] *vi* faire un signe de tête (*affirmatif
ou amical*); (*sleep*) somnoler ♦ *vt*: **to ~
one's head** faire un signe de (la) tête; (*in
agreement*) faire signe que oui ♦ *n* signe *m*
de (la) tête; **~ off** *vi* s'assoupir
noise [nɔɪz] *n* bruit *m*; **noisy** ['nɔɪzɪ] *adj*
bruyant(e)

nominal ['nɒmɪnl] *adj* (*rent, leader*) symbolique
nominate ['nɒmɪneɪt] *vt* (*propose*) proposer; (*appoint*) nommer; **nominee** [nɒmɪ'niː]
n candidat agréé; personne nommée
non... *prefix* non-; **~alcoholic** *adj* nonalcoolisé(e); **~committal** *adj* évasif(ive)
nondescript ['nɒndɪskrɪpt] *adj* quelconque,
indéfinissable
none [nʌn] *pron* aucun(e); **~ of you** aucun
d'entre vous, personne parmi vous; **I've ~
left** je n'en ai plus; **he's ~ the worse for it**
il ne s'en porte pas plus mal
nonentity [nɒ'nentɪtɪ] *n* personne insignifiante
nonetheless [nʌnðə'les] *adv* néanmoins
non-existent [nɒnɪg'zɪstənt] *adj* inexistant(e)
non-fiction [nɒn'fɪkʃən] *n* littérature *f*
non-romanesque
nonplussed ['nɒn'plʌst] *adj* perplexe
nonsense ['nɒnsəns] *n* absurdités *fpl*, idioties *fpl*; **~!** ne dites pas d'idioties!
non: **~-smoker** *n* non-fumeur *m*; **~-stick**
adj qui n'attache pas; **~-stop** *adj* direct(e),
sans arrêt (*d'un escale*) ♦ *adv* sans arrêt
noodles ['nuːdlz] *npl* nouilles *fpl*
nook [nʊk] *n*: **~s and crannies** recoins *mpl*
noon [nuːn] *n* midi *m*
no one ['nəuwʌn] *pron* = **nobody**
noose [nuːs] *n* nœud coulant; (*hangman's*)
corde *f*
nor [nɔː*] *conj* = **neither** ♦ *adv see* **neither**
norm [nɔːm] *n* norme *f*
normal ['nɔːməl] *adj* normal(e); **~ly** *adv*
normalement
Normandy ['nɔːməndɪ] *n* Normandie *f*
north [nɔːθ] *n* nord *m* ♦ *adj* du nord, nord
inv ♦ *adv* au or vers le nord; **N~ America**
n Amérique *f* du Nord; **~-east** *n* nord-est
m; **~erly** ['nɔːðəlɪ] *adj* du nord; **~ern**
['nɔːðən] *adj* du nord, septentrional(e);
N~ern Ireland *n* Irlande *f* du Nord; **N~
Pole** *n* pôle *m* Nord; **N~ Sea** *n* mer *f* du
Nord; **~ward(s)** ['nɔːθwəd(z)] *adv* vers le
nord; **~-west** *n* nord-ouest *m*
Norway ['nɔːweɪ] *n* Norvège *f*
Norwegian [nɔː'wiːdʒən] *adj* norvégien(ne)
♦ *n* Norvégien(ne); (*LING*) norvégien *m*
nose [nəuz] *n* nez *m*; **~ about, around** *vi*
fouiner or fureter (partout); **~bleed** *n* saignement *m* du nez; **~-dive** *n* (descente *f*
en) piqué *m*; **~y** (*inf*) *adj* = **nosy**
nostalgia [nɒs'tældʒɪə] *n* nostalgie *f*
nostril ['nɒstrɪl] *n* narine *f*; (*of horse*) naseau *m*
nosy ['nəuzɪ] (*inf*) *adj* curieux(euse)
not [nɒt] *adv* (ne ...) pas; **he is ~ or isn't
here** il n'est pas ici; **you must ~ or you
mustn't do that** tu ne dois pas faire ça;
it's too late, isn't it or is it ~? c'est trop
tard, n'est-ce pas?; **~ yet/now** pas

encore/maintenant; *see also* **all; only**

notably ['nəʊtəblɪ] *adv* (*particularly*) en particulier; (*markedly*) spécialement

notary ['nəʊtərɪ] *n* notaire *m*

notch [nɒtʃ] *n* encoche *f*

note [nəʊt] *n* note *f*; (*letter*) mot *m*; (*banknote*) billet *m* ♦ *vt* (*also*: ~ *down*) noter; (*observe*) constater; ~**book** *n* carnet *m*; ~**d** ['nəʊtɪd] *adj* réputé(e); ~**pad** *n* blocnotes *m*; ~**paper** *n* papier *m* à lettres

nothing ['nʌθɪŋ] *n* rien *m*; **he does** ~ il ne fait rien; ~ **new** rien de nouveau; **for** ~ pour rien

notice ['nəʊtɪs] *n* (*announcement, warning*) avis *m*; (*period of time*) délai *m*; (*resignation*) démission *f*; (*dismissal*) congé *m* ♦ *vt* remarquer, s'apercevoir de; **to take** ~ **of** prêter attention à; **to bring sth to sb's** ~ porter qch à la connaissance de qn; **at short** ~ dans un délai très court; **until further** ~ jusqu'à nouvel ordre; **to hand in one's** ~ donner sa démission, démissionner; ~**able** *adj* visible; ~ **board** (*BRIT*) *n* panneau *m* d'affichage

notify ['nəʊtɪfaɪ] *vt*: **to** ~ **sth to sb** notifier qch à qn; **to** ~ **sb (of sth)** avertir qn (de qch)

notion ['nəʊʃən] *n* idée *f*; (*concept*) notion *f*

notorious [nəʊ'tɔːrɪəs] *adj* notoire (*souvent en mal*)

notwithstanding [nɒtwɪθ'stændɪŋ] *adv* néanmoins ♦ *prep* en dépit de

nought [nɔːt] *n* zéro *m*

noun [naʊn] *n* nom *m*

nourish ['nʌrɪʃ] *vt* nourrir; ~**ing** *adj* nourrissant(e); ~**ment** *n* nourriture *f*

novel ['nɒvəl] *n* roman *m* ♦ *adj* nouveau(velle), original(e); ~**ist** *n* romancier *m*; ~**ty** *n* nouveauté *f*

November [nəʊ'vembə*] *n* novembre *m*

now [naʊ] *adv* maintenant ♦ *conj*: ~ (**that**) maintenant que; **right** ~ tout de suite; **by** ~ à l'heure qu'il est; **just** ~: **that's the fashion just** ~: c'est la mode en ce moment; ~ **and then,** ~ **and again** de temps en temps; **from** ~ **on** dorénavant; ~**adays** ['naʊədeɪz] *adv* de nos jours

nowhere ['nəʊwɛə*] *adv* nulle part

nozzle ['nɒzl] *n* (*of hose etc*) ajutage *m*; (*of vacuum cleaner*) suceur *m*

nuclear ['njuːklɪə*] *adj* nucléaire

nucleus ['njuːklɪəs, pl 'njuːklɪaɪ] (*pl* **nuclei**) *n* noyau *m*

nude [njuːd] *adj* nu(e) ♦ *n* nu *m*; **in the** ~ (tout(e)) nu(e)

nudge [nʌdʒ] *vt* donner un (petit) coup de coude à

nudist ['njuːdɪst] *n* nudiste *m/f*

nuisance ['njuːsns] *n*: **it's a** ~ c'est (très) embêtant; **he's a** ~ il est assommant *or* casse-pieds; **what a** ~! quelle barbe!

null [nʌl] *adj*: ~ **and void** nul(le) et non avenu(e)

numb [nʌm] *adj* engourdi(e); (*with fear*) paralysé(e)

number ['nʌmbə*] *n* nombre *m*; (*numeral*) chiffre *m*; (*of house, bank account etc*) numéro *m* ♦ *vt* numéroter; (*amount to*) compter; **a** ~ **of** un certain nombre de; **to be** ~**ed among** compter parmi; **they were seven in** ~ ils étaient (au nombre de) sept; ~ **plate** *n* (*AUT*) plaque *f* minéralogique *or* d'immatriculation

numeral ['njuːmərəl] *n* chiffre *m*

numerate ['njuːmərɪt] (*BRIT*) *adj*: **to be** ~ avoir des notions d'arithmétique

numerical [njuː'merɪkəl] *adj* numérique

numerous ['njuːmərəs] *adj* nombreux(euse)

nun [nʌn] *n* religieuse *f*, sœur *f*

nurse [nɜːs] *n* infirmière *f* ♦ *vt* (*patient, cold*) soigner

nursery ['nɜːsərɪ] *n* (*room*) nursery *f*; (*institution*) crèche *f*; (*for plants*) pépinière *f*; ~ **rhyme** *n* comptine *f*, chansonnette *f* pour enfants; ~ **school** *n* école maternelle; ~ **slope** *n* (*SKI*) piste *f* pour débutants

nursing ['nɜːsɪŋ] *n* (*profession*) profession *f* d'infirmière; (*care*) soins *mpl*; ~ **home** *n* clinique *f*; maison *f* de convalescence; ~ **mother** *n* mère *f* qui allaite

nut [nʌt] *n* (*of metal*) écrou *m*; (*fruit*) noix *f*, noisette *f*; cacahuète *f*; ~**crackers** ['nʌtkrækəz] *npl* casse-noix *m inv*, cassenoisette(s) *m*

nutmeg ['nʌtmeg] *n* (*noix f*) muscade *f*

nutritious [njuː'trɪʃəs] *adj* nutritif(ive), nourrissant(e)

nuts (*inf*) *adj* dingue

nutshell ['nʌtʃel] *n*: **in a** ~ en un mot

nylon ['naɪlɒn] *n* nylon *m* ♦ *adj* de *or* en nylon

O o

oak [əʊk] *n* chêne *m* ♦ *adj* de *or* en (bois de) chêne

OAP (*BRIT*) *n abbr* = **old age pensioner**

oar [ɔː*] *n* aviron *m*, rame *f*

oasis [əʊ'eɪsɪs, pl əʊ'eɪsiːz] (*pl* **oases**) *n* oasis *f*

oath [əʊθ] *n* serment *m*; (*swear word*) juron *m*; **under** ~, (*BRIT*) **on** ~ sous serment

oatmeal ['əʊtmiːl] *n* flocons *mpl* d'avoine

oats [əʊts] *n* avoine *f*

obedience [ə'biːdɪəns] *n* obéissance *f*; **ob-**

edient [ə'biːdɪənt] *adj* obéissant(e)
obey [ə'beɪ] *vt* obéir à; *(instructions)* se conformer à
obituary [ə'bɪtjʊərɪ] *n* nécrologie *f*
object [*n* 'ɒbdʒɪkt, *vb* əb'dʒekt] *n* objet *m*; *(purpose)* but *m*, objet; *(LING)* complément *m* d'objet ♦ *vi*: **to ~ to** *(attitude)* désapprouver; *(proposal)* protester contre; **expense is no ~** l'argent n'est pas un problème; **he ~ed that ...** il a fait valoir *or* a objecté que ...; **I ~!** je proteste!; **~ion** [əb'dʒekʃən] *n* objection *f*, **~ionable** [əb'dʒekʃnəbl] *adj* très désagréable; *(language)* choquant(e); **~ive** [əb'dʒektɪv] *n* objectif *m* ♦ *adj* objectif(ive)
obligation [ɒblɪ'geɪʃən] *n* obligation *f*, devoir *m*; **without ~** sans engagement
oblige [ə'blaɪdʒ] *vt (force)*: **to ~ sb to do** obliger *or* forcer qn à faire; *(do a favour)* rendre service à, obliger; **to be ~d to sb for sth** être obligé(e) à qn de qch; **obliging** [ə'blaɪdʒɪŋ] *adj* obligeant(e), serviable
oblique [ə'bliːk] *adj* oblique; *(allusion)* indirect(e)
obliterate [ə'blɪtəreɪt] *vt* effacer
oblivion [ə'blɪvɪən] *n* oubli *m*; **oblivious** [ə'blɪvɪəs] *adj*: **oblivious of** oublieux(euse) de
oblong ['ɒblɒŋ] *adj* oblong(ue) ♦ *n* rectangle *m*
obnoxious [əb'nɒkʃəs] *adj* odieux (euse); *(smell)* nauséabond(e)
oboe ['əʊbəʊ] *n* hautbois *m*
obscene [əb'siːn] *adj* obscène
obscure [əb'skjʊə*] *adj* obscur(e) ♦ *vt* obscurcir; *(hide: sun)* cacher
observant [əb'zɜːvənt] *adj* observateur(trice)
observation [ɒbzə'veɪʃən] *n (remark)* observation *f*, *(watching)* surveillance *f*; **observatory** [əb'zɜːvətrɪ] *n* observatoire *m*
observe [əb'zɜːv] *vt* observer; *(remark)* faire observer *or* remarquer; **~r** *n* observateur(trice)
obsess [əb'ses] *vt* obséder; **~ive** *adj* obsédant(e)
obsolescence [ɒbsə'lesns] *n* vieillissement *m*
obsolete ['ɒbsəliːt] *adj* dépassé(e); démodé(e)
obstacle ['ɒbstəkl] *n* obstacle *m*; **~ race** *n* course *f* d'obstacles
obstinate ['ɒbstɪnət] *adj* obstiné(e)
obstruct [əb'strʌkt] *vt (block)* boucher, obstruer; *(hinder)* entraver
obtain [əb'teɪn] *vt* obtenir; **~able** *adj* qu'on peut obtenir
obvious ['ɒbvɪəs] *adj* évident(e), manifeste; **~ly** *adv* manifestement; **~ly not!** bien sûr que non!
occasion [ə'keɪʒən] *n* occasion *f*, *(event)* événement *m*; **~al** *adj* pris(e) *or* fait(e) etc

de temps en temps; occasionnel(le); **~ally** *adv* de temps en temps, quelquefois
occupation [ɒkju'peɪʃən] *n* occupation *f*; *(job)* métier *m*, profession *f*; **~al hazard** *n* risque *m* du métier
occupier ['ɒkjʊpaɪə*] *n* occupant(e)
occupy ['ɒkjʊpaɪ] *vt* occuper; **to ~ o.s. in** *or* **with doing** s'occuper à faire
occur [ə'kɜː*] *vi (event)* se produire; *(phenomenon, error)* se rencontrer; **to ~ to sb** venir à l'esprit de qn; **~rence** *n (existence)* présence *f*, existence *f*; *(event)* cas *m*, fait *m*
ocean ['əʊʃən] *n* océan *m*; **~-going** *adj* de haute mer
o'clock [ə'klɒk] *adv*: **it is 5 ~** il est 5 heures
OCR *n abbr* = **optical character reader; optical character recognition**
October [ɒk'təʊbə*] *n* octobre *m*
octopus ['ɒktəpəs] *n* pieuvre *f*
odd [ɒd] *adj (strange)* bizarre, curieux(euse); *(number)* impair(e); *(not of a set)* dépareillé(e); **60-odd** 60 et quelques; **at ~ times** de temps en temps; **the ~ one out** l'exception *f*; **~ity** *n (person)* excentrique *m/f*; *(thing)* curiosité *f*; **~-job man** *n* homme à tout faire; **~ jobs** *npl* petits travaux divers; **~ly** *adv* bizarrement, curieusement; **~ments** *npl (COMM)* fins *fpl* de série; **~s** *npl (in betting)* cote *f*; **it makes no ~s** cela n'a pas d'importance; **at ~s** en désaccord; **~s and ends** de petites choses
odour ['əʊdə*] *(US* **odor)** *n* odeur *f*

───── *KEYWORD*

of [ɒv, əv] *prep* **1** *(gen)* de; **a friend ~ ours** un de nos amis; **a boy ~ 10** un garçon de 10 ans; **that was kind ~ you** c'était gentil de votre part
2 *(expressing quantity, amount, dates etc)* de; **a kilo ~ flour** un kilo de farine; **how much ~ this do you need?** combien vous en faut-il?; **there were 3 ~ them** *(people)* ils étaient 3; *(objects)* il y en avait 3; **3 ~ us went** 3 d'entre nous y sont allé(e)s; **the 5th ~ July** le 5 juillet
3 *(from, out of)* en, de; **a statue ~ marble** une statue de *or* en marbre; **made ~ wood** (fait) en bois

off [ɒf] *adj, adv (engine)* coupé(e); *(tap)* fermé(e); *(BRIT: food: bad)* mauvais(e); *(: milk)* tourné(e); *(absent)* absent(e); *(cancelled)* annulé(e) ♦ *prep* de; sur; **to be ~** *(to leave)* partir, s'en aller; **to be ~ sick** être absent pour cause de maladie; **a day ~** un jour de congé; **to have an ~ day** n'être pas en forme; **he had his coat ~** il avait enlevé son manteau; **10% ~** *(COMM)* 10% de rabais; **~ the coast** au large de la côte; **I'm ~ meat** je ne mange plus de viande, je n'aime plus la viande; **on the ~ chance** à tout hasard

offal ['ɒfəl] n (CULIN) abats mpl

off-colour ['ɒf'kʌlə*] (BRIT) adj (ill) malade, mal fichu(e)

offence [ə'fens] (US **offense**) n (crime) délit m, infraction f; **to take ~** se vexer de, s'offenser de

offend [ə'fend] vt (person) offenser, blesser; **~er** n délinquant(e)

offense [ə'fens] (US) n = **offence**

offensive [ə'fensɪv] adj offensant(e), choquant(e); (smell etc) très déplaisant(e); (weapon) offensif(ive) ♦ n (MIL) offensive f

offer ['ɒfə*] n offre f, proposition f ♦ vt offrir, proposer; **"on ~"** (COMM) "en promotion"; **~ing** n offrande f

offhand ['ɒf'hænd] adj désinvolte ♦ adv spontanément

office ['ɒfɪs] n (place, room) bureau m; (position) charge f, fonction f; **doctor's ~** (US) cabinet (médical); **to take ~** entrer en fonctions; **~ automation** n bureautique f; **~ block** (US **~ building**) n immeuble m de bureaux; **~ hours** npl heures fpl de bureau; (US: MED) heures de consultation

officer ['ɒfɪsə*] n (MIL etc) officier m; (also: **police ~**) agent m (de police); (of organization) membre m du bureau directeur

office worker n employé(e) de bureau

official [ə'fɪʃəl] adj officiel(le) ♦ n officiel m; (civil servant) fonctionnaire m/f; employé(e); **~dom** n administration f, bureaucratie f

officiate [ə'fɪʃɪeɪt] vi (REL) officier; **to ~ at a marriage** célébrer un mariage

officious [ə'fɪʃəs] adj trop empressé(e)

offing ['ɒfɪŋ] n: **in the ~** (fig) en perspective

off: ~-licence (BRIT) n (shop) débit m de vins et de spiritueux; **~-line** adj, adv (COMPUT) (en mode) autonome; (: switched off) non connecté(e); **~-peak** adj aux heures creuses; (electricity, heating, ticket) au tarif heures creuses; **~-putting** (BRIT) adj (remark) rébarbatif(ive); (person) rebutant(e), peu engageant(e); **~-season** adj, adv hors-saison inv

offset ['ɒfset] (irreg) vt (counteract) contrebalancer, compenser

offshoot ['ɒfʃuːt] n (fig) ramification f, antenne f

offshore ['ɒf'ʃɔː*] adj (breeze) de terre; (fishing) côtier(ère)

offside ['ɒf'saɪd] adj (SPORT) hors jeu; (AUT: with right-hand drive) de droite; (: with left-hand drive) de gauche

offspring ['ɒfsprɪŋ] n inv progéniture f

off: ~stage adv dans les coulisses; **~-the-peg** (US **~-the-rack**) adv en prêt-à-porter; **~-white** adj blanc cassé inv

often ['ɒfən] adv souvent; **how ~ do you**

go? vous y allez tous les combien?; **how ~ have you gone there?** vous y êtes allé combien de fois?

ogle ['əʊgl] vt lorgner

oh [əʊ] excl ô!, oh!, ah!

oil [ɔɪl] n huile f; (petroleum) pétrole m; (for central heating) mazout m ♦ vt (machine) graisser; **~can** n burette f de graissage; (for storing) bidon m à huile; **~field** n gisement m de pétrole; **~ filter** n (AUT) filtre m à huile; **~ painting** n peinture f à l'huile; **~ refinery** n raffinerie f; **~ rig** n derrick m; (at sea) plate-forme pétrolière; **~skins** npl ciré m; **~ tanker** n (ship) pétrolier m; (truck) camion-citerne m; **~ well** n puits m de pétrole; **~y** adj huileux(euse); (food) gras(se)

ointment ['ɔɪntmənt] n onguent m

O.K., okay ['əʊ'keɪ] excl d'accord! ♦ adj (average) pas mal ♦ vt approuver, donner son accord à; **is it ~?, are you ~?** ça va?

old [əʊld] adj vieux(vieille); (person) vieux, âgé(e); (former) ancien(ne), vieux; **how ~ are you?** quel âge avez-vous?; **he's 10 years ~** il a 10 ans, il est âgé de 10 ans; **~er brother/sister** frère/sœur aîné(e); **~ age** n vieillesse f; **~ age pensioner** (BRIT) n retraité(e); **~-fashioned** adj démodé(e); (person) vieux jeu inv

olive ['ɒlɪv] n (fruit) olive f; (tree) olivier m ♦ adj (also: **~-green**) (vert) olive inv; **~ oil** n huile f d'olive

Olympic [əʊ'lɪmpɪk] adj olympique; **the ~ Games, the ~s** les Jeux mpl olympiques

omelet(te) ['ɒmlət] n omelette f

omen ['əʊmən] n présage m

ominous ['ɒmɪnəs] adj menaçant(e), inquiétant(e); (event) de mauvais augure

omit [əʊ'mɪt] vt omettre; **to ~ to do** omettre de faire

KEYWORD

on [ɒn] prep **1** (indicating position) sur; **~ the table** sur la table; **~ the wall** sur le or au mur; **~ the left** à gauche

2 (indicating means, method, condition etc): **~ foot** à pied; **~ the train/plane** (be) dans le train/l'avion; (go) en train/avion; **~ the telephone/radio/television** au téléphone/à la radio/à la télévision; **to be ~ drugs** se droguer; **~ holiday** en vacances

3 (referring to time): **~ Friday** vendredi; **~ Fridays** le vendredi; **~ June 20th** le 20 juin; **a week ~ Friday** vendredi en huit; **~ arrival** à l'arrivée; **~ seeing this** en voyant cela

4 (about, concerning) sur, de; **a book ~ Balzac/physics** un livre sur Balzac/de physique

♦ adv **1** (referring to dress, covering): **to have one's coat ~** avoir (mis) son manteau; **to put one's coat ~** mettre son manteau; **what's she got ~?** qu'est-ce qu'elle

porte?; **screw the lid ~ tightly** vissez bien le couvercle
2 *(further, continuously)*: **to walk** etc **~** continuer à marcher etc; **~ and off** de temps à autre
♦ adj **1** *(in operation: machine)* en marche; (: *radio, TV, light*) allumé(e); (: *tap, gas*) ouvert(e); (: *brakes*) mis(e); **is the meeting still ~?** *(not cancelled)* est-ce que la réunion a bien lieu?; *(in progress)* la réunion dure-t-elle encore?; **when is this film ~?** quand passe ce film?
2 *(inf)*: **that's not ~!** *(not acceptable)* cela ne se fait pas!; *(not possible)* pas question!

once [wʌns] *adv* une fois; *(formerly)* autrefois ♦ *conj* une fois que; **~ he had left/it was done** une fois qu'il fut parti/que ce fut terminé; **at ~** tout de suite, immédiatement; *(simultaneously)* à la fois; **~ a week** une fois par semaine; **~ more** encore une fois; **~ and for all** une fois pour toutes; **~ upon a time** il y avait une fois, il était une fois
oncoming ['ɒnkʌmɪŋ] *adj (traffic)* venant en sens inverse

─────────── KEYWORD

one [wʌn] *num* un(e); **~ hundred and fifty** cent cinquante; **~ day** un jour
♦ *adj* **1** *(sole)* seul(e), unique; **the ~ book which** l'unique *or* le seul livre qui; **the ~ man who** le seul (homme) qui
2 *(same)* même; **they came in the ~ car** ils sont venus dans la même voiture
♦ *pron* **1**: **this ~** celui-ci(celle-ci); **that ~** celui-là(celle-là); **I've already got ~/a red ~** j'en ai déjà un(e)/un(e) rouge; **~ by ~** un(e) à *or* par un(e)
2: **~ another** l'un(e) l'autre; **to look at ~ another** se regarder
3 *(impersonal)* on; **~ never knows** on ne sait jamais; **to cut ~'s finger** se couper le doigt

─────────────

one: **~-day excursion** *(US)* n billet m d'aller-retour *(valable pour la journée)*; **~-man** *adj (business)* dirigé(e) etc par un seul homme; **~-man band** n homme-orchestre m; **~-off** *(BRIT: inf)* n exemplaire m unique
oneself [wʌn'self] *pron (reflexive)* se; *(after prep)* soi(-même); *(emphatic)* soi-même; **to hurt ~** se faire mal; **to keep sth for ~** garder qch pour soi; **to talk to ~** se parler à soi-même
one: **~-sided** *adj (argument)* unilatéral; **~-to-~** *adj (relationship)* univoque; **~-upmanship** n: **the art of ~-upmanship** l'art de faire mieux que les autres; **~-way** *adj (street, traffic)* à sens unique
ongoing ['ɒngəʊɪŋ] *adj* en cours; *(relationship)* suivi(e)

onion ['ʌnjən] n oignon m
on-line ['ɒn'laɪn] *adj, adv (COMPUT)* en ligne; (: *switched on*) connecté(e)
onlooker ['ɒnlʊkə*] n spectateur(trice)
only ['əʊnlɪ] *adv* seulement ♦ *adj* seul(e), unique ♦ *conj* seulement, mais; **an ~ child** un enfant unique; **not ~ ... but also** non seulement ... mais aussi
onset ['ɒnset] n début m; *(of winter, old age)* approche f
onshore ['ɒnʃɔː*] *adj (wind)* du large
onslaught ['ɒnslɔːt] n attaque f, assaut m
onto ['ɒntʊ] *prep* = **on to**
onus ['əʊnəs] n responsabilité f
onward(s) ['ɒnwəd(z)] *adv (move)* en avant; **from that time ~** à partir de ce moment
ooze [uːz] *vi* suinter
opaque [əʊ'peɪk] *adj* opaque
OPEC ['əʊpek] n abbr (= Organization of Petroleum Exporting Countries) O.P.E.P. f
open ['əʊpən] *adj* ouvert(e); *(car)* découvert(e); *(road, view)* dégagé(e); *(meeting)* public(ique); *(admiration)* manifeste ♦ *vt* ouvrir ♦ *vi (flower, eyes, door, debate)* s'ouvrir; *(shop, bank, museum)* ouvrir; *(book etc: commence)* commencer, débuter; **in the ~ (air)** en plein air; **~ on to** *vt fus (subj: room, door)* donner sur; **~ up** *vt* ouvrir; *(blocked road)* dégager ♦ *vi* s'ouvrir; **~ing** n ouverture f; *(opportunity)* occasion f ♦ *adj (remarks)* préliminaire; **~ly** *adv* ouvertement; **~-minded** *adj* à l'esprit ouvert; **~-necked** *adj* à col ouvert; **~-plan** *adj* sans cloisons
opera ['ɒpərə] n opéra m; **~ singer** n chanteur(euse) d'opéra
operate ['ɒpəreɪt] *vt (machine)* faire marcher, faire fonctionner ♦ *vi* fonctionner; *(MED)*: **to ~ (on sb)** opérer (qn)
operatic [ɒpə'rætɪk] *adj* d'opéra
operating: **~-table** n table f d'opération; **~ theatre** n salle f d'opération
operation [ɒpə'reɪʃən] n opération f; *(of machine)* fonctionnement m; **to be in ~** *(system, law)* être en vigueur; **to have an ~** *(MED)* se faire opérer
operative ['ɒpərətɪv] *adj (measure)* en vigueur
operator ['ɒpəreɪtə*] n *(of machine)* opérateur(trice); *(TEL)* téléphoniste m/f
opinion [ə'pɪnjən] n opinion f, avis m; **in my ~** à mon avis; **~ated** *adj* aux idées bien arrêtées; **~ poll** n sondage m d'opinion)
opponent [ə'pəʊnənt] n adversaire m/f
opportunity [ɒpə'tjuːnɪtɪ] n occasion f; **to take the ~ of doing** profiter de l'occasion pour faire; en faire plus pour faire
oppose [ə'pəʊz] *vt* s'opposer à; **~d to** opposé(e) à; **as ~d to** par opposition à; **opposing** [ə'pəʊzɪŋ] *adj (side)* opposé(e)

opposite ['ɒpəzɪt] *adj* opposé(e); *(house etc)* en face ♦ *adv* en face ♦ *prep* en face de ♦ *n* opposé *m*, contraire *m*; **the ~ sex** l'autre sexe, le sexe opposé

opposition [ɒpə'zɪʃən] *n* opposition *f*

oppress [ə'pres] *vt* opprimer

oppressive *adj (political regime)* oppressif(ive); *(weather)* lourd(e); *(heat)* accablant(e)

opt [ɒpt] *vi*: **to ~ for** opter pour; **to ~ to do** choisir de faire; **~ out** *vi*: **to ~ out of** choisir de ne pas participer à *or* de ne pas faire

optical ['ɒptɪkəl] *adj* optique; *(instrument)* d'optique; **~ character recognition/ reader** *n* lecture *f*/lecteur *m* optique

optician [ɒp'tɪʃən] *n* opticien(ne)

optimist ['ɒptɪmɪst] *n* optimiste *m/f*; **~ic** *adj* optimiste

option ['ɒpʃən] *n* choix *m*, option *f*; *(SCOL)* matière *f* à option; *(COMM)* option; **~al** *adj* facultatif(ive); *(COMM)* en option

or [ɔː*] *conj* ou; *(with negative)*: **he hasn't seen ~ heard anything** il n'a rien vu ni entendu; **~ else** sinon; ou bien

oral ['ɔːrəl] *adj* oral(e) ♦ *n* oral *m*

orange ['ɒrɪndʒ] *n (fruit)* orange *f* ♦ *adj* orange *inv*

orator ['ɒrətə*] *n* orateur(trice)

orbit ['ɔːbɪt] *n* orbite *f* ♦ *vt* graviter autour de

orchard ['ɔːtʃəd] *n* verger *m*

orchestra ['ɔːkɪstrə] *n* orchestre *m*; *(US: seating)* (fauteuils *mpl* d')orchestre

orchid ['ɔːkɪd] *n* orchidée *f*

ordain [ɔː'deɪn] *vt (REL)* ordonner

ordeal [ɔː'diːl] *n* épreuve *f*

order ['ɔːdə*] *n* ordre *m*; *(COMM)* commande *f* ♦ *vt* ordonner; *(COMM)* commander; **in ~** en ordre; *(document)* en règle; **in (working) ~** en état de marche; **out of ~** *(not in correct order)* en désordre; *(not working)* en dérangement; **in ~ to do/that** pour faire/ que *+sub*; **on ~** *(COMM)* en commande; **to ~ sb to do** ordonner à qn de faire; **~ form** *n* bon *m* de commande; **~ly** *n (MIL)* ordonnance *f*; *(MED)* garçon *m* de salle ♦ *adj (room)* en ordre; *(person)* qui a de l'ordre

ordinary ['ɔːdnrɪ] *adj* ordinaire, normal(e); *(pej)* ordinaire, quelconque; **out of the ~** exceptionnel(le)

Ordnance Survey map *n* ≈ carte *f* d'Etat-Major

ore [ɔː*] *n* minerai *m*

organ ['ɔːgən] *n* organe *m*; *(MUS)* orgue *m*, orgues *fpl*; **~ic** [ɔː'gænɪk] *adj* organique

organization [ɔːgənaɪ'zeɪʃən] *n* organisation *f*

organize ['ɔːgənaɪz] *vt* organiser; **~r** *n* organisateur(trice)

orgasm ['ɔːgæzəm] *n* orgasme *m*

Orient ['ɔːrɪənt] *n*: **the ~** l'Orient *m*; **o~al** [ɔːrɪ'entəl] *adj* oriental(e)

origin ['ɒrɪdʒɪn] *n* origine *f*

original [ə'rɪdʒɪnl] *adj* original(e); *(earliest)* originel(le) ♦ *n* original *m*; **~ly** *adv (at first)* à l'origine

originate [ə'rɪdʒɪneɪt] *vi*: **to ~ from** *(person)* être originaire de; *(suggestion)* provenir de; **to ~ in** prendre naissance dans; avoir son origine dans

Orkneys ['ɔːknɪz] *npl*: **the ~** *(also: the Orkney Islands)* les Orcades *fpl*

ornament ['ɔːnəmənt] *n* ornement *m*; *(trinket)* bibelot *m*; **~al** [ɔːnə'mentl] *adj* décoratif(ive); *(garden)* d'agrément

ornate [ɔː'neɪt] *adj* très orné(e)

orphan ['ɔːfən] *n* orphelin(e); **~age** *n* orphelinat *m*

orthopaedic [ɔːθəʊ'piːdɪk] *(US* **orthopedic)** *adj* orthopédique

ostensibly [ɒs'tensəblɪ] *adv* en apparence

ostentatious [ɒsten'teɪʃəs] *adj* prétentieux(euse)

ostracize ['ɒstrəsaɪz] *vt* frapper d'ostracisme

ostrich ['ɒstrɪtʃ] *n* autruche *f*

other ['ʌðə*] *adj* autre ♦ *pron*: **the ~ (one)** l'autre; **~s** *(~ people)* d'autres; **~ than** autrement que; à part; **~wise** *adv*, *conj* autrement

otter ['ɒtə*] *n* loutre *f*

ouch [autʃ] *excl* aïe!

ought [ɔːt] *(pt* ought) *aux vb*: **I ~ to do it** je devrais le faire, il faudrait que je le fasse; **this ~ to have been corrected** cela aurait dû être corrigé; **he ~ to win** il devrait gagner

ounce [auns] *n* once *f* (= 28.35g; 16 in a pound)

our [auə*] *adj* notre, nos *pl*; *see also* **my**; **~s** *pron* le(la) nôtre, les nôtres; *see also* **mine**[1]; **~selves** *pron pl (reflexive, after preposition)* nous; *(emphatic)* nous-mêmes; *see also* **oneself**

oust [aust] *vt* évincer

out [aut] *adv* dehors; *(published, not at home etc)* sorti(e); *(light, fire)* éteint(e); **~ here** ici; **~ there** là-bas; **he's ~** *(absent)* il est sorti; *(unconscious)* il est sans connaissance; **to be ~ in one's calculations** s'être trompé dans ses calculs; **to run/back** *etc* **~** sortir en courant/en reculant *etc*; **~ loud** à haute voix; **~ of** *(outside)* en dehors de; *(because of: anger etc)* par; *(from among)*: **~ of 10** sur 10; **~ of**; *(without)*: **~ of petrol** sans essence, à court d'essence; **~ of order** *(machine)* en panne; *(TEL: line)* en dérangement; **~-and-out** *adj (liar, thief etc)* véritable

outback ['autbæk] *n (in Australia)*: **the ~** l'intérieur *m*

outboard ['autbɔːd] *n (also: ~ motor)* (mo-

teur m) hors-bord m;
out: ~break ['autbreɪk] n (of war, disease) début m; (of violence) éruption f; **~burst** ['autbɜːst] n explosion f, accès m; **~cast** ['autkɑːst] n exilé(e); (socially) paria m; **~come** ['autkʌm] n issue f, résultat m; **~crop** ['autkrɒp] n (of rock) affleurement m; **~cry** ['autkraɪ] n tollé (général); **~dated** [aut'deɪtɪd] adj démodé(e); **~do** [aut'duː] (irreg) vt surpasser

outdoor ['autdɔː*] adj de or en plein air; **~s** adv dehors; au grand air

outer ['autə*] adj extérieur(e); **~ space** n espace m cosmique

outfit ['autfɪt] n (clothes) tenue f

outgoing ['autgəuɪŋ] adj (character) ouvert(e), extraverti(e); (retiring) sortant(e); **~s** (BRIT) npl (expenses) dépenses fpl

outgrow [aut'grəu] (irreg) vt (clothes) devenir trop grand(e) pour

outhouse ['authaus] n appentis m, remise f

outing ['autɪŋ] n sortie f; excursion f

outlandish [aut'lændɪʃ] adj étrange

outlaw ['autlɔː] n hors-la-loi m inv ♦ vt mettre hors-la-loi

outlay ['autleɪ] n dépenses fpl; (investment) mise f de fonds

outlet ['autlet] n (for liquid etc) issue f, sortie f; (US: ELEC) prise f de courant; (also: retail ~) point m de vente

outline ['autlaɪn] n (shape) contour m; (summary) esquisse f, grandes lignes ♦ vt (fig: theory, plan) exposer à grands traits

out: ~live [aut'lɪv] vt survivre à; **~look** ['autluk] n perspective f; **~lying** ['autlaɪɪŋ] adj écarté(e); **~moded** [aut'məudɪd] adj démodé(e); dépassé(e); **~number** [aut'nʌmbə*] vt surpasser en nombre

out-of-date [autəv'deɪt] adj (passport) périmé(e); (theory etc) dépassé(e); (clothes etc) démodé(e)

out-of-the-way [autəvðə'weɪ] adj (place) loin de tout

outpatient ['autpeɪʃənt] n malade m/f en consultation externe

outpost ['autpəust] n avant-poste m

output ['autput] n rendement m, production f; (COMPUT) sortie f

outrage ['autreɪdʒ] n (anger) indignation f; (violent act) atrocité f; (scandal) scandale m ♦ vt outrager; **~ous** [aut'reɪdʒəs] adj atroce; scandaleux(euse)

outright [adv 'autraɪt, adj aut'raɪt] adv complètement; (deny, refuse) catégoriquement; (ask) carrément; (kill) sur le coup ♦ adj complet(ète); catégorique

outset ['autset] n début m

outside ['aut'saɪd] n extérieur m ♦ adj extérieur(e) ♦ adv (au) dehors, à l'extérieur ♦ prep hors de, à l'extérieur de; **at the ~** (fig) au plus or maximum; **~ lane** n (AUT: in Britain) voie f de droite; (: in US, Europe)

voie de gauche; **~ line** n (TEL) ligne extérieure; **~r** n (stranger) étranger(ère)

out: ~size ['autsaɪz] adj énorme; (clothes) grande taille inv; **~skirts** ['autskɜːts] npl faubourgs mpl; **~spoken** [aut'spəukən] adj très franc(franche)

outstanding [aut'stændɪŋ] adj remarquable, exceptionnel(le); (unfinished) en suspens; (debt) impayé(e); (problem) non réglé(e)

outstay [aut'steɪ] vt: **to ~ one's welcome** abuser de l'hospitalité de son hôte

out: ~stretched ['autstretʃt] adj (hand) tendu(e); **~strip** [aut'strɪp] vt (competitors, demand) dépasser; **~ tray** n courrier m "départ"

outward ['autwəd] adj (sign, appearances) extérieur(e); (journey) (d')aller; **~ly** adv extérieurement; en apparence

outweigh [aut'weɪ] vt l'emporter sur

outwit [aut'wɪt] vt se montrer plus malin que

oval ['əuvəl] adj ovale ♦ n ovale m

ovary ['əuvərɪ] n ovaire m

oven ['ʌvn] n four m; **~proof** adj allant au four

over ['əuvə*] adv (par-)dessus ♦ adj (finished) fini(e), terminé(e); (too much) en plus ♦ prep sur; par-dessus; (above) au-dessus de; (on the other side of) de l'autre côté de; (more than) plus de; (during) pendant; **~ here** ici; **~ there** là-bas; **all ~** (everywhere) partout; (finished) fini(e); **~ and ~ (again)** à plusieurs reprises; **~ and above** en plus de; **to ask sb ~** inviter qn (à passer)

overall [adj, n 'əuvərɔːl, adv əuvər'ɔːl] adj (length, cost etc) total(e); (study) d'ensemble ♦ n (BRIT) blouse f ♦ adv dans l'ensemble, en général; **~s** npl bleus mpl (de travail)

overawe [əuvər'ɔː] vt impressionner

over: ~balance [əuvə'bæləns] vi basculer; **~bearing** [əuvə'beərɪŋ] adj impérieux(euse), autoritaire; **~board** ['əuvəbɔːd] adv (NAUT) par-dessus bord; **~book** [əuvə'buk] vt faire du surbooking; **~cast** ['əuvəkɑːst] adj couvert(e)

overcharge [əuvə'tʃɑːdʒ] vt: **to ~ sb for sth** faire payer qch trop cher à qn

overcoat ['əuvəkəut] n pardessus m

overcome [əuvə'kʌm] (irreg) vt (defeat) triompher de; (difficulty) surmonter

overcrowded [əuvə'kraudɪd] adj bondé(e)

overdo [əuvə'duː] (irreg) vt exagérer; (overcook) trop cuire; **to ~ it** (work etc) se surmener

overdose ['əuvədəus] n dose excessive

overdraft ['əuvədrɑːft] n découvert m; **overdrawn** ['əuvə'drɔːn] adj (account) à découvert; (person) dont le compte est à découvert

overdue ['əuvə'djuː] adj en retard; (change,

reform) qui tarde

overestimate [əuvər'ɛstɪmeɪt] *vt* surestimer

overexcited [əuvərɪk'saɪtɪd] *adj* surexcité(e)

overflow [*vb* əuvə'fləu, *n* 'əuvəfləu] *vi* déborder ♦ *n* (*also*: ~ **pipe**) tuyau *m* d'écoulement, trop-plein *m*

overgrown ['əuvə'grəun] *adj* (*garden*) envahi(e) par la végétation

overhaul [*vb* əuvə'hɔːl, *n* 'əuvəhɔːl] *vt* réviser ♦ *n* révision *f*

overhead [*adv* əuvə'hed, *adj, n* 'əuvəhed] *adv* au-dessus ♦ *adj* aérien(ne); (*lighting*) vertical(e) ♦ ~**s** *npl*, (*US*) *n* frais généraux

overhear [əuvə'hɪə*] (*irreg*) *vt* entendre (par hasard)

overheat [əuvə'hiːt] *vi* (*engine*) chauffer

overjoyed [əuvə'dʒɔɪd] *adj*: ~ (**at**) ravi(e) (de), enchanté(e) (de)

overkill ['əuvəkɪl] *n*: **that would be** ~ ce serait trop

overland *adj, adv* par voie de terre

overlap [*vb* əuvə'læp, *n* 'əuvəlæp] *vi* se chevaucher

overleaf [əuvə'liːf] *adv* au verso

overload ['əuvə'ləud] *vt* surcharger

overlook [əuvə'luk] *vt* (*have view of*) donner sur; (*miss: by mistake*) oublier; (*forgive*) fermer les yeux sur

overnight [*adv* 'əuvə'naɪt, *adj* 'əuvənaɪt] *adv* (*happen*) durant la nuit; (*fig*) soudain ♦ *adj* d'une (*or* de) nuit; **he stayed there** ~ il y a passé la nuit

overpass *n* pont autoroutier

overpower [əuvə'pauə*] *vt* vaincre; (*fig*) accabler; ~**ing** *adj* (*heat, stench*) suffocant(e)

overrate ['əuvə'reɪt] *vt* surestimer

override [əuvə'raɪd] (*irreg: like* ride) *vt* (*order, objection*) passer outre à; **overriding** [əuvə'raɪdɪŋ] *adj* prépondérant(e)

overrule [əuvə'ruːl] *vt* (*decision*) annuler; (*claim*) rejeter; (*person*) rejeter l'avis de

overrun [əuvə'rʌn] (*irreg: like* run) *vt* (*country*) occuper; (*time limit*) dépasser

overseas ['əuvə'siːz] *adv* outre-mer; (*abroad*) à l'étranger ♦ *adj* (*trade*) extérieur(e); (*visitor*) étranger(ère)

overshadow [əuvə'ʃædəu] *vt* (*fig*) éclipser

oversight ['əuvəsaɪt] *n* omission *f*, oubli *m*

oversleep ['əuvə'sliːp] (*irreg*) *vi* se réveiller (trop) tard

overstate *vt* exagérer

overstep [əuvə'step] *vt*: **to** ~ **the mark** dépasser la mesure

overt [əu'vɜːt] *adj* non dissimulé(e)

overtake [əuvə'teɪk] (*irreg*) *vt* (*AUT*) dépasser, doubler

overthrow [əuvə'θrəu] (*irreg*) *vt* (*government*) renverser

overtime ['əuvətaɪm] *n* heures *fpl* supplémentaires

overtone ['əuvətəun] *n* (*also*: ~**s**) note *f*,

sous-entendus *mpl*

overture ['əuvətʃuə*] *n* (*MUS, fig*) ouverture *f*

overturn [əuvə'tɜːn] *vt* renverser ♦ *vi* se retourner

overweight ['əuvə'weɪt] *adj* (*person*) trop gros(se)

overwhelm [əuvə'welm] *vt* (*subj: emotion*) accabler; (*enemy, opponent*) écraser; ~**ing** *adj* (*victory, defeat*) écrasant(e); (*desire*) irrésistible

overwork ['əuvə'wɜːk] *n* surmenage *m*

overwrought ['əuvə'rɔːt] *adj* excédé(e)

owe [əu] *vt*: **to** ~ **sb sth, to** ~ **sth to sb** devoir qch à qn; **owing to** ['əuɪŋ-] *prep* à cause de, en raison de

owl [aul] *n* hibou *m*

own [əun] *vt* posséder ♦ *adj* propre; **a room of my** ~ une chambre à moi, ma propre chambre; **to get one's** ~ **back** prendre sa revanche; **on one's** ~ tout(e) seul(e); ~ **up** *vi* avouer; ~**er** *n* propriétaire *m/f*; ~**ership** *n* possession *f*

ox [ɒks] (*pl* **oxen**) *n* bœuf *m*

oxtail ['ɒksteɪl] *n*: ~ **soup** soupe *f* à la queue de bœuf

oxygen ['ɒksɪdʒən] *n* oxygène *m*; ~ **mask** *n* masque *m* à oxygène

oyster ['ɔɪstə*] *n* huître *f*

oz. *abbr* = **ounce(s)**

ozone hole *n* trou *m* d'ozone

ozone layer *n* couche *f* d'ozone

P p

p [piː] *abbr* = **penny; pence**

PA *n abbr* = **personal assistant; public address system**

pa [pɑː] (*inf*) *n* papa *m*

p.a. *abbr* = **per annum**

pace [peɪs] *n* pas *m*; (*speed*) allure *f*; vitesse *f* ♦ *vi*: **to** ~ **up and down** faire les cent pas; **to keep** ~ **with** aller à la même vitesse que; ~**maker** *n* (*MED*) stimulateur *m* cardiaque; (*SPORT: also*: pacesetter) meneur(euse) de train

Pacific *n*: **the** ~ (**Ocean**) le Pacifique, l'océan *m* Pacifique

pack [pæk] *n* (*packet; US: of cigarettes*) paquet *m*; (*of hounds*) meute *f*; (*of thieves etc*) bande *f*; (*back pack*) sac *m* à dos; (*of cards*) jeu *m* ♦ *vt* (*goods*) empaqueter, emballer; (*box*) remplir; (*cram*) entasser; **to** ~ **one's**

suitcase faire sa valise; **to ~ (one's bags)** faire ses bagages; **to ~ sb off** to expédier qn à; **~ it in!** laisse tomber!, écrase!

package ['pækɪdʒ] *n* paquet *m*; (*also: ~ deal*) forfait *m*; **~ tour** (*BRIT*) *n* voyage organisé

packed lunch ['pækt-] (*BRIT*) *n* repas froid

packet ['pækɪt] *n* paquet *m*

packing ['pækɪŋ] *n* emballage *m*; **~ case** *n* caisse *f* (d'emballage)

pact [pækt] *n* pacte *m*; traité *m*

pad [pæd] *n* bloc(-notes) *m*; (*to prevent friction*) tampon *m*; (*inf: home*) piaule *f* ♦ *vt* rembourrer; **~ding** *n* rembourrage *m*

paddle ['pædl] *n* (*oar*) pagaie *f*; (*US: for table tennis*) raquette *f* de ping-pong ♦ *vt*: **to ~ a canoe** *etc* pagayer ♦ *vi* barboter, faire trempette; **~ steamer** *n* bateau *m* à aubes; **paddling pool** (*BRIT*) *n* petit bassin

paddock ['pædək] *n* enclos *m*; (*RACING*) paddock *m*

paddy field ['pædɪ-] *n* rizière *f*

padlock ['pædlɒk] *n* cadenas *m*

paediatrics [piːdɪ'ætrɪks] (*US* **pediatrics**) *n* pédiatrie *f*

pagan ['peɪgən] *adj, n* païen(ne)

page [peɪdʒ] *n* (*of book*) page *f*; (*also: ~ boy*) groom *m*, chasseur *m*; (*at wedding*) garçon *m* d'honneur ♦ *vt* (*in hotel etc*) (faire) appeler

pageant ['pædʒənt] *n* spectacle *m* historique; **~ry** *n* apparat *m*, pompe *f*

pager ['peɪdʒə*], **paging device** *n* (*TEL*) récepteur *m* d'appels

paid [peɪd] *pt, pp of* **pay** ♦ *adj* (*work, official*) rémunéré(e); (*holiday*) payé(e); **to put ~ to** (*BRIT*) mettre fin à, régler; **~ gunman** *n* tueur *m* à gages

pail [peɪl] *n* seau *m*

pain [peɪn] *n* douleur *f*; **to be in ~** souffrir, avoir mal; **to take ~s to do** se donner du mal pour faire; **~ed** *adj* peiné(e), chagrin(e); **~ful** *adj* douloureux(euse); (*fig*) difficile, pénible; **~fully** *adv* (*fig: very*) terriblement; **~killer** *n* analgésique *m*; **~less** *adj* indolore

painstaking ['peɪnzteɪkɪŋ] *adj* (*person*) soigneux(euse); (*work*) soigné(e)

paint [peɪnt] *n* peinture *f* ♦ *vt* peindre; **to ~ the door blue** peindre la porte en bleu; **~brush** *n* pinceau *m*; **~er** *n* peintre *m*; **~ing** *n* peinture *f*; (*picture*) tableau *m*; **~work** *n* peinture *f*

pair [pɛə*] *n* (*of shoes, gloves etc*) paire *f*; (*of people*) couple *m*; **~ of scissors** (paire de) ciseaux *mpl*; **~ of trousers** pantalon *m*

pajamas [pə'dʒɑːməz] (*US*) *npl* pyjama(s) *m(pl)*

Pakistan [pɑːkɪ'stɑːn] *n* Pakistan *m*; **~i** *adj* pakistanais(e) ♦ *n* Pakistanais(e)

pal [pæl] (*inf*) *n* copain(copine)

palace ['pæləs] *n* palais *m*

palatable ['pælətəbl] *adj* bon(bonne), agréable au goût

palate ['pælɪt] *n* palais *m* (*ANAT*)

pale [peɪl] *adj* pâle ♦ *n*: **beyond the ~** (*behaviour*) inacceptable; **to grow ~** pâlir

Palestine ['pælɪstaɪn] *n* Palestine *f*; **Palestinian** *adj* palestinien(ne) ♦ *n* Palestinien(ne)

palette ['pælɪt] *n* palette *f*

pall [pɔːl] *n* (*of smoke*) voile *m* ♦ *vi* devenir lassant(e)

pallet ['pælɪt] *n* (*for goods*) palette *f*

pallid ['pælɪd] *adj* blême

palm [pɑːm] *n* (*of hand*) paume *f*; (*also: ~ tree*) palmier *m* ♦ *vt*: **to ~ sth off on sb** (*inf*) refiler qch à qn; **P~ Sunday** *n* le dimanche des Rameaux

palpable ['pælpəbl] *adj* évident(e), manifeste

paltry ['pɔːltrɪ] *adj* dérisoire

pamper ['pæmpə*] *vt* gâter, dorloter

pamphlet ['pæmflət] *n* brochure *f*

pan [pæn] *n* (*also: sauce~*) casserole *f*; (: *frying ~*) poêle *f*

pancake ['pænkeɪk] *n* crêpe *f*

panda ['pændə] *n* panda *m*; **~ car** (*BRIT*) *n* ≈ voiture *f* pie *inv* (*de police*)

pandemonium [pændɪ'məunɪəm] *n* tohu-bohu *m*

pander ['pændə*] *vi*: **to ~ to** flatter bassement; obéir servilement à

pane [peɪn] *n* carreau *m*, vitre *f*

panel ['pænl] *n* (*of wood, cloth etc*) panneau *m*; (*RADIO, TV*) experts *mpl*; (*for interview, exams*) jury *m*; **~ling** (*US* **~ing**) *n* boiseries *fpl*

pang [pæŋ] *n*: **~s of remorse/jealousy** affres *mpl* du remords/de la jalousie; **~s of hunger/conscience** tiraillements *mpl* d'estomac/de la conscience

panic ['pænɪk] *n* panique *f*, affolement *m* ♦ *vi* s'affoler, paniquer; **~ky** *adj* (*person*) qui panique *or* s'affole facilement; **~-stricken** *adj* affolé(e)

pansy ['pænzɪ] *n* (*BOT*) pensée *f*; (*inf: pej*) tapette *f*, pédé *m*

pant [pænt] *vi* haleter

panther ['pænθə*] *n* panthère *f*

panties ['pæntɪz] *npl* slip *m*

pantomime ['pæntəmaɪm] (*BRIT*) *n* spectacle *m* de Noël

pantry ['pæntrɪ] *n* garde-manger *m inv*

pants [pænts] *npl* (*BRIT: woman's*) slip *m*; (: *man's*) slip, caleçon *m*; (*US: trousers*) pantalon *m*

pantyhose ['pæntɪhəuz] (*US*) *npl* collant *m*

paper ['peɪpə*] *n* papier *m*; (*also: wall~*) papier peint; (: *news~*) journal *m*; (*academic essay*) article *m*; (*exam*) épreuve écrite ♦ *adj* en or de papier ♦ *vt* tapisser (de papier peint); **~s** *npl* (*also: identity ~s*) papiers (d'identité); **~back** *n* livre *m* de poche; livre broché *or* non relié; **~ bag** *n* sac

m en papier; ~ **clip** *n* trombone *m*; ~
hankie *n* mouchoir *m* en papier; ~**weight**
n presse-papiers *m inv*; ~**work** *n* papiers
mpl; *(pej)* paperasserie *f*

par [pɑː*] *n* pair *m*; *(GOLF)* normale *f* du
parcours; **on a** ~ **with** à égalité avec, au
même niveau que

parable ['pærəbl] *n* parabole *f (REL)*

parachute ['pærəʃuːt] *n* parachute *m*

parade [pə'reɪd] *n* défilé *m* ♦ *vt (fig)* faire
étalage de ♦ *vi* défiler

paradise ['pærədaɪs] *n* paradis *m*

paradox ['pærədɒks] *n* paradoxe *m*; ~**ical-
ly** [pærə'dɒksɪkəlɪ] *adv* paradoxalement

paraffin ['pærəfɪn] *(BRIT) n (also:* ~ *oil)* pétrole (lampant)

paragon ['pærəgən] *n* modèle *m*

paragraph ['pærəgrɑːf] *n* paragraphe *m*

parallel ['pærəlel] *adj* parallèle; *(fig)* semblable ♦ *n (line)* parallèle *f*, *(fig, GEO)* parallèle *m*

paralyse ['pærəlaɪz] *(BRIT) vt* paralyser

paralysis [pə'ræləsɪs] *n* paralysie *f*

paralyze ['pærəlaɪz] *(US) vt* = **paralyse**

paramount ['pærəmaunt] *adj*: **of** ~ **importance** de la plus haute *or* grande importance

paranoid ['pærənɔɪd] *adj (PSYCH)* para-
noïaque

paraphernalia ['pærəfə'neɪlɪə] *n* attirail *m*

parasol ['pærəsɒl] *n* ombrelle *f*, *(over table)*
parasol *m*

paratrooper ['pærətruːpə*] *n* parachutiste
m (soldat)

parcel ['pɑːsl] *n* paquet *m*, colis *m* ♦ *vt
(also:* ~ *up)* empaqueter

parch [pɑːtʃ] *vt* dessécher; ~**ed** *adj (person)* assoiffé(e)

parchment ['pɑːtʃmənt] *n* parchemin *m*

pardon ['pɑːdn] *n* pardon *m*; grâce *f* ♦ *vt*
pardonner à; ~ **me!, I beg your** ~! pardon!, je suis désolé!; **(I beg your)** ~?, *(US)*
~ **me?** pardon?

parent ['pɛərənt] *n* père *m or* mère *f*; ~**s**
npl parents *mpl*

Paris ['pærɪs] *n* Paris

parish ['pærɪʃ] *n* paroisse *f*, *(BRIT: civil)* ≈
commune *f*

Parisian [pə'rɪzɪən] *adj* parisien(ne) ♦ *n* Pa-
risien(ne)

park [pɑːk] *n* parc *m*, jardin public ♦ *vt* garer ♦ *vi* se garer

parking ['pɑːkɪŋ] *n* stationnement *m*; "**no**
~" "stationnement interdit"; ~ **lot** *(US) n*
parking *m*, parc *m* de stationnement; ~
meter *n* parcomètre *m*; ~ **ticket** *n* P.V. *m*

parlance ['pɑːləns] *n* langage *m*

parliament ['pɑːləmənt] *n* parlement *m*;
~**ary** [pɑːlə'mentərɪ] *adj* parlementaire

parlour ['pɑːlə*] *(US* **parlor**) *n* salon *m*

parochial [pə'rəʊkɪəl] *(pej) adj* à l'esprit de
clocher

parody ['pærədɪ] *n* parodie *f*

parole [pə'rəʊl] *n*: **on** ~ en liberté condi-
tionnelle

parrot ['pærət] *n* perroquet *m*

parry ['pærɪ] *vt (blow)* esquiver

parsley ['pɑːslɪ] *n* persil *m*

parsnip ['pɑːsnɪp] *n* panais *m*

parson ['pɑːsn] *n* ecclésiastique *m*; *(Church
of England)* pasteur *m*

part [pɑːt] *n* partie *f*, *(of machine)* pièce *f*,
(THEATRE etc) rôle *m*; *(of serial)* épisode *m*;
(US: in hair) raie *f* ♦ *adv* = **partly** ♦ *vt* séparer ♦ *vi (people)* se séparer; *(crowd)* s'ouvrir; **to take** ~ **in** participer à, prendre part
à; **to take sth in good** ~ prendre qch du
bon côté; **to take sb's** ~ prendre le parti
de qn, prendre parti pour qn; **for my** ~ en
ce qui me concerne; **for the most** ~ dans
la plupart des cas; ~ **with** *vt fus* se séparer
de; ~ **exchange** *(BRIT) n*: **in** ~ **exchange**
en reprise

partial ['pɑːʃəl] *adj (not complete)* par-
tiel(le); **to be** ~ **to** avoir un faible pour

participate [pɑː'tɪsɪpeɪt] *vi*: **to** ~ **(in)** participer (à), prendre part (à); **participation**
[pɑːtɪsɪ'peɪʃən] *n* participation *f*

participle ['pɑːtɪsɪpl] *n* participe *m*

particle ['pɑːtɪkl] *n* particule *f*

particular [pə'tɪkjʊlə*] *adj* particulier(ère);
(special) spécial(e); *(fussy)* difficile; méti-
culeux(euse); ~**s** *npl (details)* détails *mpl*;
(personal) nom, adresse etc; **in** ~ en particulier; ~**ly** *adv* particulièrement

parting ['pɑːtɪŋ] *n* séparation *f*, *(BRIT: in
hair)* raie *f* ♦ *adj* d'adieu

partisan [pɑːtɪ'zæn] *n* partisan(e) ♦ *adj* par-
tisan(e); de parti

partition [pɑː'tɪʃən] *n (wall)* cloison *f*,
(POL) partition *f*, division *f*

partly ['pɑːtlɪ] *adv* en partie, partiellement

partner ['pɑːtnə*] *n* partenaire *m/f*; *(in marriage)* conjoint(e); *(boyfriend, girlfriend)*
ami(e); *(COMM)* associé(e); *(at dance)* cava-
lier(ère); ~**ship** *n* association *f*

partridge ['pɑːtrɪdʒ] *n* perdrix *f*

part-time ['pɑːt'taɪm] *adj, adv* à mi-temps,
à temps partiel

party ['pɑːtɪ] *n (POL)* parti *m*; *(group)* groupe *m*; *(LAW)* partie *f*, *(celebration)* réception
f, soirée *f*, fête *f* ♦ *cpd (POL)* de *or* du parti;
~ **dress** *n* robe habillée; ~ **line** *n (TEL)* ligne partagée

pass [pɑːs] *vt* passer; *(place)* passer devant;
(friend) croiser; *(overtake)* dépasser; *(exam)*
être reçu(e) à, réussir; *(approve)* approuver,
accepter ♦ *vi* passer; *(SCOL)* être reçu(e) or
admis(e), réussir ♦ *n (permit)* laissez-passer
m inv; carte *f* d'accès *or* d'abonnement; *(in
mountains)* col *m*; *(SPORT)* passe *f*, *(SCOL:
also:* ~ *mark)*: **to get a** ~ être reçu(e) (sans
mention); **to make a** ~ **at sb** *(inf)* faire des
avances à qn; ~ **away** *vi* mourir; ~ **by** *vi*

passer ♦ vt négliger; ~ **on** vt (news, object) transmettre; (illness) passer; ~ **out** vi s'évanouir; ~ **up** vt (opportunity) laisser passer; ~**able** adj (road) praticable; (work) acceptable

passage ['pæsɪdʒ] n (also: ~**way**) couloir m; (gen, in book) passage m; (by boat) traversée f

passbook ['pɑːsbʊk] n livret m

passenger ['pæsɪndʒə*] n passager(ère)

passer-by ['pɑːsə'baɪ] (pl ~**s-by**) n passant(e)

passing ['pɑːsɪŋ] adj (fig) passager(ère); **in** ~ en passant

passing place n (AUT) aire f de croisement

passion ['pæʃən] n passion f; ~**ate** adj passionné(e)

passive ['pæsɪv] adj (also LING) passif(ive); ~ **smoking** n tabagisme m passif

Passover ['pɑːsəʊvə*] n Pâque f (juive)

passport ['pɑːspɔːt] n passeport m; ~ **control** n contrôle m des passeports

password ['pɑːswɜːd] n mot m de passe

past [pɑːst] prep (in front of) devant; (further than) au delà de, plus loin que; après; (later than) après ♦ adj passé(e); (president etc) ancien(ne) ♦ n passé m; **he's** ~ **forty** il a dépassé la quarantaine, il a plus de or passé quarante ans; **for the** ~ **few/3 days** depuis quelques/3 jours; ces derniers/3 derniers jours; **ten/quarter** ~ **eight** huit heures dix/un or et quart

pasta ['pæstə] n pâtes fpl

paste [peɪst] n pâte f; (meat ~) pâté m (à tartiner); (tomato ~) purée f, concentré m; (glue) colle f (de pâte) ♦ vt coller

pasteurized ['pæstəraɪzd] adj pasteurisé(e)

pastille ['pæstl] n pastille f

pastime ['pɑːstaɪm] n passe-temps m inv

pastry ['peɪstrɪ] n pâte f; (cake) pâtisserie f

pasture ['pɑːstʃə*] n pâturage m

pasty [n 'pæstɪ, adj 'peɪstɪ] n petit pâté (en croûte) ♦ adj (complexion) terreux(euse)

pat [pæt] vt tapoter; (dog) caresser

patch [pætʃ] n (of material) pièce f; (eye ~) cache m; (spot) tache f; (on tyre) rustine f ♦ vt (clothes) rapiécer; **(to go through) a bad** ~ (passer par) une période difficile; ~ **up** vt réparer (grossièrement); **to** ~ **up a quarrel** se raccommoder; ~**y** adj inégal(e); (incomplete) fragmentaire

pâté ['pæteɪ] n pâté m, terrine f

patent ['peɪtənt] n brevet m (d'invention) ♦ vt faire breveter ♦ adj patent(e), manifeste; ~ **leather** n cuir verni

paternal [pə'tɜːnl] adj paternel(le)

path [pɑːθ] n chemin m, sentier m; (in garden) allée f; (trajectory) trajectoire f

pathetic [pə'θetɪk] adj (pitiful) pitoyable; (very bad) lamentable, minable

pathological [pæθə'lɒdʒɪkl] adj pathologique

pathos ['peɪθɒs] n pathétique m

pathway ['pɑːθweɪ] n sentier m, passage m

patience ['peɪʃəns] n patience f; (BRIT: CARDS) réussite f

patient ['peɪʃənt] n patient(e); malade m/f ♦ adj patient(e)

patriotic [pætrɪ'ɒtɪk] adj patriotique; (person) patriote

patrol [pə'trəʊl] n patrouille f ♦ vt patrouiller dans; ~ **car** n voiture f de police; ~**man** (irreg: US) n agent m de police

patron ['peɪtrən] n (in shop) client(e); (of charity) patron(ne); ~ **of the arts** mécène m; ~**ize** vt (pej) traiter avec condescendance; (shop, club) être (un) client or un habitué de

patter ['pætə*] n crépitement m, tapotement m; (sales talk) boniment m

pattern ['pætən] n (design) motif m; (SEWING) patron m

paunch [pɔːntʃ] n gros ventre, bedaine f

pauper ['pɔːpə*] n indigent(e)

pause [pɔːz] n pause f, arrêt m ♦ vi faire une pause, s'arrêter

pave [peɪv] vt paver, daller; **to** ~ **the way for** ouvrir la voie à; ~**ment** ['peɪvmənt] (BRIT) n trottoir m

pavilion [pə'vɪlɪən] n pavillon m; tente f

paving ['peɪvɪŋ] n (material) pavé m, dalle f; ~ **stone** n pavé m

paw [pɔː] n patte f

pawn [pɔːn] n (CHESS, also fig) pion m ♦ vt mettre en gage; ~**broker** n prêteur f sur gages; ~**shop** n mont-de-piété m

pay [peɪ] (pt, pp **paid**) n salaire m; paie f ♦ vt payer ♦ vi payer; (be profitable) être rentable; **to** ~ **attention (to)** prêter attention (à); **to** ~ **sb a visit** rendre visite à qn; **to** ~ **one's respects to sb** présenter ses respects à qn; ~ **back** vt rembourser; ~ **for** vt fus payer; ~ **in** vt verser; ~ **off** vt régler, acquitter; (person) rembourser ♦ vi (scheme, decision) se révéler payant(e); ~ **up** vt (money) payer; ~**able** adj: ~**able to sb** (cheque) à l'ordre de qn; ~**ee** [peɪ'iː] n bénéficiaire m/f; ~ **envelope** (US) n = pay packet; ~**ment** n paiement m; règlement m; **monthly** ~**ment** mensualité f; ~ **packet** (BRIT) n paie f; ~ **phone** n cabine f téléphonique, téléphone public; ~**roll** n registre m du personnel; ~ **slip** (BRIT) n bulletin m de paie; ~ **television** n chaînes fpl payantes

PC n abbr = **personal computer**

p.c. abbr = **per cent**

pea [piː] n (petit) pois

peace [piːs] n paix f; (calm) calme m, tranquillité f; ~**ful** adj paisible, calme

peach [piːtʃ] n pêche f

peacock ['piːkɒk] n paon m

peak [piːk] n (mountain) pic m, cime f; (of

cap) visière f; (fig: highest level) maximum m; (: of career, fame) apogée m; ~ **hours** npl heures fpl de pointe

peal [pi:l] n (of bells) carillon m; ~ **of laughter** éclat m de rire

peanut ['pi:nʌt] n arachide f, cacahuète f

pear [pɛə*] n poire f

pearl [pɜ:l] n perle f

peasant ['pezənt] n paysan(ne)

peat [pi:t] n tourbe f

pebble ['pebl] n caillou m, galet m

peck [pek] vt (also: ~ **at**) donner un coup de bec à ♦ n coup m de bec; (kiss) bise f; ~**ing** order n ordre m des préséances; ~**ish** (BRIT: inf) adj: **I feel** ~**ish** je mangerais bien quelque chose

peculiar [pɪ'kju:lɪə*] adj étrange, bizarre, curieux(euse); ~ **to** particulier(ère) à

pedal ['pedl] n pédale f ♦ vi pédaler

pedantic [pɪ'dæntɪk] adj pédant(e)

peddler ['pedlə*] n (of drugs) revendeur(euse)

pedestal ['pedɪstl] n piédestal m

pedestrian [pɪ'destrɪən] n piéton m; ~ **crossing** (BRIT) n passage clouté

pediatrics [pi:dɪ'ætrɪks] (US) n = **paediatrics**

pedigree ['pedɪgri:] n ascendance f; (of animal) pedigree m ♦ cpd (animal) de race

pee [pi:] (inf) vi faire pipi, pisser

peek [pi:k] vi jeter un coup d'œil (furtif)

peel [pi:l] n pelure f, épluchure f; (of orange, lemon) écorce f ♦ vt peler, éplucher ♦ vi (paint etc) s'écailler; (wallpaper) se décoller; (skin) peler

peep [pi:p] n (BRIT: look) coup d'œil furtif; (sound) pépiement m ♦ vi (BRIT) jeter un coup d'œil (furtif); ~ **out** (BRIT) vi se montrer (furtivement); ~**hole** n judas m

peer [pɪə*] vi: **to** ~ **at** regarder attentivement, scruter ♦ n (noble) pair m; (equal) pair, égal(e); ~**age** n pairie f

peeved [pi:vd] adj irrité(e), fâché(e)

peg [peg] n (for coat etc) patère f; (BRIT: also: clothes ~) pince f à linge

Peking [pi:'kɪŋ] n Pékin; **Pekin(g)ese** [pi:kɪ'ni:z] n (dog) pékinois m

pelican ['pelɪkən] n pélican m; ~ **crossing** (BRIT) n (AUT) feu m à commande manuelle

pellet ['pelɪt] n boulette f; (of lead) plomb m

pelt [pelt] vt: **to** ~ **sb (with)** bombarder qn (de) ♦ vi (rain) tomber à seaux; (inf: run) courir à toutes jambes ♦ n peau f

pelvis ['pelvɪs] n bassin m

pen [pen] n (for writing) stylo m; (for sheep) parc m

penal ['pi:nl] adj pénal(e); (system, colony) pénitentiaire; ~**ize** vt pénaliser

penalty ['penəltɪ] n pénalité f; sanction f; (fine) amende f; (SPORT) pénalisation f;

(FOOTBALL) penalty m; (RUGBY) pénalité f

penance ['penəns] n pénitence f

pence [pens] (BRIT) npl of **penny**

pencil ['pensl] n crayon m; ~ **case** n trousse f (d'écolier); ~ **sharpener** n taille-crayon(s) m inv

pendant ['pendənt] n pendentif m

pending ['pendɪŋ] prep en attendant ♦ adj en suspens

pendulum ['pendjuləm] n (of clock) balancier m

penetrate ['penɪtreɪt] vt pénétrer dans; pénétrer

penfriend ['penfrend] (BRIT) n correspondant(e)

penguin ['peŋgwɪn] n pingouin m

penicillin [penɪ'sɪlɪn] n pénicilline f

peninsula [pɪ'nɪnsjulə] n péninsule f

penis ['pi:nɪs] n pénis m, verge f

penitentiary [penɪ'tenʃərɪ] n prison f

penknife ['pennaɪf] n canif m

pen name n nom m de plume, pseudonyme m

penniless ['penɪləs] adj sans le sou

penny ['penɪ] (pl **pennies** or (BRIT) **pence**) n penny m; (US) = **cent**

penpal ['penpæl] n correspondant(e)

pension ['penʃən] n pension f; (from company) retraite f; ~**er** (BRIT) n retraité(e); ~ **fund** n caisse f de pension

Pentecost ['pentɪkɒst] n Pentecôte f

penthouse ['penthaus] n appartement m (de luxe) (en attique)

pent-up ['pentʌp] adj (feelings) refoulé(e)

penultimate [pɪ'nʌltɪmɪt] adj avant-dernier(ère)

people ['pi:pl] npl gens mpl; personnes fpl; (inhabitants) population f; (POL) peuple m ♦ n (nation, race) peuple m; **several** ~ **came** plusieurs personnes sont venues; ~ **say that** ... on dit que ...

pep [pep] (inf) n entrain m, dynamisme m; ~ **up** vt remonter

pepper ['pepə*] n poivre m; (vegetable) poivron m ♦ vt (fig): **to** ~ **with** bombarder de; ~**mint** n (sweet) pastille f de menthe

peptalk ['pepto:k] (inf) n (petit) discours d'encouragement

per [pɜ:*] prep par; ~ **hour** (miles etc) à l'heure; (fee) (de) l'heure; ~ **kilo** etc le kilo etc; ~ **annum** adv par an; ~ **capita** adj, adv par personne, par habitant

perceive [pə'si:v] vt percevoir; (notice) remarquer, s'apercevoir de

per cent [pə'sent] adv pour cent

percentage [pə'sentɪdʒ] n pourcentage m

perception [pə'sepʃən] n perception f; (insight) perspicacité f

perceptive [pə'septɪv] adj pénétrant(e); (person) perspicace

perch [pɜ:tʃ] n (fish) perche f; (for bird) perchoir m ♦ vi: **to** ~ **on** se percher sur

percolator ['pɜːkəleɪtə*] n cafetière f (électrique)

perennial [pə'renɪəl] adj perpétuel(le); (BOT) vivace

perfect [adj, n 'pɜːfɪkt, vb pə'fekt] adj parfait(e) ♦ n (also: ~ tense) parfait m ♦ vt parfaire; mettre au point; **~ly** adv parfaitement

perforate ['pɜːfəreɪt] vt perforer, percer; **perforation** [pɜːfə'reɪʃən] n perforation f

perform [pə'fɔːm] vt (carry out) exécuter; (concert etc) jouer, donner ♦ vi jouer; **~ance** n représentation f, spectacle m; (of an artist) interprétation f; (SPORT) performance f; (of car, engine) fonctionnement m; (of company, economy) résultats mpl; **~er** n artiste m/f, interprète m/f

perfume ['pɜːfjuːm] n parfum m

perfunctory [pə'fʌŋktərɪ] adj négligent(e), pour la forme

perhaps [pə'hæps] adv peut-être

peril ['perɪl] n péril m

perimeter [pə'rɪmɪtə*] n périmètre m

period ['pɪərɪəd] n période f; (HISTORY) époque f; (SCOL) cours m; (full stop) point m; (MED) règles fpl ♦ adj (costume, furniture) d'époque; **~ic(al)** [pɪərɪ'ɒdɪk(əl)] adj périodique; **~ical** n périodique m

peripheral [pə'rɪfərəl] adj périphérique ♦ n (COMPUT) périphérique m

perish ['perɪʃ] vi périr; (decay) se détériorer; **~able** adj périssable

perjury ['pɜːdʒərɪ] n parjure m, faux serment

perk [pɜːk] n avantage m; accessoire, à-côté m; ~ **up** vi (cheer up) se ragaillardir; **~y** adj (cheerful) guilleret(te)

perm [pɜːm] n (for hair) permanente f

permanent ['pɜːmənənt] adj permanent(e)

permeate ['pɜːmɪeɪt] vi s'infiltrer ♦ vt s'infiltrer dans; pénétrer

permissible [pə'mɪsəbl] adj permis(e), acceptable

permission [pə'mɪʃən] n permission f, autorisation f

permissive [pə'mɪsɪv] adj tolérant(e), permissif(ive)

permit [n 'pɜːmɪt, vb pə'mɪt] n permis m ♦ vt permettre

perpendicular [pɜːpən'dɪkjʊlə*] adj perpendiculaire

perplex [pə'pleks] vt (person) rendre perplexe

persecute ['pɜːsɪkjuːt] vt persécuter

persevere [pɜːsɪ'vɪə*] vi persévérer

Persian ['pɜːʃən] adj persan(e) ♦ n (LING) persan m; **the (~)** Gulf le golfe Persique

persist [pə'sɪst] vi: to ~ **(in doing)** persister or s'obstiner (à faire); **~ent** adj persistant(e), tenace

person ['pɜːsn] n personne f; **in** ~ en personne; **~al** adj personnel(le); **~al assis-**tant n secrétaire privé(e); **~al call** n communication privée; **~al column** n annonces personnelles; **~al computer** n ordinateur personnel; **~ality** [pɜːsə'nælɪtɪ] n personnalité f; **~ally** adv personnellement; **to take sth ~ally** se sentir visé(e) (par qch); **~al organizer** n filofax m (®); **~al stereo** n balladeur m

personnel [pɜːsə'nel] n personnel m

perspective [pə'spektɪv] n perspective f; **to get things into ~** faire la part des choses

Perspex ['pɜːspeks] (®) n plexiglas m (®)

perspiration [pɜːspə'reɪʃən] n transpiration f

persuade [pə'sweɪd] vt: to ~ **sb to do sth** persuader qn de faire qch

persuasion [pə'sweɪʒən] n persuasion f; (creed) religion f

pertaining [pɜː'teɪnɪŋ] : ~ **to** prép relatif(ive) à

peruse [pə'ruːz] vt lire (attentivement)

pervade [pɜː'veɪd] vt se répandre dans, envahir

perverse [pə'vɜːs] adj pervers(e); (contrary) contrariant(e); **pervert** [n 'pɜːvɜːt, vb pə'vɜːt] n perverti(e) ♦ vt pervertir; (words) déformer

pessimist ['pesɪmɪst] n pessimiste m/f; **~ic** [pesɪ'mɪstɪk] adj pessimiste

pest [pest] n animal m (or insecte m) nuisible; (fig) fléau m

pester ['pestə*] vt importuner, harceler

pet [pet] n animal familier ♦ cpd (favourite) favori(te) ♦ vt (stroke) caresser, câliner ♦ vi (inf) se peloter; **teacher's ~** chouchou m du professeur, ~ **hate** bête noire

petal ['petl] n pétale m

peter out ['piːtə-] vi (stream, conversation) tarir; (meeting) tourner court; (road) se perdre

petite [pə'tiːt] adj menu(e)

petition [pə'tɪʃən] n pétition f

petrified ['petrɪfaɪd] adj (fig) mort(e) de peur

petrol ['petrəl] (BRIT) n essence f; **two-star** ~ essence f ordinaire; **four-star** ~ super m; ~ **can** n bidon m à essence

petroleum [pɪ'trəʊlɪəm] n pétrole m

petrol: ~ **pump** (BRIT) n pompe f à essence; ~ **station** (BRIT) n station-service f; ~ **tank** (BRIT) n réservoir m (d'essence)

petticoat ['petɪkəʊt] n combinaison f

petty ['petɪ] adj (mean) mesquin(e); (unimportant) insignifiant(e), sans importance; ~ **cash** n caisse f des dépenses courantes; ~ **officer** n second-maître m

petulant ['petjʊlənt] adj boudeur(euse), irritable

pew [pjuː] n banc m (d'église)

pewter ['pjuːtə*] n étain m

phantom ['fæntəm] n fantôme m

pharmacy ['fɑːməsɪ] n pharmacie f

phase [feɪz] n phase f ♦ vt: **to ~ sth in/out** introduire/supprimer qch progressivement

PhD abbr = Doctor of Philosophy n (title) ≈ docteur m (en droit or lettres etc) ≈ doctorat m; titulaire m/f d'un doctorat

pheasant ['feznt] n faisan m

phenomenon [fɪ'nɒmɪnən] n (pl **phenomena**) n phénomène m

philosophical [fɪlə'sɒfɪkl] adj philosophique

philosophy [fɪ'lɒsəfɪ] n philosophie f

phobia ['fəubjə] n phobie f

phone [fəun] n téléphone m ♦ vt téléphoner; **to be on the ~** avoir le téléphone; (be calling) être au téléphone; **~ back** vt, vi rappeler; **~ up** vt téléphoner à ♦ vi téléphoner; **~ book** n annuaire m; **~ booth** n = **phone box**; **~ box** (BRIT) n cabine f téléphonique; **~ call** n coup m de fil or de téléphone; **~ card** n carte f de téléphone; **~-in** (BRIT) n (RADIO, TV) programme m à ligne ouverte

phonetics [fə'netɪks] n phonétique f

phoney ['fəunɪ] adj faux(fausse), factice; (person) pas franc(he), poseur(euse)

photo ['fəutəu] n photo f

photo...: **~copier** [-'kɒpɪə*] n photocopieuse f; **~copy** [-kɒpɪ] n photocopie f ♦ vt photocopier; **~graph** [-grɑːf] n photographie f ♦ vt photographier; **~grapher** [-grəfə*] n photographe m/f; **~graphy** [-grəfɪ] n photographie f

phrase [freɪz] n expression f; (LING) locution f ♦ vt exprimer; **~ book** n recueil m d'expressions (pour touristes)

physical ['fɪzɪkəl] adj physique; **~ education** n éducation f physique; **~ly** adv physiquement

physician [fɪ'zɪʃən] n médecin m

physicist ['fɪzɪsɪst] n physicien(ne)

physics ['fɪzɪks] n physique f

physiotherapy [fɪzɪə'θerəpɪ] n kinésithérapie f

physique [fɪ'ziːk] n physique m; constitution f

pianist ['pɪənɪst] n pianiste m/f

piano [pɪ'ænəu] n piano m

pick [pɪk] n (tool: also: **~axe**) pic m, pioche f ♦ vt choisir; (fruit etc) cueillir; (remove) prendre; (lock) forcer; **take your ~** faites votre choix; **the ~ of** le(la) meilleur(e) de; **to ~ one's nose** se mettre les doigts dans le nez; **to ~ one's teeth** se curer les dents; **to ~ a quarrel with sb** chercher noise à qn; **~ at** vt fus: **to ~ at one's food** manger du bout des dents, chipoter; **~ on** vt fus (person) harceler; **~ out** vt choisir; (distinguish) distinguer; **~ up** vi (improve) s'améliorer ♦ vt ramasser; (collect) passer prendre; (AUT: give lift to) prendre, emmener; (learn) apprendre; (RADIO) capter; **to ~ up speed** prendre de la vitesse; **to ~**

o.s. up se relever

picket ['pɪkɪt] n (in strike) piquet m de grève ♦ vt mettre un piquet de grève devant

pickle ['pɪkl] n (also: **~s**: as condiment) pickles mpl, petits légumes macérés dans du vinaigre ♦ vt conserver dans du vinaigre or dans de la saumure; **to be in a ~** (mess) être dans le pétrin

pickpocket ['pɪkpɒkɪt] n pickpocket m

pick-up ['pɪkʌp] n (small truck) pick-up m inv

picnic ['pɪknɪk] n pique-nique m

picture ['pɪktʃə*] n image f; (painting) peinture f, tableau m; (etching) gravure f; (photograph) photo(graphie) f; (drawing) dessin m; (film) film m; (fig) description f; tableau m ♦ vt se représenter; **the ~s** (BRIT: inf) le cinéma; **~ book** n livre d'images

picturesque [pɪktʃə'resk] adj pittoresque

pie [paɪ] n tourte f; (of fruit) tarte f; (of meat) pâté m en croûte

piece [piːs] n morceau m; (item): **a ~ of furniture/advice** un meuble/conseil ♦ vt: **to ~ together** rassembler; **to take to ~s** démonter; **~meal** adv (irregularly) au coup par coup; (bit by bit) par bouts; **~work** n travail m aux pièces

pie chart n graphique m circulaire, camembert m

pier [pɪə*] n jetée f

pierce [pɪəs] vt percer, transpercer

pig [pɪg] n cochon m, porc m

pigeon ['pɪdʒən] n pigeon m; **~hole** n casier m

piggy bank ['pɪgɪ-] n tirelire f

pig: **~headed** [-'hedɪd] adj entêté(e), têtu(e); **~let** n porcelet m, petit cochon; **~skin** [-skɪn] n peau m de porc; **~sty** [-staɪ] n porcherie f; **~tail** [-teɪl] n natte f, tresse f

pike [paɪk] n (fish) brochet m

pilchard ['pɪltʃəd] n pilchard m (sorte de sardine)

pile [paɪl] n (pillar, of books) pile f; (heap) tas m; (of carpet) poils mpl ♦ vt (also: ~ up) empiler, entasser ♦ vi (also: ~up) s'entasser, s'accumuler; **to ~ into** (car) s'entasser dans

piles [paɪlz] npl hémorroïdes fpl

pile-up ['paɪlʌp] n (AUT) télescopage m, collision f en série

pilfering ['pɪlfərɪŋ] n chapardage m

pilgrim ['pɪlgrɪm] n pèlerin m

pill [pɪl] n pilule f

pillage ['pɪlɪdʒ] vt piller

pillar ['pɪlə*] n pilier m; **~ box** (BRIT) n boîte f aux lettres

pillion ['pɪljən] n: **to ride ~** (on motorcycle) monter derrière

pillow ['pɪləu] n oreiller m; **~case** n taie f d'oreiller

pilot ['paɪlət] n pilote m ♦ cpd (scheme etc)

pilote, expérimental(e) ♦ vt piloter; ~ **light** n veilleuse f

pimp ['pɪmp] n souteneur m, maquereau m

pimple ['pɪmpl] n bouton m

pin [pɪn] n épingle f; (*TECH*) cheville f ♦ vt épingler; ~**s and needles** fourmis fpl; **to ~ sb down** (fig) obliger qn à répondre; **to ~ sth on sb** (fig) mettre qch sur le dos de qn

pinafore ['pɪnəfɔː*] n tablier m

pinball ['pɪnbɔːl] n flipper m

pincers ['pɪnsəz] npl tenailles fpl; (of crab etc) pinces fpl

pinch [pɪntʃ] n (of salt etc) pincée f ♦ vt pincer; (inf: steal) piquer, chiper; **at a ~** à la rigueur

pincushion ['pɪnkuʃən] n pelote f à épingles

pine [paɪn] n (also: ~ **tree**) pin m ♦ vi: **to ~ for** s'ennuyer de, désirer ardemment; ~ **away** vi dépérir

pineapple ['paɪnæpl] n ananas m

ping [pɪŋ] n (noise) tintement m; ~-**pong** ® n ping-pong m ®

pink [pɪŋk] adj rose ♦ n (colour) rose m; (*BOT*) œillet m, mignardise f

PIN (number) n code m confidentiel

pinpoint ['pɪnpɔɪnt] vt indiquer or localiser (avec précision); (problem) mettre le doigt sur

pint [paɪnt] n pinte f (BRIT = 0.57l; US = 0.47l); (*BRIT: inf*) ≈ demi m

pioneer [paɪə'nɪə*] n pionnier m

pious ['paɪəs] adj pieux(euse)

pip [pɪp] n (seed) pépin m; **the ~s** npl (*BRIT: time signal on radio*) le(s) top(s) sonore(s)

pipe [paɪp] n tuyau m, conduite f; (for smoking) pipe f ♦ vt amener par tuyau; ~**s** npl (also: bag~s) cornemuse f; ~ **down** (inf) vi se taire; ~ **cleaner** n cure-pipe m; ~ **dream** n chimère f, château m en Espagne; ~**line** n pipe-line m; ~**r** n joueur(euse) de cornemuse

piping ['paɪpɪŋ] adv: ~ **hot** très chaud(e)

pique [piːk] n dépit m

pirate ['paɪərɪt] n pirate m

Pisces ['paɪsiːz] n les Poissons mpl

piss [pɪs] (inf!) vi pisser; ~**ed** (inf!) adj (drunk) bourré(e)

pistol ['pɪstl] n pistolet m

piston ['pɪstən] n piston m

pit [pɪt] n trou m, fosse f; (also: coal ~) puits m de mine; (quarry) carrière f ♦ vt: **to ~ one's wits against sb** se mesurer à qn; ~**s** npl (*AUT*) aire f de service

pitch [pɪtʃ] n (*MUS*) ton m; (*BRIT: SPORT*) terrain m; (tar) poix f; (fig) degré m; point m ♦ vt (throw) lancer ♦ vi (fall) tomber; **to ~ a tent** dresser une tente; ~-**black** adj noir(e) (comme du cirage); ~**ed battle** n bataille rangée

piteous ['pɪtɪəs] adj pitoyable

pitfall ['pɪtfɔːl] n piège m

pith [pɪθ] n (of orange etc) intérieur m de l'écorce

pithy ['pɪθɪ] adj piquant(e)

pitiful ['pɪtɪful] adj (touching) pitoyable

pitiless ['pɪtɪləs] adj impitoyable

pittance ['pɪtəns] n salaire m de misère

pity ['pɪtɪ] n pitié f ♦ vt plaindre; **what a ~!** quel dommage!

pizza ['piːtsə] n pizza f

placard ['plækɑːd] n affiche f; (in march) pancarte f

placate [plə'keɪt] vt apaiser, calmer

place [pleɪs] n endroit m, lieu m; (proper position, job, rank, seat) place f; (home): **at/to his ~** chez lui ♦ vt (object) placer, mettre; (identify) situer; reconnaître; **to take ~** avoir lieu; **out of ~** (not suitable) déplacé(e), inopportun(e); **to change ~s with sb** changer de place avec qn; **in the first ~** d'abord, en premier

plague [pleɪg] n fléau m; (*MED*) peste f ♦ vt (fig) tourmenter

plaice [pleɪs] n inv carrelet m

plaid [plæd] n tissu écossais

plain [pleɪn] adj (in one colour) uni(e); (simple) simple; (clear) clair(e), évident(e); (not handsome) quelconque, ordinaire ♦ adv franchement, carrément ♦ n plaine f; ~ **chocolate** n chocolat m à croquer; ~ **clothes** adj (police officer) en civil; ~**ly** adv clairement; (frankly) carrément, sans détours

plaintiff ['pleɪntɪf] n plaignant(e)

plait [plæt] n tresse f, natte f

plan [plæn] n plan m; (scheme) projet m ♦ vt (think in advance) projeter; (prepare) organiser; (house) dresser les plans de, concevoir ♦ vi faire des projets; **to ~ to do** prévoir de faire

plane [pleɪn] n (*AVIAT*) avion m; (*ART, MATH etc*) plan m; (fig) niveau m, plan; (tool) rabot m; (also: ~ **tree**) platane m ♦ vt raboter

planet ['plænɪt] n planète f

plank [plæŋk] n planche f

planner ['plænə*] n planificateur(trice); (town ~) urbaniste m/f

planning ['plænɪŋ] n planification f; **family ~** planning familial; ~ **permission** n permis m de construire

plant [plɑːnt] n plante f; (machinery) matériel m; (factory) usine f ♦ vt planter; (bomb) poser; (microphone, incriminating evidence) cacher

plaster ['plɑːstə*] n plâtre m; (also: ~ **of Paris**) plâtre à mouler; (*BRIT: also: sticking* ~) pansement adhésif ♦ vt plâtrer; (cover): **to ~ with** couvrir de; ~**ed** (inf) adj soûl(e)

plastic ['plæstɪk] n plastique m ♦ adj (made of ~) en plastique; ~ **bag** n sac m en plastique

Plasticine ['plæstɪsiːn] (®) n pâte f à modeler

plastic surgery n chirurgie f esthétique

plate [pleɪt] n (dish) assiette f; (in book) gravure f, planche f; (dental ~) dentier m

plateau ['plætəʊ] (pl ~s or ~x) n plateau m

plate glass n verre m (de vitrine)

platform ['plætfɔːm] n (stage) plate-forme f; (at meeting) tribune f; (stage) estrade f; (RAIL) quai m

platinum ['plætɪnəm] n platine m

platter ['plætə*] n plat m

plausible ['plɔːzɪbl] adj plausible; (person) convaincant(e)

play [pleɪ] n (THEATRE) pièce f (de théâtre) ♦ vt (game) jouer à; (team, opponent) jouer contre; (instrument) jouer de; (part, piece of music, note) jouer; (record etc) passer ♦ vi jouer; **to ~ safe** ne prendre aucun risque; **~ down** vt minimiser; **~ up** vi (cause trouble) faire des siennes; **~boy** n playboy m; **~er** n joueur(euse); (THEATRE) acteur(trice); (MUS) musicien(ne); **~ful** adj enjoué(e); **~ground** n cour f de récréation; (in park) aire f de jeux; **~group** n garderie f; **~ing card** n carte f à jouer; **~ing field** n terrain m de sport; **~mate** n camarade m/f, copain(copine); **~-off** n (SPORT) belle f; **~pen** n parc m (pour bébé); **~thing** n jouet m; **~time** n récréation f; **~wright** n dramaturge m

plc abbr (= public limited company) ≈ SARL f

plea [pliː] n (request) appel m; (LAW) défense f

plead [pliːd] vt plaider; (give as excuse) invoquer ♦ vi (LAW) plaider; (beg): **to ~ with sb** implorer qn

pleasant ['pleznt] adj agréable; **~ries** npl (polite remarks) civilités fpl

please [pliːz] excl s'il te (or vous) plaît ♦ vt plaire à ♦ vi plaire; (think fit): **do as you ~** faites ce qu'il vous plaira; **~ yourself!** à ta (or votre) guise!; **~d** adj: **~d (with)** content(e) (de); **~d to meet you** enchanté (de faire votre connaissance); **pleasing** ['pliːzɪŋ] adj agréable(e), qui fait plaisir

pleasure ['pleʒə*] n plaisir m; "**it's a ~**" "je vous en prie"; **~ boat** n bateau m de plaisance

pleat [pliːt] n pli m

pledge [pledʒ] n (promise) promesse f ♦ vt engager; promettre

plentiful ['plentɪfʊl] adj abondant(e), copieux(euse)

plenty ['plentɪ] n: **~ of** beaucoup de; (bien) assez de

pliable ['plaɪəbl] adj flexible; (person) malléable

pliers ['plaɪəz] npl pinces fpl

plight [plaɪt] n situation f critique

plimsolls ['plɪmsəlz] (BRIT) npl chaussures

fpl de tennis, tennis mpl

plinth [plɪnθ] n (of statue) socle m

PLO n abbr (= Palestine Liberation Organization) OLP f

plod [plɒd] vi avancer péniblement; (fig) peiner

plonk [plɒŋk] (inf) n (BRIT: wine) pinard m, piquette f ♦ vt: **to ~ sth down** poser brusquement qch

plot [plɒt] n complot m, conspiration f; (of story, play) intrigue f; (of land) lot m de terrain, lopin m ♦ vt (sb's downfall) comploter; (mark out) pointer; relever, déterminer ♦ vi comploter

plough [plaʊ] (US **plow**) n charrue f ♦ vt (earth) labourer; **to ~ money into** investir dans; **~ through** vt fus (snow etc) avancer péniblement dans; **~man's lunch** (BRIT) n assiette froide avec du pain, du fromage et des pickles

ploy [plɔɪ] n stratagème m

pluck [plʌk] vt (fruit) cueillir; (musical instrument) pincer; (bird) plumer; (eyebrow) épiler ♦ n courage m, cran m; **to ~ up courage** prendre son courage à deux mains

plug [plʌg] n (ELEC) prise f de courant; (stopper) bouchon m, bonde f; (AUT: also: sparking ~) bougie f ♦ vt (hole) boucher; (inf: advertise) faire du battage pour; **~ in** vt (ELEC) brancher

plum [plʌm] n (fruit) prune f ♦ cpd: **~ job** (inf) travail m en or

plumber ['plʌmə*] n plombier m

plumbing ['plʌmɪŋ] n (trade) plomberie f; (piping) tuyauterie f

plummet ['plʌmɪt] vi: **to ~ (down)** plonger, dégringoler

plump [plʌmp] adj rondelet(te), dodu(e), bien en chair ♦ vi: **to ~ for** (col: choose) se décider pour

plunder ['plʌndə*] n pillage m (loot) butin m ♦ vt piller

plunge [plʌndʒ] n plongeon m; (fig) chute f ♦ vt plonger ♦ vi (dive) plonger (fall) tomber, dégringoler; **to take the ~** se jeter à l'eau; **~r** n (for drain) (débouchoir m à) ventouse f; **plunging** adj: **plunging neckline** décolleté plongeant

pluperfect [pluːˈpɜːfɪkt] n plus-que-parfait m

plural ['plʊərəl] adj pluriel(le) ♦ n pluriel m

plus [plʌs] n (also: ~ sign) signe m plus ♦ prep plus; **ten/twenty ~** plus de dix/vingt

plush [plʌʃ] adj somptueux(euse)

ply [plaɪ] vt (a trade) exercer ♦ vi (ship) faire la navette ♦ n (of wool, rope) fil m, brin m; **to ~ sb with drink** donner continuellement à boire à qn; **to ~ sb with questions** presser qn de questions; **~wood** n contre-plaqué m

PM *abbr* = **Prime Minister**

p.m. *adv abbr* (= *post meridiem*) de l'après-midi

pneumatic drill [nju:'mætɪk-] *n* marteau-piqueur *m*

pneumonia [nju:'məunɪə] *n* pneumonie *f*

poach [pəutʃ] *vt* (*cook*) pocher; (*steal*) pêcher (*or* chasser) sans permis ♦ *vi* braconner; ~**ed egg** *n* œuf poché; ~**er** *n* braconnier *m*

P.O. Box *n abbr* = **Post Office Box**

pocket ['pɔkɪt] *n* poche *f* ♦ *vt* empocher; **to be out of** ~ (*BRIT*) en être de sa poche; ~**book** (*US*) *n* (*wallet*) portefeuille *m*; ~ **knife** *n* canif *m*; ~ **money** *n* argent *m* de poche

pod [pɔd] *n* cosse *f*

podgy ['pɔdʒɪ] *adj* rondelet(te)

podiatrist [pɔ'di:ətrɪst] (*US*) *n* pédicure *m/f*, podologue *m/f*

poem ['pəuəm] *n* poème *m*

poet ['pəuɪt] *n* poète *m*; ~**ic** *adj* poétique; ~ **laureate** *n* poète lauréat (*nommé par la Cour royal*); ~**ry** *n* poésie *f*

poignant ['pɔɪnjənt] *adj* poignant(e); (*sharp*) vif(vive)

point [pɔɪnt] *n* point *m*; (*tip*) pointe *f*, (*in time*) moment *m*; (*in space*) endroit *m*; (*subject, idea*) point, sujet *m*; (*purpose*) sens *m*; (*ELEC*) prise *f*; (*also: decimal* ~): **2** ~ **3 (2.3)** 2 virgule 3 (2,3) ♦ *vt* (*show*) indiquer; (*gun etc*): **to** ~ **sth at** braquer *or* diriger qch sur ♦ *vi*: **to** ~ **at** montrer du doigt; ~**s** *npl* (*AUT*) vis platinées; (*RAIL*) aiguillage *m*; **to be on the** ~ **of doing sth** être sur le point de faire qch; **to make a** ~ **of doing** ne pas manquer de faire; **to get the** ~ comprendre, saisir; **to miss the** ~ ne pas comprendre; **to come to the** ~ en venir au fait; **there's no** ~ (**in doing**) cela ne sert à rien (de faire); ~ **out** *vt* faire remarquer, souligner; ~ **to** *vt fus* (*fig*) indiquer; ~**-blank** *adv* (*fig*) catégoriquement; (*also: at* ~*-blank range*) à bout portant; ~**ed** *adj* (*shape*) pointu(e); (*remark*) plein(e) de sous-entendus; ~**er** *n* (*needle*) aiguille *f*; (*piece of advice*) conseil *m*; (*clue*) indice *m*; ~**less** *adj* inutile, vain(e); ~ **of view** *n* point *m* de vue

poise [pɔɪz] *n* (*composure*) calme *m*

poison ['pɔɪzn] *n* poison *m* ♦ *vt* empoisonner; ~**ous** *adj* (*snake*) venimeux(euse); (*plant*) vénéneux(euse); (*fumes etc*) toxique

poke [pəuk] *vt* (*fire*) tisonner; (*jab with finger, stick etc*) piquer; pousser du doigt; (*put*): **to** ~ **sth in(to)** fourrer *or* enfoncer qch dans; ~ **about** *vi* fureter

poker ['pəukə*] *n* tisonnier *m*; (*CARDS*) poker *m*

poky ['pəukɪ] *adj* exigu(ë)

Poland ['pəulənd] *n* Pologne *f*

polar ['pəulə*] *adj* polaire; ~ **bear** *n* ours blanc

Pole [pəul] *n* Polonais(e)

pole [pəul] *n* poteau *m*; (*of wood*) mât *m*, perche *f*, (*GEO*) pôle *m*; ~ **bean** (*US*) *n* haricot *m* (à rames); ~ **vault** *n* saut *m* à la perche

police [pə'li:s] *npl* police *f* ♦ *vt* maintenir l'ordre dans; ~ **car** *n* voiture *f* de police; ~**man** (*irreg*) *n* agent *m* de police, policier *m*; ~ **station** *n* commissariat *m* de police; ~**woman** (*irreg*) *n* femme-agent *f*

policy ['pɔlɪsɪ] *n* politique *f*; (*also: insurance* ~) police *f* (d'assurance)

polio ['pəulɪəu] *n* polio *f*

Polish ['pəulɪʃ] *adj* polonais(e) ♦ *n* (*LING*) polonais *m*

polish ['pɔlɪʃ] *n* (*for shoes*) cirage *m*; (*for floor*) cire *f*, encaustique *f*; (*shine*) éclat *m*, poli *m*; (*fig: refinement*) raffinement *m* ♦ *vt* (*put polish on shoes, wood*) cirer; (*make shiny*) astiquer, faire briller; ~ **off** *vt* (*work*) expédier; (*food*) liquider; ~**ed** *adj* (*fig*) raffiné(e)

polite [pə'laɪt] *adj* poli(e); **in** ~ **society** dans la bonne société; ~**ness** *n* politesse *f*

political [pə'lɪtɪkəl] *adj* politique

politician [pɔlɪ'tɪʃən] *n* homme *m* politique, politicien *m*

politics ['pɔlɪtɪks] *npl* politique *f*

poll [pəul] *n* scrutin *m*, vote *m*; (*also: opinion* ~) sondage *m* (d'opinion) ♦ *vt* obtenir

pollen ['pɔlən] *n* pollen *m*

polling day ['pəulɪŋ-] (*BRIT*) *n* jour *m* des élections

polling station (*BRIT*) *n* bureau *m* de vote

pollute [pə'lu:t] *vt* polluer; **pollution** *n* pollution *f*

polo ['pəuləu] *n* polo *m*; ~**-necked** *adj* à col roulé; ~ **shirt** *n* polo *m*

poltergeist ['pɔltəgaɪst] *n* esprit frappeur

polyester [pɔlɪ'estə*] *n* polyester *m*

polytechnic [pɔlɪ'teknɪk] (*BRIT*) *n* (*college*) I.U.T. *m*, Institut *m* Universitaire de Technologie

polythene ['pɔlɪθi:n] *n* polyéthylène *m*; ~ **bag** *n* sac *m* en plastique

pomegranate ['pɔmǝgrænɪt] *n* grenade *f*

pomp [pɔmp] *n* pompe *f*, faste *f*, apparat *m*; ~**ous** ['pɔmpəs] *adj* pompeux(euse)

pond [pɔnd] *n* étang *m*; mare *f*

ponder ['pɔndə*] *vt* considérer, peser; ~**ous** *adj* pesant(e), lourd(e)

pong [pɔŋ] (*BRIT: inf*) *n* puanteur *f*

pony ['pəunɪ] *n* poney *m*; ~**tail** *n* queue *f* de cheval; ~ **trekking** (*BRIT*) *n* randonnée *f* à cheval

poodle ['pu:dl] *n* caniche *m*

pool [pu:l] *n* (*of rain*) flaque *f*; (*pond*) mare *f*; (*also: swimming* ~) piscine *f*; (*billiards*) poule *f* ♦ *vt* mettre en commun; ~**s** *npl* (*football pools*) ≈ loto sportif

poor [puə*] *adj* pauvre; (*mediocre*) médiocre, faible, mauvais(e) ♦ npl: **the** ~ les pauvres mpl; **~ly** adj souffrant(e), malade ♦ adv mal; médiocrement

pop [pɒp] n (MUS) musique f pop; (drink) boisson gazeuse; (US: inf: father) papa m; (noise) bruit sec ♦ vt (put) mettre (rapidement) ♦ vi éclater; (cork) sauter; ~ **in** vi entrer en passant; ~ **out** vi sortir (brièvement); ~ **up** vi apparaître, surgir

pope [pəʊp] n pape m

poplar ['pɒplə*] n peuplier m

popper ['pɒpə*] (BRIT: inf) n bouton-pression m

poppy ['pɒpɪ] n coquelicot m; pavot m

Popsicle ['pɒpsɪkl] (®: US) n esquimau m (glace)

popular ['pɒpjʊlə*] adj populaire; (fashionable) à la mode

population [pɒpjʊ'leɪʃən] n population f

porcelain ['pɔːslɪn] n porcelaine f

porch [pɔːtʃ] n porche m; (US) véranda f

porcupine ['pɔːkjʊpaɪn] n porc-épic m

pore [pɔː*] n pore m ♦ vi: **to** ~ **over** s'absorber dans, être plongé(e) dans

pork [pɔːk] n porc m

pornography [pɔː'nɒgrəfɪ] n pornographie f

porpoise ['pɔːpəs] n marsouin m

porridge ['pɒrɪdʒ] n porridge m

port [pɔːt] n (harbour) port m; (NAUT: left side) bâbord m; (wine) porto m; ~ **of call** escale f

portable ['pɔːtəbl] adj portatif(ive)

porter ['pɔːtə*] n (for luggage) porteur m; (doorkeeper) gardien(ne); portier m

portfolio [pɔːt'fəʊlɪəʊ] n portefeuille m; (of artist) portfolio m

porthole ['pɔːthəʊl] n hublot m

portion ['pɔːʃən] n portion f, part f

portly ['pɔːtlɪ] adj corpulent(e)

portrait ['pɔːtrɪt] n portrait m

portray [pɔː'treɪ] vt faire le portrait de; (in writing) dépeindre, représenter; (subj: actor) jouer; **~al** n portrait m, représentation f

Portugal ['pɔːtjʊgəl] n Portugal m

Portuguese [pɔːtjuˈgiːz] adj portugais(e) ♦ n inv Portugais(e); (LING) portugais m

pose [pəʊz] n pose f ♦ vi (pretend): **to** ~ **as** se poser en ♦ vt poser; (problem) créer

posh [pɒʃ] (inf) adj chic inv

position [pə'zɪʃən] n position f; (job) situation f ♦ vt placer

positive ['pɒzɪtɪv] adj positif(ive); (certain) sûr(e), certain(e); (definite) formel(le), catégorique

posse ['pɒsɪ] (US) n détachement m

possess [pə'zes] vt posséder; **~ion** [pə'zeʃən] n possession f

possibility [pɒsə'bɪlɪtɪ] n possibilité f; éventualité f

possible ['pɒsəbl] adj possible; **as big as** ~ aussi gros que possible

possibly ['pɒsəblɪ] adv (perhaps) peut-être; **if you** ~ **can** si cela vous est possible; **I cannot** ~ **come** il m'est impossible de venir

post [pəʊst] n poste f; (BRIT: letters, delivery) courrier m; (job, situation, MIL) poste m; (pole) poteau m ♦ vt (BRIT: send by ~) poster; (: appoint): **to** ~ **to** affecter à; **~age** n tarifs mpl d'affranchissement; **~al order** n mandat(-poste) m; **~box** (BRIT) n boîte f aux lettres; **~card** n carte postale; **~code** (BRIT) n code postal

poster ['pəʊstə*] n affiche f

poste restante ['pəʊst'restɑːnt] (BRIT) n poste restante

postgraduate ['pəʊst'grædjuɪt] n ≈ étudiant(e) de troisième cycle

posthumous ['pɒstjʊməs] adj posthume

postman ['pəʊstmən] (irreg) n facteur m

postmark ['pəʊstmɑːk] n cachet m (de la poste)

postmortem ['pəʊst'mɔːtəm] n autopsie f

post office n (building) poste f; (organization): **the Post Office** les Postes; **Post Office Box** n boîte postale

postpone [pə'spəʊn] vt remettre (à plus tard)

posture ['pɒstʃə*] n posture f; (fig) attitude f

postwar ['pəʊst'wɔː*] adj d'après-guerre

posy ['pəʊzɪ] n petit bouquet

pot [pɒt] n pot m; (for cooking) marmite f; casserole f; (tea~) théière f; (coffee~) cafetière f; (inf: marijuana) herbe f ♦ vt (plant) mettre en pot; **to go to** ~ (inf: work, performance) aller à vau-l'eau

potato [pə'teɪtəʊ] (pl ~es) n pomme f de terre; ~ **peeler** n épluche-légumes m inv

potent ['pəʊtənt] adj puissant(e); (drink) fort(e), très alcoolisé(e); (man) viril

potential [pəʊ'tenʃəl] adj potentiel(le) ♦ n potentiel m

pothole ['pɒthəʊl] n (in road) nid m de poule; (BRIT: underground) gouffre m, caverne f; **potholing** ['pɒthəʊlɪŋ] (BRIT) n: **to go potholing** faire de la spéléologie

potluck ['pɒt'lʌk] n: **to take** ~ tenter sa chance

potted ['pɒtɪd] adj (food) en conserve; (plant) en pot; (abbreviated) abrégé(e)

potter ['pɒtə*] n potier m ♦ vi: **to** ~ **around**, ~ **about** (BRIT) bricoler; **~y** n poterie f

potty ['pɒtɪ] adj (inf: mad) dingue ♦ n (child's) pot m

pouch [paʊtʃ] n (ZOOL) poche f; (for tobacco) blague f; (for money) bourse f

poultry ['pəʊltrɪ] n volaille f

pounce [paʊns] vi: **to** ~ **(on)** bondir (sur), sauter (sur)

pound [paʊnd] n (unit of money) livre f; (unit of weight) livre ♦ vt (beat) bourrer de

coups, marteler; (*crush*) piler, pulvériser ♦
vi (*heart*) battre violemment, taper

pour [pɔ:*] vt verser ♦ vi couler à flots; **to
~ (with rain)** pleuvoir à verse; **to ~ sb a
drink** verser *or* servir à boire à qn; **~
away** vt vider; **~ in** vi (*people*) affluer, se
précipiter; (*news, letters etc*) arriver en masse; **~ off** vt = **pour away**; **~ out** vi (*people*) sortir en masse ♦ vt vider; (*fig*) déverser; (*serve: a drink*) verser; **~ing** adj; **~ing
rain** pluie torrentielle

pout [paut] vi faire la moue

poverty ['pɔvətɪ] n pauvreté f, misère f; **~-
stricken** adj pauvre, déshérité(e)

powder ['paudə*] n poudre f ♦ vt: **to ~
one's face** se poudrer; **~ compact** n poudrier m; **~ed milk** n lait m en poudre; **~
puff** n houppette f; **~ room** n toilettes fpl
(pour dames)

power ['pauə*] n (*strength*) puissance f,
force f; (*ability, authority*) pouvoir m; (*of
speech, thought*) faculté f; (ELEC) courant
m; **to be in ~** (POL *etc*) être au pouvoir; **~
cut** (BRIT) n coupure f de courant; **~ed**
adj: **~ed by** actionné(e) par, fonctionnant
à; **~ failure** n panne f de courant; **~ful**
adj puissant(e); **~less** adj impuissant(e); **~
point** (BRIT) n prise f de courant; **~ station** n centrale f électrique

p.p. abbr (= *per procurationem*): **~ J. Smith**
pour M. J. Smith

PR n abbr = **public relations**

practical ['præktɪkəl] adj pratique; **~ities**
npl (*of situation*) aspect m pratique; **~ity**
(*no pl*) n (*of person*) sens m pratique; **~
joke** n farce f; **~ly** adv (*almost*) pratiquement

practice ['præktɪs] n pratique f; (*of profession*) exercice m; (*at football etc*) entraînement m; (*business*) cabinet m ♦ vt, vi
(US) = **practise**; **in ~** (*in reality*) en pratique; **out of ~** rouillé(e)

practise ['præktɪs] (US **practice**) vt (*musical
instrument*) travailler; (*train for: sport*) s'entraîner à; (*a sport, religion*) pratiquer; (*profession*) exercer ♦ vi s'exercer, travailler;
(*train*) s'entraîner; (*lawyer, doctor*) exercer;
practising ['præktɪsɪŋ] adj (*Christian etc*)
pratiquant(e); (*lawyer*) en exercice

practitioner [præk'tɪʃənə*] n praticien(ne)

prairie ['prɛərɪ] n steppe f, prairie f

praise [preɪz] n éloge(s) m(pl), louange(s)
f(pl) ♦ vt louer, faire l'éloge de; **~worthy**
adj digne d'éloges

pram [præm] (BRIT) n landau m, voiture f
d'enfant

prance [prɑ:ns] vi (*also: to ~ about: person*)
se pavaner

prank [præŋk] n farce f

prawn [prɔ:n] n crevette f (rose)

pray [preɪ] vi prier; **~er** [prɛə*] n prière
f

preach [pri:tʃ] vt, vi prêcher

precaution [prɪ'kɔ:ʃən] n précaution f

precede [prɪ'si:d] vt précéder

precedent ['presɪdənt] n précédent m

precinct ['pri:sɪŋkt] n (US) circonscription
f, arrondissement m; **~s** npl (*neighbourhood*) alentours mpl, environs mpl; **pedestrian ~** (BRIT) zone piétonnière; **shopping
~** (BRIT) centre commercial

precious ['preʃəs] adj précieux(euse)

precipitate [vb prɪ'sɪpɪteɪt] vt précipiter

precise [prɪ'saɪs] adj précis(e); **~ly** adv précisément

preclude [prɪ'klu:d] vt exclure

precocious [prɪ'kəuʃəs] adj précoce

precondition ['pri:kən'dɪʃən] n condition f
nécessaire

predecessor ['pri:dɪsesə*] n prédécesseur
m

predicament [prɪ'dɪkəmənt] n situation f
difficile

predict [prɪ'dɪkt] vt prédire; **~able** adj prévisible

predominantly [prɪ'dɒmɪnəntlɪ] adv en
majeure partie; surtout

preempt vt anticiper, devancer

preen [pri:n] vt: **to ~ itself** (*bird*) se lisser
les plumes; **to ~ o.s.** s'admirer

prefab ['pri:fæb] n bâtiment préfabriqué

preface ['prefɪs] n préface f

prefect ['pri:fekt] (BRIT) n (*in school*) élève
chargé(e) de certaines fonctions de discipline

prefer [prɪ'fɜ:*] vt préférer; **~ably** adv de
préférence; **~ence** n préférence f; **~ential**
adj: **~ential treatment** traitement m de faveur *or* préférentiel

prefix ['pri:fɪks] n préfixe m

pregnancy ['pregnənsɪ] n grossesse f

pregnant ['pregnənt] adj enceinte; (*animal*)
pleine

prehistoric ['pri:hɪs'tɔrɪk] adj préhistorique

prejudice ['predʒudɪs] n préjugé m; **~d** adj
(*person*) plein(e) de préjugés; (*in a matter*)
partial(e)

premarital ['pri:'mærɪtl] adj avant le mariage

premature ['premətʃuə*] adj prématuré(e)

premier ['premɪə*] adj premier(ère), princi-
pal(e) ♦ n (POL) Premier ministre

première [premɪ'ɛə*] n première f

premise ['premɪs] n prémisse f; **~s** npl
(*building*) locaux mpl; **on the ~s** sur les
lieux; sur place

premium ['pri:mɪəm] n prime f; **to be at a
~** faire prime; **~ bond** (BRIT) n bon m à
lot, obligation f à prime

premonition [premə'nɪʃən] n prémonition
f

preoccupied [pri:'ɒkjupaɪd] adj préoc-
cupé(e)

prep [prep] n (SCOL: *study*) étude f

prepaid ['priː'peɪd] *adj* payé(e) d'avance

preparation [prepə'reɪʃən] *n* préparation *f*; ~s *npl* (*for trip, war*) préparatifs *mpl*

preparatory [prɪ'pærətərɪ] *adj* préliminaire; ~ **school** (*BRIT*) *n* école primaire privée

prepare [prɪ'peə*] *vt* préparer ♦ *vi*: **to ~ for** se préparer à; ~**d to** prêt(e) à

preposition [prepə'zɪʃən] *n* préposition *f*

preposterous [prɪ'postərəs] *adj* absurde

prep school *n* = **preparatory school**

prerequisite ['priː'rekwɪzɪt] *n* condition *f* préalable

prescribe [prɪs'kraɪb] *vt* prescrire

prescription [prɪs'krɪpʃən] *n* (*MED*) ordonnance *f*; (: *medicine*) médicament (obtenu sur ordonnance)

presence ['prezns] *n* présence *f*; ~ **of mind** présence d'esprit

present [*adj, n* 'preznt, *vb* prɪ'zent] *adj* présent(e) ♦ *n* (*gift*) cadeau *m*; (*actuality*) présent *m* ♦ *vt* présenter; (*prize, medal*) remettre; (*give*): **to ~ sb with sth** *or* **sth to sb** offrir qch à qn; **to give sb a ~** offrir un cadeau à qn; **at ~** en ce moment; ~**ation** *n* présentation *f*; (*ceremony*) remise *f* du cadeau (*or* de la médaille *etc*); ~**-day** *adj* contemporain(e), actuel(le); ~**er** *n* (*RADIO, TV*) présentateur(trice); ~**ly** *adv* (*with verb in past*) peu après; (*soon*) tout à l'heure, bientôt; (*at present*) en ce moment

preservative [prɪ'zɜːvətɪv] *n* agent *m* de conservation

preserve [prɪ'zɜːv] *vt* (*keep safe*) préserver, protéger; (*maintain*) conserver, garder; (*food*) mettre en conserve ♦ *n* (*often pl:* jam) confiture *f*

president ['prezɪdənt] *n* président(e); ~**ial** *adj* présidentiel(le)

press [pres] *n* presse *f*; (*for wine*) pressoir *m* ♦ *vt* (*squeeze*) presser, serrer; (*push*) appuyer sur; (*clothes: iron*) repasser; (*put pressure on*) faire pression sur; (*insist*): **to ~ sth on sb** presser qn d'accepter qch ♦ *vi* appuyer, peser; **to ~ for sth** faire pression pour obtenir qch; **we are ~ed for time/ money** le temps/l'argent nous manque; ~ **on** *vi* continuer; ~ **conference** *n* conférence *f* de presse; ~**ing** *adj* urgent(e), pressant(e); ~ **stud** (*BRIT*) *n* bouton-pression *m*; ~**-up** (*BRIT*) *n* traction *f*

pressure ['preʃə*] *n* pression *f*; (*stress*) tension *f*; **to put ~ on sb (to do)** faire pression sur qn (pour qu'il/elle fasse); ~ **cooker** *n* cocotte-minute *f*; ~ **gauge** *n* manomètre *m*; ~ **group** *n* groupe *m* de pression

prestige [pres'tiːʒ] *n* prestige *m*

presumably [prɪ'zjuːməblɪ] *adv* vraisemblablement

presume [prɪ'zjuːm] *vt* présumer, supposer

pretence [prɪ'tens] (*US* **pretense**) *n* (*claim*) prétention *f*; **under false ~s** sous des prétextes fallacieux

pretend [prɪ'tend] *vt* (*feign*) feindre, simuler ♦ *vi* faire semblant

pretext ['priːtekst] *n* prétexte *m*

pretty ['prɪtɪ] *adj* joli(e) ♦ *adv* assez

prevail [prɪ'veɪl] *vi* (*be usual*) avoir cours; (*win*) l'emporter, prévaloir; ~**ing** *adj* dominant(e)

prevalent ['prevələnt] *adj* répandu(e), courant(e)

prevent [prɪ'vent] *vt*: **to ~ (from doing)** empêcher (de faire); ~**ative** *adj* = **preventive**; ~**ive** *adj* préventif(ive)

preview ['priːvjuː] *n* (*of film etc*) avant-première *f*

previous ['priːvɪəs] *adj* précédent(e); antérieur(e); ~**ly** *adv* précédemment, auparavant

prewar ['priː'wɔː*] *adj* d'avant-guerre

prey [preɪ] *n* proie *f* ♦ *vi*: **to ~ on** s'attaquer à; **it was ~ing on his mind** cela le travaillait

price [praɪs] *n* prix *m* ♦ *vt* (*goods*) fixer le prix de; ~**less** *adj* sans prix, inestimable; ~ **list** *n* liste *f* des prix, tarif *m*

prick [prɪk] *n* piqûre *f* ♦ *vt* piquer; **to ~ up one's ears** dresser *or* tendre l'oreille

prickle ['prɪkl] *n* (*of plant*) épine *f*; (*sensation*) picotement *m*; **prickly** ['prɪklɪ] *adj* piquant(e), épineux(euse); **prickly heat** *n* fièvre *f* miliaire

pride [praɪd] *n* orgueil *m*; fierté *f* ♦ *vt*: **to ~ o.s. on** se flatter de; s'enorgueillir de

priest [priːst] *n* prêtre *m*; ~**hood** *n* prêtrise *f*, sacerdoce *m*

prim [prɪm] *adj* collet monté *inv*, guindé(e)

primarily ['praɪmərɪlɪ] *adv* principalement, essentiellement

primary ['praɪmərɪ] *adj* (*first in importance*) premier(ère), primordial(e), principal(e) ♦ *n* (*US: election*) (élection *f*) primaire *f*; ~ **school** (*BRIT*) *n* école primaire *f*

prime [praɪm] *adj* primordial(e), fondamental(e); (*excellent*) excellent(e) ♦ *n*: **in the ~ of life** dans la fleur de l'âge ♦ *vt* (*wood*) apprêter; (*fig*) mettre au courant; **P~ Minister** *n* Premier ministre *m*

primeval [praɪ'miːvəl] *adj* primitif(ive); ~ **forest** forêt *f* vierge

primitive ['prɪmɪtɪv] *adj* primitif(ive)

primrose ['prɪmrəuz] *n* primevère *f*

primus (stove) ['praɪməs-] (®:*BRIT*) *n* réchaud *m* de camping

prince [prɪns] *n* prince *m*

princess [prɪn'ses] *n* princesse *f*

principal ['prɪnsəpl] *adj* principal(e) ♦ *n* (*headmaster*) directeur(trice), principal *m*

principle ['prɪnsəpl] *n* principe *m*; **in/on ~** en/par principe

print [prɪnt] *n* (*mark*) empreinte *f*; (*letters*) caractères *mpl*; (*ART*) gravure *f*, estampe *f*; (: *photograph*) photo *f* ♦ *vt* imprimer;

(*publish*) publier; (*write in block letters*) écrire en caractères d'imprimerie; **out of ~** épuisé(e); **~ed matter** n imprimé(s) m(pl); **~er** n imprimeur m; (*machine*) imprimante f; **~ing** n impression f; **~-out** n copie f papier

prior ['praɪə*] adj antérieur(e), précédent(e); (*more important*) prioritaire ♦ adv: **~ to doing** avant de faire

priority [praɪ'ɒrɪtɪ] n priorité f

prise [praɪz] vt: **to ~ open** forcer

prison ['prɪzn] n prison f ♦ cpd pénitentiaire; **~er** n prisonnier(ère)

pristine ['prɪstiːn] adj parfait(e)

privacy ['prɪvəsɪ] n intimité f, solitude f

private ['praɪvɪt] adj privé(e); (*personal*) personnel(le); (*house, lesson*) particulier(ère); (*quiet: place*) tranquille; (*reserved: person*) secret(ète) ♦ n soldat m de deuxième classe; **"~"** (*on envelope*) "personnelle"; **in ~** en privé; **~ enterprise** n l'entreprise privée; **~ eye** n détective privé; **~ property** n propriété privée; **privatize** vt privatiser

privet ['prɪvɪt] n troène m

privilege ['prɪvɪlɪdʒ] n privilège m

privy ['prɪvɪ] adj: **to be ~ to** être au courant de

prize [praɪz] n prix m ♦ adj (*example, idiot*) parfait(e); (*bull, novel*) primé(e) ♦ vt priser, faire grand cas de; **~-giving** n distribution f des prix; **~winner** n gagnant(e)

pro [prəʊ] n (SPORT) professionnel(le); **the ~s and cons** le pour et le contre

probability [prɒbə'bɪlɪtɪ] n probabilité f; **probable** ['prɒbəbl] adj probable; **probably** adv probablement

probation [prə'beɪʃən] n: **on ~** (LAW) en liberté surveillée, en sursis; (*employee*) à l'essai

probe [prəʊb] n (MED, SPACE) sonde f; (*enquiry*) enquête f, investigation f ♦ vt sonder, explorer

problem ['prɒbləm] n problème m

procedure [prə'siːdʒə*] n (ADMIN, LAW) procédure f; (*method*) marche f à suivre, façon f de procéder

proceed [prə'siːd] vi continuer; (*go forward*) avancer; **to ~ (with)** continuer, poursuivre; **to ~ to do** se mettre à faire; **~ings** npl (LAW) poursuites fpl; (*meeting*) réunion f, séance f; **~s** ['prəʊsiːdz] npl produit m, recette f

process ['prəʊses] n processus m; (*method*) procédé m ♦ vt traiter; **~ing** n (PHOT) développement m; **~ion** [prə'seʃən] n défilé m, cortège m; (REL) procession f; **funeral ~ion** (*on foot*) cortège m funèbre; (*in cars*) convoi m mortuaire

proclaim [prə'kleɪm] vt déclarer, proclamer

procrastinate [prəʊ'kræstɪneɪt] vi faire traîner les choses, vouloir tout remettre au lendemain

procure [prə'kjʊə*] vt obtenir

prod [prɒd] vt pousser

prodigal ['prɒdɪgəl] adj prodigue

prodigy ['prɒdɪdʒɪ] n prodige m

produce [n 'prɒdjuːs, vb prə'djuːs] n (AGR) produits mpl ♦ vt produire; (*to show*) présenter; (*cause*) provoquer, causer; (THEATRE) monter, mettre en scène; **~r** n producteur m; (THEATRE) metteur m en scène

product ['prɒdʌkt] n produit m

production [prə'dʌkʃən] n production f; (THEATRE) mise f en scène; **~ line** n chaîne f (de fabrication)

productivity [prɒdʌk'tɪvɪtɪ] n productivité f

profession [prə'feʃən] n profession f; **~al** n professionnel(le) ♦ adj professionnel(le); (*work*) de professionnel

professor [prə'fesə*] n professeur m (*titulaire d'une chaire*)

proficiency [prə'fɪʃənsɪ] n compétence f, aptitude f

profile ['prəʊfaɪl] n profil m

profit ['prɒfɪt] n bénéfice m; profit m ♦ vi: **to ~ (by or from)** profiter (de); **~able** adj lucratif(ive), rentable

profound [prə'faʊnd] adj profond(e)

profusely [prə'fjuːslɪ] adv abondamment; avec effusion

prognosis [prɒg'nəʊsɪs] (pl **prognoses**) n pronostic m

programme ['prəʊgræm] (US **program**) n programme m; (RADIO, TV) émission f ♦ vt programmer; **~r** (US **programer**) n programmeur(euse)

progress [n 'prəʊgres, vb prə'gres] n progrès m(pl) ♦ vi progresser, avancer; **in ~** en cours; **~ive** adj progressif(ive); (*person*) progressiste

prohibit [prə'hɪbɪt] vt interdire, défendre

project [n 'prɒdʒekt, vb prə'dʒekt] n (*plan*) projet m, plan m; (*venture*) opération f, entreprise f; (*research*) étude f, dossier m ♦ vt projeter ♦ vi (*stick out*) faire saillie, s'avancer; **~ion** [prə'dʒekʃən] n projection f; (*overhang*) saillie f; **~or** [prə'dʒektə*] n projecteur m

prolong [prə'lɒŋ] vt prolonger

prom [prɒm] n abbr = **promenade**; (US: *ball*) bal m d'étudiants

promenade [prɒmɪ'nɑːd] n (*by sea*) esplanade f, promenade f; **~ concert** (BRIT) n concert m populaire (de musique classique)

prominent ['prɒmɪnənt] adj (*standing out*) proéminent(e); (*important*) important(e)

promiscuous [prə'mɪskjʊəs] adj (*sexually*) de mœurs légères

promise ['prɒmɪs] n promesse f ♦ vt, vi promettre; **promising** ['prɒmɪsɪŋ] adj prometteur(euse)

promote [prə'məʊt] vt promouvoir; (*new product*) faire la promotion de; **~r** n (of *event*) organisateur(trice); (*of cause, idea*) promoteur(trice); **promotion** [prə'məʊʃən] n promotion f

prompt [prɒmpt] *adj* rapide ♦ *adv* (*punctually*) à l'heure ♦ n (COMPUT) message m (de guidage) ♦ *vt* provoquer; (*person*) inciter, pousser; (THEATRE) souffler (son rôle *or* ses répliques) à; **~ly** *adv* rapidement, sans délai; ponctuellement

prone [prəʊn] *adj* (*lying*) couché(e) (face contre terre); **~ to** enclin(e) à

prong [prɒŋ] n (*of fork*) dent f

pronoun ['prəʊnaʊn] n pronom m

pronounce [prə'naʊns] *vt* prononcer

pronunciation [prənʌnsɪ'eɪʃən] n prononciation f

proof [pruːf] n preuve f; (TYP) épreuve f ♦ *adj*: **~ against** à l'épreuve de

prop [prɒp] n support m, étai m; (*fig*) soutien m ♦ *vt* (*also:* ~ **up**) étayer, soutenir; (*lean*): **to ~ sth against** appuyer qch contre *or* à

propaganda [prɒpə'gændə] n propagande f

propel [prə'pel] *vt* propulser, faire avancer; **~ler** n hélice f

propensity [prə'pensɪtɪ] n: **a ~ for** *or* **to/ to do** une propension à/à faire

proper ['prɒpə*] *adj* (*suited, right*) approprié(e), bon(bonne); (*seemly*) correct(e), convenable; (*authentic*) vrai(e), véritable; (*referring to place*): **the village ~** le village proprement dit; **~ly** *adv* correctement, convenablement; **~ noun** n nom m propre

property ['prɒpətɪ] n propriété f; (*things owned*) biens mpl; propriété(s) f(pl); (*land*) terres fpl

prophecy ['prɒfɪsɪ] n prophétie f

prophesy ['prɒfɪsaɪ] *vt* prédire

prophet ['prɒfɪt] n prophète m

proportion [prə'pɔːʃən] n proportion f; (*share*) part f; partie f; **~al, ~ate** *adj* proportionnel(le)

proposal [prə'pəʊzl] n proposition f, offre f; (*plan*) projet m; (*of marriage*) demande f en mariage

propose [prə'pəʊz] *vt* proposer, suggérer ♦ *vi* faire sa demande en mariage; **to ~ to do** avoir l'intention de faire; **proposition** [prɒpə'zɪʃən] n proposition f

propriety [prə'praɪətɪ] n (*seemliness*) bienséance f, convenance f

prose [prəʊz] n (*not poetry*) prose f

prosecute ['prɒsɪkjuːt] *vt* poursuivre; **prosecution** [prɒsɪ'kjuːʃən] n poursuites fpl judiciaires; (*accusing side*) partie plaignante; **prosecutor** ['prɒsɪkjuːtə*] n (US: *plaintiff*) plaignant(e); (*also:* public ~) procureur m, ministère public

prospect [n 'prɒspekt, vb prə'spekt] n perspective f ♦ *vt, vi* prospecter; **~s** npl (*for work etc*) possibilités fpl d'avenir, débouchés mpl; **~ing** n (*for gold, oil etc*) pros-

pection f; **~ive** *adj* (*possible*) éventuel(le); (*future*) futur(e)

prospectus [prə'spektəs] n prospectus m

prosperity [prɒ'sperɪtɪ] n prospérité f

prostitute ['prɒstɪtjuːt] n prostitué(e)

protect [prə'tekt] *vt* protéger; **~ion** n protection f; **~ive** *adj* protecteur(trice); (*clothing*) de protection

protein ['prəʊtiːn] n protéine f

protest [n 'prəʊtest, vb prə'test] n protestation f ♦ *vi, vt*: **to ~ (that)** protester (que)

Protestant ['prɒtɪstənt] *adj, n* protestant(e)

protester [prə'testə*] n manifestant(e)

protracted [prə'træktɪd] *adj* prolongé(e)

protrude [prə'truːd] *vi* avancer, dépasser

proud [praʊd] *adj* fier(ère); (*pej*) orgueilleux(euse)

prove [pruːv] *vt* prouver, démontrer ♦ *vi*: **to ~ (to be) correct** *etc* s'avérer juste *etc*; **to ~ o.s.** montrer ce dont on est capable

proverb ['prɒvɜːb] n proverbe m

provide [prə'vaɪd] *vt* fournir; **to ~ sb with sth** fournir qch à qn; **~ for** *vt fus* (*person*) subvenir aux besoins de; (*future event*) prévoir; **~d (that)** *conj* à condition que +*sub*; **providing** [prə'vaɪdɪŋ] *conj*: **providing (that)** à condition que +*sub*

province ['prɒvɪns] n province f; (*fig*) domaine m; **provincial** [prə'vɪnʃəl] *adj* provincial(e)

provision [prə'vɪʒən] n (*supplying*) fourniture f; approvisionnement m; (*stipulation*) disposition f; **~s** npl (*food*) provisions fpl; **~al** *adj* provisoire

proviso [prə'vaɪzəʊ] n condition f

provocative [prə'vɒkətɪv] *adj* provocateur(trice), provocant(e)

provoke [prə'vəʊk] *vt* provoquer

prow [praʊ] n proue f

prowess ['praʊes] n prouesse f

prowl [praʊl] *vi* (*also:* ~ **about**, ~ **around**) rôder ♦ n: **on the ~** à l'affût; **~er** n rôdeur(euse)

proxy ['prɒksɪ] n procuration f

prudent ['pruːdənt] *adj* prudent(e)

prune [pruːn] n pruneau m ♦ *vt* élaguer

pry [praɪ] *vi*: **to ~ into** fourrer son nez dans

PS n abbr (= *postscript*) p.s.

psalm [sɑːm] n psaume m

pseudo- ['sjuːdəʊ] *prefix* pseudo-; **~nym** ['sjuːdənɪm] n pseudonyme m

psyche ['saɪkɪ] n psychisme m

psychiatrist [saɪ'kaɪətrɪst] n psychiatre m/f

psychic ['saɪkɪk] *adj* (*also:* ~**al**) (méta)psychique; (*person*) doué(e) d'un sixième sens

psychoanalyst [saɪkəʊ'ænəlɪst] n psychanalyste m/f

psychological [saɪkə'lɒdʒɪkəl] *adj* psychologique; **psychologist** [saɪ'kɒlədʒɪst] n psychologue m/f; **psychology** [saɪ'kɒlədʒɪ] n psychologie f

PTO *abbr* (= *please turn over*) T.S.V.P.

pub [pʌb] *n* (= *public house*) pub *m*

public ['pʌblɪk] *adj* public(ique) ♦ *n* public *m*; **in** ~ en public; **to make** ~ rendre public; ~ **address system** *n* (système *m* de) sonorisation *f*; **hauts-parleurs** *mpl*

publican ['pʌblɪkən] *n* patron *m* de pub

public: ~ **company** *n* société *f* anonyme (cotée en Bourse); ~ **convenience** (*BRIT*) *n* toilettes *fpl*; ~ **holiday** *n* jour férié; ~ **house** (*BRIT*) *n* pub *m*

publicity [pʌb'lɪsɪtɪ] *n* publicité *f*

publicize ['pʌblɪsaɪz] *vt* faire connaître, rendre public(ique)

public: ~ **opinion** *n* opinion publique; ~ **relations** *n* relations publiques; ~ **school** *n* (*BRIT*) école (secondaire) privée; (*US*) école publique; ~-**spirited** *adj* qui fait preuve de civisme; ~ **transport** *n* transports *mpl* en commun

publish ['pʌblɪʃ] *vt* publier; ~**er** *n* éditeur *m*; ~**ing** *n* édition *f*

pucker ['pʌkə*] *vt* plisser

pudding ['pudɪŋ] *n* pudding *m*; (*BRIT*: *sweet*) dessert *m*, entremets *m*; **black** ~, (*US*) **blood** ~ boudin (noir)

puddle ['pʌdl] *n* flaque *f* (d'eau)

puff [pʌf] *n* bouffée *f* ♦ *vt*: **to** ~ **one's pipe** tirer sur sa pipe ♦ *vi* (*pant*) haleter; ~ **out** *vt* (*fill with air*) gonfler; ~**ed** (**out**) (*inf*) *adj* (*out of breath*) tout(e) essoufflé(e); ~ **pastry** (*US* = **paste**) *n* pâte feuilletée; ~**y** *adj* bouffi(e), boursouflé(e)

pull [pul] *n* (*tug*): **to give sth a** ~ tirer sur qch ♦ *vt* tirer; (*trigger*) presser ♦ *vi* tirer; **to** ~ **to pieces** mettre en morceaux; **to** ~ **one's punches** ménager son adversaire; **to** ~ **one's weight** faire sa part (du travail); **to** ~ **o.s. together** se ressaisir; **to** ~ **sb's leg** (*fig*) faire marcher qn; ~ **apart** *vt* (*break*) mettre en pièces, démantibuler; ~ **down** *vt* (*house*) démolir; ~ **in** *vi* (*AUT*) entrer; (*RAIL*) entrer en gare; ~ **off** *vt* enlever, ôter; (*deal etc*) mener à bien, conclure; ~ **out** *vi* démarrer, partir ♦ *vt* sortir; arracher; ~ **over** *vi* (*AUT*) se ranger; ~ **through** *vi* s'en sortir; ~ **up** *vi* (*stop*) s'arrêter ♦ *vt* remonter; (*uproot*) déraciner, arracher

pulley ['pulɪ] *n* poulie *f*

pullover ['puləuvə*] *n* pull-(over) *m*, tricot *m*

pulp [pʌlp] *n* (*of fruit*) pulpe *f*

pulpit ['pulpɪt] *n* chaire *f*

pulsate [pʌl'seɪt] *vi* battre, palpiter; (*music*) vibrer

pulse [pʌls] *n* (*of blood*) pouls *m*; (*of heart*) battement *m*; (*of music, engine*) vibrations *fpl*; (*BOT, CULIN*) légume sec

pump [pʌmp] *n* pompe *f*; (*shoe*) escarpin *m* ♦ *vt* pomper; ~ **up** *vt* gonfler

pumpkin ['pʌmpkɪn] *n* potiron *m*, citrouille *f*

pun [pʌn] *n* jeu *m* de mots, calembour *m*

punch [pʌntʃ] *n* (*blow*) coup *m* de poing; (*tool*) poinçon *m*; (*drink*) punch *m* ♦ *vt* (*hit*): **to** ~ **sb/sth** donner un coup de poing à qn/sur qch; ~-**line** *n* (*of joke*) conclusion *f*; ~-**up** (*BRIT*: *inf*) *n* bagarre *f*

punctual ['pʌŋktjuəl] *adj* ponctuel(le)

punctuation [pʌŋktju'eɪʃən] *n* ponctuation *f*

puncture ['pʌŋktʃə*] *n* crevaison *f*

pundit ['pʌndɪt] *n* individu *m* qui pontifie, pontife *m*

pungent ['pʌndʒənt] *adj* piquant(e), âcre

punish ['pʌnɪʃ] *vt* punir; ~**ment** *n* punition *f*, châtiment *m*

punk [pʌŋk] *n* (also: ~ **rocker**) punk *m/f*; (: ~ **rock**) le punk rock; (*US*: *inf*: *hoodlum*) voyou *m*

punt [pʌnt] *n* (*boat*) bachot *m*

punter ['pʌntə*] *n* (*BRIT*) *n* (*gambler*) parieur(euse); (*inf*): **the** ~**s** le public

puny ['pjuːnɪ] *adj* chétif(ive); (*effort*) piteux(euse)

pup [pʌp] *n* chiot *m*

pupil ['pjuːpl] *n* (*SCOL*) élève *m/f*; (*of eye*) pupille *f*

puppet ['pʌpɪt] *n* marionnette *f*, pantin *m*

puppy ['pʌpɪ] *n* chiot *m*, jeune chien(ne)

purchase ['pɜːtʃɪs] *n* achat *m* ♦ *vt* acheter; ~**r** *n* acheteur(euse)

pure [pjuə*] *adj* pur(e); ~**ly** ['pjuəlɪ] *adv* purement

purge [pɜːdʒ] *n* purge *f*

purple ['pɜːpl] *adj* violet(te); (*face*) cramoisi(e)

purport [pɜː'pɔːt] *vi*: **to** ~ **to be/do** prétendre être/faire

purpose ['pɜːpəs] *n* intention *f*, but *m*; **on** ~ exprès; ~**ful** *adj* déterminé(e), résolu(e)

purr [pɜː*] *vi* ronronner

purse [pɜːs] *n* (*BRIT*: *for money*) porte-monnaie *m inv*; (*US*: *handbag*) sac *m* à main ♦ *vt* serrer, pincer

purser ['pɜːsə*] *n* (*NAUT*) commissaire *m* du bord

pursue [pə'sjuː] *vt* poursuivre

pursuit [pə'sjuːt] *n* poursuite *f*; (*occupation*) occupation *f*, activité *f*

push [puʃ] *n* poussée *f* ♦ *vt* pousser; (*button*) appuyer sur; (*thrust*): **to** ~ **sth (into)** enfoncer qch (dans); (*product*) faire de la publicité pour ♦ *vi* pousser; (*demand*): **to** ~ **for** exiger, demander avec insistance; ~ **aside** *vt* écarter; ~ **off** (*inf*) *vi* filer, ficher le camp; ~ **on** *vi* (*continue*) continuer; ~ **through** *vi* se frayer un chemin ♦ *vt* (*measure*) faire accepter; ~ **up** *vt* (*total, prices*) faire monter; ~**chair** (*BRIT*) *n* poussette *f*; ~**er** *n* (*drug* ~**er**) revendeur(euse) (de drogue), ravitailleur(euse) (en drogue); ~**over**

(*inf*) n: **it's a ~over** c'est un jeu d'enfant; **~-up** (*US*) n traction f; **~y** (*pej*) adj arriviste

puss [pus] (*inf*) n minet m

pussy (cat) ['pusɪ (kæt)] (*inf*) n minet m

put [put] (*pt, pp* **put**) vt mettre, poser, placer; (*say*) dire, exprimer; (*a question*) poser; (*case, view*) exposer, présenter; (*estimate*) estimer; **~ about** vt (*rumour*) faire courir; **~ across** vt (*ideas etc*) communiquer; **~ away** vt (*store*) ranger; **~ back** vt (*replace*) remettre, replacer; (*postpone*) remettre; (*delay*) retarder; **~ by** vt (*money*) mettre de côté, économiser; **~ down** vt (*parcel etc*) poser, déposer; (*in writing*) mettre par écrit, inscrire; (*suppress: revolt etc*) réprimer, faire cesser; (*animal*) abattre; (*dog, cat*) faire piquer; (*attribute*) attribuer; **~ forward** vt (*ideas*) avancer; **~ in** vt (*gas, electricity*) installer; (*application, complaint*) soumettre; (*time, effort*) consacrer; **~ off** vt (*light etc*) éteindre; (*postpone*) remettre à plus tard, ajourner; (*discourage*) dissuader; **~ on** vt (*clothes, lipstick, record*) mettre; (*light etc*) allumer, (*play etc*) monter; (*food: cook*) mettre à cuire or à chauffer; (*gain*): **to ~ on weight** prendre du poids, grossir; **to ~ the brakes on** freiner; **to ~ the kettle on** mettre l'eau à chauffer; **~ out** vt (*take out*) mettre dehors; (*one's hand*) tendre; (*light etc*) éteindre; (*person: inconvenience*) déranger, gêner; **~ through** vt (*TEL: call*) passer; (*: person*) mettre en communication; (*plan*) faire accepter; **~ up** vt (*raise*) lever, relever, remonter; (*pin up*) afficher; (*hang*) accrocher; (*build*) construire, ériger; (*tent*) monter; (*umbrella*) ouvrir; (*increase*) augmenter; (*accommodate*) loger; **~ up with** vt fus supporter

putt [pʌt] n coup roulé; **~ing green** n green m

putty ['pʌtɪ] n mastic m

put-up ['putʌp] (*BRIT*) adj: **~ job** coup monté

puzzle ['pʌzl] n énigme f, mystère m; (*jigsaw*) puzzle m ♦ vt intriguer, rendre perplexe ♦ vi se creuser la tête; **puzzling** adj déconcertant(e)

pyjamas [pɪ'dʒɑːməz] (*BRIT*) npl pyjama(s) m(pl)

pyramid ['pɪrəmɪd] n pyramide f

Pyrenees [pɪrɪ'niːz] npl: **the ~** les Pyrénées fpl

Q q

quack [kwæk] n (*of duck*) coin-coin m inv; (*pej: doctor*) charlatan m

quad [kwɒd] n abbr = **quadrangle** ♦ abbr = **quadruplet**

quadrangle ['kwɒdræŋgl] n (*courtyard*) cour f

quadruple [kwɒ'druːpl] vt, vi quadrupler; **~ts** [kwɒ'druːpləts] npl quadruplés

quagmire ['kwæɡmaɪə*] n bourbier m

quail [kweɪl] n (*ZOOL*) caille f ♦ vi: **to ~ at** or **before** reculer devant

quaint [kweɪnt] adj bizarre; (*house, village*) au charme vieillot, pittoresque

quake [kweɪk] vi trembler

qualification [kwɒlɪfɪ'keɪʃən] n (*often pl: degree etc*) diplôme m; (*: training*) qualification(s) f(pl); expérience f; (*ability*) compétence(s) f(pl); (*limitation*) réserve f, restriction f

qualified ['kwɒlɪfaɪd] adj (*trained*) qualifié(e); (*professionally*) diplômé(e); (*fit, competent*) compétent(e), qualifié(e); (*limited*) conditionnel(le)

qualify ['kwɒlɪfaɪ] vt qualifier; (*modify*) atténuer, nuancer ♦ vi: **to ~ (as)** obtenir son diplôme (de); **to ~ (for)** remplir les conditions requises (pour); (*SPORT*) se qualifier (pour)

quality ['kwɒlɪtɪ] n qualité f

qualm [kwɑːm] n doute m; scrupule m

quandary ['kwɒndərɪ] n: **in a ~** devant un dilemme, dans l'embarras

quantity ['kwɒntɪtɪ] n quantité f; **~ surveyor** n métreur m vérificateur

quarantine ['kwɒrəntiːn] n quarantaine f

quarrel ['kwɒrəl] n querelle f, dispute f ♦ vi se disputer, se quereller; **~some** adj querelleur(euse)

quarry ['kwɒrɪ] n (*for stone*) carrière f; (*animal*) proie f, gibier m

quart [kwɔːt] n ≈ litre m

quarter ['kwɔːtə*] n quart m; (*US: coin: 25 cents*) quart de dollar; (*of year*) trimestre m; (*district*) quartier m ♦ vt (*divide*) partager en quartiers or en quatre; **~s** npl (*living ~*) logement m; (*MIL*) quartiers mpl, cantonnement m; **a ~ of an hour** un quart d'heure; **~ final** n quart m de finale; **~ly** adj trimestriel(le) ♦ adv tous les trois mois

quartet(te) [kwɔ:'tet] *n* quatuor *m*; (*jazz players*) quartette *m*

quartz [kwɔ:ts] *n* quartz *m*

quash [kwɒʃ] *vt* (*verdict*) annuler

quaver ['kweɪvə*] *n* (*BRIT: MUS*) croche *f* ♦ *vi* trembler

quay [ki:] *n* (*also: ~side*) quai *m*

queasy ['kwi:zɪ] *adj*: **to feel ~** avoir mal au cœur

queen [kwi:n] *n* reine *f*; (*CARDS etc*) dame *f*; **~ mother** *n* reine mère *f*

queer [kwɪə*] *adj* étrange, curieux(euse); (*suspicious*) louche ♦ *n* (*inf!*) homosexuel *m*

quell [kwel] *vt* réprimer, étouffer

quench [kwentʃ] *vt*: **to ~ one's thirst** se désaltérer

querulous ['kwerʊləs] *adj* (*person*) récriminateur(trice); (*voice*) plaintif(ive)

query ['kwɪərɪ] *n* question *f* ♦ *vt* remettre en question, mettre en doute

quest [kwest] *n* recherche *f*, quête *f*

question ['kwestʃən] *n* question *f* ♦ *vt* (*person*) interroger; (*plan, idea*) remettre en question, mettre en doute; **beyond ~** sans aucun doute; **out of the ~** hors de question; **~able** *adj* discutable; **~ mark** *n* point *m* d'interrogation; **~naire** [kwestʃə'nɛə*] *n* questionnaire *m*

queue [kju:] (*BRIT*) *n* queue *f*, file *f* ♦ *vi* (*also: ~ up*) faire la queue

quibble ['kwɪbl] *vi*: **~ (about)** *or* **(over)** *or* **(with sth)** ergoter (sur qch)

quick [kwɪk] *adj* rapide; (*agile*) agile, vif(vive) ♦ *n*: **cut to the ~** (*fig*) touché(e) au vif; **be ~!** dépêche-toi!; **~en** *vt* accélérer, presser ♦ *vi* s'accélérer, devenir plus rapide; **~ly** *adv* vite, rapidement; **~sand** *n* sables mouvants; **~-witted** *adj* à l'esprit vif

quid [kwɪd] (*BRIT: inf*) *n, pl inv* livre *f*

quiet ['kwaɪət] *adj* tranquille, calme; (*voice*) bas(se); (*ceremony, colour*) discret(ète) ♦ *n* tranquillité *f*, calme *m*; (*silence*) silence *m* ♦ *vt, vi* (*US*) **= quieten; keep ~!** tais-toi!; **~en** *vi* (*also: ~ down*) se calmer, s'apaiser ♦ *vt* calmer, apaiser; **~ly** *adv* tranquillement, calmement; (*silently*) silencieusement; **~ness** *n* tranquillité *f*, calme *m*; (*silence*) silence *m*

quilt [kwɪlt] *n* édredon *m*; (*continental ~*) couette *f*

quin [kwɪn] *n abbr* **= quintuplet**

quintuplets [kwɪn'tju:pləts] *npl* quintuplé(e)s

quip [kwɪp] *n* remarque piquante *or* spirituelle, pointe *f*

quirk [kwɜ:k] *n* bizarrerie *f*

quit [kwɪt] (*pt, pp* **~** *or* **~ted**) *vt* quitter; (*smoking, grumbling*) arrêter de ♦ *vi* (*give up*) abandonner, renoncer; (*resign*) démissionner

quite [kwaɪt] *adv* (*rather*) assez, plutôt; (*entirely*) complètement, tout à fait; (*following a negative = almost*): **that's not ~ big enough** ce n'est pas tout à fait assez grand; **I ~ understand** je comprends très bien; **~ a few of them** un assez grand nombre d'entre eux; **~ (so)!** exactement!

quits [kwɪts] *adj*: **~ (with)** quitte (envers); **let's call it ~** restons-en là

quiver ['kwɪvə*] *vi* trembler, frémir

quiz [kwɪz] *n* (*game*) jeu-concours *m* ♦ *vt* interroger; **~zical** *adj* narquois(e)

quota ['kwəʊtə] *n* quota *m*

quotation [kwəʊ'teɪʃən] *n* citation *f*; (*estimate*) devis *m*; **~ marks** *npl* guillemets *mpl*

quote [kwəʊt] *n* citation *f*; (*estimate*) devis *m* ♦ *vt* citer; (*price*) indiquer; **~s** *npl* guillemets *mpl*

R r

rabbi ['ræbaɪ] *n* rabbin *m*

rabbit ['ræbɪt] *n* lapin *m*; **~ hutch** *n* clapier *m*

rabble ['ræbl] (*pej*) *n* populace *f*

rabies ['reɪbɪz] *n* rage *f*

RAC *n abbr* (*BRIT*) **= Royal Automobile Club**

rac(c)oon [rə'ku:n] *n* raton laveur

race [reɪs] *n* (*species*) race *f*; (*competition, rush*) course *f* ♦ *vt* (*horse*) faire courir ♦ *vi* (*compete*) faire la course, courir; (*hurry*) aller à toute vitesse, courir; (*engine*) s'emballer; (*pulse*) augmenter; **~ car** (*US*) *n* **= racing car; ~ car driver** (*US*) *n* **= racing driver; ~course** *n* champ *m* de courses; **~horse** *n* cheval *m* de course; **~track** *n* piste *f*

racial ['reɪʃəl] *adj* racial(e)

racing ['reɪsɪŋ] *n* courses *fpl*; **~ car** (*BRIT*) *n* voiture *f* de course; **~ driver** (*BRIT*) *n* pilote *m* de course

racism ['reɪsɪzəm] *n* racisme *m*; **racist** *adj* raciste ♦ *n* raciste *m/f*

rack [ræk] *n* (*for guns, tools*) râtelier *m*; (*also: luggage ~*) porte-bagages *m inv*, filet *m* à bagages; (*: roof ~*) galerie *f*; (*dish ~*) égouttoir *m* ♦ *vt* tourmenter; **to ~ one's brains** se creuser la cervelle

racket ['rækɪt] *n* (*for tennis*) raquette *f*; (*noise*) tapage *m*; vacarme *m*; (*swindle*) escroquerie *f*

racquet ['rækɪt] *n* raquette *f*

racy ['reɪsɪ] *adj* plein(e) de verve; (*slightly indecent*) osé(e)

radar ['reɪdɑ:*] *n* radar *m*

radial ['reɪdɪəl] *adj* (*also: ~-ply*) à carcasse radiale

radiant ['reɪdɪənt] *adj* rayonnant(e)

radiate ['reɪdɪeɪt] *vt* (*heat*) émettre, dégager; (*emotion*) rayonner de ♦ *vi* (*lines*) rayonner

radiation [reɪdɪ'eɪʃən] *n* rayonnement *m*; (*radioactive*) radiation *f*

radiator ['reɪdɪeɪtə*] *n* radiateur *m*

radical ['rædɪkəl] *adj* radical(e)

radii ['reɪdɪaɪ] *npl of* **radius**

radio ['reɪdɪəʊ] *n* radio *f* ♦ *vt* appeler par radio; **on the ~** à la radio; **~active** [reɪdɪəʊ'æktɪv] *adj* radioactif(ive); **~ station** *f* de radio

radish ['rædɪʃ] *n* radis *m*

radius ['reɪdɪəs] (*pl* **radii**) *n* rayon *m*

RAF *n abbr* = **Royal Air Force**

raffle ['ræfl] *n* tombola *f*

raft [rɑːft] *n* (*craft; also: life ~*) radeau *m*

rafter ['rɑːftə*] *n* chevron *m*

rag [ræg] *n* chiffon *m*; (*pej: newspaper*) feuille *f* de chou, torchon *m*; (*student ~*) attractions organisées au profit d'œuvres de charité; **~s** *npl* (*torn clothes etc*) haillons *mpl*; **~ doll** *n* poupée *f* de chiffon

rage [reɪdʒ] *n* (*fury*) rage *f*, fureur *f* ♦ *vi* (*person*) être furieux(euse) de rage; (*storm*) faire rage, être déchaîné(e); **it's all the ~** cela fait fureur

ragged ['rægɪd] *adj* (*edge*) inégal(e); (*clothes*) en loques; (*appearance*) déguenillé(e)

raid [reɪd] *n* (*attack, also: MIL*) raid *m*; (*criminal*) hold-up *m inv*; (*by police*) descente *f*, rafle *f* ♦ *vt* faire un raid sur *or* un hold-up *or* une descente dans

rail [reɪl] *n* (*on stairs*) rampe *f*; (*on bridge, balcony*) balustrade *f*; (*of ship*) bastingage *m*; **~s** *npl* (*track*) rails *mpl*, voie ferrée; **by ~** par chemin de fer, en train; **~ing(s)** *n(pl)* grille *f*, **~road** (*US*), **~way** (*BRIT*) *n* (*track*) voie ferrée; (*company*) chemin *m* de fer; **~way line** (*BRIT*) *n* ligne *f* de chemin de fer; **~wayman** (*BRIT: irreg*) *n* cheminot *m*; **~way station** (*BRIT*) *n* gare *f*

rain [reɪn] *n* pluie *f* ♦ *vi* pleuvoir; **in the ~** sous la pluie; **it's ~ing** il pleut; **~bow** *n* arc-en-ciel *m*; **~coat** *n* imperméable *m*; **~drop** *n* goutte *f* de pluie; **~fall** *n* chute *f* de pluie; (*measurement*) hauteur *f* des précipitations; **~forest** *n* forêt *f* tropicale humide; **~y** *adj* pluvieux(euse)

raise [reɪz] *n* augmentation *f* ♦ *vt* (*lift*) lever; hausser; (*increase*) augmenter; (*morale*) remonter; (*standards*) améliorer; (*question, doubt*) provoquer, soulever; (*cattle, family*) élever; (*crop*) faire pousser; (*funds*) rassembler; (*loan*) obtenir; (*army*) lever; **to ~ one's voice** élever la voix

raisin ['reɪzən] *n* raisin sec

rake [reɪk] *n* (*tool*) râteau *m* ♦ *vt* (*garden, leaves*) ratisser; (*with machine gun*) balayer

rally ['rælɪ] *n* (*POL etc*) meeting *m*, rassemblement *m*; (*AUT*) rallye *m*; (*TENNIS*) échange *m* ♦ *vt* (*support*) gagner ♦ *vi* (*sick person*) aller mieux; (*Stock Exchange*) reprendre; **~ round** *vt fus* venir en aide à

RAM [ræm] *n abbr* (= *random access memory*) mémoire vive

ram [ræm] *n* bélier *m* ♦ *vt* enfoncer; (*crash into*) emboutir; percuter

ramble ['ræmbl] *n* randonnée *f* ♦ *vi* (*walk*) se promener, faire une randonnée; (*talk: also: ~ on*) discourir, pérorer; **~r** *n* promeneur(euse), randonneur(euse); (*BOT*) rosier grimpant; **rambling** ['ræmblɪŋ] *adj* (*speech*) décousu(e); (*house*) plein(e) de coins et de recoins; (*BOT*) grimpant(e)

ramp [ræmp] *n* (*incline*) rampe *f*; dénivellation *f*; **on ~, off ~** (*US: AUT*) bretelle *f* d'accès

rampage [ræm'peɪdʒ] *n*: **to be on the ~** se déchaîner

rampant ['ræmpənt] *adj* (*disease etc*) qui sévit

ramshackle ['ræmʃækl] *adj* (*house*) délabré(e); (*car etc*) déglingué(e)

ran [ræn] *pt of* **run**

ranch [rɑːntʃ] *n* ranch *m*; **~er** *n* propriétaire *m* de ranch

rancid ['rænsɪd] *adj* rance

rancour ['ræŋkə*] (*US* **rancor**) *n* rancune *f*

random ['rændəm] *adj* fait(e) *or* établi(e) au hasard; (*MATH*) aléatoire ♦ *n*: **at ~** au hasard; **~ access** *n* (*COMPUT*) accès sélectif

randy ['rændɪ] (*BRIT: inf*) *adj* excité(e); lubrique

rang [ræŋ] *pt of* **ring**

range [reɪndʒ] *n* (*of mountains*) chaîne *f*; (*of missile, voice*) portée *f*; (*of products*) choix *m*, gamme *f*; (*MIL: also: shooting ~*) champ *m* de tir; (*indoor*) stand *m* de tir; (*also: kitchen ~*) fourneau *m* (de cuisine) ♦ *vt* (*place in a line*) mettre en rang, ranger ♦ *vi*: **to ~ over** (*extend*) couvrir; **to ~ from ... to** aller de ... à; **a ~ of** (*series: of proposals etc*) divers(e)

ranger ['reɪndʒə*] *n* garde forestier

rank [ræŋk] *n* rang *m*; (*MIL*) grade *m*; (*BRIT: also: taxi ~*) station *f* de taxis ♦ *vi*: **to ~ among** compter *or* se classer parmi ♦ *adj* (*stinking*) fétide, puant(e); **the ~ and file** (*fig*) la masse, la base

rankle ['ræŋkl] *vi* (*insult*) rester sur le cœur

ransack ['rænsæk] *vt* fouiller (à fond); (*plunder*) piller

ransom ['rænsəm] *n* rançon *f*; **to hold to ~** (*fig*) exercer un chantage sur

rant [rænt] *vi* fulminer

rap [ræp] *vt* frapper sur *or* à; taper sur; *n*: **~** (*music*) rap *m*

rape [reɪp] *n* viol *m*; (*BOT*) colza *m* ♦ *vt*

violer; ~**(seed) oil** n huile f de colza

rapid ['ræpɪd] adj rapide; ~**s** npl (GEO) rapides mpl

rapist ['reɪpɪst] n violeur m

rapport [ræ'pɔ:*] n entente f

rapture ['ræptʃə*] n extase f, ravissement m; **rapturous** ['ræptʃərəs] adj enthousiaste, frénétique

rare [rɛə*] adj rare; (CULIN: steak) saignant(e)

raring ['rɛərɪŋ] adj: ~ **to go** (inf) très impatient(e) de commencer

rascal ['rɑːskəl] n vaurien m

rash [ræʃ] adj imprudent(e), irréfléchi(e) ♦ n (MED) rougeur f, éruption f; (spate: of events) série (noire)

rasher ['ræʃə*] n fine tranche (de lard)

raspberry ['rɑːzbərɪ] n framboise f; ~ **bush** n framboisier m

rasping ['rɑːspɪŋ] adj: ~ **noise** grincement m

rat [ræt] n rat m

rate [reɪt] n taux m; (speed) vitesse f, rythme m; (price) tarif m ♦ vt classer; évaluer; ~**s** npl (BRIT: tax) impôts locaux; (fees) tarifs mpl; to ~ **sb/sth as** considérer qn/qch comme; ~**able value** (BRIT) n valeur locative imposable; ~**payer** (BRIT) n contribuable m/f (payant les impôts locaux)

rather ['rɑːðə*] adv plutôt; **it's** ~ **expensive** c'est assez cher; (too much) c'est un peu cher; **there's** ~ **a lot** il y en a beaucoup; **I would** or **I'd** ~ **go** j'aimerais mieux or je préférerais partir

rating ['reɪtɪŋ] n (assessment) évaluation f; (score) classement m; (NAUT: BRIT: sailor) matelot m; ~**s** npl (RADIO, TV) indice m d'écoute

ratio ['reɪʃɪəu] n proportion f

ration ['ræʃən] n (gen pl) ration(s) f(pl)

rational ['ræʃənl] adj raisonnable, sensé(e); (solution, reasoning) logique; ~**e** [ræʃə'nɑːl] n raisonnement m; ~**ize** ['ræʃnəlaɪz] vt rationaliser; (conduct) essayer d'expliquer or de motiver

rat race n foire f d'empoigne

rattle ['rætl] n (of door, window) battement m; (of coins, chain) cliquetis m; (of train, engine) bruit m de ferraille; (object: for baby) hochet m ♦ vi cliqueter; (car, bus): **to ~ along** rouler dans un bruit de ferraille ♦ vt agiter (bruyamment); (unnerve) décontenancer; ~**snake** n serpent m à sonnettes

raucous ['rɔːkəs] adj rauque; (noisy) bruyant(e), tapageur(euse)

rave [reɪv] vi (in anger) s'emporter; (with enthusiasm) s'extasier; (MED) délirer

raven ['reɪvn] n corbeau m

ravenous ['rævənəs] adj affamé(e)

ravine [rə'viːn] n ravin m

raving ['reɪvɪŋ] adj: ~ **lunatic** n fou(folle) furieux(euse)

ravishing ['rævɪʃɪŋ] adj enchanteur(eresse)

raw [rɔː] adj (uncooked) cru(e); (not processed) brut(e); (sore) à vif, irrité(e); (inexperienced) inexpérimenté(e); (weather, day) froid(e) et humide; ~ **deal** (inf) n sale coup m; ~ **material** n matière première

ray [reɪ] n rayon m; ~ **of hope** lueur f d'espoir

raze [reɪz] vt (also: ~ **to the ground**) raser, détruire

razor ['reɪzə*] n rasoir m; ~ **blade** n lame f de rasoir

Rd abbr = **road**

re [riː] prep concernant

reach [riːtʃ] n portée f, atteinte f; (of river etc) étendue f ♦ vt atteindre; (conclusion, decision) parvenir à ♦ vi s'étendre, étendre le bras; **out of/within** ~ hors de/à portée; **within** ~ **of the shops** pas trop loin des or à proximité des magasins; ~ **out** vt tendre ♦ vi: **to** ~ **out (for)** allonger le bras (pour prendre)

react [riː'ækt] vi réagir; ~**ion** [riː'ækʃən] n réaction f

reactor [riː'æktə*] n réacteur m

read[1] [riːd] (pt, pp **read**) vi lire ♦ vt lire; (understand) comprendre, interpréter; (study) étudier; (meter) relever; ~ **out** vt lire à haute voix; ~**able** adj facile or agréable à lire; (writing) lisible; ~**er** n lecteur(trice); (book) livre m de lecture; (BRIT: at university) chargé(e) d'enseignement; ~**ership** n (of paper etc) (nombre m de) lecteurs mpl

read[2] [red] pt, pp of **read**[1]

readily ['redɪlɪ] adv volontiers, avec empressement; (easily) facilement

readiness ['redɪnəs] n empressement m; **in** ~ (prepared) prêt(e)

reading ['riːdɪŋ] n lecture f; (understanding) interprétation f; (on instrument) indications fpl

ready ['redɪ] adj prêt(e); (willing) prêt, disposé(e); (available) disponible ♦ n: **at the** ~ (MIL) prêt à faire feu; **to get** ~ se préparer ♦ vt préparer; ~**-made** adj tout(e) fait(e); ~ **money** n (argent m) liquide m; ~**-to-wear** adj prêt(e) à porter

real [rɪəl] adj véritable; réel(le); **in** ~ **terms** dans la réalité; ~ **estate** n biens fonciers or immobiliers; ~**istic** adj réaliste; ~**ity** [riː'ælɪtɪ] n réalité f

realization [rɪəlaɪ'zeɪʃən] n (awareness) prise f de conscience; (fulfilment; also: of asset) réalisation f

realize ['rɪəlaɪz] vt (understand) se rendre compte de; (a project, COMM: asset) réaliser

really ['rɪəlɪ] adv vraiment; ~? vraiment?, c'est vrai?

realm [relm] n royaume m; (fig) domaine m

realtor ['rɪəltɔː*] (®:US) n agent immobilier

reap [riːp] vt moissonner; (fig) récolter

reappear ['riːə'pɪə*] *vi* réapparaître, reparaître

rear [rɪə*] *adj* de derrière, arrière *inv*; (AUT: wheel etc) arrière ♦ *n* arrière *m* ♦ *vt* (cattle, family) élever ♦ *vi* (also: ~ up: animal) se cabrer; **~guard** *n* (MIL) arrière-garde *f*

rear-view mirror ['rɪəvjuː-] *n* (AUT) rétroviseur *m*

reason ['riːzn] *n* raison *f* ♦ *vi*: **to ~ with sb** raisonner qn, faire entendre raison à qn; **to have ~ to think** avoir lieu de penser; **it stands to ~ that** il va sans dire que; **~able** *adj* raisonnable; (not bad) acceptable; **~ably** *adv* raisonnablement; **~ing** *n* raisonnement *m*

reassurance ['riːə'ʃʊərəns] *n* réconfort *m*; (factual) assurance *f*, garantie *f*, **reassure** ['riːə'ʃʊə*] *vt* rassurer

rebate ['riːbeɪt] *n* (on tax etc) dégrèvement *m*

rebel [*n* 'rebl, *vb* rɪ'bel] *n* rebelle *m/f* ♦ *vi* se rebeller, se révolter; **~lious** *adj* rebelle

rebound [*vb* rɪ'baund, *n* 'riːbaund] *vi* (ball) rebondir ♦ *n* rebond *m*; **to marry on the ~** se marier immédiatement après une déception amoureuse

rebuff [rɪ'bʌf] *n* rebuffade *f*

rebuke [rɪ'bjuːk] *vt* réprimander

rebut [rɪ'bʌt] *vt* réfuter

recall [rɪ'kɔːl] *vt* rappeler, (remember) se rappeler, se souvenir de ♦ *n* rappel *m*; (ability to remember) mémoire *f*

recant [rɪ'kænt] *vi* se rétracter; (REL) abjurer

recap ['riːkæp], **recapitulate** [riːkə'pɪtjuleɪt] *vt, vi* récapituler

rec'd *abbr* = received

recede [rɪ'siːd] *vi* (tide) descendre; (disappear) disparaître peu à peu; (memory, hope) s'estomper; **receding** [rɪ'siːdɪŋ] *adj* (chin) fuyant(e); **receding hairline** front dégarni

receipt [rɪ'siːt] *n* (document) reçu *m*; (for parcel etc) accusé *m* de réception; (act of receiving) réception *f*, **~s** *npl* (COMM) recettes *fpl*

receive [rɪ'siːv] *vt* recevoir

receiver [rɪ'siːvə*] *n* (TEL) récepteur *m*, combiné *m*; (RADIO) récepteur *m*; (of stolen goods) receleur *m*; (LAW) administrateur *m* judiciaire

recent ['riːsnt] *adj* récent(e); **~ly** *adv* récemment

receptacle [rɪ'septəkl] *n* récipient *m*

reception [rɪ'sepʃən] *n* réception *f*; (welcome) accueil *m*, réception; **~ desk** *n* réception *f*; **~ist** *n* réceptionniste *m/f*

recess [rɪ'ses] *n* (in room) renfoncement *m*, alcôve *f*; (secret place) recoin *m*; (POL etc: holiday) vacances *fpl*

recession [rɪ'seʃən] *n* récession *f*

recipe ['resɪpɪ] *n* recette *f*

recipient [rɪ'sɪpɪənt] *n* (of payment) bénéfi-

ciaire *m/f*; (of letter) destinataire *m/f*

recital [rɪ'saɪtl] *n* récital *m*

recite [rɪ'saɪt] *vt* (poem) réciter

reckless ['rekləs] *adj* (driver etc) imprudent(e)

reckon ['rekən] *vt* (count) calculer, compter; (think): **I ~ that ...** je pense que ...; **~ on** *vt fus* compter sur, s'attendre à; **~ing** *n* compte *m*, calcul *m*; estimation *f*

reclaim [rɪ'kleɪm] *vt* (demand back) réclamer (le remboursement or la restitution de); (land: from sea) assécher; (waste materials) récupérer

recline [rɪ'klaɪn] *vi* être allongé(e) or étendu(e); **reclining** [rɪ'klaɪnɪŋ] *adj* (seat) à dossier réglable

recluse [rɪ'kluːs] *n* reclus(e), ermite *m*

recognition [rekəg'nɪʃən] *n* reconnaissance *f*; **to gain ~** être reconnu(e); **transformed beyond ~** méconnaissable

recognize ['rekəgnaɪz] *vt*: **to ~ (by/as)** reconnaître (à/comme étant)

recoil [rɪ'kɔɪl] *vi* (person): **to ~ (from sth/ doing sth)** reculer (devant qch/l'idée de faire qch) ♦ *n* (of gun) recul *m*

recollect [rekə'lekt] *vt* se rappeler, se souvenir de; **~ion** [rekə'lekʃən] *n* souvenir *m*

recommend [rekə'mend] *vt* recommander

reconcile ['rekənsaɪl] *vt* (two people) réconcilier; (two facts) concilier, accorder; **to ~ o.s. to** se résigner à

recondition ['riːkən'dɪʃən] *vt* remettre à neuf; réviser entièrement

reconnoitre [rekə'nɔɪtə*] (US **reconnoiter**) *vt* (MIL) reconnaître

reconstruct ['riːkən'strʌkt] *vt* (building) reconstruire; (crime, policy, system) reconstituer

record [*n* 'rekɔːd, *vb* rɪ'kɔːd] *n* rapport *m*, récit *m*; (of meeting etc) procès-verbal *m*; (register) registre *m*; (file) dossier *m*; (also: criminal ~) casier *m* judiciaire; (MUS: disc) disque *m*; (SPORT) record *m*; (COMPUT) article *m* ♦ *vt* (set down) noter; (MUS: song etc) enregistrer; **in ~ time** en un temps record *inv*; **off the ~** *adj* officieux(euse) ♦ *adv* officieusement; **~ card** *n* (in file) fiche *f*; **~ed delivery** [rɪ'kɔːdɪd-] *n* (BRIT: POST): **~ed delivery letter** *etc* lettre *etc* recommandée; **~er** [rɪ'kɔːdə*] *n* (MUS) flûte *f* à bec; **~ holder** *n* (SPORT) détenteur(trice) du record; **~ing** [rɪ'kɔːdɪŋ] *n* (MUS) enregistrement *m*; **~ player** *n* tourne-disque *m*

recount [rɪ'kaunt] *vt* raconter

re-count ['riːkaunt] *n* (POL: of votes) deuxième compte *m* ♦ *vt* recompter

recoup [rɪ'kuːp] *vt*: **to ~ one's losses** récupérer ce qu'on a perdu, se refaire

recourse [rɪ'kɔːs] *n*: **to have ~ to** avoir recours à

recover [rɪ'kʌvə*] *vt* récupérer ♦ *vi*: **to ~ (from)** (illness) se rétablir (de); (from shock) se remettre (de); **~y** [rɪ'kʌvərɪ] *n* récupération *f*; rétablissement *m*; (ECON) redressement *m*

recreation [rekrɪ'eɪʃən] *n* récréation *f*, détente *f*; **~al** *adj* pour la détente, récréatif(ive)

recruit [rɪ'kruːt] *n* recrue *f* ♦ *vt* recruter

rectangle ['rektæŋgl] *n* rectangle *m*; **rectangular** [rek'tæŋgjulə*] *adj* rectangulaire

rectify ['rektɪfaɪ] *vt* (error) rectifier, corriger

rector ['rektə*] *n* (REL) pasteur *m*

recuperate [rɪ'kuːpəreɪt] *vi* récupérer; (from illness) se rétablir

recur [rɪ'kɜː*] *vi* se reproduire; (symptoms) réapparaître; **~rence** *n* répétition *f*; réapparition *f*; **~rent** *adj* périodique, fréquent(e)

recycle *vt* recycler

red [red] *n* rouge *m*; (POL: pej) rouge *m/f* ♦ *adj* rouge; (hair) roux(rousse); **in the ~** (account) à découvert; (business) en déficit; **~ carpet treatment** *n* réception *f* en grande pompe; **R~ Cross** *n* Croix-Rouge *f*; **~currant** *n* groseille *f* (rouge); **~den** *vt, vi* rougir; **~dish** *adj* rougeâtre; (hair) qui tirent sur le roux

redeem [rɪ'diːm] *vt* (debt) rembourser; (sth in pawn) dégager; (fig, also REL) racheter; **~ing** *adj* (feature) qui sauve, qui rachète (le reste)

redeploy ['riːdɪ'plɔɪ] *vt* (resources) réorganiser

redevelopment [riːdɪ'veləpmənt] *n* rénovation *f*, reconstruction *f*

red: **~-haired** ['heəd] *adj* roux(rousse); **~-handed** [-'hændɪd] *adj*: **to be caught ~-handed** être pris(e) en flagrant délit *or* la main dans le sac; **~head** [-'hed] *n* roux (rousse); **~ herring** *n* (fig) diversion *f*, fausse piste; **~-hot** [-'hɒt] *adj* chauffé(e) au rouge, brûlant(e)

redirect ['riːdaɪ'rekt] *vt* (mail) faire suivre

red light *n*: **to go through a ~** (AUT) brûler un feu rouge; **red-light district** *n* quartier *m* des prostituées

redo ['riː'duː] (irreg) *vt* refaire

redolent ['redəʊlənt] *adj*: **~ of** qui sent; (fig) qui évoque

redress [rɪ'dres] *n* réparation *f* ♦ *vt* redresser

Red Sea *n*: **the ~** la mer Rouge

redskin ['redskɪn] *n* Peau-Rouge *m/f*

red tape *n* (fig) paperasserie (administrative)

reduce [rɪ'djuːs] *vt* réduire; (lower) abaisser; **"~ speed now"** (AUT) "ralentir"; **reduction** [rɪ'dʌkʃən] *n* réduction *f*; (discount) rabais *m*

redundancy [rɪ'dʌndənsɪ] (BRIT) *n* licenciement *m*, mise *f* au chômage

redundant [rɪ'dʌndənt] *adj* (BRIT: worker) mis(e) au chômage, licencié(e); (detail, ob-

ject) superflu(e); **to be made ~** être licencié(e), être mis(e) au chômage

reed [riːd] *n* (BOT) roseau *m*; (MUS: of clarinet etc) anche *f*

reef [riːf] *n* (at sea) récif *m*, écueil *m*

reek [riːk] *vi*: **to ~ (of)** puer, empester

reel [riːl] *n* bobine *f*; (FISHING) moulinet *m*; (CINEMA) bande *f*; (dance) quadrille écossais ♦ *vi* (sway) chanceler; **~ in** *vt* (fish, line) ramener

ref [ref] (inf) *n abbr* (= referee) arbitre *m*

refectory [rɪ'fektərɪ] *n* réfectoire *m*

refer [rɪ'fɜː*] *vt*: **to ~ sb to** (inquirer: for information, patient: to specialist) adresser qn à; (reader: to text) renvoyer qn à; (dispute, decision): **to ~ sth to** soumettre qch à ♦ *vi*: **~ to** (allude to) parler de, faire allusion à; (consult) se reporter à

referee [refə'riː] *n* arbitre *m*; (TENNIS) juge-arbitre *m*; (BRIT: for job application) répondant(e)

reference ['refrəns] *n* référence *f*, renvoi *m*; (mention) allusion *f*, mention *f*; (for job application: letter) références, lettre *f* de recommandation; **with ~ to** (COMM: in letter) me référant à, suite à; **~ book** *n* ouvrage *m* de référence

refill [*vb* 'riː'fɪl, *n* 'riːfɪl] *vt* remplir à nouveau; (pen, lighter etc) recharger ♦ *n* (for pen etc) recharge *f*

refine [rɪ'faɪn] *vt* (sugar, oil) raffiner; (taste) affiner; (theory, idea) fignoler (inf); **~d** *adj* (person, taste) raffiné(e)

reflect [rɪ'flekt] *vt* (light, image) réfléchir, refléter; (fig) refléter ♦ *vi* (think) réfléchir, méditer; **it ~s badly on him** cela te discrédite; **it ~s well on him** c'est tout à son honneur; **~ion** [rɪ'flekʃən] *n* réflexion *f*; (image) reflet *m*; (criticism): **~ion on** critique *f* de; atteinte *f* à; **on ~ion** réflexion faite

reflex ['riːfleks] *adj* réflexe ♦ *n* réflexe *m*; **~ive** [rɪfleksɪv] *adj* (LING) réfléchi(e)

reform [rɪ'fɔːm] *n* réforme *f* ♦ *vt* réformer; **R~ation** [refə'meɪʃən] *n*: **the R~ation** la Réforme; **~atory** (US) *n* ≈ centre *m* d'éducation surveillée

refrain [rɪ'freɪn] *vi*: **to ~ from doing** s'abstenir de faire ♦ *n* refrain *m*

refresh [rɪ'freʃ] *vt* rafraîchir; (subj: sleep) reposer; **~er course** (BRIT) *n* cours *m* de recyclage; **~ing** *adj* (drink) rafraîchissant(e); (sleep) réparateur(trice); **~ments** *npl* rafraîchissements *mpl*

refrigerator [rɪ'frɪdʒəreɪtə*] *n* réfrigérateur *m*, frigidaire *m* (®)

refuel ['riː'fjuəl] *vi* se ravitailler en carburant

refuge ['refjuːdʒ] *n* refuge *m*; **to take ~ in** se réfugier dans

refugee [refju'dʒiː] *n* réfugié(e)

refund [*n* 'riːfʌnd, *vb* rɪ'fʌnd] *n* rembourse-

ment *m* ♦ *vt* rembourser
refurbish ['riː'fɜːbɪʃ] *vt* remettre à neuf
refusal [rɪ'fjuːzəl] *n* refus *m*; **to have first ~ on** avoir droit de préemption sur
refuse¹ [rɪ'fjuːz] *vt, vi* refuser
refuse² ['refjuːs] *n* ordures *fpl*, détritus *mpl*; **~ collection** *n* ramassage *m* d'ordures
regain [rɪ'geɪn] *vt* regagner; retrouver
regal ['riːgəl] *adj* royal(e)
regard [rɪ'gɑːd] *n* respect *m*, estime *f*, considération *f* ♦ *vt* considérer; **to give one's ~s to** faire ses amitiés à; **"with kindest ~s"** "bien amicalement"; **as ~s, with ~ to = regarding; ~ing** *prep* en ce qui concerne; **~less** *adv* quand même; **~less of** sans se soucier de
régime [reɪ'ʒiːm] *n* régime *m*
regiment [*n* 'redʒɪmənt, *vb* 'redʒɪment] *n* régiment *m*; **~al** [redʒɪ'mentl] *adj* d'un *or* du régiment
region ['riːdʒən] *n* région *f*; **in the ~ of** (*fig*) aux alentours de; **~al** *adj* régional(e)
register ['redʒɪstə*] *n* registre *m*; (*also: electoral ~*) liste électorale ♦ *vt* enregistrer; (*birth, death*) déclarer; (*vehicle*) immatriculer; (*POST: letter*) envoyer en recommandé; (*subj: instrument*) marquer ♦ *vi* s'inscrire; (*at hotel*) signer le registre; (*make impression*) être (bien) compris(e); **~ed** *adj* (*letter, parcel*) recommandé(e); **~ed trademark** *n* marque déposée; **registrar** [redʒɪs'trɑː*] *n* officier *m* de l'état civil; **registration** [redʒɪs'treɪʃən] *n* enregistrement *m*; (*BRIT AUT: also: ~ number*) numéro *m* d'immatriculation
registry ['redʒɪstrɪ] *n* bureau *m* de l'enregistrement; **~ office** (*BRIT*) *n* bureau *m* de l'état civil; **to get married in a ~ office** ≈ se marier à la mairie
regret [rɪ'gret] *n* regret *m* ♦ *vt* regretter; **~fully** *adv* à *or* avec regret
regular ['regjʊlə*] *adj* régulier(ère); (*usual*) habituel(le); (*soldier*) de métier ♦ *n* (*client etc*) habitué(e); **~ly** *adv* régulièrement
regulate ['regjʊleɪt] *vt* régler; **regulation** [regjʊ'leɪʃən] *n* (*rule*) règlement *m*; (*adjustment*) réglage *m*
rehabilitation ['riːhəbɪlɪ'teɪʃən] *n* (*of offender*) réinsertion *f*; (*of addict*) réadaptation *f*
rehearsal [rɪ'hɜːsəl] *n* répétition *f*
rehearse [rɪ'hɜːs] *vt* répéter
reign [reɪn] *n* règne *m* ♦ *vi* régner
reimburse [riːɪm'bɜːs] *vt* rembourser
rein [reɪn] *n* (*for horse*) rêne *f*
reindeer ['reɪndɪə*] *n, pl inv* renne *m*
reinforce [riːɪn'fɔːs] *vt* renforcer; **~d concrete** *n* béton armé; **~ments** *npl* (*MIL*) renfort(s) *m(pl)*
reinstate ['riːɪn'steɪt] *vt* rétablir, réintégrer
reject [*n* 'riːdʒekt, *vb* rɪ'dʒekt] *n* (*COMM*) article *m* de rebut ♦ *vt* refuser; (*idea*) reje-

ter; **~ion** ['riːdʒekʃən] *n* rejet *m*, refus *m*
rejoice [rɪ'dʒɔɪs] *vi*: **to ~** (*at or over*) se réjouir (de)
rejuvenate [rɪ'dʒuːvɪneɪt] *vt* rajeunir
relapse [rɪ'læps] *n* (*MED*) rechute *f*
relate [rɪ'leɪt] *vt* (*tell*) raconter; (*connect*) établir un rapport entre ♦ *vi*: **this ~s to** cela se rapporte à; **to ~ to sb** entretenir des rapports avec qn; **~d** *adj* apparenté(e); **relating to** *prep* concernant
relation [rɪ'leɪʃən] *n* (*person*) parent(e); (*link*) rapport *m*, lien *m*; **~ship** *n* rapport *m*, lien *m*; (*personal ties*) relations *fpl*, rapports; (*also: family ~ship*) lien de parenté
relative ['relətɪv] *n* parent(e) ♦ *adj* relatif(ive); **all her ~s** toute sa famille; **~ly** *adv* relativement
relax [rɪ'læks] *vi* (*muscle*) se relâcher; (*person: unwind*) se détendre ♦ *vt* relâcher; (*mind, person*) détendre; **~ation** [riːlæk'seɪʃən] *n* relâchement *m*; (*of mind*) détente *f*, relaxation *f*; (*recreation*) détente, délassement *m*; **~ed** *adj* détendu(e); **~ing** *adj* délassant(e)
relay ['riːleɪ] *n* (*SPORT*) course *f* de relais ♦ *vt* (*message*) retransmettre, relayer
release [rɪ'liːs] *n* (*from prison, obligation*) libération *f*; (*of gas etc*) émission *f*; (*of film etc*) sortie *f*; (*new recording*) disque *m* ♦ *vt* (*prisoner*) libérer; (*gas etc*) émettre, dégager; (*free: from wreckage etc*) dégager; (*TECH: catch, spring etc*) faire jouer; (*book, film*) sortir; (*report, news*) rendre public, publier
relegate ['relɪgeɪt] *vt* reléguer; (*BRIT SPORT*): **to be ~d** descendre dans une division inférieure
relent [rɪ'lent] *vi* se laisser fléchir; **~less** *adj* implacable; (*unceasing*) continuel(le)
relevant ['reləvənt] *adj* (*question*) pertinent(e); (*fact*) significatif(ive); (*information*) utile; **~ to** ayant rapport à, approprié à
reliable [rɪ'laɪəbl] *adj* (*person, firm*) sérieux(euse), fiable; (*method, machine*) fiable; (*news, information*) sûr(e); **reliably** *adv*: **to be reliably informed** savoir de source sûre
reliance [rɪ'laɪəns] *n*: **~ (on)** (*person*) confiance *f* (en); (*drugs, promises*) besoin *m* (de), dépendance *f* (de)
relic ['relɪk] *n* (*REL*) relique *f*; (*of the past*) vestige *m*
relief [rɪ'liːf] *n* (*from pain, anxiety etc*) soulagement *m*; (*help, supplies*) secours *m(pl)*; (*ART, GEO*) relief *m*
relieve [rɪ'liːv] *vt* (*pain, patient*) soulager; (*fear, worry*) dissiper; (*bring help*) secourir; (*take over from: gen*) relayer; (: *guard*) relever; **to ~ sb of sth** débarrasser qn de qch; **to ~ o.s.** se soulager
religion [rɪ'lɪdʒən] *n* religion *f*; **religious** [rɪ'lɪdʒəs] *adj* religieux(euse); (*book*) de piété
relinquish [rɪ'lɪŋkwɪʃ] *vt* abandonner;

(*plan, habit*) renoncer à

relish ['relɪʃ] n (CULIN) condiment m; (*enjoyment*) délectation f ♦ vt (*food etc*) savourer; **to ~ doing** se délecter à faire

relocate ['ri:ləʊ'keɪt] vt installer ailleurs ♦ vi déménager, s'installer ailleurs

reluctance [rɪ'lʌktəns] n répugnance f

reluctant [rɪ'lʌktənt] adj peu disposé(e), qui hésite; **~ly** adv à contrecœur

rely on [rɪlaɪ] vt fus (*be dependent*) dépendre de; (*trust*) compter sur

remain [rɪ'meɪn] vi rester; **~der** n reste m; **~ing** adj qui reste; **~s** npl restes mpl

remand [rɪ'mɑːnd] n: **on ~** en détention préventive ♦ vt: **to be ~ed in custody** être placé(e) en détention préventive; **~ home** (BRIT) n maison f d'arrêt

remark [rɪ'mɑːk] n remarque f, observation f ♦ vt (faire) remarquer, dire; **~able** adj remarquable

remedial [rɪ'miːdɪəl] adj (*tuition, classes*) de rattrapage; **~ exercises** gymnastique corrective

remedy ['remədɪ] n: **~ (for)** remède m (contre or à) ♦ vt remédier à

remember [rɪ'membə*] vt se rappeler, se souvenir de; (*send greetings*): **~ me to him** saluez-le de ma part; **remembrance** [rɪ'membrəns] n souvenir m; mémoire f

remind [rɪ'maɪnd] vt: **to ~ sb of** rappeler à qn; **to ~ sb to do** faire penser à qn à faire, rappeler à qn qu'il doit faire; **~er** n (*souvenir*) souvenir m; (*letter*) rappel m

reminisce [remɪ'nɪs] vi: **to ~ (about)** évoquer ses souvenirs (de)

reminiscent [remɪ'nɪsnt] adj: **to be ~ of** rappeler, faire penser à

remiss [rɪ'mɪs] adj négligent(e)

remission [rɪ'mɪʃən] n (*of illness, sins*) rémission f; (*of debt, prison sentence*) remise f

remit [rɪ'mɪt] vt (*send: money*) envoyer; **~tance** n paiement m

remnant ['remnənt] n reste m, restant m; (*of cloth*) coupon m; **~s** npl (COMM) fins fpl de série

remorse [rɪ'mɔːs] n remords m; **~ful** adj plein(e) de remords; **~less** adj (*fig*) impitoyable

remote [rɪ'məʊt] adj éloigné(e), lointain(e); (*person*) distant(e); (*possibility*) vague; **~ control** n télécommande f; **~ly** adv au loin; (*slightly*) très vaguement

remould ['riːməʊld] (BRIT) n (*tyre*) pneu rechapé

removable [rɪ'muːvəbl] adj (*detachable*) amovible

removal [rɪ'muːvəl] n (*taking away*) enlèvement m; suppression f; (BRIT: *from house*) déménagement m; (*from office: dismissal*) renvoi m; (*of stain*) nettoyage m; (MED) ablation f; **~ van** (BRIT) n camion m de déménagement

remove [rɪ'muːv] vt enlever, retirer; (*employee*) renvoyer; (*stain*) faire partir; (*abuse*) supprimer; (*doubt*) chasser

render ['rendə*] vt rendre; **~ing** n (MUS etc) interprétation f

rendezvous n rendez-vous m inv

renew [rɪ'njuː] vt renouveler; (*negotiations*) reprendre; (*acquaintance*) renouer; **~able** adj (*energy*) renouvelable; **~al** n renouvellement m; reprise f

renounce [rɪ'naʊns] vt renoncer à

renovate ['renəveɪt] vt rénover; (*art work*) restaurer

renown [rɪ'naʊn] n renommée f; **~ed** adj renommé(e)

rent [rent] n loyer m ♦ vt louer; **~al** n (*for television, car*) (prix m de) location f

rep [rep] n abbr = **representative**; = **repertory**

repair [rɪ'pɛə*] n réparation f ♦ vt réparer; **in good/bad ~** en bon/mauvais état; **~ kit** n trousse f de réparation

repatriate [riː'pætrɪeɪt] vt rapatrier

repay [riː'peɪ] (*irreg*) vt (*money, creditor*) rembourser; (*sb's efforts*) récompenser; **~ment** n remboursement m

repeal [rɪ'piːl] n (*of law*) abrogation f ♦ vt (*law*) abroger

repeat [rɪ'piːt] n (RADIO, TV) reprise f ♦ vt répéter (COMM: *order*) renouveler; (SCOL: *a class*) redoubler ♦ vi répéter; **~edly** adv souvent, à plusieurs reprises

repel [rɪ'pel] vt repousser; **~lent** adj repoussant(e) ♦ n: **insect ~lent** insectifuge m

repent [rɪ'pent] vi: **to ~ (of)** se repentir (de); **~ance** n repentir m

repertory ['repətərɪ] n (*also: ~ theatre*) théâtre m de répertoire

repetition [repə'tɪʃən] n répétition f

repetitive [rɪ'petɪtɪv] adj (*movement, work*) répétitif(ive); (*speech*) plein(e) de redites

replace [rɪ'pleɪs] vt (*put back*) remettre, replacer; (*take the place of*) remplacer; **~ment** n (*substitution*) remplacement m; (*person*) remplaçant(e)

replay ['riːpleɪ] n (*of match*) match rejoué; (*of tape, film*) répétition f

replenish [rɪ'plenɪʃ] vt (*glass*) remplir (de nouveau); (*stock etc*) réapprovisionner

replica ['replɪkə] n réplique f, copie exacte

reply [rɪ'plaɪ] n réponse f ♦ vi répondre; **~ coupon** n coupon-réponse m

report [rɪ'pɔːt] n rapport m; (PRESS etc) reportage m; (BRIT: *also: school ~*) bulletin m (scolaire); (*of gun*) détonation f ♦ vt rapporter, faire un compte rendu de; (PRESS etc) faire un reportage sur; (*bring to notice: occurrence*) signaler ♦ vi (*make a ~*) faire un rapport (or un reportage); (*present o.s.*): **to ~ (to sb)** se présenter (chez qn); (*be responsible to*): **to ~ to sb** être sous les ordres de qn; ~ **card** (US, SCOTTISH) n bulletin m scolaire; ~**edly** adv: **she is** ~**edly living in ...** elle habiterait ...; **he** ~**edly told them to ...** il leur aurait ordonné de ...; ~**er** n reporter m

repose [rɪ'pəuz] n: **in** ~ en or au repos

represent [reprɪ'zent] vt représenter; (view, belief) présenter, expliquer; (describe): **to** ~ **sth as** présenter or décrire qch comme; ~**ation** [reprɪzen'teɪʃən] n représentation f; ~**ations** npl (protest) démarche f; ~**ative** n représentant(e); (US: POL) député m ♦ adj représentatif(ive), caractéristique

repress [rɪ'pres] vt réprimer; ~**ion** [rɪ'preʃən] n répression f

reprieve [rɪ'priːv] n (LAW) grâce f; (fig) sursis m, délai m

reprisal [rɪ'praɪzəl] n: ~**s** npl représailles fpl

reproach [rɪ'prəutʃ] vt: **to** ~ **sb with sth** reprocher qch à qn; ~**ful** adj de reproche

reproduce [riːprə'djuːs] vt reproduire ♦ vi se reproduire; **reproduction** [riːprə'dʌkʃən] n reproduction f

reproof [rɪ'pruːf] n reproche m

reptile ['reptaɪl] n reptile m

republic [rɪ'pʌblɪk] n république f; ~**an** adj républicain(e)

repudiate [rɪ'pjuːdɪeɪt] vt répudier, rejeter

repulsive [rɪ'pʌlsɪv] adj repoussant(e), répulsif(ive)

reputable ['repjutəbl] adj de bonne réputation; (occupation) honorable

reputation [repju'teɪʃən] n réputation f

reputed [rɪ'pjuːtɪd] adj (supposed) supposé(e); ~**ly** adv d'après ce qu'on dit

request [rɪ'kwest] n demande f; (formal) requête f ♦ vt: **to** ~ (**of** or **from sb**) demander (à qn); ~ **stop** (BRIT) n (for bus) arrêt facultatif

require [rɪ'kwaɪə*] vt (need: subj: person) avoir besoin de; (: thing, situation) demander; (want) exiger; (order): **to** ~ **sb to do sth/sth of sb** exiger que qn fasse qch/qch de qn; ~**ment** n exigence f; besoin m; condition requise

requisite ['rekwɪzɪt] n chose f nécessaire ♦ adj requis(e), nécessaire; **toilet** ~**s** accessoires mpl de toilette

requisition [rekwɪ'zɪʃən] n: ~ (**for**) demande f (de) ♦ vt (MIL) réquisitionner

rescue ['reskjuː] n (from accident) sauvetage m; (help) secours mpl ♦ vt sauver; ~ **party** n équipe f de sauvetage; ~**r** n sauveteur m

research [rɪ'sɜːtʃ] n recherche(s) f(pl) ♦ vt faire des recherches sur

resemblance [rɪ'zembləns] n ressemblance f

resemble [rɪ'zembl] vt ressembler à

resent [rɪ'zent] vt être contrarié(e) par; ~**ful** adj irrité(e), plein(e) de ressentiment; ~**ment** n ressentiment m

reservation [rezə'veɪʃən] n (booking) réser-

vation f; (doubt) réserve f; (for tribe) réserve; **to make a** ~ (**in a hotel/a restaurant/ on a plane**) réserver or retenir une chambre/une table/une place

reserve [rɪ'zɜːv] n réserve f; (SPORT) remplaçant(e) ♦ vt (seats etc) réserver, retenir; ~**s** npl (MIL) réservistes mpl; **in** ~ en réserve; ~**d** adj réservé(e)

reshuffle ['riː'ʃʌfl] n: **Cabinet** ~ (POL) remaniement ministériel

residence ['rezɪdəns] n résidence f; ~ **permit** (BRIT) n permis m de séjour

resident ['rezɪdənt] n résident(e) ♦ adj résidant(e); ~**ial** [rezɪ'denʃəl] adj (area) résidentiel(le); (course) avec hébergement sur place; ~**ial school** n internat m

residue ['rezɪdjuː] n reste m; (CHEM, PHYSICS) résidu m

resign [rɪ'zaɪn] vt (one's post) démissionner de ♦ vi démissionner; **to** ~ **o.s. to** se résigner à; ~**ation** [rezɪg'neɪʃən] n (of post) démission f; (state of mind) résignation f; ~**ed** adj résigné(e)

resilient [rɪ'zɪlɪənt] adj (material) élastique; (person) qui réagit, qui a du ressort

resist [rɪ'zɪst] vt résister à; ~**ance** n résistance f

resolution [rezə'luːʃən] n résolution f

resolve [rɪ'zɒlv] n résolution f ♦ vt (problem) résoudre ♦ vi: **to** ~ **to do** résoudre or décider de faire

resort [rɪ'zɔːt] n (town) station f; (recourse) recours m ♦ vi: **to** ~ **to** avoir recours à; **in the last** ~ en dernier ressort

resound [rɪ'zaund] vi: **to** ~ (**with**) retentir or résonner (de); ~**ing** [rɪ'zaundɪŋ] adj retentissant(e)

resource [rɪ'sɔːs] n ressource f; ~**s** npl (supplies, wealth etc) ressources; ~**ful** adj ingénieux(euse), débrouillard(e)

respect [rɪs'pekt] n respect m ♦ vt respecter; ~**s** npl (compliments) respects, hommages mpl; **with** ~ **to** en ce qui concerne; **in this** ~ à cet égard; ~**able** adj respectable; ~**ful** adj respectueux(euse)

respite ['respaɪt] n répit m

resplendent [rɪs'plendənt] adj resplendissant(e)

respond [rɪs'pɒnd] vi répondre; (react) réagir; **response** [rɪs'pɒns] n réponse f; réaction f

responsibility [rɪspɒnsə'bɪlɪtɪ] n responsabilité f

responsible [rɪs'pɒnsəbl] adj (liable): ~ (**for**) responsable (de); (person) digne de confiance; (job) qui comporte des responsabilités

responsive [rɪs'pɒnsɪv] adj qui réagit; (person) qui n'est pas réservé(e) or indifférent(e)

rest [rest] n repos m; (stop) arrêt m, pause f; (MUS) silence m; (support) support m, appui *m*; *(remainder)* reste *m*, restant *m* ♦ *vi* se reposer; *(be supported)*: **to ~ on** appuyer *or* reposer sur; *(remain)* rester ♦ *vt* *(lean)*: **to ~ sth on/against** appuyer qch sur/contre; **the ~ of them** les autres; **it ~s with him to ...** c'est à lui de ...

restaurant ['rɛstərɒŋ] *n* restaurant *m*; **~ car** *(BRIT)* *n* wagon-restaurant *m*

restful ['rɛstful] *adj* reposant(e)

restive ['rɛstɪv] *adj* agité(e), impatient(e); *(horse)* rétif(ive)

restless ['rɛstləs] *adj* agité(e)

restoration [rɛstə'reɪʃən] *n* restauration *f*; restitution *f*; rétablissement *m*

restore [rɪ'stɔ:*] *vt (building)* restaurer; *(sth stolen)* restituer; *(peace, health)* rétablir; **to ~ to** *(former state)* ramener à

restrain [rɪs'treɪn] *vt* contenir; *(person)*: **to ~ (from doing)** retenir (de faire); **~ed** *adj (style)* sobre; *(manner)* mesuré(e); **~t** *n (restriction)* contrainte *f*; *(moderation)* retenue *f*

restrict [rɪs'trɪkt] *vt* restreindre, limiter; **~ion** [rɪs'trɪkʃən] *n* restriction *f*, limitation *f*

rest room *(US)* *n* toilettes *fpl*

result [rɪ'zʌlt] *n* résultat *m* ♦ *vi*: **to ~ in** aboutir à, se terminer par; **as a ~ of** à la suite de

resume [rɪ'zju:m] *vt, vi (work, journey)* reprendre

résumé ['reɪzju:meɪ] *n* résumé *m*; *(US)* curriculum vitae *m*

resumption [rɪ'zʌmpʃən] *n* reprise *f*

resurgence [rɪ'sɜ:dʒəns] *n (of energy, activity)* regain *m*

resurrection [rɛzə'rɛkʃən] *n* résurrection *f*

resuscitate [rɪ'sʌsɪteɪt] *vt (MED)* réanimer

retail [*n, adj* 'ri:teɪl, *vb* 'ri:'teɪl] *adj* de *or* au détail ♦ *adv* au détail; **~er** ['ri:teɪlə*] *n* détaillant(e); **~ price** *n* prix *m* de détail

retain [rɪ'teɪn] *vt (keep)* garder, conserver; **~er** *n (fee)* acompte *m*, provision *f*

retaliate [rɪ'tælɪeɪt] *vi*: **to ~ (against)** se venger (de); **retaliation** [rɪtælɪ'eɪʃən] *n* représailles *fpl*, vengeance *f*

retarded [rɪ'tɑ:dɪd] *adj* retardé(e)

retch [rɛtʃ] *vi* avoir des haut-le-cœur

retentive [rɪ'tɛntɪv] *adj*: **~ memory** excellente mémoire

retina ['rɛtɪnə] *n* rétine *f*

retire [rɪ'taɪə*] *vi (give up work)* prendre sa retraite; *(withdraw)* se retirer, partir; *(go to bed)* (aller) se coucher; **~d** *adj (person)* retraité(e); **~ment** *n* retraite *f*; **retiring** [rɪ'taɪərɪŋ] *adj (shy)* réservé(e); *(leaving)* sortant(e)

retort [rɪ'tɔ:t] *vi* riposter

retrace [rɪ'treɪs] *vt*: **to ~ one's steps** revenir sur ses pas

retract [rɪ'trækt] *vt (statement, claws)* rétracter; *(undercarriage, aerial)* rentrer, escamoter

retrain ['ri:'treɪn] *vt (worker)* recycler

retread ['ri:trɛd] *n (tyre)* pneu rechapé

retreat [rɪ'tri:t] *n* retraite *f* ♦ *vi* battre en retraite

retribution [rɛtrɪ'bju:ʃən] *n* châtiment *m*

retrieval [rɪ'tri:vəl] *n (see vb)* récupération *f*, réparation *f*

retrieve [rɪ'tri:v] *vt (sth lost)* récupérer; *(situation, honour)* sauver; *(error, loss)* réparer; **~r** *n* chien *m* d'arrêt

retrospect ['retrəuspɛkt] *n*: **in ~** rétrospectivement, après coup; **~ive** [retrəu'spɛktɪv] *adj* rétrospectif(ive); *(law)* rétroactif(ive)

return [rɪ'tɜ:n] *n (going or coming back)* retour *m*; *(of sth stolen etc)* restitution *f*; *(FINANCE: from land, shares)* rendement *m*, rapport *m* ♦ *cpd (journey)* de retour; *(BRIT: ticket)* aller et retour; *(match)* retour ♦ *vi (come back)* revenir; *(go back)* retourner ♦ *vt* rendre; *(bring back)* rapporter; *(send back; also: ball)* renvoyer; *(put back)* remettre; *(POL: candidate)* élire; **~s** *npl (COMM)* recettes *fpl*; *(FINANCE)* bénéfices *mpl*; **in ~ (for)** en échange (de); **by ~ (of post)** par retour (du courrier); **many happy ~s (of the day)!** bon anniversaire!

reunion [ri:'ju:njən] *n* réunion *f*

reunite ['ri:ju:'naɪt] *vt* réunir

rev [rev] *n abbr (AUT: = revolution)* tour *m* ♦ *vt (also: ~ up)* emballer

revamp ['ri:'væmp] *vt (firm, system etc)* réorganiser

reveal [rɪ'vi:l] *vt (make known)* révéler; *(display)* laisser voir; **~ing** *adj* révélateur(trice); *(dress)* au décolleté généreux *or* suggestif

revel ['rɛvl] *vi*: **to ~ in sth/in doing** se délecter de qch/à faire

revelry ['rɛvlrɪ] *n* festivités *fpl*

revenge [rɪ'vɛndʒ] *n* vengeance *f*; **to take ~ on** *(enemy)* se venger sur

revenue ['rɛvənju:] *n* revenu *m*

reverberate [rɪ'vɜ:bəreɪt] *vi (sound)* retentir, se répercuter; *(fig: shock etc)* se propager

reverence ['rɛvərəns] *n* vénération *f*, révérence *f*

Reverend ['rɛvərənd] *adj (in titles)*: **the ~ John Smith** *(Anglican)* le révérend John Smith; *(Catholic)* l'abbé (John) Smith; *(Protestant)* le pasteur (John) Smith

reversal [rɪ'vɜ:səl] *n (of opinion)* revirement *m*; *(of order)* renversement *m*; *(of direction)* changement *m*

reverse [rɪ'vɜ:s] *n* contraire *m*, opposé *m*; *(back)* dos *m*, envers *m*; *(of paper)* verso *m*; *(of coin; also: setback)* revers *m*; *(AUT: also: ~ gear)* marche *f* arrière ♦ *adj (order, direction)* opposé(e), inverse ♦ *vt (order, position)* changer, inverser; *(direction, policy)* changer complètement de; *(decision)* annuler; *(roles)* renverser; *(car)* faire marche arrière avec ♦ *vi (BRIT: AUT)* faire marche arrière; **he ~d (the car) into a wall** il a embouti un mur en marche arrière; **~d charge call** (*BRIT*) *n* (*TEL*) communication *f* en PCV; **reversing lights** (*BRIT*) *npl* (*AUT*) feux *mpl* de marche arrière *or* de recul

revert [rɪ'vɜːt] *vi*: **to ~ to** revenir à, retourner à

review [rɪ'vjuː] *n* revue *f*; (*of book, film*) critique *f*, compte rendu; (*of situation, policy*) examen *m*, bilan *m* ♦ *vt* passer en revue; faire la critique de; examiner; **~er** *n* critique *m*

revile [rɪ'vaɪl] *vt* injurier

revise [rɪ'vaɪz] *vt* réviser, modifier; (*manuscript*) revoir, corriger ♦ *vi* (*study*) réviser; **revision** [rɪ'vɪʒən] *n* révision *f*

revival [rɪ'vaɪvəl] *n* reprise *f*; (*recovery*) rétablissement *m*; (*of faith*) renouveau *m*

revive [rɪ'vaɪv] *vt* (*person*) ranimer; (*custom*) rétablir; (*economy*) relancer; (*hope, courage*) raviver, faire renaître; (*play*) reprendre ♦ *vi* (*person*) reprendre connaissance; (*: from ill health*) se rétablir; (*hope etc*) renaître; (*activity*) reprendre

revoke [rɪ'vəuk] *vt* révoquer; (*law*) abroger

revolt [rɪ'vəult] *n* révolte *f* ♦ *vi* se révolter, se rebeller ♦ *vt* révolter, dégoûter; **~ing** *adj* dégoûtant(e)

revolution [revə'luːʃən] *n* révolution *f*; (*of wheel etc*) tour *m*, révolution; **~ary** *adj* révolutionnaire ♦ *n* révolutionnaire *m/f*

revolve [rɪ'vɒlv] *vi* tourner

revolver [rɪ'vɒlvə*] *n* revolver *m*

revolving [rɪ'vɒlvɪŋ] *adj* tournant(e); (*chair*) pivotant(e); **~ door** (porte *f* à) tambour *m*

revulsion [rɪ'vʌlʃən] *n* dégoût *m*, répugnance *f*

reward [rɪ'wɔːd] *n* récompense *f* ♦ *vt*: **to ~ (for)** récompenser (de); **~ing** *adj* (*fig*) qui (en) vaut la peine, gratifiant(e)

rewind ['riː'waɪnd] (*irreg*) *vt* (*tape*) rembobiner

rewire ['riː'waɪə*] *vt* (*house*) refaire l'installation électrique de

rheumatism ['ruːmətɪzəm] *n* rhumatisme *m*

Rhine [raɪn] *n*: **the ~** le Rhin

rhinoceros [raɪ'nɒsərəs] *n* rhinocéros *m*

Rhone [rəun] *n*: **the ~** le Rhône

rhubarb ['ruːbɑːb] *n* rhubarbe *f*

rhyme [raɪm] *n* rime *f*; (*verse*) vers *mpl*

rhythm ['rɪðəm] *n* rythme *m*

rib [rɪb] *n* (*ANAT*) côte *f*

ribbon ['rɪbən] *n* ruban *m*; **in ~s** (*torn*) en lambeaux

rice [raɪs] *n* riz *m*; **~ pudding** *n* riz au lait

rich [rɪtʃ] *adj* riche; (*gift, clothes*) somptueux(euse) ♦ *npl*: **the ~** les riches *mpl*; **~es** *npl* richesses *fpl*; **~ly** *adv* richement; (*deserved, earned*) largement

rickets ['rɪkɪts] *n* rachitisme *m*

rickety ['rɪkɪtɪ] *adj* branlant(e)

rickshaw ['rɪkʃɔː] *n* pousse-pousse *m inv*

rid [rɪd] (*pt, pp* **rid**) *vt*: **to ~ sb of** débarrasser qn de; **to get ~ of** se débarrasser de

riddle ['rɪdl] *n* (*puzzle*) énigme *f* ♦ *vt*: **to be ~d with** être criblé(e) de; (*fig: guilt, corruption, doubts*) être en proie à

ride [raɪd] (*pt* **rode**, *pp* **ridden**) *n* promenade *f*, tour *m*; (*distance covered*) trajet *m* ♦ *vi* (*as sport*) monter (à cheval), faire du cheval; (*go somewhere: on horse, bicycle*) aller (à cheval *or* bicyclette *etc*); (*journey: on bicycle, motorcycle, bus*) rouler ♦ *vt* (*a certain horse*) monter; (*distance*) parcourir, faire; **to take sb for a ~** (*fig*) faire marcher qn; **to ~ a horse/bicycle** monter à cheval/à bicyclette; **~r** *n* cavalier(ère); (*in race*) jockey *m*; (*on bicycle*) cycliste *m/f*; (*on motorcycle*) motocycliste *m/f*

ridge [rɪdʒ] *n* (*of roof, mountain*) arête *f*; (*of hill*) faîte *m*; (*on object*) strie *f*

ridicule ['rɪdɪkjuːl] *n* ridicule *m*; dérision *f*

ridiculous [rɪ'dɪkjuləs] *adj* ridicule

riding ['raɪdɪŋ] *n* équitation *f*; **~ school** *n* manège *m*, école *f* d'équitation

rife [raɪf] *adj* répandu(e); **~ with** abondant(e) en, plein(e) de

riffraff ['rɪfræf] *n* racaille *f*

rifle ['raɪfl] *n* fusil *m* (à canon rayé) ♦ *vt* vider, dévaliser; **~ through** *vt* (*belongings*) fouiller; (*papers*) feuilleter; **~ range** *n* champ *m* de tir; (*at fair*) stand *m* de tir

rift [rɪft] *n* fente *f*, fissure *f*; (*fig: disagreement*) désaccord *m*

rig [rɪg] *n* (*also: oil ~: at sea*) plate-forme pétrolière ♦ *vt* (*election etc*) truquer; **~ out** (*BRIT*) *vt*: **to ~ out as/in** habiller en/de; **~ up** *vt* arranger, faire avec des moyens de fortune; **~ging** *n* (*NAUT*) gréement *m*

right [raɪt] *adj* (*correctly chosen: answer, road etc*) bon(bonne); (*true*) juste, exact(e); (*suitable*) approprié(e), convenable; (*just*) juste, équitable; (*morally good*) bien; (*not left*) droit(e) ♦ *n* (*what is morally right*) bien *m*; (*title, claim*) droit *m*; (*not left*) droite *f* ♦ *adv* (*answer*) correctement, juste; (*treat*) bien, comme il faut; (*not on the left*) à droite ♦ *vt* redresser ♦ *excl* bon!; **to be ~** (*person*) avoir raison; (*answer*) être juste *or* correct(e); (*clock*) être à l'heure (juste); **by ~s** en toute justice; **on the ~** à droite; **to be in the ~** avoir raison; **~ now** en ce moment même; tout de suite; **~ in the middle** en plein milieu; **~ away** immédiatement; **~ angle** *n* (*MATH*) angle droit; **~eous** ['raɪtʃəs] *adj* droit(e), vertueux(euse); (*anger*) justifié(e); **~ful** *adj* légitime; **~-handed** *adj* (*person*) droitier(ère); **~-hand man** *n* bras droit (*fig*); **~-hand side** *n* côté droit; **~ly** *adv* (*with reason*) à juste titre; **~ of way** *n* droit *m* de passage; (*AUT*)

priorité f; ~**-wing** adj (POL) de droite
rigid ['rɪdʒɪd] adj rigide; (principle, control) strict(e)
rigmarole ['rɪgmərəʊl] n comédie f
rigorous ['rɪgərəs] adj rigoureux(euse)
rile [raɪl] vt agacer
rim [rɪm] n bord m; (of spectacles) monture f; (of wheel) jante f
rind [raɪnd] n (of bacon) couenne f; (of lemon etc) écorce f, zeste m; (of cheese) croûte f
ring [rɪŋ] (pt **rang**, pp **rung**) n anneau m; (on finger) bague f; (also: wedding ~) alliance f; (of people, objects) cercle m; (of spies) réseau m; (of smoke etc) rond m; (arena) piste f, arène f; (for boxing) ring m; (sound of bell) bourdonner ♦ vt (BRIT: TEL: also: ~ up) téléphoner à, appeler; (bell) faire sonner; **to ~ the bell** sonner; **to give sb a ~** (BRIT: TEL) appeler qn; ~ **back** (BRIT) vt, vi (TEL) rappeler; ~ **off** (BRIT) vi (TEL) raccrocher; ~ **up** (BRIT) vt (TEL) appeler; ~**ing** n (of telephone) sonnerie f; (of bell) tintement m; (in ears) bourdonnement m; ~**ing tone** (BRIT) n (TEL) sonnerie f; ~**leader** n (of gang) chef m, meneur m
ringlets ['rɪŋlɪts] npl anglaises fpl
ring road: (BRIT) n route f de ceinture; (motorway) périphérique m
rink [rɪŋk] n (also: ice ~) patinoire f
rinse [rɪns] vt rincer
riot ['raɪət] n émeute f, (of flowers, colour) profusion f ♦ vi faire une émeute, manifester avec violence; **to run ~** se déchaîner; ~**ous** adj (mob, assembly) séditieux(euse), déchaîné(e); (living, behaviour) débauché(e); (party) très animé(e); (welcome) délirant(e)
rip [rɪp] n déchirure f ♦ vt déchirer ♦ vi se déchirer; ~**cord** ['rɪpkɔːd] n poignée f d'ouverture
ripe [raɪp] adj (fruit) mûr(e); (cheese) fait(e); ~**n** vt mûrir ♦ vi mûrir
ripple ['rɪpl] n ondulation f, (of applause, laughter) cascade f ♦ vi onduler
rise [raɪz] (pt **rose**, pp **risen**) n (slope) côte f, pente f; (hill) hauteur f; (increase: in wages: BRIT) augmentation f; (: in prices, temperature) hausse f, augmentation f; (fig: to power etc) ascension f ♦ vi s'élever, monter; (prices, numbers) augmenter; (waters) monter; (sun; person: from chair, bed) se lever; (also: ~ up: tower, building) s'élever; (: rebel) se révolter; (in rank) s'élever; **to give ~ to** donner lieu à; **to ~ to the occasion** se montrer à la hauteur; **rising** adj (increasing: number, prices) en hausse; (tide) montant(e); (sun, moon) levant(e)
risk [rɪsk] n risque m ♦ vt risquer; **at ~ en**

danger; **at one's own ~** à ses risques et périls; ~**y** adj risqué(e)
rissole ['rɪsəʊl] n croquette f
rite [raɪt] n rite m; **last ~s** derniers sacrements; **ritual** ['rɪtjʊəl] adj rituel(le) ♦ n rituel m
rival ['raɪvəl] adj, n rival(e); (in business) concurrent(e) ♦ vt (match) égaler; ~**ry** n rivalité f, concurrence f
river ['rɪvə*] n rivière f, (major, also fig) fleuve m ♦ cpd (port, traffic) fluvial(e); **up/down** ~ en amont/aval; ~**bank** n rive f, berge f
rivet ['rɪvɪt] n rivet m ♦ vt (fig) river, fixer
Riviera [rɪvɪ'eərə] n: **the (French)** ~ la Côte d'Azur; **the Italian** ~ la Riviera (italienne)
road [rəʊd] n route f; (in town) rue f; (fig) chemin, voie f; **major/minor** ~ route principale or à priorité/voie secondaire; ~ **accident** n accident m de la circulation; ~**block** n barrage routier; ~**hog** n chauffard m; ~ **map** n carte routière; ~ **safety** n sécurité routière; ~**side** n bord m de la route, bas-côté m; ~**sign** n panneau m de signalisation; ~**way** n chaussée f; ~ **works** npl travaux mpl (de réfection des routes); ~**worthy** adj en bon état de marche
roam [rəʊm] vi errer, vagabonder
roar [rɔː*] n rugissement m; (of crowd) hurlements mpl; (of vehicle, thunder, storm) grondement m ♦ vi rugir; hurler; gronder; **to ~ with laughter** éclater de rire; **to do a ~ing trade** faire des affaires d'or
roast [rəʊst] n rôti m ♦ vt (faire) rôtir; (coffee) griller, torréfier; ~ **beef** n rôti m de bœuf, rosbif m
rob [rɒb] vt (person) voler; (bank) dévaliser; **to ~ sb of sth** voler or dérober qch à qn; (fig: deprive) priver qn de qch; ~**ber** n bandit m, voleur m; ~**bery** n vol m
robe [rəʊb] n (for ceremony etc) robe f; (also: bath~) peignoir m; (US) couverture f
robin ['rɒbɪn] n rouge-gorge m
robust [rəʊ'bʌst] adj robuste; (material, appetite) solide
rock [rɒk] n (substance) roche f, roc m; (boulder) rocher m; (US: small stone) caillou m; (BRIT: sweet) ≈ sucre m d'orge ♦ vt (swing gently: cradle) balancer; (: child) bercer; (shake) ébranler, secouer ♦ vi (se) balancer; être ébranlé(e) or secoué(e); **on the** ~**s** (drink) avec des glaçons; (marriage etc) en train de craquer; ~ **and roll** n rock (and roll) m, rock'n'roll m; ~**-bottom** adj (fig: prices) sacrifié(e); ~**ery** n (jardin m de) rocaille f
rocket ['rɒkɪt] n fusée f; (MIL) fusée, roquette f
rocking chair ['rɒkɪŋ-] n fauteuil m à bascule

rocking horse n cheval m à bascule
rocky ['rɒkɪ] adj (hill) rocheux(euse); (path) rocailleux(euse)
rod [rɒd] n (wooden) baguette f; (metallic) tringle f; (TECH) tige f; (also: fishing ~) canne f à pêche
rode [rəud] pt of **ride**
rodent ['rəudənt] n rongeur m
rodeo ['rəudɪəu] (US) n rodéo m
roe [rəu] n (species: also: ~ deer) chevreuil m; (of fish, also: hard ~) œufs mpl de poisson; **soft** ~ laitance f
rogue [rəug] n coquin(e)
role [rəul] n rôle m
roll [rəul] n rouleau m; (of banknotes) liasse f; (also: bread ~) petit pain; (register) liste f; (sound: of drums etc) roulement m ♦ vt rouler; (also: ~ up: string) enrouler; (: sleeves) retrousser; (: ~ out: pastry) étendre au rouleau, abaisser ♦ vi rouler; ~ **about** vi rouler çà et là; (person) se rouler par terre; ~ **around** vi = **roll about**; ~ **by** vi (time) s'écouler, passer; ~ **in** vi (mail, cash) affluer; ~ **over** vi se retourner; ~ **up** vi (inf: arrive) arriver, s'amener ♦ vt rouler; ~ **call** n appel m; ~**er** n rouleau m; (wheel) roulette f; (for road) rouleau compresseur; ~**er coaster** n montagnes fpl russes; ~**er skates** npl patins mpl à roulettes; ~**ing** ['rəulɪŋ] adj (landscape) onduleux(euse); ~**ing pin** n rouleau m à pâtisserie; ~**ing stock** n (RAIL) matériel roulant
ROM [rɒm] n abbr (= read only memory) mémoire morte
Roman ['rəumən] adj romain(e); ~ **Catholic** adj, n catholique (m/f)
romance [rə'mæns] n (love affair) idylle f; (charm) poésie f; (novel) roman m à l'eau de rose
Romania [rəu'meɪnɪə] n Roumanie f; ~**n** adj roumain(e) ♦ n Roumain(e); (LING) roumain m
Roman numeral n chiffre romain
romantic [rə'mæntɪk] adj romantique; sentimental(e)
Rome [rəum] n Rome
romp [rɒmp] n jeux bruyants ♦ vi (also: ~ about) s'ébattre, jouer bruyamment; ~**ers** ['rɒmpəz] npl barboteuse f
roof [ru:f] (pl ~s) n toit m ♦ vt couvrir (d'un toit); **the** ~ **of the mouth** la voûte du palais; ~**ing** n toiture f; ~ **rack** n (AUT) galerie f
rook [ruk] n (bird) freux m; (CHESS) tour f
room [rum] n (in house) pièce f; (also: bed~) chambre f (à coucher); (in school etc) salle f; (space) place f; ~**s** npl (lodging) meublé m; "~**s to let**" (BRIT) or "~**s for rent**" (US) "chambres à louer"; **single/double** ~ chambre pour une personne/deux personnes; **there is** ~ **for improvement** cela lais-

se à désirer; ~**ing house** (US) n maison f or immeuble m de rapport; ~**mate** m/f de chambre; ~ **service** n service m des chambres (dans un hôtel); ~**y** adj spacieux(euse); (garment) ample
roost [ru:st] vi se jucher
rooster ['ru:stə*] n (esp US) coq m
root [ru:t] n (BOT, MATH) racine f; (fig: of problem) origine f, fond m ♦ vi (plant) s'enraciner; ~ **about** vi (fig) fouiller; ~ **for** vt fus encourager, applaudir; ~ **out** vt (find) dénicher
rope [rəup] n corde f; (NAUT) cordage m ♦ vt (tie up or together) attacher; (climbers: also: ~ together) encorder; (area: ~ off) interdire l'accès de; (divide off) séparer; **to know the** ~**s** (fig) être au courant, connaître les ficelles; ~ **in** vt (fig: person) embringuer
rosary ['rəuzərɪ] n chapelet m
rose [rəuz] pt of **rise** ♦ n rose f; (also: ~bush) rosier m; (on watering can) pomme f
rosé ['rəuzeɪ] n rosé m
rosebud ['rəuzbʌd] n bouton m de rose
rosemary ['rəuzmərɪ] n romarin m
roster ['rɒstə*] n: **duty** ~ tableau m de service
rostrum ['rɒstrəm] n tribune f (pour un orateur etc)
rosy ['rəuzɪ] adj rose; **a** ~ **future** un bel avenir
rot [rɒt] n (decay) pourriture f; (fig: pej) idioties fpl ♦ vt, vi pourrir
rota ['rəutə] n liste f, tableau m de service; **on a** ~ **basis** par roulement
rotary ['rəutərɪ] adj rotatif(ive)
rotate [rəu'teɪt] vt (revolve) faire tourner; (change round: jobs) faire à tour de rôle ♦ vi (revolve) tourner; **rotating** adj (movement) tournant(e)
rote [rəut] n: **by** ~ machinalement, par cœur
rotten ['rɒtn] adj (decayed) pourri(e); (dishonest) corrompu(e); (inf: bad) mauvais(e), moche; **to feel** ~ (ill) être mal fichu(e)
rotund [rəu'tʌnd] adj (person) rondelet(te)
rough [rʌf] adj (cloth, skin) rêche, rugueux(euse); (terrain) accidenté(e); (path) rocailleux(euse); (voice) rauque, rude; (person, manner: coarse) rude, fruste; (: violent) brutal(e); (district, weather) mauvais(e); (sea) houleux(euse); (plan etc) ébauché(e); (guess) approximatif(ive) ♦ n (GOLF) rough m; **to** ~ **it** vivre à la dure; **to sleep** ~ (BRIT) coucher à la dure; ~**age** n fibres fpl alimentaires; ~-**and-ready** adj rudimentaire; ~ **copy**, ~**draft** n brouillon m; ~**ly** adv (handle) rudement, brutalement; (speak) avec brusquerie; (make) grossièrement; (approximately) à peu près, en gros
roulette [ru:'let] n roulette f

Roumania [ruːˈmeɪnɪə] *n* = **Romania**
round [raʊnd] *adj* rond(e) ♦ *n* (BRIT: *of toast*) tranche *f*; (*duty: of policeman, milkman etc*) tournée *f*; (: *of doctor*) visites *fpl*; (*game: of cards, in competition*) partie *f*; (*BOXING*) round *m*; (*of talks*) série *f* ♦, *vt* (*corner*) tourner ♦ *prep* autour de ♦ *adv*: **all ~ tout** autour; **the long way ~** (par) le chemin le plus long; **all the year ~** toute l'année; **it's just ~ the corner** (*fig*) c'est tout près; **~ the clock** 24 heures sur 24; **to go ~ to sb's (house)** aller chez qn; **go ~ the back** passez par derrière; **to go ~ a house** visiter une maison, faire le tour d'une maison; **enough to go ~** assez pour tout le monde; **~ of ammunition** cartouche *f*; **~ of applause** ban *m*, applaudissements *mpl*; **~ of drinks** tournée *f*; **~ of sandwiches** sandwich *m*; **~ off** *vt* (*speech etc*) terminer; **~ up** *vt* rassembler; (*criminals*) effectuer une rafle de; (*price, figure*) arrondir (au chiffre supérieur); **~about** *n* (*BRIT: AUT*) rond-point *m* (à sens giratoire); (: *at fair*) manège *m* (de chevaux de bois) ♦ *adj* (*route, means*) détourné(e); **~ers** *n* (*game*) sorte de baseball; **~ly** *adv* (*fig*) tout net, carrément; **~-shouldered** *adj* au dos rond; **~ trip** *n* (voyage *m*) aller et retour *m*; **~up** *n* rassemblement *m*; (*of criminals*) rafle *f*
rouse [raʊz] *vt* (*wake up*) réveiller; (*stir up*) susciter; provoquer; éveiller.
rousing [ˈraʊzɪŋ] *adj* (*welcome*) enthousiaste
rout [raʊt] *n* (*MIL*) déroute *f*
route [ruːt] *n* itinéraire *m*; (*of bus*) parcours *m*; (*of trade, shipping*) route *f*; **~ map** (*BRIT*) *n* (for journey) croquis *m* d'itinéraire
routine [ruːˈtiːn] *adj* (*work*) ordinaire, courant(e); (*procedure*) d'usage ♦ *n* (*habits*) habitudes *fpl*; (*pej*) train-train *m*; (*THEATRE*) numéro *m*
rove [rəʊv] *vt* (*area, streets*) errer dans
row[1] [rəʊ] *n* (*line*) rangée *f*; (*of people, seats, KNITTING*) rang *m*; (*behind one another: of cars, people*) file *f* ♦ *vi* (*in boat*) ramer; (*as sport*) faire de l'aviron ♦ *vt* (*boat*) faire aller à la rame *or* à l'aviron; **in a row** (*fig*) d'affilée
row[2] [raʊ] *n* (*noise*) vacarme *m*; (*dispute*) dispute *f*, querelle *f*; (*scolding*) réprimande *f*, savon *m* ♦ *vi* se disputer, se quereller
rowboat [ˈrəʊbəʊt] (*US*) *n* canot *m* (à rames)
rowdy [ˈraʊdɪ] *adj* chahuteur(euse); (*occasion*) tapageur(euse)
rowing [ˈrəʊɪŋ] *n* canotage *m*; (*as sport*) aviron *m*; **~ boat** (*BRIT*) *n* canot *m* (à rames)
royal [ˈrɔɪəl] *adj* royal(e); **R~ Air Force** (*BRIT*) *n* armée de l'air britannique
royalty [ˈrɔɪəltɪ] *n* (*royal persons*) (membres

mpl de la) famille royale; (*payment: to author*) droits *mpl* d'auteur; (: *to inventor*) royalties *fpl*
rpm *abbr* (*AUT*: = revs per minute*) tr/mn
RSVP *abbr* (= *répondez s'il vous plaît*) R.S.V.P.
Rt Hon. *abbr* (*BRIT*: = Right Honourable*) titre donné aux députés de la Chambre des communes
rub [rʌb] *vt* frotter; frictionner; (*hands*) se frotter ♦ *n* (*with cloth*) coup *m* chiffon *or* de torchon; **to give sth a ~** donner un coup de chiffon *or* de torchon à; **to ~ sb up** (*BRIT*) *or* **to ~ sb** (*US*) **the wrong way** prendre qn à rebrousse-poil; **~ off** *vi* partir; **~ off on** *vt fus* déteindre sur; **~ out** *vt* effacer
rubber [ˈrʌbə*] *n* caoutchouc *m*; (*BRIT*: *eraser*) gomme *f* (à effacer); **~ band** *n* élastique *m*; **~ plant** *n* caoutchouc *m* (*plante verte*)
rubbish [ˈrʌbɪʃ] *n* (*from household*) ordures *fpl*; (*fig: pej*) camelote *f*; (: *nonsense*) bêtises *fpl*, idioties *fpl*; **~ bin** (*BRIT*) *n* poubelle *f*; **~ dump** *n* décharge publique, dépotoir *m*
rubble [ˈrʌbl] *n* décombres *mpl*; (*smaller*) gravats *mpl*; (*CONSTR*) blocage *m*
ruby [ˈruːbɪ] *n* rubis *m*
rucksack [ˈrʌksæk] *n* sac *m* à dos
rudder [ˈrʌdə*] *n* gouvernail *m*
ruddy [ˈrʌdɪ] *adj* (*face*) coloré(e); (*inf: damned*) sacré(e), fichu(e)
rude [ruːd] *adj* (*impolite*) impoli(e); (*coarse*) grossier(ère); (*shocking*) indécent(e), inconvenant(e)
ruffian [ˈrʌfɪən] *n* brute *f*, voyou *m*
ruffle [ˈrʌfl] *vt* (*hair*) ébouriffer; (*clothes*) chiffonner; (*fig: person*): **to get ~d** s'énerver
rug [rʌg] *n* petit tapis *m*; (*BRIT*: *blanket*) couverture *f*
rugby [ˈrʌgbɪ] *n* (*also*: ~ **football**) rugby *m*
rugged [ˈrʌgɪd] *adj* (*landscape*) accidenté(e); (*features, character*) rude
rugger [ˈrʌgə*] (*BRIT*: *inf*) *n* rugby *m*
ruin [ˈruːɪn] *n* ruine *f* ♦ *vt* ruiner; (*spoil, clothes*) abîmer; (*event*) gâcher; **~s** *npl* (*of building*) ruine(s)
rule [ruːl] *n* règle *f*; (*regulation*) règlement *m*; (*government*) autorité *f*, gouvernement *m* ♦ *vt* (*country*) gouverner; (*person*) dominer ♦ *vi* commander; (*LAW*) statuer; **as a ~** normalement, en règle générale; **~ out** *vt* exclure; **~d** *adj* (*paper*) réglé(e); **~r** *n* (*sovereign*) souverain(e); (*for measuring*) règle *f*, **ruling** *adj* (*party*) au pouvoir; (*class*) dirigeant(e) ♦ *n* (*LAW*) décision *f*
rum [rʌm] *n* rhum *m*
Rumania [ruːˈmeɪnɪə] *n* = **Romania**
rumble [ˈrʌmbl] *vi* gronder; (*stomach, pipe*) gargouiller

rummage ['rʌmɪdʒ] *vi* fouiller
rumour ['ruːmə*] (*US* rumor) *n* rumeur *f*, bruit *m* (qui court) ♦ *vt*: **it is ~ed that** le bruit court que
rump [rʌmp] *n* (*of animal*) croupe *f*; (*inf: of person*) postérieur *m*; ~ **steak** *n* rumsteck *m*
rumpus ['rʌmpəs] (*inf*) *n* tapage *m*, chahut *m*
run [rʌn] (*pt* ran, *pp* run) *n* (*fast pace*) (pas *m* de) course *f*; (*outing*) tour *m* or promenade *f* (en voiture); (*distance travelled*) parcours *m*, trajet *m*; (*series*) suite *f*, série *f*; (*THEATRE*) série de représentations; (*SKI*) piste *f*; (*CRICKET, BASEBALL*) point *m*; (*in tights, stockings*) maille filée, échelle *f* ♦ *vt* (*operate: business*) diriger; (: *competition, course*) organiser; (: *hotel, house*) tenir; (*race*) participer à; (*COMPUT*) exécuter; (*to pass: hand, finger*) passer; (*water, bath*) faire couler; (*PRESS: feature*) publier ♦ *vi* courir; (*flee*) s'enfuir; (*work: machine, factory*) marcher; (*bus, train*) circuler; (*continue: play*) se jouer; (: *contract*) être valide; (*flow: river, bath; nose*) couler; (*colours, washing*) déteindre; (*in election*) être candidat, se présenter; **to go for a ~** faire un peu de course à pied; **there was a ~ on ...** (*meat, tickets*) les gens se sont rués sur ...; **in the long ~** à longue échéance; à la longue; **on the ~** en fuite; **I'll ~ you to the station** je vais vous emmener *or* conduire à la gare; **to ~ a risk** courir un risque; ~ **about** *vi* (*children*) courir çà et là; ~ **across** *vt fus* (*find*) trouver par hasard; ~ **around** *vi* = run about; ~ **down** *vt* (*production*) réduire progressivement; (*factory*) réduire progressivement la production de; (*AUT*) renverser; (*criticize*) critiquer, dénigrer; **to be ~ down** (*person: tired*) être fatigué(e) *or* à plat; ~ **in** (*BRIT*) *vt* (*car*) roder; ~ **into** *vt fus* (*meet: person*) rencontrer par hasard; (: *trouble*) se heurter à; (*collide with*) heurter; ~ **off** *vi* s'enfuir ♦ *vt* (*water*) laisser s'écouler; (*copies*) tirer; ~ **out** *vi* (*person*) sortir en courant; (*liquid*) couler; (*lease*) expirer; (*money*) être épuisé(e); ~ **out of** *vt fus* se trouver à court de; ~ **over** *vt* (*AUT*) écraser ♦ *vt fus* (*revise*) revoir, reprendre; ~ **through** *vt fus* (*recapitulate*) reprendre; (*play*) répéter; ~ **up** *vt*: **to ~ up against** (*difficulties*) se heurter à; **to ~ up a debt** s'endetter; **~away** *adj* (*horse*) emballé(e); (*truck*) fou(folle); (*person*) fugitif(ive); (*teenager*) fugueur(euse)
rung [rʌŋ] *pp of* ring ♦ *n* (*of ladder*) barreau *m*
runner ['rʌnə*] *n* (*in race: person*) coureur(euse); (: *horse*) partant *m*; (*on sledge*) patin *m*; (*for drawer etc*) coulisseau *m*; ~ **bean** (*BRIT*) *n* haricot *m* (à rames); **~-up** *n* second(e)

running ['rʌnɪŋ] *n* course *f*; (*of business, organization*) gestion *f*, direction *f* ♦ *adj* (*water*) courant(e); **to be in/out of the ~ for sth** être/ne pas être sur les rangs pour qch; **6 days** ~ 6 jours de suite; ~ **commentary** *n* commentaire détaillé; ~ **costs** *npl* frais *mpl* d'exploitation
runny ['rʌnɪ] *adj* qui coule
run-of-the-mill ['rʌnəvðə'mɪl] *adj* ordinaire, banal(e)
runt [rʌnt] (*also pej*) *n* avorton *m*
run-up ['rʌnʌp] *n*: ~ **to sth** (*election etc*) période *f* précédant qch
runway ['rʌnweɪ] *n* (*AVIAT*) piste *f*
rupee [ruː'piː] *n* roupie *f*
rupture ['rʌptʃə*] *n* (*MED*) hernie *f*
rural ['rʊərəl] *adj* rural(e)
rush [rʌʃ] *n* (*hurry*) hâte *f*, précipitation *f*; (*of crowd; COMM: sudden demand*) ruée *f*; (*current*) flot *m*; (*of emotion*) vague *f*; (*BOT*) jonc *m* ♦ *vt* (*hurry*) transporter *or* envoyer d'urgence ♦ *vi* se précipiter; ~ **hour** *n* heures *fpl* de pointe
rusk [rʌsk] *n* biscotte *f*
Russia ['rʌʃə] *n* Russie *f*; **~n** *adj* russe ♦ *n* Russe *m/f*; (*LING*) russe *m*
rust [rʌst] *n* rouille *f* ♦ *vi* rouiller
rustic ['rʌstɪk] *adj* rustique
rustle ['rʌsl] *vi* bruire, produire un bruissement ♦ *vt* (*paper*) froisser; (*US: cattle*) voler
rustproof ['rʌstpruːf] *adj* inoxydable
rusty ['rʌstɪ] *adj* rouillé(e)
rut [rʌt] *n* ornière *f*; (*ZOOL*) rut *m*; **to be in a ~** suivre l'ornière, s'encroûter
ruthless ['ruːθləs] *adj* sans pitié, impitoyable
rye [raɪ] *n* seigle *m*; ~ **bread** *n* pain de seigle

S s

Sabbath ['sæbəθ] *n* (*Jewish*) sabbat *m*; (*Christian*) dimanche *m*
sabotage ['sæbətɑːʒ] *n* sabotage *m* ♦ *vt* saboter
saccharin(e) ['sækərɪn] *n* saccharine *f*
sachet ['sæʃeɪ] *n* sachet *m*
sack [sæk] *n* (*bag*) sac *m* ♦ *vt* (*dismiss*) renvoyer, mettre à la porte; (*plunder*) piller, mettre à sac; **to get the ~** être renvoyé(e), être mis(e) à la porte; **~ing** *n* (*material*) toile *f* à sac; (*dismissal*) renvoi *m*

sacrament ['sækrəmənt] *n* sacrement *m*
sacred ['seɪkrɪd] *adj* sacré(e)
sacrifice ['sækrɪfaɪs] *n* sacrifice *m* ♦ *vt* sacrifier
sad [sæd] *adj* triste; (*deplorable*) triste, fâcheux(euse)
saddle ['sædl] *n* selle *f* ♦ *vt* (*horse*) seller; **to be ~d with sth** (*inf*) avoir qch sur les bras; **~bag** *n* sacoche *f*
sadistic [sə'dɪstɪk] *adj* sadique
sadly *adv* tristement; (*unfortunately*) malheureusement; (*seriously*) fort
sadness ['sædnəs] *n* tristesse *f*
s.a.e. *n abbr* = **stamped addressed envelope**
safe [seɪf] *adj* (*out of danger*) hors de danger, en sécurité; (*not dangerous*) sans danger; (*unharmed*) indemne; **~ journey!** bon voyage!; (*cautious*) prudent(e); (*sure: bet etc*) assuré(e) ♦ *n* coffre-fort *m*; **~ from** à l'abri de; **~ and sound** sain(e) et sauf(sauve); (*just*) **to be on the ~ side** pour plus de sûreté, par précaution; **~-conduct** *n* sauf-conduit *m*; **~-deposit** *n* (*vault*) dépôt *m* de coffres-forts; (*box*) coffre-fort *m*; **~guard** *n* sauvegarde *f*, protection *f* ♦ *vt* sauvegarder, protéger; **~keeping** *n* bonne garde; **~ly** *adv* (*assume, say*) sans risque d'erreur; (*drive, arrive*) sans accident; **~ sex** *n* rapports *mpl* sexuels sans risque, sexe *m* sans risques
safety ['seɪftɪ] *n* sécurité *f*; **~ belt** *n* ceinture *f* de sécurité; **~ pin** *n* épingle *f* de sûreté *or* de nourrice; **~ valve** *n* soupape *f* de sûreté
sag [sæg] *vi* s'affaisser; (*hem, breasts*) pendre
sage [seɪdʒ] *n* (*herb*) sauge *f*; (*person*) sage *m*
Sagittarius [sædʒɪ'tɛərɪəs] *n* le Sagittaire
Sahara [sə'hɑːrə] *n*: **the ~ (Desert)** le (désert du) Sahara
said [sed] *pt, pp of* **say**
sail [seɪl] *n* (*on boat*) voile *f*; (*trip*): **to go for a ~** faire un tour en bateau ♦ *vt* (*boat*) manœuvrer, piloter ♦ *vi* (*travel: ship*) avancer, naviguer; (*set off*) partir, prendre la mer; (*SPORT*) faire de la voile; **they ~ed into Le Havre** ils sont entrés dans le port du Havre; **~ through** *vi, vt fus* (*fig*) réussir haut la main; **~boat** (*US*) *n* bateau *m* à voiles, voilier *m*; **~ing** *n* (*SPORT*) voile *f*; **to go ~ing** faire de la voile; **~ing boat** *n* bateau *m* à voiles, voilier *m*; **~ing ship** *n* grand voilier *m*; **~or** *n* marin *m*, matelot *m*
saint [seɪnt] *n* saint(e)
sake [seɪk] *n*: **for the ~ of** pour (l'amour de), dans l'intérêt de; par égard pour
salad ['sæləd] *n* salade *f*; **~ bowl** *n* saladier *m*; **~ cream** (*BRIT*) *n* (sorte *f* de) mayonnaise *f*; **~ dressing** *n* vinaigrette *f*
salary ['sælərɪ] *n* salaire *m*

sale [seɪl] *n* vente *f*; (*at reduced prices*) soldes *mpl*; **"for ~"** "à vendre"; **on ~** en vente; **on ~ or return** vendu(e) avec faculté de retour; **~room** *n* salle *f* des ventes; **~s assistant** *n* vendeur(euse); **~s clerk** (*US*) *n* vendeur(euse); **~sman** (*irreg*) *n* vendeur *m*; (*representative*) représentant *m* de commerce; **~swoman** (*irreg*) *n* vendeuse *f*; (*representative*) représentante *f* de commerce
sallow ['sæləʊ] *adj* cireux(euse)
salmon ['sæmən] *n inv* saumon *m*
saloon [sə'luːn] *n* (*US*) bar *m*; (*BRIT: AUT*) berline *f*; (*ship's lounge*) salon *m*
salt [sɔːlt] *n* sel *m* ♦ *vt* saler; **~ cellar** *n* salière *f*; **~water** *adj* de mer; **~y** *adj* salé(e)
salute [sə'luːt] *n* salut *m* ♦ *vt* saluer
salvage ['sælvɪdʒ] *n* (*saving*) sauvetage *m*; (*things saved*) biens sauvés *or* récupérés ♦ *vt* sauver, récupérer
salvation [sæl'veɪʃən] *n* salut *m*; **S~ Army** *n* armée *f* du Salut
same [seɪm] *adj* même ♦ *pron*: **the ~** le(la) même, les mêmes; **the ~ book as** le même livre que; **at the ~ time** en même temps; **all** *or* **just the ~** tout de même, quand même; **to do the ~** faire de même, en faire autant; **to do the ~ as sb** faire comme qn; **the ~ to you!** à vous de même!; (*after insult*) toi-même!
sample ['sɑːmpl] *n* échantillon *m*; (*blood*) prélèvement *m* ♦ *vt* (*food, wine*) goûter
sanctimonious [sæŋktɪ'məʊnɪəs] *adj* moralisateur(trice)
sanction ['sæŋkʃən] *n* approbation *f*, sanction *f*
sanctity ['sæŋktɪtɪ] *n* sainteté *f*, caractère sacré
sanctuary ['sæŋktjʊərɪ] *n* (*holy place*) sanctuaire *m*; (*refuge*) asile *m*; (*for wild life*) réserve *f*
sand [sænd] *n* sable *m* ♦ *vt* (*furniture: also:* **~ down**) poncer
sandal ['sændl] *n* sandale *f*
sand: **~box** (*US*) *n* tas *m* de sable; **~castle** *n* château *m* de sable; **~paper** *n* papier *m* de verre; **~pit** (*BRIT*) *n* (*for children*) tas *m* de sable; **~stone** *n* grès *m*
sandwich ['sænwɪdʒ] *n* sandwich *m*; **cheese/ham ~** sandwich au fromage/jambon; **~ course** (*BRIT*) *n* cours *m* de formation professionnelle
sandy ['sændɪ] *adj* sablonneux(euse); (*colour*) sable *inv*, blond roux *inv*
sane [seɪn] *adj* (*person*) sain(e) d'esprit; (*outlook*) sensé(e), sain(e)
sang [sæŋ] *pt of* **sing**
sanitary ['sænɪtərɪ] *adj* (*system, arrangements*) sanitaire; (*clean*) hygiénique; **~ towel** (*US* **~ napkin**) *n* serviette *f* hygiénique
sanitation [sænɪ'teɪʃən] *n* (*in house*) installations *fpl* sanitaires; (*in town*) système *m* sanitaire; **~ department** (*US*) *n* service *m*

de voirie

sanity ['sænɪtɪ] n santé mentale; (common sense) bon sens

sank [sæŋk] pt of **sink**

Santa Claus [sæntə'klɔːz] n le père Noël

sap [sæp] n (of plants) sève f ♦ vt (strength) saper, miner

sapling ['sæplɪŋ] n jeune arbre m

sapphire ['sæfaɪə*] n saphir m

sarcasm ['sɑːkæzəm] n sarcasme m, raillerie f

sardine [sɑː'diːn] n sardine f

Sardinia [sɑː'dɪnɪə] n Sardaigne f

sash [sæʃ] n écharpe f

sat [sæt] pt, pp of **sit**

satchel ['sætʃəl] n cartable m

satellite ['sætəlaɪt] n satellite m; ~ **dish** n antenne f parabolique; ~ **television** n télévision f par câble

satin ['sætɪn] n satin m ♦ adj en or de satin, satiné(e)

satisfaction [sætɪs'fækʃən] n satisfaction f; **satisfactory** [sætɪs'fæktərɪ] adj satisfaisant(e)

satisfy ['sætɪsfaɪ] vt satisfaire, contenter; (convince) convaincre, persuader; ~**ing** adj satisfaisant(e)

Saturday ['sætədeɪ] n samedi m

sauce [sɔːs] n sauce f; ~**pan** n casserole f

saucer ['sɔːsə*] n soucoupe f

saucy ['sɔːsɪ] adj impertinent(e)

Saudi ['saudɪ]: ~ **Arabia** n Arabie Saoudite; ~ **(Arabian)** adj saoudien(ne)

sauna ['sɔːnə] n sauna m

saunter ['sɔːntə*] vi: **to** ~ **along/in/out** etc marcher/entrer/sortir etc d'un pas nonchalant

sausage ['sɒsɪdʒ] n saucisse f; (cold meat) saucisson m; ~ **roll** n ≈ friand m

savage ['sævɪdʒ] adj (cruel, fierce) brutal(e), féroce; (primitive) primitif(ive), sauvage ♦ n sauvage m/f

save [seɪv] vt (person, belongings) sauver; (money) mettre de côté, économiser; (time) (faire) gagner, (keep) garder; (COMPUT) sauvegarder; (SPORT: stop) arrêter; (avoid: trouble) éviter ♦ vi (also: ~ **up**) mettre de l'argent de côté ♦ n (SPORT) arrêt m (du ballon) ♦ prep sauf, à l'exception de

saving ['seɪvɪŋ] n économie f ♦ adj: **the** ~ **grace of sth** ce qui rachète qch; ~**s** npl (money saved) économies fpl; ~**s account** n compte m d'épargne; ~**s bank** n caisse f d'épargne

saviour ['seɪvjə*] (US **savior**) n sauveur m

savour ['seɪvə*] (US **savor**) vt savourer; ~**y** (US **savory**) adj (dish: not sweet) salé(e)

saw [sɔː] (pt ~**ed**, pp ~**ed** or **sawn**) vt scier ♦ n (tool) scie f ♦ pt of **see**; ~**dust** n sciure f; ~**mill** n scierie f; ~**n-off** adj: ~**n-off shotgun** carabine f à canon scié

saxophone ['sæksəfəun] n saxophone m

say [seɪ] (pt, pp **said**) n: **to have one's** ~ dire ce qu'on a à dire ♦ vt dire; **to have a** or **some** ~ **in sth** avoir voix au chapitre; **could you** ~ **that again?** pourriez-vous répéter ce que vous venez de dire?; **that goes without** ~**ing** cela va sans dire, cela va de soi; ~**ing** n dicton m, proverbe m

scab [skæb] n croûte f; (pej) jaune m

scaffold ['skæfəuld] n échafaud m; ~**ing** n échafaudage m

scald [skɔːld] n brûlure f ♦ vt ébouillanter

scale [skeɪl] n (of fish) écaille f; (MUS) gamme f; (of ruler, thermometer etc) graduation f, échelle (graduée); (of salaries, fees etc) barème m; (of map, also size, extent) échelle ♦ vt (mountain) escalader; ~**s** npl (for weighing) balance f; (also: bathroom ~) pèse-personne m inv; **on a large** ~ sur une grande échelle, en grand; ~ **of charges** tableau m des tarifs; ~ **down** vt réduire

scallop ['skɔləp] n coquille f Saint-Jacques; (SEWING) feston m

scalp [skælp] n cuir chevelu ♦ vt scalper

scamper ['skæmpə*] vi: **to** ~ **away** or **off** détaler

scampi ['skæmpɪ] npl langoustines (frites), scampi mpl

scan [skæn] vt scruter, examiner; (glance at quickly) parcourir; (TV, RADAR) balayer ♦ n (MED) scanographie f

scandal ['skændl] n scandale m; (gossip) ragots mpl

Scandinavian [skændɪ'neɪvɪən] adj scandinave

scant [skænt] adj insuffisant(e); ~**y** adj peu abondant(e), insuffisant(e); (underwear) minuscule

scapegoat ['skeɪpgəut] n bouc m émissaire

scar [skɑː*] n cicatrice f ♦ vt marquer (d'une cicatrice)

scarce ['skɛəs] adj rare, peu abondant(e); **to make o.s.** ~ (inf) se sauver; ~**ly** adv à peine; **scarcity** n manque m, pénurie f

scare ['skɛə*] n peur f, panique f ♦ vt effrayer, faire peur à; **to** ~ **sb stiff** faire une peur bleue à qn; **bomb** ~ alerte f à la bombe; ~ **away** vt faire fuir; ~ **off** vt = **scare away**; ~**crow** n épouvantail m; ~**d** adj: **to be** ~**d** avoir peur

scarf [skɑːf] (pl ~**s** or **scarves**) n (long) écharpe f; (square) foulard m

scarlet ['skɑːlət] adj écarlate; ~ **fever** n scarlatine f

scary ['skɛərɪ] (inf) adj effrayant(e)

scathing ['skeɪðɪŋ] adj cinglant(e), acerbe

scatter ['skætə*] vt éparpiller, répandre; (crowd) disperser ♦ vi se disperser; ~**brained** adj écervelé(e), étourdi(e)

scavenger ['skævɪndʒə*] n (person: in bins etc) pilleur m de poubelles

scene [siːn] n scène f; (of crime, accident) lieu(x) m(pl); (sight, view) spectacle m, vue f; **~ry** ['sɪːnərɪ] n (THEATRE) décor(s) m(pl); (landscape) paysage m; **scenic** ['siːnɪk] adj (picturesque) offrant de beaux paysages or panoramas

scent [sent] n parfum m, odeur f; (track) piste f

sceptical ['skeptɪkəl] (US **skeptical**) adj sceptique

schedule ['ʃedjuːl, (US) 'skedʒuːl] n programme m, plan m; (of trains) horaire m; (of prices etc) barème m, tarif m ♦ vt prévoir; **on** ~ à l'heure (prévue); à la date prévue; **to be ahead of/behind** ~ avoir de l'avance/du retard; **~d flight** n vol régulier

scheme [skiːm] n plan m, projet m; (dishonest plan, plot) complot m, combine f, (arrangement) arrangement m, classification f; (pension ~ etc) régime m ♦ vi comploter, manigancer; **scheming** ['skiːmɪŋ] adj rusé(e), intrigant(e) ♦ n manigances fpl, intrigues fpl

scholar ['skɒlə*] n érudit(e); (pupil) boursier(ière); **~ly** adj érudit(e), savant(e); **~ship** n (knowledge) érudition f; (grant) bourse f (d'études)

school [skuːl] n école f; (secondary ~) collège m, lycée m; (US: university) université f; (in university) faculté f ♦ cpd scolaire; **~book** n livre m scolaire or de classe; **~boy** n écolier m; collégien m, lycéen m; **~children** npl écoliers mpl; collégiens mpl, lycéens mpl; **~days** npl années fpl de scolarité; **~girl** n écolière f; collégienne f, lycéenne f; **~ing** n instruction f, études fpl; **~master** n (primary) instituteur m; (secondary) professeur m; **~mistress** n institutrice f; professeur m; **~teacher** n instituteur(trice); professeur m

sciatica [saɪˈætɪkə] n sciatique f

science ['saɪəns] n science f; ~ **fiction** n science-fiction f; **scientific** [saɪənˈtɪfɪk] adj scientifique; **scientist** ['saɪəntɪst] n scientifique m/f; (eminent) savant m

scissors ['sɪzəz] npl ciseaux mpl

scoff [skɒf] vt (BRIT: inf: eat) avaler, bouffer ♦ vi: **to** ~ **(at)** (mock) se moquer (de)

scold [skəʊld] vt gronder

scone [skɒn] n sorte de petit pain rond au lait

scoop [skuːp] n pelle f (à main); (for ice cream) boule f à glace; (PRESS) scoop m; ~ **out** vt évider, creuser; ~ **up** vt ramasser

scooter ['skuːtə*] n (also: motor ~) scooter m; (toy) trottinette f

scope [skəʊp] n (capacity: of plan, undertaking) portée f, envergure f; (: of person) compétence f, capacités fpl; (opportunity) possibilités fpl; **within the** ~ **of** dans les limites de

scorch [skɔːtʃ] vt (clothes) brûler (légèrement), roussir; (earth, grass) dessécher, brûler

score [skɔː*] n score m, décompte m des points; (MUS) partition f; (twenty) vingt ♦ vt (goal, point) marquer; (success) remporter ♦ vi marquer des points; (FOOTBALL) marquer un but; (keep ~) compter les points; **~s of** (very many) beaucoup de, un tas de (fam); **on that** ~ sur ce chapitre, à cet égard; **to** ~ **6 out of 10** obtenir 6 sur 10; ~ **out** vt rayer, barrer, biffer; **~board** n tableau m

scorn ['skɔːn] n mépris m, dédain m

Scorpio ['skɔːpɪəʊ] n le Scorpion

Scot [skɒt] n Écossais(e)

Scotch [skɒtʃ] n whisky m, scotch m

scotch vt (plan) faire échouer; (rumour) étouffer

scot-free ['skɒtˈfriː] adv: **to get off** ~ s'en tirer sans être puni(e)

Scotland ['skɒtlənd] n Écosse f

Scots [skɒts] adj écossais(e); **~man** (irreg) n Écossais; **~woman** (irreg) n Écossaise f

Scottish ['skɒtɪʃ] adj écossais(e)

scoundrel ['skaʊndrəl] n vaurien m

scour ['skaʊə*] vt (search) battre, parcourir

scourge [skɜːdʒ] n fléau m

scout [skaʊt] n (MIL) éclaireur m; (also: boy ~) scout m; **girl** ~ (US) guide f; ~ **around** vi explorer, chercher

scowl [skaʊl] vi se renfrogner, avoir l'air maussade; **to** ~ **at** regarder de travers

scrabble ['skræbl] vi (also: ~ around: search) chercher à tâtons; (claw): **to** ~ **(at)** gratter ♦ n: **S~** ® Scrabble m ®

scram [skræm] (inf) vi ficher le camp

scramble ['skræmbl] n (rush) bousculade f, ruée f ♦ vi: **to** ~ **up/down** grimper/descendre tant bien que mal; **to** ~ **out** sortir or descendre à toute vitesse; **to** ~ **through** se frayer un passage (à travers); **to** ~ **for** se bousculer or se disputer pour (avoir); **~d eggs** npl œufs brouillés

scrap [skræp] n bout m, morceau m; (fight) bagarre f; (also: ~ iron) ferraille f ♦ vt jeter, mettre au rebut; (fig) abandonner, laisser tomber ♦ vi (fight) se bagarrer; **~s** npl (waste) déchets mpl; **~book** n album m; ~ **dealer** n marchand m de ferraille

scrape [skreɪp] vt, vi gratter, racler ♦ n: **to get into a** ~ s'attirer des ennuis; **to** ~ **through** réussir de justesse; ~ **together** vt (money) racler ses fonds de tiroir pour réunir

scrap: ~ **heap** n: **on the** ~ **heap** (fig) au rancart or rebut; ~ **merchant** (BRIT) n marchand m de ferraille; ~ **paper** n papier m brouillon; **~py** adj décousu(e)

scratch [skrætʃ] n égratignure f, rayure f; éraflure f; (from claw) coup m de griffe ♦ cpd: ~ **team** équipe de fortune or improvisée ♦ vt (rub) (se) gratter; (record) rayer; (paint etc) érafler; (with claw, nail) griffer ♦ vi (se) gratter; **to start from** ~ partir de zéro; **to be up to** ~ être à la hauteur

scrawl [skrɔ:l] vi gribouiller

scrawny ['skrɔ:nɪ] adj décharné(e)

scream [skri:m] n cri perçant, hurlement m ♦ vi crier, hurler

screech [skri:tʃ] vi hurler; (tyres) crisser; (brakes) grincer

screen [skri:n] n écran m; (in room) paravent m; (fig) écran, rideau m ♦ vt (conceal) masquer, cacher; (from the wind etc) abriter, protéger; (film) projeter; (candidates etc) filtrer; ~**ing** n (MED) test m (or tests) de dépistage; ~**play** n scénario m

screw [skru:] n vis f ♦ vt (also: ~ in) visser; ~ **up** vt (paper etc) froisser; **to** ~ **up one's eyes** plisser les yeux; ~**driver** n tournevis m

scribble ['skrɪbl] vt, vi gribouiller, griffonner

script [skrɪpt] n (CINEMA etc) scénario m, texte m; (system of writing) (écriture f) script m

Scripture(s) ['skrɪptʃə*(z)] n(pl) (Christian) Écriture sainte; (other religions) écritures saintes

scroll [skrəul] n rouleau m

scrounge [skraundʒ] (inf) vt: **to** ~ **sth off or from sb** taper qn de qch; ~**r** (inf) n parasite m

scrub [skrʌb] n (land) broussailles fpl ♦ vt (floor) nettoyer à la brosse; (pan) récurer; (washing) frotter; (inf: cancel) annuler

scruff [skrʌf] n: **by the** ~ **of the neck** par la peau du cou

scruffy ['skrʌfɪ] adj débraillé(e)

scrum(mage) ['skrʌm(ɪdʒ)] n (RUGBY) mêlée f

scruple ['skru:pl] n scrupule m

scrutiny ['skru:tɪnɪ] n examen minutieux

scuff [skʌf] vt érafler

scuffle ['skʌfl] n échauffourée f, rixe f

sculptor ['skʌlptə*] n sculpteur m

sculpture ['skʌlptʃə*] n sculpture f

scum [skʌm] n écume f, mousse f; (pej: people) rebut m, lie f

scurrilous ['skʌrɪləs] adj calomnieux(euse)

scurry ['skʌrɪ] vi filer à toute allure; **to** ~ **off** détaler, se sauver

scuttle ['skʌtl] n (also: coal ~) seau m (à charbon) ♦ vt (ship) saborder ♦ vi (scamper): **to** ~ **away** or **off** détaler

scythe [saɪð] n faux f

sea [si:] n mer f ♦ cpd marin(e), de (la) mer; **by** ~ (travel) par mer, en bateau; **on the** ~ (boat) en mer; (town) au bord de la mer; **to be all at** ~ (fig) nager complètement; **out to** ~ au large; (out) **at** ~ en mer; ~**board** n côte f; ~**food** n fruits mpl de mer; ~**front** n bord m de mer; ~**going** adj (ship) de mer; ~**gull** n mouette f

seal [si:l] n (animal) phoque m; (stamp) sceau m, cachet m ♦ vt sceller; (envelope) coller; (: with seal) cacheter; ~ **off** vt (forbid entry to) interdire l'accès de

sea level n niveau m de la mer

sea lion n otarie f

seam [si:m] n couture f; (of coal) veine f, filon m

seaman ['si:mən] (irreg) n marin m

seance ['seɪɑ̃s] n séance f de spiritisme

seaplane ['si:pleɪn] n hydravion m

search [sɜ:tʃ] n (for person, thing, COMPUT) recherche(s) f(pl); (LAW: at sb's home) perquisition f ♦ vt fouiller; (examine) examiner minutieusement; scruter ♦ vi: **to** ~ **for** chercher; **in** ~ **of** à la recherche de; ~ **through** vt fus fouiller; ~**ing** adj pénétrant(e); ~**light** n projecteur m; ~ **party** n expédition f de secours; ~ **warrant** n mandat m de perquisition

sea: ~**shore** [si:ʃɔ:*] n rivage m, plage f, bord m de (la) mer; ~**sick** ['si:sɪk] adj: **to be** ~**sick** avoir le mal de mer; ~**side** ['si:saɪd] n bord m de la mer; ~**side resort** n station f balnéaire

season ['si:zn] n saison f ♦ vt assaisonner, relever; **to be in/out of** ~ être/ne pas être de saison; ~**al** adj (work) saisonnier(ère); ~**ed** adj (fig) expérimenté(e); ~ **ticket** n carte f d'abonnement

seat [si:t] n siège m; (in bus, train: place) place f; (buttocks) postérieur m; (of trousers) fond m ♦ vt faire asseoir, placer; (have room for) avoir des places assises pour, pouvoir accueillir; ~ **belt** n ceinture f de sécurité

sea: ~ **water** n eau f de mer; ~**weed** ['si:wi:d] n algues fpl; ~**worthy** ['si:wɜ:ðɪ] adj en état de naviguer

sec. abbr = **second(s)**

secluded [sɪ'klu:dɪd] adj retiré(e), à l'écart

seclusion [sɪ'klu:ʒən] n solitude f

second1 [sɪ'kɒnd] (BRIT) vt (employee) affecter provisoirement

second2 ['sekənd] adj deuxième, second(e) ♦ adv (in race etc) en seconde position ♦ n (unit of time) seconde f; (AUT: ~ gear) seconde; (COMM: imperfect) article m de second choix; (BRIT: UNIV) licence f avec mention ♦ vt (motion) appuyer; ~**ary** adj secondaire; ~**ary school** n collège m, lycée m; ~**-class** adj de deuxième classe; (RAIL) de seconde (classe) (POST) au tarif réduit (pej) de qualité inférieure ♦ adv (RAIL) en seconde; (POST) au tarif réduit; ~**hand** adj d'occasion; de seconde main; ~ **hand** n (on clock) trotteuse f; ~**ly** adv deuxièmement; ~**ment** [sɪ'kɒndmənt] (BRIT) n détachement m; ~**-rate** adj de deuxième ordre, de qualité inférieure; ~ **thoughts** npl doutes mpl; **on** ~ **thoughts** or (US) **thought** à la réflexion

secrecy ['si:krəsɪ] n secret m

secret ['si:krət] *adj* secret(ète) ♦ *n* secret *m*; **in ~** en secret, secrètement, en cachette

secretary ['sekrətrı] *n* secrétaire *m/f*; (COMM) secrétaire général; **S~ of State (for)** (BRIT: POL) ministre *m* (de)

secretive ['si:krətıv] *adj* dissimulé

sectarian [sek'teərıən] *adj* sectaire

section ['sekʃən] *n* section *f*; (of document) section, article *m*, paragraphe *m*; (cut) coupe *f*

sector ['sektə*] *n* secteur *m*

secular ['sekjulə*] *adj* profane; laïque; séculier(ère)

secure [sı'kjuə*] *adj* (free from anxiety) sans inquiétude, sécurisé(e); (firmly fixed) solide, bien attaché(e) (or fermé(e) etc); (in safe place) en lieu sûr, en sûreté ♦ *vt* (fix) fixer, attacher; (get) obtenir, se procurer

security [sı'kjuərıtı] *n* sécurité *f*, mesures *fpl* de sécurité; (for loan) caution *f*, garantie *f*

sedan [sı'dæn] (US) *n* (AUT) berline *f*

sedate [sı'deıt] *adj* calme; posé(e) ♦ *vt* (MED) donner des sédatifs à

sedative ['sedətıv] *n* calmant *m*, sédatif *m*

seduce [sı'dju:s] *vt* séduire; **seduction** [sı'dʌkʃən] *n* séduction *f*; **seductive** [sı'dʌktıv] *adj* séduisant(e); (smile) séducteur(trice), (fig: offer) alléchant(e)

see [si:] (pt **saw**, pp **seen**) *vt* voir; (accompany): **to ~ sb to the door** reconduire or raccompagner qn jusqu'à la porte ♦ *vi* voir ♦ *n* évêché *m*; **to ~ that** (ensure) veiller à ce que +sub, faire en sorte que +sub, s'assurer que; ~ **you soon!** à bientôt!; ~ **about** *vt fus* s'occuper de; ~ **off** *vt* accompagner (à la gare or à l'aéroport etc); ~ **through** *vt* mener à bonne fin ♦ *vt fus* voir clair dans; ~ **to** *vt fus* s'occuper de, se charger de

seed [si:d] *n* graine *f*; (sperm) semence *f*; (fig) germe *m*; (TENNIS) tête *f* de série; **to go to ~** monter en graine; (fig) se laisser aller; ~**ling** *n* jeune plant *m*, semis *m*; ~**y** *adj* (shabby) minable, miteux(euse)

seeing ['si:ıŋ] *conj*: ~ **(that)** vu que, étant donné que

seek [si:k] (pt, pp **sought**) *vt* chercher, rechercher

seem [si:m] *vi* sembler, paraître; **there ~s to be ...** il semble qu'il y a ...; on dirait qu'il y a ...; ~**ingly** *adv* apparemment

seen [si:n] *pp of* **see**

seep [si:p] *vi* suinter, filtrer

seesaw ['si:sɔ:] *n* (jeu *m* de) bascule *f*

seethe [si:ð] *vi* être en effervescence; **to ~ with anger** bouillir de colère

see-through ['si:θru:] *adj* transparent(e)

segment *n* segment *m*; (of orange) quartier *m*

segregate ['segrıgeıt] *vt* séparer, isoler

seize [si:z] *vt* saisir, attraper; (take posses-

sion of) s'emparer de; (opportunity) saisir; ~ **up** *vi* (TECH) se gripper; ~ **(up)on** *vt fus* saisir, sauter sur

seizure ['si:ʒə*] *n* (MED) crise *f*, attaque *f*; (of power) prise *f*

seldom ['seldəm] *adv* rarement

select [sı'lekt] *adj* choisi(e), d'élite ♦ *vt* sélectionner, choisir; ~**ion** [sı'lekʃən] *n* sélection *f*, choix *m*

self [self] (pl **selves**) *n*: **the ~** le moi *inv* ♦ *prefix* auto-; ~**assured** *adj* sûr(e) de soi; ~**catering** (BRIT) *adj* avec cuisine, où l'on peut faire sa cuisine; ~**centred** (US ~**centered**) *adj* égocentrique; ~**confidence** *n* confiance *f* en soi; ~**conscious** *adj* timide, qui manque d'assurance; ~**contained** (BRIT) *adj* (flat) avec entrée particulière, indépendant(e); ~**control** *n* maîtrise *f* de soi; ~**defence** (US ~**defense**) *n* autodéfense *f*; (LAW) légitime défense *f*; ~**discipline** *n* discipline personnelle; ~**employed** *adj* qui travaille à son compte; ~**evident** *adj*: **to be ~evident** être évident(e), aller de soi; ~**governing** *adj* autonome; ~**indulgent** *adj* qui ne se refuse rien; ~**interest** *n* intérêt personnel; ~**ish** *adj* égoïste; ~**ishness** *n* égoïsme *m*; ~**less** *adj* désintéressé(e); ~**pity** *n* apitoiement *m* sur soimême; ~**possessed** *adj* assuré(e); ~**preservation** *n* instinct *m* de conservation; ~**respect** *n* respect *m* de soi, amour-propre *m*; ~**righteous** *adj* suffisant(e); ~**sacrifice** *n* abnégation *f*; ~**satisfied** *adj* content(e) de soi, suffisant(e); ~**service** *adj* libre-service, self-service; ~**sufficient** *adj* autosuffisant(e); (person: independent) indépendant(e); ~**taught** *adj* (artist, pianist) qui a appris par lui-même

sell [sel] (pt, pp **sold**) *vt* vendre ♦ *vi* se vendre; **to ~ at or for 10 F** se vendre 10 F; ~ **off** *vt* liquider; ~ **out** *vi*: **to ~ out (of sth)** (use up stock) vendre tout son stock (de qch); **the tickets are all sold out** il ne reste plus de billets; ~**by date** *n* date *f* limite de vente; ~**er** *n* vendeur(euse), marchand(e); ~**ing price** *n* prix *m* de vente

Sellotape ['seləuteıp] (®: BRIT) *n* papier collant *m*, scotch *m* (®)

selves [selvz] *npl of* **self**

semblance ['sembləns] *n* semblant *m*

semen ['si:mən] *n* sperme *m*

semester [sı'mestə*] *n* (esp US) semestre *m*

semi ['semı] *prefix* semi-, demi-; à demi, à moitié; ~**circle** *n* demi-cercle *m*; ~**colon** *n* point-virgule *m*; ~**detached** (house) (BRIT) *n* maison jumelée or jumelle; ~**final** *n* demi-finale *f*

seminar ['semınɑ:*] *n* séminaire *m*

seminary ['semınərı] *n* (REL: for priests) séminaire *m*

semiskilled ['semɪ'skɪld] adj: ~ **worker** ouvrier(ère) spécialisé(e)

semi-skimmed milk n lait demi-écrémé

senate ['senɪt] n sénat m; **senator** n sénateur m

send [send] (pt, pp **sent**) vt envoyer; ~ **away** vt (letter, goods) envoyer, expédier; (unwelcome visitor) renvoyer; ~ **away for** vt fus commander par correspondance, se faire envoyer; ~ **back** vt renvoyer; ~ **for** vt fus envoyer chercher; faire venir; ~ **off** vt (goods) envoyer, expédier; (BRIT: SPORT: player) expulser or renvoyer du terrain; ~ **out** vt (invitation) envoyer (par la poste); (light, heat, signal) émettre; ~ **up** vt faire monter; (BRIT: parody) mettre en boîte, parodier; ~**er** n expéditeur(trice); ~**-off** n: a good ~**-off** des adieux chaleureux

senior ['siːnɪə*] adj (high-ranking) de haut niveau; (of higher rank): **to be** ~ **to sb** être le supérieur de qn ♦ n (older): **she is 15 years his** ~ elle est son aînée de 15 ans, elle est plus âgée que lui de 15 ans; ~ **citizen** n personne âgée; ~**ity** [siːnɪ'ɒrɪtɪ] n (in service) ancienneté f

sensation [sen'seɪʃən] n sensation f; ~**al** adj qui fait sensation; (marvellous) sensationnel(le)

sense [sens] n sens m; (feeling) sentiment m; (meaning) sens, signification f; (wisdom) bon sens ♦ vt sentir, pressentir; **it makes** ~ c'est logique; ~**less** adj insensé(e), stupide; (unconscious) sans connaissance

sensible ['sensəbl] adj sensé(e), raisonnable; sage

sensitive ['sensɪtɪv] adj sensible

sensual ['sensjuəl] adj sensuel(le)

sensuous ['sensjuəs] adj voluptueux(euse), sensuel(le)

sent [sent] pt, pp of **send**

sentence ['sentəns] n (LING) phrase f; (LAW: judgment) condamnation f, sentence f; (: punishment) peine f ♦ vt: **to** ~ **sb to death/to 5 years in prison** condamner qn à mort/à 5 ans de prison

sentiment ['sentɪmənt] n sentiment m; (opinion) opinion f, avis m; ~**al** [sentɪ'mentl] adj sentimental(e)

sentry ['sentrɪ] n sentinelle f

separate [adj 'seprət, vb 'sepəreɪt] adj séparé(e), indépendant(e), différent(e) ♦ vt séparer; (make a distinction between) distinguer ♦ vi se séparer; ~**ly** adv séparément; ~**s** npl (clothes) coordonnés mpl; **separation** [sepə'reɪʃən] n séparation f

September [sep'tembə*] n septembre m

septic ['septɪk] adj (wound) infecté(e); ~ **tank** n fosse f septique

sequel ['siːkwəl] n conséquence f; séquelles fpl; (of story) suite f

sequence ['siːkwəns] n ordre m, suite f; (film ~) séquence f; (dance ~) numéro m

sequin ['siːkwɪn] n paillette f

serene [sə'riːn] adj serein(e), calme, paisible

sergeant ['sɑːdʒənt] n sergent m; (POLICE) brigadier m

serial ['sɪərɪəl] n feuilleton m; ~ **number** n numéro m de série

series ['sɪəriz] n inv série f; (PUBLISHING) collection f

serious ['sɪərɪəs] adj sérieux(euse); (illness) grave; ~**ly** adv sérieusement; (hurt) gravement

sermon ['sɜːmən] n sermon m

serrated [se'reɪtɪd] adj en dents de scie

servant ['sɜːvənt] n domestique m/f; (fig) serviteur/servante

serve [sɜːv] vt (employer etc) servir, être au service de; (purpose) servir à; (customer, food, meal) servir; (subj: train) desservir; (apprenticeship) faire, accomplir; (prison term) purger ♦ vi servir; (be useful): **to** ~ **as/for/to do** servir de/à/à faire ♦ n (TENNIS) service m; **it** ~**s him right** c'est bien fait pour lui; ~ **out, ~ up** vt (food) servir

service ['sɜːvɪs] n service m; (AUT: maintenance) révision f ♦ vt (car, washing machine) réviser; **the S**~**s** les forces armées; **to be of** ~ **to sb** rendre service à qn; ~**able** adj pratique, commode; ~ **charge** (BRIT) n service m; ~**man** (irreg) n militaire m; ~ **station** n station-service f

serviette [sɜːvɪ'et] (BRIT) n serviette f (de table)

session ['seʃən] n séance f

set [set] (pt, pp **set**) n série f, assortiment m; (of tools etc) jeu m; (RADIO, TV) poste m; (TENNIS) set m; (group of people) cercle m, milieu m; (THEATRE: stage) scène f; (: scenery) décor m; (MATH) ensemble m; (HAIRDRESSING) mise f en plis ♦ adj (fixed) fixe, déterminé(e); (ready) prêt(e) ♦ vt (place) poser, placer; (fix, establish) fixer; (: record) établir; (adjust) régler; (decide: rules etc) fixer, choisir; (task) donner; (exam) composer ♦ vi (sun) se coucher; (jam, jelly, concrete) prendre; (bone) se ressouder; **to be** ~ **on doing** être résolu à faire; **to** ~ **the table** mettre la table; **to** ~ **(to music)** mettre en musique; **to** ~ **on fire** mettre le feu à; **to** ~ **free** libérer; **to** ~ **sth going** déclencher qch; **to** ~ **sail** prendre la mer; ~ **about** vt fus (task) entreprendre, se mettre à; ~ **aside** vt mettre de côté; (time) garder; ~ **back** vt (in time): **to** ~ **back (by)** retarder (de); (cost): **to** ~ **sb back £5** coûter 5 livres à qn; ~ **off** vi se mettre en route, partir ♦ vt (bomb) faire exploser; (cause to start) déclencher; (show up well) mettre en valeur, faire valoir; ~ **out** vi se mettre en route, partir ♦ vt (arrange) disposer; (arguments) présenter, exposer; **to** ~ **out to do**

entreprendre de faire, avoir pour but *or* intention de faire; **~ up** *vt* (*organization*) fonder, créer; **~back** *n* (*hitch*) revers *m*, contretemps *m*; **~ menu** *n* menu *m*

settee ['se'ti:] *n* canapé *m*

setting ['setɪŋ] *n* cadre *m*; (*of jewel*) monture *f*, (*position: of controls*) réglage *m*

settle ['setl] *vt* (*argument, matter, account*) régler; (*problem*) résoudre; (*MED: calm*) calmer ♦ *vi* (*bird, dust etc*) se poser; (*also:* **~ down**) s'installer, se fixer; (*calm down*) se calmer; **to ~ for sth** accepter qch, se contenter de qch; **to ~ on sth** opter *or* se décider pour qch; **~ in** *vi* s'installer; **~ up** *vi:* **to ~ up with sb** régler (ce que l'on doit à) qn; **~ment** *n* (*payment*) règlement *m*; (*agreement*) accord *m*; (*village etc*) établissement *m*; hameau *m*; **~r** *n* colon *m*

setup ['setʌp] *n* (*arrangement*) manière *f* dont les choses sont organisées; (*situation*) situation *f*

seven ['sevn] *num* sept; **~teen** *num* dix-sept; **~th** *num* septième; **~ty** *num* soixante-dix

sever ['sevə*] *vt* couper, trancher; (*relations*) rompre

several ['sevrəl] *adj, pron* plusieurs *m/fpl*; **~ of us** plusieurs d'entre nous

severance ['sevərəns] *n* (*of relations*) rupture *f*; **~ pay** *n* indemnité *f* de licenciement

severe [sɪ'vɪə*] *adj* (*stern*) sévère, strict(e); (*serious*) grave, sérieux(euse); (*plain*) sévère, austère; **severity** [sɪ'verɪtɪ] *n* sévérité *f*; gravité *f*, rigueur *f*

sew [səu] (*pt* **sewed**, *pp* **sewn**) *vt, vi* coudre; **~ up** *vt* (re)coudre

sewage ['sju:ɪdʒ] *n* vidange(s) *f(pl)*

sewer ['sjuə*] *n* égout *m*

sewing ['səuɪŋ] *n* couture *f*; (*item(s)*) ouvrage *m*; **~ machine** *n* machine *f* à coudre

sewn [səun] *pp of* **sew**

sex [seks] *n* sexe *m*; **to have ~ with** avoir des rapports (sexuels) avec; **~ist** *adj* sexiste; **~ual** ['seksjuəl] *adj* sexuel(le); (*~y* ['seksɪ] *adj* sexy *inv*

shabby ['ʃæbɪ] *adj* miteux(euse); (*behaviour*) mesquin(e), méprisable

shack [ʃæk] *n* cabane *f*, hutte *f*

shackles ['ʃæklz] *npl* chaînes *fpl*, entraves *fpl*

shade [ʃeɪd] *n* ombre *f*; (*for lamp*) abat-jour *m inv*; (*of colour*) nuance *f*, ton *m* ♦ *vt* abriter du soleil, ombrager; **in the ~** à l'ombre; **a ~ too large/more** un tout petit peu trop grand(e)/plus

shadow ['ʃædəu] *n* ombre *f* ♦ *vt* (*follow*) filer; **~ cabinet** *n* (BRIT) (POL) cabinet parallèle formé par l'Opposition; **~y** *adj* ombragé(e); (*dim*) vague, indistinct(e)

shady ['ʃeɪdɪ] *adj* ombragé(e); (*fig: dishonest*) louche, véreux(euse)

shaft [ʃɑ:ft] *n* (*of arrow, spear*) hampe *f*;

(*AUT, TECH*) arbre *m*; (*of mine*) puits *m*; (*of lift*) cage *f*; (*of light*) rayon *m*, trait *m*

shaggy ['ʃægɪ] *adj* hirsute; en broussaille

shake [ʃeɪk] (*pt* **shook**, *pp* **shaken**) *vt* secouer; (*bottle, cocktail*) agiter; (*house, confidence*) ébranler ♦ *vi* trembler; **to ~ one's head** (*in refusal*) dire *or* faire non de la tête; (*in dismay*) secouer la tête; **to ~ hands with sb** serrer la main à qn; **~ off** *vt* secouer; (*pursuer*) se débarrasser de; **~ up** *vt* secouer; **~n** ['ʃeɪkn] *pp of* **shake**; **shaky** ['ʃeɪkɪ] *adj* (*hand, voice*) tremblant(e); (*building*) branlant(e), peu solide

shall [ʃæl] *aux vb:* **I ~ go** j'irai; **~ I open the door?** j'ouvre la porte?; **I'll get the coffee, ~ I?** je vais chercher le café, d'accord?

shallow ['ʃæləu] *adj* peu profond(e); (*fig*) superficiel(le)

sham [ʃæm] *n* frime *f* ♦ *vt* simuler

shambles ['ʃæmblz] *n* (*muddle*) confusion *f*, pagaïe *f*, fouillis *m*

shame [ʃeɪm] *n* honte *f* ♦ *vt* faire honte à; **it is a ~ (that/to do)** c'est dommage (que +*sub*/de faire); **what a ~!** quel dommage!; **~faced** *adj* honteux(euse), penaud(e); **~ful** *adj* honteux(euse), scandaleux(euse); **~less** *adj* éhonté(e), effronté(e)

shampoo [ʃæm'pu:] *n* shampooing *m* ♦ *vt* faire un shampooing à; **~ and set** *n* shampooing *m* (et) mise *f* en plis

shamrock ['ʃæmrɒk] *n* trèfle *m* (*emblème de l'Irlande*)

shandy ['ʃændɪ] *n* bière panachée

shan't [ʃɑ:nt] = **shall not**

shanty town ['ʃæntɪ-] *n* bidonville *m*

shape [ʃeɪp] *n* forme *f* ♦ *vt* façonner, modeler; (*sb's ideas*) former; (*sb's life*) déterminer ♦ *vi* (*also:* **~ up:** *events*) prendre tournure; (*: person*) faire des progrès, s'en sortir; **to take ~** prendre forme *or* tournure; **-shaped** *suffix:* **heart-shaped** en forme de cœur; **~less** *adj* informe, sans forme; **~ly** *adj* bien proportionné(e), beau(belle)

share [ʃɛə*] *n* part *f*; (COMM) action *f* ♦ *vt* partager; (*have in common*) avoir en commun; **~ out** *vt* partager; **~holder** *n* actionnaire *m/f*

shark [ʃɑ:k] *n* requin *m*

sharp [ʃɑ:p] *adj* (*razor, knife*) tranchant(e), bien aiguisé(e); (*point, voice*) aigu(guë); (*nose, chin*) pointu(e); (*outline, increase*) net(te); (*cold, pain*) vif(vive); (*taste*) piquant(e), âcre; (MUS) dièse; (*person: quick-witted*) vif(vive), éveillé(e); (*: unscrupulous*) malhonnête ♦ *n* (MUS) dièse *m* ♦ *adv* (*precisely*): **at 2 o'clock ~** à 2 heures pile *or* précises; **~en** *vt* aiguiser; (*pencil*) tailler; **~ener** *n* (*also:* **pencil ~ener**) taille-crayon(s) *m inv*; **~-eyed** *adj* à qui rien n'échappe; **~ly** *adv* (*turn, stop*) brusquement; (*stand out*) nettement; (*criticize, re-*

tort) sèchement, vertement

shatter ['ʃætə*] *vt* briser; (*fig: upset*) bouleverser; (: *ruin*) briser, ruiner ♦ *vi* voler en éclats, se briser

shave [ʃeɪv] *vt* raser ♦ *vi* se raser ♦ *n*: **to have a ~** se raser; **~r** *n* (*also*: **electric ~r**) rasoir *m* électrique

shaving ['ʃeɪvɪŋ] *n* (*action*) rasage *m*; **~s** *npl* (*of wood etc*) copeaux *mpl*; **~ brush** *n* blaireau *m*; **~ cream** *n* crème *f* à raser; **~ foam** *n* mousse *f* à raser

shawl [ʃɔːl] *n* châle *m*

she [ʃiː] *pron* elle ♦ *prefix*: **~-cat** chatte *f*; **~-elephant** éléphant *m* femelle

sheaf [ʃiːf] (*pl* **sheaves**) *n* gerbe *f*; (*of papers*) liasse *f*

shear [ʃɪə*] (*pt* **~ed**, *pp* **shorn**) *vt* (*sheep*) tondre; **~ off** *vi* (*branch*) partir, se détacher; **~s** *npl* (*for hedge*) cisaille(s) *f(pl)*

sheath [ʃiːθ] *n* gaine *f*, fourreau *m*, étui *m*; (*contraceptive*) préservatif *m*

shed [ʃed] (*pt, pp* **shed**) *n* remise *f*, resserre *f* ♦ *vt* perdre; (*tears*) verser, répandre; (*workers*) congédier

she'd [ʃiːd] = **she had; she would**

sheen [ʃiːn] *n* lustre *m*

sheep [ʃiːp] *n inv* mouton *m*; **~dog** *n* chien *m* de berger; **~ish** *adj* penaud(e); **~skin** *n* peau *f* de mouton

sheer [ʃɪə*] *adj* (*utter*) pur(e), pur et simple; (*steep*) à pic, abrupt(e); (*almost transparent*) extrêmement fin(e) ♦ *adv* à pic, abruptement

sheet [ʃiːt] *n* (*on bed*) drap *m*; (*of paper*) feuille *f*; (*of glass, metal etc*) feuille, plaque *f*

sheik(h) [ʃeɪk] *n* cheik *m*

shelf [ʃelf] (*pl* **shelves**) *n* étagère *f*, rayon *m*

shell [ʃel] *n* (*on beach*) coquillage *m*; (*of egg, nut etc*) coquille *f*; (*explosive*) obus *m*; (*of building*) carcasse *f* ♦ *vt* (*peas*) écosser; (*MIL*) bombarder (d'obus)

she'll [ʃiːl] = **she will; she shall**

shellfish ['ʃelfɪʃ] *n inv* (*crab etc*) crustacé *m*; (*scallop etc*) coquillage *m* ♦ *npl* (*as food*) fruits *mpl* de mer

shell suit *n* survêtement *m* (en synthétique froissé)

shelter ['ʃeltə*] *n* abri *m*, refuge *m* ♦ *vt* abriter, protéger; (*give lodging to*) donner asile à ♦ *vi* s'abriter, se mettre à l'abri; **~ed** **housing** *n* foyers *mpl* (*pour personnes âgées ou handicapées*)

shelve [ʃelv] *vt* (*fig*) mettre en suspens or en sommeil; **~s** *npl* of **shelf**

shepherd ['ʃepəd] *n* berger *m* ♦ *vt* (*guide*) guider, escorter; **~'s pie** (*BRIT*) *n* ≈ hachis *m* Parmentier

sheriff ['ʃerɪf] (*US*) *n* shérif *m*

sherry ['ʃerɪ] *n* xérès *m*, sherry *m*

she's [ʃiːz] = **she is; she has**

Shetland ['ʃetlənd] *n* (*also*: **the ~s, the ~** **Islands**) les îles *fpl* Shetland

shield [ʃiːld] *n* bouclier *m*; (*protection*) écran *m* de protection ♦ *vt*: **to ~ (from)** protéger (de or contre)

shift [ʃɪft] *n* (*change*) changement *m*; (*work period*) période *f* de travail; (*of workers*) équipe *f*, poste *m* ♦ *vt* déplacer, changer de place; (*remove*) enlever ♦ *vi* changer de place, bouger; **~less** *adj* (*person*) fainéant(e); **~ work** *n* travail *m* en équipe or par relais or par roulement; **~y** *adj* sournois(e); (*eyes*) fuyant(e)

shilly-shally ['ʃɪlɪʃælɪ] *vi* tergiverser, atermoyer

shimmer ['ʃɪmə*] *vi* miroiter, chatoyer

shin [ʃɪn] *n* tibia *m*

shine [ʃaɪn] (*pt, pp* **shone**) *n* éclat *m*, brillant *m* ♦ *vi* briller ♦ *vt* (*torch etc*): **to ~ on** braquer sur; (*polish: pt, pp* **~d**) faire briller or reluire

shingle ['ʃɪŋgl] *n* (*on beach*) galets *mpl*; **~s** *n* (*MED*) zona *m*

shiny ['ʃaɪnɪ] *adj* brillant(e)

ship [ʃɪp] *n* bateau *m*; (*large*) navire *m* ♦ *vt* transporter (par mer); (*send*) expédier (par mer); **~building** *n* construction navale; **~ment** *n* cargaison *f*; **~per** *n* affréteur *m*; **~ping** *n* (*ships*) navires *mpl*; (*the industry*) industrie navale; (*transport*) transport *m*; **~wreck** *n* (*ship*) épave *f*; (*event*) naufrage *m* ♦ *vt*: **to be ~wrecked** faire naufrage; **~yard** *n* chantier naval

shire ['ʃaɪə*] (*BRIT*) *n* comté *m*

shirk [ʃɜːk] *vt* esquiver, se dérober à

shirt [ʃɜːt] *n* (*man's*) chemise *f*; (*woman's*) chemisier *m*; **in (one's) ~ sleeves** en bras de chemise

shit [ʃɪt] (*inf!*) *n, excl* merde *f* (*!*)

shiver ['ʃɪvə*] *n* frisson *m* ♦ *vi* frissonner

shoal [ʃəul] *n* (*of fish*) banc *m*; (*fig: also*: **~s**) masse *f*, foule *f*

shock [ʃɒk] *n* choc *m*; (*ELEC*) secousse *f*; (*MED*) commotion *f*, choc ♦ *vt* (*offend*) choquer, scandaliser; (*upset*) bouleverser; **~ absorber** *n* amortisseur *m*; **~ing** *adj* (*scandalizing*) choquant(e), scandaleux(euse); (*appalling*) épouvantable

shod [ʃɒd] *pt, pp* of **shoe**

shoddy ['ʃɒdɪ] *adj* de mauvaise qualité, mal fait(e)

shoe [ʃuː] (*pt, pp* **shod**) *n* chaussure *f*, soulier *m*; (*also*: **horse~**) fer *m* à cheval ♦ *vt* (*horse*) ferrer; **~lace** *n* lacet *m* (de soulier); **~ polish** *n* cirage *m*; **~ shop** *n* magasin *m* de chaussures; **~string** *n* (*fig*): **on a ~string** avec un budget dérisoire

shone [ʃɒn] *pt, pp* of **shine**

shoo [ʃuː] *excl* ouste!

shook [ʃuk] *pt* of **shake**

shoot [ʃuːt] (*pt, pp* **shot**) *n* (*on branch, seedling*) pousse *f* ♦ *vt* (*game*) chasser; tirer; abattre; (*person*) blesser (or tuer) d'un coup de fusil (or de revolver); (execute) fusiller; (arrow) tirer; (gun) tirer un coup de; (film) tourner ♦ vi (with gun, bow): to ~ (at) tirer (sur); (FOOTBALL) shooter, tirer; ~ **down** vt (plane) abattre; ~ **in** vi entrer comme une flèche; ~ **out** vi sortir comme une flèche; ~ **up** vi (fig) monter en flèche; ~**ing** n (shots) coups mpl de feu, fusillade f; (HUNTING) chasse f; ~**ing star** n étoile filante

shop [ʃɔp] n magasin m; (workshop) atelier m ♦ vi (also: go ~ping) faire ses courses or ses achats; ~ **assistant** (BRIT) n vendeur(euse); ~ **floor** (BRIT) n (INDUSTRY: fig) ouvriers mpl; ~**keeper** n commerçant(e); ~**lifting** n vol m à l'étalage; ~**per** n personne f qui fait ses courses, acheteur(euse); ~**ping** n (goods) achats mpl, provisions fpl; ~**ping bag** n sac m (à provisions); ~**ping centre** (US ~**ping center**) n centre commercial; ~**soiled** adj défraîchi(e), qui a fait la vitrine; ~ **steward** (BRIT) n (INDUSTRY) délégué(e) syndical(e); ~ **window** n vitrine f

shore [ʃɔ:*] n (of sea, lake) rivage m, rive f ♦ vt: to ~ (up) étayer; on ~ à terre

shorn [ʃɔ:n] pp of **shear**

short [ʃɔ:t] adj (not long) court(e); (soon finished) court, bref(brève); (person, step) petit(e); (curt) brusque, sec(sèche); (insufficient) insuffisant(e); **to be/run ~ of** sth être à court de or manquer de qch; **in** ~ bref, en bref; ~ **of doing** ... à moins de faire ...; **everything ~ of** tout sauf; **it is** ~ **for** c'est l'abréviation or le diminutif de; **to cut** ~ (speech, visit) abréger, écourter; **to fall** ~ **of** ne pas être à la hauteur de; **to run** ~ **of** arriver à court de, venir à manquer de; **to stop** ~ s'arrêter net; **to stop** ~ **of** ne pas aller jusqu'à; ~**age** n manque m, pénurie f; ~**bread** n ≈ sablé m; ~**-change** vt ne pas rendre assez à; ~**circuit** n court-circuit m; ~**coming** n défaut m; ~**(crust) pastry** (BRIT) n pâte brisée; ~**cut** n raccourci m; ~**en** vt raccourcir; (text, visit) abréger; ~**fall** n déficit m; ~**hand** (BRIT) n sténo(graphie) f; ~**hand typist** (BRIT) n sténodactylo m/f; ~**list** (BRIT) n (for job) liste f des candidats sélectionnés; ~**lived** adj de courte durée; ~**ly** adv bientôt, sous peu; ~**s** npl: **(a pair of)** ~**s** un short; ~**sighted** adj (BRIT) myope; (fig) qui manque de clairvoyance; ~**staffed** adj à court de personnel; ~**story** n nouvelle f; ~**tempered** adj qui s'emporte facilement; ~**term** adj (effect) à court terme; ~ **wave** n (RADIO) ondes courtes

shot [ʃɔt] pt, pp of **shoot** ♦ n coup m (de feu); (try) coup, essai m; (injection) piqûre f; (PHOT) photo f; **he's a good/poor** ~ **il** tire bien/mal; **like a** ~ comme une flèche; (very readily) sans hésiter; ~**gun** n fusil m

de chasse

should [ʃud] aux vb: **I** ~ **go now** je devrais partir maintenant; **he** ~ **be there now** il devrait être arrivé maintenant; **I** ~ **go if I were you** si j'étais vous, j'irais; **I** ~ **like to** j'aimerais bien, volontiers

shoulder ['ʃəuldə*] n épaule f ♦ vt (fig) endosser, se charger de; ~ **bag** n sac m à bandoulière; ~ **blade** n omoplate f; ~ **strap** n bretelle f

shouldn't ['ʃudnt] = **should not**

shout [ʃaut] n cri m ♦ vt crier ♦ vi (also: ~ out) crier, pousser des cris; ~ **down** vt huer; ~**ing** n cris mpl

shove [ʃʌv] vt pousser; (inf: put): **to** ~ **sth in** fourrer or ficher qch dans; ~ **off** (inf) vi ficher le camp

shovel [ʃʌvl] n pelle f

show [ʃəu] (pt ~**ed**, pp **shown**) n (of emotion) manifestation f, démonstration f; (semblance) semblant m, apparence f; (exhibition) exposition f, salon m; (THEATRE, TV) spectacle m ♦ vt montrer; (film) donner; (courage etc) faire preuve de, manifester; (exhibit) exposer ♦ vi se voir, être visible; **for** ~ pour l'effet; **on** ~ (exhibits etc) exposé(e); ~ **in** vt (person) faire entrer; ~ **off** vi (pej) crâner ♦ vt (display) faire valoir; ~ **out** vt (person) reconduire (jusqu'à la porte); ~ **up** vi (stand out) ressortir; (inf: turn up) se montrer ♦ vt (flaw) faire ressortir; ~ **business** n le monde du spectacle; ~**down** n épreuve f de force

shower ['ʃauə*] n (rain) averse f; (of stones etc) pluie f, grêle f; (also: ~**bath**) douche f ♦ vi prendre une douche, se doucher ♦ vt: **to** ~ **sb with** (gifts etc) combler qn de; **to have** or **take a** ~ prendre une douche; ~**proof** adj imperméabilisé(e)

showing ['ʃəuɪŋ] n (of film) projection f

show jumping n concours m hippique

shown [ʃəun] pp of **show**

show: ~**-off** ['ʃəuɔf] (inf) n (person) crâneur(euse), m'as-tu-vu(e); ~**piece** n (of exhibition) trésor m; ~**room** ['ʃəurum] n magasin m or salle f d'exposition

shrank [ʃræŋk] pt of **shrink**

shrapnel [ʃ'ræpnl] n éclats mpl d'obus

shred [ʃred] n (gen pl) lambeau m, petit morceau m ♦ vt mettre en lambeaux, déchirer; (CULIN) râper; couper en lanières; ~**der** n (for vegetables) râpeur m; (for documents) déchiqueteuse f

shrewd [ʃru:d] adj astucieux(euse), perspicace; (businessman) habile

shriek [ʃri:k] vi hurler, crier

shrill [ʃrɪl] adj perçant(e), aigu(guë), strident(e)

shrimp [ʃrɪmp] n crevette f

shrine [ʃraɪn] n (place) lieu m de pèlerinage

shrink [ʃrɪŋk] (pt **shrank**, pp **shrunk**) vi rétrécir; (fig) se réduire, diminuer; (move:

also: ~ **away**) reculer ♦ *vt* (*wool*) (faire) rétrécir ♦ *n* (*inf: pej*) psychiatre *m/f*, psy *mf*; **to ~ from** (**doing**) **sth** reculer devant (la pensée de faire) qch; ~**age** *n* rétrécissement *m*; ~**wrap** *vt* emballer sous film plastique

shrivel ['ʃrɪvl] *vt* (*also*: ~ **up**) ratatiner, flétrir ♦ *vi* se ratatiner, se flétrir

shroud [ʃraʊd] *n* linceul *m* ♦ *vt*: ~**ed in mystery** enveloppé(e) de mystère

Shrove Tuesday ['ʃrəʊv-] *n* (le) Mardi gras

shrub [ʃrʌb] *n* arbuste *m*; ~**bery** *n* massif *m* d'arbustes

shrug [ʃrʌg] *vt, vi*: **to ~** (**one's shoulders**) hausser les épaules; ~ **off** *vt* faire fi de

shrunk [ʃrʌŋk] *pp of* **shrink**

shudder ['ʃʌdə*] *vi* frissonner, frémir

shuffle ['ʃʌfl] *vt* (*cards*) battre ♦ *vt, vi*: **to ~** (**one's feet**) traîner les pieds

shun [ʃʌn] *vt* éviter, fuir

shunt [ʃʌnt] *vt* (*RAIL*) aiguiller

shut [ʃʌt] (*pt, pp* **shut**) *vt* fermer ♦ *vi* (se) fermer; ~ **down** *vt, vi* fermer définitivement; ~ **off** *vt* couper, arrêter; ~ **up** *vi* (*inf: keep quiet*) se taire ♦ *vt* (*close*) fermer; (*silence*) faire taire; ~**ter** *n* volet *m*; (*PHOT*) obturateur *m*

shuttle ['ʃʌtl] *n* navette *f*; (*also*: ~ **service**) (service *m* de) navette *f*

shuttlecock ['ʃʌtlkɒk] *n* volant *m* (*de badminton*)

shy [ʃaɪ] *adj* timide

sibling ['sɪblɪŋ] *n*: ~**s** enfants *mpl* de mêmes parents

Sicily ['sɪsɪlɪ] *n* Sicile *f*

sick [sɪk] *adj* (*ill*) malade; (*vomiting*): **to be ~** vomir; (*humour*) noir(e), macabre; **to feel ~** avoir envie de vomir, avoir mal au cœur; **to be ~ of** (*fig*) en avoir assez de; ~ **bay** *n* infirmerie *f*; ~**en** *vt* écœurer; ~**ening** *adj* (*fig*) écœurant(e), dégoûtant(e)

sickle ['sɪkl] *n* faucille *f*

sick: ~ **leave** *n* congé *m* de maladie; ~**ly** *adj* maladif(ive), souffreteux(euse); (*causing nausea*) écœurant(e); ~**ness** *n* maladie *f*; (*vomiting*) vomissement(s) *m(pl)*; ~ **pay** *n* indemnité *f* de maladie

side [saɪd] *n* côté *m*; (*of lake, road*) bord *m*; (*team*) camp *m*, équipe *f* ♦ *adj* (*door, entrance*) latéral(e) ♦ *vi*: **to ~ with sb** prendre le parti de qn, se ranger du côté de qn; **by the ~ of** au bord de; ~ **by ~** côte à côte; **from ~ to ~** d'un côté à l'autre; **to take ~s** (**with**) prendre parti (pour); ~**board** *n* buffet *m*; ~**boards** (*BRIT*), ~**burns** *npl* (*whiskers*) pattes *fpl*; ~ **drum** *n* tambour plat; ~ **effect** *n* effet *m* secondaire; ~**light** *n* (*AUT*) veilleuse *f*; ~**line** *n* (*SPORT*) (ligne *f* de) touche *f*; (*fig*) travail *m* secondaire; ~**long** *adj* oblique; ~**saddle** *adv* en amazone; ~**show** *n* attrac-

tion *f*; ~**step** *vt* (*fig*) éluder; éviter; ~ **street** *n* (petite) rue transversale; ~**track** *vt* (*fig*) faire dévier de son sujet; ~**walk** (*US*) *n* trottoir *m*; ~**ways** *adv* de côté

siding ['saɪdɪŋ] *n* (*RAIL*) voie *f* de garage

sidle ['saɪdl] *vi*: **to ~ up** (**to**) s'approcher furtivement (de)

siege [siːdʒ] *n* siège *m*

sieve [sɪv] *n* tamis *m*, passoire *f*

sift [sɪft] *vt* (*fig: also*: ~ *through*) passer en revue; (*lit: flour etc*) passer au tamis

sigh [saɪ] *n* soupir *m* ♦ *vi* soupirer, pousser un soupir

sight [saɪt] *n* (*faculty*) vue *f*; (*spectacle*) spectacle *m*; (*on gun*) mire *f* ♦ *vt* apercevoir; **in ~** visible; **out of ~** hors de vue; ~**seeing** *n* tourisme *m*; **to go ~seeing** faire du tourisme

sign [saɪn] *n* signe *m*; (*with hand etc*) signe, geste *m*; (*notice*) panneau *m*, écriteau *m* ♦ *vt* signer; ~ **on** *vi* (*MIL*) s'engager; (*as unemployed*) s'inscrire au chômage; (*for course*) s'inscrire ♦ *vt* (*MIL*) engager; (*employee*) embaucher; ~ **over** *vt*: **to ~ sth over to sb** céder qch pour écrit à qn; ~ **up** *vt* engager ♦ *vi* (*MIL*) s'engager; (*for course*) s'inscrire

signal ['sɪgnl] *n* signal *m* ♦ *vi* (*AUT*) mettre son clignotant ♦ *vt* (*person*) faire signe à; (*message*) communiquer par signaux; ~**man** (*irreg*) *n* (*RAIL*) aiguilleur *m*

signature ['sɪgnətʃə*] *n* signature *f*; ~ **tune** *n* indicatif musical

signet ring ['sɪgnət-] *n* chevalière *f*

significance [sɪg'nɪfɪkəns] *n* signification *f*; importance *f*; **significant** [sɪg'nɪfɪkənt] *adj* significatif(ive); (*important*) important(e), considérable

signpost ['saɪnpəʊst] *n* poteau indicateur

silence ['saɪləns] *n* silence *m* ♦ *vt* faire taire, réduire au silence; ~**r** *n* (*on gun, BRIT: AUT*) silencieux *m*

silent ['saɪlənt] *adj* silencieux(euse); (*film*) muet(te); **to remain ~** garder le silence, ne rien dire; ~ **partner** *n* (*COMM*) bailleur *m* de fonds, commanditaire *m*

silhouette [sɪluː'et] *n* silhouette *f*

silicon chip ['sɪlɪkən-] *n* puce *f* électronique

silk [sɪlk] *n* soie *f* ♦ *cpd* de *or* en soie; ~**y** *adj* soyeux(euse)

silly ['sɪlɪ] *adj* stupide, sot(te), bête

silt [sɪlt] *n* vase *f*; limon *m*

silver ['sɪlvə*] *n* argent *m*; (*money*) monnaie *f* (en pièces d'argent); (*also*: ~*ware*) argenterie *f* ♦ *adj* d'argent, en argent; ~ **paper** (*BRIT*) *n* papier *m* d'argent *or* d'étain; ~-**plated** *adj* plaqué(e) argent; ~**smith** *n* orfèvre *m/f*; ~**y** *adj* argenté(e)

similar ['sɪmɪlə*] *adj*: ~ (**to**) semblable (à); ~**ly** *adv* de la même façon, de même

simile ['sɪmɪlɪ] *n* comparaison *f*

simmer ['sɪmə*] *vi* cuire à feu doux, mijoter

simple ['sɪmpl] *adj* simple; **simplicity** [sɪm'plɪsɪtɪ] *n* simplicité *f*; **simply** *adv* (*without fuss*) avec simplicité

simultaneous [sɪməl'teɪnɪəs] *adj* simultané(e)

sin [sɪn] *n* péché *m* ♦ *vi* pécher

since [sɪns] *adv, prep* depuis ♦ *conj* (*time*) depuis que; (*because*) puisque, étant donné que, comme; ~ **then, ever** ~ depuis ce moment-là

sincere [sɪn'sɪə*] *adj* sincère; ~**ly** *adv see* **yours**; **sincerity** [sɪn'serɪtɪ] *n* sincérité *f*

sinew ['sɪnjuː] *n* tendon *m*

sinful ['sɪnful] *adj* coupable; (*person*) pécheur(eresse)

sing [sɪŋ] (*pt* **sang**, *pp* **sung**) *vt, vi* chanter

singe [sɪndʒ] *vt* brûler légèrement; (*clothes*) roussir

singer ['sɪŋə*] *n* chanteur(euse)

singing ['sɪŋɪŋ] *n* chant *m*

single ['sɪŋgl] *adj* seul(e), unique; (*unmarried*) célibataire; (*not double*) simple ♦ *n* (*BRIT: also*: ~ **ticket**) aller *m* (simple); (*record*) 45 tours *m*; ~ **out** *vt* choisir; (*distinguish*) distinguer; ~**-breasted** *adj* droit(e); ~ **file** *n*: **in** ~ **file** en file indienne; ~**handed** *adv* tout(e) seul(e), sans (aucune) aide; ~**-minded** *adj* résolu(e), tenace; ~**room** *n* chambre *f* à un lit *or* pour une personne; ~**s** *n* (*TENNIS*) simple *m*; **singly** *adv* séparément

singular ['sɪŋgjʊlə*] *adj* singulier(ère), étrange; (*outstanding*) remarquable; (*LING*) (au) singulier, du singulier ♦ *n* singulier *m*

sinister ['sɪnɪstə*] *adj* sinistre

sink [sɪŋk] (*pt* **sank**, *pp* **sunk**) *n* évier *m* ♦ *vt* (*ship*) (faire) couler, faire sombrer; (*foundations*) creuser ♦ *vi* couler, sombrer; (*ground etc*) s'affaisser; (*also*: ~ **back**, ~ **down**) se laisser retomber; to ~ **sth into** enfoncer qch dans; **my heart sank** j'ai complètement perdu courage; ~ **in** *vi* (*fig*) pénétrer, être compris(e)

sinner ['sɪnə*] *n* pécheur(eresse)

sinus ['saɪnəs] *n* sinus *m inv*

sip [sɪp] *n* gorgée *f* ♦ *vt* boire à petites gorgées

siphon ['saɪfən] *n* siphon *m*; ~ **off** *vt* siphonner; (*money: illegally*) détourner

sir [sɜː*] *n* monsieur *m*; **S~ John Smith** sir John Smith; **yes** ~ oui, Monsieur

siren ['saɪərən] *n* sirène *f*

sirloin ['sɜːlɔɪn] *n* (*also*: ~ **steak**) aloyau *m*

sissy ['sɪsɪ] (*inf*) *n* (*coward*) poule mouillée

sister ['sɪstə*] *n* sœur *f*; (*nun*) religieuse *f*, sœur; (*BRIT: nurse*) infirmière *f* en chef; ~**-in-law** *n* belle-sœur *f*

sit [sɪt] (*pt, pp* **sat**) *vi* s'asseoir; (*be sitting*) être assis(e); (*assembly*) être en séance, siéger; (*for painter*) poser ♦ *vt* (*exam*) passer,

se présenter à; ~ **down** *vi* s'asseoir; ~ **in on** *vt fus* assister à; ~ **up** *vi* s'asseoir; (*straight*) se redresser; (*not go to bed*) rester debout, ne pas se coucher

sitcom ['sɪtkɒm] *n abbr* (= *situation comedy*) comédie *f* de situation

site [saɪt] *n* emplacement *m*, site *m*; (*also: building* ~) chantier *m* ♦ *vt* placer

sit-in ['sɪtɪn] *n* (*demonstration*) sit-in *m inv*, occupation *f* (de locaux)

sitting ['sɪtɪŋ] *n* (*of assembly etc*) séance *f*; (*in canteen*) service *m*; ~ **room** *n* salon *m*

situated ['sɪtjʊeɪtɪd] *adj* situé(e)

situation [sɪtjʊ'eɪʃən] *n* situation *f*; "~**s vacant"** (*BRIT*) "offres d'emploi"

six [sɪks] *num* six; ~**teen** *num* seize; ~**th** *num* sixième; ~**ty** *num* soixante

size [saɪz] *n* taille *f*, dimensions *fpl*; (*of clothing*) taille *f*; (*of shoes*) pointure *f*; (*fig*) ampleur *f*, (*glue*) colle *f*; ~ **up** *vt* juger, jauger; ~**able** *adj* assez grand(e); assez important(e)

sizzle ['sɪzl] *vi* grésiller

skate [skeɪt] *n* patin *m*; (*fish: pl inv*) raie *f* ♦ *vi* patiner; ~**board** *n* skateboard *m*, planche *f* à roulettes; ~**r** *n* patineur(euse); **skating** ['skeɪtɪŋ] *n* patinage *m*; **skating rink** *n* patinoire *f*

skeleton ['skelɪtn] *n* squelette *m*; (*outline*) schéma *m*; ~ **staff** *n* effectifs réduits

skeptical ['skeptɪkl] (*US*) *adj* = **sceptical**

sketch [sketʃ] *n* (*drawing*) croquis *m*, esquisse *f*; (*THEATRE*) sketch *m*, saynète *f* ♦ *vt* esquisser, faire un croquis *or* une esquisse de; ~ **book** *n* carnet *m* à dessin; ~**y** *adj* incomplet(ète), fragmentaire

skewer ['skjuə*] *n* brochette *f*

ski [skiː] *n* ski *m* ♦ *vi* skier, faire du ski; ~ **boot** *n* chaussure *f* de ski

skid [skɪd] *vi* déraper

ski: ~**er** ['skiːə*] *n* skieur(euse); ~**ing** ['skiːɪŋ] *n* ski *m*; ~ **jump** *n* saut *m* à skis

skilful ['skɪlful] (*US* **skillful**) *adj* habile, adroit(e)

ski lift *n* remonte-pente *m inv*

skill [skɪl] *n* habileté *f*, adresse *f*, talent *m*; (*requiring training: gen pl*) compétences *fpl*; ~**ed** *adj* habile, adroit(e); (*worker*) qualifié(e)

skim [skɪm] *vt* (*milk*) écrémer; (*glide over*) raser; , effleurer ♦ *vi*: **to** ~ **through** (*fig*) parcourir; ~**med milk** *n* lait écrémé

skimp [skɪmp] *vt* (*also*: ~ **on**: *work*) bâcler, faire à la va-vite; (*cloth etc*) lésiner sur; ~**y** *adj* maigre; (*skirt*) étriqué(e)

skin [skɪn] *n* peau *f* ♦ *vt* (*fruit etc*) éplucher; (*animal*) écorcher; ~ **cancer** *n* cancer *m* de la peau; ~**-deep** *adj* superficiel(le); ~ **diving** *n* plongée sous-marine; ~**ny** *adj* maigre, maigrichon(ne); ~**tight** *adj* (*jeans etc*) collant(e), ajusté(e)

skip [skɪp] *n* petit bond *or* saut *m*; (*BRIT*:

container) benne f ♦ *vi* gambader, sautiller; (*with rope*) sauter à la corde ♦ *vt* sauter

ski pants *npl* fuseau *m* (de ski)

ski pole *n* bâton *m* de ski

skipper ['skɪpə*] *n* capitaine *m*; (*in race*) skipper *m*

skipping rope ['skɪpɪŋ-] (*BRIT*) *n* corde f à sauter

skirmish ['skɜ:mɪʃ] *n* escarmouche f, accrochage *m*

skirt [skɜ:t] *n* jupe f ♦ *vt* longer, contourner; **~ing board** (*BRIT*) *n* plinthe f

ski slope *n* piste f de ski

ski suit *n* combinaison f (de ski)

skittle ['skɪtl] *n* quille f; **skittles** *n* (*game*) (jeu *m* de) quilles *fpl*

skive [skaɪv] (*BRIT: inf*) *vi* tirer au flanc

skulk [skʌlk] *vi* rôder furtivement

skull [skʌl] *n* crâne *m*

skunk [skʌŋk] *n* mouffette f

sky [skaɪ] *n* ciel *m*; **~light** *n* lucarne f; **~scraper** *n* gratte-ciel *m inv*

slab [slæb] *n* (*of stone*) dalle f; (*of food*) grosse tranche

slack [slæk] *adj* (*loose*) lâche, desserré(e); (*slow*) stagnant(e); (*careless*) négligent(e), peu sérieux(euse) *or* consciencieux(euse); **~s** *npl* (*trousers*) pantalon *m*; **~en** *vi* ralentir, diminuer ♦ *vt* (*speed*) réduire; (*grip*) relâcher; (*clothing*) desserrer

slag heap [slæg-] *n* crassier *m*

slag off (*BRIT: inf*) *vt* dire du mal de

slain [sleɪn] *pp of* **slay**

slam [slæm] *vt* (*door*) (faire) claquer; (*throw*) jeter violemment, flanquer (*fam*); (*criticize*) démolir ♦ *vi* claquer

slander ['slɑ:ndə*] *n* calomnie f; diffamation f

slang [slæŋ] *n* argot *m*

slant [slɑ:nt] *n* inclinaison f; (*fig*) angle *m*, point *m* de vue; **~ed** *adj* = **slanting**; **~ing** *adj* en pente, incliné(e); **~ing eyes** yeux bridés

slap [slæp] *n* claque f, gifle f; tape f ♦ *vt* donner une claque *or* une gifle *or* une tape à; (*paint*) appliquer rapidement ♦ *adv* (*directly*) tout droit, en plein; **~dash** *adj* fait(e) sans soin *or* à la va-vite; (*person*) insouciant(e), négligent(e); **~stick** *n* (*comedy*) grosse farce, style *m* tarte à la crème; **~-up** (*BRIT*) *adj*: **a ~-up meal** un repas extra *or* fameux

slash [slæʃ] *vt* entailler, taillader; (*fig: prices*) casser

slat [slæt] *n* latte f, lame f

slate [sleɪt] *n* ardoise f ♦ *vt* (*fig: criticize*) éreinter, démolir

slaughter ['slɔ:tə*] *n* carnage *m*, massacre *m* ♦ *vt* (*animal*) abattre; (*people*) massacrer; **~house** *n* abattoir *m*

slave [sleɪv] *n* esclave *m/f* ♦ *vi* (*also: ~ away*) trimer, travailler comme un forçat;

~ry *n* esclavage *m*; **slavish** *adj* servile

slay [sleɪ] (*pt* **slew**, *pp* **slain**) *vt* tuer

sleazy ['sli:zɪ] *adj* miteux(euse), minable

sledge [sledʒ] *n* luge f

sledgehammer *n* marteau *m* de forgeron

sleek [sli:k] *adj* (*hair, fur etc*) brillant(e), lisse; (*car, boat etc*) aux lignes pures *or* élégantes

sleep [sli:p] (*pt, pp* **slept**) *n* sommeil *m* ♦ *vi* dormir; (*spend night*) dormir, coucher; **to go to ~** s'endormir; **~ around** *vi* coucher à droite et à gauche; **~ in** *vi* (*over~*) se réveiller trop tard; **~er** (*BRIT*) *n* (*RAIL: train*) train-couchettes *m*; (: *berth*) couchette f; **~ing bag** *n* sac *m* de couchage; **~ing car** *n* (*RAIL*) wagon-lit *m*, voiture-lit f; **~ing partner** (*BRIT*) *n* associé *m* commanditaire; **~ing pill** *n* somnifère *m*; **~less** *adj*: **a ~less night** une nuit blanche; **~walker** *n* somnambule *m/f*; **~y** *adj* qui a sommeil; (*fig*) endormi(e)

sleet [sli:t] *n* neige fondue

sleeve [sli:v] *n* manche f; (*of record*) pochette f

sleigh [sleɪ] *n* traîneau *m*

sleight [slaɪt] *n*: **~ of hand** tour *m* de passe-passe

slender ['slendə*] *adj* svelte, mince; (*fig*) faible, ténu(e)

slept [slept] *pt, pp of* **sleep**

slew [slu:] *vi* (*also: ~ around*) virer, pivoter ♦ *pt of* **slay**

slice [slaɪs] *n* tranche f; (*round*) rondelle f; (*utensil*) spatule f, truelle f ♦ *vt* couper en tranches (*or* en rondelles)

slick [slɪk] *adj* (*skilful*) brillant(e) (en apparence); (*salesman*) qui a du bagout ♦ *n* (*also: oil ~*) nappe f de pétrole, marée noire

slide [slaɪd] (*pt, pp* **slid**) *n* (*in playground*) toboggan *m*; (*PHOT*) diapositive f; (*BRIT: also: hair ~*) barrette f; (*in prices*) chute f, baisse f ♦ *vt* (*faire*) glisser ♦ *vi* glisser; **sliding** ['slaɪdɪŋ] *adj* (*door*) coulissant(e); **sliding scale** *n* échelle f mobile

slight [slaɪt] *adj* (*slim*) mince, menu(e); (*frail*) frêle; (*trivial*) faible, insignifiant(e); (*small*) petit(e), léger(ère) (*before n*) ♦ *n* offense f, affront *m*; **not in the ~est** pas le moins du monde, pas du tout; **~ly** *adv* légèrement, un peu

slim [slɪm] *adj* mince ♦ *vi* maigrir; (*diet*) suivre un régime amaigrissant

slime [slaɪm] *n* (*mud*) vase f; (*other substance*) substance visqueuse

slimming ['slɪmɪŋ] *adj* (*diet, pills*) amaigrissant(e); (*foodstuff*) qui ne fait pas grossir

sling [slɪŋ] (*pt, pp* **slung**) *n* (*MED*) écharpe f; (*for baby*) porte-bébé *m*; (*weapon*) fronde f, lance-pierre *m* ♦ *vt* lancer, jeter

slip [slɪp] *n* faux pas; (*mistake*) erreur f, étourderie f, bévue f; (*underskirt*) combinai-

son f; (of paper) petite feuille, fiche f ♦ vt
(slide) glisser ♦ vi glisser; (decline) baisser;
(move smoothly): **to ~ into/out of** se glisser or se faufiler dans/hors de; **to ~ sth
on/off** enfiler/enlever qch; **to give sb the
~** fausser compagnie à qn; **a ~ of the
tongue** un lapsus; **~ away** vi s'esquiver;
~ in vt glisser ♦ vi (errors) s'y glisser; **~
out** vi sortir; **~ up** vi faire une erreur, gaf-
fer; **~ped disc** n déplacement m de vertèbre

slipper ['slɪpə*] n pantoufle f

slippery ['slɪpərɪ] adj glissant(e)

slip road (BRIT) n (to motorway) bretelle f
d'accès

slipshod ['slɪpʃɒd] adj négligé(e), peu soi-
gné(e)

slip-up ['slɪpʌp] n bévue f

slipway ['slɪpweɪ] n cale f (de construction
or de lancement)

slit [slɪt] (pt, pp slit) n fente f; (cut) incision
f ♦ vt fendre; couper; inciser

slither ['slɪðə*] vi glisser; (snake) onduler

sliver ['slɪvə*] n (of glass, wood) éclat m;
(of cheese etc) petit morceau, fine tranche

slob [slɒb] (inf) n rustaud(e)

slog [slɒg] (BRIT) vi travailler très dur ♦ n
gros effort; tâche fastidieuse

slogan ['sləʊgən] n slogan m

slop [slɒp] vi (also: ~ over) se renverser; déborder ♦ vt répandre; renverser

slope [sləʊp] n pente f, côte f; (side of
mountain) versant m; (slant) inclinaison f ♦
vi: **to ~ down** être or descendre en pente;
to ~ up monter; **sloping** adj en pente;
(writing) penché(e)

sloppy ['slɒpɪ] adj (work) peu soigné(e),
bâclé(e); (appearance) négligé(e), dé-
braillé(e)

slot [slɒt] n fente f ♦ vt: **to ~ sth into** encastrer or insérer qch dans

sloth [sləʊθ] n (laziness) paresse f

slot machine n (BRIT: vending machine)
distributeur m (automatique); (for gambling) machine f à sous

slouch [slaʊtʃ] vi avoir le dos rond, être
voûté(e)

slovenly ['slʌvnlɪ] adj sale, débraillé(e);
(work) négligé(e)

slow [sləʊ] adj lent(e); (watch): **to be ~** retarder ♦ adv lentement ♦ vt, vi (also: ~
down, ~ up) ralentir; "~" (road sign) "ralentir"; **~ly** adv lentement; ~ **motion** n:
in ~ motion au ralenti

sludge [slʌdʒ] n boue f

slue [sluː] (US) vi = slew

slug [slʌg] n limace f; (bullet) balle f

sluggish ['slʌgɪʃ] adj (person) mou(molle),
lent(e); (stream, engine, trading) lent

sluice [sluːs] n (also: ~ gate) vanne f

slum [slʌm] n (house) taudis m

slump [slʌmp] n baisse soudaine, effondre-

ment m; (ECON) crise f ♦ vi s'effondrer,
s'affaisser

slung [slʌŋ] pt, pp of sling

slur [slɜː*] n (fig: smear): ~ **(on)** atteinte f
(à); insinuation f (contre) ♦ vt mal articuler

slush [slʌʃ] n neige fondue; ~ **fund** n caisse noire, fonds secrets

slut [slʌt] (pej) n souillon f

sly [slaɪ] adj (person) rusé(e); (smile, expression, remark) sournois(e)

smack [smæk] n (slap) tape f; (on face) gifle
f ♦ vt donner une tape à; (on face) gifler;
(on bottom) donner la fessée à ♦ vi: **to ~
of** avoir des relents de, sentir

small [smɔːl] adj petit(e); ~ **ads** (BRIT) npl
petites annonces; ~ **change** n petite or
menue monnaie; ~ **fry** n (fig) menu fretin;
~holder (BRIT) n petit cultivateur; ~
hours npl: **in the ~ hours** au petit matin;
~pox n variole f; ~ **talk** n menus propos

smart [smɑːt] adj (neat, fashionable) élé-
gant(e), chic inv; (clever) intelligent(e), as-
tucieux(euse), futé(e); (quick) rapide,
vif(vive), prompt(e) ♦ vi faire mal, brûler;
(fig) être piqué(e) au vif; **~en up** vi devenir plus élégant(e), se faire beau(belle) ♦ vt
rendre plus élégant(e)

smash [smæʃ] n (also: ~-up) collision f, accident m; (: ~ hit) succès foudroyant ♦ vt
casser, briser, fracasser; (opponent) écraser;
(SPORT: record) pulvériser ♦ vi se briser, se
fracasser; s'écraser; **~ing** (inf) adj formidable

smattering ['smætərɪŋ] n: **a ~ of** quelques
notions de

smear [smɪə*] n tache f, salissure f; trace f;
(MED) frottis m ♦ vt enduire; (make dirty)
salir; ~ **campaign** n campagne f de diffamation

smell [smel] (pt, pp smelt or smelled) n
odeur f; (sense) odorat m ♦ vt sentir ♦ vi
(food etc): **to ~ (of)** sentir (de); (pej) sentir
mauvais

smelly ['smelɪ] adj qui sent mauvais, malo-
dorant(e)

smile [smaɪl] n sourire m ♦ vi sourire

smirk [smɜːk] n petit sourire suffisant or af-
fecté

smock [smɒk] n blouse f

smog [smɒg] n brouillard mêlé de fumée,
smog m

smoke [sməʊk] n fumée f ♦ vt, vi fumer;
~d adj (bacon, glass) fumé(e); **~r** n (person) fumeur(euse); (RAIL) wagon m fu-
meurs; ~ **screen** n rideau m or écran m
de fumée; (fig) paravent m; **smoking**
['sməʊkɪŋ] n tabagisme m; **"no smoking"**
(sign) "défense de fumer"; **to give up
smoking** arrêter de fumer; **smoky**
['sməʊkɪ] adj enfumé(e); (taste) fumé(e)

smolder ['sməʊldə*] (US) vi = smoulder

smooth [smuːð] adj lisse; (sauce) onctueux(euse); (flavour, whisky) moelleux(euse); (movement) régulier(ère), sans à-coups or heurts; (pej: person) douce-reux(euse), mielleux(euse) ♦ vt (also: ~ out: skirt, paper) lisser, défroisser; (: creases, difficulties) faire disparaître

smother ['smʌðə*] vt étouffer

smoulder ['sməuldə*] (US **smolder**) vi couver

smudge [smʌdʒ] n tache f, bavure f ♦ vt salir, maculer

smug [smʌg] adj suffisant(e)

smuggle ['smʌgl] vt passer en contrebande or en fraude; ~r n contrebandier(ère); **smuggling** ['smʌglɪŋ] n contrebande f

smutty ['smʌtɪ] adj (fig) grossier(ère), obscène

snack [snæk] n casse-croûte m inv; ~ **bar** n snack(-bar) m

snag [snæg] n inconvénient m, difficulté f

snail [sneɪl] n escargot m

snake [sneɪk] n serpent m

snap [snæp] n (sound) claquement m, bruit sec; (photograph) photo f, instantané m ♦ adj subit(e); fait(e) sans réfléchir ♦ vt (break) casser net; (fingers) faire claquer ♦ vi se casser net or avec un bruit sec; (speak sharply) parler d'un ton brusque; **to ~ shut** se refermer brusquement; ~ **at** vt fus (subj: dog) essayer de mordre; ~ **off** vi (break) casser net; ~ **up** vt sauter sur, saisir; ~**py** (inf) adj prompt(e); (slogan) qui a du punch; **make it ~py!** grouille-toi!, et que ça saute!; ~**shot** n photo f, instantané m

snare [snɛə*] n piège m

snarl [snɑːl] vi gronder

snatch [snætʃ] n (small amount): ~**es of** des fragments mpl or bribes fpl de ♦ vt saisir (d'un geste vif); (steal) voler

sneak [sniːk] (pt (US) also **snuck**) vi: **to ~ in/out** entrer/sortir furtivement or à la dérobée ♦ n (inf, pej: informer) faux jeton; **to ~ up on sb** s'approcher de qn sans faire de bruit; ~**ers** ['sniːkəz] npl tennis mpl or baskets mpl

sneer [snɪə*] vi ricaner; **to ~ at** traiter avec mépris

sneeze [sniːz] vi éternuer

sniff [snɪf] vi renifler ♦ vt renifler, flairer; (glue, drugs) sniffer, respirer

snigger ['snɪgə*] vi ricaner; pouffer de rire

snip [snɪp] n (cut) petit coup; (BRIT: inf: bargain) (bonne) occasion or affaire ♦ vt couper

sniper ['snaɪpə*] n tireur embusqué

snippet ['snɪpɪt] n bribe(s) f(pl)

snivelling ['snɪvlɪŋ] adj larmoyant(e), pleurnicheur(euse)

snob [snɔb] n snob m/f; ~**bish** adj snob inv

snooker ['snuːkə*] n sorte de jeu de billard

snoop [snuːp] vi: **to ~ about** fureter

snooty ['snuːtɪ] adj snob inv

snooze [snuːz] n petit somme ♦ vi faire un petit somme

snore [snɔː*] vi ronfler

snorkel ['snɔːkl] n tuba m

snort [snɔːt] vi grogner; (horse) renâcler

snout [snaut] n museau m

snow [snəu] n neige f ♦ vi neiger; ~**ball** n boule f de neige; ~**bound** adj enneigé(e), bloqué(e) par la neige; ~**drift** n congère f; ~**drop** n perce-neige or f; ~**fall** n chute f de neige; ~**flake** n flocon m de neige; ~**man** (irreg) n bonhomme m de neige; ~**plough** (US ~**plow**) n chasse-neige m inv; ~**shoe** n raquette f (pour la neige); ~**storm** n tempête f de neige

snub [snʌb] vt repousser, snober ♦ n rebuffade f; ~**-nosed** adj au nez retroussé

snuff [snʌf] n tabac m à priser

snug [snʌg] adj douillet(te), confortable; (person) bien au chaud

snuggle ['snʌgl] vi: **to ~ up to sb** se serrer or se blottir contre qn

---

KEYWORD

so [səu] adv 1 (thus, likewise) ainsi; **if** ~ si oui; ~ **do** or **have I** moi aussi; **it's 5 o'clock** - ~ **it is!** il est 5 heures - en effet! or c'est vrai!; **I hope/think** ~ je l'espère/le crois; ~ **far** jusqu'ici, jusqu'à maintenant; (in past) jusque-là

2 (in comparisons etc: to such a degree) si, tellement; ~ **big (that)** si or tellement grand (que); **she's not** ~ **clever as her brother** elle n'est pas aussi intelligente que son frère

3: ~ **much** adj, adv tant (de); **I've got** ~ **much work** tant de travail; **I love you** ~ **much** je vous aime tant; ~ **many** tant (de)

4 (phrases): **10 or** ~ à peu près or environ 10; ~ **long!** (inf: goodbye) au revoir!, à un de ces jours!

♦ conj 1 (expressing purpose): ~ **as to do** pour faire or afin de faire; ~ **(that)** pour que or afin que +sub

2 (expressing result) donc, par conséquent; ~ **that** si bien que, de (telle) sorte que

---

soak [səuk] vt faire tremper; (drench) tremper ♦ vi tremper; ~ **in** vi être absorbé(e); ~ **up** vt absorber

soap [səup] n savon m; ~**flakes** npl paillettes fpl de savon; ~ **opera** n feuilleton télévisé; ~ **powder** n lessive f; ~**y** adj savonneux(euse)

soar [sɔː*] vi monter (en flèche), s'élancer; (building) s'élancer

sob [sɔb] n sanglot m ♦ vi sangloter

sober ['səubə*] adj qui n'est pas (or plus) ivre; (serious) sérieux(euse), sensé(e); (colour, style) sobre, discret(ète); ~ **up** vt des-

soûler (*inf*) ♦ *vi* dessoûler (*inf*)
so-called ['səʊ'kɔːld] *adj* soi-disant *inv*
soccer ['sɒkə*] *n* football *m*
social ['səʊʃəl] *adj* social(e); (*sociable*) sociable ♦ *n* (petite) fête; ~ **club** *n* amicale *f*, foyer *m*; ~**ism** *n* socialisme *m*; ~**ist** *adj* socialiste ♦ *n* socialiste *m/f*; ~**ize** *vi*: **to** ~**ize (with)** lier connaissance (avec); parler (avec); ~ **security** (*BRIT*) *n* aide sociale; ~ **work** *n* assistance sociale, travail social; ~ **worker** *n* assistant(e) social(e)
society [sə'saɪətɪ] *n* société *f*; (*club*) société, association *f*; (*also:* high ~) (haute) société, grand monde
sociology [səʊsɪ'ɒlədʒɪ] *n* sociologie *f*
sock [sɒk] *n* chaussette *f*
socket ['sɒkɪt] *n* cavité *f*; (*BRIT: ELEC: also:* wall ~) prise *f* de courant
sod [sɒd] *n* (*of earth*) motte *f*; (*BRIT: inf!*) con *m* (*!*); salaud *m* (*!*)
soda ['səʊdə] *n* (*CHEM*) soude *f*; (*also:* ~ *water*) eau *f* de Seltz; (*US: also:* ~ *pop*) soda *m*
sodden ['sɒdn] *adj* trempé(e); détrempé(e)
sofa ['səʊfə] *n* sofa *m*, canapé *m*
soft [sɒft] *adj* (*not rough*) doux(douce); (*not hard*) doux; mou(molle); (*not loud*) doux, léger(ère); (*kind*) doux, gentil(le); ~ **drink** *n* boisson non alcoolisée; ~**en** ['sɒfn] *vt* (r)amollir; (*fig*) adoucir; atténuer ♦ *vi* se ramollir; s'adoucir; s'atténuer; ~**ly** *adv* doucement; gentiment; ~**ness** *n* douceur *f*; ~ **spot** *n*: **to have a** ~ **spot for sb** avoir un faible pour qn; ~**ware** *n* ['sɒftwɛə*] *n* (*COMPUT*) logiciel *m*, software *m*
soggy ['sɒgɪ] *adj* trempé(e); détrempé(e)
soil [sɔɪl] *n* (*earth*) sol *m*, terre *f* ♦ *vt* salir; (*fig*) souiller
solace ['sɒləs] *n* consolation *f*
solar ['səʊlə*] *adj* solaire; ~ **panel** *n* panneau *m* solaire; ~ **power** *n* énergie *f* solaire
sold [səʊld] *pt, pp* *of* **sell**
solder ['səʊldə*] *vt* souder (*au fil à souder*) ♦ *n* soudure *f*
soldier ['səʊldʒə*] *n* soldat *m*, militaire *m*
sole [səʊl] *n* (*of foot*) plante *f*; (*of shoe*) semelle *f*; (*fish: pl inv*) sole *f* ♦ *adj* seul(e), unique
solemn ['sɒləm] *adj* solennel(le); (*person*) sérieux(euse), grave
sole trader *n* (*COMM*) chef *m* d'entreprise individuelle
solicit [sə'lɪsɪt] *vt* (*request*) solliciter ♦ *vi* (*prostitute*) racoler
solicitor [sə'lɪsɪtə*] *n* (*for wills etc*) ≈ notaire *m*; (*in court*) ≈ avocat *m*
solid ['sɒlɪd] *adj* solide; (*not hollow*) plein(e), compact(e), massif(ive); (*entire*): **3** ~ **hours** 3 heures entières ♦ *n* solide *m*
solidarity [sɒlɪ'dærɪtɪ] *n* solidarité *f*
solitary ['sɒlɪtərɪ] *adj* solitaire; ~ **confinement** *n* (*LAW*) isolement *m*

solo ['səʊləʊ] *n* solo *m* ♦ *adv* (*fly*) en solitaire; ~**ist** *n* soliste *m/f*
soluble ['sɒljʊbl] *adj* soluble
solution [sə'luːʃən] *n* solution *f*
solve [sɒlv] *vt* résoudre
solvent ['sɒlvənt] *adj* (*COMM*) solvable ♦ *n* (*CHEM*) (dis)solvant *m*

─────────── *KEYWORD*

some [sʌm] *adj* **1** (*a certain amount or number of*): ~ **tea/water/ice cream** du thé/de l'eau/de la glace; ~ **children/apples** des enfants/pommes
2 (*certain: in contrasts*): ~ **people say that** ... il y a des gens qui disent que ...; ~ **films were excellent, but most** ... certains films étaient excellents, mais la plupart ...
3 (*unspecified*): ~ **woman was asking for you** il y avait une dame qui vous demandait; **he was asking for** ~ **book (or other)** il demandait un livre quelconque; ~ **day** un de ces jours; ~ **day next week** un jour la semaine prochaine
♦ *pron* **1** (*a certain number*) quelques-un(e)s, certain(e)s; **I've got** ~ (*books etc*) j'en ai (quelques-uns); ~ (**of them**) **have been sold** certains ont été vendus
2 (*a certain amount*) un peu; **I've got** ~ (*money, milk*) j'en ai un peu
♦ *adv*: ~ **10 people** quelque 10 personnes, 10 personnes environ

─────────────

some: ~**body** ['sʌmbədɪ] *pron* = **someone**; ~**how** ['sʌmhaʊ] *adv* d'une façon ou d'une autre; (*for some reason*) pour une raison ou une autre; ~**one** ['sʌmwʌn] *pron* quelqu'un; ~**place** ['sʌmpleɪs] (*US*) *adv* = **somewhere**
somersault ['sʌməsɔːlt] *n* culbute *f*, saut périlleux ♦ *vi* faire la culbute *or* un saut périlleux; (*car*) faire un tonneau
something ['sʌmθɪŋ] *pron* quelque chose; ~ **interesting** quelque chose d'intéressant
sometime ['sʌmtaɪm] *adv* (*in future*) un de ces jours, un jour ou l'autre; (*in past*): ~ **last month** au cours du mois dernier
some: ~**times** ['sʌmtaɪmz] *adv* quelquefois, parfois; ~**what** ['sʌmwɒt] *adv* quelque peu, un peu; ~**where** ['sʌmwɛə*] *adv* quelque part
son [sʌn] *n* fils *m*
song [sɒŋ] *n* chanson *f*; (*of bird*) chant *m*
son-in-law ['sʌnɪnlɔː] *n* gendre *m*, beau-fils *m*
sonny ['sʌnɪ] (*inf*) *n* fiston *m*
soon [suːn] *adv* bientôt; (*early*) tôt; ~ **afterwards** peu après; **as** ~ **as possible** dès possible, aussitôt possible; *see also* **as**; ~**er** *adv* (*time*) plus tôt; (*preference*): **I would** ~**er do** j'aimerais autant *or* je préférerais faire; ~**er or later** tôt ou tard
soot [sʊt] *n* suie *f*

soothe [suːð] *vt* calmer, apaiser

sophisticated [sə'fɪstɪkeɪtɪd] *adj* raffiné(e); sophistiqué(e); (*machinery*) hautement perfectionné(e), très complexe

sophomore ['sɔfəmɔː*] (*US*) *n* étudiant(e) de seconde année

sopping ['sɔpɪŋ] *adj* (*also:* ~ *wet*) complètement trempé(e)

soppy ['sɔpɪ] (*pej*) *adj* sentimental(e)

soprano [sə'prɑːnəʊ] *n* (*singer*) soprano *m/f*

sorcerer ['sɔːsərə*] *n* sorcier *m*

sore [sɔː*] *adj* (*painful*) douloureux(euse), sensible ♦ *n* plaie *f*; **~ly** *adv* (*tempted*) fortement

sorrow ['sɔrəʊ] *n* peine *f*, chagrin *m*

sorry ['sɔrɪ] *adj* désolé(e); (*condition, excuse*) triste, déplorable; **~!** pardon!, excusez-moi!; **~?** pardon?; **to feel ~ for sb** plaindre qn

sort [sɔːt] *n* genre *m*, espèce *f*, sorte *f* ♦ *vt* (*also:* ~ *out*) trier; classer; ranger; (*: problems*) résoudre, régler; **~ing office** *n* bureau *m* de tri

SOS *n abbr* (= *save our souls*) S.O.S. *m*

so-so ['səʊ'səʊ] *adv* comme ci comme ça

sought [sɔːt] *pt, pp of* **seek**

soul [səʊl] *n* âme *f*; **~-destroying** *adj* démoralisant(e); **~ful** *adj* sentimental(e); (*eyes*) expressif(ive)

sound [saʊnd] *adj* (*healthy*) en bonne santé, sain(e); (*safe, not damaged*) solide, en bon état; (*reliable, not superficial*) sérieux(euse), solide; (*sensible*) sensé(e) ♦ *adv:* ~ **asleep** profondément endormi(e) ♦ *n* son *m*; bruit *m*; (*GEO*) détroit *m*, bras *m* de mer ♦ *vt* (*alarm*) sonner ♦ *vi* sonner, retentir; (*fig: seem*) sembler (être); **to** ~ **like** ressembler à; ~ **out** *vt* sonder; ~ **barrier** *n* mur *m* du son; ~ **effects** *npl* bruitage *m*; **~ly** *adv* (*sleep*) profondément; (*beat*) complètement, à plate couture; **~proof** *adj* insonorisé(e); **~track** *n* (*of film*) bande *f* sonore

soup [suːp] *n* soupe *f*, potage *m*; **in the** ~ (*fig*) dans le pétrin; ~ **plate** *n* assiette creuse or à soupe; **~spoon** *n* cuiller *f* à soupe

sour ['saʊə*] *adj* aigre; **it's** ~ **grapes** (*fig*) c'est du dépit

source [sɔːs] *n* source *f*

south [saʊθ] *n* sud *m* ♦ *adj* sud *inv*, du sud ♦ *adv* au sud, vers le sud; **S~ Africa** *n* Afrique *f* du Sud; **S~ African** *adj* sud-africain(e) ♦ *n* Sud-Africain(e); **S~ America** *n* Amérique *f* du Sud; **S~ American** *adj* sud-américain(e) ♦ *n* Sud-Américain(e); **~-east** *n* sud-est *m*; **~erly** ['sʌðəlɪ] *adj* du sud; au sud; **~ern** ['sʌðən] *adj* (du) sud (e); méridional(e); **S~ Pole** *n* Pôle *m* Sud; **~ward(s)** *adv* vers le sud; **~-west** *n* sud-ouest *m*

souvenir [suːvə'nɪə*] *n* (*objet*) souvenir *m*

sovereign ['sɔvrɪn] *n* souverain(e)

soviet ['səʊvɪət] *adj* soviétique; **the S~ Union** l'Union *f* soviétique

sow[1] [saʊ] *n* truie *f*

sow[2] [səʊ] (*pt* ~**ed**, *pp* **sown** [səʊn]) *vt* semer; ~**n** [səʊn] *pp of* **sow**[2]

soya ['sɔɪə] (*US* **soy**) *n:* ~ **bean** graine *f* de soja; ~ **sauce** sauce *f* de soja

spa [spɑː] *n* (*town*) station thermale; (*US: also:* **health** ~) établissement *m* de cure de rajeunissement *etc*

space [speɪs] *n* espace *m*; (*room*) place *f*, espace; (*length of time*) laps *m* de temps ♦ *cpd* spatial(e) ♦ *vt* (*also:* ~ *out*) espacer; ~**craft** *n* engin spatial; ~**man** (*irreg*) *n* astronaute *m*, cosmonaute *m*; ~**ship** *n* = **spacecraft**; ~**woman** (*irreg*) *n* astronaute *f*, cosmonaute *f*; **spacing** *n* espacement *m*

spade [speɪd] *n* (*tool*) bêche *f*, pelle *f*; (*child's*) pelle; ~**s** *npl* (*CARDS*) pique *m*

Spain [speɪn] *n* Espagne *f*

span [spæn] *n* (*of bird, plane*) envergure *f*; (*of arch*) portée *f*; (*in time*) espace *m* de temps, durée *f* ♦ *vt* enjamber, franchir; (*fig*) couvrir, embrasser

Spaniard ['spænjəd] *n* Espagnol(e)

spaniel ['spænjəl] *n* épagneul *m*

Spanish ['spænɪʃ] *adj* espagnol(e) ♦ *n* (*LING*) espagnol *m*; **the** ~ *npl* les Espagnols *mpl*

spank [spæŋk] *vt* donner une fessée à

spanner ['spænə*] (*BRIT*) *n* clé *f* (de mécanicien)

spar [spɑː*] *n* espar *m* ♦ *vi* (*BOXING*) s'entraîner

spare [spɛə*] *adj* de réserve, de rechange; (*surplus*) de or en trop, de reste ♦ *n* (*part*) pièce *f* de rechange, pièce détachée ♦ *vt* (*do without*) se passer de; (*afford to give*) donner, accorder; (*refrain from hurting*) épargner; **to** ~ (*surplus*) en surplus, de trop; ~ **part** *n* pièce *f* de rechange, pièce détachée; ~ **time** *n* moments *mpl* de loisir, temps *m* libre; ~ **wheel** *n* (*AUT*) roue *f* de secours; **sparing** ['spɛərɪŋ] *adj:* **to be sparing with** ménager; **sparingly** *adv* avec modération

spark [spɑːk] *n* étincelle *f*; ~**(ing) plug** *n* bougie *f*

sparkle ['spɑːkl] *n* scintillement *m*, éclat *m* ♦ *vi* étinceler, scintiller; **sparkling** ['spɑːklɪŋ] *adj* (*wine*) mousseux(euse), pétillant(e); (*water*) pétillant(e); (*fig: conversation, performance*) étincelant(e), pétillant(e)

sparrow ['spærəʊ] *n* moineau *m*

sparse [spɑːs] *adj* clairsemé(e)

spartan ['spɑːtən] *adj* (*fig*) spartiate

spasm ['spæzəm] *n* (*MED*) spasme *m*; ~**odic** [spæz'mɔdɪk] *adj* (*fig*) intermittent(e)

spastic ['spæstɪk] *n* handicapé(e) moteur

spat [spæt] *pt, pp of* **spit**

spate [speɪt] *n* (*fig*): **a** ~ **of** une avalanche *or* un torrent de

spatter ['spætə*] vt éclabousser
spawn [spɔ:n] vi frayer ♦ n frai m
speak [spi:k] (pt **spoke**, pp **spoken**) vt parler; (truth) dire ♦ vi parler; (make a speech) prendre la parole; **to ~ to sb/of** or **about sth** parler à qn/de qch; **~ up!** parle plus fort!; **~er** n (in public) orateur m; (also: loud~er) haut-parleur m; **the S~er** (BRIT POL) le président de la chambre des Communes; (US POL) le président de la chambre des Représentants
spear [spɪə*] n lance f ♦ vt transpercer; **~head** vt (attack etc) mener
spec [spek] (inf) n: **on ~** à tout hasard
special ['speʃəl] adj spécial(e); **~ist** n spécialiste m/f; **~ity** n spécialité f; **~ize** vi: **to ~ize (in)** se spécialiser (dans); **~ly** adv spécialement, particulièrement; **~ty** (esp US) n = **speciality**
species ['spi:ʃi:z] n inv espèce f
specific [spə'sɪfɪk] adj précis(e); particulier(ère); (BOT, CHEM etc) spécifique; **~ally** adv expressément, explicitement; **~ation** n (TECH) spécification f; (requirement) stipulation f
specimen ['spesɪmɪn] n spécimen m, échantillon m; (of blood) prélèvement m
speck [spek] n petite tache, petit point; (particle) grain m; **~led** ['spekld] adj tacheté(e), moucheté(e)
specs [speks] (inf) npl lunettes fpl
spectacle ['spektəkl] n spectacle m; **~s** npl (glasses) lunettes fpl
spectacular [spek'tækjulə*] adj spectaculaire
spectator [spek'teɪtə*] n spectateur(trice)
spectrum ['spektrəm] (pl **spectra**) n spectre m
speculation [spekju'leɪʃən] n spéculation f
speech [spi:tʃ] n (faculty) parole f; (talk) discours m, allocution f; (manner of speaking) façon f de parler, langage m; (enunciation) élocution f; **~less** adj muet(te)
speed [spi:d] n vitesse f; (promptness) rapidité f ♦ vi: **to ~ along/past** etc aller/passer etc à toute vitesse; **at full** or **top ~** à toute vitesse or allure; **~ up** vi aller plus vite, accélérer ♦ vt accélérer; **~boat** n vedette f, hors-bord m inv; **~ily** adv rapidement, promptement; **~ing** n (AUT) excès m de vitesse; **~ limit** n limitation f de vitesse, vitesse maximale permise; **~ometer** [spɪ'dɒmɪtə*] n compteur m (de vitesse); **~way** n (SPORT: also: ~way racing) épreuve(s) f(pl) de vitesse de motos; **~y** adj rapide, prompt(e)
spell [spel] (pt, pp **spelt** (BRIT) or **~ed**) n (also: magic ~) sortilège m, charme m; (period of time) (courte) période ♦ vt (in writing) écrire, orthographier; (aloud) épeler; (fig) signifier; **to cast a ~ on sb** jeter un sort à qn; **he can't ~** il fait des fautes d'or-

thographe; **~bound** adj envoûté(e), subjugué(e); **~ing** n orthographe f
spend [spend] (pt, pp **spent**) vt (money) dépenser; (time, life) passer; consacrer; **~thrift** n dépensier(ère)
sperm [spɜ:m] n sperme m
spew [spju:] vt (also: ~ out) vomir
sphere [sfɪə*] n sphère f
spice [spaɪs] n épice f
spick-and-span ['spɪkən'spæn] adj impeccable
spicy ['spaɪsɪ] adj épicé(e), relevé(e); (fig) piquant(e)
spider ['spaɪdə*] n araignée f
spike [spaɪk] n pointe f; (BOT) épi m
spill [spɪl] (pt, pp **spilt** or **~ed**) vt renverser; répandre ♦ vi se répandre; **~ over** vi déborder
spin [spɪn] (pt **spun** or **span**, pp **spun**) n (revolution of wheel) tour m; (AVIAT) (chute f en) vrille f, (trip in car) petit tour, balade f ♦ vt (wool etc) filer; (wheel) faire tourner ♦ vi filer; (turn) tourner, tournoyer; **~ out** vt faire durer
spinach ['spɪnɪtʃ] n épinard m; (as food) épinards
spinal ['spaɪnl] adj vertébral(e), spinal(e); **~ cord** n moelle épinière
spindly ['spɪndlɪ] adj grêle, filiforme
spin-dryer ['spɪn'draɪə*] (BRIT) n essoreuse f
spine [spaɪn] n colonne vertébrale; (thorn) épine f; **~less** adj (fig) mou(molle)
spinning ['spɪnɪŋ] n (of thread) filature f; **~ top** n toupie f; **~ wheel** n rouet m
spin-off ['spɪnɒf] n avantage inattendu; sous-produit m
spinster ['spɪnstə*] n célibataire f; vieille fille (péj)
spiral ['spaɪərl] n spirale f ♦ vi (fig) monter en flèche; **~ staircase** n escalier m en colimaçon
spire ['spaɪə*] n flèche f, aiguille f
spirit ['spɪrɪt] n esprit m; (mood) état m d'esprit; (courage) courage m, énergie f; **~s** npl (drink) spiritueux mpl, alcool m; **in good ~s** de bonne humeur; **~ed** adj vif(vive), fougueux(euse), plein(e) d'allant; **~ual** ['spɪrɪtjuəl] adj spirituel(le); (religious) religieux(euse)
spit [spɪt] (pt, pp **spat**) n (for roasting) broche f; (saliva) salive f ♦ vi cracher; (sound) crépiter
spite [spaɪt] n rancune f, dépit m ♦ vt contrarier, vexer; **in ~ of** en dépit de, malgré; **~ful** adj méchant(e), malveillant(e)
spittle ['spɪtl] n salive f; (of animal) bave f, (spat out) crachat m
splash [splæʃ] n (sound) plouf m; (of colour) tache f ♦ vt éclabousser ♦ vi (also: ~ about) barboter, patauger
spleen [spli:n] n (ANAT) rate f

splendid ['splendɪd] *adj* splendide, superbe, magnifique

splint [splɪnt] *n* attelle *f*, éclisse *f*

splinter ['splɪntə*] *n* (*wood*) écharde *f*; (*glass*) éclat *m* ♦ *vi* se briser, se fendre

split [splɪt] (*pt, pp* split) *n* fente *f*, déchirure *f*; (*fig: POL*) scission *f* ♦ *vt* diviser; (*work, profits*) partager, répartir ♦ *vi* (*divide*) se diviser; ~ **up** *vi* (*couple*) se séparer, rompre; (*meeting*) se disperser

splutter ['splʌtə*] *vi* bafouiller; (*spit*) postillonner

spoil [spɔɪl] (*pt, pp* spoilt *or* ~ed) *vt* (*damage*) abîmer; (*mar*) gâcher; (*child*) gâter; ~**s** *npl* butin *m*; (*fig: profits*) bénéfices *npl*; ~**sport** *n* trouble-fête *m*, rabat-joie *m*

spoke [spəuk] *pt* speak ♦ *n* (*of wheel*) rayon *m*; ~**n** ['spəukn] *pp of* **speak**; ~**sman** ['spəuksmən] (*irreg*) *n* porte-parole *m inv*; ~**swoman** ['spəukswumən] (*irreg*) *n* porte-parole *m inv*

sponge [spʌndʒ] *n* éponge *f*; (*also:* ~ *cake*) ≈ biscuit *m* de Savoie ♦ *vt* éponger ♦ *vi:* **to** ~ **off** *or* **on** vivre aux crochets de; ~ **bag** (*BRIT*) *n* trousse *f* de toilette

sponsor ['spɒnsə*] *n* (*RADIO, TV, SPORT*) sponsor *m*; (*for application*) parrain *m*, marraine *f*; (*BRIT: for fund-raising event*) donateur(trice) ♦ *vt* sponsoriser, parrainer; faire un don à; ~**ship** *n* sponsoring *m*; parrainage *m*; dons *mpl*

spontaneous [spɒn'teɪnɪəs] *adj* spontané(e)

spooky ['spuːkɪ] (*inf*) *adj* qui donne la chair de poule

spool [spuːl] *n* bobine *f*

spoon [spuːn] *n* cuiller *f*; ~**-feed** *vt* nourrir à la cuiller; (*fig*) mâcher le travail à; ~**ful** *n* cuillerée *f*

sport [spɔːt] *n* sport *m*; (*person*) chic type(fille) ♦ *vt* arborer; ~**ing** *adj* sportif(ive); **to give sb a** ~**ing chance** donner sa chance à qn; ~ **jacket** (*US*) *n* = **sports jacket**; ~**s car** *n* voiture *f* de sport; ~**s jacket** (*BRIT*) *n* veste *f* de sport; ~**sman** (*irreg*) *n* sportif *m*; ~**smanship** *n* esprit sportif, sportivité *f*; ~**swear** *n* vêtements *mpl* de sport; ~**swoman** (*irreg*) *n* sportive *f*; ~**y** *adj* sportif(ive)

spot [spɒt] *n* tache *f*; (*dot: on pattern*) pois *m*; (*pimple*) bouton *m*; (*place*) endroit *m*, coin *m*; (*RADIO, TV: in programme: for person*) numéro *m*; (: *for activity*) rubrique *f*; (*small amount*): **a** ~ **of** un peu de ♦ *vt* (*notice*) apercevoir, repérer; **on the** ~ sur place, sur les lieux; (*immediately*) sur-le-champ; (*in difficulty*) dans l'embarras; ~ **check** *n* sondage *m*, vérification ponctuelle; ~**less** *adj* immaculé(e); ~**light** *n* projecteur *m*; ~**ted** *adj* (*fabric*) à pois; ~**ty** *adj* (*face, person*) boutonneux(euse)

spouse [spauz] *n* époux(épouse)

spout [spaut] *n* (*of jug*) bec *m*; (*of pipe*) orifice *m* ♦ *vi* jaillir

sprain [spreɪn] *n* entorse *f*, foulure *f* ♦ *vt:* **to** ~ **one's ankle** *etc* se fouler *or* se tordre la cheville *etc*

sprang [spræŋ] *pt of* **spring**

sprawl [sprɔːl] *vi* s'étaler

spray [spreɪ] *n* jet *m* (en fines gouttelettes); (*from sea*) embruns *mpl*; (*container*) vaporisateur *m*; (*for garden*) pulvérisateur *m*; (*aerosol*) bombe *f*; (*of flowers*) petit bouquet ♦ *vt* vaporiser, pulvériser; (*crops*) traiter

spread [spred] (*pt, pp* spread) *n* (*distribution*) répartition *f*; (*CULIN*) pâte *f* à tartiner; (*inf: meal*) festin *m* ♦ *vt* étendre, étaler; répandre; (*wealth, workload*) distribuer ♦ *vi* (*disease, news*) se propager; (*also:* ~ *out:* *stain*) s'étaler; ~ **out** *vi* (*people*) se disperser; ~**-eagled** ['spredi:gld] *adj* étendu(e) bras et jambes écartés; ~**sheet** *n* (*COMPUT*) tableur *m*

spree [spriː] *n:* **to go on a** ~ faire la fête

sprightly ['spraɪtlɪ] *adj* alerte

spring [sprɪŋ] (*pt* sprang, *pp* sprung) *n* (*leap*) bond *m*, saut *m*; (*coiled metal*) ressort *m*; (*season*) printemps *m*; (*of water*) source *f* ♦ *vi* (*leap*) bondir, sauter; **in** ~ au printemps; **to** ~ **from** provenir de; ~ **up** *vi* (*problem*) se présenter, surgir; (*plant, buildings*) surgir de terre; ~**board** *n* tremplin *m*; ~**-clean(ing)** *n* grand nettoyage de printemps; ~**time** *n* printemps *m*

sprinkle ['sprɪŋkl] *vt:* **to** ~ **water** *etc* **on,** ~ **with water** *etc* asperger d'eau *etc*; **to** ~ **sugar** *etc* **on,** ~ **with sugar** *etc* saupoudrer de sucre *etc*; ~**r** ['sprɪŋklə*] *n* (*for lawn*) arroseur *m*; (*to put out fire*) diffuseur *m* d'extincteur automatique d'incendie

sprint [sprɪnt] *n* sprint *m* ♦ *vi* courir à toute vitesse; (*SPORT*) sprinter

sprout [spraut] *vi* germer, pousser; ~**s** *npl* (*also:* Brussels ~s) choux *mpl* de Bruxelles

spruce [spruːs] *n inv* épicéa *m* ♦ *adj* net(te), pimpant(e)

sprung [sprʌŋ] *pp of* **spring**

spry [spraɪ] *adj* alerte, vif(vive)

spun [spʌn] *pt, pp of* **spin**

spur [spɜː*] *n* éperon *m*; (*fig*) aiguillon *m* ♦ *vt* (*also:* ~ **on**) éperonner; aiguillonner; **on the** ~ **of the moment** sous l'impulsion du moment

spurious ['spjuərɪəs] *adj* faux(fausse)

spurn [spɜːn] *vt* repousser avec mépris

spurt [spɜːt] *n* (*of blood*) jaillissement *m*; (*of energy*) regain *m*, sursaut *m* ♦ *vi* jaillir, gicler

spy [spaɪ] *n* espion(ne) ♦ *vi:* **to** ~ **on** espionner, épier; (*see*) apercevoir; ~**ing** *n* espionnage *m*

sq. *abbr* = **square**

squabble ['skwɒbl] *vi* se chamailler

squad [skwɒd] n (MIL, POLICE) escouade f, groupe m; (FOOTBALL) contingent m

squadron ['skwɒdrən] n (MIL) escadron m; (AVIAT, NAUT) escadrille f

squalid ['skwɒlɪd] adj sordide

squall [skwɔːl] n rafale f, bourrasque f

squalor ['skwɒlə*] n conditions fpl sordides

squander ['skwɒndə*] vt gaspiller, dilapider

square [skwɛə*] n carré m; (in town) place f ♦ adj carré(e); (inf: ideas, tastes) vieux jeu inv ♦ vt (arrange) régler; arranger; (MATH) élever au carré ♦ vi (reconcile) concilier; **all ~** quitte; à égalité; **a ~ meal** un repas convenable; **2 metres ~** (de) 2 mètres sur 2; **2 ~ metres** 2 mètres carrés; **~ly** adv carrément

squash [skwɒʃ] n (BRIT: drink): **lemon/ orange ~** citronnade f/orangeade f; (US: marrow) courge f; (SPORT) squash m ♦ vt écraser

squat [skwɒt] adj petit(e) et épais(se), ramassé(e) ♦ vi (also: ~ **down**) s'accroupir; **~ter** n squatter m

squawk [skwɔːk] vi pousser un or des gloussement(s)

squeak [skwiːk] vi grincer, crier; (mouse) pousser un petit cri

squeal [skwiːl] vi pousser un or des cri(s) aigu(s) or perçant(s); (brakes) grincer

squeamish ['skwiːmɪʃ] adj facilement dégoûté(e)

squeeze [skwiːz] n pression f; (ECON) restrictions fpl de crédit ♦ vt presser; (hand, arm) serrer; **~ out** vt exprimer

squelch [skweltʃ] vi faire un bruit de succion

squid [skwɪd] n calmar m

squiggle ['skwɪɡl] n gribouillis m

squint [skwɪnt] vi loucher ♦ n: **he has a ~** il louche, il souffre de strabisme

squirm [skwɜːm] vi se tortiller

squirrel ['skwɪrəl] n écureuil m

squirt [skwɜːt] vi jaillir, gicler

Sr abbr = **senior**

St abbr = **saint; street**

stab [stæb] n (with knife etc) coup m (de couteau etc); (of pain) lancée f; (inf: try): **to have a ~ at (doing) sth** s'essayer à (faire) qch ♦ vt poignarder

stable ['steɪbl] n écurie f ♦ adj stable

stack [stæk] n tas m, pile f ♦ vt (also: ~ **up**) empiler, entasser

stadium ['steɪdɪəm] n (pl stadia or ~s) n stade m

staff [stɑːf] n (workforce) personnel m; (BRIT: SCOL) professeurs mpl ♦ vt pourvoir en personnel

stag [stæɡ] n cerf m

stage [steɪdʒ] n scène f; (platform) estrade f ♦ n; (profession): **the ~** le théâtre; (point) étape f, stade m ♦ vt (play) monter, mettre en scène; (demonstration) organiser; **in ~s**

par étapes, par degrés; **~coach** n diligence f; **~ manager** n régisseur m

stagger ['stæɡə*] vi chanceler, tituber ♦ vt (person: amaze) stupéfier; (hours, holidays) étaler, échelonner; **~ing** adj (amazing) stupéfiant(e), renversant(e)

stagnate [stæɡ'neɪt] vi stagner, croupir

stag party n enterrement m de vie de garçon

staid [steɪd] adj posé(e), rassis(e)

stain [steɪn] n tache f; (colouring) colorant m ♦ vt tacher; (wood) teindre; **~ed glass window** n vitrail m; **~less steel** n acier m inoxydable, inox m; **~ remover** n détachant m

stair [stɛə*] n (step) marche f; **~s** npl (flight of steps) escalier m; **~case** n escalier m; **~way** n = **staircase**

stake [steɪk] n pieu m, poteau m; (BETTING) enjeu m; (COMM: interest) intérêts mpl ♦ vt risquer, jouer; **to be at ~** être en jeu; **to ~ one's claim (to)** revendiquer

stale [steɪl] adj (bread) rassis(e); (food) pas frais(fraîche); (beer) éventé(e); (smell) de renfermé; (air) confiné(e)

stalemate ['steɪlmeɪt] n (CHESS) pat m; (fig) impasse f

stalk [stɔːk] n tige f ♦ vt traquer ♦ vi: **to ~ out/off** sortir/partir d'un air digne

stall [stɔːl] n (BRIT: in street, market etc) éventaire m, étal m; (in stable) stalle f ♦ vt (AUT) caler; (delay) retarder ♦ vi (AUT) caler; (fig) essayer de gagner du temps; **~s** npl (BRIT: in cinema, theatre) orchestre m

stallion ['stælɪən] n étalon m (cheval)

stalwart ['stɔːlwət] adj dévoué(e); fidèle

stamina ['stæmɪnə] n résistance f, endurance f

stammer ['stæmə*] n bégaiement m ♦ vi bégayer

stamp [stæmp] n timbre m; (rubber ~) tampon m; (mark, also fig) empreinte f ♦ vi (also: ~ **one's foot**) taper du pied ♦ vt (letter) timbrer; (with rubber ~) tamponner; **~ album** n album m de timbres(-poste); **~ collecting** n philatélie f

stampede [stæm'piːd] n ruée f

stance [stæns] n position f

stand [stænd] n (pt, pp **stood**) n (position) position f; (for taxis) station f (de taxis); (music ~) pupitre m à musique; (COMM) étalage m, stand m; (SPORT) tribune f ♦ vi être or se tenir (debout); (rise) se lever, se mettre debout; (be placed) se trouver; (remain: offer etc) rester valable; (BRIT: in election) être candidat(e), se présenter ♦ vt (place) mettre, poser; (tolerate, withstand) supporter; (treat, invite to) offrir (treat, invite), payer; **to make** or **take a ~** prendre position; **to ~ at** (score, value etc) être de; **to ~ for parliament** (BRIT) se présenter aux élections législatives; **~ by** vi (be ready) se tenir prêt(e) ♦ *vt fus (opinion)* s'en tenir à; *(person)* ne pas abandonner, soutenir; ~ **down** *vi (withdraw)* se retirer; ~ **for** *vt fus (signify)* représenter, signifier; *(tolerate)* supporter, tolérer; ~ **in for** *vt fus* remplacer; ~ **out** *vi (be prominent)* ressortir; ~ **up** *vi (rise)* se lever, se mettre debout; ~ **up for** *vt fus* défendre; ~ **up to** *vt fus* tenir tête à, résister à

standard ['stændəd] *n (level)* niveau (voulu); *(norm)* norme *f*, étalon *m*; *(criterion)* critère *m*; *(flag)* étendard *m* ♦ *adj (size etc)* ordinaire, normal(e); courant(e); *(text)* de base; ~**s** *npl (morals)* morale *f*, principes *mpl*; ~ **lamp** *(BRIT)* n lampadaire *m*; ~ **of living** *n* niveau *m* de vie

stand-by ['stændbaɪ] *n* remplaçant(e); **to be on** ~ se tenir prêt(e) (à intervenir); être de garde; ~ **ticket** *n (AVIAT)* billet *m* stand-by

stand-in ['stændɪn] *n* remplaçant(e)

standing ['stændɪŋ] *adj* debout *inv*; *(permanent)* permanent(e) ♦ *n* réputation *f*, rang *m*, standing *m*; **of many years'** ~ qui dure or existe depuis longtemps; ~ **joke** *n* vieux sujet de plaisanterie; ~ **order** *(BRIT) n (at bank)* virement *m* automatique, prélèvement *m* bancaire; ~ **room** *n* places *fpl* debout

standoffish [-'ɒfɪʃ] *adj* distant(e), froid(e)

standpoint ['stændpɔɪnt] *n* point *m* de vue

standstill ['stændstɪl] *n*: **at a** ~ paralysé(e); **to come to a** ~ s'immobiliser, s'arrêter

stank [stæŋk] *pt of* **stink**

staple ['steɪpl] *n (for papers)* agrafe *f* ♦ *adj (food etc)* de base ♦ *vt* agrafer; ~**r** *n* agrafeuse *f*

star [stɑː*] *n* étoile *f*; *(celebrity)* vedette *f* ♦ *vi*: **to** ~ **(in)** être la vedette (de) ♦ *vt (CINEMA etc)* avoir pour vedette; **the** ~**s** *npl* l'horoscope *m*

starboard ['stɑːbəd] *n* tribord *m*

starch [stɑːtʃ] *n* amidon *m*; *(in food)* fécule *f*

stardom ['stɑːdəm] *n* célébrité *f*

stare [steə*] *n* regard *m* fixe ♦ *vi*: **to** ~ **at** regarder fixement

starfish ['stɑːfɪʃ] *n* étoile *f* de mer

stark [stɑːk] *adj (bleak)* désolé(e), morne ♦ *adv*: ~ **naked** complètement nu(e)

starling ['stɑːlɪŋ] *n* étourneau *m*

starry ['stɑːrɪ] *adj* étoilé(e); ~**-eyed** *adj (innocent)* ingénu(e)

start [stɑːt] *n* commencement *m*, début *m*; *(of race)* départ *m*; *(sudden movement)* sursaut *m*; *(advantage)* avance *f*, avantage *m* ♦ *vt* commencer; *(found)* créer; *(engine)* mettre en marche ♦ *vi* partir, se mettre en route; *(jump)* sursauter; **to** ~ **doing** or **to do sth** se mettre à faire qch; ~ **off** *vi* commencer; *(leave)* partir; ~ **up** *vi* commencer; *(car)* démarrer ♦ *vt (business)* créer; *(car)* mettre en marche; ~**er** *n (AUT)*

démarreur *m*; *(SPORT: official)* starter *m*; *(BRIT: CULIN)* entrée *f*; ~**ing point** *n* point *m* de départ

startle ['stɑːtl] *vt* faire sursauter; donner un choc à; **startling** *adj (news)* surprenant(e)

starvation [stɑː'veɪʃən] *n* faim *f*, famine *f*;

starve [stɑːv] *vi* mourir de faim; être affamé(e) ♦ *vt* affamer

state [steɪt] *n* état *m*; *(POL)* État ♦ *vt* déclarer, affirmer; **the S**~**s** *npl (America)* les États-Unis *mpl*; **to be in a** ~ être dans tous ses états; ~**ly** *adj* majestueux(euse), imposant(e); ~**ment** *n* déclaration *f*; ~**sman** *(irreg) n* homme *m* d'État

static ['stætɪk] *n (RADIO, TV)* parasites *mpl* ♦ *adj* statique

station ['steɪʃən] *n* gare *f*; *(police* ~*)* poste *m* de police ♦ *vt* placer, poster

stationary ['steɪʃənərɪ] *adj* à l'arrêt, immobile

stationer ['steɪʃənə*] *n* papetier(ère); ~'**s (shop)** *n* papeterie *f*; ~**y** *n* papier *m* à lettres, petit matériel de bureau

stationmaster ['steɪʃənmɑːstə*] *n (RAIL)* chef *m* de gare

station wagon *(US) n* break *m*

statistic [stə'tɪstɪk] *n* statistique *f*; ~**s** *n (science)* statistique *f*

statue ['stætjuː] *n* statue *f*

status ['steɪtəs] *n* position *f*, situation *f*; *(official)* statut *m*; *(prestige)* prestige *m*; ~ **symbol** *n* signe extérieur de richesse

statute ['stætjuːt] *n* loi *f*, statut *m*; **statutory** *adj* statutaire, prévu(e) par un article de loi

staunch [stɔːntʃ] *adj* sûr(e), loyal(e)

stave off [steɪv] *vt (attack)* parer; *(threat)* conjurer

stay [steɪ] *n (period of time)* séjour *m* ♦ *vi* rester; *(reside)* loger; *(spend some time)* séjourner; **to** ~ **put** ne pas bouger; **to** ~ **with friends** loger chez des amis; **to** ~ **the night** passer la nuit; ~ **behind** *vi* rester en arrière; ~ **in** *vi (at home)* rester à la maison; ~ **on** *vi* rester; ~ **out** *vi (of house)* ne pas rentrer; ~ **up** *vi (at night)* ne pas se coucher; ~**ing power** *n* endurance *f*

stead [sted] *n*: **in sb's** ~ à la place de qn; **to stand sb in good** ~ être très utile à qn

steadfast ['stedfəst] *adj* ferme, résolu(e)

steadily ['stedɪlɪ] *adv (regularly)* progressivement; *(firmly)* fermement; *(: walk)* d'un pas ferme; *(fixedly: look)* sans détourner les yeux

steady ['stedɪ] *adj* stable, solide, ferme; *(regular)* constant(e), régulier(ère); *(person)* calme, pondéré(e) ♦ *vt* stabiliser; *(nerves)* calmer; **a** ~ **boyfriend** un petit ami

steak [steɪk] *n (beef)* bifteck *m*, steak *m*; *(fish, pork)* tranche *f*

steal [stiːl] *(pt* **stole**, *pp* **stolen***) vt* voler ♦ *vi* voler; *(move secretly)* se faufiler, se déplacer furtivement

stealth [stelθ] n: by ~ furtivement

steam [sti:m] n vapeur f ♦ vt (CULIN) cuire à la vapeur ♦ vi fumer; ~ **engine** n locomotive f à vapeur; ~**er** n (bateau m à) vapeur m; ~**ship** n = **steamer**; ~**y** adj embué(e), humide

steel [sti:l] n acier m ♦ adj d'acier; ~**works** n aciérie f

steep [sti:p] adj raide, escarpé(e); (price) excessif(ive)

steeple ['sti:pl] n clocher m

steer [stɪə*] vt diriger; (boat) gouverner; (person) guider, conduire ♦ vi tenir le gouvernail; ~**ing** n (AUT) conduite f; ~**ing wheel** n volant m

stem [stem] n (of plant) tige f; (of glass) pied m ♦ vt contenir, arrêter, juguler; ~ **from** vt fus provenir de, découler de

stench [stentʃ] n puanteur f

stencil ['stensl] n stencil m; (pattern used) pochoir m ♦ vt polycopier

stenographer [ste'nɒgrəfə*] (US) n sténographe m/f

step [step] n pas m; (stair) marche f; (action) mesure f, disposition f ♦ vi: to ~ **forward/back** faire un pas en avant/arrière, avancer/reculer; ~**s** npl (BRIT) = **stepladder**; **to be in/out of** ~ (**with**) (fig) aller dans le sens (de)/être déphasé(e) (par rapport à); ~ **down** vi (fig) se retirer, se désister; ~ **up** vt augmenter; intensifier; ~**brother** n demi-frère m; ~**daughter** n belle-fille f; ~**father** n beau-père m; ~**ladder** (BRIT) n escabeau m; ~**mother** n belle-mère f; ~**ping stone** n pierre f de gué; (fig) tremplin m; ~**sister** n demi-sœur f; ~**son** n beau-fils m

stereo ['sterɪəʊ] n (sound) stéréo f; (hi-fi) chaîne f stéréo inv ♦ adj (also: ~**phonic**) stéréo(phonique)

sterile ['steraɪl] adj stérile; **sterilize** ['sterɪlaɪz] vt stériliser

sterling ['stɜ:lɪŋ] adj (silver) de bon aloi, fin(e) ♦ n (ECON) livres fpl sterling inv; **a pound** ~ une livre sterling

stern [stɜ:n] adj sévère ♦ n (NAUT) arrière m, poupe f

stew [stju:] n ragoût m ♦ vt, vi cuire (à la casserole)

steward ['stju:əd] n (on ship, plane, train) steward m; ~**ess** n hôtesse f (de l'air)

stick [stɪk] (pt, pp **stuck**) n bâton m; (walking ~) canne f ♦ vt (glue) coller; (inf: put) mettre, fourrer; (: tolerate) supporter; (thrust): **to** ~ **sth into** planter or enfoncer qch dans ♦ vi (become attached) rester collé(e) or fixé(e); (be unmoveable: wheels etc) se bloquer; (remain) rester; ~ **out** vi dépasser, sortir; ~ **up** vi = **stick out**; ~ **up for** vt fus défendre; ~**er** n auto-collant m; ~**ing plaster** n sparadrap m, pansement

adhésif

stickler ['stɪklə*] n: **to be a** ~ **for** être pointilleux(euse) sur

stick-up ['stɪkʌp] (inf) n braquage m, hold-up m inv

sticky ['stɪkɪ] adj poisseux(euse); (label) adhésif(ive); (situation) délicat(e)

stiff [stɪf] adj raide; rigide; dur(e); (difficult) difficile, ardu(e); (cold) froid(e), distant(e); (strong, high) fort(e), élevé(e) ♦ adv: **to be bored/scared/frozen** s'ennuyer à mort/ être mort(e) de peur/froid; ~**en** vi se raidir; ~ **neck** n torticolis m

stifle ['staɪfl] vt étouffer, réprimer

stigma ['stɪgmə] n stigmate m

stile [staɪl] n échalier m

stiletto [stɪ'letəʊ] (BRIT) n (also: ~ **heel**) talon m aiguille

still [stɪl] adj immobile ♦ adv (up to this time) encore, toujours; (even) encore; (nonetheless) quand même, tout de même; ~**born** adj mort-né(e); ~ **life** n nature morte

stilt [stɪlt] n (for walking on) échasse f; (pile) pilotis m

stilted ['stɪltɪd] adj guindé(e), emprunté(e)

stimulate ['stɪmjʊleɪt] vt stimuler

stimulus ['stɪmjʊləs] (pl **stimuli**) n stimulant m; (BIOL, PSYCH) stimulus m

sting [stɪŋ] (pt, pp **stung**) n piqûre f; (organ) dard m ♦ vt, vi piquer

stingy ['stɪndʒɪ] adj avare, pingre

stink [stɪŋk] (pt **stank**, pp **stunk**) n puanteur f ♦ vi puer, empester; ~**ing** (inf) adj (fig) infect(e), vache; **a** ~**ing** ... un(e) foutu(e) ...

stint [stɪnt] n part f de travail ♦ vi: **to** ~ **on** lésiner sur, être chiche de

stir [stɜ:*] n agitation f, sensation f ♦ vt remuer ♦ vi remuer, bouger; ~ **up** vt (trouble) fomenter, provoquer

stirrup ['stɪrəp] n étrier m

stitch [stɪtʃ] n (SEWING) point m; (KNITTING) maille f; (MED) point de suture; (pain) point de côté ♦ vt coudre, piquer; (MED) suturer

stoat [stəʊt] n hermine f (avec son pelage d'été)

stock [stɒk] n réserve f, provision f; (COMM) stock m; (AGR) cheptel m, bétail m; (CULIN) bouillon m; (descent, origin) souche f; (FINANCE) valeurs fpl, titres mpl ♦ adj (fig: reply etc) classique ♦ vt (have in ~) avoir, vendre; ~**s and shares** valeurs (mobilières), titres; **in/out of** ~ en stock or en magasin/épuisé(e); **to take** ~ **of** (fig) faire le point de; ~ **up** vi: **to** ~ **up** (**with**) s'approvisionner (en); ~**broker** ['stɒkbrəʊkə*] n agent m de change; ~ **cube** n bouillon-cube m; ~ **exchange** n Bourse f

stocking ['stɒkɪŋ] n bas m

stock: ~ **market** n Bourse f, marché financier; ~ **phrase** n cliché m; ~**pile** n stock m, réserve f ♦ vt stocker, accumuler; ~**taking** (BRIT) n (COMM) inventaire m

stocky ['stɒkɪ] adj trapu(e), râblé(e)

stodgy ['stɒdʒɪ] adj bourratif(ive), lourd(e)

stoke [stəuk] vt (fire) garnir, entretenir; (boiler) chauffer

stole [stəul] pt of **steal** ♦ n étole f

stolen ['stəulən] pp of **steal**

stolid ['stɒlɪd] adj impassible, flegmatique

stomach ['stʌmək] n estomac m; (abdomen) ventre m ♦ vt digérer, supporter; ~**ache** n mal m à l'estomac or au ventre

stone [stəun] n pierre f; (pebble) caillou m, galet m; (in fruit) noyau m; (MED) calcul m; (BRIT: weight) n = 6,348 kg ♦ adj de or en pierre ♦ vt (person) lancer des pierres sur, lapider; ~**cold** adj complètement froid(e); ~**deaf** adj sourd(e) comme un pot; ~**work** n maçonnerie f

stood [stud] pt, pp of **stand**

stool [stuːl] n tabouret m

stoop [stuːp] vi (also: have a ~) être voûté(e); (: ~ down: bend) se baisser

stop [stɒp] n arrêt m; halte f; (in punctuation: also: full ~) point m ♦ vt arrêter, bloquer; (break off) interrompre; (also: put a ~ to) mettre fin à ♦ vi s'arrêter; (rain, noise etc) cesser, s'arrêter; **to ~ doing sth** cesser or arrêter de faire qch; ~ **dead** vi s'arrêter net; ~ **off** vi faire une courte halte; ~ **up** vt (hole) boucher; ~**gap** n (person) bouche-trou m; (measure) mesure f intérimaire; ~**over** n halte f; (AVIAT) escale f; ~**page** n (strike) arrêt de travail; (blockage) obstruction f; ~**per** ['stɒpə*] n bouchon m; ~ **press** n nouvelles fpl de dernière heure; ~**watch** ['stɒpwɒtʃ] n chronomètre m

storage ['stɔːrɪdʒ] n entreposage m; ~ **heater** n radiateur m électrique par accumulation

store [stɔː*] n (stock) provision f, réserve f; (depot) entrepôt m; (BRIT: large shop) grand magasin; (US) magasin m ♦ vt emmagasiner; (information) enregistrer; ~**s** npl (food) provisions f; **in** ~ en réserve; ~ **up** vt mettre en réserve; accumuler; ~**room** n réserve f, magasin m

storey ['stɔːrɪ] (US **story**) n étage m

stork [stɔːk] n cigogne f

storm [stɔːm] n tempête f; (thunder~) orage m ♦ vi (fig) fulminer ♦ vt prendre d'assaut; ~**y** adj orageux(euse)

story ['stɔːrɪ] n histoire f; récit m; (US) = **storey**; ~**book** n livre m d'histoires or de contes

stout [staut] adj solide; (fat) gros(se), corpulent(e) ♦ n bière brune

stove [stəuv] n (for cooking) fourneau m; (: small) réchaud m; (for heating) poêle m

stow [stəu] vt (also: ~ **away**) ranger; ~**away** n passager(ère) clandestin(e)

straddle ['strædl] vt enjamber, être à cheval sur

straggle ['strægl] vi être (or marcher) en désordre; (houses) être disséminé(e)

straight [streɪt] adj droit(e); (hair) raide; (frank) honnête, franc(franche); (simple) simple ♦ adv (tout) droit; (drink) sec, sans eau; **to put** or **get** ~ (fig) mettre au clair; ~ **away**, ~ **off** (at once) tout de suite; ~**en** vt ajuster; (bed) arranger; ~**en out** vt (fig) débrouiller; ~**faced** adj impassible; ~**forward** adj simple; (honest) honnête, direct(e)

strain [streɪn] n tension f; pression f; (physical) effort m; (mental) tension (nerveuse); (breed) race f ♦ vt (stretch: resources etc) mettre à rude épreuve, grever; (hurt: back etc) se faire mal à; (vegetables) égoutter; ~**s** npl (MUS) accords mpl, accents mpl; **back** ~ tour m de rein; ~**ed** adj (muscle) froissé(e); (laugh etc) forcé(e), contraint(e); (relations) tendu(e); ~**er** n passoire f

strait [streɪt] n (GEO) détroit m; ~**s** npl: **to be in dire** ~**s** avoir de sérieux ennuis (d'argent); ~**jacket** n camisole f de force; ~**laced** adj collet monté inv

strand [strænd] n (of thread) fil m, brin m; (of rope) toron m; (of hair) mèche f; ~**ed** adj en rade, en plan

strange [streɪndʒ] adj (not known) inconnu(e); (odd) étrange, bizarre; ~**ly** adv étrangement, bizarrement; see also **enough**; ~**r** n inconnu(e); (from another area) étranger(ère)

strangle ['stræŋgl] vt étrangler; ~**hold** n (fig) emprise totale, mainmise f

strap [stræp] n lanière f, courroie f, sangle f; (of slip, dress) bretelle f

strapping ['stræpɪŋ] adj costaud(e)

strategic [strə'tiːdʒɪk] adj stratégique.

strategy ['strætədʒɪ] n stratégie f

straw [strɔː] n paille f; **that's the last** ~! ça, c'est le comble!

strawberry ['strɔːbərɪ] n fraise f

stray [streɪ] adj (animal) perdu(e), errant(e); (scattered) isolé(e) ♦ vi s'égarer; ~ **bullet** n balle perdue

streak [striːk] n bande f, filet m; (in hair) raie f ♦ vt zébrer, strier ♦ vi: **to ~ past** passer à toute allure

stream [striːm] n ruisseau m; courant m, flot m; (of people) défilé ininterrompu, flot ♦ vt (SCOL) répartir par niveau ♦ vi ruisseler; **to ~ in/out** entrer/sortir à flots; ~**er** ['striːmə*] n serpentin m; (banner) banderole f; ~**lined** ['striːmlaɪnd] adj aérodynamique; (fig) rationalisé(e)

street [striːt] n rue f; ~**car** (US) n tramway m; ~ **lamp** n réverbère m; ~ **plan** n plan m (des rues); ~**wise** (inf) adj futé(e), réaliste

strength [strɛŋθ] n force f; (of girder, knot etc) solidité f; **~en** vt fortifier; renforcer; consolider

strenuous ['strɛnjʊəs] adj vigoureux(euse), énergique

stress [strɛs] n (force, pressure) pression f; (mental strain) tension (nerveuse), stress m; (accent) accent m ♦ vt insister sur, souligner

stretch [strɛtʃ] n (of sand etc) étendue f ♦ vi s'étirer; (extend): **to ~ to** or **as far as** s'étendre jusqu'à ♦ vt tendre, étirer; (fig) pousser (au maximum); **~ out** vi s'étendre ♦ vt (arm etc) allonger, tendre; (spread) étendre

stretcher ['strɛtʃə*] n brancard m, civière f

strewn [struːn] adj: **~ with** jonché(e) de

stricken ['strɪkən] adj (person) très éprouvé(e); (city, industry etc) dévasté(e); **~ with** (disease etc) frappé(e) or atteint(e) de

strict [strɪkt] adj strict(e)

stride [straɪd] (pt **strode**, pp **stridden**) n grand pas, enjambée f ♦ vi marcher à grands pas

strife [straɪf] n conflit m, dissensions fpl

strike [straɪk] (pt, pp **struck**) n grève f; (of oil etc) découverte f; (attack) raid m ♦ vt frapper; (oil etc) trouver, découvrir; (deal) conclure ♦ vi faire grève; (attack) attaquer; (clock) sonner; **on ~** (workers) en grève; **to ~ a match** frotter une allumette; **~ down** vt terrasser; **~ up** vt (MUS) se mettre à jouer; **to ~ up a friendship with** se lier d'amitié avec; **to ~ up a conversation (with)** engager une conversation (avec); **~r** n gréviste m/f; (SPORT) buteur m; **striking** ['straɪkɪŋ] adj frappant(e), saisissant(e); (attractive) éblouissant(e)

string [strɪŋ] (pt, pp **strung**) n ficelle f; (row of beads) rang m; (: of onions) chapelet m; (MUS) corde f ♦ vt: **to ~ out** échelonner; **the ~s** npl (MUS) les instruments mpl à cordes; **to ~ together** enchaîner; **to pull ~s** (fig) faire jouer le piston; **~ bean** n haricot vert; **~(ed) instrument** n (MUS) instrument m à cordes

stringent ['strɪndʒənt] adj rigoureux(euse)

strip [strɪp] n bande f ♦ vt (undress) déshabiller; (paint) décaper; (also: **~ down**: machine) démonter ♦ vi se déshabiller; **~ cartoon** n bande dessinée

stripe [straɪp] n raie f, rayure f; (MIL) galon m; **~d** adj rayé(e), à rayures

strip lighting (BRIT) n éclairage m au néon or fluorescent

stripper ['strɪpə*] n strip-teaseuse f

strive [straɪv] (pt **strove**, pp **striven**) vi: **to ~ to do/for sth** s'efforcer de faire/d'obtenir qch

strode [strəʊd] pt of **stride**

stroke [strəʊk] n coup m; (SWIMMING)

nage f; (MED) attaque f ♦ vt caresser; **at a ~** d'un (seul) coup

stroll [strəʊl] n petite promenade ♦ vi flâner, se promener nonchalamment; **~er** (US) n (pushchair) poussette f

strong [strɒŋ] adj fort(e); vigoureux(euse); (heart, nerves) solide; **they are 50 ~** ils sont au nombre de 50; **~hold** n bastion m; **~ly** adv fortement, avec force; vigoureusement; solidement; **~room** n chambre forte

strove [strəʊv] pt of **strive**

struck [strʌk] pt, pp of **strike**

structural ['strʌktʃərəl] adj structural(e); (CONSTR: defect) de construction; (damage) affectant les parties portantes

structure ['strʌktʃə*] n structure f; (building) construction f

struggle ['strʌgl] n lutte f ♦ vi lutter, se battre

strum [strʌm] vt (guitar) jouer (en sourdine) de

strung [strʌŋ] pt, pp of **string**

strut [strʌt] n étai m, support m ♦ vi se pavaner

stub [stʌb] n (of cigarette) bout m, mégot m; (of cheque etc) talon m ♦ vt: **to ~ one's toe** se cogner le doigt de pied; **~ out** vt écraser

stubble ['stʌbl] n chaume m; (on chin) barbe f de plusieurs jours

stubborn ['stʌbən] adj têtu(e), obstiné(e), opiniâtre

stuck [stʌk] pt, pp of **stick** ♦ adj (jammed) bloqué(e), coincé(e); **~-up** (inf) adj prétentieux(euse)

stud [stʌd] n (on boots etc) clou m; (on collar) bouton m de col; (earring) petite boucle d'oreille; (of horses: also: **~ farm**) écurie f, haras m; (also: **~ horse**) étalon m ♦ vt (fig): **~ded with** parsemé(e) or criblé(e) de

student ['stjuːdənt] n étudiant(e) ♦ adj estudiantin(e); d'étudiant; **~ driver** (US) n (conducteur(trice)) débutant(e)

studio ['stjuːdɪəʊ] n studio m, atelier m; (TV etc) studio

studious ['stjuːdɪəs] adj studieux(euse), appliqué(e); (attention) soutenu(e); **~ly** adv (carefully) soigneusement

study ['stʌdɪ] n étude f; (room) bureau m ♦ vt étudier; (examine) examiner ♦ vi étudier, faire ses études

stuff [stʌf] n chose(s) f(pl); affaires fpl, trucs mpl; (substance) substance f ♦ vt rembourrer; (CULIN) farcir; (inf: push) fourrer; **~ing** n bourre f, rembourrage m; (CULIN) farce f; **~y** adj (room) mal ventilé(e) or aéré(e); (ideas) vieux jeu inv

stumble ['stʌmbl] vi trébucher; **to ~ across** or **on** (fig) tomber sur; **stumbling block** n pierre f d'achoppement

stump [stʌmp] n souche f; (of limb) moignon m ♦ vt: **to be ~ed** sécher, ne pas savoir que répondre

stun [stʌn] *vt* étourdir; abasourdir

stung [stʌŋ] *pt, pp of* **sting**

stunk [stʌŋk] *pp of* **stink**

stunning *adj* (*news etc*) stupéfiant(e); (*girl etc*) éblouissant(e)

stunt [stʌnt] *n* (*in film*) cascade *f*, acrobatie *f*; (*publicity* ~) truc *m* publicitaire ♦ *vt* retarder, arrêter(r) ♦ ~**ed** *adj* rabougri(e); (*growth*) retardé(e); ~**man** (*irreg*) *n* cascadeur *m*

stupendous [stju:'pendəs] *adj* prodigieux(euse), fantastique

stupid ['stju:pɪd] *adj* stupide, bête; ~**ity** [stju:'pɪdɪtɪ] *n* stupidité *f*, bêtise *f*

sturdy ['stɜːdɪ] *adj* robuste; solide

stutter ['stʌtə*] *vi* bégayer

sty [staɪ] *n* (*for pigs*) porcherie *f*

stye [staɪ] *n* (*MED*) orgelet *m*

style [staɪl] *n* style *m*; (*distinction*) allure *f*, cachet *m*, style; **stylish** ['staɪlɪʃ] *adj* élégant(e), chic *inv*

stylus ['staɪləs] (*pl* **styli** *or* ~**es**) *n* (*of record player*) pointe *f* de lecture

suave [swɑːv] *adj* doucereux(euse), onctueux(euse)

sub... [sʌb] *prefix* sub..., sous-; ~**conscious** *adj* subconscient(e); ~**contract** *vt* sous-traiter

subdue [səb'dju:] *vt* subjuguer, soumettre; ~**d** *adj* (*light*) tamisé(e); (*person*) qui a perdu de son entrain

subject [*n* 'sʌbdʒɪkt, *vb* səb'dʒekt] *n* sujet *m*; (*SCOL*) matière *f* ♦ *vt*: **to ~ to** soumettre à; exposer à; **to be ~ to** (*law*) être soumis(e) à; (*disease*) être sujet(te) à; ~**ive** [səb'dʒektɪv] *adj* subjectif(ive); ~ **matter** *n* (*content*) contenu *m*

sublet ['sʌb'let] *vt* sous-louer

submarine [sʌbmə'ri:n] *n* sous-marin *m*

submerge [səb'mɜːdʒ] *vt* submerger ♦ *vi* plonger

submission [səb'mɪʃən] *n* soumission *f*; **submissive** [səb'mɪsɪv] *adj* soumis(e)

submit [səb'mɪt] *vt* soumettre ♦ *vi* se soumettre

subnormal ['sʌb'nɔːməl] *adj* au-dessous de la normale

subordinate [sə'bɔːdɪnət] *adj* subalterne ♦ *n* subordonné(e)

subpoena [sə'piːnə] *n* (*LAW*) citation *f*, assignation *f*

subscribe [səb'skraɪb] *vi* cotiser; **to ~ to** (*opinion, fund*) souscrire à; (*newspaper*) s'abonner à; être abonné(e) à; ~**r** *n* (*to periodical, telephone*) abonné(e); **subscription** [səb'skrɪpʃən] *n* (*to magazine etc*) abonnement *m*

subsequent ['sʌbsɪkwənt] *adj* ultérieur(e), suivant(e); consécutif(ive); ~**ly** *adv* par la suite

subside [səb'saɪd] *vi* (*flood*) baisser; (*wind,*

feelings) tomber; ~**nce** [sʌb'saɪdəns] *n* affaissement *m*

subsidiary [səb'sɪdɪərɪ] *adj* subsidiaire; accessoire ♦ *n* (*also*: ~ *company*) filiale *f*

subsidize ['sʌbsɪdaɪz] *vt* subventionner; **subsidy** ['sʌbsɪdɪ] *n* subvention *f*

substance ['sʌbstəns] *n* substance *f*

substantial [səb'stænʃəl] *adj* substantiel(le); (*fig*) important(e); ~**ly** *adv* considérablement; (*in essence*) en grande partie

substantiate [səb'stænʃɪeɪt] *vt* étayer, fournir des preuves à l'appui de

substitute ['sʌbstɪtjuːt] *n* (*person*) remplaçant(e); (*thing*) succédané *m* ♦ *vt*: **to ~ sth/sb for** substituer qch/qn à, remplacer par qch/qn

subterranean [sʌbtə'reɪnɪən] *adj* souterrain(e)

subtitle ['sʌbtaɪtl] *n* (*CINEMA*) sous-titre *m*

subtle ['sʌtl] *adj* subtil(e)

subtotal [sʌb'təʊtl] *n* total partiel

subtract [səb'trækt] *vt* soustraire, retrancher; ~**ion** *n* soustraction *f*

suburb ['sʌbɜːb] *n* faubourg *m*; **the ~s** *npl* la banlieue; ~**an** [sə'bɜːbən] *adj* de banlieue, suburbain(e); ~**ia** [sə'bɜːbɪə] *n* la banlieue

subway ['sʌbweɪ] *n* (*US: railway*) métro *m*; (*BRIT: underpass*) passage souterrain

succeed [sək'siːd] *vi* réussir ♦ *vt* succéder à; **to ~ in doing** réussir à faire; ~**ing** *adj* (*following*) suivant(e)

success [sək'ses] *n* succès *m*; réussite *f*; ~**ful** *adj* (*venture*) couronné(e) de succès; **to be ~ful (in doing)** réussir (à faire); ~**fully** *adv* avec succès

succession [sək'seʃən] *n* succession *f*; **3 days in ~** 3 jours de suite

successive [sək'sesɪv] *adj* successif(ive); consécutif(ive)

such [sʌtʃ] *adj* tel(telle); (*of that kind*): ~ **a book** un livre de ce genre, un livre pareil, un tel livre; (*so much*): ~ **courage** un tel courage ♦ *adv* si; ~ **books** des livres de ce genre, des livres pareils, de tels livres; ~ **a long trip** un si long voyage; ~ **a lot of** tellement *or* tant de; ~ **as** (*like*) tel que, comme; **as** ~ en tant que tel, à proprement parler; ~**-and-such** *adj* tel ou tel

suck [sʌk] *vt* sucer; (*breast, bottle*) téter; ~**er** *n* ventouse *f*; (*inf*) poire *f*

suction ['sʌkʃən] *n* succion *f*

sudden ['sʌdn] *adj* soudain(e), subit(e); **all of a ~** soudain, tout à coup; ~**ly** *adv* brusquement, tout à coup, soudain

suds [sʌdz] *npl* eau savonneuse

sue [su:] *vt* poursuivre en justice, intenter un procès à

suede [sweɪd] *n* daim *m*

suet [suɪt] *n* graisse *f* de rognon

suffer ['sʌfə*] *vt* souffrir, subir; (*bear*) tolérer, supporter ♦ *vi* souffrir; ~**er** *n* (*MED*) malade *m/f*; ~**ing** *n* souffrance(s) *f(pl)*

sufficient [səˈfɪʃənt] *adj* suffisant(e); ~ **money** suffisamment d'argent; ~**ly** *adv* suffisamment, assez

suffocate [ˈsʌfəkeɪt] *vi* suffoquer; étouffer

sugar [ˈʃugə*] *n* sucre *m* ♦ *vt* sucrer; ~ **beet** *n* betterave sucrière; ~ **cane** *n* canne f à sucre

suggest [səˈdʒest] *vt* suggérer, proposer; (*indicate*) dénoter; ~**ion** *n* suggestion f

suicide [ˈsuɪsaɪd] *n* suicide *m*; *see also* **commit**

suit [suːt] *n* (*man's*) costume *m*, complet *m*; (*woman's*) tailleur *m*, ensemble *m*; (*LAW*) poursuite(s) *f* procès *m*; (*CARDS*) couleur f ♦ *vt* aller à; convenir à; (*adapt*): **to ~ sth to** adapter *or* approprier qch à; **well ~ ed** (*couple*) faits l'un pour l'autre, très bien assortis; ~**able** *adj* qui convient; approprié(e); ~**ably** *adv* comme il se doit (*or se devait etc*), convenablement

suitcase [ˈsuːtkeɪs] *n* valise f

suite [swiːt] *n* (*of rooms, also MUS*) suite f; (*furniture*): **bedroom/dining room** ~ (ensemble *m* de) chambre f à coucher/salle f à manger

suitor [ˈsuːtə*] *n* soupirant *m*, prétendant *m*

sulfur [ˈsʌlfə*] (*US*) *n* = **sulphur**

sulk [sʌlk] *vi* bouder; ~**y** *adj* boudeur(euse), maussade

sullen [ˈsʌlən] *adj* renfrogné(e), maussade

sulphur [ˈsʌlfə*] (*US* **sulfur**) *n* soufre *m*

sultana [sʌlˈtɑːnə] *n* (*CULIN*) raisin (sec) de Smyrne

sultry [ˈsʌltrɪ] *adj* étouffant(e)

sum [sʌm] *n* somme f; (*SCOL etc*) calcul *m*; ~ **up** *vt, vi* résumer

summarize [ˈsʌməraɪz] *vt* résumer

summary [ˈsʌmərɪ] *n* résumé *m*

summer [ˈsʌmə*] *n* été *m* ♦ *adj* d'été, estival(e); ~**house** *n* (*in garden*) pavillon *m*; ~**time** *n* été *m*; ~ **time** *n* (*by clock*) heure f d'été

summit [ˈsʌmɪt] *n* sommet *m*

summon [ˈsʌmən] *vt* appeler, convoquer; ~ **up** *vt* rassembler, faire appel à; ~**s** *n* citation f, assignation f

sump [sʌmp] (*BRIT*) *n* (*AUT*) carter *m*

sun [sʌn] *n* soleil *m*; **in the** ~ au soleil; ~**bathe** *vi* prendre un bain de soleil; ~**burn** *n* coup *m* de soleil; ~**burned** *adj* = **sunburnt**; ~**burnt** *adj* (*tanned*) bronzé(e)

Sunday [ˈsʌndeɪ] *n* dimanche *m*; ~ **school** *n* ≈ catéchisme *m*

sundial [ˈsʌndaɪəl] *n* cadran *m* solaire

sundown [ˈsʌndaʊn] *n* coucher *m* du (*or de*) soleil

sundries [ˈsʌndrɪz] *npl* articles divers

sundry [ˈsʌndrɪ] *adj* divers(e), différent(e) ♦ *n*: **all and** ~ tout le monde, n'importe qui

sunflower [ˈsʌnflaʊə*] *n* tournesol *m*

sung [sʌŋ] *pp of* **sing**

sunglasses [ˈsʌnglɑːsɪz] *npl* lunettes *fpl* de soleil

sunk [sʌŋk] *pp of* **sink**

sun: ~**light** *n* (lumière f du) soleil *m*; ~**lit** *adj* ensoleillé(e); ~**ny** *adj* ensoleillé(e); ~**rise** *n* lever *m* du (*or de*) soleil; ~ **roof** *n* (*AUT*) toit ouvrant; ~**set** *n* coucher *m* du (*or de*) soleil; ~**shade** *n* (*over table*) parasol *m*; ~**shine** *n* (lumière f du) soleil *m*; ~**stroke** *n* insolation f; ~**tan** *n* bronzage *m*; ~**tan lotion** *n* lotion f *or* lait *m* solaire; ~**tan oil** *n* huile f solaire

super [ˈsuːpə*] (*inf*) *adj* formidable

superannuation [ˈsuːpərænjuˈeɪʃən] *n* (*contribution*) cotisations *fpl* pour la pension

superb [suːˈpɜːb] *adj* superbe, magnifique

supercilious [suːpəˈsɪlɪəs] *adj* hautain(e), dédaigneux(euse)

superficial [suːpəˈfɪʃəl] *adj* superficiel(le)

superimpose [suːpərɪmˈpəʊz] *vt* superposer

superintendent [suːpərɪnˈtendənt] *n* directeur(trice); (*POLICE*) ≈ commissaire *m*

superior [sʊˈpɪərɪə*] *adj*, *n* supérieur(e); ~**ity** [sʊpɪərɪˈɒrɪtɪ] *n* supériorité f

superlative [suːˈpɜːlətɪv] *n* (*LING*) superlatif *m*

superman [ˈsuːpəmæn] (*irreg*) *n* surhomme *m*

supermarket [ˈsuːpəmɑːkɪt] *n* supermarché *m*

supernatural [suːpəˈnætʃərəl] *adj* surnaturel(le)

superpower [ˈsuːpəpaʊə*] *n* (*POL*) superpuissance f

supersede [suːpəˈsiːd] *vt* remplacer, supplanter

superstitious [suːpəˈstɪʃəs] *adj* superstitieux(euse)

supervise [ˈsuːpəvaɪz] *vt* surveiller; diriger; **supervision** [suːpəˈvɪʒən] *n* surveillance f; contrôle *m*; **supervisor** [ˈsuːpəvaɪzə*] *n* surveillant(e); (*in shop*) chef *m* de rayon

supine [ˈsuːpaɪn] *adj* couché(e) *or* étendu(e) sur le dos

supper [ˈsʌpə*] *n* dîner *m*; (*late*) souper *m*

supple [ˈsʌpl] *adj* souple

supplement [*n* ˈsʌplɪmənt, *vb* sʌplɪˈment] *n* supplément *m* ♦ *vt* compléter; ~**ary** *adj* supplémentaire; ~**ary benefit** (*BRIT*) *n* allocation f (supplémentaire) d'aide sociale

supplier [səˈplaɪə*] *n* fournisseur *m*

supply [səˈplaɪ] *vt* (*provide*) fournir; (*equip*): **to ~ (with)** approvisionner *or* ravitailler (en); fournir (en) provision f, réserve f; (~**ing**) approvisionnement *m*; **supplies** *npl* (*food*) vivres *mpl*; (*MIL*) subsistances *fpl*; ~ **teacher** (*BRIT*) *n* suppléant(e)

support [səˈpɔːt] *n* (*moral, financial etc*)

soutien *m*, appui *m*; (*TECH*) support *m*,
soutien ♦ *vt* soutenir; supporter; (*financially*)
subvenir aux besoins de; (*uphold*) être
pour, être partisan de, appuyer; ~**er** *n* (*POL
etc*) partisan(e); (*SPORT*) supporter *m*

suppose [sə'pəuz] *vt* supposer; imaginer; **to
be** ~**d to do** être censé(e) faire; ~**dly**
[sə'pəuzɪdlɪ] *adv* soi-disant; **supposing**
[sə'pəuzɪŋ] *conj* si, à supposer que +*sub*

suppress [sə'prɛs] *vt* (*revolt*) réprimer; (*information*) supprimer; (*yawn*) étouffer;
(*feelings*) refouler

supreme [su'priːm] *adj* suprême

surcharge ['sɜːtʃɑːdʒ] *n* surcharge *f*

sure [ʃuə*] *adj* sûr(e); (*definite, convinced*)
sûr, certain(e); ~**!** (*of course*) bien sûr!; ~
enough effectivement; **to make** ~ **of sth**
s'assurer de *or* vérifier qch; **to make** ~
that s'assurer *or* vérifier que; ~**ly** *adv*
sûrement; certainement

surety ['ʃuərətɪ] *n* caution *f*

surf [sɜːf] *n* (*waves*) ressac *m*

surface ['sɜːfɪs] *n* surface *f* ♦ *vt* (*road*) poser un revêtement sur ♦ *vi* remonter à la
surface; faire surface; ~ **mail** *n* courrier *m*
par voie de terre (*or* maritime)

surfboard ['sɜːfbɔːd] *n* planche *f* de surf

surfeit ['sɜːfɪt] *n*: **a** ~ **of** un excès de; une
indigestion de

surfing ['sɜːfɪŋ] *n* surf *m*

surge [sɜːdʒ] *n* vague *f*, montée *f* ♦ *vi* déferler

surgeon ['sɜːdʒən] *n* chirurgien *m*

surgery ['sɜːdʒərɪ] *n* chirurgie *f*, (*BRIT*:
room) cabinet *m* (de consultation); (: *also*:
~ **hours**) heures *fpl* de consultation

surgical ['sɜːdʒɪkəl] *adj* chirurgical(e); ~
spirit (*BRIT*) *n* alcool *m* à 90°

surly ['sɜːlɪ] *adj* revêche, maussade

surname ['sɜːneɪm] *n* nom *m* de famille

surplus ['sɜːpləs] *n* surplus *m*, excédent *m*
♦ *adj* en surplus, de trop; (*COMM*) excédentaire

surprise [sə'praɪz] *n* surprise *f*; (*astonishment*) étonnement *m* ♦ *vt* surprendre; (*astonish*) étonner; **surprising** [sə'praɪzɪŋ] *adj*
surprenant(e), étonnant(e); **surprisingly**
adv (*easy, helpful*) étonnamment

surrender [sə'rɛndə*] *n* reddition *f*, capitulation *f* ♦ *vi* se rendre, capituler

surreptitious [sʌrəp'tɪʃəs] *adj* subreptice,
furtif(ive)

surrogate ['sʌrəgɪt] *n* substitut *m*; ~
mother *n* mère porteuse *or* de substitution

surround [sə'raund] *vt* entourer; (*MIL etc*)
encercler; ~**ing** *adj* environnant(e); ~**ings**
npl environs *mpl*, alentours *mpl*

surveillance [sɜː'veɪləns] *n* surveillance *f*

survey [*n* 'sɜːveɪ, *vb* sɜː'veɪ] *n* enquête *f*,
étude *f*; (*in housebuying etc*) inspection *f*,
(rapport *m* d')expertise *f*; (*of land*) levé *m* ♦
vt enquêter sur; inspecter; (*look at*) embras-

ser du regard; ~**or** [sə'veɪə*] *n* (*of house*)
expert *m*; (*of land*) (arpenteur *m*) géomètre
m

survival [sə'vaɪvəl] *n* survie *f*; (*relic*) vestige
m

survive [sə'vaɪv] *vi* survivre; (*custom etc*)
subsister ♦ *vt* survivre à; **survivor**
[sə'vaɪvə*] *n* survivant(e); (*fig*) battant(e)

susceptible [sə'sɛptəbl] *adj*: ~ **(to)** sensible
(à); (*disease*) prédisposé(e) (à)

suspect [*n, adj* 'sʌspɛkt, *vb* səs'pɛkt] *adj, n*
suspect(e) ♦ *vt* soupçonner, suspecter

suspend [səs'pɛnd] *vt* suspendre; ~**ed
sentence** *n* condamnation *f* avec sursis;
~**er belt** *n* porte-jarretelles *m inv*; ~**ers**
npl (*BRIT*) jarretelles *fpl*; (*US*) bretelles *fpl*

suspense [səs'pɛns] *n* attente *f*, incertitude
f; (*in film etc*) suspense *m*

suspension [səs'pɛnʃən] *n* suspension *f*;
(*of driving licence*) retrait *m* provisoire; ~
bridge *n* pont suspendu

suspicion [səs'pɪʃən] *n* soupçon(s) *m(pl)*

suspicious [səs'pɪʃəs] *adj* (*suspecting*)
soupçonneux(euse), méfiant(e); (*causing
suspicion*) suspect(e)

sustain [səs'teɪn] *vt* soutenir; (*food etc*)
nourrir, donner des forces à; (*suffer*) subir;
recevoir; ~**able** *adj* (*development, growth
etc*) viable; ~**ed** *adj* (*effort*) soutenu(e),
prolongé(e)

sustenance ['sʌstɪnəns] *n* nourriture *f*;
(*money*) moyens *mpl* de subsistance

swab [swɒb] *n* (*MED*) tampon *m*

swagger ['swægə*] *vi* plastronner

swallow ['swɒləu] *n* (*bird*) hirondelle *f* ♦ *vt*
avaler; ~ **up** *vt* engloutir

swam [swæm] *pt of* **swim**

swamp [swɒmp] *n* marais *m*, marécage *m* ♦
vt submerger

swan [swɒn] *n* cygne *m*

swap [swɒp] *vt*: **to** ~ **(for)** échanger
(contre), troquer (contre)

swarm [swɔːm] *n* essaim *m* ♦ *vi* fourmiller,
grouiller

swarthy ['swɔːðɪ] *adj* basané(e), bistré(e)

swastika ['swɒstɪkə] *n* croix gammée

swat [swɒt] *vt* écraser

sway [sweɪ] *vi* se balancer, osciller ♦ *vt* (*influence*) influencer

swear [swɛə*] (*pt* **swore**, *pp* **sworn**) *vt, vi*
jurer; ~**word** *n* juron *m*, gros mot

sweat [swɛt] *n* sueur *f*, transpiration *f* ♦ *vi*
suer

sweater ['swɛtə*] *n* tricot *m*, pull *m*

sweaty ['swɛtɪ] *adj* en sueur, moite *or*
mouillé(e) de sueur

Swede [swiːd] *n* Suédois(e)

swede [swiːd] (*BRIT*) *n* rutabaga *m*

Sweden ['swiːdn] *n* Suède *f*; **Swedish**
['swiːdɪʃ] *adj* suédois(e) ♦ *n* (*LING*) suédois
m

sweep [swiːp] (*pt, pp* **swept**) *n* coup *m* de

balai; (*also: chimney* ~) ramoneur m ♦ vt balayer; (*subj: current*) emporter ♦ vi (*hand, arm*) faire un mouvement; (*wind*) souffler; ~ **away** vt balayer; entraîner; emporter; ~ **past** vi passer majestueusement or rapidement; ~ **up** vi balayer; ~**ing** adj (*gesture*) large; circulaire; **a** ~**ing statement** une généralisation hâtive

sweet [swiːt] n (*candy*) bonbon m; (*BRIT: pudding*) dessert m ♦ adj doux(douce); (*not savoury*) sucré(e); (*fig: kind*) gentil(le); (*baby*) mignon(ne); ~**corn** n maïs m; ~**en** vt adoucir; (*with sugar*) sucrer; ~**heart** n amoureux(euse); ~**ness** n goût sucré; douceur f; ~**pea** n pois m de senteur

swell [swel] (*pt* ~**ed**, *pp* **swollen** or ~**ed**) n (*of sea*) houle f ♦ adj (*US: inf: excellent*) chouette ♦ vi grossir, augmenter; (*sound*) s'enfler; (*MED*) enfler; ~**ing** n (*MED*) enflure f; (*lump*) grosseur f

sweltering ['sweltərɪŋ] adj étouffant(e), oppressant(e)

swept [swept] pt, pp of **sweep**

swerve [swɜːv] vi faire une embardée or un écart; dévier

swift [swɪft] n (*bird*) martinet m ♦ adj rapide, prompt(e)

swig [swɪɡ] n (*inf*) n (*drink*) lampée f

swill [swɪl] vt (*also:* ~ **out**, ~ **down**) laver à grande eau

swim [swɪm] (*pt* **swam**, *pp* **swum**) n: **to go for a** ~ aller nager or se baigner ♦ vi nager; (*SPORT*) faire de la natation; (*head, room*) tourner ♦ vt traverser (à la nage); (*a length*) faire (à la nage); ~**mer** n nageur(euse); ~**ming** n natation f; ~**ming cap** n bonnet m de bain; ~**ming costume** (*BRIT*) n maillot m (de bain); ~**ming pool** n piscine f; ~**ming trunks** npl caleçon m or slip m de bain; ~**suit** n maillot m (de bain)

swindle ['swɪndl] n escroquerie f

swine [swaɪn] (*infl*) n inv salaud m (*!*)

swing [swɪŋ] (*pt, pp* **swung**) n balançoire f; (*movement*) balancement m, oscillations fpl; (*MUS: also rhythm*) rythme m; (*change: in opinion etc*) revirement m ♦ vt balancer, faire osciller; (*also:* ~ *round*) tourner, faire virer ♦ vi se balancer, osciller; (*also:* ~ *round*) virer, tourner; **to be in full** ~ battre son plein; ~ **bridge** n pont tournant; ~**door** (*US* ~**ing door**) n porte battante

swingeing ['swɪndʒɪŋ] (*BRIT*) adj écrasant(e); (*cuts etc*) considérable

swipe [swaɪp] (*inf*) vt (*steal*) piquer

swirl [swɜːl] vi tourbillonner, tournoyer

swish [swɪʃ] vi (*tail*) remuer; (*clothes*) froufrouter

Swiss [swɪs] adj suisse ♦ n inv Suisse m/f

switch [swɪtʃ] n (*for light, radio etc*) bouton m; (*change*) changement m, revirement m ♦ vt changer; ~ **off** vt éteindre; (*engine*) arrêter; ~ **on** vt allumer; (*engine, machine*)

mettre en marche; ~**board** n (*TEL*) standard m

Switzerland ['swɪtsələnd] n Suisse f

swivel ['swɪvl] vi (*also:* ~ *round*) pivoter, tourner

swollen ['swəʊlən] pp of **swell**

swoon [swuːn] vi se pâmer

swoop [swuːp] n (*by police*) descente f ♦ vi (*also:* ~ *down*) descendre en piqué, piquer

swop [swɒp] vt = **swap**

sword [sɔːd] n épée f; ~**fish** n espadon m

swore [swɔː*] pt of **swear**

sworn [swɔːn] pp of **swear** ♦ adj (*statement, evidence*) donné(e) sous serment

swot [swɒt] vi bûcher, potasser

swum [swʌm] pp of **swim**

swung [swʌŋ] pt, pp of **swing**

syllable ['sɪləbl] n syllabe f

syllabus ['sɪləbəs] n programme m

symbol ['sɪmbəl] n symbole m

symmetry ['sɪmɪtrɪ] n symétrie f

sympathetic [sɪmpə'θetɪk] adj compatissant(e); bienveillant(e), compréhensif(ive); (*likeable*) sympathique; ~ **towards** bien disposé(e) envers

sympathize ['sɪmpəθaɪz] vi: **to** ~ **with sb** plaindre qn; (*in grief*) s'associer à la douleur de qn; **to** ~ **with sth** comprendre qch; ~**r** n (*POL*) sympathisant(e)

sympathy ['sɪmpəθɪ] n (*pity*) compassion f; **sympathies** npl (*support*) soutien m; **left-wing etc sympathies** penchants mpl à gauche etc; **in** ~ **with** (*strike*) en or par solidarité avec; **with our deepest** ~ **en** vous priant d'accepter nos sincères condoléances

symphony ['sɪmfənɪ] n symphonie f

symptom ['sɪmptəm] n symptôme m; indice m

syndicate ['sɪndɪkət] n syndicat m, coopérative f

synonym ['sɪnənɪm] n synonyme m

synopsis [sɪ'nɒpsɪs, *pl* -siːz] (*pl* **synopses**) n résumé m

syntax ['sɪntæks] n syntaxe f

synthetic [sɪn'θetɪk] adj synthétique

syphon ['saɪfən] n, vb = **siphon**

Syria ['sɪrɪə] n Syrie f

syringe [sɪ'rɪndʒ] n seringue f

syrup ['sɪrəp] n sirop m; (*also: golden* ~) mélasse raffinée

system ['sɪstəm] n système m; (*ANAT*) organisme m; ~**atic** [sɪstə'mætɪk] adj systématique; méthodique; ~ **disk** n (*COMPUT*) disque m système; ~**s analyst** n analyste fonctionnel(le)

T t

ta [tɑː] (BRIT: inf) excl merci!

tab [tæb] n (label) étiquette f; (on drinks can etc) languette f; **to keep ~s on** (fig) surveiller

tabby ['tæbɪ] n (also: ~ cat) chat(te) tigré(e)

table ['teɪbl] n table f ♦ vt (BRIT: motion etc) présenter; **to lay** or **set the ~** mettre le couvert or la table; **~cloth** ['-klɔθ] n nappe f; **~ d'hôte** ['tɑːbl'dəʊt] adj (meal) à prix fixe; **~ lamp** n lampe f de table; **~mat** ['teɪblmæt] n (for plate) napperon m, set m; (for hot dish) dessous-de-plat m inv; **~ of contents** n table f des matières; **~spoon** ['teɪblspuːn] n cuiller f de service; (also: **~spoonful**: as measurement) cuillerée f à soupe

table football n baby-foot m.

tablet ['tæblət] n (MED) comprimé m; (of stone) plaque f

table tennis n ping-pong m ®, tennis m de table

table wine n vin m de table

tabloid ['tæblɔɪd] n quotidien m populaire

tabulate ['tæbjʊleɪt] vt (data, figures) présenter sous forme de table(s)

tack [tæk] n (nail) petit clou ♦ vt clouer; (fig) direction f; (BRIT: stitch) faufiler ♦ vi tirer un or des bord(s)

tackle ['tækl] n matériel m, équipement m; (for lifting) appareil m de levage; (RUGBY) plaquage m ♦ vt (difficulty, animal, burglar etc) s'attaquer à; (person: challenge) s'expliquer avec; (RUGBY) plaquer

tacky ['tækɪ] adj collant(e); (pej: of poor quality) miteux(euse)

tact [tækt] n tact m; **~ful** adj plein(e) de tact

tactical ['tæktɪkəl] adj tactique

tactics ['tæktɪks] npl tactique f

tactless ['tæktləs] adj qui manque de tact

tadpole ['tædpəʊl] n têtard m

taffy ['tæfɪ] (US) n (bonbon m au) caramel m

tag [tæg] n étiquette f; **~ along** vi suivre

tail [teɪl] n queue f; (of shirt) pan m ♦ vt (follow) suivre, filer; **~s** npl habit m; **~ away**, **~ off** vi (in size, quality etc) baisser peu à peu; **~back** (BRIT) n (AUT) bouchon m; **~ end** n bout m, fin f; **~gate** n (AUT) hayon m arrière

tailor ['teɪlə*] n tailleur m; **~ing** n (cut) coupe f; **~-made** adj fait(e) sur mesure; (fig) conçu(e) spécialement

tailwind ['teɪlwɪnd] n vent m arrière inv

tainted ['teɪntɪd] adj (food) gâté(e); (water, air) infecté(e); (fig) souillé(e)

take [teɪk] (pt **took**, pp **taken**) vt prendre; (gain: prize) remporter; (require: effort, courage) demander; (tolerate) accepter, supporter; (hold: passengers etc) contenir; (accompany) emmener, accompagner; (bring, carry) apporter, emporter; (exam) passer, se présenter à; **to ~ sth from** (drawer etc) prendre qch dans; (person) prendre qch à; **I ~ it that ...** je suppose que ...; **~ after** vt fus ressembler à; **~ apart** vt démonter; **~ away** vt enlever; (carry off) emporter; **~ back** vt (return) rendre, rapporter; (one's words) retirer; **~ down** vt (building) démolir; (letter etc) prendre, écrire; **~ in** vt (deceive) tromper, rouler; (understand) comprendre, saisir; (include) comprendre, inclure; (lodger) prendre; **~ off** vi (AVIAT) décoller ♦ vt (go away) s'en aller; (remove) enlever; **~ on** vt (work) accepter, se charger de; (employee) prendre, embaucher; (opponent) accepter de se battre contre; **~ out** vt (invite) emmener, sortir; (remove) enlever; **to ~ sth out of sth** (drawer, pocket etc) prendre qch dans qch; **~ over** vt (business) reprendre ♦ vi: **to ~ over from sb** prendre la relève de qn; **~ to** vt fus (person) se prendre d'amitié pour; (thing) prendre goût à; **~ up** vt (activity) se mettre à; (dress) raccourcir; (occupy: time, space) prendre, occuper; **to ~ sb up on an offer** accepter la proposition de qn; **~away** (BRIT) adj (food) à emporter ♦ n (shop, restaurant) qui vend des plats à emporter; **~off** n (AVIAT) décollage m; **~over** n (COMM) rachat m; **takings** ['teɪkɪŋz] npl (COMM) recette f

talc [tælk] n (also: **~um powder**) talc m

tale [teɪl] n (story) conte m, histoire f; (account) récit m; **to tell ~s** (fig) rapporter

talent ['tælənt] n talent m, don m; **~ed** adj doué(e), plein(e) de talent

talk [tɔːk] n (a speech) causerie f, exposé m; (conversation) discussion f, entretien m; (gossip) racontars mpl ♦ vi parler; **~s** npl (POL etc) entretiens mpl; **to ~ about** parler de; **to ~ sb into/out of doing** persuader qn de faire/ne pas faire; **to ~ shop** parler métier or affaires; **~ over** vt discuter (de); **~ative** ['tɔːkətɪv] adj bavard(e); **~ show** n causerie (télévisée or radiodiffusée)

tall [tɔːl] adj (person) grand(e); (building, tree) haut(e); **to be 6 feet ~** ≈ mesurer 1 mètre 80; **~ story** n histoire f invraisemblable

tally ['tælɪ] n compte m ♦ vi: **to ~ (with)** correspondre (à)

talon ['tælən] n griffe f; (of eagle) serre f

tame [teɪm] adj apprivoisé(e); (fig: story, style) insipide

tamper ['tæmpə*] vi: **to ~ with** toucher à

tampon ['tæmpən] n tampon m (hygiénique or périodique)

tan [tæn] n (also: sun~) bronzage m ♦ vt, vi bronzer ♦ adj (colour) brun roux inv

tang [tæŋ] n odeur (or saveur) piquante

tangent ['tændʒənt] n (MATH) tangente f; **to go off at a ~** (fig) changer de sujet

tangerine [tændʒə'ri:n] n mandarine f

tangle ['tæŋgl] n enchevêtrement m; **to get in(to) a ~** s'embrouiller

tank [tæŋk] n (water ~) réservoir m; (for fish) aquarium m; (MIL) char m d'assaut, tank m

tanker ['tæŋkə*] n (ship) pétrolier m, tanker m; (truck) camion-citerne m

tantalizing ['tæntəlaɪzɪŋ] adj (smell) extrêmement appétissant(e); (offer) terriblement tentant(e)

tantamount ['tæntəmaunt] adj: **~ to** qui équivaut à

tantrum ['tæntrəm] n accès m de colère

tap [tæp] n (on sink etc) robinet m; (gentle blow) petite tape ♦ vt frapper or taper légèrement; (resources) exploiter, utiliser; (telephone) mettre sur écoute; **on ~** (fig: resources) disponible; **~-dancing** ['tæpdɑːnsɪŋ] n claquettes fpl

tape [teɪp] n ruban m; (also: magnetic ~) bande f (magnétique); (cassette) cassette f; (sticky) scotch m ♦ vt (record) enregistrer; (stick with ~) coller avec du scotch; **~ deck** n platine f d'enregistrement; **~ measure** n mètre m à ruban

taper ['teɪpə*] n cierge m ♦ vi s'effiler

tape recorder n magnétophone m

tapestry ['tæpɪstrɪ] n tapisserie f

tar [tɑː*] n goudron m

target ['tɑːgɪt] n cible f; (fig) objectif m

tariff ['tærɪf] n (COMM) tarif m; (taxes) tarif douanier

tarmac ['tɑːmæk] n (BRIT: on road) macadam m; (AVIAT) piste f

tarnish ['tɑːnɪʃ] vt ternir

tarpaulin [tɑː'pɔːlɪn] n bâche (goudronnée)

tarragon ['tærəgən] n estragon m

tart [tɑːt] n (CULIN) tarte f; (BRIT: inf: prostitute) putain f ♦ adj (flavour) âpre, aigrelet(te); **~ up** (BRIT: inf) vt (object) retaper; **to ~ o.s. up** se faire beau(belle), s'attifer (pej)

tartan ['tɑːtən] n tartan m ♦ adj écossais(e)

tartar ['tɑːtə*] n (on teeth) tartre m; **~(e) sauce** n sauce f tartare

task [tɑːsk] n tâche f; **to take sb to ~** prendre qn à partie; **~ force** n (MIL, POLICE) détachement spécial

tassel ['tæsəl] n gland m; pompon m

taste [teɪst] n goût m; (fig: glimpse, idea) idée f, aperçu m ♦ vt goûter ♦ vi: **to ~ of** or like (fish etc) avoir le or un goût de; **you can ~ the garlic (in it)** on sent bien l'ail; **can I have a ~ of this wine?** puis-je goûter un peu de ce vin?; **in good/bad ~** de bon/mauvais goût; **~ful** adj de bon goût; **~less** adj (food) fade; (remark) de mauvais goût; **tasty** ['teɪstɪ] adj savoureux(euse), délicieux(euse)

tatters ['tætəz] npl: **in ~** en lambeaux

tattoo [tə'tuː] n tatouage m; (spectacle) parade f militaire ♦ vt tatouer

tatty (BRIT: inf) adj (clothes) frippé(e); (shop, area) délabré(e)

taught [tɔːt] pt, pp of **teach**

taunt [tɔːnt] n raillerie f ♦ vt railler

Taurus ['tɔːrəs] n le Taureau

taut [tɔːt] adj tendu(e)

tax [tæks] n (on goods etc) taxe f; (on income) impôts mpl, contributions fpl ♦ vt taxer; imposer; (fig: patience etc) mettre à l'épreuve; **~able** adj (income) imposable; **~ation** [tæk'seɪʃən] n taxation f; impôts mpl, contributions fpl; **~ avoidance** n dégrèvement fiscal; **~ disc** (BRIT) n (AUT) vignette f (automobile); **~ evasion** n fraude fiscale; **~-free** adj exempt(e) d'impôts

taxi ['tæksɪ] n taxi m ♦ vi (AVIAT) rouler (lentement) au sol; **~ driver** n chauffeur m de taxi; **~ rank** (BRIT) n station f de taxis; **~ stand** n = **taxi rank**

tax: ~ payer n contribuable m/f; **~ relief** n dégrèvement fiscal; **~ return** n déclaration f d'impôts or de revenus

TB n abbr = **tuberculosis**

tea [tiː] n thé m; (BRIT: snack: for children) goûter m; **high ~** collation combinant goûter et dîner; **~ bag** n sachet m de thé; **~ break** (BRIT) n pause-thé f

teach [tiːtʃ] (pt, pp taught) vt: **to ~ sb sth**, **~ sth to sb** apprendre qch à qn; (in school etc) enseigner qch à qn enseigner; **~er** n (in secondary school) professeur m; (in primary school) instituteur(trice); **~ing** n enseignement m

tea cosy n cloche f à thé

teacup ['tiːkʌp] n tasse f à thé

teak [tiːk] n teck m

team [tiːm] n équipe f; (of animals) attelage m; **~work** n travail m d'équipe

teapot ['tiːpɔt] n théière f

tear¹ [tɛə*] (pt tore, pp torn) n déchirure f ♦ vt déchirer ♦ vi se déchirer; **~ along** vi (rush) aller à toute vitesse; **~ up** vt (sheet of paper etc) déchirer, mettre en morceaux or pièces

tear² [tɪə*] n larme f; **in ~s** en larmes; **~ful** adj larmoyant(e); **~ gas** n gaz m lacrymogène

tearoom ['tiːrum] n salon m de thé

tease [tiːz] vt taquiner; (unkindly) tourmenter

tea set n service m à thé

teaspoon ['tiːspuːn] *n* petite cuiller; (*also:* ~*ful: as measurement*) ≈ cuillerée f à café
teat [tiːt] *n* tétine f
teatime ['tiːtaɪm] *n* l'heure f du thé
tea towel (*BRIT*) *n* torchon m (à vaisselle)
technical ['teknɪkəl] *adj* technique; ~**ity** [teknɪ'kælɪtɪ] *n* (*detail*) détail m technique; (*point of law*) vice m de forme; ~**ly** *adv* techniquement; (*strictly speaking*) en théorie
technician [tek'nɪʃən] *n* technicien(ne)
technique [tek'niːk] *n* technique f
technological [teknə'lɒdʒɪkəl] *adj* technologique; **technology** [tek'nɒlədʒɪ] *n* technologie f
teddy (bear) ['tedɪ-] *n* ours m en peluche
tedious ['tiːdɪəs] *adj* fastidieux(euse)
tee [tiː] *n* (*GOLF*) tee m
teem [tiːm] *vi*: **to ~ (with)** grouiller (de); **it is** ~**ing (with rain)** il pleut à torrents
teenage ['tiːneɪdʒ] *adj* (*fashions etc*) pour jeunes, pour adolescents; (*children*) adolescent(e); ~**r** *n* adolescent(e)
teens [tiːnz] *npl*: **to be in one's** ~ être adolescent(e)
tee-shirt ['tiːʃɜːt] *n* = T-shirt
teeter ['tiːtə*] *vi* chanceler, vaciller
teeth [tiːθ] *npl of* **tooth**
teethe [tiːð] *vi* percer ses dents
teething ring ['tiːðɪŋ-] *n* anneau pour bébé qui perce ses dents
teething troubles *npl* (*fig*) difficultés initiales
teetotal ['tiːtəʊtl] *adj* (*person*) qui ne boit jamais d'alcool
telegram ['telɪgræm] *n* télégramme m
telegraph ['telɪgrɑːf] *n* télégraphe m; ~ **pole** *n* poteau m télégraphique
telephone ['telɪfəʊn] *n* téléphone m ♦ *vt* (*person*) téléphoner à; (*message*) téléphoner; **on the** ~ au téléphone; **to be on the** ~ (*BRIT: have a* ~) avoir le téléphone; ~ **booth** (*BRIT*) *n* = **telephone box**; ~ **box** *n* cabine f téléphonique; ~ **call** *n* coup m de téléphone, appel m téléphonique; ~ **directory** *n* annuaire m (du téléphone); ~ **number** *n* numéro m de téléphone; **telephonist** [tə'lefənɪst] (*BRIT*) *n* téléphoniste m/f
telescope ['telɪskəʊp] *n* télescope m
television ['telɪvɪʒən] *n* télévision f; **on** ~ à la télévision; ~ **set** *n* (poste f de) télévision m
telex ['teleks] *n* télex m
tell [tel] (*pt, pp* **told**) *vt* dire; (*relate: story*) raconter; (*distinguish*): **to ~ sth from** distinguer qch de ♦ *vi* (*talk*): **to ~ (of)** parler (de); (*have effect*) se faire sentir, se voir; **to ~ sb to do** dire à qn de faire; ~ **off** *vt* réprimander, gronder; ~**er** *n* (*in bank*) caissier(ère); ~**ing** *adj* (*remark, detail*) révélateur(trice); ~**tale** *adj* (*sign*) éloquent(e), révélateur(trice)

telly ['telɪ] (*BRIT: inf*) *n abbr* (= *television*) télé f
temp [temp] *n abbr* (= *temporary*) (secrétaire f) intérimaire f
temper ['tempə*] *n* (*nature*) caractère m; (*mood*) humeur f; (*fit of anger*) colère f ♦ *vt* (*moderate*) tempérer, adoucir; **to be in a** ~ être en colère; **to lose one's** ~ se mettre en colère
temperament ['temprəmənt] *n* (*nature*) tempérament m; ~**al** [temprə'mentl] *adj* capricieux(euse)
temperate ['tempərət] *adj* (*climate, country*) tempéré(e)
temperature ['temprɪtʃə*] *n* température f; **to have** *or* **run a** ~ avoir de la fièvre
temple ['templ] *n* (*building*) temple m; (*ANAT*) tempe f
temporary ['tempərərɪ] *adj* temporaire, provisoire; (*job, worker*) temporaire
tempt [tempt] *vt* tenter; **to ~ sb into doing** persuader qn de faire; ~**ation** [temp'teɪʃən] *n* tentation f
ten [ten] *num* dix
tenacity [tə'næsɪtɪ] *n* ténacité f
tenancy ['tenənsɪ] *n* location f; état m de locataire
tenant ['tenənt] *n* locataire m/f
tend [tend] *vt* s'occuper de ♦ *vi*: **to ~ to do** avoir tendance à faire
tendency ['tendənsɪ] *n* tendance f
tender ['tendə*] *adj* tendre; (*delicate*) délicat(e); (*sore*) sensible ♦ *n* (*COMM: offer*) soumission f ♦ *vt* offrir
tenement ['tenəmənt] *n* immeuble m
tenet ['tenət] *n* principe m
tennis ['tenɪs] *n* tennis m; ~ **ball** *n* balle f de tennis; ~ **court** *n* (court m de) tennis; ~ **player** *n* joueur(euse) de tennis; ~ **racket** *n* raquette f de tennis; ~ **shoes** *npl* (chaussures *fpl* de) tennis *mpl*
tenor ['tenə*] *n* (*MUS*) ténor m
tenpin bowling (*BRIT*) *n* bowling m (à dix quilles)
tense [tens] *adj* tendu(e) ♦ *n* (*LING*) temps m
tension ['tenʃən] *n* tension f
tent [tent] *n* tente f
tentative ['tentətɪv] *adj* timide, hésitant(e); (*conclusion*) provisoire
tenterhooks ['tentəhʊks] *npl*: **on** ~ sur des charbons ardents
tenth [tenθ] *num* dixième
tent peg *n* piquet m de tente
tent pole *n* montant m de tente
tenuous ['tenjʊəs] *adj* ténu(e)
tenure ['tenjʊə*] *n* (*of property*) bail m; (*of job*) période f de jouissance
tepid ['tepɪd] *adj* tiède
term [tɜːm] *n* terme m; (*SCOL*) trimestre m ♦ *vt* appeler; ~**s** *npl* (*conditions*) conditions *fpl*; (*COMM*) tarif m; **in the short/long** ~ à

court/long terme; **to come to ~s with** (*problem*) faire face à

terminal ['tɜːmɪnl] *adj* (*disease*) dans sa phase terminale; (*patient*) incurable ♦ *n* (*ELEC*) borne *f*; (*for oil, ore etc, COMPUT*) terminal *m*; (*also*: *air* ~) aérogare *f*; (*BRIT: also*: *coach* ~) gare routière

terminate ['tɜːmɪneɪt] *vt* mettre fin à; (*pregnancy*) interrompre

terminus ['tɜːmɪnəs] (*pl* **termini**) *n* terminus *m inv*

terrace ['terəs] *n* terrasse *f*; (*BRIT: row of houses*) rangée *f* de maisons (*attenantes*); **the ~s** *npl* (: *SPORT*) les gradins *mpl*; **~d** *adj* (*garden*) en terrasses

terracotta ['terə'kɔtə] *n* terre cuite

terrain [te'reɪn] *n* terrain *m* (*sol*)

terrible ['terəbl] *adj* terrible, atroce; (*weather, conditions*) affreux(euse), épouvantable; **terribly** ['terəblɪ] *adv* terriblement; (*very badly*) affreusement mal

terrier ['terɪə*] *n* terrier *m* (*chien*)

terrific [tə'rɪfɪk] *adj* fantastique, incroyable, terrible; (*wonderful*) formidable, sensationnel(le)

terrify ['terɪfaɪ] *vt* terrifier

territory ['terɪtərɪ] *n* territoire *m*

terror ['terə*] *n* terreur *f*; **~ism** *n* terrorisme *m*; **~ist** *n* terroriste *m/f*

terse [tɜːs] *adj* (*style*) concis(e); (*reply*) sec(sèche)

Terylene ['terɪliːn] (®) *n* tergal *m* (®)

test [test] *n* (*trial, check*) essai *m*; (*of courage etc*) épreuve *f*; (*MED*) examen *m*; (*CHEM*) analyse *f*; (*SCOL*) interrogation *f*; (*also: driving* ~) (examen du) permis *m* de conduire ♦ *vt* essayer; mettre à l'épreuve; examiner; analyser; faire subir une interrogation à

testament ['testəmənt] *n* testament *m*; **the Old/New T~** l'Ancien/le Nouveau Testament

testicle ['testɪkl] *n* testicule *m*

testify ['testɪfaɪ] *vi* (*LAW*) témoigner, déposer; **to ~ to sth** attester qch

testimony ['testɪmənɪ] *n* témoignage *m*; (*clear proof*): **to be (a) ~ to** être la preuve de

test: ~ match *n* (*CRICKET, RUGBY*) match international; **~ pilot** *n* teste *m* d'essai; **~ tube** *n* éprouvette *f*

tetanus ['tetənəs] *n* tétanos *m*

tether ['teðə*] *vt* attacher ♦ *n*: **at the end of one's ~** à bout (de patience)

text [tekst] *n* texte *m*; **~book** *n* manuel *m*

textile *n* textile *m*

texture ['tekstʃə*] *n* texture *f*; (*of skin, paper etc*) grain *m*

Thames [temz] *n*: **the ~** la Tamise

than [ðæn, ðən] *conj* que; (*with numerals*): **more ~ 10/once** plus de 10/d'une fois; **I have more/less ~ you** j'en ai plus/moins

que toi; **she has more apples ~ pears** elle a plus de pommes que de poires

thank [θæŋk] *vt* remercier, dire merci à; **~s** *npl* (*gratitude*) remerciements *mpl* ♦ *excl* merci!; **~ you (very much)** merci (beaucoup); **~s to** grâce à; **~ God!** Dieu merci!; **~ful** *adj*: **~ful (for)** reconnaissant(e) (de); **~less** *adj* ingrat(e); **T~sgiving (Day)** *n* jour *m* d'action de grâce (*fête américaine*)

────────────────── *KEYWORD*

that [ðæt] *adj* (*demonstrative: pl those*) ce, cet +*vowel or h mute*, *f* cette; **~ man/woman/book** cet homme/cette femme/ce livre; (*not this*) cet homme-là/cette femme-là/ce livre-là; **~ one** celui-là(celle-là)

♦ *pron* **1** (*demonstrative: pl those*) ce; (*not this one*) cela, ça; **who's ~?** qui est-ce?; **what's ~?** qu'est-ce que c'est?; **is ~ you?** c'est toi?; **I prefer this to ~** je préfère ceci à cela *or* ça; **~'s what he said** c'est *or* voilà ce qu'il a dit; **~ is (to say)** c'est-à-dire, à savoir

2 (*relative: subject*) qui; (: *object*) que; (: *indirect*) lequel(laquelle), lesquels(lesquelles) *pl*; **the book ~ I read** le livre que j'ai lu; **the books ~ are in the library** les livres qui sont dans la bibliothèque; **all ~ I have** tout ce que j'ai; **the box ~ I put it in** la boîte dans laquelle je l'ai mis; **the people ~ I spoke to** les gens auxquels *or* à qui j'ai parlé

3 (*relative: of time*) où; **the day ~ he came** le jour où il est venu

♦ *conj* que; **he thought ~ I was ill** il pensait que j'étais malade

♦ *adv* (*demonstrative*): **I can't work ~ much** je ne peux pas travailler autant que cela; **I didn't know it was ~ bad** je ne savais pas que c'était si *or* aussi mauvais; **it's about ~ high** c'est à peu près de cette hauteur

────────────────────────────

thatched [θætʃt] *adj* (*roof*) de chaume; **~ cottage** chaumière *f*

thaw [θɔː] *n* dégel *m* ♦ *vi* (*ice*) fondre; (*food*) dégeler ♦ *vt* (: *also*: ~ **out**) (faire) dégeler

────────────────── *KEYWORD*

the [ðiː, ðə] *def art* **1** (*gen*) le, la *f*, l' +*vowel or h mute*, les *pl*; **~ boy/girl/ink** le garçon/la fille/l'encre; **~ children** les enfants; **~ history of the world** l'histoire du monde; **give it to ~ postman** donne-le au facteur; **to play ~ piano/flute** jouer du piano/de la flûte; **~ rich and ~ poor** les riches et les pauvres

2 (*in titles*): **Elizabeth ~ First** Elisabeth première; **Peter ~ Great** Pierre le Grand

3 (*in comparisons*): **~ more he works, ~ more he earns** plus il travaille, plus il gagne de l'argent

theatre ['θɪətə*] *n* théâtre *m*; (*also: lecture* ~) amphi(théâtre) *m*; (*MED: also: operating* ~) salle *f* d'opération; **~-goer** *n* habitué(e) du théâtre; **theatrical** [θɪ'ætrɪkəl] *adj* théâtral(e)

theft [θeft] *n* vol *m* (*larcin*)

their [ðɛə*] *adj* leur; (*pl*) leurs; *see also* my; **~s** *pron* le(la) leur; (*pl*) les leurs; *see also* **mine**[1]

them [ðem, ðəm] *pron* (*direct*) les; (*indirect*) leur; (*stressed, after prep*) eux(elles); *see also* **me**

theme [θiːm] *n* thème *m*; ~ **park** *n* parc *m* (d'attraction) à thème; ~ **song** *n* chanson principale

themselves [ðəm'selvz] *pl pron* (*reflexive*) se; (*emphatic, after prep*) eux-mêmes(elles-mêmes); *see also* **oneself**

then [ðen] *adv* (*at that time*) alors, à ce moment-là; (*next*) puis, ensuite; (*and also*) et puis ♦ *conj* (*therefore*) alors, dans ce cas ♦ *adj*: **the ~ president** le président d'alors *or* de l'époque; **by ~** (*past*) à ce moment-là; (*future*) d'ici là; **from ~ on** dès lors

theology [θɪ'ɒlədʒɪ] *n* théologie *f*

theoretical [θɪə'retɪkəl] *adj* théorique

theorize ['θɪəraɪz] *vi* faire des théories

theory ['θɪərɪ] *n* théorie *f*

therapy ['θerəpɪ] *n* thérapie *f*

─────────── KEYWORD ───────────

there [ðɛə*] *adv 1*: ~ **is**, ~ **are** il y a; ~ **are 3 of them** (*people, things*) il y en a 3; ~ **has been an accident** il y a eu un accident

2 (*referring to place*) là, là-bas; **it's** ~ c'est là(-bas); **in/on/up/down** ~ là-dedans/là-dessus/là-haut/en bas; **he went** ~ **on Friday** il y est allé vendredi; **I want that book** ~ je veux ce livre-là; ~ **he is!** le voilà!

3: ~, ~ (*esp to child*) allons, allons!

thereabouts [ðɛərə'bauts] *adv* (*place*) par là, près de là; (*amount*) environ, à peu près

thereafter [ðɛər'ɑːftə*] *adv* par la suite

thereby [ðɛə'baɪ] *adv* ainsi

therefore ['ðɛəfɔː*] *adv* donc, par conséquent

there's ['ðɛəz] = **there is**; **there has**

thermal ['θəːml] *adj* (*springs*) thermal(e); (*underwear*) en thermolactyl (®); (*COMPUT: paper*) thermosensible; (: *printer*) thermique

thermometer [θə'mɒmɪtə*] *n* thermomètre *m*

Thermos ['θəːməs] (®) *n* (*also:* ~ **flask**) thermos *m or f inv* (®)

thermostat ['θəːməustæt] *n* thermostat *m*

thesaurus [θɪ'sɔːrəs] *n* dictionnaire *m* des synonymes

these [ðiːz] *pl adj* ces; (*not "those"*): ~ **books** ces livres-ci ♦ *pl pron* ceux-ci(celles-ci)

thesis ['θiːsɪs] (*pl* **theses**) *n* thèse *f*

they [ðeɪ] *pl pron* ils(elles); (*stressed*) eux(elles); ~ **say that ...** (*it is said that*) on dit que ...; **~'d** = ~ **had**; ~ **would**; **~'ll** = **they shall**; ~ **will**; **~'re** = ~ **are**; **~'ve** = **they have**

thick [θɪk] *adj* épais(se); (*stupid*) bête, borné(e) ♦ *n*: **in the** ~ **of** au beau milieu de, en plein cœur de; **it's 20 cm** ~ il/elle a 20 cm d'épaisseur; **~en** *vi* s'épaissir ♦ *vt* (*sauce etc*) épaissir; **~ness** *n* épaisseur *f*; **~set** *adj* trapu(e), costaud(e); **~skinned** *adj* (*fig*) peu sensible

thief [θiːf] (*pl* **thieves**) *n* voleur(euse)

thigh [θaɪ] *n* cuisse *f*

thimble ['θɪmbl] *n* dé *m* (à coudre)

thin [θɪn] *adj* mince; (*skinny*) maigre; (*soup, sauce*) peu épais(se), clair(e); (*hair, crowd*) clairsemé(e) ♦ *vt*: **to** ~ (**down**) (*sauce, paint*) délayer

thing [θɪŋ] *n* chose *f*; (*object*) objet *m*; (*contraption*) truc *m*; (*mania*): **to have a** ~ **about** être obsédé(e) par; **~s** *npl* (*belongings*) affaires *fpl*; **poor ~!** le(la) pauvre!; **the best** ~ **would be to** le mieux serait de; **how are ~s?** comment ça va?

think [θɪŋk] (*pt, pp* **thought**) *vi* penser, réfléchir; (*believe*) penser ♦ *vt* (*imagine*) imaginer; **what did you** ~ **of them?** qu'avez-vous pensé d'eux?; **to** ~ **about sth/sb** penser à qch/qn; **I'll** ~ **about it** je vais y réfléchir; **to** ~ **of doing** avoir l'idée de faire; **I** ~ **so/not** je crois *or* pense que oui/non; **to** ~ **well of** avoir une haute opinion de; ~ **over** *vt* bien réfléchir à; ~ **up** *vt* inventer, trouver; ~ **tank** *n* groupe *m* de réflexion

thinly *adv* (*cut*) en fines tranches; (*spread*) en une couche mince

third [θəːd] *num* troisième ♦ *n* (*fraction*) tiers *m*; (*AUT*) troisième (vitesse) *f*; (*BRIT: SCOL: degree*) ≈ licence *f* sans mention; **~ly** *adv* troisièmement; ~ **party insurance** (*BRIT*) *n* assurance *f* au tiers; **~-rate** *adj* de qualité médiocre; **the T~ World** *n* le tiers monde

thirst [θəːst] *n* soif *f*; **~y** *adj* (*person*) qui a soif, assoiffé(e); (*work*) qui donne soif; **to be ~y** avoir soif

thirteen ['θəː'tiːn] *num* treize

thirty ['θəːtɪ] *num* trente

─────────── KEYWORD ───────────

this [ðɪs] *adj* (*demonstrative: pl* **these**) ce, cet +*vowel or h mute*, cette *f*; ~ **man/woman/book** cet homme/cette femme/ce livre; (*not that*) cet homme-ci/cette femme-ci/ce livre-ci; ~ **one** celui-ci(celle-ci)

♦ *pron* (*demonstrative: pl* **these**) ce; (*not that*

one) celui-ci(celle-ci), ceci; **who's ~?** qui est-ce?; **what's ~?** qu'est-ce que c'est?; **I prefer ~ to that** je préfère ceci à cela; **~ is what he said** voici ce qu'il a dit; **~ is Mr Brown** (*in introductions*) je vous présente Mr Brown; (*in photo*) c'est Mr Brown; (*on telephone*) ici Mr Brown
♦ *adv* (*demonstrative*): **it was about ~ big** c'était à peu près de cette grandeur *or* grand comme ça; **I didn't know it was ~ bad** je ne savais pas que c'était si *or* aussi mauvais

thistle ['θɪsl] *n* chardon *m*
thorn [θɔːn] *n* épine *f*
thorough ['θʌrə] *adj* (*search*) minutieux(euse); (*knowledge, research*) approfondi(e); (*work, person*) consciencieux(euse); (*cleaning*) à fond; **~bred** *n* (*horse*) pursang *m inv*; **~fare** *n* route *f*; **"no ~fare" "passage interdit"**; **~ly** *adv* minutieusement; en profondeur; à fond; (*very*) tout à fait
those [ðəuz] *pl adj* ces; (*not "these"*): **~ books** ces livres-là ♦ *pl pron* ceux-là(celles-là)
though [ðəu] *conj* bien que +*sub*, quoique +*sub* ♦ *adv* pourtant
thought [θɔːt] *pt, pp of* think ♦ *n* pensée *f*; (*idea*) idée *f*; (*opinion*) avis *m*; **~ful** *adj* (*deep in thought*) pensif(ive); (*serious*) réfléchi(e); (*considerate*) prévenant(e); **~less** *adj* étourdi(e); qui manque de considération
thousand ['θauzənd] *num* mille; **two ~** deux mille; **~s of** des milliers de; **~th** *num* millième
thrash [θræʃ] *vt* rouer de coups; donner une correction à; (*defeat*) battre à plate couture; **~ about, ~ around** *vi* se débattre; **~ out** *vt* débattre de
thread [θred] *n* fil *m*; (*of screw*) pas *m*, filetage *m* ♦ *vt* (*needle*) enfiler; **~bare** *adj* râpé(e), élimé(e)
threat [θret] *n* menace *f*; **~en** *vi* menacer ♦ *vt*: **to ~en sb with sth/to do** menacer qn de qch/de faire
three [θriː] *num* trois; **~-dimensional** *adj* à trois dimensions; **~-piece suit** *n* complet *m* (avec gilet); **~-piece suite** *n* salon *m* comprenant un canapé et deux fauteuils assortis; **~-ply** *adj* (*wool*) trois fils *inv*
thresh [θreʃ] *vt* (*AGR*) battre
threshold ['θreʃhəuld] *n* seuil *m*
threw [θruː] *pt of* throw
thrift [θrɪft] *n* économie *f*; **~y** *adj* économe
thrill [θrɪl] *n* (*excitement*) émotion *f*, sensation forte; (*shudder*) frisson *m* ♦ *vt* (*audience*) électriser; **to be ~ed** (*with gift etc*) être ravi(e); **~er** *n* film *m* (*or* roman *m or* pièce *f*) à suspense; **~ing** *adj* saisissant(e),

palpitant(e)
thrive [θraɪv] (*pt* **~d, throve,** *pp* **~d**) *vi* pousser, se développer; (*business*) prospérer; **he ~s on it** cela lui réussit; **thriving** ['θraɪvɪŋ] *adj* (*business, community*) prospère
throat [θrəut] *n* gorge *f*; **to have a sore ~** avoir mal à la gorge
throb [θrɒb] *vi* (*heart*) palpiter; (*engine*) vibrer; **my head is ~bing** j'ai des élancements dans la tête
throes [θrəuz] *npl*: **in the ~ of** au beau milieu de
throne [θrəun] *n* trône *m*
throng [θrɒŋ] *n* foule *f* ♦ *vt* se presser dans
throttle ['θrɒtl] *n* (*AUT*) accélérateur *m* ♦ *vt* étrangler
through [θruː] *prep* à travers; (*time*) pendant, durant; (*by means of*) par, par l'intermédiaire de; (*owing to*) à cause de ♦ *adj* (*ticket, train, passage*) direct(e) ♦ *adv* à travers; **to put sb ~ to sb** (*BRIT: TEL*) passer qn à qn; **to be ~** avoir la communication; (*esp US: have finished*) avoir fini; **to be ~ with sb** (*relationship*) avoir rompu avec qn; **"no ~ road"** (*BRIT*) "impasse"; **~out** [θruː'aut] *prep* (*place*) partout dans; (*time*) durant tout(e) le(la) ♦ *adv* partout
throve [θrəuv] *pt of* thrive
throw [θrəu] (*pt* **threw,** *pp* **thrown**) *n* jet *m*; (*SPORT*) lancer *m* ♦ *vt* lancer, jeter; (*SPORT*) lancer; (*rider*) désarçonner; (*fig*) décontenancer; **to ~ a party** donner une réception; **~ away** *vt* jeter; **~ off** *vt* se débarrasser de; **~ out** *vt* jeter; (*reject*) rejeter; (*person*) mettre à la porte; **~ up** *vi* vomir; **~away** *adj* à jeter; (*remark*) fait(e) en passant; **~-in** *n* (*SPORT*) remise *f* en jeu
thru [θruː] (*US*) = **through**
thrush [θrʌʃ] *n* (*bird*) grive *f*
thrust [θrʌst] (*pt, pp* **thrust**) *n* (*TECH*) poussée *f* ♦ *vt* pousser brusquement; (*push in*) enfoncer
thud [θʌd] *n* bruit sourd
thug [θʌg] *n* voyou *m*
thumb [θʌm] *n* (*ANAT*) pouce *m*, arrêter une voiture; **to ~ a lift** faire de l'auto-stop; **~ through** *vt* (*book*) feuilleter; **~tack** (*US*) *n* punaise *f* (*clou*)
thump [θʌmp] *n* grand coup; (*sound*) bruit sourd ♦ *vt* cogner sur ♦ *vi* cogner, battre fort
thunder ['θʌndə*] *n* tonnerre *m* ♦ *vi* tonner; (*train etc*): **to ~ past** passer dans un grondement *or* un bruit de tonnerre; **~bolt** *n* foudre *f*; **~clap** *n* coup *m* de tonnerre; **~storm** *n* orage *m*; **~y** *adj* orageux(euse)
Thursday ['θɜːzdeɪ] *n* jeudi *m*
thus [ðʌs] *adv* ainsi
thwart [θwɔːt] *vt* contrecarrer
thyme [taɪm] *n* thym *m*
tiara [tɪ'ɑːrə] *n* (*woman's*) diadème *m*

tick [tɪk] n (sound: of clock) tic-tac m; (mark) coche f; (ZOOL) tique f; (BRIT: inf): **in a ~** dans une seconde ♦ vi faire tic-tac ♦ vt (item on list) cocher; **~ off** vt (item on list) cocher; (person) réprimander, attraper; **~ over** vi (engine) tourner au ralenti; (fig) aller or marcher doucettement

ticket ['tɪkɪt] n billet m; (for bus, tube) ticket m; (in shop: on goods) étiquette f; (for library) carte f; (parking ~) papillon m, p.-v. m; **~ collector** n contrôleur(euse); **~ office** n guichet m, bureau m de vente des billets

tickle ['tɪkl] vt, vi chatouiller; **ticklish** adj (person) chatouilleux(euse); (problem) épineux(euse)

tidal ['taɪdl] adj (force) de la marée; (estuary) à marée; **~ wave** n raz-de-marée m inv

tidbit ['tɪdbɪt] (US) n = **titbit**

tiddlywinks ['tɪdlɪwɪŋks] n jeu m de puce

tide [taɪd] n marée f; (fig: of events) cours m ♦ vt: **to ~ sb over** dépanner qn; **high/low ~** marée haute/basse

tidy ['taɪdɪ] adj (room) bien rangé(e); (dress, work) net(te), soigné(e); (person) ordonné(e), qui a de l'ordre ♦ vt (also: ~ up) ranger

tie [taɪ] n (string etc) cordon m; (BRIT: also: neck~) cravate f; (fig: link) lien m; (SPORT: draw) égalité f de points; match nul ♦ vt (parcel) attacher; (ribbon, shoelaces) nouer ♦ vi (SPORT) faire match nul; finir à égalité de points; **to ~ sth in a bow** faire un nœud à or avec qch; **to ~ a knot in sth** faire un nœud à qch; **~ down** vt (fig): **to ~ sb down (to)** contraindre qn (à accepter); **to be ~d down** (by relationship) se fixer; **~ up** vt (parcel) ficeler; (dog, boat) attacher; (prisoner) ligoter; (arrangements) conclure; **to be ~d up** (busy) être pris(e) or occupé(e)

tier [tɪə*] n gradin m; (of cake) étage m

tiger ['taɪgə*] n tigre m

tight [taɪt] adj (rope) tendu(e), raide; (clothes) étroit(e), très juste; (budget, programme, bend) serré(e); (control) strict(e), sévère; (inf: drunk) ivre, rond(e) ♦ adv (squeeze) très fort; (shut) hermétiquement, bien; **~en** vt (rope) tendre; (screw) resserrer; (control) renforcer ♦ vi se tendre, se resserrer; **~-fisted** adj avare; **~ly** adv (grasp) bien, très fort; **~rope** n corde f raide; **~s** (BRIT) npl collant m

tile [taɪl] n (on roof) tuile f; (on wall or floor) carreau m; **~d** adj en tuiles; carrelé(e)

till [tɪl] n caisse (enregistreuse) ♦ vt (land) cultiver ♦ prep, conj = **until**

tiller ['tɪlə*] n (NAUT) barre f (du gouvernail)

tilt [tɪlt] vt pencher, incliner ♦ vi pencher, être incliné(e)

timber ['tɪmbə*] n (material) bois m (de construction); (trees) arbres mpl

time [taɪm] n temps m; (epoch: often pl) époque f, temps; (by clock) heure f; (moment) moment m; (occasion, also MATH) fois f; (MUS) mesure f ♦ vt (race) chronométrer; (programme) minuter; (visit) fixer; (remark etc) choisir le moment de; **a long ~** un long moment, longtemps; **for the ~ being** pour le moment; **4 at a ~** 4 à la fois; **from ~ to ~** de temps en temps; **at ~s** parfois; **in ~** (soon enough) à temps; (after some ~) avec le temps, à la longue; (MUS) en mesure; **in a week's ~** dans une semaine; **in no ~** en un rien de temps; **any ~** n'importe quand; **on ~** à l'heure; **5 ~s 5** 5 fois 5; **what ~ is it?** quelle heure est-il?; **to have a good ~** bien s'amuser; **~ bomb** n bombe f à retardement; **~ lag** (BRIT) n décalage m; (in travel) décalage horaire; **~less** adj éternel(le); **~ly** adj opportun(e); **~ off** n temps m libre; **~r** n (TECH) minuteur m; (in kitchen) compte-minutes m inv; **~scale** n délais mpl; **~-share** n maison f (or appartement m) en multipropriété; **~ switch** (BRIT) n minuteur m; (for lighting) minuterie f; **~table** n (RAIL) (indicateur m) horaire m; (SCOL) emploi m du temps; **~ zone** n fuseau m horaire

timid ['tɪmɪd] adj timide; (easily scared) peureux(euse)

timing ['taɪmɪŋ] n minutage m; chronométrage m; **the ~ of his resignation** le moment choisi pour sa démission

timpani ['tɪmpənɪ] npl timbales fpl

tin [tɪn] n étain m; (also: ~ plate) fer-blanc m; (BRIT: can) boîte f (de conserve); (for storage) boîte f; **~foil** n papier m d'étain or aluminium

tinge [tɪndʒ] n nuance f ♦ vt: **~d with** teinté(e) de

tingle ['tɪŋgl] vi picoter; (person) avoir des picotements

tinker ['tɪŋkə*] n (gipsy) romanichel m; **~ with** vt fus bricoler, rafistoler

tinkle ['tɪŋkl] vi tinter

tinned [tɪnd] (BRIT) adj (food) en boîte, en conserve

tin opener ['-əupnə*] (BRIT) n ouvre-boîte(s) m

tinsel ['tɪnsəl] n guirlandes fpl de Noël (argentées)

tint [tɪnt] n teinte f; (for hair) shampooing colorant; **~ed** adj (hair) teint(e); (spectacles, glass) teinté(e)

tiny ['taɪnɪ] adj minuscule

tip [tɪp] n (end) bout m; (gratuity) pourboire m; (BRIT: for rubbish) décharge f; (advice) tuyau m ♦ vt (waiter) donner un pourboire à; (tilt) incliner; (overturn: also: ~ over) renverser; (empty: ~ out) déverser; **~-off** n *(hint)* tuyau m; **~ped** *(BRIT)* adj *(cigarette)* (à bout) filtre *inv*

tipsy ['tɪpsɪ] *(inf)* adj un peu ivre, éméché(e)

tiptoe ['tɪptəʊ] n: **on ~** sur la pointe des pieds

tiptop ['tɪp'tɒp] adj: **in ~ condition** en excellent état

tire ['taɪə*] n *(US)* = **tyre** ♦ vt fatiguer ♦ vi se fatiguer; **~d** adj fatigué(e); **to be ~d of** en avoir assez de, être las(lasse) de; **~less** adj *(person)* infatigable; *(efforts)* inlassable; **~some** adj ennuyeux(euse); **tiring** ['taɪərɪŋ] adj fatigant(e)

tissue ['tɪʃuː] n tissu m; *(paper handkerchief)* mouchoir m en papier, kleenex m (®); **~ paper** n papier m de soie

tit [tɪt] n *(bird)* mésange f; **to give ~ for tat** rendre la pareille

titbit ['tɪtbɪt] n *(food)* friandise f; *(news)* potin m

title ['taɪtl] n titre m; **~ deed** n *(LAW)* titre (constitutif) de propriété; **~ role** n rôle principal

titter ['tɪtə*] vi rire (bêtement)

TM abbr = **trademark**

─────── *KEYWORD*

to [tuː, tə] prep **1** *(direction)* à; **~ go to France/Portugal/London/school** aller en France/au Portugal/à Londres/à l'école; **~ go to Claude's/the doctor's** aller chez Claude/le docteur; **the road ~ Edinburgh** la route d'Édimbourg

2 *(as far as)* (jusqu')à; **~ count ~ 10** compter jusqu'à 10; **from 40 ~ 50 people** de 40 à 50 personnes

3 *(with expressions of time)*: **a quarter ~ 5** 5 heures moins le quart; **it's twenty ~ 3** il est 3 heures moins vingt

4 *(for, of)* de; **the key ~ the front door** la clé de la porte d'entrée; **a letter ~ his wife** une lettre (adressée) à sa femme

5 *(expressing indirect object)* à; **~ give sth ~ sb** donner qch à qn; **~ talk ~ sb** parler à qn

6 *(in relation to)* à; **3 goals ~ 2** 3 (buts) à 2; **30 miles ~ the gallon** ≈ 9,4 litres aux cent (km)

7 *(purpose, result)*: **~ come ~ sb's aid** venir au secours de qn, porter secours à qn; **~ sentence sb ~ death** condamner qn à mort; **~ my surprise** à ma grande surprise ♦ *with vb* **1** *(simple infinitive)*: **~ go/eat** aller/manger

2 *(following another vb)*: **~ want/try/start ~ do** vouloir/essayer de/commencer à faire

3 *(with vb omitted)*: **I don't want ~** je ne veux pas

4 *(purpose, result)* pour; **I did it ~ help you** je l'ai fait pour vous aider

5 *(equivalent to relative clause)*: **I have** things **~ do** j'ai des choses à faire; **the main thing is ~ try** l'important est d'essayer

6 *(after adjective etc)*: **ready ~ go** prêt(e) à partir; **too old/young ~ ...** trop vieux/jeune pour ...

♦ adv: **push/pull the door ~** tirez/poussez la porte

─────────────────

toad [təʊd] n crapaud m

toadstool n champignon (vénéneux)

toast [təʊst] n *(CULIN)* pain grillé, toast m; *(drink, speech)* toast ♦ vt *(CULIN)* faire griller; *(drink to)* porter un toast à; **~er** n grille-pain m *inv*

tobacco [tə'bækəʊ] n tabac m; **~nist** [tə'bækənɪst] n marchand(e) de tabac; **~nist's (shop)** n (bureau m de) tabac m

toboggan [tə'bɒgən] n toboggan m; *(child's)* luge f

today [tə'deɪ] adv *(also fig)* aujourd'hui ♦ n aujourd'hui m

toddler ['tɒdlə*] n enfant m/f qui commence à marcher, bambin m

to-do [tə'duː] n *(fuss)* histoire f, affaire f

toe [təʊ] n doigt m de pied, orteil m; *(of shoe)* bout m ♦ vt: **to ~ the line** *(fig)* obéir, se conformer; **~nail** n ongle m du pied

toffee ['tɒfɪ] n caramel m; **~ apple** *(BRIT)* n pomme caramélisée

toga ['təʊgə] n toge f

together [tə'geðə*] adv ensemble; *(at same time)* en même temps; **~ with** avec

toil [tɔɪl] n dur travail, labeur m ♦ vi peiner

toilet ['tɔɪlət] n *(BRIT: lavatory)* toilettes fpl ♦ cpd *(accessories etc)* de toilette; **~ paper** n papier m hygiénique; **~ries** ['tɔɪlətrɪz] npl articles mpl de toilette; **~ roll** n rouleau m de papier hygiénique; **~ water** n eau f de toilette

token ['təʊkən] n *(sign)* marque f, témoignage m; *(metal disc)* jeton m ♦ adj *(strike, payment etc)* symbolique; **book/record ~** *(BRIT)* chèque-livre/-disque m; **gift ~** n bon-cadeau m

told [təʊld] pt, pp of **tell**

tolerable ['tɒlərəbl] adj *(bearable)* tolérable; *(fairly good)* passable

tolerant ['tɒlərnt] adj: **~ (of)** tolérant(e) (à l'égard de)

tolerate ['tɒləreɪt] vt supporter, tolérer

toll [təʊl] n *(tax, charge)* péage m ♦ vi *(bell)* sonner; **the accident ~ on the roads** le nombre des victimes de la route

tomato [tə'mɑːtəʊ] *(pl ~es)* n tomate f

tomb [tuːm] n tombe f

tomboy ['tɒmbɔɪ] n garçon manqué

tombstone ['tuːmstəʊn] n pierre tombale

tomcat ['tɒmkæt] n matou m

tomorrow [tə'mɒrəʊ] adv *(also fig)* demain ♦ n demain m; **the day after ~** après-demain; ~ **morning** demain matin

ton [tʌn] *n* tonne *f* (*BRIT* = 1016kg; *US* = 907kg); (*metric*) tonne (= 1000 kg); ~**s** of (*inf*) des tas de

tone [təʊn] *n* ton *m* ♦ *vi* (*also*: ~ *in*) s'harmoniser; ~ **down** *vt* (*colour, criticism*) adoucir; (*sound*) baisser; ~ **up** *vt* (*muscles*) tonifier; ~**-deaf** *adj* qui n'a pas d'oreille

tongs [tɒŋz] *npl* (*for coal*) pincettes *fpl*; (*for hair*) fer *m* à friser

tongue [tʌŋ] *n* langue *f*; ~ **in cheek** ironiquement; ~**-tied** *adj* (*fig*) muet(te); ~ **twister** *n* phrase *f* très difficile à prononcer

tonic ['tɒnɪk] *n* (*MED*) tonique *m*; (*also*: ~ *water*) tonic *m*, Schweppes *m* (®)

tonight [tə'naɪt] *adv, n* cette nuit; (*this evening*) ce soir

tonsil ['tɒnsl] *n* amygdale *f*; ~**litis** *n* angine *f*

too [tuː] *adv* (*excessively*) trop; (*also*) aussi; ~ **much** *adv* trop de ♦ *adj* trop; ~ **many** trop de; ~ **bad!** tant pis!

took [tʊk] *pt of* **take**

tool [tuːl] *n* outil *m*; ~ **box** *n* boîte *f* à outils

toot [tuːt] *n* (*of car horn*) coup *m* de klaxon; (*of whistle*) coup de sifflet ♦ *vi* (*with car horn*) klaxonner

tooth [tuːθ] (*pl* **teeth**) *n* (*ANAT, TECH*) dent *f*; ~**ache** *n* mal *m* de dents; ~**brush** *n* brosse *f* à dents; ~**paste** *n* (*pâte f*) dentifrice *m*; ~**pick** *n* cure-dent *m*

top [tɒp] *n* (*of mountain, head*) sommet *m*; (*of page, ladder, garment*) haut *m*; (*of box, cupboard, table*) dessus *m*; (*lid: of box, jar*) couvercle *m*; (: *of bottle*) bouchon *m*; (*toy*) toupie *f* ♦ *adj* du haut; (*in rank*) premier(ère); (*best*) meilleur(e) ♦ *vt* (*exceed*) dépasser; (*be first in*) être en tête de; **on** ~ **of** sur; (*in addition to*) en plus de; **from** ~ **to bottom** de fond en comble; ~ **up** (*US* ~ **off**) *vt* (*bottle*) remplir; (*salary*) compléter; ~ **floor** *n* dernier étage; ~ **hat** *n* haut-de-forme *m*; ~**-heavy** *adj* (*object*) trop lourd(e) du haut

topic ['tɒpɪk] *n* sujet *m*, thème *m*; ~**al** *adj* d'actualité

top: ~**less** ['tɒpləs] *adj* (*bather etc*) aux seins nus; ~**-level** ['tɒp'levl] *adj* (*talks*) au plus haut niveau; ~**most** ['tɒpməʊst] *adj* le(la) plus haut(e)

topple ['tɒpl] *vt* renverser, faire tomber ♦ *vi* basculer; tomber

top-secret ['tɒp'siːkrət] *adj* top secret(ète)

topsy-turvy ['tɒpsɪ'tɜːvɪ] *adj, adv* sens dessus dessous

torch [tɔːtʃ] *n* torche *f*; (*BRIT: electric*) lampe *f* de poche

tore [tɔː*] *pt of* **tear**[1]

torment [*n* 'tɔːment, *vb* tɔː'ment] *n* tourment *m* ♦ *vt* tourmenter; (*fig: annoy*) harce-

ler

torn [tɔːn] *pp of* **tear**[1]

tornado [tɔː'neɪdəʊ] (*pl* ~**es**) *n* tornade *f*

torpedo [tɔː'piːdəʊ] (*pl* ~**es**) *n* torpille *f*

torrent ['tɒrənt] *n* torrent *m*

tortoise ['tɔːtəs] *n* tortue *f*; ~**shell** *adj* en écaille

torture ['tɔːtʃə*] *n* torture *f* ♦ *vt* torturer

Tory ['tɔːrɪ] (*BRIT POL*) *adj* tory, conservateur(trice) ♦ *n* tory *m/f*, conservateur(trice)

toss [tɒs] *vt* lancer, jeter; (*pancake*) faire sauter; (*head*) rejeter en arrière; **to** ~ **a coin** jouer à pile ou face; **to** ~ **up for sth** jouer qch à pile ou face; **to** ~ **and turn** (*in bed*) se tourner et se retourner

tot [tɒt] *n* (*BRIT: drink*) petit verre; (*child*) bambin *m*

total ['təʊtl] *adj* total(e) ♦ *n* total *m* ♦ *vt* (*add up*) faire le total de, additionner; (*amount to*) s'élever à; ~**ly** ['təʊtəlɪ] *adv* totalement

totter ['tɒtə*] *vi* chanceler

touch [tʌtʃ] *n* contact *m*, toucher *m*; (*sense, also skill: of pianist etc*) toucher ♦ *vt* toucher; (*tamper with*) toucher à; **a** ~ **of** (*fig*) un petit peu de; une touche de; **to get in** ~ **with** prendre contact avec; **to lose** ~ (*friends*) se perdre de vue; ~ **on** *vt fus* (*topic*) effleurer, aborder; ~ **up** *vt* (*paint*) retoucher; ~**-and-go** *adj* incertain(e); ~**down** *n* atterrissage *m*; (*on sea*) amerrissage *m*; (*US: FOOTBALL*) touché-en-but *m*; ~**ed** *adj* (*moved*) touché(e); ~**ing** *adj* touchant(e), attendrissant(e); ~**line** *n* (*SPORT*) (ligne *f* de) touche *f*; ~**y** *adj* (*person*) susceptible

tough [tʌf] *adj* dur(e); (*resistant*) résistant(e), solide; (*meat*) dur, coriace; (*firm*) inflexible; (*task*) dur, pénible; ~**en** *vt* (*character*) endurcir; (*glass etc*) renforcer

toupee ['tuːpeɪ] *n* postiche *m*

tour [tʊə*] *n* voyage *m*; (*also: package* ~) voyage organisé; (*of town, museum*) tour *m*, visite *f*; (*by artist*) tournée *f* ♦ *vt* visiter

tourism ['tʊərɪzm] *n* tourisme *m*

tourist ['tʊərɪst] *n* touriste *m/f* ♦ *cpd* touristique; ~ **office** *n* syndicat *m* d'initiative

tournament ['tʊənəmənt] *n* tournoi *m*

tousled ['tauzld] *adj* (*hair*) ébouriffé(e)

tout [taut] *vi*: **to** ~ **for** essayer de raccrocher, racoler (*also: ticket* ~) revendeur *m* de billets

tow [təʊ] *vt* remorquer; (*caravan, trailer*) tracter; "**on** (*BRIT*) **or in** (*US*) ~" (*AUT*) "véhicule en remorque"

toward(s) [tə'wɔːd(z)] *prep* vers; (*of attitude*) envers, à l'égard de; (*of purpose*) pour

towel ['tauəl] *n* serviette *f* (de toilette); ~**ling** *n* (*fabric*) tissu éponge *m*; ~ **rail** (*US* ~ **rack**) *n* porte-serviettes *m inv*

tower ['tauə*] *n* tour *f*; ~ **block** (*BRIT*) *n* tour *f* (d'habitation); ~**ing** *adj* très haut(e), imposant(e)

town [taun] *n* ville *f*; **to go to** ~ aller en ville; *(fig)* y mettre le paquet; ~ **centre** *n* centre *m* de la ville, centre-ville *m*; ~ **council** *n* conseil municipal; ~ **hall** *n* ≈ mairie *f*; ~ **plan** *n* plan *m* de ville; ~ **planning** *n* urbanisme *m*

towrope ['təurəup] *n* (câble *m* de) remorque *f*

tow truck *(US) n* dépanneuse *f*

toy [tɔɪ] *n* jouet *m*; ~ **with** *vt fus* jouer avec; *(idea)* caresser

trace [treɪs] *n* trace *f* ♦ *vt (draw)* tracer, dessiner; *(follow)* suivre la trace de; *(locate)* retrouver; **tracing paper** *n* papier-calque *m*

track [træk] *n (mark)* trace *f*; *(path: gen)* chemin *m*, piste *f*; *(: of bullet etc)* trajectoire *f*; *(: of suspect, animal)* piste *f*; *(RAIL)* voie ferrée, rails *mpl*; *(on tape, SPORT)* piste; *(on record)* plage *f* ♦ *vt* suivre la trace *or* la piste de; **to keep** ~ **of** suivre; ~ **down** *vt (prey)* trouver et capturer; *(sth lost)* finir par retrouver; ~**suit** *n* survêtement *m*

tract [trækt] *n (GEO)* étendue *f*, zone *f*; *(pamphlet)* tract *m*

traction ['trækʃən] *n* traction *f*; *(MED)*: **in** ~ en extension

tractor ['træktə*] *n* tracteur *m*

trade [treɪd] *n* commerce *m*; *(skill, job)* métier *m* ♦ *vi* faire du commerce ♦ *vt (exchange)*: **to** ~ **sth (for sth)** échanger qch (contre qch); ~ **in** *vt (old car etc)* faire reprendre; ~ **fair** *n* foire(-exposition) commerciale; ~**-in price** *n* prix *m* à la reprise; ~**mark** *n* marque *f* de fabrique; ~**name** *n* nom *m* de marque; ~**r** *n* commerçant(e), négociant(e); ~**sman** *(irreg) n (shopkeeper)* commerçant; ~ **union** *n* syndicat *m*; ~ **unionist** *n* syndicaliste *m/f*

tradition [trə'dɪʃən] *n* tradition *f*; ~**al** *adj* traditionnel(le)

traffic ['træfɪk] *n* trafic *m*; *(cars)* circulation *f* ♦ *vi*: **to** ~ **in** *(pej: liquor, drugs)* faire le trafic de; ~ **circle** *(US) n* rond-point *m*; ~ **jam** *n* embouteillage *m*; ~ **lights** *npl* feux *mpl* (de signalisation); ~ **warden** *n* contractuel(le)

tragedy ['trædʒədɪ] *n* tragédie *f*

tragic ['trædʒɪk] *adj* tragique

trail [treɪl] *n (tracks)* trace *f*, piste *f*; *(path)* chemin *m*, piste; *(of smoke etc)* traînée *f* ♦ *vt* traîner, tirer; *(follow)* suivre ♦ *vi* traîner; *(in game, contest)* être en retard; ~ **behind** *vi* traîner, être à la traîne; ~**er** *n (AUT)* remorque *f*; *(US)* caravane *f*; *(CINEMA)* bande-annonce *f*; ~**er truck** *(US) n* (camion *m*) semi-remorque *m*

train [treɪn] *n* train *m*; *(in underground)* rame *f*; *(of dress)* traîne *f* ♦ *vt (apprentice, doctor etc)* former; *(sportsman)* entraîner; *(dog)* dresser; *(memory)* exercer; *(point: gun etc)*: **to** ~ **sth on** braquer qch sur ♦ *vi* sui-

vre une formation; *(SPORT)* s'entraîner; **one's** ~ **of thought** le fil de sa pensée; ~**ed** *adj* qualifié(e), qui a reçu une formation; *(animal)* dressé(e); ~**ee** *n* stagiaire *m/f*; *(in trade)* apprenti(e); ~**er** *n (SPORT: coach)* entraîneur(euse); *(: shoe)* chaussure *f* de sport; *(of dogs etc)* dresseur(euse); ~**ing** *n* formation *f*; entraînement *m*; **in** ~**ing** *(SPORT)* à l'entraînement; *(fit)* en forme; ~**ing college** *n* école professionnelle; *(for teachers)* ≈ école normale; ~**ing shoes** *npl* chaussures *fpl* de sport

traipse [treɪps] *vi*: **to** ~ **in/out** entrer/sortir d'un pas traînant

trait [treɪ(t)] *n* trait *m* (de caractère)

traitor ['treɪtə*] *n* traître *m*

tram [træm] *(BRIT) n (also:* ~**car)** tram(way) *m*

tramp [træmp] *n (person)* vagabond(e), clochard(e); *(inf: pej: woman)*: **to be a** ~ être coureuse ♦ *vi* marcher d'un pas lourd

trample ['træmpl] *vt*: **to** ~ **(underfoot)** piétiner

trampoline ['træmpəliːn] *n* trampoline *m*

tranquil ['træŋkwɪl] *adj* tranquille; ~**lizer** *(US* ~**izer)** *n (MED)* tranquillisant *m*

transact [træn'zækt] *vt (business)* traiter; ~**ion** *n* transaction *f*

transatlantic ['trænzət'læntɪk] *adj* transatlantique

transfer [*n* 'trænsfə*, *vt* træns'fɜː*] *n (gen, also SPORT)* transfert *m*; *(POL: of power)* passation *f*; *(picture, design)* décalcomanie *f*; *(: stick-on)* autocollant *m* ♦ *vt* transférer; passer; **to** ~ **the charges** *(BRIT: TEL)* téléphoner en P.C.V.

transform [træns'fɔːm] *vt* transformer

transfusion [træns'fjuːʒən] *n* transfusion *f*

transient ['trænzɪənt] *adj* transitoire, éphémère

transistor [træn'zɪstə*] *n (ELEC, also:* ~ **radio)** transistor *m*

transit ['trænzɪt] *n*: **in** ~ en transit

transitive ['trænzɪtɪv] *adj (LING)* transitif(ive)

transit lounge *n* salle *f* de transit

translate [trænz'leɪt] *vt* traduire; **translation** [trænz'leɪʃən] *n* traduction *f*; **translator** [trænz'leɪtə*] *n* traducteur(trice)

transmission [trænz'mɪʃən] *n* transmission *f*

transmit [trænz'mɪt] *vt* transmettre; *(RADIO, TV)* émettre

transparency [træns'pærənsɪ] *n (of glass etc)* transparence *f*; *(BRIT: PHOT)* diapositive *f*; **transparent** [træns'pærənt] *adj* transparent(e)

transpire [træns'paɪə*] *vi (turn out)*: **it** ~**d that ...** on a appris que ...; *(happen)* arriver

transplant [*vb* træns'plɑːnt, *n* 'trænsplɑːnt] *vt* transplanter; *(seedlings)* repiquer ♦ *n (MED)* transplantation *f*

transport [*n* 'trænspɔːt, *vb* træns'pɔːt] *n* transport *m*; (*car*) moyen *m* de transport, voiture *f* ♦ *vt* transporter; **~ation** [trænspɔː'teɪʃən] *n* transport *m*; (*means of* ~) moyen *m* de transport; **~ café** (*BRIT*) *n* ≈ restaurant *m* de routiers

trap [træp] *n* (*snare, trick*) piège *m*; (*carriage*) cabriolet *m* ♦ *vt* prendre au piège; (*confine*) coincer; **~ door** *n* trappe *f*

trapeze [trə'piːz] *n* trapèze *m*

trappings ['træpɪŋz] *npl* ornements *mpl*; attributs *mpl*

trash [træʃ] (*pej*) *n* (*goods*) camelote *f*; (*nonsense*) sottises *fpl*; **~ can** (*US*) *n* poubelle *f*

trauma ['trɔːmə] *n* traumatisme *m*; **~tic** *adj* traumatisant(e)

travel ['trævl] *n* voyage(s) *m(pl)* ♦ *vi* voyager; (*news, sound*) circuler, se propager ♦ *vt* (*distance*) parcourir; **~ agency** *n* agence *f* de voyages; **~ agent** *n* agent *m* de voyages; **~ler** (*US* **~er**) *n* voyageur(euse); **~ler's cheque** (*US* **~er's check**) *n* chèque *m* de voyage; **~ling** (*US* **~ing**) *n* voyage(s) *m(pl)*; **~ sickness** *n* mal *m* de la route (*or* de mer *or* de l'air)

travesty ['trævəstɪ] *n* parodie *f*

trawler ['trɔːlə*] *n* chalutier *m*

tray [treɪ] *n* (*for carrying*) plateau *m*; (*on desk*) corbeille *f*

treacherous *adj* (*person, look*) traître(esse); (*ground, tide*) dont il faut se méfier

treachery ['tretʃərɪ] *n* traîtrise *f*

treacle ['triːkl] *n* mélasse *f*

tread [tred] (*pt* **trod**, *pp* **trodden**) *n* pas *m*; (*sound*) bruit *m* de pas; (*of tyre*) chape *f*, bande *f* de roulement ♦ *vi* marcher; **~ on** *vt fus* marcher sur

treason ['triːzn] *n* trahison *f*

treasure ['treʒə*] *n* trésor *m* ♦ *vt* (*value*) tenir beaucoup à

treasurer ['treʒərə*] *n* trésorier(ère)

treasury ['treʒərɪ] *n*: **the T~**, (*US*) **the T~ Department** le ministère des Finances

treat [triːt] *n* petit cadeau, petite surprise ♦ *vt* traiter; **to ~ sb to sth** offrir qch à qn

treatment ['triːtmənt] *n* traitement *m*

treaty ['triːtɪ] *n* traité *m*

treble ['trebl] *adj* triple ♦ *vt, vi* tripler; **~ clef** *n* (*MUS*) clé *f* de sol

tree [triː] *n* arbre *m*

trek [trek] *n* (*long*) voyage; (*on foot*) (longue) marche, tirée *f*

tremble ['trembl] *vi* trembler

tremendous [trə'mendəs] *adj* (*enormous*) énorme, fantastique; (*excellent*) formidable

tremor ['tremə*] *n* tremblement *m*; (*also: earth* ~) secousse *f* sismique

trench [trentʃ] *n* tranchée *f*

trend [trend] *n* (*tendency*) tendance *f*; (*of events*) cours *m*; (*fashion*) mode *f*; **~y** *adj* (*idea, person*) dans le vent; (*clothes*) dernier

cri *inv*

trepidation [trepɪ'deɪʃən] *n* vive agitation *or* inquiétude *f*

trespass ['trespəs] *vi*: **to ~ on** s'introduire sans permission dans; **"no ~ing"** "propriété privée", "défense d'entrer"

trestle ['tresl] *n* tréteau *m*

trial ['traɪəl] *n* (*LAW*) procès *m*, jugement *m*; (*test: of machine etc*) essai *m*; **~s** *npl* (*unpleasant experiences*) épreuves *fpl*; **to be on ~** (*LAW*) passer en jugement; **by ~ and error** par tâtonnements; **~ period** *n* période *f* d'essai

triangle ['traɪæŋgl] *n* (*MATH, MUS*) triangle *m*

tribe [traɪb] *n* tribu *f*; **~sman** (*irreg*) *n* membre *m* d'une tribu

tribunal [traɪ'bjuːnl] *n* tribunal *m*

tributary ['trɪbjutərɪ] *n* (*river*) affluent *m*

tribute ['trɪbjuːt] *n* tribut *m*, hommage *m*; **to pay ~ to** rendre hommage à

trice [traɪs] *n*: **in a ~** en un clin d'œil

trick [trɪk] *n* (*magic* ~) tour *m*; (*joke, prank*) tour, farce *f*; (*skill, knack*) astuce *f*, truc *m*; (*CARDS*) levée *f* ♦ *vt* attraper, rouler; **to play a ~ on sb** jouer un tour à qn; **that should do the ~** ça devrait faire l'affaire; **~ery** *n* ruse *f*

trickle ['trɪkl] *n* (*of water etc*) filet *m* ♦ *vi* couler en un filet *or* goutte à goutte

tricky ['trɪkɪ] *adj* difficile, délicat(e)

tricycle ['traɪsɪkl] *n* tricycle *m*

trifle ['traɪfl] *n* bagatelle *f*; (*CULIN*) ≈ diplomate *m* ♦ *adv*: **a ~ long** un peu long

trifling ['traɪflɪŋ] *adj* insignifiant(e)

trigger ['trɪgə*] *n* (*of gun*) gâchette *f*; **~ off** *vt* déclencher

trim [trɪm] *adj* (*house, garden*) bien tenu(e); (*figure*) svelte ♦ *n* (*haircut etc*) légère coupe; (*on car*) garnitures *fpl* ♦ *vt* (*cut*) couper légèrement; (*NAUT: a sail*) gréer; (*decorate*): **to ~ (with)** décorer (de); **~mings** *npl* (*CULIN*) garniture *f*

trinket ['trɪŋkɪt] *n* bibelot *m*; (*piece of jewellery*) colifichet *m*

trip [trɪp] *n* voyage *m*; (*excursion*) excursion *f*; (*stumble*) faux pas ♦ *vi* faire un faux pas, trébucher; (*go lightly*) marcher d'un pas léger; **on a ~** en voyage; **~ up** *vi* trébucher ♦ *vt* faire un croc-en-jambe à

tripe [traɪp] *n* (*CULIN*) tripes *fpl*; (*pej: rubbish*) idioties *fpl*

triple ['trɪpl] *adj* triple

triplets ['trɪplɪts] *npl* triplés(ées)

triplicate ['trɪplɪkɪt] *n*: **in ~** en trois exemplaires

tripod ['traɪpɒd] *n* trépied *m*

trite [traɪt] (*pej*) *adj* banal(e)

triumph ['traɪʌmf] *n* triomphe *m* ♦ *vi*: **to ~ (over)** triompher (de)

trivia ['trɪvɪə] (*pej*) *npl* futilités *fpl*

trivial ['trɪvɪəl] *adj* insignifiant(e); (*common-*

place) banal(e)

trod [trɔd] *pt of* **tread**

trodden ['trɔdn] *pp of* **tread**

trolley ['trɔlɪ] *n* chariot *m*

trombone [trɔm'bəun] *n* trombone *m*

troop [tru:p] *n* bande *f*, groupe *m* ♦ *vi*: ~ **in/out** entrer/sortir en groupe; ~**s** *npl* (MIL) troupes *fpl*; (: *men*) hommes *mpl*, soldats *mpl*; ~**ing the colour** (BRIT) *n* (*ceremony*) le salut au drapeau

trophy ['trəufɪ] *n* trophée *m*

tropic ['trɔpɪk] *n* tropique *m*; ~**al** *adj* tropical(e)

trot [trɔt] *n* trot *m* ♦ *vi* trotter; **on the** ~ (BRIT: *fig*) d'affilée

trouble ['trʌbl] *n* difficulté(s) *f(pl)*, problème(s) *m(pl)*; (*worry*) ennuis *mpl*, soucis *mpl*; (*bother, effort*) peine *f*; (POL) troubles *mpl*; (MED): **stomach** *etc* ~ troubles gastriques *etc* ♦ *vt* (*disturb*) déranger, gêner; (*worry*) inquiéter ♦ *vi*: **to** ~ **to do** prendre la peine de faire; ~**s** *npl* (POL *etc*) troubles *mpl*; (*personal*) ennuis, soucis; **to be in** ~ avoir des ennuis; (*ship, climber etc*) être en difficulté; **what's the** ~? qu'est-ce qui ne va pas?; ~**d** *adj* (*person*) inquiet(ète); (*epoch, life*) agité(e); ~**maker** *n* élément perturbateur, fauteur *m* de troubles; ~**shooter** *n* (*in conflict*) médiateur *m*; ~**some** *adj* (*child*) fatigant(e), difficile; (*cough etc*) gênant(e)

trough [trɔf] *n* (*also*: *drinking* ~) abreuvoir *m*; (: *feeding* ~) auge *f*; (*depression*) creux *m*

trousers ['trauzəz] *npl* pantalon *m*; **short** ~ culottes courtes

trout [traut] *n inv* truite *f*

trowel ['trauəl] *n* truelle *f*; (*garden tool*) déplantoir *m*

truant ['truənt] (BRIT) *n*: **to play** ~ faire l'école buissonnière

truce [tru:s] *n* trêve *f*

truck [trʌk] *n* camion *m*; (RAIL) wagon *m* à plate-forme; ~ **driver** *n* camionneur *m*; ~ **farm** (US) *n* jardin maraîcher

trudge [trʌdʒ] *vi* marcher lourdement, se traîner

true [tru:] *adj* vrai(e); (*accurate*) exact(e); (*genuine*) vrai, véritable; (*faithful*) fidèle; **to come** ~ se réaliser

truffle ['trʌfl] *n* truffe *f*

truly ['tru:lɪ] *adv* vraiment, réellement; (*truthfully*) sans mentir; *see also* **yours**

trump [trʌmp] *n* (*also*: ~ *card*) atout *m*; ~**ed up** *adj* inventé(e) (de toutes pièces)

trumpet ['trʌmpɪt] *n* trompette *f*

truncheon ['trʌntʃən] (BRIT) *n* bâton *m* (d'agent de police); matraque *f*

trundle ['trʌndl] *vt, vi*: **to** ~ **along** rouler lentement et bruyamment

trunk [trʌŋk] *n* (*of tree, person*) tronc *m*; (*of elephant*) trompe *f*; (*case*) malle *f*; (*US*:

AUT) coffre *m*; ~**s** *npl* (*also*: *swimming* ~**s**) maillot *m or* slip *m* de bain

truss [trʌs] *n* (MED) bandage *m* herniaire ♦ *vt*: **to** ~ (**up**) (CULIN) brider, trousser

trust [trʌst] *n* confiance *f*; (*responsibility*) charge *f*; (LAW) fidéicommis *m* ♦ *vt* (*rely on*) avoir confiance en; (*hope*) espérer; (*entrust*): **to** ~ **sth to sb** confier qch à qn; **to take sth on** ~ accepter qch les yeux fermés; ~**ed** *adj* en qui l'on a confiance; ~**ee** *n* (LAW) fidéicommissaire *m/f*; (*of school etc*) administrateur(trice); ~**ful**, ~**ing** *adj* confiant(e); ~**worthy** *adj* digne de confiance

truth [tru:θ, *pl* tru:ðz] *n* vérité *f*; ~**ful** *adj* (*person*) qui dit la vérité; (*answer*) sincère

try [traɪ] *n* essai *m*, tentative *f*; (RUGBY) essai ♦ *vt* (*attempt*) essayer, tenter; (*test: sth new: also*: ~ *out*) essayer, tester; (LAW: *person*) juger; (*strain*) éprouver ♦ *vi* essayer; **to have a** ~ essayer; **to** ~ **to do** essayer de faire; (*seek*) chercher à faire; ~ **on** *vt* (*clothes*) essayer; ~**ing** *adj* pénible

T-shirt ['ti:ʃə:t] *n* tee-shirt *m*

T-square ['ti:skwɛə*] *n* équerre *f* en T, té *m*

tub [tʌb] *n* cuve *f*; (*for washing clothes*) baquet *m*; (*bath*) baignoire *f*

tubby ['tʌbɪ] *adj* rondelet(te)

tube [tju:b] *n* tube *m*; (BRIT: *underground*) métro *m*; (*for tyre*) chambre *f* à air

TUC *n abbr* (BRIT: = *Trades Union Congress*) confédération *f* des syndicats britanniques

tuck [tʌk] *vt* (*put*) mettre; ~ **away** *vt* cacher, ranger; ~ **in** *vt* rentrer; (*child*) border ♦ *vi* (*eat*) manger (de bon appétit); ~ **up** *vt* (*child*) border; ~ **shop** (BRIT) *n* boutique *f* à provisions (*dans une école*)

Tuesday ['tju:zdeɪ] *n* mardi *m*

tuft [tʌft] *n* touffe *f*

tug [tʌg] *n* (*ship*) remorqueur *m* ♦ *vt* tirer (sur); ~**-of-war** *n* lutte *f* à la corde; (*fig*) lutte acharnée

tuition [tju:'ɪʃən] *n* (BRIT) leçons *fpl*; (: *private* ~) cours particuliers; (US: *school fees*) frais *mpl* de scolarité

tulip ['tju:lɪp] *n* tulipe *f*

tumble ['tʌmbl] *n* (*fall*) chute *f*, culbute *f* ♦ *vi* tomber, dégringoler; **to** ~ **to sth** (*inf*) réaliser qch; ~**down** *adj* délabré(e); ~ **dryer** (BRIT) *n* séchoir *m* à air chaud

tumbler ['tʌmblə*] *n* (*glass*) verre (droit), gobelet *m*

tummy ['tʌmɪ] (*inf*) *n* ventre *m*

tumour ['tju:mə*] (US **tumor**) *n* tumeur *f*

tuna ['tju:nə] *n inv* (*also*: ~ *fish*) thon *m*

tune [tju:n] *n* (*melody*) air *m* ♦ *vt* (MUS) accorder; (RADIO, TV, AUT) régler; **to be in/out of** ~ (*instrument*) être accordé/désaccordé; (*singer*) chanter juste/faux; **to be in/out of** ~ **with** (*fig*) être en accord/

désaccord avec; ~ **in** vi (RADIO, TV): **to ~ in (to)** se mettre à l'écoute (de); ~ **up** vi (musician) accorder son instrument; ~**ful** adj mélodieux(euse); ~**r** n: **piano ~r** accordeur m (de pianos)

tunic ['tjuːnɪk] n tunique f

Tunisia [tjuːˈnɪzɪə] n Tunisie f

tunnel ['tʌnl] n tunnel m; (in mine) galerie f ♦ vi percer un tunnel

turbulence ['tɜːbjʊləns] n (AVIAT) turbulence f

tureen [tjʊˈriːn] n (for soup) soupière f; (for vegetables) légumier m

turf [tɜːf] n gazon m; (clod) motte f (de gazon) ♦ vt gazonner; ~ **out** (inf) vt (person) jeter dehors

turgid ['tɜːdʒɪd] adj (speech) pompeux(euse)

Turk [tɜːk] n Turc(Turque) m(f)

Turkey ['tɜːkɪ] n Turquie f

turkey ['tɜːkɪ] n dindon m, dinde f

Turkish ['tɜːkɪʃ] adj turc(turque) ♦ n (LING) turc m

turmoil ['tɜːmɔɪl] n trouble m, bouleversement m; **in ~** en émoi, en effervescence

turn [tɜːn] n tour m; (in road) tournant m; (of mind, events) tournure f; (performance) numéro m; (MED) crise f, attaque f ♦ vt tourner; (collar, steak) retourner; (change): **to ~ sth into** changer qch en ♦ vi (object, wind, milk) tourner; (person: look back) se (re)tourner; (reverse direction) faire demi-tour; (become) devenir; (age) atteindre; **to ~ into** se changer en; **a good ~** un service; **it gave me quite a ~** ça m'a fait un coup; **"no left ~"** (AUT) "défense de tourner à gauche"; **it's your ~** c'est (à) votre tour; **in ~** à son tour; à tour de rôle; **to take ~s (at)** se relayer (pour or à); ~ **away** vi se détourner ♦ vt (applicants) refuser; ~ **back** vi revenir, faire demi-tour ♦ vt (person, vehicle) faire faire demi-tour à; (clock) reculer; ~ **down** vt (refuse) rejeter, refuser; (reduce) baisser; (fold) rabattre; ~ **in** vi (inf: go to bed) aller se coucher ♦ vt (fold) rentrer; ~ **off** vi (from road) tourner ♦ vt (light, radio etc) éteindre; (tap) fermer; (engine) arrêter; ~ **on** vt (light, radio etc) allumer; (tap) ouvrir; (engine) mettre en marche; ~ **out** vt (light, gas) éteindre; (produce) produire ♦ vi (voters, troops etc) se présenter; **to ~ out to be ...** s'avérer ..., se révéler ...; ~ **over** vi (person) se retourner ♦ vt (object) retourner; (page) tourner; ~ **round** vi faire demi-tour, (rotate) tourner; ~ **up** vi (person) arriver, se pointer (inf); (lost object) être retrouvé(e) ♦ vt (collar) remonter; (radio, heater) mettre plus fort; ~**ing** n (in road) tournant m; ~**ing point** n (fig) tournant m, moment décisif

turnip ['tɜːnɪp] n navet m

turnout ['tɜːnaʊt] n (of voters) taux m de participation

turnover ['tɜːnəʊvə*] n (COMM: amount of money) chiffre m d'affaires; (: of goods) roulement m; (of staff) renouvellement m, changement m

turnpike ['tɜːnpaɪk] (US) n autoroute f à péage

turnstile ['tɜːnstaɪl] n tourniquet m (d'entrée)

turntable ['tɜːnteɪbl] n (on record player) platine f

turn-up ['tɜːnʌp] (BRIT) n (on trousers) revers m

turpentine ['tɜːpəntaɪn] n (also: **turps**) (essence f de) térébenthine f

turquoise ['tɜːkwɔɪz] n (stone) turquoise f ♦ adj turquoise inv

turret ['tʌrɪt] n tourelle f

turtle ['tɜːtl] n tortue marine or d'eau douce; ~**neck (sweater)** n (BRIT) pullover m à col montant; (US) pullover à col roulé

tusk [tʌsk] n défense f

tussle ['tʌsl] n bagarre f, mêlée f

tutor ['tjuːtə*] n (in college) directeur(trice) d'études; (private teacher) précepteur(trice); ~**ial** [tjuːˈtɔːrɪəl] n (SCOL) (séance f de) travaux mpl pratiques

tuxedo [tʌkˈsiːdəʊ] (US) n smoking m

TV ['tiːˈviː] n abbr (= television) télé f

twang [twæŋ] n (of instrument) son vibrant; (of voice) ton nasillard

tweed [twiːd] n tweed m

tweezers ['twiːzəz] npl pince f à épiler

twelfth [twelfθ] num douzième

twelve [twelv] num douze; **at ~ (o'clock)** à midi; (midnight) à minuit

twentieth ['twentɪɪθ] num vingtième

twenty ['twentɪ] num vingt

twice [twaɪs] adv deux fois; ~ **as much** deux fois plus

twiddle ['twɪdl] vt, vi: **to ~ (with) sth** tripoter qch; **to ~ one's thumbs** (fig) se tourner les pouces

twig [twɪg] n brindille f ♦ vi (inf) piger

twilight ['twaɪlaɪt] n crépuscule m

twin [twɪn] adj, n jumeau(elle) ♦ vt jumeler; ~**(-bedded) room** n chambre f à deux lits

twine [twaɪn] n ficelle f ♦ vi (plant) s'enrouler

twinge [twɪndʒ] n (of pain) élancement m; **a ~ of conscience** un certain remords; **a ~ of regret** un pincement au cœur

twinkle ['twɪŋkl] vi scintiller; (eyes) pétiller

twirl [twɜːl] vt faire tournoyer ♦ vi tournoyer

twist [twɪst] n torsion f, tour m; (in road) virage m; (in wire, flex) tortillon m; (in story) coup m de théâtre ♦ vt tordre; (weave) entortiller; (roll around) enrouler; (fig) déformer ♦ vi (road, river) serpenter

twit [twɪt] (inf) n crétin(e)

twitch [twɪtʃ] n (pull) coup sec, saccade f;

(*nervous*) tic *m* ♦ *vi* se convulser; avoir un tic

two [tuː] *num* deux; **to put ~ and ~ together** (*fig*) faire le rapprochement; **~-door** *adj* (*AUT*) à deux portes; **~-faced** (*pej*) *adj* (*person*) faux(fausse); **~-fold** *adv*: **to increase ~fold** doubler; **~-piece (suit)** *n* (*man's*) costume *m* (deux-pièces); (*woman's*) (tailleur *m*) deux-pièces *m inv*; **~-piece (swimsuit)** *n* (maillot *m* de bain) deux-pièces *m inv*; **~some** *n* (*people*) couple *m*; **~-way** *adj* (*traffic*) dans les deux sens

tycoon [taɪˈkuːn] *n*: (**business**) **~** gros homme d'affaires

type [taɪp] *n* (*category*) type *m*, genre *m*, espèce *f*; (*model, example*) type *m*, modèle *m*; (*TYP*) type, caractère *m* ♦ *vt* (*letter etc*) taper (à la machine); **~-cast** *adj* (*actor*) condamné(e) à toujours jouer le même rôle; **~face** *n* (*TYP*) œil *m* de caractère; **~script** *n* texte dactylographié; **~writer** *n* machine *f* à écrire; **~written** *adj* dactylographié(e)

typhoid [ˈtaɪfɔɪd] *n* typhoïde *f*

typical [ˈtɪpɪkəl] *adj* typique, caractéristique

typing [ˈtaɪpɪŋ] *n* dactylo(graphie) *f*

typist [ˈtaɪpɪst] *n* dactylo *m/f*

tyrant [ˈtaɪərnt] *n* tyran *m*

tyre [taɪə*] (*US* **tire**) *n* pneu *m*; **~ pressure** *n* pression *f* (de gonflage)

U u

U-bend [ˈjuːˈbend] *n* (*in pipe*) coude *m*

ubiquitous *adj* omniprésent(e)

udder [ˈʌdə*] *n* pis *m*, mamelle *f*

UFO [ˈjuːfəʊ] *n abbr* (= *unidentified flying object*) ovni *m*

Uganda [juːˈgændə] *n* Ouganda *m*

ugh [ɜːh] *excl* pouah!

ugly [ˈʌglɪ] *adj* laid(e), vilain(e); (*situation*) inquiétant(e)

UK *n abbr* = **United Kingdom**

ulcer [ˈʌlsə*] *n* ulcère *m*; (*also*: **mouth ~**) aphte *f*

Ulster [ˈʌlstə*] *n* Ulster *m*; (*inf*: *Northern Ireland*) Irlande *f* du Nord

ulterior [ʌlˈtɪərɪə*] *adj*: **~ motive** arrière-pensée *f*

ultimate [ˈʌltɪmət] *adj* ultime, final(e); (*authority*) suprême; **~ly** *adv* en fin de compte; finalement

ultrasound [ˈʌltrəˈsaʊnd] *n* ultrason *m*

umbilical cord [ʌmˈbɪlɪkl-] *n* cordon ombilical

umbrella [ʌmˈbrelə] *n* parapluie *m*; (*for sun*) parasol *m*

umpire [ˈʌmpaɪə*] *n* arbitre *m*; (*TENNIS*) juge *m* de chaise

umpteen [ˈʌmptiːn] *adj* je ne sais combien de; **~th** *adj*: **for the ~th time** pour la nième fois

UN *n abbr* = **United Nations**

unable [ʌnˈeɪbl] *adj*: **to be ~ to** ne pas pouvoir, être dans l'impossibilité de; (*incapable*) être incapable de

unaccompanied [ˈʌnəˈkʌmpənɪd] *adj* (*child, lady*) non accompagné(e); (*song*) sans accompagnement

unaccountably [ˈʌnəˈkaʊntəblɪ] *adv* inexplicablement

unaccustomed [ˈʌnəˈkʌstəmd] *adj*: **to be ~ to sth** ne pas avoir l'habitude de qch

unanimous [juːˈnænɪməs] *adj* unanime; **~ly** *adv* à l'unanimité

unarmed [ʌnˈɑːmd] *adj* (*without a weapon*) non armé(e); (*combat*) sans armes

unashamed [ʌnəˈʃeɪmd] *adj* effronté(e), impudent(e)

unassuming [ʌnəˈsjuːmɪŋ] *adj* modeste, sans prétentions

unattached [ʌnəˈtætʃt] *adj* libre, sans attaches; (*part*) non attaché(e), indépendant(e)

unattended [ˈʌnəˈtendɪd] *adj* (*car, child, luggage*) sans surveillance

unattractive [ʌnəˈtræktɪv] *adj* peu attrayant(e); (*character*) peu sympathique

unauthorized [ʌnˈɔːθəraɪzd] *adj* non autorisé(e), sans autorisation

unavoidable [ʌnəˈvɔɪdəbl] *adj* inévitable

unaware [ˈʌnəˈweə*] *adj*: **to be ~ of** ignorer, être inconscient(e) de; **~s** *adv* à l'improviste, au dépourvu

unbalanced [ˈʌnˈbælənst] *adj* déséquilibré(e); (*report*) peu objectif(ive)

unbearable [ʌnˈbeərəbl] *adj* insupportable

unbeatable [ʌnˈbiːtəbl] *adj* imbattable

unbeknown(st) [ˈʌnbɪˈnəʊn(st)] *adv*: **~ to me/Peter** à mon insu/l'insu de Peter

unbelievable [ʌnbɪˈliːvəbl] *adj* incroyable

unbend [ˈʌnˈbend] (*irreg*) *vi* se détendre ♦ *vt* (*wire*) redresser, détordre

unbiased [ʌnˈbaɪəst] *adj* impartial(e)

unborn [ʌnˈbɔːn] *adj* à naître, qui n'est pas encore né(e)

unbreakable [ˈʌnˈbreɪkəbl] *adj* incassable

unbroken [ˈʌnˈbrəʊkən] *adj* intact(e); (*fig*) continu(e), ininterrompu(e)

unbutton [ˈʌnˈbʌtn] *vt* déboutonner

uncalled-for [ʌnˈkɔːldfɔː*] *adj* déplacé(e), injustifié(e)

uncanny [ʌnˈkænɪ] *adj* étrange, troublant(e)

unceasing [ʌnˈsiːsɪŋ] *adj* incessant(e), continu(e)

unceremonious [ˈʌnserɪˈməʊnɪəs]   adj
(abrupt, rude) brusque
uncertain [ʌnˈsɜːtn]   adj incertain(e); (hesitant) hésitant(e); **in no ~ terms** sans équivoque possible; **~ty** n incertitude f, doute(s) m(pl)
unchecked [ʌnˈtʃekt]   adv sans contrôle or opposition
uncivilized [ʌnˈsɪvɪlaɪzd]   adj (gen) non civilisé(e); (fig: behaviour etc) barbare; (hour) indu(e)
uncle [ˈʌŋkl]   n oncle m
uncomfortable [ʌnˈkʌmfətəbl]   adj inconfortable, peu confortable; (uneasy) mal à l'aise, gêné(e); (situation) désagréable
uncommon [ʌnˈkɒmən]   adj rare, singulier(ère), peu commun(e)
uncompromising [ʌnˈkɒmprəmaɪzɪŋ]   adj intransigeant(e), inflexible
unconcerned [ʌnkənˈsɜːnd]   adj: **to be ~ (about)** ne pas s'inquiéter (de)
unconditional [ʌnkənˈdɪʃənl]   adj sans conditions
unconscious [ʌnˈkɒnʃəs]   adj sans connaissance, évanoui(e); (unaware): **~ of** inconscient(e) de ♦ n: **the ~** l'inconscient m; **~ly** adv inconsciemment
uncontrollable [ʌnkənˈtrəʊləbl]   adj indiscipliné(e); (temper, laughter) irrépressible
unconventional [ʌnkənˈvenʃənl]   adj peu conventionnel(le)
uncouth [ʌnˈkuːθ]   adj grossier(ère), fruste
uncover [ʌnˈkʌvə*]   vt découvrir
undecided [ʌndɪˈsaɪdɪd]   adj indécis(e), irrésolu(e)
under [ˈʌndə*]   prep sous; (less than) (de) moins de; au-dessous de; (according to) selon, en vertu de ♦ adv au-dessous; en dessous; **~ there** là-dessous; **~ repair** en (cours de) réparation
under: **~age** adj (person) qui n'a pas l'âge réglementaire; **~carriage** n (AVIAT) train m d'atterrissage; **~charge** vt ne pas faire payer assez à; **~coat** n (paint) couche f de fond; **~cover** adj secret(ète), clandestin(e); **~current** n courant or sentiment sous-jacent; **~cut** (irreg) vt vendre moins cher que; **~dog** n opprimé m; **~done** adj (CULIN) saignant(e); (pej) pas assez cuit(e); **~estimate** vt sous-estimer; **~fed** sous-alimenté(e); **~foot** adv sous les pieds; **~go** (irreg) vt subir; (treatment) suivre; **~graduate** n étudiant(e) (qui prépare la licence); **~ground** n (BRIT: railway) métro m; (POL) clandestinité f ♦ adj souterrain(e); (fig) clandestin(e) ♦ adv dans la clandestinité, clandestinement; **~growth** n broussailles fpl, sous-bois m; **~hand(ed)** adj (fig: behaviour, method etc) en dessous; **~lie** (irreg) vt être à la base de; **~line** vt souligner; **~ling** (pej) n sous-fifre m, subalterne m; **~mine** vt saper, miner; **~neath**

[ˈʌndəˈniːθ]   adv (en) dessous ♦ prep sous, au-dessous de; **~paid** adj sous-payé(e); **~pants** npl caleçon m, slip m; **~pass** (BRIT) n passage souterrain; (on motorway) passage inférieur; **~privileged** [ˈʌndəˈprɪvɪlɪdʒd]   adj défavorisé(e), économiquement faible; **~rate** vt sous-estimer; **~shirt** (US) n tricot m de corps; **~shorts** (US) npl caleçon m, slip m; **~side** n dessous m; **~skirt** (BRIT) n jupon m
understand [ʌndəˈstænd]   (irreg: like stand) vt, vi comprendre; **I ~ that ...** je me suis laissé dire que ...; je crois comprendre que ...; **~able** adj compréhensible; **~ing** adj compréhensif(ive) ♦ n compréhension f, (agreement) accord m
understatement [ˈʌndəsteɪtmənt]   n: **that's an ~** c'est (bien) peu dire, le terme est faible
understood [ʌndəˈstʊd]   pt, pp of **understand** ♦ adj entendu(e); (implied) sous-entendu(e)
understudy [ˈʌndəstʌdɪ]   n doublure f
undertake [ʌndəˈteɪk]   (irreg) vt entreprendre; se charger de; **to ~ to do sth** s'engager à faire qch
undertaker [ˈʌndəteɪkə*]   n entrepreneur m des pompes funèbres, croque-mort m
undertaking [ʌndəˈteɪkɪŋ]   n entreprise f; (promise) promesse f
undertone [ˈʌndətəʊn]   n: **in an ~** à mi-voix
under: **~water** [ˈʌndəˈwɔːtə*]   adv sous l'eau ♦ adj sous-marin(e); **~wear** [ˈʌndəweə*]   n sous-vêtements mpl; (women's only) dessous mpl; **~world** [ˈʌndəwɜːld]   n (of crime) milieu m, pègre f; **~writer** [ˈʌndəraɪtə*]   n (INSURANCE) assureur m
undies [ˈʌndɪz]   (inf) npl dessous mpl, lingerie f
undiplomatic [ʌndɪpləˈmætɪk]   adj peu diplomatique
undo [ʌnˈduː]   (irreg) vt défaire; **~ing** n ruine f, perte f
undoubted [ʌnˈdaʊtɪd]   adj indubitable, certain(e); **~ly** adv sans aucun doute
undress [ʌnˈdres]   vi se déshabiller
undue [ʌnˈdjuː]   adj indu(e), excessif(ive)
undulating [ˈʌndjʊleɪtɪŋ]   adj ondoyant(e), onduleux(euse)
unduly [ʌnˈdjuːlɪ]   adv trop, excessivement
unearth [ʌnˈɜːθ]   vt déterrer; (fig) dénicher
unearthly [ʌnˈɜːθlɪ]   adj (hour) indu(e), impossible
uneasy [ʌnˈiːzɪ]   adj mal à l'aise, gêné(e); (worried) inquiet(ète); (feeling) désagréable; (peace, truce) fragile
uneconomic(al) [ʌniːkəˈnɒmɪk(l)]   adj peu économique
uneducated [ʌnˈedjʊkeɪtɪd]   adj (person) sans instruction

unemployed ['ʌnɪm'plɔɪd] adj sans travail, en or au chômage ♦ n: **the ~** les chômeurs mpl; **unemployment** ['ʌnɪm'plɔɪmənt] n chômage m

unending [ʌn'endɪŋ] adj interminable, sans fin

unerring ['ʌn'ɜːrɪŋ] adj infaillible, sûr(e)

uneven ['ʌn'iːvən] adj inégal(e); irrégulier(ère)

unexpected [ʌnɪk'spektɪd] adj inattendu(e), imprévu(e); **~ly** adv (arrive) à l'improviste; (succeed) contre toute attente

unfailing [ʌn'feɪlɪŋ] adj inépuisable; infaillible

unfair ['ʌn'fɛə*] adj: **~ (to)** injuste (envers)

unfaithful ['ʌn'feɪθful] adj infidèle

unfamiliar [ʌnfə'mɪlɪə*] adj étrange, inconnu(e); **to be ~ with** mal connaître

unfashionable [ʌn'fæʃnəbl] adj (clothes) démodé(e); (place) peu chic inv

unfasten ['ʌn'fɑːsn] vt défaire; détacher; (open) ouvrir

unfavourable ['ʌn'feɪvərəbl] (US **unfavorable**) adj défavorable

unfeeling [ʌn'fiːlɪŋ] adj insensible, dur(e)

unfinished [ʌn'fɪnɪʃt] adj inachevé(e)

unfit ['ʌn'fɪt] adj en mauvaise santé; pas en forme; (incompetent): **~ (for)** impropre (à); (work, service) inapte (à)

unfold [ʌn'fəuld] vt déplier ♦ vi se dérouler

unforeseen ['ʌnfɔː'siːn] adj imprévu(e)

unforgettable [ʌnfə'getəbl] adj inoubliable

unfortunate [ʌn'fɔːtʃnət] adj malheureux(euse), (event, remark) malencontreux(euse); **~ly** adv malheureusement

unfounded { ʌn'faundɪd] adj sans fondement

unfriendly ['ʌn'frendlɪ] adj inamical(e), peu aimable

ungainly [ʌn'geɪnlɪ] adj gauche, dégingandé(e)

ungodly [ʌn'gɒdlɪ] adj (hour) indu(e)

ungrateful [ʌn'greɪtful] adj ingrat(e)

unhappiness [ʌn'hæpɪnəs] n tristesse f, peine f

unhappy [ʌn'hæpɪ] adj triste, malheureux(euse); **~ about** or **with** (arrangements etc) mécontent(e) de, peu satisfait(e) de

unharmed ['ʌn'hɑːmd] adj indemne, sain(e) et sauf(sauve)

unhealthy [ʌn'helθɪ] adj malsain(e); (person) maladif(ive)

unheard-of [ʌn'hɜːdɒv] adj inouï(e), sans précédent

unhurt [ʌn'hɜːt] adj indemne

unidentified [ʌnaɪ'dentɪfaɪd] adj non identifié(e); see also **UFO**

uniform ['juːnɪfɔːm] n uniforme m ♦ adj uniforme

uninhabited [ʌnɪn'hæbɪtɪd] adj inhabité(e)

unintentional [ʌnɪn'tenʃənəl] adj involontaire

union ['juːnjən] n union f; (also: **trade ~**) syndicat m ♦ cpd du syndicat, syndical(e); **U~ Jack** n drapeau du Royaume-Uni

unique [juː'niːk] adj unique

unison ['juːnɪsn] n: **in ~** (sing) à l'unisson; (say) en chœur

unit ['juːnɪt] n unité f; (section: of furniture etc) élément m, bloc m; **kitchen ~** élément de cuisine

unite [juː'naɪt] vt unir ♦ vi s'unir; **~d** uni(e); unifié(e); (effort) conjugué(e); **U~d Kingdom** n Royaume-Uni m; **U~d Nations (Organization)** n (Organisation f des) Nations unies; **U~d States (of America)** n États-Unis mpl

unit trust (BRIT) n fonds commun de placement

unity ['juːnɪtɪ] n unité f

universal [juːnɪ'vɜːsəl] adj universel(le)

universe ['juːnɪvɜːs] n univers m

university [juːnɪ'vɜːsɪtɪ] n université f

unjust ['ʌn'dʒʌst] adj injuste

unkempt ['ʌn'kempt] adj négligé(e), débraillé(e); (hair) mal peigné(e)

unkind [ʌn'kaɪnd] adj peu gentil(le), méchant(e)

unknown ['ʌn'nəun] adj inconnu(e)

unlawful [ʌn'lɔːful] adj illégal(e)

unleaded [ʌn'ledɪd] adj (petrol, fuel) sans plomb

unleash ['ʌn'liːʃ] vt (fig) déchaîner, déclencher

unless [ən'les] conj: **~ he leaves** à moins qu'il ne parte

unlike ['ʌn'laɪk] adj dissemblable, différent(e) ♦ prep contrairement à

unlikely [ʌn'laɪklɪ] adj improbable; invraisemblable

unlimited [ʌn'lɪmɪtɪd] adj illimité(e)

unlisted ['ʌn'lɪstɪd] (US) adj (TEL) sur la liste rouge

unload ['ʌn'ləud] vt décharger

unlock ['ʌn'lɒk] vt ouvrir

unlucky [ʌn'lʌkɪ] adj (person) malchanceux(euse); (object, number) qui porte malheur; **to be ~** (person) ne pas avoir de chance

unmarried ['ʌn'mærɪd] adj célibataire

unmistak(e)able [ʌnmɪs'teɪkəbl] adj indubitable; qu'on ne peut pas ne pas reconnaître

unmitigated [ʌn'mɪtɪgeɪtɪd] adj non mitigé(e), absolu(e), pur(e)

unnatural [ʌn'nætʃrəl] adj non naturel(le); (habit) contre nature

unnecessary ['ʌn'nesəsərɪ] adj inutile, superflu(e)

unnoticed [ʌn'nəutɪst] adj: **(to go** or **pass) ~** (passer) inaperçu(e)

UNO ['juːnəu] n abbr = **United Nations Organization**

unobtainable ['ʌnəb'teɪnəbl] adj impossible à obtenir

unobtrusive [ʌnəb'truːsɪv] *adj* discret(ète)

unofficial [ʌnə'fɪʃl] *adj* (*news*) officieux(euse); (*strike*) sauvage

unorthodox [ʌn'ɔːθədɔks] *adj* peu orthodoxe; (*REL*) hétérodoxe

unpack ['ʌn'pæk] *vi* défaire sa valise ♦ *vt* (*suitcase*) défaire; (*belongings*) déballer

unpalatable [ʌn'pælətəbl] *adj* (*meal*) mauvais(e); (*truth*) désagréable (à entendre)

unparalleled [ʌn'pærəleld] *adj* incomparable, sans égal

unpleasant [ʌn'pleznt] *adj* déplaisant(e), désagréable

unplug ['ʌn'plʌg] *vt* débrancher

unpopular [ʌn'pɔpjulə*] *adj* impopulaire

unprecedented [ʌn'presidəntid] *adj* sans précédent

unpredictable [ʌnprɪ'dɪktəbl] *adj* imprévisible

unprofessional [ʌnprə'feʃənl] *adj*: ~ **conduct** manquement *m* aux devoirs de la profession

unqualified ['ʌn'kwɔlifaɪd] *adj* (*teacher*) non diplômé(e), sans titres; (*success, disaster*) sans réserve, total(e)

unquestionably [ʌn'kwestʃənəblɪ] *adv* incontestablement

unravel [ʌn'rævəl] *vt* démêler

unreal ['ʌn'rɪəl] *adj* irréel(le); (*extraordinary*) incroyable; ~**istic** [ʌnrɪə'lɪstɪk] *adj* irréaliste; peu réaliste

unreasonable [ʌn'riːznəbl] *adj* qui n'est pas raisonnable

unrelated [ʌnrɪ'leɪtɪd] *adj* sans rapport; sans lien de parenté

unrelenting [ʌnrɪ'lentɪŋ] *adj* implacable

unreliable [ʌnrɪ'laɪəbl] *adj* sur qui (*or* quoi) on ne peut pas compter, peu fiable

unremitting [ʌnrɪ'mɪtɪŋ] *adj* inlassable, infatigable, acharné(e)

unreservedly [ʌnrɪ'zɜːvɪdlɪ] *adv* sans réserve

unrest [ʌn'rest] *n* agitation *f*, troubles *mpl*

unroll ['ʌn'rəul] *vt* dérouler

unruly [ʌn'ruːlɪ] *adj* indiscipliné(e)

unsafe ['ʌn'seɪf] *adj* (*in danger*) en danger; (*journey, car*) dangereux(euse)

unsaid ['ʌn'sed] *adj*: **to leave sth** ~ passer qch sous silence

unsatisfactory ['ʌnsætɪs'fæktərɪ] *adj* peu satisfaisant(e)

unsavoury ['ʌn'seɪvərɪ] (*US* **unsavory**) *adj* (*fig*) peu recommandable

unscathed [ʌn'skeɪðd] *adj* indemne

unscrew ['ʌn'skruː] *vt* dévisser

unscrupulous [ʌn'skruːpjuləs] *adj* sans scrupules

unsettled ['ʌn'setld] *adj* perturbé(e); instable

unshaven ['ʌn'ʃeɪvn] *adj* non *or* mal rasé(e)

unsightly [ʌn'saɪtlɪ] *adj* disgracieux(euse), laid(e)

unskilled ['ʌn'skɪld] *adj*: ~ **worker** manœuvre *m*

unspeakable [ʌn'spiːkəbl] *adj* indicible; (*awful*) innommable

unstable [ʌn'steɪbl] *adj* instable

unsteady [ʌn'stedɪ] *adj* mal assuré(e), chancelant(e), instable

unstuck ['ʌn'stʌk] *adj*: **to come** ~ se décoller; (*plan*) tomber à l'eau

unsuccessful ['ʌnsək'sesful] *adj* (*attempt*) infructueux(euse), vain(e); (*writer, proposal*) qui n'a pas de succès; **to be** ~ (*in attempting sth*) ne pas réussir; ne pas avoir de succès; (*application*) ne pas être retenu(e)

unsuitable ['ʌn'suːtəbl] *adj* qui ne convient pas, peu approprié(e); inopportun(e)

unsure [ʌn'ʃuə*] *adj* pas sûr(e); **to be** ~ **of o.s.** manquer de confiance en soi

unsuspecting [ʌnsə'spektɪŋ] *adj* qui ne se doute de rien

unsympathetic ['ʌnsɪmpə'θetɪk] *adj* (*person*) antipathique; (*attitude*) peu compatissant(e)

untapped ['ʌn'tæpt] *adj* (*resources*) inexploité(e)

unthinkable [ʌn'θɪŋkəbl] *adj* impensable, inconcevable

untidy [ʌn'taɪdɪ] *adj* (*room*) en désordre; (*appearance, person*) débraillé(e); (*person: in character*) sans ordre, désordonné

untie ['ʌn'taɪ] *vt* (*knot, parcel*) défaire; (*prisoner, dog*) détacher

until [ən'tɪl] *prep* jusqu'à; (*after negative*) avant ♦ *conj* jusqu'à ce que +*sub*; (*in past, after negative*) avant que +*sub*; ~ **he comes** jusqu'à ce qu'il vienne, jusqu'à son arrivée; ~ **now** jusqu'à présent, jusqu'ici; ~ **then** jusque-là

untimely [ʌn'taɪmlɪ] *adj* inopportun(e); (*death*) prématuré(e)

untold ['ʌn'təuld] *adj* (*story*) jamais raconté(e); (*wealth*) incalculable; (*joy, suffering*) indescriptible

untoward [ʌntə'wɔːd] *adj* fâcheux(euse), malencontreux(euse)

unused[1]   [ʌn'juːzd]   *adj*   (*clothes*) neuf(neuve)

unused[2] [ʌn'juːst] *adj*: **to be unused to sth/to doing sth** ne pas avoir l'habitude de qch/de faire qch

unusual [ʌn'juːʒuəl] *adj* insolite, exceptionnel(le), rare

unveil [ʌn'veɪl] *vt* dévoiler

unwanted [ʌn'wɔntɪd] *adj* (*child, pregnancy*) non désiré(e); (*clothes etc*) à donner

unwelcome [ʌn'welkəm] *adj* importun(e); (*news*) fâcheux(euse)

unwell [ʌn'wel] *adj* souffrant(e); **to feel** ~ ne pas se sentir bien

unwieldy [ʌn'wiːldɪ] *adj* (*object*) difficile à

manier; (*system*) lourd(e)

unwilling [ʌnˈwɪlɪŋ] *adj*: **to be ~ to do** ne pas vouloir faire; **~ly** *adv* à contrecœur, contre son gré

unwind [ʌnˈwaɪnd] (*irreg*) *vt* dérouler ♦ *vi* (*relax*) se détendre

unwise [ʌnˈwaɪz] *adj* irréfléchi(e), imprudent(e)

unwitting [ʌnˈwɪtɪŋ] *adj* involontaire

unworkable [ʌnˈwɜːkəbl] *adj* (*plan*) impraticable

unworthy [ʌnˈwɜːðɪ] *adj* indigne

unwrap [ʌnˈræp] *vt* défaire; ouvrir

unwritten [ʌnˈrɪtn] *adj* (*agreement*) tacite

--------------------------- *KEYWORD*

up [ʌp] *prep*: **he went ~ the stairs/the hill** il a monté l'escalier/la colline; **the cat was ~ a tree** le chat était dans un arbre; **they live further ~ the street** ils habitent plus haut dans la rue
♦ *adv* **1** (*upwards, higher*): **~ in the sky/ the mountains** (là-haut) dans le ciel/les montagnes; **put it a bit higher ~** mettez-le un peu plus haut; **~ there** là-haut; **~ above** au-dessus
2: **to be ~** (*out of bed*) être levé(e); (*prices*) avoir augmenté *or* monté
3: **~ to** (*as far as*) jusqu'à; **~ to now** jusqu'à présent
4: **to be ~ to** (*depending on*): **it's ~ to you** c'est à vous de décider; (*equal to*): **he's not ~ to it** (*job, task etc*) il n'en est pas capable; (*inf: be doing*): **what is he ~ to?** qu'est-ce qu'il peut bien faire?
♦ *n*: **~s and downs** hauts et bas *mpl*

up-and-coming [ʌpəndˈkʌmɪŋ] *adj* plein(e) d'avenir *or* de promesses

upbringing [ˈʌpbrɪŋɪŋ] *n* éducation *f*

update [ʌpˈdeɪt] *vt* mettre à jour

upgrade *vt* (*house*) moderniser; (*job*) revaloriser; (*employee*) promouvoir

upheaval [ʌpˈhiːvəl] *n* bouleversement *m*; branle-bas *m*; crise *f*

uphill [ˈʌpˈhɪl] *adj* qui monte; (*fig: task*) difficile, pénible ♦ *adv* (*face, look*) en amont; **to go ~** monter

uphold [ʌpˈhəʊld] (*irreg*) *vt* (*law, decision*) maintenir

upholstery [ʌpˈhəʊlstərɪ] *n* rembourrage *m*; (*cover*) tissu *m* d'ameublement; (*of car*) garniture *f*

upkeep [ˈʌpkiːp] *n* entretien *m*

upon [əˈpɒn] *prep* sur

upper [ˈʌpə*] *adj* supérieur(e); du dessus ♦ *n* (*of shoe*) empeigne *f*; **~-class** *adj* de la haute société, aristocratique; **~ hand** *n*: **to have the ~ hand** avoir le dessus; **~most** *adj* le(la) plus haut(e); **what was ~most in my mind** ce à quoi je pensais surtout

upright [ˈʌpraɪt] *adj* droit(e); vertical(e);

(*fig*) droit, honnête

uprising [ˈʌpraɪzɪŋ] *n* soulèvement *m*, insurrection *f*

uproar [ˈʌprɔː*] *n* tumulte *m*; (*protests*) tempête *f* de protestations

uproot [ʌpˈruːt] *vt* déraciner

upset [*n* ˈʌpset, *vb, adj* ʌpˈset] (*irreg: like set*) *n* bouleversement *m*; (*stomach ~*) indigestion *f* ♦ *vt* (*glass etc*) renverser; (*plan*) déranger; (*person: offend*) contrarier; (*: grieve*) faire de la peine à; bouleverser ♦ *adj* contrarié(e); peiné(e); (*stomach*) dérangé(e)

upshot [ˈʌpʃɒt] *n* résultat *m*

upside-down [ˈʌpsaɪdˈdaʊn] *adv* à l'envers; **to turn ~** mettre sens dessus dessous

upstairs [ˈʌpˈstɛəz] *adv* en haut ♦ *adj* (*room*) du dessus, d'en haut ♦ *n*: **the ~** l'étage *m*

upstart [ˈʌpstɑːt] (*pej*) *n* parvenu(e)

upstream [ˈʌpˈstriːm] *adv* en amont

uptake [ˈʌpteɪk] *n*: **to be quick/slow on the ~** comprendre vite/être lent à comprendre

uptight [ˈʌpˈtaɪt] (*inf*) *adj* très tendu(e), crispé(e)

up-to-date [ˈʌptəˈdeɪt] *adj* moderne; (*information*) très récent(e)

upturn [ˈʌptɜːn] *n* (*in luck*) retournement *m*; (*COMM: in market*) hausse *f*

upward [ˈʌpwəd] *adj* ascendant(e); vers le haut; **~(s)** *adv* vers le haut; **~(s) of 200** 200 et plus

urban [ˈɜːbən] *adj* urbain(e)

urbane [ɜːˈbeɪn] *adj* urbain(e), courtois(e)

urchin [ˈɜːtʃɪn] *n* polisson *m*

urge [ɜːdʒ] *n* besoin *m*; envie *f*; forte envie, désir *m* ♦ *vt*: **to ~ sb to do** exhorter qn à faire, pousser qn à faire; recommander vivement à qn de faire

urgency [ˈɜːdʒənsɪ] *n* urgence *f*; (*of tone*) insistance *f*

urgent [ˈɜːdʒənt] *adj* urgent(e); (*tone*) insistant(e), pressant(e)

urinal [ˈjʊərɪnl] *n* urinoir *m*; (*vessel*) urinal *m*

urine [ˈjʊərɪn] *n* urine *f*

urn [ɜːn] *n* urne *f*; (*also: tea ~*) fontaine *f* à thé

US *n abbr* = **United States**

us [ʌs] *pron* nous; *see also* **me**

USA *n abbr* = **United States of America**

use [*n* juːs, *vb* juːz] *n* emploi *m*, utilisation *f*; usage *m*; (*usefulness*) utilité *f* ♦ *vt* se servir de, utiliser, employer; **in ~** en usage; **out of ~** hors d'usage; **to be of ~** servir, être utile; **it's no ~** ça ne sert à rien; **she ~d to do it** elle le faisait (autrefois), elle avait coutume de le faire; **~d to**: **to be ~d to** avoir l'habitude de, être habitué(e) à; **~ up** *vt* finir, épuiser; consommer; **~d** *adj* (*car*) d'occasion; **~ful** *adj* utile; **~fulness** *n* utilité *f*; **~less** *adj* inutile; (*person: hope-*

less) nul(le); **~r** _n_ utilisateur(trice), usager _m_; **~r-friendly** _adj_ (_computer_) convivial(e), facile d'emploi

usher ['ʌʃə*] _n_ (_at wedding ceremony_) placeur _m_; **~ette** [ʌʃə'ret] _n_ (_in cinema_) ouvreuse _f_

usual ['juːʒuəl] _adj_ habituel(le); **as ~** comme d'habitude; **~ly** _adv_ d'habitude, d'ordinaire

utensil [juːˈtɛnsl] _n_ ustensile _m_

uterus ['juːtərəs] _n_ utérus _m_

utility [juːˈtɪlɪtɪ] _n_ utilité _f_; (_also: public ~_) service public; **~ room** _n_ buanderie _f_

utmost ['ʌtməust] _adj_ extrême, le(la) plus grand(e) ♦ _n_: **to do one's ~** faire tout son possible

utter ['ʌtə*] _adj_ total(e), complet(ète) ♦ _vt_ (_words_) prononcer, proférer; (_sounds_) émettre; **~ance** _n_ paroles _fpl_; **~ly** _adv_ complètement, totalement

U-turn ['juːˈtɜːn] _n_ demi-tour _m_

V v

v. _abbr_ = **verse; versus; volt;** (= _vide_) voir

vacancy ['veɪkənsɪ] _n_ (_BRIT: job_) poste vacant; (_room_) chambre _f_ disponible

vacant ['veɪkənt] _adj_ (_seat etc_) libre, disponible; (_expression_) distrait(e); **~ lot** (_US_) _n_ terrain inoccupé; (_for sale_) terrain à vendre

vacate [vəˈkeɪt] _vt_ quitter

vacation [vəˈkeɪʃən] _n_ vacances _fpl_

vaccinate ['væksɪneɪt] _vt_ vacciner

vacuum ['vækjum] _n_ vide _m_; **~ cleaner** _n_ aspirateur _m_; **~-packed** _adj_ emballé(e) sous vide

vagina [vəˈdʒaɪnə] _n_ vagin _m_

vagrant ['veɪɡrənt] _n_ vagabond(e)

vague [veɪɡ] _adj_ (_useless_) vague, imprécis(e); (_blurred: photo, outline_) flou(e); **~ly** _adv_ vaguement

vain [veɪn] _adj_ (_useless_) vain(e); (_conceited_) vaniteux(euse); **in ~** en vain

valentine ['væləntaɪn] _n_ (_also: ~ card_) carte _f_ de la Saint-Valentin; (_person_) bien-aimé(e) (_le jour de la Sainte-Valentin_)

valiant ['væliənt] _adj_ vaillant(e)

valid ['vælɪd] _adj_ valable; (_document_) valable, valide

valley ['vælɪ] _n_ vallée _f_

valour ['vælə*] (_US_ **valor**) _n_ courage _m_

valuable ['væljuəbl] _adj_ (_jewel_) de valeur; (_time, help_) précieux(euse); **~s** _npl_ objets _mpl_ de valeur

valuation [væljuˈeɪʃən] _n_ (_price_) estimation _f_; (_quality_) appréciation _f_

value ['væljuː] _n_ valeur _f_ ♦ _vt_ (_fix price_) évaluer, expertiser; (_appreciate_) apprécier; **~ added tax** (_BRIT_) _n_ taxe _f_ à la valeur ajoutée; **~d** _adj_ (_person_) estimé(e); (_advice_) précieux(euse)

valve [vælv] _n_ (_in machine_) soupape _f_, valve _f_; (_MED_) valve, valvule _f_

van [væn] _n_ (_AUT_) camionnette _f_

vandal ['vændl] _n_ vandale _m/f_; **~ism** _n_ vandalisme _m_; **~ize** ['vændəlaɪz] _vt_ saccager

vanguard ['vænɡɑːd] _n_ (_fig_): **in the ~ of** à l'avant-garde de

vanilla [vəˈnɪlə] _n_ vanille _f_

vanish ['vænɪʃ] _vi_ disparaître

vanity ['vænɪtɪ] _n_ vanité _f_

vantage point ['vɑːntɪdʒ-] _n_ bonne position

vapour ['veɪpə*] (_US_ **vapor**) _n_ vapeur _f_; (_on window_) buée _f_

variable ['vɛərɪəbl] _adj_ variable; (_mood_) changeant(e)

variance ['vɛərɪəns] _n_: **to be at ~ (with)** être en désaccord (avec); (_facts_) être en contradiction (avec)

varicose ['værɪkəus] _adj_: **~ veins** varices _fpl_

varied ['vɛərɪd] _adj_ varié(e), divers(e)

variety [vəˈraɪətɪ] _n_ variété _f_; (_quantity_) nombre _m_, quantité _f_; **~ show** _n_ (spectacle _m_ de) variétés _fpl_

various ['vɛərɪəs] _adj_ divers(e), différent(e); (_several_) divers, plusieurs

varnish ['vɑːnɪʃ] _n_ vernis _m_ ♦ _vt_ vernir

vary ['vɛərɪ] _vt, vi_ varier, changer

vase [vɑːz] _n_ vase _m_

Vaseline ['væsɪliːn] (®) _n_ vaseline _f_

vast [vɑːst] _adj_ vaste, immense; (_amount, success_) énorme

VAT [væt] _n abbr_ (= _value added tax_) TVA _f_

vat [væt] _n_ cuve _f_

vault [vɔːlt] _n_ (_of roof_) voûte _f_; (_tomb_) caveau _m_; (_in bank_) salle _f_ des coffres; chambre forte ♦ _vt_ (_also: ~ over_) sauter (d'un bond)

vaunted ['vɔːntɪd] _adj_: **much-vaunted** tant vanté(e)

VCR _n abbr_ = **video cassette recorder**

VD _n abbr_ = **venereal disease**

VDU _n abbr_ = **visual display unit**

veal [viːl] _n_ veau _m_

veer [vɪə*] _vi_ tourner; virer

vegetable ['vedʒətəbl] _n_ légume _m_ ♦ _adj_ végétal(e)

vegetarian [vedʒɪˈtɛərɪən] _adj, n_ végétarien(ne)

vehement ['viːɪmənt] _adj_ violent(e), impétueux(euse); (_impassioned_) ardent(e)

vehicle ['viːɪkl] _n_ véhicule _m_

veil [veɪl] _n_ voile _m_

vein [veɪn] *n* veine *f*; (*on leaf*) nervure *f*

velocity [vɪ'lɒsɪtɪ] *n* vitesse *f*

velvet ['vɛlvɪt] *n* velours *m*

vending machine ['vɛndɪŋ-] *n* distributeur *m* automatique

veneer [və'nɪə*] *n* (*on furniture*) placage *m*; (*fig*) vernis *m*

venereal [vɪ'nɪərɪəl] *adj*: ~ **disease** maladie vénérienne

Venetian blind [vɪ'niːʃən-] *n* store vénitien

vengeance ['vɛndʒəns] *n* vengeance *f*; **with a** ~ (*fig*) vraiment, pour de bon

venison ['vɛnɪsn] *n* venaison *f*

venom ['vɛnəm] *n* venin *m*

vent [vɛnt] *n* conduit *m* d'aération; (*in dress, jacket*) fente *f* ♦ *vt* (*fig: one's feelings*) donner libre cours à

ventilator ['vɛntɪleɪtə*] *n* ventilateur *m*

ventriloquist [vɛn'trɪləkwɪst] *n* ventriloque *m/f*

venture ['vɛntʃə*] *n* entreprise *f* ♦ *vt* risquer, hasarder ♦ *vi* s'aventurer, se risquer

venue ['vɛnjuː] *n* lieu *m*

verb [vɜːb] *n* verbe *m*; ~**al** *adj* verbal(e); (*translation*) littéral(e)

verbatim [vɜː'beɪtɪm] *adj, adv* mot pour mot

verdict ['vɜːdɪkt] *n* verdict *m*

verge [vɜːdʒ] *n* (*BRIT*) bord *m*, bas-côté *m*; "**soft** ~**s**"(: *AUT*) "accotement non stabilisé"; **on the** ~ **of doing** sur le point de faire; ~ **on** *vt fus* approcher de

verify ['vɛrɪfaɪ] *vt* vérifier; (*confirm*) confirmer

vermin ['vɜːmɪn] *npl* animaux *mpl* nuisibles; (*insects*) vermine *f*

vermouth ['vɜːməθ] *n* vermouth *m*

versatile ['vɜːsətaɪl] *adj* polyvalent(e)

verse [vɜːs] *n* (*poetry*) vers *mpl*; (*stanza*) strophe *f*; (*in Bible*) verset *m*

version ['vɜːʃən] *n* version *f*

versus ['vɜːsəs] *prep* contre

vertical ['vɜːtɪkəl] *adj* vertical(e) ♦ *n* verticale *f*

vertigo ['vɜːtɪɡəʊ] *n* vertige *m*

verve [vɜːv] *n* brio *m*; enthousiasme *m*

very ['vɛrɪ] *adv* très ♦ *adj*: **the** ~ **book which** le livre même que; **the** ~ **last** le tout dernier; **at the** ~ **least** tout au moins; ~ **much** beaucoup

vessel ['vɛsl] *n* (*ANAT, NAUT*) vaisseau *m*; (*container*) récipient *m*

vest [vɛst] *n* (*BRIT*) tricot *m* de corps; (*US: waistcoat*) gilet *m*

vested interest ['vɛstɪd-] *n* (*COMM*) droits acquis

vet [vɛt] *n abbr* (*BRIT*: = *veterinary surgeon*) vétérinaire *m/f* ♦ *vt* examiner soigneusement

veteran ['vɛtərn] *n* vétéran *m*; (*also*: war ~) ancien combattant

veterinarian [vɛtrə'nɛərɪən] (*US*) *n* = **veterinary surgeon**

veterinary surgeon ['vɛtrɪnərɪ-] (*BRIT*) *n* vétérinaire *m/f*

veto ['viːtəʊ] (*pl* ~es) *n* veto *m* ♦ *vt* opposer son veto à

vex [vɛks] *vt* fâcher, contrarier; ~**ed** *adj* (*question*) controversé(e)

via ['vaɪə] *prep* par, via

viable ['vaɪəbl] *adj* viable

vibrate [vaɪ'breɪt] *vi* vibrer

vicar ['vɪkə*] *n* pasteur *m* (*de l'Église anglicane*); ~**age** *n* presbytère *m*

vicarious [vɪ'kɛərɪəs] *adj* indirect(e)

vice [vaɪs] *n* (*evil*) vice *m*; (*TECH*) étau *m*

vice- *prefix* vice-

vice squad *n* ≈ brigade mondaine

vice versa ['vaɪsɪ'vɜːsə] *adv* vice versa

vicinity [vɪ'sɪnɪtɪ] *n* environs *mpl*, alentours *mpl*

vicious ['vɪʃəs] *adj* (*remark*) cruel(le), méchant(e); (*blow*) brutal(e); (*dog*) méchant(e), dangereux(euse); (*horse*) vicieux(euse); ~ **circle** *n* cercle vicieux

victim ['vɪktɪm] *n* victime *f*

victor ['vɪktə*] *n* vainqueur *m*

Victorian [vɪk'tɔːrɪən] *adj* victorien(ne)

victory ['vɪktərɪ] *n* victoire *f*

video ['vɪdɪəʊ] *cpd* vidéo *inv* ♦ *n* (~ *film*) vidéo *f*; (*also*: ~ *cassette*) vidéocassette *f*; (: ~ *cassette recorder*) magnétoscope *m*; ~ **tape** *n* bande *f* vidéo *inv*; (*cassette*) vidéocassette *f*

vie [vaɪ] *vi*: **to** ~ **with** rivaliser avec

Vienna [vɪ'enə] *n* Vienne

Vietnam [vjɛt'næm] *n* Viêt-nam *m*, Vietnam *m*; ~**ese** [vjɛtnə'miːz] *adj* vietnamien(ne) ♦ *n inv* Vietnamien(ne); (*LING*) vietnamien *m*

view [vjuː] *n* vue *f*; (*opinion*) avis *m*, vue ♦ *vt* voir, regarder; (*situation*) considérer; (*house*) visiter; **in full** ~ **of** sous les yeux de; **in** ~ **of the weather/the fact that** étant donné le temps/que; **in my** ~ à mon avis; ~**er** *n* (*TV*) téléspectateur(trice); ~**finder** *n* viseur *m*; ~**point** *n* point *m* de vue

vigorous ['vɪɡərəs] *adj* vigoureux(euse)

vile [vaɪl] *adj* (*action*) vil(e); (*smell, food*) abominable; (*temper*) massacrant(e)

villa ['vɪlə] *n* villa *f*

village ['vɪlɪdʒ] *n* village *m*; ~**r** *n* villageois(e)

villain ['vɪlən] *n* (*scoundrel*) scélérat *m*; (*BRIT: criminal*) bandit *m*; (*in novel etc*) traître *m*

vindicate ['vɪndɪkeɪt] *vt* (*person*) innocenter; (*action*) justifier

vindictive [vɪn'dɪktɪv] *adj* vindicatif(ive), rancunier(ère)

vine [vaɪn] *n* vigne *f*; (*climbing plant*) plante grimpante

vinegar ['vɪnɪgə*] n vinaigre m
vineyard ['vɪnjəd] n vignoble m
vintage ['vɪntɪdʒ] n (year) année f, millésime m; ~ **car** n voiture f d'époque; ~
wine n vin m de grand cru
viola [vɪ'əulə] n (MUS) alto m
violate ['vaɪəleɪt] vt violer
violence ['vaɪələns] n violence f
violent ['vaɪələnt] adj violent(e)
violet ['vaɪələt] adj violet(te) ♦ n (colour)
violet m; (plant) violette f
violin [vaɪə'lɪn] n violon m; ~**ist** n violoniste m/f
VIP n abbr (= very important person) V.I.P.
m
virgin ['vɜːdʒɪn] n vierge f ♦ adj vierge
Virgo ['vɜːgəu] n la Vierge
virile ['vɪraɪl] adj viril(e)
virtually ['vɜːtjuəlɪ] adv (almost) pratiquement
virtual reality n (COMPUT) réalité virtuelle
virtue ['vɜːtjuː] n vertu f; (advantage) mérite
m, avantage m; **by** ~ **of** en vertu or en raison de; **virtuous** ['vɜːtjuəs] adj ver-
tueux(euse)
virus ['vaɪərəs] n (also: COMPUT) virus m
visa ['viːzə] n visa m
visibility [vɪzɪ'bɪlɪtɪ] n visibilité f
visible ['vɪzəbl] adj visible
vision ['vɪʒən] n (sight) vue f, vision f;
(foresight, in dream) vision
visit ['vɪzɪt] n visite f; (stay) séjour m ♦ vt
(person) rendre visite à; (place) visiter;
~**ing hours** npl (in hospital etc) heures fpl
de visite; ~**or** n visiteur(euse) f; (to one's
house) visite f, invité(e)
visor ['vaɪzə*] n visière f
vista ['vɪstə] n vue f
visual ['vɪzjuəl] adj visuel(le); ~ **aid** n support visuel; ~ **display unit** n console f de
visualisation, visuel m; ~**ize** ['vɪzjuəlaɪz] vt
se représenter, s'imaginer
vital ['vaɪtl] adj vital(e); (person) plein(e)
d'entrain; ~**ly** adv (important) absolument;
~ **statistics** npl (fig) mensurations fpl
vitamin ['vɪtəmɪn] n vitamine f
vivacious [vɪ'veɪʃəs] adj animé(e), qui a de
la vivacité
vivid ['vɪvɪd] adj (account) vivant(e); (light,
imagination) vif(vive); ~**ly** adv (describe)
d'une manière vivante; (remember) de façon précise
V-neck ['viːnek] n décolleté m en V
vocabulary [vəu'kæbjuləri] n vocabulaire m
vocal ['vəukəl] adj vocal(e); (articulate) qui
sait s'exprimer; ~ **cords** npl cordes vocales
vocation [vəu'keɪʃən] n vocation f; ~**al** adj
professionnel(le)
vociferous [vəu'sɪfərəs] adj bruyant(e)
vodka ['vodkə] n vodka f
vogue [vəug] n: **in** ~ en vogue f

voice [vɔɪs] n voix f ♦ vt (opinion) exprimer,
formuler
void [vɔɪd] n vide m ♦ adj nul(le); ~ **of**
vide de, dépourvu(e) de
volatile ['volətaɪl] adj volatil(e); (person)
versatile; (situation) explosif(ive)
volcano [vol'keɪnəu] (pl ~**es**) n volcan m
volition [və'lɪʃən] n: **of one's own** ~ de
son propre gré
volley ['volɪ] n (of gunfire) salve f; (of
stones etc) grêle f, volée f; (of questions)
multitude f, série f; (TENNIS etc) volée f;
~**ball** n volley(-ball) m
volt [vəult] n volt m; ~**age** n tension f, vol-
tage m
volume ['voljuːm] n volume m
voluntarily adv volontairement
voluntary ['voləntəri] adj volontaire; (unpaid) bénévole
volunteer [volən'tɪə*] n volontaire m/f ♦ vt
(information) fournir (spontanément) ♦ vi
(MIL) s'engager comme volontaire; **to** ~ **to**
do se proposer pour faire
vomit ['vomɪt] vt, vi vomir
vote [vəut] n vote m, suffrage m; (cast) voix
f, vote; (franchise) droit m de vote ♦ vt
(elect): **to be** ~**d chairman** etc être élu président etc; (propose): **to** ~ **that** proposer
que ♦ vi voter; ~ **of thanks** discours m de
remerciement; ~**r** n électeur(trice); **voting**
['vəutɪŋ] n scrutin m, vote m
voucher ['vautʃə*] n (for meal, petrol, gift)
bon m
vouch for [vautʃ] vt fus se porter garant de
vow [vau] n vœu m, serment m ♦ vi jurer
vowel ['vauəl] n voyelle f
voyage ['vɔɪɪdʒ] n voyage m par mer, traversée f; (by spacecraft) voyage
vulgar ['vʌlgə*] adj vulgaire
vulnerable ['vʌlnərəbl] adj vulnérable
vulture ['vʌltʃə*] n vautour m

W w

wad [wod] n (of cotton wool, paper) tampon
m; (of banknotes etc) liasse f
waddle ['wodl] vi se dandiner
wade [weɪd] vi: **to** ~ **through** marcher
dans, patauger dans; (fig: book) s'évertuer à
lire
wafer ['weɪfə*] n (CULIN) gaufrette f
waffle ['wofl] n (CULIN) gaufre f; (inf) ver-
biage m, remplissage m ♦ vi parler pour ne

rien dire, faire du remplissage

waft [wɑːft] *vt* porter ♦ *vi* flotter

wag [wæg] *vt* agiter, remuer ♦ *vi* remuer

wage [weɪdʒ] *n* (*also*: ~s) salaire *m*, paye *f* ♦ *vt*: **to ~ war** faire la guerre; ~ **earner** *n* salarié(e); ~ **packet** *n* (enveloppe *f* de) paye *f*

wager ['weɪdʒə*] *n* pari *m*

waggle ['wægl] *vt, vi* remuer

wag(g)on ['wægən] *n* (*horse-drawn*) chariot *m*; (*BRIT: RAIL*) wagon *m* (de marchandises)

wail [weɪl] *vi* gémir; (*siren*) hurler

waist [weɪst] *n* taille *f*; ~**coat** (*BRIT*) *n* gilet *m*; ~**line** *n* (tour *m* de) taille *f*

wait [weɪt] *n* attente *f* ♦ *vi* attendre; **to keep sb ~ing** faire attendre qn; **to ~ for** attendre; **I can't ~ to ...** (*fig*) je meurs d'envie de ...; ~ **behind** *vi* rester (à attendre); ~ **on** *vt fus* servir; ~**er** *n* garçon *m* (de café), serveur *m*; ~**ing** *n*: "**no ~ing**" (*BRIT: AUT*) "stationnement interdit"; ~**ing list** *n* liste *f* d'attente; ~**ing room** *n* salle *f* d'attente; ~**ress** *n* serveuse *f*

waive [weɪv] *vt* renoncer à, abandonner

wake [weɪk] (*pt* woke, ~d, *pp* woken, ~d) *vt* (*also*: ~ **up**) réveiller ♦ *vi* (*also*: ~ **up**) se réveiller ♦ *n* (*for dead person*) veillée *f* mortuaire; (*NAUT*) sillage *m*

Wales [weɪlz] *n* pays *m* de Galles; **the Prince of ~** le prince de Galles

walk [wɔːk] *n* promenade *f*; (*short*) petit tour; (*gait*) démarche *f*; (*path*) chemin *m*; (*in park etc*) allée *f* ♦ *vi* marcher; (*for pleasure, exercise*) se promener ♦ *vt* (*distance*) faire à pied; (*dog*) promener; **10 minutes' ~ from** à 10 minutes à pied de; **from all ~s of life** de toutes conditions sociales; ~ **out** *vi* (*audience*) sortir, quitter la salle; (*workers*) se mettre en grève; ~ **out on** (*inf*) *vt fus* quitter, plaquer; ~**er** *n* (*person*) marcheur(euse); ~**ie-talkie** *n* talkie-walkie *m*; ~**ing** *n* marche *f* à pied; ~**ing shoes** *npl* chaussures *fpl* de marche; ~**ing stick** *n* canne *f*; ~**out** *n* (*of workers*) grève-surprise *f*; ~**over** (*inf*) *n* victoire *f* ou examen *m* etc facile; ~**way** *n* promenade *f*, cheminement *m* piéton

wall [wɔːl] *n* mur *m*; (*of tunnel, cave etc*) paroi *m*; ~**ed** *adj* (*city*) fortifié(e); (*garden*) entouré(e) d'un mur, clos(e)

wallet ['wɒlɪt] *n* portefeuille *m*

wallflower ['wɔːlflauə*] *n* giroflée *f*; **to be a ~** (*fig*) faire tapisserie

wallop ['wɒləp] (*BRIT: inf*) *vt* donner un grand coup à

wallow ['wɒləu] *vi* se vautrer

wallpaper ['wɔːlpeɪpə*] *n* papier peint ♦ *vt* tapisser

walnut ['wɔːlnʌt] *n* noix *f*; (*tree, wood*) noyer *m*

walrus ['wɔːlrəs] (*pl* ~ *or* ~**es**) *n* morse *m*

waltz [wɔːlts] *n* valse *f* ♦ *vi* valser

wan [wɒn] *adj* pâle; triste

wand [wɒnd] *n* (*also*: **magic ~**) baguette *f* (magique)

wander ['wɒndə*] *vi* (*person*) errer; (*thoughts*) vagabonder, errer ♦ *vt* errer dans

wane [weɪn] *vi* (*moon*) décroître; (*reputation*) décliner

wangle ['wæŋgl] (*BRIT: inf*) *vt* se débrouiller pour avoir; carotter

want [wɒnt] *vt* vouloir; (*need*) avoir besoin de ♦ *n*: **for ~ of** par manque de, faute de; ~**s** *npl* (*needs*) besoins *mpl*; **to ~ to do** vouloir faire; **to ~ sb to do** vouloir que qn fasse; ~**ed** *adj* (*criminal*) recherché(e) par la police; "**cook ~ed**" "on recherche un cuisinier"; ~**ing** *adj*: **to be found ~ing** ne pas être à la hauteur

wanton ['wɒntən] *adj* (*gratuitous*) gratuit(e); (*promiscuous*) dévergondé(e)

war [wɔː*] *n* guerre *f*; **to make ~ (on)** faire la guerre (à)

ward [wɔːd] *n* (*in hospital*) salle *f*; (*POL*) canton *m*; (*LAW: child*) pupille *m/f*; ~ **off** *vt* (*attack, enemy*) repousser, éviter

warden ['wɔːdn] *n* gardien(ne); (*BRIT: of institution*) directeur(trice); (: *also*: **traffic ~**) contractuel(le); (*of youth hostel*) père *m* ou mère *f* aubergiste

warder ['wɔːdə*] (*BRIT*) *n* gardien *m* de prison

wardrobe ['wɔːdrəub] *n* (*cupboard*) armoire *f*; (*clothes*) garde-robe *f*; (*THEATRE*) costumes *mpl*

warehouse ['wεəhaus] *n* entrepôt *m*

wares [wεəz] *npl* marchandises *fpl*

warfare ['wɔːfεə*] *n* guerre *f*

warhead ['wɔːhed] *n* (*MIL*) ogive *f*

warily ['wεərɪlɪ] *adv* avec prudence

warm [wɔːm] *adj* chaud(e); (*thanks, welcome, applause, person*) chaleureux(euse); **it's ~** il fait chaud; **I'm ~** j'ai chaud; ~ **up** *vi* (*person, room*) se réchauffer; (*water*) chauffer; (*athlete*) s'échauffer ♦ *vt* (*food*) (faire) réchauffer, (faire) chauffer; (*engine*) faire chauffer; ~**-hearted** *adj* affectueux(euse); ~**ly** *adv* chaudement; chaleureusement; ~**th** *n* chaleur *f*

warn [wɔːn] *vt* avertir, prévenir; **to ~ sb (not) to do** conseiller à qn de (ne pas) faire; ~**ing** *n* avertissement *m*; (*notice*) avis *m*; (*signal*) avertisseur *m*; ~**ing light** *n* avertisseur lumineux; ~**ing triangle** *n* (*AUT*) triangle *m* de présignalisation

warp [wɔːp] *vi* (*wood*) travailler, se déformer ♦ *vt* (*fig: character*) pervertir

warrant ['wɒrənt] *n* (*guarantee*) garantie *f*; (*LAW: to arrest*) mandat *m* d'arrêt; (: *to search*) mandat de perquisition

warranty ['wɒrəntɪ] *n* garantie *f*

warren ['wɒrən] *n* (*of rabbits*) terrier *m*; (*fig: of streets etc*) dédale *m*

warrior ['wɒrɪə*] n guerrier(ère)

Warsaw ['wɔːsɔː] n Varsovie

warship ['wɔːʃɪp] n navire m de guerre

wart [wɔːt] n verrue f

wartime ['wɔːtaɪm] n: **in ~** en temps de guerre

wary ['wɛərɪ] adj prudent(e)

was [wɒz, wəz] pt of **be**

wash [wɒʃ] vt laver ♦ vi se laver; (sea): **to ~ over/against sth** inonder/baigner qch ♦ n (clothes) lessive f; (~ing programme) lavage m; (of ship) sillage m; **to have a ~** se laver, faire sa toilette; **to give sth a ~** laver qch; **~ away** vt (stain) enlever au lavage; (subj: river etc) emporter; **~ off** vi partir au lavage; **~ up** vi (BRIT) faire la vaisselle; (US) se débarbouiller; **~basin** (US **~bowl**) n lavabo m; **~cloth** (US) n gant m de toilette; **~er** n (TECH) rondelle f, joint m; **~ing** n (dirty) linge m; (clean) lessive f; **~ing machine** n machine f à laver; **~ing powder** (BRIT) n lessive f (en poudre); **~ing-up** n vaisselle f; **~ing-up liquid** n produit m pour la vaisselle; **~-out** (inf) n désastre m; **~room** (US) n toilettes fpl

wasn't ['wɒznt] = **was not**

wasp [wɒsp] n guêpe f

wastage ['weɪstɪdʒ] n gaspillage m; (in manufacturing, transport etc) pertes fpl, déchets mpl; **natural ~** départs naturels

waste [weɪst] n gaspillage m; (of time) perte f; (rubbish) déchets mpl; (also: household ~) ordures fpl ♦ adj (leftover): **~ material** déchets mpl; (land, ground: in city) à l'abandon ♦ vt gaspiller; (time, opportunity) perdre; **~s** npl (area) étendue f désertique; **~ away** vi dépérir; **~ disposal unit** (BRIT) n broyeur m d'ordures; **~ful** adj gaspilleur(euse); (process) peu économique; **~ ground** (BRIT) n terrain m vague; **~paper basket** n corbeille f à papier; **~ pipe** n (tuyau m de) vidange f

watch [wɒtʃ] n montre f; (act of ~ing) surveillance f; guet m; (MIL: guards) garde f; (NAUT: guards, spell of duty) quart m ♦ vt (look at) observer; (: match, programme, TV) regarder; (spy on, guard) surveiller; (be careful of) faire attention à ♦ vi regarder; (keep guard) monter la garde; **~ out** vi faire attention; **~dog** n chien m de garde; (fig) gardien(ne); **~ful** adj attentif(ive), vigilant(e); **~maker** n horloger(ère); **~man** (irreg) n see **night**; **~strap** n bracelet m de montre

water ['wɔːtə*] n eau f ♦ vt (plant, garden) arroser ♦ vi (eyes) larmoyer; (mouth): **it makes my mouth ~** j'en ai l'eau à la bouche; **in British ~s** dans les eaux territoriales britanniques; **~ down** vt (milk) couper d'eau; (fig: story) édulcorer; **~colour** (US **~color**) n aquarelle f; **~cress** n cresson m

(de fontaine); **~fall** n chute f d'eau; **~ heater** n chauffe-eau m; **~ing can** n arrosoir m; **~ lily** n nénuphar m; **~line** n (NAUT) ligne f de flottaison; **~logged** adj (ground) détrempé(e); **~ main** n canalisation f d'eau; **~melon** n pastèque f; **~proof** adj imperméable; **~shed** n (GEO) ligne f de partage des eaux; (fig) moment m critique, point décisif; **~-skiing** n ski m nautique; **~tight** adj étanche; **~way** n cours m d'eau navigable; **~works** n (building) station f hydraulique; **~y** adj (coffee, soup) trop faible; (eyes) humide, larmoyant(e)

watt [wɒt] n watt m

wave [weɪv] n vague f; (of hand) geste m, signe m; (RADIO) onde f; (in hair) ondulation f ♦ vi faire signe de la main; (flag) flotter au vent; (grass) ondoyer ♦ vt (handkerchief) agiter; (stick) brandir; **~length** n longueur f d'ondes

waver ['weɪvə*] vi vaciller; (voice) trembler; (person) hésiter

wavy ['weɪvɪ] adj ondulé(e); onduleux(euse)

wax [wæks] n cire f; (for skis) fart m ♦ vt cirer; (car) lustrer; (skis) farter ♦ vi (moon) croître; **~works** npl personnages mpl de cire ♦ n musée m de cire

way [weɪ] n chemin m, voie f; (distance) distance f; (direction) chemin m, direction f; (manner) façon f, manière f; (habit) habitude f, façon; **which ~? - this ~** par où? - par ici; **on the ~** (en route) en route; **to be on one's ~** être en route; **to go out of one's ~ to do** (fig) se donner du mal pour faire; **to be in the ~** bloquer le passage; (fig) gêner; **to lose one's ~** perdre son chemin; **under ~** en cours; **in a ~** dans un sens; **in some ~s** à certains égards; **no ~!** (inf) pas question!; **by the ~ ...** à propos ...; **"~ in"** (BRIT) "entrée"; **"~ out"** (BRIT) "sortie"; **the ~ back** le chemin du retour; **"give ~"** (BRIT: AUT) "cédez le passage"; **~lay** ['weɪleɪ] (irreg) vt attaquer

wayward ['weɪwəd] adj capricieux(euse), entêté(e)

we [wiː] pl pron nous

weak [wiːk] adj faible; (health) fragile; (beam etc) peu solide; **~en** vi faiblir, décliner ♦ vt affaiblir; **~ling** n (physically) gringalet m; (morally etc) faible m/f; **~ness** n faiblesse f; (fault) point m faible; **to have a ~ness for** avoir un faible pour

wealth [welθ] n (money, resources) richesse(s) f(pl); (of details) profusion f; **~y** adj riche

wean [wiːn] vt sevrer

weapon ['wepən] n arme f

wear [wɛə*] (pt **wore**, pp **worn**) n (use) usage m; (deterioration through use) usure f; (clothing): **sports/baby~** vêtements mpl de sport/pour bébés ♦ vt (clothes) porter; (put on) mettre; (*damage: through use*) user ♦ *vi* (*last*) faire de l'usage; (*rub etc through*) s'user; **town/evening** ~ tenue *f* de ville/soirée; ~ **away** *vt* user, ronger ♦ *vi* (*inscription*) s'effacer; ~ **down** *vt* (*strength, person*) épuiser; ~ **off** *vi* disparaître; ~ **out** *vt* user; (*person, strength*) épuiser; ~ **and tear** *n* usure *f*

weary ['wɪərɪ] *adj* (*tired*) épuisé(e); (*dispirited*) las(lasse); abattu(e) ♦ *vi*: **to ~ of** se lasser de

weasel ['wiːzl] *n* (*ZOOL*) belette *f*

weather ['weðə*] *n* temps *m* ♦ *vt* (*tempest, crisis*) essuyer, réchapper à, survivre à; **under the ~** (*fig: ill*) mal fichu(e); **~-beaten** *adj* (*person*) hâlé(e); (*building*) dégradé(e) par les intempéries; **~cock** *n* girouette *f*; **~ forecast** *n* prévisions *fpl* météorologiques, météo *f*; **~ man** (*irreg: inf*) *n* météorologue *m*; **~ vane** *n* = **~cock**

weave [wiːv] (*pt* **wove**, *pp* **woven**) *vt* (*cloth*) tisser; (*basket*) tresser; **~r** *n* tisserand(e)

web [web] *n* (*of spider*) toile *f*; (*on foot*) palmure *f*; (*fabric, also fig*) tissu *m*

wed [wed] (*pt, pp* **wedded**) *vt* épouser ♦ *vi* se marier

we'd [wiːd] = **we had**; **we would**

wedding ['wedɪŋ] *n* mariage *m*; **silver/golden** ~ (**anniversary**) noces *fpl* d'argent/d'or; ~ **day** *n* jour *m* du mariage; ~ **dress** *n* robe *f* de mariée; ~ **ring** *n* alliance *f*

wedge [wedʒ] *n* (*of wood etc*) coin *m*, cale *f*; (*of cake*) part *f* ♦ *vt* (*fix*) caler; (*pack tightly*) enfoncer

Wednesday ['wenzdeɪ] *n* mercredi *m*

wee [wiː] *adj* (*SCOTTISH*) petit(e); tout(e) petit(e)

weed [wiːd] *n* mauvaise herbe ♦ *vt* désherber; **~killer** *n* désherbant *m*; **~y** *adj* (*man*) gringalet

week [wiːk] *n* semaine *f*; **a ~ today/on Friday** aujourd'hui/vendredi en huit; **~day** *n* jour *m* de semaine; (*COMM*) jour ouvrable; **~end** *n* week-end *m*; **~ly** *adv* une fois par semaine, chaque semaine ♦ *adj* hebdomadaire ♦ *n* hebdomadaire *m*

weep [wiːp] (*pt, pp* **wept**) *vi* (*person*) pleurer; **~ing willow** *n* saule pleureur

weigh [weɪ] *vt, vi* peser; **to ~ anchor** lever l'ancre; ~ **down** *vt* (*person, animal*) écraser; (*fig: with worry*) accabler; ~ **up** *vt* examiner

weight [weɪt] *n* poids *m*; **to lose/put on** ~ maigrir/grossir; **~ing** *n* (*allowance*) indemnité *f*, allocation *f*; **~-lifter** *n* haltérophile *m*; **~y** *adj* lourd(e); (*important*) de poids, important(e)

weir [wɪə*] *n* barrage *m*

weird [wɪəd] *adj* bizarre

welcome ['welkəm] *adj* bienvenu(e) ♦ *n* accueil *m* ♦ *vt* accueillir; (*also: bid* ~) souhaiter la bienvenue à; (*be glad of*) se réjouir de; **thank you - you're** ~! merci - de rien *or* il n'y a pas de quoi!

weld [weld] *vt* souder; **~er** *n* soudeur(euse)

welfare ['welfɛə*] *n* (*well-being*) bien-être *m*; (*social aid*) assistance sociale; ~ **state** *n* Etat-providence *m*; ~ **work** *n* travail social

well [wel] *n* puits *m* ♦ *adv* bien ♦ *adj*: **to be** ~ aller bien ♦ *excl* eh bien!; bon!; enfin!; **as** ~ aussi, également; **as** ~ **as** (*in addition to*) en plus de; ~ **done!** bravo!; **get** ~ **soon** remets-toi vite!; **to do** ~ bien réussir; (*business*) prospérer; ~ **up** *vi* monter

we'll [wiːl] = **we will**; **we shall**

well: **~-behaved** ['welbɪ'heɪvd] *adj* sage, obéissant(e); **~-being** ['welbiːɪŋ] *n* bien-être *m*; **~-built** ['wel'bɪlt] *adj* (*person*) bien bâti(e); **~-deserved** *adj* (bien) mérité(e); **~-dressed** *adj* bien habillé(e); **~-heeled** (*inf*) *adj* (*wealthy*) nanti(e)

wellingtons ['welɪŋtənz] *npl* (*also: wellington boots*) bottes *fpl* de caoutchouc

well: **~-known** ['wel'nəun] *adj* (*person*) bien connu(e); **~-mannered** ['wel'mænəd] *adj* bien élevé(e); **~-meaning** ['wel'miːnɪŋ] *adj* bien intentionné(e); **~-off** ['wel'ɒf] *adj* aisé(e); **~-read** ['wel'red] *adj* cultivé(e); **~-to-do** ['weltə'duː] *adj* aisé(e); **~-wishers** ['welwɪʃəz] *npl* amis *mpl* et admirateurs *mpl*; (*friends*) amis *mpl*

Welsh [welʃ] *adj* gallois(e) ♦ *n* (*LING*) gallois *m*; **the** ~ *npl* (*people*) les Gallois *mpl*; **~man** (*irreg*) *n* Gallois *m*; ~ **rarebit** *n* toast *m* au fromage; **~woman** (*irreg*) *n* Galloise *f*

went [went] *pt* of **go**

wept [wept] *pt, pp* of **weep**

were [wɜː*] *pt* of **be**

we're [wɪə*] = **we are**

weren't [wɜːnt] = **were not**

west [west] *n* ouest *m* ♦ *adj* ouest *inv*, de *or* à l'ouest ♦ *adv* à *or* vers l'ouest; **the W~** *n* l'Occident *m*, l'Ouest; **the W~ Country** (*BRIT*) *n* le sud-ouest de l'Angleterre; **~erly** *adj* (*wind*) d'ouest; (*point*) à l'ouest; **~ern** *adj* occidental(e), de *or* à l'ouest ♦ *n* (*CINEMA*) western *m*; **W~ Indian** *adj* antillais(e) ♦ *n* Antillais(e); **W~ Indies** *npl* Antilles *fpl*; **~ward(s)** *adv* vers l'ouest

wet [wet] *adj* mouillé(e); (*damp*) humide; (*soaked*) trempé(e); (*rainy*) pluvieux(euse) ♦ *n* (*BRIT: POL*) modéré *m* du parti conservateur; **to get** ~ se mouiller; "~ **paint**" "attention peinture fraîche"; ~ **blanket** *n* (*fig*) rabat-joie *m inv*; ~ **suit** *n* combinaison *f* de plongée

we've [wiːv] = **we have**

whack [wæk] *vt* donner un grand coup à

whale [weɪl] *n* (*ZOOL*) baleine *f*

wharf [wɔːf] (*pl* **wharves**) *n* quai *m*

KEYWORD

what [wɒt] *adj* quel(le); ~ **size is he?** quelle taille fait-il?; ~ **colour is it?** de quelle couleur est-ce?; ~ **books do you need?** quels livres vous faut-il?; ~ **a mess!** quel désordre!

♦ *pron* **1** (*interrogative*) que, *prep* +quoi; ~ **are you doing?** que faites-vous?, qu'est-ce que vous faites?; ~ **is happening?** qu'est-ce qui se passe?, que se passe-t-il?; ~ **are you talking about?** de quoi parlez-vous?; ~ **is it called?** comment est-ce que ça s'appelle?; ~ **about me?** et moi?; ~ **about doing ...?** et si on faisait ...?

2 (*relative: subject*) ce qui; (: *direct object*) ce que; (: *indirect object*) ce +*prep* +quoi, ce dont; **I saw** ~ **you did/was on the table** j'ai vu ce que vous avez fait/ce qui était sur la table; **tell me** ~ **you remember** dites-moi ce dont vous vous souvenez

♦ *excl* (*disbelieving*) quoi!, comment!

whatever [wɒt'evə*] *adj*: ~ **book** quel que soit le livre que (*or* qui) +*sub*; n'importe quel livre ♦ *pron*: **do** ~ **is necessary** faites (tout) ce qui est nécessaire; ~ **happens** quoi qu'il arrive; **no reason** ~ pas la moindre raison; **nothing** ~ rien du tout

whatsoever [wɒt'sɔuevə*] *adj* = **whatever**

wheat [wiːt] *n* blé *m*, froment *m*

wheedle ['wiːdl] *vt*: **to** ~ **sb into doing sth** cajoler *or* enjôler qn pour qu'il fasse qch; **to** ~ **sth out of sb** obtenir qch de qn par des cajoleries

wheel [wiːl] *n* roue *f*; (*also: steering* ~) volant *m*; (*NAUT*) gouvernail *m* ♦ *vt* (*pram etc*) pousser ♦ *vi* (*birds*) tournoyer; (*also:* ~ *round: person*) virevolter; ~**barrow** *n* brouette *f*, ~**chair** *n* fauteuil roulant; ~ **clamp** *n* (*AUT*) sabot *m* (de Denver)

wheeze [wiːz] *vi* respirer bruyamment

KEYWORD

when [wen] *adv* quand; ~ **did he go?** quand est-ce qu'il est parti?

♦ *conj* **1** (*at, during, after the time that*) quand, lorsque; **she was reading** ~ **I came in** elle lisait quand *or* lorsque je suis entré

2 (*on, at which*): **on the day** ~ **I met him** le jour où je l'ai rencontré

3 (*whereas*) alors que; **I thought I was wrong** ~ **in fact I was right** j'ai cru que j'avais tort alors qu'en fait j'avais raison

whenever [wen'evə*] *adv* quand donc ♦ *conj* quand; (*every time that*) chaque fois que

where [wɛə*] *adv, conj* où; **this is** ~ c'est là que; ~**abouts** ['wɛərə'bauts] *adv* où donc ♦ *n*: **nobody knows his** ~**abouts** personne ne sait où il se trouve; ~**as**

[wɛər'æz] *conj* alors que; ~**by** *adv* par lequel (*or* laquelle *etc*); ~**upon** *adv* sur quoi

wherever [wɛər'evə*] *adv* où donc ♦ *conj* où que +*sub*

wherewithal ['wɛəwɪðɔːl] *n* moyens *mpl*

whet [wet] *vt* aiguiser

whether ['weðə*] *conj* si; **I don't know** ~ **to accept or not** je ne sais pas si je dois accepter ou non; **it's doubtful** ~ il est peu probable que +*sub*; ~ **you go or not** que vous y alliez ou non

---

KEYWORD

which [wɪtʃ] *adj* **1** (*interrogative: direct, indirect*) quel(le); ~ **picture do you want?** quel tableau voulez-vous?; ~ **one?** lequel(laquelle)?

2: **in** ~ **case** auquel cas

♦ *pron* **1** (*interrogative*) lequel(laquelle), lesquels(lesquelles) *pl*; **I don't mind** ~ peu importe lequel; ~ (**of these**) **are yours?** lesquels sont à vous?; **tell me** ~ **you want** dites-moi lesquels *or* ceux que vous voulez

2 (*relative: subject*) qui; (: *object*) que, *prep* +lequel(laquelle); **the apple** ~ **you ate/** ~ **is on the table** la pomme que vous avez mangée/qui est sur la table; **the chair on** ~ **you are sitting** la chaise sur laquelle vous êtes assis; **the book of** ~ **you spoke** le livre dont vous avez parlé; **he knew,** ~ **is true/I feared** il le savait, ce qui est vrai/ce que je craignais; **after** ~ après quoi

---

whichever [wɪtʃ'evə*] *adj*: **take** ~ **book you prefer** prenez le livre que vous préférez, peu importe lequel; ~ **book you take** quel que soit le livre que vous preniez

whiff [wɪf] *n* bouffée *f*

while [waɪl] *n* moment *m* ♦ *conj* pendant que; (*as long as*) tant que; (*whereas*) alors que; **bien que** +*sub*; **for a** ~ pendant quelque temps; ~ **away** *vt* (*time*) (faire) passer

whim [wɪm] *n* caprice *m*

whimper ['wɪmpə*] *vi* geindre

whimsical ['wɪmzɪkəl] *adj* (*person*) capricieux(euse); (*look, story*) étrange

whine [waɪn] *vi* gémir, geindre

whip [wɪp] *n* fouet *m*; (*for riding*) cravache *f*; (*POL: person*) chef de file assurant la discipline dans son groupe parlementaire ♦ *vt* fouetter; (*eggs*) battre; (*move quickly*) enlever (*or* sortir) brusquement; ~**ped cream** *n* crème fouettée; ~**-round** (*BRIT*) *n* collecte *f*

whirl [wɜːl] *vt* faire tourbillonner; faire tournoyer ♦ *vi* tourbillonner; (*dancers*) tournoyer; ~**pool** *n* tourbillon *m*; ~**wind** *n* tornade *f*

whirr [wɜː*] *vi* (*motor etc*) ronronner; (: *louder*) vrombir

whisk [wɪsk] *n* (*CULIN*) fouet *m* ♦ *vt* fouetter; (*eggs*) battre; **to** ~ **sb away** *or* **off** emmener qn rapidement

whiskers ['wɪskəz] *npl* (*of animal*) moustaches *fpl*; (*of man*) favoris *mpl*

whisky ['wɪskɪ] (*IRELAND, US* **whiskey**) *n* whisky *m*

whisper ['wɪspə*] *vt, vi* chuchoter

whistle ['wɪsl] *n* (*sound*) sifflement *m*; (*object*) sifflet *m* ♦ *vi* siffler

white [waɪt] *adj* blanc(blanche); (*with fear*) blême ♦ *n* blanc *m*; (*person*) blanc(blanche); ~ **coffee** (*BRIT*) *n* café *m* au lait, (café) crème *m*; ~-**collar worker** *n* employé(e) de bureau; ~ **elephant** *n* (*fig*) objet dispendieux et superflu; ~ **lie** *n* pieux mensonge; ~ **paper** *n* (*POL*) livre blanc; ~**wash** *vt* blanchir à la chaux; (*fig*) blanchir ♦ *n* (*paint*) blanc *m* de chaux

whiting ['waɪtɪŋ] *n inv* (*fish*) merlan *m*

Whitsun ['wɪtsn] *n* la Pentecôte

whittle ['wɪtl] *vt*: **to** ~ **away**, ~ **down** (*costs*) réduire

whizz [wɪz] *vi*: **to** ~ **past** *or* **by** passer à toute vitesse; ~ **kid** (*inf*) *n* petit prodige

who [hu:] *pron* qui; ~**dunit** [hu:'dʌnɪt] (*inf*) *n* roman policier

whoever [hu:'evə*] *pron*: ~ **finds it** celui(celle) qui le trouve(, qui que ce soit), quiconque le trouve; **ask** ~ **you like** demandez à qui vous voulez; ~ **he marries** quelle que soit la personne qu'il épouse; ~ **told you that?** qui a bien pu vous dire ça?

whole [həul] *adj* (*complete*) entier(ère), tout(e); (*not broken*) intact(e), complet(ète) ♦ *n* (*all*): **the** ~ **of** la totalité de, tout(e) le(la); (*entire unit*) tout *m*; **the** ~ **of the town** la ville tout entière; **on the** ~, **as a** ~ dans l'ensemble; ~**food(s)** *n(pl)* aliments complets; ~**hearted** *adj* sans réserve(s); ~**meal** (*BRIT*) *adj* (*bread, flour*) complet(ète); ~**sale** *n* (vente *f* en) gros *m* ♦ *adj* (*price*) de gros; (*destruction*) systématique ♦ *adv* en gros; ~**saler** *n* grossiste *m/f*; ~**some** *adj* sain(e); ~**wheat** *adj* = ~**meal**; **wholly** ['həulɪ] *adv* entièrement, tout à fait

whom [hu:m] *pron* **1** (*interrogative*) qui; ~ **did you see?** qui avez-vous vu?; **to** ~ **did you give it?** à qui l'avez-vous donné?

2 (*relative*) que, *prep* + qui; **the man** ~ **I saw/to** ~ **I spoke** l'homme que j'ai vu/à qui j'ai parlé

whooping cough ['hu:pɪŋ-] *n* coqueluche *f*

whore ['hɔ:*] (*inf: pej*) *n* putain *f*

whose [hu:z] *adj* **1** (*possessive: interrogative*): ~ **book is this?** à qui est ce livre?; ~ **pencil have you taken?** à qui est le crayon que vous avez pris?, c'est le crayon de qui

que vous avez pris?; ~ **daughter are you?** de qui êtes-vous la fille?

2 (*possessive: relative*): **the man** ~ **son you rescued** l'homme dont *or* de qui vous avez sauvé le fils; **the girl** ~ **sister you were speaking to** la fille à la sœur de qui *or* de laquelle vous parliez; **the woman** ~ **car was stolen** la femme dont la voiture a été volée

♦ *pron* à qui; ~ **is this?** à qui est ceci?; **I know** ~ **it is** je sais à qui c'est

why [waɪ] *adv* pourquoi ♦ *excl* eh bien!, tiens!; **the reason** ~ la raison pour laquelle; **tell me** ~ dites-moi pourquoi; ~ **not?** pourquoi pas?; ~**ever** *adv* pourquoi donc, mais pourquoi

wicked ['wɪkɪd] *adj* mauvais(e), méchant(e); (*crime*) pervers(e); (*mischievous*) malicieux(euse)

wicket ['wɪkɪt] *n* (*CRICKET*) guichet *m*; terrain *m* (*entre les deux guichets*)

wide [waɪd] *adj* large; (*area, knowledge*) vaste, très étendu(e); (*choice*) grand(e) ♦ *adv*: **to open** ~ ouvrir tout grand; **to shoot** ~ tirer à côté; ~-**angle lens** *n* objectif *m* grand angle; ~-**awake** *adj* bien éveillé(e); ~**ly** *adv* (*differing*) radicalement; (*spaced*) sur une grande étendue; (*believed*) généralement; (*travel*) beaucoup; ~**n** *vt* élargir ♦ *vi* s'élargir; ~ **open** *adj* grand(e) ouvert(e); ~**spread** *adj* (*belief etc*) très répandu(e)

widow ['wɪdəu] *n* veuve *f*; ~**ed** *adj* veuf(veuve); ~**er** *n* veuf *m*

width [wɪdθ] *n* largeur *f*

wield [wi:ld] *vt* (*sword*) manier; (*power*) exercer

wife [waɪf] (*pl* **wives**) *n* femme *f*, épouse *f*

wig [wɪg] *n* perruque *f*

wiggle ['wɪgl] *vt* agiter, remuer

wild [waɪld] *adj* sauvage; (*sea*) déchaîné(e); (*idea, life*) fou(folle); (*behaviour*) extravagant(e), déchaîné(e); ~**s** *npl* (*remote area*) régions *fpl* sauvages; **to make a** ~ **guess** émettre une hypothèse à tout hasard; ~**erness** ['wɪldənəs] *n* désert *m*, région *f* sauvage; ~-**goose chase** *n* (*fig*) fausse piste; ~**life** *n* (*animals*) faune *f*; ~**ly** *adv* (*behave*) de manière déchaînée; (*applaud*) frénétiquement; (*hit, guess*) au hasard; (*happy*) follement

wilful ['wɪlful] (*US* **willful**) *adj* (*person*) obstiné(e); (*action*) délibéré(e)

will [wɪl] (*vt: pt, pp* **willed**) *aux vb* **1** (*forming future tense*): **I** ~ **finish it tomorrow** je le finirai demain; **I** ~ **have finished it by tomorrow** je l'aurai fini d'ici demain; ~ **you do it? - yes I** ~/**no I won't** le ferez-vous? - oui/non

2 (*in conjectures, predictions*): **he** ~ *or* **he'll**

be there by now il doit être arrivé à l'heure qu'il est; **that ~ be the postman** ça doit être le facteur
3 *(in commands, requests, offers)*: **~ you be quiet!** voulez-vous bien vous taire!; **~ you help me?** est-ce que vous pouvez m'aider?; **~ you have a cup of tea?** voulez-vous une tasse de thé?; **I won't put up with it!** je ne le tolérerai pas!
♦ *vt*: **to ~ sb to do** souhaiter ardemment que qn fasse; **he ~ed himself to go on** par un suprême effort de volonté, il continua
♦ *n* volonté *f*; testament *m*

willing ['wɪlɪŋ] *adj* de bonne volonté, serviable; **he's ~ to do it** il est disposé à le faire, il veut bien le faire; **~ly** *adv* volontiers; **~ness** *n* bonne volonté
willow ['wɪləu] *n* saule *m*
willpower ['wɪl'pauə*] *n* volonté *f*
willy-nilly ['wɪlɪ'nɪlɪ] *adv* bon gré mal gré
wilt [wɪlt] *vi* dépérir; *(flower)* se faner
wily ['waɪlɪ] *adj* rusé(e)
win [wɪn] *(pt, pp won) n (in sports etc)* victoire *f* ♦ *vt* gagner; *(prize)* remporter; *(popularity)* acquérir ♦ *vi* gagner; **~ over** *vt* convaincre; **~ round** *(BRIT) vt* = **~ over**
wince [wɪns] *vi* tressaillir
winch [wɪntʃ] *n* treuil *m*
wind¹ [wɪnd] *n (also MED)* vent *m*; *(breath)* souffle *m* ♦ *vt (take breath)* couper le souffle à
wind² [waɪnd] *(pt, pp wound) vt* enrouler; *(wrap)* envelopper; *(clock, toy)* remonter ♦ *vi (road, river)* serpenter; **~ up** *vt (clock)* remonter; *(debate)* terminer, clôturer
windfall ['wɪndfɔːl] *n* coup *m* de chance
winding ['waɪndɪŋ] *adj (road)* sinueux(euse); *(staircase)* tournant(e)
wind instrument *n (MUS)* instrument *m* à vent
windmill ['wɪndmɪl] *n* moulin *m* à vent
window ['wɪndəu] *n* fenêtre *f*; *(in car, train, also: ~ pane)* vitre *f*; *(in shop etc)* vitrine *f*; **~ box** *n* jardinière *f*; **~ cleaner** *n (person)* laveur(euse) de vitres; **~ ledge** *n* rebord *m* de la fenêtre; **~ pane** *n* vitre *f*, carreau *m*; **~-shopping** *n*: **to go ~-shopping** faire du lèche-vitrines; **~sill** *n (inside)* appui *m* de la fenêtre; *(outside)* rebord *m* de la fenêtre
windpipe ['wɪndpaɪp] *n* trachée *f*
wind power *n* énergie éolienne
windscreen ['wɪndskriːn] *n* pare-brise *m* *inv*; **~ washer** *n* lave-glace *m inv*; **~ wiper** *n* essuie-glace *m inv*
windshield ['wɪndʃiːld] *(US) n* = **windscreen**
windswept ['wɪndswept] *adj* balayé(e) par le vent; *(person)* ébouriffé(e)
windy ['wɪndɪ] *adj* venteux(euse); **it's ~** il y a du vent
wine [waɪn] *n* vin *m*; **~ bar** *n* bar *m* à vin;

~ cellar *n* cave *f* à vin; **~ glass** *n* verre *m* à vin; **~ list** *n* carte *f* des vins; **~ waiter** *n* sommelier *m*
wing [wɪŋ] *n* aile *f*; **~s** *npl (THEATRE)* coulisses *fpl*; **~er** *n (SPORT)* ailier *m*
wink [wɪŋk] *n* clin *m* d'œil ♦ *vi* faire un clin d'œil; *(blink)* cligner des yeux
winner ['wɪnə*] *n* gagnant(e)
winning ['wɪnɪŋ] *adj (team)* gagnant(e); *(goal)* décisif(ive); **~s** *npl* gains *mpl*
winter ['wɪntə*] *n* hiver *m*; **in ~** en hiver; **~ sports** *npl* sports *mpl* d'hiver; **wintry** ['wɪntrɪ] *adj* hivernal(e)
wipe [waɪp] *n*: **to give sth a ~** donner un coup de torchon *(or* de chiffon *or* d'éponge) à qch ♦ *vt* essuyer; *(erase: tape)* effacer; **~ off** *vt* enlever; **~ out** *vt (debt)* éteindre, amortir; *(memory)* effacer; *(destroy)* anéantir; **~ up** *vt* essuyer
wire [waɪə*] *n* fil *m (de fer)*; *(ELEC)* fil électrique; *(TEL)* télégramme *m* ♦ *vt (house)* faire l'installation électrique de; *(also: ~ up)* brancher; *(person: send telegram to)* télégraphier à; **~less** *n (BRIT)* poste *m* de radio; **wiring** ['waɪərɪŋ] *n* installation *f* électrique
wiry ['waɪərɪ] *adj* noueux(euse), nerveux(euse); *(hair)* dru(e)
wisdom ['wɪzdəm] *n* sagesse *f*; *(of action)* prudence *f*; **~ tooth** *n* dent *f* de sagesse
wise [waɪz] *adj* sage, prudent(e); *(remark)* judicieux(euse) ♦ *suffix*: **...wise:** timewise *etc* en ce qui concerne le temps *etc*; **~crack** *n* remarque *f* ironique
wish [wɪʃ] *n (desire)* désir *m*; *(specific desire)* souhait *m*, vœu *m* ♦ *vt* souhaiter, désirer, vouloir; **best ~es** *(on birthday etc)* meilleurs vœux; **with best ~es** *(in letter)* bien amicalement; **to ~ sb goodbye** dire au revoir à qn; **he ~ed me well** il m'a souhaité bonne chance; **to ~ to do/sb to do** désirer *or* vouloir faire/que qn fasse; **to ~ for** souhaiter; **~ful** *adj*: **it's ~ful thinking** c'est prendre ses désirs pour des réalités
wistful ['wɪstful] *adj* mélancolique
wit [wɪt] *n (gen pl)* intelligence *f*, esprit *m*; *(presence of mind)* présence *f* d'esprit; *(wittiness)* esprit; *(person)* homme/femme d'esprit
witch [wɪtʃ] *n* sorcière *f*; **~craft** *n* sorcellerie *f*

--- *KEYWORD*

with [wɪð, wɪθ] *prep* **1** *(in the company of)* avec; *(at the home of)* chez; **we stayed ~ friends** nous avons logé chez des amis; **I'll be ~ you in a minute** je suis à vous dans un instant
2 *(descriptive)*: **a room ~ a view** une chambre avec vue; **the man ~ the grey hat/blue eyes** l'homme au chapeau gris/

aux yeux bleus
3 (*indicating manner, means, cause*): ~
tears in her eyes les larmes aux yeux; **to**
walk ~ a stick marcher avec une canne; **red ~ anger** rouge de colère; **to shake ~**
fear trembler de peur; **to fill sth ~ water**
remplir qch d'eau
4: **I'm ~ you** (*I understand*) je vous suis; **to**
be ~ it (*inf. up to-date*) être dans le vent

withdraw [wɪθˈdrɔː] (*irreg*) *vt* retirer ♦ *vi* se
retirer; ~**al** *n* retrait *m*; ~**al symptoms**
npl (*MED*): **to have ~al symptoms** être en
état de manque; ~**n** *adj* (*person*) renfer-
mé(e)
wither [ˈwɪðə*] *vi* (*plant*) se faner
withhold [wɪθˈhəʊld] (*irreg*) *vt* (*money*) retenir; **to ~** (**from**) (*information*) cacher (à);
(*permission*) refuser (à)
within [wɪðˈɪn] *prep* à l'intérieur de ♦ *adv* à
l'intérieur; ~ **his reach** à sa portée; ~
sight of en vue de; ~ **a kilometre of** à
moins d'un kilomètre de; ~ **the week**
avant la fin de la semaine
without [wɪðˈaʊt] *prep* sans; ~ **a coat** sans
manteau; ~ **speaking** sans parler; **to go ~**
sth se passer de qch
withstand [wɪθˈstænd] (*irreg*) *vt* résister à
witness [ˈwɪtnɪs] *n* (*person*) témoin *m* ♦ *vt*
(*event*) être témoin de; (*document*) attester
l'authenticité de; **to bear ~** (**to**) (*fig*) attester; ~ **box** *n* barre *f* des témoins; ~ **stand**
(*US*) *n* = ~ **box**
witticism [ˈwɪtɪsɪzəm] *n* mot *m* d'esprit;
witty [ˈwɪtɪ] *adj* spirituel(le), plein(e) d'esprit
wives [waɪvz] *npl of* **wife**
wizard [ˈwɪzəd] *n* magicien *m*
wk *abbr* = **week**
wobble [ˈwɒbl] *vi* trembler; (*chair*) branler
woe [wəʊ] *n* malheur *m*
woke [wəʊk] *pt of* **wake**
woken [ˈwəʊkən] *pp of* **wake**
wolf [wʊlf, *pl* wʊlvz] (*pl* **wolves**) *n* loup *m*
woman [ˈwʊmən] (*pl* **women**) *n* femme *f*;
~ **doctor** *n* femme *f* médecin; ~**ly** *adj* fé-
minin(e)
womb [wuːm] *n* (*ANAT*) utérus *m*
women [ˈwɪmɪn] *npl of* **woman**; ~**'s lib**
(*inf*) *n* MLF *m*; **W~'s (Liberation) Move-**
ment *n* mouvement *m* de libération de la
femme
won [wʌn] *pt, pp of* **win**
wonder [ˈwʌndə*] *n* merveille *f*, miracle *m*;
(*feeling*) émerveillement *m* ♦ *vi*: **to ~**
whether/why se demander si/pourquoi; **to**
~ **at** (*marvel*) s'émerveiller de; **to ~ about**
songer à; **it's no ~** (**that**) il n'est pas étonnant (que +*sub*); ~**ful** *adj* mer-
veilleux(euse)
won't [wəʊnt] = **will not**
woo [wuː] *vt* (*woman*) faire la cour à;

(*audience etc*) chercher à plaire à
wood [wʊd] *n* (*timber, forest*) bois *m*; ~
carving *n* sculpture *f* en or sur bois; ~**ed**
adj boisé(e); ~**en** *adj* en bois; (*fig*) raide;
inexpressif(ive); ~**pecker** *n* pic *m* (*oiseau*);
~**wind** *n* (*MUS*): **the ~wind** les bois *mpl*;
~**work** *n* menuiserie *f*; ~**worm** *n* ver *m*
du bois
wool [wʊl] *n* laine *f*; **to pull the ~ over**
sb's eyes (*fig*) en faire accroire à qn; ~**len**
(*US* ~**en**) *adj* de or en laine; (*industry*) lai-
nier(ère); ~**lens** *npl* (*clothes*) lainages *mpl*;
~**ly** (*US* ~**y**) *adj* laineux(euse); (*fig: ideas*)
confus(e)
word [wɜːd] *n* mot *m*; (*promise*) parole *f*;
(*news*) nouvelles *fpl* ♦ *vt* rédiger, formuler;
in other ~s en d'autres termes; **to break/**
keep one's ~ manquer à sa parole/tenir
parole; ~**ing** *n* termes *mpl*; libellé *m*; ~
processing *n* traitement *m* de texte; ~
processor *n* machine *f* de traitement de
texte
wore [wɔː*] *pt of* **wear**
work [wɜːk] *n* travail *m*; (*ART, LITERATU-*
RE) œuvre *f* ♦ *vi* travailler; (*mechanism*)
marcher, fonctionner; (*plan etc*) marcher;
(*medicine*) agir ♦ *vt* (*clay, wood etc*) travailler; (*mine etc*) exploiter; (*machine*) faire
marcher or fonctionner; (*miracles, wonders*
etc) faire; **to be out of ~** être sans emploi;
to ~ loose se défaire, se desserrer; ~ **on**
vt fus travailler à; (*principle*) se baser sur;
(*person*) (essayer d')influencer; ~ **out** *vi*
(*plans etc*) marcher ♦ *vt* (*problem*) résoudre;
(*plan*) élaborer; **it ~s out at £100** ça fait
100 livres; ~ **up** *vt*: **to get ~ed up** se mettre dans tous ses états; ~**able** *adj* (*solution*)
réalisable; ~**aholic** [wɜːkəˈhɒlɪk] *n* bourreau *m* de travail; ~**er** *n* travailleur(euse),
ouvrier(ère); ~**force** *n* main-d'œuvre *f*;
~**ing class** *n* classe ouvrière; ~**ing-class**
adj. ouvrière(ère); ~**ing order** *n*: **in ~ing or-**
der en état de marche; ~**man** (*irreg*) *n* ouvrier *m*; ~**manship** *n* (*skill*) métier *m*, habileté *f*; ~**s** *n* (*BRIT: factory*) usine *f* ♦ *npl*
(*of clock, machine*) mécanisme *m*; ~ **sheet**
n (*COMPUT*) feuille *f* de programmation;
~**shop** *n* atelier *m*; ~ **station** *n* poste *m*
de travail; ~**-to-rule** (*BRIT*) *n* grève *f* du
zèle
world [wɜːld] *n* monde *m* ♦ *cpd* (*champion*)
du monde; (*power, war*) mondial(e); **to**
think the ~ of sb (*fig*) ne jurer que par
qn; ~**ly** *adj* de ce monde; (*knowledgeable*)
qui a l'expérience du monde; ~**wide** *adj*
universel(le)
worm [wɜːm] *n* ver *m*
worn [wɔːn] *pp of* **wear** ♦ *adj* usé(e); ~**-**
out *adj* (*object*) complètement usé(e); (*per-*
son) épuisé(e)
worried [ˈwʌrɪd] *adj* inquiet(ète)
worry [ˈwʌrɪ] *n* souci *m* ♦ *vt* inquiéter ♦ *vi*

s'inquiéter, se faire du souci

worse [wɜːs] *adj* pire, plus mauvais(e) ♦ *adv* plus mal ♦ *n* pire *m*; **a change for the ~** une détérioration; **~n** *vt, vi* empirer; **~ off** *adj* moins à l'aise financièrement; *(fig)*: **you'll be ~ off this way** ça ira moins bien de cette façon

worship ['wɜːʃɪp] *n* culte *m* ♦ *vt (God)* rendre un culte à; *(person)* adorer; **Your W~** *(BRIT: to mayor)* Monsieur le maire; (: *to judge)* Monsieur le juge

worst [wɜːst] *adj* le(la) pire, le(la) plus mauvais(e) ♦ *adv* le plus mal ♦ *n* pire *m*; **at ~** au pis aller

worth [wɜːθ] *n* valeur *f* ♦ *adj*: **to be ~** valoir; **it's ~ it** cela en vaut la peine, ça vaut la peine; **it is ~ one's while (to do)** on gagne (à faire); **~less** *adj* qui ne vaut rien; **~while** *adj (activity, cause)* utile, louable

worthy [wɜːðɪ] *adj (person)* digne; *(motive)* louable; **~ of** digne de

─────────────── KEYWORD

would [wʊd] *aux vb* **1** *(conditional tense)*: **if you asked him he ~ do it** si vous le lui demandiez, il le ferait; **if you had asked him he ~ have done it** si vous le lui aviez demandé, il l'aurait fait

2 *(in offers, invitations, requests)*: **~ you like a biscuit?** voulez-vous *or* voudriez-vous un biscuit?; **~ you close the door please?** voulez-vous fermer la porte, s'il vous plaît?

3 *(in indirect speech)*: **I said I ~ do it** j'ai dit que je le ferais

4 *(emphatic)*: **it WOULD have to snow today!** naturellement il neige aujourd'hui! *or* il faut qu'il neige aujourd'hui!

5 *(insistence)*: **she ~n't do it** elle n'a pas voulu *or* elle a refusé de le faire

6 *(conjecture)*: **it ~ have been midnight** il devait être minuit

7 *(indicating habit)*: **he ~ go there on Mondays** il y allait le lundi

would-be ['wʊdbiː] *(pej) adj* soi-disant
wouldn't ['wʊdnt] = **would not**
wound¹ [wuːnd] *n* blessure *f* ♦ *vt* blesser
wound² [waʊnd] *pt, pp of* **wind²**
wove [wəʊv] *pt of* **weave**
woven ['wəʊvən] *pp of* **weave**
wrap [ræp] *vt (also: ~ up)* envelopper, emballer; *(wind)* enrouler; **~per** *n (BRIT: of book)* couverture *f*; *(on chocolate)* emballage *m*, papier *m*; **~ping paper** *n* papier *m* d'emballage; *(for gift)* papier cadeau
wrath [rɒθ] *n* courroux *m*
wreak [riːk] *vt*: **to ~ havoc (on)** avoir un effet désastreux (sur)
wreath [riːθ, *pl* riːðz] *(pl* ~s) *n* couronne *f*
wreck [rek] *n (ship)* épave *f*; *(vehicle)* véhicule accidenté; *(pej: person)* loque humaine

♦ *vt* démolir; *(fig)* briser, ruiner; **~age** *n* débris *mpl*; *(of building)* décombres *mpl*; *(of ship)* épave *f*
wren [ren] *n (ZOOL)* roitelet *m*
wrench [rentʃ] *n (TECH)* clé *f* (à écrous); *(tug)* violent mouvement de torsion; *(fig)* déchirement *m* ♦ *vt* tirer violemment sur, tordre; **to ~ sth from** arracher qch à *or* de
wrestle ['resl] *vi*: **to ~ (with sb)** lutter (avec qn); **~r** *n* lutteur(euse); **wrestling** *n* lutte *f*; *(also: all-in wrestling)* catch *m*
wretched ['retʃɪd] *adj* misérable; *(inf)* maudit(e)
wriggle ['rɪgl] *vi (also: ~ about)* se tortiller
wring [rɪŋ] *(pt, pp* **wrung)** *vt* tordre; *(wet clothes)* essorer; *(fig)*: **to ~ sth out of sb** arracher qch à qn
wrinkle ['rɪŋkl] *n (on skin)* ride *f*; *(on paper etc)* pli *m* ♦ *vt* plisser ♦ *vi* se plisser
wrist [rɪst] *n* poignet *m*; **~watch** *n* montre-bracelet *f*
writ [rɪt] *n* acte *m* judiciaire
write [raɪt] *(pt* **wrote,** *pp* **written)** *vt, vi* écrire; *(prescription)* rédiger; **~ down** *vt* noter; *(put in writing)* mettre par écrit; **~ off** *vt (debt)* passer aux profits et pertes; *(project)* mettre une croix sur; **~ out** *vt* écrire; **~ up** *vt* rédiger; **~-off** *n* perte totale; **~r** *n* auteur *m*, écrivain *m*
writhe [raɪð] *vi* se tordre
writing ['raɪtɪŋ] *n* écriture *f*; *(of author)* œuvres *fpl*; **in ~** par écrit; **~ paper** *n* papier *m* à lettres
wrong [rɒŋ] *adj (incorrect: answer, information)* faux(fausse); *(inappropriate: choice, action etc)* mauvais(e); *(wicked)* mal; *(unfair)* injuste ♦ *adv* mal ♦ *n* tort *m* ♦ *vt* faire du tort à, léser; **you are ~ to do it** tu as tort de le faire; **you are ~ about that, you've got it ~** tu te trompes; **what's ~?** qu'est-ce qui ne va pas?; **to go ~** *(person)* se tromper; *(plan)* mal tourner; *(machine)* tomber en panne; **to be in the ~** avoir tort; **~ful** *adj* injustifié(e); **~ly** *adv* mal, incorrectement; **~ side** *n (of material)* envers *m*
wrote [rəʊt] *pt of* **write**
wrought [rɔːt] *adj*: **~ iron** fer forgé
wrung [rʌŋ] *pt, pp of* **wring**
wry [raɪ] *adj* désabusé(e)
wt. *abbr* = **weight**

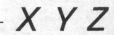

─────────────── X Y Z

Xmas ['eksməs] *n abbr* = **Christmas**
X-ray ['eks'reɪ] *n (ray)* rayon *m* X; *(photo)*

radio(graphie) f

xylophone ['zaɪləfəʊn] n xylophone m

yacht [jɒt] n yacht m; voilier m; ~**ing** n yachting m, navigation f de plaisance; ~**sman** (irreg) n plaisancier m

Yank(ee) [jæŋk(ɪ)] (pej) n Amerloque m/f

yap [jæp] vi (dog) japper

yard [jɑːd] n (of house etc) cour f; (measure) yard m (= 91,4 cm); ~**stick** n (fig) mesure f, critères mpl

yarn [jɑːn] n fil m; (tale) longue histoire

yawn [jɔːn] n bâillement m ♦ vi bâiller; ~**ing** adj (gap) béant(e)

yd. abbr = **yard(s)**

yeah [jɛə] (inf) adv ouais

year [jɪə*] n an m, année f; **to be 8 ~s old** avoir 8 ans; **an eight-~-old child** un enfant de huit ans; ~**ly** adj annuel(le) ♦ adv annuellement

yearn [jɜːn] vi: **to ~ for sth** aspirer à qch, languir après qch; **to ~ to do** aspirer à faire

yeast [jiːst] n levure f

yell [jel] vi hurler

yellow ['jeləʊ] adj jaune

yelp [jelp] vi japper; glapir

yeoman ['jəʊmən] (irreg) n: ~ **of the guard** hallebardier m de la garde royale

yes [jes] adv oui; (answering negative question) si ♦ n oui m; **to say/answer** ~ dire/répondre oui

yesterday ['jestədeɪ] adv hier ♦ n hier m; ~ **morning/evening** hier matin/soir; **all day** ~ toute la journée d'hier

yet [jet] adv encore; déjà ♦ conj pourtant, néanmoins; **it is not finished** ~ ce n'est pas encore fini or toujours pas fini; **the best** ~ le meilleur jusqu'ici or jusque-là; **as** ~ jusqu'ici, encore

yew [juː] n if m

yield [jiːld] n production f, rendement m; rapport m ♦ vt produire, rendre, rapporter; (surrender) céder ♦ vi céder; (US: AUT) céder la priorité

YMCA n abbr (= Young Men's Christian Association) YMCA m

yoghourt ['jɒgət] n yaourt m

yog(h)urt ['jɒgət] n = **yoghourt**

yoke [jəʊk] n joug m

yolk [jəʊk] n jaune m (d'œuf)

c'est à toi or vous que j'ai dit de le faire
4 (after prep, in comparisons) toi; vous; **it's for ~** c'est pour toi or vous; **she's younger than ~** elle est plus jeune que toi or vous
5 (impersonal: one) on; **fresh air does ~ good** l'air frais fait du bien; ~ **never know** on ne sait jamais

you'd [juːd] = **you had**; **you would**

you'll [juːl] = **you will**; **you shall**

young [jʌŋ] adj jeune ♦ npl (of animal) petits mpl; (people): **the** ~ les jeunes, la jeunesse; ~**er** adj (brother etc) cadet(te); ~**ster** n jeune m (garçon m); (child) enfant m/f

your ['jɔː*] adj ton(ta), tes pl; (polite form, pl) votre, vos pl; see also **my**

you're ['jʊə*] = **you are**

yours [jɔːz] pron le(la) tien(ne), les tiens(tiennes); (polite form, pl) le(la) vôtre, les vôtres; ~ **sincerely/faithfully/truly** veuillez agréer l'expression de mes sentiments les meilleurs; see also **mine**[1]

yourself [jɔː'self] pron (reflexive) te; (: polite form) vous; (after prep) toi; vous; (emphatic) toi-même; vous-même; see also **oneself**; **yourselves** pl pron vous; (emphatic) vous-mêmes

youth [juːθ, pl juːðz] n jeunesse f; (young man: pl youths) jeune homme m; ~ **club** n centre m de jeunes; ~**ful** adj jeune; (enthusiasm) de jeunesse, juvénile; ~ **hostel** n auberge f de jeunesse

you've [juːv] = **you have**

YTS (BRIT) n abbr (= Youth Training Scheme) ≈ TUC m

Yugoslav adj yougoslave ♦ n Yougoslave m/f; ~**ia** n Yougoslavie f

yuppie ['jʌpɪ] (inf) n yuppie m/f

YWCA n abbr (= Young Women's Christian Association) YWCA m

zany ['zeɪnɪ] adj farfelu(e), loufoque

zap [zæp] vt (COMPUT) effacer

zeal [ziːl] n zèle m, ferveur f; empressement m

zebra ['ziːbrə] n zèbre m; ~ **crossing** (BRIT) n passage clouté or pour piétons

zero ['zɪərəʊ] n zéro m

zest [zest] n entrain m, élan m; (of orange) zeste m

Zimbabwe [zɪm'bɑːbwɪ] n Zimbabwe m

zinc [zɪŋk] n zinc m

zip [zɪp] n (also: ~ **fastener**) fermeture f éclair (®) ♦ vt (: ~ **up**) fermer avec une fermeture éclair (®); ~ **code** (US) n code postal; ~**per** (US) n = **zip**

zodiac ['zəʊdɪæk] n zodiaque m

zone [zəʊn] n zone f

zoo [zuː] n zoo m

zoom [zuːm] vi: **to ~ past** passer en trombe; ~ **lens** n zoom m

zucchini [zuː'kiːnɪ] n(pl) courgette(s) f(pl)

─── KEYWORD

you [juː] pron **1** (subject) tu; (polite form) vous; (plural) vous; ~ **French enjoy your food** vous autres Français, vous aimez bien manger; ~ **and I will go** toi et moi or vous et moi, nous irons
2 (object: direct, indirect) te, t' +vowel; vous; **I know** ~ je te or vous connais; **I gave it to** ~ je te l'ai donné, je te l'ai donné
3 (stressed) toi; vous; **I told YOU to do it**

Grammar

Using the Grammar

The Grammar section deals systematically and comprehensively with all the information you will need in order to communicate accurately in French. The user-friendly layout explains the grammar point on a left-hand page, leaving the facing page free for illustrative examples. The bracketed numbers, (→1) etc, direct you to the relevant example in every case.

The Grammar section also provides invaluable guidance on the danger of translating English structures by identical structures in French. Use of Numbers and Punctuation are important areas covered towards the end of the section. Finally, the index lists the main words and grammatical terms in both English and French.

Abbreviations

ctd.	continued	**p(p)**	page(s)	**qu**	quelqu'un
fem.	feminine	**perf.**	perfect	**sb**	somebody
infin.	infinitive	**plur.**	plural	**sing.**	singular
masc.	masculine	**qch**	quelque chose	**sth**	something

4 CONTENTS

VERBS
Simple tenses: formation 6
      : first conjugation 8
      : second conjugation 10
      : third conjugation 12
First conjugation spelling irregularities 14
The imperative 20
Compound tenses: formation 22
Reflexive verbs 30
The passive 36
Impersonal verbs 40
The infinitive 44
The present participle 48
Past participle agreement 50
Modal auxiliary verbs 52
Use of tenses 54
The subjunctive: when to use it 58
Verbs governing *à* and *de* 64
Irregular verbs 74

NOUNS
The gender of nouns 132
Formation of feminines 134
Regular feminine endings 136
Formation of plurals 138

ARTICLES
The definite article 140
The partitive article 144
The indefinite article 146

ADJECTIVES
Formation of feminines and plurals 148
Regular feminine endings 150
Irregular feminine forms 152
Comparatives and superlatives 154
Demonstrative adjectives 156
Interrogative and exclamatory adjectives 158
Possessive adjectives 160

Position of adjectives 162

PRONOUNS
Personal pronouns 164
The pronoun *en* 174
The pronoun *y* 176
Indefinite pronouns 178
Relative pronouns 180
Interrogative pronouns 186
Possessive pronouns 192
Demonstrative pronouns 194

ADVERBS
Formation 198
Irregular adverbs 198
Position 200
Comparatives and superlatives 200
Common adverbs and their usage 202

PREPOSITIONS 204

CONJUNCTIONS 212

SENTENCE STRUCTURE
Word order 214
Negatives 216
Question forms 220

USE OF NUMBERS
Cardinal and ordinal numbers 224
Calendar 227
The time 228

TRANSLATION PROBLEMS 230

PRONUNCIATION 236
From spelling to sounds 240
Pronunciation of feminines and plurals 244

ALPHABET 246

INDEX 247

6 VERBS

Simple Tenses: formation

In French the simple tenses are:

Present	(→ 1)
Imperfect	(→ 2)
Future	(→ 3)
Conditional	(→ 4)
Past Historic	(→ 5)
Present Subjunctive	(→ 6)
Imperfect Subjunctive	(→ 7)

They are formed by adding endings to a verb stem. The endings show the number and person of the subject of the verb (→ 8)

The stem and endings of regular verbs are totally predictable. The following sections show all the patterns for regular verbs. For irregular verbs see pp. 74 ff.

Regular Verbs

There are three regular verb patterns (called conjugations), each identifiable by the ending of the infinitive:

● First conjugation verbs end in **-er** e.g. **donner** to give

● Second conjugation verbs end in **-ir** e.g. **finir** to finish

● Third conjugation verbs end in **-re** e.g. **vendre** to sell

These three conjugations are treated in order on the following pages.

Continued

1 **je donne**
I give, I am giving, I do give

2 **je donnais**
I gave, I was giving, I used to give

3 **je donnerai**
I shall give, I shall be giving

4 **je donnerais**
I should/would give, I should/would be giving

5 **je donnai**
I gave

6 **(que) je donne**
(that) I give/gave

7 **(que) je donnasse**
(that) I gave

8 | | |
|---|---|
| **je donne** | I give |
| **nous donnons** | we give |
| **je donnerais** | I would give |
| **nous donnerions** | we would give |

Simple Tenses: First Conjugation

● The stem is formed as follows:

TENSE	FORMATION	EXAMPLE
Present		
Imperfect		
Past Historic	infinitive minus **-er**	**donn-**
Present Subjunctive		
Imperfect Subjunctive		
Future	infinitive	**donner-**
Conditional		

● To the appropriate stem add the following endings:

		PRESENT (→1)	IMPERFECT (→2)	PAST HISTORIC (→3)
sing.	1st person	-e	-ais	-ai
	2nd person	-es	-ais	-as
	3rd person	-e	-ait	-a
plur.	1st person	-ons	-ions	-âmes
	2nd person	-ez	-iez	-âtes
	3rd person	-ent	-aient	-èrent

		PRESENT SUBJUNCTIVE (→4)	IMPERFECT SUBJUNCTIVE (→5)
sing.	1st person	-e	-asse
	2nd person	-es	-asses
	3rd person	-e	-ât
plur.	1st person	-ions	-assions
	2nd person	-iez	-assiez
	3rd person	-ent	-assent

		FUTURE (→6)	CONDITIONAL (→7)
sing.	1st person	-ai	-ais
	2nd person	-as	-ais
	3rd person	-a	-ait
plur.	1st person	-ons	-ions
	2nd person	-ez	-iez
	3rd person	-ont	-aient

1 *PRESENT*		**2** *IMPERFECT*		**3** *PAST HISTORIC*	
je	donne	je	donnais	je	donnai
tu	donnes	tu	donnais	tu	donnas
il	donne	il	donnait	il	donna
elle	donne	elle	donnait	elle	donna
nous	donnons	nous	donnions	nous	donnâmes
vous	donnez	vous	donniez	vous	donnâtes
ils	donnent	ils	donnaient	ils	donnèrent
elles	donnent	elles	donnaient	elles	donnèrent

4 *PRESENT SUBJUNCTIVE*		**5** *IMPERFECT SUBJUNCTIVE*	
je	donne	je	donnasse
tu	donnes	tu	donnasses
il	donne	il	donnât
elle	donne	elle	donnât
nous	donnions	nous	donnassions
vous	donniez	vous	donnassiez
ils	donnent	ils	donnassent
elles	donnent	elles	donnassent

6 *FUTURE*		**7** *CONDITIONAL*	
je	donnerai	je	donnerais
tu	donneras	tu	donnerais
il	donnera	il	donnerait
elle	donnera	elle	donnerait
nous	donnerons	nous	donnerions
vous	donnerez	vous	donneriez
ils	donneront	ils	donneraient
elles	donneront	elles	donneraient

Simple Tenses: Second Conjugation

● The stem is formed as follows:

TENSE	FORMATION	EXAMPLE
Present		
Imperfect		
Past Historic	infinitive minus **-ir**	**fin-**
Present Subjunctive		
Imperfect Subjunctive		
Future	infinitive	**finir-**
Conditional		

● To the appropriate stem add the following endings:

		PRESENT (→**1**)	IMPERFECT (→**2**)	PAST HISTORIC (→**3**)
sing.	1st person	-is	-issais	-is
	2nd person	-is	-issais	-is
	3rd person	-it	-issait	-it
plur.	1st person	-issons	-issions	-îmes
	2nd person	-issez	-issiez	-îtes
	3rd person	-issent	-issaient	-irent

		PRESENT SUBJUNCTIVE (→**4**)	IMPERFECT SUBJUNCTIVE (→**5**)
sing.	1st person	-isse	-isse
	2nd person	-isses	-isses
	3rd person	-isse	-ît
plur.	1st person	-issions	-issions
	2nd person	-issiez	-issiez
	3rd person	-issent	-issent

		FUTURE (→**6**)	CONDITIONAL (→**7**)
sing.	1st person	-ai	-ais
	2nd person	-as	-ais
	3rd person	-a	-ait
plur.	1st person	-ons	-ions
	2nd person	-ez	-iez
	3rd person	-ont	-aient

1	PRESENT	**2**	IMPERFECT	**3**	PAST HISTORIC
je	fin**is**	je	fin**issais**	je	fin**is**
tu	fin**is**	tu	fin**issais**	tu	fin**is**
il	fin**it**	il	fin**issait**	il	fin**it**
elle	fin**it**	elle	fin**issait**	elle	fin**it**
nous	fin**issons**	nous	fin**issions**	nous	fin**îmes**
vous	fin**issez**	vous	fin**issiez**	vous	fin**îtes**
ils	fin**issent**	ils	fin**issaient**	ils	fin**irent**
elles	fin**issent**	elles	fin**issaient**	elles	fin**irent**

4	PRESENT SUBJUNCTIVE	**5**	IMPERFECT SUBJUNCTIVE
je	fin**isse**	je	fin**isse**
tu	fin**isses**	tu	fin**isses**
il	fin**isse**	il	fin**ît**
elle	fin**isse**	elle	fin**ît**
nous	fin**issions**	nous	fin**issions**
vous	fin**issiez**	vous	fin**issiez**
ils	fin**issent**	ils	fin**issent**
elles	fin**issent**	elles	fin**issent**

6	FUTURE	**7**	CONDITIONAL
je	fin**irai**	je	fin**irais**
tu	fin**iras**	tu	fin**irais**
il	fin**ira**	il	fin**irait**
elle	fin**ira**	elle	fin**irait**
nous	fin**irons**	nous	fin**irions**
vous	fin**irez**	vous	fin**iriez**
ils	fin**iront**	ils	fin**iraient**
elles	fin**iront**	elles	fin**iraient**

Simple Tenses: Third Conjugation

● The stem is formed as follows:

TENSE	FORMATION	EXAMPLE
Present		
Imperfect		
Past Historic	infinitive minus -re	vend-
Present Subjunctive		
Imperfect Subjunctive		
Future	infinitive minus -e	vendr-
Conditional		

● To the appropriate stem add the following endings:

		PRESENT (→1)	IMPERFECT (→2)	PAST HISTORIC (→3)
sing.	1st person	-s	-ais	-is
	2nd person	-s	-ais	-is
	3rd person	–	-ait	-it
plur.	1st person	-ons	-ions	-îmes
	2nd person	-ez	-iez	-îtes
	3rd person	-ent	-aient	-irent

		PRESENT SUBJUNCTIVE (→4)	IMPERFECT SUBJUNCTIVE (→5)
sing.	1st person	-e	-isse
	2nd person	-es	-isses
	3rd person	-e	-ît
plur.	1st person	-ions	-issions
	2nd person	-iez	-issiez
	3rd person	-ent	-issent

		FUTURE (→6)	CONDITIONAL (→7)
sing.	1st person	-ai	-ais
	2nd person	-as	-ais
	3rd person	-a	-ait
plur.	1st person	-ons	-ions
	2nd person	-ez	-iez
	3rd person	-ont	-aient

1	*PRESENT*	**2**	*IMPERFECT*	**3**	*PAST HISTORIC*
je	vends	je	vendais	je	vendis
tu	vends	tu	vendais	tu	vendis
il	vend	il	vendait	il	vendit
elle	vend	elle	vendait	elle	vendit
nous	vendons	nous	vendions	nous	vendîmes
vous	vendez	vous	vendiez	vous	vendîtes
ils	vendent	ils	vendaient	ils	vendirent
elles	vendent	elles	vendaient	elles	vendirent

4	*PRESENT SUBJUNCTIVE*	**5**	*IMPERFECT SUBJUNCTIVE*
je	vende	je	vendisse
tu	vendes	tu	vendisses
il	vende	il	vendît
elle	vende	elle	vendît
nous	vendions	nous	vendissions
vous	vendiez	vous	vendissiez
ils	vendent	ils	vendissent
elles	vendent	elles	vendissent

6	*FUTURE*	**7**	*CONDITIONAL*
je	vendrai	je	vendrais
tu	vendras	tu	vendrais
il	vendra	il	vendrait
elle	vendra	elle	vendrait
nous	vendrons	nous	vendrions
vous	vendrez	vous	vendriez
ils	vendront	ils	vendraient
elles	vendront	elles	vendraient

First Conjugation Spelling Irregularities

Before certain endings, the stems of some '-er' verbs may change slightly.

Below, and on subsequent pages, the verb types are identified, and the changes described are illustrated by means of a representative verb.

Verbs ending:	**-cer**
Change:	**c** becomes **ç** before **a** or **o**
Tenses affected:	Present, Imperfect, Past Historic, Imperfect Subjunctive, Present Participle
Model:	**lancer** *to throw* (→ **1**)

● Why the change occurs:
   A cedilla is added to the **c** to retain its soft [s] pronunciation before the vowels **a** and **o**

Verbs ending:	**-ger**
Change:	**g** becomes **ge** before **a** or **o**
Tenses affected:	Present, Imperfect, Past Historic, Imperfect Subjunctive, Present Participle
Model:	**manger** *to eat* (→ **2**)

● Why the change occurs:
   An **e** is added after the **g** to retain its soft [ʒ] pronunciation before the vowels **a** and **o**

Continued

1   *INFINITIVE*   *PRESENT PARTICIPLE*
     lancer   **lançant**

     PRESENT   *IMPERFECT*
     je lance   **je lançais**
     tu lances   **tu lançais**
     il/elle lance   **il/elle lançait**
     nous lançons   nous lancions
     vous lancez   vous lanciez
     ils/elles lancent   **ils/elles lançaient**

     PAST HISTORIC   *IMPERFECT SUBJUNCTIVE*
     je lançai   **je lançasse**
     tu lanças   **tu lançasses**
     il/elle lança   **il/elle lançât**
     nous lançâmes   **nous lançassions**
     vous lançâtes   **vous lançassiez**
     ils/elles lancèrent   **ils/elles lançassent**

2   *INFINITIVE*   *PRESENT PARTICIPLE*
     manger   **mangeant**

     PRESENT   *IMPERFECT*
     je mange   **je mangeais**
     tu manges   **tu mangeais**
     il/elle mange   **il/elle mangeait**
     nous mangeons   nous mangions
     vous mangez   vous mangiez
     ils/elles mangent   **ils/elles mangeaient**

     PAST HISTORIC   *IMPERFECT SUBJUNCTIVE*
     je mangeai   **je mangeasse**
     tu mangeas   **tu mangeasses**
     il/elle mangea   **il/elle mangeât**
     nous mangeâmes   **nous mangeassions**
     vous mangeâtes   **vous mangeassiez**
     ils/elles mangèrent   **ils/elles mangeassent**

First Conjugation Spelling Irregularities (ctd.)

Verbs ending	**-eler**
Change:	**-l** doubles before **-e**, **-es**, **-ent** and throughout the Future and Conditional tenses
Tenses affected:	Present, Present Subjunctive, Future, Conditional
Model:	**appeler** *to call* (→ **1**)

● Exceptions: **geler** *to freeze*
 peler *to peel* } like **mener** (p. 18)

Verbs ending	**-eter**
Change:	**-t** doubles before **-e**, **es**, **-ent** and throughout the Future and Conditional tenses
Tenses affected:	Present, Present Subjunctive, Future, Conditional
Model:	**jeter** *to throw* (→ **2**)

● Exceptions: **acheter** *to buy*
 haleter *to pant* } like **mener** (p. 18)

Verbs ending	**-yer**
Change:	**y** changes to **i** before **-e**, **-es**, **-ent** and throughout the Future and Conditional tenses
Tenses affected:	Present, Present Subjunctive, Future, Conditional
Model:	**essuyer** *to wipe* (→ **3**)

● The change described is optional for verbs ending in **-ayer** e.g. **payer** *to pay*, **essayer** *to try*

Continued

1 *PRESENT (+ SUBJUNCTIVE)*

j'**appelle**
tu **appelles**
il/elle **appelle**
nous appelons
(appelions)
vous appelez
(appeliez)
ils/elles **appellent**

FUTURE

j'**appellerai**
tu **appelleras**
il **appellera** *etc.*

CONDITIONAL

j'**appellerais**
tu **appellerais**
il **appellerait** *etc.*

2 *PRESENT (+ SUBJUNCTIVE)*

je **jette**
tu **jettes**
il/elle **jette**
nous jetons
(jetions)
vous jetez
(jetiez)
ils/elles **jettent**

FUTURE

je **jetterai**
tu **jetteras**
il **jettera** *etc.*

CONDITIONAL

je **jetterais**
tu **jetterais**
il **jetterait** *etc.*

3 *PRESENT (+ SUBJUNCTIVE)*

j'**essuie**
tu **essuies**
il/elle **essuie**
nous essuyons
(essuyions)
vous essuyez
(**essuyiez**)
ils/elles **essuient**

FUTURE

j'**essuierai**
tu **essuieras**
il **essuiera** *etc.*

CONDITIONAL

j'**essuierais**
tu **essuierais**
il **essuierait** *etc.*

First Conjugation Spelling Irregularities (ctd.)

Verbs ending	**mener, peser, lever** etc
Change:	**e** changes to **è**, before **-e, -es, -ent** and throughout the Future and Conditional tenses
Tenses affected:	Present, Present Subjunctive, Future, Conditional
Model:	**mener** *to lead* (→ **1**)

Verbs like:	**céder, régler, espérer** etc
Change:	**é** changes to **è** before **-e, -es, -ent**
Tenses affected:	Present, Present Subjunctive
Model:	**céder** *to yield* (→ **2**)

1   *PRESENT (+ SUBJUNCTIVE)*

je	**mène**
tu	**mènes**
il/elle	**mène**
nous	menons
	(menions)
vous	menez
	(meniez)
ils/elles	**mènent**

FUTURE

je	**mènerai**
tu	**mèneras**
il	**mènera** *etc.*

CONDITIONAL

je	**mènerais**
tu	**mènerais**
il	**mènerait** *etc.*

2   *PRESENT (+ SUBJUNCTIVE)*

je	**cède**
tu	**cèdes**
il/elle	**cède**
nous	cédons
	(cédions)
vous	cédez
	(cédiez)
ils/elles	**cèdent**

The Imperative

The imperative is the form of the verb used to give commands or orders. It can be used politely, as in English 'Shut the door, please'.

The imperative is the same as the present tense **tu**, **nous** and **vous** forms without the subject pronouns:

> **donne***   **finis**   **vends**
> *give*   *finish*   *sell*
> *The final 's' of the present tense of first conjugation verbs is dropped, except before **y** and **en** (→ **1**)

> **donnons**   **finissons**   **vendons**
> *let's give*   *let's finish*   *let's sell*

> **donnez**   **finissez**   **vendez**
> *give*   *finish*   *sell*

● The imperative of irregular verbs is given in the verb tables, pp. 74 ff.

● Position of object pronouns with the imperative:
　in POSITIVE commands: they follow the verb and are attached to it
　　　　　　　　　by hyphens (→ **2**)
　in NEGATIVE commands: they precede the verb and are not
　　　　　　　　　attached to it (→ **3**)

● For the order of object pronouns, see p. 170

● For reflexive verbs – e.g. **se lever** *to get up* – the object pronoun is the reflexive pronoun (→ **4**)

1 Compare: **Tu donnes de l'argent à Paul**
You give (some) money to Paul
and: **Donne de l'argent à Paul**
Give (some) money to Paul

2 **Excusez-moi**
Excuse me
Crois-nous
Believe us
Attendons-la
Let's wait for her/it

Envoyons-les-leur
Let's send them to them
Expliquez-le-moi
Explain it to me
Rends-la-lui
Give it back to him/her

3 **Ne me dérange pas**
Don't disturb me
Ne les négligeons pas
Let's not neglect them
Ne leur répondez pas
Don't answer them

Ne leur en parlons pas
Let's not speak to them about it
N'y pense plus
Don't think about it any more
Ne la lui rends pas
Don't give it back to him/her

4 **Lève-toi**
Get up
Dépêchons-nous
Let's hurry
Levez-vous
Get up

Ne te lève pas
Don't get up
Ne nous affolons pas
Let's not panic
Ne vous levez pas
Don't get up

Compound Tenses: formation

In French the compound tenses are:

Perfect	(→ **1**)
Pluperfect	(→ **2**)
Future Perfect	(→ **3**)
Conditional Perfect	(→ **4**)
Past Anterior	(→ **5**)
Perfect Subjunctive	(→ **6**)
Pluperfect Subjunctive	(→ **7**)

They consist of the past participle of the verb together with an auxiliary verb. Most verbs take the auxiliary **avoir**, but some take **être** (see p. 28).

Compound tenses are formed in exactly the same way for both regular and irregular verbs, the only difference being that irregular verbs may have an irregular past participle.

The Past Participle

For all compound tenses you need to know how to form the past participle of the verb. For regular verbs this is as follows:
● 1st conjugation: replace the **-er** of the infinitive by **-é** (→ **8**)
● 2nd conjugation: replace the **-ir** of the infinitive by **-i** (→ **9**)
● 3rd conjugation: replace the **-re** of the infinitive by **-u** (→ **10**)

● See p. 50 for agreement of past participles.

Continued

with **avoir**

with **être**

1 **j'ai donné**
I gave, have given

je suis tombé
I fell, have fallen

2 **j'avais donné**
I had given

j'étais tombé
I had fallen

3 **j'aurai donné**
I shall have given

je serai tombé
I shall have fallen

4 **j'aurais donné**
I should/would have given

je serais tombé
I should/would have fallen

5 **j'eus donné**
I had given

je fus tombé
I had fallen

6 **(que) j'aie donné**
(that) I gave, have given

(que) je sois tombé
(that) I fell, have fallen

7 **(que) j'eusse donné**
(that) I had given

(que) je fusse tombé
(that) I had fallen

8 **donner → donné**
to give   given

9 **finir → fini**
to finish   finished

10 **vendre → vendu**
to sell   sold

Compound Tenses: formation (ctd.)

Verbs taking the auxiliary avoir

Perfect tense:	the present tense of **avoir** plus the past participle (→ **1**)
Pluperfect tense:	the imperfect tense of **avoir** plus the past participle (→ **2**)
Future Perfect:	the future tense of **avoir** plus the past participle (→ **3**)
Conditional Perfect:	the conditional of **avoir** plus the past participle (→ **4**)
Past Anterior:	the past historic of **avoir** plus the past participle (→ **5**)
Perfect Subjunctive:	the present subjunctive of **avoir** plus the past participle (→ **6**)
Pluperfect Subjunctive:	the imperfect subjunctive of **avoir** plus the past participle (→ **7**)

● For how to form the past participle of regular verbs see p. 22. The past participle of irregular verbs is given for each verb in the verb tables, pp. 74 ff.

● The past participle must agree in number and in gender with any preceding direct object (see p. 50)

Continued

1 *PERFECT*
j'ai donné   nous avons donné
tu as donné   vous avez donné
il/elle a donné   ils/elles ont donné

2 *PLUPERFECT*
j'avais donné   nous avions donné
tu avais donné   vous aviez donné
il/elle avait donné   ils/elles avaient donné

3 *FUTURE PERFECT*
j'aurai donné   nous aurons donné
tu auras donné   vous aurez donné
il/elle aura donné   ils/elles auront donné

4 *CONDITIONAL PERFECT*
j'aurais donné   nous aurions donné
tu aurais donné   vous auriez donné
il/elle aurait donné   ils/elles auraient donné

5 *PAST ANTERIOR*
j'eus donné   nous eûmes donné
tu eus donné   vous eûtes donné
il/elle eut donné   ils/elles eurent donné

6 *PERFECT SUBJUNCTIVE*
j'aie donné   nous ayons donné
tu aies donné   vous ayez donné
il/elle ait donné   ils/elles aient donné

7 *PLUPERFECT SUBJUNCTIVE*
j'eusse donné   nous eussions donné
tu eusses donné   vous eussiez donné
il/elle eût donné   ils/elles eussent donné

Compound Tenses: formation (ctd.)

Verbs taking the auxiliary être

Perfect tense:	the present tense of **être** plus the past participle (→ **1**)
Pluperfect tense:	the imperfect tense of **être** plus the past participle (→ **2**)
Future Perfect:	the future tense of **être** plus the past participle (→ **3**)
Conditional Perfect:	the conditional of **être** plus the past participle (→ **4**)
Past Anterior:	the past historic of **être** plus the past participle (→ **5**)
Perfect Subjunctive:	the present subjunctive of **être** plus the past participle (→ **6**)
Pluperfect Subjunctive:	the imperfect subjunctive of **être** plus the past participle (→ **7**)

● For how to form the past participle of regular verbs see p. 22. The past participle of irregular verbs is given for each verb in the verb tables, pp. 74 ff.

● For agreement of past participles, see p. 50

● For a list of verbs and verb types that take the auxiliary **être**, see p. 28

Continued

1 *PERFECT*

je suis tombé(e)	nous sommes tombé(e)s
tu es tombé(e)	vous êtes tombé(e)(s)
il est tombé	ils sont tombés
elle est tombée	elles sont tombées

2 *PLUPERFECT*

j'étais tombé(e)	nous étions tombé(e)s
tu étais tombé(e)	vous étiez tombé(e)(s)
il était tombé	ils étaient tombés
elle était tombée	elles étaient tombées

3 *FUTURE PERFECT*

je serai tombé(e)	nous serons tombé(e)s
tu seras tombé(e)	vous serez tombé(e)(s)
il sera tombé	ils seront tombés
elle sera tombée	elles seront tombées

4 *CONDITIONAL PERFECT*

je serais tombé(e)	nous serions tombé(e)s
tu serais tombé(e)	vous seriez tombé(e)(s)
il serait tombé	ils seraient tombés
elle serait tombée	elles seraient tombées

5 *PAST ANTERIOR*

je fus tombé(e)	nous fûmes tombé(e)s
tu fus tombé(e)	vous fûtes tombé(e)(s)
il fut tombé	ils furent tombés
elle fut tombée	elles furent tombées

6 *PERFECT SUBJUNCTIVE*

je sois tombé(e)	nous soyons tombé(e)s
tu sois tombé(e)	vous soyez tombé(e)(s)
il soit tombé	ils soient tombés
elle soit tombée	elles soient tombées

7 *PLUPERFECT SUBJUNCTIVE*

je fusse tombé(e)	nous fussions tombé(e)s
tu fusses tombé(e)	vous fussiez tombé(e)(s)
il fût tombé	ils fussent tombés
elle fût tombée	elles fussent tombées

Compound Tenses (ctd.)

The following verbs take the auxiliary être

● Reflexive verbs (see p. 30) (→ **1**)

● The following intransitive verbs (i.e. verbs which cannot take a direct object), largely expressing motion or a change of state:

aller	to go (→ **2**)	**passer**	to pass
arriver	to arrive; to happen	**rentrer**	to go back/in
descendre	to go/come down	**rester**	to stay (→ **5**)
devenir	to become	**retourner**	to go back
entrer	to go/come in	**revenir**	to come back
monter	to go/come up	**sortir**	to go/come out
mourir	to die (→ **3**)	**tomber**	to fall
naître	to be born	**venir**	to come (→ **6**)
partir	to leave (→ **4**)		

● Of these, the following are conjugated with **avoir** when used transitively (i.e. with a direct object):

descendre	to bring/take down
entrer	to bring/take in
monter	to bring/take up (→ **7**)
passer	to pass; to spend (→ **8**)
rentrer	to bring/take in
retourner	to turn over
sortir	to bring/take out (→ **9**)

● Note that the past participle must show an agreement in number and gender whenever the auxiliary is **être** EXCEPT FOR REFLEXIVE VERBS WHERE THE REFLEXIVE PRONOUN IS THE INDIRECT OBJECT (see p. 50)

1 **je me suis arrêté(e)**
I stopped
tu t'es levé(e)
you got up

   elle s'est trompée
   she made a mistake
   ils s'étaient battus
   they had fought (one another)

2 **elle est allée**
she went

3 **ils sont morts**
they died

4 **vous êtes partie**
you left (*addressing a female person*)
vous êtes parties
you left (*addressing more than one female person*)

5 **nous sommes resté(e)s**
we stayed

6 **elles étaient venues**
they [female] had come

7 **Il a monté les valises**
He's taken up the cases

8 **Nous avons passé trois semaines chez elle**
We spent three weeks at her place

9 **Avez-vous sorti la voiture?**
Have you taken the car out?

Reflexive Verbs

A reflexive verb is one accompanied by a reflexive pronoun, e.g. **se lever** to get up; **se laver** to wash (oneself). The pronouns are:

PERSON	SINGULAR	PLURAL
1st	**me (m')**	**nous**
2nd	**te (t')**	**vous**
3rd	**se (s')**	**se (s')**

The forms shown in brackets are used before a vowel, an **h** 'mute', or the pronoun **y** (→ **1**)

● In positive commands, **te** changes to **toi** (→ **2**)

● The reflexive pronoun 'reflects back' to the subject, but it is not always translated in English (→ **3**)
The plural pronouns are sometimes translated as *one another*, *each other* (the 'reciprocal' meaning) (→ **4**)
The reciprocal meaning may be emphasised by **l'un(e) l'autre (les un(e)s les autres)** (→ **5**)

● Simple tenses of reflexive verbs are conjugated in exactly the same way as those of non-reflexive verbs except that the reflexive pronoun is always used. Compound tenses are formed with the auxiliary **être**. A sample reflexive verb is conjugated in full on pp. 34 and 35.

For agreement of past participles, see p. 32

Position of Reflexive Pronouns

● In constructions other than the imperative affirmative the pronoun comes before the verb (→ **6**)

● In the imperative affirmative, the pronoun follows the verb and is attached to it by a hyphen (→ **7**)

Continued

1 **Je m'ennuie**
  I'm bored
  Elle s'habille
  She's getting dressed
  Ils s'y intéressent
  They are interested in it

2 **Assieds-toi**
  Sit down
  Tais-toi
  Be quiet

3 **Je me prépare**
  I'm getting (myself) ready
  Nous nous lavons
  We're washing (ourselves)
  Elle se lève
  She gets up

4 **Nous nous parlons**
  We speak to each other
  Ils se ressemblent
  They resemble one another

5 **Ils se regardent l'un l'autre**
  They are looking at each other

6 **Je me couche tôt**
  I go to bed early
  Comment vous appelez-vous?
  What is your name?
  Il ne s'est pas rasé
  He hasn't shaved
  Ne te dérange pas pour nous
  Don't put yourself out on our account

7 **Dépêche-toi**
  Hurry (up)
  Renseignons-nous
  Let's find out
  Asseyez-vous
  Sit down

Reflexive Verbs (ctd.)

Past Participle Agreement

● In most reflexive verbs the reflexive pronoun is a DIRECT object pronoun (→ **1**)

● When a direct object accompanies the reflexive verb the pronoun is then the INDIRECT object (→ **2**)

● The past participle of a reflexive verb agrees in number and gender with a direct object which *precedes* the verb (usually, but not always, the reflexive pronoun) (→ **3**)
The past participle does not change if the direct object follows the verb (→ **4**)

Here are some common reflexive verbs:

s'en aller	to go away	**se hâter**	to hurry
s'amuser	to enjoy oneself	**se laver**	to wash (oneself)
s'appeler	to be called	**se lever**	to get up
s'arrêter	to stop	**se passer**	to happen
s'asseoir	to sit (down)	**se promener**	to go for a walk
se baigner	to go swimming	**se rappeler**	to remember
se blesser	to hurt oneself	**se ressembler**	to resemble each other
se coucher	to go to bed	**se retourner**	to turn round
se demander	to wonder	**se réveiller**	to wake up
se dépêcher	to hurry	**se sauver**	to run away
se diriger	to make one's way	**se souvenir de**	to remember
s'endormir	to fall asleep	**se taire**	to be quiet
s'ennuyer	to be/get bored	**se tromper**	to be mistaken
se fâcher	to get angry	**se trouver**	to be (situated)
s'habiller	to dress (oneself)		

Continued

1 Je m'appelle
I'm called (*literally: I call myself*)
Asseyez-vous
Sit down (*literally: Seat yourself*)
Ils se lavent
They wash (themselves)

2 Elle se lave les mains
She's washing her hands (*literally: She's washing to herself the hands*)
Je me brosse les dents
I brush my teeth
Nous nous envoyons des cadeaux à Noël
We send presents to each other at Christmas

3 'Je me suis endormi' s'est-il excusé
'I fell asleep', he apologized
Pauline s'est dirigée vers la sortie
Pauline made her way towards the exit
Ils se sont levés vers dix heures
They got up around ten o'clock
Elles se sont excusées de leur erreur
They apologised for their mistake
Est-ce que tu t'es blessée, Cécile?
Have you hurt yourself, Cécile?

4 Elle s'est lavé les cheveux
She (has) washed her hair
Nous nous sommes serré la main
We shook hands
Christine s'est cassé la jambe
Christine has broken her leg

Reflexive Verbs (ctd.)

Conjugation of: **se laver** to wash (oneself)

| SIMPLE TENSES

PRESENT
je me lave	nous nous lavons
tu te laves	vous vous lavez
il/elle se lave	ils/elles se lavent

IMPERFECT
je me lavais	nous nous lavions
tu te lavais	vous vous laviez
il/elle se lavait	ils/elles se lavaient

FUTURE
je me laverai	nous nous laverons
tu te laveras	vous vous laverez
il/elle se lavera	ils/elles se laveront

CONDITIONAL
je me laverais	nous nous laverions
tu te laverais	vous vous laveriez
il/elle se laverait	ils/elles se laveraient

PAST HISTORIC
je me lavai	nous nous lavâmes
tu te lavas	vous vous lavâtes
il/elle se lava	ils/elles se lavèrent

PRESENT SUBJUNCTIVE
je me lave	nous nous lavions
tu te laves	vous vous laviez
il/elle se lave	ils/elles se lavent

IMPERFECT SUBJUNCTIVE
je me lavasse	nous nous lavassions
tu te lavasses	vous vous lavassiez
il/elle se lavât	ils/elles se lavassent

Reflexive Verbs (ctd.)

Conjugation of: **se laver** to wash (oneself)

II   *COMPOUND TENSES*

PERFECT
  je me suis lavé(e)
  tu t'es lavé(e)
  il/elle s'est lavé(e)

  nous nous sommes lavé(e)s
  vous vous êtes lavé(e)(s)
  ils/elles se sont lavé(e)s

PLUPERFECT
  je m'étais lavé(e)
  tu t'étais lavé(e)
  il/elle s'était lavé(e)

  nous nous étions lavé(e)s
  vous vous étiez lavé(e)(s)
  ils/elles s'étaient lavé(e)s

FUTURE PERFECT
  je me serai lavé(e)
  tu te seras lavé(e)
  il/elle se sera lavé(e)

  nous nous serons lavé(e)s
  vous vous serez lavé(e)(s)
  ils/elles se seront lavé(e)s

CONDITIONAL PERFECT
  je me serais lavé(e)
  tu te serais lavé(e)
  il/elle se serait lavé(e)

  nous nous serions lavé(e)s
  vous vous seriez lavé(e)(s)
  ils/elles se seraient lavé(e)s

PAST ANTERIOR
  je me fus lavé(e)
  tu te fus lavé(e)
  il/elle se fut lavé(e)

  nous nous fûmes lavé(e)s
  vous vous fûtes lavé(e)(s)
  ils/elles se furent lavé(e)s

PERFECT SUBJUNCTIVE
  je me sois lavé(e)
  tu te sois lavé(e)
  il/elle se soit lavé(e)

  nous nous soyons lavé(e)s
  vous vous soyez lavé(e)(s)
  ils/elles se soient lavé(e)s

PLUPERFECT SUBJUNCTIVE
  je me fusse lavé(e)
  tu te fusses lavé(e)
  il/elle se fût lavé(e)

  nous nous fussions lavé(e)s
  vous vous fussiez lavé(e)(s)
  ils/elles se fussent lavé(e)s

The Passive

In the passive, the subject *receives* the action (e.g. *I was hit*) as opposed to *performing* it (e.g. *I hit him*). In English the verb 'to be' is used with the past participle. In French the passive is formed in exactly the same way, i.e.:

a tense of **être** + past participle

The past participle agrees in number and gender with the subject (→**1**)

A sample verb is conjugated in the passive voice on pp. 38 and 39.

● The indirect object in French cannot become the subject in the passive:

in **quelqu'un m'a donné un livre** the indirect object **m'** cannot become the subject of a passive verb (unlike English: *someone gave me a book→I was given a book*)

● The passive meaning is often expressed in French by:
  – **on** plus a verb in the active voice (→**2**)
  – a reflexive verb (see p. 30) (→**3**)

Continued

1 **Philippe a été récompensé**
  Phillip has been rewarded
  Cette peinture est très admirée
  This painting is greatly admired
  Ils le feront pourvu qu'ils soient payés
  They'll do it provided they're paid
  Les enfants seront félicités
  The children will be congratulated
  Cette mesure aurait été critiquée si . . .
  This measure would have been criticized if . . .
  Les portes avaient été fermées
  The doors had been closed

2 **On leur a envoyé une lettre**
  They were sent a letter
  On nous a montré le jardin
  We were shown the garden
  On m'a dit que . . .
  I was told that . . .

3 **Ils se vendent 30 francs (la) pièce**
  They are sold for 30 francs each
  Ce mot ne s'emploie plus
  This word is no longer used

The Passive (ctd.)

Conjugation of: **être aimé** *to be liked*

PRESENT

je suis aimé(e)	**nous sommes aimé(e)s**
tu es aimé(e)	**vous êtes aimé(e)(s)**
il/elle est aimé(e)	**ils/elles sont aimé(e)s**

IMPERFECT

j'étais aimé(e)	**nous étions aimé(e)s**
tu étais aimé(e)	**vous étiez aimé(e)(s)**
il/elle était aimé(e)	**ils/elles étaient aimé(e)s**

FUTURE

je serai aimé(e)	**nous serons aimé(e)s**
tu seras aimé(e)	**vous serez aimé(e)(s)**
il/elle sera aimé(e)	**ils/elles seront aimé(e)s**

CONDITIONAL

je serais aimé(e)	**nous serions aimé(e)s**
tu serais aimé(e)	**vous seriez aimé(e)(s)**
il/elle serait aimé(e)	**ils/elles seraient aimé(e)s**

PAST HISTORIC

je fus aimé(e)	**nous fûmes aimé(e)s**
tu fus aimé(e)	**vous fûtes aimé(e)(s)**
il/elle fut aimé(e)	**ils/elles furent aimé(e)s**

PRESENT SUBJUNCTIVE

je sois aimé(e)	**nous soyons aimé(e)s**
tu sois aimé(e)	**vous soyez aimé(e)(s)**
il/elle soit aimé(e)	**ils/elles soient aimé(e)s**

IMPERFECT SUBJUNCTIVE

je fusse aimé(e)	**nous fussions aimé(e)s**
tu fusses aimé(e)	**vous fussiez aimé(e)(s)**
il/elle fût aimé(e)	**ils/elles fussent aimé(e)s**

The Passive (ctd.)

Conjugation of: **être aimé** *to be liked*

PERFECT
j'ai été aimé(e)
tu as été aimé(e)
il/elle a été aimé(e)

nous avons été aimé(e)s
vous avez été aimé(e)(s)
ils/elles ont été aimé(e)s

PLUPERFECT
j'avais été aimé(e)
tu avais été aimé(e)
il/elle avait été aimé(e)

nous avions été aimé(e)s
vous aviez été aimé(e)(s)
ils/elles avaient été aimé(e)s

FUTURE PERFECT
j'aurai été aimé(e)
tu auras été aimé(e)
il/elle aura été aimé(e)

nous aurons été aimé(e)s
vous aurez été aimé(e)(s)
ils/elles auront été aimé(e)s

CONDITIONAL PERFECT
j'aurais été aimé(e)
tu aurais été aimé(e)
il/elle aurait été aimé(e)

nous aurions été aimé(e)s
vous auriez été aimé(e)(s)
ils/elles auraient été aimé(e)s

PAST ANTERIOR
j'eus été aimé(e)
tu eus été aimé(e)
il/elle eut été aimé(e)

nous eûmes été aimé(e)s
vous eûtes été aimé(e)(s)
ils/elles eurent été aimé(e)s

PERFECT SUBJUNCTIVE
j'aie été aimé(e)
tu aies été aimé(e)
il/elle ait été aimé(e)

nous ayons été aimé(e)s
vous ayez été aimé(e)(s)
ils/elles aient été aimé(e)s

PLUPERFECT SUBJUNCTIVE
j'eusse été aimé(e)
tu eusses été aimé(e)
il/elle eût été aimé(e)

nous eussions été aimé(e)s
vous eussiez été aimé(e)(s)
ils/elles eussent été aimé(e)s

Impersonal Verbs

Impersonal verbs are used only in the infinitive and in the third person singular with the subject pronoun **il**, generally translated *it*.

    e.g. **il pleut**
    it's raining
    il est facile de dire que ...
    it's easy to say that ...

The most common impersonal verbs are:

INFINITIVE	CONSTRUCTIONS
s'agir	**il s'agit de** + noun (→**1**) *it's a question/matter of something,* *it's about something* **il s'agit de** + infinitive (→**2**) *it's a question/matter of doing; somebody must do*
falloir	**il faut** + noun object (+ indirect object) (→**3**) *(somebody) needs something, something is necessary (to somebody)* **il faut** + infinitive (+ indirect object) (→**4**) *it is necessary to do* **il faut que** + subjunctive (→**5**) *it is necessary to do, somebody must do*
grêler	**il grêle** *it's hailing*
neiger	**il neige** *it's snowing*
pleuvoir	**il pleut** *it's raining*
tonner	**il tonne** *it's thundering*
valoir mieux	**il vaut mieux** + infinitive (→**7**) *it's better to do* **il vaut mieux que** + subjunctive (→**8**) *it's better to do/that somebody does*

The entries grêler, neiger, pleuvoir and tonner are grouped with a brace marked (→**6**).

Continued

1 **Il ne s'agit pas d'argent**
   It isn't a question/matter of money
   De quoi s'agit-il?
   What is it about?
   Il s'agit de la vie d'une famille au début du siècle
   It's about the life of a family at the turn of the century

2 **Il s'agit de faire vite**
   We must act quickly

3 **Il faut du courage pour faire ça**
   One needs courage to do that; Courage is needed to do that
   Il me faut une chaise de plus
   I need an extra chair

4 **Il faut partir**
   It is necessary to leave; We/I/You must leave*
   Il me fallait prendre une décision
   I had to make a decision

5 **Il faut que vous partiez**
   You have to leave/You must leave
   Il faudrait que je fasse mes valises
   I should have to/ought to pack my cases

6 **Il pleuvait à verse**
   It was raining heavily/It was pouring

7 **Il vaut mieux refuser**
   It's better to refuse; You/He/I had better refuse*
   Il vaudrait mieux rester
   You/We/She had better stay*

8 **Il vaudrait mieux que nous ne venions pas**
   It would be better if we didn't come; We'd better not come

   The translation here obviously depends on context

Impersonal Verbs (ctd.)

The following verbs are also commonly used in impersonal constructions:

INFINITIVE	CONSTRUCTIONS
avoir	**il y a** + noun (→**1**) *there is/are*
être	**il est** + noun (→**2**) *it is; there are* (very literary style) **il est** + adjective + **de** + infinitive (→**3**) *it is*
faire	**il fait** + adjective of weather (→**4**) *it is* **il fait** + noun depicting weather/dark/light etc. *it is* (→**5**)
manquer	**il manque** + noun (+ indirect object) (→**6**) *there is/are ... missing, something is missing/lacking*
paraître	**il paraît que** + subjunctive (→**7**) *it seems/appears that* **il paraît** + indirect object + **que** + indicative (→**8**) *it seems/appears to somebody that*
rester	**il reste** + noun (+ indirect object) (→**9**) *there is/are ... left, (somebody) has something left*
sembler	**il semble que** + subjunctive (→**10**) *it seems/appears that* **il semble** + indirect object + **que** + indicative (→**11**) *it seems/appears to somebody that*
suffire	**il suffit de** + infinitive (→**12**) *it is enough to do* **il suffit de** + noun (→**13**) *something is enough, it only takes something*

Continued

1 **Il y a du pain (qui reste)**
There is some bread (left)
Il n'y avait pas de lettres ce matin
There were no letters this morning

2 **Il est dix heures**
It's ten o'clock
Il est des gens qui ...
There are (some) people who ...

3 **Il était inutile de protester**
It was useless to protest
Il est facile de critiquer
Criticizing is easy

4 **Il fait beau/mauvais**
It's lovely/horrible weather

5 **Il faisait du soleil/du vent**
It was sunny/windy
Il fait jour/nuit
It's light/dark

6 **Il manque deux tasses**
There are two cups missing; Two cups are missing
Il manquait un bouton à sa chemise
His shirt had a button missing

7 **Il paraît qu'ils partent demain**
It appears they are leaving tomorrow

8 **Il nous paraît certain qu'il aura du succès**
It seems certain to us that he'll be successful

9 **Il reste deux miches de pain**
There are two loaves left
Il lui restait cinquante francs
He/She had fifty francs left

10 **Il semble que vous ayez raison**
It seems that you are right

11 **Il me semblait qu'il conduisait trop vite**
It seemed to me (that) he was driving too fast

12 **Il suffit de téléphoner pour réserver une place**
You need only phone to reserve a seat

13 **Il suffit d'une seule erreur pour tout gâcher**
One single error is enough to ruin everything

The Infinitive

The infinitive is the form of the verb found in dictionary entries meaning 'to ...', e.g. **donner** *to give*, **vivre** *to live*.

There are three main types of verbal construction involving the infinitive:

> – with no linking preposition (→**1**)
> – with the linking preposition **à** (→**2**)
>   (see also p. 64)
> – with the linking preposition **de** (→**3**)
>   (see also p. 64)

Verbs followed by an infinitive with no linking preposition

● **devoir, pouvoir, savoir, vouloir** and **falloir** (i.e. modal auxiliary verbs: p. 52) (→**1**)
● **valoir mieux:** see Impersonal Verbs, p. 40
● verbs of seeing or hearing e.g. **voir** *to see*, **entendre** *to hear* (→**4**)
● intransitive verbs of motion e.g. **aller** *to go*, **descendre** *to come/go down* (→**5**)
● **envoyer** *to send* (→**6**)
● **faillir** (→**7**)
● **faire** (→**8**)
● **laisser** *to let, allow* (→**9**)
● The following common verbs:

adorer	*to love*	
aimer	*to like, love*	(→**10**)
aimer mieux	*to prefer*	(→**11**)
compter	*to expect*	
désirer	*to wish, want*	(→**12**)
détester	*to hate*	(→**13**)
espérer	*to hope*	(→**14**)
oser	*to dare*	(→**15**)
préférer	*to prefer*	
sembler	*to seem*	(→**16**)
souhaiter	*to wish*	

Continued

1 **Voulez-vous attendre?**
   Would you like to wait?
2 **J'apprends à nager**
   I'm learning to swim
3 **Essayez de venir**
   Try to come
4 **Il nous a vus arriver**
   He saw us arriving
5 **Allez voir Nicolas**
   Go and see Nicholas
   Descends leur demander
   Go down and ask them
6 **Je l'ai envoyé les voir**
   I sent him to see them
7 **J'ai failli tomber**
   I almost fell
8 **Ne me faites pas rire!**
   Don't make me laugh!
   J'ai fait réparer ma valise
   I've had my case repaired
9 **Laissez-moi passer**
   Let me pass
10 **Il aime nous accompagner**
   He likes to come with us
11 **J'aimerais mieux le choisir moi-même**
   I'd rather choose it myself
12 **Elle ne désire pas venir**
   She doesn't wish to come
13 **Je déteste me lever le matin**
   I hate getting up in the morning
14 **Espérez-vous aller en vacances?**
   Are you hoping to go on holiday?
15 **Nous n'avons pas osé y retourner**
   We haven't dared go back
16 **Vous semblez être inquiet**
   You seem to be worried

On les entend chanter
You can hear them singing

The Infinitive: Set Expressions

The following are set in French with the meaning shown:

aller chercher	*to go for, to go and get*	(→**1**)
envoyer chercher	*to send for*	(→**2**)
entendre dire que	*to hear it said that*	(→**3**)
entendre parler de	*to hear of/about*	(→**4**)
faire entrer	*to show in*	(→**5**)
faire sortir	*to let out*	(→**6**)
faire venir	*to send for*	(→**7**)
laisser tomber	*to drop*	(→**8**)
vouloir dire	*to mean*	(→**9**)

The Perfect Infinitive

● The perfect infinitive is formed using the auxiliary verb **avoir** or **être** as appropriate with the past participle of the verb (→**10**)

● The perfect infinitive is found:
  – following the preposition **après** *after* (→**11**)
  – following certain verbal constructions (→**12**)

1   **Va chercher tes photos**
    Go and get your photos
    Il est allé chercher Alexandre
    He's gone to get Alexander
2   **J'ai envoyé chercher un médecin**
    I've sent for a doctor
3   **J'ai entendu dire qu'il est malade**
    I've heard it said that he's ill
4   **Je n'ai plus entendu parler de lui**
    I didn't hear anything more (said) of him
5   **Fais entrer nos invités**
    Show our guests in
6   **J'ai fait sortir le chat**
    I've let the cat out
7   **Je vous ai fait venir parce que ...**
    I sent for you because ...
8   **Il a laissé tomber le vase**
    He dropped the vase
9   **Qu'est-ce que cela veut dire?**
    What does that mean?
10 **avoir fini**
    to have finished
    être allé   **s'être levé**
    to have gone   to have got up
11 **Après avoir pris cette décision, il nous a appelé**
    After making/having made that decision, he called us
    Après être sorties, elles se sont dirigées vers le parking
    After leaving/having left, they headed for the car park
    Après nous être levé(e)s, nous avons lu les journaux
    After getting up/having got up, we read the papers
12 **pardonner à qn d'avoir fait**
    to forgive sb for doing/having done
    remercier qn d'avoir fait
    to thank sb for doing/having done
    regretter d'avoir fait
    to be sorry for doing/having done

The Present Participle

Formation

- 1st conjugation
  Replace the **-er** of the infinitive by **-ant** (→**1**)

  - Verbs ending in **-cer**: **c** changes to **ç** (→**2**)
  - Verbs ending in **-ger**: **g** changes to **ge** (→**3**)

- 2nd conjugation
  Replace the **-ir** of the infinitive by **-issant** (→**4**)

- 3rd conjugation
  Replace the **-re** of the infinitive by **-ant** (→**5**)

- For irregular present participles, see irregular verbs, p. 74 ff.

Uses

The present participle has a more restricted use in French than in English.

- Used as a verbal form, the present participle is invariable. It is found:
  - on its own, where it corresponds to the English present participle (→**6**)
  - following the preposition **en** (→**7**)
  Note, in particular, the construction:
  verb + **en** + present participle
  which is often translated by an English phrasal verb, i.e. one followed by a preposition like *to run down, to bring up* (→**8**)

- Used as an adjective, the present participle agrees in number and gender with the noun or pronoun (→**9**)

- Note, in particular, the use of **ayant** and **étant** – the present participles of the auxiliary verbs **avoir** and **être** – with a past participle (→**10**)

Continued

1 **donner**   → **donnant**
  to give   giving
2 **lancer**   → **lançant**
  to throw   throwing
3 **manger**   → **mangeant**
  to eat   eating
4 **finir**   → **finissant**
  to finish   finishing
5 **vendre**   → **vendant**
  to sell   selling
6 **David, habitant près de Paris, a la possibilité de ...**
  David, living near Paris, has the opportunity of ...
  Elle, pensant que je serais fâché, a dit '...'
  She, thinking that I would be angry, said '...'
  Ils m'ont suivi, criant à tue-tête
  They followed me, shouting at the top of their voices
7 **En attendant sa sœur, Richard s'est endormi**
  While waiting for his sister, Richard fell asleep
  Téléphone-nous en arrivant chez toi
  Telephone us when you get home
  En appuyant sur ce bouton, on peut ...
  By pressing this button, you can ...
  Il s'est blessé en essayant de sauver un chat
  He hurt himself trying to rescue a cat
8 **sortir en courant**
  to run out (*literally: to go out running*)
  avancer en boîtant
  to limp along (*literally: to go forward limping*)
9 **le soleil couchant**   **une lumière éblouissante**
  the setting sun   a dazzling light
  ils sont déroutants   **elles étaient étonnantes**
  they are disconcerting   they were surprising
10 **Ayant mangé plus tôt, il a pu ...**
  Having eaten earlier, he was able to ...
  Etant arrivée en retard, elle a dû ...
  Having arrived late, she had to ...

Past Participle Agreement

Like adjectives, a past participle must sometimes agree in number and gender with a noun or pronoun. For the rules of agreement, see below. Example: **donné**

	MASCULINE	FEMININE
SING.	donné	donnée
PLUR.	donnés	données

● When the masculine singular form already ends in **-s**, no further **s** is added in the masculine plural, e.g. **pris** *taken*

Rules of Agreement in Compound Tenses

● When the auxiliary verb is **avoir**
The past participle remains in the masculine singular form, unless a direct object precedes the verb. The past participle then agrees in number and gender with the preceding direct object (→**1**)

● When the auxiliary verb is **être**
The past participle of a non-reflexive verb agrees in number and gender with the subject (→**2**)
The past participle of a reflexive verb agrees in number and gender with the reflexive pronoun, if the pronoun is a direct object (→**3**)
No agreement is made if the reflexive pronoun is an indirect object (→**4**)

The Past Participle as an adjective
The past participle agrees in number and gender with the noun or pronoun (→**5**)

1   **Voici le livre que vous avez demandé**
    Here's the book you asked for
    Laquelle avaient-elles choisie?
    Which one had they chosen?
    Ces amis? Je les ai rencontrés à Edimbourg
    Those friends? I met them in Edinburgh
    Il a gardé toutes les lettres qu'elle a écrites
    He has kept all the letters she wrote

2   **Est-ce que ton frère est allé à l'étranger?**
    Did your brother go abroad?
    Elle était restée chez elle
    She had stayed at home
    Ils sont partis dans la matinée
    They left in the morning
    Mes cousines sont revenues hier
    My cousins came back yesterday

3   **Tu t'es rappelé d'acheter du pain, Georges?**
    Did you remember to buy bread, George?
    Martine s'est demandée pourquoi il l'appelait
    Martine wondered why he was calling her
    'Lui et moi nous nous sommes cachés' a-t-elle dit
    'He and I hid,' she said
    Les vendeuses se sont mises en grève
    Shop assistants have gone on strike
    Vous vous êtes brouillés?
    Have you fallen out with each other?
    Les ouvrières s'étaient entraidées
    The workers had helped one another

4   **Elle s'est lavé les mains**
    She washed her hands
    Ils se sont parlé pendant des heures
    They talked to each other for hours

5   **à un moment donné**   **la porte ouverte**
    at a given time   the open door
    ils sont bien connus   **elles semblent fatiguées**
    they are well-known   they seem tired

Modal Auxiliary Verbs

● In French, the modal auxiliary verbs are: **devoir**, **pouvoir**, **savoir**, **vouloir** and **falloir**.

● They are followed by a verb in the infinitive and have the following meanings:

devoir
to have to, must (→**1**)
to be due to (→**2**)
in the conditional/conditional perfect:
should/should have, ought/ought to have (→**3**)

pouvoir
to be able to, can (→**4**)
to be allowed to, can, may (→**5**)
indicating possibility: *may/might/could* (→**6**)

savoir
to know how to, can (→**7**)

vouloir
to want/wish to (→**8**)
to be willing to, will (→**9**)
in polite phrases (→**10**)

falloir
to be necessary: see Impersonal Verbs, p. 40

1 **Je dois leur rendre visite**
I must visit them
Elle a dû partir
She (has) had to leave
Il a dû regretter d'avoir parlé
He must have been sorry he spoke

2 **Vous devez revenir demain**
You're due (to come) back tomorrow
Je devais attraper le train de neuf heures mais ...
I was (supposed) to catch the nine o'clock train but ...

3 **Je devrais le faire**
I ought to do it
J'aurais dû m'excuser
I ought to have apologised

4 **Il ne peut pas lever le bras**
He can't raise his arm
Pouvez-vous réparer cette montre?
Can you mend this watch?

5 **Puis-je les accompagner?**
May I go with them?

6 **Il peut encore changer d'avis**
He may change his mind yet
Cela pourrait être vrai
It could/might be true

7 **Savez-vous conduire?**
Can you drive?
Je ne sais pas faire une omelette
I don't know how to make an omelette

8 **Elle veut rester encore un jour**
She wants to stay another day

9 **Ils ne voulaient pas le faire**
They wouldn't do it/They weren't willing to do it
Ma voiture ne veut pas démarrer
My car won't start

10 **Voulez-vous boire quelque chose?**
Would you like something to drink?

Use of Tenses

The Present

- Unlike English, French does not distinguish between the simple present (e.g. *I smoke, he reads*, we live) and the continuous present (e.g. *I am smoking, he is reading, we are living*) (→ **1**)
- To emphasise continuity, the following constructions may be used:
  être en train de faire ⎫
  être à faire ⎭ *to be doing* (→ **2**)
- French uses the present tense where English uses the perfect in the following cases:
  - with certain prepositions of time – notably **depuis** *for/since* – when an action begun in the past is continued in the present (→ **3**) Note, however, that the perfect is used as in English when the verb is negative or the action has been completed (→ **4**)
  - in the construction **venir de faire** *to have just done* (→ **5**)

The Future

The future is generally used as in English, but note the following:
- Immediate future time is often expressed by means of the present tense of **aller** plus an infinitive (→ **6**)
- In time clauses expressing future action, French uses the future where English uses the present (→ **7**)

The Future Perfect

- Used as in English to mean *shall/will have done* (→ **8**)
- In time clauses expressing future action, where English uses the perfect tense (→ **9**)

Continued

1 **Je fume** I smoke OR I am smoking
  Il lit He reads OR He is reading
  Nous habitons We live OR We are living
2 **Il est en train de travailler**
  He's (busy) working
3 **Paul apprend à nager depuis six mois**
  Paul's been learning to swim for six months (*and still is*)
  Je suis debout depuis sept heures
  I've been up since seven
  Il y a longtemps que vous attendez?
  Have you been waiting long?
  Voilà deux semaines que nous sommes ici
  That's two weeks we've been here (now)
4 **Ils ne se sont pas vus depuis des mois**
  They haven't seen each other for months
  Elle est revenue il y a un an
  She came back a year ago
5 **Elisabeth vient de partir**
  Elizabeth has just left
6 **Tu vas tomber si tu ne fais pas attention**
  You'll fall if you're not careful
  Il va manquer le train
  He's going to miss the train
  Ça va prendre une demi-heure
  It'll take half an hour
7 **Quand il viendra vous serez en vacances**
  When he comes you'll be on holiday
  Faites-nous savoir aussitôt qu'elle arrivera
  Let us know as soon as she arrives
8 **J'aurai fini dans une heure**
  I shall have finished in an hour
9 **Quand tu auras lu ce roman, rends-le-moi**
  When you've read the novel, give it back to me
  Je partirai dès que j'aurai fini
  I'll leave as soon as I've finished

Use of Tenses (ctd.)

The Imperfect
● The imperfect describes:
  – an action (or state) in the past without definite limits in time (→ **1**)
  – habitual action(s) in the past (often translated by means of *would* or *used to*) (→ **2**)
● French uses the imperfect tense where English uses the pluperfect in the following cases:
  – with certain prepositions of time – notably **depuis** *for/ since* – when an action begun in the remoter past was continued in the more recent past (→ **3**)
    Note, however, that the pluperfect *is* used as in English, when the verb is negative or the action has been completed (→ **4**)
  – in the construction **venir de faire** *to have just done* (→ **5**)

The Perfect
● The perfect is used to recount a completed action or event in the past. Note that this corresponds to a perfect tense or a simple past tense in English (→ **6**)

The Past Historic
● Only ever used in *written*, *literary* French, the past historic recounts a completed action in the past, corresponding to a simple past tense in English (→ **7**)

The Past Anterior
This tense is used instead of the pluperfect when a verb in another part of the sentence is in the past historic. That is
● in time clauses, after conjunctions like: **quand**, **lorsque** *when*, **dès que**, **aussitôt que** *as soon as*, **après que** *after* (→ **8**)
● after **à peine** *hardly, scarcely* (→ **9**)

The Subjunctive
● In spoken French, the present subjunctive generally replaces the imperfect subjunctive. See also pp. 58 ff.

1 **Elle regardait par la fenêtre**
She was looking out of the window
Il pleuvait quand je suis sorti de chez moi
It was raining when I left the house
Nos chambres donnaient sur la plage
Our rooms overlooked the beach

2 **Dans sa jeunesse il se levait à l'aube**
In his youth he got up at dawn
Nous causions des heures entières
We would talk for hours on end
Elle te taquinait, n'est-ce pas?
She used to tease you, didn't she?

3 **Nous habitions à Londres depuis deux ans**
We had been living in London for two years (*and still were*)
Il était malade depuis 1985
He had been ill since 1985
Il y avait assez longtemps qu'il le faisait
He had been doing it for quite a long time

4 **Voilà un an que je ne l'avais pas vu**
I hadn't seen him for a year
Il y avait une heure qu'elle était arrivée
She had arrived one hour before

5 **Je venais de les rencontrer**
I had just met them

6 **Nous sommes allés au bord de la mer**
We went/have been to the seaside
Il a refusé de nous aider
He (has) refused to help us
La voiture ne s'est pas arrêtée
The car didn't stop/hasn't stopped

7 **Le roi mourut en 1592**
The king died in 1592

8 **Quand il eut fini, il se leva**
When he had finished, he got up

9 **A peine eut-il parlé qu'on frappa à la porte**
He had scarcely spoken when there was a knock at the door

The Subjunctive: when to use it

(For how to form the subjunctive see pp. 6 ff.)

● After certain conjunctions

quoique
bien que } *although* (→ **1**)

pour que
afin que } *so that* (→ **2**)

pourvu que   *provided that* (→ **3**)
jusqu'à ce que   *until* (→ **4**)
avant que (... ne)   *before* (→ **5**)
à moins que (... ne)   *unless* (→ **6**)
de peur que (... ne)
de crainte que (... ne) } *for fear that, lest* (→ **7**)

Note that the **ne** following the conjunctions in examples **5** to **7** has no translation value. It is often omitted in spoken informal French.

● After the conjunctions

de sorte que
de façon que } *so that* (indicating a *purpose*) (→ **8**)
de manière que

When these conjunctions introduce a *result* and not a *purpose*, the subjunctive is not used (→ **9**)

● After impersonal constructions which express necessity, possibility etc

il faut que
il est nécessaire que } *it is necessary that* (→ **10**)

il est possible que   *it is possible that* (→ **11**)
il semble que   *it seems that* (→ **12**)
il vaut mieux que   *it is better that* (→ **13**)
il est dommage que   *it's a pity that* (→ **14**)

Continued

1 **Bien qu'il fasse beaucoup d'efforts, il est peu récompensé**
Although he makes a lot of effort, he isn't rewarded for it

2 **Demandez un reçu afin que vous puissiez être remboursé**
Ask for a receipt so that you can get a refund

3 **Nous partirons ensemble pourvu que Sylvie soit d'accord**
We'll leave together provided Sylvie agrees

4 **Reste ici jusqu'à ce que nous revenions**
Stay here until we come back

5 **Je le ferai avant que tu ne partes**
I'll do it before you leave

6 **Ce doit être Paul, à moins que je ne me trompe**
That must be Paul, unless I'm mistaken

7 **Parlez bas de peur qu'on ne vous entende**
Speak softly lest anyone hears you

8 **Retournez-vous de sorte que je vous voie**
Turn round so that I can see you

9 **Il refuse de le faire de sorte que je dois le faire moi-même**
He refuses to do it so that I have to do it myself

10 **Il faut que je vous parle immédiatement**
I must speak to you right away/It is necessary that I speak …

11 **Il est possible qu'ils aient raison**
They may be right/It's possible that they are right

12 **Il semble qu'elle ne soit pas venue**
It appears that she hasn't come

13 **Il vaut mieux que vous restiez chez vous**
It's better that you stay at home

14 **Il est dommage qu'elle ait perdu cette adresse**
It's a shame/a pity that she's lost the address

The Subjunctive: when to use it (ctd.)

● After verbs of:
- 'wishing'
  vouloir que
  désirer que } *to wish that, want* (→ **1**)
  souhaiter que

- 'fearing'
  craindre que } *to be afraid that* (→ **2**)
  avoir peur que

Note that **ne** in the first phrase of example 2 has no translation value. It is often omitted in spoken informal French.

- 'ordering', 'forbidding', 'allowing'
  ordonner que *to order that* (→ **3**)
  défendre que *to forbid that* (→ **4**)
  permettre que *to allow that* (→ **5**)

- opinion, expressing uncertainty
  croire que } *to think that* (→ **6**)
  penser que
  douter que *to doubt that* (→ **7**)

- emotion (e.g. regret, shame, pleasure)
  regretter que *to be sorry that* (→ **8**)
  être content/surpris etc **que**
  to be pleased/ surprised etc that (→ **9**)

● After a superlative (→ **10**)

● After certain adjectives expressing some sort of 'uniqueness'
dernier ... **qui/que**	*last* ... *who/that*	
premier ... **qui/que**	*first* ... *who/that*	
meilleur ... **qui/que**	*best* ... *who/that*	(→ **11**)
seul } ... **qui/que**	*only* ... *who/that*	
unique		

Continued

1 **Nous voulons qu'elle soit contente**
  We want her to be happy (*literally: We want that she is happy*)
  Désirez-vous que je le fasse?
  Do you want me to do it?

2 **Il craint qu'il ne soit trop tard**
  He's afraid it may be too late
  Avez-vous peur qu'il ne revienne pas?
  Are you afraid that he won't come back?

3 **Il a ordonné qu'ils soient désormais à l'heure**
  He has ordered that they be on time from now on

4 **Elle défend que vous disiez cela**
  She forbids you to say that

5 **Permettez que nous vous aidions**
  Allow us to help you

6 **Je ne pense pas qu'ils soient venus**
  I don't think they came

7 **Nous doutons qu'il ait dit la vérité**
  We doubt that he told the truth

8 **Je regrette que vous ne puissiez pas venir**
  I'm sorry that you cannot come

9 **Je suis content que vous les aimiez**
  I'm pleased that you like them

10 **la personne la plus sympathique que je connaisse**
   the nicest person I know
   l'article le moins cher que j'aie jamais acheté
   the cheapest item I have ever bought

11 **Voici la dernière lettre qu'elle m'ait écrite**
   This is the last letter she wrote to me
   David est la seule personne qui puisse me conseiller
   David is the only person who can advise me

The Subjunctive: when to use it (ctd.)

● After

si (...) que	*however (...)*	(→ **1**)
qui que	*whoever*	(→ **2**)
quoi que	*whatever*	(→ **3**)

   ● After **que** in the following:
     – to form the 3rd person imperative or to express a wish (→ **4**)
     – when **que** has the meaning *if*, replacing **si** in a clause (→ **5**)
     – when **que** has the meaning *whether* (→ **6**)

● In relative clauses following certain types of indefinite and negative construction (→ **7/8**)

● In set expressions (→ **9**)

1 **si courageux qu'il soit**
   however brave he may be
   si peu que ce soit
   however little it is

2 **Qui que vous soyez, allez-vous-en!**
   Whoever you are, go away!

3 **Quoi que nous fassions, ...**
   Whatever we do, ...

4 **Qu'il entre!**
   Let him come in!
   Que cela vous serve de leçon!
   Let that be a lesson to you!

5 **S'il fait beau et que tu te sentes mieux, nous irons ...**
   If it's nice and you're feeling better, we'll go ...

6 **Que tu viennes ou non, je ...**
   Whether you come or not, I ...

7 **Il cherche une maison qui ait deux caves**
   He's looking for a house which has two cellars
   (*subjunctive used since such a house may or may not exist*)
   J'ai besoin d'un livre qui décrive l'art du mime
   I need a book which describes the art of mime
   (*subjunctive used since such a book may or may not exist*)

8 **Je n'ai rencontré personne qui la connaisse**
   I haven't met anyone who knows her
   Il n'y a rien qui puisse vous empêcher de ...
   There's nothing that can prevent you from ...

9 **Vive le roi!**
   Long live the king!
   Que Dieu vous bénisse!
   God bless you!

Verbs governing à and de

The following lists (pp. 64 to 72) contain common verbal constructions using the prepositions **à** and **de**

Note the following abbreviations:

infin.	infinitive
perf. infin.	perfect infinitive*
qch	quelque chose
qn	quelqu'un
sb	somebody
sth	something

*For formation see p. 46

accuser qn de qch/de + perf. infin.	*to accuse sb of sth/of doing, having done* (→ **1**)
accoutumer qn à qch/à + infin.	*to accustom sb to sth/to doing*
acheter qch à qn	*to buy sth from sb/for sb* (→ **2**)
achever de + infin.	*to end up doing*
aider qn à + infin.	*to help sb to do* (→ **3**)
s'amuser à + infin.	*to have fun doing*
s'apercevoir de qch	*to notice sth* (→ **4**)
apprendre qch à qn	*to teach sb sth*
apprendre à + infin.	*to learn to do* (→ **5**)
apprendre à qn à + infin.	*to teach sb to do* (→ **6**)
s'approcher de qn/qch	*to approach sb/sth* (→ **7**)
arracher qch à qn	*to snatch sth from sb* (→ **8**)
(s')arrêter de + infin.	*to stop doing* (→ **9**)
arriver à + infin.	*to manage to do* (→ **10**)
assister à qch	*to attend sth, be at sth*
s'attendre à + infin.	*to expect to do* (→ **11**)
blâmer qn de qch/de + perf. infin.	*to blame sb for sth/for having done* (→ **12**)
cacher qch à qn	*to hide sth from sb* (→ **13**)
cesser de + infin.	*to stop doing* (→ **14**)

Continued

1 **Il m'a accusé d'avoir menti**
He accused me of lying

2 **Marie-Christine leur a acheté deux billets**
Marie-Christine bought two tickets from/for them

3 **Aidez-moi à porter ces valises**
Help me to carry these cases

4 **Il ne s'est pas aperçu de son erreur**
He didn't notice his mistake

5 **Elle apprend à lire**
She's learning to read

6 **Je lui apprends à nager**
I'm teaching him/her to swim

7 **Elle s'est approchée de moi, en disant '...'**
She came up to me, saying '...'

8 **Le voleur lui a arraché l'argent**
The thief snatched the money from him/her

9 **Arrêtez de faire du bruit!**
Stop being (so) noisy!

10 **Je n'arrive pas à le comprendre**
I can't understand it

11 **Est-ce qu'elle s'attendait à le voir?**
Was she expecting to see him?

12 **Je ne la blâme pas de l'avoir fait**
I don't blame her for doing it

13 **Cache-les-leur!**
Hide them from them!

14 **Est-ce qu'il a cessé de pleuvoir?**
Has it stopped raining?

Verbs governing à and de (ctd.)

changer de qch	to change sth (→ **1**)
se charger de qch/**de** + infin.	to see to sth/undertake to do
chercher à + infin.	to try to do
commander à qn **de** + infin.	to order sb to do (→ **2**)
commencer à/de + infin.	to begin to do (→ **3**)
conseiller à qn **de** + infin.	to advise sb to do (→ **4**)
consentir à qch/**à** + infin.	to agree to sth/to do (→ **5**)
continuer à/de + infin.	to continue to do
craindre de + infin.	to be afraid to do/of doing
décider de + infin.	to decide to (→ **6**)
se décider à + infin.	to make up one's mind to do
défendre à qn **de** + infin.	to forbid sb to do (→ **7**)
demander qch **à** qn	to ask sb sth/for sth (→ **8**)
demander à qn **de** + infin.	to ask sb to do (→ **9**)
se dépêcher de + infin.	to hurry to do
dépendre de qn/qch	to depend on sb/sth
déplaire à qn	to displease sb (→ **10**)
désobéir à qn	to disobey sb (→ **11**)
dire à qn **de** + infin.	to tell sb to do (→ **12**)
dissuader qn **de** + infin.	to dissuade sb from doing
douter de qch	to doubt sth
se douter de qch	to suspect sth
s'efforcer de + infin.	to strive to do
empêcher qn **de** + infin.	to prevent sb from doing (→ **13**)
emprunter qch **à** qn	to borrow sth from sb (→ **14**)
encourager qn **à** + infin.	to encourage sb to do (→ **15**)
enlever qch **à** qn	to take sth away from sb
enseigner qch **à** qn	to teach sb sth
enseigner à qn **à** + infin.	to teach sb to do
entreprendre de + infin.	to undertake to do
essayer de + infin.	to try to do (→ **16**)
éviter de + infin.	to avoid doing (→ **17**)

Continued

1 **J'ai changé d'avis/de robe**
  I changed my mind/my dress
  Il faut changer de train à Toulouse
  You have to change trains at Toulouse

2 **Il leur a commandé de tirer**
  He ordered them to shoot

3 **Il commence à neiger**
  It's starting to snow

4 **Il leur a conseillé d'attendre**
  He advised them to wait

5 **Je n'ai pas consenti à l'aider**
  I haven't agreed to help him/her

6 **Qu'est-ce que vous avez décidé de faire?**
  What have you decided to do?

7 **Je leur ai défendu de sortir**
  I've forbidden them to go out

8 **Je lui ai demandé l'heure**
  I asked him/her the time
  Il lui a demandé un livre
  He asked him/her for a book

9 **Demande à Alain de le faire**
  Ask Alan to do it

10 **Leur attitude lui déplaît**
   He/She doesn't like their attitude

11 **Ils lui désobéissent souvent**
   They often disobey him/her

12 **Dites-leur de se taire**
   Tell them to be quiet

13 **Le bruit m'empêche de travailler**
   The noise is preventing me from working

14 **Puis-je vous emprunter ce stylo?**
   May I borrow this pen from you?

15 **Elle encourage ses enfants à être indépendants**
   She encourages her children to be independent

16 **Essayez d'arriver à l'heure**
   Try to arrive on time

17 **Il évite de lui parler**
   He avoids speaking to him/her

Verbs governing à and de (ctd.)

s'excuser de qch/de + (perf.) infin.	*to apologise for sth/for doing, having done (→ 1)*
exceller à + infin.	*to excel at doing*
se fâcher de qch	*to be annoyed at sth*
feindre de + infin.	*to pretend to do (→ 2)*
féliciter qn **de** qch/de + (perf.) infin.	*to congratulate sb on sth/on doing, having done (→ 3)*
se fier à qn	*to trust sb (→ 4)*
finir de + infin.	*to finish doing (→ 5)*
forcer qn **à** + infin.	*to force sb to do*
habituer qn **à** + infin.	*to accustom sb to doing*
s'habituer à + infin.	*to get/be used to doing (→ 6)*
se hâter de + infin.	*to hurry to do*
hésiter à + infin.	*to hesitate to do*
interdire à qn **de** + infin.	*to forbid sb to do (→ 7)*
s'intéresser à qn/qch/à + infin.	*to be interested in sb/sth/in doing (→ 8)*
inviter qn **à** + infin.	*to invite sb to do (→ 9)*
jouer à (+ sports, games)	*to play (→ 10)*
jouer de (+ musical instruments)	*to play (→ 11)*
jouir de qch	*to enjoy sth (→ 12)*
jurer de + infin.	*to swear to do*
louer qn **de** qch	*to praise sb for sth*
manquer à qn	*to be missed by sb (→ 13)*
manquer de qch	*to lack sth*
manquer de + infin.	*to fail to do (→ 14)*
se marier à qn	*to marry sb*
se méfier de qn	*to distrust sb*
menacer de + infin.	*to threaten to do (→ 15)*
mériter de + infin.	*to deserve to do (→ 16)*
se mettre à + infin.	*to begin to do*
se moquer de qn/qch	*to make fun of sb/sth*
négliger de + infin.	*to fail to do*

Continued

1 **Je m'excuse d'être (arrivé) en retard**
I apologise for being (arriving) late

2 **Elle feint de dormir**
She's pretending to be asleep

3 **Je l'ai félicitée d'avoir gagné**
I congratulated her on winning

4 **Je ne me fie pas à ces gens-là**
I don't trust those people

5 **Avez-vous fini de lire ce journal?**
Have you finished reading this newspaper?

6 **Il s'est habitué à boire moins de café**
He got used to drinking less coffee

7 **Il a interdit aux enfants de jouer avec des allumettes**
He's forbidden the children to play with matches

8 **Elle s'intéresse beaucoup au sport**
She's very interested in sport

9 **Il m'a invitée à danser**
He asked me to dance

10 **Elle joue au tennis et au hockey**
She plays tennis and hockey

11 **Il joue du piano et de la guitare**
He plays the piano and the guitar

12 **Il jouit d'une santé solide**
He enjoys good health

13 **Tu manques à tes parents**
Your parents miss you

14 **Je ne manquerai pas de le lui dire**
I'll be sure to tell him/her about it

15 **Elle a menacé de démissionner tout de suite**
She threatened to resign at once

16 **Ils méritent d'être promus**
They deserve to be promoted

Verbs governing à and de (ctd.)

nuire à qch	*to harm sth (→ 1)*
obéir à qn	*to obey sb*
obliger qn à + infin.	*to oblige sb to do (→ 2)*
s'occuper de qch/qn	*to look after sth/sb (→ 3)*
offrir de + infin.	*to offer to do (→ 4)*
omettre de + infin.	*to fail to do*
ordonner à qn de + infin.	*to order sb to do (→ 5)*
ôter qch à qn	*to take sth away from sb*
oublier de + infin.	*to forget to do*
pardonner qch à qn	*to forgive sb for sth*
pardonner à qn de + perf. infin.	*to forgive sb for having done (→ 6)*
parvenir à + infin.	*to manage to do*
se passer de qch	*to do/go without sth (→ 7)*
penser à qn/qch	*to think about sb/sth (→ 8)*
permettre qch à qn	*to allow sb sth*
permettre à qn de + infin.	*to allow sb to do (→ 9)*
persister à + infin.	*to persist in doing*
persuader qn de + infin.	*to persuade sb to do (→ 10)*
se plaindre de qch	*to complain about sth*
plaire à qn	*to please sb (→ 11)*
pousser qn à + infin.	*to urge sb to do*
prendre qch à qn	*to take sth from sb (→ 12)*
préparer qn à + infin.	*to prepare sb to do*
se préparer à + infin.	*to get ready to do*
prier qn de + infin.	*to beg sb to do*
profiter de qch/de + infin.	*to take advantage of sth/of doing*
promettre à qn de + infin.	*to promise sb to do (→ 13)*
proposer de + infin.	*to suggest doing (→ 14)*
punir qn de qch	*to punish sb for sth (→ 15)*
récompenser qn de qch	*to reward sb for sth*
réfléchir à qch	*to think about sth*
refuser de + infin.	*to refuse to do (→ 16)*

Continued

1 **Ce mode de vie va nuire à sa santé**
This lifestyle will damage her health
2 **Il les a obligés à faire la vaisselle**
He made them do the washing-up
3 **Je m'occupe de ma nièce**
I'm looking after my niece
4 **Stuart a offert de nous accompagner**
Stuart has offered to go with us
5 **Les soldats leur ont ordonné de se rendre**
The soldiers ordered them to give themselves up
6 **Est-ce que tu as pardonné à Charles de t'avoir menti?**
Have you forgiven Charles for lying to you?
7 **Nous nous sommes passés d'électricité pendant plusieurs jours**
We did without electricity for several days
8 **Je pense souvent à toi**
I often think about you
9 **Permettez-moi de continuer, s'il vous plaît**
Allow me to go on, please
10 **Elle nous a persuadés de rester**
She persuaded us to stay
11 **Est-ce que ce genre de film lui plaît?**
Does he/she like this kind of film?
12 **Je lui ai pris son baladeur**
I took his personal stereo from him
13 **Ils ont promis à Pascale de venir**
They promised Pascale that they would come
14 **J'ai proposé de les inviter**
I suggested inviting them
15 **Il a été puni de sa malhonnêteté**
He has been punished for his dishonesty
16 **Il a refusé de coopérer**
He has refused to cooperate

Verbs governing à and de (ctd.)

regretter de + perf. infin.	*to regret doing, having done (→ 1)*
remercier qn de qch/de + perf. infin.	*to thank sb for sth/for doing, having done (→ 2)*
renoncer à qch/à + infin.	*to give sth up/give up doing*
reprocher qch à qn	*to reproach sb with/for sth (→ 3)*
résister à qch	*to resist sth (→ 4)*
résoudre de + infin.	*to resolve to do*
ressembler à qn/qch	*to look/be like sb/sth (→ 5)*
réussir à + infin.	*to manage to do (→ 6)*
rire de qn/qch	*to laugh at sb/sth*
risquer de + infin.	*to risk doing (→ 7)*
servir à qch/à + infin.	*to be used for sth/for doing (→ 8)*
se servir de qch	*to use sth; to help oneself to sth (→ 9)*
songer à + infin.	*to think of doing*
se souvenir de qn/qch/de + perf. infin.	*to remember sb/sth/doing, having done (→ 10)*
succéder à qn	*to succeed sb*
survivre à qn	*to outlive sb (→ 11)*
tâcher de + infin.	*to try to do (→ 12)*
tarder à + infin.	*to delay doing (→ 13)*
tendre à + infin.	*to tend to do*
tenir à + infin.	*to be keen to do (→ 14)*
tenter de + infin.	*to try to do (→ 15)*
se tromper de qch	*to be wrong about sth (→ 16)*
venir de* + infin.	*to have just done (→ 17)*
vivre de qch	*to live on sth*
voler qch à qn	*to steal sth from sb*

*See also Use of Tenses, pp. 54 and 56

1 **Je regrette de ne pas vous avoir écrit plus tôt**
   I'm sorry for not writing to you sooner

2 **Nous les avons remerciés de leur gentillesse**
   We thanked them for their kindness

3 **On lui reproche son manque d'enthousiasme**
   They're reproaching him for his lack of enthusiasm

4 **Comment résistez-vous à la tentation?**
   How do you resist temptation?

5 **Elles ressemblent beaucoup à leur mère**
   They look very like their mother

6 **Vous avez réussi à me convaincre**
   You've managed to convince me

7 **Vous risquez de tomber en faisant cela**
   You risk falling doing that

8 **Ce bouton sert à régler le volume**
   This knob is (used) for adjusting the volume

9 **Il s'est servi d'un tournevis pour l'ouvrir**
   He used a screwdriver to open it

10 **Vous vous souvenez de Lucienne?**
   Do you remember Lucienne?
   Il ne se souvient pas de l'avoir perdu
   He doesn't remember losing it

11 **Elle a survécu à son mari**
   She outlived her husband

12 **Tâchez de ne pas être en retard!**
   Try not to be late!

13 **Il n'a pas tardé à prendre une décision**
   He was not long in taking a decision

14 **Elle tient à le faire elle-même**
   She's keen to do it herself

15 **J'ai tenté de la comprendre**
   I've tried to understand her

16 **Je me suis trompé de route**
   I took the wrong road

17 **Mon père vient de téléphoner**   **Nous venions d'arriver**
   My father's just phoned   We had just arrived

Irregular Verbs

The verbs listed opposite and conjugated on pp. 76 to 131 provide the main patterns for irregular verbs. The verbs are grouped opposite according to their infinitive ending (except **avoir** and **être**), and are shown in the following tables in alphabetical order.

In the tables, the most important irregular verbs are given in their most common simple tenses, together with the imperative and the present participle.

The auxiliary (**avoir** or **être**) is also shown for each verb, together with the past participle, to enable you to form all the compound tenses, as on pp. 24 and 26.

● For a fuller list of irregular verbs, the reader is referred to Collins Gem French Verb Tables, which shows you how to conjugate some 2000 French verbs.

Continued

avoir
être

'-er':	aller	'-re':	battre
	envoyer		boire
			connaître
'-ir':	acquérir		coudre
	bouillir		craindre
	courir		croire
	cueillir		croître
	dormir		cuire
	fuir		dire
	haïr		écrire
	mourir		faire
	ouvrir		lire
	partir		mettre
	sentir		moudre
	servir		naître
	sortir		paraître
	tenir		plaire
	venir		prendre
	vêtir		résoudre
			rire
'-oir':	s'asseoir		rompre
	devoir		suffire
	falloir		suivre
	pleuvoir		se taire
	pouvoir		vaincre
	recevoir		vivre
	savoir		
	valoir		
	voir		
	vouloir		

acquérir *to acquire*

Auxiliary: **avoir**

PAST PARTICIPLE
acquis

PRESENT PARTICIPLE
acquérant

IMPERATIVE
acquiers
acquérons
acquérez

PRESENT

j'	**acquiers**
tu	**acquiers**
il	**acquiert**
nous	**acquérons**
vous	**acquérez**
ils	**acquierent**

FUTURE

j'	**acquerrai**
tu	**acquerras**
il	**acquerra**
nous	**acquerrons**
vous	**acquerrez**
ils	**acquerront**

PRESENT SUBJUNCTIVE

j'	**acquière**
tu	**acquières**
il	**acquière**
nous	**acquérions**
vous	**acquériez**
ils	**acquièrent**

IMPERFECT

j'	**acquérais**
tu	**acquérais**
il	**acquérait**
nous	**acquérions**
vous	**acquériez**
ils	**acquéraient**

CONDITIONAL

j'	**acquerrais**
tu	**acquerrais**
il	**acquerrait**
nous	**acquerrions**
vous	**acquerriez**
ils	**acquerraient**

PAST HISTORIC

j'	**acquis**
tu	**acquis**
il	**acquit**
nous	**acquîmes**
vous	**acquîtes**
ils	**acquirent**

aller *to go*   Auxiliary: **être**

PAST PARTICIPLE
  allé

PRESENT PARTICIPLE
  allant

IMPERATIVE
  va
  allons
  allez

PRESENT		IMPERFECT	
je	**vais**		j'allais
tu	**vas**	tu	allais
il	**va**	il	allait
nous	allons	nous	allions
vous	allez	vous	alliez
ils	**vont**	ils	allaient

FUTURE		CONDITIONAL	
	j'irai		j'irais
tu	iras	tu	irais
il	ira	il	irait
nous	irons	nous	irions
vous	irez	vous	iriez
ils	iront	ils	iraient

PRESENT SUBJUNCTIVE		PAST HISTORIC	
	j'aille		j'allai
tu	ailles	tu	allas
il	aille	il	alla
nous	allions	nous	allâmes
vous	alliez	vous	allâtes
ils	aillent	ils	allèrent

s'asseoir *to sit down* Auxiliary: **être**

PAST PARTICIPLE
assis

PRESENT PARTICIPLE
s'asseyant

IMPERATIVE
assieds-toi
asseyons-nous
asseyez-vous

PRESENT
je	m'assieds *or* assois
tu	t'assieds *or* assois
il	s'assied *or* assoit
nous	nous asseyons *or* assoyons
vous	vous asseyez *or* assoyez
ils	s'asseyent *or* assoient

IMPERFECT
je	m'asseyais
tu	t'asseyais
il	s'asseyait
nous	nous asseyions
vous	vous asseyiez
ils	s'asseyaient

FUTURE
je	m'assiérai
tu	t'assiéras
il	s'assiéra
nous	nous assiérons
vous	vous assiérez
ils	s'assiéront

CONDITIONAL
je	m'assiérais
tu	t'assiérais
il	s'assiérait
nous	nous assiérions
vous	vous assiériez
ils	s'assiéraient

PRESENT SUBJUNCTIVE
je	m'asseye
tu	t'asseyes
il	s'asseye
nous	nous asseyions
vous	vous asseyiez
ils	s'asseyent

PAST HISTORIC
je	m'assis
tu	t'assis
il	s'assit
nous	nous assîmes
vous	vous assîtes
ils	s'assirent

avoir *to have*　　　　　Auxiliary: **avoir**

PAST PARTICIPLE
eu

PRESENT PARTICIPLE
ayant

IMPERATIVE
aie
ayons
ayez

PRESENT
j'**ai**
tu **as**
il **a**
nous **avons**
vous **avez**
ils **ont**

IMPERFECT
j'**avais**
tu **avais**
il **avait**
nous **avions**
vous **aviez**
ils **avaient**

FUTURE
j'**aurai**
tu **auras**
il **aura**
nous **aurons**
vous **aurez**
ils **auront**

CONDITIONAL
j'**aurais**
tu **aurais**
il **aurait**
nous **aurions**
vous **auriez**
ils **auraient**

PRESENT SUBJUNCTIVE
j'**aie**
tu **aies**
il **ait**
nous **ayons**
vous **ayez**
ils **aient**

PAST HISTORIC
j'**eus**
tu **eus**
il **eut**
nous **eûmes**
vous **eûtes**
ils **eurent**

battre *to beat*   Auxiliary: **avoir**

PAST PARTICIPLE
  battu

IMPERATIVE
  bats
  battons
  battez

PRESENT PARTICIPLE
  battant

PRESENT

je	**bats**
tu	**bats**
il	**bat**
nous	battons
vous	battez
ils	battent

IMPERFECT

je	battais
tu	battais
il	battait
nous	battions
vous	battiez
ils	battaient

FUTURE

je	battrai
tu	battras
il	battra
nous	battrons
vous	battrez
ils	battront

CONDITIONAL

je	battrais
tu	battrais
il	battrait
nous	battrions
vous	battriez
ils	battraient

PRESENT SUBJUNCTIVE

je	batte
tu	battes
il	batte
nous	battions
vous	battiez
ils	battent

PAST HISTORIC

je	battis
tu	battis
il	battit
nous	battîmes
vous	battîtes
ils	battirent

boire *to drink*　　　　　　　　Auxiliary: **avoir**

PAST PARTICIPLE
bu

PRESENT PARTICIPLE
buvant

IMPERATIVE
bois
buvons
buvez

PRESENT
je	bois
tu	bois
il	boit
nous	**buvons**
vous	**buvez**
ils	**boivent**

IMPERFECT
je	**buvais**
tu	**buvais**
il	**buvait**
nous	**buvions**
vous	**buviez**
ils	**buvaient**

FUTURE
je	boirai
tu	boiras
il	boira
nous	boirons
vous	boirez
ils	boiront

CONDITIONAL
je	boirais
tu	boirais
il	boirait
nous	boirions
vous	boiriez
ils	boiraient

PRESENT SUBJUNCTIVE
je	**boive**
tu	**boives**
il	**boive**
nous	**buvions**
vous	**buviez**
ils	**boivent**

PAST HISTORIC
je	**bus**
tu	**bus**
il	**but**
nous	**bûmes**
vous	**bûtes**
ils	**burent**

bouillir *to boil*   Auxiliary: **avoir**

PAST PARTICIPLE bouilli	*IMPERATIVE* **bous** **bouillons** **bouillez**
PRESENT PARTICIPLE **bouillant**	

PRESENT
je **bous**
tu **bous**
il **bout**
nous **bouillons**
vous **bouillez**
ils **bouillent**

IMPERFECT
je **bouillais**
tu **bouillais**
il **bouillait**
nous **bouillions**
vous **bouilliez**
ils **bouillaient**

FUTURE
je bouillirai
tu bouilliras
il bouillira
nous bouillirons
vous bouillirez
ils bouilliront

CONDITIONAL
je bouillirais
tu bouillirais
il bouillirait
nous bouillirions
vous bouilliriez
ils bouilliraient

PRESENT SUBJUNCTIVE
je **bouille**
tu **bouilles**
il **bouille**
nous **bouillions**
vous **bouilliez**
ils **bouillent**

PAST HISTORIC
je bouillis
tu bouillis
il bouillit
nous bouillîmes
vous bouillîtes
ils bouillirent

connaître *to know*   Auxiliary: **avoir**

PAST PARTICIPLE
connu

PRESENT PARTICIPLE
connaissant

IMPERATIVE
connais
connaissons
connaissez

PRESENT
je	**connais**
tu	**connais**
il	connaît
nous	**connaissons**
vous	**connaissez**
ils	**connaissent**

IMPERFECT
je	**connaissais**
tu	**connaissais**
il	**connaissait**
nous	**connaissions**
vous	**connaissiez**
ils	**connaissaient**

FUTURE
je	connaîtrai
tu	connaîtras
il	connaîtra
nous	connaîtrons
vous	connaîtrez
ils	connaîtront

CONDITIONAL
je	connaîtrais
tu	connaîtrais
il	connaîtrait
nous	connaîtrions
vous	connaîtriez
ils	connaîtraient

PRESENT SUBJUNCTIVE
je	**connaisse**
tu	**connaisses**
il	**connaisse**
nous	**connaissions**
vous	**connaissiez**
ils	**connaissent**

PAST HISTORIC
je	**connus**
tu	**connus**
il	**connut**
nous	**connûmes**
vous	**connûtes**
ils	**connurent**

coudre *to sew* Auxiliary: **avoir**

PAST PARTICIPLE
cousu

PRESENT PARTICIPLE
cousant

IMPERATIVE
couds
cousons
cousez

PRESENT
je	couds
tu	couds
il	coud
nous	**cousons**
vous	**cousez**
ils	**cousent**

IMPERFECT
je	**cousais**
tu	**cousais**
il	**cousait**
nous	**cousions**
vous	**cousiez**
ils	**cousaient**

FUTURE
je	coudrai
tu	coudras
il	coudra
nous	coudrons
vous	coudrez
ils	coudront

CONDITIONAL
je	coudrais
tu	coudrais
il	coudrait
nous	coudrions
vous	coudriez
ils	coudraient

PRESENT SUBJUNCTIVE
je	**couse**
tu	**couses**
il	**couse**
nous	**cousions**
vous	**cousiez**
ils	**cousent**

PAST HISTORIC
je	**cousis**
tu	**cousis**
il	**cousit**
nous	**cousîmes**
vous	**cousîtes**
ils	**cousirent**

courir *to run*   Auxiliary: **avoir**

PAST PARTICIPLE
couru

PRESENT PARTICIPLE
courant

IMPERATIVE
cours
courons
courez

PRESENT
je	**cours**
tu	**cours**
il	**court**
nous	**courons**
vous	**courez**
ils	**courent**

IMPERFECT
je	**courais**
tu	**courais**
il	**courait**
nous	**courions**
vous	**couriez**
ils	**couraient**

FUTURE
je	**courrai**
tu	**courras**
il	**courra**
nous	**courrons**
vous	**courrez**
ils	**courront**

CONDITIONAL
je	**courrais**
tu	**courrais**
il	**courrait**
nous	**courrions**
vous	**courriez**
ils	**courraient**

PRESENT SUBJUNCTIVE
je	**coure**
tu	**coures**
il	**coure**
nous	**courions**
vous	**couriez**
ils	**courent**

PAST HISTORIC
je	**courus**
tu	**courus**
il	**courut**
nous	**courûmes**
vous	**courûtes**
ils	**coururent**

craindre *to fear*   Auxiliary: **avoir**

PAST PARTICIPLE
craint

PRESENT PARTICIPLE
craignant

IMPERATIVE
crains
craignons
craignez

PRESENT
je	**crains**
tu	**crains**
il	**craint**
nous	**craignons**
vous	**craignez**
ils	**craignent**

IMPERFECT
je	**craignais**
tu	**craignais**
il	**craignait**
nous	**craignions**
vous	**craigniez**
ils	**craignaient**

FUTURE
je	craindrai
tu	craindras
il	craindra
nous	craindrons
vous	craindrez
ils	craindront

CONDITIONAL
je	craindrais
tu	craindrais
il	craindrait
nous	craindrions
vous	craindriez
ils	craindraient

PRESENT SUBJUNCTIVE
je	**craigne**
tu	**craignes**
il	**craigne**
nous	**craignions**
vous	**craigniez**
ils	**craignent**

PAST HISTORIC
je	**craignis**
tu	**craignis**
il	**craignit**
nous	**craignîmes**
vous	**craignîtes**
ils	**craignirent**

Verbs ending in **-eindre** and **-oindre** are conjugated similarly

croire *to believe*   Auxiliary: **avoir**

PAST PARTICIPLE
cru

PRESENT PARTICIPLE
croyant

IMPERATIVE
crois
croyons
croyez

PRESENT		IMPERFECT	
je	crois	**je**	**croyais**
tu	crois	**tu**	**croyais**
il	**croit**	**il**	**croyait**
nous	**croyons**	**nous**	**croyions**
vous	**croyez**	**vous**	**croyiez**
ils	croient	**ils**	**croyaient**

FUTURE		CONDITIONAL	
je	croirai	je	croirais
tu	croiras	tu	croirais
il	croira	il	croirait
nous	croirons	nous	croirions
vous	croirez	vous	croiriez
ils	croiront	ils	croiraient

PRESENT SUBJUNCTIVE		PAST HISTORIC	
je	croie	**je**	**crus**
tu	croies	**tu**	**crus**
il	croie	**il**	**crut**
nous	**croyions**	**nous**	**crûmes**
vous	**croyiez**	**vous**	**crûtes**
ils	croient	**ils**	**crurent**

croître *to grow* Auxiliary: **avoir**

PAST PARTICIPLE
crû

PRESENT PARTICIPLE
croissant

IMPERATIVE
crois
croissons
croissez

PRESENT	
je	**croîs**
tu	**croîs**
il	**croît**
nous	**croissons**
vous	**croissez**
ils	**croissent**

IMPERFECT	
je	**croissais**
tu	**croissais**
il	**croissait**
nous	**croissions**
vous	**croissiez**
ils	**croissaient**

FUTURE	
je	croîtrai
tu	croîtras
il	croîtra
nous	croîtrons
vous	croîtrez
ils	croîtront

CONDITIONAL	
je	croîtrais
tu	croîtrais
il	croîtrait
nous	croîtrions
vous	croîtriez
ils	croîtraient

PRESENT SUBJUNCTIVE	
je	**croisse**
tu	**croisses**
il	**croisse**
nous	**croissions**
vous	**croissiez**
ils	**croissent**

PAST HISTORIC	
je	**crûs**
tu	**crûs**
il	**crût**
nous	**crûmes**
vous	**crûtes**
ils	**crûrent**

cueillir *to pick*   Auxiliary: **avoir**

PAST PARTICIPLE
  cueilli

PRESENT PARTICIPLE
  cueillant

IMPERATIVE
  cueille
  cueillons
  cueillez

PRESENT

je	**cueille**
tu	**cueilles**
il	**cueille**
nous	**cueillons**
vous	**cueillez**
ils	**cueillent**

IMPERFECT

je	**cueillais**
tu	**cueillais**
il	**cueillait**
nous	**cueillions**
vous	**cueilliez**
ils	**cueillaient**

FUTURE

je	**cueillerai**
tu	**cueilleras**
il	**cueillera**
nous	**cueillerons**
vous	**cueillerez**
ils	**cueilleront**

CONDITIONAL

je	**cueillerais**
tu	**cueillerais**
il	**cueillerait**
nous	**cueillerions**
vous	**cueilleriez**
ils	**cueilleraient**

PRESENT SUBJUNCTIVE

je	**cueille**
tu	**cueilles**
il	**cueille**
nous	**cueillions**
vous	**cueilliez**
ils	**cueillent**

PAST HISTORIC

je	cueillis
tu	cueillis
il	cueillit
nous	cueillîmes
vous	cueillîtes
ils	cueillirent

cuire *to cook*   Auxiliary: **avoir**

PAST PARTICIPLE   *IMPERATIVE*
  cuit   cuis
                                              cuisons
PRESENT PARTICIPLE   **cuisez**
  cuisant

PRESENT		*IMPERFECT*	
je	cuis	**je**	**cuisais**
tu	cuis	**tu**	**cuisais**
il	**cuit**	**il**	**cuisait**
nous	**cuisons**	**nous**	**cuisions**
vous	**cuisez**	**vous**	**cuisiez**
ils	**cuisent**	**ils**	**cuisaient**

FUTURE		*CONDITIONAL*	
je	cuirai	je	cuirais
tu	cuiras	tu	cuirais
il	cuira	il	cuirait
nous	cuirons	nous	cuirions
vous	cuirez	vous	cuiriez
ils	cuiront	ils	cuiraient

PRESENT SUBJUNCTIVE		*PAST HISTORIC*	
je	**cuise**	**je**	**cuisis**
tu	**cuises**	**tu**	**cuisis**
il	**cuise**	**il**	**cuisit**
nous	**cuisions**	**nous**	**cuisîmes**
vous	**cuisiez**	**vous**	**cuisîtes**
ils	**cuisent**	**ils**	**cuisirent**

---

nuire *to harm*, conjugated similarly, but past participle **nui**

devoir *to have to; to owe* Auxiliary: **avoir**

PAST PARTICIPLE
dû

PRESENT PARTICIPLE
devant

IMPERATIVE
dois
devons
devez

PRESENT		IMPERFECT	
je	dois	je	devais
tu	dois	tu	devais
il	doit	il	devait
nous	devons	nous	devions
vous	devez	vous	deviez
ils	doivent	ils	devaient

FUTURE		CONDITIONAL	
je	devrai	je	devrais
tu	devras	tu	devrais
il	devra	il	devrait
nous	devrons	nous	devrions
vous	devrez	vous	devriez
ils	devront	ils	devraient

PRESENT SUBJUNCTIVE		PAST HISTORIC	
je	doive	je	dus
tu	doives	tu	dus
il	doive	il	dut
nous	devions	nous	dûmes
vous	deviez	vous	dûtes
ils	doivent	ils	durent

dire *to say, tell* Auxiliary: **avoir**

PAST PARTICIPLE
  dit

IMPERATIVE
  dis
  disons
  dites

PRESENT PARTICIPLE
  disant

PRESENT		IMPERFECT	
je	dis	je	disais
tu	dis	tu	disais
il	dit	il	disait
nous	disons	nous	disions
vous	dites	vous	disiez
ils	disent	ils	disaient

FUTURE		CONDITIONAL	
je	dirai	je	dirais
tu	diras	tu	dirais
il	dira	il	dirait
nous	dirons	nous	dirions
vous	direz	vous	diriez
ils	diront	ils	diraient

PRESENT SUBJUNCTIVE		PAST HISTORIC	
je	**dise**	je	dis
tu	**dises**	tu	dis
il	**dise**	il	dit
nous	**disions**	nous	dîmes
vous	**disiez**	vous	dîtes
ils	**disent**	ils	dirent

interdire *to forbid*, conjugated similarly, but 2nd person plural of the present tense is **vous interdisez**

dormir *to sleep*   Auxiliary: **avoir**

PAST PARTICIPLE
dormi

IMPERATIVE
dors
dormons
dormez

PRESENT PARTICIPLE
dormant

PRESENT

je	**dors**
tu	**dors**
il	**dort**
nous	**dormons**
vous	**dormez**
ils	**dorment**

IMPERFECT

je	**dormais**
tu	**dormais**
il	**dormait**
nous	**dormions**
vous	**dormiez**
ils	**dormaient**

FUTURE

je	dormirai
tu	dormiras
il	dormira
nous	dormirons
vous	dormirez
ils	dormiront

CONDITIONAL

je	dormirais
tu	dormirais
il	dormirait
nous	dormirions
vous	dormiriez
ils	dormiraient

PRESENT SUBJUNCTIVE

je	**dorme**
tu	**dormes**
il	**dorme**
nous	**dormions**
vous	**dormiez**
ils	**dorment**

PAST HISTORIC

je	dormis
tu	dormis
il	dormit
nous	dormîmes
vous	dormîtes
ils	dormirent

écrire *to write* Auxiliary: **avoir**

PAST PARTICIPLE
écrit

PRESENT PARTICIPLE
écrivant

IMPERATIVE
écris
écrivons
écrivez

PRESENT
j'écris
tu écris
il écrit
nous écrivons
vous écrivez
ils écrivent

IMPERFECT
j'écrivais
tu écrivais
il écrivait
nous écrivions
vous écriviez
ils écrivaient

FUTURE
j'écrirai
tu écriras
il écrira
nous écrirons
vous écrirez
ils écriront

CONDITIONAL
j'écrirais
tu écrirais
il écrirait
nous écririons
vous écririez
ils écriraient

PRESENT SUBJUNCTIVE
j'écrive
tu écrives
il écrive
nous écrivions
vous écriviez
ils écrivent

PAST HISTORIC
j'écrivis
tu écrivis
il écrivit
nous écrivîmes
vous écrivîtes
ils écrivirent

envoyer *to send*   Auxiliary: **avoir**

PAST PARTICIPLE
envoyé

PRESENT PARTICIPLE
envoyant

IMPERATIVE
envoie
envoyons
envoyez

PRESENT
       j'envoie
tu   envoies
il   envoie
nous   envoyons
vous   envoyez
ils   envoient

IMPERFECT
       j'envoyais
tu   envoyais
il   envoyait
nous   envoyions
vous   envoyiez
ils   envoyaient

FUTURE
       j'enverrai
tu   enverras
il   enverra
nous   enverrons
vous   enverrez
ils   enverront

CONDITIONAL
       j'enverrais
tu   enverrais
il   enverrait
nous   enverrions
vous   enverriez
ils   enverraient

PRESENT SUBJUNCTIVE
       j'envoie
tu   envoies
il   envoie
nous   envoyions
vous   envoyiez
ils   envoient

PAST HISTORIC
       j'envoyai
tu   envoyas
il   envoya
nous   envoyâmes
vous   envoyâtes
ils   envoyèrent

être *to be*   Auxiliary: **avoir**

PAST PARTICIPLE
  été

PRESENT PARTICIPLE
  étant

IMPERATIVE
  sois
  soyons
  soyez

PRESENT
je	suis
tu	es
il	est
nous	sommes
vous	êtes
ils	sont

IMPERFECT
j'	étais
tu	étais
il	était
nous	étions
vous	étiez
ils	étaient

FUTURE
je	serai
tu	seras
il	sera
nous	serons
vous	serez
ils	seront

CONDITIONAL
je	serais
tu	serais
il	serait
nous	serions
vous	seriez
ils	seraient

PRESENT SUBJUNCTIVE
je	sois
tu	sois
il	soit
nous	soyons
vous	soyez
ils	soient

PAST HISTORIC
je	fus
tu	fus
il	fut
nous	fûmes
vous	fûtes
ils	furent

faire *to do; to make*   Auxiliary: **avoir**

PAST PARTICIPLE
fait

IMPERATIVE
fais
faisons
faites

PRESENT PARTICIPLE
faisant

PRESENT
je	fais
tu	fais
il	fait
nous	faisons
vous	faites
ils	font

IMPERFECT
je	faisais
tu	faisais
il	faisait
nous	faisions
vous	faisiez
ils	faisaient

FUTURE
je	ferai
tu	feras
il	fera
nous	ferons
vous	ferez
ils	feront

CONDITIONAL
je	ferais
tu	ferais
il	ferait
nous	ferions
vous	feriez
ils	feraient

PRESENT SUBJUNCTIVE
je	fasse
tu	fasses
il	fasse
nous	fassions
vous	fassiez
ils	fassent

PAST HISTORIC
je	fis
tu	fis
il	fit
nous	fîmes
vous	fîtes
ils	firent

falloir *to be necessary*   Auxiliary: **avoir**

PAST PARTICIPLE
fallu

IMPERATIVE
not used

PRESENT PARTICIPLE
not used

PRESENT
  il **faut**

IMPERFECT
  il **fallait**

FUTURE
  il **faudra**

CONDITIONAL
  il **faudrait**

PRESENT SUBJUNCTIVE
  il **faille**

PAST HISTORIC
  il **fallut**

fuir *to flee* Auxiliary: **avoir**

PAST PARTICIPLE
fui

PRESENT PARTICIPLE
fuyant

IMPERATIVE
fuis
fuyons
fuyez

PRESENT
je	fuis
tu	fuis
il	fuit
nous	**fuyons**
vous	**fuyez**
ils	**fuient**

IMPERFECT
je	**fuyais**
tu	**fuyais**
il	**fuyait**
nous	**fuyions**
vous	**fuyiez**
ils	**fuyaient**

FUTURE
je	fuirai
tu	fuiras
il	fuira
nous	fuirons
vous	fuirez
ils	fuiront

CONDITIONAL
je	fuirais
tu	fuirais
il	fuirait
nous	fuirions
vous	fuiriez
ils	fuiraient

PRESENT SUBJUNCTIVE
je	**fuie**
tu	**fuies**
il	**fuie**
nous	**fuyions**
vous	**fuyiez**
ils	**fuient**

PAST HISTORIC
je	fuis
tu	fuis
il	fuit
nous	fuîmes
vous	fuîtes
ils	fuirent

haïr _to hate_   Auxiliary: **avoir**

PAST PARTICIPLE
  haï

PRESENT PARTICIPLE
  haïssant

IMPERATIVE
  hais
  haïssons
  haïssez

PRESENT		IMPERFECT	
je	hais	**je**	**haïssais**
tu	hais	**tu**	**haïssais**
il	hait	**il**	**haïssait**
nous	**haïssons**	**nous**	**haïssions**
vous	**haïssez**	**vous**	**haïssiez**
ils	**haïssent**	**ils**	**haïssaient**

FUTURE		CONDITIONAL	
je	haïrai	je	haïrais
tu	haïras	tu	haïrais
il	haïra	il	haïrait
nous	haïrons	nous	haïrions
vous	haïrez	vous	haïriez
ils	haïront	ils	haïraient

PRESENT SUBJUNCTIVE		PAST HISTORIC	
je	**haïsse**	**je**	**haïs**
tu	**haïsses**	**tu**	**haïs**
il	**haïsse**	**il**	**haït**
nous	**haïssions**	**nous**	**haïmes**
vous	**haïssiez**	**vous**	**haïtes**
ils	**haïssent**	**ils**	**haïrent**

lire *to read*   Auxiliary: **avoir**

PAST PARTICIPLE
  lu

IMPERATIVE
  lis
  lisons
  lisez

PRESENT PARTICIPLE
  lisant

PRESENT
je	lis
tu	lis
il	**lit**
nous	**lisons**
vous	**lisez**
ils	**lisent**

IMPERFECT
je	**lisais**
tu	**lisais**
il	**lisait**
nous	**lisions**
vous	**lisiez**
ils	**lisaient**

FUTURE
je	lirai
tu	liras
il	lira
nous	lirons
vous	lirez
ils	liront

CONDITIONAL
je	lirais
tu	lirais
il	lirait
nous	lirions
vous	liriez
ils	liraient

PRESENT SUBJUNCTIVE
je	**lise**
tu	**lises**
il	**lise**
nous	**lisions**
vous	**lisiez**
ils	**lisent**

PAST HISTORIC
je	**lus**
tu	**lus**
il	**lut**
nous	**lûmes**
vous	**lûtes**
ils	**lurent**

mettre *to put*   Auxiliary: **avoir**

PAST PARTICIPLE
 mis

IMPERATIVE
 mets
 mettons
 mettez

PRESENT PARTICIPLE
 mettant

PRESENT
 je **mets**
 tu **mets**
 il **met**
 nous mettons
 vous mettez
 ils mettent

IMPERFECT
 je mettais
 tu mettais
 il mettait
 nous mettions
 vous mettiez
 ils mettaient

FUTURE
 je mettrai
 tu mettras
 il mettra
 nous mettrons
 vous mettrez
 ils mettront

CONDITIONAL
 je mettrais
 tu mettrais
 il mettrait
 nous mettrions
 vous mettriez
 ils mettraient

PRESENT SUBJUNCTIVE
 je mette
 tu mettes
 il mette
 nous mettions
 vous mettiez
 ils mettent

PAST HISTORIC
 je **mis**
 tu **mis**
 il **mit**
 nous **mîmes**
 vous **mîtes**
 ils **mirent**

moudre _to grind_

Auxiliary: **avoir**

PAST PARTICIPLE
moulu

PRESENT PARTICIPLE
moulant

IMPERATIVE
mouds
moulons
moulez

PRESENT		IMPERFECT	
je	mouds	**je**	**moulais**
tu	mouds	**tu**	**moulais**
il	moud	**il**	**moulait**
nous	**moulons**	**nous**	**moulions**
vous	**moulez**	**vous**	**mouliez**
ils	**moulent**	**ils**	**moulaient**

FUTURE		CONDITIONAL	
je	moudrai	je	moudrais
tu	moudras	tu	moudrais
il	moudra	il	moudrait
nous	moudrons	nous	moudrions
vous	moudrez	vous	moudriez
ils	moudront	ils	moudraient

PRESENT SUBJUNCTIVE		PAST HISTORIC	
je	**moule**	**je**	**moulus**
tu	**moules**	**tu**	**moulus**
il	**moule**	**il**	**moulut**
nous	**moulions**	**nous**	**moulûmes**
vous	**mouliez**	**vous**	**moulûtes**
ils	**moulent**	**ils**	**moulurent**

mourir *to die*   Auxiliary: **être**

PAST PARTICIPLE
  mort

PRESENT PARTICIPLE
  mourant

IMPERATIVE
  meurs
  mourons
  mourez

PRESENT		*IMPERFECT*	
je	meurs	je	mourais
tu	meurs	tu	mourais
il	meurt	il	mourait
nous	mourons	nous	mourions
vous	mourez	vous	mouriez
ils	meurent	ils	mouraient

FUTURE		*CONDITIONAL*	
je	mourrai	je	mourrais
tu	mourras	tu	mourrais
il	mourra	il	mourrait
nous	mourrons	nous	mourrions
vous	mourrez	vous	mourriez
ils	mourront	ils	mourraient

PRESENT SUBJUNCTIVE		*PAST HISTORIC*	
je	meure	je	mourus
tu	meures	tu	mourus
il	meure	il	mourut
nous	mourions	nous	mourûmes
vous	mouriez	vous	mourûtes
ils	meurent	ils	moururent

naître *to be born*   Auxiliary: **être**

PAST PARTICIPLE
né

IMPERATIVE
nais
naissons
naissez

PRESENT PARTICIPLE
naissant

PRESENT
je	nais
tu	nais
il	naît
nous	naissons
vous	naissez
ils	naissent

IMPERFECT
je	naissais
tu	naissais
il	naissait
nous	naissions
vous	naissiez
ils	naissaient

FUTURE
je	naîtrai
tu	naîtras
il	naîtra
nous	naîtrons
vous	naîtrez
ils	naîtront

CONDITIONAL
je	naîtrais
tu	naîtrais
il	naîtrait
nous	naîtrions
vous	naîtriez
ils	naîtraient

PRESENT SUBJUNCTIVE
je	naisse
tu	naisses
il	naisse
nous	naissions
vous	naissiez
ils	naissent

PAST HISTORIC
je	naquis
tu	naquis
il	naquit
nous	naquîmes
vous	naquîtes
ils	naquirent

---

ouvrir *to open*   Auxiliary: **avoir**

PAST PARTICIPLE
  ouvert

PRESENT PARTICIPLE
  ouvrant

IMPERATIVE
  ouvre
  ouvrons
  ouvrez

PRESENT		IMPERFECT	
	j'ouvre		j'ouvrais
tu	ouvres	tu	ouvrais
il	ouvre	il	ouvrait
nous	ouvrons	nous	ouvrions
vous	ouvrez	vous	ouvriez
ils	ouvrent	ils	ouvraient

FUTURE		CONDITIONAL	
	j'ouvrirai		j'ouvrirais
tu	ouvriras	tu	ouvrirais
il	ouvrira	il	ouvrirait
nous	ouvrirons	nous	ouvririons
vous	ouvrirez	vous	ouvririez
ils	ouvriront	ils	ouvriraient

PRESENT SUBJUNCTIVE		PAST HISTORIC	
	j'ouvre		j'ouvris
tu	ouvres	tu	ouvris
il	ouvre	il	ouvrit
nous	ouvrions	nous	ouvrîmes
vous	ouvriez	vous	ouvrîtes
ils	ouvrent	ils	ouvrirent

---

offrir *to offer*, **souffrir** *to suffer* are conjugated similarly

paraître *to appear*　　　　Auxiliary: **avoir**

PAST PARTICIPLE
paru

PRESENT PARTICIPLE
paraissant

IMPERATIVE
parais
paraissons
paraissez

PRESENT

je	**parais**
tu	**parais**
il	paraît
nous	**paraissons**
vous	**paraissez**
ils	**paraissent**

IMPERFECT

je	**paraissais**
tu	**paraissais**
il	**paraissait**
nous	**paraissions**
vous	**paraissiez**
ils	**paraissaient**

FUTURE

je	paraîtrai
tu	paraîtras
il	paraîtra
nous	paraîtrons
vous	paraîtrez
ils	paraîtront

CONDITIONAL

je	paraîtrais
tu	paraîtrais
il	paraîtrait
nous	paraîtrions
vous	paraîtriez
ils	paraîtraient

PRESENT SUBJUNCTIVE

je	**paraisse**
tu	**paraisses**
il	**paraisse**
nous	**paraissions**
vous	**paraissiez**
ils	**paraissent**

PAST HISTORIC

je	**parus**
tu	**parus**
il	**parut**
nous	**parûmes**
vous	**parûtes**
ils	**parurent**

partir *to leave*   Auxiliary: **être**

PAST PARTICIPLE
parti

IMPERATIVE
pars
partons
partez

PRESENT PARTICIPLE
partant

PRESENT
je	**pars**
tu	**pars**
il	**part**
nous	**partons**
vous	**partez**
ils	**partent**

IMPERFECT
je	**partais**
tu	**partais**
il	**partait**
nous	**partions**
vous	**partiez**
ils	**partaient**

FUTURE
je	partirai
tu	partiras
il	partira
nous	partirons
vous	partirez
ils	partiront

CONDITIONAL
je	partirais
tu	partirais
il	partirait
nous	partirions
vous	partiriez
ils	partiraient

PRESENT SUBJUNCTIVE
je	**parte**
tu	**partes**
il	**parte**
nous	**partions**
vous	**partiez**
ils	**partent**

PAST HISTORIC
je	partis
tu	partis
il	partit
nous	partîmes
vous	partîtes
ils	partirent

plaire *to please*   Auxiliary: **avoir**

PAST PARTICIPLE
plu

IMPERATIVE
plais
plaisons
plaisez

PRESENT PARTICIPLE
plaisant

PRESENT
je	plais
tu	plais
il	**plaît**
nous	**plaisons**
vous	**plaisez**
ils	**plaisent**

IMPERFECT
je	**plaisais**
tu	**plaisais**
il	**plaisait**
nous	**plaisions**
vous	**plaisiez**
ils	**plaisaient**

FUTURE
je	plairai
tu	plairas
il	plaira
nous	plairons
vous	plairez
ils	plairont

CONDITIONAL
je	plairais
tu	plairais
il	plairait
nous	plairions
vous	plairiez
ils	plairaient

PRESENT SUBJUNCTIVE
je	**plaise**
tu	**plaises**
il	**plaise**
nous	**plaisions**
vous	**plaisiez**
ils	**plaisent**

PAST HISTORIC
je	**plus**
tu	**plus**
il	**plut**
nous	**plûmes**
vous	**plûtes**
ils	**plurent**

pleuvoir *to rain*   Auxiliary: **avoir**

PAST PARTICIPLE
plu

IMPERATIVE
not used

PRESENT PARTICIPLE
pleuvant

PRESENT	*IMPERFECT*
il **pleut**	il **pleuvait**
FUTURE	*CONDITIONAL*
il **pleuvra**	il **pleuvrait**
PRESENT SUBJUNCTIVE	*PAST HISTORIC*
il **pleuve**	il **plut**

pouvoir to be able to   Auxiliary: **avoir**

PAST PARTICIPLE
pu

IMPERATIVE
not used

PRESENT PARTICIPLE
pouvant

PRESENT

je	peux*
tu	peux
il	peut
nous	pouvons
vous	pouvez
ils	peuvent

IMPERFECT

je	pouvais
tu	pouvais
il	pouvait
nous	pouvions
vous	pouviez
ils	pouvaient

FUTURE

je	pourrai
tu	pourras
il	pourra
nous	pourrons
vous	pourrez
ils	pourront

CONDITIONAL

je	pourrais
tu	pourrais
il	pourrait
nous	pourrions
vous	pourriez
ils	pourraient

PRESENT SUBJUNCTIVE

je	puisse
tu	puisses
il	puisse
nous	puissions
vous	puissiez
ils	puissent

PAST HISTORIC

je	pus
tu	pus
il	put
nous	pûmes
vous	pûtes
ils	purent

*In questions: **puis-je?**

prendre *to take*   Auxiliary: **avoir**

PAST PARTICIPLE
pris

IMPERATIVE
prends
prenons
prenez

PRESENT PARTICIPLE
prenant

PRESENT
je	prends
tu	prends
il	prend
nous	**prenons**
vous	**prenez**
ils	**prennent**

IMPERFECT
je	**prenais**
tu	**prenais**
il	**prenait**
nous	**prenions**
vous	**preniez**
ils	**prenaient**

FUTURE
je	prendrai
tu	prendras
il	prendra
nous	prendrons
vous	prendrez
ils	prendront

CONDITIONAL
je	prendrais
tu	prendrais
il	prendrait
nous	prendrions
vous	prendriez
ils	prendraient

PRESENT SUBJUNCTIVE
je	**prenne**
tu	**prennes**
il	**prenne**
nous	**prenions**
vous	**preniez**
ils	**prennent**

PAST HISTORIC
je	**pris**
tu	**pris**
il	**prit**
nous	**prîmes**
vous	**prîtes**
ils	**prirent**

recevoir *to receive*   Auxiliary: **avoir**

PAST PARTICIPLE
reçu

PRESENT PARTICIPLE
recevant

IMPERATIVE
reçois
recevons
recevez

PRESENT

je	reçois
tu	reçois
il	reçoit
nous	recevons
vous	recevez
ils	reçoivent

IMPERFECT

je	recevais
tu	recevais
il	recevait
nous	recevions
vous	receviez
ils	recevaient

FUTURE

je	recevrai
tu	recevras
il	recevra
nous	recevrons
vous	recevrez
ils	recevront

CONDITIONAL

je	recevrais
tu	recevrais
il	recevrait
nous	recevrions
vous	recevriez
ils	recevraient

PRESENT SUBJUNCTIVE

je	reçoive
tu	reçoives
il	reçoive
nous	recevions
vous	receviez
ils	reçoivent

PAST HISTORIC

je	reçus
tu	reçus
il	reçut
nous	reçûmes
vous	reçûtes
ils	reçurent

résoudre *to solve*   Auxiliary: **avoir**

PAST PARTICIPLE
résolu

IMPERATIVE
résous
résolvons
résolvez

PRESENT PARTICIPLE
résolvant

PRESENT		*IMPERFECT*	
je	**résous**	je	**résolvais**
tu	**résous**	tu	**résolvais**
il	**résout**	il	**résolvait**
nous	**résolvons**	nous	**résolvions**
vous	**résolvez**	vous	**résolviez**
ils	**résolvent**	ils	**résolvaient**

FUTURE		*CONDITIONAL*	
je	résoudrai	je	résoudrais
tu	résoudras	tu	résoudrais
il	résoudra	il	résoudrait
nous	résoudrons	nous	résoudrions
vous	résoudrez	vous	résoudriez
ils	résoudront	ils	résoudraient

PRESENT SUBJUNCTIVE		*PAST HISTORIC*	
je	**résolve**	je	**résolus**
tu	**résolves**	tu	**résolus**
il	**résolve**	il	**résolut**
nous	**résolvions**	nous	**résolûmes**
vous	**résolviez**	vous	**résolûtes**
ils	**résolvent**	ils	**résolurent**

rire *to laugh*   Auxiliary: **avoir**

PAST PARTICIPLE
ri

IMPERATIVE
ris
rions
riez

PRESENT PARTICIPLE
riant

PRESENT
    je   ris
    tu   ris
    il   **rit**
  nous rions
  vous riez
   ils rient

IMPERFECT
    je   riais
    tu   riais
    il   riait
  nous riions
  vous riiez
   ils riaient

FUTURE
    je   rirai
    tu   riras
    il   rira
  nous rirons
  vous rirez
   ils riront

CONDITIONAL
    je   rirais
    tu   rirais
    il   rirait
  nous ririons
  vous ririez
   ils riraient

PRESENT SUBJUNCTIVE
    je   rie
    tu   ries
    il   rie
  nous riions
  vous riiez
   ils rient

PAST HISTORIC
    je   **ris**
    tu   **ris**
    il   **rit**
  nous **rîmes**
  vous **rîtes**
   ils **rirent**

rompre *to break*   Auxiliary: **avoir**

PAST PARTICIPLE
rompu

IMPERATIVE
romps
rompons
rompez

PRESENT PARTICIPLE
rompant

PRESENT
je	romps
tu	romps
il	**rompt**
nous	rompons
vous	rompez
ils	rompent

IMPERFECT
je	rompais
tu	rompais
il	rompait
nous	rompions
vous	rompiez
ils	rompaient

FUTURE
je	romprai
tu	rompras
il	rompra
nous	romprons
vous	romprez
ils	rompront

CONDITIONAL
je	romprais
tu	romprais
il	romprait
nous	romprions
vous	rompriez
ils	rompraient

PRESENT SUBJUNCTIVE
je	rompe
tu	rompes
il	rompe
nous	rompions
vous	rompiez
ils	rompent

PAST HISTORIC
je	rompis
tu	rompis
il	rompit
nous	rompîmes
vous	rompîtes
ils	rompirent

savoir _to know_   Auxiliary: **avoir**

PAST PARTICIPLE
su

PRESENT PARTICIPLE
sachant

IMPERATIVE
sache
sachons
sachez

PRESENT

je	sais
tu	sais
il	sait
nous	savons
vous	savez
ils	savent

IMPERFECT

je	savais
tu	savais
il	savait
nous	savions
vous	saviez
ils	savaient

FUTURE

je	saurai
tu	sauras
il	saura
nous	saurons
vous	saurez
ils	sauront

CONDITIONAL

je	saurais
tu	saurais
il	saurait
nous	saurions
vous	sauriez
ils	sauraient

PRESENT SUBJUNCTIVE

je	sache
tu	saches
il	sache
nous	sachions
vous	sachiez
ils	sachent

PAST HISTORIC

je	sus
tu	sus
il	sut
nous	sûmes
vous	sûtes
ils	surent

sentir *to feel; to smell*   Auxiliary: **avoir**

PAST PARTICIPLE
senti

IMPERATIVE
sens
sentons
sentez

PRESENT PARTICIPLE
sentant

PRESENT		IMPERFECT	
je	**sens**	je	**sentais**
tu	**sens**	tu	**sentais**
il	**sent**	il	**sentait**
nous	**sentons**	nous	**sentions**
vous	**sentez**	vous	**sentiez**
ils	**sentent**	ils	**sentaient**

FUTURE		CONDITIONAL	
je	sentirai	je	sentirais
tu	sentiras	tu	sentirais
il	sentira	il	sentirait
nous	sentirons	nous	sentirions
vous	sentirez	vous	sentiriez
ils	sentiront	ils	sentiraient

PRESENT SUBJUNCTIVE		PAST HISTORIC	
je	**sente**	je	sentis
tu	**sentes**	tu	sentis
il	**sente**	il	sentit
nous	**sentions**	nous	sentîmes
vous	**sentiez**	vous	sentîtes
ils	**sentent**	ils	sentirent

servir *to serve* Auxiliary: **avoir**

PAST PARTICIPLE
servi

IMPERATIVE
sers
servons
servez

PRESENT PARTICIPLE
servant

PRESENT		IMPERFECT	
je	**sers**	je	**servais**
tu	**sers**	tu	**servais**
il	**sert**	il	**servait**
nous	**servons**	nous	**servions**
vous	**servez**	vous	**serviez**
ils	**servent**	ils	**servaient**

FUTURE		CONDITIONAL	
je	servirai	je	servirais
tu	serviras	tu	servirais
il	servira	il	servirait
nous	servirons	nous	servirions
vous	servirez	vous	serviriez
ils	serviront	ils	serviraient

PRESENT SUBJUNCTIVE		PAST HISTORIC	
je	**serve**	je	servis
tu	**serves**	tu	servis
il	**serve**	il	servit
nous	**servions**	nous	servîmes
vous	**serviez**	vous	servîtes
ils	**servent**	ils	servirent

sortir *to go/come out* Auxiliary: être

PAST PARTICIPLE
sorti

IMPERATIVE
sors
sortons
sortez

PRESENT PARTICIPLE
sortant

PRESENT
je	**sors**
tu	**sors**
il	**sort**
nous	**sortons**
vous	**sortez**
ils	**sortent**

IMPERFECT
je	**sortais**
tu	**sortais**
il	**sortait**
nous	**sortions**
vous	**sortiez**
ils	**sortaient**

FUTURE
je	sortirai
tu	sortiras
il	sortira
nous	sortirons
vous	sortirez
ils	sortiront

CONDITIONAL
je	sortirais
tu	sortirais
il	sortirait
nous	sortirions
vous	sortiriez
ils	sortiraient

PRESENT SUBJUNCTIVE
je	**sorte**
tu	**sortes**
il	**sorte**
nous	**sortions**
vous	**sortiez**
ils	**sortent**

PAST HISTORIC
je	sortis
tu	sortis
il	sortit
nous	sortîmes
vous	sortîtes
ils	sortirent

suffire *to be enough*   Auxiliary: **avoir**

PAST PARTICIPLE
  suffi

IMPERATIVE
  , suffis .
  suffisons
  suffisez

PRESENT PARTICIPLE
  suffisant

PRESENT
je	suffis
tu	suffis
il	suffit
nous	**suffisons**
vous	**suffisez**
ils	**suffisent**

IMPERFECT
je	**suffisais**
tu	**suffisais**
il	**suffisait**
nous	**suffisions**
vous	**suffisiez**
ils	**suffisaient**

FUTURE
je	suffirai
tu	suffiras
il	suffira
nous	suffirons
vous	suffirez
ils	suffiront

CONDITIONAL
je	suffirais
tu	suffirais
il	suffirait
nous	suffirions
vous	suffiriez
ils	suffiraient

PRESENT SUBJUNCTIVE
je	**suffise**
tu	**suffises**
il	**suffise**
nous	**suffisions**
vous	**suffisiez**
ils	**suffisent**

PAST HISTORIC
je	**suffis**
tu	**suffis**
il	**suffit**
nous	**suffîmes**
vous	**suffîtes**
ils	**suffirent**

suivre *to follow*   Auxiliary: **avoir**

PAST PARTICIPLE
suivi

PRESENT PARTICIPLE
suivant

IMPERATIVE
suis
suivons
suivez

PRESENT		IMPERFECT	
je	**suis**	je	suivais
tu	**suis**	tu	suivais
il	**suit**	il	suivait
nous	suivons	nous	suivions
vous	suivez	vous	suiviez
ils	suivent	ils	suivaient

FUTURE		CONDITIONAL	
je	suivrai	je	suivrais
tu	suivras	tu	suivrais
il	suivra	il	suivrait
nous	suivrons	nous	suivrions
vous	suivrez	vous	suivriez
ils	suivront	ils	suivraient

PRESENT SUBJUNCTIVE		PAST HISTORIC	
je	suive	je	suivis
tu	suives	tu	suivis
il	suive	il	suivit
nous	suivions	nous	suivîmes
vous	suiviez	vous	suivîtes
ils	suivent	ils	suivirent

se taire *to stop talking*   Auxiliary: **être**

PAST PARTICIPLE
 tu

PRESENT PARTICIPLE
 se taisant

IMPERATIVE
 tais-toi
 taisons-nous
 taisez-vous

PRESENT
 je me tais
 tu te tais
 il se tait
 nous nous taisons
 vous vous taisez
 ils se taisent

FUTURE
 je me tairai
 tu te tairas
 il se taira
 nous nous tairons
 vous vous tairez
 ils se tairont

PRESENT SUBJUNCTIVE
 je me taise
 tu te taises
 il se taise
 nous nous taisions
 vous vous taisiez
 ils se taisent

IMPERFECT
 je me taisais
 tu te taisais
 il se taisait
 nous nous taisions
 vous vous taisiez
 ils se taisaient

CONDITIONAL
 je me tairais
 tu te tairais
 il se tairait
 nous nous tairions
 vous vous tairiez
 ils se tairaient

PAST HISTORIC
 je me tus
 tu te tus
 il se tut
 nous nous tûmes
 vous vous tûtes
 ils se turent

tenir *to hold*   Auxiliary: **avoir**

PAST PARTICIPLE
  tenu

PRESENT PARTICIPLE
  tenant

IMPERATIVE
  tiens
  tenons
  tenez

PRESENT		IMPERFECT	
je	tiens	je	tenais
tu	tiens	tu	tenais
il	tient	il	tenait
nous	tenons	nous	tenions
vous	tenez	vous	teniez
ils	tiennent	ils	tenaient

FUTURE		CONDITIONAL	
je	tiendrai	je	tiendrais
tu	tiendras	tu	tiendrais
il	tiendra	il	tiendrait
nous	tiendrons	nous	tiendrions
vous	tiendrez	vous	tiendriez
ils	tiendront	ils	tiendraient

PRESENT SUBJUNCTIVE		PAST HISTORIC	
je	tienne	je	tins
tu	tiennes	tu	tins
il	tienne	il	tint
nous	tenions	nous	tînmes
vous	teniez	vous	tîntes
ils	tiennent	ils	tinrent

vaincre *to defeat*   Auxiliary: **avoir**

PAST PARTICIPLE
vaincu

IMPERATIVE
vaincs
vainquons
vainquez

PRESENT PARTICIPLE
vainquant

PRESENT
- je vaincs
- tu vaincs
- il vainc
- **nous vainquons**
- **vous vainquez**
- **ils vainquent**

IMPERFECT
- **je vainquais**
- **tu vainquais**
- **il vainquait**
- **nous vainquions**
- **vous vainquiez**
- **ils vainquaient**

FUTURE
- je vaincrai
- tu vaincras
- il vaincra
- nous vaincrons
- vous vaincrez
- ils vaincront

CONDITIONAL
- je vaincrais
- tu vaincrais
- il vaincrait
- nous vaincrions
- vous vaincriez
- ils vaincraient

PRESENT SUBJUNCTIVE
- **je vainque**
- **tu vainques**
- **il vainque**
- **nous vainquions**
- **vous vainquiez**
- **ils vainquent**

PAST HISTORIC
- **je vainquis**
- **tu vainquis**
- **il vainquit**
- **nous vainquîmes**
- **vous vainquîtes**
- **ils vainquirent**

valoir *to be worth* Auxiliary: **avoir**

PAST PARTICIPLE
valu

PRESENT PARTICIPLE
valant

IMPERATIVE
vaux
valons
valez

PRESENT		IMPERFECT	
je	vaux	je	valais
tu	vaux	tu	valais
il	vaut	il	valait
nous	valons	nous	valions
vous	valez	vous	valiez
ils	valent	ils	valaient

FUTURE		CONDITIONAL	
je	vaudrai	je	vaudrais
tu	vaudras	tu	vaudrais
il	vaudra	il	vaudrait
nous	vaudrons	nous	vaudrions
vous	vaudrez	vous	vaudriez
ils	vaudront	ils	vaudraient

PRESENT SUBJUNCTIVE		PAST HISTORIC	
je	vaille	je	valus
tu	vailles	tu	valus
il	vaille	il	valut
nous	valions	nous	valûmes
vous	valiez	vous	valûtes
ils	vaillent	ils	valurent

venir *to come*   Auxiliary: être

PAST PARTICIPLE
venu

PRESENT PARTICIPLE
venant

IMPERATIVE
viens
venons
venez

PRESENT		IMPERFECT	
je	**viens**	je	**venais**
tu	**viens**	tu	**venais**
il	**vient**	il	**venait**
nous	**venons**	nous	**venions**
vous	**venez**	vous	**veniez**
ils	**viennent**	ils	**venaient**

FUTURE		CONDITIONAL	
je	**viendrai**	je	**viendrais**
tu	**viendras**	tu	**viendrais**
il	**viendra**	il	**viendrait**
nous	**viendrons**	nous	**viendrions**
vous	**viendrez**	vous	**viendriez**
ils	**viendront**	ils	**viendraient**

PRESENT SUBJUNCTIVE		PAST HISTORIC	
je	**vienne**	je	**vins**
tu	**viennes**	tu	**vins**
il	**vienne**	il	**vint**
nous	**venions**	nous	**vînmes**
vous	**veniez**	vous	**vîntes**
ils	**viennent**	ils	**vinrent**

vêtir *to dress*　　　　　　Auxiliary: **avoir**

PAST PARTICIPLE
vêtu

IMPERATIVE
vêts
vêtons
vêtez

PRESENT PARTICIPLE
vêtant

PRESENT		IMPERFECT	
je	**vêts**	je	**vêtais**
tu	**vêts**	tu	**vêtais**
il	**vêt**	il	**vêtait**
nous	**vêtons**	nous	**vêtions**
vous	**vêtez**	vous	**vêtiez**
ils	**vêtent**	ils	**vêtaient**

FUTURE		CONDITIONAL	
je	vêtirai	je	vêtirais
tu	vêtiras	tu	vêtirais
il	vêtira	il	vêtirait
nous	vêtirons	nous	vêtirions
vous	vêtirez	vous	vêtiriez
ils	vêtiront	ils	vêtiraient

PRESENT SUBJUNCTIVE		PAST HISTORIC	
je	**vête**	je	vêtis
tu	**vêtes**	tu	vêtis
il	**vête**	il	vêtit
nous	**vêtions**	nous	vêtîmes
vous	**vêtiez**	vous	vêtîtes
ils	**vêtent**	ils	vêtirent

vivre *to live*   Auxiliary: **avoir**

PAST PARTICIPLE
vécu

PRESENT PARTICIPLE
vivant

IMPERATIVE
vis
vivons
vivez

PRESENT		IMPERFECT	
je	**vis**	je	vivais
tu	**vis**	tu	vivais
il	**vit**	il	vivait
nous	vivons	nous	vivions
vous	vivez	vous	viviez
ils	vivent	ils	vivaient

FUTURE		CONDITIONAL	
je	vivrai	je	vivrais
tu	vivras	tu	vivrais
il	vivra	il	vivrait
nous	vivrons	nous	vivrions
vous	vivrez	vous	vivriez
ils	vivront	ils	vivraient

PRESENT SUBJUNCTIVE		PAST HISTORIC	
je	vive	je	**vécus**
tu	vives	tu	**vécus**
il	vive	il	**vécut**
nous	vivions	nous	**vécûmes**
vous	viviez	vous	**vécûtes**
ils	vivent	ils	**vécurent**

voir *to see*   Auxiliary: **avoir**

PAST PARTICIPLE	IMPERATIVE
vu	vois
	voyons
PRESENT PARTICIPLE	voyez
voyant	

PRESENT		IMPERFECT	
je	vois	je	voyais
tu	vois	tu	voyais
il	voit	il	voyait
nous	voyons	nous	voyions
vous	voyez	vous	voyiez
ils	voient	ils	voyaient

FUTURE		CONDITIONAL	
je	verrai	je	verrais
tu	verras	tu	verrais
il	verra	il	verrait
nous	verrons	nous	verrions
vous	verrez	vous	verriez
ils	verront	ils	verraient

PRESENT SUBJUNCTIVE		PAST HISTORIC	
je	voie	je	vis
tu	voies	tu	vis
il	voie	il	vit
nous	voyions	nous	vîmes
vous	voyiez	vous	vîtes
ils	voient	ils	virent

vouloir *to wish, want* Auxiliary: **avoir**

PAST PARTICIPLE
voulu

PRESENT PARTICIPLE
voulant

IMPERATIVE
veuille
veuillons
veuillez

PRESENT

je	veux
tu	veux
il	veut
nous	voulons
vous	voulez
ils	veulent

FUTURE

je	voudrai
tu	voudras
il	voudra
nous	voudrons
vous	voudrez
ils	voudront

PRESENT SUBJUNCTIVE

je	veuille
tu	veuilles
il	veuille
nous	voulions
vous	vouliez
ils	veuillent

IMPERFECT

je	voulais
tu	voulais
il	voulait
nous	voulions
vous	vouliez
ils	voulaient

CONDITIONAL

je	voudrais
tu	voudrais
il	voudrait
nous	voudrions
vous	voudriez
ils	voudraient

PAST HISTORIC

je	voulus
tu	voulus
il	voulut
nous	voulûmes
vous	voulûtes
ils	voulurent

The Gender of Nouns

In French, all nouns are either masculine or feminine, whether denoting people, animals or things. Unlike English, there is no neuter gender for inanimate objects and abstract nouns.

Gender is largely unpredictable and has to be learnt for each noun. However, the following guidelines will help you determine the gender for certain types of nouns.

● Nouns denoting male people and animals are usually – but not always – masculine, e.g.

un homme   **un taureau**
a man   *a bull*
un infirmier   **un cheval**
a (male) nurse   *a horse*

● Nouns denoting female people and animals are usually – but not always – feminine, e.g.

une fille   **une vache**
a girl   *a cow*
une infirmière   **une brebis**
a nurse   *a ewe*

● Some nouns are masculine OR feminine depending on the sex of the person to whom they refer, e.g.

un camarade   **une camarade**
a (male) friend   *a (female) friend*
un Belge   **une Belge**
a Belgian (man)   *a Belgian (woman)*

● Other nouns referring to either men or women have only one gender which applies to both, e.g.

un professeur   **une personne**   **une sentinelle**
a teacher   *a person*   *a sentry*
un témoin   **une victime**   **une recrue**
a witness   *a victim*   *a recruit*

● Sometimes the ending of the noun indicates its gender. Shown below are some of the most important to guide you:

Masculine endings

-age   **le courage** *courage*, **le rinçage** *rinsing*
         EXCEPTIONS: **une cage** *a cage*, **une image** *a picture*, **la nage** *swimming*, **une page** *a page*, **une plage** *a beach*, **une rage** *a rage*

-ment   **le commencement** *the beginning*
         EXCEPTION: **une jument** *a mare*

-oir   **un couloir** *a corridor*, **un miroir** *a mirror*

-sme   **le pessimisme** *pessimism*, **l'enthousiasme** *enthusiasm*

Feminine endings

-ance, anse   **la confiance** *confidence*, **la danse** *dancing*

-ence, -ense   **la prudence** *caution*, **la défense** *defence*
         EXCEPTION: **le silence** *silence*

-ion   **une région** *a region*, **une addition** *a bill*
         EXCEPTIONS: **un pion** *a pawn*, **un espion** *a spy*

-oire   **une baignoire** *a bath(tub)*

-té, -tié   **la beauté** *beauty*, **la moitié** *half*

● Suffixes which differentiate between male and female are shown on pp. 134 and 136

● The following words have different meanings depending on gender:

le crêpe	crêpe	**la crêpe**	pancake
le livre	book	**la livre**	pound
le manche	handle	**la manche**	sleeve
le mode	method	**la mode**	fashion
le moule	mould	**la moule**	mussel
le page	page(boy)	**la page**	page (in book)
le physique	physique	**la physique**	physics
le poêle	stove	**la poêle**	frying pan
le somme	nap	**la somme**	sum
le tour	turn	**la tour**	tower
le voile	veil	**la voile**	sail

Gender: the formation of feminines

As in English, male and female are sometimes differentiated by the use of two quite separate words, e.g.

mon oncle	**ma tante**
my uncle	*my aunt*
un taureau	**une vache**
a bull	*a cow*

There are, however, some words in French which show this distinction by the form of their ending

● Some nouns add an **e** to the masculine singular form to form the feminine (→ **1**)

● If the masculine singular form already ends in **-e**, no further **e** is added in the feminine (→ **2**)

● Some nouns undergo a further change when **e** is added. These changes occur regularly and are shown on p. 136

Feminine forms to note

MASCULINE	FEMININE	
un âne	**une ânesse**	*donkey*
le comte	**la comtesse**	*count/countess*
le duc	**la duchesse**	*duke/duchess*
un Esquimau	**une Esquimaude**	*Eskimo*
le fou	**la folle**	*madman/madwoman*
le Grec	**la Grecque**	*Greek*
un hôte	**une hôtesse**	*host/hostess*
le jumeau	**la jumelle**	*twin*
le maître	**la maîtresse**	*master/mistress*
le prince	**la princesse**	*prince/princess*
le tigre	**la tigresse**	*tiger/tigress*
le traître	**la traîtresse**	*traitor*
le Turc	**la Turque**	*Turk*
le vieux	**la vieille**	*old man/old woman*

Continued

1   **un ami**
   a (male) friend
   un employé
   a (male) employee
   un Français
   a Frenchman

        une amie
        a (female) friend
        une employée
        a (female) employee
        une Française
        a Frenchwoman

2   **un élève**
   a (male) pupil
   un collègue
   a (male) colleague
   un camarade
   a (male) friend

        une élève
        a (female) pupil
        une collègue
        a (female) colleague
        une camarade
        a (female) friend

Regular feminine endings

MASC. SING.	FEM. SING.	
-f	-ve	(→ 1)
-x	-se	(→ 2)
-eur	-euse	(→ 3)
-teur	-teuse	(→ 4)
	-trice	(→ 5)

Some nouns double the final consonant before adding **e**:

MASC. SING.	FEM. SING.	
-an	-anne	(→ 6)
-en	-enne	(→ 7)
-on	-onne	(→ 8)
-et	-ette	(→ 9)
-el	-elle	(→ 10)

Some nouns add an accent to the final syllable before adding **e**:

MASC. SING.	FEM. SING.	
-er	-ère	(→ 11)

Pronunciation and feminine endings

This is dealt with on p. 244.

1 **un sportif**   **une sportive**
   a sportsman   a sportswoman
   un veuf   **une veuve**
   a widower   a widow

2 **un époux**   **une épouse**
   a husband   a wife
   un amoureux   **une amoureuse**
   a man in love   a woman in love

3 **un danseur**   **une danseuse**
   a dancer   a dancer
   un voleur   **une voleuse**
   a thief   a thief

4 **un menteur**   **une menteuse**
   a liar   a liar
   un chanteur   **une chanteuse**
   a singer   a singer

5 **un acteur**   **une actrice**
   an actor   an actress
   un conducteur   **une conductrice**
   a driver   a driver

6 **un paysan**   **une paysanne**
   a countryman   a countrywoman

7 **un Parisien**   **une Parisienne**
   a Parisian   a Parisian (woman)

8 **un baron**   **une baronne**
   a baron   a baroness

9 **le cadet**   **la cadette**
   the youngest (child)   the youngest (child)

10 **un intellectuel**   **une intellectuelle**
   an intellectual   an intellectual

11 **un étranger**   **une étrangère**
   a foreigner   a foreigner
   le dernier   **la dernière**
   the last (one)   the last (one)

The formation of plurals

● Most nouns add **s** to the singular form (→ **1**)

● When the singular form already ends in **-s**, **-x** or **-z**, no further **s** is added (→ **2**)

● For nouns ending in **-au**, **-eau** or **-eu**, the plural ends in **-aux**, **-eaux** or **-eux** (→ **3**)

Exceptions:			
	pneu	*tyre*	(plur: **pneus**)
	bleu	*bruise*	(plur: **bleus**)

● For nouns ending in **-al** or **-ail**, the plural ends in **-aux** (→ **4**)

Exceptions:			
	bal	*ball*	(plur: **bals**)
	festival	*festival*	(plur: **festivals**)
	chandail	*sweater*	(plur: **chandails**)
	détail	*detail*	(plur: **détails**)

● Forming the plural of compound nouns is complicated and you are advised to check each one individually in a dictionary

Irregular plural forms

● Some masculine nouns ending in **-ou** add **x** in the plural. These are:

bijou	*jewel*	**genou**	*knee*	**joujou**	*toy*
caillou	*pebble*	**hibou**	*owl*	**pou**	*louse*
chou	*cabbage*				

● Some other nouns are totally unpredictable. Chief among these are:

SINGULAR	PLURAL
œil *eye*	**yeux**
ciel *sky*	**cieux**
Monsieur *Mr.*	**Messieurs**
Madame *Mrs.*	**Mesdames**
Mademoiselle *Miss*	**Mesdemoiselles**

Pronunciation of plural forms
This is dealt with on p. 244

1 le jardin
the garden
une voiture
a car
l'hôtel
the hotel

les jardins
the gardens
des voitures
(some) cars
les hôtels
the hotels

2 un tas
a heap
une voix
a voice
le gaz
the gas

des tas
(some) heaps
des voix
(some) voices
les gaz
the gases

3 un tuyau
a pipe
le chapeau
the hat
le feu
the fire

des tuyaux
(some) pipes
les chapeaux
the hats
les feux
the fires

4 le journal
the newspaper
un travail
a job

les journaux
the newspapers
des travaux
(some) jobs

The Definite Article

	WITH MASC. NOUN	WITH FEM. NOUN	
SING.	le (l')	la (l')	the
PLUR.	les	les	the

● The gender and number of the noun determines the form of the article (→ **1**)

● **le** and **la** change to **l'** before a vowel or an **h** 'mute' (→ **2**)

● For uses of the definite article see p. 142

● à + le/la (l'), à + les

	WITH MASC. NOUN	WITH FEM. NOUN	
SING.	au (à l')	à la (à l')	(→ **3**)
PLUR.	aux	aux	

● The definite article combines with the preposition **à**, as shown above. You should pay particular attention to the masculine singular form **au**, and both plural forms **aux**, since these are not visually the sum of their parts

● de + le/la (l'), de + les

	WITH MASC. NOUN	WITH FEM. NOUN	
SING.	du (de l')	de la (de l')	(→ **4**)
PLUR.	des	des	

● The definite article combines with the preposition **de**, as shown above. You should pay particular attention to the masculine singular form **du**, and both plural forms **des**, since these are not visually the sum of their parts

Continued

MASCULINE	FEMININE
1 le train	**la gare**
the train	the station
le garçon	**la fille**
the boy	the girl
les hôtels	**les écoles**
the hotels	the schools
les professeurs	**les femmes**
the teachers	the women
2 l'acteur	**l'actrice**
the actor	the actress
l'effet	**l'eau**
the effect	the water
l'ingrédient	**l'idée**
the ingredient	the idea
l'objet	**l'ombre**
the object	the shadow
l'univers	**l'usine**
the universe	the factory
l'hôpital	**l'heure**
the hospital	the time
3 au cinéma	**à la bibliothèque**
at/to the cinema	at/to the library
à l'employé	**à l'infirmière**
to the employee	to the nurse
à l'hôpital	**à l'hôtesse**
at/to the hospital	to the hostess
aux étudiants	**aux maisons**
to the students	to the houses
4 du bureau	**de la réunion**
from/of the office	from/of the meeting
de l'auteur	**de l'Italienne**
from/of the author	from/of the Italian woman
de l'hôte	**de l'horloge**
from/of the host	of the clock
des Etats-Unis	**des vendeuses**
from/of the United States	from/of the saleswomen

Uses of the definite article

While the definite article is used in much the same way in French as it is in English, its use is more widespread in French. Unlike English the definite article is also used:

● with abstract nouns, except when following certain prepositions (→ **1**)

● in generalisations, especially with plural or uncountable* nouns (→ **2**)

● with names of countries (→ **3**)
  Exceptions: no article with countries following **en** *to/in* (→ **4**)

● with parts of the body (→ **5**)
  'Ownership' is often indicated by an indirect object pronoun or a reflexive pronoun (→ **6**)

● in expressions of quantity/rate/price (→ **7**)

● with titles/ranks/professions followed by a proper name (→ **8**)

● The definite article is NOT used with nouns in apposition (→ **9**)

*An uncountable noun is one which cannot be used in the plural or with an indefinite article, e.g. **l'acier** *steel*, **le lait** *milk*

1 **Les prix montent**
  Prices are rising
  L'amour rayonne dans ses yeux
  Love shines in his eyes
  BUT   **avec plaisir**   **sans espoir**
           with pleasure   without hope

2 **Je n'aime pas le café**
  I don't like coffee
  Les enfants ont besoin d'être aimés
  Children need to be loved

3 **le Japon**   **la France**   **l'Italie**   **les Pays-Bas**
  Japan   France   Italy   The Netherlands

4 **aller en Ecosse**   **Il travaille en Allemagne**
  to go to Scotland   He works in Germany

5 **Tournez la tête à gauche**
  Turn your head to the left
  J'ai mal à la gorge
  My throat is sore, I have a sore throat

6 **La tête me tourne**
  My head is spinning
  Elle s'est brossé les dents
  She brushed her teeth

7 **40 francs le mètre/le kilo/la douzaine/la pièce**
  40 francs a metre/a kilo/a dozen/each
  rouler à 80 km à l'heure
  to go at 50 m.p.h.
  payé à l'heure/au jour/au mois
  paid by the hour/by the day/by the month

8 **le roi Georges III**   **le capitaine Darbeau**
  King George III   Captain Darbeau
  le docteur Rousseau   **Monsieur le président**
  Dr. Rousseau   Mr. Chairman/President

9 **Victor Hugo, grand écrivain du dix-neuvième siècle**
  Victor Hugo, a great author of the nineteenth century
  Joseph Leblanc, inventeur et entrepreneur, a été le premier ...
  Joseph Leblanc, an inventor and entrepreneur, was the first ...

The Partitive Article

The partitive article has the sense of *some* or *any*, although the French is not always translated in English.

Forms of the partitive

	WITH MASC. NOUN	WITH FEM. NOUN	
SING.	**du (de l')**	**de la (de l')**	*some, any*
PLUR.	**des**	**des**	*some, any*

● The gender and number of the noun determines the form of the partitive (→ **1**)

● The forms shown in brackets are used before a vowel or an **h** 'mute' (→ **2**)

● **des** becomes **de** (**d'** + vowel) before an adjective (→ **3**), unless the adjective and noun are seen as forming one unit (→ **4**)

● In negative sentences **de** (**d'** + vowel) is used for both genders, singular and plural (→ **5**)
  Exception: after **ne ... que** *only*, the positive forms above are used (→ **6**)

1 Avez-vous du sucre?
Have you any sugar?
J'ai acheté de la farine et de la margarine
I bought (some) flour and margarine
Il a mangé des gâteaux
He ate some cakes
Est-ce qu'il y a des lettres pour moi?
Are there (any) letters for me?

2 Il me doit de l'argent   **C'est de l'histoire ancienne**
He owes me (some) money   That's ancient history

3 Il a fait de gros efforts pour nous aider
He made a great effort to help us
Cette région a de belles églises
This region has some beautiful churches

4 des grandes vacances   **des jeunes gens**
summer holidays   young people

5 Je n'ai pas de nourriture/d'argent
I don't have any food/money
Vous n'avez pas de timbres/d'œufs?
Have you no stamps/eggs?
Je ne mange jamais de viande/d'omelettes
I never eat meat/omelettes
Il ne veut plus de visiteurs/d'eau
He doesn't want any more visitors/water

6 Il ne boit que du thé/de la bière/de l'eau
He only drinks tea/beer/water
Je n'ai que des problèmes avec cette machine
I have nothing but problems with this machine

The Indefinite Article

	WITH MASC. NOUN	WITH FEM. NOUN	
SING.	**un**	**une**	*a*
PLUR.	**des**	**des**	*some*

● **des** is also the plural of the partitive article (see p. 144)

● In negative sentences, **de** (**d'** + vowel) is used for both singular and plural (→ **1**)

● The indefinite article is used in French largely as it is in English EXCEPT:

  – there is no article when a person's profession is being stated (→ **2**)
    The article *is* present however, following **ce** (**c'** + vowel) (→ **3**)

  – the English article is not translated by **un/une** in constructions like *what a surprise, what an idiot* (→ **4**)

  – in structures of the type given in example **5** the article **un/une** is used in French and not translated in English (→ **5**)

1 Je n'ai pas de livre/d'enfants
I don't have a book/(any) children

2 Il est professeur   **Ma mère est infirmière**
He's a teacher   My mother's a nurse

3 C'est un médecin
He's/She's a doctor
Ce sont des acteurs
They're actors

4 Quelle surprise!   **Quel dommage!**
What a surprise!   What a shame!

5 avec une grande sagesse/un courage admirable
with great wisdom/admirable courage
Il a fait preuve d'un sang-froid incroyable
He showed incredible coolness
Un produit d'une qualité incomparable
A product of incomparable quality

Adjectives

Most adjectives agree in number and in gender with the noun or pronoun.

The formation of feminines

● Most adjectives add an **e** to the masculine singular form (→ **1**)

● If the masculine singular form already ends in **-e**, no further **e** is added (→ **2**)

● Some adjectives undergo a further change when **e** is added. These changes occur regularly and are shown on p. 150

● Irregular feminine forms are shown on p. 152

The formation of plurals

● The plural of both regular and irregular adjectives is formed by adding an **s** to the masculine or feminine singular form, as appropriate (→ **3**)

● When the masculine singular form already ends in **-s** or **-x**, no further **s** is added (→ **4**)

● For masculine singulars ending in **-au** and **-eau**, the masculine plural is **-aux** and **-eaux** (→ **5**)

● For masculine singulars ending in **-al**, the masculine plural is **-aux** (→ **6**)

Exceptions:	**final**	(masculine plural **finals**)
	fatal	(masculine plural **fatals**)
	naval	(masculine plural **navals**)

Pronunciation of feminine and plural adjectives
This is dealt with on p. 244

1   **mon frère aîné**   **ma sœur aînée**
    my elder brother   my elder sister
    le petit garçon   **la petite fille**
    the little boy   the little girl
    un sac gris   **une chemise grise**
    a grey bag   a grey shirt
    un bruit fort   **une voix forte**
    a loud noise   a loud voice

2   **un jeune homme**   **une jeune femme**
    a young man   a young woman
    l'autre verre   **l'autre assiette**
    the other glass   the other plate

3   **le dernier train**   **les derniers trains**
    the last train   the last trains
    une vieille maison   **de vieilles maisons**
    an old house   old houses
    un long voyage   **de longs voyages**
    a long journey   long journeys
    la rue étroite   **les rues étroites**
    the narrow street   the narrow streets

4   **un diplomate français**   **des diplomates français**
    a French diplomat   French diplomats
    un homme dangereux   **des hommes dangereux**
    a dangerous man   dangerous men

5   **le nouveau professeur**   **les nouveaux professeurs**
    the new teacher   the new teachers
    un chien esquimau   **des chiens esquimaux**
    a husky (Fr. = an Eskimo dog)   huskies (Fr. = Eskimo dogs)

6   **un ami loyal**   **des amis loyaux**
    a loyal friend   loyal friends
    un geste amical   **des gestes amicaux**
    a friendly gesture   friendly gestures

Regular feminine endings

MASC. SING.	FEM. SING.	EXAMPLES	
-f	-ve	neuf, vif	(→ 1)
-x	-se	heureux, jaloux	(→ 2)
-eur	-euse	travailleur, flâneur	(→ 3)
-teur	{ -teuse	flatteur, menteur	(→ 4)
	{ -trice	destructeur, séducteur	(→ 5)

Exceptions:

    bref: see p. 152

    doux, faux, roux, vieux: see p. 152

    extérieur, inférieur, intérieur, meilleur, supérieur: all add **e** to the masculine

    enchanteur: fem. = **enchanteresse**

MASC. SING.	FEM. SING.	EXAMPLES	
-an	-anne	paysan	(→ 6)
-en	-enne	ancien, parisien	(→ 7)
-on	-onne	bon, breton	(→ 8)
-as	-asse	bas, las	(→ 9)
-et*	-ette	muet, violet	(→ 10)
-el	-elle	annuel, mortel	(→ 11)
-eil	-eille	pareil, vermeil	(→ 12)

Exception:

    ras: fem. = **rase**

MASC. SING.	FEM. SING.	EXAMPLES	
-et*	-ète	secret, complet	(→ 13)
-er	-ère	étranger, fier	(→ 14)

*Note that there are two feminine endings for masculine adjectives ending in **-et**.

1 **un résultat positif**
  a positive result

  une attitude positive
  a positive attitude

2 **d'un ton sérieux**
  in a serious tone (of voice)

  une voix sérieuse
  a serious voice

3 **un enfant trompeur**
  a deceitful child

  une déclaration trompeuse
  a misleading statement

4 **un tableau flatteur**
  a flattering picture

  une comparaison flatteuse
  a flattering comparison

5 **un geste protecteur**
  a protective gesture

  une couche protectrice
  a protective layer

6 **un problème paysan**
  a farming problem

  la vie paysanne
  country life

7 **un avion égyptien**
  an Egyptian plane

  une statue égyptienne
  an Egyptian statue

8 **un bon repas**
  a good meal

  de bonne humeur
  in a good mood

9 **un plafond bas**
  a low ceiling

  à voix basse
  in a low voice

10 **un travail net**
  a clean piece of work

  une explication nette
  a clear explanation

11 **un homme cruel**
  a cruel man

  une remarque cruelle
  a cruel remark

12 **un livre pareil**
  such a book

  en pareille occasion
  on such an occasion

13 **un regard inquiet**
  an anxious look

  une attente inquiète
  an anxious wait

14 **un goût amer**
  a bitter taste

  une amère déception
  a bitter disappointment

Adjectives with irregular feminine forms

MASC. SING.	FEM. SING.		
aigu	aiguë	*sharp; high-pitched*	(→ 1)
ambigu	ambiguë	*ambiguous*	
beau (bel)*	belle	*beautiful*	
bénin	bénigne	*benign*	
blanc	blanche	*white*	
bref	brève	*brief, short*	(→ 2)
doux	douce	*soft; sweet*	
épais	épaisse	*think*	
esquimau	esquimaude	*Eskimo*	
faux	fausse	*wrong*	
favori	favorite	*favourite*	(→ 3)
fou (fol)*	folle	*mad*	
frais	fraîche	*fresh*	(→ 4)
franc	franche	*frank*	
gentil	gentille	*kind*	
grec	grecque	*Greek*	
gros	grosse	*big*	
jumeau	jumelle	*twin*	(→ 5)
long	longue	*long*	
malin	maligne	*malignant*	
mou (mol)*	molle	*soft*	
nouveau (nouvel)*	nouvelle	*new*	
nul	nulle	*no*	
public	publique	*public*	(→ 6)
roux	rousse	*red-haired*	
sec	sèche	*dry*	
sot	sotte	*foolish*	
turc	turque	*Turkish*	
vieux (vieil)*	vieille	*old*	

*This form is used when the following word begins with a vowel or an **h** 'mute' (→ 7)

1 **un son aigu**
a high-pitched sound

une douleur aiguë
a sharp pain

2 **un bref discours**
a short speech

une brève rencontre
a short meeting

3 **mon sport favori**
my favourite sport

ma chanson favorite
my favourite song

4 **du pain frais**
fresh bread

de la crème fraîche
fresh cream

5 **mon frère jumeau**
my twin brother

ma sœur jumelle
my twin sister

6 **un jardin public**
a (public) park

l'opinion publique
public opinion

7 **un bel appartement**
a beautiful flat
le nouvel inspecteur
the new inspector
un vieil arbre
an old tree

un bel habit
a beautiful outfit
un nouvel harmonica
a new harmonica
un vieil hôtel
an old hotel

Comparatives and Superlatives

Comparatives

These are formed using the following constructions:

plus ... (que)	*more ... (than)*	(→ **1**)
moins ... (que)	*less ... (than)*	(→ **2**)
aussi ... que	*as ... as*	(→ **3**)
si ... que*	*as ... as*	(→ **4**)

*used mainly after a negative

Superlatives

These are formed using the following constructions:

le/la/les plus ... (que)	*the most ... (that)*	(→ **5**)
le/la/les moins ... (que)	*the least ... (that)*	(→ **6**)

- When the possessive adjective is present, two constructions are possible (→ **7**)
- After a superlative the preposition **de** is often translated as *in* (→ **8**)
- If a clause follows a superlative, the verb is in the subjunctive (→ **9**)

Adjectives with irregular comparatives/superlatives

ADJECTIVE	COMPARATIVE	SUPERLATIVE
bon	**meilleur**	**le meilleur**
good	*better*	*the best*
mauvais	**pire** OR	**le pire** OR
bad	**plus mauvais**	**le plus mauvais**
	worse	*the worst*
petit	**moindre*** OR	**le moindre*** OR
small	**plus petit**	**le plus petit**
	smaller;	*the smallest;*
	lesser	*the least*

*used only with abstract nouns

- Comparative and superlative adjectives agree in number and in gender with the noun, just like any other adjective (→ **10**)

1 **une raison plus grave**
a more serious reason
Elle est plus petite que moi
She is smaller than me

2 **un film moins connu**
a less well-known film
C'est moins cher qu'il ne pense
It's cheaper than he thinks

3 **Robert était aussi inquiet que moi**
Robert was as worried as I was
Cette ville n'est pas aussi grande que Bordeaux
This town isn't as big as Bordeaux

4 **Ils ne sont pas si contents que ça**
They aren't as happy as all that

5 **le guide le plus utile**   **la voiture la plus petite**
the most useful guidebook   the smallest car
les plus grandes maisons
the biggest houses

6 **le mois le moins agréable**   **la fille la moins forte**
the least pleasant month   the weakest girl
les moins belles peintures
the least attractive paintings

7 **Mon désir le plus cher** ⎫
                ⎬ **est de voyager**
Mon plus cher désir ⎭
My dearest wish is to travel

8 **la plus grande gare de Londres**
the biggest station in London
l'habitant le plus âgé du village/de la région
the oldest inhabitant in the village/in the area

9 **la personne la plus gentille que je connaisse**
the nicest person I know

10 **les moindres difficultés**
the least difficulties
la meilleure qualité
the best quality

Demonstrative Adjectives

	MASCULINE	FEMININE	
SING.	**ce (cet)**	**cette**	*this; that*
FLUR.	**ces**	**ces**	*these; those*

● Demonstrative adjectives agree in number and gender with the noun (→ **1**)

● **cet** is used when the following word begins with a vowel or an **h** 'mute' (→ **2**)

● For emphasis or in order to distinguish between people or objects, **-ci** or **-là** is added to the noun: **-ci** indicates proximity (usually translated *this*) and **là** distance (*that*) (→ **3**)

1 Ce stylo ne marche pas
This/That pen isn't working
Comment s'appelle cette entreprise?
What's this/that company called?
Ces livres sont les miens
These/Those books are mine
Ces couleurs sont plus jolies
These/Those colours are nicer

2 cet oiseau
this/that bird
cet article
this/that article
cet homme
this/that man

3 Combien coûte ce manteau-ci?
How much is this coat?
Je voudrais cinq de ces pommes-là
I'd like five of those apples
Est-ce que tu reconnais cette personne-là?
Do you recognize that person?
Mettez ces vêtements-ci dans cette valise-là
Put these clothes in that case
Ce garçon-là appartient à ce groupe-ci
That boy belongs to this group

Interrogative Adjectives

	MASCULINE	FEMININE	
SING.	quel?	quelle?	what?; which?
PLUR.	quels?	quelles?	what?; which?

- Interrogative adjectives agree in number and gender with the noun (→ **1**)

- The forms shown above are also used in indirect questions (→ **2**)

Exclamatory Adjectives

	MASCULINE	FEMININE	
SING.	quel!	quelle!	what (a)!
PLUR.	quels!	quelles!	what!

- Exclamatory adjectives agree in number and gender with the noun (→ **3**)

- For other exclamations, see p. 214

1 Quel genre d'homme est-ce?
What type of man is he?
Quelle est leur décision?
What is their decision?
Vous jouez de quels instruments?
What instruments do you play?
Quelles offres avez-vous reçues?
What offers have you received?
Quel vin recommandez-vous?
Which wine do you recommend?
Quelles couleurs préférez-vous?
Which colours do you prefer?

2 Je ne sais pas à quelle heure il est arrivé
I don't know what time he arrived
Dites-moi quels sont les livres les plus intéressants
Tell me which books are the most interesting

3 Quel dommage!
What a pity!
Quelle idée!
What an idea!
Quels beaux livres vous avez!
What fine books you have!
Quelles jolies fleurs!
What nice flowers!

Possessive Adjectives

WITH SING. NOUN		WITH PLUR. NOUN	
MASC.	*FEM.*	*MASC./FEM.*	
mon	ma (mon)	mes	*my*
ton	ta (ton)	tes	*your*
son	sa (son)	ses	*his; her; its*
notre	notre	nos	*our*
votre	votre	vos	*your*
leur	leur	leurs	*their*

- Possessive adjectives agree in number and gender with the noun, NOT WITH THE OWNER (→ **1**)

- The forms shown in brackets are used when the following word begins with a vowel or an **h** 'mute' (→ **2**)

- **son, sa, ses** have the additional meaning of *one's* (→ **3**)

1 **Catherine a oublié son parapluie**
   Catherine has left her umbrella
   Paul cherche sa montre
   Paul's looking for his watch
   Mon frère et ma sœur habitent à Glasgow
   My brother and sister live in Glasgow
   Est-ce que tes voisins ont vendu leur voiture?
   Did your neighbours sell their car?
   Rangez vos affaires
   Put your things away

2 **mon appareil-photo**
   my camera
   ton histoire
   your story
   son erreur
   his/her mistake
   mon autre sœur
   my other sister

3 **perdre son équilibre**
   to lose one's balance
   présenter ses excuses
   to offer one's apologies

Position of Adjectives

● French adjectives usually follow the noun (→ **1**)

● Adjectives of colour or nationality *always* follow the noun (→ **2**)

● As in English, demonstrative, possessive, numerical and interrogative adjectives precede the noun (→ **3**)

● The adjectives **autre** *other* and **chaque** *each, every* precede the noun (→ **4**)

● The following common adjectives can precede the noun:

beau	*beautiful*	**jeune**	*young*
bon	*good*	**joli**	*pretty*
court	*short*	**long**	*long*
dernier	*last*	**mauvais**	*bad*
grand	*great*	**petit**	*small*
gros	*big*	**tel**	*such (a)*
haut	*high*	**vieux**	*old*

● The meaning of the following adjectives varies according to their position:

	BEFORE NOUN	AFTER NOUN	
ancien	*former*	*old, ancient*	(→ **5**)
brave	*good*	*brave*	(→ **6**)
cher	*dear (beloved)*	*expensive*	(→ **7**)
grand	*great*	*tall*	(→ **8**)
même	*same*	*very*	(→ **9**)
pauvre	*poor (wretched)*	*poor (not rich)*	(→ **10**)
propre	*own*	*clean*	(→ **11**)
seul	*single, sole*	*on one's own*	(→ **12**)
simple	*mere, simple*	*simple, easy*	(→ **13**)
vrai	*real*	*true*	(→ **14**)

● Adjectives following the noun are linked by **et** (→ **15**)

1 **le chapitre suivant**
the following chapter

    l'heure exacte
    the right time

2 **une cravate rouge**
a red tie

    un mot français
    a French word

3 **ce dictionnaire**
this dictionary

    mon père
    my father

  le premier étage
the first floor

    deux exemples
    two examples

  quel homme?
which man?

4 **une autre fois**
another time

    chaque jour
    every day

5 **un ancien collègue**
a former colleague

    l'histoire ancienne
    ancient history

6 **un brave homme**
a good man

    un homme brave
    a brave man

7 **mes chers amis**
my dear friends

    une robe chère
    an expensive dress

8 **un grand peintre**
a great painter

    un homme grand
    a tall man

9 **la même réponse**
the same answer

    vos paroles mêmes
    your very words

10 **cette pauvre femme**
that poor woman

    une nation pauvre
    a poor nation

11 **ma propre vie**
my own life

    une chemise propre
    a clean shirt

12 **une seule réponse**
a single reply

    une femme seule
    a woman on her own

13 **un simple regard**
a mere look

    un problème simple
    a simple problem

14 **la vraie raison**
the real reason

    les faits vrais
    the true facts

15 **un acte lâche et trompeur**
a cowardly, deceitful act

  un acte lâche, trompeur et ignoble
a cowardly, deceitful and ignoble act

Personal Pronouns

	SUBJECT PRONOUNS	
PERSON	*SINGULAR*	*PLURAL*
1st	**je (j')**	**nous**
	I	*we*
2nd	**tu**	**vous**
	you	*you*
3rd (masc.)	**il**	**ils**
	he; it	*they*
(fem.)	**elle**	**elles**
	she; it	*they*

je changes to **j'** before a vowel, an **h** 'mute', or the pronoun **y** (→ **1**)

● **tu/vous**

Vous, as well as being the second person plural, is also used when addressing one person. As a general rule, use **tu** only when addressing a friend, a child, a relative, someone you know very well, or when invited to do so. In all other cases use **vous**. For singular and plural uses of **vous**, see example **2**.

● **il/elle; ils/elles**

The form of the 3rd person pronouns reflects the number and gender of the noun(s) they replace, referring to animals and things as well as to people. **Ils** also replaces a combination of masculine and feminine nouns (→ **3**)

● Sometimes stressed pronouns replace the subject pronouns, see p. 172

Continued

1 J'arrive!
I'm just coming!
J'en ai trois
I've got 3 of them
J'hésite à le déranger
I hesitate to disturb him
J'y pense souvent
I often think about it

2 Compare: **Vous êtes certain, Monsieur Leclerc?**
Are you sure, Mr Leclerc?
and: **Vous êtes certains, les enfants?**
Are you sure, children?
Compare: **Vous êtes partie quand, Estelle?**
When did you leave, Estelle?
and: **Estelle et Sophie – vous êtes parties quand?**
Estelle and Sophie – when did you leave?

3 Où logent ton père et ta mère quand ils vont à Rome?
Where do your father and mother stay when they go to Rome?
Donne-moi le journal et les lettres quand ils arriveront
Give me the newspaper and the letters when they arrive

Personal Pronouns (ctd.)

DIRECT OBJECT PRONOUNS

PERSON	SINGULAR	PLURAL
1st	**me (m')**	**nous**
	me	*us*
2nd	**te (t')**	**vous**
	you	*you*
3rd (masc.)	**le (l')**	**les**
	him; it	*them*
(fem.)	**la (l')**	**les**
	her; it	*them*

The forms shown in brackets are used before a vowel, an **h** 'mute', or the pronoun **y** (→ **1**)

● In positive commands **me** and **te** change to **moi** and **toi** except before **en** or **y** (→ **2**)

● **le** sometimes functions as a 'neuter' pronoun, referring to an idea or information contained in a previous statement or question. It is often not translated (→ **3**)

Position of direct object pronouns
● In constructions other than the imperative affirmative the pronoun comes before the verb (→ **4**)
The same applies when the verb is in the infinitive (→ **5**)
In the imperative affirmative, the pronoun follows the verb and is attached to it by a hyphen (→ **6**)

● For further information, see Order of Object Pronouns, p. 170

Reflexive Pronouns
These are dealt with under reflexive verbs, p. 30

Continued

1 Il m'a vu
He saw me
Je ne t'oublierai jamais
I'll never forget you
Ça l'habitue à travailler seul
That gets him/her used to working on his/her own
Je veux l'y accoutumer
I want to accustom him/her to it

2 Avertis-moi de ta décision → Avertis-m'en
Inform me of your decision   Inform me of it

3 Il n'est pas là. – Je le sais bien.
He isn't there. – I know that.
Aidez-moi si vous le pouvez
Help me if you can
Elle viendra demain. – Je l'espère bien.
She'll come tomorrow. – I hope so.

4 Je t'aime
I love you
Les voyez-vous?
Can you see them?
Elle ne nous connaît pas
She doesn't know us
Est-ce que tu ne les aimes pas?
Don't you like them?
Ne me faites pas rire
Don't make me laugh

5 Puis-je vous aider?
May I help you?

6 Aidez-moi   **Suivez-nous**
Help me   Follow us

Personal Pronouns (ctd.)

INDIRECT OBJECT PRONOUNS

PERSON	SINGULAR	PLURAL
1st	**me (m')**	**nous**
2nd	**te (t')**	**vous**
3rd (masc.)	**lui**	**leur**
(fem.)	**lui**	**leur**

me and **te** change to **m'** and **t'** before a vowel or an **h** 'mute' (→**1**)

● In positive commands, **me** and **te** change to **moi** and **toi** except before **en** (→**2**)

● The pronouns shown in the above table replace the preposition **à** + noun, where the noun is a person or an animal (→**3**)

● The verbal construction affects the translation of the pronoun (→**4**)

Position of indirect object pronouns
● In constructions other than the imperative affirmative, the pronoun comes before the verb (→**5**)
The same applies when the verb is in the infinitive (→**6**)
In the imperative affirmative, the pronoun follows the verb and is attached to it by a hyphen (→**7**)

● For further information, see Order of Object Pronouns, p. 170

Reflexive Pronouns
These are dealt with under reflexive verbs, p. 30

Continued

1 Tu m'as donné ce livre
You gave me this book
Ils t'ont caché les faits
They hid the facts from you

2 Donnez-moi du sucre   → **Donnez-m'en**
Give me some sugar   Give me some
Garde-toi assez d'argent   → **Garde-t'en assez**
Keep enough money for   Keep enough for yourself
yourself

3 J'écris à Suzanne   → **Je lui écris**
I'm writing to Suzanne   I'm writing to her
Donne du lait au chat   ⇢ **Donne-lui du lait**
Give the cat some milk   Give it some milk

4 arracher qch à qn   to snatch sth from sb:
      Un voleur m'a arraché mon porte-monnaie
      A thief snatched my purse from me
promettre qch à qn   to promise sb sth:
      Il leur a promis un cadeau
      He promised them a present
demander à qn de faire   to ask sb to do:
      Elle nous avait demandé de revenir
      She had asked us to come back

5 Elle vous a écrit   **Vous a-t-elle écrit?**
She's written to you   Has she written to you?
Il ne nous parle pas
He doesn't speak to us
Est-ce que cela ne vous intéresse pas?
Doesn't it interest you?
Ne leur répondez pas
Don't answer them

6 Voulez-vous leur envoyer l'adresse?
Do you want to send them the address?

7 Répondez-moi   **Donnez-nous la réponse**
Answer me   Tell us the answer

Personal Pronouns (ctd.)

Order of object pronouns

- When two object pronouns of different persons come before the verb, the order is: indirect before direct, i.e.

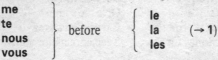

me			
te	before	le	
nous		la	(→ 1)
vous		les	

- When two 3rd person object pronouns come before the verb, the order is: direct before indirect, i.e.

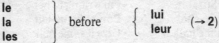

le			
la	before	lui	(→ 2)
les		leur	

- When two object pronouns come after the verb (i.e. in the imperative affirmative), the order is: direct before indirect, i.e.

le		moi	
la	before	toi	
les		lui	(→ 3)
		nous	
		vous	
		leur	

- The pronouns **y** and **en** (see pp. 176 and 174) always come last (→ 4)

Continued

1 Dominique vous l'envoie demain
Dominique's sending it to you tomorrow
Est-ce qu'il te les a montrés?
Has he shown them to you?
Ne me le dis pas
Don't tell me (it)
Il ne veut pas nous la prêter
He won't lend it to us

2 Elle le leur a emprunté
She borrowed it from them
Je les lui ai lus
I read them to him/her
Ne la leur donne pas
Don't give it to them
Je voudrais les lui rendre
I'd like to give them back to him/her

3 Rends-les-moi
Give them back to me
Donnez-le-nous
Give it to us
Apportons-les-leur
Let's take them to them

4 Donnez-leur-en
Give them some
Je l'y ai déposé
I dropped him there
Ne nous en parlez plus
Don't speak to us about it any more

Personal Pronouns (ctd.)

STRESSED OR DISJUNCTIVE PRONOUNS

PERSON	SINGULAR	PLURAL
1st	**moi**	**nous**
	me	*us*
2nd	**toi**	**vous**
	you	*you*
3rd (masc.)	**lui**	**eux**
	him; it	*them*
(fem.)	**elle**	**elles**
	her; it	*them*
('reflexive')	**soi**	
	oneself	

● These pronouns are used:
  – after prepositions (→ **1**)
  – on their own (←→ **2**)
  – following **c'est**, **ce sont** *it is* (→ **3**)
  – for emphasis, especially where contrast is involved (→ **4**)
  – when the subject consists of two or more pronouns (→ **5**)
  – when the subject consists of a pronoun and a noun (→ **6**)
  – in comparisons (→ **7**)
  – before relative pronouns (→ **8**)

● For particular emphasis -**même** (singular) or -**mêmes** (plural) is added to the pronoun (→ **9**)

moi-même	*myself*	**nous-mêmes**	*ourselves*
toi-même	*yourself*	**vous-même**	*yourself*
lui-même	*himself; itself*	**vous-mêmes**	*yourselves*
elle-même	*herself; itself*	**eux-mêmes**	*themselves*
soi-même	*oneself*	**elles-mêmes**	*themselves*

1 **Je pense à toi**
   I think about you
   C'est pour elle
   This is for her
   Venez avec moi
   Come with me

   Partez sans eux
   Leave without them
   Assieds-toi à côté de lui
   Sit beside him
   Il a besoin de nous
   He needs us

2 **Qui a fait cela? – Lui.**
   Who did that? – He did.
   Qui est-ce qui gagne? – Moi
   Who's winning? – Me

3 **C'est toi, Simon? – Non, c'est moi, David.**
   Is that you, Simon? – No, it's me, David
   Qui est-ce? – Ce sont eux.
   Who is it? – It's them.

4 **Ils voyagent séparément: lui par le train, elle en autobus**
   They travel separately: he by train and she by bus
   Toi, tu ressembles à ton père, eux pas
   You look like your father, *they* don't
   Il n'a pas l'air de s'ennuyer, lui!
   He doesn't look bored!

5 **Lui et moi partons demain**
   He and I are leaving tomorrow
   Ni vous ni elles ne pouvez rester
   Neither you nor they can stay

6 **Mon père et elle ne s'entendent pas**
   My father and she don't get on

7 **plus jeune que moi**
   younger than me

   Il est moins grand que toi
   He's smaller than you (are)

8 **Moi, qui étais malade, je n'ai pas pu les accompagner**
   I, who was ill, couldn't go with them
   Ce sont eux qui font du bruit, pas nous
   They're the ones making the noise, not us

9 **Je l'ai fait moi-même**
   I did it myself

The pronoun en

● **en** replaces the preposition **de** + noun (→ **1**)
The verbal construction can affect the translation (→ **2**)

● **en** also replaces the partitive article (*English = some, any*) + noun
(→ **3**)

In expressions of quantity **en** represents the noun (→ **4**)

● Position:
en comes before the verb, except in positive commands when it
follows and is attached to the verb by a hyphen (→ **5**)

● **en** follows other object pronouns (→ **6**)

1 **Il est fier de son succès**   → **Il en est fier**
   He's proud of his success   He's proud of it
   Elle est sortie du cinéma   → **Elle en est sortie**
   She came out of the cinema   She came out (of it)
   Je suis couvert de peinture → **J'en suis couvert**
   I'm covered in paint   I'm covered in it
   Il a beaucoup d'amis   → **Il en a beaucoup**
   He has lots of friends   He has lots (of them)

2 **avoir besoin de qch**   to need sth:
   J'en ai besoin
   I need it/them
   avoir peur de qch   to be afraid of sth:
   J'en ai peur
   I'm afraid of it/them

3 **Avez-vous de l'argent?**   → **En avez-vous?**
   Have you any money?   Do you have any?
   Je veux acheter des timbres → **Je veux en acheter**
   I want to buy some stamps   I want to buy some

4 **J'ai deux crayons**   → **J'en ai deux**
   I've two pencils   I've two (of them)
   Combien de sœurs as-tu? – J'en ai trois.
   How many sisters do you have? – I have three.

5 **Elle en a discuté avec moi**
   She discussed it with me
   En êtes-vous content?
   Are you pleased with
   it/them?
   Je veux en garder trois
   I want to keep three of them
   N'en parlez plus
   Don't talk about it any more
   Prenez-en   **Soyez-en fier**
   Take some   Be proud of it/them
6 **Donnez-leur-en**   **Il m'en a parlé**
   Give them some   He spoke to me about it

The pronoun y

● **y** replaces the preposition **à** + noun (→ **1**)
  The verbal construction can affect the translation (→ **2**)

● **y** also replaces the prepositions **dans** and **sur** + noun (→ **3**)

● **y** can also mean *there* (→ **4**)

● Position:
  y comes before the verb, except in positive commands when it follows and is attached to the verb by a hyphen (→ **5**)

● **y** follows other object pronouns (→ **6**)

1 **Ne touchez pas à ce bouton** → **N'y touchez pas**
  Don't touch this switch   Don't touch it
  Il participe aux concerts → **Il y participe**
  He takes part in the concerts He takes part (in them)

2 **penser à qch**   to think about sth:
    J'y pense souvent
    I often think about it
  consentir à qch   to agree to sth:
    Tu y as consenti?
    Have you agreed to it?

3 **Mettez-les dans la boîte** → **Mettez-les-y**
  Put them in the box   Put them in it
  Il les a mis sur les étagères → **Il les y a mis**
  He put them on the shelves   He put them on them
  J'ai placé de l'argent sur ce
  compte   → **J'y ai placé de l'argent**
  I've put money into this   I've put money into it
  account

4 **Elle y passe tout l'été**
  She spends the whole summer there

5 **Il y a ajouté du sucre**
  He added sugar to it
  Elle n'y a pas écrit son nom
  She hasn't written her name on it
  Comment fait-on pour y aller?
  How do you get there?
  N'y pense plus!
  Don't give it another thought!
  Restez-y   **Réfléchissez-y**
  Stay there   Think it over

6 **Elle m'y a conduit**   **Menez-nous-y**
  She drove me there   Take us there

Indefinite Pronouns

aucun(e)	*none, not any*	(→1)
certain(e)s	*some, certain*	(→2)
chacun(e)	*each (one)* *everybody*	(→3)
on	*one, you* *somebody* *they, people* *we* (informal use)	(→4)
personne	*nobody*	(→5)
plusieurs	*several*	(→6)
quelque chose	*something; anything*	(→7)
quelques-un(e)s	*some, a few*	(→8)
quelqu'un	*somebody; anybody*	(→9)
rien	*nothing*	(→10)
tout	*all; everything*	(→11)
tous (toutes)	*all*	(→12)
l'un(e) ... l'autre	*(the) one ... the other*	
les un(e)s ... les autres	*some ...others*	(→13)

● **aucun(e), personne, rien**

When used as subject or object of the verb, these require the word **ne** placed immediately before the verb. Note that **aucun** further needs the pronoun **en** when used as an object (→14)

● **quelque chose, rien**

When qualified by an adjective, these pronouns require the preposition **de** before the adjective (→15)

1 **Combien en avez-vous? – Aucun**
How many have you got? – None

2 **Certains pensent que ...**
Some (people) think that ...

3 **Chacune de ces boîtes est pleine**　　**Chacun son tour!**
Each of these boxes is full　　　　　　Everybody in turn!

4 **On voit l'église de cette fenêtre**
You can see the church from this window
À la campagne on se couche tôt
In the country they/we go to bed early
Est-ce qu'on lui a permis de rester?
Was he/she allowed to stay?

5 **Qui voyez-vous? – Personne**
Who can you see? – Nobody

6 **Ils sont plusieurs**
There are several of them

7 **Mange donc quelque chose!**　　**Tu as vu quelque chose?**
Eat something!　　　　　　　　　Did you see anything?

8 **Je connais quelques-uns de ses amis**
I know some of his/her friends

9 **Quelqu'un a appelé**　　　　　**Tu as vu quelqu'un?**
Somebody called (out)　　　　　Did you see anybody?

10 **Qu'est-ce que tu as dans la main? – Rien**
What have you got in your hand? – Nothing

11 **Il a tout gâché**　　　　　　　**Tout va bien**
He has spoiled everything　　　All's well

12 **Tu les as tous?**　　　　　　　**Elles sont toutes venues**
Do you have all of them?　　　They all came

13 **Les uns sont satisfaits, les autres pas**
Some are satisfied, (the) others aren't

14 **Je ne vois personne**　　　　　**Rien ne lui plaît**
I can't see anyone　　　　　　　Nothing pleases him/her
Aucune des entreprises ne veut ...　**Il n'en a aucun**
None of the companies wants ...　　He hasn't any (of them)

15 **quelque chose de grand**　　　**rien d'intéressant**
something big　　　　　　　　　nothing interesting

Relative Pronouns

qui   *who; which*
que   *who(m); which*

These are subject and direct object pronouns that introduce a clause and refer to people or things.

	PEOPLE	THINGS
SUBJECT	**qui** (→1)	**qui** (→3)
	who, that	*which, that*
DIRECT	**que (qu')** (→2)	**que (qu')** (→4)
OBJECT	*who(m), that*	*which, that*

● **que** changes to **qu'** before a vowel (→2/4)
● You cannot omit the object relative pronoun in French as you can in English (→2/4)

After a preposition:
● When referring to people, use **qui** (→5)
    Exceptions: after **parmi** *among* and **entre** *between* use **lesquels/lesquelles** (see below) (→6)
● When referring to things, use forms of **lequel**:

	MASCULINE	FEMININE	
SING.	**lequel**	**laquelle**	*which*
PLUR.	**lesquels**	**lesquelles**	*which*

The pronoun agrees in number and gender with the noun (→7)

● After the prepositions **à** and **de**, **lequel** and **lesquel(le)s** contract as follows:

> à + lequel → auquel
> à + lesquels → auxquels   (→8)
> à + lesquelles → auxquelles

> de + lequel → duquel
> de + lesquels → desquels   (→9)
> de + lesquelles → desquelles

Continued

1 **Mon frère, qui a vingt ans, est à l'université**
  My brother, who's twenty, is at university

2 **Les amis que je vois le plus sont ...**
  The friends (that) I see most are ...
  Lucienne, qu'il connaît depuis longtemps, est ...
  Lucienne, whom he has known for a long time, is ...

3 **Il y a un escalier qui mène au toit**
  There's a staircase which leads to the roof

4 **La maison que nous avons achetée a ...**
  The house (which) we've bought has ...
  Voici le cadeau qu'elle m'a envoyé
  This is the present (that) she sent me

5 **la personne à qui il parle**
  the person he's talking to
  la personne avec qui je voyage
  the person with whom I travel
  les enfants pour qui je l'ai acheté
  the children for whom I bought it

6 **Il y avait des jeunes, parmi lesquels Robert**
  There were some young people, Robert among them
  les filles entre lesquelles j'étais assis
  the girls between whom I was sitting

7 **le torchon avec lequel il l'essuie**
  the cloth he's wiping it with
  la table sur laquelle je l'ai mis
  the table on which I put it
  les moyens par lesquels il l'accomplit
  the means by which he achieves it
  les pièces pour lesquelles elle est connue
  the plays for which she is famous

8 **le magasin auquel il livre ces marchandises**
  the shop to which he delivers these goods

9 **les injustices desquelles il se plaint**
  the injustices he's complaining about

Relative Pronouns (ctd.)

quoi   *which, what*

● When the relative pronoun does not refer to a specific noun, **quoi** is used after a preposition (→**1**)

dont   *whose, of whom, of which*

● **dont** often (but not always) replaces **de qui, duquel, de laquelle**, and **desquel(le)s** (→**2**)

● It cannot replace **de qui**, **duquel** etc in the construction preposition + noun + **de qui / duquel** (→**3**)

Continued

1 C'est en quoi vous vous trompez
That's where you're wrong
A quoi, j'ai répondu '...'
To which I replied, '...'

2 la femme dont (= de qui) la voiture est garée en face
the woman whose car is parked opposite
un prix dont (= de qui) je suis fier
an award I am proud of
un ami dont (= de qui) je connais le frère
a friend whose brother I know
les enfants dont (= de qui) vous vous occupez
the children you look after
le film dont (= duquel) il a parlé
the film of which he spoke
la fenêtre dont (= de laquelle) les rideaux sont tirés
the window whose curtains are drawn
des livres dont (= desquels) j'ai oublié les titres
books whose titles I've forgotten
les maladies dont (= desquelles) il souffre
the illnesses he suffers from

3 une personne sur l'aide de qui on peut compter
a person whose help one can rely on
les enfants aux parents de qui j'écris
the children to whose parents I'm writing
la maison dans le jardin de laquelle il y a ...
the house in whose garden there is ...

Relative Pronouns (ctd.)

ce qui, ce que   *that which, what*
These are used when the relative pronoun does not refer to a specific noun, and they are often translated as *what* (literally: *that which*)

> **ce qui**   is used as the subject (→**1**)
> **ce que***   is used as the direct object (→**2**)
>
> ***que** changes to **qu'** before a vowel (→**2**)

● Note the construction

> **tout ce qui** }
> **tout ce que** }   *everything/all that*   (→**3**)

● **de + ce que → ce dont** (→**4**)

● preposition + **ce que → ce** + preposition + **quoi** (→**5**)

● When **ce qui**, **ce que** etc, refers to a previous CLAUSE the translation is *which* (→**6**)

Continued

1 **Ce qui m'intéresse ne l'intéresse pas forcément**
  What interests me doesn't necessarily interest him
  Je n'ai pas vu ce qui s'est passé
  I didn't see what happened

2 **Ce que j'aime c'est la musique classique**
  What I like is classical music
  Montrez-moi ce qu'il vous a donné
  Show me what he gave you

3 **Tout ce qui reste c'est ...**
  All that's left is ...
  Donnez-moi tout ce que vous avez
  Give me everything you have

4 **Il risque de perdre ce dont il est si fier**
  He risks losing what he's so proud of
  Voilà ce dont il s'agit
  That's what it's about

5 **Ce n'est pas ce à quoi je m'attendais**
  It's not what I was expecting
  Ce à quoi je m'intéresse particulièrement c'est ...
  What I'm particularly interested in is ...

6 **Il est d'accord, ce qui m'étonne**
  He agrees, which surprises me
  Il a dit qu'elle ne venait pas, ce que nous savions déjà
  He said she wasn't coming, which we already knew

Interrogative Pronouns

qui? *who?; whom?*
que? *what?*
quoi? *what?*

These pronouns are used in direct questions.
The form of the pronoun depends on:
- whether it refers to people or to things
- whether it is the subject or object of the verb, or if it comes after a preposition

Qui and **que** have longer forms, as shown in the tables below.

● Referring to people:

SUBJECT	**qui?**	
	qui est-ce qui?	(→**1**)
	who?	
OBJECT	**qui?**	
	qui est-ce que*?	(→**2**)
	who(m)?	
AFTER PREPOSITIONS	**qui?**	(→**3**)
	who(m)?	

● Referring to things:

SUBJECT	**qu'est-ce qui?**	(→**4**)
	what?	
OBJECT	**que*?**	
	qu'est-ce que*?	(→**5**)
	what?	
AFTER PREPOSITIONS	**quoi?**	(→**6**)
	what?	

***que** changes to **qu'** before a vowel (→**2, 5**)

Continued

1 **Qui vient?**
  Qui est-ce qui vient?
  Who's coming?

2 **Qui vois-tu?**
  Qui est-ce que tu vois?
  Who(m) can you see?
  Qui a-t-elle rencontré?
  Qui est-ce qu'elle a rencontré?
  Who(m) did she meet?

3 **De qui parle-t-il?**
  Who's he talking about?
  Pour qui est ce livre?
  Who's this book for?
  A qui avez-vous écrit?
  To whom did you write?

4 **Qu'est-ce qui se passe?**
  What's happening?
  Qu'est-ce qui a vexé Paul?
  What upset Paul?

5 **Que faites-vous?**
  Qu'est-ce que vous faites?
  What are you doing?
  Qu'a-t-il dit?
  Qu'est-ce qu'il a dit?
  What did he say?

6 **A quoi cela sert-il?**
  What's that used for?
  De quoi a-t-on parlé?
  What was the discussion about?
  Sur quoi vous basez-vous?
  What do you base it on?

Interrogative Pronouns (ctd.)

qui *who; whom*
ce qui *what*
ce que *what*
quoi *what*

These pronouns are used in indirect questions.
The form of the pronoun depends on:

> – whether it refers to people or to things
> – whether it is the subject or object of the verb, or if it comes after a preposition

● Referring to people: use **qui** in all instances (→**1**)

● Referring to things:

SUBJECT	**ce qui**	(→**2**)
	what	
OBJECT	**ce que***	(→**3**)
	what	
AFTER	**quoi**	(→**4**)
PREPOSITIONS	*what*	

***que** changes to **qu'** before a vowel (→**3**)

Continued

1 **Demande-lui qui est venu**
  Ask him who came
  Je me demande qui ils ont vu
  I wonder who they saw
  Dites-moi qui vous préférez
  Tell me who you prefer
  Elle ne sait pas à qui s'adresser
  She doesn't know who to apply to
  Demandez-leur pour qui elles travaillent
  Ask them who they work for

2 **Il se demande ce qui se passe**
  He's wondering what's happening
  Je ne sais pas ce qui vous fait croire que ...
  I don't know what makes you think that ...

3 **Raconte-nous ce que tu as fait**
  Tell us what you did
  Je me demande ce qu'elle pense
  I wonder what she's thinking

4 **On ne sait pas de quoi vivent ces animaux**
  We don't know what these animals live on
  Je vais lui demander à quoi il fait allusion
  I'm going to ask him what he's hinting at

Interrogative Pronouns (ctd.)

lequel?, laquelle?; lesquels?, lesquelles?

	MASCULINE	FEMININE	
SING.	**lequel?**	**laquelle?**	*which (one)?*
PLUR.	**lesquels?**	**lesquelles?**	*which (ones)?*

● The pronoun agrees in number and gender with the noun it refers to (→**1**)

● The same forms are used in indirect questions (→**2**)

● After the prepositions **à** and **de**, **lequel** and **lesquel(le)s** contract as follows:

> à + lequel? → auquel?
> à + lesquels? → auxquels?
> à + lesquelles? → auxquelles?
>
> de + lequel? → duquel?
> de + lesquels? → desquels?
> de + lesquelles? → desquelles?

1 J'ai choisi un livre. – Lequel?
I've chosen a book. – Which one?
Laquelle de ces valises est la vôtre?
Which of these cases is yours?
Amenez quelques amis. – Lesquels?
Bring some friends. – Which ones?
Lesquelles de vos sœurs sont mariées?
Which of your sisters are married?

2 Je me demande laquelle des maisons est la leur
I wonder which is their house
Dites-moi lesquels d'entre eux étaient là
Tell me which of them were there

Possessive Pronouns

	SINGULAR	
MASCULINE	*FEMININE*	
le mien	**la mienne**	*mine*
le tien	**la tienne**	*yours*
le sien	**la sienne**	*his; hers; its*
le nôtre	**la nôtre**	*ours*
le vôtre	**la vôtre**	*yours*
le leur	**la leur**	*theirs*

	PLURAL	
MASCULINE	*FEMININE*	
les miens	**les miennes**	*mine*
les tiens	**les tiennes**	*yours*
les siens	**les siennes**	*his; hers; its*
les nôtres	**les nôtres**	*ours*
les vôtres	**les vôtres**	*yours*
les leurs	**les leurs**	*theirs*

● The pronoun agrees in number and gender with the noun it replaces, NOT WITH THE OWNER (→**1**)

● Alternative translations are *my own, your own* etc; **le sien, la sienne** etc. may also mean *one's own* (→**2**)

● After the prepositions **à** and **de** the articles **le** and **les** are contracted in the normal way (see p. 140):

> **à + le mien → au mien**
> **à + les miens → aux miens**   (→**3**)
> **à + les miennes → aux miennes**
>
> **de + le mien → du mien**
> **de + les miens → des miens**   (→**4**)
> **de + les miennes → des miennes**

1 **Demandez à Carole si ce stylo est le sien**
Ask Carol if this pen is hers
Quelle équipe a gagné – la leur ou la nôtre?
Which team won – theirs or ours?
Mon stylo marche mieux que le tien
My pen writes better than yours
Richard a pris mes affaires pour les siennes
Richard mistook my belongings for his
Si tu n'as pas de disques, emprunte les miens
If you don't have any records, borrow mine
Nos maisons sont moins grandes que les vôtres
Our houses are smaller than yours

2 **Est-ce que leur entreprise est aussi grande que la vôtre?**
Is their company as big as your own?
Leurs prix sont moins élevés que les nôtres
Their prices are lower than our own
Le bonheur des autres importe plus que le sien
Other people's happiness matters more than one's own

3 **Pourquoi préfères-tu ce manteau au mien?**
Why do you prefer this coat to mine?
Quelles maisons ressemblent aux leurs?
Which houses resemble theirs?

4 **Leur car est garé**
Their coach is parked
Vos livres sont au-dessus des miens
Your books are on top of mine

Demonstrative Pronouns

celui, celle; ceux, celles

	MASCULINE	FEMININE	
SING.	**celui**	**celle**	*the one*
PLUR.	**ceux**	**celles**	*the ones*

● The pronoun agrees in number and gender with the noun it replaces (→**1**)

● Uses:
  – preceding a relative pronoun, meaning *the one(s) who/which* (→**1**)
  – preceding the preposition **de**, meaning *the one(s) belonging to, the one(s) of* (→**2**)
  – with **-ci** and **-là**, for emphasis or to distinguish between two things:

	MASCULINE	FEMININE		
SING.	**celui-ci**	**celle-ci**	*this (one)*	(→**3**)
PLUR.	**ceux-ci**	**celles-ci**	*these (ones)*	

	MASCULINE	FEMININE		
SING.	**celui-là**	**celle-là**	*that (one)*	(→**3**)
PLUR.	**ceux-là**	**celles-là**	*those (ones)*	

  – an additional meaning of **celui-ci/celui-là** etc. is *the former/the latter*

Continued

1 **Lequel? – Celui qui parle à Anne**
Which man? – The one who's talking to Anne
Quelle robe désirez-vous? – Celle qui est en vitrine
Which dress do you want? – The one which is in the window
Est-ce que ces livres sont ceux qu'il t'a donnés?
Are these the books that he gave you?
Quelles filles? – Celles que nous avons vues hier
Which girls? – The ones we saw yesterday
Cet article n'est pas celui dont vous m'avez parlé
This article isn't the one you spoke to me about

2 **Ce jardin est plus grand que celui de mes parents**
This garden is bigger than my parents' (garden)
Est-ce que ta fille est plus âgée que celle de Gabrielle?
Is your daughter older than Gabrielle's (daughter)?
Je préfère les enfants de Paul à ceux de Roger
I prefer Paul's children to Roger's (children)
Comparez vos réponses à celles de votre voisin
Compare your answers with your neighbours (answers)
les montagnes d'Écosse et celles du pays de Galles
the mountains of Scotland and those of Wales

3 **Quel tailleur préférez-vous: celui-ci ou celui-là?**
Which suit do you prefer: this one or that one?
Cette chemise a deux poches mais celle-la n'en a pas
This shirt has two pockets but that one has none
Quels œufs choisirais-tu: ceux-ci ou ceux-là?
Which eggs would you choose: these (ones) or those (ones)?
De toutes mes jupes, celle-ci me va le mieux
Of all my skirts, this one fits me best

Demonstrative Pronouns (ctd.)

ce (c')   *it, that*

● Usually used with **être**, in the expressions **c'est**, **c'était**, **ce sont** etc. (→**1**)

● Note the spelling **ç** when followed by the letter **a** (→**2**)

● Uses:
  – to identify a person or object (→**3**)
  – for emphasis (→**4**)
  – as a neuter pronoun, referring to a statement, idea etc. (→**5**)

ce qui, ce que, ce dont   etc.: see Relative Pronouns (p. 184), Interrogative Pronouns (p. 188)

cela, ça   *it, that*

● **cela** and **ça** are used as 'neuter' pronouns, referring to a statement, an idea, an object (→**6**)

● In everyday spoken language **ça** is used in preference to **cela**

ceci   *this* (→**7**)

● **ceci** is not used as often as 'this' in English; **cela**, **ça** are often used where we use 'this'

1 C'est ...
It's/That's ...

C'était moi
It was me

2 Ça a été la cause de ...
It has been cause of ...

3 Qui est-ce?
Who is it?; Who's this/that?; Who's he/she?

C'est lui/mon frère/nous
It's/That's him/my brother/us

C'est une infirmière*
She's a nurse

Qu'est-ce que c'est?
What's this/that?

C'est une agrafeuse
It's a stapler

Ce sont eux
It's them

Ce sont des professeurs*
They're teachers

Qu'est-ce que c'est que ça?
What's that?

Ce sont des trombones
They're paper clips

4 C'est moi qui ai téléphoné
It was me who phoned

Ce sont les enfants qui importent le plus
It's the children who matter most

5 C'est très intéressant
That's/It's very interesting

Ce serait dangereux
That/It would be dangerous

6 Ça ne fait rien
It doesn't matter

A quoi bon faire ça?
What's the use of doing that?

Cela ne compte pas
That doesn't count

Cela demande du temps
It/That takes time

7 A qui est ceci?
Whose is this?

Ouvrez-le comme ceci
Open it like this

*See pp. 146 and 147 for the use of the article when stating a person's profession

Adverbs

Formation

● Most adverbs are formed by adding **-ment** to the feminine form of the adjective (→**1**)

● **-ment** is added to the *masculine* form when the masculine form ends in **-é, -i** or **-u** (→**2**)
Exception: **gai** (→**3**)
Occasionally the **u** changes to **û** before **-ment** is added (→**4**)

● If the adjective ends in **-ant** or **-ent**, the adverb ends in **-amment** or **-emment** (→**5**)
Exceptions: **lent, présent** (→**6**)

Irregular Adverbs

ADJECTIVE		ADVERB		
aveugle	*blind*	**aveuglément**	blindly	
bon	*good*	**bien**	well	(→**7**)
bref	*brief*	**brièvement**	briefly	
énorme	*enormous*	**énormément**	enormously	
exprès	*express*	**expressément**	expressly	(→**8**)
gentil	*kind*	**gentiment**	kindly	
mauvais	*bad*	**mal**	badly	(→**9**)
meilleur	*better*	**mieux**	better	
pire	*worse*	**pis**	worse	
précis	*precise*	**précisément**	precisely	
profond	*deep*	**profondément**	deeply	(→**10**)
traître	*treacherous*	**traîtreusement**	treacherously	

Adjectives used as adverbs

Certain adjectives are used adverbially. These include: **bas, bon, cher, clair, court, doux, droit, dur, faux, ferme, fort, haut, mauvais** and **net** (→**11**)

1 *MASC/FEM. ADJECTIVE*   *ADVERB*
heureux/heureuse fortunate   **heureusement** fortunately
franc/franche frank   **franchement** frankly
extrême/extrême extreme   **extrêmement** extremely

2 *MASC. ADJECTIVE*   *ADVERB*
désespéré desperate   **désespérément** desperately
vrai true   **vraiment** truly
résolu resolute   **résolument** resolutely

3 gai cheerful   **gaiement** *OR* **gaîment** cheerfully

4 continu continuous   **continûment** continuously

5 constant constant   **constamment** constantly
courant fluent   **couramment** fluently
évident obvious   **évidemment** obviously
fréquent frequent   **fréquemment** frequently

6 lent slow   **lentement** slowly
présent present   **présentement** presently

7 Elle travaille bien
She works well

8 Il a expressément défendu qu'on parte
He has expressly forbidden us to leave

9 Un emploi mal payé
A badly paid job

10 J'ai été profondément ému
I was deeply moved

11 parler bas/haut
to speak softly/loudly
coûter cher
to be expensive
voir clair
to see clearly
travailler dur
to work hard
chanter faux
to sing off key
sentir bon/mauvais
to smell nice/horrible

Position of Adverbs

● When the adverb accompanies a verb in a simple tense, it generally follows the verb (→ **1**)
● When the adverb accompanies a verb in a compound tense, it generally comes between the auxiliary verb and the past participle (→ **2**)
  Some adverbs, however, follow the past participle (→ **3**)
● When the adverb accompanies an adjective or another adverb it generally precedes the adjective/adverb (→ **4**)

Comparatives of Adverbs

These are formed using the following constructions:

plus ... (que)	*more ... (than)*	(→ **5**)
moins ... (que)	*less ... (than)*	(→ **6**)
aussi ... que	*as ... as*	(→ **7**)
si ... que*	*as ... as*	(→ **8**)

*used mainly after a negative

Superlatives of Adverbs

These are formed using the following constructions:

le plus ... (que)	*the most ... (that)*	(→ **9**)
le moins ... (que)	*the least ... (that)*	(→ **10**)

Adverbs with irregular comparatives/superlatives

ADVERB	COMPARATIVE	SUPERLATIVE
beaucoup	**plus**	**le plus**
a lot	*more*	*(the) most*
bien	**mieux**	**le mieux**
well	*better*	*(the) best*
mal	**pis** OR	**le pis** OR
	plus mal	**le plus mal**
badly	*worse*	*(the) worst*
peu	**moins**	**le moins**
little	*less*	*(the) least*

1 **Il dort encore**   **Je pense souvent à toi**
   He's still asleep   I often think about you

2 **Ils sont déjà partis**   **J'ai toujours cru que ...**
   They've already gone   I've always thought that ...
   J'ai presque fini   **Il a trop mangé**
   I'm almost finished   He's eaten too much

3 **On les a vus partout**   **Elle est revenue hier**
   We saw them everywhere   She came back yesterday

4 **un très beau chemisier**   **une femme bien habillée**
   a very nice blouse   a well-dressed woman
   beaucoup plus vite   **peu souvent**
   much faster   not very often

5 **plus vite**   **plus régulièrement**
   more quickly   more regularly
   Elle chante plus fort que moi
   She sings louder than I do

6 **moins facilement**   **moins souvent**
   less easily   less often
   Nous nous voyons moins fréquemment qu'auparavant
   We see each other less frequently than before

7 **Faites-le aussi vite que possible**
   Do it as quickly as possible
   Il en sait aussi long que nous
   He knows as much about it as we do

8 **Ce n'est pas si loin que je pensais**
   It's not as far as I thought

9 **Marianne court le plus vite**
   Marianne runs fastest
   Le plus tôt que je puisse venir c'est samedi
   The earliest that I can come is Saturday

10 **C'est l'auteur que je connais le moins bien**
   It's the writer I'm least familiar with

Common adverbs and their usage

assez	*enough; quite*	(→ 1) See also below
aussi	*also, too; as*	(→ 2)
autant	*as much*	(→ 3) See also below
beaucoup	*a lot; much*	(→ 4) See also below
bien	*well; very*	(→ 5) See also below
	very much; 'indeed'	
combien	*how much; how many*	(→ 6) See also below
comme	*how; what*	(→ 7)
déjà	*already; before*	(→ 8)
encore	*still; yet*	(→ 9)
	more; even	
moins	*less*	(→ 10) See also below
peu	*little, not much; not very*	(→ 11) See also below
plus	*more*	(→ 12) See also below
si	*so; such*	(→ 13)
tant	*so much*	(→ 14) See also below
toujours	*always; still*	(→ 15)
trop	*too much; too*	(→ 16) See also below

● **assez, autant, beaucoup, combien** etc. are used in the construction *adverb* + **de** + *noun* with the following meanings:

assez de	*enough*	(→17)
autant de	*as much; as many*	
	so much; so many	
beaucoup de	*a lot of*	
combien de	*how much; how many*	
moins de	*less; fewer*	(→17)
peu de	*little, not much; few,*	
	not many	
plus de	*more*	
tant de	*so much; so many*	
trop de	*too much; too many*	

● **bien** can be followed by a partitive article (see p. 144) plus a noun to mean *a lot of; a good many* (→ 18)

1 **Avez-vous assez chaud?**   **Il est assez tard**
Are you warm enough?   It's quite late

2 **Je préfère ça aussi**   **Elle est aussi grande que moi**
I prefer it too   She is as tall as I am

3 **Je voyage autant que lui**   I have as much as him

4 **Tu lis beaucoup?**   **C'est beaucoup plus loin?**
Do you read a lot?   Is it much further?

5 **Bien joué!**   **Je suis bien content que ...**
Well played!   I'm very pleased that ...
Il s'est bien amusé   **Je l'ai bien fait**
He enjoyed himself very much   I DID do it

6 **Combien coûte ce livre?**   **Vous êtes combien?**
How much is this book?   How many of you are there?

7 **Comme tu es jolie!**   **Comme il fait beau!**
How pretty you look!   What lovely weather!

8 **Je l'ai déjà fait**   **Êtes-vous déjà allé en France?**
I've already done it   Have you been to France before?

9 **J'en ai encore deux**   **Elle n'est pas encore là**
I've still got two   She isn't there yet
Encore du café, Alain?   **Encore mieux!**
More coffee, Alain?   Even better!

10 **Travaillez moins**   **Je suis moins étonné que toi**
Work less   I'm less surprised than you are

11 **Elle mange peu**   **C'est peu important**
She doesn't eat very much   It's not very important

12 **Il se détend plus**   **Elle est plus timide que Sophie**
He relaxes more   She is shyer than Sophie

13 **Simon est si charmant**   **une si belle vue**
Simon is so charming   such a lovely view

14 **Elle l'aime tant**   She loves him so much

15 **Il dit toujours ça!**   **Tu le vois toujours?**
He always says that!   Do you still see him?

16 **J'ai trop mangé**   **C'est trop cher**
I've eaten too much   It's too expensive

17 **assez d'argent/de livres**   **moins de temps/d'amis**
enough money/books   less time/fewer friends

18 **bien du mal/des gens**   a lot of harm/a good many people

On the following pages you will find some of the most frequent uses of prepositions in French. Particular attention is paid to cases where usage differs markedly from English. It is often difficult to give an English equivalent for French prepositions, since usage *does* vary so much between the two languages.

In the list below, the broad meaning of the preposition is given on the left, with examples of usage following.

Prepositions are dealt with in alphabetical order, except **à**, **de** and **en** which are shown first.

à

at	**lancer qch à qn**	*to throw sth at sb*
	il habite à St. Pierre	*he lives at St. Pierre*
	à 5 francs (la) pièce	*(at) 5 francs each*
	à 100 km à l'heure	*at 100 km per hour*
in	**à la campagne**	*in the country*
	à Londres	*in London*
	au lit	*in bed* (also *to bed*)
	un livre à la main	*with a book in his/her hand*
on	**un tableau au mur**	*a picture on the wall*
to	**aller au cinéma**	*to go to the cinema*
	donner qch à qn	*to give sth to sb*
	le premier / dernier à faire	*the first/last to do*
	demander qch à qn	*to ask sb sth*
from	**arracher qch à qn**	*to snatch sth from sb*
	acheter qch à qn	*to buy sth from sb*
	cacher qch à qn	*to hide sth from sb*
	emprunter qch à qn	*to borrow sth from sb*
	prendre qch à qn	*to take sth from sb*
	voler qch à qn	*to steal sth from sb*

descriptive	**la femme au chapeau vert**	*the woman with the green hat*
	un garçon aux yeux bleus	*a boy with blue eyes*
manner, means	**à l'anglaise**	*in the English manner*
	fait à la main	*handmade*
	à bicyclette/cheval	*by bicycle/on horseback* (BUT note other forms of transport used with **en** and **par**)
	à pied	*on foot*
	chauffer au gaz	*to heat with/by gas*
	à pas lents	*with slow steps*
	cuisiner au beurre	*to cook with butter*
time, date: *at, in*	**à minuit**	*at midnight*
	à trois heures cinq	*at five past three*
	au 20ème siècle	*in the 20th century*
	à Noël/Pâques	*at Christmas/Easter*
distance	**à 6 km d'ici**	*(at a distance of) 6 km from here*
	à deux pas de chez moi	*just a step from my place*
destined for	**une tasse à thé**	*a teacup* (compare **une tasse de thé**)
	un service à café	*a coffee service*
after certain adjectives	**son écriture est difficile à lire**	*his writing is difficult to read* (compare the usage with **de**, p. 206)
	prêt à tout	*ready for anything*
after certain verbs *Continued*	see p. 64	

de

from	venir de Londres	to come from London
	du matin au soir	from morning till night
	du 21 juin au 5 juillet	from 21st June till 5th July
	de 10 à 15	from 10 to 15
belonging to, *of*	un ami de la famille	a family friend
	les vents d'automne	the autumn winds
contents, composition, material	une boîte d'allumettes	a box of matches
	une tasse de thé	a cup of tea (compare **une tasse à thé**)
	une robe de soie	a silk dress
manner	d'une façon irrégulière	in an irregular way
	d'un coup de couteau	with the blow of a knife
quality	la société de consommation	the consumer society
	des objets de valeur	valuable items
comparative + a number	il y avait plus/moins de cent personnes	there were more/fewer than a hundred people
after superlatives: *in*	la plus/moins belle ville du monde	the most/least beautiful city in the world
after certain adjectives	surpris de voir	surprised to see
	il est difficile d'y accéder	access is difficult (compare the usage with **à**, p. 205)
after certain verbs	see p. 64	

en

place: *to, in, on*	**en ville**	*in/to town*
	en pleine mer	*on the open sea*
	en France	*in/to France* (note that masculine countries use **à**)
dates, months: *in*	**en 1923**	*in 1923*
	en janvier	*in January*
transport	**en voiture**	*by car*
	en avion	*by plane* (but note usage of **à** and **par** in other expressions)
language	**en français**	*in French*
duration	**je le ferai en trois jours**	*I'll do it in three days* (i.e. *I'll take 3 days to do it*: compare **dans trois jours**)
material	**un bracelet en or**	*a bracelet made of gold* (note that the use of **en** stresses the material more than the use of **de**)
	consister en	*to consist of*
in the manner of, like a	**parler en vrai connaisseur**	*to speak like a real connoisseur*
	déguisé en cowboy	*dressed up as a cowboy*
+ present participle	**il l'a vu en passant devant la porte**	*he saw it as he came past the door*

Continued

avant

before	**il est arrivé avant toi**	*he arrived before you*
+ infinitive (add **de**)	**je vais finir ça avant de manger**	*I'm going to finish this before eating*
preference	**la santé avant tout**	*health above all things*

chez

at the home of	**chez lui/moi**	*at his/my house*
	être chez soi	*to be at home*
	venez chez nous	*come round to our place*
at/to a shop	**chez le boucher**	*at/to the butcher's*
in a person, *among* a group of people or animals	**ce que je n'aime pas chez lui c'est son ...**	*what I don't like in him is his ...*
	chez les fourmis	*among ants*

dans

position	**dans une boîte**	*in(to) a box*
circumstance	**dans son enfance**	*in his childhood*
future time	**dans trois jours**	*in three days' time* (compare **en trois jours**, p. 207)

depuis

since: time	**depuis mardi**	*since Tuesday*
place	**il pleut depuis Paris**	*it's been raining since Paris*
for	**il habite cette maison depuis 3 ans**	*he's been living in this house for 3 years* (NOTE TENSE)

dès

past time	**dès mon enfance**	*since my childhood*
future time	**je le ferai dès mon retour**	*I'll do it as soon as I get back*

entre

between	**entre 8 et 10**	*between 8 and 10*
among	**Jean et Pierre, entre autres**	*Jean and Pierre, among others*
reciprocal	**s'aider entre eux**	*to help each other (out)*

d'entre

of, among	**trois d'entre eux**	*three of them*

par

agent of passive: *by*	**renversé par une voiture**	*knocked down by a car*
	tué par la foudre	*killed by lightning*
weather conditions	**par un beau jour d'été**	*on a lovely summer's day*
by (means of)	**par un couloir/sentier**	*by a corridor/path*
	par le train	by train (but see also **à** and **en**)
	par l'intermédiaire de M. Duval	*through Mr. Duval*
distribution	**deux par deux**	*two by two*
	par groupes de dix	*in groups of ten*
	deux fois par jour	*twice a day*

Continued

pour

for	c'est pour vous	it's for you
	c'est pour demain	it's for tomorrow
	une chambre pour 2 nuits	a room for 2 nights
	pour un enfant, il se débrouille bien	for a child he manages very well
	il part pour l'Espagne	he's leaving for Spain
	il l'a fait pour vous	he did it for you
	il lui a donné 50 francs pour ce livre	he gave him 50 francs for this book
	je ne suis pas pour cette idée	I'm not for that idea
	pour qui me prends-tu?	who do you take me for?
	il passe pour un idiot	he's taken for a fool
+ infinitive: (in order) to	elle se pencha pour le ramasser	she bent down to pick it up
	c'est trop fragile pour servir de siège	it's too fragile to be used as a seat
to(wards)	être bon/gentil pour qn	to be kind to sb
with prices, time	pour 200 francs d'essence	200 francs' worth of petrol
	j'en ai encore pour une heure	I'll be another hour (at it) yet

sans

without	sans eau	without water
	sans ma femme	without my wife
+ infinitive	sans compter les autres	without counting the others

sauf

except (for)	**tous sauf lui**	*all except him*
	sauf quand il pleut	*except when its raining*
barring	**sauf imprévu**	*barring the unexpected*
	sauf avis contraire	*unless you hear to the contrary*

sur

on	**sur le siège**	*on the seat*
	sur l'armoire	*on top of the wardrobe*
	sur le mur	*on (top of) the wall (if the meaning is hanging on the wall use à, p. 204)*
	sur votre gauche	*on your left*
	être sur le point de faire	*to be on the point of doing*
on (to)	**mettez-le sur la table**	*put it on the table*
proportion: out of, by	**8 sur 10**	*8 out of 10*
	un automobiliste sur 5	*one motorist in 5*
	la pièce fait 2 mètres sur 3	*the room measures 2 metres by 3*

Conjunctions

There are conjunctions which introduce a main clause, such as **et** *and*, **mais** *but*, **si** *if*, **ou** *or* etc., and those which introduce subordinate clauses like **parce que** *because*, **pendant que** *while*, **après que** *after* etc. They are all used in much the same way as in English, but the following points are of note:

● Some conjunctions in French require a following subjunctive, see p. 58

● Some conjunctions are 'split' in French like *both ... and, either ... or* in English:

et ... et	*both ... and*	(→ **1**)
ni ... ni ... ne	*neither ... nor*	(→ **2**)
ou (bien) .. ou (bien)	*either ... or (else)*	(→ **3**)
soit ... soit	*either ... or*	(→ **4**)

● **si + il(s) → s'il(s)** (→ **5**)

● **que**
  – meaning *that* (→ **6**)
  – replacing another conjunction (→ **7**)
  – replacing **si**, see p. 62
  – in comparisons, meaning *as, than* (→ **8**)
  – followed by the subjunctive, see p. 62

● **aussi** *so, therefore*: the subject and verb are inverted if the subject is a pronoun (→ **9**)

1 **Ces fleurs poussent et en été et en hiver**
These flowers grow in both summer and winter

2 **Ni lui ni elle ne sont venus**
Neither he nor she came
Ils n'ont ni argent ni nourriture
They have neither money nor food

3 **Elle doit être ou naïve ou stupide**
She must be either naïve or stupid
Ou bien il m'évite ou bien il ne me reconnaît pas
Either he's avoiding me or else he doesn't recognise me

4 **Il faut choisir soit l'un soit l'autre**
You have to choose either one or the other

5 **Je ne sais pas s'il vient/s'ils viennent**
I don't know if he's coming/if they're coming
Dis-moi s'il y a des erreurs
Tell me if there are any mistakes
Votre passeport, s'il vous plaît
Your passport, please

6 **Il dit qu'il t'a vu**
He says (that) he saw you
Est-ce qu'elle sait que vous êtes là?
Does she know that you're here?

7 **Quand tu seras plus grand et que tu auras une maison à toi, ...**
When you're older and you have a house of your own, ...
Comme il pleuvait et que je n'avais pas de parapluie, ...
As it was raining and I didn't have an umbrella, ...

8 **Ils n'y vont pas aussi souvent que nous**
They don't go there as often as we do
Il les aime plus que jamais
He likes them more than ever
L'argent est moins lourd que le plomb
Silver is lighter than lead

9 **Ceux-ci sont plus rares, aussi coûtent-ils cher**
These ones are rarer, so they're expensive

Word Order

Word order in French is largely the same as in English, except for the following. Most of these have already been dealt with under the appropriate part of speech, but are summarised here along with other instances not covered elsewhere.

- Object pronouns nearly always come before the verb (→ **1**)
  For details, see pp. 166 to 170

- Certain adjectives come after the noun (→ **2**)
  For details, see p. 162

- Adverbs accompanying a verb in a simple tense usually follow the verb (→ **3**)
  For details, see p. 200

- After **aussi** *so, therefore*, **à peine** *hardly*, **peut-être** *perhaps*, the verb and subject are inverted (→ **4**)

- After the relative pronoun **dont** *whose* (→ **5**)
  For details, see p. 182

- In exclamations, **que** and **comme** do not affect the normal word order (→ **6**)

- Following direct speech:
  - the *verb + subject* order is inverted to become *subject + verb* (→ **7**)
  - with a pronoun subject, the verb and pronoun are linked by a hyphen (→ **8**)
  - when the verb ends in a vowel in the 3rd person singular, **-t-** is inserted between the pronoun and the verb (→ **9**)

For word order in negative sentences, see p. 216
For word order in interrogative sentences, see pp. 220 and 222

1 **Je les vois!**
I can see them!

Il me l'a donné
He gave it to me

2 **une ville française**
a French town

du vin rouge
some red wine

3 **Il pleut encore**
It's still raining

Elle m'aide quelquefois
She sometimes helps me

4 **Il vit tout seul, aussi fait-il ce qu'il veut**
He lives alone, so he does what he likes

A peine la pendule avait-elle sonné trois heures que ...
Hardly had the clock struck three when ...

Peut-être avez-vous raison
Perhaps you're right

5 Compare: **un homme dont je connais la fille**
a man whose daughter I know

and: **un homme dont la fille me connaît**
a man whose daughter knows me

If the person (or object) 'owned' is the *object* of the verb, the order is:

dont + verb + noun (1st sentence)

If the person (or object) 'owned' is the *subject* of the verb, the order is:

dont + noun + verb (2nd sentence)

Note also: **l'homme dont elle est la fille**
the man whose daughter she is

6 **Qu'il fait chaud!**
How warm it is!

Que je suis content de vous voir!
How pleased I am to see you!

Comme c'est cher
How expensive it is!

Que tes voisins sont gentils!
How kind your neighbours are!

7 **'Je pense que oui' a dit Luc**
'I think so,' said Luke

'Ça ne fait rien' répondit Jean
'It doesn't matter,' John replied

8 **'Quelle horreur!' me suis-je exclamé**
'How awful!' I exclaimed

9 **'Pourquoi pas?' a-t-elle demandé**
'Why not?' she asked

'Si c'est vrai,' continua-t-il '...'
'If it's true,' he went on '...'

Negatives

ne ... pas	*not*
ne ... point (literary)	*not*
ne ... rien	*nothing*
ne ... personne	*nobody*
ne ... plus	*no longer, no more*
ne ... jamais	*never*
ne ... que	*only*
ne ... aucun(e)	*no*
ne ... nul(le)	*no*
ne ... nulle part	*nowhere*
ne ... ni	*neither ... nor*
ne ... ni ... ni	*neither ... nor*

● **Word order**

– In simple tenses and the imperative:
  ne precedes the verb (and any object pronouns) and the second
  element follows the verb (→ **1**)

– In compound tenses:
  i **ne ... pas, ne ... point, ne ... rien, ne ... plus, ne ...
     jamais, ne ... guère** follow the pattern:
     ne + auxiliary verb + **pas** + past participle (→ **2**)
  ii **ne ... personne, ne ... que, ne ... aucun(e), ne ... nul(le),
     ne ... nulle part, ne ... ni (... ni)** follow the pattern:
     ne + auxiliary verb + past participle + **personne** (→ **3**)

– With a verb in the infinitive:
  ne ... pas, ne ... point (etc. see i above) come together (→ **4**)

● For use of **rien**, **personne** and **aucun** as pronouns, see p. 178

Continued

1 **Je ne fume pas**
   I don't smoke
   Ne changez rien
   Don't change anything
   Je ne vois personne
   I can't see anybody
   Nous ne nous verrons plus
   We won't see each other any more
   Il n'arrive jamais à l'heure
   He never arrives on time
   Il n'avait qu'une valise
   He only had one suitcase
   Je n'ai reçu aucune réponse
   I have received no reply
   Il ne boit ni ne fume
   He neither drinks nor smokes
   Ni mon fils ni ma fille ne les connaissaient
   Neither my son nor my daughter knew them

2 **Elle n'a pas fait ses devoirs**
   She hasn't done her homework
   Ne vous a-t-il rien dit?
   Didn't he say anything to you?
   Ils n'avaient jamais vu une si belle maison
   They had never seen such a beautiful house
   Tu n'as guère changé
   You've hardly changed

3 **Je n'ai parlé à personne**
   I haven't spoken to anybody
   Il n'avait mangé que la moitié du repas
   He had only eaten half the meal
   Elle ne les a trouvés nulle part
   She couldn't find them anywhere
   Il ne l'avait ni vu ni entendu
   He had neither seen nor heard him

4 **Il essayait de ne pas rire**
   He was trying not to laugh

Negatives (ctd.)

● Combination of negatives.
These are the most common combinations of negative particles:

ne ... plus jamais	(→ 1)
ne ... plus personne	(→ 2)
ne ... plus rien	(→ 3)
ne ... plus ni ... ni ...	(→ 4)
ne ... jamais personne	(→ 5)
ne ... jamais rien	(→ 6)
ne ... jamais que	(→ 7)
ne ... jamais ni ... ni ...	(→ 8)
(ne ... pas) non plus	(→ 9)

non and **pas**

● **non** *no* is the usual negative response to a question (→ 10)
It is often translated as *not* (→ 11)
● **pas** is generally used when a distinction is being made, or for emphasis (→ 12)
It is often translated as *not* (→ 13)

1 **Je ne le ferai plus jamais**
   I'll never do it again

2 **Je ne connais plus personne à Rouen**
   I don't know anybody in Rouen any more

3 **Ces marchandises ne valaient plus rien**
   Those goods were no longer worth anything

4 **Ils n'ont plus ni chats ni chiens**
   They no longer have either cats or dogs

5 **On n'y voit jamais personne**
   You never see anybody there

6 **Ils ne font jamais rien d'intéressant**
   They never do anything interesting

7 **Je n'ai jamais parlé qu'à sa femme**
   I've only ever spoken to his wife

8 **Il ne m'a jamais ni écrit ni téléphoné**
   He has never either written to me or phoned me

9 **Ils n'ont pas d'enfants et nous non plus**
   They don't have any children and neither do we
   Je ne les aime pas – Moi non plus
   I don't like them – Neither do I; I don't either

10 **Vous voulez nous accompagner? – Non**
   Do you want to come with us? – No (I don't)

11 **Tu viens ou non?**
   Are you coming or not?
   J'espère que non
   I hope not

12 **Ma sœur aime le ski, moi pas**
   My sister likes skiing, I don't

13 **Qui a fait ça? – Pas moi!**
   Who did that? – Not me!
   Est-il de retour? – Pas encore
   Is he back? – Not yet
   Tu as froid? – Pas du tout
   Are you cold? – Not at all

Question forms: direct

There are four ways of forming direct questions in French:

- by inverting the normal word order so that
  pronoun subject + *verb* → *verb* + *pronoun subject*.
  A hyphen links the verb and pronoun (→ **1**)

  – When the subject is a noun, a pronoun is inserted after the verb
  and linked to it by a hyphen (→ **2**)

  – When the verb ends in a vowel in the third person singular, **-t-** is
  inserted before the pronoun (→ **3**)
- by maintaining the word order *subject* + *verb*, but by using a rising
  intonation at the end of the sentence (→ **4**)

- by inserting **est-ce que** before the construction *subject* + *verb* (→ **5**)

- by using an interrogative word at the beginning of the sentence,
  together with inversion *or* the **est-ce que** form above (→ **6**)

1 **Aimez-vous la France?**
   Do you like France?
   Est-ce possible?
   Is it possible?
   Part-on tout de suite?
   Are we leaving right away?

   Avez-vous fini?
   Have you finished?
   Est-elle restée?
   Did she stay?

2 **Tes parents sont-ils en vacances?**
   Are your parents on holiday?
   Jean-Benoît est-il parti?
   Has Jean-Benoît left?

3 **A-t-elle de l'argent?**
   Has she any money?
   La pièce dure-t-elle longtemps?
   Does the play last long?
   Mon père a-t-il téléphoné?
   Has my father phoned?

4 **Il l'a fini**
   He's finished it
   Robert va venir
   Robert's coming

   Il l'a fini?
   Has he finished it?
   Robert va venir?
   Is Robert coming?

5 **Est-ce que tu la connais?**
   Do you know her?
   Est-ce que tes parents sont revenus d'Italie?
   Have your parents come back from Italy?

6 **Quel train** { **prends-tu?**
                    est-ce que tu prends?
   What train are you getting?
   Lequel { **est-ce que ta sœur préfère?**
               ta sœur préfère-t-elle?
   Which one does your sister prefer?
   Quand { **êtes-vous arrivé?**
              est-ce que vous êtes arrivé?
   When did you arrive?
   Pourquoi { **ne sont-ils pas venus?**
                 est-ce qu'ils ne sont pas venus?
   Why haven't they come?

Question forms: indirect

An indirect question is one that is 'reported', e.g. he asked me *what the time was*, tell me *which way to go*. Word order in indirect questions is as follows:

- *interrogative word* + *subject* + *verb* (→ **1**)

- when the subject is a noun, and not a pronoun, the subject and verb are often inverted (→ **2**)

n'est-ce pas

This is used wherever English would use *isn't it?, don't they?, weren't we?, is it?* etc. tagged on to the end of a sentence (→ **3**)

oui and si

Oui is the word for *yes* in answer to a question put in the affirmative (→ **4**)

Si is the word for *yes* in answer to a question put in the negative or to contradict a negative statement (→ **5**)

1 **Je me demande s'il viendra**
   I wonder if he'll come
   Je ne sais pas à quoi ça sert
   I don't know what it's for
   Dites-moi quel autobus va à la gare
   Tell me which bus goes to the station
   Il m'a demandé combien d'argent j'avais
   He asked me how much money I had

2 **Elle ne sait pas à quelle heure commence le film**
   She doesn't know what time the film starts
   Je me demande où sont mes clés
   I wonder where my keys are
   Elle nous a demandé comment allait notre père
   She asked us how our father was
   je ne sais pas ce que veulent dire ces mots
   I don't know what these words mean

3 **Il fait chaud, n'est-ce pas?**
   It's warm, isn't it?
   Vous n'oublierez pas, n'est-ce pas?
   You won't forget, will you?

4 **Tu l'as fait? – Oui**
   Have you done it? – Yes (I have)

5 **Tu ne l'as pas fait? – Si**
   Haven't you done it? – Yes (I have)

Numbers

Cardinal (*one, two etc.*)		Ordinal (*first, second etc.*)	
zéro	0		
un (une)	1	premier (première)	1er, 1ère
deux	2	deuxième, second(e)	2ème
trois	3	troisième	3ème
quatre	4	quatrième	4ème
cinq	5	cinquième	5ème
six	6	sixième	6ème
sept	7	septième	7ème
huit	8	huitième	8ème
neuf	9	neuvième	9ème
dix	10	dixième	10ème
onze	11	onzième	11ème
douze	12	douzième	12ème
treize	13	treizième	13ème
quatorze	14	quatorzième	14ème
quinze	15	quinzième	15ème
seize	16	seizième	16ème
dix-sept	17	dix-septième	17ème
dix-huit	18	dix-huitième	18ème
dix-neuf	19	dix-neuvième	19ème
vingt	20	vingtième	20ème
vingt et un (une)	21	vingt et unième	21ème
vingt-deux	22	vingt-deuxième	22ème
vingt-trois	23	vingt-troisième	23ème
trente	30	trentième	30ème
quarante	40	quarantième	40ème
cinquante	50	cinquantième	50ème
soixante	60	soixantième	60ème
soixante-dix	70	soixante-dixième	70ème
soixante et onze	71	soixante-onzième	71ème
soixante-douze	72	soixante-douzième	72ème
quatre-vingts	80	quatre-vingtième	80ème
quatre-vingt-un (une)	81	quatre-vingt-unième	81ème
quatre-vingt-dix	90	quatre-vingt-dixième	90ème
quatre-vingt-onze	91	quatre-vingt-onzième	91ème

Numbers (ctd.)

Cardinal		Ordinal	
cent	100	centième	100ème
cent un (une)	101	cent unième	101ème
cent deux	102	cent deuxième	102ème
cent dix	110	cent dixième	110ème
cent quarante-deux	142	cent quarante-deuxième	142ème
deux cents	200	deux centième	200ème
duex cent un (une)	201	deux cent unième	201ème
duex cent deux	202	deux cent-deuxième	202ème
trois cents	300	trois centième	300ème
quatre cents	400	quatre centième	400ème
cinq cents	500	cinq centième	500ème
six cents	600	six centième	600ème
sept cents	700	sept centième	700ème
huit cents	800	huit centième	800ème
neuf cents	900	neuf centième	900ème
mille	1000	millième	1000ème
mille un (une)	1001	mille unième	1001ème
mille deux	1002	mille deuxième	1002ème
deux mille	2000	deux millième	2000ème
cent mille	100.000	cent millième	100.000ème
un million	1.000.000	millionième	1.000.000ème
deux millions	2.000.000	deux millionième	2.000.000ème

Fractions		Others	
un demi, une demie	½	zéro virgule cinq	0,5
un tiers	⅓	un virgule trois	1,3
deux tiers	⅔	dix pour cent	10%
un quart	¼	deux plus deux	2 + 2
trois quarts	¾	deux moins deux	2 − 2
un cinquième	⅕	deux fois deux	2 × 2
cinq et trois quarts	5¾	deux divisé par deux	2 ÷ 2

Note the use of points with large numbers and commas with fractions, i.e. the opposite of English usage.

Numbers: Other Uses

● **-aine** denoting approximate numbers:

une douzaine (de pommes)	about a dozen (apples)
une quinzaine (d'hommes)	about fifteen (men)
des centaines de personnes	hundreds of people
BUT: **un millier (de voitures)**	about a thousand (cars)

● measurements:

vingt mètres carrés	20 square metres
vingt mètres cubes	20 cubic metres
un pont long de quarante mètres	a bridge 40 metres long
avoir trois mètres de large / de haut	to be 3 metres wide / high

● miscellaneous:

Il habite au dix	He lives at number 10
C'est au chapitre sept	It's in chapter 7
(C'est) à la page 17	(It's) on page 17
(Il habite) au septième étage	(He lives) on the 7th floor
Il est arrivé le septième	He came in 7th
échelle au vingt-cinq millième	scale 1:25,000

Telephone numbers

Je voudrais Edimbourg trois cent trente, vingt-deux, dix
I would like Edinburgh 330 22 10

Je voudrais le soixante-cinq, treize, vingt-deux, zéro deux
Could you get me 65 13 22 02

Poste trois cent trente-cinq
Extension number 335

Poste vingt-deux, trente-trois
Extension number 22 33

N.B. In French, telephone numbers are broken down into groups of two or three numbers (never four), and are not spoken separately as in English. They are also written in groups of two or three numbers.

The calendar

Dates

Quelle est la date d'aujourd'hui?
Quel jour sommes-nous? } What's the date today?

C'est ...
Nous sommes ... } It's the ...

    le premier février   1st of February
    le deux février   2nd of February
    le vingt-huit février   28th of February

Il vient le sept mars   He's coming on the 7th of March

N.B. Use cardinal numbers except for the first of the month.

Years

Je suis né en 1971
I was born in 1971

le douze février { **dix-neuf cent soixante et onze**
                { **mil neuf cent soixante et onze**
(on) 12th February 1971

N.B. There are two ways of expressing the year (see last example).
Note the spelling of **mil** *one thousand* in dates.

Other expressions

dans les années cinquante	during the fifties
au vingtième siècle	in the twentieth century
en mai	in May
lundi (quinze)	on Monday (the 15th)
le lundi	on Mondays
dans dix jours	in 10 days' time
il y a dix jours	10 days ago

The Time

Quelle heure est-il?	*What time is it?*
Il est . . .	*It's . . .*

00.00	**minuit** *midnight, twelve o'clock*
00.10	**minuit dix, zéro heure dix**
00.15	**minuit et quart, zéro heure quinze**
00.30	**minuit et demi, zéro heure trente**
00.45	**une heure moins (le) quart, zéro heure quarante-cinq**
01.00	**une heure du matin** *one a.m., one o'clock in the morning*
01.10	**une heure dix (du matin)**
01.15	**une heure et quart, une heure quinze**
01.30	**une heure et demie, une heure trente**
01.45	**deux heures moins (le) quart, une heure quarante-cinq**
01.50	**deux heures moins dix, une heure cinquante**
01.59	**deux heures moins une, une heure cinquante-neuf**
12.00	**midi, douze heures** *noon, twelve o'clock*
12.30	**midi et demi, douze heures trente**
13.00	**une heure de l'après-midi, treize heures** *one p.m., one o'clock in the afternoon*
01.30	**une heure et demie (de l'après-midi), treize heures trente**
19.00	**sept heures du soir, dix-neuf heures** *seven p.m., seven o'clock in the evening*
19.30	**sept heures et demie (du soir), dix-neuf heures trente**

A quelle heure venez-vous? – A sept heures
What time are you coming? – At seven o'clock
Les bureaux sont fermés de midi à quatorze heures
The offices are closed from twelve until two
à deux heures du matin/de l'après-midi
at two o'clock in the morning/afternoon, at two a.m./p.m.
à sept heures du soir
at seven o'clock in the evening, at seven p.m.
à cinq heures précises *or* **pile**
at five o'clock sharp
vers neuf heures
about nine o'clock
peu avant/après midi
shortly before/after noon
entre huit et neuf heures
between eight and nine o'clock
Il est plus de trois heures et demie
It's after half past three
Il faut y être à dix heures au plus tard/au plus tôt
You have to be there by ten o'clock at the latest/earliest
Ne venez pas plus tard que onze heures moins le quart
Come no later than a quarter to eleven
Il en a pour une demi-heure
He'll be half an hour (at it)
Elle est restée sans connaissance pendant un quart d'heure
She was unconscious for a quarter of an hour
Je les attends depuis une heure
I've been waiting for them for an hour/since one o'clock
Ils sont partis il y a quelques minutes
They left a few minutes ago
Je l'ai fait en vingt minutes
I did it in twenty minutes
Le train arrive dans une heure
The train arrives in an hour('s time)
Combien de temps dure ce film?
How long does this film last?

Beware of translating word for word. While on occasion this is quite possible, quite often it is not. The need for caution is illustrated by the following:

● English phrasal verbs (i.e. verbs followed by a preposition) e.g. *to run away, to fall down* are often translated by one word in French (→ **1**)

● English verbal constructions often contain a preposition where none exists in French, or vice versa (→ **2**)

● Two or more prepositions in English may have a single rendering in French (→ **3**)

● A word which is singular in English may be plural in French, or vice versa (→ **4**)

● French has no equivalent of the possessive construction denoted by *--'s/--'s* (→ **5**)
See also *at/in/to*, p. 234

Specific problems

-ing

This is translated in a variety of ways in French:

● *to be ...-ing* is translated by a simple verb (→ **6**)
Exception: when a physical position is denoted, a past participle is used (→ **7**)

● in the construction *to see/hear sb ...-ing*, use an infinitive or **qui** + verb (→ **8**)

-ing can also be translated by:
  – an infinitive (→ **9**)
    (see p. 44)
  – a perfect infinitive (→ **10**)
    (see p. 46)
  – a present participle (→ **11**)
    (see p. 48)
  – a noun (→ **12**)
Continued

1 **s'enfuir**   **tomber**   **céder**
to run away   to fall down   to give in

2 **payer**   **regarder**   **écouter**
to pay for   to look at   to listen to
obéir à   **nuire à**   **manquer de**
to obey   to harm   to lack

3 **s'étonner de**   **satisfait de**
to be surprised at   satisfied with
voler qch à   **apte à**
to steal sth from   capable of; fit for

4 **les bagages**   **ses cheveux**
the luggage   his/her hair
le bétail   **mon pantalon**
the cattle   my trousers

5 **la voiture de mon frère**   **la chambre des enfants**
my brother's car   the children's bedroom
(*literally: . . . of my brother*)   (*literally: . . . of the children*)

6 **Il part demain**   **Je lisais un roman**
He's leaving tomorrow   I was reading a novel

7 **Elle est assise là-bas**   **Il était couché par terre**
She's sitting over there   He was lying on the ground

8 **Je les vois** { **venir** / **qui viennent** } I can see them coming

Je l'ai entendue { **chanter** / **qui chantait** } I heard her singing

9 **J'aime aller au cinéma**   **Arrêtez de parler!**
I like going to the cinema   Stop talking!
Au lieu de répondre   **Avant de partir**
Instead of answering   Before leaving

10 **Après avoir ouvert la boîte, il . . .**
After opening the box, he . . .

11 **Etant plus timide que moi, elle . . .**
Being shyer than me, she . . .

12 **Le ski me maintient en forme**
Skiing keeps me fit

to be

- Generally translated by **être** (→ **1**)
  When physical location is implied, **se trouver** may be used (→ **2**)

- In set expressions, describing physical and emotional conditions, **avoir** is used:

avoir chaud/froid	to be warm/cold
avoir faim/soif	to be hungry/thirsty
avoir peur/honte	to be afraid/ashamed
avoir tort/raison	to be wrong/right

- Describing the weather, e.g. *what's the weather like?*, *it's windy/sunny*, use **faire** (→ **3**)

- For ages, e.g. *he is 6*, use **avoir** (→ **4**)

- For state of health, e.g. *he's unwell, how are you?*, use **aller** (→ **5**)

it is, it's

- Usually **il/elle est**, when referring to a noun (→ **6**)

- For expressions of time, also use **il est** (→ **7**)

- To describe the weather, e.g. *it's windy*, see above

- In the construction: *it is difficult/easy to do sth*, use **il est** (→ **8**)

- In all other constructions, use **c'est** (→ **9**)

there is/there are

- Both are translated by **il y a** (→ **10**)

can, be able

- Physical ability is expressed by **pouvoir** (→ **11**)

- If the meaning is *to know how to*, use **savoir** (→ **12**)

- *Can* + a 'verb of hearing or seeing etc.' in English is not translated in French (→ **13**)

1 Il est tard
It's late

C'est peu probable
It's not very likely

2 Où se trouve la gare?
Where's the station?

3 Quel temps fait-il?
What's the weather like?

Il fait beau/mauvais/du vent
It's lovely/miserable/windy

4 Quel âge avez-vous?
How old are you?

J'ai quinze ans
I'm fifteen

5 Comment allez-vous?
How are you?

Je vais très bien
I'm very well

6 Où est mon parapluie? – Il est là, dans le coin
Where's my umbrella? – It's there, in the corner

Descends la valise si elle n'est pas trop lourde
Bring down the case if it isn't too heavy

7 Quelle heure est-il? – Il est sept heures et demie
What's the time? – It's half past seven

8 Il est difficile de répondre à cette question
It's difficult to reply to this question

9 C'est moi qui ne l'aime pas
It's me who doesn't like him

C'est Charles/ma mère qui l'a dit
It's Charles/my mother who said so

C'est ici que je les ai achetés
It's here that I bought them

C'est parce que la poste est fermée que ...
It's because the post office is closed that ...

10 Il y a quelqu'un à la porte
There's somebody at the door

Il y a cinq livres sur la table
There are five books on the table

11 Pouvez-vous atteindre cette étagère?
Can you reach up to that shelf?

12 Elle ne sait pas nager
She can't swim

13 Je ne vois rien
I can't see anything

Il les entendait
He could hear them

to (see also below)

● Generally translated by **à** (→ **1**)
(See p. 204)

● In time expressions, e.g. *10 to 6*, use **moins** (→ **2**)

● When the meaning is *in order to*, use **pour** (→ **3**)

● Following a verb, as in *to try to do*, *to like to do*, see pp. 44 and 64

● *easy/difficult/impossible* etc. *to do*:
The preposition used depends on whether a specific noun is referred to (→ **4**) or not (→ **5**)

at/in/to

● With feminine countries, use **en** (→ **6**)
With masculine countries, use **au** (**aux** with plural countries) (→ **7**)

● With towns, use **à** (→ **8**)

● *at/to the butcher's/grocer's* etc.: use **à** + noun designating the shop, or **chez** + noun designating the shopkeeper (→ **9**)

● *at/to the dentist's/doctor's* etc.: use **chez** (→ **10**)

● *at/to …'s/…s' house*: use **chez** (→ **11**)

1 **Donne le livre à Patrick**
Give the book to Patrick

2 **dix heures moins cinq**   **à sept heures moins le quart**
five to ten   at a quarter to seven

3 **Je l'ai fait pour vous aider**
I did it to help you
Il se pencha pour nouer son lacet
He bent down to tie his shoelace

4 **Ce livre est difficile à lire**
This book is difficult to read

5 **Il est difficile de comprendre leurs raisons**
It's difficult to understand their reasons

6 **Il est allé en France/en Suisse**
He has gone to France/to Switzerland
un village en Norvège/en Belgique
a village in Norway/in Belgium

7 **Etes-vous allé au Canada/au Danemark/aux Etats-Unis?**
Have you been to Canada/to Denmark/to the United States?
une ville au Japon/au Brésil
a town in Japan/in Brazil

8 **Il est allé à Vienne/à Bruxelles**
He has gone to Vienna/to Brussels
Il habite à Londres/à Genève
He lives in London/in Geneva
Ils logent dans un hôtel à St. Pierre
They're staying in a hotel at St. Pierre

9 **Je l'ai acheté** { **à l'épicerie** / **chez l'épicier** }   I bought it at the grocer's
Elle est allée { **à la boulangerie** / **chez le boulanger** }   She's gone to the baker's

10 **J'ai un rendez-vous chez le dentiste**
I've an appointment at the dentist's
Il est allé chez le médecin
He has gone to the doctor's

11 **chez Christian**   **chez les Pagot**
at/to Christian's house   at/to the Pagots' house

General Points

● Activity of the lips

The lips play a very important part in French. When a vowel is described as having 'rounded' lips, the lips are slightly drawn together and pursed, as when an English speaker expresses exaggerated surprise with the vowel 'ooh!'. Equally, if the lips are said to be 'spread', the corners are pulled firmly back towards the cheeks, tendng to reveal the front teeth.

In English, lip position is not important, and vowel sounds tend to merge because of this. In French, the activity of the lips means that every vowel sound is clearly distinct from every other.

● No diphthongs

A diphthong is a glide between two vowel sounds in the same syllable. In English, there are few 'pure' vowel sounds, but largely diphthongs instead. Although speakers of English may *think* they produce one vowel sound in the word 'day', in fact they use a diphthong, which in this instance is a glide between the vowels [e] and [ɪ]: [deɪ]. In French the tension maintained in the lips, tongue and the mouth in general prevents diphthongs occurring, as the vowel sound is kept constant throughout. Hence the French word corresponding to the above example, 'dé', is pronounced with no final [ɪ] sound, but is phonetically represented thus: [de].

● Consonants

In English, consonants are often pronounced with a degree of laxness that can result in their practically disappearing altogether although not strictly 'silent'. In a relaxed pronunciation of a word such as 'hat', the 't' is often scarcely heard, or is replaced by a 'glottal stop' (a sort of jerk in the throat). This never occurs in French, where consonants are always given their full value.

Pronunciation of Consonants

Some consonants are pronounced almost exactly as in English: [b, p, f, v, g, k, m, w].

Most others are similar to English, but slight differences should be noted.

EXAMPLES	HINTS ON PRONUNCIATION
[d] di**n**de	
[t] **t**ente	The tip of the tongue touches the upper front teeth and not the roof of the mouth as in English
[n] **n**o**nn**e	
[l] Li**ll**e	
[s] tou**s ç**a	The tip of the tongue is down behind the bottom front teeth, lower than in English
[z] **z**éro ro**s**e	
[ʃ] **ch**ose ta**ch**e	Like the *sh* of English *shout*
[ʒ] **j**e **g**ilet bei**g**e	Like the *s* of English *measure*
[j] **y**eux pai**ll**e	Like the *y* of English *yes*

Three consonants are not heard in English:

[ʀ] **r**a**r**e veni**r**	*R* is often silent in English, e.g. fa*r*m. In French the [ʀ] is never silent, unless it follows an **e** at the end of a word e.g. cherch**er**. To pronounce it, try to make a short sound like gargling. Similar, too, to the Scottish pronunciation of lo*ch*
[ɲ] vi**gn**e a**gn**eau	Similar to the *ni* of Spa*ni*ard
[ɥ] h**u**ile l**u**eur	Like a very rapid [y] (see p. 239) followed immediately by the next vowel of the word

Pronunciation of Vowels

EXAMPLES	HINTS ON PRONUNCIATION
[a] pa**tte** pl**at a**mour	Similar to the vowel in English *pat*
[ɑ] b**as** p**â**te	Longer than the sound above, it resembles the English exclamation of surprise *ah!* Similar, too, to the English vowel in *car* without the final *r* sound
[ɛ] l**ait j**ou**et m**e**rci	Similar to the English vowel in *pet*. Beware of using the English diphthong [eɪ] as in *pay*
[e] **été j**ou**er**	A pure vowel, again quite different from the diphthong in English *pay*
[ə] l**e** pr**e**mier	Similar to the English sound in butt*er* when the *r* is not pronounced
[i] **ici v**ie **l**ycée	The lips are well spread towards the cheeks while uttering this sound. Shorter than the English vowel in *see*
[ɔ] m**ort h**omme	The lips are well rounded while producing a sound similar to the *o* of English *cot*
[o] m**ot d**ô**me eau**	A pure vowel with strongly rounded lips; quite different from the diphthong in English *bone*, *low*

[u] gen**ou** r**ou**e	A pure vowel with strongly rounded lips. Similar to the English *ooh!* of surprise
[y] r**ue** v**ê**tu	Often the most difficult for English speakers to produce: round your lips and try to pronounce [i] (see above). There is no [j] sound (see p. 237) as there is in English *pure*
[œ] s**œu**r b**eu**rre	Similar to the vowel in English *fir* or *murmur*, but without the *r* sound and with the lips more strongly rounded
[ø] p**eu** d**eux**	To pronounce this, try to say [e] (see above) with the lips strongly rounded

Nasal Vowels

These are spelt with a vowel followed by a 'nasal' consonant – **n** or **m**. The production of nasal vowels really requires the help of a teacher or a recording of the sound. However, to help you, the vowel is pronounced by allowing the air from the lungs to come partly down the nose and partly through the mouth, and the **n** or **m** is not pronounced at all.

[ɑ̃] l**en**t s**an**g d**an**s

[ɛ̃] mat**in** pl**ein**

[ɔ̃] n**on** p**on**t

[œ̃] br**un** **un** parf**um**

In each case, the vowel shown in the phonetic symbol is pronounced as described above, but air is allowed to come through the nose as well as the mouth

From Spelling to Sounds

Although it may not seem so at first sight, there are some fairly precise 'rules' which can help you to know how to pronounce French words from their spelling.

Vowels

SPELLING	PRONOUNCED	EXAMPLES
a, à	[a]	cha**tt**e, t**a**ble
a, â	[ɑ]	p**â**te, p**a**s
e, é	[e]	**é**t**é**, march**e**r
e, é, ê	[ɛ]	fen**ê**tre, f**e**rmer, ch**è**re
e	[ɔ]	doubl**e**, f**e**nêtre
i, î, y	[i]	l**i**t. ab**î**mer, lyc**é**e
o, ô	[o]	p**o**t, tr**o**p, d**ô**me
o	[ɔ]	s**o**tte, **o**range
u, û	[y]	batt**u**, f**û**t, p**u**r

Vowel Groups

There are several groups of vowels in French spelling which are regularly pronounced in the same way:

ai	[ɛ] or [e]	m**ai**son, march**ai**, f**ai**re
ail	[aj]	port**ail**
ain, aim, (c)in, im	[ɛ̃]	p**ain**, f**aim**, fr**ein**, **im**pair
au	[o]	**au**berge, land**au**
an, am, en, em	[ɑ̃]	pl**an**, **am**ple, **en**trer, t**em**ps
eau	[o]	bat**eau**, **eau**
eu	[œ] or [ø]	f**eu**, p**eu**r
euil(le), ueil	[œj]	f**euil**le, rec**ueil**
oi, oy	[wa]	v**oi**re, v**oy**age
on, om	[ɔ̃]	t**on**, c**om**pter
ou	[u]	hib**ou**, **ou**til
œu	[œ]	s**œu**r, c**œu**r
ue	[y]	r**ue**
un, um	[œ̃]	br**un**, parf**um**

Added to these are the many groups of letters occurring at the end of words, where their pronunciation is predictable, bearing in mind the tendency (see p. 242) of final consonants to remain silent:

TYPICAL WORDS	PRONUNCIATION OF FINAL SYLLABLE
pas, mât, chat	[ɑ] or [a]
marcher, marchez marchais, marchait, baie, valet, mes, fumée	[e] or [ɛ]
nid	[i]
chaud, vaut, faux, sot, tôt, Pernod, dos, croc	[o]
bout, bijoux, sous, boue	[u]
fut, fût, crus, crûs	[y]
queue, heureux, bleus	[ø]
en, vend, vent, an, sang, grand, dans	[ã]
fin, feint, frein, vain	[ɛ̃]
on, pont, fond, avons	[ɔ̃]
brun, parfum	[œ̃]

Continued

From Spelling to Sounds (ctd.)

Consonants

● Final consonants are usually silent (→**1**)

● **n** or **m** at the end of a syllable or word are silent, but they have the effect of 'nasalizing' the preceding vowel(s) (see p. 239 on Nasal Vowels)

● The letter **h** is either 'silent' ('mute') or 'aspirate' when it begins a word. When silent, the word behaves as though it started with a vowel and takes a liaison with the preceding word where appropriate.
When the **h** is aspirate, no liaison is made (→**2**)
There is no way of predicting which words start with which sort of **h** – this simply has to be learnt with each word

● The following consonants in spelling have predictable pronunciations: b, d, f, k, l, p, r, t, v, w, x, y, z. Others vary:

SPELLING	PRONOUNCED	ENGLISH EXAMPLES	
c + a, o, u	[k]	**c**an, **c**ot, **c**ut	
+ l, r		**c**lass, **c**ram	(→**3**)
c + e, i, y	[s]	**c**eiling, i**c**e	(→**4**)
ç + a, o, u	[s]	**c**eiling, i**c**e	(→**5**)
ch	[ʃ]	**sh**op, la**sh**	(→**6**)
g + a, o, u	[g]	**g**ate, **g**ot, **g**un	
+ l, r		**g**lass, **g**ramme	(→**7**)
g + e, i, y	[ʒ]	lei**s**ure	(→**8**)
gn	[ɲ]	compa**ni**on, o**ni**on	(→**9**)
j	[ʒ]	mea**s**ure	(→**10**)
q, qu	[k]	**qu**ay, **k**it	(→**11**)
s between vowels:	[z]	ro**s**e	
elsewhere	[s]	**s**it	(→**12**)
th	[t]	**Th**omas	(→**13**)
t in **-tion**	[s]	**s**it	(→**14**)

1 **éclat**
[ekla]
chaud
[ʃo]

nez
[ne]
aider
[ɛde]

2 silent **h**:
des hôtels
[de zotɛl]

aspirate **h**:
des haricots
[de aʀiko]

3 **café**
[kafe]
classe
[klas]

côte
[kot]
croûte
[kʀut]

culture
[kyltyʀ]

4 **ceci**
[səsi]

cil
[sil]

cycliste
[siklist]

5 **ça**
[sɑ]

garçon
[gaʀsɔ̃]

déçu
[desy]

6 **chat**
[ʃa]

riche
[ʀiʃ]

7 **gare**
[gaʀ]
glaise
[glɛz]

gourde
[guʀd]
gramme
[gʀam]

aigu
[ɛgy]

8 **gemme**
[ʒɛm]

gilet
[ʒilɛ]

gymnaste
[ʒimnast]

9 **vigne**
[viɲ]

oignon
[ɔɲɔ̃]

10 **joli**
[ʒɔli]

Jules
[ʒyl]

11 **quiche**
[kiʃ]

quitter
[kite]

12 **sable**
[sablə]

maison
[mɛzɔ̃]

13 **théâtre**
[teɑtʀ]

Thomas
[tɔma]

14 **nation**
[nasjɔ̃]

action
[aksjɔ̃]

Feminine Forms and Pronunciation

● For adjectives and nouns ending in a vowel in the masculine, the addition of an **e** to form the feminine does not alter the pronunciation (→**1**)

● If the masculine ends with a silent consonant, generally **-d**, **-s**, **-r** or **-t**, the consonant is sounded in the feminine (→**2**)
This also applies when the final consonant is doubled before the addition of the feminine **e** (→**3**)

● If the masculine ends in a nasal vowel and a silent **n**, e.g. **-an**, **-on**, **-in**, the vowel is no longer nasalized and the **-n** is pronounced in the feminine (→**4**)
This also applies when the final **-n** is doubled before the addition of the feminine **e** (→**5**)

● Where the masculine and feminine forms have totally different endings (see pp. 136 and 150), the pronunciation of course varies accordingly (→**6**)

Plural Forms and Pronunciation

● The addition of **s** or **x** to form regular plurals generally does not affect pronunciation (→**7**)

● Where liaison has to be made, the final **-s** or **-x** of the plural form is pronounced (→**8**)

● Where the masculine singular and plural forms have totally different endings (see pp. 138 and 148), the pronunciation of course varies accordingly (→**9**)

● Note the change in pronunciation in the following nouns:

SINGULAR		PLURAL		
bœuf	[bœf]	**bœufs**	[bø]	ox/oxen
œuf	[œf]	**œufs**	[ø]	egg/eggs
os	[ɔs]	**os**	[o]	bone/bones

ADJECTIVES		NOUNS	
1 joli → **jolie**		**un ami** → **une amie**	
[ʒɔli] [ʒɔli]		[ami] [ami]	
déçu → **déçue**		**un employé** → **une employée**	
[desy] [desy]		[ɑ̃plwaje] [ɑ̃plwaje]	
2 chaud → **chaude**		**un étudiant** → **une étudiante**	
[ʃo] [ʃod]		[etydjɑ̃] [etydjɑ̃t]	
français → **française**		**un Anglais** → **une Anglaise**	
[frɑ̃sɛ] [frɑ̃sɛz]		[ɑ̃glɛ] [ɑ̃glɛz]	
inquiet → **inquiète**		**un étranger** → **une étrangère**	
[ɛ̃kjɛ] [ɛ̃kjɛt]		[etrɑ̃ʒe] [etrɑ̃ʒɛr]	
3 violet → **violette**		**le cadet** → **la cadette**	
[vjɔlɛ] [vjɔlɛt]		[kadɛ] [kadɛt]	
gras → **grasse**		→	
[grɑ] [grɑs]			
4 plein → **pleine**		**le souverain** → **la souveraine**	
[plɛ̃] [plɛn]		[suvrɛ̃] [suvrɛn]	
fin → **fine**		**Le Persan** → **la Persane**	
[fɛ̃] [fin]		[pɛrsɑ̃] [pɛrsan]	
brun → **brune**		**le voisin** → **la voisine**	
[brœ̃] [bryn]		[vwazɛ̃] [vwazin]	
5 canadien → **canadienne**		**le paysan** → **la paysanne**	
[kanadjɛ̃] [kanadjɛn]		[peizɑ̃] [peizan]	
breton → **bretonne**		**le baron** → **la baronne**	
[brətɔ̃] [brətɔn]		[barɔ̃] [barɔn]	
6 vif → **vive**		**le veuf** → **la veuve**	
[vif] [viv]		[vœf] [vœv]	
traître → **traîtresse**		**le maître** → **la maîtresse**	
[trɛtrə] [trɛtrɛs]		[mɛtrə] [mɛtrɛs]	
7 beau → **beaux**		**la maison** → **les maisons**	
[bo] [bo]		[mɛzɔ̃] [mɛzɔ̃]	
8 des anciens élèves			
[de zɑ̃sjɛ̃ zelɛv]			
de beaux arbres			
[də bo zarbr(ə)]			
9 amical → **amicaux**		**un journal** → **des journaux**	
[amikal] [amiko]		[ʒurnal] [ʒurno]	

The Alphabet

A, a	[ɑ]	**J, j**	[ʒi]	**S, s**	[ɛs]
B, b	[be]	**K, k**	[ka]	**T, t**	[te]
C, c	[se]	**L, l**	[ɛl]	**U, u**	[y]
D, d	[de]	**M, m**	[ɛm]	**V, v**	[ve]
E, e	[ə]	**N, n**	[ɛn]	**W, w**	[dubləve]
F, f	[ɛf]	**O, o**	[o]	**X, x**	[iks]
G, g	[ʒe]	**P, p**	[pe]	**Y, y**	[igʀɛk]
H, h	[aʃ]	**Q, q**	[ky]	**Z, z**	[zɛd]
I, i	[i]	**R, r**	[ɛr]		

Capital letters are used as in English *except* for the following:

- adjectives of nationality
  e.g. **une ville espagnole**   **un auteur français**
       a Spanish town   a French author

- languages
  e.g. **Parlez-vous anglais?**   **Il parle français et allemand**
       Do you speak English?   He speaks French and German

- days of the week:
lundi	Monday
mardi	Tuesday
mercredi	Wednesday
jeudi	Thursday
vendredi	Friday
samedi	Saturday
dimanche	Sunday

- months of the year:
janvier	January	**juillet**	July
février	February	**août**	August
mars	March	**septembre**	September
avril	April	**octobre**	October
mai	May	**novembre**	November
juin	June	**décembre**	December

The following index lists comprehensively both grammatical terms and key words in French and English contained in this book.

a 146
à 204, 234
à governed by verbs 64
à with infinitives 44
à + le/les 140
à moins que 58
à peine 56, 214
ability 232
acheter 16
acquérir 76
address forms 164
adjectives 148
  position 162
  used as adverbs 198
adorer 44
adverbs 198
afin que 58
age 232
agent 209
agir s' 40
agreement:
  of adjectives 148, 154, 156, 158, 160
  of past participle 28, 32, 50
ago 227
aigu 152
aimer 44
aimer mieux 44
aller 28, 44, 232

to express future 54
  conjugated 77
aller chercher 46
alphabet 246
among 180, 209
ancien 162
any 144
appeler 16
apposition, nouns in 142
après with perfect infinitive 46
arriver 28
articles 140
as 212
as ... as 154, 200
asseoir s' 32
  conjugated 78
assez 202
at 204, 234
au 140, 234
aucun 178
auquel 180, 190
aussi 202, 212, 214
aussi ... que 154, 200
autant 202
autre 162
aux 140, 234
auxiliary verbs 22
auxquelles 180, 190

auxquels 180, 190
avant 208
avant que 58
avoir 42, 232
auxiliary, 22, 46, 50
  conjugated 79
avoir peur (que) 60, 232
ayant 48
bad 154, 198
badly 198
barring 211
battre 80
be, to 232
beau 152, 162
beaucoup 200, 202
before 58, 208
bel 152
belle 152
belonging to 194, 206
best 60, 154, 200
better 154, 198, 200
between 180, 209
bien 198, 200, 202
bien que 58
bijou 138
blanc 152
blanche 152
bleu noun 138

bœuf(s) 244
boire 81
bouillir 82
brave 162
bref 152, 198
brève 152
brièvement 198
by 209, 211
by (means of) 209
c'est 196, 232
c'était 196
ça 196
cage 133
caillou 138
calendar 227, 246
capitals, use of 246
cardinal numbers
  224
ce demonstrative
  adjective 156
  pronoun 184, 196
  use of article
    following 146
ce que 184, 188
ce qui 184, 188
ce sont 196
ceci 196
céder 18
cela 196
celle 194
celles 194
celui 194
-cer verbs 14
certain pronouns
  178
ces 156

cet 156
cette 156
ceux 194
chacun 178
chaque 162
cher 162
chez 208, 234
chou 138
-ci 156, 194
ciel, cieux 138
circumstance,
  expressing 208
colour adjectives
  162
combien 202
commands, 20
comme 202, 214
comparative of
  adjectives 154,
  212
comparative of
  adverbs 200, 212
compound tenses
  22, 50
compter 44
conditional 6
conditional perfect
  22, 24, 26
conjunctions 212
connaître 83
consonants:
  pronunciation 237
coucher se 32
coudre 84
countries 142, 234
courir 85
court 162

craindre 86, 60
crêpe 133
croire 87, 60
croître 88
cueillir 89
cuire 90
d'entre 209
dans 208
date 205, 207
days of the week
  246
de preposition 206
  governed by verbs
    64
  with infinitives 44
  after superlative
    154, 206
  indefinite article
    146
  partitive 144
de + le/les 140
de crainte que 58
de façon que 58
de manière que
  58
de peur que 58
de sorte que 58
défendre que 60
definite article 140
  uses 142
déjà 202
demonstrative
  adjectives 156
demonstrative
  pronouns 194
depuis 208
  use of tense fol-

lowing 54, 56
dernier 60, 162
des 140
  indefinite 146
  partitive 144
dés 209
descendre 28, 44
désirer 44, 60
desquelles 180, 190
desquels 180, 190
détester 44
devenir 28
devoir 44, 52
  conjugated 91
dire 92
direct object
  pronouns 166
direct questions
  220
direct speech 214
disjunctive
  pronouns 172
distance 156, 205
distribution 209
donner 6
dont 182
  word order
  following 214
dormir 93
douter que 60
doux 152
du 140
  partitive 144
duquel 180, 190
duration 207
each other 30

écrire 94
-eler verbs 16
elle 164, 172
elle-même 172
elles 164, 172
elles-mêmes 172
emotion, verbs of
  60
emphasis 172, 196
en 207, 234
  with present
  participle 48
  pronoun 170, 174
encore 202
énorme 198
énormément 198
entendre 44
entendre dire que
  46
entendre parler de
  46
entre 180, 209
entrer 28
envoyer 44, 95
envoyer chercher
  46
épais 152
-er verbs 6
espérer 18, 44
essayer 16
essuyer 16
est-ce que 220
et 212
et ... et 212
étant 48
-eter verbs 16
être 232

auxiliary 22, 46
  in passive 36
  conjugated 96
être en train de
  54
eux 172
eux-mêmes 172
except (for) 211
exclamatory
  adjectives 158
faillir 44
faire 44
  conjugated 97
  to express the
  weather 42, 232
faire entrer 46
faire venir 46
falloir 40, 44, 52
  conjugated 98
faut, il 40, 58
faux 152
favori 152
fear 60
feminine:
  formation 134,
  148
  nouns 132, 244
  endings 133, 136,
  150
  pronunciation of
  244
final 148
finir 6
first 60
first conjugation 6,
  8
  spelling irregu-

larities 14
fol 152
folle 152
for 210
  in time
    expressions 54,
      56, 208
former, the 194
fou 152
fractions 225
fraîche 152
frais 152
franc(he) 152
from 204, 206
fuir 99
future perfect 22,
  24, 26
  use of 54
future tense 6
  use of 54
future time,
  expressing 208
geler 16
gender 132
  and meaning 133
generalisations 142
genou 138
-**ger** verbs 14
good 154, 198
grand 162
grec(que) 152
grêler 40
gros 152, 162
grosse 152
haïr 100
haleter 16
haut 162

he 164
hearing, verbs of
  44, 230
her adjective 160
  pronoun 166, 172
hers 192
herself 172
hibou 138
him 166, 172
himself 172
his adjective 160
  pronoun 192
I 164
il 164
  impersonal 40
il y a 42, 227, 232
ils 164
image 133
imperative 20
imperative
  affirmative 30,
    166, 168, 170
imperfect tense 6
  use of 56
impersonal
  constructions 58
impersonal verbs
  40
in 204, 205, 206,
  207
in order to 210
indefinite article
  146
indefinite pronouns
  178
indirect object
  pronouns 168

indirect questions
  222
infinitive 44, 230
infirmier/ière 132
interrogatives 220
interrogative
  adjectives 158
interrogative
  pronouns 186
intonation 220
intransitive verbs
  28, 44
inversion 220
-**ir** verbs 6
irregular
  comparatives 154,
    200
irregular
  superlatives 154,
    200
irregular verbs 74
it 40, 164, 166, 172,
  196
its 192
je, j' 164
jeter 16
jeune 162
joli 162
joujou 138
jusqu'à ce que 58
l' see **le, la**
l'un ... l'autre 30,
  178
la article 140
  pronoun 166
-**là** 156, 194
laisser 44

laisser tomber 46
lancer 14
languages 207, 246
laquelle 180, 190
last 60
latter, the 194
laver se 32, 34
le article 140
  pronoun 166
le moins ... (que) 154
le plus ... (que) 154
least 154, 200
least, the 154
lequel 180, 190
les article 140
  pronoun 166
lesquelles 180, 190
lesquelles 180, 190
less 200, 202
less than 154, 200
leur possessive 160
  pronoun 168
leur, le/la 192
leurs 160
leurs, les 192
lever 18
lever se 32
lire 101
livre 133
long(ue) 152, 162
lui 168, 172
lui-même 172
m' see me
ma 160

mal 198, 200
manche 133
manger 14
manner 205, 206
manquer 42
masculine endings 133
masculine adjectives before vowel 152
masculine nouns 132
material 206, 207
mauvais 154, 162, 198
me 30, 166, 168
me 166, 172
means 205
meilleur 60, 150, 154, 198
même 162
mener 18
mes 160
mettre 102
mien, le 192
mienne, la 192
miennes, les 192
miens, les 192
mieux 198, 200
mine 192
modal auxiliary verbs 52
mode 133
moi 166, 168, 172
moi-même 172
moindre 154
moins 200, 202, 234

moins ... (que) 154, 200
mol 152
molle 152
mon 160
monter 28
months 207, 246
more 200, 202
more than 154, 200
most 200
most, the 154
mou 152
moudre 103
moule 133
mourir 28
  conjugated 104
my 160
myself 172
nage 133
naître 28
  conjugated 105
nasal vowels 239
nationality 162, 246
ne used with subjunctive 58, 60
ne ... aucun 216
ne ... guère 216
ne ... jamais 216
ne ... ni 216
ne ... nul 216
ne ... nulle part 216
ne ... pas 216
ne ... personne 216
ne ... plus 216

ne ... point 216
ne ... que 216
ne ... rien 216
n'est-ce pas 222
necessity 58
negative commands 20
negatives 216
 combination of 218
 form of article following 146
 form of partitive following 144
neiger 40
neuter pronoun 166, 196
ni ... ni 212
nos 160
notre 160
nôtre, le/la 192
nôtres, les 192
noun endings 133
nouns 132, 244
nous 30, 164, 166, 168, 172
nous-mêmes 172
nouveau 152
nouvel 152
nouvelle 152
numbers 224
object pronouns 166, 168
œil 138
œuf(s) 244
of 206
on 36, 178

on 204, 207, 211
one's 160
oneself 172
only 60, 216
onto 211
opinion 60
order of object pronouns 170
orders 20, 60
ordinal numbers 224
ordonner 60
os 244
oser 44
ou ... ou 212
oui 222
our 160
ours 192
ourselves 172
out of 211
ouvrir 106
page 133
par 209
paraître 42
 conjugated 107
parmi 180
partir 28
 conjugated 108
partitive article 144
parts of the body 142
passer 28
passive 36, 209
past anterior 22, 24, 26
 use of 56
past historic 6

use of 56
past participle:
 formation 22
 agreement 28, 32, 50
pauvre 162
payer 16
peler 16
penser que 60
perfect infinitive 46, 230
perfect tense 22, 24, 26
 use of 56
permettre que 60
personal pronouns 164
personne 178
peser 18
petit 154, 162
peu 200, 202
peut-être 214
phrasal verbs 48, 230
physique 133
pire 154, 198
pis 198, 200
plage 133
plaire 109
pleut, il 40
pleuvoir 40, 110
pluperfect 22, 24, 26
plurals:
 formation 138, 148
 pronunciation 244

plus 202
plus … (que) 154, 200
plusieurs 178
pneu 138
poêle 133
position:
  of adjectives 162
  of adverbs 200
  of object pronouns 166
  of indirect object pronouns 168
  of **en** 174
  of **y** 176
positive commands 20
possession 182, 230
possessive adjectives 160
possessive pronouns 192
possibility 58
pour 210
pour que 58
pourvu que 58
pouvoir 44, 52, 232
  conjugated 111
préférer 44
premier 60
prendre 112
prepositions 204
present participle 48, 230
  used with **en** 207

present tense 6
  use of 54
prices 142, 210
professeur 132
pronoun objects:
  position 20, 166, 168
pronouns 164
  position 166, 168
pronunciation 236
proportion 211
propre 162
proximity 156
public 152
publique 152
purpose 58
qu' see **que**
quality 206
que 186, 212, 214
  pronoun 180
  replacing **si** 62
  to form an imperative 62
quel 158
quelle 158
quelles 158
quelque chose 178
quelques-uns 178
quelqu'un 178
quels 158
qu'est-ce que 186
qu'est-ce qui 186
question forms 220
qui 180, 186, 188, 230
qui est-ce que 186

qui est-ce qui 186
qui que 62
quoi 182, 184, 186, 188
quoi que 62
quoique 58
rage 133
ras 150
-re verbs 6
recevoir 113
reflexive pronouns 30
  position 30
reflexive verbs 30, 36
régler 18
regretter que 60
regular verbs 6
relative clauses 62
realtive pronouns 180
rentrer 28
résoudre 114
ressembler se 32
rester 28, 42
result 58
retourner 28
revenir 28
rien 178
rire 115
rompre 116
s' see **se, si**
sa 160
sans 210
sauf 211
savoir 44, 52, 232
  conjugated 117

se 30
sec 152
sèche 152
second conjugation 6, 10
seeing, verbs of 44, 230
sembler 42, 44
sentence structure 214
sentir 118
servir 119
ses 160
seul 60, 162
she 164
si 202, 212
si ... (que) 62, 154, 200
si yes 222
sien, le 192
sienne, la 192
siennes, les 192
siens, les 192
silence 133
simple 162
simple tenses 6
since 54, 56, 208
small 154
soi 172
soi-même 172
soit ... soit 212
some 144
somme 133
son 160
sortir 28, 120
sot(te) 152
souhaiter 44, 60

spelling 240
stem 6
stressed pronouns 172
subject pronouns 164
subjective:
  present 6
  imperfect 6
  perfect 22, 24, 26
  pluperfect 22, 24, 26
  use of 58
suffire 42, 121
suffixes 133
suivre 122
superlative of adjectives 154
superlative of adverbs 200
superlatives: use of subjunctive after 60
sur 211
t' see **te**
ta 160
taire se 123
tant 202
te 30, 166, 168
tel 162
telephone numbers 226
témoin 132
tenir 124
tenses: use of 54
tes 160
that adjective 156

relative pronoun 180
demonstrative pronoun 194, 196
conjunction 212
the 140
their 160
theirs 192
them 66, 172
themselves 172
there 176
there is/are 232
these adjective 156
  pronoun 194
they 164
third conjugation 6, 12
this adjective 156
  pronoun 194, 196
these adjective 156
  pronoun 194
tien, le 192
tienne, la 192
tiennes, les 192
tiens, les 192
time 205, 210, 228
to 204, 207, 234
toi 30, 166, 168, 172
toi-même 172
tomber 28
ton 160
tonner 40
toujours 202
tour 133
tous 178

tout 178
tout ce que 184
tout ce qui 184
toutes 178
towards 210
transport 207
trop 202
trouver se 32, 232
tu 164
un article 146
uncertainty 60
une article 146
unique 60
us 166, 172
vaincre 125
valoir 126
valoir mieux 40, 44
vapeur 133
vaut mieux, il 40
vendre 6
venir 28
  conjugated 127
venir de 54, 56
verb endings 6
verbs of motion 28, 44

verbs taking **être** 28
vêtir 128
vieil 152
vieille 152
vieux 152, 162
vivre 129
voile 133
voir 44, 130
vos 160
votre 160
vôtre, le/la 192
vôtres, les 192
vouloir 44, 52, 60
  conjugated 131
vouloir dire 46
vous 30, 164, 166, 168, 172
vous-même(s) 172
vowels:
  pronunciation 238
vrai 162
want 60
we 164
weather 42, 209, 232
well 198

what 184, 186
what a . . . 146, 158
which 184
  pronoun 180, 190
  adjective 54
who 180, 186
whom 180, 186
whose 182
wishing, verbs of 60
without 210
word order 212, 214
  indirect questions 222
  negatives 216
worse 154, 198, 200
worst 154, 200
y 170, 176
years 227
-yer verbs 16
yeux 138
you 164, 166, 172
your 160
yours 192
yourself 172
yourselves 172